Introducing
Psychology

When we first saw this sculpture of the human body by Antony Gormley, we didn't know that he became interested in the body because he views it as intimately connected to memory and emotion—topics of great interest to us psychologists. We only discovered that later. But we did know right away that we were drawn in by the sheer energy that this wonderful sculpture seems to radiate. Like Gormley, we're extremely interested in the connection between mind and body, and we're pleased that the artist whose striking work we have chosen for our cover has focused on expressing artistically his perspective on matters that are central to our text.

Antony Gormley has explored the relationship between the individual and the community in large-scale installations such as *Allotment* (1995), *Domain Field* (2003), and *Another Place* (1997). *Angel of the North* (1995/98), one of his most celebrated works, is a landmark in contemporary British sculpture. *Field* (1991), an installation of hundreds or thousands of small clay figures sculpted by the local population, has been enacted in various locations throughout the world, involving local communities across four continents. "I am interested in the body," he says, "because it is the place where emotions are most directly registered. When you feel frightened, when you feel excited, happy, depressed somehow the body registers it."

Antony Gormley was born in 1950 in London, England, where he lives and works. He has participated in major group exhibitions, including the Venice Biennale (1982 and 1986); Documenta VIII, Kassel, Germany (1987); and the Sydney Biennale (2006). Solo exhibitions include Fundação Calouste Gulbenkian, Lisbon (2004), Baltic Centre for Contemporary Art, Gateshead, England (2003), and the National History Museum, Beijing, China (2003). He was awarded the Turner Prize in 1994 and made an Order of the British Empire (OBE) in 1997. He is an Honorary Fellow of the Royal Institute of British Architects and has been a Royal Academician since 2003. Gormley exhibits his work at the White Cube studio in London, England.

Introducing Psychology

•DANIEL L. SCHACTER•

HARVARD UNIVERSITY

•DANIEL T. GILBERT•

HARVARD UNIVERSITY

•DANIEL M. WEGNER•

HARVARD UNIVERSITY

WORTH PUBLISHERS

Senior Publisher: Catherine Woods
Senior Acquisitions Editor: Charles Linsmeier
Executive Marketing Manager: Katherine Nurre
Development Editors: Valerie Raymond, Mimi Melek
Media Editor: Christine Burak
Associate Managing Editor: Tracey Kuehn
Project Editor: Leo Kelly, MPS Limited, A Macmillan Company
Photo Editor: Ted Szczepanski
Photo Researcher: Elyse Rieder
Illustration Researcher: Lyndall Culbertson
Art Director and Cover Designer: Babs Reingold
Text Designer: Babs Reingold
Layout Designer: Paul Lacy
Illustration Coordinator: Eleanor Jaekel
Illustrations: Matt Holt, Christy Krames, Don Stewart, and Todd Buck
Cover Photograph: Antony Gormley Studio
Production Manager: Sarah Segal
Composition: MPS Limited, A Macmillan Company
Printing and Binding: Worldcolor Versailles

Credits for art denoting the beginnings of chapters: pp. viii and xxxii: Scott Laumann/
theISpot.com; pp. viii and 32: Neil Leslie/Ikon Images/Masterfile; pp. ix and 54: Stephanie
Dalton Cowan/www.daltoncowan.com; pp. ix and 88: John Singer Illustration; pp. x and 126:
Ian Dodds; pp. x and 160: Andrew Steward/Artmarket; pp. xi and 196: Noma Bliss; pp. xi
and 232: Eric Field/ericfield.com; pp. xii and 268: Jonathan Barkat/Bernstein & Andriulli;
pp. xii and 296: Boris Semeniako/borissemeniako.com; pp. xiii and 332: Boris Semeniako/
borissemeniako.com; pp. xiii and 362: Jay Koelzer; pp. xiv and 396: Rob Day; pp. xiv and 426:
Katelan V. Foisey/Langley Creative; pp. xv and 456: Shonagh Rae/Heart USA

Library of Congress Control Number: 2009940264

ISBN-13: 978-1-4292-1821-4
ISBN-10: 1-4292-1821-5

Printed in the United States of America

First printing

Worth Publishers
41 Madison Avenue
New York, NY 10010
www.worthpublishers.com

To our children and their children

Hannah Schacter

Emily Schacter

Arlo Gilbert

Shona Gilbert

Daylyn Gilbert

Sari Gilbert

Kelsey Wegner

Haley Wegner

About the Authors

DANIEL L. SCHACTER is a professor of psychology at Harvard University. Schacter received his BA degree from the University of North Carolina at Chapel Hill in 1974. He subsequently developed a keen interest in memory disorders. He continued his research and education at the University of Toronto, where he received his PhD in 1981. He taught on the faculty at Toronto for the next 6 years before joining the psychology department at the University of Arizona in 1987. In 1991, he joined the faculty at Harvard University. His research explores the relation between conscious and unconscious forms of memory, the nature of memory distortions, and how individuals use memory to think about future events. He has received the Phi Beta Kappa Teaching Prize and several research awards, including the Troland Award from the National Academy of Sciences and the 2009 Howard Crosby Warren Medal from the Society of Experimental Psychologists. Many of Schacter's studies are summarized in his 1996 book, *Searching for Memory: The Brain, the Mind, and the Past,* and his 2001 book, *The Seven Sins of Memory: How the Mind Forgets and Remembers,* both winners of the APA's William James Book Award. While his adolescent dreams of becoming a professional golfer may be dashed, Dan nonetheless spends as much of his spare time (perhaps more than he should) on golf courses in the Boston area and anywhere his travels take him.

DANIEL T. GILBERT is a professor of psychology at Harvard University. After attending the Community College of Denver and completing his BA at the University of Colorado at Denver in 1981, he earned his PhD from Princeton University in 1985. He taught on the faculty of the University of Texas at Austin for the next 11 years. In 1996, he joined the faculty at Harvard University. Gilbert received the APA's Distinguished Scientific Award for Early Career Contribution to Psychology. He has also won numerous teaching awards, including the Phi Beta Kappa Teaching Prize. His research on "affective forecasting" is an attempt to understand how and how well people predict their emotional reactions to future events. He is the author of the 2006 national best seller *Stumbling on Happiness,* winner of the Royal Society General Book Prize given for the year's best popular science book. He has been a guest on many television shows, including *20/20, The Today Show, and The Colbert Report*, and he is the host of PBS television series "*This Emotional Life.*" Earlier in his life, Dan was a science fiction writer, but these days his hobbies are limited to playing guitar (badly) and listening to jazz (well).

DANIEL M. WEGNER is a professor of psychology at Harvard University. He received his BS in 1970 and PhD in 1974, both from Michigan State University. He began his teaching career at Trinity University in San Antonio, Texas, before his appointments at the University of Virginia in 1990 and at Harvard University in 2000. He is Fellow of the American Association for the Advancement of Science and former associate editor of *Psychological Review.* His research focuses on thought suppression and mental control, social memory in relationships and groups, and the experience of conscious will. His seminal work in thought suppression and consciousness served as the basis for two popular books, *White Bears and Other Unwanted Thoughts* and the *Illusion of Conscious Will,* both of which were named *Choice* Outstanding Academic Books. In his free time, Dan enjoys food and cooking, playing the blues on keyboards, and being with his family—and thinks there is nothing better than a summer morning spent paddling around a lake in a kayak annoying the ducks.

Brief Contents

Contents

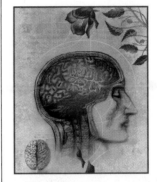

Preface

As professors, we have done many of the things that psychology professors do: we've taught classes, we've written articles for professional journals, we've published trade books for the general public, we've worn sweater vests long after they stopped being fashionable. And then, about ten years ago, we decided to write the textbook that we wished our professors had given us when we were in college.

We finished that book in 2008 and—in a moment of unparalleled creativity—we named it *Psychology*. It was our first venture into textbook writing and we didn't know quite what to expect, so we were thrilled by the responses of teachers who used it. But to be honest, we were even more thrilled by the responses of students who read it, many of whom wrote to us just to say how much they enjoyed our book.

The terrific response to the first edition of our textbook motivated us to write a brief edition, which we've named *Introducing Psychology*. (Okay, so we aren't very original when it comes to titles.) We wrote this brief edition with a few things in mind. First, we felt that a textbook should be as much fun to read as a trade book—or at least *almost* as much fun. We understand why students have to slam espresso to get through a chapter of organic chemistry, but psychology is the most fascinating subject in the world—so why should reading about it ever be dull? Second, in our brief edition we've tried to capture the essence of what psychologists know about the mind, the brain, and behavior by focusing on key ideas and central themes in psychology without losing the quirky asides and interesting details that make the book a pleasure to read. We initially worried that trimming our book would make it worse, but in fact, we think it made it better.

Less Is More: A Focus on Core Topics

For any of us, it is much easier to prepare an hour-long talk than a five-minute one. Trained in our respective fields, we are all comfortable carrying on about our interests in psychology. But asked to deliver a talk with a conciseness demanded by a time restriction and we are forced to make hard decisions about what is important, how it can be conveyed with interest, and how the benefit to the audience can be maximized. These are challenges we faced in writing *Introducing Psychology*. We found that you cannot say all the same things, but you can say them in the same way. For us, that meant retaining the aides, the touches of humor, and the broader story of psychology that is so important to understanding its influence. We have always felt that in presenting psychology to a new audience, the stories need to carry the facts, not vice versa. So, we have stayed true to the approach that so many found appealing in *Psychology*, asking the students to read, engage, think, and inevitably enjoy this first encounter with psychology.

A Stronger Emphasis on Culture

In *Introducing Psychology*, we have given special attention to the influence of culture and gender psychology, which place human behavior in the context of nations, ethnicities, communities, and cultures. Much of psychology celebrates the hard-won facts that characterize human nature, so we thought it made sense to pause and celebrate its diversity. Cultures influence our lives

Culture & Community

Expecting a Helping Hand? It Depends Where You Are

Robert Levine of California State University–Fresno sent his students to 23 large international cities for an observational study in the field. Their task was to observe helping behaviors in a naturalistic context. In two versions of the experiment, students pretended to be either blind or injured while trying to cross a street, while another student stood by to observe whether anyone would come to help. A third version involved a student dropping a pen to see if anyone would pick it up.

The results showed that people helped in all three events fairly evenly within cities, but there was a wide range of response between cities. Rio de Janeiro, Brazil, came out on top as the most helpful city in the study with an overall helping score of 93%. Kuala Lampur, Malaysia, came in last with a score of 40%, while New York City placed next to last with a score of 45%. On average, Latin American cities ranked most helpful (Levine, Norenzayan, & Philbrick, 2001).

and guide what we do and value—and not all cultures are the same. We explore the rich diversity of human cultures throughout the book, but especially in our new "Culture & Community" sections.

Selected Examples of Research in Cultural and Gender Psychology

Aggression, pp. 459–460	Health risks, pp. 442, 449	Motivation, p. 294
Anxiety disorder, p. 372	Helpfulness, p. 35	Obesity, pp. 298, 451
Attachment, p. 312	History of psychology, pp. 24–25	Obsessive compulsive disorder, p. 374
Attractiveness, pp. 466–467	Intelligence: pp. 173, 191, 213–214, 220, 224–226	Panic disorder, p. 374
Bipolar disorder, p. 381	genetics, pp. 221–222, 224	Perception, pp. 11, 91
Close relationships, pp. 464–465, 468–470	group performance, pp. 220, 225–226	Personality disorder, p. 391
Cognitive development, p. 309	learning, pp. 173, 191	Personality, p. 351
Color deficiency, p. 102	measurement, 213–214, 221	Phobias, p. 373
Coping, p. 439	Language:	Prejudice, pp. 23, 27, 430
Depression, pp. 25, 380, 442	bilingualism, pp. 200, 205	Research methods, p. 47
Development, p. 227	memory, p. 138	Sexual activity, pp. 290–291, 320, 452, 464
Dissociative identity disorder, p. 376	sign language, p. 200	Sexual orientation, pp. 121, 320
Dreams, p. 251	structure, pp. 198, 200	Smell, p. 121
Drugs, pp. 256, 265	Learning, pp. 173, 191, 310	Stereotyping, pp. 225, 483, 487
Eating disorders, pp. 288, 451	Maturation, pp. 318, 320	Stress, pp. 430, 443
Emotional expressions, pp. 25, 279, 282	Meditation, p. 263	Suicide, p. 382
Ethics, p. 51	Memory:	Treatment, pp. 399, 401, 404
Fear, p. 276	earliest, pp. 25, 157	Work, pp. 26–27, 314
Genetics, pp. 76, 222, 224, 320	language, p. 138	
	Mental disorder, p. 369	

Forgetting is a highly adaptive property of memory. Information that is used infrequently is less likely to be needed in the future than information that is used more frequently over the same period of time.

Forgetting is a highly adaptive property of memory. Information that is used infrequently is less likely to be needed in the future than information that is used more frequently over the same period of time (Anderson & Schooler, 1991, 2000). Memory, in essence, makes a bet that when we haven't used information recently, we probably won't need it in the future. We win this bet more often than we lose it, making transience an adaptive property of memory. But we are acutely aware of the losses—the frustrations of forgetting—and are never aware of the wins. This may be why people are often quick to complain about their memories: the drawbacks of forgetting are painfully evident but the benefits of forgetting are hidden.

Your immediate awareness of thoughts, sensations, memories, and the world around you represents the experience of consciousness. That the experience of consciousness varies enormously from moment to moment is easy to illustrate. Imagine that we could videotape three one-minute segments of your conscious activities at different times which ...

● **What is the benefit of forgetting?**

... the influential American psychologist ... as a "river" or "stream." Although ... described as unified and unbroken, ... awareness, our experience of consciousness ... of personal identity that has ...

... topics to be tackled by the fledgling science of psychology in the late 1800s (Schneider, 1993). In Chapter 1, we discussed how the first psychologists tried to determine the nature of the human mind through introspection—verbal self-reports that tried to capture the "structure" of conscious experiences (see page 5). But because such self-reports were not objectively verifiable, many of the leading psychologists at the turn of the century emphasized the scientific study of behavior, which could be directly observed, measured, and verified. What happens when people leave the free-running condition and are once again exposed to normal daylight and darkness cues? Within days, sunlight "resets" the biological clock. Circadian rhythms become synchronized again,

An Emphasis on Critical Thinking: Cue Questions

We have placed a stronger emphasis on critical thinking in *Introducing Psychology*. Telling the story of psychology is a great joy for us, and part of our joy comes from thinking creatively and critically about it. Introductory psychology students are also faced with absorbing the facts, concepts, and applications of psychology across a wide variety of subfields in psychology. This challenge is made easier if the textbook supports their learning with thoughtful pedagogy to help students get closer to the ideas they encounter. We've written "cue questions," which are questions that encourage critical thinking and help identify the most important concepts on every page. We hope this tool makes it easier for students to grasp and remember the takeaway points in every section.

An Emphasis on Retention: Summary Quizzes

In addition to the addition of "cue questions," we've added summary quizzes to the end of every major section. These short 3–5 question multiple-choice quizzes provide students with an opportunity to assess their understanding of the broader concepts in the chapter. Taken in themselves, they provide a quick glimpse at comprehension of the major topics. Taken with the "cue questions," they provide a built-in measure of students' retention of the key concepts within the chapter. We encourage students to review their progress with the summary quizzes, but also to return to the chapter and walk through the "cue questions" on each page.

An Engaging New Design

We live in an image rich, boldly colored media world. Textbooks have evolved greatly over the years to reflect these qualities, without sacrificing the essential clarity necessary in a learning tool. In *Introducing Psychology*, we've created a design that is both visually enticing and pedagogically effective. The addition of people and situation-specific photos, a hallmark of our books, continues with *Introducing Psychology*. You will notice that many of the photos deal with real people, demonstrating real psychological phenomena, with captions that both entertain and inform. Several of the figures have also been revised, providing more detail for greater context. Visually appealing but never at the expense of accuracy, the artwork teaches in a way that text alone cannot.

summary quiz [10.2]

4. In terms of motor development, babies gain control over their _____ before they gain control over their _____.
   a. extremities; trunk
   c. head; trunk
   b. legs; arms
   d. arms; shoulders

5. Little Isabel sees a butterfly and exclaims "Bird!" "No, that's a butterfly," says her grandmother. The next time Isabel sees a butterfly, she says "Butterfly." According to Piaget, Isabel has just shown
   a. habituation.
   c. assimilation.
   b. concrete operations.
   d. accommodation.

6. Baby Maria plays without a fuss when her mother leaves and, upon her return, ignores her. Maria is demonstrating which type of attachment style?
   a. avoidant
   c. disorganized
   b. ambivalent
   d. secure

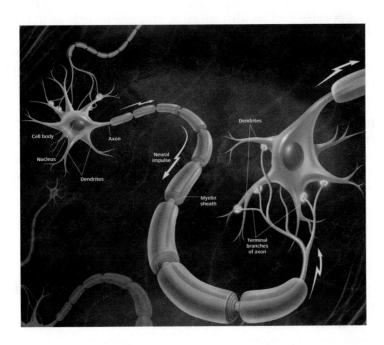

Most people are upset by the suffering of others, and research suggests that even young children have this response, which may be the basis of their emerging morality.

Supplemental Resources & Media
Web/CD-ROM

NEW! **Worth Publishers Student Video Tool Kit for Introductory Psychology**
With its superb collection of 51 brief clips (1 to 13 minutes) and emphasis on the biological basis of behavior, the **Student Video Tool Kit for Introductory Psychology CD-Rom** gives students a fresh way to experience both the classic experiments at the

heart of psychological science and cutting-edge research conducted by the field's most influential investigators.

The balance of contemporary news footage and classic experiments (both original and re-created) helps bring key concepts of the introductory psychology course to life. The **Student Video Tool Kit for Introductory Psychology** is correlated to each Worth introductory psychology textbook. Each clip is accompanied by multiple-choice questions that focus on the ideas students need to learn. Students can submit their answers online or print their answers and hand them in during class.

NEW! The Online Video Tool Kit for Introductory Psychology
The online version of the **Video Tool Kit for Introductory Psychology** includes the 51 video clips found on the student CD-Rom and more! It is easily accessible through an access code packaged with *Introducing Psychology*. Fully customizable, the **Online Video Tool Kit** offers instructors the option of incorporating videos into assignments as well as annotating each video with notes or instructions, making the tool kit an integral part of the introductory course. Instructors also have the option of assigning the tool kit to students without instructor involvement. Videos are correlated to the textbook, and each video is accompanied by multiple-choice questions so that students can assess their understanding of what they have seen. Student responses/grades are sent to an online grade book, so instructors can assess class performance.

NEW! PsychInvestigator: Laboratory Learning in Introductory Psychology by Arthur Kohn, Ph.D, Dark Blue Morning Productions
This exciting new Web-based product is a virtual laboratory environment that enables students to participate in real experiments. Students are introduced to psychological experiments in a dynamic environment featuring hosts video-streamed for the most realistic portrayal possible. In **PsychInvestigator**, students participate in classic psychology experiments, generate real data, and analyze their findings. In each experiment, students participate in compelling video tutorials that are displayed before *and* after the actual experiment. **PsychInvestigator** requires no additional faculty time. Students' quiz scores can be automatically uploaded into an online grade book if instructors wish to monitor students' progress.

Introducing Psychology **Book Companion Website at www.worthpublishers.com/schacterbrief1e**
The *Introducing Psychology* **Book Companion Website** offers students a virtual study guide 24 hours a day, 7 days a week. Best of all, these resources are free and do not require any special access codes or passwords. The site includes:

- Chapter Objectives
- Chapter Outlines
- Online quizzes
- Interactive flashcards
- Online version of 20 PsychSim 5.0 modules (by Thomas Ludwig, Hope College), accompanied by worksheets and multiple-choice quizzes for each activity
- A **password-protected Instructor site** offers a full array of teaching resources, including Illustration and Lecture PowerPoint™ slides, iClicker™ Questions, electronic Instructor's Resources and Faculty Guides, an online quiz grade book, and more.

Course Management

NEW! PsychPortal—One click. One place. For all the psychology tools you need!
Created BY psychologists FOR psychologists, Worth Publishers' PsychPortal is an innovative course space that combines a powerful quizzing engine with unparalleled

media resources. It contains all the functionality you expect from a site that can serve as an independent online course, but the core teaching and learning components are what make PsychPortal truly unique.

A multimedia-enhanced eBook

The eBook integrates the text, a rich assortment of media-powered learning opportunities, and a variety of customization features for students and instructors. Worth's acclaimed eBook platform was developed by cognitive psychologist Pepper Williams (Ph.D., Yale University) who taught undergraduate psychology at the University of Massachusetts. The eBook is also available in a stand-alone version.

- **Easy Customization.** Students can customize their eBook with highlighting, bookmarking, and take their own notes just as they would with a printed textbook. Instructors can assign and annotate chapters, sections, or pages.

- **Concepts in Action.** Embedded throughout the eBook, new Concepts in Action help students solidify their understanding of key concepts as they encounter them in the text. These Flash-based activities, created by award-winning multimedia author Tom Ludwig (Hope College), incorporate video and demonstrations, plus dynamic animations by Terry Bazzett (SUNY College at Geneseo).

Diagnostic Quizzing and Personalized Study Plans

Students can take advantage of PsychPortal's research-based diagnostic quizzing to focus their studying where it's needed the most. Students can take Pre-Lecture Quizzes or Mastery Quizzes to test their understanding of a chapter. They receive feedback to their quiz results through a Personalized Study Plan, which provides direct links to resources that will help them focus on the questions they answered incorrectly.

Assignment Center

The Assignment Center lets instructors easily construct and administer tests and quizzes based on the book's Test Bank or their own questions. Quizzes are randomized and timed, and instructors can receive summaries of student results in reports that follow the section order of the chapters. Through PsychPortal's Assignment Center, you can create and customize meaningful assignments with the online version of Worth's Video Tool Kit for Introductory Psychology, as well as countless other multimedia activities and resources.

Course Materials

This central location provides access to all student and instructor interactive media associated with the book. Within this tab are three groundbreaking sets of interactive student materials created by Tom Ludwig: PsychSim, PsychInquiry, and the brand new Concepts in Action. Psych Investigator, a virtual laboratory experience, and the Online Video Tool Kit can also be accessed here.

NEW! Online Study Center

www.worthpublishers.com/osc/shcacterbrief1e

Available 24/7, this robust resource helps students focus their study and exam prep time. Students can take Pre-Lecture Quizzes to assess how well they understand a particular chapter before coming to class. Or, they can take Mastery Quizzes to test their knowledge whenever they choose. Students receive feedback on their quiz results through a Personalized Study Plan, which provides direct links to resources that will help them focus on the questions they answered incorrectly.

- Students and instructors alike can browse the library of Course Materials to access the myriad of interactive demonstrations and review materials.

- Instructors can view reports indicating their students' strengths and weaknesses, allowing them to focus their teaching efforts accordingly. Student quiz results report to a fully customizable gradebook.

Enhanced Course Management Solutions: Superior Content All in One Place
www.bfwpub.com/lms

The most powerful course management tools are worthless without solid teaching and learning resources that have been meaningfully integrated. Our enhanced *Introducing Psychology* turnkey course in Blackboard, WebCT (Campus Edition and Vista), and Angel course management systems offers a completely integrated solution that you can easily customize and adapt to meet your teaching goals and course objectives. Student content is organized by book chapters and instructor content by content type (e.g., PowerPoint™ slides). On demand, we can also provide our enhanced *Introducing Psychology* solution to those using Desire2Learn, Sakai, and Moodle.

Sample Instructor Content

- Video clip library of more than 40 digitized video clips organized by the text chapters
- Complete test bank
- Complete instructor's resources (PDF)
- Chapter art PowerPoint slides
- Lecture PowerPoint™ slides
- iClicker™ questions
- PsychSim 5.0 worksheet answer key

Sample Student Content

- PsychSim 5.0 (20 activities, work sheets, and quizzes)
- Interactive flashcards
- Online Quizzes
- Chapter Objectives
- Chapter Outlines

To learn more about the course management solution to accompany *Introducing Psychology,* go to www.bfwpub.com/lms.

NEW! We Now Offer Customized ePacks and Course Cartridges

Through the custom program, we can also help you tailor *Introducing Psychology* content to meet your course needs as well as provide you with technical support and services such as customizing your tests and quizzes, adding new student premium resources, adding Web links, reorganizing content, and adding a customized course banner. For more details, contact your Worth representative.

Assessment

Printed Test Bank by Claire Etaugh, Bradley University, et al.

The **Test Bank** provides more than 2,500 multiple-choice, true/false, and essay questions. Each question is keyed to a chapter objective and APA Outcome, and referenced to the textbook pages. Web quizzes from the Book Companion site are also included.

Diploma Computerized Test Bank (available in Windows and Macintosh on one CD-ROM)

The CD-ROM allows you to add an unlimited number of questions, edit questions, format a test, scramble questions, and include pictures, equations, or multimedia links. With the accompanying grade book, you can record students' grades throughout a course, sort student records and view detailed analyses of test items, curve tests, generate reports, and add weights to grades. This CD-ROM is the access point for **Diploma Online Testing**. Blackboard- and WebCT-formatted versions of the **Test Bank** are also available in the Course Cartridge and ePack.

Diploma Online Testing at www.thetestingcenter.com
With **Diploma**, you can easily create and administer exams over the Internet with questions that incorporate multimedia and interactivity. Students receive instant feedback and can take the quizzes multiple times. Instructors can sort and view results and can take advantage of various grade-book and result-analysis features as well as restrict tests to specific computers or time blocks.

Online Quizzing at www.worthpublishers.com/schacterbrief1e
Now you can easily and securely quiz students online using prewritten multiple-choice questions for each chapter. Students receive instant feedback and can take the quizzes multiple times. As the instructor, you can view results by quiz, student, or question or you can get weekly results via e-mail.

iClicker Radio Frequency Classroom Response System

Offered by Worth Publishers in partnership with iClicker
iClicker is Worth's hassle-free new polling system, created by educators for educators. This radio frequency system makes your class time more efficient and interactive. **iClicker** allows you to pause to ask questions and instantly record responses as well as take attendance, direct students through lectures, and gauge students' understanding of the material.

Presentation

ActivePsych: Classroom Activities Project and Video Teaching Modules
Recognizing that professors want out-of-the-box tools to make introductory psychology more applied and class presentations more interactive, Worth Publishers is proud to launch **ActivePsych**, a suite of instructor presentation CD-ROMs that include the following:

- Interactive activities designed for in-class presentation and group participation. **ActivePsych** activities require very little instructor preparation (allowing adopters to simply load the CD-ROM and launch the activity) and are designed to foster class discussion. Activities include animations, video clips, illustrations and photographs, and critical thinking questions. A number of activities have been adapted from Martin Bolt's Instructor's Resources and Thomas Ludwig's PsychSim 5.0 (and are now classroom-presentation friendly). **ActivePsych** also includes a significant number of completely original, creative activities all written (and class-tested) by veteran introductory psychology teachers.

- **ActivePsych: Classroom Activities Project** This segment of ActivePsych includes

  32 flash-based interactive demonstrations designed to promote classroom discussion and critical thinking.

  22 PowerPoint-based demonstrations, inventories, and surveys designed to assess student understanding of various psychological topics. These demonstrations can easily work with the iClicker classroom response systems.

NEW! **Digital Media Archive, Second Edition** Housed in **ActivePsych** and edited by Joe Morrissey, State University of New York at Binghamton (with the assistance of Ann Merriwether, State University of New York at Binghamton and Meredith Woitach, University of Rochester), the second edition offers 33 sections of completely new short video clips and animations drawn from a variety of sources.

NEW! *Scientific American Frontiers* **Teaching Modules, Third Edition** Housed in **ActivePsych** and edited by Martin Bolt, Calvin College, the third edition offers 15 edited clips from *Scientific American* Frontiers segments produced between 2003 and 2005.

Instructor's Resource CD-ROM
Customized for *Introducing Psychology,* this CD-ROM contains prebuilt PowerPoint presentation slide sets for each chapter, all the figures, photos and tables from the book, and an electronic version of the Instructor's Resources.

- **Chapter Art PowerPoint Slides** feature all of the text art and illustrations (including tables, charts, and graphs) in a PowerPoint format.
- **Lecture PowerPoint Presentation Slides** focus on key concepts and themes from the text and feature tables, graphs, and figures from both the text and outside sources.

Video/DVD Resources

NEW! **Worth Publishers Instructor Video Tool Kit for Introductory Psychology • Available in Dual Platform CD-ROM, and closed-captioned DVD**
With its superb collection of brief (1 to 13 minutes) video clips and emphasis on the biological bases of behavior, the **Instructor Video Tool Kit** allows you to introduce central topics, illustrate and reinforce specific core concepts, or stimulate small-group and full-classroom discussions. The **Instructor Video Tool Kit** includes a set of 72 digitized video clips combining both research and news footage from the BBC Motion Gallery, CBS News, and other sources. The CD version provides the clips in MPEG format, which can be easily incorporated into PowerPoint® or run in a video player application and is accompanied by a faculty guide by Martin Bolt (Calvin College).

Worth Digital Media Archive • Available in Dual Platform CD-ROMs, VHS, and DVD
This rich presentation tool contains 42 digitized video clips of classic experiments and research. Footage includes Bandura's Bobo doll experiment, Takooshian's bystander studies, Piaget's conservation experiment, Harlow's monkey experiments, and Milgram's obedience studies. The **Digital Media Archive** CD-ROM clips are available in MPEG for optimal visual presentation and are compatible with PowerPoint.

***Psychology: The Human Experience* Teaching Modules • Available in VHS and DVD**
This series includes more than 3 hours of footage from the introductory psychology telecourse *Psychology: The Human Experience*, produced by Coast Learning Systems in collaboration with Worth Publishers. Footage contains noted scholars, the latest research, and striking animations.

***The Many Faces of Psychology* Video**
Created and written by Frank J. Vattano, Colorado State University, and Martin Bolt, Calvin College (Produced by the Office of Instructional Services, Colorado State University) • Available in VHS and DVD
A terrific way to begin your psychology course, *The Many Faces of Psychology* introduces psychology as a science and a profession, illustrating basic and applied methods. This 22-minute video presents some of the major areas in which psychologists work and teach.

***The Brain* Video Teaching Modules, Second Edition**
Edited by Frank J. Vattano and Thomas L. Bennet, Colorado State University, and Michelle Butler, United States Air Force Academy • Available in VHS and DVD
This collection of 32 short clips provides vivid examples for myriad topics in introductory psychology.

***The Mind* Video Teaching Modules, Second Edition**
Edited by Frank J. Vattano, Colorado State University, in consultation with Charles Brewer, Furman University, and David Myers, Hope College, in association with WNET • Available in VHS and DVD
These 35 brief, engaging video clips will dramatically enhance and illustrate your lectures. Examples include segments on language processing, infant cognitive development, genetic factors in alcoholism, and living without memory (featuring a dramatic interview with Clive Wearing).

Scientific American Frontiers Video Collection, Second Edition • Available in VHS and DVD

Hosted by Alan Alda, these 8- to-12-minute teaching modules from the highly praised *Scientific American* series feature the work of such notable researchers as Steve Sumi, Renee Baillargeon, Carl Rosengren, Laura Pettito, Steven Pinker, Barbara Rothbaum, Bob Stickgold, Irene Pepperberg, Marc Hauser, Linda Bartoshuk, and Michael Gazzaniga.

Print Supplements

For Instructors

Instructor's Resources by Russell Frohardt, Helen Just, and Alan Swinkels, St. Edwards University

Written and compiled by experienced instructors of introductory psychology, the **Instructor's Resources** includes the following:

- An **Outline of Resources** for each chapter, organized by text section, includes the relevant Instructor's Resources items by type (classroom exercise, lecture/discussion topic, etc.) with a cross-reference to its appropriate Instructor Resource page number.

- **Chapter Outlines** follow the major text section headings, providing relevant instructional materials for each topic—including dozens of ready-to-use, detailed lecture/discussion ideas, student projects, classroom exercises (many with hand-outs for in-class or out-of-class use), multimedia resource suggestions provided by Worth Publishers (see *Using Multimedia in the Classroom*), and feature films (as they apply to psychological concepts discussed in the text). Other film resources are listed at the end of each chapter of the Instructor's Resources.

- **Chapter Objectives** from the text highlight main concepts and terms and detail the key points of each text chapter. They can be used as essay questions in class-room examinations.

Instructor's Media Guide

This handy guide organizes the extensive instructor and student media resources available for *Introducing Psychology*, including every video, Web activity (including Psych-Sim and the Video Tool Kit), PowerPoint, and more—all organized by introductory psychology topic.

For Students

Study Guide by Russell Frohardt and Helen Just, St. Edwards University

Following the text's content, the **Study Guide** offers the following for each main chapter:

- **The Big Picture**, a brief wrap-up of the chapter's main ideas and concepts

- **Chapter Objectives**, which also appear in the Instructor's Resources and Test Bank

- **Chapter Overview**, a fill-in-the-blank summary that is divided by major section

- Three 10-question **"Quick Quizzes"**

- **Hey, Guess What I Learned in Psychology Today**, an essay question asking students to apply what they have learned

- **Things to Ponder,** a section that helps students extend and apply knowledge and think about where the material might be going.

- **Web Links and Suggested Reading**

- **Answers section** which includes full explanations of why an answer choice is cor-rect or incorrect

Pursuing Human Strengths: A Positive Psychology Guide by Martin Bolt, Calvin College

By using the scientific method in its efforts to assess, understand, and then build human strengths, positive psychology balances the investigation of weakness and damage with a study of strength and virtue. This brief positive psychology guide gives instructors and students alike the means to learn more about this relevant approach to psychology.

***Critical Thinking Companion,* Second Edition by Jane Halonen, University of West Florida, and Cynthia Gray, Alverno College**
Tied to the main topics in psychology, this engaging handbook includes six categories of critical thinking exercises: pattern recognition, practical problem solving, creative problem solving, scientific critical thinking, psychological reasoning, and perspective taking, which connect to the six categories used in the Critical Thinking Exercises available in the student Study Guide.

***Scientific American* Reader to Accompany *Introducing Psychology* by Daniel L. Schacter, Daniel T. Gilbert, and Daniel M. Wegner**
Exclusive to Worth Publishers and in partnership with *Scientific American*, this collection of articles features pioneering and cutting-edge research across the fields of psychology. Selected by the authors themselves, this collection provides further insight into the fields of psychology through articles written for a popular audience.

Scientific American Mind
Scientific American Mind is a new magazine from the editors of *Scientific American*. The magazine explores riveting breakthroughs in psychology, neuroscience, and related fields. *Scientific American Mind* investigates, analyzes, and reveals new thinking on a variety of contemporary psychological theories and ideas.

***Improving the Mind and Brain:* A *Scientific American* Special Issue**
This single-topic issue from *Scientific American* magazine features findings from the most distinguished researchers in the field.

***Scientific American Explores the Hidden Mind:* A Collector's Edition**
This collector's edition includes feature articles that explore and reveal the mysterious inner workings of our minds and brains.

Acknowledgments

Despite what you might guess by looking at our photographs, we all found women who were willing to marry us. We thank Susan McGlynn, Marilynn Oliphant, and Toni Wegner for that particular miracle and also for their love and support during the years when we were busy writing this book.

Although ours are the names on the cover, writing a textbook is a team sport, and we were lucky to have an amazing group of professionals in our dugout. One in particular—Catherine E. Myers of *Rutgers University-Newark*—provided invaluable assistance in helping us to identify and communicate the essential parts of each chapter. We owe her a significant debt of thanks. We also greatly appreciate the contributions of Martin M. Antony, Mark Baldwin, Patricia Csank, Denise D. Cummins, Ian J. Deary, Howard Eichenbaum, Paul Harris, Arthur S. Reber, Alan Swinkels, Richard M. Wenzlaff, and Steven Yantis.

We are grateful for the editorial, clerical, and research assistance we received from Celeste Beck, Amy Cameron, Beth Mela, Betsy Sparrow, Adrian Gilmore, and Alana Wong.

In addition, we would like to thank our core supplements authors. They provided insight into the role our book can play in the classroom and adeptly developed the materials to support it. Helen Just, Russ Frohardt, Alan Swinkels, and Claire Etaugh, we appreciate your tireless work in the classroom and the experience you brought to the book's supplements.

Over 1,000 students have class-tested chapters of *Introducing Psychology* in various stages of development. Not only are we encouraged by the overwhelmingly positive responses to *Introducing Psychology,* but we are also pleased to incorporate these students' insightful and constructive comments. In particular, we would like to thank the faculty who reviewed the manuscript in design, many of whom class-tested chapters with their introductory psychology students. They showed a level of engagement we have come to expect from our best colleagues and students:

Erica Altomare,
University of Pittsburgh at Titusville

Stephanie Anderson,
Central Community College

Jo Ann Armstrong,
Patrick Henry Community College

Harold Arnold,
Judson College

Cynthia Bane,
Wartburg College

Maida Berenblatt,
Suffolk County Community College

Cheryl Bluestone,
Queensborough Community College

Richard Brewer,
Southwest Baptist University

Wayne Briner,
University of Nebraska at Kearney

Rita Butterfield,
Sonoma State University

Shawn Charlton,
University of Central Arkansas

Veda Charlton,
University of Central Arkansas

Arthur Cherdack,
Los Angeles Valley College

Diana Ciesko,
Valencia Community College

Shirley Clay,
Northeast Texas Community College

David Devonis,
Graceland University

Adria DiBenedetto,
Quinnipiac University

Dale Doty,
St. John Fisher College

Dewitt Drinkard,
Danville Community College

Mirari Elcoro,
Armstrong Atlantic State University

Michael Feiler,
Merritt College

Carie Forden,
Clarion University

Pamela Frazier-Anderson,
Lincoln University

Danielle Gagne,
Alfred University

Michael Gardner,
Los Angeles Valley College

Marilyn Gibbons-Arhelger,
Texas State University

Sandra Gibbs,
Muskegon Community College

Arthur Gonchar,
University of La Verne

Dan Grangaard,
Austin Community College

Gary Greenberg,
Univeristy of Illinois at Chicago

Robert Guttentag,
University of North Carolina at Greensboro

Shawn Haake, *Iowa Central Community College*

Charles Hallock, *Pima County Community College*

Scot Hamilton,
University of West Georgia

Christopher Hayashi,
Southwestern College

Holly Haynes,
Georgia Gwinnett College

Ann Hennessey,
Pierce College

Stacie Herzog,
University of Wisconsin-Green Bay

James Higley,
Brigham Young University

Elizabeth Hood,
North Carolina Wesleyan College

Linda Jones,
Blinn College

Diane Kobrynowicz,
Austin Community College

Susan Lacke,
Concordia University Wisconsin

Cindy Lahar,
York County Community College

Christopher Long,
Ouachita Baptist University

Karsten Look,
Columbus State Community College

Judith Luna Meyer,
Beaufort County Community College

Sher'ri Madden Turner,
Illinois Central College

Elizabeth Maloney,
San Joaquin Delta College

John Marazita,
Ohio Dominican University

Christopher Mayhorn,
North Carolina State University

Dawn McBride,
Illinois State University

Jason McCoy,
Cape Fear Community College

Margaret McDevitt,
McDaniel College

Marcia McKinley,
Mount St. Mary's University

Barbara McMillan,
Alabama Southern Community College

Glenn Meyer,
Trinity University

Daniel Miller,
Wayne State College

Ronald Mossler,
Los Angeles Valley College

Paulina Multhaupt,
Macomb Community College

Bryan Neighbors,
Southwestern University

Caroline Olko,
Nassau Community College

Jennifer Ortiz Garza,
The Victoria College

Randall Osborne,
Texas State University

Carol Pandey,
Pierce College

Richard Pare,
University of Maine at Bangor

David Payne,
Wallace Community College

Kathleen Petrill,
Ashland University

Linda Petroff,
Central Community College

James Previte,
Victor Valley College

Frank Provenzano,
Greenville Technical College

Michael Rodman,
Middlesex Community College

Beverly Salzman,
Housatonic Community College

Patricia Sawyer,
Middlesex Community College

Nathan Saxon,
Somerset Community College

Asani Seawell,
Grinnell College

Leslie Sekerka,
Menlo College

Brian Siers,
Roosevelt University

Jerry Snead,
Coastal Carolina Community College

Jason Spiegelman,
Community College of Beaver County

Susan Spooner,
McLennan Community College

Jonathan Springer,
Kean University

David Steitz,
Nazareth College of Rochester

Krishna Stilianos,
Oakland Community College

Eva Szeli,
Arizona State University

Kathleen Taylor,
Sierra College

Jeri Thompson,
Hastings College

Michelle Tomaszycki,
Wayne State University

Meral Topcu,
Ferris State University

Sandra Trafalis,
San Jose State University

Sarah Trost,
Cardinal Stritch University

Ayme Turnbull,
Adelpi University

Jyotsna Vaid,
Texas A&M University

Linda Walsh,
University of Northern Iowa

Mary Waterstreet,
St. Ambrose University

Linda Weldon,
Community College of Baltimore County

Jan Wertz,
Centre College

Melissa Weston,
El Centro College

Nancy White,
Coastal Carolina Community College

Judith Wightman,
Kirkwood Community College

Peter Wooldridge,
Durham Technical Community College

Jennifer Yates,
Ohio Wesleyan University

Erin Young,
Texas A&M University

Lee Zasloff,
American River College

We learned a lot during the development of *Introducing* Psychology from focus group attendees, survey respondents, chapter reviewers, and class testers who read parts of our book, and we thank them for their time and insights, both of which were considerable. They include:

Art Beaman,
University of Kentucky

John Best,
Eastern Illinois University

Lyn T. Boulter,
Catawaba College

Kate Byerwalter,
Grand Rapids Community College

Dave Carroll,
University of Wisconsin, Superior

Elaine Cassel,
Lord Fairfax Community College

Heather Chabot,
New England College

Susan Cloninger,
The Sage Colleges

Nathalie Cote,
Belmont Abbey College

Catherine C. Crain,
Cascadia Community College

Christopher Cronin,
Saint Leo University

Robert DaPrato,
Solano Community College

Peggy DeCooke,
Purchase College

Wendy Domjan,
University of Texas, Austin

Evelyn Doody,
College of Southern Nevada

Kimberley Duff,
Cerritos College

Anne Duran,
California State University, Bakersfield

Claire Etaugh,
Bradley University

Kimberly Fairchild,
Manhattan College

Bryan D. Fantie,
American University

Meredyth Fellows,
West Chester University of Pennsylvania

Kevin Filter,
Minnesota State University

Krista Forrest,
University of Nebraska

Daniel Fox,
Sam Houston State University

Nelson Freedman,
Queen's University

Elizabeth Freeman,
Young Bentley University

Andrew Guest,
University of Portland

Rob Guttentag,
University of North Carolina at Greensboro

David Haaga,
American University

Gordon Hammerle,
Adrian College

Christine Homen,
Bristol Community College

Suzy Horton,
Mesa Community College

David Hothersall,
The Ohio State University

Allen Huffcutt,
Bradley University

Charles Huffman,
James Madison University

Annette Kujawski-Taylor,
University of San Diego

Fred Leavitt,
California State University, East Bay

Douglas Lenz,
Metropolitan Community College of Omaha

Mike Levine,
University of Illinois at Chicago

Nancey Lobb,
Alvin Community College

Cynthia Lofaso,
Central Virginia Community College

Anthony A. Lopez,
Cerritos College

Christopher May,
Carroll University

Kyla McKay,
Bristol Community College

Ann McKay,
Bristol Community College

Mitchell Metzger,
Ashland University

Judith Meyer,
Beaufort County Community College

Caroline Olko,
Nassau Community College

Barb Philibert,
Ashford University

Karyn Plumm,
University of North Dakota

Julia Raehpour,
Chippewa Valley Technical College

Dr. Bryan Raudenbush,
Wheeling Jesuit University

Vicki M. Ritts,
St. Louis Community College

Ana Ruiz,
Alvernia University

Deirdre Slavik,
Northwest Arkansas Community College

Helen Taylor,
Bellevue College Washington

Melissa Terlecki,
Cabrini College

Eleanor Webber,
Johnson State College

Paul Wellman,
Texas A&M University

Jamie Workman,
University of North Carolina Greensboro

We are especially grateful to the extraordinary people of Worth Publishers. They include our publisher, Catherine Woods, who provided guidance and encouragement at all stages of the project; our acquisitions editor, Charles Linsmeier, who managed the project with intelligence, grace, and good humor; our development editors, Valerie Raymond and Mimi Melek; our associate managing editor Tracey Kuehn, project editor Leo Kelly, production manager Sarah Segal, and assistant editor Jaclyn Castaldo, who through some remarkable alchemy turned a manuscript into a book; our art director Babs Reingold, layout designer Paul Lacy, photo editor Ted Szczepanski, and photo researcher Elyse Rieder, who made that book an aesthetic delight; our media editor Christine Burak, and production manager Stacey Alexander, who guided the development and creation of a superb supplements package; and our executive marketing manager Kate Nurre, and associate director of market development Carlise Stembridge, who served as tireless public advocates for our vision. Thank you one and all. We look forward to working with you again.

Daniel L. Schacter   Daniel T. Gilbert   Daniel M. Wegner
                                                          Cambridge, 2009

CHAPTER ONE

Psychology: The Evolution of a Science

A LOT WAS HAPPENING IN 1860. Abraham Lincoln had just been elected president, the Pony Express had just begun to deliver mail between Missouri and California, and a woman named Anne Kellogg had just given birth to a child who would one day grow up to invent the cornflake. But none of this mattered very much to William James, a bright, taciturn, 18-year-old who had no idea what to do with his life. He loved to paint and draw but worried that he wasn't talented enough to become a serious artist. He had enjoyed studying biology in school but doubted that a naturalist's salary would ever allow him to get married and have a family of his own. And so like many young people who are faced with difficult decisions about their futures, William abandoned his dreams and chose to do something in which he had little interest but of which his family heartily approved. Alas, within a few months of arriving at Harvard Medical School, his initial disinterest in medicine blossomed into a troubling lack of enthusiasm. With a bit of encouragement from the faculty, he put his medical studies on hold to join a biological expedition to the Amazon. When he returned to medical school, both his physical and mental health began to deteriorate. It was clear to everyone that William James was not the sort of person who should be put in charge of a scalpel and a bag of drugs.

James became so depressed that he was once again forced to leave medical school. He decided to travel around Europe, where he learned about a new science called *psychology* (from a combination of the Greek *psyche,* which means "soul," and *logos,* which means "to study"), which was just beginning to develop. As William read about psychology and talked with those who were developing it, he began to see that this new field was taking a modern, scientific approach to age-old questions about human nature—questions that had become painfully familiar to him during his personal search for meaning, but questions to which only poets and philosophers had ever before offered answers (Bjork, 1983; Simon, 1998). Excited about the new discipline, William returned to America and quickly finished his medical degree. But he never practiced medicine. Rather, he became a professor at Harvard University and devoted the rest of his life to psychology. His landmark book—*The Principles of Psychology*—is still widely read and remains one of the most influential books ever written on the subject (James, 1890). ■

Over the years, many young people, like this happy pair, have turned to travel as they considered their next step in life. Thankfully, for the young William James, his travels led him to psychology.

MIKE HARRINGTON/GETTY IMAGES

William James (1842—1910) was excited by the new field of psychology, which allowed him to apply a scientific approach to age-old questions about the nature of human beings.

A lot has happened since then. Abraham Lincoln has become the face on a penny, the Pony Express has been replaced by a somewhat slower mail system, and the Kellogg Company sells about $9 billion worth of cornflakes every year. If William James (1842–1910) were alive today, he would be amazed by all of these things. But he would probably be even more amazed by the intellectual advances that have taken place in the science that he helped create. Indeed, the sophistication and diversity of modern psychology are nothing short of staggering: Psychologists today are exploring perception, memory, creativity, consciousness, love, anxiety, addictions, and more. They use state-of-the-art technologies to examine what happens in the brain when people feel anger, recall a past experience, undergo hypnosis, or take an intelligence test. They examine the impact of culture on individuals, the origins and uses of language, the ways in which groups form and dissolve, and the similarities and differences between people from different backgrounds. Their research advances the frontiers of basic knowledge and has practical applications as well—from new treatments for depression and anxiety to new systems that allow organizations to function more effectively.

Psychology is *the scientific study of **mind** and **behavior.** The **mind** refers to our *private inner experience,* the ever-flowing stream of consciousness that is made of perceptions, thoughts, memories, and feelings. **Behavior** refers to *observable actions of human beings and nonhuman animals,* the things that we do in the world, by ourselves or with others. As you will see in the chapters to come, psychology is an attempt to use scientific methods to address fundamental questions about mind and behavior that have puzzled people for millennia. For example, psychologists would like to understand how the mind usually functions so effectively in the world, allowing us to accomplish tasks as mundane as tying our shoes, as extraordinary as sending astronauts to the moon, or as sublime as painting the *Mona Lisa.* Psychologists also want to understand why the mind occasionally functions so *in*effectively in the world, causing us to experience illusions in perception and gaps in memory. Let's take a look at some examples:

■ *What are the bases of perceptions, thoughts, memories, and feelings, or our subjective sense of self?* For thousands of years, philosophers tried to understand how the objective, physical world of the body was related to the subjective, psychological world of the mind, and some philosophers even suggested that the pineal gland in the brain might function as the magic tunnel between these two worlds. Today, psychologists know that there is no magic tunnel, and no need for one, because all of our subjective experiences arise from the electrical and chemical activities of our brains.

● **What are the bases of perceptions, thoughts, memories, and feelings, or our subjective sense of self?**

As you will see throughout this book, some of the most exciting developments in psychological research focus on how our perceptions, thoughts, memories, and feelings are related to activity in the brain. Psychologists and neuroscientists are using new technologies to explore this relationship in ways that would have seemed like science fiction only 20 years ago. For example, the technique known as *functional magnetic resonance imaging,* or fMRI, allows scientists to "scan" a living brain and see which parts are active when a person reads a word, sees a face, learns a new skill, or remembers a personal experience. What William James could only ponder, modern psychologists can observe.

■ *How does the mind usually allow us to function effectively in the world?* Scientists sometimes say that form follows function; that is, if we want to understand *how* something works (e.g., an engine or a thermometer), we need to know what it is working *for* (e.g., powering vehicles or measuring temperature). Psychological processes are said to be *adaptive,* which means that they promote the welfare and reproduction of organisms that engage in those processes.

For instance, perception allows us to recognize our families, see predators before they see us, and avoid stumbling into oncoming traffic. Language allows us

psychology The scientific study of mind and behavior.

mind Our private inner experience of perceptions, thoughts, memories, and feelings.

behavior Observable actions of human beings and nonhuman animals.

to organize our thoughts and communicate them to others, which enables us to form social groups and cooperate. Memory allows us to avoid solving the same problems over again every time we encounter them and to keep in mind what we are doing and why. Emotions allow us to react quickly to events that have "life or death" significance, and they enable us to form strong social bonds. The list goes on and on.

● **How does the mind usually allow us to function effectively in the world?**

Given the adaptiveness of psychological processes, it is not surprising that people with deficiencies in those processes often have a pretty tough time. Consider Elliot, a middle-aged husband and father with a good job, whose life was forever changed when surgeons discovered a tumor in the middle of his brain (Damasio, 1994). The surgeons were able to remove the tumor and save his life, but as time went on, Elliot started having trouble making decisions—and the decisions he did make were increasingly bad. He couldn't prioritize tasks at work because he couldn't decide what to do first, and when he did, he got it wrong. Eventually he was fired, so he pursued a series of risky business ventures—all of which failed, and he lost his life's savings. His wife divorced him, he married again, and his second wife divorced him. too. So what ruined Elliot's life? Elliot's brain had been damaged in a way that left him no longer able to experience emotions. For example, Elliot didn't experience anxiety when he poured his entire bank account into a foolish business venture, he didn't experience any sorrow when his wives left him, and he didn't experience any regret or anger when his boss showed him the door. Most of us have wished from time to time that we could be as stoic and unflappable as that; after all, who needs anxiety, sorrow, regret, and anger? The answer is that we all do. Emotions are adaptive because they function as signals that tell us when we are putting ourselves in harm's way. If you felt no anxiety when you thought about taking an upcoming exam, about borrowing your friend's car without permission, or about cheating on your taxes, you would probably make a string of poor decisions that would leave you without a degree and without a friend, except perhaps for your cellmate. Elliot didn't have those feelings, and he paid a big price for it.

SUPERSTUDIO/GETTY IMAGES

■ *Why does the mind occasionally function so ineffectively in the world?* The mind is an amazing machine that can do a great many things quickly. We can drive a car while talking to a passenger while recognizing the street address while remembering the name of the song that just came on the radio. But like all machines, the mind often trades accuracy for speed and versatility. This can produce "bugs" in the system, such as when a doughnut-making machine occasionally spews out gobs of gooey mush rather than dozens of delicious doughnuts. Our mental life is just as susceptible to *mind-bugs,* or occasional malfunctions in our otherwise-efficient

● **Why does the mind occasionally function so ineffectively in the world?**

mental processing. One of the most fascinating aspects of psychology is that we are *all* prone to a variety of errors and illusions. Indeed, if thoughts, feelings, and actions were error free, then human behavior would be orderly, predictable, and dull, which it clearly is not. Rather, it is endlessly surprising, and its surprises often derive from our ability to do precisely the wrong thing at the wrong time. Consider a few examples from diaries of people who took part in a study concerning mindbugs in everyday life (Reason & Mycielska, 1982, pp. 70–73):

■ *I meant to get my car out, but as I passed the back porch on my way to the garage, I stopped to put on my boots and gardening jacket as if to work in the yard.*

■ *I put some money into a machine to get a stamp. When the stamp appeared, I took it and said, "Thank you."*

■ *On leaving the room to go to the kitchen, I turned the light off, although several people were there.*

If these lapses seem amusing, it is because, in fact, they are. But they are also potentially important as clues to human nature. For example, notice that the person who bought a stamp said, "Thank you," to the machine and not, "How do I find the subway?" In other words, the person did not just do *any* wrong thing; rather, he did something that would have been perfectly right in a real social interaction. As each of these examples suggest, people often operate on "autopilot," or behave automatically, relying on well-learned habits that they execute without really thinking. When we are not actively focused on what we are saying or doing, these habits may be triggered inappropriately. William James thought that the influence of habit could help explain the seemingly bizarre actions of "absentminded" people: "Very absent-minded persons," he wrote in *The Principles of Psychology,* "on going into their bedroom to dress for dinner have been known to take off one garment after another and finally get into bed."

James understood that the mind's mistakes are as instructive as they are intriguing, and modern psychology has found it quite useful to study such mindbugs. Cars that are whole and unbroken cruise along nicely while leaving no clue about how they do their jobs. It is only when they break down that we learn about their engines, water pumps, and other fine pieces and processes that normally work together to produce the ride. In the same way, understanding lapses, errors, mistakes, and the occasionally buggy nature of human behavior provides a vantage point for understanding the normal operation of mental life and behavior. The story of Elliot, whose behavior broke down after he had brain surgery, is an example that highlights the role that emotions play in guiding normal judgment and behavior.

Psychology is exciting because it addresses fundamental questions about human experience and behavior, and the three questions we've just considered are merely the tip of the iceberg. Think of this book as a guide to exploring the rest of the iceberg. But before we don our parkas and grab our pick axes, we need to understand how the iceberg got here in the first place. To understand psychology in the 21st century, we need to become familiar with the psychology of the past.

Psychology's Roots: The Path to a Science of Mind

When the young William James interrupted his medical studies to travel in Europe during the late 1860s, he wanted to learn about human nature. But he confronted a very different situation than a similarly curious student would confront today, largely because psychology did not yet exist as an independent field of study. As James cheekily wrote, "The first lecture in psychology that I ever heard was the first I ever gave." Of course, that doesn't mean no one had ever thought about human nature before. For 2,000 years, philosophers had pondered such questions.

Psychology's Ancestors: The Great Philosophers

The desire to understand ourselves is not new. Greek thinkers such as Plato (428 BC–347 BC) and Aristotle (384 BC–322 BC) were among the first to struggle with fundamental questions about how the mind works (Robinson, 1995). For example, are cognitive abilities and knowledge inborn, or are they acquired only through experience? Plato argued in favor of **nativism**, which maintains that *certain kinds of knowledge are innate or inborn.* Children in every culture figure out early on that sounds can have meanings that can be arranged into words, which then can be arranged into sentences. Is the propensity to learn language "hardwired"—something that children are born with—or does the ability to learn language depend on the child's experience? Aristotle believed that the child's mind was

● **What fundamental question has puzzled philosophers ever since humans began thinking about behavior?**

nativism The philosophical view that certain kinds of knowledge are innate or inborn.

philosophical empiricism The philosophical view that all knowledge is acquired through experience.

phrenology A now defunct theory that specific mental abilities and characteristics, ranging from memory to the capacity for happiness, are localized in specific regions of the brain.

a *"tabula rasa"* (a blank slate) on which experiences were written, and he argued for **philo-sophical empiricism**, which holds that *all knowledge is acquired through experience.*

Although few modern psychologists believe that nativism or empiricism is entirely correct, the issue of just how much "nature" and "nurture" explain any given behavior is still a matter of controversy. In some ways, it is quite amazing that ancient philosophers were able to articulate so many of the important questions in psychology and offer many excellent insights into their answers without any access to scientific evidence. Their ideas came from personal observations, intuition, and speculation. Unfortunately, their approach provided no means of settling disputes, such as the nativism-empiricism debate, because they had no way of testing their theories. As you will see in Chapter 2, the ability to test a theory is the cornerstone of the scientific approach and the basis for reaching conclusions in modern psychology.

How do young children learn about the world? Plato believed that certain kinds of knowledge are innate, whereas Aristotle believed that the mind is a blank slate on which experiences are written.

From the Brain to the Mind: The French Connection

We all know that the brain and the body are physical objects that we can see and touch and that the subjective contents of our minds—our perceptions, thoughts, and feelings—are not. The French philosopher René Descartes (1596–1650) argued that body and mind are fundamentally different things—that the body is made of a material substance, whereas the mind (or soul) is made of an immaterial or spiritual substance. But if the mind and the body are different things made of different substances, then how do they interact? This is the problem of *dualism,* or how mental activity can be reconciled and coordinated with physical behavior.

Other philosophers, such as the British philosopher Thomas Hobbes (1588–1679), argued that the mind and body aren't different things at all; rather, the mind *is* what the brain *does*. From this perspective, looking for a place in the brain where the mind meets the body is like looking for the place in a television where the picture meets the flat panel display.

The French physician Franz Joseph Gall (1758–1828) also thought that brains and minds were linked. He examined the brains of animals and of people who had died of disease, or as healthy adults, or as children, and observed that mental ability often increases with larger brain size and decreases with damage to the brain. These aspects of Gall's findings were generally accepted (and the part about brain damage still is today). But Gall went far beyond his evidence to develop a psychological theory known as **phrenology**, which held that *specific mental abilities and characteristics, ranging from memory to the capacity for happiness, are localized in specific regions of the brain* (**FIGURE 1.1**). The idea that different parts of the brain are specialized for specific psychological functions turned out to be right; as you'll learn later in the book, a part of the brain called the hippocampus is intimately involved in memory, just as a structure called the amygdala is intimately involved in fear. But phrenology took this idea to an absurd extreme. Gall asserted that the size of bumps or indentations on the skull reflected the size of the brain regions beneath them and that by feeling those bumps, one could tell whether a person was friendly, cautious, assertive, idealistic, and so on. What Gall didn't realize was that bumps on the skull do not necessarily reveal anything about the shape of the brain underneath.

Phrenology made for a nice parlor game and gave young people a good excuse for touching each other, but in the end it amounted to a series of strong claims based on weak evidence and was quickly discredited (Fancher, 1979).

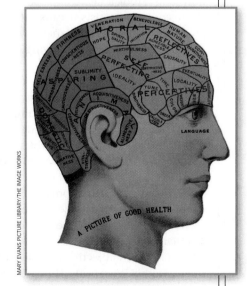

FIGURE 1.1 • • • • • • • • • • • • •
Phrenology *Francis Gall (1758–1828) developed a theory called phrenology, which suggested that psychological capacities (e.g., the capacity for friendship) and traits (e.g., cautiousness and mirth) were located in particular parts of the brain. The more of these capacities and traits a person had, the larger the corresponding bumps on the skull.*

● Surgeon Paul Broca (1824–1880) worked with a brain-damaged person who could comprehend but not produce spoken language. Broca suggested that the mind is grounded in the material processes of the brain.

While Gall was busy playing bumpologist, other French scientists were beginning to link the brain and the mind in a more convincing manner. Biologists began to conduct experiments in which they surgically removed specific parts of the brain from dogs, birds, and other animals and found (not surprisingly!) that their actions and movements differed from those of animals with intact brains. Although no one conducted similar experiments on humans, clues were emerging on that front as well. The surgeon Paul Broca (1825–1880) worked with a patient who had suffered damage to a small part of the left side of the brain (now known as Broca's area). The patient was virtually unable to speak and could utter only the single syllable "tan." Yet the patient understood everything that was said to him and was able to communicate using gestures. Broca had the crucial insight that damage to a specific part of the brain impaired a specific mental function, clearly demonstrating that the brain and mind are closely linked. This was important in the 19th century because at that time many people accepted Descartes' idea that the mind is separate from, but interacts with, the brain and the body. These studies were beginning to demonstrate that the mind is grounded in a material substance; namely, the brain. Their work jump-started the scientific investigation of mental processes.

● How did work involving patients with brain damage help demonstrate the mind-brain connection?

From Physiology to Psychology: A New Science Is Born

In the middle of the 19th century, psychology benefited from the work of German scientists who were trained in the field of **physiology**, which is *the study of biological processes, especially in the human body*. Physiologists had developed methods that allowed them to measure such things as the speed of nerve impulses, and some of them had begun to use these methods to measure mental abilities. William James was drawn to the work of two such physiologists: Hermann von Helmholtz (1821–1894) and Wilhelm Wundt (1832–1920). "It seems to me that perhaps the time has come for psychology to begin to be a science," wrote James in a letter written in 1867 during his visit to Berlin. "Helmholtz and a man called Wundt at Heidelberg are working at it."

The first of these men, Helmholtz, had developed a method for measuring the speed of nerve impulses in a frog's leg, a technique that he then adapted to the study of human beings. Helmholtz trained participants to respond when he applied a **stimulus**—*sensory input from the environment*—to different parts of the leg, and recorded his participants' **reaction time**, or *the amount of time taken to respond to a specific stimulus*. Helmholtz found that people generally took longer to respond when their toe was stimulated than when their thigh was stimulated, and the difference between these reaction times allowed him to estimate how long it took a nerve impulse to travel to the brain. These results were astonishing to 19th-century scientists because at that time just about everyone thought that mental processes occurred instantaneously. Helmholtz showed that this wasn't true; in fact, the neurological processes underlying mental events are not instantaneous, just very fast—so fast that no one before Helmholtz had been able to measure their speed.

Although Helmholtz's contributions were important, historians generally credit the official emergence of psychology to Helmholtz's research assistant, Wilhelm Wundt (Rieber, 1980). In 1867, Wundt taught what was probably the first university-level course in physiological psychology. A decade later, Wundt opened the first university laboratory ever to be exclusively devoted to psychological studies, and this event marked the official birth of psychology as an independent field of study. The new lab was full of graduate students carrying out research on topics assigned by Wundt, and it soon attracted young scholars from all over the world who were eager to learn about the new science that Wundt had developed.

Wundt believed that scientific psychology should focus on analyzing **consciousness**, *a person's subjective experience of the world and the mind*. Consciousness encompasses a broad range of subjective experiences. We may be conscious of sights, sounds, tastes, smells, bodily sensations, thoughts, or feelings.

physiology The study of biological processes, especially in the human body.

stimulus Sensory input from the environment.

reaction time The amount of time taken to respond to a specific stimulus.

consciousness A person's subjective experience of the world and the mind.

As Wundt tried to figure out a way to study consciousness scientifically, he noted that chemists try to understand the structure of matter by breaking down natural substances into basic elements. So he and his students adopted an approach called **structuralism**, or *the analysis of the basic elements that constitute the mind*. This approach involved breaking consciousness down into elemental sensations and feelings. Some of Wundt's studies involved **introspection**, which involves *the subjective observation of one's own experience*. In these studies, observers would be presented with a stimulus and asked to report their own introspections, or sensory experience.

Wundt also tried to provide objective measurements of conscious processes by using reaction time techniques similar to those first developed by Helmholtz. His research participants were instructed to press a button as soon as a tone sounded.

● **How did the work of chemists influence early psychology?**

Some participants were told to concentrate on perceiving the tone before pressing the button, whereas others were told to concentrate only on pressing the button. Those people who concentrated on the tone responded about one tenth of a second more slowly than those told to concentrate only on pressing the button. Wundt reasoned that both fast and slow participants had to register the tone in consciousness (perception), but only the slower participants had to also interpret the significance of the tone. The faster research participants, focusing only on the response they were to make, could respond automatically to the tone because they didn't have to engage in the additional step of interpretation (Fancher, 1979). This type of experimentation broke new ground by showing that psychologists could use scientific techniques to disentangle even subtle conscious processes. In fact, as you'll see in later chapters, reaction time procedures have proven extremely useful in modern research.

The pioneering efforts of Wundt's laboratory launched psychology as an independent science and profoundly influenced the field for the remainder of the 19th century. Many psychologists journeyed to Leipzig to study with Wundt. Among the most eminent was the British-born Edward Titchener (1867–1927), who studied with Wundt and then came to the United States and set up a psychology laboratory at Cornell University (where, if you'd like to see it, his brain is still on display in the psychology department). Titchener brought some parts of Wundt's approach to America, but whereas Wundt emphasized the relationship between elements of consciousness, Titchener focused on identifying the basic elements themselves. Titchener put forward a list of more than 44,000 elemental qualities of conscious experience, most of them visual (32,820) or auditory (11,600) (Schultz & Schultz, 1987).

structuralism The analysis of the basic elements that constitute the mind.

introspection The subjective observation of one's own experience.

ARCHIVES OF THE HISTORY OF AMERICAN PSYCHOLOGY

Wilhelm Wundt (1832–1920), far right, founded the first laboratory devoted exclusively to psychology at the University of Leipzig in Germany.

The influence of the structuralist approach gradually faded, due mostly to the introspective method. Science requires replicable observations; we could never determine the structure of DNA or the life span of a dust mite if every scientist who looked through a microscope saw something different. Alas, even trained observers provided conflicting introspections about their conscious experiences ("I see a cloud that looks like a duck"—"No, *I* think that cloud looks like a horse"), thus making it difficult for different psychologists to agree on the basic elements of conscious experience. Indeed, some psychologists had doubts about whether it was even possible to identify such elements through introspection alone. One of the most prominent skeptics was someone you've already met—a young man with a bad attitude and a useless medical degree—William James.

James and the Functional Approach

By the time James returned from his European tour, he was inspired by the idea of approaching psychological issues from a scientific perspective. He received a teaching appointment at Harvard (primarily because the president of the university was a neighbor and family friend) and taught the first course at an American university to draw on the new experimental psychology developed by Wundt and his German followers (Schultz & Schultz, 1987). These courses and experiments led James to write his masterpiece, *The Principles of Psychology* (James, 1890).

James disagreed with Wundt's claim that consciousness could be broken down into separate elements. James believed that trying to isolate and analyze a particular moment of consciousness (as the structuralists did) distorted the essential nature of consciousness. Consciousness, he argued, was more like a flowing stream than a bundle of separate elements. So James decided to approach psychology from a different perspective entirely, and he developed an approach known as **functionalism:** *the study of the purpose mental processes serve in enabling people to adapt to their environment.* In contrast to structuralism, which examined the structure of mental processes, functionalism set out to understand the functions those mental processes served. (See the Real World box for some strategies to enhance one of those functions—learning.)

James's thinking was inspired by the ideas in Charles Darwin's (1809–1882) recently published book on biological evolution, *The Origin of Species* (1859). Darwin

● **How does functionalism relate to Darwin's theory of natural selection?**

proposed the principle of **natural selection**, which states that *the features of an organism that help it survive and reproduce are more likely than other features to be passed on to subsequent generations.* From this perspective, James reasoned, mental abilities must have evolved because they were adaptive—that is, because they helped people solve problems and increased their chances of survival. Like other animals, people have always needed to avoid predators, locate food, build shelters, and attract mates. Applying Darwin's principle of natural selection, James (1890) reasoned that consciousness must serve an important biological function and the task for psychologists was to understand what those functions are. Wundt and the other structuralists worked in laboratories, and James felt that such work was limited in its ability to tell us how consciousness functioned in the natural environment. Wundt, in turn, felt that James did not focus enough on new findings from the laboratory that he and the structuralists had begun to produce. Commenting on *The Principles of Psychology*, Wundt conceded that James was a topflight writer but disapproved of his approach: "It is literature, it is beautiful, but it is not psychology" (Bjork, 1983, p. 12).

The rest of the world did not agree, and James's functionalist psychology quickly gained followers, especially in North America, where Darwin's ideas were influencing many thinkers.

functionalism The study of the purpose mental processes serve in enabling people to adapt to their environment.

natural selection Charles Darwin's theory that the features of an organism that help it survive and reproduce are more likely than other features to be passed on to subsequent generations.

[THE REAL WORLD] •

Improving Study Skills

Psychologists have progressed a great deal in understanding how we remember and learn. We'll explore the science of memory and learning in Chapters 5 and 6, but here we focus on the practical implications of psychological research for everyday life: how you can use psychology to improve your study skills. Such knowledge should help you perform your best in this course and others, but perhaps more importantly, it can help prepare you for challenges after graduation. With the rapid pace of technological change in our society, learning and memory skills are more important than ever. Experts estimate that the knowledge and skills required for success in a job will change completely every 3 to 7 years during an individual's career (Herrmann, Raybeck, & Gruneberg, 2002). Enhancing your learning and memory skills now should pay off for you later in life in ways we can't even yet predict.

Psychologists have focused on mental strategies that can enhance your ability to *acquire* information, to *retain* it over time, and to *retrieve* what you have acquired and retained. Let's begin with the process of acquiring information—that is, transforming what you see and hear into an enduring memory. Our minds don't work like video cameras, passively recording everything that happens around us. To acquire information effectively, you need to actively manipulate it. A particularly effective strategy is called *spaced rehearsal*, where you repeat information to yourself at increasingly long intervals. For example, suppose that you want to learn the name of a person you've just met named Eric. Repeat the name to yourself right away, wait a few seconds and think of it again, wait for a bit longer (maybe 30 seconds) and bring the name to mind once more, and then rehearse the name again after a minute and once more after 2 or 3 minutes. Studies show that this

"As I get older, I find I rely more and more on these sticky notes to remind me."

type of rehearsal improves long-term learning more than rehearsing the name without any spacing between rehearsals (Landauer & Bjork, 1978). You can apply this technique to names, dates, definitions, and many other kinds of information, including concepts presented in this textbook.

Another important lesson from psychological research is that we acquire information most effectively when we think about its meaning and reflect on its significance. For example, later in this chapter you'll read about Skinner's approach to behaviorism. As you read, ask yourself the following kinds of questions: How did behaviorism differ from previous approaches in psychology? What would a behaviorist like Skinner think about whether a mentally disturbed individual should be held responsible for committing a crime? In attempting to answer such questions, you will need to review what you've learned about behaviorism and then relate it to other things you already know about. This active review will help you remember the new information.

Another tip is to take some of the load off your memory by developing effective note-taking and outlining skills. Students often scribble down vague and

fragmentary notes during lectures, figuring that the notes will be good enough to jog memory later. But when the time comes to study, the notes are no longer clear. Realize that you can't write down everything an instructor says, and try to focus on making detailed notes about the main ideas, facts, and people mentioned in the lecture. Then, after the lecture, organize your notes into an outline that clearly highlights the major concepts. The act of organizing an outline will force you to reflect on the information in a way that promotes retention and will also provide you with a helpful study guide to promote self-testing and review.

Anxious feelings about an upcoming exam may be unpleasant, but as you've probably experienced yourself, they can motivate much-needed study.

The stage was set for functionalism to develop as a major school of psychological thought in North America. Psychology departments that embraced a functionalist approach started to spring up at many major American universities, and in a struggle for survival that would have made Darwin proud, functionalism became more influential than structuralism had ever been. By the time Wundt and Titchener died in the 1920s, functionalism was the dominant approach to psychology in North America.

summary quiz [1.1]

1. The notion that all knowledge is acquired through experience was proposed by
    a. Aristotle.
    b. Plato.
    c. Descartes.
    d. Hobbes.

2. Methods for measuring reaction time were first developed by
    a. Gall.
    b. Helmholtz.
    c. Wundt.
    d. Titchener.

3. The analysis of the basic elements that constitute the mind is called
    a. philosophical empiricism.
    b. phrenology.
    c. introspection.
    d. structuralism.

4. The study of how mental processes help people adapt to their environment is called
    a. nativism.
    b. structuralism.
    c. functionalism.
    d. natural selection.

············ FIGURE 1.2

The Mueller-Lyer Line Illusion
Although they do not appear to be, these two horizontal lines are actually the same length. The Gestalt psychologists used illusions like this to show how the perception of a whole object or scene can influence judgments about its individual elements.

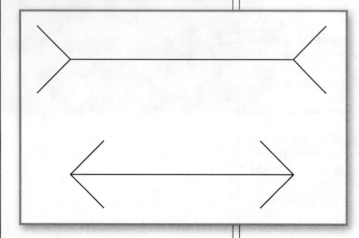

Errors and Illusions Reveal Psychology

At about the same time that some psychologists were developing structuralism and functionalism, other psychologists were beginning to think about how illusions and disorders might illuminate psychological functioning. They began to realize that one can often understand how something works by examining how it breaks. A careful examination of some mindbugs led to a clearer understanding of human mental functioning.

Illusions of Movement and the Birth of Gestalt Psychology

Magicians and artists could not earn a living unless people were susceptible to **illusions**—that is, *errors of perception, memory, or judgment in which subjective experience differs from objective reality.* For example, if you measure the dark horizontal lines shown in **FIGURE 1.2** with a ruler, you'll see that they are of equal length. And yet, for most of us, the top line appears longer than the bottom one. As you'll learn in Chapter 4, this is because the surrounding vertical lines influence your perception of the horizontal lines. A similar visual illusion fired the imagination of a German psychologist named Max Wertheimer (1880–1943), who was enjoying a train ride during his vacation when he had a sudden insight into the nature of visual perception. In Wertheimer's illusion, a person was shown two lines that flashed quickly on a screen, one after the other. One light was flashed through a vertical slit, the other through a diagonal slit. When the time between two flashes was relatively long (one fifth of a second or more), an observer would see two lights flashing in alternation. But when Wertheimer reduced the time between flashes to around one twentieth of a second, observers saw a single flash of light moving back and forth (Fancher, 1979; Sarris, 1989).

Creating the illusion of motion was not new. Turn-of-the-century moviemakers already understood that quickly flashing a series of still images, one after the other, could fool people into perceiving motion where none actually existed. But Wertheimer's *interpretation* of this illusion was the novel element that contributed to the

Max Wertheimer's (1880–1943) insights about the perception of motion offered a scientific explanation of why we see movement when viewing a series of rapidly flashed still pictures, a method used by moviemakers in the early 1900s.

Culture & Community

Why Is It That Most of Us, but Not All of Us, See the Top Line in Figure 1.2 as Longer Than the Bottom Line?

In the classic study, two groups of people classified culturally as European and non-European were asked to evaluate the length of the Mueller-Lyer lines (Segall, Campbell, & Herskovits, 1963). Europeans came to the wrong conclusion that the lines are of different lengths considerably more times than non-Europeans. The authors of the study inferred that people living in cities built of primarily rectangular shapes, as in European cities, see acute and obtuse angles drawn on paper as representative of three-dimensional space. The non-Europeans in this study, primarily from rural hunting and gathering groups from southern Africa, did not make this mental leap, and so were more likely to see the lines as they truly are: of the same length.

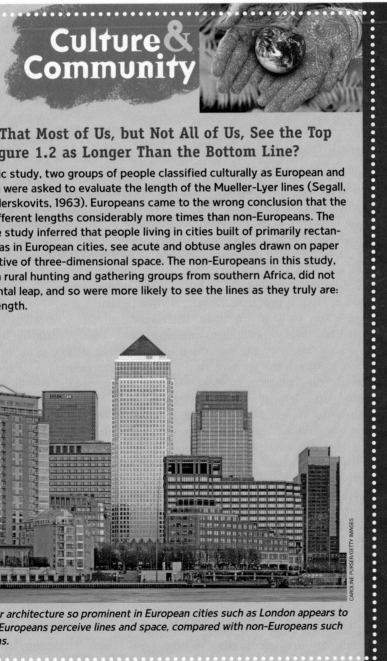

The rectangular architecture so prominent in European cities such as London appears to influence how Europeans perceive lines and space, compared with non-Europeans such as rural Africans.

illusions Errors of perception, memory, or judgment in which subjective experience differs from objective reality.

growth of psychology (Benjamin, 1988; Steinman, Pizlo, & Pizlo, 2000). He reasoned that the perceived motion could not be explained in terms of the separate elements that cause the illusion (the two flashing lights) but instead that the moving flash of light is perceived as a *whole* rather than as the sum of its two parts. This unified whole, which in German is called *Gestalt,* makes up the perceptual experience. Wertheimer's interpretation of the illusion led to the development of **Gestalt psychology**, *a psychological approach that emphasizes that we often perceive the whole rather than the sum of the parts.*

● **How did the earliest movies influence Gestalt psychology?**

In other words, the mind imposes organization on what it perceives, so people don't see what the experimenter actually shows them (two separate lights); instead, they see the elements as a unified whole (one moving light). This analysis provides an excellent illustration of how illusions can offer clues about the basic principles of the mind.

The Gestaltists' claim was diametrically opposed to the structuralists' claim that experience can be broken down into separate elements. Although Gestalt psychology no longer exists today as a distinct school of thought, its basic claims have influenced the modern study of object perception (as you'll see in Chapter 4) as well as social perception (as you'll see in Chapter 16). Indeed, the notion that the mind imposes structure and organization remains one of modern psychology's most widely accepted principles.

Mental Disorders and Multiple Selves

While the Gestalt psychologists were discovering that illusions in visual perception can help us understand how the eye and the brain normally work so well, other psychologists were discovering how the bizarre behaviors of patients with psychological disorders could shed light on the workings of the ordinary mind. For example, French physicians Jean-Marie Charcot (1825–1893) and Pierre Janet (1859–1947) interviewed patients who had developed a condition known then as **hysteria**, or a *temporary loss of cognitive or motor functions, usually as a result of emotionally upsetting experiences.* Hysterical patients became blind, paralyzed, or lost their memories, even though there was no known physical cause of their problems. However, when the patients were put into a trancelike state through the use of hypnosis (an altered state of consciousness characterized by suggestibility), their symptoms disappeared: Blind patients could see, paralyzed patients could walk, and forgetful patients could remember. After coming out of the hypnotic trance, however, the patients forgot what had happened under hypnosis and again showed their symptoms. In short, the patients behaved like two different people in the waking versus hypnotic states.

Such psychological disorders were ignored by Wundt, Titchener, and other laboratory scientists, who did not consider them a proper subject for scientific psychology (Bjork, 1983). But William James believed such mental disruptions reflected mindbugs at work, which had important implications for understanding the nature of the mind (Taylor, 2001). During our ordinary conscious experience, we are only aware of a single " or "self," but the aberrations described by Charcot,

● **What do mindbugs teach us about the mind?**

Janet, and others suggested that the brain can create many conscious selves that are not aware of each other's existence (James, 1890, p. 400). These striking observations also fueled the imagination of a young physician from Vienna, Austria, who studied with Charcot in Paris in 1885. His name was Sigmund Freud (1856–1939).

Freud and Psychoanalytic Theory

After his visit to Charcot's clinic in Paris, Freud returned to Vienna, where he continued his work with hysteric patients. (The word *hysteria,* by the way, comes from the Latin word *hyster,* which means "womb." It was once thought that only women suffered from

---

Gestalt psychology A psychological approach that emphasizes that we often perceive the whole rather than the sum of the parts.

hysteria A temporary loss of cognitive or motor functions, usually as a result of emotionally upsetting experiences.

unconscious The part of the mind that operates outside of conscious awareness but influences conscious thoughts, feelings, and actions.

psychoanalytic theory Sigmund Freud's approach to understanding human behavior that emphasizes the importance of unconscious mental processes in shaping feelings, thoughts, and behaviors.

psychoanalysis A therapeutic approach that focuses on bringing unconscious material into conscious awareness to better understand psychological disorders.

In this photograph, Sigmund Freud (1856—1939) sits by the couch reserved for his psychoanalytic patients.

hysteria, which was thought to be caused by a "wandering womb.") Freud began to make his own observations of hysteric patients and develop theories to explain their strange behaviors and symptoms. Freud theorized that many of the patients' problems could be traced to the effects of painful childhood experiences that the person could not remember, and he suggested that the powerful influence of these seemingly lost memories revealed the presence of an unconscious mind. According to Freud, the **unconscious** is *the part of the mind that operates outside conscious awareness but influences conscious thoughts, feelings, and actions.* This idea led Freud to develop **psychoanalytic theory**, *an approach that emphasizes the importance of unconscious mental processes in shaping feelings, thoughts, and behaviors.* From a psychoanalytic perspective, it is important to uncover a person's early experiences and to illuminate a person's unconscious anxieties, conflicts, and desires. Psychoanalytic theory formed the basis for a therapy that Freud called **psychoanalysis**, which focuses on *bringing unconscious material into conscious awareness.* During psychoanalysis, patients recalled past experiences ("When I was a toddler, I was frightened by a masked man on a black horse") and related their dreams and fantasies ("Sometimes I close my eyes and imagine not having to pay for this session"). Psychoanalysts used Freud's theoretical approach to interpret what their patients said. In the early 1900s, Freud and a growing number of followers formed a psychoanalytic movement. Carl Gustav Jung (1875–1961) and Alfred Adler (1870–1937) were prominent in the movement, but both were independent thinkers, and Freud apparently had little tolerance for individuals who challenged his ideas. Soon enough, Freud broke off his relationships with both men so that he could shape the psychoanalytic movement himself (Sulloway, 1992). Psychoanalytic theory became quite controversial because it suggested that understanding a person's thoughts, feelings, and behavior required a thorough exploration of the person's early sexual experiences and unconscious sexual desires. In those days these topics were considered far too racy for scientific discussion.

Freud, and most of his early followers, were trained as physicians and did not conduct psychological experiments in the laboratory (though early in his career, Freud did do some nice laboratory work on the sexual organs of eels). By and large, psychoanalysts did not hold positions in universities and developed their ideas in isolation from the research-based approaches of James and others. Although James worked in an academic setting and Freud worked with clinical patients, both men believed that mental aberrations provide important clues into the nature of mind. Each thinker, in his own way, recognized the value of pursuing mindbugs as a clue to human functioning.

humanistic psychology An approach to understanding human nature that emphasizes the positive potential of human beings.

Influence of Psychoanalysis and the Humanistic Response

Most historians consider Freud to be one of the most influential thinkers of the 20th century, and the psychoanalytic movement influenced everything from literature and history to politics and art. Within psychology, psychoanalysis had its greatest impact on clinical practice, but that influence has been considerably diminished over the past 40 years.

This is partly because Freud's vision of human nature was a dark one, emphasizing limitations and problems rather than possibilities and potentials. He saw people as hostages to their forgotten childhood experiences and primitive sexual impulses, and the inherent pessimism of his perspective frustrated those psychologists who had a more optimistic view of human nature. Freud's ideas were also difficult to test, and a theory that can't be tested is of limited use in psychology or other sciences. Though Freud's emphasis on unconscious processes has had an enduring impact on psychology, psychologists began to have serious misgivings about many aspects of Freud's theory.

● Why are Freud's ideas less influential today?

In the years after World War II, psychologists such as Abraham Maslow (1908–1970) and Carl Rogers (1902–1987) pioneered a new movement called **humanistic psychology**, *an approach to understanding human nature that emphasizes the positive potential of human beings.* Humanistic psychologists focused on the highest aspirations that people had for themselves. Rather than viewing people as prisoners of events in their remote pasts, humanistic psychologists viewed people as free agents who have an inherent need to develop, grow, and attain their full potential. This movement reached its peak in the 1960s when a generation of "flower children" found it easy to see psychological life as a kind of blossoming of the spirit. Humanistic therapists sought to help people realize their full potential; in fact, they called them "clients" rather than "patients." In this relationship, the therapist and the client (unlike the psychoanalyst and the patient) were on equal footing. In fact, the development of the humanistic perspective was one more reason why Freud's ideas became less influential.

Carl Rogers (1902–1987) (left) and Abraham Maslow (1908–1970) (right) introduced a positive, humanistic psychology in response to what they viewed as the overly pessimistic view of psychoanalysis.

UNIVERSITY OF CALIFORNIA, SANTA BARBARA

BETTMANN/CORBIS

summary quiz [1.2]

5. The approach that emphasizes that we often perceive the whole rather than the sum of its parts is called
   a. introspection.
   b. humanistic psychology.
   c. psychoanalytic theory.
   d. gestalt psychology.

6. The temporary loss of cognitive or motor function, usually resulting from emotional upsetting experiences, is called
   a. reaction time.
   b. the unconscious.
   c. hysteria.
   d. split personality.

7. Which psychological theory emphasizes the importance of the unconscious in determining behavior?
   a. psychoanalytic theory
   b. humanistic psychology
   c. Gestalt psychology
   d. functionalism

8. The psychological theory that emphasizes the positive potential of human beings is known as
   a. psychoanalytic theory.
   b. humanistic psychology.
   c. Gestalt psychology.
   d. structuralism.

behaviorism An approach that advocates that psychologists restrict themselves to the scientific study of objectively observable behavior.

Psychology in the 20th Century: Behaviorism Takes Center Stage

The schools of psychological thought that had developed by the early 20th century—structuralism, functionalism, psychoanalysis, Gestalt psychology, and humanism—differed substantially from one another. But they shared an important similarity: Each tried to understand the inner workings of the mind by examining conscious perceptions, thoughts, memories, and feelings or by trying to elicit previously unconscious material, all of which were reported by participants in experiments or patients in a clinical setting. In each case, it proved difficult to establish with much certainty just what was going on in people's minds, due to the unreliable nature of the method-

● **How did behaviorism help psychology advance as a science?**

ology. As the 20th century unfolded, a new approach developed as psychologists challenged the idea that psychology should focus on mental life at all. This new approach was called **behaviorism**, which advocated that psychologists should restrict themselves to *the scientific study of objectively observable behavior.* Behaviorism represented a dramatic departure from previous schools of thought.

Watson and the Emergence of Behaviorism

John Watson (1878–1958) believed that private experience was too idiosyncratic and vague to be an object of scientific inquiry. Science required replicable, objective measurements of phenomena that were accessible to all observers, and the introspective methods used by structuralists and functionalists were far too subjective for that. So instead of describing conscious experiences, Watson proposed that psychologists focus entirely on the study of behavior—what people *do*, rather than what people *experience*—because behavior can be observed by anyone and can be measured objectively.

At the time, animal behavior specialists such as Margaret Floy Washburn were arguing that nonhuman animals, much like human animals, have conscious mental experiences (Scarborough & Furumoto, 1987). Watson reacted to this claim with venom. Because we cannot ask pigeons about their private, inner experiences (well, we can *ask*, but they never tell us), Watson decided that the only way to understand how animals learn and adapt was to focus solely on their behavior, and he suggested that the study of human beings should proceed on the same basis. Watson was influenced by the work of the Russian physiologist Ivan Pavlov (1849–1936), who carried out pioneering research on the physiology of digestion. In the course of this work, Pavlov noticed something interesting about the dogs he was studying (Fancher, 1979). Not only did the dogs salivate at the sight of food; they also salivated at the sight of the person who fed them.

In 1894, Margaret Floy Washburn (1871–1939), a student of Edward Titchener at Cornell, became the first woman to receive a PhD degree in psychology. Washburn went on to a highly distinguished career, spent mainly in teaching and research at Vassar College in Poughkeepsie, New York. Washburn wrote an influential book, The Animal Mind, developed a theory of consciousness, and contributed to the development of psychology as a profession.

The feeders were not dressed in Alpo suits, so why should the mere sight of them trigger a basic digestive response in the dogs? To answer this question, Pavlov developed a procedure in which he sounded a tone every time he fed the dogs, and after a while he observed that the dogs would salivate when they heard the tone alone. In Pavlov's experiments, the sound of the tone was a stimulus—sensory input from the environment—that influenced the salivation of the dogs, which was a **response**—*an action or physiological change elicited by a stimulus.* Watson and other behaviorists made these two notions the building blocks of their theories, which is why behaviorism is sometimes called "stimulus-response" or "S-R" psychology.

B. F. Skinner and the Development of Behaviorism

In 1926, Burrhus Frederick Skinner (1904–1990) graduated from Hamilton College. Like William James, Skinner couldn't decide what to do with his life. He aspired to become a writer and wondered whether a novelist could portray a character without understanding why the character behaved as he or she did. When he came across Watson's books, he knew he had the answer. Skinner completed his PhD studies in psychology at Harvard (Wiener, 1996) and began to develop a new kind of behaviorism. In Pavlov's experiments, the dogs had been passive participants that stood around, listened to tones, and drooled. Skinner recognized that in everyday life, animals don't just stand there—they do something! Animals *act* on their environments in order to find shelter, food, or mates, and. Skinner wondered if he could develop behaviorist principles that would explain how they *learned* to act in those situations.

Skinner built what he called a "conditioning chamber" but what the rest of the world would forever call a "Skinner box." The box has a lever and a food tray, and a hungry rat could get food delivered to the tray by pressing the lever. Skinner observed that when a rat was put in the box, it would wander around, sniffing and exploring, and would usually press the bar by accident, at which point a food pellet would drop into the tray. After that happened, the rate of bar pressing would increase dramatically and remain high until the rat was no longer hungry. Skinner saw evidence for what he called the principle of **reinforcement**, which states that *the consequences of a behavior determine whether it will be more or less likely to occur again.* The concept of reinforcement became the foundation for Skinner's new approach to behaviorism (see Chapter 6), which he formulated in a landmark book, *The Behavior of Organisms* (Skinner, 1938).

Skinner set out to use his ideas about reinforcement to help improve the quality of everyday life. He was visiting his daughter's fourth-grade class when he realized that he might be able to improve classroom instruction by breaking a complicated task into small bits and then using the principle of reinforcement to teach children each bit (Bjork, 1993). He developed automatic devices known as "teaching machines" that did exactly that (Skinner, 1958). The teaching machine asked a series of increasingly difficult questions that built on the students' answers to the simpler ones. To learn a complicated math problem, for instance, students would first be asked an easy question about the simplest part of the problem. They would then be told whether the answer was right or wrong, and if a correct response was made, the machine would move on to a more difficult question. Skinner thought that the satisfaction of knowing they were correct would be reinforcing and help students learn.

If fourth graders and rats could be successfully trained, then why stop there? In the controversial books *Beyond Freedom and Dignity* (1971) and *Walden II* (1948/ 1986), Skinner put forth the simple but stunning claim that our subjective sense of free will is an illusion and that when we think we are exercising free will, we are actually responding to present and past patterns of reinforcement. We do things in the present that have been rewarding in the past, and our sense of "choosing" to do them is nothing more than an illusion. Not surprisingly, Skinner's claims sparked an outcry from critics who believed that Skinner

● **Which of Skinner's claims provoked an outcry?**

@ ONLY HUMAN

"A" TRAIN FROM THE COOP TO HEATHROW A full page of letters from readers in an issue of *New Scientist* magazine reported sightings by London, England, subway riders of pigeons boarding, and disembarking from, subway cars in "purposeful" ways that suggest they have figured out where they are going.

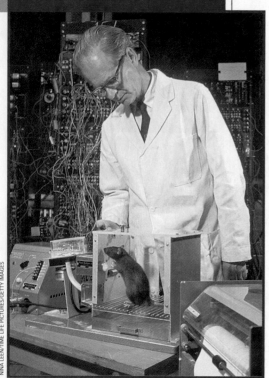

● *Inspired by Watson's behaviorism, B. F. Skinner (1904–1990) investigated the way an animal learns by interacting with its environment. Here, he demonstrates the "Skinner box," in which rats learn to press a lever to receive food.*

NINA LEEN/TIME LIFE PICTURES/GETTY IMAGES

was giving away one of our most cherished attributes—free will—and calling for a repressive society that manipulated people for its own ends. Given the nature of Skinner's ideas, the critics' attacks were understandable—he had seriously underestimated how much people cherish the idea of free will—but in the sober light of hindsight, the attacks were clearly overblown. Skinner did not want to turn society into a "dog obedience school" or strip people of their personal freedoms. Rather, he argued that an understanding of the principles by which behavior is generated could be used to increase the social welfare, which is precisely what happens when a government launches advertisements to encourage citizens to drink milk or quit smoking. The result of all the controversy, however, was that Skinner's fame reached a level rarely attained by psychologists. A popular magazine that listed the 100 most important people who ever lived ranked Skinner just 39 points below Jesus Christ (Herrnstein, 1977).

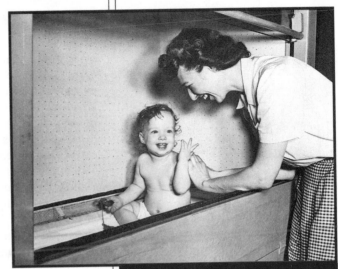

Skinner's well-publicized questioning of such cherished notions as free will led to a rumor that he had raised his own daughter in a Skinner box. This urban legend, while untrue, likely originated from the climate-controlled, glass-encased crib that he invented to protect his daughter from the cold Minnesota winter. Skinner marketed the crib under various names, including the "Air-crib" and the "Heir Conditioner," but it failed to catch on with parents.

summary quiz [1.3]

9. The approach that stresses the scientific study of objectively observable behavior is known as

   a. conditioning.
       c. behaviorism.

   b. reinforcement.
       d. stimulus-reaction time theory.

10. The person who studied why dogs salivate at the sight of the person who feeds them was

   a. John Watson.
       c. Margaret Floy Washburn.

   b. Ivan Pavlov.
       d. B. F. Skinner.

11. The notion that the consequences of a behavior determine whether it will be likely to occur again was formulated by

   a. B. F. Skinner.
       c. Ivan Pavlov.

   b. Margaret Floy Washburn.
       d. John Watson.

Beyond Behaviorism: Psychology Expands

Watson, Skinner, and the behaviorists dominated psychology from the 1930s to the 1950s. The psychologist Ulric Neisser recalled the atmosphere when he was a student at Swarthmore in the early 1950s:

> Behaviorism was the basic framework for almost all of psychology at the time. It was what you had to learn. That was the age when it was supposed that no psychological phenomenon was real unless you could demonstrate it in a rat (quoted in Baars, 1986, p. 275).

But although behaviorism allowed psychologists to measure, predict, and control behavior, it did this by ignoring some important things. First, it ignored the mental processes that had fascinated psychologists such as Wundt and James and, in so doing, found itself unable to explain some very important phenomena, such as how children learn language. Second, it ignored the evolutionary history of the organisms it studied and was thus unable to explain why, for example, a rat could learn to associate nausea with food much more quickly than it could learn to associate nausea with a tone or a light.

response An action or physiological change elicited by a stimulus.

reinforcement The consequences of a behavior that determine whether it will be more likely that the behavior will occur again.

"What about that! His brain still uses the old vacuum tubes."

The Emergence of Cognitive Psychology

Even at the height of behaviorist domination, there were a few quiet revolutionaries whose research and writings were focused on mental processes. For example, Sir Frederic Bartlett (1886–1969) was a British psychologist interested in memory. Dissatisfied with existing research, he believed that it was more important to examine memory for the kinds of information people actually encounter in everyday life. Bartlett gave people stories to remember and carefully observed the kinds of errors they made when they tried to recall them some time later (Bartlett, 1932). Bartlett discovered that research participants often remembered what *should* have happened or what they *expected* to happen rather than what actually *did* happen. These and other errors led Bartlett to suggest that memory is not a photographic reproduction of past experience and that our attempts to recall the past are powerfully influenced by our knowledge, beliefs, hopes, aspirations, and desires.

Another researcher who focused on mental processes was Jean Piaget (1896–1980), who studied the perceptual and cognitive errors of children in order to gain insight into the nature and development of the human mind. For example, in one of his tasks, Piaget would give a 3-year-old child a large and a small mound of clay and tell the child to make the two mounds equal. Then Piaget would break one of the clay mounds into smaller pieces and ask the child which mound now had more clay. Although the amount of clay remained the same, of course, 3-year-old children usually said that the mound that was broken into smaller pieces was bigger, but by the age of 6 or 7, they no longer made this error. As you'll see in Chapter 9, Piaget theorized that younger children lack a particular cognitive ability that allows older children to appreciate the fact that the mass of an object remains constant even when it is divided. For Piaget, mindbugs such as these provided key insights into the mental world of the child (Piaget & Inhelder, 1969).

The German psychologist Kurt Lewin (1890–1947) was also a pioneer in the study of thought at a time when thought had been banished from psychology. Lewin (1936) argued that one could best predict a person's behavior in the world by understanding the person's subjective experience of the world. A television soap opera is a meaningless series of unrelated physical movements unless one thinks about the characters' experiences—how Karen feels about Bruce; what Van was planning to say to Kathy about Emily; and whether Linda's sister, Nancy, will always hate their mother for meddling in the marriage. Lewin realized that it was not the stimulus, but rather the person's *construal* of the stimulus, that determined the person's subsequent behavior. A pinch on the cheek can be pleasant or unpleasant depending on who administers it, under what circumstances, and to which set of cheeks. Lewin used a special kind of mathematics called *topology* to model the person's subjective experience, and although his topological theories were not particularly influential, his attempts to model mental life and his insistence that psychologists study how people construe their worlds would have a lasting impact on psychology.

● **How did computers influence the study of psychology?**

But, aside from a handful of pioneers such as these, most psychologists happily ignored mental processes until the 1950s, when something important happened: the computer. The advent of computers had enormous practical impact, of course, but it also had a giant conceptual impact on psychology. People and computers differ in many ways, but both seem to register, store, and retrieve information, leading psychologists to wonder whether the computer might be used as a model for the human mind. Computers are information-processing systems, and the flow of information through their circuits is clearly no fairy tale. If psychologists could think of mental events—such as remembering, attending, thinking, believing, evaluating,

Jean Piaget (1896—1980) studied and theorized about the developing mental lives of children, a marked departure from the observations of external behavior dictated by the methods of the behaviorists.

BETTMANN/CORBIS

This 1950s computer was among the first generation of digital computers. Although different in many ways, computers and the human brain both process and store information, which led many psychologists at the time to think of the mind as a computer. Researchers currently adopt a more sophisticated view of the mind and the brain, but the computer analogy was helpful in the early days of cognitive psychology.

feeling, and assessing—as the flow of information through the mind, then they might be able to study the mind scientifically after all. The emergence of the computer led to a reemergence of interest in mental processes all across the discipline of psychology, and it spawned a new approach called **cognitive psychology**, which is *the scientific study of mental processes, including perception, thought, memory, and reasoning.*

Ironically, the emergence of cognitive psychology was also energized by the appearance of a book by B. F. Skinner called *Verbal Behavior,* which offered a behaviorist analysis of language (Skinner, 1957). A linguist at the Massachusetts Institute of Technology (MIT), Noam Chomsky (b. 1928), published a devastating critique of the book in which he argued that Skinner's insistence on observable behavior had caused him to miss some of the most important features of language. According to Chomsky, language relies on mental rules that allow people to understand and produce novel words and sentences. The ability of even the youngest child to generate new sentences that he or she had never heard before flew in the face of the behaviorist claim that children learn to use language by reinforcement. Chomsky provided a clever, detailed, and thoroughly cognitive account of language that could explain many of the phenomena that the behaviorist account could not (Chomsky, 1959).

These developments during the 1950s set the stage for an explosion of cognitive studies during the 1960s. Cognitive psychologists did not return to the old introspective procedures used during the 19th century, but instead they developed new and ingenious methods that allowed them to study cognitive processes.

RICK FRIEDMAN/CORBIS

Noam Chomsky's (b. 1928) critique of Skinner's theory of language signaled the end of behaviorism's dominance in psychology and helped spark the development of cognitive psychology.

The Brain Meets the Mind: The Rise of Cognitive Neuroscience

If cognitive psychologists studied the software of the mind, they had little to say about the hardware of the brain. And yet, as any computer scientist knows, the relationship between software and hardware is crucial: Our mental activities depend on intricate operations carried out by the brain. This dependence is revealed by dramatic cases in which damage to a particular part of the brain causes a person to lose a specific cognitive ability. Recall Broca's patient who, after damage to a limited area in the left side of the brain, could not produce words—even though he could understand them perfectly well. As you'll see later in the book, damage to other parts of the brain can also result in syndromes that are characterized by the loss of specific mental abilities (e.g.,

cognitive psychology The scientific study of mental processes, including perception, thought, memory, and reasoning.

behavioral neuroscience An approach to psychology that links psychological processes to activities in the nervous system and other bodily processes.

cognitive neuroscience A field that attempts to understand the links between cognitive processes and brain activity.

evolutionary psychology A psychological approach that explains mind and behavior in terms of the adaptive value of abilities that are preserved over time by natural selection.

prosopagnosia, in which the person cannot recognize human faces) or by the emergence of bizarre behavior or beliefs (e.g., Capgras syndrome, in which the person believes that a close family member has been replaced by an imposter). These striking—sometimes startling—cases remind us that even the simplest cognitive processes depend on the brain.

Karl Lashley (1890–1958), a psychologist who studied with Watson, conducted a famous series of studies in which he trained rats to run mazes, surgically removed parts of their brains, and then measured how well they could run the maze again. Lashley hoped to find the precise spot in the brain where the rat's memories for how to navigate through the maze were stored. Alas, no one spot seemed to uniquely and reliably eliminate memory (Lashley, 1960). Rather, Lashley simply found that the more of the rat's brain he removed, the more poorly the rat ran the maze. Lashley was frustrated by his inability to identify a specific site of learning, but his efforts inspired other scientists to take up the challenge. They developed a research area called *physiological psychology*. Today, this area has grown into **behavioral neuroscience**, which *links psychological processes to activities in the nervous system and other bodily processes*. To learn about the relationship between brain and behavior, behavioral neuroscientists observe animals' responses as the animals perform specially constructed tasks, such as running through a maze to obtain food rewards. The neuroscientists can record electrical or chemical responses in the brain as the task is being performed or remove specific parts of the brain to see how performance is affected (**FIGURE 1.3**).

Of course, experimental brain surgery cannot ethically be performed on human beings, and thus psychologists who want to study how damage affects the human brain have to rely on nature's cruel and inexact experiments. Birth defects, accidents, and illnesses often cause damage to particular brain regions, and if this damage disrupts a particular ability, then psychologists deduce that the damaged region is involved in producing the ability. (Broca's patient, about whom you read earlier, and whose brain damage devastated the ability to use language, was one such example.) But in the late 1980s, technological breakthroughs led to the development of noninvasive "brain-scanning" techniques that made it possible for psychologists to watch what happens inside a human brain as a person performs a task such as reading, imagining, listening, or remembering. Brain scanning is an invaluable tool because it allows us to observe the brain in action and to see which parts are involved in which operations (see Chapter 3).

● What have we learned by watching the brain at work?

For example, researchers used scanning technology to identify the parts of the brain in the left hemisphere that are involved in specific aspects of language, such as understanding or producing words (Peterson et al., 1989). Later scanning studies showed that people who are deaf from birth but who learn to communicate using American

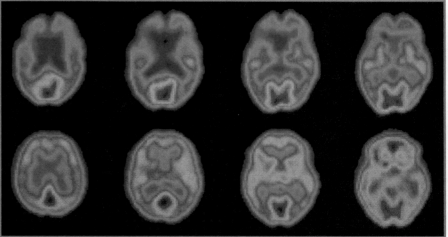

FIGURE 1.3

PET Scans of Healthy and Alzheimer's Brains *PET scans are one of a variety of brain-imaging technologies that psychologists use to observe the living brain. The four brain images on the top each come from a person suffering from Alzheimer's disease; the four on the bottom each come from a healthy person of similar age. The red and green areas reflect higher levels of brain activity compared to the blue areas, which reflect lower levels of activity. In each image, the front of the brain is on the top, and the back of the brain is on the bottom. You can see that the patient with Alzheimer's disease, compared with the healthy person, shows more extensive areas of lowered activity toward the front of the brain.*

ROGER RESSMEYER/CORBIS

Sign Language (ASL) rely on regions in the right hemisphere (as well as the left) when using ASL. In contrast, people with normal hearing who learned ASL after puberty seem to rely only on the left hemisphere when using ASL (Newman et al., 2002). These findings suggest that although both spoken and signed language usually rely on the left hemisphere, the right hemisphere also can become involved—but only for a limited period (perhaps until puberty). The findings also provide a nice example of how psychologists can now use scanning techniques to observe people with various kinds of cognitive capacities and use their observations to unravel the mysteries of the mind and the brain (**FIGURE 1.4**). In fact, there's a name for this area of research. **Cognitive neuroscience** is the *field that attempts to understand the links between cognitive processes and brain activity* (Gazzaniga, 2000).

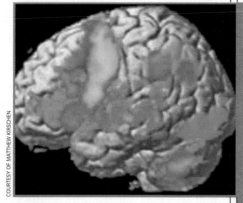

COURTESY OF MATTHEW KIRSCHEN

The Adaptive Mind: The Emergence of Evolutionary Psychology

Psychology's renewed interest in mental processes and its growing interest in the brain were two developments that led psychologists away from behaviorism. A third development also pointed them in a different direction. Recall that one of behaviorism's key claims was that organisms are blank slates on which experience writes its lessons, and hence any one lesson should be as easily written as another. But in experiments conducted during the 1960s and 1970s, the psychologist John Garcia and his colleagues showed that rats can learn to associate nausea with the smell of food much more quickly than they can learn to associate nausea with a flashing light (Garcia, 1981). Why should this be? In the real world of forests, sewers, and garbage cans, nausea is usually caused by spoiled food and not by lightning, and although these particular rats had been born in a laboratory and had never left their cages, millions of years of evolution had "prepared" their brains to learn the natural association more quickly than the artificial one. In other words, it was not only the rat's learning history but the rat's *ancestors'* learning histories that determined the rat's ability to learn. Although that fact was at odds with the behaviorist doctrine, it was the credo for a new kind of psychology.

Evolutionary psychology *explains mind and behavior in terms of the adaptive value of abilities that are preserved over time by natural selection.* Evolutionary psychology has its roots in Charles Darwin's theory of natural selection, which inspired William James's functionalist approach. But it is only since the publication in 1975 of *Sociobiology,* by the biologist E. O. Wilson, that evolutionary thinking has had an identifiable presence in psychology. That presence is steadily increasing (Buss, 1999; Pinker, 1997b; Tooby & Cosmides, 2000). Evolutionary psychologists think of the mind as a collection of specialized "modules" that are designed to solve the problems our ancestors faced as they attempted to eat, mate, and reproduce over millions of years. According to evolutionary psychology, the brain is not an all-purpose computer that can do or learn one thing just as easily as it can do or learn another; rather, it is a computer that was built to do a few things well and everything else not at all. It is a computer that comes with a small suite of built-in applications that are designed to do the things that previous versions of that computer needed to have done.

Consider, for example, how evolutionary psychology treats the emotion of jealousy. All of us who have been in romantic relationships have been jealous, if only because we noticed our partner noticing someone else. Jealousy can be a powerful, overwhelming emotion that we might wish to avoid, but according to evolutionary

TIME LIFE PICTURES/GETTY IMAGES

Today's evolutionary psychologists ● ● ● ● ● ● ● ● ● ● ●
embrace Charles Darwin's (1809–1882) ideas, just as William James did 100 years ago. Darwin's theories of evolution, adaptation, and natural selection have provided insight into why brains and minds work the way they do.

psychology, it exists today because it once served an adaptive function. If some of our hominid ancestors experienced jealousy and others did not, then the ones who experienced it might have been more likely to guard their mates and aggress against

● **Why might so many of us have inherited "jealous genes"?**

their rivals and thus may have been more likely to reproduce their "jealous genes" (Buss, 2000).

Critics of the evolutionary approach point out that many current traits of people and other animals probably evolved to serve different functions than those they currently serve. For example, biologists believe that the feathers of birds probably evolved initially to perform such functions as regulating body temperature or capturing prey and only later served the entirely different function of flight. Likewise, people are reasonably adept at learning to drive a car, but nobody would argue that such an ability is the result of natural selection; the learning abilities that allow us to become skilled car drivers must have evolved for purposes other than driving cars.

Complications like these have led the critics to wonder how evolutionary hypotheses can ever be tested (Coyne, 2000; Sterelny & Griffiths, 1999). We don't have a record of our ancestors' thoughts, feelings, and actions, and fossils won't provide much information about the evolution of mind and behavior. Testing ideas about the evolutionary origins of psychological phenomena is indeed a challenging task, but not an impossible one (Buss et al., 1998; Pinker, 1997a). Start with the assumption that evolutionary adaptations should also increase reproductive success. So, if a specific trait or feature has been favored by natural selection, it should be possible to find some evidence of this in the numbers of offspring that are produced by the trait's bearers. Consider, for instance, the hypothesis that men tend to be tall because women prefer to mate with tall men. To investigate this hypothesis, researchers conducted a study in which they compared the numbers of offspring from short and tall men. They did their best to equate other factors that might affect the results, such as the level of education attained by short and tall men. Consistent with the evolutionary hypothesis, they found that tall men do indeed bear more offspring than short men (Pawlowski, Dunbar, & Lipowicz, 2000). This kind of study provides evidence that allows evolutionary psychologists to test their ideas. Not every evolutionary hypothesis can be tested, of course, but evolutionary psychologists are becoming increasingly inventive in their attempts.

Beyond the Individual: The Development of Social Psychology

The psychological approaches discussed so far may vaguely suggest a scene from some 1950s science-fiction film in which the protagonist is a living brain that thinks, feels, hopes, and worries while suspended in a vat of pink jelly in a basement laboratory. Although psychologists often do focus on the brain and the mind of the individual, they have not lost sight of the fact that human beings are fundamentally social animals who are part of a vast network of family, friends, teachers, and coworkers. Trying to understand people in the absence of that fact is a bit like trying to understand an ant or a bee without considering the function and influence of the colony or hive. People are the most important and most complex objects that we ever encounter, and thus it is not surprising that our behavior is strongly influenced by their presence—or their absence.

Social psychology is *the study of the causes and consequences of interpersonal behavior.* This broad definition allows social psychologists to address a remarkable variety of topics. Historians trace the birth of social psychology to an experiment conducted in 1895 by the psychologist and bicycle enthusiast, Norman Triplett, who noticed that cyclists seemed to ride faster when they rode with others. Intrigued by this observation, he conducted an experiment that showed that children reeled in a fishing line faster when tested in the presence of other children than when tested alone. Triplett was not trying to improve the fishing abilities of American children, of course, but rather was trying to show that the mere presence of other people can influence performance on even the most mundane kinds of tasks.

social psychology A subfield of psychology that studies the causes and consequences of interpersonal behavior.

AHN YOUNG-JOON/AP PHOTO

Social psychology studies how the thoughts, feelings, and behaviors of individuals can be influenced by the presence of others. Members of Reverend Sun Myung Moon's Unification Church are often married to one another in ceremonies of 10,000 people or more; in some cases, couples don't know each other before the wedding begins. Social movements such as this have the power to sway individuals.

Social psychology's development began in earnest in the 1930s, and was strongly influenced by Gestalt psychology. You'll recall that Gestalt psychologists held that "the whole is greater than the sum of its parts," and though the Gestaltists had been talking about the visual perception of objects, social psychologists felt that the phrase also captured a basic truth about the relationship between social groups and the individuals who constitute them. Philosophers had speculated about the nature of sociality for thousands of years, and political scientists, economists, anthropologists, and sociologists had been studying social life scientifically for some time. But social psychologists began to generate theories of social behavior that resembled the theories generated by natural scientists, and more importantly, they were the first to conduct experiments to test their social theories.

Historical events also shaped social psychology in its early years. The rise of Nazism in Germany in the 1930s, and the Holocaust in which millions of Jews and others were killed, brought the problems of conformity and obedience into sharp focus, leading psychologists to examine the conditions under which people can influence each other to think and act in inhuman or irrational ways. The civil rights movement of the 1960s and the rising tensions between Black and White Americans led psychologists such as Gordon Allport (1897–1967) to study stereotyping, prejudice, and racism and to shock the world of psychology by suggesting that prejudice was the result of a perceptual error that was every bit as natural and unavoidable as an optical illusion (Allport, 1954). Allport identified a mindbug at work: The same perceptual processes that allow us to efficiently categorize elements of our social and physical world allow us to erroneously categorize entire groups of people. Social psychologists today study a wider variety of topics (from social memory to social relationships) and use a wider variety of techniques (from opinion polls to neuroimaging) than did their forebears, but this field of psychology remains dedicated to understanding the brain as a social organ, the mind as a social adaptation, and the individual as a social creature.

The Emergence of Cultural Psychology

North Americans and Western Europeans are sometimes surprised to realize that most of the people on the planet are members of neither culture. Although we're all more alike than we are different, there is nonetheless considerable diversity within

cultural psychology The study of how cultures reflect and shape the psychological processes of their members.

the human species in social practices, customs, and ways of living. *Culture* refers to the values, traditions, and beliefs that are shared by a particular group of people. Although we usually think of culture in terms of nationality and ethnic groups, cultures can also be defined by age (youth culture), sexual orientation (gay culture), religion (Jewish culture), or occupation (academic culture). **Cultural psychology** is *the study of how cultures reflect and shape the psychological processes of their members* (Shweder & Sullivan, 1993). Cultural psychologists study a wide range of phenomena, ranging from visual perception to social interaction, as they seek to understand which of these phenomena are universal and which vary from place to place and time to time.

Perhaps surprisingly, one of the first psychologists to pay attention to the influence of culture was someone recognized today for pioneering the development of experimental psychology: Wilhelm Wundt. He believed that a complete psychology would have to combine a laboratory approach with a broader cultural perspective. But Wundt's ideas failed to spark much interest from other psychologists, who had their hands full trying to make sense of results from laboratory experiments and formulating general laws of human behavior. Outside psychology, anthropologists such as Margaret Mead (1901–1978) and Gregory Bateson (1904–1980) attempted to understand the workings of culture by traveling to far-flung regions of the world and carefully observing child-rearing patterns, rituals, religious ceremonies, and the like. Such studies revealed practices—some bizarre from a North American perspective—that served important functions in a culture, such as the painful ritual of violent body mutilation and bloodletting in mountain tribes of New Guinea, which initiates young boys into training to become warriors (Mead, 1935/1968; Read, 1965). Yet at the time, most anthropologists paid as little attention to psychology as psychologists did to anthropology. Cultural psychology only began to emerge as a strong force in psychology during the 1980s and 1990s, when psychologists and anthropologists began to communicate with each other about their ideas and methods (Stigler, Shweder, & Herdt, 1990).

● **Why are psychological conclusions so often relative to the person, place or culture described?**

The laws of physics and chemistry are assumed to be universal: water is made of hydrogen and oxygen whether that water is located in Cleveland, Moscow, or the Orion Nebula. For much of psychology's history, the same assumption was made about the principles that govern human behavior (Shweder, 1991). *Absolutism* holds that culture makes little or no difference for most psychological phenomena—that "honesty is honesty

The Namgay family from Shingkhey, Bhutan (left), and the Skeen family from Texas, United States (right), display their respective family possessions in these two photos, both taken in 1993. Cultural psychology studies the similarities and differences in psychological processes that arise between people living in different cultures.

© PETER MENZEL PHOTOGRAPHY

© PETER MENZEL PHOTOGRAPHY

and depression is depression, no matter where one observes it" (Segall, Lonner, & Berry, 1998, p. 1103). And yet, as any world traveler knows, cultures differ in exciting, delicious, and frightening ways, and things that are true of people in one culture are not necessarily true of people in another. *Relativism* holds that psychological phenomena are likely to vary considerably across cultures and should be viewed only in the context of a specific culture (Berry et al., 1992). Although depression is observed in nearly every culture, the symptoms associated with it vary dramatically from one place to another. For example, in Western cultures, depressed people tend to devalue themselves, whereas depressed people in Eastern cultures do not (Draguns, 1980).

Today, most cultural psychologists fall somewhere between these two extremes. Most psychological phenomena can be influenced by culture, some are completely determined by it, and others seem to be entirely unaffected. For example, the age of a person's earliest memory differs dramatically across cultures (MacDonald, Uesiliana, & Hayne, 2000), whereas judgments of facial attractiveness do not (Cunningham et al., 1995).

As noted when we discussed evolutionary psychology, it seems likely that the most universal phenomena are those that are closely associated with the basic biology that all human beings share. Conversely, the least universal phenomena are those rooted in the varied socialization practices that different cultures evolve. Of course, the only way to determine whether a phenomenon is variable or constant across cultures is to design research to investigate these possibilities, and cultural psychologists do just that (Cole, 1996; Segall et al., 1998).

summary quiz [1.4]

12. The scientific study of mental processes, including perception, thought, memory, and reasoning is called
    a. social psychology.
    b. evolutionary.
    c. cognitive psychology.
    d. cultural psychology.

13. The explanation of mind and behavior that focuses on the adaptive value of abilities that are preserved over time by natural selection is called
    a. cultural psychology.
    b. evolutionary psychology.
    c. functionalism.
    d. cognitive neuroscience.

14. The field that studies causes and consequences of people interacting with each other is known as
    a. social psychology.
    b. cognitive psychology.
    c. cultural psychology.
    d. Gestalt psychology.

15. The field that studies how behaviors vary among people of different ethnicities, nationalities, religions, and so on, is known as _____ psychology.
    a. relativistic
    b. evolutionary
    c. social
    d. cultural

The Profession of Psychology: Past and Present

You'll recall that when we last saw William James, he was wandering around the greater Boston area, expounding the virtues of the new science of psychology. In July 1892, James and five other psychologists traveled to Clark University to attend a meeting. Each worked at a large university where they taught psychology courses, performed research, and wrote textbooks. Although they were too few to make up a jury or even a respectable hockey team, these men decided that it was time to form an organization that represented psychology as a profession, and on that day the American Psychological Association (APA) was born. The psychologists could scarcely have imagined that today their little club would have more than 150,000 members—approximately the population of a decent-sized city in the United States. Although all of the original members were employed by universities or colleges, today academic psychologists make up only 20% of the membership, while nearly 70% of the members work in clinical and health-related settings. Because the APA is no longer as focused on academic psychology as it once was, the American Psychological Society (APS) was formed in 1988 by academic psychologists who wanted an organization that focused specifically on the needs of psychologists carrying out scientific research. The APS, renamed the Association for Psychological Science in 2006, grew quickly; today it comprises nearly 12,000 psychologists.

The Growing Role of Women and Minorities

In 1892, APA had 31 members, all of whom were White and all of whom were male. Today, about half of all APA members are women, and the percentage of non-White members continues to grow. Surveys of recent PhD recipients reveal a picture of increasing diversification in the field. The proportion of women receiving PhDs in psychology increased nearly 20% between the mid-1980s and mid-1990s, and the proportion of minorities receiving PhDs in psychology nearly doubled during that same period. Clearly, psychology is increasingly reflecting the diversity of American society.

● **How has the face of psychology changed as the field has evolved?**

The current involvement of women and minorities in the APA, and psychology more generally, can be traced to early pioneers who blazed a trail that others followed. One such pioneer was Mary Calkins (1863–1930), who studied with William James at Harvard and later became a professor of psychology at Wellesley College. In 1905, Calkins became the first woman to serve as president of the APA. In her presidential address, Calkins described her theory of the role of the "self" in psychological function. Arguing against Wundt's and Titchener's structuralist ideas that the mind can be dissected into components, Calkins claimed that the self is a single unit that cannot be broken down into individual parts. She wrote four books and published over 100 articles during her illustrious career (Calkins, 1930; Scarborough & Furumoto, 1987; Stevens & Gardner, 1982).

Today, women play leading roles in all areas of psychology. Some of the men who formed the APA might have been surprised by the prominence of women in the field today, but we suspect that William James, a strong supporter of Mary Calkins, would not be one of them.

Just as there were no women at the first meeting of the APA, there weren't any non-White people, either. The first member of a minority group to become president of the

Mary Whiton Calkins (1863–1930), the first woman elected APA president, suffered from the sex discrimination that was common during her lifetime. Despite academic setbacks (e.g., Harvard University refusing to grant women an official PhD), Calkins went on to a distinguished career in research and teaching at Wellesley College.

WELLESLEY COLLEGE ARCHIVES—MARGARET CLAPP LIBRARY

APA was Kenneth Clark (1914–2005), who was elected in 1970. Clark worked extensively on the self-image of African American children and argued that segregation of the races creates great psychological harm. Clark's conclusions had a large influence on public policy, and his research contributed to the Supreme Court's 1954 ruling (*Brown v. Board of Education*) to outlaw segregation in public schools (Guthrie, 2000). Clark's interest in psychology was sparked as an undergraduate at Howard University when he took a course from Francis Cecil Sumner (1895–1954), who was the first African American to receive a PhD in psychology (from Clark University, in 1920). Little known today, Sumner's work focused on the education of African American youth (Sawyer, 2000).

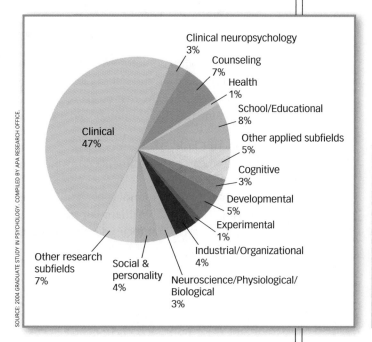

WILLIAM E. SAURO/NEW YORK TIMES CO./GETTY IMAGES

A student of Francis Cecil Sumner's, Kenneth B. Clark (1914–2005) studied the developmental effects of prejudice, discrimination, and segregation on children. In one classic study from the 1950s, he found that African American preschoolers preferred white dolls to black ones. Clark's research was cited by the U.S. Supreme Court in its decision for the landmark Brown v. Board of Education *case that ended school segregation.*

What Psychologists Do

So what should you do if you want to become a psychologist and conduct research in the tradition of James, Wundt, Calkins, and Clark? You can become "a psychologist" by a variety of routes, and the people who call themselves psychologists may hold a variety of different degrees. Typically, students finish college and enter graduate school to obtain a PhD (or doctor of philosophy) degree in some particular area of psychology (e.g., social, cognitive, developmental). During graduate school, students gain exposure to the field by taking classes and learn to conduct research by collaborating with their professors. Although William James was able to master every area of psychology because the areas were so small during his lifetime, today a student can spend the better part of a decade mastering just one.

After receiving a PhD, you can go on for more specialized research training by pursuing a postdoctoral fellowship under the supervision of an established researcher in their area or apply for a faculty position at a college or university or a research position in government or industry. Academic careers usually involve a combination of teaching and research, whereas careers in government or industry are typically dedicated to research alone.

But research is not the only career option for a psychologist (**FIGURE 1.5**). Most of the people who call themselves psychologists neither teach nor do research; rather, they assess or treat people with psychological problems. Such *clinical psychologists* hold a doctorate with a specialization in clinical psychology (a PhD or PsyD); this degree provides extensive training in assessment and treatment of clinical disorders. Clinical psychologists

ONLY HUMAN

A TREASURY OF THERAPEUTIC TECHNIQUES The *Austin American-Statesman* reported that then Texas treasurer Martha Whitehead had hired a psychologist, for $1,000, to counsel several employees of her office who were despondent about Whitehead's recommendation to abolish her agency.

SOURCE: 2004 GRADUATE STUDY IN PSYCHOLOGY, COMPILED BY APA RESEARCH OFFICE.

Clinical neuropsychology
3%
Counseling
7%
Health
1%
School/Educational
8%
Other applied subfields
5%
Cognitive
3%
Developmental
5%
Experimental
1%
Industrial/Organizational
4%
Neuroscience/Physiological/Biological
3%
Social & personality
4%
Other research subfields
7%
Clinical
47%

FIGURE 1.5
The Major Subfields in Psychology
Psychologists are drawn to many different subfields in psychology. Here are the percentages of people receiving PhDs in various subfields. Clinical psychology makes up almost half of the doctorates awarded in psychology.

must then be licensed by the state; most states require 2 years of supervised practical training and a competency exam. Most clinical psychologists work in private practice, but some work in hospitals or medical schools, some have faculty positions at universities or colleges, and some combine private practice with an academic job. Many clinical psychologists focus on specific problems or disorders, such as depression or anxiety, whereas others focus on specific populations, such as children, ethnic minority groups, or elderly adults.

Just over 10% of APA members are counseling psychologists, who assist people in dealing with work or career issues and changes or help people deal with common crises such as divorce, the loss of a job, or the death of a loved one. Counseling psychologists may have a PhD or an MA (master's degree) in counseling psychology or an MSW (master of social work).

Psychologists are also quite active in educational settings. About 5% of APA members are *school psychologists,* who offer guidance to students, parents, and teachers. A similar proportion of APA members, known as *industrial/organizational psychologists,* focus on issues in the workplace. These psychologists typically work in business or industry and may be involved in assessing potential employees, finding ways to improve productivity, or helping staff and management to develop effective planning strategies for coping with change or anticipated future developments.

● **In what ways does psychology contribute to society?**

Even this brief and incomplete survey of the APA membership provides a sense of the wide variety of contexts in which psychologists operate. You can think of psychology as an international community of professionals devoted to advancing scientific knowledge; assisting people with psychological problems and disorders; and trying to enhance the quality of life in work, school, and other everyday settings.

summary quiz [1.5]

16. The largest organization of psychologists in the United States is the
    a. American Psychological Society.
    b. American Psychological Association.
    c. Association for Psychological Science.
    d. Psychonomic Society.

17. Mary Calkins
    a. studied with Wilhelm Wundt in the first psychology laboratory.
    b. did research on the self-image of African American children.
    c. was present at the first meeting of the APA.
    d. became the first woman president of the APA.

18. Kenneth Clark
    a. did research that influenced the Supreme Court decision to ban segregation in public schools.
    b. was one of the founders of the American Psychological Society.
    c. was a student of William James.
    d. did research that focused on the education of African American youth.

WhereDoYouStand?

The Perils of Procrastination

As you've read in this chapter, the human mind and behavior are fascinating in part because they are not error free. Mindbugs interest us primarily as paths to achieving a better understanding of mental activity and behavior, but they also have practical consequences. Let's consider a mindbug that can have significant consequences in your own life: procrastination.

At one time or another, most of us have avoided carrying out a task or put it off to a later time. The task may be unpleasant, difficult, or just less entertaining than other things we could be doing at the moment. Over 70% of college students report that they engage in some form of procrastination, such as putting off writing a term paper or preparing for a test (Schouwenburg, 1995). Procrastination can be thought of as a mindbug because it prevents the completion of tasks in a timely manner.

Some procrastinators defend the practice by claiming that they tend to work best under pressure or by noting that as long as a task gets done, it doesn't matter all that much if it is completed just before the deadline. Is there any merit to such claims, or are they just feeble excuses for counterproductive behavior?

A study of 60 undergraduate psychology college students provides some intriguing answers (Tice & Baumeister, 1997). At the beginning of the semester, the instructor announced a due date for the term paper and told students that if they could not meet the date, they would receive an extension to a later date. About a month later, students completed a scale that measures tendencies toward procrastination. At that same time, and then again during the last week of class, students recorded health symptoms they had experienced during the past week, the amount of stress they had experienced during that week, and the number of visits they had made to a health care center during the previous month.

Students who scored high on the procrastination scale tended to turn in their papers late. One month into the semester, these procrastinators reported less stress and fewer symptoms of physical illness than did nonprocrastinators. But at the end of the semester, the procrastinators reported *more* stress and *more* health symptoms than did the nonprocrastinators and also reported more visits to the health center. Furthermore, the study found no evidence to support the idea that procrastinators do their "best work under pressure," since procrastinators received lower grades on their papers and on course exams.

Where do you stand on procrastination? Calculate your procrastination score by rating the following statements on a scale of 1-5, where

1 = not at all;
2 = incidentally;
3 = sometimes;
4 = most of the time;
5 = always.

How frequently last week did you engage in the following behaviors or thoughts?

1. Drifted off into daydreams while studying
2. Studied the subject matter that you had planned to do
3. Had no energy to study
4. Prepared to study at some point but did not get any further
5. Gave up when studying was not going well
6. Gave up studying early in order to do more pleasant things
7. Put off the completion of a task
8. Allowed yourself to be distracted from your work
9. Experienced concentration problems when studying
10. Interrupted studying for a while in order to do other things
11. Forgot to prepare things for studying
12. Did so many other things that there was insufficient time left for studying
13. Thought that you had enough time left, so that there was really no need to start studying

CHAPTER REVIEW

Summary

Psychology's Roots: The Path to a Science of Mind

- Early philosophers pondered ideas about human nature, but their approach did not allow them to provide empirical evidence to support their claims.

- Some of the earliest successful efforts to develop a *science* linking mind and behavior came from studies showing that damage to the brain can result in impairments in behavior and mental functions.

- Helmholtz furthered the science of the mind by developing methods for measuring reaction time; he and his followers (including Wundt, who is credited with the founding of psychology as a scientific discipline) espoused structuralism—the idea that the mind could be studied by understanding its basic elements.

- James and his followers emphasized the functions of consciousness and applied Darwin's theory of natural selection to the study of the mind.

Errors and Illusions Reveal Psychology

- Psychologists have often focused on mindbugs as a way of understanding human behavior.

- Gestalt psychology examines illusions that cause us to see the whole instead of its parts.

- Clinicians studying unusual cases in which patients act like different people under hypnosis raise the possibility that each of us has more than one self.

- Freud developed psychoanalysis, which emphasized the importance of unconscious influences and childhood experiences in shaping thoughts, feelings, and behavior.

- Humanistic psychologists suggest that people are inherently disposed toward growth and can reach their full potential with a little help from their friends.

Psychology in the 20th Century: Behaviorism Takes Center Stage

- For much of the early 20th century, the dominant approach in psychology was behaviorism, which advocated that psychologists should restrict themselves to the scientific study of observable behavior.

- Watson and Pavlov studied how organisms learn associations between a stimulus and a response.

- Skinner formulated the principle of reinforcement, which states that the consequences of a behavior determine whether it will be likely to occur again.

Beyond Behaviorism: Psychology Expands

- Cognitive psychologists defied the behavioral doctrine and studied inner mental processes such as perception, attention, memory, and reasoning.

- Cognitive neuroscience attempts to link the brain with the mind through studies of brain-damaged and healthy people.

- Evolutionary psychology focuses on the adaptive function that minds and brains serve, and it seeks to understand the nature and origin of psychological processes in terms of natural selection.

- Social psychology recognizes that people exist as part of a network of other people, examining how individuals influence and interact with one another.

- Cultural psychology is concerned with the effects of broader culture on individuals and studies similarities and differences among people in different cultures.

The Profession of Psychology: Past and Present

- The American Psychological Association (APA) was formed in 1892 by James and others, and it now includes over 150,000 members working in clinical, academic, and applied settings.

- Through the efforts of pioneers such as Calkins, women are now as well represented in the field as men. Minority involvement took longer, but the efforts of Sumner, Clark, and others have led to increased participation of minorities in psychology.

- Psychologists prepare for careers through graduate and postgraduate training, and thy work in a variety of settings, including research, clinical settings, schools, and industry.

Key Terms

psychology (p. 2)

mind (p. 2)

behavior (p. 2)

nativism (p. 4)

philosophical empiricism (p. 5)

phrenology (p. 5)

physiology (p. 6)

stimulus (p. 6)

reaction time (p. 6)

consciousness (p. 6)

structuralism (p. 7)

introspection (p. 7)

functionalism (p. 8)

natural selection (p. 8)

illusions (p. 10)

Gestalt psychology (p. 12)

hysteria (p. 12)

unconscious (p. 13)

psychoanalytic theory (p. 13)

psychoanalysis (p. 13)

humanistic psychology (p. 14)

behaviorism (p. 15)

response (p. 16)

reinforcement (p. 16)

cognitive psychology (p. 19)

behavioral neuroscience (p. 20)

cognitive neuroscience (p. 21)

evolutionary psychology (p. 21)

social psychology (p. 22)

cultural psychology (p. 24)

Critical Thinking Questions

1. William James thought Darwin's theory of natural selection might explain how mental abilities evolve, by conferring survival advantages on individuals who were better able to solve problems.

   How might a specific mental ability, such as the ability to recognize the facial expressions of others as signaling their emotional state, help an individual survive longer and produce more offspring?

2. Behaviorists explain behavior in terms of organisms learning to make particular responses that are paired with reinforcement (and to avoid responses that are paired with punishment). Evolutionary psychology focuses on how abilities are preserved over time if they contribute to an organism's ability to survive and reproduce.

   How might a proponent of each approach explain the fact that a rat placed in an unfamiliar environment will tend to stay in dark corners and to avoid brightly lit open areas?

Answers to Summary Quizzes

Summary Quiz 1.1	Summary Quiz 1.2	Summary Quiz 1.3	Summary Quiz 1.4	Summary Quiz 1.5
1. a; 2. b; 3. d; 4. c	5. d; 6. c; 7. a; 8. b	9. c; 10. b; 11. a	12. c; 13. b; 14. a; 15. d	6. b; 17. d; 18. a

Need more help? Additional resources are located at the book's free companion Web site at: www.worthpublishers.com/schacterbriefle

The Methods of Psychology

LORI AND REBA SCHAPPELL ARE HAPPY to be twins. One is an award-winning country music singer; one is a wisecracking hospital worker who likes strawberry daiquiris. Despite their different interests and different temperaments, they get along quite well and love each other dearly. That's a good thing because Lori and Reba share more than the same parents and the same birthday. Lori and Reba are conjoined twins who have been attached at the forehead since birth. When asked whether they would ever consider being surgically separated, Reba seems perplexed: "Our point of view is no, straight-out no. You'd be ruining two lives in the process" (Angier, 1997). If you find this hard to believe, then welcome to the club. Conjoined twins are routinely separated at birth even when this means crippling both or killing one of them because surgeons and parents—like most of us—can't imagine that a conjoined life is really worth living. And yet, conjoined twins don't seem to share that view. As one medical historian noted, "The desire to remain together is so widespread among communicating conjoined twins as to be practically universal. . . .I have yet to find an instance in which conjoined twins have sought out separation" (Dreger, 1998).

Are conjoined twins really as happy as they claim, or are they simply fooling themselves? Do parents and doctors have the right to impose dangerous surgery on infants who would otherwise grow up to refuse it? Such questions have moral, religious, and philosophical answers, but they can have scientific answers as well. If we could find some way to measure a psychological property such as happiness, then we could use scientific methods to determine who has it and who doesn't and to discover what kinds of lives promote or preclude it. Is a conjoined life a wonderful life, or is it society's responsibility to separate conjoined twins whenever possible? As you are about to see, psychological methods are designed to provide answers to questions like this one. ■

Are conjoined twins less happy than singletons? Reba (left) and Lori (right) Schappell are sisters who say that the answer is no.

Empiricism: How to Know Things

When ancient Greeks sprained their ankles, caught the flu, or accidentally set their togas on fire, they had to choose between two kinds of doctors: dogmatists (from *dogmatikos,* meaning "belief"), who thought that the best way to understand illness was to develop theories about the body's functions, and empiricists (from *empeirikos,* meaning "experience"), who thought that the best way to understand illness was to observe sick people. The rivalry between these two schools of medicine didn't last long, however, because the people who chose to see dogmatists tended to die, which wasn't very good for repeat business. It is little wonder that today we use the word *dogmatism* to describe the tendency for people to cling to their assumptions and the word **empiricism** to describe *the belief that accurate knowledge of the world requires observation of it.* The fact that we can answer questions about the world by observation may seem obvious to you, but this obvious fact is actually a relatively new discovery. Throughout most of human history, people have trusted authority to answer important questions about the world, and it is only in the last millennium (and especially in the past three centuries) that people have begun to trust their eyes and ears more than their elders. Empiricism has proved to be a profitable approach to understanding natural phenomena, but using this approach requires a **method**, which is *a set of rules and techniques for observation that allow observers to avoid the illusions, mistakes, and erroneous conclusions that simple observation can produce.*

"Are you just pissing and moaning, or can you verify what you're saying with data?"

● **Why is it so hard to study people scientifically?**

Human behavior is relatively easy to observe, so you might expect psychology's methods to be relatively simple. In fact, the empirical challenges facing psychologists are among the most daunting in all of modern science, and thus psychological methods are among the most sophisticated. Three things make people especially difficult to study:

- *Complexity:* Psychologists study the single most complex object in the known universe. No galaxy, particle, molecule, or machine is as complicated as the human brain. Scientists can barely begin to say how the 500 million interconnected neurons that constitute the brain give rise to the thoughts, feelings, and actions that are psychology's core concerns.

- *Variability:* In almost all the ways that matter, one *E. coli* bacterium is pretty much like another. But people are as varied as their fingerprints. No two individuals ever do, say, think, or feel exactly the same thing under exactly the same circumstances.

- *Reactivity:* An atom of cesium-133 oscillates 9,192,631,770 times per second regardless of who's watching. But people often think, feel, and act one way when they are being observed and a different way when they are not.

In short, human beings are tremendously complex, endlessly variable, and uniquely reactive, and these attributes present a major challenge to the scientific study of their behavior. As you'll see, psychologists have developed a variety of methods that are designed to meet these challenges head-on.

The Science of Observation: Saying What

There is no escaping the fact that you have to observe *what* people do before you can try to explain *why* they do it. To *observe* something means to use your senses to learn about its properties. For example, when you observe a round, red apple, your brain is using the pattern of light that is falling on your eyes to draw an inference about the apple's identity, shape, and color. That kind of informal observation is fine for buying fruit but not for doing science. Why? First, casual observations are notoriously unstable. The same apple

● *The fish are probably annoyed by the wide variety of people who invade their territory on Labor Day, but hey ... life's a beach.*

may appear red in the daylight and crimson at night or spherical to one person and elliptical to another. Second, casual observations can't tell us about many of the properties in which we might be interested. No matter how long and hard you look, you will never be able to discern an apple's crunchiness or pectin content simply by watching it. If you want to know about those properties, you must do more than observe. You must *measure*.

Measurement

You probably think you know what *length* is. But if you try to define it without using the word *long*, you get tongue-tied pretty quickly. We use words such as *weight, speed,* or *length* all the time in ordinary conversation without realizing that each of these terms has an **operational definition**, which is a *description of a property in measurable terms*. For example, the operational definition of the property we casually refer to as *length* is "the change in the location of light over time." When we say that a bookshelf is "a meter in length," we are actually saying how long it takes a particle of light to travel from one end of the shelf to the other. (In case you're interested, the answer is 1/299,792,458th of a second.) Operational definitions specify the concrete events that count as instances of an abstract property. The first step in making any measurement is to define the property we want to measure in concrete terms.

The second step is to find a way to detect the concrete terms that our definition describes. To do this we must use a **measure**, which is *a device that can detect the events to which an operational definition refers*. For example, length is the change in the location of light over time, and we can detect such changes by using a photon detector (which tells us the location of a particle of light) and a clock (which tells us how long it took the particle of light to travel from one location to another). Once we have determined just how far a photon travels in 1/299,792,458th of a second, we can make our next measurement a lot less expensive by marking that distance on a piece of wood and calling it a ruler.

Defining and *detecting* are the two tasks that allow us to measure physical properties, and these same two tasks allow us to measure psychological properties as well. If we wanted to measure Lori Schappell's happiness, for example, our first task would

● **How could you measure happiness?**

be to develop an operational definition of that property—that is, to specify some concrete, measurable event that will count as an instance of happiness. For example, we might define happiness as the simultaneous contraction of the *zygomatic major* (which is the muscle that makes your mouth turn up when you smile) and the *orbicularis oculi* (which is the muscle that makes your eyes crinkle when you smile). After defining happiness as a specific set of muscular contractions, we would then need to measure those contractions, and the **electromyograph (EMG)**—which is *a device that measures muscle contractions under the surface of a person's skin*—would do splendidly. Once we have defined happiness and found a way to detect the concrete events that our definition supplies, we are in a position to measure it (**FIGURE 2.1**).

Culture & Community

Expecting a Helping Hand? It Depends Where You Are

Robert Levine of California State University–Fresno sent his students to 23 large international cities for an observational study in the field. Their task was to observe helping behaviors in a naturalistic context. In two versions of the experiment, students pretended to be either blind or injured while trying to cross a street, while another student stood by to observe whether anyone would come to help. A third version involved a student dropping a pen to see if anyone would pick it up.

The results showed that people helped in all three events fairly evenly within cities, but there was a wide range of response between cities. Rio de Janeiro, Brazil, came out on top as the most helpful city in the study with an overall helping score of 93%. Kuala Lampur, Malaysia, came in last with a score of 40%, while New York City placed next to last with a score of 45%. On average, Latin American cities ranked most helpful (Levine, Norenzayan, & Philbrick, 2001).

empiricism Originally a Greek school of medicine that stressed the importance of observation, and now generally used to describe any attempt to acquire knowledge by observing objects or events.

method A set of rules and techniques for observation that allow researchers to avoid the illusions, mistakes, and erroneous conclusions that simple observation can produce.

operational definition A description of an abstract property in terms of a concrete condition that can be measured.

measure A device that can detect the measurable events to which an operational definition refers.

electromyograph (EMG) A device that measures muscle contractions under the surface of a person's skin.

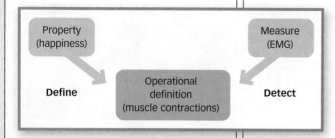

FIGURE 2.1

Sources of Invalidity. *The process of defining links properties to operational definitions, and the process of detecting links operational definitions to measures. Invalidity can result from problems in either of these links.*

"Are you (a) contented, (b) happy, (c) very happy, (d) wildly happy, (e) deliriously happy?"

But is this the *right* way to measure happiness? That's hard to say. There are many ways to define the same property and many ways to detect the events that this definition supplies. For instance, we could detect the muscular contractions involved in smiling by using EMG, or we could detect them by asking a human observer to watch a participant's face and tell us how often the participant smiled. We could even define happiness as a person's self-assessment of his or her own emotional state, in which case we could measure it by asking people how happy they feel and recording their answers. With so many options for defining and detecting happiness, how are we to choose among them?

The best kinds of measurements share three properties: validity, reliability, and power. **Validity** is *the characteristic of an observation that allows one to draw accurate inferences from it*. There are two kinds of validity. First, the operational definition must adequately define the property ("construct validity"). In other words, the distance that a proton travels is a good way to define length, but it's not a valid way to define happiness. Second, the operational definition must be related to other operational definitions of the same property ("predictive validity"). In other words, if an operational definition such as smiling is linked to a property such as happiness, then it should also be linked to other operational definitions of the same property—such as a person's likelihood of saying, "I sure am happy right now."

The other important property of a good measurement is **reliability**, which is *the tendency for a measure to produce the same result whenever it is used to measure the same thing*. For example, if a person's zygomatic muscle did not move for 10 minutes, we would expect the EMG to produce the same reading for 10 minutes. If the EMG produced different readings from one minute to the next, then it would be an unreliable measure that was detecting differences that weren't really there. A good measure must be reliable. The flip side of reliability is **power**, which is *the tendency for a measure to produce different results when it is used to measure different things*. If a person's zygomatic muscle moved continuously for 10 minutes, we would expect the EMG to produce different readings in those 10 minutes. If the EMG instead produced the same reading from one minute to the next, then it would be a weak or powerless measure that was failing to detect differences that were really there. Reliable and powerful measures are those that detect the conditions specified by an operational definition (a) when they happen and (b) *only* when they happen.

Validity, reliability, and power are prerequisites for accurate measurement. But once you've got a good ruler in hand, the next step is to find something to measure with it. Psychologists have developed techniques for doing that, too.

A bathroom scale and a laboratory balance both measure weight, but the balance is more likely to provide exactly the same measurement when it is used to weigh the same object twice (reliability) and more likely to provide different measurements when it is used to weigh two objects that differ by just a fraction of a gram (power). Not surprisingly, the bathroom scale sells for around $30 and the balance for around $3,000. Power and reliability don't come cheap.

MEDIABAKERY

Samples

If a pig flew over the White House, it wouldn't matter whether other pigs could do the same trick. The fact that just one pig flew just one time would challenge our most cherished assumptions about animal physiology, aerodynamics, and national security and would thus be an observation well worth making. Similarly, individuals sometimes do remarkable things that deserve close study, and when psychologists study them closely, they are using the **case method**, which is *a method of gathering scientific knowledge by studying a single individual.* For example, the physician Oliver Sacks described his observations of a brain-damaged patient in a book titled *The Man Who Mistook His Wife for a Hat,* and those observations were worth making because this is a rather unusual mistake for a man to make. As you saw in Chapter 1, people with unusual abilities, unusual experiences, or unusual deficits often provide important insights about human psychology.

● **How can an exceptional case teach us about normal behavior?**

But exceptional cases are the exception, and more often than not, psychologists are in the business of observing *un*exceptional people and trying to explain why they think, feel, and act as they do. Of course, it's not possible to observe every ordinary person in the world. Even if we consider a subset (e.g., every pair of conjoined twins currently alive), it's still not possible to observe everyone who meets those criteria—if only because these people may be spread across many different continents. Instead of observing the entire **population**, *the complete collection of objects or events that might be measured,* psychologists observe a **sample**, *a partial collection of objects or events that is measured.* If the sample is relatively large and well chosen, then the behavior of individuals in the sample should be representative of the larger population. (For more on sampling techniques, see the appendix.)

Demand Characteristics

Once psychologists have settled on a valid and reliable measurement, and constructed a representative sample to study, the next problem is to figure out how to apply that measurement to the sample in the most accurate way possible. One problem is that, while psychologists are trying to discover how people really *do* behave, people are often trying to behave as they think they *should* behave. People pick their noses, exceed the speed limit, read each other's mail, and skip over major sections of *War and Peace,* and they are especially likely to do these things when they think no one is looking. They are much less likely to indulge in these behaviors if they are aware that someone is observing them and taking notes. **Demand characteristics** are *those aspects of a setting that cause people to behave as they think an observer wants or expects them to behave.* They are called demand characteristics because they seem to "demand" or require that people say and do things that they normally might not. If you have ever been asked the question "Do you think these jeans make me look fat?," then you have experienced a demand characteristic. Demand characteristics hinder our attempts to measure behavior as it normally unfolds.

● **Why do people act differently when they know they're being observed?**

One way psychologists try to avoid this problem is to observe people without their knowledge. **Naturalistic observation** is *a technique for gathering scientific knowledge by unobtrusively observing people in their natural environments.* For example, naturalistic observation reveals that the biggest groups tend to leave the smallest tips in restaurants (Freeman et al., 1975), that hungry shoppers buy the most impulse items at the grocery store (Gilbert, Gill, & Wilson, 2002), and that Olympic athletes smile more when they win the bronze rather than the silver medal (Medvec, Madey, & Gilovich, 1995). All of these conclusions are the result of measurements made by psychologists who observed people who didn't know they were being observed. It is unlikely that any of these things would have

"This fundamentally changes everything we know about elephants!"

 **ONLY HUMAN**

MAYBE THEY COULD PASS A LAW OF LARGE NUMBERS? In 1997, David Cook of Caledonian University in Glasgow, Scotland, told the British Psychological Society's annual conference that his 3-year study shows that politicians have significant behavior patterns in common with criminal psychopaths. Cook said that criminals were relatively easy to analyze but that he did not have as much data as he would like on politicians. "They don't like to be studied," he said.

validity The characteristic of an observation that allows one to draw accurate inferences from it.

reliability The tendency for a measure to produce the same result whenever it is used to measure the same thing.

power The tendency for a measure to produce different results when it is used to measure different things.

case method A method of gathering scientific knowledge by studying a single individual.

population The complete collection of participants who might possibly be measured.

sample The partial collection of people who actually were measured in a study.

demand characteristics Those aspects of an observational setting that cause people to behave as they think an observer wants or expects them to behave.

naturalistic observation A method of gathering scientific knowledge by unobtrusively observing people in their natural environments.

DANIEL PEEBLES PHOTO

This bar on 10th Avenue in New York City has a "one-way" mirror in its unisex restroom. Customers see their reflections in the restroom's mirror, and people who are walking down the street see the customers. Are the customers influenced by the fact that pedestrians may be watching them? Hard to say, but one observer did notice a suspiciously "high percentage of people who wash their hands" (Wolf, 2003).

happened in exactly the same way if the diners, shoppers, and athletes had known that they were being scrutinized.

Unfortunately, there are two reasons why naturalistic observation cannot by itself solve the problem of demand characteristics. First, some of the things psychologists want to observe simply don't occur naturally. For example, if we wanted to know whether people who have undergone sensory deprivation perform poorly on motor tasks, we would have to hang around the shopping mall for a very long time before a few dozen blindfolded people with earplugs just happened to wander by and start typing. Second, some of the things that psychologists want to observe can only be gathered from direct interaction with a person—for example, by administering a survey, giving tests, conducting an interview, or hooking someone up to an EEG. If we wanted to know how often people worried about dying, how accurately they could remember their high school graduation, how quickly they could solve a logic puzzle, or how much electrical activity their brain produced when they felt happy, then simply observing them would not do the trick.

When psychologists cannot avoid demand characteristics by hiding in the bushes, they often avoid them by hiding other things instead. For instance, people are less likely to be influenced by demand characteristics when they cannot be identified as the originators of their actions, and psychologists often take advantage of this fact by allowing people to respond privately (e.g., by having them complete questionnaires when they are alone) or anonymously (e.g., by failing to collect personal information, such as the person's name or address). Another technique that psychologists use to avoid demand characteristics is to measure behaviors that are not susceptible to demand. For instance, behaviors can't be influenced by demand characteristics if they aren't under voluntary control. You may not want a psychologist to know that you are feeling excited, but you can't prevent your pupils from dilating when you feel aroused. Behaviors are also unlikely to be influenced by demand characteristics when people don't know that the demand and the behavior are related. You may want a psychologist to believe that you are concentrating on a task, but you probably don't know that your blink rate slows when you are concentrating and thus you won't fake a slow blink.

All of these tricks of the trade are useful, of course, but the very best way to avoid demand characteristics is to keep the people who are being observed (known as *participants*) from knowing the true purpose of the observation. When participants are kept "blind" to the observer's expectations—that is, when they do not know what the observer expects them to do—then they cannot strive to meet those expectations. If you did not know that a psychologist was studying the effects of baroque music on mood, then you would not feel compelled to smile when the psychologist played Bach's *Air on*

WIN MCNAMEE/GETTY IMAGES

One way to avoid demand characteristics is to measure behaviors that people are unable or unlikely to control, such as facial expressions, reaction times, eye blink rate, and so on. For example, when people feel anxious, they tend to involuntarily compress their lips, as President George W. Bush did in this 2006 photo taken as he gave a speech in the Rose Garden.

G String. This is why psychologists often do not reveal the true purpose of a study to the participants until the study is over.

Of course, people are clever and curious, and when psychologists don't tell them the purpose of their observations, participants generally try to figure it out for themselves ("I wonder why the psychologist is playing the violin and watching me"). That's why psychologists sometimes use *cover stories,* or misleading explanations that are meant to keep participants from discerning the true purpose of an observation. For example, if a psychologist wanted to know how baroque music influenced your mood, he or she might tell you that the purpose of the study was to determine how quickly people can do logic puzzles while music plays in the background. (We will discuss the ethical implications of deceiving people later in this chapter.) In addition, the psychologist might use *filler items,* or pointless measures that are meant to mask the true purpose of the observation. So, for example, he or she might ask you a few questions that are relevant to the study ("How happy are you right now?") and a few that are not ("Do you like cats more or less than dogs?"), which would make it difficult for you to guess the purpose of the study from the nature of the questions you were asked. These are just a few of the techniques that psychologists use to avoid demand characteristics.

● **Why is it sometimes important that participants not be aware of an experiment's true purpose?**

The Blind Observer

Participants aren't the only ones whose behavior can interfere with valid and reliable measurement. The behavior of the observers can interfere, too. After all, observers are human beings, and like all human beings, they tend to see what they expect to see. This fact was demonstrated in a classic study in which a group of psychology students were asked to measure the speed with which a rat learned to run through a maze (Rosenthal & Fode, 1963). Some students were told that their rat had been specially bred to be "maze dull" (i.e., slow to learn a maze), and others were told that their rat had been specially bred to be "maze bright" (i.e., quick to learn a maze). Although all the rats were actually the same breed, the students who *thought* they were measuring the speed of a dull rat reported that their rats took longer to learn the maze than did the students who *thought* they were measuring the speed of a bright rat. In other words, the rats seemed to do just what the students who observed them expected them to do.

Why did this happen? *First, expectations can influence observations.* It is easy to make errors when measuring the speed of a rat, and expectations often determine the kinds of errors people make. Does putting one paw over the finish line count as "learning the maze"? If the rat falls asleep, should the stopwatch be left running or should the rat be awakened and given a second chance? If a rat runs a maze in 18.5 seconds, should that number be rounded up or rounded down before it is recorded in the log book? The answers to these questions may depend on whether one thinks the rat is bright or dull. The students who timed the rats probably tried to be honest, vigilant, fair, and objective, but their expectations influenced their observations in subtle ways that they could neither detect nor control. Second, *expectations can influence reality.* Students who expected their rats to learn quickly may have unknowingly done things to help that learning along— for example, by muttering, "Oh, no!" when the bright rat turned the wrong way in the maze or by petting the bright rat more affectionately than the dull rat and so on. (We shall discuss these phenomena more extensively in Chapter 16.)

Observers' expectations, then, can have a powerful influence on both their observations and on the behavior of those whom they observe. Psychologists use many techniques to avoid these influences, and one of the most common is the **double-blind observation,** which is *an observation whose true purpose is hidden from both the observer and the participant.* For example, if the students had not been told which rats were bright and which were dull,

● **When might a computer run a better experiment than a human being?**

double-blind observation An observation whose true purpose is hidden from the researcher as well as from the participant.

AP PHOTO/TIMES RECORD, KAIA LARSEN

People's expectations can influence ● ● ● ● their observations. On September 10, 2002, Gurdeep Wander boarded an airplane with three other dark-skinned men who had no luggage, switched seats, and got up several times to use the restroom. This was enough to convince the pilot to make an emergency landing in Arkansas and have Mr. Wander arrested as a potential terrorist. Mr. Wander is an American citizen who works at Exxon and was on his way to a convention.

Worried customers lined up in 2008 after the IndyMac bank failed (above). Only the intervention of federal government prevented a repeat of the events of 1929. People's expectations can cause the phenomena they expect. In 1929, investors who expected the stock market to collapse sold their stocks and thereby caused the very crisis they feared. The New York Times attributed the crash to "mob psychology" (right).

then they would not have *had* any expectations about their rats. It is common practice in psychology to keep the observers as blind as the participants. For example, measurements are often made by research assistants who do not know what a particular participant is expected to say or do and who only learn about the nature of the study when it is concluded. Indeed, many modern studies are carried out by the world's blindest experimenter: a computer, which presents information to participants and measures their responses without any expectations whatsoever.

summary quiz [2.1]

1. The belief that accurate knowledge of the world requires observation of it is called
   a. measurement.
   b. empiricism.
   c. validity.
   d. naturalistic observation.

2. A set of rules and techniques for observation necessary to avoid mistakes that simple observation can produce is called
   a. a method.
   b. a measure.
   c. an operational definition.
   d. empiricism.

3. A device that can detect the event to which an operational definition refers is called
   a. empiricism.
   b. the case method.
   c. a measure.
   d. a detector.

4. Professor Craig developed a new test that supposedly measured IQ. When many individuals were given this test on two separate occasions, their scores showed little consistency from the first testing to the second. Professor Craig's test apparently lacked
   a. validity.
   b. reliability.
   c. power.
   d. demand characteristics.

correlation The "co-relationship" or pattern of covariation between two variables, each of which has been measured several times.

variable A property whose value can vary or change.

The Science of Explanation: Saying Why

The techniques discussed so far allow us to construct valid, reliable, powerful, and unbiased measures of properties such as happiness; to use those instruments to measure the happiness of a sample without demand characteristics; and to draw conclusions about the happiness of a population. Although scientific research always begins with the careful measurement of properties, its ultimate goal is typically the discovery of *causal relationships between properties.* We may find that happy people are more altruistic than unhappy people, but what we really want to know is whether their happiness is the cause of their altruism. Measurements can tell us how *much* happiness and altruism occur in a particular sample, but they cannot tell us (a) whether these properties are related and, (b) if so, whether their relationship is causal. As you will see, scientists have developed some clever ways of using measurement to answer these questions.

Correlation and Causation

If you wanted to determine whether there is any sort of relationship between happiness and altruism, you'd have to collect some data. (You are an empiricist, after all). You might, for example, measure the happiness and altruism of a few dozen people and make a table like the one shown in **TABLE 2.1**. Inspecting the table, you would quickly notice that altruism and happiness tend to occur together far more often than not. When two properties occur together, often we say they are **correlated**, which means that *the value of one is systematically related to the value of the other.* When the value of altruism is high, then the value of happiness tends to be high, too. *Correlation* is short for *co-relationship.*

● Televised violence and aggression are correlated. Does that mean televised violence causes aggressiveness?

As you look at Table 2.1, you might be tempted to conclude that the reason why happiness and altruism are correlated is that happiness causes altruism. You should resist that temptation. The fact that two **variables,** *properties whose values can vary across individuals or over time,* such as altruism and happiness are correlated does not mean that one necessarily causes the other.

Consider an example. Many studies (see Huesmann et al., 2003) have found a positive correlation between the amount of violence a child sees on television (let's call this variable *X*) and the aggressiveness of the child's behavior (let's call this variable *Y*). The more violence a child sees, the more aggressive that child is likely to be. But does that mean that seeing violence *causes* aggression? Not necessarily. It may be that watching violence on TV (*X*) causes aggressiveness (*Y*), but it may also be that aggressiveness (*Y*) causes children to watch televised violence (*X*). For example, children who are naturally aggressive may enjoy televised violence more than those who aren't and therefore may seek opportunities to watch it.

To make matters more complicated, it could even be the case that a third variable (*Z*) causes children both to be aggressive (*Y*)

TABLE 2.1		
Hypothetical Data of the Relationship between Happiness and Altruism		
Participant	Happiness	Level of Altruism
1	Happy	High
2	Happy	High
3	Unhappy	Low
4	Unhappy	Low
5	Happy	High
6	Happy	High
7	Unhappy	Low
8	Unhappy	Low
9	Happy	High
10	Happy	High
11	Unhappy	Low
12	Unhappy	Low
13	Happy	High
14	Happy	High
15	Unhappy	Low
16	Unhappy	Low
17	Happy	High
18	Happy	High
19	Unhappy	Low
20	Unhappy	Low

Climate change is destroying the ● ● ● ● ● ● ● ● ● ● *polar bear's habitat and may well drive it to extinction. Human activity is not just correlated with global warming; it is one of the causes.*

STUART YATES/ALAMY

· FIGURE 2.2

Causes of Correlation. *If X (watching televised violence) and Y (aggressiveness) are correlated, then there are exactly three possible explanations: X causes Y, Y causes X, or Z (some other factor, such as lack of adult supervision) causes both Y and X, neither of which causes the other.*

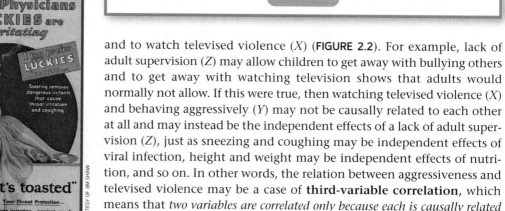

Although people have smoked tobacco for centuries, only recently has the causal relationship between cigarette smoke and lung disease been detected. By the way, how many physicians said the opposite? And "less irritating" than what?

and to watch televised violence (*X*) (**FIGURE 2.2**). For example, lack of adult supervision (*Z*) may allow children to get away with bullying others and to get away with watching television shows that adults would normally not allow. If this were true, then watching televised violence (*X*) and behaving aggressively (*Y*) may not be causally related to each other at all and may instead be the independent effects of a lack of adult supervision (*Z*), just as sneezing and coughing may be independent effects of viral infection, height and weight may be independent effects of nutrition, and so on. In other words, the relation between aggressiveness and televised violence may be a case of **third-variable correlation**, which means that *two variables are correlated only because each is causally related to a third variable.* How can we tell whether this is the case?

Matched Samples and Matched Pairs

The most straightforward way to determine whether a third variable such as lack of adult supervision (*Z*) causes children to watch televised violence (*X*) and to behave aggressively (*Y*) is to eliminate differences in adult supervision (*Z*) among a sample of children and see if the correlation between televised violence (*X*) and aggressiveness (*Y*) remains. For example, you could observe children using the **matched samples technique**, which is *a technique whereby the participants in two samples are identical in terms of a third variable.* For instance, we could measure only children who are supervised by an adult exactly 87% of the time, thus ensuring that every child who watched a lot of televised violence had exactly the same amount of adult supervision as every child who did not watch a lot of televised violence. Alternatively, you could observe children using the **matched pairs technique**, which is *a technique whereby each participant in a sample is identical to one other participant in that sample in terms of a third variable.* For instance, you could measure children who experience different amounts of adult supervision, but you could make sure that for every child you measure who watches a lot of televised violence and is supervised 24% of the time, you also observe a child who watches little

third-variable correlation The fact that two variables may be correlated only because they are both caused by a third variable.

matched samples An observational technique that involves matching the average of the participants in the experimental and control groups in order to eliminate the possibility that a third variable (and not the independent variable) caused changes in the dependent variable.

matched pairs An observational technique that involves matching each participant in the experimental group with a specific participant in the control group in order to eliminate the possibility that a third variable (and not the independent variable) caused changes in the dependent variable.

third-variable problem The fact that the causal relationship between two variables cannot be inferred from the correlation between them because of the ever-present possibility of third-variable correlation.

televised violence and is supervised 24% of the time, thus ensuring that the children who do and do not watch a lot of televised violence have the same amount of adult supervision *on average*. Regardless of which technique you used, you would know that the children who do and don't watch televised violence have equal amounts of adult supervision on average; as such, if those who watch a lot of televised violence were more aggressive on average than those who didn't, then lack of adult supervision could not possibly be the cause.

A woman's age is correlated with the number of children she has borne, but age does not cause women to become pregnant, and pregnancy does not cause women to age.

[HOT SCIENCE]

Establishing Causality in the Brain

Sometimes the best way to learn about something is to see what happens when it breaks, and the human brain is no exception. Scientists have studied the effects of brain damage for centuries, and those studies reveal a lot about how the brain normally works so well. But the problem with studying brain-damaged patients, of course, is the problem with studying any naturally occurring variable: Brain damage may be related to particular patterns of behavior, but that relationship may or may not be causal. Experimentation is the premiere method for establishing causal relationships between variables, but scientists cannot ethically cause brain damage in human beings, and thus they have not been able to establish causal relationships between particular kinds of brain damage and particular patterns of behavior.

Until now. Scientists have recently discovered a way to mimic brain damage with a benign technique called *transcranial magnetic stimulation* (or TMS) (Barker, Jalinous, & Freeston, 1985; Hallett, 2000). If you've ever held a magnet under a piece of paper and used it to drag a pin across the paper's surface,

you know that magnetic fields can pass through material such as paper and wood. They can pass through bone, too. TMS delivers a magnetic pulse that passes through the skull and deactivates neurons in the cerebral cortex for a short period. Researchers can direct TMS pulses to particular brain regions—essentially turning them "off"—and then measure temporary changes in the way a person moves, sees, thinks, remembers, speaks, or feels. By manipulating the state of the brain, scientists can perform experiments that establish causal relationships. For example, scientists have recently discovered that magnetic stimulation of the visual cortex temporarily impairs a person's ability to detect the motion of an object, without impairing the person's ability to recognize that object (Beckers & Zeki, 1995). This intriguing discovery suggests that motion perception and object recognition are accomplished by different parts of the brain, but moreover, it establishes that the activity of these brain regions *causes* motion perception and object recognition.

For the first time in human history, the causal relationships between particular brain regions

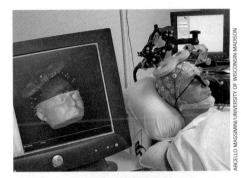

Transcranial magnetic stimulation activates and deactivates regions of the brain with a magnetic pulse, temporarily mimicking brain damage.

and particular behaviors have been unequivocally established. Rather than relying on observational studies of brain-damaged patients or the snapshots provided by MRI or PET scans, researchers can now manipulate brain activity and measure its effects. Studies suggest that TMS has no harmful side effects (Pascual-Leone et al., 1993), and this new tool promises to revolutionize the study of how our brains create our thoughts, feelings, and actions.

Although both the matched samples and matched pairs techniques can be useful, neither would allow you to dismiss the possibility of third-variable correlation entirely. Why? Because even if you used these techniques to dismiss a *particular* third variable (e.g., lack of adult supervision), you would not be able to dismiss *all* third variables. For example, as soon as you finished making these observations, it might suddenly occur to you that emotional instability (*Z*) might cause children to gravitate toward violent television programs (*X*) and to behave aggressively (*Y*). Emotional instability would be a new third variable, and you would have to design a new test to dismiss it. The problem is that you could dream up new third variables all day long without ever breaking a sweat, and every time you dreamed one up, you would have to rush out and do a new test using matched samples or matched pairs to determine whether *this* third variable was the cause of watching televised violence and of behaving aggressively.

The fact is that there are an infinite number of third variables out there and thus an infinite number of reasons why *X* and *Y* might be correlated. Because most of us don't have the time to perform an infinite number of studies with matched samples or matched pairs, we can never be sure that the correlation we observe between *X* and *Y* is evidence of a causal relationship between them. The **third-variable problem** refers to the fact that *a causal relationship between two variables cannot be inferred from the*

How can third-variable correlation explain the fact that the more tattoos a person has, the more likely he or she is to be involved in a motorcycle accident?

naturally occurring correlation between them because of the ever-present possibility of third-variable correlation. In other words, if we care about causality, then naturally occuring correlations can never tell us what we really want to know.

Experimentation

The third-variable problem prevents us from using naturally occuring correlations to learn about causal relationships, and so we have to find another method that will. Let's start by considering once again the source of all our troubles. We cannot conclude that watching televised violence causes children to behave aggressively because there is some chance that both behaviors are caused by a third variable, such as lack of adult supervision or emotional instability, and there are so many third variables in the world that we could never do enough tests to dismiss them all. Another way of saying this is that children who do watch and don't watch televised violence differ in countless ways, and any one of these countless differences could be the real cause of their different levels of aggressiveness and their different levels of violence watching. Of course, if we could somehow eliminate *all* of these count-less differences at once—somehow find a sample of children who were perfect clones of each other, with identical amounts of adult supervi-sion, identical amounts of emotional stability, identical histories, iden-tical physiologies, identical neighborhoods, siblings, toys, schools, teeth, dreams, and so on—then we *could* conclude that televised violence and aggressiveness have a causal relationship. If we could only find a sam-ple of children, some of whom watch televised violence and some of whom don't, but all of whom are identical in terms of *every possible* third variable, then we would know that watching tele-vised violence and behaving aggressively are not just correlated but causally related.

Finding a sample of clones is not very likely, and so scientists have developed a tech-nique that can eliminate all the countless differences between people in a sample. It is called an experiment. An **experiment** is *a technique for establishing the causal relationship between variables.* The most important thing to know about experiments is that you al-ready know the most important thing about experiments because you've been doing them all your life. Imagine, for instance, what you would do if you were surfing the web on a laptop that used a wireless connection when all of a sudden the connection stopped working. You might suspect that another device, such as your roommate's new cordless phone, was interfering with your connection. Your first step would be to observe and measure carefully, noting whether you had a connection when your roommate was and was not using his cordless phone. But even if you observed a correlation between the failure to connect and your room-mate's phone usage, the third-variable problem would prevent you from drawing a causal conclusion. For example, maybe your roommate is afraid of loud noises and calls his mommy for comfort whenever there is an electrical storm. And maybe the storm somehow interrupts your wireless connection. In other words, it is possible that a storm (Z) is the cause of both your roommate's phone calls (X) and your laptop's failure to con-nect to the internet (Y).

How could you solve the third-variable problem? Rather than *observing* the correla-tion between telephone usage and connection failure, you could try to *create* a correla-tion by intentionally switching your roommate's phone on and off a few times and observing changes in your laptop's connection. If you noticed that "telephone on" and "connection failed" occurred together more often than not, then you would conclude that your roommate's telephone was the *cause* of your failed connection, and you would put the phone in the trash compactor and deny it when your roommate asked.

The technique you might intuitively use to solve your connection problem is the same technique that psychologists use to solve scientific problems. Consider again the

> ● In what ways do we perform experiments in everyday life?

● *Children's aggressiveness is correlated with the amount of violence they see on TV, but that doesn't mean that one of these things causes the other.*

experiment A technique for establishing the causal relationship between variables.

independent variable The variable that is manipulated in an experiment.

experimental group One of the two groups of participants created by the manipulation of an independent variable in an experiment: the experimental group is exposed to the stimulus being studied and the *control group* is not.

control group One of the two groups of participants created by the manipulation of an independent variable in an experiment that is not exposed to the stimulus being studied.

dependent variable The variable that is measured in a study.

internal validity The characteristic of an experiment that allows one to draw accurate inferences about the causal relationship between an independent and dependent variable.

correlation between aggressiveness and tele-vised violence. How can you determine why these variables are correlated? Well, rather than *measuring* how much televised violence a child watches (as you did when you used the matched pairs or matched sample tech-niques), you could *manipulate* how much tel-evised violence a child watches. For example, you could find a sample of children, expose half of them to 2 hours of televised violence every day for a month, and make sure that the other half saw no televised violence at all (see **FIGURE 2.3**). At the end of a month, you could measure the aggressiveness of the children in the two groups. In essence, you would be computing the correlation between a variable that you measured (aggressiveness) and a variable that you manipulated (televised vio-lence), and in so doing, you would have solved the third-variable problem. Because you *ma-nipulated* rather than *measured* how much tel-evised violence a child saw, you would never have to wonder whether a third variable (such as lack of adult supervision) might have caused it. Why? Because you already *know* what caused the child to watch or not watch televised vio-lence. You did!

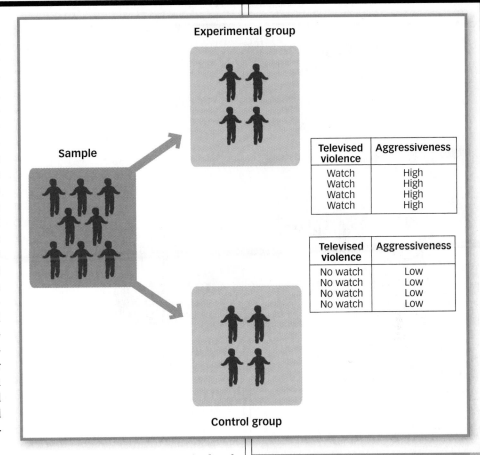

Experiments always involves manipulation. We call *the variable that is manipulated* the **independent variable** because it is under our control, and thus it is "indepen-dent" of what the participant says or does. When we manipulate an independent variable (e.g., watching televised violence), we create at least two groups of partici-pants: an **experimental group**, which is *the group of people who are treated in a partic-ular way,* such as being exposed to two hours of televised violence per day for a month, and a **control group**, which is *the group of people who are not treated in this particular way.* Then we measure another variable, and we call *the variable that is measured* the **dependent variable** because its value "depends" on what the participant says or does.

FIGURE 2.3 • • • • • • • • • • • • • • • • • •

Manipulation. *The independent variable is televised violence and the dependent variable is aggressiveness. Manipulation of the independent variable results in an experimental group and a control group. When we compare the behavior of participants in these two groups, we are actually computing the correlation between the independent variable and the dependent variable.*

Drawing Conclusions

If you were to apply the techniques discussed so far, you could design an experiment that has **internal validity**, which is *the characteristic of an experiment that allows one to draw accurate inferences about the causal relationship between an independent and dependent variable.* When we say that an experiment is internally valid, we mean that everything *inside* the experiment is working exactly as it must in order for us to draw conclusions about causal relationships. Specifically, an experiment is internally valid when

- An independent variable has been effectively manipulated.
- A dependent variable has been measured in an unbiased way with a valid, powerful, and reliable measure.
- A correlation has been observed between the independent and the dependent variable.

If we do these things, then we may conclude that manipulated changes in the inde-pendent variable caused measured changes in the dependent variable. For example, our imaginary experiment on televised violence and aggressiveness would allow us conclude that televised violence (as we defined it) caused aggressiveness (as we defined it) in the

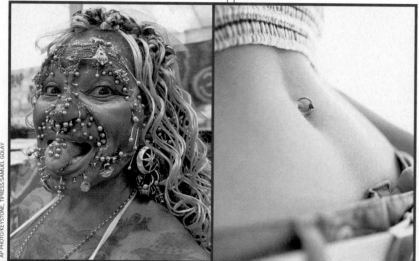

● *Does piercing make a person more or less attractive? The answer, of course, depends entirely on how you operationally define piercing.*

people whom we measured. Notice that the phrase "as we defined it" represents an important restriction on the kinds of conclusions we can draw from this experiment. Our experiment does not allow us to draw the sweeping conclusion that "televised violence causes aggressiveness" because as you saw when we discussed operational definitions, there are many different ways to define "televised violence" (should a shouting match between a Democratic and Republican strategist count as violence?) and many different ways to define "aggressiveness" (does cutting someone off midsentence count as aggressiveness?). Whether we observe a correlation between the violence we manipulated and the aggressiveness we measured will surely depend on how we defined them in the first place.

So what is the right way to define such variables? One obvious answer is that we should define them as they are typically defined in the real world. **External validity** is *a property of an experiment in which variables have been operationally defined in a normal, typical, or realistic way*. It seems fairly clear that *interrupting* is not the kind of aggressive behavior with which teachers and parents are normally concerned and that most instances of aggression among children lie somewhere between an insult and a chain saw massacre. If the goal of an experiment is to determine whether the kinds of programs children typically watch cause the kinds of aggression in which children typically engage, then external validity is essential.

● **Should variables be defined as they typically are in the real world?**

But that isn't what many experiments are meant to do. Psychologists are rarely trying to learn about the real world by creating tiny replicas of it in their laboratories. Rather, they are usually trying to learn about the real world by using experiments to test theories and hypotheses (Mook, 1983). A **theory** is *a hypothetical account of how and why a phenomenon occurs*, and a **hypothesis** is *a testable prediction made by a theory*. For example, physicists have a theory stating that heat is the result of the rapid movement of molecules. This theory suggests a hypothesis—namely, that if the molecules that constitute an object are slowed, the object should become cooler. Now imagine that a physicist tested this hypothesis by performing an experiment in which a laser was used to slow the movement of the molecules in a rubber ball, whose temperature was then measured. Would we criticize this experiment by saying, "Sorry, but your experiment teaches us nothing about the real world because in the real world, no one actually uses lasers to slow the movement of the molecules in rubber balls"? Let's hope not. The physicist's theory (molecular motion causes heat) led to a hypothesis about what would happen in the laboratory (slowing the molecules in a rubber ball should cool it), and thus the events that the physicist manipulated and measured in the laboratory served to test the theory. Similarly, a good theory about the causal relationship between watching violence on television and behaving aggressively should lead to hypotheses about how children will behave after watching 2 minutes of Road Runner cartoons or all five *Nightmare on Elm Street* movies back to back. As such, even these this unrepresentative forms of television watching can serve to test the theory. In short, theories allow us to generate hypotheses about what *can* happen, or what *must* happen, or what *will* happen under particular circumstances, and experiments are typically meant to create these circumstances, test the hypotheses, and thereby provide evidence for or against the theories that generated them. Experiments are not meant to be miniature versions of everyday life, and thus external invalidity is not necessarily a problem.

"Hi. You've been randomly selected to participate in a sex survey upstairs in fifteen minutes."

Our imaginary experiment on televised violence and aggressiveness would allow us to conclude that televised violence (as we defined it) caused aggressiveness (as we defined it) in the people whom we measured. The phrase "the people whom we measured" represents another important restriction on the kinds of conclusions we can draw from this experiment. All experiments are done with a sample of participants who are drawn from a larger population. How can we know whether the conclusions we draw about the sample are also true of the larger population? The best way to do this is to use **random sampling**, which is *a technique for choosing participants that ensures that every member of a population has an equal chance of being included in the sample*. When we randomly sample participants from a population, we earn the right to *generalize*—that is, to conclude that what we observed in our sample would also have been observed if we had measured the entire population. You already have good intuitions about the importance of random sampling. For example, if you stopped at a farm stand to buy a bag of cherries and the farmer offered to let you taste a few that he had specially handpicked from the bag, you'd be reluctant to generalize from that nonrandom sample to the population of cherries in the bag. But if the farmer invited you to pull a few cherries from the bag without looking, you'd probably be willing to take those cherries as reasonably representative of the cherry population, and you'd be reasonably sure that your conclusions about these randomly sampled cherries would apply to the rest of the cherries in the bag.

Given the importance of random sampling, you may be surprised to learn that psychologists almost never do it. Indeed, virtually every participant in every psychology experiment you will ever read about was a volunteer, and most were college students who were significantly younger, smarter, healthier, wealthier, and whiter than the average earthling. Psychologists sample their participants the "wrong way" (by nonrandom sampling) because it is just about impossible to do it the "right way" (by random sampling). Even if there were an alphabetized list of all the world's human inhabitants from which we could randomly choose our research participants, the likelihood that we could actually perform experiments on those whom we sampled would be depressingly slim. After all, how would we find the 72-year-old Bedouin woman whose family roams the desert so that we could measure the electrical activity in her brain while she watched cartoons? How would we convince the 3-week-old infant in New Delhi to complete a lengthy questionnaire about his political beliefs? Most psychology experiments are conducted by professors and graduate students at colleges and universities in the Western Hemisphere, and as much as they might like to randomly sample the population of the planet, the practical truth is that they are pretty much stuck studying the folks who volunteer for their studies.

● **When can a sample teach us about a population?**

So how can we learn *anything* from psychology experiments? Isn't the failure to randomly sample a fatal flaw? No, it's not. Although we can't automatically generalize from nonrandom samples, there are three reasons why this is not a lethal problem for the science of psychology:

■ Sometimes generality does not matter. One flying pig utterly disproves most people's theories of porcine locomotion. Similarly, in psychology it often doesn't matter if *everyone* does something as long as *someone* does it. If watching a violent television show for 1 hour caused a nonrandomly selected group of children to start shoving in the lunch line, then this fact would utterly disprove every theory that claimed that televised violence cannot cause aggression—and it might even provide important clues about when aggression will and won't occur. An experimental result can be illuminating even when its generality is severely limited.

■ Sometimes generality can be determined. When the generality of an experimental result *is* important, psychologists often perform a new experiment that uses the same procedures on a different sample.

external validity A characteristic of an experiment in which the independent and dependent variables are operationally defined in a normal, typical, or realistic way.

theory A hypothetical account of how and why a phenomenon occurs, usually in the form of a statement about the causal relationship between two or more properties. Theories lead to *hypotheses*.

hypothesis A specific and testable prediction that is usually derived from a *theory*.

random sampling A technique for choosing participants that ensures that every member of a population has an equal chance of being included in the sample.

GETTY IMAGES

*College students are the traditional ● ● ● ●
"guinea pigs" of psychological research.*

For example, if we were to measure how some American children behaved after watching televised violence for 2 hours, we could then replicate the experiment with Japanese children, or with teenagers, or with adults. In essence, we could treat the attributes of our sample, such as culture and age, as independent variables and do experiments to determine whether these attributes influenced our dependent variable. If the results of our study were replicated in numerous nonrandom samples, we could be more confident (though never completely confident) that the results would generalize to the population at large.

■ Sometimes generality can be assumed. Instead of asking, "Is there a compelling reason to generalize from a nonrandom sample?" we might just as easily ask, "Is there a compelling reason not to?" For example, few of us would be willing to take an experimental drug that could potentially make us smarter and happier if a nonrandom sample of seven participants took the drug and died a slow, painful death. Indeed, we would probably refuse the drug even if the seven subjects were mice. Although the study used a nonrandom sample of participants who are different from us in many ways, we are willing to generalize from their experience to ours because we know that even mice share enough of our basic biology to make it a good bet that what harms them can harm us, too. By this same reasoning, if a psychology experiment demonstrated that some American children behaved violently after watching televised violence for 1 hour, we might ask whether there is a compelling reason to suspect that Ecuadorian college students or middle-aged Australians would behave any differently. If we had a reason to suspect they would, then the experimental method would provide a way for us to investigate that possibility.

summary quiz [2.2]

5. Your friend tells you that she has just heard that there is a positive correlation between pizza consumption and children's intelligence. If this were in fact true, it would mean that
   a. the more intelligent children are, the more pizza they eat.
   b. pizza ingredients enhance brain development.
   c. intelligent children realize that pizza is a healthful food.
   d. parents of intelligent children encourage them to eat lots of pizza.

6. Marie Rodriquez divides her seventh-grade gifted class in half during study hour. Half watch a video encouraging volunteer activities, while the other half watch an MTV video. She then records how aggressively students behave at recess later that day. What is the independent variable in this study?
   a. students' aggressive behavior   c. giftedness of the students
   b. recess   d. type of video

7. Dr. Shondra Jones administers to female and male students at both northern universities and southern universities a questionnaire that measures attitudes towards women's rights. The dependent variable in this study is
   a. gender of the students.   c. attitudes toward women's rights.
   b. geographic location of the students. d. the majors of the students.

8. The characteristic of an experiment that allows one to draw accurate inferences about the causal relationship between an independent and dependent variable is called
   a. external validity.   c. third-variable correlation.
   b. internal validity.   d. matched sample technique.

The Ethics of Science: Saying Please and Thank You

Somewhere along the way, someone probably told you that it isn't nice to treat people like objects. And yet, it may seem that psychologists do just that—creating situations that cause people to feel fearful or sad, to do things that are embarrassing or immoral, and to learn things about themselves that they might not really want to know. Why do psychologists treat people so shabbily? In fact, psychologists go to great lengths to ensure the safety and well-being of their research participants, and they are bound by a code of ethics that is as detailed and demanding as the professional codes that bind physicians, lawyers, and members of the clergy. This code of ethics was formalized by the American Psychological Association in 1958 and offers a number of rules that govern all research conducted with human beings. Here are a few of the most important ones:

- *Informed consent:* Participants may not take part in a psychological study unless they have given **informed consent**, which is a *written agreement to participate in a study made by an adult who has been informed of all the risks that participation may entail.* This doesn't mean that the person must know everything about the study (the hypothesis), but it does mean that the person must know about anything that might potentially be harmful, painful, embarrassing, or unpleasant. If people cannot give informed consent (perhaps because they are minors or are mentally incapable), then informed consent must be obtained from their legal guardians.

- *Freedom from coercion:* Psychologists may not coerce participation. Coercion not only means physical and psychological coercion but monetary coercion as well. It is unethical to offer people large amounts of money to persuade them to do something that they might otherwise decline to do. College students may be invited to participate in studies as part of their training in psychology, but they are ordinarily offered the option of learning the same things by other means.

- *Protection from harm:* Psychologists must take every possible precaution to protect their research participants from physical or psychological harm. If there are two equally effective ways to study something, the psychologist must use the safer method. If no safe method is available, the psychologist may not perform the study.

- *Risk-benefit analysis:* Although participants may be asked to accept small risks, such as a minor shock or a small embarrassment, they may not even be *asked* to accept large risks, such as severe pain or psychological trauma, or risks that are greater than those they would ordinarily take in their everyday lives. Furthermore, even when participants are asked to take small risks, the psychologist must first demonstrate that these risks are outweighed by the social benefits of the new knowledge that might be gained from the study.

- *Debriefing:* Although psychologists need not divulge everything about a study before a person participates, they must divulge it after the person participates. If a participant is deceived in any way before or during a study, the psychologist must provide a **debriefing**, which is *a verbal description of the true nature and purpose of a study.* If the participant was changed in any way (e.g., made to feel sad), the psychologist must attempt to undo that change (e.g., ask the person to do a task that will make them happy) and restore the participant to the state he or she was in before the study.

These rules require that psychologists show extraordinary concern for their participants' welfare, but how are they enforced? Almost all psychology studies are done by psychologists who work at colleges and universities. These institutions have institutional review boards (IRBs) that are composed of instructors and researchers, university

informed consent A written agreement to participate in a study made by a person who has been informed of all the risks that participation may entail.

debriefing A verbal description of the true nature and purpose of a study that psychologists provide to people after they have participated in the study.

"I don't usually volunteer for experiments, but I'm kind of a puzzle freak."

😀 ONLY HUMAN

THE WELL-BEING OF PARTICIPANTS ALWAYS COMES FIRST! In 1997 in Mill Valley, California, 10th-grade student Ari Hoffman won first place in the Marin County science fair for doing a study that found that exposure to radiation decreased the offspring of fruitflies. However, he was quickly disqualified for cruelty when it was learned that about 35 of his 200 flies died during the 3-month experiment. Hoffman was disappointed because he had used extraordinary efforts to keep the flies alive, for example, by maintaining a tropical temperature for his flies during the entire experiment.

staff, and laypeople from the community (e.g., business leaders or members of the clergy). A psychologist may conduct a study only after the IRB has reviewed and approved it. As you can imagine, the code of ethics and the procedure for approval are so strict that many studies simply cannot be performed anywhere, by anyone, at any time. For example, psychologists have long wondered how growing up without exposure to language affects a person's subsequent ability to speak and think, but they cannot ethically manipulate such a variable in an experiment. As such, they must be content to study the natural correlations between variables such as language exposure and speaking ability, and they must forever forgo the possibility of firmly establishing causal relationships between these variables. There are many questions that psychologists will never be able to answer definitively because doing so would require unethical experimentation. This is an unavoidable consequence of studying creatures who have fundamental human rights.

● **Is it ever justifiable to harm a human or nonhuman research participant?**

Of course, not all research participants have human rights because not all research participants are human. Some are chimpanzees, rats, pigeons, or other nonhuman animals. How does the ethical code of the psychologist apply to nonhuman participants? The question of animal rights is one of the most hotly debated issues of our time, and people on opposite sides of the debate rarely have much good to say about each other. And yet, consider three points on which every reasonable person would agree:

■ A very small percentage of psychological experiments are performed on nonhuman animals, and a very small percentage of these experiments cause discomfort or death.

■ Nonhuman animals deserve good care, should never be subjected to more discomfort than is absolutely necessary, and should be protected by federal and institutional guidelines.

■ Some experiments on nonhuman animals have had tremendous benefits for human beings, and many have not.

None of these points is in dispute among thoughtful advocates of different positions, so what exactly is the controversy? The controversy lies in the answer to a single question: Is it morally acceptable to force nonhuman animals to pay certain costs so that human animals can reap uncertain benefits? Although compelling arguments may be made on both sides of this moral dilemma, it is clearly just that—a *moral* dilemma and not a scientific controversy that one can hope to answer with evidence and facts. Anyone who has ever loved a pet can empathize with the plight of the nonhuman animal that is being forced to participate in an experiment, feel pain, or even die when it would clearly prefer not to. Anyone who has ever loved a person with a debilitating illness can understand the desire of researchers to develop drugs and medical procedures by doing to nonhuman animals the same things that farmers and animal trainers do every day. Do animals have rights, and if so, do they ever outweigh the rights of people? This is a difficult question with which individuals and societies are currently wrestling. For now, at least, there is no easy answer.

Some people consider it unethical to use animals for clothing or research. Others see an important distinction between these two purposes.

summary quiz [2.3]

9. A written agreement to participate in a study made by an adult who has been informed of all the risks that participation may entail is known as
   a. a memorandum of understanding.
   b. informed consent.
   c. a signature of authorization.
   d. debriefing.

10. Participants in a psychology study

　　a.　can be asked to accept risks such as severe pain or psychological trauma.

　　b.　can be asked to accept risks that are greater than those they would ordinarily take in their everyday lives.

　　c.　can be asked to accept small risks, whether or not these are outweighed by the social benefits of gaining new knowledge.

　　d.　can be asked to accept small risks, but only if these risks are outweighed by the social benefits of gaining new knowledge.

11. A verbal description of the true nature and purpose of a study provided to the participant after the study is done is called

　　a.　informed consent. 　　　　　　　c.　debriefing.

　　b.　risk-benefit analysis. 　　　　　　d.　harm-protection follow-up.

12. According to the textbook, reasonable people would agree on which of the following points regarding research performed on nonhuman animals?

　　a.　Some experiments on nonhuman animals have had tremendous benefits for humans.

　　b.　Nonhuman animals should never be subjected to discomfort or death even if the results would greatly benefit humans.

　　c.　Although human research participants are protected by federal and institutional guidelines, nonhuman animals do not need these protections.

　　d.　It can be demonstrated scientifically that the rights of humans always outweigh the rights of nonhuman animals.

WhereDoYouStand?

The Morality of Immoral Experiments

Is it wrong to benefit from someone else's wrongdoing? Although this may seem like an abstract question for moral philosophers, it is a very real question that scientists must ask when they consider the results of unethical experiments. During World War II, Nazi doctors conducted barbaric medical studies on prisoners in concentration camps. They placed prisoners in decompression chambers and then dissected their living brains, in order to determine how similar decompression at high altitude might affect pilots. They irradiated and chemically mutilated the reproductive organs of men and women in order to find inexpensive methods for the mass sterilization of "racially inferior" people. They infected prisoners with streptococcus and tetanus in order to devise treatments for soldiers who had been exposed to these bacteria. And in one of the most horrible experiments, prisoners were immersed in tanks of ice water so that the doctors could discover how long pilots would survive if they bailed out over the North Sea. The prisoners were frozen, thawed, and frozen again until they died. During these experiments, the doctors carefully recorded the prisoners' physiological responses.

These experiments were crimes, but the records of these experiments remain, and in some cases they provide valuable information that could never be obtained ethically. For example, because researchers cannot perform controlled studies that would expose volunteers to dangerously cold temperatures, there is still controversy among doctors about the best treatment for hypothermia. In 1988, Robert Pozos, a physiologist who had spent a lifetime studying hypothermia, came across an unpublished report written in 1945 titled "The Treatment of Shock from Prolonged Exposure to Cold, Especially in Water." The report described the results of the horrible freezing experiments performed on prisoners at the Dachau concentration camp, and it suggested that contrary to the conventional medical wisdom, rapid rewarming (rather than slow rewarming) might be the best way to treat hypothermia.

Should the Nazi medical studies have been published so that modern doctors might more effectively treat hypothermia? Many scientists and ethicists thought they should. "The prevention of a death outweighs the protection of a memory. The victims' dignity was irrevocably lost in vats of freezing liquid forty years ago. Nothing can change that," argued bioethicist Arthur Caplan. Others disagreed. "I don't see how any credence can be given to the work of unethical investigators," wrote Arnold Relman, editor of the *New England Journal of Medicine*. "It goes to legitimizing the evil done," added Abraham Foxman, national director of the Anti-Defamation League (Siegel, 1988). The debate about this issue rages on (Caplan, 1992). If we use data that were obtained unethically, are we rewarding those who collected it and legitimizing their actions? Or can we condemn such investigations but still learn from them? Where do you stand?

CHAPTER REVIEW

Summary

Empiricism: How to Know Things

- An empiricist believes observation is key to accurate knowledge.
- A method is a set of rules and techniques for observation necessary to avoid mistakes that simple observation can produce.

The Science of Observation: Saying What

- Measurement is a scientific means of observation that involves defining an abstract property in terms of some concrete condition, called an operational definition, and then constructing a device, or a measure, that can detect the conditions that the operational definition specifies.
- Psychologists sometimes use the case method to study single, exceptional individuals, but more often they use samples of many people drawn from a population.
- When people know they are being observed, they may behave as they think they should; psychologists try to reduce or eliminate such demand characteristics by observing participants in their natural habitat or by hiding their expectations from people.
- In double-blind observations, the experiment's purpose is hidden from the experimenter and the participants, ensuring that observers neither see what they want to see nor cause participants to behave as the observers expect them to behave.

The Science of Explanation: Saying Why

- To determine whether two variables are causally related, we must first determine whether they are related at all.

- Even when we find a correlation between two variables, we can't conclude that they are causally related, because an infinite number of "third variables" might be causing them both.
- Experiments solve the third-variable problem by manipulating an independent variable, assigning participants to the experimental and control groups that this manipulation creates, and measuring a dependent variable which is then compared across groups.
- An internally valid experiment establishes a causal relationship between variables as they were operationally defined and among the participants whom they included. When an experiment is externally valid—that is, when the variables mimic the real world and participants are randomly sampled—we may generalize from its results. Internal validity is essential; external validity is not.

The Ethics of Science: Saying Please and Thank You

- Psychologists have the responsibility of making sure that human research participants give their informed and voluntary consent to participate in studies, and that these studies pose minimal or no risk.
- Similar principles guide the human treatment of nonhuman research subjects.
- Enforcement of these principles by federal, institutional, and professional governing agencies ensures that the research process is a meaningful one that can lead to significant increases in knowledge.

Key Terms

empiricism (p. 34)

method (p. 34)

operational definition (p. 35)

measure (p. 35)

electromyograph (EMG) (p. 35)

validity (p. 36)

reliability (p. 36)

power (p. 36)

case method (p. 37)

population (p. 37)

sample (p. 37)

demand characteristics (p. 37)

naturalistic observation (p. 37)

double-blind observation (p. 39)

correlated (p. 41)

variable (p. 41)

third-variable correlation (p. 42)

matched samples (p. 42)

matched pairs (p. 42)

third-variable problem (p. 43)

experiment (p. 44)

independent variable (p. 45)

experimental group (p. 45)

control group (p. 45)

dependent variable (p. 45)

internal validity (p. 45)

external validity (p. 46)

theory (p. 46)

hypothesis (p. 46)

random sampling (p. 47)

informed consent (p. 49)

debriefing (p. 49)

Critical Thinking Questions

1. Among the ancient Greeks, the dogmatists were healers who tried to understand the body by developing theories about its function; in contrast, the empiricists tried to understand the body by observing sick people.

   Today, our modern word *dogmatic* is used to describe someone who authoritatively states his opinions as if they were facts, while an unqualified physician who trusts his own experience without regard to established theory or standard practice can be called a quack, a charlatan, or an "empiric."

   How do you think these modern definitions grew out of the ancient ones?

2. Demand characteristics are those aspects of a setting or experiment that cause people to behave as they think an observer wants or expects them to behave. Experimental results can also be skewed because the experimenter's expectations can influence observations.

   Suppose you are a medical researcher conducting a study to see if a new trial drug called Relievia is more or less effective than aspirin at relieving pain. On the one hand, although you plan to run the study fairly, you hope that Relievia will work, because you've invested so much time in developing this drug. On the other hand, the study participants may feel pressured to report that the fancy-sounding, expensive new drug works better than plain old aspirin. Both these demand characteristics and your own preconceptions could influence the results.

   How would you design your experiment to minimize the effects of these preconceptions on your study?

3. A fundamental idea in psychology is that correlation (two things that tend to occur together) does not necessarily imply causation (one thing causing the other). This is an idea that confuses many people (including some psychologists).

   For example, many newspaper articles have now noted that people who live in houses located under high-voltage power lines have a heightened risk of developing certain kinds of cancer. In other words, living under power lines and cancer risk may be statistically correlated.

   Does this mean that long-term exposure to power lines causes cancer? If not, what else might explain the correlation?

Answers to Summary Quizzes

Summary Quiz 2.1
1. b; 2. a; 3. c; 4. b

Summary Quiz 2.2
5. a; 6. d; 7. c; 8. b

Summary Quiz 2.3
9. b; 10. d; 11. c; 12. a

Need more help? Additional resources are located at the book's free companion Web site at: www.worthpublishers.com/schacterbriefle

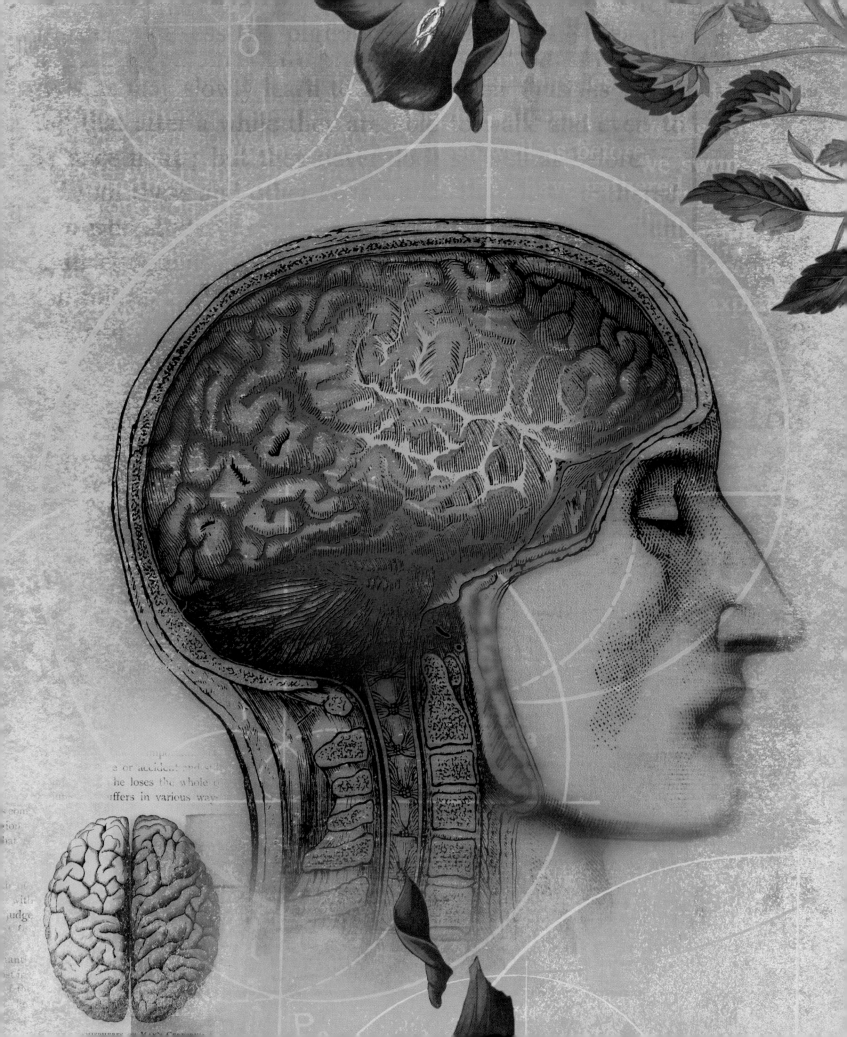

Neuroscience and Behavior

TWO PATIENTS WERE ADMITTED TO A hospital emergency room late one evening, complaining of problems with their vision. One patient was a 17-year-old named David, and the other was a 75-year-old named Betty. David saw people who weren't there and Betty didn't recognize her own husband, but these weren't problems with their eyes: They were disorders of their brains.

David was brought in by some fellow members of his gang. They told the doctors that David had become frantic, believing he kept seeing members of a rival gang sneaking up on him. At first David's friends listened to his warnings and searched for their rivals. After repeated scares and false alarms, they decided David had gone crazy. The doctors didn't find any problems with David's eyes. Instead, they discovered he was suffering from hallucinations—a side effect of abusing methamphetamine (McKetin et al., 2006). David's prolonged crystal meth habit altered the normal functioning of some chemicals in his brain, distorting his perception of reality and "fooling" his brain into perceiving things that were not actually there. After he stopped taking the drug, the hallucinations disappeared, and David was back to his normal calm self.

The second patient, Betty, had fainted earlier in the day. After she was revived, Betty no longer recognized her husband, George. She didn't recognize her two sons, either, but she insisted it was just a problem with her eyes and had the family bring her to the emergency room for examination. The doctor who examined Betty's eyes found her vision to be perfectly normal. A brain scan showed that Betty had suffered a stroke that damaged a small area on the right side of her brain. Doctors diagnosed Betty with a rare disorder called *prosopagnosia*, which is an inability to recognize familiar faces (Duchaine et al., 2006; Yin, 1970)—a result of the brain damage caused by her stroke.

David and Betty both complained of problems with their vision, but their symptoms were actually caused by disorders in the brain. David's problem resulted from a malfunction in the brain's system for passing chemical messages between cells. Betty's problem resulted from damage to an area of the brain that integrates and interprets visual information. Our ability to perceive the world around us and recognize familiar people depends not only on information we take in through our senses but, perhaps more importantly, on the interpretation of this information performed by the brain. ■

Betty and David both complained of problems with their vision, but their symptoms were actually caused by disorders in the brain. Brain disorders, whether caused by taking drugs or suffering from a stroke, can produce bizarre and sometimes dangerous distortions of perception.

HOMESTUDIO/DREAMSTIME.COM

Neurons: The Origin of Behavior

Humans have thoughts, feelings, and behaviors that are often accompanied by visible signals. For example, anticipating seeing a friend waiting up the block for you in the movie ticket line may elicit a range of behaviors. An observer might see a smile on your face or notice how fast you are walking; internally, you might mentally rehearse what you'll say to your friend and feel a surge of happiness as you approach her. But all those visible and experiential signs are produced by an underlying invisible physical component coordinated by the activity of your brain cells. The anticipation you have, the happiness you feel, and the speed of your feet are the result of information processing in your brain. In a way, all of your thoughts, feelings, and behaviors spring from cells in the brain that take in information and produce some kind of output.

The cells that perform this function trillions of times a day are called neurons. **Neurons** are *cells in the nervous system that communicate with one another to perform information-processing tasks* (see **FIGURE 3.1**). There are approximately *100 billion* neurons

•••••••••••••••••••••••••• **FIGURE 3.1**

Components of a Neuron *A neuron is made up of three parts: a cell body that houses the chromosomes with the organism's DNA and maintains the health of the cell, dendrites that receive information from other neurons, and an axon that transmits information to other neurons, muscles, and glands.*

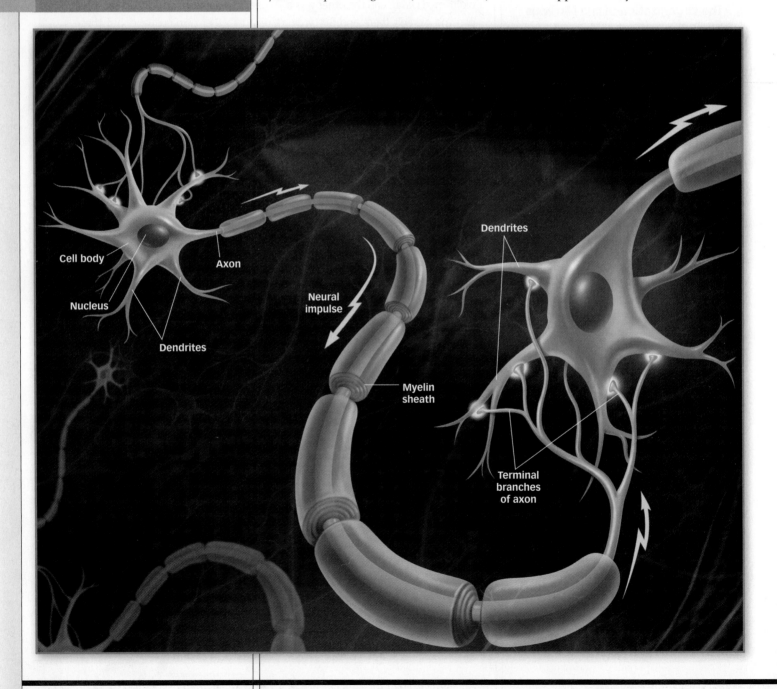

in your brain. To give you a sense of just how big that number is, it's more than five times the estimated 6.5 billion people currently living on Earth. These neurons come in different shapes and sizes, and they perform a variety of tasks that allow you to function as a human being.

Like cells in all organs of the body, neurons have a **cell body** (also called the *soma*), the component of the neuron that *coordinates the information-processing tasks and keeps the cell alive*. Functions such as protein synthesis, energy production, and metabolism take place here. The cell body contains a *nucleus;* this structure houses chromosomes that contain your DNA, the genetic blueprint of who you are. The cell body is surrounded by a porous cell membrane that allows molecules to flow into and out of the cell. Unlike other cells in the body, neurons have two types of specialized extensions of the cell membrane that allow them to communicate: dendrites and axons. **Dendrites** *receive information from other neurons and relay it to the cell body.* The term *dendrite* comes from the Greek word for "tree"; indeed, most neurons have many dendrites that look like tree branches. The **axon** *transmits information to other neurons, muscles, or glands.* Each neuron has a single axon that sometimes can be very long, even stretching up to a meter from the base of the spinal cord down to the big toe.

In addition to the 100 billion neurons processing information in your brain, there are 10 to 50 times as many **glial cells**, which are *support cells found in the nervous system.* Some glial cells digest parts of dead neurons; others provide physical and nutritional support for neurons. Some glial cells form **myelin sheaths**, *insulating layers of fatty material around the axons of some neurons.* Axons insulated with myelin can more efficiently transmit signals to other neurons, organs, or muscles.

In fact, in *demyelinating diseases,* such as multiple sclerosis, the myelin sheath deteriorates, causing a slowdown in the transmission of information from one neuron to another (Schwartz & Westbrook, 2000). This condition leads to a variety of problems, including loss of feeling in the limbs, partial blindness, and difficulties in coordinated movement. Multiple sclerosis often entails cycles of myelin loss and subsequent recovery.

Although neurons look like they form a continuously connected lattice in the brain, the dendrites and axons of neurons do not actually touch each other. There's a small gap between the axon of one neuron and the dendrites or cell body of another. This gap is part of the **synapse:** *the junction or region between the axon of one neuron and the dendrites or cell body of another* (see **FIGURE 3.2** on the next page). Many of the 100 billion neurons in your brain have a few thousand synaptic junctions, so most adults have between 100 trillion and 500 trillion synapses. As you'll read shortly, the transmission of information across the synapse is fundamental to communication between neurons, a process that allows us to think, feel, and behave.

● **How do the three types of neurons work together to transmit information?**

There are three major types of neurons, each performing a distinct function: sensory neurons, motor neurons, and interneurons. **Sensory neurons** *receive information from the external world and convey this information to the brain via the spinal cord.* Sensory neurons have specialized endings on their dendrites that receive signals for light, sound, touch, taste, and smell. For example, in our eyes, sensory neurons' endings are sensitive to light. **Motor neurons** *carry signals from the spinal cord to the muscles to produce movement.* These neurons often have long axons that can stretch to muscles at our extremities. However, most of the nervous system is composed of the third type of neuron, **interneurons**, which *connect sensory neurons, motor neurons, or other interneurons.* Some interneurons carry information from sensory neurons into the nervous system, others carry information from the nervous system to motor neurons, and still others perform a variety of information-processing functions within the nervous system. Interneurons work together in small circuits to perform simple tasks, such as identifying the location of a sensory signal, and much more complicated ones, such as recognizing a familiar face.)

neurons Cells in the nervous system that communicate with one another to perform information-processing tasks.

cell body The part of a neuron that coordinates information-processing tasks and keeps the cell alive.

dendrites The part of a neuron that receives information from other neurons and relays it to the cell body.

axon The part of a neuron that transmits information to other neurons, muscles, or glands.

myelin sheath An insulating layer of fatty material.

glial cells Support cells found in the nervous system.

synapse The junction or region between the axon of one neuron and the dendrites or cell body of another.

sensory neurons Neurons that receive information from the external world and convey this information to the brain via the spinal cord.

motor neurons Neurons that carry signals from the spinal cord to the muscles to produce movement.

interneurons Neurons that connect sensory neurons, motor neurons, or other interneurons.

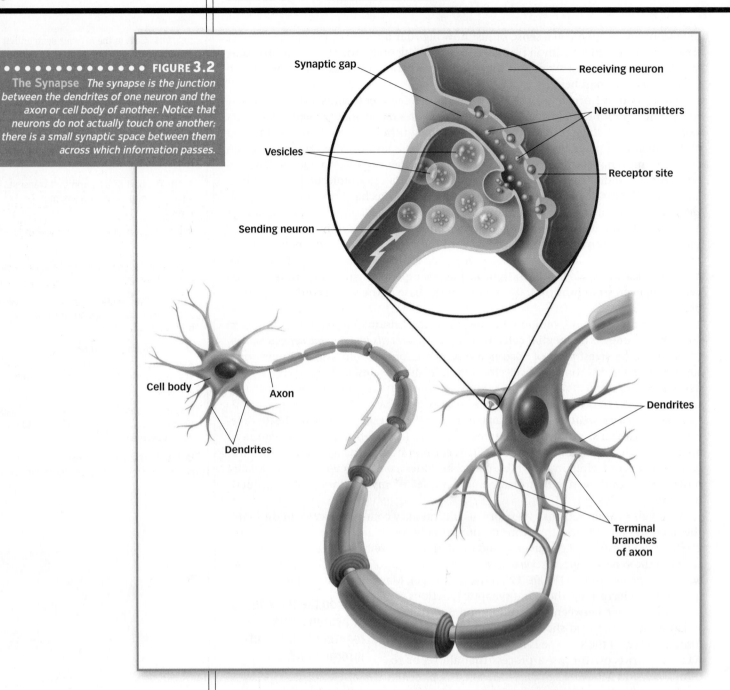

•••••••••••••••••••••••• FIGURE **3.2**

The Synapse *The synapse is the junction between the dendrites of one neuron and the axon or cell body of another. Notice that neurons do not actually touch one another: there is a small synaptic space between them across which information passes.*

Synaptic gap

Vesicles

Sending neuron

Receiving neuron

Neurotransmitters

Receptor site

Cell body

Axon

Dendrites

Dendrites

Terminal branches of axon

Electric Signaling: Communicating Information within a Neuron

Understanding how neurons process information is key to appreciating how the brain works—that is, how these tiny cells make it possible for us to think, feel, and act. The communication of information within and between neurons proceeds in two stages—*conduction* and *transmission*. The first stage is the conduction of an electric signal over relatively long distances within neurons, from the dendrites to the cell body, then throughout the axon. The second stage is the transmission of electric signals between neurons over the synapse.

The neuron's cell membrane is porous: It allows small electrically charged molecules, called *ions,* to flow in and out of the cell. The idea is similar to using a strainer while you're preparing spaghetti: The pasta is trapped inside but small particles of water can still seep in and out of it. Similarly, the neuron's cell membrane has small channels that allow different ions to flow in and out. When the neuron is at rest, the channels that allow small, positively charged potassium ions (K^+) to pass are open; channels that

resting potential The difference in electric charge between the inside and outside of a neuron's cell membrane.

action potential An electric signal that is conducted along an axon to a synapse.

allow the flow of other molecules are normally closed. There is naturally a higher concentration of potassium ions *inside* the neuron, and so some K⁺ ions flow out—like water out of a strainer. This leaves the neuron with fewer positively charged molecules on the inside relative to the outside. This natural electric charge or **resting potential** is *the difference in electric charge between the inside and outside of a neuron's cell membrane* (Kandel,

● **Why is an action potential an all-or-nothing event?**

2000). The resting potential is about –70 millivolts, or roughly 1/200 of the charge of an AA battery.

The neuron maintains its resting potential most of the time. However, biologists working with neurons from the squid (which has particularly large, easy-to-study neurons) noticed that they could stimulate the axon with a brief electric shock, which resulted in the conduction of a large electric impulse down the length of the axon (Hausser, 2000; Hodgkin & Huxley, 1939). This electric impulse is called an **action potential**, which is *an electric signal that is conducted along the length of a neuron's axon to the synapse* (see **FIGURE 3.3**). The action potential occurs only when the electric shock reaches a certain level, or *threshold*. When the shock was below this threshold, the researchers recorded only tiny signals, which dissipated rapidly. Interestingly, increases in the electric shock above the threshold did *not* increase the strength of the action potential. The action potential is *all or none*: Electric stimulation below the threshold fails to produce an action potential, whereas electric stimulation at or above the threshold always produces the action potential. The action potential always occurs with exactly the same characteristics and at the same magnitude regardless of whether the stimulus is at or above the threshold.

The action potential occurs when there is a change in the state of the axon's membrane channels. Remember, during the resting potential, only the K⁺ channels are open. However, when an electric charge is raised to the threshold value, the K⁺ channels briefly shut down, and other channels that allow the flow of another positively charged ion, sodium (Na⁺), are opened. Na⁺ is typically much more concentrated outside the axon than inside. When the Na⁺ channels open, those positively charged ions flow inside, increasing the positive charge inside the axon relative to that outside. This flow of Na⁺ into the axon pushes the neuron's electrical charge all the way from its resting potential of –70 millivolts all the way to +40 millivolts.

Biologists Alan Hodgkin and Andrew ● ● ●
Huxley worked with the squid giant axon because it is 100 times longer than the biggest axon in humans. They discovered the neuron's resting potential.

MAREVISION/AGEFOTOSTOCK/PHOTOLIBRARY

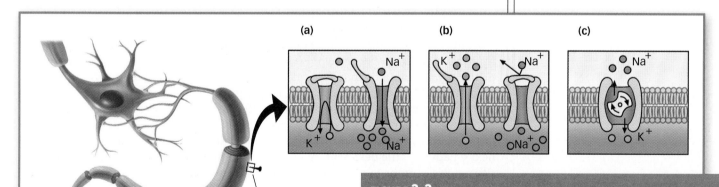

FIGURE 3.3 ●
The Action Potential *(a) Electric stimulation of the neuron shuts down the K+ channels and opens the Na+ channels, allowing Na+ to enter the axon. The increase of Na+ inside the neuron results in an action potential. (b) In the refractory period after the action potential, the channels return to their original state, allowing K+ to flow out of the axon. This leaves an abundance of K+ outside and Na+ inside the cell. (c) A chemical pump then reverses the ion balance of ions by moving Na+ out of the axon and K+ into the axon. The neuron can now generate another action potential.*

Stimulating electrode

(a) (b) (c)

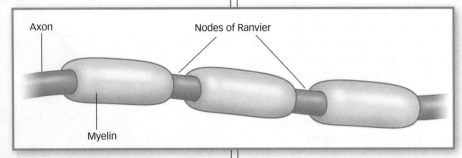

Axon
Nodes of Ranvier
Myelin

●●●●●●●●●●●●●●●●●●●● FIGURE 3.4

Myelin and Nodes of Ranvier *Myelin is formed by a type of glial cell, and it wraps around a neuron's axon to speed the transmission of the action potential along the length of the axon. Breaks in the myelin sheath are called the nodes of Ranvier. The electric impulse jumps from node to node, thereby speeding the conduction of information down the axon.*

When an action potential is generated at the beginning of the axon, it spreads a short distance, which generates an action potential at a nearby location on the axon (see Figure 3.5). That action potential also spreads, initiating an action potential at another nearby location, and so on, thus transmitting the charge down the length of the axon. This simple mechanism ensures that the action potential travels the full length of the axon and that it achieves its full intensity at each step, regardless of the distance traveled.

The myelin sheath, which is made up of glial cells that coat and insulate the axon, facilitates the transmission of the action potential. Myelin doesn't cover the entire axon; rather, it clumps around the axon with little break points between clumps, looking kind of like sausage links. These breakpoints are called the *nodes of Ranvier*, after French pathologist Louis-Antoine Ranvier, who discovered them (see **FIGURE 3.4**). When an electric current passes down the length of a myelinated axon, the charge "jumps" from node to node rather than having to traverse the entire axon. This jumping helps speed the flow of information down the axon.

After the action potential reaches its maximum, the membrane channels return to their original state, and K^+ flows out until the axon returns to its resting potential. This leaves a lot of extra Na^+ ions inside the axon and a lot of extra K^+ ions outside the axon. During this period where the ions are imbalanced, the neuron cannot initiate another action potential, so it is said to be in a **refractory period**, *the time following an action potential during which a new action potential cannot be initiated*. The imbalance in ions eventually is reversed by an active chemical "pump" in the cell membrane that moves Na^+ outside the axon and moves K^+ inside the axon.

Chemical Signaling: Synaptic Transmission between Neurons

When the action potential reaches the end of an axon, the electric charge of the action potential takes a form that can cross the relatively small synaptic gap by relying on a bit of chemistry. Axons usually end in **terminal buttons**, *which are knoblike structures that branch out from an axon*. When the action potential reaches the terminal button, it stimulates the release of **neurotransmitters**, *chemicals that transmit information across the synapse to a receiving neuron's dendrites*. These neurotransmitters float across the synapse and bind to sites on the dendrites of the receiving neuron called **receptors**, *parts of the cell membrane that receive neurotransmitters and initiate a new electric signal*. Just as a particular key will only fit in a particular lock, so too will only some neurotransmitters bind to specific receptor sites on a dendrite. The molecular structure of the neurotransmitter must "fit" the molecular structure of the receptor site. Activation of receptors on the receiving neuron, or *postsynaptic neuron*, can cause a new electric potential to be initiated in that neuron, and the process continues down that neuron's axon to the next synapse and the next neuron. This electrochemical action, called *synaptic transmission*, allows neurons to communicate with one another and ultimately underlies your thoughts, emotions, and behavior (see **FIGURE 3.5**).

● **How does a neuron communicate with another neuron?**

Neurotransmitters left in the synapse after the chemical message is relayed to the postsynaptic neuron have to be cleared up; otherwise, there would be no end to the signals that they send. Neurotransmitters leave the synapse through three processes. First, *reuptake* occurs when neurotransmitters are reabsorbed by the terminal buttons of the presynaptic neuron's axon. Second, neurotransmitters can be destroyed by enzymes in the synapse in a process called *enzyme deactivation*; specific enzymes break down specific neurotransmitters. Finally, neurotransmitters can bind to the receptor sites

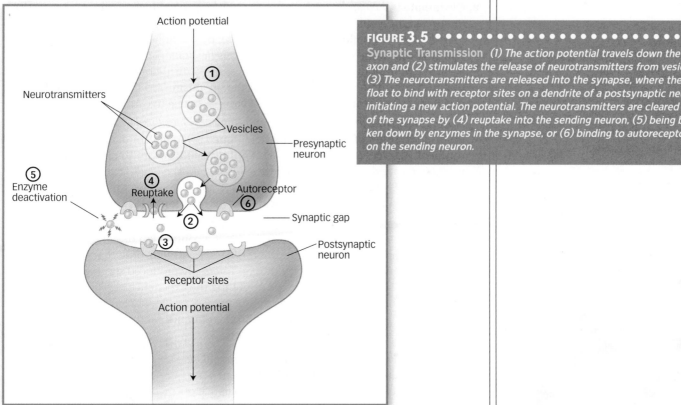

FIGURE 3.5 •
Synaptic Transmission *(1) The action potential travels down the axon and (2) stimulates the release of neurotransmitters from vesicles. (3) The neurotransmitters are released into the synapse, where they float to bind with receptor sites on a dendrite of a postsynaptic neuron, initiating a new action potential. The neurotransmitters are cleared out of the synapse by (4) reuptake into the sending neuron, (5) being broken down by enzymes in the synapse, or (6) binding to autoreceptors on the sending neuron.*

called *autoreceptors* on the presynaptic neurons. Autoreceptors detect how much of a neurotransmitter has been released into a synapse and signal the neuron to stop releasing the neurotransmitter when an excess is present.

Types of Neurotransmitters

Given that different kinds of neurotransmitters can activate different kinds of receptors, like a lock and key, you might wonder how many types of neurotransmitters are floating across synapses in your brain right now. Today, we know that some 60 chemicals play a role in transmitting information throughout the brain and body, each differently affecting thought, feeling, and behavior. But a few major classes seem particularly important. We'll summarize those here, and you'll meet some of these neurotransmitters again, in later chapters.

- **Acetylcholine (Ach)**, *a neurotransmitter involved in a number of functions, including voluntary motor control*, was one of the first neurotransmitters discovered. Acetylcholine is found in neurons of the brain and in the synapses where axons connect to muscles and body organs, such as the heart. Acetylcholine activates muscles to initiate motor behavior, but it also contributes to the regulation of attention, learning, sleeping, dreaming, and memory (Gais & Born, 2004; Hasselmo, 2006; Wrenn et al., 2006). Alzheimer's disease, a medical condition involving severe memory impairments, is associated with the deterioration of Ach-producing neurons.

- **Dopamine** is *a neurotransmitter that regulates motor behavior, motivation, pleasure, and emotional arousal*. Because of its role in basic motivated behaviors, such as seeking pleasure or associating actions with rewards, dopamine plays a role in drug addiction (Baler & Volkow, 2006). High levels of dopamine have been linked to schizophrenia (Winterer & Weinberger, 2004), while low levels have been linked to Parkinson's disease.

refractory period The time following an action potential during which a new action potential cannot be initiated.

terminal buttons Knoblike structures that branch out from an axon.

neurotransmitters Chemicals that transmit information across the synapse to a receiving neuron's dendrites.

receptors Parts of the cell membrane that receive the neurotransmitter and initiate a new electric signal.

- **Glutamate** is *a major excitatory neurotransmitter involved in information transmission throughout the brain*. This means that glutamate enhances the transmission of information. Too much glutamate can overstimulate the brain, causing seizures. **GABA (gamma-aminobutyric acid)**, in contrast, is *the primary inhibitory neurotransmitter in the brain*. Inhibitory neurotransmitters stop the firing of neurons, an activity that also contributes to the function of the organism. Too little GABA, just like too much glutamate, can cause neurons to become overactive, causing seizures.

- **Norepinephrine**, *a neurotransmitter that influences mood and arousal*, is particularly involved in states of vigilance, or a heightened awareness of dangers in the environment (Ressler & Nemeroff, 1999). Another neurotransmitter, **serotonin** is *involved in the regulation of sleep and wakefulness, eating, and aggressive behavior* (Kroeze & Roth, 1998). Because both of these neurotransmitters affect mood and arousal, low levels of each have been implicated in mood disorders (Tamminga et al., 2002).

- **Endorphins** are *chemicals that act within the pain pathways and emotion centers of the brain* (Keefe et al., 2001). The term *endorphin* is a contraction of *endogenous morphine*, and that's a pretty apt description. Morphine is a synthetic drug that has a calming and pleasurable effect; an endorphin is an internally produced substance that has similar properties, such as dulling the experience of pain and elevating moods. The "runner's high" experienced by many athletes as they push their bodies to painful limits of endurance can be explained by the release of endorphins in the brain.

● **How do neurotransmitters create the feeling of a "runner's high"?**

Each of these neurotransmitters affects thought, feeling, and behavior in different ways, so normal functioning involves a delicate balance of each. Even a slight imbalance—too much of one neurotransmitter or not enough of another—can dramatically affect behavior. These imbalances sometimes occur naturally. The brain doesn't produce enough serotonin, for example, which contributes to depressed or anxious moods. Other times a person may actively seek to cause imbalances. People who smoke, drink alcohol, or take drugs, legal or not, are altering the balance of neurotransmitters in their brains. The drug LSD, for example, is structurally very similar to serotonin, so it binds very easily with serotonin receptors in the brain, producing similar effects on thoughts, feelings, or behavior. In the next section, we'll look at how some drugs are able to "trick" receptor sites in just this way.

How Drugs Mimic Neurotransmitters

Many drugs that affect the nervous system operate by increasing, interfering with, or mimicking the manufacture or function of neurotransmitters (Cooper, Bloom, & Roth, 2003; Sarter, 2006). *Agonists* are drugs that increase the action of a neurotransmitter. *Antagonists* are drugs that block the function of a neurotransmitter. Some drugs alter a step in the production or release of the neurotransmitter, whereas others have a chemical structure so similar to a neurotransmitter that the drug is able to bind to that neuron's receptor. If, by binding to a receptor, a drug activates the neurotransmitter, it is an agonist; if it blocks the action of the neurotransmitter, it is an antagonist. For example, Parkinson's disease is a movement disorder characterized by tremors and difficulty initiating movement, and it is caused by the loss of neurons that produce the neurotransmitter dopamine. Dopamine is created in neurons by a modification of a common molecule called L-dopa. Ingesting L-dopa will elevate the amount of L-dopa in the brain and spur the surviving neurons to produce more dopamine. In other words, L-dopa acts as an agonist for dopamine. The use of L-dopa has become a major success in alleviating Parkinson's disease symptoms (Muenter & Tyce, 1971).

DIGITAL VISION/PHOTOLIBRARY

Individuals who take part in extreme sports such as skydiving are probably seeking the kind of pleasurable effect associated with the release of endorphins. Individuals who avoid such sports, such as your textbook authors, take considerable pleasure from remaining in contact with Mother Earth.

Some unexpected evidence also highlights the central role of dopamine in regulating movement and motor performance. In 1982, six people ranging in age from 25 to 45 from the San Francisco Bay Area were admitted to emergency rooms with a bizarre set of symptoms: paralysis, drooling, and an inability to speak (Langston, 1995). A diagnosis of advanced Parkinson's disease was made, as these symptoms are consistent with the later stages of this degenerative disease. It was unusual for six fairly young people to come down with advanced Parkinson's at the same time in the same geographic area. Indeed, none of the patients had Parkinson's, but they were all heroin addicts.

● **How does giving patients L-dopa alleviate symptoms of Parkinson's disease?**

These patients thought they were ingesting a synthetic form of heroin (called MPPP), but instead they ingested a close derivative called MPTP, which unfortunately had the effects of destroying dopamine-producing neurons in an area of the brain crucial for motor performance. Hence, these "frozen addicts" exhibited paralysis and masklike expressions. The patients experienced a remarkable recovery after they were given L-dopa. Just as L-dopa acts as an agonist by enhancing the production of dopamine, drugs such as MPTP act as antagonists by destroying dopamine-producing neurons.

Like MPTP, other street drugs can alter neurotransmitter function. Amphetamine, for example, is a popular drug that stimulates the release of norepinephrine and dopamine and also prevents the reuptake of norepinephrine and dopamine. The result is to flood the synapse with those neurotransmitters, resulting in increased activation of their receptors. Thus, it is a strong agonist. Cocaine acts through similar mechanisms to amphetamine, although the psychological effects of the two drugs differ somewhat because of subtle distinctions in where and how they act on the brain. Norepinephrine and dopamine play a critical role in mood control, such that increases in either neurotransmitter result in euphoria, wakefulness, and a burst of energy. However, norepinephrine also increases heart rate. An overdose of amphetamine or cocaine can cause the heart to contract so rapidly that heartbeats do not last long enough to pump blood effectively, leading to fainting and sometimes to death.

Prozac, a drug commonly used to treat depression, is another example of a neurotransmitter agonist. Prozac blocks the reuptake of the neurotransmitter serotonin, making it part of a category of drugs called *selective serotonin reuptake inhibitors*, or *SSRIs* (Wong, Bymaster, & Engelman, 1995). Patients suffering from clinical depression typically have reduced levels of serotonin in their brains. By blocking reuptake, more of the neurotransmitter remains in the synapse longer and produces greater activation of serotonin receptors. Serotonin elevates mood, which can help relieve depression.

As you've read, many drugs alter the actions of neurotransmitters. Think back to David, whom you met at the beginning of this chapter: His paranoid hallucinations were induced by his crystal meth habit. The actions of methamphetamine involve a complex interaction at the neuron's synapses—it affects pathways for dopamine, serotonin, and norepinephrine—making it difficult to interpret exactly how it works. But the combination of its agonist and antagonist effects alters the functions of neurotransmitters that help us perceive and interpret visual images. In David's case, it led to hallucinations that called his eyesight, and his sanity, into question.

summary quiz [3.1]

1. The gap between the axon of one neuron and the dendrites of another is called the
   a. glial cell.
   b. interneuron.
   c. myelin sheath.
   d. synapse.

2. The neurons that receive information from the external world and convey this information to the brain are called
   a. sensory neurons.
   b. motor neurons.
   c. interneurons.
   d. glial cells.

3. An action potential occurs when an electric charge causes
   a. potassium ions to flow into the neuron.
   b. potassium ions to flow out of the neuron.
   c. sodium ions to flow into the neuron.
   d. sodium ions to flow out of the neuron.

4. One way to clear up an overflow of neurotransmitters in the synapse is reabsortion of the excess by the terminal buttons of the presynaptic neuron's axon. This process is called
   a. enzyme deactivation.
   b. uptake.
   c. autoreceptor action.
   d. agonistic action.

5. Depression is often treated by a class of drugs that inhibits the reuptake of which neurotransmitter?
   a. serotonin
   b. endorphins
   c. glutamate
   d. GABA

The Organization of the Nervous System

Neurons work by forming circuits and pathways in the brain, which in turn influence circuits and pathways in other areas of the body. Without this kind of organization and delegation, neurons would be churning away with little purpose. Neurons are the building blocks that form *nerves,* or bundles of axons and the glial cells that support them. The **nervous system** *is an interacting network of neurons that conveys electrochemical information throughout the body.* In this section, we'll look at the major divisions of the nervous system, focusing particularly on structures in the brain and their specific functions.

Divisions of the Nervous System

There are two major divisions of the nervous system: the central nervous system and the peripheral nervous system (see **FIGURE 3.6** on the following page). The **central nervous system (CNS)** *is composed of the brain and spinal cord.* The central nervous system receives sensory information from the external world, processes and coordinates this information, and sends commands to the skeletal and muscular systems for action.

The **peripheral nervous system (PNS)** *connects the central nervous system to the body's organs and muscles.* The peripheral nervous system is itself composed of two major subdivisions, the somatic nervous system and the autonomic nervous system. The **somatic nervous system** *is a set of nerves that conveys information into and out of the central nervous system.* Humans have conscious control over this system and use it to perceive, think, and coordinate their behaviors. For example, directing your hand to reach out and pick

---

nervous system An interacting network of neurons that conveys electrochemical information throughout the body.

central nervous system (CNS) The part of the nervous system that is composed of the brain and spinal cord.

peripheral nervous system (PNS) The part of the nervous system that connects the central nervous system to the body's organs and muscles.

somatic nervous system A set of nerves that conveys information into and out of the central nervous system.

autonomic nervous system (ANS) A set of nerves that carries involuntary and automatic commands that control blood vessels, body organs, and glands.

sympathetic nervous system A set of nerves that prepares the body for action in threatening situations.

parasympathetic nervous system A set of nerves that helps the body return to a normal resting state.

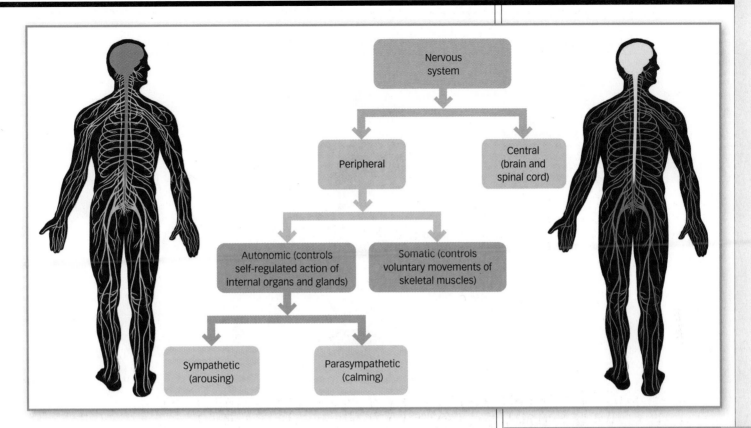

FIGURE 3.6 • • • • • • • • • • • • •
The Human Nervous System *The nervous system is organized into the peripheral and central nervous systems. The peripheral nervous system is further divided into the automatic and somatic nervous systems.*

up a coffee cup involves the elegantly orchestrated activities of the somatic nervous system: Information from the receptors in your eyes travels to your brain, registering that a cup is on the table; signals from your brain travel to the muscles in your arm and hand; feedback from those muscles tells your brain that the cup has been grasped; and so on.

In contrast, the **autonomic nervous system (ANS)** is *a set of nerves that carries involuntary and automatic commands that control blood vessels, body organs, and glands.* As suggested by its name, this system works on its own to regulate bodily systems, largely outside conscious control. The ANS has two major subdivisions, which each exerts a different type of control on the body. The **sympathetic nervous system** is *a set of nerves that prepares the body for action in threatening situations* (see **FIGURE 3.7** on the next page).

When danger threatens, your sympathetic nervous system kicks into action: It dilates your pupils to let in more light, increases your heart rate and respiration to pump more oxygen to muscles, diverts blood flow to your brain and muscles, and activates sweat glands to cool your body. To conserve energy, the sympathetic nervous system inhibits salivation and bowel movements, suppresses the body's immune responses, and suppresses responses to pain and injury. The sum total of these fast, automatic responses is that they increase the likelihood that you can escape from or fight off the threat.

● What triggers the increase in your heart rate when you feel threatened?

The **parasympathetic nervous system** *helps the body return to a normal resting state.* Once the threat has been eliminated or avoided, your body doesn't need to remain on red alert. Now the parasympathetic nervous system kicks in to reverse the effects of the sympathetic nervous system and return your body to its normal state. The parasympathetic nervous system generally mirrors the connections of the sympathetic nervous system. For example, the parasympathetic nervous system constricts your pupils, slows your heart rate and respiration, diverts blood flow to your digestive system, and decreases activity in your sweat glands.

•••••••••••••••••••••••• • • • FIGURE **3.7**
Sympathetic and Parasympathetic Systems *The autonomic nervous system is composed of two subsystems that complement each other. Activation of the sympathetic system serves several aspects of arousal, whereas the parasympathetic nervous system returns the body to its normal resting state.*

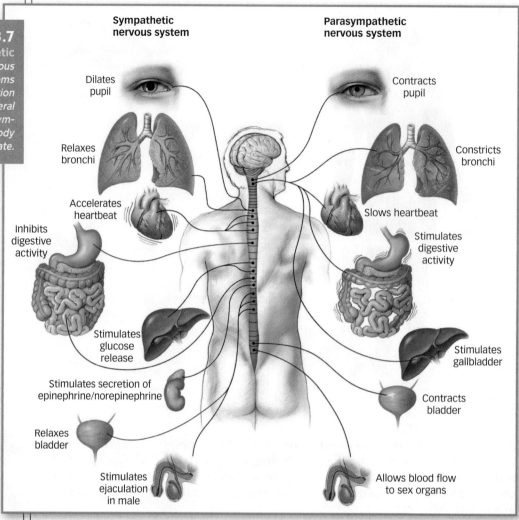

As you might imagine, the sympathetic and parasympathetic nervous systems coordinate to control many bodily functions. One example is sexual behavior. In men, the parasympathetic nervous system engorges the blood vessels of the penis to produce an erection, but the sympathetic nervous system is responsible for ejaculation. In women, the parasympathetic nervous system produces vaginal lubrication, but the sympathetic nervous system underlies orgasm. In both men and women, a successful sexual experience depends on a delicate balance of these two systems; in fact, anxiety about sexual performance can disrupt this balance. For example, sympathetic nervous system activation caused by anxiety can lead to premature ejaculation in males and lack of lubrication in females.

Components of the Central Nervous System

Compared to the many divisions of the peripheral nervous system, the central nervous system may seem simple. After all, it has only two elements: The brain and the spinal cord. But those two elements are ultimately responsible for most of what we do as humans.

The spinal cord often seems like the brain's poor relation: The brain gets all the glory, and the spinal cord just hangs around, doing relatively simple tasks. Those tasks, however, are pretty important: keeping you breathing, responding to pain, moving your muscles, allowing you to walk. What's more, without the spinal cord, the brain would not be able to put any of its higher processing into action.

For some very basic behaviors, the spinal cord doesn't need input from the brain at all. Connections between the sensory inputs and motor neurons in the spinal cord mediate

spinal reflexes Simple pathways in the nervous system that rapidly generate muscle contractions.

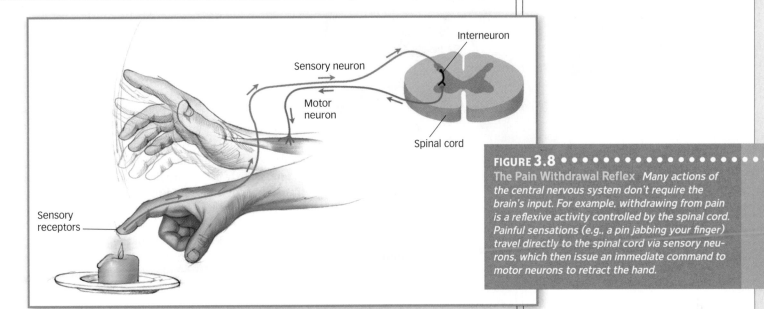

Interneuron

Sensory neuron

Motor neuron

Spinal cord

Sensory receptors

FIGURE 3.8
The Pain Withdrawal Reflex *Many actions of the central nervous system don't require the brain's input. For example, withdrawing from pain is a reflexive activity controlled by the spinal cord. Painful sensations (e.g., a pin jabbing your finger) travel directly to the spinal cord via sensory neurons, which then issue an immediate command to motor neurons to retract the hand.*

spinal reflexes, *simple pathways in the nervous system that rapidly generate muscle contractions.* For example, if you touch a hot stove, the sensory neurons that register pain send inputs directly into the spinal cord (see **FIGURE 3.8,** above). Through just a few synaptic connections within the spinal cord, interneurons relay these sensory inputs to motor neurons that connect to your arm muscles and direct you to quickly retract your hand. In other words, you don't need a whole lot of brainpower to rapidly pull your hand off a hot stove!

More elaborate tasks require the collaboration of the spinal cord and the brain. The peripheral nervous system communicates with the central nervous system through nerves that conduct sensory information into the brain, carry commands out of the brain, or both. Damage to the spinal cord severs the connection from the brain to sensory and motor neurons that are essential to sensory perception and movement. The location of the spinal injury often determines the extent of the abilities that are lost. Patients with damage at a particular level of the spinal cord lose sensation of touch and pain in body parts below the level of the injury as well as a loss of motor control of the muscles in the same areas. A spinal injury higher up the cord usually predicts a much poorer prognosis, such as quadriplegia (the loss of sensation and motor control over all limbs), breathing through a respirator, and lifelong immobility.

● **What important functions does the spinal cord perform on its own?**

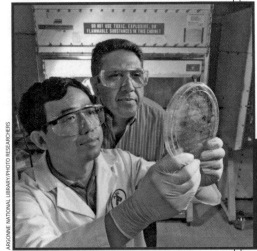

Research using embryonic stem cells, ● *which has the potential to advance understanding and treatment of serious brain diseases, should be enhanced by President Obama's executive order in early 2009 lifting previous restrictions on this research.*

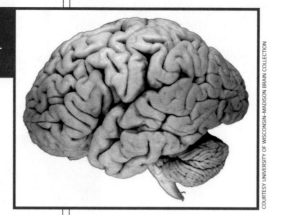

The human brain weighs only three pounds and isn't much to look at, but its accomplishments are staggering.

COURTESY UNIVERSITY OF WISCONSIN-MADISON BRAIN COLLECTION

Exploring the Brain

The human brain is really not much to look at. It's about three pounds of slightly slimy, pinkish grayish stuff that sits there like a lump. You already know, of course, that the neurons and glial cells that make up that lump are busy humming away, giving you consciousness, feelings, and potentially brilliant ideas. But to find out which neurons in which parts of the brain control which functions, scientists first had to divide and conquer—that is, find a way of describing the brain that allows researchers to communicate with one another.

Neuroscientists divide up the brain in several ways. Although these divisions make it easier to understand areas of the brain and their functions, keep in mind that none of these structures or areas in the brain can act alone: They are all part of one big, interacting, interdependent whole. Often, it's convenient to divide the brain into three parts: the hindbrain, the midbrain, and the forebrain (see **FIGURE 3.9**).

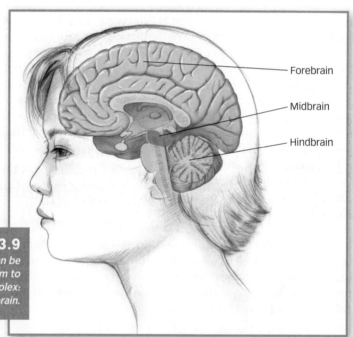

— Forebrain

— Midbrain

— Hindbrain

FIGURE 3.9
The Major Divisions of the Brain *The brain can be organized into three parts moving from the bottom to the top, from simpler functions to the more complex: the hindbrain, the midbrain, and the forebrain.*

The Hindbrain

If you follow the spinal cord from your tailbone to where it enters your skull, you'll find it difficult to determine where your spinal cord ends and your brain begins. That's because the spinal cord is continuous with the **hindbrain**, *an area of the brain that coordinates information coming into and out of the spinal cord.* The hindbrain is sometimes called the *brain stem;* indeed, it looks like a stalk on which the rest of the brain sits. The hindbrain controls the most basic functions of life: respiration, alertness, and motor skills (see **FIGURE 3.10** on the next page). The **medulla** is *an extension of the spinal cord into the skull that coordinates heart rate, circulation, and respiration.* Inside the medulla is a small cluster of neurons called the **reticular formation**, *which regulates sleep, wakefulness, and levels of arousal.*

● **Which part of the brain helps to orchestrate movements that keep you steady on your bike?**

hindbrain An area of the brain that coordinates information coming into and out of the spinal cord.

medulla An extension of the spinal cord into the skull that coordinates heart rate, circulation, and respiration.

reticular formation A brain structure that regulates sleep, wakefulness, and levels of arousal.

Behind the medulla is the **cerebellum**, *a large structure of the hindbrain that controls fine motor skills*. The cerebellum orchestrates the proper sequence of movements when we ride a bike, play the piano, or maintain balance while walking and running. It is important for "fine-tuning" or smoothing our actions, rather than initiating them; accordingly, damage to the cerebellum produces impairments in coordination and balance, although not paralysis or immobility.

The last major area of the hindbrain is the **pons**, *a structure that relays information from the cerebellum to the rest of the brain*. Pons means "bridge" in Latin. Although the detailed functions of the pons remain poorly understood, it essentially acts as a "relay station" or bridge between the cerebellum and other structures in the brain.

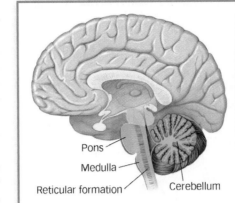

FIGURE **3.10**
The Hindbrain *The hindbrain coordinates information coming into and out of the spinal cord and controls the basic functions of life. It includes the medulla, the reticular formation, the cerebellum, and the pons.*

Pons
Medulla
Reticular formation
Cerebellum

The Midbrain

Sitting on top of the hindbrain is the *midbrain,* which is relatively small in humans. As you can see in **FIGURE 3.11** (below), the midbrain contains two main structures: the tectum and the tegmentum. The **tectum** *orients an organism in the environment*. The tectum receives stimulus input from the eyes, ears, and skin and moves the organism in a coordinated way toward the stimulus. The **tegmentum** *is involved in movement and arousal; it also helps orient an organism toward sensory stimuli*. The midbrain may be relatively small, but it is a central location of neurotransmitters such as *dopamine* and *serotonin* that are involved in arousal, mood, and motivation and the brain structures that rely on them (White, 1996).

Olympic medalist Apolo Anton Ohno relies on his cerebellum to execute graceful, coordinated motions on the ice. The cerebellum, part of the hindbrain, helps direct the smooth action of a variety of motor behaviors.

AP PHOTO/KEVORK DJANSEZIAN

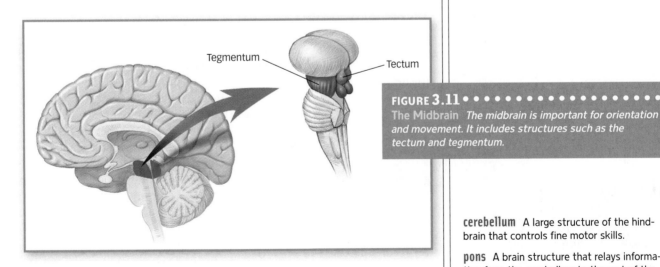

Tegmentum
Tectum

FIGURE **3.11**
The Midbrain *The midbrain is important for orientation and movement. It includes structures such as the tectum and tegmentum.*

The Forebrain

You could survive if you had only a hindbrain and a midbrain. The structures in the hindbrain would take care of all the bodily functions necessary to sustain life, and the structures in the midbrain would orient you toward or away from pleasurable or threatening stimuli in the environment. But this wouldn't be much of a life. To understand

cerebellum A large structure of the hindbrain that controls fine motor skills.

pons A brain structure that relays information from the cerebellum to the rest of the brain.

tectum A part of the midbrain that orients an organism in the environment.

tegmentum A part of the midbrain that is involved in movement and arousal.

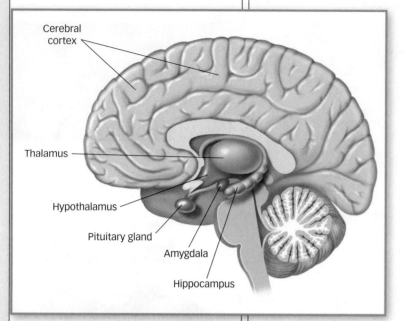

Cerebral cortex

Thalamus

Hypothalamus

Pituitary gland

Amygdala

Hippocampus

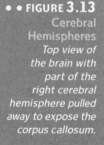

FIGURE 3.12

The Forebrain *The forebrain, the highest level of the brain, is critical for complex cognitive, emotional, sensory, and motor functions. The forebrain is divided into two parts: the cerebral cortex and the underlying subcortical structures. These include the thalamus, hypothalamus, pituitary gland, amygdala, and hippocampus.*

where the abilities that make us fully human come from, you need a forebrain. The *forebrain* is the highest level of the brain—literally and figuratively—and controls complex cognitive, emotional, sensory, and motor functions (see **FIGURE 3.12**). The forebrain itself is divided into two main sections: the cerebral cortex and the subcortical structures. The **cerebral cortex** is *the outermost layer of the brain*; the **subcortical structures** are *areas of the forebrain housed under the cerebral cortex near the very center of the brain.* You'll meet many key subcortical structures in later chapters, but for now, let's just review a few of the most critical.

The **thalamus** *relays and filters information from the senses and transmits the information to the cerebral cortex.* The thalamus receives inputs from all the major senses except smell, which has direct connections to the cerebral cortex. More than just a relay station, the thalamus actively filters incoming sensory information, giving more weight to some inputs and less weight to others. The thalamus also closes the pathways of incoming sensations during sleep, providing a valuable function in *not* allowing information to pass to the rest of the brain.

The **hypothalamus**, located below the thalamus (*hypo-* is Greek for "under"), *regulates body temperature, hunger, thirst, and sexual behavior.* For example, the hypothalamus makes sure that body temperature, blood sugar levels, and metabolism are kept within an optimal range for normal human functioning. Also, when you think about sex, messages from your cerebral cortex are sent to the hypothalamus to trigger the release of hormones. It's been suggested, then, that the hypothalamus is in charge of the "four Fs" of behavior: (a) fighting, (b) fleeing, (c) feeding, and (d) mating.

Other important subcortical structures, shown in Figure 3.12 and covered in more depth in later chapters, are the **pituitary gland,** *which releases hormones that direct the functions of many other glands* (such as the hypothalamus); the **hippocampus,** *which is critical for the creation and storage of new memories;* the **amygdala,** *which plays a central role in many emotional processes*; and the *basal ganglia,* a set of structures that direct intentional movement.

The Cerebral Cortex

Perched atop all these subcortical areas in the forebrain lies the cerebral cortex. The cortex is responsible for the most complex aspects of perception, emotion, movement, and thought (Fuster, 2003). It sits over the rest of the brain, like a mushroom cap shielding the underside and stem, and it is the wrinkled surface you see when looking at the brain

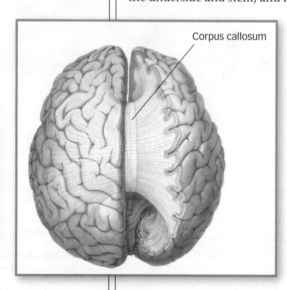

Corpus callosum

FIGURE 3.13

Cerebral Hemispheres *Top view of the brain with part of the right cerebral hemisphere pulled away to expose the corpus callosum.*

with the naked eye. The cerebral cortex can be divided down the middle into two halves, the left hemisphere and the right hemisphere. The two hemispheres are more or less symmetrical in their appearance and, to some extent, in their functions. However, each hemisphere controls the functions of the opposite side of the body: Your right cerebral hemisphere perceives stimuli from and controls movements on the left side of your body, whereas your left cerebral hemisphere perceives stimuli from and controls movement on the right side of your body. The cerebral hemispheres are connected to each other by *commissures,* bundles of axons that make possible communication between parallel areas of the cortex in each half. The largest of these commissures is the **corpus callosum,** which *connects large areas of the cerebral cortex on each side of the brain and supports communication of information across the hemispheres* (see **FIGURE 3.13**). This means that information received in the right hemisphere, for example, can pass across the corpus callosum and be registered, virtually instantaneously, in the left hemisphere.

The hemispheres themselves can be subdivided into four areas or *lobes*. From back to front, these are the occipital lobe, the parietal lobe, the temporal lobe, and the frontal lobe, as shown in **FIGURE 3.14**. We'll examine the functions of these lobes in more detail later; for now, here's a quick review. The **occipital lobe**, located at the back of the cerebral cortex, *processes visual information*. The **parietal lobe**, located in front of the occipital lobe, carries out functions that include *processing information about touch*. The parietal lobe contains the *somatosensory cortex*, a strip of brain tissue running from the top of the brain down to the sides (see Figure 3.14). Each part of the somatosensory cortex maps onto a particular part of the body. If a body area is more sensitive, a larger part of the somatosensory cortex is devoted to it. For example, the part of the somatosensory cortex that corresponds to the lips and tongue is larger than the area corresponding to the feet. The **temporal lobe**, located on the lower side of each hemisphere, is *responsible for hearing and language*. The *primary auditory cortex* in the temporal lobe is analogous to the somatosensory cortex in the parietal lobe and the primary visual areas of the occipital lobe; it receives sensory information from the ears based on the frequencies of sounds. Secondary areas of the temporal lobe then process the information into meaningful units, such as speech and words. The temporal lobe also houses the visual association areas that interpret the meaning of visual stimuli and help us recognize common objects in the environment (Martin, 2007).

● **What types of thinking occur in the frontal lobe?**

The **frontal lobe**, which sits behind the forehead, has *specialized areas for movement, abstract thinking, planning, memory, and judgment*. Lying just in front of the somatosensory cortex, at the back of the frontal lobe, is a parallel strip of brain tissue called the *motor cortex* (see **FIGURE 3.15** on the next page). Like the somatosensory cortex, different parts of the motor cortex correspond to different body parts. The motor cortex initiates voluntary movements and sends messages to the basal ganglia, cerebellum, and spinal cord. Other areas in the frontal lobe coordinate thought processes that help us manipulate information and retrieve memories, which we can use to plan our behaviors and interact socially with others. In short, the frontal cortex allows us to do the kind of thinking, imagining, planning, and anticipating that sets humans apart from most other species (Stuss & Benson, 1986).

Within each of the cortical lobes are areas specialized for processing particular types of information. Other areas, called **association areas**, *help provide sense and meaning to information registered in the cortex*. For example, neurons in the primary visual cortex are highly specialized; some detect features of the environment that are in a horizontal orientation, others detect movement, and still others process information about human versus nonhuman forms. The association areas of the occipital lobe interpret the information extracted by these primary areas—shape, motion, and so on—to help stitch together the threads of information in the various parts of the cortex to produce a meaningful understanding of what's being registered in the brain. Neurons in the association areas are usually less specialized and more flexible than neurons in the primary areas. As such, they can be shaped by

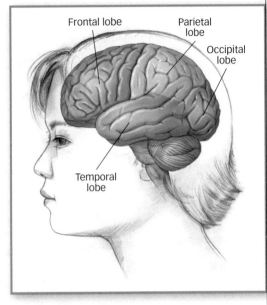

Frontal lobe   Parietal lobe

Occipital lobe

Temporal lobe

FIGURE 3.14 ● ● ● ● ● ● ● ● ● ● ● ● ● ● ●
Cerebral Cortex and Lobes *The four major lobes of the cerebral cortex are the occipital lobe, the parietal lobe, the temporal lobe, and the frontal lobe.*

cerebral cortex The outermost layer of the brain, visible to the naked eye and divided into two hemispheres.

subcortical structures Areas of the forebrain housed under the cerebral cortex near the very center of the brain.

thalamus A subcortical structure that relays and filters information from the senses and transmits the information to the cerebral cortex.

hypothalamus A subcortical structure that regulates body temperature, hunger, thirst, and sexual behavior.

pituitary gland The "master gland" of the body's hormone-producing system, which releases hormones that direct the functions of many other glands in the body.

hippocampus A structure critical for creating new memories and integrating them into a network of knowledge so that they can be stored indefinitely in other parts of the cerebral cortex.

amygdala A part of the subcortical system that plays a central role in many emotional processes, particularly the formation of emotional memories.

corpus callosum A thick band of nerve fibers that connects large areas of the cerebral cortex on each side of the brain and supports communication of information across the hemispheres.

occipital lobe A region of the cerebral cortex that processes visual information.

parietal lobe A region of the cerebral cortex whose functions include processing information about touch.

temporal lobe A region of the cerebral cortex responsible for hearing and language.

frontal lobe A region of the cerebral cortex that has specialized areas for movement, abstract thinking, planning, memory, and judgment.

association areas Areas of the cerebral cortex that are composed of neurons that help provide sense and meaning to information registered in the cortex.

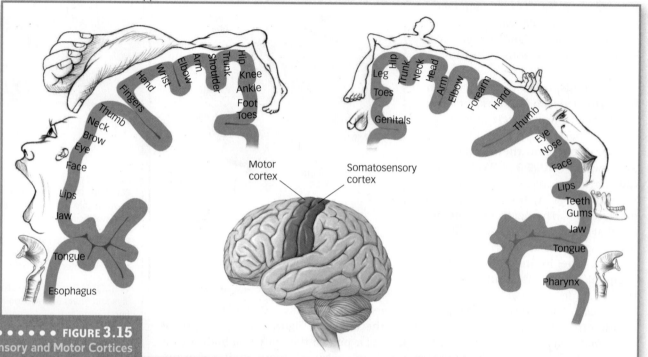

Motor cortex

Somatosensory cortex

● **FIGURE 3.15**

Somatosensory and Motor Cortices
The motor cortex, a strip of brain tissue in the frontal lobe, represents and controls different skin and body areas on the contralateral side of the body. Directly behind the motor cortex, in the parietal lobe, lies the somatosensory cortex. Like the motor cortex, the somatosensory cortex represents skin areas of particular parts on the contralateral side of the body.

● ● ● ● ● ● ● ● ● ● *The homunculus is a rendering of the body in which each part is shown in proportion to how much of the somatosensory cortex is devoted to it.*

learning and experience to do their job more effectively, a quality researchers call *plasticity* (i.e., "the ability to be molded"). As an example, if you lose your middle finger in an accident, the part of the somatosensory area that represents that finger is initially unresponsive (Kaas, 1991). After all, there's no longer any sensory input going from that location to that part of the brain. You might expect the "left middle finger neurons" of the somatosensory cortex to wither away. However, over time, that area in the somatosensory cortex becomes responsive to stimulation of the fingers *adjacent* to the missing finger. The brain is plastic: Functions that were assigned to certain areas of the brain may be capable of being reassigned to other areas of the brain to accommodate changing input from the environment. This suggests that sensory inputs "compete" for representation in each cortical area.

Plasticity doesn't only occur to compensate for missing digits or limbs, however. An extraordinary amount of stimulation of one finger can result in that finger "taking over" the representation of the part of the cortex that usually represents other, adjacent fingers (Merzenich et al., 1990). For example, concert pianists have highly developed cortical areas for finger control: The continued input from the fingers commands a larger area of representation in the somatosensory cortices in the brain. Similar findings have been obtained with quilters (who may have highly developed areas for the thumb and forefinger, which are critical to their profession) and taxi drivers (who have overdeveloped brain areas in the hippocampus that are used during spatial navigation; Maguire, Woollett, & Spiers, 2006).

summary quiz [3.2]

6. When you feel threatened, your _____ nervous system prepares you to either fight or run away.
   a. central
   b. somatic
   c. sympathetic
   d. parasympathetic

7. The proper sequence of movements when we walk, run, ride a bike, or play the piano is controlled by the
   a. medulla.
   b. cerebellum.
   c. pons.
   d. thalamus.

8. Jim was in a bad car accident, and his occipital lobe was severely damaged. After that, he had difficulty recognizing
   a. faces.
   b. odors.
   c. familiar melodies.
   d. tastes.

9. According to the textbook, which part of the cerebral cortex sets humans apart from most other species?
   a. occipital lobe
   b. parietal lobe
   c. temporal lobe
   d. frontal lobe

The Evolution of Nervous Systems

Another way to understand the organization of the nervous system is to consider its evolution over time. This approach reveals how the nervous system in humans evolved and adapted from other species to be the way it is, which is surprisingly imperfect. Far from being a single, elegant machine—the enchanted loom philosophers wrote so poetically about—the human brain is instead a system composed of many distinct components that have been added at different times during the course of evolution. The human species has retained what worked best in earlier versions of the brain, then added bits and pieces to get us to our present state through evolution.

Evolutionary Development of the Central Nervous System

The nervous system evolved from the very simple one found in simple animals to the elaborate one in humans today. Even the simplest animals have sensory neurons and motor neurons for responding to the environment (Shepherd, 1988). For example, single-celled protozoa have molecules in their cell membrane that are sensitive to food in the water. These molecules trigger the movement of tiny threads called *cilia*, which help propel the protozoa toward the food source. The first neurons appeared in simple invertebrates, such as jellyfish; the sensory neurons in the jellyfish's tentacles can feel the touch of a potentially dangerous predator, which prompts the jellyfish to swim to safety. If you're a jellyfish, this simple neural system is sufficient to keep you alive.

The first central nervous system worthy of the name, though, appeared in flatworms. The flatworm has a collection of neurons in the head—a simple kind of brain—that includes sensory neurons for vision and taste and motor neurons that control feeding behavior. Emerging from the brain are a pair of tracts that form a spinal cord. The tracts are also connected by smaller collections of neurons called *ganglia*, which integrate information and coordinate motor behavior in the body region near each ganglion.

● Flatworms don't have much of a brain, but then again, they don't need much of a brain. The rudimentary brain areas found in simple invertebrates eventually evolved into the complex brain structures found in humans.

During the course of evolution, a major split in the organization of the nervous system occurred between invertebrate animals (those without a spinal column) and vertebrate animals (those with a spinal column). In all vertebrates, the central nervous system is a organized into a hierarchy: The lower levels of the brain and spinal cord execute simpler functions, while the higher levels of the nervous system perform more complex functions. As you saw earlier, in humans, reflexes are accomplished in the spinal cord. At the next level, the midbrain executes the more complex task of orienting toward an important stimulus in the environment. Finally, a more complex task, such as imagining what your life will be like 20 years from now, is performed in the forebrain (Addis, Wong, & Schacter, 2007; Szpunar, Watson, & McDermott, 2007).

The forebrain undergoes further evolutionary advances in vertebrates. In lower vertebrate species such as amphibians (frogs and newts), the forebrain consists only of small clusters of neurons. In higher vertebrates, including reptiles, birds, and mammals, the forebrain is much larger, and it evolves in two different patterns. Reptiles and birds have almost no cerebral cortex. By contrast, mammals have highly developed cerebral cortex, which develops multiple areas that serve a broad range of higher mental functions. This forebrain development has reached its peak—so far—in humans; the human forebrain allows for some remarkable, uniquely human abilities: self-awareness, sophisticated language use, social interaction, abstract reasoning, imagining, and empathy, among others.

● **Are our brains still evolving?**

Intriguing evidence indicates that the human brain evolved more quickly than the brains of other species (Dorus et al., 2004). Researchers compared the sequences of 200 brain-related genes in mice, rats, monkeys, and humans and discovered a collection of genes that evolved more rapidly among primates. What's more, they found that this evolutionary process was more rapid along the lineage that led to humans. That is, primate brains evolved quickly compared to those of other species, but the brains of the primates who eventually became humans evolved even more rapidly. These results suggest that in addition to the normal adaptations that occur over the process of evolution, the genes for human brains took particular advantage of a variety of mutations (changes in a gene's DNA) along the evolutionary pathway. These results also suggest that the human brain is still evolving—becoming bigger and more adapted to the demands of the environment (Evans et al., 2005; Mekel-Bobrov et al., 2005).

Genes may direct the development of the brain on a large, evolutionary scale, but they also guide the development of an individual and, generally, the development of a species. Let's take a brief look at how genes and the environment contribute to the biological bases of behavior.

"You're making more at this firm than anyone else whose brain is the size of a walnut."

Genes and the Environment

A **gene** is *the unit of hereditary transmission*. Genes are built from strands of DNA (deoxyribonucleic acid) and are organized into large threads called **chromosomes**, which are *strands of DNA wound around each other in a double-helix configuration* (see **FIGURE 3.16**). Chromosomes come in pairs, and humans have 23 pairs each. These pairs of chromosomes are similar but not identical: You inherit one of each pair from your father and one from your mother. For example, the 23rd pair of chromosomes determine an individual's biological sex. Each chromosome in the 23rd pair can be either an X chromosome or a Y chromosome. Females have two X chromosomes, whereas males have one X and one Y chromosome. You inherited an X chromosome from your mother since she has only X chromosomes to give. Your biological sex, therefore, was determined by whether you received an additional X chromosome or a Y chromosome from your father.

gene The unit of hereditary transmission.

chromosomes Strands of DNA wound around each other in a double-helix configuration.

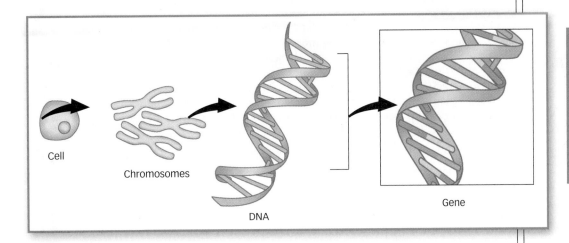

Cell

Chromosomes

DNA

Gene

FIGURE 3.16 • • • • • • • • • • • • • • • •
Genes, Chromosomes, and Their Recombination *The cell nucleus houses chromosomes, which are made up of double-helix strands of DNA. Every cell in our bodies has 23 pairs of chromosomes. Genes are segments on a strand of DNA with codes that make us who we are.*

There is considerable variability in the genes that individual offspring receive. Nonetheless, children share a higher proportion of their genes with their parents than with more distant relatives or with nonrelatives. Children share half their genes with each parent, a quarter of their genes with their grandparents, an eighth of their genes with cousins, and so on. The probability of sharing genes is called *degree of relatedness*. The most genetically related people are *monozygotic twins* (also called *identical twins*), who develop from the splitting of a single fertilized egg and therefore share 100% of their genes. *Dizygotic twins* (*fraternal twins*) develop from two separate fertilized eggs and share 50% of their genes, the same as any two siblings born separately.

Monozygotic twins (left) share 100% • • • • • • • • • • •
of their genes in common, while dizygotic twins (right) share 50% of their genes, the same as other siblings. Studies of monozygotic and dizygotic twins help researchers estimate the relative contributions of genes and environmental influences on behavior.

Culture & Community

Is the Desire to Explore New Lands in the Genes?

Psychologists have found an intriguing correlation between the migratory patterns of various populations of people and the dopamine D4 receptor gene (DRD4) (Chen et al., 1999). They found that (a) the DRD4 genotype varies considerably across populations and (b) that the distance each group moved from their original place of settlement was associated with the frequency of the long allele of DRD4 (see the graph).

For example, Native Americans in the United States, whose ancestors traveled from northern Asia, have a higher proportion of long allele of DRD4, which has been associated with novelty seeking, whereas Han Chinese have traveled little and have very few long allele DRD4.

Although it's tempting to want to reach conclusions based on this relationship, causal links have not been demonstrated. Still, it has potentially interesting implications for our understanding of the link between biology and culture.

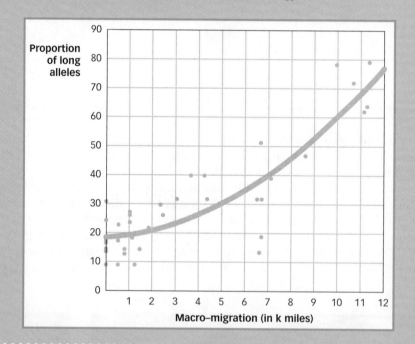

Many researchers have tried to determine the relative influence of genetics on behavior. One way to do this is to compare a trait shown by monozygotic twins with that same trait among dizygotic twins. This type of research usually enlists twins who were raised in the same household, so that the impact of their environment—their socioeconomic status, access to education, parental child-rearing practices, environmental stressors, and so forth—remains relatively constant. Finding that monozygotic twins have a higher prevalence of a specific trait suggests a genetic influence (Boomsma, Busjahn, & Peltonen, 2002).

As an example, the likelihood that the dizygotic twin of a person who has schizophrenia (a mental disorder we'll discuss in greater detail in Chapter 13) will *also* develop schizophrenia is 27%. However, this statistic rises to 50% for monozygotic twins. This observation suggests a substantial genetic influence on the likelihood of developing schizophrenia. Monozygotic twins share 100% of their genes, and if one assumes environmental influences are relatively consistent for both members of the twin pair, the 50% likelihood can be traced to genetic factors. That sounds scarily high . . . until you realize that the remaining 50% probability must be due to environmental influences. In short, genetics can contribute to the development, likelihood, or onset of a variety of traits. But a more complete picture of genetic influences on behavior must always take the environmental context into consideration. Genes express themselves within an environment, not in isolation.

"The title of my science project is My Little Brother: Nature or Nurture.'"

With these parameters in mind, behavioral geneticists use calculations based on relatedness to compute the heritability of behaviors (Plomin et al., 2001a). *Heritability* is a measure of the variability of behavioral traits among individuals that can be accounted for by genetic factors. It's calculated as a proportion, and its numerical value (index) ranges from 0 to 1.00. A heritability of 0 means that genes do not contribute to individual differences in the behavioral trait; a heritability of 1.00 means that genes are the *only* reason for the individual differences. As you might guess, scores of 0 or 1.00 occur so infrequently that they serve more as theoretical limits than realistic values; almost nothing in human behavior is completely due to the environment or *completely* to genetic inheritance. Scores between 0 and 1.00, then, indicate that individual differences are caused by varying degrees of genetic and environmental contributions—a little stronger influence of genetics here, a little stronger influence of the environment there, but each always within the context of the other.

For human behavior, almost all estimates of heritability are in the moderate range, between 0.30 and 0.60. For example, a heritability index of 0.50 for intelligence indicates that half of the variability in intelligence test scores is attributable to genetic influences, and the remaining half is due to environmental influences. Smart parents often (but not always) produce smart children; genetics certainly plays a role. But smart and not-so-smart children attend good or not-so-good schools, practice their piano lessons with more or less regularity, study or not study as hard as they might, have good and not-so-good teachers and role models, and so on. Genetics is only half the story in intelligence. Environmental influences also play a significant role in predicting the basis of intelligence (see Chapter 7).

● **Are abilities, such as intelligence and memory, inherited through our genes?**

Heritability has proven to be a theoretically useful and statistically sound concept in helping scientists understand the relative genetic and environmental influences on behavior. However, there are four important points about heritability to bear in mind.

First, *heritability is an abstract concept*: It tells us nothing about the *specific* genes that contribute to a trait. Second, *heritability is a population concept*: It tells us nothing about an individual. For example, a 0.50 heritability of intelligence means that, on average, about 50% of the differences in intellectual performance are attributable to genetic differences among individuals in the population. It does *not* mean that 50% of any given person's intelligence is due to her or his genetic makeup. Third, *heritability is dependent on the environment*. Just as behavior occurs within certain contexts, so do genetic influences. For example, intelligence isn't an unchanging quality: People are intelligent within a particular learning context, a social setting, a family environment, a socioeconomic class, and so on. Heritability, therefore, is meaningful only for the environmental conditions in which it was computed, and heritability estimates may change dramatically under other environmental conditions. Finally, *heritability is not fate*. It tells us nothing about the degree to which interventions can change a behavioral trait. Heritability is useful for identifying behavioral traits that are influenced by genes, but it is not useful for determining how individuals will respond to particular environmental conditions or treatments.

summary quiz [3.3]

10. The first central nervous system appeared in
   a. protozoa.
   b. jellyfish.
   c. flatworms.
   d. frogs.

11. Which is true of forebrain development in vertebrates?
   a. Amphibians have no forebrain at all.
   b. Reptiles have a large cerebral cortex.
   c. The cerebral cortex of mammals is smaller than that of birds.
   d. Birds have almost no cerebral cortex

12. A heritability index of 0.50 for intelligence indicates that
   a. half of each person's intelligence is due to her or his genetic makeup, and half is due to environment.
   b. among individuals in the population, half of the variability in intellectual performance is attributable to genetic influence, and half is due to environment.
   c. no matter how the environment changes, heritability of intelligence will remain at 0.50.
   d. half of the specific genes that cause intelligence have been identified.

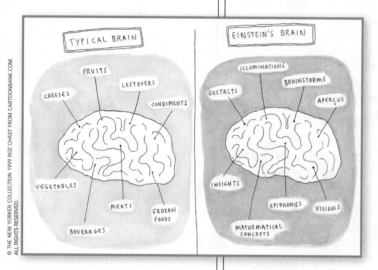

Investigating the Brain

So far, you've read a great deal about the nervous system: how it's organized, how it works, what its components are, and what those components do. But one question remains largely unanswered: *How* do we know all of this? Anatomists can dissect a human brain and identify its structures, but this cannot tell us which structures play a role in producing which behaviors. To study function, scientists use a variety of methods to understand how the brain affects behavior. Let's consider three of the main ones: testing people with brain damage and observing their deficits, studying electrical activity in the brain during behavior, and conducting brain scans while people perform various tasks.

Learning about Brain Organization by Studying the Damaged Brain

Remember Betty, the 75-year-old woman admitted to the emergency room because she couldn't recognize her own husband? She had suffered a stroke from a blood clot that deprived her brain of oxygen and caused the death of neurons in the afflicted area. Betty's stroke affected part of the association area in her temporal lobe, where complex visual objects are identified. Betty's occipital lobe, the main area where visual processing takes place, was unaffected, so Betty could see her husband and two sons, but because of the damage to her temporal lobe, she could not recognize them.

Much research in neuroscience correlates the loss of specific perceptual, motor, emotional, or cognitive functions with specific areas of brain damage (Andrewes, 2001; Kolb & Whishaw, 2003). By studying these mindbugs, neuroscientists can theorize

● **How have brain disorders been central to our study of specific areas of the brain?**

about the functions those brain areas normally perform. The modern history of neuroscience can be dated to the work of Paul Broca (see Chapter 1). In 1861, Broca described a patient who had lost the capacity to produce spoken language (but not the ability to understand language) due to damage in a small area in the left frontal lobe. In 1874, Carl Wernicke (1848–1905) described a patient with an impairment in language comprehension (but not the ability to produce speech) associated with damage to an area in the upper-left temporal lobe. These areas were named, respectively, *Broca's area* and *Wernicke's area,* and they provided the earliest evidence that the brain locations for speech production and speech comprehension are separate and that for most people, the left hemisphere is critical to producing and understanding language (Young, 1990).

The Emotional Functions of the Frontal Lobes

Individuals with brain damage have also given us important insight into the functions of the frontal lobes. One famous case was Phineas Gage, a muscular 25-year-old railroad worker who, in 1848, was packing an explosive charge into a crevice in a rock when the powder exploded, driving a 3-foot, 13-pound iron rod through his head at high speed. As **FIGURE 3.17** shows, the rod entered through his lower left jaw and exited through the middle top of his head. Incredibly, Gage lived to tell the tale. But his personality underwent a significant change.

Before the accident, Gage had been mild mannered, quiet, conscientious, and a hard worker. After the accident, he became irritable, irresponsible, indecisive, and given to profanity. The sad decline of Gage's personality and emotional life nonetheless provided an unexpected benefit to psychology. His case study was the first to allow researchers to investigate the hypothesis that the frontal lobe is involved in emotion regulation, planning, and decision making. Furthermore, because the connections between the frontal lobe and subcortical structures concerned with emotion and motivation were affected, scientists were able to better understand how the amygdala, hippocampus, and related subcortical structures interacted with the cerebral cortex (Damasio, 2005).

FROM DAMASIO ET AL. (1994).

FIGURE 3.17 ● ● ● ● ● ● ● ● ● ● ● ●
Phineas Gage *Phineas Gage's traumatic accident allowed researchers to investigate the functions of the frontal lobe and its connections with emotion centers in the subcortical structures. The likely path of the metal rod through Gage's skull is reconstructed here.*

The Distinct Roles of the Left and Right Hemispheres

The study of patients with brain damage has even yielded clues about the different functions of the left and right hemispheres of the cerebral cortex. Some of these studies focus on patients who suffer from severe, intractable epilepsy. Seizures that begin in one hemisphere cross the corpus callosum (the thick band of nerve fibers that allows the two hemispheres to communicate) to the opposite hemisphere and start a feedback loop that results in a kind of firestorm in the brain. To alleviate the severity of the seizures, surgeons can sever the corpus callosum in a procedure called a *split-brain procedure.* This meant that a seizure that starts in one hemisphere is isolated in that hemisphere since there is no longer a connection to the other side. This procedure helps the patients with epilepsy but also produces some unusual, if not unpredictable, behaviors. Normally, any information that initially enters the left hemisphere is also registered in the right hemisphere and vice versa. The information comes in and

THIS IS THE RIGHT SIDE OF THE BRAIN CALLING THE LEFT SIDE OF THE BRAIN. COME IN, LEFT SIDE...

Yo!

SCHWADRON

WWW.CARTOONSTOCK.COM

Roger Wolcott Sperry (1913–1994) received the Nobel Prize in Physiology in 1981 for his pioneering work investigating the independent functions of the cerebral hemisphere.

travels across the corpus callosum, and both hemispheres understand what's going on. But in a split-brain patient, information entering one hemisphere stays there. Without an intact corpus callosum, there's no way for that information to reach the other hemisphere.

To investigate this phenomenon, Roger Sperry and his colleagues had split-brain patients look at a spot in the center of a screen and then projected a stimulus on one side of the screen, isolating the stimulus to one hemisphere (Sperry et al. 1964). For example, they could project a picture of an object to the left hemisphere of a split-brain patient and ask her to verbally describe what it was. Typically, the left hemisphere is specialized for language processing, and so the patient would have no difficulty verbally describing what she saw. But suppose the patient was instead asked to reach behind a screen with her left hand and pick up the object she just saw. Remember that the hemispheres exert contralateral control over the body, meaning that the left hand is controlled by the right hemisphere. But this patient's right hemisphere has no clue what the object was because that information was received in the left hemisphere and was unable to travel to the right hemisphere! So, even though the split-brain patient saw the object and could verbally describe it, she would be unable to use the right hemisphere to perform other tasks regarding that object, such as correctly selecting it from a group with her left hand (see **FIGURE 3.18**).

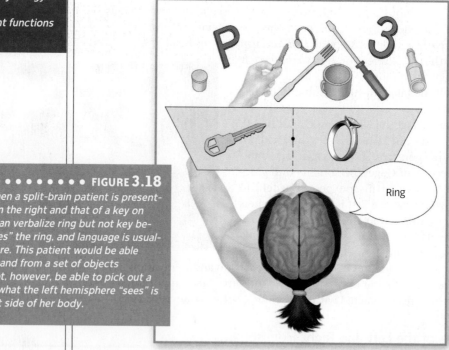

FIGURE 3.18

Split-Brain Experiment *When a split-brain patient is presented with the picture of a ring on the right and that of a key on the left side of a screen, she can verbalize ring but not key because the left hemisphere "sees" the ring, and language is usually located in the left hemisphere. This patient would be able to choose a key with her left hand from a set of objects behind a screen. She would not, however, be able to pick out a ring with her right hand since what the left hemisphere "sees" is not communicated to the right side of her body.*

Such split-brain studies reveal that the two hemispheres perform different functions and can work together seamlessly as long as the corpus callosum is intact. Without a way to transmit information from one hemisphere to the other, information gets "stuck" in the hemisphere it initially entered, and we become acutely aware of the different functions of each hemisphere. Of course, a split-brain patient can adapt to this by simply moving her eyes a little so that the same information independently enters both hemispheres. Split-brain studies have continued over the past few decades and play an important role in shaping our understanding of how the brain works (Gazzaniga, 2006).

Listening to the Brain: Single Neurons and the EEG

A second approach to studying the link between brain structures and behavior involves recording the pattern of electrical activity of neurons. An *electroencephalogram (EEG)* is a device used to record electrical activity in the brain. Typically, electrodes are placed on the outside of the head, and even though the source of electrical activity in synapses and action potentials is far removed from these wires, the electric signals can be amplified several thousand times by the EEG to provide a visual record of the underlying electrical activity, as shown in **FIGURE 3.19**. Using this technique, researchers can determine the amount of brain activity when individuals engage in a variety of psychological functions, such as perceiving, learning, and remembering.

A different approach to recording electrical activity resulted in a more refined understanding of the brain's division of responsibilities, even at a cellular level. Nobel

● **How does the EEG record electrical activity in the brain?**

laureates David Hubel and Torsten Wiesel used a technique that inserted electrodes into the occipital lobes of anesthetized cats and observed the patterns of action potentials of individual neurons (Hubel, 1988). Hubel and Wiesel amplified the action potential signals through a loudspeaker so that the signals could be heard as clicks as well as seen on an oscilloscope. While flashing lights in front of the animal's eye, Hubel and Wiesel recorded the resulting activity of neurons in the occipital cortex. They discovered that neurons in the primary visual cortex are activated whenever a contrast between light and dark occurs in part of the visual field, seen particularly well when the visual stimulus was a thick line of light against a dark background. They then found that each neuron responded vigorously only when presented with a contrasting edge at a particular orientation. Since then, many studies have shown that neurons in the primary visual cortex represent particular features of visual stimuli, such as contrast, shape, and color (Zeki, 1993). These dimensions can then be combined during a later stage of processing to allow recognition and perception of a stimulus.

Other studies have identified a variety of features that are detected by sensory neurons. For example, some visual processing neurons in the temporal lobe are activated only when detecting faces (Kanwisher, 2000; Perrett, Rolls, & Caan, 1982). These neurons lie in the same area of the temporal cortex that was damaged in Betty's stroke. Neurons in this area are specialized for processing faces; damage to this area results in an inability to perceive faces. These complementary observations—showing that the type of function that is lost or altered when a brain area is damaged corresponds to the kind of information processed by neurons in that cortical area—provide the most compelling evidence linking the brain to behavior. (See the Hot Science box on the next page.)

FIGURE 3.19 ● ● ● ● ● ● ● ● ● ● ● ● ●
EEG *The electroencephalogram (EEG) records electrical activity in the brain. Many states of consciousness, such as wakefulness and stages of sleep, are characterized by particular types of brainwaves.*

David Hubel (left, b. 1926) and Torsten ● ● ● ● ● ● ● ● ● ●
Wiesel (right, b. 1924) received the Nobel Prize in Physiology in 1981 for their work on mapping the visual cortex.

Brain Imaging: Watching the Brain in Action

The third major way that neuroscientists can peer into the workings of the human brain has only become possible within the past several decades. *Neuroimaging techniques* use advanced technology to create images of the living, healthy brain (Posner & Raichle, 1994; Raichle & Mintun, 2006).

Mirror, Mirror, in My Brain

You've no doubt heard the expression "Monkey see, monkey do." In fact, you may have taunted a sibling or playmate with that line more than once in your life. You probably didn't realize that you were *that close* to making one of the major discoveries in neuroscience when you uttered those prophetic words!

One of the most exciting recent advances in neuroscience is the discovery of the mirror-neuron system. Mirror neurons are found in the frontal lobe (near the motor cortex) and in the parietal lobe (Rizzolatti & Craighero, 2004). They have been identified in birds, monkeys, and humans, and their name reflects the function they serve. Mirror neurons are active when an animal performs a behavior, such as reaching for or manipulating an object. However, mirror neurons are also activated whenever another animal *observes* this animal performing the behavior. In other words, mirror neurons are active both in the animal reaching for the food and in the animal observing this behavior. This kind of mirroring—one monkey sees, one monkey does, but both monkeys' mirror neurons fire—holds intriguing implications for understanding the brain's role in complex social behavior.

A recent study on mirror neurons used fMRI, a technique discussed later in the chapter, to monitor the brains of humans as they watched each of three presentations (Iacoboni et al., 2005). Sometimes participants saw a hand making grasping motions in midair with no "props" or background. Sometimes they saw only the context: coffee cups or scrubbing sponges but no hands making motions to go with them. Other times they saw hand motions in two different contexts, either grasping and moving a coffee cup to drink, or cleaning dishes with a sponge.

When actions were embedded in a context, such as in the last set of presentations, the participants' mirror neurons responded more strongly than in either of the other two conditions. This suggests that the same set of neurons involved in action recognition are also involved in understanding the intentions of others. Recognizing another person's intentions means that the observer has inferred something about that person's goals, wants, or wishes ("Oh, she must be thirsty"). These fMRI results suggest that this kind of recognition occurs effortlessly at a neural level.

Why is this interesting? For one thing, these results suggest a possible inborn neural basis for empathy. Grasping the intentions of another person—indeed, having your brain respond in kind as another person acts—is critical to smooth social interaction. It allows us to understand other people's possible motivations and anticipate their future actions. In fact, these are the kinds of skills that people suffering from autism severely lack. Autism is a developmental disorder charac-

PHOTO/DAVID LONGSTREATH

When one animal observes another engaging in a particular behavior, some of the same neurons become active in the observer as well as in the animal exhibiting the behavior. These mirror neurons, documented in monkeys, birds, and humans, seem to play an important role in the social behavior.

terized by impoverished social interactions and communication skills (Frith, 2001). Psychologists who study autism focus on trying to understand the nature of the disorder and devise ways to help people with autism cope with and function in human society. Research on mirror neurons may offer one avenue for better understanding the origin and prognosis of this disorder (Iacoboni & Dapretto, 2006).

Off The Mark

© MARK PARISI/ATLANTIC FEATURE SYNDICATE

One of the first neuroimaging techniques developed was the *computerized axial tomography (CT) scan*. In a CT scan, a scanner rotates a device around a person's head and takes a series of x-ray photographs from different angles. Computer programs then combine these images to provide views from any angle. CT scans show different densities of tissue in the brain. For example, the higher-density skull looks white on a CT scan, the cortex shows up as gray, and the least dense fissures and ventricles in the brain look dark (see **FIGURE 3.20** on the next page). CT scans are used to locate lesions or tumors, which typically appear darker because they are less dense than the cortex.

Magnetic resonance imaging (MRI) involves applying brief but powerful magnetic pulses to the head and recording how these pulses are absorbed throughout the brain. For very short periods, these magnetic pulses cause molecules in the brain tissue to twist slightly and then relax, which releases a small amount of energy. Differently charged molecules respond differently to the magnetic pulses, so the energy signals reveal brain structures with different molecular compositions. Magnetic resonance imaging produces pictures of soft tissue at a better resolution than a CT scan, as you can see in Figure 3.20. These techniques give psychologists a clearer picture of the structure of the brain and can help localize brain damage (as when someone suffers a stroke), but they reveal nothing about the functions of the brain.

Two newer techniques show researchers much more than just the structure of the brain. *Functional-brain-imaging* techniques allow us to actually watch the brain in action. These techniques rely on the fact that activated brain areas demand more energy for their neurons to work. This energy is supplied through increased blood flow to the activated areas. Functional-imaging techniques can detect such changes in blood flow. In *positron emission tomography* (*PET*), a harmless radioactive substance is injected into a person's bloodstream. Then the brain is scanned by radiation detectors as the person performs perceptual or cognitive tasks, such as reading or speaking. Areas of the brain that are activated during these tasks demand more energy and greater blood flow, resulting in a higher amount of the radioactivity in that region. The radiation detectors record the level of radioactivity in each region, producing a computerized image of the activated areas (see **FIGURE 3.21**, below).

For psychologists, the most widely used functional-brain-imaging technique nowadays is *functional magnetic resonance imaging* (*fMRI*), which detects the twisting of

● **What does an fMRI track in an active brain?**

oxygen-carrying hemoglobin molecules in the blood when they are exposed to magnetic pulses. When active neurons demand more energy and blood flow, oxygenated hemoglobin concentrates in the active areas. fMRI detects the oxygenated hemoglobin and provides a picture of the level of activation in each brain area. Both fMRI and PET allow researchers to localize changes in the brain very accurately. However, fMRI has a couple of advantages over PET. First, fMRI does not require any exposure to a radioactive substance. Second, fMRI can localize changes in brain activity across briefer periods than PET, which makes it more useful for analyzing psychological processes that occur extremely quickly, such as reading a word or recognizing a face.

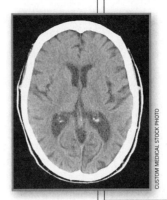
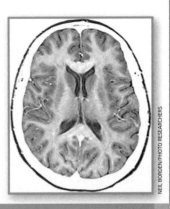

FIGURE 3.20 ● ● ● ● ● ● ● ● ● ● ● ● ● ● ● ● ●
Structural Imaging Techniques (CT and MRI) *CT (left) and MRI (right) scans are used to provide information about the structure of the brain and can help spot tumors and other kinds of damage. Each scan shown here provides a snapshot of a single slice in the brain. Note that the MRI scan provides a clearer, higher-resolution image than the CT scan (see the text for further discussion of how these images are constructed and what they depict).*

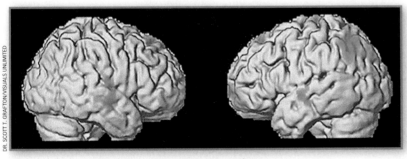

Gesture preparation

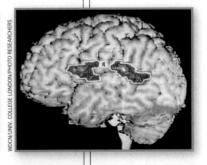

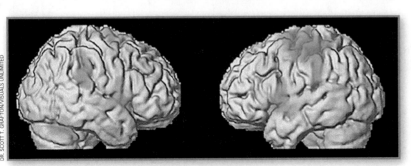

Gesture production

FIGURE 3.21 ● ● ● ● ● ● ● ● ● ● ● ● ● ● ● ● ●
Functional-Imaging Techniques (PET fMRI) *PET and fMRI scans provide information about the functions of the brain by revealing which brain areas become more or less active in different conditions. The PET scan (directly above) shows areas in the left hemisphere (Broca's area, left; lower parietal-upper temporal area, right) that become active when people hold in mind a string of letters for a few seconds. The fMRI scans (all views to the left) show several different regions in both hemispheres that become active when someone is thinking about a gesture (top) and when performing a gesture (bottom).*

PET and fMRI provide remarkable insights into the types of information processing that take place in specific areas of the brain. For example, when a person performs a simple perceptual task, such as looking at a circular checkerboard, the primary visual areas are activated. But when people perform a task that engages emotional processing, such as looking at sad pictures, researchers observe significant activation in the amygdala, which is linked with emotional arousal (Phelps, 2006). There is also increased activation in parts of the frontal lobe that are involved in emotional regulation—in fact, in the same areas that were most likely damaged in the case of Phineas Gage (Wang et al., 2005). It's always nice when independent methods—in these instances, very old case studies and very recent technology—arrive at the same conclusions. As you'll also see at various points in the text, brain-imaging techniques such as fMRI are also revealing new and surprising findings, such as the insights described in the Where Do You Stand? box (on the next page). Although the human brain still holds many mysteries, researchers are developing increasingly sophisticated ways of unraveling them.

summary quiz [3.4]

13. The earliest evidence that separate brain locations control speech comprehension and speech production was provided by
   a. Phineas Gage.
   b. David Hubel and Torsten Wiesel.
   c. Roger Sperry and his colleagues.
   d. Paul Broca and Carl Wernicke.

14. Split-brain studies have revealed that
   a. neurons in the primary visual cortex represent features of visual stimuli such as contrast, shape, and color.
   b. the two hemispheres perform different functions but can work together by means of the corpus callosum.
   c. when people perform a task that involves emotional processing, the amygdala is activated.
   d. brain locations for vision, touch, and hearing are separate.

15. The activity of specific neurons in the brain can best be detected by means of
   a. brain-imaging techniques.
   b. split-brain procedures.
   c. inserting electrodes into brain cells.
   d. studying the behaviors of individuals with brain damage.

16. Researchers can observe relationships between energy consumption in certain brain areas and specific cognitive and behavioral events using which technique?
   a. functional brain imaging
   b. electroencephalographs
   c. inserting electrodes into individual cells
   d. CT scans

WhereDoYouStand?

Brain Death

A story shrouded in mystery follows the memory of Andreas Vesalius (1514–1564), a Belgian physician regarded as one of the founders of modern anatomy. According to the story, Vesalius conducted an autopsy in 1564 in front of a large crowd in Madrid, Spain. When the cadaver's chest was opened, the audience saw that the man's heart was still beating! The possibility that the patient was still alive created a scandal that forced Vesalius to leave Spain, where he was serving as the imperial physician at the time. He died during his exodus in a shipwreck.

We may never know whether this story is accurate. However, it raises a question related to the brain and behavior that is still fiercely debated today. In Vesalius's time, if a patient didn't appear to be breathing, was generally unresponsive, or gave no strong evidence of a heartbeat, the person could safely be considered dead (despite the occasional misdiagnosis). Modern resuscitative techniques can keep the heart, lungs, and other organs functioning for days, months, or even years, so physicians have identified measures of brain function that allow them to decide more definitively when someone is dead.

In 1981, the President's Commission for the Study of Ethical Problems in Medicine and Biomedical and Behavioral Research defined brain death as the *irreversible loss of all functions of the brain*. Contrary to what you may think, brain death is not the same as being in a coma or being unresponsive to stimulation. Respiration is controlled by structures in the hindbrain, such as the medulla, and will continue as long as this area is intact. A heartbeat does not require input from any area of the brain, so the heart will continue to beat as long it continues to receive oxygen, either by intact respiration or if the patient is artificially ventilated. Also, a patient who is brain dead may continue to have muscle spasms, twitches, or even sit up. This so-called *Lazarus reflex* is coordinated solely by the spinal cord.

Brain death came to the forefront of national attention during March 2005 in the case of Terri Schiavo, a woman who had been kept alive on a respirator for nearly 15 years in a Florida nursing home. A person like Schiavo is commonly referred to as brain dead, but such an individual is more accurately described as being in a *persistent vegetative state*. In fact, some people consider patients in a persistent vegetative state to still be alive.

Terri Schiavo's parents thought she had a substantial level of voluntary consciousness; they felt that she appeared to smile, cry, and turn toward the source of a voice. Terri's parents hired physicians who claimed that she had a primitive type of consciousness. However, neurologists who specialize in these cases emphasized that these responses could be automatic reflexes supported by circuits in the thalamus and midbrain. These neurologists failed to see conclusive evidence of consciousness or voluntary behavior.

Terri's husband, Michael, agreed with the neurologists and asked the courts to remove the feeding tube that kept her alive, a decision a Florida court accepted. Nonetheless, Florida governor Jeb Bush decreed in 2003 that doctors retain Terri's feeding tube and continue to provide medical care. Eventually, in 2005, the court again ordered her feeding tube removed, and this time it was not replaced, resulting in her death.

Where do you stand on this issue? Should Terri Schiavo have been kept alive indefinitely? The definition of brain death includes the term *irreversible*, suggesting that as long as *any* component of the brain can still function—with or without the aid of a machine—the person should be considered alive. But does a persistent vegetative state qualify as "life"? Is a simple consensus of qualified professionals–doctors, nurses, social workers, specialists–sufficient to decide whether someone is "still living" or at least "still living enough" to maintain whatever treatments may be in place? How should the wishes of family members be considered? What is your position on these questions of the brain and the ultimate behavior: staying alive?

After you've thought about your answers to these questions, consider this: A recent study found evidence that a person diagnosed as being in a vegetative state showed intentional mental activity (Owen et al., 2006). Researchers used fMRI to observe the patterns of brain activity in a 25-year-old woman with severe brain injuries as the result of a traffic accident. When the researchers spoke ambiguous sentences ("The creak came from a beam in the ceiling") and unambiguous sentences ("There was milk and sugar in his coffee"), fMRI revealed that the activated areas in the woman's brain were comparable to those areas activated in the brains of normal volunteers. What's more, when the woman was instructed to imagine playing a game of tennis and then imagine walking through the rooms of her house, the areas of her brain that showed activity were again indistinguishable from those brain areas in normal, healthy volunteers.

The researchers suggest that these findings are evidence for, at least, conscious understanding of spoken commands and, at best, a degree of intentionality in an otherwise vegetative person. The patient's brain activity while "playing tennis" and "walking through her house" revealed that she could both understand the researchers' instructions and willfully complete them. Unfortunately, it's too early to tell how these and other research findings may impact decisions regarding the brain and when life ends (Laureys et., 2006).

CHAPTER REVIEW

Summary

Neurons: The Origin of Behavior

- Neurons process information, communicate with each other, and send messages to the body's muscles and organs. They contain three major parts: cell body, dendrites, and axon.

- Action potentials occur when sodium channels in the axon membrane open, allowing sodium ions to rush inside, changing the cell's electrical potential.

- When it reaches the end of the axon, the action potential triggers a release of neurotransmitters into the synapse, where they may bind to receptors on the receiving neuron's dendrite, completing transmission of the message.

- Some major neurotransmitters are acetylcholine, dopamine, glutamate, GABA, norepinephrine, serotonin, and the endorphins.

- Drugs can affect behavior by facilitating or increasing, or by blocking, the actions of neurotransmitters.

The Organization of the Nervous System

- The nervous system can be divided into the central nervous system (brain and spinal cord) and the peripheral nervous system (somatic nervous system and autonomic nervous system). The autonomic nervous system can be further divided into the sympathetic nervous system, which oversees arousal to prepare the body to fight or run away, and the parasympathetic nervous system, which helps calm the body after the threat has passed.

- The brain can be divided into the hindbrain (medulla, cerebellum, and pons), the midbrain (tectum and tegmentum), and the forebrain, which includes the cerebral cortex and subcortical structures such as the thalamus, hypothalamus, pituitary gland, hippocampus, and amygdala.

- The cerebral cortex contains two symmetrical hemispheres. Each can be divided into four major lobes: the occipital lobe, which processes visual information; the parietal lobe, which processes sensory (touch) information; the temporal lobe, which is responsible for hearing and language; and the frontal lobe, which has specialized areas for movement, abstract

thinking, planning, memory, and judgment. Each lobe also has association areas, which help integrate information across different modalities.

The Evolution of Nervous Systems

- Even the simplest animals have sensory neurons and motor neurons for responding to the environment. The first central nervous system appeared in flatworms.

- Animals can be divided into vertebrates (those with a spinal column) and invertebrates (those without a spinal column). Among vertebrates, reptiles, birds, and mammals have large forebrains; and in mammals, the cerebral cortex is particularly large.

- An individual's behavior is determined by both genetics ("nature") and environment ("nurture"). Heritability is a measure of the degree to which variations in behavior across individuals can be accounted for by genetic factors, but it tells us nothing about specific individuals, about what specific genes cause the behavior, or about how interventions might alter a trait.

Investigating the Brain

- There are three major approaches to studying the link between brain and behavior.

- By studying how perceptual, intellectual, motor, and emotional capabilities are altered in patients with damage to particular areas of the brain, researchers can better understand how those brain areas normally play a role in producing those behaviors.

- Global activity in the brain can be observed from outside the skull (using electroencephalographs), and activity of specific neurons can be recorded to determine whether they respond to particular kinds of stimuli or control particular aspects of behavior.

- With brain imaging, researchers can see the structure of the living brain; with functional brain imaging, researchers can observe correlations energy consumption in particular brain areas with specific cognitive and behavioral events, suggesting that those brain areas are involved in those events.

Key Terms

neurons (p. 56)
cell body (p. 57)
dendrites (p. 57)
axon (p. 57)
glial cell (p. 57)
myelin sheath (p. 57)
synapse (p. 57)
sensory neurons (p. 57)

motor neurons (p. 57)
interneurons (p. 57)
resting potential (p. 59)
action potential (p. 59)
refractory period (p. 60)
terminal buttons (p. 60)
neurotransmitters (p. 60)
receptors (p. 60)

nervous system (p. 64)
central nervous system (CNS) (p. 64)
peripheral nervous system (PNS) (p. 64)
somatic nervous system (p. 64)
autonomic nervous system (p. 65)

sympathetic nervous system (p. 65)
parasympathetic nervous system (p. 65)
spinal reflexes (p. 67)
hindbrain (p. 68)
medulla (p. 68)
reticular formation (p. 68)
cerebellum (p. 69)

pons (p. 69)

tectum (p. 69)

tegmentum (p. 69)

cerebral cortex (p. 70)

subcortical structures (p. 70)

thalamus (p. 70)

hypothalamus (p. 70)

pituitary gland (p. 70)

hippocampus (p. 70)

amygdala (p. 70)

corpus callosum (p. 70)

occipital lobe (p. 71)

parietal lobe (p. 71)

temporal lobe (p. 71)

frontal lobe (p. 71)

association areas (p. 71)

gene (p. 75)

chromosomes, (p. 75)

Critical Thinking Questions

1. In this chapter, you read about the various functions of different areas of the human cerebral cortex. Reptiles and birds have almost no cerebral cortex, while mammals such as rats and cats do have a cerebral cortex, but their frontal lobes are proportionately much smaller than the frontal lobes of humans and other primates.

   How might this explain the fact that only humans have developed complex language, computer technology, and calculus?

2. Different parts of the human cerebral cortex specialize in processing different types of information: The occipital lobe processes visual information, the parietal lobe processes information about touch, the temporal lobe is responsible for hearing and language, and the frontal lobe is involved in planning and judgment.

   Suppose a toddler is playing with the remote control and accidentally pushes the big red button, at which point her favorite cartoon disappears from the television screen. How

would the different parts of her cortex encode information about this event so that she may learn not to make the same mistake twice?

3. In Chapter 2, you learned about the difference between correlation and causation, and that even if two events are correlated, it does not necessarily mean that one causes the other. In this chapter, you read about techniques such as fMRI and PET, which researchers can use to measure blood flow or activity in different regions while people perform particular tasks.

   Suppose a researcher designs an experiment in which participants view words on a screen and are asked to pronounce each word aloud, while the researcher uses fMRI to examine brain activity. First, what areas of the brain would you expect to show activity on fMRI while participants complete this task? Second, can the researcher now safely conclude that those brain areas are required for humans to perform word pronunciation?

Answers to Summary Quizzes

Summary Quiz 3.1
1. d; 2. a; 3. c; 4. b; 5. a

Summary Quiz 3.2
6. c; 7. b; 8. a; 9. d

Summary Quiz 3.3
10. c; 11. d; 12. b

Summary Quiz 3.4
13. d; 14. b; 15. c; 16. a

Need more help? Additional resources are located at the book's free companion Web site at: www.worthpublishers.com/schacterbriefle

Sensation and Perception

N *is sort of . . . rubbery . . . smooth,* L *is sort of the consistency of watery paint . . . Letters also have vague personalities, but not as strongly as numerals do.*
—Julieta

The letter A *is blue,* B *is red,* C *is kind of a light gray,* D *is orange. . . .*
—Karen

I hear a note by one of the fellows in the band and it's one color. I hear the same note played by someone else and it's a different color. When I hear sustained musical tones, I see just about the same colors that you do, but I see them in textures.
—Jazz musician Duke Ellington (George, 1981, p. 226)

Basically, I taste words.
—Amelia

THESE COMMENTS ARE NOT FROM A recent meeting of the Slightly Odd Society. They're the remarks of otherwise perfectly normal people describing what seem to be perfectly bizarre experiences except to them; they think these experiences are quite common-place and genuine. After all, if you can't trust Duke Ellington, an internationally acclaimed jazz composer and bandleader, who can you trust? Perhaps Stevie Wonder? Eddie Van Halen? Vladimir Nabokov, the author of *Lolita*? Franz Liszt, the classical composer? Richard Feynman, the Nobel Prize–winning physicist? Take your pick because these and many other notable people have at least one thing in common: Their perceptual worlds seem to be quite different from most of ours. ■

What do these people have in common? Duke Ellington, Stevie Wonder, Eddie Van Halen, and Franz Liszt are all musicians, but Richard Feynman was a physicist. All of these people are men, but that has little to do with it. Some are living; some are dead. In fact, all of these people have fairly well-documented experiences of synesthesia, the experience of one sense that is evoked by a different sense.

These unusual perceptual events are varieties of *synesthesia*, the perceptual experience of one sense that is evoked by another sense (Hubbard & Ramachandran, 2003). For some synesthetes, musical notes evoke the visual sensation of color. Other people with synesthesia see printed letters (**FIGURE 4.1**) or numbers in specific, consistent colors (always seeing the digit 2 as pink and 3 as green, for example). Still others experience specific tastes when certain sounds are heard.

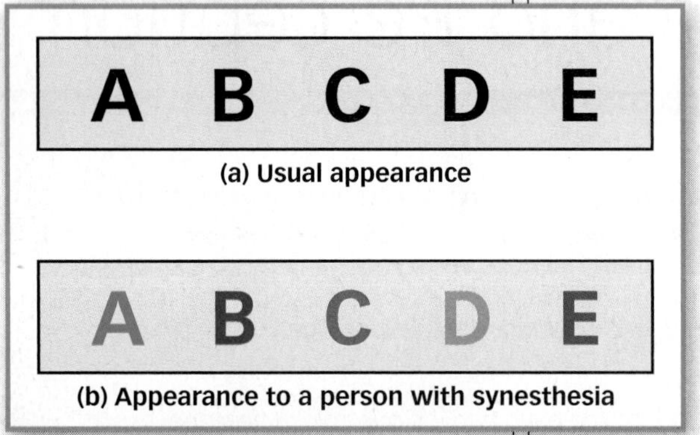

For those of us who don't experience synesthesia, the prospect of tasting sounds or hearing colors may seem unbelievable or the product of some hallucinogenic experience. Indeed, for many years scientists dismissed synesthesia as either a rare curiosity or a case of outright faking. But recent research indicates that synesthesia is far more common than previously believed: some forms of synesthesia may be found in as many as 1 in every 100 people (Hubbard & Ramachandran, 2005).

Recent research has documented the psychological and neurobiological reality of synesthesia. For example, a synesthete who sees the digits 2 and 4 as pink and 3 as green will find it easier to pick out a 2 among a bunch of 3s than among a bunch of 4s, whereas a nonsynesthete will perform these two tasks equally well (Palmieri, Ingersoll, & Stone, 2002). Brain-imaging studies also show that in some synesthetes, areas of the brain involved in processing colors are more active when they hear words that evoke color than when they hear tones that don't evoke color; no such differences are seen among people in a control group (Nunn, Gregory, & Brammer, 2002).

So, synesthesia may indicate that in some people, the brain is "wired" differently than in most, so that brain regions for different sensory modalities cross-activate one another (Ramachandran & Hubbard, 2003). Whatever the ultimate explanations for these fascinating phenomena, this recent wave of research shows that synesthesia is a mindbug that can shed new light on how the brain is organized and how we sense and perceive the world.

In this chapter, we'll explore key insights into the nature of sensation and perception. These experiences are basic to survival and reproduction; we wouldn't last long without the ability to accurately make sense of the world around us. Indeed, research on sensation and perception is the basis for much of psychology, a pathway toward understanding more complex cognition and behavior such as memory, emotion, motivation, or decision making. Yet sensation and perception also sometimes reveal mindbugs, ranging from the complexities of synesthesia to various kinds of perceptual illusions that you might see at a science fair or in a novelty shop. These mindbugs are reminders that the act of perceiving the world is not as simple or straightforward as it might seem.

The Doorway to Psychology

Sensation is *simple awareness due to the stimulation of a sense organ*. It is the basic registration of light, sound, pressure, odor, or taste as parts of your body interact with the physical world. After a sensation registers in your central nervous system, **perception** takes place at the level of your brain: It is *the organization, identification, and interpretation of a sensation in order to form a mental representation*. As an example, your eyes are coursing across these sentences right now. The sensory receptors in your eyeballs are registering different patterns of light reflecting off the page. Your brain, however, is integrating and processing that light information into the meaningful perception of words, such as *meaningful, perception,* and *words*. Your eyes—the sensory organ—aren't really seeing words; they're simply encoding different shapes and patterns of ink on a page. Your brain—the perceptual organ—is transforming those shapes into a coherent mental representation of words and concepts.

| **A** | **B** | **C** | **D** | **E** |

(a) Usual appearance

| A | B | C | D | E |

(b) Appearance to a person with synesthesia

FIGURE 4.1

Synesthesia *Most of us see letters printed in black as they appear in (a). Some people with synesthesia link their perceptions of letters with certain colors and perceive letters as printed in different colors, as shown in (b). In synesthesia, brain regions for different sensory modalities cross-activate one another.*

sensation Simple awareness due to the stimulation of a sense organ.

perception The organization, identification, and interpretation of a sensation in order to form a mental representation.

transduction What takes place when many sensors in the body convert physical signals from the environment into neural signals sent to the central nervous system.

If all of this sounds a little peculiar, it's because from the vantage point of your conscious experience, it *seems* as if you're reading words directly; sensation and perception feel like one continuous, seamless event. If you think of the discussion of brain damage in Chapter 3, however, you'll recall that sometimes a person's eyes can work just fine, yet the individual is still "blind" to faces she has seen for many years. Damage to the visual-processing centers in the brain can interfere with the interpretation of information coming from the eyes. The senses are intact, but perceptual ability is compromised. Sensation and perception are related—but separate—events.

We all know that sensory events involve vision, hearing, touch, taste, and smell. Arguably, we possess several more senses besides these five. Touch, for example,

● **What role does the brain play in what we see and hear?**

encompasses distinct body senses, including sensitivity to pain and temperature, joint position and balance, and even the state of the gut—perhaps to sense nausea via the autonomic nervous system. Despite the variety of our senses, they all depend on the process of **transduction**, which is *the conversion, by sensors in the body, of physical signals from the environment into neural signals sent to the central nervous system.*

In vision, light reflected from surfaces provides the eyes with information about the shape, color, and position of objects. In audition, vibrations (from vocal cords or a guitar string, perhaps) cause changes in air pressure that propagate through space to a listener's ears. In touch, the pressure of a surface against the skin signals its shape, texture, and temperature. In taste and smell, molecules dispersed in the air or dissolved in saliva reveal the identity of substances that we may or may not want to eat. In each case physical energy from the world is converted to neural energy inside the central nervous system. We've already seen that synesthetes experience a mixing of these perceptions; however, even during synesthesia the processes of transduction that begin those perceptions are the same. Despite "hearing colors," your eyes simply can't transduce sound waves, no matter how long you stare at your stereo speakers!

Psychophysics

It's intriguing to consider the possibility that our basic perceptions of sights or sounds might differ fundamentally from those of other people. One reason we find synesthetes fascinating is because their perceptual experiences are so different from most of ours. But we won't get very far in understanding such differences by simply relying on casual self-reports. As you learned in Chapter 2, to understand a behavior, researchers must first *operationalize* it, and that involves finding a reliable way to measure it.

Any type of scientific investigation requires objective measurements. Measuring the physical energy of a stimulus, such as the color and brightness of a light, is easy enough: You can probably

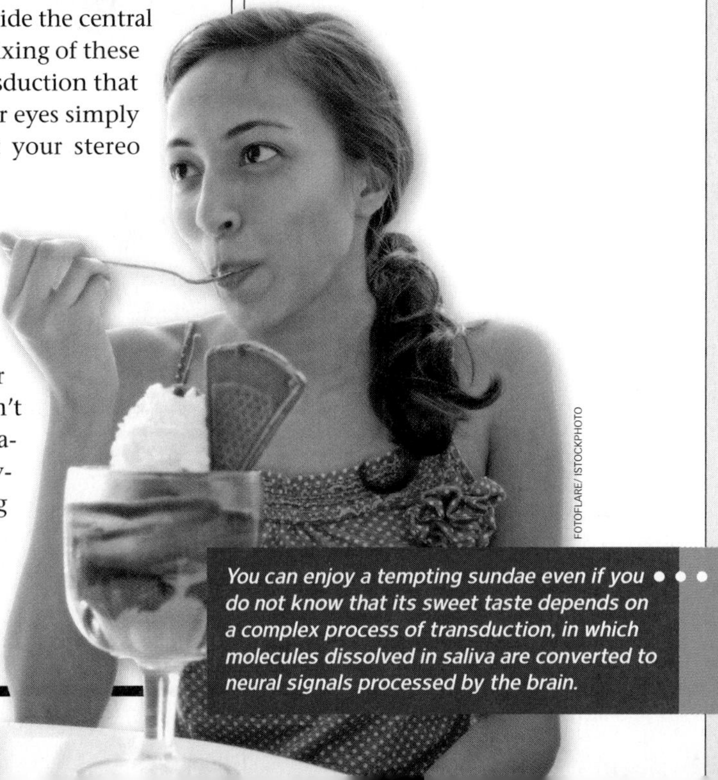

Culture & Community

Our Brains Interpret Messages from Our Senses and Transform Them into Meaningful Words, Images, and Concepts. Is This Process Universal, or Might Culture Influence Perception?

In an experiment, researchers gave Japanese and American participants a sheet of paper with a square drawn on it, within which was printed a single vertical line (Kitayama et al., 2003). The participants were then given the task of reproducing the single line within a second, smaller box in (a) absolute terms (reproducing the exact length of the line from the original box) and (b) relative terms (reproducing a line proportional to the new height of the surrounding box).

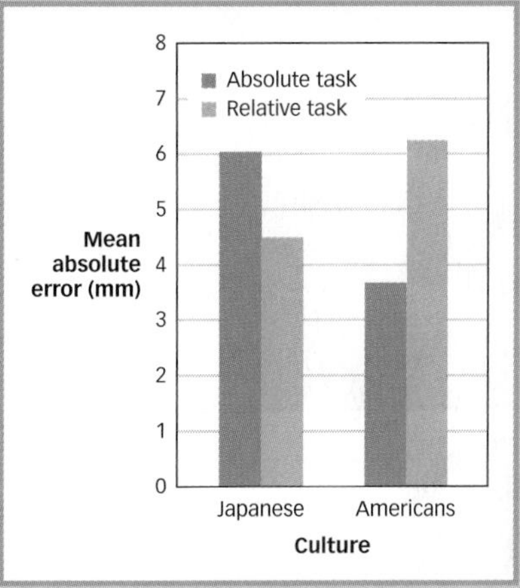

In support of the researchers' hypothesis, Japanese were significantly more accurate at the relative task than the absolute task, whereas Americans were significantly more accurate at the absolute task than the relative task. Interestingly, when testing Americans living in Japan or Japanese living in America, the participants tended to show an increase in the skill appropriate to their host nation.

Bar chart: Mean absolute error (mm), y-axis from 0 to 8. Legend: ■ Absolute task, ■ Relative task. x-axis: Japanese, Americans (Culture).

You can enjoy a tempting sundae even if you do not know that its sweet taste depends on a complex process of transduction, in which molecules dissolved in saliva are converted to neural signals processed by the brain.

FOTOFLARE/ISTOCKPHOTO

buy the necessary instruments online to do that yourself. But how do you quantify a person's private, subjective *perception* of that light? The structuralists, led by Wilhelm Wundt, tried using introspection to measure perceptual experiences (see Chapter 1). They failed miserably at this task. After all, you can describe your experience to another

● **Why is the perception of any event unique to yourself?**

person in words, but that person cannot know directly what you perceive when you look at a sunset. You both may call the sunset "orange" and "beautiful," but neither of you can directly perceive the other's experience of the same event. Evoked memories and emotions intertwine with what you are hearing, seeing, and smelling, making your perception of an event—and therefore your experience of that event—unique.

Given that perception is different for each of us, how could we ever hope to measure it? This question was answered in the mid-1800s by the German scientist and philosopher Gustav Fechner (1801–1887). Fechner developed an approach to measuring sensation and perception called **psychophysics**: *methods that measure the strength of a stimulus and the observer's sensitivity to that stimulus* (Fechner, 1966/1860). In a typical psychophysics experiment, researchers ask people to make a simple judgment—whether or not they saw a flash of light, for example. The psychophysicist then relates the measured stimulus, such as the brightness of the light flash, to each observer's yes-or-no response.

Measuring Thresholds

The simplest quantitative measurement in psychophysics is the **absolute threshold**, *the minimal intensity needed to just barely detect a stimulus*. A *threshold* is a boundary. The doorway that separates the inside from the outside of a house is a threshold, as is the boundary between two psychological states ("awareness" and "unawareness," for example). In finding the absolute threshold for sensation, the two states in question are *sensing* and *not sensing* some stimulus. **TABLE 4.1** lists the approximate sensory thresholds for each of the five senses.

To measure the absolute threshold for detecting a sound, for example, an observer sits in a soundproof room wearing headphones linked to a computer. The experimenter presents a pure tone (the sort of sound made by striking a tuning fork), using the computer to vary the loudness or the length of time each tone lasts and recording how often the observer reports hearing that tone under each condition. Investigators typically define the absolute threshold as the loudness required for the listener to say she or he has heard the tone on 50% of the trials.

If we repeat this experiment for many different tones, we can observe and record the thresholds for tones ranging from very low pitch to very high. It turns out that people tend to be most sensitive to the range of tones corresponding to human conversation. If the tone is low enough, such as the lowest note on a pipe organ, most humans cannot hear it at all; we can only feel it. If the tone is high enough, we likewise cannot hear it, but dogs and many other animals can.

● **Why can parents identify their own child's cry over others?**

The absolute threshold is useful for assessing how sensitive we are to faint stimuli, but most everyday perception involves detecting differences among stimuli that are well above the absolute threshold. Most people are pretty adept at noticing that a couch is red, but they're likely to want to know if the couch is redder than the drapes they're considering. Similarly, parents can usually detect their own infant's cry from the cries

TABLE 4.1

Approximate Sensory Thresholds

Sense	Absolute Threshold	
Vision	A candle flame 30 miles away on a clear, dark night	 JANOS MISETA FEATUREPICS
Hearing	A clock's tick 20 feet away when all is quiet	 RAINFORESTAUSTRALIA ISTOCKPHOTO
Touch	A fly's wing falling on the cheek from one centimeter away	TYLER OLSON FEATUREPICS
Smell	A single drop of perfume diffused through an area equivalent to the volume of six rooms	 MARCO ANDRAS EST AGEFOTOSTOCK
Taste	A teaspoon of sugar dissolved in two gallons of water	FOODFOLIO ALAMY

Source: Adapted from Galanter (1962).

of other babies, but it's probably more useful to be able to differentiate the "I'm hungry" cry from the "I'm cranky" cry from the "Something is biting my toes" cry. In short, the human perceptual system excels at detecting *changes* in stimulation rather than the simple onset or offset of stimulation.

As a way of measuring this difference threshold, Fechner proposed the **just noticeable difference**, or JND—*the minimal change in a stimulus that can just barely be detected.* The JND is not a fixed quantity; rather, it is roughly proportional to the magnitude of the standard stimulus. This relationship was first noticed in 1834 by a German physiologist named Ernst Weber, and it is now called **Weber's law,** which states that *the just noticeable difference of a stimulus is a constant proportion despite variations in intensity.* As an example, the JND for weight is about 2%. If you picked up a one-ounce envelope, then a two-ounce envelope, you'd probably notice the difference between them. But if you picked up a five-pound package, then a five-pound, one-ounce package, you'd probably detect no difference at all between them. In fact, you'd probably need about a five-and-a-half-pound package to detect a JND. When calculating a difference threshold, it is the proportion between stimuli that is important; the measured size of the difference, whether in brightness, loudness, or weight, is irrelevant.

Signal Detection

Measuring absolute and difference thresholds requires a critical assumption: that a threshold exists! But much of what scientists know about biology suggests that such a discrete, all-or-none change in the brain is unlikely. Humans don't suddenly and rapidly switch between perceiving and not perceiving; in fact, the transition from *not sensing* to *sensing* is gradual. The very same physical stimulus, such as a dim light or a quiet tone, presented on several different occasions, may be perceived by the same person on some occasions but not on others. Remember, an absolute threshold is operationalized as perceiving the stimulus 50% of the time . . . which means the other 50% of the time it might go undetected.

Our accurate perception of a sensory stimulus, then, can be somewhat haphazard. Whether in the psychophysics lab or out in the world, sensory signals face a lot of competition, or *noise,* which refers to all the other stimuli coming from the internal and external environment. Memories, moods, and motives intertwine with what you are seeing, hearing, and smelling at any given time. This internal "noise" competes with your ability to detect a stimulus with perfect, focused attention. Other sights, sounds, and smells in the world at large also compete for attention; you rarely have the luxury of attending to just one stimulus apart from everything else. As a consequence of noise, you may not perceive everything that you sense, and you may even perceive things that you haven't sensed.

● **How accurate and complete are our perceptions of the world?**

An approach to psychophysics called **signal detection theory** holds that *the response to a stimulus depends both on a person's sensitivity to the stimulus in the presence of noise and on a person's response criterion.* That is, observers consider the sensory evidence evoked by the stimulus and compare it to an internal decision criterion (Green & Swets, 1966; Macmillan & Creelman, 2005). If the sensory evidence exceeds the criterion, the observer responds by saying, "Yes, I detected the stimulus"; if it falls short of the criterion, the observer responds by saying, "No, I did not detect the stimulus."

Signal detection theory is a more sophisticated approach than was used in the early days of establishing absolute thresholds. Back then, it might have been assumed that everyone (or at least a majority of observers)

psychophysics Methods that measure the strength of a stimulus and the observer's sensitivity to that stimulus.

absolute threshold The minimal intensity needed to just barely detect a stimulus.

just noticeable difference (JND) The minimal change in a stimulus that can just barely be detected.

Weber's law The just noticeable difference of a stimulus is a constant proportion despite variations in intensity.

signal detection theory An observation that the response to a stimulus depends both on a person's sensitivity to the stimulus in the presence of noise and on a person's response criterion.

Cluttered environments such as this promenade in Venice Beach, California, present our visual system with a challenging signal detection task.

ERNST WRBA/ALAMY

sensory adaptation Sensitivity to prolonged stimulation tends to decline over time as an organism adapts to current conditions.

heard a tone or saw a flickering candle flame with equal facility. Signal detection theory, in contrast, explicitly takes into account observers' response tendencies, such as liberally saying, "Yes," or reserving identifications only for obvious instances of the stimulus.

For example, a radiologist may have to decide whether a mammogram shows that a patient has breast cancer. The radiologist knows that certain features, such as a mass of a particular size and shape, are associated with the presence of cancer. But noncancerous features can have a very similar appearance to cancerous ones. The radiologist may decide on a strictly liberal criterion and check every possible case of cancer with a biopsy. This decision strategy minimizes the possibility of missing a true cancer but leads to many false alarms. A strictly conservative criterion will cut down on false alarms but will miss some treatable cancers.

These different types of errors have to be weighed against one another in setting the decision criterion. Signal detection theory offers a practical way to choose among criteria that permit decision makers to take into account the consequences of hits, misses, false alarms, and correct rejections (McFall & Treat, 1999; Swets, Dawes, & Monahan, 2000). (For an example of a common everyday task that can interfere with signal detection, see the Real World box, on the next page.)

Sensory Adaptation

When you walk into a bakery, the aroma of freshly baked bread overwhelms you, but after a few minutes the smell fades. If you dive into cold water, the temperature is shocking at first, but after a few minutes you get used to it. When you wake up in the middle of the night for a drink of water, the bathroom light blinds you, but after a few minutes you no longer squint. These are all examples of **sensory adaptation**, the observation that *sensitivity to prolonged stimulation tends to decline over time as an organism adapts to current conditions.*

Sensory adaptation is a useful process for most organisms. Imagine what your sensory and perceptual world would be like without it. When you put on your jeans in the morning, the feeling of rough cloth against your bare skin would be as noticeable hours later as it was in the first few minutes. The stink of garbage in your apartment when you first walk in would never dissipate. If you had to constantly be aware of how your tongue feels while it is resting in your mouth, you'd be driven to distraction. Our perceptual systems respond more strongly to changes in stimulation rather than to constant stimulation. A stimulus that doesn't change usually doesn't require any action; your car probably emits a certain hum all the time that you've gotten used to. But a change in stimulation often signals a need for action. If your car starts making different kinds of noises, you're not only more likely to notice them, but you're also more likely to do something about it.

● **What conditions have you already adapted to today? Sounds? Smells?**

summary quiz [4.1]

1. Sensation and perception
   a. are basically the same process.
   b. are two completely different and unrelated processes.
   c. are related but separate events.
   d. feel like two distinct events.

2. The minimal intensity needed to just barely detect a stimulus is called the
   a. just noticeable difference.
   b. receptive field.
   c. absolute threshold.
   d. difference threshold.

3. Dr. Gonzalez, a radiologist, uses a very liberal criterion when she reads mammograms. She recommends a biopsy for every possible case of cancer. This decision strategy

a. maximizes the chances of missing a true cancer and also leads to many false alarms.

b. minimizes the chances of missing a true cancer but also minimizes false alarms.

c. minimizes the chances of missing a true cancer but also leads to many false alarms.

d. maximizes the chances of missing a true cancer but minimizes the chances of false alarms.

4. If you dive into cold water, the temperature seems chilling at first, but after a few minutes you don't notice it. This is an example of

a. accommodation.

b. Weber's law.

c. sensory adaption.

d. signal detection.

[THE REAL WORLD] ●

Multitasking

By one estimate, using a cell phone while driving makes having an accident four times more likely (McEvoy et al., 2005). In response to highway safety experts and statistics such as this, state legislatures are passing laws that restrict, and sometimes ban, using mobile phones while driving. You might think that's a fine idea . . . for everyone else on the road. But surely *you* can manage to punch in a number on a phone, carry on a conversation, or maybe even text-message while simultaneously driving in a safe and courteous manner. Right?

In a word, *wrong*. The issue here is *selective attention*, or perceiving only what's currently relevant to you. Try this. Without moving a muscle, think about the pressure of your skin against your chair right now. Effortlessly you shifted your attention to allow a sensory signal to enter your awareness. This simple shift shows that your perception of the world depends both on what sensory signals are present and on your choice of which signals to attend to and which to ignore. Perception is an active, moment-to-moment exploration for relevant or interesting information, not a passive receptacle for whatever happens to come along.

Talking on a cell phone while driving demands that you juggle two independent sources of sensory input—vision and audition—the same time. Normally this kind of *multitasking* works rather well. It's only when you need to react suddenly that your driving performance may suffer. Researchers have tested experienced drivers in a highly realistic driving simulator, measuring their response times to brake lights and stop signs while they listened to the radio or carried on phone conversations about a political issue, among other tasks (Strayer, Drews, & Johnston, 2003)

These experienced drivers reacted significantly slower during phone conversations than during the other tasks. This is because a phone conversation requires memory retrieval, deliberation, and planning what to say and often carries an emotional stake in the conversation topic. Tasks such as listening to the radio require far less attention or none at all.

The tested drivers became so engaged in their conversations that their minds no longer seemed to be in the car. Their slower braking response translated into an increased stopping distance that, depending on the driver's speed, would have resulted in a rear-end collision. Whether the phone was handheld or hands free made little difference. This suggests that laws requiring drivers to use hands-free phones may have little effect on reducing accidents.

Other researchers have measured brain activity using fMRI while people were shifting attention between visual and auditory information. When attention was directed to audition, activity in visual areas decreased compared to when attention was directed to vision (Shomstein & Yantis, 2004). It was as if the participants could adjust a mental "volume knob" to regulate the flow of incoming information according to which task they were attending to at the moment.

So how well do we multitask in several thousand pounds of metal hurtling down the highway? Experienced drivers can handle divided attention to a degree, yet most of us have to acknowledge that we have had close calls due to driving while distracted. Unless you have two heads with one brain each—one to talk and one to concentrate on driving—you might do well to keep your eyes on the road and not on the phone.

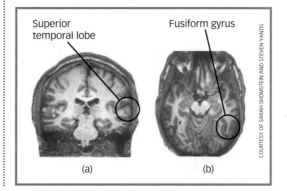

Shifting Attention Participants received fMRI scans as they performed tasks that required them to shift their attention between visual and auditory information. (a) When focusing on auditory information, a region in the superior (upper) temporal lobe involved in auditory processing showed increased activity (yellow/orange). (b) In striking contrast, a visual region, the fusiform gyrus, showed decreased activity when participants focused on auditory information (blue).

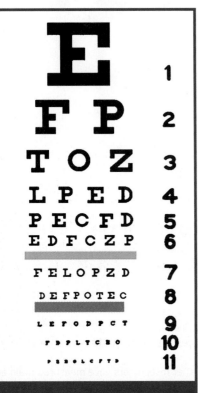

The Snellen chart is commonly used to measure visual acuity. Chances are good you've seen one yourself on more than one occasion.

Vision: More Than Meets the Eye

You might be proud of your 20/20 vision, even if it is corrected by glasses or contact lenses. *20/20* refers to a measurement associated with a Snellen chart, named after Hermann Snellen (1834–1908), the Dutch ophthalmologist who developed it as a means of assessing **visual acuity**, *the ability to see fine detail;* it is the smallest line of letters that a typical person can read from a distance of 20 feet. By comparison, hawks, eagles, owls, and other raptors have much greater visual acuity than humans—in many cases, about eight times greater, or the equivalent of 20/2 vision. That's handy if you want to spot a mouse from a mile away, but if you simply need to see where your roommate left the big bag of Fritos, you can probably live with the fact that no one ever calls you "Ol' Eagle Eye."

Although you won't win any I Spy contests against a hawk, your sophisticated visual system has evolved to transduce visual energy in the world into neural signals in the brain. Humans have sensory receptors in their eyes that respond to wavelengths of light energy. Understanding vision, then, starts with understanding light.

Sensing Light

Visible light is simply the portion of the electromagnetic spectrum that we can see, and it is an extremely small slice. You can think about light as waves of energy. Like ocean waves, light waves vary in height and in the distance between their peaks, or *wavelengths,* as **TABLE 4.2** (below) shows.

Light waves have three properties, each of which has a physical dimension that produces a corresponding psychological dimension. The *length* of a light wave determines its hue, or what humans perceive as color. The intensity or *amplitude* of a light wave—how high the peaks are—determines what we perceive as the brightness of light. The third property is *purity,* or the number of wavelengths that make up the light. Purity corresponds to what humans perceive as saturation, or the richness of colors (see **FIGURE 4.2**, on page 97). In other words, light doesn't need a human to have the properties it does: Length, amplitude, and purity are properties of the light waves themselves. What humans perceive from those properties are color, brightness, and saturation.

visual acuity The ability to see fine detail.

retina Light-sensitive tissue lining the back of the eyeball.

TABLE **4.2**	
Properties of Light Waves	
Physical Dimension	Psychological Dimension
Length	Hue, or what we perceive as color
Amplitude	Brightness
Purity	Saturation or richness of color

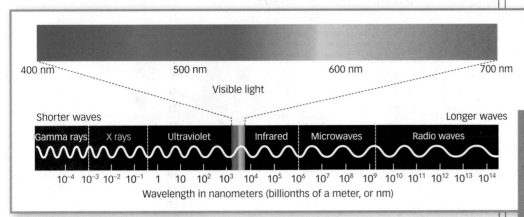

FIGURE **4.2** • • • • • • • • • • • • • • •
Electromagnetic Spectrum *The sliver of light waves visible to humans as a rainbow of colors from violet-blue to red is bounded on the short end by ultraviolet rays, which honeybees can see, and on the long end by infrared waves, on which night vision equipment operates. Someone wearing night vision goggles, for example, can detect another person's body heat in complete darkness. Light waves are minute, but the scale along the bottom of this chart offers a glimpse of their varying lengths, measured in nanometers (nm; 1 nm = 1 billionth of a meter).*

The Human Eye

Eyes have evolved as specialized organs to detect light. Light that reaches the eyes passes first through a clear, smooth outer tissue called the *cornea*, which bends the light wave and sends it through the *pupil*, a hole in the colored part of the eye (**FIGURE 4.3**, below). This colored part is the *iris*, which is a translucent, doughnut-shaped muscle that controls the size of the pupil and hence the amount of light that can enter the eye.

Immediately behind the iris, muscles inside the eye control the shape of the *lens* to bend the light again and focus it onto the **retina**, *light-sensitive tissue lining the back of the eyeball*. The muscles change the shape of the lens to focus objects at different distances, making the lens flatter for objects that are far away or rounder for nearby objects. This is called *accommodation*, the process by which the eye maintains a clear image on the retina. **FIGURE 4.4a** (page 98) shows how accommodation works.

If your eyeballs are a little too long or a little too short, the lens will not focus images properly on the retina. If the eyeball is too long, images are focused in front of the retina, leading to nearsightedness (*myopia*), which is shown in **FIGURE 4.4b** (page 98). If the eyeball is too short, images are focused behind the retina, and the result is farsightedness (*hyperopia*), as shown in **FIGURE 4.4c** (page 98).

● **How do eyeglasses actually correct vision?**

Eyeglasses, contact lenses, and surgical procedures can correct either condition. For example, eyeglasses and contacts both provide an additional lens to help focus light more appropriately, and procedures such as LASIK physically reshape the cornea.

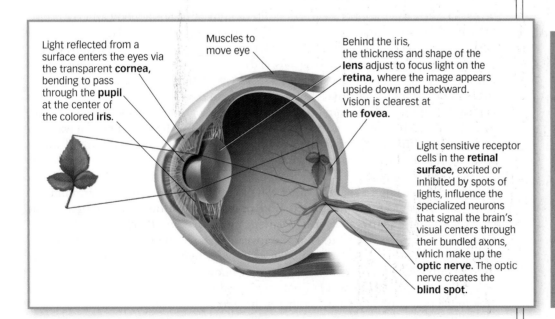

Light reflected from a surface enters the eyes via the transparent **cornea,** bending to pass through the **pupil** at the center of the colored **iris.**

Muscles to move eye

Behind the iris, the thickness and shape of the **lens** adjust to focus light on the **retina,** where the image appears upside down and backward. Vision is clearest at the **fovea.**

Light sensitive receptor cells in the **retinal surface,** excited or inhibited by spots of lights, influence the specialized neurons that signal the brain's visual centers through their bundled axons, which make up the **optic nerve.** The optic nerve creates the **blind spot.**

FIGURE **4.3** • • • • • • • • • • • • • •
Anatomy of the Human Eye
Light reflected from a surface enters the eye via the transparent cornea, bending to pass through the pupil at the center of the colored iris. Behind the iris, the thickness and shape of the lens adjust to focus the light on the retina, where the image appears upside down and backward. Basically, this is how a camera lens works. Light-sensitive receptor cells in the retinal surface, excited or inhibited by spots of light, influence the specialized neurons that convey nerve impulses to the brain's visual centers through their axons, which make up the optic nerve.

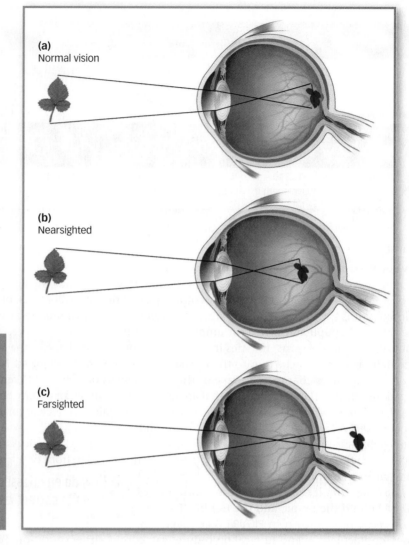

FIGURE 4.4

Accommodation *Inside the eye, the lens changes shape to focus nearby or faraway objects on the retina. (a) People with normal vision focus the image on the retina at the back of the eye, both for near and far objects. (b) Nearsighted people see clearly what's nearby, but distant objects are blurry because light from them is focused in front of the retina, a condition called myopia. (c) Farsighted people have the opposite problem: Distant objects are clear, but those nearby are blurry because their point of focus falls beyond the surface of the retina, a condition called hyperopia.*

cones Photoreceptors that detect color, operate under normal daylight conditions, and allow us to focus on fine detail.

rods Photoreceptors that become active only under low-light conditions for night vision.

fovea An area of the retina where vision is the clearest and there are no rods at all.

blind spot An area of the retina that contains neither rods nor cones and therefore has no mechanism to sense light.

Phototransduction in the Retina

The retina is the interface between the world of light outside the body and the world of vision inside the central nervous system. Two types of *photoreceptor cells* in the retina contain light-sensitive pigments that transduce light into neural impulses. **Cones** *detect color, operate under normal daylight conditions, and allow us to focus on fine detail.* **Rods** *become active only under low-light conditions for night vision* (see **FIGURE 4.5**, on the next page).

Rods are much more sensitive photoreceptors than cones, but this sensitivity comes at a cost. Because all rods contain the same photopigment, they provide no information about color, and sense only shades of gray. Think about this the next time you wake up in the middle of the night and make your way to the bathroom for a drink of water. Using only the moonlight from the window to light your way, do you see the room in color or in shades of gray?

Rods and cones differ in several other ways as well, most notably in their numbers. About 120 million rods are distributed more or less evenly around each retina except in the very center, the **fovea**, *an area of the retina where vision is the clearest and there are no rods at all.* The absence of rods in the fovea decreases the sharpness of vision in reduced light, but it can be overcome. For example, when amateur astronomers view dim stars through their telescopes at night, they know to look a little off to the side of the target so that the image will fall not on the rod-free fovea but on some other part of the retina that contains many highly sensitive rods.

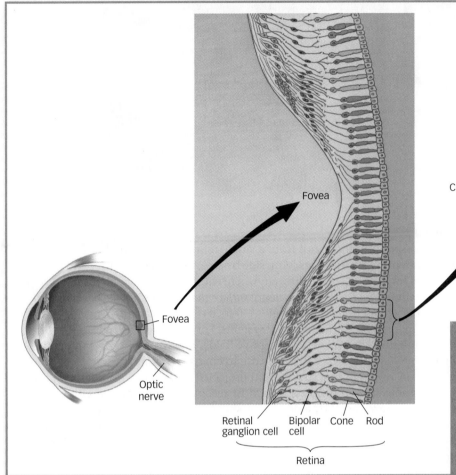

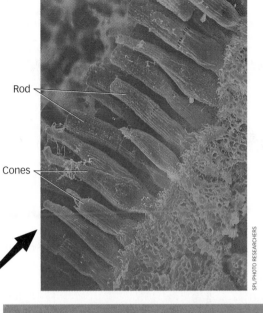

Fovea

Optic nerve

Fovea

Rod

Cones

Retinal ganglion cell   Bipolar cell   Cone   Rod

Retina

SPL/PHOTO RESEARCHERS

FIGURE 4.5 ● ● ● ● ● ● ● ● ● ● ● ● ● ● ●
Close-up of the Retina *The surface of the retina is composed of photoreceptor cells, the rods and cones, beneath a layer of transparent neurons, the bipolar and retinal ganglion cells, connected in sequence. Viewed close up in this cross-sectional diagram is the area of greatest visual acuity, the fovea, where most color-sensitive cones are concentrated, allowing us to see fine detail as well as color. Rods, the predominant photoreceptors activated in low-light conditions, are distributed everywhere else on the retina.*

In contrast to rods, each retina contains only about 6 million cones, which are densely packed in the fovea and much more sparsely distributed over the rest of the retina, as you can see in **FIGURE 4.5**. The high concentration of cones in the fovea directly affects visual acuity and explains why objects off to the side, in your *peripheral vision,* aren't so clear. The light reflecting from those peripheral objects has a difficult time landing in the fovea, making the resulting image less clear. The more fine detail encoded and represented in the visual system, the clearer the perceived image. The process is analogous to the quality of photographs taken with a six-megapixel digital camera versus a two-megapixel camera.

The retina is thick with cells. The photoreceptor cells (rods and cones) form the innermost layer. The middle layer contains *bipolar cells,* which collect neural signals from the rods and cones and transmit them to the outermost layer of the retina, where neurons called *retinal ganglion cells* (RGCs) organize the signals and send them to the brain. The bundled RGC axons—about 1.5 million per eye—form the *optic nerve,* which leaves the eye through a hole in the retina called the **blind spot,** which *contains neither rods nor cones and therefore has no mechanism to sense light.* Try the demonstration in **FIGURE 4.6** to find the blind spot in each of your own eyes.

MIKE SONNENBERG/ISTOCKPHOTO

The full-color image on the left is what you'd ● ● ● ● ● ● ● ● ● ● ●
see when your rods and cones were fully at work. The grayscale image on the right is what you'd see if only your rods were functioning.

······· • FIGURE 4.6

Blind Spot Demonstration *To find your blind spot, close your left eye and stare at the cross with your right eye. Hold the book 6 to 12 inches (15 to 30 centimeters) away from your eyes, and move it slowly toward and away from you until the dot disappears. The dot is now in your blind spot and so is not visible. At this point the vertical lines may appear as one continuous line because the visual system fills in the area occupied by the missing dot. To test your left-eye blind spot, turn the book upside down and repeat with your right eye closed.*

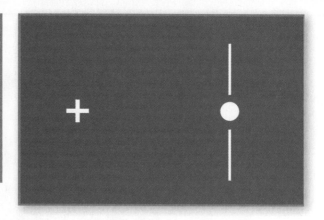

Receptive Fields

Most RGCs respond to input not from a single retinal cone or rod but from an entire patch of adjacent photoreceptors lying side by side, or laterally, in the retina. A particular RGC will respond to light falling anywhere within that small patch, which is called its **receptive field**, *the region of the sensory surface that, when stimulated, causes a change in the firing rate of that neuron.* Although we'll focus on vision here, the general concept of receptive fields applies to all sensory systems. For example, the cells that connect to the touch centers of the brain have receptive fields, which are the part of the skin that, when stimulated, causes that cell's response to change in some way.

A given RGC responds to a spot of light projected anywhere within a small, roughly circular patch of retina (Kuffler, 1953). Most receptive fields contain either a central excitatory zone surrounded by a doughnut-shaped inhibitory zone, which is called an *on-center cell*, or a central inhibitory zone surrounded by an excitatory zone, which is called an *off-center cell* (see **FIGURE 4.7**). The doughnut-shaped regions represent patches of retina.

Think about the response of an on-center retinal ganglion cell when its receptive field is stimulated with spots of light of different sizes (**FIGURE 4.7a**). A small spot shining on the central excitatory zone increases the RGC's firing rate. When the spot exactly fills the excitatory zone, it elicits the strongest response, whereas light falling on the surrounding inhibitory zone elicits the weakest response or none at all. The response of an

········· • FIGURE 4.7

RGC Receptive Fields Viewed End-on *(a) An on-center ganglion cell increases its firing rate when the receptive field is stimulated by light in the central area but decreases its firing rate when the light strikes the surrounding area. Both neural response levels are shown in the right column. (b) The off-center ganglion cell decreases its firing rate when its receptive field is stimulated by light in the central area but increases its firing rate when the light strikes the surrounding area. Both responses are shown at the right.*

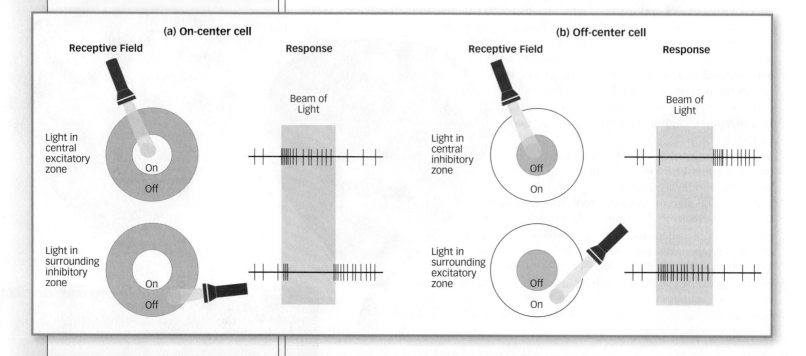

off-center cell, shown in **FIGURE 4.7b** (previous page), is just the opposite. A small spot shining on the central inhibitory zone elicits a weak response, and a spot shining on the surrounding excitatory zone elicits a strong response in the RGC. The retina is organized in this way to detect edges—abrupt transitions from light to dark or vice versa. Edges are of supreme importance in vision. They define the shapes of objects, and anything that highlights such boundaries improves our ability to see an object's shape, particularly in low-light situations.

receptive field The region of the sensory surface that, when stimulated, causes a change in the firing rate of that neuron.

Perceiving Color

We thrill to the burst of colors during a fireworks display, "ooh" and "aah" at nature's palette during sunset, and marvel at the vibrant hues of a peacock's tail feathers. These rich experiences of color depend critically on our perception of light's wavelength (see **FIGURE 4.8**). We perceive the shortest visible wavelengths as deep purple. As wavelengths increase, the color perceived changes gradually and continuously to blue, then green, yellow, orange, and, with the longest visible wavelengths, red. This rainbow of hues and accompanying wavelengths is called the *visible spectrum,* illustrated in **FIGURE 4.8**.

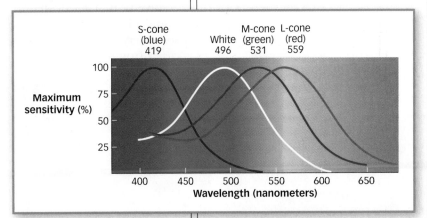

You'll recall that all rods contain the same photopigment, which makes them ideal for low-light vision but bad at distinguishing colors. Cones, by contrast, contain any one of three types of pigment. Each cone absorbs light over a range of wavelengths, but its pigment type is especially sensitive to visible wavelengths that correspond to red (long-wavelength), green (medium-wavelength), or blue (short-wavelength) light. Red, green, and blue are the primary colors of light; color perception results from different combinations of the three basic elements in the retina that respond to the wavelengths corresponding to the three primary colors of light. For example, lighting designers add primary colors of light together, such as shining red and green spotlights on a surface to create a yellow light, as shown in **FIGURE 4.9a** (below). Notice that in the center of the figure, where the red, green, and blue lights overlap, the surface looks white. This demonstrates that a white surface really is reflecting all visible wavelengths of light. Increasing light to create color in this way is called *additive color mixing.*

You may have discovered a similar process for yourself when mixing paints: you can re-create any color found in nature simply by mixing only three colors: red, blue, and yellow. This *subtractive color mixing* works by removing light from the mix, such as when you combine yellow and red to make orange or blue and yellow to make green, shown in **FIGURE 4.9b**. The darker the color, the less light it contains, which is why black surfaces reflect no light.

FIGURE 4.8 • • • • • • • • • • • • • • • • •
Seeing in Color *We perceive a spectrum of color because objects selectively absorb some wavelengths of light and reflect others. Color perception corresponds to the summed activity of the three types of cones. Each type is most sensitive to a narrow range of wavelengths in the visible spectrum—short (bluish light), medium (greenish light), or long (reddish light). Rods, represented by the white curve, are most sensitive to the medium wavelengths of visible light but do not contribute to color perception.*

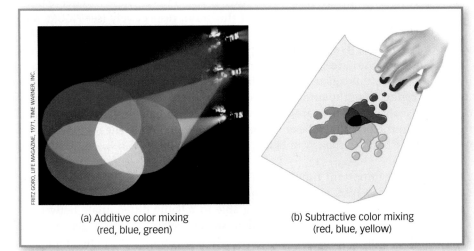

(a) Additive color mixing
(red, blue, green)

(b) Subtractive color mixing
(red, blue, yellow)

FRITZ GORO, LIFE MAGAZINE, 1971, TIME WARNER, INC.

FIGURE 4.9 •
Color Mixing *The millions of shades of color that humans can perceive are products not only of a light's wavelength but also of the mixture of wavelengths a stimulus absorbs or reflects. We see a ripe banana as yellow because the banana skin reflects the light waves that we perceive as yellow but absorbs the wavelengths that we perceive as shades of blue to green and those that make us see red. (a) Additive color mixing works by increasing the reflected wavelengths—by adding light to stimulate the red, blue, or green photopigments in the cones. When all visible wavelengths are present, we see white. (b) Subtractive color mixing removes wavelengths, thus absorbing light waves we see as red, blue, or yellow. When all visible wavelengths are absorbed, we see black.*

Light striking the retina causes a specific pattern of response in the three cone types (Schnapf, Kraft, & Baylor, 1987). The pattern of responding across the three types of cones provides a unique code for each color. Researchers can "read out" the wavelength of the light entering the eye by working backward from the relative firing rates of the three types of cones. A genetic disorder in which one of the cone types is missing—and, in some very rare cases, two or all three—causes a *color deficiency* (sometimes referred to as *color blindness,* although

● What happens when the cones in your eyes get fatigued?

people missing only one type of cone can still distinguish many colors). Color deficiency is sex linked, affecting men much more often than women.

You can create a sort of temporary color deficiency by exploiting the idea of sensory adaptation. Just like the rest of your body, cones need an occasional break, too. Staring too long at one color fatigues the cones that respond to that color, producing a form of sensory adaptation called *color afterimage.* To demonstrate this effect for yourself, follow these instructions for **FIGURE 4.10**:

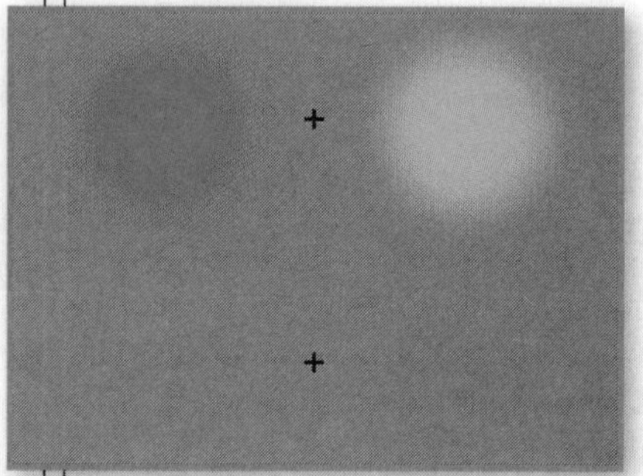

●●●●●●●●● ● ● ● ● ● ● ● ● ● ● ● ● **FIGURE 4.10**
Color Afterimage Demonstration *Follow the accompanying instructions in the text, and sensory adaptation will do the rest. When the afterimage fades, you can get back to reading the chapter.*

- Stare at the small cross between the two color patches for about 1 minute. Try to keep your eyes as still as possible.

- After a minute, look at the lower cross. You should see a vivid color aftereffect that lasts for a minute or more. Pay particular attention to the colors in the afterimage.

Were you puzzled that the red patch produces a green afterimage and the green patch produces a red afterimage? This result may seem like nothing more than a curious mind-bug, but in fact it reveals something important about color perception. When you view a color—let's say, green—the cones that respond most strongly to green become fatigued over time. Fatigue leads to an imbalance in the inputs to the red-green color-opponent neurons, beginning with the retinal ganglion cells. The weakened signal from the green-responsive cones leads to an overall response that emphasizes red.

The Visual Brain

A great deal of visual processing takes place within the retina itself, including the encoding of simple features such as spots of light, edges, and color. More complex aspects of vision, however, require more powerful processing, and that enlists the brain.

Streams of action potentials containing information encoded by the retina travel to the brain along the optic nerve. Half of the axons in the optic nerve that leave each eye come from retinal ganglion cells that code information in the right visual field, whereas the other half code information in the left visual field. These two nerve bundles link to the left and right hemispheres of the brain, respectively (see **FIGURE 4.11**, on page 103). The optic nerve travels from each eye to the *lateral geniculate nucleus (LGN),* located in the thalamus. As you will recall from Chapter 3, the thalamus receives inputs from all of the senses except smell. From there the visual signal travels to the back of the brain, to a location called **area V1**, the *part of the occipital lobe that contains the primary visual cortex.* Here the information is systematically mapped into a representation of the visual scene. There are about 30 to 50 brain areas specialized for vision, located mainly in the occipital lobe at the back of the brain and in the temporal lobes on the sides of the brain (Orban, Van Essen, & Vanduffel, 2004; Van Essen, Anderson, & Felleman, 1992).

One of the most important functions of vision involves perceiving the shapes of objects; our day-to-day lives would be a mess if we couldn't distinguish individual shapes from one another. Imagine not being able to reliably differentiate between a warm doughnut with glazed icing and a straight stalk of celery and you'll get the idea; breakfast could become a traumatic experience if you couldn't distinguish shapes.

area V1 The part of the occipital lobe that contains the primary visual cortex.

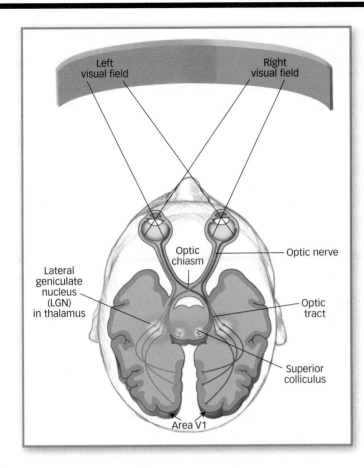

FIGURE **4.11** • • • • • • • • • • • • • • • •
Visual Pathway from Eye through Brain   *Objects in the right visual field stimulate the left half of each retina, and objects in the left visual field stimulate the right half of each retina. The optic nerves, one exiting each eye, are formed by the axons of retinal ganglion cells emerging from the retina. Just before they enter the brain at the optic chiasm, about half the nerve fibers from each eye cross. The left half of each optic nerve, representing the right visual field, runs through the brain's left hemisphere via the thalamus, and the right halves, representing the left visual field, travel this route through the right hemisphere. So information from the right visual field ends up in the left hemisphere, and information from the left visual field ends up in the right hemisphere.*

Perceiving shape depends on the location and orientation of an object's edges. It is not surprising, then, that area V1 is specialized for encoding edge orientation.

As you read in Chapter 3, neurons in the visual cortex selectively respond to bars and edges in specific orientations in space (Hubel & Weisel, 1962, 1998). In effect, area V1 contains populations of neurons, each "tuned" to respond to edges oriented at each position in the visual field. This means that some neurons fire when an object in a vertical orientation is perceived, other neurons fire when an object in a horizontal orientation is perceived, still other neurons fire when objects in a diagonal orientation of 45 degrees are perceived, and so on (see **FIGURE 4.12**). The outcome of the coordinated response of all these feature detectors contributes to a sophisticated visual system that can detect where a doughnut ends and celery begins.

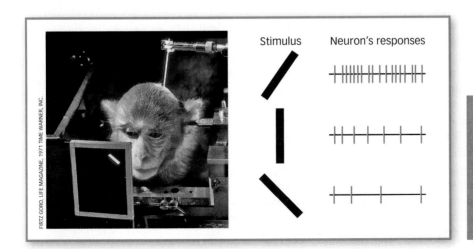

Stimulus   Neuron's responses

FIGURE **4.12** •
Single Neuron Feature Detectors   *Area V1 contains neurons that respond to specific orientations of edges. Here a single neuron's responses are recorded (at right) as the monkey views bars at different orientations (left). This neuron fires continuously when the bar is pointing to the right at 45 degrees, less often when it is vertical, and not at all when it is pointing to the left at 45 degrees.*

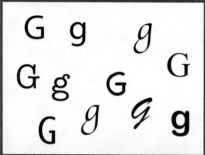

A quick glance and you recognize all these letters as G, but their varying sizes, shapes, angles, and orientations ought to make this recognition task difficult. What is it about the process of object recognition that allows us to perform this task effortlessly?

Recognizing Objects by Sight

Take a quick look at the letters in the accompanying illustration. Even though they're quite different from one another, you probably effortlessly recognized them as all being examples of the letter *G*. Now consider the same kind of demonstration using your best friend's face. Suppose one day your friend gets a dramatic new haircut—or adds glasses, hair dye, or a nose ring. Even though your friend now looks strikingly different, you still recognize that person with ease. Just like the variability in *G*s, you somehow are able to extract the underlying features of the face that allow you to accurately identify your friend.

This thought exercise may seem trivial, but it's no small perceptual feat. If the visual system were somehow stumped each time a minor variation occurred in an object being perceived, the inefficiency of it all would be overwhelming. We'd have to effortfully process information just to perceive our friend as the same person from one meeting to another, not to mention laboring through the process of knowing when a *G* is really a *G*. In general, though, object recognition proceeds fairly smoothly, in large part due to the operation of the feature detectors we discussed earlier.

Representing Objects and Faces in the Brain

How do feature detectors help the visual system get from a spatial array of light hitting the eye to the accurate perception of an object, such as your friend's face? Some researchers argue for a *modular view:* that specialized brain areas, or modules, detect and represent faces or houses or even body parts. Using fMRI to examine visual processing in healthy young adults, researchers found a subregion in the temporal lobe that responds selectively to faces compared to just about any other object category, while a nearby area responds selectively to buildings and landscapes (Kanwisher, McDermott, & Chun, 1997). This view suggests that we not only have detectors to aid in visual perception but also "face detectors," "building detectors," and possibly other types of neurons specialized for particular types of object perception (Kanwisher & Yovel, 2006).

Other researchers argue for a more *distributed representation* of object categories. In this view, it is the pattern of activity across multiple brain regions that identifies any viewed object, including faces (Haxby et al., 2001). Each of these views explains some data better than the other one, and researchers are continuing to debate their relative merits.

One perspective on this issue is provided by experiments designed to measure precisely where epileptic seizures originate; these experiments have provided insights on how single neurons in the human brain respond to objects and faces (Quiroga et al., 2005). Electrodes were placed in the temporal lobes of people who suffer from epilepsy. Then the volunteers were shown photographs of faces and objects as the researchers recorded their neural responses. The researchers found that neurons in the temporal lobe respond to specific objects viewed from multiple angles and to people wearing different clothing and facial expressions and photographed from various angles. In some cases, the neurons also respond to the words for the objects they prefer. For example, a neuron that responded to photographs of the Sydney Opera House also responded when the words *Sydney Opera* were displayed but not when the words *Eiffel Tower* were displayed (Quiroga et al., 2005).

● **How do we recognize our friends, even when they're hidden behind sunglasses?**

Taken together, these experiments demonstrate the principle of **perceptual constancy:** *Even as aspects of sensory signals change, perception remains consistent.* Think back once again to our discussion of difference thresholds early in this chapter. Our perceptual systems are sensitive to relative differences in changing stimulation and make allowances for varying sensory input. This general principle helps explain why you still recognize your friend despite changes in hair color or style or the addition of facial jewelry. It's not as though your visual perceptual system responds to a change with "Here's a new and unfamiliar face to perceive." Rather, it's as though it responds with "Interesting . . . here's a deviation from the way this face usually looks." Perception is sensitive to changes in stimuli, but perceptual constancies allow us to notice the differences in the first place.

ONLY HUMAN

I KNOW IT'S AROUND HERE SOMEPLACE
A 44-year-old man was arrested for DUI in Australia's Northern Territory after he asked a police officer how to get to the hard-to-miss Uluru (Ayers Rock, the huge, 1,000-foot-high rock formation that appears red in sunlight), which was about 300 feet in front of him, illuminated in his headlights.

Principles of Perceptual Organization

Of course, before object recognition can even kick in, the visual system must perform another important task: to group the image regions that belong together into a representation of an object. The idea that we tend to perceive a unified, whole object rather than a collection of separate parts is the foundation of Gestalt psychology, which you read about in Chapter 1. Gestalt principles characterize many aspects of human perception. Among the foremost are the Gestalt *perceptual grouping rules,* which govern how the features and regions of things fit together (Koffka, 1935). Here's a sampling:

- *Simplicity:* A basic rule in science is that the simplest explanation is usually the best. When confronted with two or more possible interpretations of an object's shape, the visual system tends to select the simplest or most likely interpretation: It's easier to interpret the object in **FIGURE 4.13a** (below) as a single arrow than as a triangle placed carefully on top of a rectangle.

- *Closure:* We tend to fill in missing elements of a visual scene, allowing us to perceive edges that are separated by gaps as belonging to complete objects. Thus, in **FIGURE 4.13b** we see a single arrow shape, not four unrelated sets of bent lines.

- *Continuity:* Edges or contours that have the same orientation have what the Gestaltists called "good continuation," and we tend to group them together perceptually. Thus, in **FIGURE 4.13c**, we see one curved line crossing another curved line.

- *Similarity:* Regions that are similar in color, lightness, shape, or texture are perceived a belonging to the same object; thus, in **FIGURE 4.13d**, we tend to see one column of circles, surrounded by two columns of triangles, rather than three rows each containing two triangles and a circle.

- *Proximity:* Objects that are close together tend to be grouped together. Thus, in **FIGURE 4.13e**, we tend to see three clusters of dots.

- *Common fate:* Elements of a visual image that move together are perceived as parts of a single moving object. Thus, a sign such as the one shown **FIGURE 4.13f**, where the blinking arrows come on and off in a sequence from left to right, we tend to see an arrow moving from left to right.

Perceptual grouping is a powerful aid to our ability to recognize objects by sight. Grouping involves visually separating an object from its surroundings. In Gestalt terms, this means identifying a *figure* apart from the (back)*ground* in which it resides. For example, the words on this page are perceived as figural: They stand out from the ground of the sheet of paper on which they're printed. Similarly, your instructor is perceived as

perceptual constancy A perceptual principle stating that even as aspects of sensory signals change, perception remains consistent.

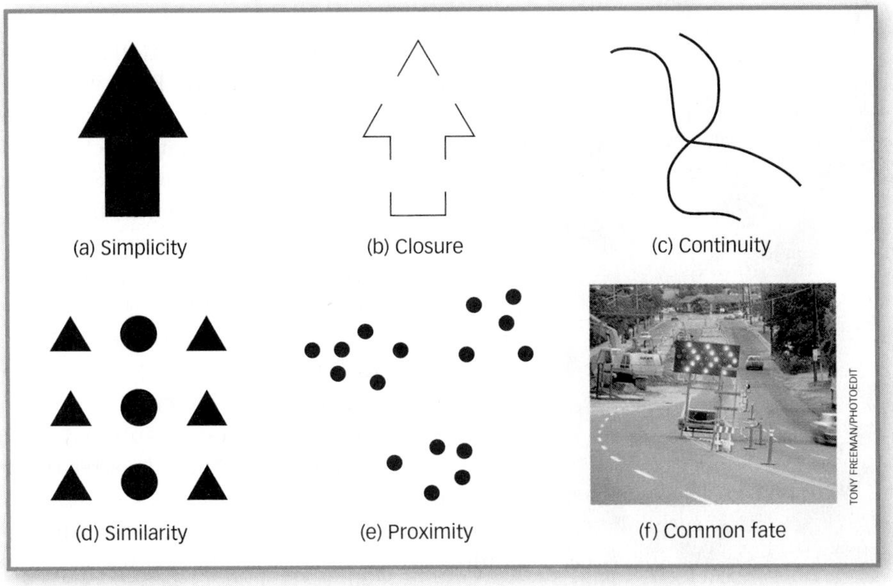

(a) Simplicity (b) Closure (c) Continuity

(d) Similarity (e) Proximity (f) Common fate

TONY FREEMAN/PHOTOEDIT

FIGURE 4.13 ● ● ● ● ● ● ● ● ● ● ● ● ● ● ● ● ●
Perceptual Grouping Rules *Principles first identified by Gestalt psychologists and now supported by experimental evidence demonstrate that the brain is predisposed to impose order on incoming sensations. One neural strategy for perception involves responding to patterns among stimuli and grouping like patterns together.*

monocular depth cues Aspects of a scene that yield information about depth when viewed with only one eye.

binocular disparity The difference in the retinal images of the two eyes that provides information about depth.

the figure against the backdrop of all the other elements in your classroom. You certainly can perceive these elements differently, of course: The words *and* the paper are all part of a thing called "a page," and your instructor *and* the classroom can all be perceived as "your learning environment." Typically, though, our perceptual systems focus attention on some objects as distinct from their environments.

Size provides one clue to what's figure and what's ground: Smaller regions are likely to be figures, such as tiny letters on a big paper. Movement also helps: Your instructor is (we hope) a dynamic lecturer, moving around in a static environment. Another critical step toward object recognition is *edge assignment.* Given an edge, or boundary, between figure and ground, to which region does that edge belong? If the edge belongs to the figure, it helps define the object's shape, and the background continues behind the edge. Sometimes, though, it's not easy to tell which is which.

This ambiguity drives the famous illusion shown in **FIGURE 4.14.** You can view this figure in two ways, either as a vase on a black background or as a pair of silhouettes facing each other. Your visual system settles on one or the other interpretation and fluctuates between them every few seconds. This happens because the edge that would normally separate figure from ground is really part of neither: It equally defines the contours of the vase as it does the contours of the faces. Evidence from fMRI scans shows, quite nicely, that when people are seeing the Rubin image as a face, there is greater activity in the face-selective region of the temporal lobe that we discussed earlier than when they are seeing it as a vase (Hasson et al., 2001).

······· • **FIGURE 4.14**
Ambiguous Edges Here's how Rubin's classic reversible figure-ground illusion works: Fixate your eyes on the center of the image, and your perception will alternate between a vase and facing silhouettes, even as the sensory stimulation remains constant.

Perceiving Depth and Size

Objects in the world are arranged in three dimensions—length, width, and depth—but the retinal image contains only two dimensions, length and width. How does the brain process a flat, two-dimensional retinal image so that we perceive the depth of an object and how far away it is? The answer lies in a collection of *depth cues* that change as you move through space. Monocular and binocular cues help visual perception (Howard, 2002).

······· • **FIGURE 4.15**
Familiar Size and Relative Size When you view images of people, such as the men in the left-hand photo (below), or of things you know well, the object you perceive as smaller appears farther away. With a little image manipulation, you can see in the right-hand photo that the relative size difference projected on your retinas is far greater than you perceive. The image of the person who is brought forward in the second photo is exactly the same size in both photos.

Monocular depth cues are *aspects of a scene that yield information about depth when viewed with only one eye.* These cues rely on the relationship between distance and size. Even with one eye closed, the retinal image of an object you're focused on grows smaller as that object moves farther away and larger as it moves closer. Our brains routinely use these differences in retinal image size, or *relative size,* to perceive distance. This works particularly well in a monocular depth cue called *familiar size.* Most adults, for example, fall within a familiar range of heights (perhaps five to seven feet tall), so retinal image size alone is usually a reliable cue to how far away they are. Our visual system automatically corrects for size differences and attributes them to differences in distance. **FIGURE 4.15** demonstrates how strong this mental correction for familiar size is. In addition to relative size and

© THE PHOTO WORKS

familiar size, there are several more monocular depth cues:

- *Linear perspective,* which describes the phenomenon that parallel lines seem to converge as they recede into the distance (see **FIGURE 4.16a**).

- *Texture gradient,* which arises when you view a more or less uniformly patterned surface because the size of the pattern elements, as well as the distance between them, grows smaller as the surface recedes from the observer (see **FIGURE 4.16b**).

- *Interposition,* which occurs when one object partly blocks another (see **FIGURE 4.16c**). You can infer that the block*ing* object is closer than the block*ed* object. However, interposition by itself cannot provide information about how far apart the two objects are.

- *Relative height in the image* depends on your field of vision (see **FIGURE 4.16d**). Objects that are closer to you are lower in your visual field, while faraway objects are higher.

We also obtain depth information through **binocular disparity**, *the difference in the retinal images of the two eyes that provides information about depth.* Because our eyes are slightly separated, each registers a slightly different view of the world. Your brain computes the disparity between the two retinal images to perceive how far away objects are, as shown in **FIGURE 4.17** (on page 108). Viewed from above in the figure, the images of the more distant square and the closer circle each fall at different points on each retina. The View-Master toy works by presenting a pair of photos, taken from two horizontally displaced locations; when viewed, one by each eye, the pairs of images evoke a vivid sense of depth. 3-D movies are based on this same idea.

(a)

(b)

(c)

(d)

FIGURE 4.16
Pictorial Depth Cues *Visual artists rely on a variety of monocular cues to make their work come to life. You can rely on cues such as (a) linear perspective, (b) texture gradient, (c) interposition, and (d) relative height in an image to infer distance, depth, and position, even if you're wearing an eye patch.*

The View-Master has been a popular toy for decades. It is based on the principle of binocular disparity: Two images taken from slightly different angles produce a stereoscopic effect.

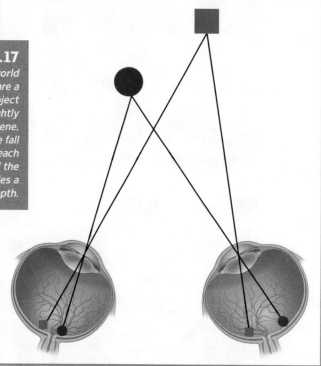

FIGURE 4.17
Binocular Disparity *We see the world in three dimensions because our eyes are a distance apart and the image of an object falls on the retinas of each eye at a slightly different place. In this two-object scene, the images of the square and the circle fall on different points of the retina in each eye. The disparity in the positions of the circle's retinal images provides a compelling cue to depth.*

Most of the time, these mechanisms for depth perception work effortlessly and well to help us compute the size and distance of objects. But we are all vulnerable to *illusions,* mindbugs in which our perceptions differ from reality. The relation between size and distance has been used to create elaborate illusions that depend on fooling the visual system about how far away objects are. One of the most famous of these is the *Ames room,* constructed by the American ophthalmologist Adelbert Ames in 1946. The room is trapezoidal in shape rather than square: Only two sides are parallel (see **FIGURE 4.18a** on page 109). A person standing in one corner of an Ames room is physically twice as far away from the viewer as a person standing in the other corner. But when viewed with one eye looking through the small peephole placed in one wall, the Ames room looks square because the shapes of the windows and the flooring tiles are carefully crafted to *look* square from the viewing port (Ittelson, 1952). The visual system perceives the far wall as perpendicular to the line of sight so that people standing at different positions along that wall appear to be at the same distance, and the viewer's judgments of their sizes are based directly on retinal image size. As a result, a person standing in the right corner appears to be much larger than a person standing in the left corner (see **FIGURE 4.18b** on page 109).

● **What does the Ames room tell us about how the brain can be fooled?**

Perceiving Motion

You should now have a good sense of how we see what and where objects are, a process made substantially easier when the objects stay in one place. But real life, of course, is full of moving targets; objects change position over time. To sense motion, the visual system must encode information about both space and time. The simplest case to consider is an observer who does not move trying to perceive an object that does.

As an object moves across an observer's stationary visual field, it first stimulates one location on the retina, and then a little later it stimulates another location on the retina. Neural circuits in the brain can detect this change in position over time and respond to specific speeds and directions of motion (Emerson, Bergen, & Adelson, 1992). A region in the middle of the temporal lobe referred to as *MT* is specialized for the visual perception of motion (Born & Bradley, 2005; Newsome & Paré, 1988), and brain damage in this area leads to a deficit in normal motion perception (Zihl, von Cramon, & Mai, 1983).

Of course, in the real world, rarely are you a stationary observer. As you move around, your head and eyes move all the time, and motion perception is not as simple. The motion-perception system must take into account the position and movement of your eyes, and ultimately of your head and body, in order to perceive the motions of objects correctly and allow you to approach or avoid them. The brain accomplishes this by monitoring your eye and head movements and "subtracting" them from the motion in the retinal image.

apparent motion The perception of movement as a result of alternating signals appearing in rapid succession in different locations.

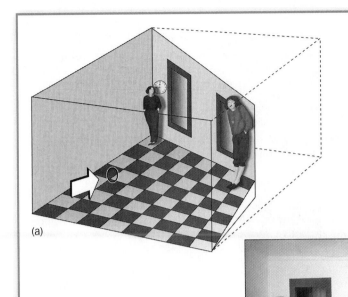

(a)

(b)

FIGURE 4.18 •
The Amazing Ames Room *(a) A diagram showing the actual propor-tions of the Ames room reveals its secrets. The sides of the room form a trapezoid with parallel sides but a back wall that's way off square. The un-even floor makes the room's height in the far back corner shorter than the other. Add misleading cues such as specially designed windows and flooring and position the room's occupants in each far corner, and you're ready to lure an unsuspecting observer. (b) Looking into the Ames room through the viewing port with only one eye, the observer infers a normal size-distance relationship—that both girls are the same distance away. But the different image sizes they project on the retina leads the viewer to conclude, based on the monocular cue of familiar size, that one girl is very small and the other very large.*

Motion perception, like color perception, is subject to sensory adaptation. A motion aftereffect called the *waterfall illusion* is analogous to color aftereffects. If you stare at the downward rush of a waterfall for several seconds, you'll experience an upward motion aftereffect when you then look at stationary objects near the waterfall such as trees or rocks. What's going on here?

The process is similar to seeing green after staring at a patch of red. Motion-sensitive neurons are connected to motion detector cells in the brain that encode motion in op-posite directions. A sense of motion comes from the difference in the strength of these two opposing sensors. If one set of motion detector cells is fatigued through adaptation to motion in one direction, then the opposing sensor will take over. The net result is that motion is perceived in the opposite direction. Evidence from fMRI indicates that when people experience the waterfall illusion while viewing a stationary stimulus, there is increased activity in region MT, which plays a key role in motion perception (Tootell et al., 1995).

● **How can flashing lights on a casino sign give the impression of movement?**

The movement of objects in the world is not the only event that can evoke the perception of motion. The suc-cessively flashing lights of a Las Vegas casino sign can evoke a strong sense of motion, exactly the sort of illusion that inspired Max Wertheimer to investigate the *phi phenom-enon,* discussed in Chapter 1. Recall, too, the Gestalt grouping rule of *common fate:* Peo-ple perceive a series of flashing lights as a whole, moving object (see **FIGURE 4.13f** on page 105). This *perception of movement is a result of alternating signals appearing in rapid succession in different locations* is called **apparent motion.**

Video technology and animation depend on apparent motion. A sequence of still im-ages sample the continuous motion in the original scene. In the case of motion pictures, the sampling rate is 24 frames per second (fps). A slower sampling rate would produce a much choppier sense of motion; a faster sampling rate would be a waste of resources be-cause we would not perceive the motion as any smoother than it appears at 24 fps.

*Want a powerful demonstration of • • •
apparent motion? Take a stroll down
the Las Vegas strip.*

summary quiz [4.2]

5. Which is the correct sequence of eye parts that light passes through on its way to the brain?

    a. pupil, lens, cornea, retina

    b. cornea, pupil, lens, retina

    c. iris, lens, pupil, cornea

    d. lens, pupil, cornea, retina

6. Objects in your peripheral vision are less clear because light reflecting from these objects has a hard time landing in

    a. the retinal ganglion cell layer.

    b. the lens.

    c. the pupil.

    d. the fovea.

7. Color deficiency (also called color blindness) is a result of a disorder in which

    a. one type of rod is missing.

    b. one type of cone is missing.

    c. the blind spot is larger than normal.

    d. the individual has synesthesia.

8. The hypothesis that specialized brain areas detect and represent various object categories is called

    a. the perceptual constancy view.

    b. signal detection theory.

    c. the distributed representation view.

    d. the modular view.

9. "When confronted with two or more possible interpretations of an object's shape, we tend to select the most likely interpretation." This is a statement of which rule?

    a. closure

    b. continuity

    c. simplicity

    d. similarity

10. You are at Niagara Falls, staring at the downward rush of the water for several seconds. When you then look at the nearby trees and rocks, they seem to be moving upward. You are experiencing

    a. the phi phenomenon.

    b. apparent motion.

    c. motion parallax.

    d. the waterfall illusion.

Audition: More Than Meets the Ear

Vision is based on the spatial pattern of light waves on the retina. The sense of hearing, by contrast, is all about *sound waves*—changes in air pressure unfolding over time. Plenty of things produce sound waves: the collision of a tree hitting the forest floor, the impact of two hands clapping, the vibration of vocal cords during a stirring speech, the resonance of a bass guitar string during a thrash metal concert. Except for synesthetes who "hear colors," understanding most people's auditory experience requires understanding how we transform changes in air pressure into perceived sounds.

Sensing Sound

Striking a tuning fork produces a *pure tone,* a simple sound wave that first increases air pressure and then creates a relative vacuum. This cycle repeats hundreds or thousands of times per second as sound waves propagate outward in all directions from the source.

    Just as there are three dimensions of light waves corresponding to three dimensions of visual perception, so too there are three physical dimensions

"The ringing in your ears—I think I can help."

TABLE 4.3

Properties of Sound Waves

Frequency Corresponds to our perception of pitch.	Low frequency (low-pitched sound)	High frequency (high-pitched sound)
Amplitude Corresponds to our perception of loudness.	High amplitude (loud sound)	Low amplitude (soft sound)
Complexity Corresponds to our perception of timbre.	Simple (pure tone)	Complex (mix of frequencies)

pitch How high or low a sound is.

loudness A sound's intensity.

timbre A listener's experience of sound quality or resonance.

of a sound wave. Frequency, amplitude, and complexity determine what we hear as the pitch, loudness, and quality of a sound (see **TABLE 4.3** above).

The *frequency* of the sound wave, or its wavelength, depends on how often the peak in air pressure passes the ear or a microphone, measured in cycles per second, or hertz (abbreviated Hz). Changes in the physical frequency of a sound wave are perceived by humans as changes in **pitch**, *how high or low a sound is.*

The *amplitude* of a sound wave refers to its height, relative to the threshold for human hearing (which is set at zero decibels, or dBs). Amplitude corresponds to **loudness**, or *a sound's intensity.* To give you an idea of amplitude and intensity, the rustling of leaves in a soft breeze is about 20 dB, normal conversation is measured at about 40 dB, shouting produces 70 dB, a Slayer concert is about 130 decibels, and the sound of the space shuttle taking off one mile away registers at 160 dB or more. That's loud enough to cause permanent damage to the auditory system and is well above the pain threshold; in fact, any sounds above 85 decibels can be enough to cause hearing damage, depending on the length and type of exposure.

● **Why does one note sound so different on a flute and a trumpet?**

Differences in the *complexity* of sound waves, or their mix of frequencies, correspond to **timbre**, *a listener's experience of sound quality or resonance.* Timbre (pronounced "TAM-ber") offers us information about the nature of sound. The same note played at the same loudness produces a perceptually different experience depending on whether it was played on a flute versus a trumpet, a phenomenon due entirely to timbre. Many "natural" sounds also illustrate the complexity of wavelengths, such as the sound of bees buzzing, the tonalities of speech, or the babbling of a brook. Unlike the purity of a tuning fork's hum, the drone of cicadas is a clamor of overlapping sound frequencies.

JEWEL SAMAD/AFP/GETTY IMAGES

Foo Fighters star Dave Grohl has revealed that his deafness is causing problems in his marriage. "I'm virtually deaf . . . my wife asks me where we should go for dinner, and it sounds like the schoolteacher from the TV show Charlie Brown!"

cochlea A fluid-filled tube that is the organ of auditory transduction.

basilar membrane A structure in the inner ear that undulates when vibrations from the ossicles reach the cochlear fluid.

hair cells Specialized auditory receptor neurons embedded in the basilar membrane.

area A1 A portion of the temporal lobe that contains the primary auditory cortex.

Of the three dimensions of sound waves, frequency provides most of the information we need to identify sounds. Amplitude and complexity contribute texture to our auditory perceptions, but it is frequency that carries their meaning. Sound-wave frequencies blend together to create countless sounds, just as different wavelengths of light blend to create the richly colored world we see. Changes in frequency over time allow us to identify the location of sounds, an ability that can be crucial to survival and also allow us to understand speech and appreciate music, skills that are valuable to our cultural survival. The focus in our discussion of hearing, then, is on how the auditory system encodes and represents sound-wave frequency (Kubovy, 1981).

The Human Ear

How does the auditory system convert sound waves into neural signals? The process is very different from the visual system, which is not surprising, given that light is a form of electromagnetic radiation, whereas sound is a physical change in air pressure over time. Different forms of energy suggest different processes of transduction. The human ear is divided into three distinct parts, as shown in **FIGURE 4.19** (below). The *outer ear* collects sound waves and funnels them toward the *middle ear,* which transmits the vibrations to the *inner ear,* embedded in the skull, where they are transduced into neural impulses.

The outer ear consists of the visible part on the outside of the head (called the *pinna*); the auditory canal; and the eardrum, an airtight flap of skin that vibrates in response to sound waves gathered by the pinna and channeled into the canal. The middle ear, a tiny, air-filled chamber behind the eardrum, contains the three smallest bones in the body, called *ossicles*. Named for their appearance as hammer, anvil, and stirrup, the ossicles fit together into a lever that mechanically transmits and intensifies vibrations from the eardrum to the inner ear.

● How do hair cells in the ear enable us to hear?

The inner ear contains the spiral-shaped **cochlea** (Latin for "snail"), *a fluid-filled tube that is the organ of auditory transduction*. The cochlea is divided along its length by the **basilar membrane**, *a structure in the inner ear that undulates when vibrations from the ossicles reach the cochlear fluid* (see **FIGURE 4.20**). Its wavelike movement stimulates thousands of tiny **hair cells**, *specialized auditory receptor neurons embedded in the basilar membrane*. The hair cells then release neurotransmitter molecules, initiating a neural signal in the auditory

●●●●●●●●●●●●●●●●●●●●●● **FIGURE 4.19**
Anatomy of the Human Ear *The pinna funnels sound waves into the auditory canal to vibrate the eardrum at a rate that corresponds to the sound's frequency. In the middle ear, the ossicles pick up the eardrum vibrations, amplify them, and pass them along by vibrating a membrane at the surface of the fluid-filled cochlea in the inner ear. Here fluid carries the wave energy to the auditory receptors that transduce it into electrochemical activity, exciting the neurons that form the auditory nerve, leading to the brain.*

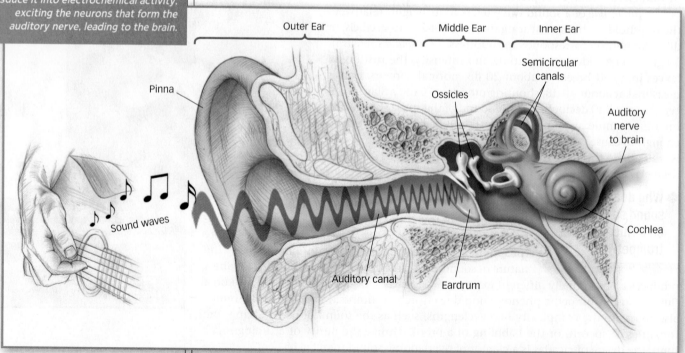

Outer Ear   Middle Ear   Inner Ear

Pinna
Semicircular canals
Ossicles
Auditory nerve to brain
Sound waves
Cochlea
Auditory canal
Eardrum

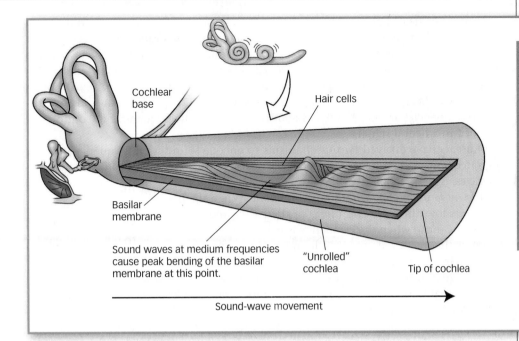

FIGURE **4.20** • • • • • • • • • • • • • • • •
Auditory Transduction *Inside the cochlea, shown here as though it were uncoiled, the basilar membrane undulates in response to wave energy in the cochlear fluid. Waves of differing frequencies ripple varying locations along the membrane, from low frequencies at its tip to high frequencies at the base, and bend the embedded hair cell receptors at those locations. The hair-cell motion generates impulses in the auditory neurons, whose axons form the auditory nerve that emerges from the cochlea .*

nerve that travels to the brain. You might not want to think that the whispered "I love you" that sends chills up your spine got a kick start from lots of little hair cells wiggling around, but the mechanics of hearing are what they are!

Perceiving Pitch

From the inner ear, action potentials in the auditory nerve travel to the thalamus and ultimately to the contralateral ("opposite side"; see Chapter 3) hemisphere of the cerebral cortex. This is called **area A1**, *a portion of the temporal lobe that contains the primary auditory cortex* (see **FIGURE 4.21**, below). For most of us, the auditory areas in the left hemisphere analyze sounds related to language and those in the right hemisphere specialize in rhythmic sounds and music.

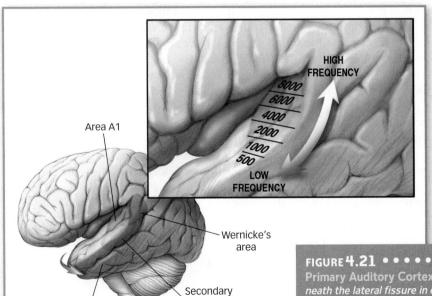

FIGURE **4.21** •
Primary Auditory Cortex *Area A1 is folded into the temporal lobe beneath the lateral fissure in each hemisphere. The left hemisphere auditory areas govern speech in most people. (inset) A1 cortex has a topographic organization, with lower frequencies mapping toward the front of the brain and higher frequencies toward the back, mirroring the organization of the basilar membrane along the cochlea (see Figure 4.20).*

place code The cochlea encodes different frequencies at different locations along the basilar membrane.

temporal code The cochlea registers low frequencies via the firing rate of action potentials entering the auditory nerve.

haptic perception The active exploration of the environment by touching and grasping objects with our hands.

Neurons in area A1 respond to simple tones, and successive auditory areas in the brain process sounds of increasing complexity (Schreiner, Read, & Sutter, 2000). Like area V1 in the visual cortex, area A1 has a topographic organization: Similar frequencies activate neurons in adjacent locations (see **FIGURE 4.21**, inset, on page 113). A young adult with normal hearing ideally can detect sounds between about 20 and 20,000 Hz, although the ability to hear at the upper range decreases with age. The human ear is most sensitive to frequencies around 1,000 to 3,500 Hz. But how is the frequency of a sound wave encoded in a neural signal?

Our ears have evolved two mechanisms to encode sound-wave frequency, one for high frequencies and one for low frequencies. The **place code**, used mainly for high frequencies, is active when *the cochlea encodes different frequencies at different locations along the basilar membrane*. When the frequency is low, the wide end (*apex*) of the basilar membrane moves the most; when the frequency is high, the narrow end (*base*) of the membrane moves the most. The movement of the basilar membrane causes hair cells to bend, initiating a neural signal in the auditory nerve. The place code works best for relatively high frequencies that resonate at the basilar membrane's base and less well for low frequencies that resonate at the apex.

● **How does the frequency of a sound wave relate to what we hear?**

A complementary process handles lower frequencies. A **temporal code** *registers low frequencies via the firing rate of action potentials entering the auditory nerve*. Action potentials from the hair cells are synchronized in time with the peaks of the incoming sound waves (Johnson, 1980). If you imagine the rhythmic *boom-boom-boom* of a bass drum, you can probably also imagine the *fire-fire-fire* of action potentials corresponding to the beats. This process provides the brain with very precise information about pitch that supplements the information provided by the place code.

However, individual neurons can produce action potentials at a maximum rate of only about 1,000 spikes per second, so the temporal code does not work as well as the place code for high frequencies. (Imagine if the action potential has to fire in time with the *rat-a-tat-a-tat-a-tat* of a snare drum roll!) Like the cones in color processing, the place code and the temporal code work together to cover the entire range of pitches that people can hear.

Localizing Sound Sources

Just as the differing positions of our eyes give us stereoscopic vision, the placement of our ears on opposite sides of the head give us stereophonic hearing. The sound arriving at the ear closer to the sound source is louder than the sound in the farther ear, mainly because the listener's head partially blocks sound energy. This loudness difference decreases as the sound source moves from a position directly to one side (maximal difference) to straight ahead (no difference).

Another cue to a sound's location arises from timing: Sound waves arrive a little sooner at the near ear than at the far ear. The timing difference can be as brief as a few microseconds, but together with the intensity difference, it is sufficient to allow us to perceive the location of a sound. When the sound source is ambiguous, you may find yourself turning your head from side to side to localize it. By doing this, you are changing the relative intensity and timing of sound waves arriving in your ears and collecting better information about the likely source of the sound.

summary quiz [4.3]

11. As the number of cycles per second of a sound wave increases, we experience a _____ sound.

 a. higher   c. louder
 b. lower   d. softer

12. The fluid filled tube that is the organ of auditory transduction is the
   a. cochlea.
   b. basilar membrane.
   c. auditory canal.
   d. eardrum.

13. The place code works best for encoding
   a. high intensities.
   b. medium frequencies.
   c. low frequencies.
   d. high frequencies.

The Body Senses: More Than Skin Deep

Vision and audition provide information about the world at a distance. By responding to light and sound energy in the environment, these "distance" senses allow us to identify and locate the objects and people around us. In comparison, the body senses, also called *somatosenses* (*soma* from the Greek for "body"), are up close and personal. **Haptic perception** results from our *active exploration of the environment by touching and grasping objects with our hands*. We use sensory receptors in our muscles, tendons, and joints as well as a variety of receptors in our skin to get a feel for the world around us.

Touch

Four types of receptors located under the skin's surface enable us to sense pressure, texture, pattern, or vibration against the skin (see **FIGURE 4.22**, below). The receptive fields of these specialized cells work together to provide a rich tactile (from Latin, "to touch") experience when you explore an object by feeling it or attempt to grasp it. In addition, *thermoreceptors,* nerve fibers that sense cold and warmth, respond when your skin temperature changes. All these sensations blend seamlessly together in perception, of course, but detailed physiological studies have successfully isolated the parts of the touch system (Johnson, 2002).

Touch begins with the transduction of skin sensations into neural signals. Like cells in the retina of each eye, touch receptors have receptive fields that, when stimulated, cause that cell's response to change. The representation of touch in the brain follows a topographic scheme, much as vision and hearing do. Think back to the homunculus

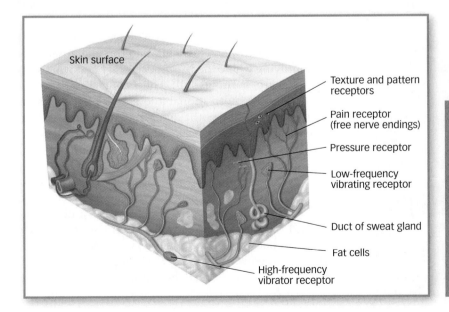

Skin surface

Texture and pattern receptors

Pain receptor (free nerve endings)

Pressure receptor

Low-frequency vibrating receptor

Duct of sweat gland

Fat cells

High-frequency vibrator receptor

FIGURE 4.22 ●
Touch Receptors *Specialized sensory neurons form distinct groups of haptic receptors that detect pressure, temperature, and vibrations against the skin. Touch receptors respond to stimulation within their receptive fields, and their long axons enter the brain via the spinal or cranial nerves. Pain receptors populate all body tissues that feel pain: They are distributed around bones and within muscles and internal organs as well as under the skin surface. Both types of pain receptors—the fibers that transmit immediate, sharp pain sensations quickly and those that signal slow, dull pain that lasts and lasts— are free nerve endings.*

you read about in Chapter 3; you'll recall that different locations on the body project sensory signals to different locations in the somatosensory cortex in the parietal lobe.

Two important principles describe the neural representation of the body's surface. First, there is contralateral organization: The left half of the body is represented in the right half of the brain and vice versa. Second, more of the tactile brain is devoted to parts of the skin surface that have greater spatial resolution. Regions such as the fingertips and lips are very good at discriminating fine spatial detail, whereas areas such as the lower back are quite poor at that task. These perceptual abilities are a natural consequence of the fact that the fingertips and lips have a relatively dense arrangement of touch receptors and a large topographical representation in the somatosensory cortex; comparatively, the lower back, hips, and calves have a relatively small representation (Penfield & Rasmussen, 1950).

● **Why might discriminating spatial detail be important for fingertips and lips?**

Pain

Although pain is arguably the least pleasant of sensations, this aspect of touch is among the most important for survival. Pain indicates damage or potential damage to the body. The possibility of a life free from pain might seem appealing, but without the ability to feel pain, we might ignore infections, broken bones, or serious burns. Congenital insensitivity to pain, a rare inherited disorder that specifically impairs pain perception, is more of a curse than a blessing: Children who experience this disorder often mutilate themselves (biting into their tongues, for example, or gouging their skin while scratching) and are at increased risk of dying during childhood (Nagasako, Oaklander, & Dworkin, 2003).

Tissue damage is transduced by pain receptors, the free nerve endings shown in **FIGURE 4.22**, on page 115. Researchers have distinguished between fast-acting *A-delta fibers,* which transmit the initial sharp pain one might feel right away from a sudden injury, and slower *C fibers,* which transmit the longer-lasting, duller pain that persists after the initial injury. If you were running barefoot outside and stubbed your toe against a rock, you would first feel a sudden stinging pain transmitted by A-delta fibers that would die down quickly, only to be replaced by the throbbing but longer-lasting pain carried by C fibers. Both the A-delta and C fibers are impaired in cases of congenital insensitivity to pain, which is one reason why the disorder can be life threatening.

As you'll remember from Chapter 3, the pain withdrawal reflex is coordinated by the spinal cord. No brainpower is required when you touch a hot stove; you retract your hand almost instantaneously. But neural signals for pain—such as wrenching your elbow as you brace yourself from falling—travel to two distinct areas in the brain and evoke two distinct psychological experiences (Treede et al., 1999). One pain pathway sends signals to the somatosensory cortex, identifying where the pain is occurring and what sort of pain it is (sharp, burning, dull). The second pain pathway sends signals to the motivational and emotional centers of the brain, such as the hypothalamus and amygdala, and to the frontal lobe. This is the aspect of pain that is unpleasant and motivates us to escape from or relieve the pain.

Pain typically feels as if it comes from the site of the tissue damage that caused it. If you burn your finger, you will perceive the pain as originating there. But we have pain receptors in many areas besides the skin—around bones and within muscles and internal organs as well. When pain originates internally, in a body organ, for example, we actually feel it on the surface of the body. This kind of **referred pain** occurs when *sensory information from internal and external areas converge on the same nerve cells in the spinal cord.* One common example is

● *Injuries are a part of football, but knowing that doesn't make them any less painful.*

AP PHOTO/THE DECATUR DAILY/DAN HENRY

a heart attack: Victims often feel pain radiating from the left arm rather than from inside the chest.

Pain intensity cannot always be predicted solely from the extent of the injury that causes the pain (Keefe, Abernathy, & Campbell, 2005). For example, *turf toe* sounds like the mildest of ailments; it is pain at the base of the big toe as a result of bending or pushing off repeatedly, as a runner or football player might do during a sporting event. This small-sounding injury in a small area of the body can nonetheless sideline an athlete for a month with considerable pain. At the same time, you've probably heard a story or two about someone treading bone-chilling water for hours on end, or dragging their shattered legs a mile down a country road to seek help after a tractor accident, or performing some other incredible feat despite searing pain and extensive tissue damage. Pain type and pain intensity show a less-than-perfect correlation, a fact that has researchers intrigued.

How do psychologists account for this puzzling variability in pain perception? According to **gate-control theory**, *signals arriving from pain receptors in the body*

● **Why does rubbing an injured area sometimes help alleviate pain?**

can be stopped, or gated, by interneurons in the spinal cord via feedback from two directions (Melzack & Wall, 1965). Pain can be gated by the skin receptors, for example, by rubbing the affected area. Rubbing your stubbed toe activates neurons that "close the gate" to stop pain signals from traveling to the brain. Pain can also be gated from the brain by modulating the activity of pain-transmission neurons. This neural feedback is elicited not by the pain itself, but rather by activity deep within the thalamus.

The neural feedback comes from a region in the midbrain called the *periaqueductal gray* (PAG). Under extreme conditions, such as high stress, naturally occurring endorphins can activate the PAG to send inhibitory signals to neurons in the spinal cord that then suppress pain signals to the brain, thereby modulating the experience of pain. The PAG is also activated through the action of opiate drugs, such as morphine.

A different kind of feedback signal can *increase* the sensation of pain. This system is activated by events such as infection and learned danger signals. When we are quite ill, what might otherwise be experienced as mild discomfort can feel quite painful. This pain facilitation signal presumably evolved to motivate people who are ill to rest and avoid strenuous activity, allowing their energy to be devoted to healing.

Gate-control theory offers strong evidence that perception is a two-way street. The senses feed information, such as pain sensations, to the brain, a pattern termed *bottom-up control* by perceptual psychologists. The brain processes this sensory data into perceptual information at successive levels to support movement, object recognition, and eventually more complex cognitive tasks, such as memory and planning. But there is ample evidence that the brain exerts plenty of control over what we sense as well. Visual illusions and the Gestalt principles of filling in, shaping up, and rounding out what isn't really there provide some examples. This kind of *top-down control* also explains the descending pain pathway initiated in the midbrain.

Body Position, Movement, and Balance

It may sound odd, but one aspect of sensation and perception is knowing where parts of your body are at any given moment. Your body needs some way to sense its position in physical space other than moving your eyes to constantly visually check the location of your limbs. Sensations related to position, movement, and balance depend on stimulation produced within our bodies.

Sensory receptors in the muscles, tendons, and joints signal the position of the body in space, providing the information we need to perceive the position and movement of our limbs, head, and body. These receptors also provide feedback about whether we are

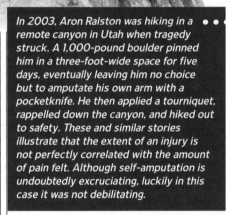

MALCOM DALY

In 2003, Aron Ralston was hiking in a ●●●●●●●●●● remote canyon in Utah when tragedy struck. A 1,000-pound boulder pinned him in a three-foot-wide space for five days, eventually leaving him no choice but to amputate his own arm with a pocketknife. He then applied a tourniquet, rappelled down the canyon, and hiked out to safety. These and similar stories illustrate that the extent of an injury is not perfectly correlated with the amount of pain felt. Although self-amputation is undoubtedly excruciating, luckily in this case it was not debilitating.

referred pain The feeling of pain when sensory information from internal and external areas converge on the same nerve cells in the spinal cord.

gate-control theory A theory of pain perception based on the idea that signals arriving from pain receptors in the body can be stopped, or *gated*, by interneurons in the spinal cord via feedback from two directions.

performing a desired movement correctly and how resistance from held objects may be influencing the movement. For example, when you swing a baseball bat, the weight of the bat affects how your muscles move your arm as well as the change in sensation when the bat hits the ball. Muscle, joint, and tendon feedback about how your arms actually moved can be used to improve performance through learning.

Maintaining balance depends primarily on the **vestibular system**, *the three fluid-filled semicircular canals and adjacent organs located next to the cochlea in each inner ear* (see **FIGURE 4.19** on page 112). The semicircular canals are arranged in three perpendicular orientations and studded with hair cells that detect movement of the fluid when the head moves or accelerates. This detected motion enables us to maintain our balance, or the position of our bodies relative to gravity. The movements of the hair cells encode these somatic sensations (Lackner & DiZio, 2005).

Vision also helps us keep our balance. If you see that you are swaying relative to a vertical orientation, such as the contours of a room, you move your legs and feet to keep from falling over. Psychologists have experimented with this visual aspect of balance by placing people in rooms that can be tilted forward and backward (Bertenthal, Rose, & Bai, 1997; Lee & Aronson, 1974). If the room tilts enough—particularly when small children are tested—people will topple over as they try to compensate for what their visual system is telling them.

● **Why is it so hard to stand on one foot with your eyes closed?**

When a mismatch occurs between the information provided by visual cues and vestibular feedback, motion sickness can result. Remember this discrepancy the next time you try reading in the backseat of a moving car!

Hitting a ball with a bat or racket provides feedback as to where your arms and body are in space as well as how the resistance of these objects affects your movement and balance. Successful athletes, such as Serena Williams, have particularly well-developed body senses.

AP PHOTO/RICK RYCROFT

summary quiz [4.4]

14. Which part of the body occupies the greatest area in the somatosensory cortex?

a. calves   c. lower back

b. lips   d. hips

15. Which is an example of referred pain?

a. A football player develops pain at the base of the big toe from pushing off repeatedly.

b. You stub your toe on a rock and feel a sudden, stinging pain.

c. You touch a hot stove and retract your hand immediately.

d. A heart attack victim feels pain radiating from the left arm.

16. A mismatch between the information processed by visual feedback and vestibular cues can cause

a. referred pain.   c. turf toe.

b. motion sickness.   d. visual-form agnosis.

vestibular system The three fluid-filled semicircular canals and adjacent organs located next to the cochlea in each inner ear.

olfactory receptor neurons (ORNs) Receptor cells that initiate the sense of smell.

The Chemical Senses: Adding Flavor

Somatosensation is all about physical changes in or on the body. Vision and audition sense energetic states of the world—light and sound waves—and touch is activated by physical changes in or on the body surface. The last set of senses we'll consider shares a chemical basis to combine aspects of distance and proximity. The chemical senses of *olfaction* (smell) and *gustation* (taste) respond to the molecular structure of substances floating into the nasal cavity as you inhale or dissolving in saliva. Smell and taste combine to produce the perceptual experience we call *flavor*.

Smell

Olfaction is the least understood sense and the only one directly connected to the forebrain, with pathways into the frontal lobe, amygdala, and other forebrain structures (recall from Chapter 3 that the other senses connect first to the thalamus). This mapping indicates that smell has a close relationship with areas involved in emotional and social behavior. Smell seems to have evolved in animals as a signaling sense for the familiar—a friendly creature, an edible food, or a sexually receptive mate.

● **How many scents can humans smell?**

Countless substances release odors into the air, and some of their *odorant molecules* make their way into our noses, drifting in on the air we breathe. Situated along the top of the nasal cavity, shown in **FIGURE 4.23**, is a mucous membrane called the *olfactory epithelium,* which contains about 10 million **olfactory receptor neurons (ORNs)**, *receptor cells that initiate the sense of smell.* Odorant molecules

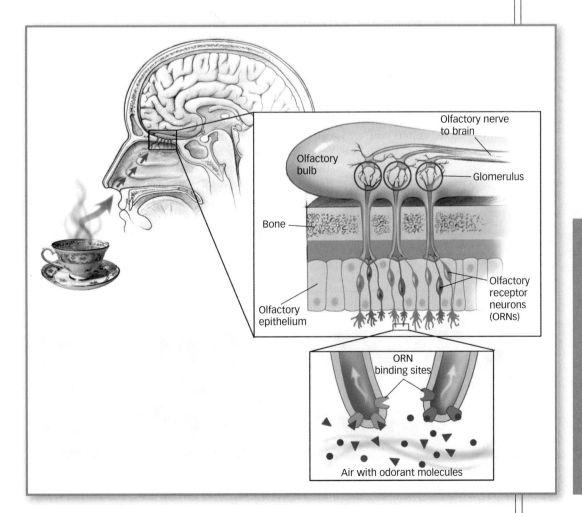

Olfactory nerve to brain

Olfactory bulb

Glomerulus

Bone

Olfactory receptor neurons (ORNs)

Olfactory epithelium

ORN binding sites

Air with odorant molecules

FIGURE 4.23 • • • • • • • • • • • • • •

Anatomy of Smell *Along the roof of the nasal cavity, odorant molecules dissolve in the mucous membrane that forms the olfactory epithelium. Odorants may then bind to olfactory receptor neurons (ORNs) embedded in the epithelium. ORNs respond to a range of odors and, once activated, relay action potentials to their associated glomeruli in the olfactory bulb, located just beneath the frontal lobes. The glomeruli synapse on neurons whose axons form the olfactory nerve, which projects directly into the forebrain.*

olfactory bulb A brain structure located above the nasal cavity beneath the frontal lobes.

pheromones Biochemical odorants emitted by other members of their species that can affect an animal's behavior or physiology.

taste buds The organ of taste transduction.

bind to sites on these specialized receptors, and if enough bindings occur, the ORNs send action potentials into the olfactory nerve (Dalton, 2003).

Each olfactory neuron has receptors that bind to some odorants but not to others, as if the receptor is a lock and the odorant is the key (see **FIGURE 4.23** on page 119). Groups of ORNs send their axons from the olfactory epithelium into the **olfactory bulb**, *a brain structure located above the nasal cavity beneath the frontal lobes.* Humans possess about 350 different ORN types that permit us to discriminate among some 10,000 different odorants through the unique patterns of neural activity each odorant evokes. This setup is similar to our ability to see a vast range of colors based on only a small number of retinal cell types or to feel a range of skin sensations based on only a handful of touch receptor cell types.

The olfactory bulb sends outputs to various centers in the brain, including the parts that are responsible for controlling basic drives, emotions, and memories. This explains why smells can have immediate strongly positive or negative effects on us. If the slightest whiff of an apple pie baking brings back fond memories of childhood or the unexpected sniff of vomit mentally returns you to a particularly bad party you once attended, you've got the idea. Thankfully, sensory adaptation is at work when it comes to smell, just as it is with the other senses. Whether the associations are good or bad, after just a few minutes the smell fades. Smell adaptation makes sense: It allows us to detect new odors that may require us to act, but after that initial evaluation has occurred, it may be best to reduce our sensitivity to allow us to detect other smells. Evidence from research using fMRI indicates that experience with a smell can modify odor perception by changing how specific parts of the brain involved in olfaction respond to that smell (Li et al., 2006).

Smell may also play a role in social behavior. Humans and other animals can detect odors from **pheromones**, *biochemical odorants emitted by other members of their species that can affect the animal's behavior or physiology.* Parents can distinguish the smell of their own children from other people's children. An infant can identify the smell of its mother's breast from the smell of other mothers. Pheromones also play a role in reproductive behavior in insects and in several mammalian species, including mice, dogs, and primates (Brennan & Zufall, 2006). Can the same thing be said of human reproductive behavior?

Studies of people's preference for the odors of individuals of the opposite sex have produced mixed results, with no consistent tendency for people to prefer them over other pleasant odors. Recent research, however, has provided a link between sexual orientation and responses to odors that may constitute human pheromones (**FIGURE 4.24**). Researchers used positron emission tomography (PET) scans to study the brain's response to two odors, one related to testosterone, which is produced in men's sweat, and the other related to estrogen, which is found in women's

•• **FIGURE 4.24**

Smell and Social Behavior *In a PET study, heterosexual women, homosexual men, and heterosexual men were scanned as they were presented with each of several odors. During the presentation of a testosterone-based odor (referred to in the figure as AND), there was significant activation in the hypothalamus for heterosexual women (left) and homosexual men (center) but not for heterosexual men (right) (Savic et al., 2005).*

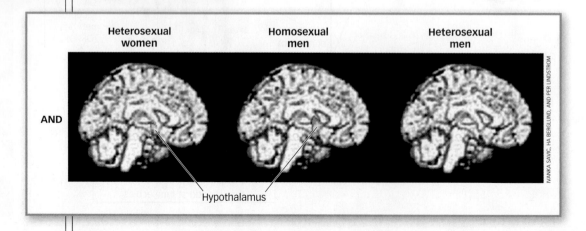

urine. The testosterone-based odor activated the hypothalamus (a part of the brain that controls sexual behavior; see Chapter 3) in heterosexual women but not heterosexual men, whereas the estrogen-based odor activated the hypothalamus in heterosexual men but not women. Strikingly, homosexual men responded to the two chemicals in the same way as women did (Savic, Berglund, & Lindstrom, 2005). Other common odors unrelated to sexual arousal were processed similarly by all three groups. A follow-up study with lesbian women showed that their responses to the testosterone- and estrogen-based odors were largely similar to those of heterosexual men (Berglund, Lindstrom, & Savic, 2006). Taken together, the two studies suggest that some human pheromones are related to sexual orientation.

Taste

One of the primary responsibilities of the chemical sense of taste is identifying things that are bad for you—as in "poisonous and lethal." Many poisons are bitter, and we avoid eating things that nauseate us for good reason, so taste aversions have a clear adaptive significance. Some aspects of taste perception are genetic, such as an aversion to extreme bitterness, and some are learned, such as an aversion to a particular food that once caused nausea. In either case, the direct contact between a tongue and possible foods allows us to anticipate whether something will be harmful or palatable.

● **Why is the sense of taste an evolutionary advantage?**

The tongue is covered with thousands of small bumps, called *papillae,* which are easily visible to the naked eye. Within each papilla are hundreds of **taste buds**, *the organ of taste transduction* (see **FIGURE 4.25**, below). Most human mouths contain between 5,000 and 10,000 taste buds fairly evenly distributed over the tongue, roof of the mouth, and upper throat (Bartoshuk & Beauchamp, 1994; Halpern, 2002). Each taste bud contains 50 to 100 taste receptor cells. Taste perception fades with age: On average, people lose half their taste receptors by the time they turn 20. This may help explain why young children seem to be "fussy eaters," because their greater number of taste buds brings with it a greater range of taste sensations.

The human eye contains millions of rods and cones, the human nose contains some 350 different types of olfactory receptors, but the taste system contains just five main types of taste receptors, corresponding to five primary taste sensations: salt, sour, bitter, sweet, and umami (savory). The first four are quite familiar, but *umami* may

ONLY HUMAN

I LOVE THE TASTE OF ASPHALT IN THE MORNING In April 2006, Jim Werych of the Wednesday Night Classics car club in Brookfield, Wisconsin, ritually dragged his tongue, in a deep lick, across Lisbon Road (with traffic stopped in both directions) to verify and proclaim that the streets were free of winter salt and thus safe for the club's delicate classics.

FIGURE 4.25 ●

A Taste Bud *(a) Taste buds stud the bumps (papillae) on your tongue, shown here, as well as the back, sides, and roof of the mouth. (b) Each taste bud contains a range of receptor cells that respond to varying chemical components of foods called tastants. Tastant molecules dissolve in saliva and stimulate the microvilli that form the tips of the taste receptor cells. (c) Each taste bud contacts the branch of a cranial nerve at its base.*

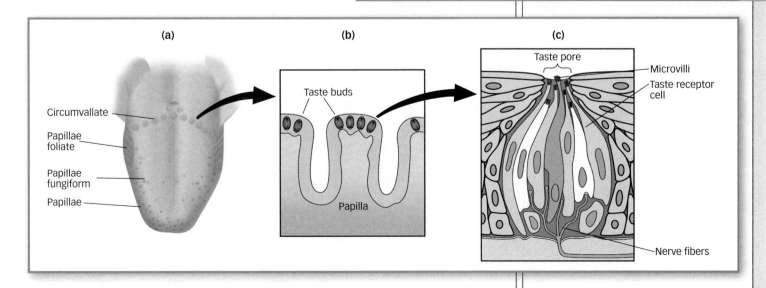

A top chef knows how to activate our various taste receptor cells in a way that puts a smile on our face.

not be. In fact, perception researchers are still debating its existence. The umami receptor was discovered by Japanese scientists who attributed it to the tastes evoked by foods containing a high concentration of protein, such as meats and cheeses (Yamaguchi, 1998). If you're a meat eater and you savor the feel of a steak topped with butter or a cheeseburger as it sits in your mouth, you've got an idea of the umami sensation.

Each taste bud contains several types of taste receptor cells whose tips, called *microvilli,* react with *tastant molecules* in food. Salt taste receptors are most strongly activated by sodium chloride—table salt. Sour receptor cells respond to acids, such as vinegar or lime juice. Bitter and sweet taste receptors are more complex. Some 50 to 80 distinct binding sites in bitter receptors are activated by an equal number of different bitter-tasting chemicals. Sweet receptor cells likewise can be activated by a wide range of substances in addition to sugars.

Although umami receptor cells are the least well understood, researchers are honing in on their key features (Chandrashekar et al., 2006). They respond most strongly to glutamate, an amino acid in many protein-containing foods. Recall from Chapter 3, glutamate acts as a neurotransmitter; in fact, it's a major excitatory neurotransmitter.

"We would like to be genetically modified to taste like Brussels sprouts."

The food additive *monosodium glutamate* (MSG), which is often used to flavor Asian foods, particularly activates umami receptors. Some people develop headaches or allergic reactions after eating MSG.

Of course, the variety of taste experiences greatly exceeds the five basic receptors discussed here. Any food molecules dissolved in saliva evoke specific, combined patterns of activity in the five taste receptor types. Although we often think of taste as the primary source for flavor, in fact, taste and smell collaborate to produce this complex perception.

You can easily demonstrate the contribution of smell to flavor by tasting a few different foods while holding your nose, preventing the olfactory system from detecting their odors. If you have a head cold, you probably already know how this turns out. Your favorite spicy burrito or zesty pasta probably tastes as bland as can be.

ALUMA IMAGES/MASTERFILE/RADIUS IMAGES

summary quiz [4.5]

17. Which is the correct sequence of transmission for the sense of smell?
a. olfactory receptor neurons; olfactory bulb; olfactory nerve
b. olfactory nerve; olfactory bulb; olfactory reception neurons
c. olfactory bulb; olfactory receptor neurons; olfactory nerve
d. olfactory receptor neurons; olfactory nerve; olfactory bulb

18. An infant can identify the smell of its mother's breast from the smell of other mothers. This is likely due to the influence of
a. taste transduction.
b. pheromones.
c. subliminal visual cues.
d. somatosensory cues.

19. People lose about half their taste buds by the time they turn
a. 20.
b. 40.
c. 60.
d. 80.

Together, taste and smell produce what we perceive as flavor. This is why smelling the "bouquet" of a wine is an essential part of the wine-tasting ritual. Without smell, it would be difficult to taste subtle differences between wines.

WhereDoYouStand?

Perception and Persuasion

In the 1950s, movie theater owners experimented with a new and controversial marketing technique: subliminal advertising. They screened films into which studios had spliced single frames containing photographs of popcorn and soda or word images such as *I'm thirsty*. At normal projection speed, these images were too brief for movie-goers to perceive consciously, but theater owners hoped that projecting the messages would register with viewers and thus increase concession sales during intermissions. However, scientific evidence for this kind of subliminal persuasion has been mixed at best.

These days, marketers advocate a more subtle form of advertising known as *sensory branding* (Lindstrom, 2005). The idea is to exploit all the senses to promote a product or a brand. We're used to seeing advertisements that feature exciting, provocative, or sexual images to sell products. In television commercials, these images are accompanied by popular music that advertisers hope will evoke an overall mood favorable to the product. The notion is that the sight and sound of exciting things will become associated with what might be an otherwise drab product.

But sensory branding goes beyond sight and sound by enlisting smell, taste, and touch as well as vision and hearing. That new-car smell you anticipate while you take a test drive? Actually, it's a manufactured fragrance sprayed into the car, carefully tested to evoke positive feelings among potential buyers. Singapore Airlines, which has consistently been rated "the world's best airline," has actually patented the smell of its airplane cabins (it's called Stefan Floridian Waters).

Is there any harm in marketing that bombards the senses or even sneaks through to perception undetected? On the one hand, advertising is a business, and like any business it is fueled by innovation in search of a profit. Perhaps these recent trends are simply the next clever step to get potential buyers to pay attention to a product message. On the other hand, is there a point when "enough is enough"? Do you want to live in a world where every sensory event is trademarked, patented, or test-marketed before reaching your perceptual system? Where do you stand?

··CHAPTER REVIEW

Summary

The Doorway to Psychology

- Sensation is the awareness that results from stimulation of a sense organ; perception organizes, identifies, and interprets sensation at the level of the brain.

- Psychophysics is an approach to measuring the strength of a stimulus and an observer's sensitivity to that stimulus.

- An observer's absolute threshold is the smallest intensity needed to detect a stimulus; the just noticeable difference (JND) is the smallest change in a stimulus that can be detected.

- Signal detection theory allows researchers to distinguish between an observer's perceptual sensitivity to a stimulus and criteria for making decisions about the stimulus.

- Sensory adaptation occurs because sensitivity to stimulation tends to decline over time.

Vision: More Than Meets the Eye

- Light passes through several layers in the eye, where two types of photoreceptor cells in the retina transduce light into neural impulses: cones, which operate under normal daylight conditions and sense color, and rods, which are active under low-light conditions for night vision.

- The outermost layer of the retina consists of retinal ganglion cells (RGCs) that collect and send signals to the brain.

- Cones are specialized to respond to short-wavelength (bluish) light, medium-wavelength (greenish) light, and long-wavelength (reddish) light; the overall pattern of response across the three cone types results in a unique code for each color.

- The outermost layer of the retina collects and sends signals along the optic nerve to the lateral geniculate nucleus in the thalamus, and then to primary visual cortex (area V1) in the occipital lobe of the brain.

- Some regions in the occipital and temporal lobes respond selectively to specific object categories; some neurons in the temporal lobe respond to specific objects when viewed from different angles or to specific objects whether presented as photos or words.

- Gestalt principles of perceptual grouping govern how the features and regions of things fit together.

- Depth perception depends on monocular cues and binocular cues.

- We experience a sense of motion through the differences in strengths of output from motion-sensitive neurons.

Audition: More Than Meets the Ear

- The frequency of a sound wave determines pitch; the amplitude determines loudness; and differences in complexity, or mix, of frequencies determine the sound quality or timbre.

- Auditory perception begins in the outer ear, which funnels sound waves toward the middle ear, which in turn sends the vibrations to the inner ear, which contains the cochlea.

- Action potentials from the inner ear travel along an auditory pathway through the thalamus to the contralateral primary auditory cortex (area A1) in the temporal lobe.

- Auditory perception depends on both a place code and a temporal code, which together cover the full range of pitches that people can hear.

- Our ability to localize sound sources depends critically on the placement of our ears on opposite sides of the head.

The Body Senses: More Than Skin Deep

- Touch is represented in the brain according to a topographic scheme in which locations on the body project sensory signals to locations in the somatosensory cortex in the parietal lobe.

- The experience of pain depends on signals that travel along two distinct pathways: one sends signals to the somatosensory cortex to indicate the location and type of pain; the other sends signals to the emotional centers of the brain, resulting in unpleasant feelings that we wish to escape.

- Balance and acceleration depend primarily on the vestibular system but are also influenced by vision.

The Chemical Senses: Adding Flavor

- Our experience of smell, or olfaction, occurs when odorant molecules bind to sites on specialized olfactory receptors, which converge at the olfactory bulb. The olfactory bulb in turn sends signals to parts of the brain that control drives, emotions, and memories.

- Sensations of taste depend on taste buds, which are distributed across the tongue, roof of the mouth, and upper throat. Taste buds contain taste receptors that correspond to the five primary taste sensations of salt, sour, bitter, sweet, and umami.

Key Terms

sensation (p. 90)
perception (p. 90)
transduction (p. 91)
psychophysics (p. 92)
absolute threshold (p. 92)

just noticeable difference (JND) (p. 93)
Weber's law (p. 93)
signal detection theory (p. 93)
sensory adaptation (p. 94)

visual acuity (p. 96)
retina (p. 97)
cones (p. 98)
rods (p. 98)
fovea (p. 98)

blind spot (p. 99)
receptive field (p. 100)
area V1 (p. 102)
perceptual constancy (p. 104)
monocular depth cues (p. 106)

Critical Thinking Questions

1. Sensory adaptation refers to the fact that sensitivity to prolonged stimulation tends to decline over time. According to the theory of natural selection, inherited characteristics that provide a survival advantage tend to spread throughout the population across generations.

   Why might sensory adaptation have evolved? What survival benefits might it confer to a small animal trying to avoid predators? To a predator trying to hunt prey?

2. When visual light (light waves with particular length, amplitude, and purity) reaches the retina, it is transduced by rods and cones into visual signals, interpreted by the brain as color, brightness and saturation.

   Many people (including about 5% of all males) inherit a common type of color blindness, in which the cones that normally process green light are mildly deficient; these people have difficulty distinguishing red from green. Unfortunately, in the United States, traffic signals use red and green lights to indicate whether cars should stop or go through an intersection. Why do drivers with red-green color blindness not risk auto accidents every time they approach an intersection?

3. Color perception and motion perception both rely partially on opponent processing, which is why we fall prey to illusions such as color aftereffects and the waterfall illusion.

   How might the concept of aftereffects account for "sea legs," in which a person who has been on a small boat for a few hours has trouble walking on land—because the ground seems to be rising and falling as if the person were still on the boat?

Answers to Summary Quizzes

Summary Quiz 4.1
1. c; 2. c; 3. c; 4. c

Summary Quiz 4.2
5. b; 6. d; 7. b; 8. d; 9. c; 10. d

Summary Quiz 4.3
11. a; 12. a; 13, d

Summary Quiz 4.4
14. b; 15. d; 16. b

Summary Quiz 4.5
17. a; 18. b; 19. a

Need more help? Additional resources are located at the book's free companion Web site at: www.worthpublishers.com/schacterbrief1e

Memory

GREG WAS A TEENAGER WHEN THE TROUBLE BEGAN. Restless and unfulfilled, he quit school, moved to New York City, and spent a few years getting high and listening to rock music. When that lifestyle didn't provide the meaning he sought, he joined the International Society for Krishna Consciousness and moved to their temple in New Orleans. At about that same time, Greg began having trouble with his vision. By the time he sought medical attention, he was completely blind. His doctors discovered a tumor the size of a small orange in Greg's brain, and although they were able to remove it, the damage had already been done. Greg lost his sight, but because the tumor had also destroyed a part of the temporal lobe that is crucial for forming and retaining memories of everyday experience, he lost much of his memory as well.

No longer able to live independently, Greg was admitted to a hospital for patients requiring long-term care. When the neurologist Oliver Sacks interviewed him, Greg had no idea why he was in the hospital but suspected that it might be due to his past drug abuse. Dr. Sacks noticed piles of rock albums in Greg's room and asked him about his interest in music, whereupon Greg launched into a version of his favorite Grateful Dead song, then shared a vivid memory of a time when he had heard the group perform in New York's Central Park. "When did you hear them in Central Park?" asked Dr. Sacks. "It's been a while, over a year maybe," Greg replied. In fact, the concert had taken place 8 years earlier (Sacks, 1995, p. 48). When asked to name the president of the United States (who at that time was Jimmy Carter), he guessed that it might be John F. Kennedy—who had been president over a decade earlier. It was as if Greg were unable to remember anything that had happened in the intervening years. Dr. Sacks conducted more tests, asking Greg to recall lists of words and simple stories. He noticed that Greg could hold on to the information for a few seconds but that within just a few minutes, he would forget nearly everything he had been told.

After Greg had spent 14 years in the hospital, Dr. Sacks took him on an outing, to a Grateful Dead reunion concert at Madison Square Garden. When the band performed their well-known songs from the 1960s, Greg sang along enthusiastically. "That was fantastic," Greg told Dr. Sacks as they left the concert. "I will always remember it. I had the time of my life." When Dr. Sacks saw Greg the next morning, he asked him about the Grateful Dead concert. "I love them. I heard them in Central Park," replied Greg. "Didn't you just hear them at Madison Square Garden?" asked Dr. Sacks. "No," replied Greg, "I've never been to the Garden" (Sacks, 1995, pp. 76–77). ■

Jerry Garcia (1943–1996) *Lead guitar player for the Grateful Dead.*

TIM MOSENFELDER/IMAGEDIRECT/GETTY IMAGES

memory The ability to store and retrieve information over time.

encoding The process by which we transform what we perceive, think, or feel into an enduring memory.

storage The process of maintaining information in memory over time.

retrieval The process of bringing to mind information that has been previously encoded and stored.

Memory is *the ability to store and retrieve information over time,* and as Greg's story suggests, it is more than just a handy device that allows us to find our car keys and schedule our dental appointments. In a very real way, our memories define us. Each of us has a unique identity that is intricately tied to the things we have thought, felt, done, and experienced. Memories are the residue of those events, the enduring changes that experience makes in our brains and leaves behind when it passes. If an experience passes without leaving a trace, it might just as well not have happened. For Greg, the last 20 years of his life have come and gone without a trace, leaving him forever frozen in 1969. He can revisit old memories, but he cannot make new ones, and so he himself can never change.

Those of us who *can* remember what we did yesterday often fail to appreciate just how complex that act of remembering really is because it occurs so easily. But just consider the role that memory plays in the simplest act, such as arranging to meet a friend at the movies. You must recall your friend's name and telephone number and how to make a call. You need to remember which movies are currently playing, as well as the types of movies that you and your friend enjoy. Eventually, you will need to remember how to get to the theater, how to drive your car, and what your friend looks like so you can recognize her among the people standing in front of the theater. And finally, you'll have to remember which movie you just saw so that you don't accidentally do this all this over again tomorrow. These are ordinary tasks, tasks so simple that you never give them a second thought. But the fact is that the most sophisticated computer could not even begin to accomplish them as efficiently as any average human.

Because memory is so remarkably complex, it is also remarkably fragile (Schacter, 1996). We all have had the experience of forgetting something we desperately wanted to remember or of remembering something that never really happened. Why does memory serve us so well in some situations and play such cruel tricks on us in other cases? When can we trust our memories and when should we view them skeptically? Is there just one kind of memory, or are there many? These are among the questions that psychologists have asked and answered.

As you've seen in other chapters, the mind's mistakes provide key insights into its fundamental operation, and there is no better illustration of these mind bugs than in the realm of memory. In this chapter, we shall consider the three key functions of memory: **encoding,** *the process by which we transform what we perceive, think, or feel into an enduring memory;* **storage,** *the process of maintaining information in memory over time;* and **retrieval,** *the process of bringing to mind information that has been previously encoded and stored.* We shall then examine several different kinds of memory and focus on the ways in which errors, distortions, and imperfections can reveal the nature of memory itself.

Greg's brain damage interfered with his ability to form new memories, so he was able to remember the Grateful Dead only as they sounded and performed in the early 1970s, not as they appeared more recently.

Encoding: Transforming Perceptions into Memories

For at least 2,000 years, people have thought of memory as a recording device that makes exact copies of information that comes in through our senses, and then stores those copies for later use. This idea is simple and intuitive. It is also thoroughly and completely incorrect. Consider the case of Bubbles P., a professional gambler with no formal education, who spent most of his time shooting craps at local clubs or playing high-stakes poker. Most people can listen to a list of numbers and then repeat them from memory—as long as the list is no more than about seven items long (try it for yourself using **FIGURE 5.1**). But Bubbles had no difficulty rattling off 20 numbers, in either forward or backward order, after just a single glance (Ceci, DeSimone, & Johnson, 1992). You might conclude that Bubbles must have had a "photographic memory" that allowed him to make an instant copy of the information that he could "look at" later. In fact, that isn't at all how he did it.

2 8
6 9 1
0 4 7 3
8 7 4 5 4
9 0 2 4 8 1
5 7 4 2 2 9 6
6 4 7 1 9 3 0 4
3 5 6 7 1 8 4 8 5
1 0 2 8 8 3 4 7 2 9
4 7 2 0 8 2 7 4 2 6 4
7 3 1 0 9 3 4 3 5 1 3 8

FIGURE 5.1 ● ● ● ● ● ● ● ● ● ● ● ● ● ● ● ● ● ●
Digit Memory Test *How many digits can you remember? Start on the first row and cover the rows below it with a piece of paper. Study the numbers in the row for 1 second and then cover that row back up again. After a couple of seconds, try to repeat the numbers. Then uncover the row to see if you were correct. If so, continue down to the next row, using the same instructions, until you can't recall all the numbers in a row. The number of digits in the last row you can remember correctly is your digit span. Bubbles P. could remember 20 random numbers, or about 5 rows deep. How did you do?*

To understand how Bubbles accomplished his astounding feats of memory, we must abandon the notion that memories are copies of sensory experience. On the contrary, memories are made by combining information we *already* have in our brains with new information that comes in through our senses. In this way memory is much less like photography and much more like cooking. Like starting from a recipe but improvising along the way, we add old information to new information, mix, shake, bake, and out pops a memory. Memories are *constructed,* not recorded, and encoding is the process by which we transform what we perceive, think, or feel into an enduring memory. Let's look at three types of encoding processes: elaborative encoding, visual imagery encoding, and organizational encoding.

● **How is making a memory unlike taking a photograph?**

Elaborative Encoding

Memories are a combination of old and new information, so the nature of any particular memory depends as much on the old information already in our memories as it does on the new information coming in through our senses. In other words, how we remember something depends on how we think about it at the time. In one study, researchers presented participants with a series of words and asked them to make one of three types of judgments (Craik & Tulving, 1975). *Semantic judgments* required the participants to think about the meaning of the words ("Is *hat* a type of clothing?"), *rhyme judgments* required the participants to think about the sound of the words ("Does *hat* rhyme with *cat*?"), and *visual judgments* required the participants to think about the appearance of the words ("Is *HAT* written uppercase or lowercase?"). The type of judgment task influenced how participants thought about each word—what old information they combined with the new—and thus had a powerful impact on their memories (**FIGURE 5.2** on the next page). Those participants who made semantic judgments (i.e., had thought about the meaning of the words) had much better memory for the words than did participants who had thought about how the word looked or sounded. The results of these and many other studies have shown that long-term retention is greatly enhanced by **elaborative encoding**, which involves *actively relating new information to knowledge that is already in memory* (Brown & Craik, 2000).

● **How do old memories influence new memories?**

elaborative encoding The process of actively relating new information to knowledge that is already in memory.

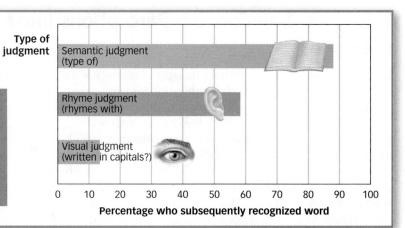

(A) COURTESY OF ANTHONY WAGNER; (B) SAVAGE ET AL., 2001, BRAIN, 124(1), PP. 219–231 FIG. 1C, P. 226. COURTESY OF C. R. SAVAGE; (C) KOSSLYN ET AL. (1999), SCIENCE, 284, PP. 167–170, FIG. 2, P. 168. COURTESY OF STEPHEN M. KOSSLYN.

FIGURE 5.2

Levels of Processing *Elaborative encoding enhances subsequent retention. Thinking about a word's meaning (making a semantic judgment) results in deeper processing—and better memory for the word later—than merely attending to its sound (rhyme judgment) or shape (visual judgment). (From Craik & Tulving, 1975)*

These findings would not have surprised Bubbles P. As a professional gambler, Bubbles found numbers unusually meaningful, so when he saw a string of digits, he tended to think about their meanings. For example, he might have thought about how they related to his latest bet at the racetrack or to his winnings after a long night at the poker table. Whereas you might try to memorize the string 22061823 by saying it over and over, Bubbles would think about betting $220 at 6 to 1 odds on horse number 8 to place 2nd in the 3rd race. Indeed, when Bubbles was tested with materials other than numbers—faces, words, objects, or locations—his memory performance was no better than average. You may consciously use Bubbles's strategy when you study for exams ("Well, if Napoleon was born in 1769, that would have made him 7 years old when America declared independence"), but you also use it automatically every day. Have you ever wondered why you can remember 20 experiences (your last summer vacation, your 16th birthday party, your first day at college) but not 20 digits? The reason is that most of the time we think of the meaning behind our experiences, and so we elaboratively encode them without even trying to (Craik & Tulving, 1975). Bubbles's amazing memory for numbers was due to elaborative encoding and not to some mysterious kind of "photographic memory."

So where does this elaborative encoding take place? What's going on in the brain when this type of information processing occurs? Studies reveal that elaborative encoding is uniquely associated with increased activity in the lower left part of the frontal lobe and the inner part of the left temporal lobe (**FIGURE 5.3 a, b**) (Demb et al., 1995; Kapur et al., 1994; Wagner et al., 1998). In fact, the amount of activity in each of these two regions during encoding is directly related to whether people later remember an item. The more activity there is in these areas, the more likely the person will remember the information.

FIGURE 5.3

Brain Activity during Different Types of Judgments *fMRI studies reveal that different parts of the brain are active during different types of judgments: (a) During semantic judgments, the lower left frontal lobe is active; (b) during organizational judgments, the upper left frontal lobe is active; and (c) during visual judgments, the occipital lobe is active.*

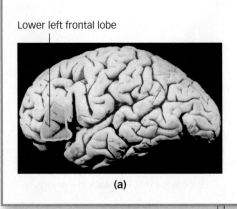

Lower left frontal lobe

(a)

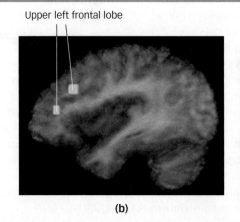

Upper left frontal lobe

(b)

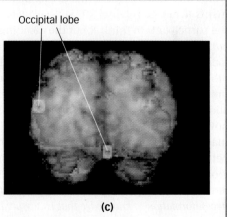

Occipital lobe

(c)

Visual Imagery Encoding

In Athens in 477 BC, the Greek poet Simonides had just left a banquet when the ceiling collapsed and killed all the people inside. Simonides was able to name every one of the dead simply by visualizing each chair around the banquet table and recalling the person who had been sitting there. Simonides wasn't the first, but he was among the most proficient, to use **visual imagery encoding**, *a form of categorization that involves storing new information by converting it into mental pictures.*

If you wanted to use Simonides' method to create an enduring memory, you could simply convert the information that you wanted to remember into a visual image and then "store it" in a familiar location. For instance, if you were going to the grocery store and wanted to remember to buy Coke, popcorn, and cheese dip, you could use the rooms in your house as locations and imagine your living room flooded in Coke, your bedroom pillows stuffed with popcorn, and your bathtub as a greasy pond of cheese dip. When you arrived at the store, you could then take a "mental walk" around your house and "look" into each room to remember the items you needed to purchase.

● **How does visual encoding influence memory?**

Numerous experiments have shown that visual imagery encoding can substantially improve memory. In one experiment, participants who studied lists of words by creating visual images of them later recalled twice as many items as participants who just mentally repeated the words (Schnorr & Atkinson, 1969). Why does visual imagery encoding work so well? First, visual imagery encoding does some of the same things that elaborative encoding does: When you create a visual image, you relate incoming information to knowledge already in memory. For example, a visual image of a parked car might help you create a link to your memory of your first kiss.

Second, when you use visual imagery to encode words and other verbal information, you end up with two different mental "placeholders" for the items—a visual one and a verbal one—which gives you more ways to remember them than just a verbal placeholder alone (Paivio, 1971, 1986). Visual imagery encoding activates visual processing regions in the occipital lobe (see **FIGURE 5.3c**), which suggests that people actually enlist the visual system when forming memories based on mental images (Kosslyn et al., 1993).

Organizational Encoding

Have you ever ordered dinner with a group of friends and watched in amazement as your server took the order without writing anything down? To find out how this is done, one researcher spent 3 months working in a restaurant where waitresses routinely wrote down orders but then left the check at the customer's table before proceeding to the kitchen and *telling* the cooks what to make (Stevens, 1988). The researcher wired each waitress with a microphone and asked her to think aloud—that is, to say what she was thinking as she walked around all day doing her job. The researcher found that as soon as the waitress left a customer's table, she immediately began *grouping* or *categorizing* the orders into hot drinks, cold drinks, hot foods, and cold foods. The waitresses grouped the items into a sequence that matched the layout of the kitchen, first placing drink orders, then hot food orders, and finally cold food orders. The waitresses remembered their orders by relying on **organizational encoding**, *a form of categorization that involves noticing the relationships among a series of items.*

visual imagery encoding The process of storing new information by converting it into mental pictures.

organizational encoding The act of categorizing information by noticing the relationships among a series of items.

Ever wonder how a server remembers who ordered the pizza and who ordered the fries without writing anything down? Some have figured out to use organizational encoding.

JEFF GREENBERG/ALAMY

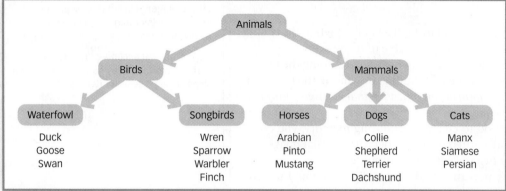

●●●●●●●●●●●●●●●●●●●●●●● FIGURE **5.4**
Organizing Words into a Hierarchy
*Organizing words into conceptual groups
and relating them to one another—such
as in this example of a hierarchy—makes
it easier to reconstruct the items from
memory later (Bower et al., 1969). Keeping
track of the 17 items in this example can
be facilitated by remembering the
hierarchical groupings they fall under.*

For example, suppose you had to memorize the words *peach, cow, chair, apple, table, cherry, lion, couch, horse,* and *desk.* The task seems difficult, but if you organized the items into three categories—fruit (*peach, apple, cherry*), animals (*cow, lion, horse*), *and furniture* (*chair, couch, desk*)—the task becomes much easier. Studies have shown that instructing people to sort items into categories like this is an effective way to enhance their subsequent recall of those items (Mandler, 1967). Even more complex organizational schemes have been used, such as the hierarchy in **FIGURE 5.4** (Bower et al., 1969). People can improve their recall of individual items by organizing them into multiple-level categories, all the way from a general category such as *animals,* through intermediate categories such as *birds* and *songbirds,* down to specific examples such as *wren* and *sparrow.*

● **Why might mentally organizing the material for an exam enhance your retrieval of that material?**

Just as elaborative and visual imagery encoding activate distinct regions of the brain, so too does organizational encoding. As you can see in Figure 5.3b, organizational encoding activates the upper surface of the left frontal lobe (Fletcher, Shallice, & Dolan, 1998; Savage et al., 2001). Different types of encoding strategies appear to rely on different areas of brain activation.

summary quiz [5.1]

1. The process of transforming information into a lasting memory is called
    a. rehearsal.
    b. sensory storage.
    c. encoding.
    d. chunking.

2. The process of actively relating new information to knowledge that is already in memory is called
    a. elaborative encoding.
    b. visual imagery encoding.
    c. organizational encoding.
    d. iconic memory.

3. Research described in the textbook found that servers in restaurants remember their orders by relying on
    a. visual imagery encoding.
    b. organizational encoding.
    c. elaborative encoding.
    d. prospective memory.

4. Visual imagery encoding occurs in which part of the brain?
    a. frontal lobe
    b. parietal lobe
    c. temporal lobe
    d. occipital lobe

Storage: Maintaining Memories over Time

Encoding is the process of turning perceptions into memories. But one of the hallmarks of a memory is that you can bring it to mind on Tuesday, not on Wednesday, and then bring it to mind again on Thursday. So where are our memories when we aren't using them? Clearly, those memories are *stored* somewhere in your brain. **Memory storage** is *the process of maintaining information in memory over time.* We can think of a memory store as a place in which memories are kept when we are not consciously experiencing them. The memory store has three major divisions: sensory, short-term, and long-term. As these names suggest, the three divisions are distinguished primarily by the amount of time in which a memory can be kept inside them.

Sensory Storage

The **sensory memory store** is *the place in which sensory information is kept for a few seconds or less.* In a series of classic experiments, research participants were asked to remember rows of letters (Sperling, 1960). In one version of the procedure, participants viewed three rows of four letters each, as shown in **FIGURE 5.5**. The researcher flashed the letters on a screen for just 1/20th of a second. When asked to remember all 12 of the letters they had just seen, participants recalled fewer than half (Sperling, 1960). There were two possible explanations for this: Either people simply couldn't encode all the letters in such a brief period of time, or they had encoded the letters but forgotten them while trying to recall everything they had seen.

To test the two ideas, the researchers relied on a clever trick. Just after the letters disappeared from the screen, a tone sounded that cued the participants to report the letters in a particular row. A *high tone* cued participants to report the contents of the top row, a *medium* tone cued participants to report the contents of the middle row, and a *low* tone cued participants to report the contents of the bottom row. When asked to report only a single row, people recalled almost all of the letters in that row! Because the tone sounded *after* the letters disappeared from the screen, the researchers concluded that people could have recalled the same number of letters from *any* of the rows had they been asked to. Participants had no way of knowing which of the three rows would be cued, so the researchers inferred that virtually all the letters had been encoded. In fact, if the tone was substantially delayed,

● **How long is information held in iconic and echoic memory before it decays?**

participants couldn't perform the task; the information had slipped away from their sensory memories. Like the afterimage of a flashlight, the 12 letters flashed on a screen are visual icons, a lingering trace stored in memory for a very short period.

Because we have more than one sense, we have more than one kind of sensory memory. **Iconic memory** is *a fast-decaying store of visual information.* A similar storage area serves as a temporary warehouse for sounds. **Echoic memory** is *a fast-decaying store of auditory information.* When you have difficulty understanding what someone has just said, you probably find yourself replaying the last few words—listening to them echo in your "mind's ear," so to speak. When you do that, you are accessing information that is being held in your echoic memory store. The hallmark of both the iconic and echoic memory stores is that they hold information for a very short time. Iconic memories usually decay in about a second or less, and echoic memories usually decay in about 5 seconds (Darwin, Turvey, & Crowder, 1972). These two sensory memory stores are a bit like doughnut shops: The products come in, they sit briefly on the shelf, and then they are discarded. If you want one, you have to grab it fast.

Short-Term Storage and Working Memory

A second kind of memory store is the **short-term memory store**, which is *a place where nonsensory information is kept for more than a few seconds but less than a minute.* For example, if someone tells you a telephone number, you can usually repeat it back with ease—

X	L	W	F
J	B	O	V
K	C	Z	R

FIGURE 5.5 ● ● ● ● ● ● ● ● ● ● ● ● ● ●
Iconic Memory Test *When a grid of letters is flashed on-screen for only 1/20th of a second, it is difficult to recall individual letters. But if prompted to remember a particular row immediately after the grid is shown, research participants will do so with high accuracy. Sperling used this procedure to demonstrate that although iconic memory stores the whole grid, the information fades away too quickly for a person to recall everything (Sperling, 1960).*

memory storage The process of maintaining information in memory over time.

sensory memory store The place in which sensory information is kept for a few seconds or less.

iconic memory A fast-decaying store of visual information.

echoic memory A fast-decaying store of auditory information.

short-term memory store A place where nonsensory information is kept for more than a few seconds but less than a minute.

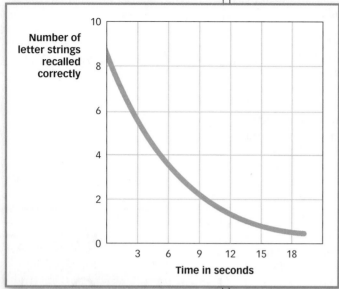

Number of letter strings recalled correctly

Time in seconds

The Decline of Short-Term Memory
A 1959 experiment showed how quickly short-term memory fades without rehearsal. On a test for memory of three-letter strings, research participants were highly accurate when tested a few seconds after exposure to each string, but if the test was delayed another 15 seconds, people barely recalled the strings at all (Peterson & Peterson, 1959).

rehearsal The process of keeping information in short-term memory by mentally repeating it.

chunking Combining small pieces of information into larger clusters or chunks that are more easily held in short-term memory.

working memory Active maintenance of information in short-term storage.

long-term memory store A place in which information can be kept for hours, days, weeks, or years.

anterograde amnesia The inability to transfer new information from the short-term store into the long-term store.

retrograde amnesia The inability to retrieve information that was acquired before a particular date, usually the date of an injury or operation.

but only for a few seconds. In one study, research participants were given consonant strings to remember, such as DBX and HLM. After seeing each string, participants were asked to count backward from 100 by 3s for varying amounts of time and were then asked to recall the strings (Peterson & Peterson, 1959). As shown in **FIGURE 5.6**, memory for the consonant strings declined rapidly, from approximately 80% after a 3-second delay to less than 20% after a 20-second delay. These results suggest that information can be held in the short-term memory store for about 15 to 20 seconds.

What if we need the information for a while longer? We can use a trick that allows us to get around the natural limitations of our short-term memories. **Rehearsal** is *the process of keeping information in short-term memory by mentally repeating it.* If someone gives you a telephone number and you don't have a pencil, you say it over and over to yourself until you find one. Each time you repeat the number, you are "reentering" it into short-term memory, thus giving it another 15 to 20 seconds of shelf life.

Short-term memory is limited in how *long* it can hold information and also in how *much* information it can hold. Most people can keep approximately seven numbers in short-term memory, and if they put in more new numbers in, then old numbers begin to fall out (Miller, 1956). Short-term memory isn't limited to numbers, of course: it can also hold about seven letters, or seven words—even though those seven words contain many more than seven letters. In fact, short-term memory can hold about seven *meaningful items* at once (Miller, 1956). Therefore, one way to increase storage is to group several letters into a single meaningful item. **Chunking** involves *combining small pieces of information into larger clusters or chunks.* Waitresses who organize customer orders into groups are essentially chunking the information, thus giving themselves less to remember.

● **Why is it helpful that local phone numbers are only seven digits long?**

Short-term memory was originally conceived of as a kind of "place" where information is kept for a limited amount of time. A more dynamic model of a limited-capacity memory system has been developed and refined over the past few decades. **Working memory** refers to *active maintenance of information in short-term storage* (Baddeley & Hitch, 1974). It differs from the traditional view that short-term memory is simply a place to hold information and instead includes the operations and processes we use to work with information in short-term memory.

Working memory includes subsystems that store and manipulate visual images or verbal information. If you wanted to keep the arrangement of pieces on a chessboard in mind as you contemplated your next move, you'd be relying on working memory. Working memory includes the visual representation of the positions of the pieces, your mental manipulation of the possible moves, and your awareness of the flow of information into and out of memory, all stored for a limited amount of time. In short, the working memory model acknowledges both the limited nature of this kind of memory storage and the activities that are commonly associated with it.

Long-Term Storage

In contrast to the time-limited sensory memory store and short-term memory stores, **long-term memory store** is *a place in which information can be kept for hours, days, weeks, or years.* In contrast to both the sensory and short-term memory stores, the long-term store has no known capacity limits (see **FIGURE 5.7**). For example, most people can recall 10,000 to 15,000 words in their native language, tens of thousands of facts ("The capital of France is Paris" and "$3 \times 3 = 9$"), and an untold number of personal experiences. Just think of all the song lyrics you can recite by heart, and you'll understand that you've got a lot of information tucked away in long-term memory!

Amazingly, people can recall items from the long-term memory store even if they haven't recalled them for years. For example, researchers have found that even 50 years after graduation, people can accurately recognize about 90% of their high school classmates from yearbook photographs (Bahrick, 2000). The feat is the more remarkable when you consider that most of this information had probably not been accessed for years before the experiment.

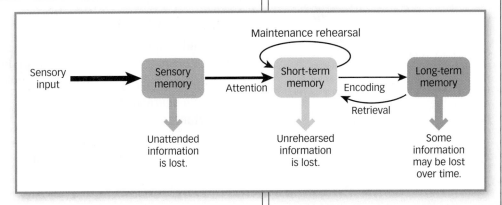

FIGURE 5.7 • • • • • • • • • • • • • • • • •
The Flow of Information through the Memory System *Information moves through several stages of memory as it gets encoded, stored, and made available for later retrieval.*

Not everyone has the same ability to put information into the long-term memory store. In 1953, a 27-year-old man, known by the initials HM, suffered from intractable epilepsy (Scoville & Milner, 1957). In a desperate attempt to stop the seizures, HM's doctors removed parts of his temporal lobes, including the hippocampus and some surrounding regions (**FIGURE 5.8**). After the operation, HM could converse easily, use and understand language, and perform well on intelligence tests—but he could not remember anything that happened to him *after* the operation. HM could repeat a telephone number with no difficulty, suggesting that his short-term memory store was just fine (Corkin, 1984, 2002; Hilts, 1995). But after information left the short-term store, it was gone forever. For example, he would often forget that he had just eaten a meal or fail to recognize the hospital staff who helped him on a daily basis. Like Greg, HM now lacked the ability to hang on to the new memories he created. Studies of HM and others have shown that the hippocampal region of the brain is critical for putting new information into the long-term store. When this region is damaged, patients suffer from a condition known as **anterograde amnesia**, which is *the inability to transfer new information from the short-term store into the long-term store.*

Some amnesic patients also suffer from **retrograde amnesia**, which is *the inability to retrieve information that was acquired before a particular date, usually the date of an injury or operation.* The fact that HM had much worse anterograde than retrograde amnesia suggests that the hippocampal region is not the site of long-term memory; indeed, research has shown that different aspects of a single memory—its sights, sounds, smells, emotional content—are stored in different places in the cortex (Damasio, 1989; Schacter, 1996; Squire & Kandel, 1999). Psychologists now believe that the hippocampal region acts as a kind of "index" that links together all of these otherwise separate bits and pieces so that we remember them as one memory (Schacter, 1996; Squire, 1992; Teyler & DiScenna, 1986). Over time, this index may become less necessary. You can think of the hippocampal-region index like a printed recipe. The first time you make a pie, you need the recipe to help you retrieve all the ingredients and then mix them together in the right amounts. As you bake more and more pies, though, you don't need to rely on the printed recipe anymore. Similarly, although the hippocampal-region index is critical when a new memory is first formed, it may become less important as the memory ages. Scientists are still debating the extent to which the hippocampal region helps us to remember details of our old memories (Bayley et al., 2005; Moscovitch et al., 2006), but the notion of the hippocampus as an index explains why people like HM *cannot* make new memories and why they *can* remember old ones.

● **How is using the hippocampal-region like learning a recipe?**

ONLY HUMAN

HELP! I'VE EATEN AND I CAN'T GET HOME! In Oslo, Norway, Jermund Slogstad, 50, was moving into his new apartment when he took a break to get something to eat. He went to a nearby café but forgot to take his wallet, which contained his new address. He was unable to find his way home. "This is embarrassing," he told a newspaper a month later, hoping word of his plight would reach his new landlady, whom he had paid a month's rent in advance.

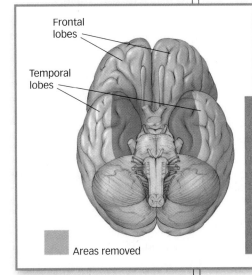

Frontal lobes

Temporal lobes

Areas removed

FIGURE 5.8 • • • • • • • • • • • • • • •
The Hippocampus Patient *HM had his hippocampus and adjacent structures of the medial temporal lobe (indicated by the shaded area) surgically removed to stop his epileptic seizures. As a result, he could not remember things that happened after the surgery.*

Memories in the Brain

If you could shrink yourself down to the size of a cell and go wandering around inside someone's brain, where exactly would you look for their memories? You'd probably be

● **Why are the spaces between neurons so important to memory?**

tempted to look at their neurons. But that isn't where you'd find them. Research suggests that the best place to look for memories is in the *spaces* between neurons. You'll recall from Chapter 3 that a *synapse* is the small space between the axon of one neuron and the dendrite of another, and neurons communicate by sending neurotransmitters across these synapses. As it turns out, sending a neurotransmitter across a synapse isn't like sending a toy boat across a pond because the act of sending actually *changes* the synapse. Specifically, it strengthens the connection between the two neurons, making it easier for them to transmit to each other the next time. This is why researchers sometimes say, "Cells that fire together wire together" (Hebb, 1949).

The idea that the connections between neurons are strengthened by their communication, thus making communication easier the next time, provides the neurological basis for long-term memory, and much of what we know about this comes from the tiny sea slug *Aplysia*. Having an extremely simple nervous system consisting of only 20,000 neurons (compared to roughly 100 billion in the human brain), *Aplysia* has been attractive to researchers because it is relatively uncomplicated. By studying these little animals, researchers have been able to observe how learning experiences result in physical changes in neurons: both by enhancing neurotransmitter release to make the messages stronger, and also by causing the growth of new synapses, to increase the number of possible communication sites (Abel et al., 1995; Squire & Kandel, 1999).

The same processes happen in larger-brained organisms, including humans. In the early 1970s, researchers applied a brief electrical stimulus to a neural pathway in a rat's hippocampus (Bliss & Lømo, 1973). They found that the electrical current produced a stronger connection between synapses that lay along the pathway and that the strengthening lasted for hours or even weeks. They called this **long-term potentiation**, more commonly known as **LTP**, which is *enhanced neural processing that results from the strengthening of synaptic connections*. Long-term potentiation has a number of properties that indicate to researchers that it plays an important role in long-term memory storage: It occurs in several pathways within the hippocampus, it can be induced rapidly, and it can last for a long time. In fact, drugs that block LTP can turn rats into rodent versions of patient HM: The animals have great difficulty remembering where they've been recently and become easily lost in a maze (Bliss, 1999; Morris, Anderson, Lynch, & Baudry, 1986). More work remains to be done in this area to conclusively show how LTP leads to the formation of long-term memories, but this line of research is giving us our first chance to "see" memories in the brain.

GERALD & BUFF CORSI/VISUALS UNLIMITED

● *The sea slug* Aplysia californica *is useful to researchers because it has an extremely simple nervous system that can be used to investigate the mechanisms of short- and long-term memory.*

long-term potentiation (LTP) Enhanced neural processing that results from the strengthening of synaptic connections.

summary quiz [5.2]

5. A fast-decaying store of visual information is called
   a. echoic memory.
   b. iconic memory.
   c. episodic memory.
   d. prospective memory.

6. Short-term memory can hold about ___ meaningful items at once.
   a. 3
   b. 5
   c. 7
   d. 12

7. The region of the brain called the _____ plays an important role in long-term memory storage.
   a. hippocampus
   b. hypothalamus
   c. amygdala
   d. temporal lobe

8. Enhanced neural processing that results from the strengthening of synaptic connections is called
   a. elaborative encoding.
   b. short-term memory store.
   c. chunking.
   d. long-term potentiation.

Retrieval: Bringing Memories to Mind

There is something fiendishly frustrating about piggy banks. You can put money in them, you can shake them around to assure yourself that the money is there, but you can't easily get the money out, which is why no one carries a piggy bank instead of a wallet. If memory were like a piggy bank, it would be similarly useless. We could make memories, we could store them, and we could even shake our heads around and listen for the telltale jingle. But if we couldn't bring our memories out of storage and use them, then what would be the point of saving them in the first place? Retrieval is the process of bringing to mind information that has been previously encoded and stored, and it is perhaps the most important of all memorial processes (Roediger, 2000; Schacter, 2001a).

Retrieval Cues: Reinstating the Past

One of the best ways to retrieve information from *inside* your head is to encounter information *outside* your head that is somehow connected to it. The information outside your head is called a **retrieval cue**, which is *external information that is associated with stored information and helps bring it to mind*. Retrieval cues can be incredibly effective.

In one experiment, undergraduates studied lists of words, such as *table, peach, bed, apple, chair, grape,* and *desk* (Tulving & Pearlstone, 1966). Later, the students were asked to write down all the words from the list that they could remember. When they were absolutely sure that they had emptied their memory stores of every last word that was in them, the experimenters again asked the students to remember the words on the list, but this time, the experimenters provided with retrieval cues, such as "furniture" or "fruit." The students who were sure that they had done all the remembering they possibly could were suddenly able to remember more words (Tulving & Pearlstone, 1966). These results suggest that information is sometimes *available* in memory even when it is momentarily *inaccessible* and that retrieval cues help us bring inaccessible information to mind. Of course, this is something you already knew. How many times have you said something like, "I *know* who starred in *Charlie and the Chocolate Factory,* but I just can't remember it"? only to have a friend give you a hint ("Wasn't he in *Pirates of the Caribbean*?"), which instantly brings the answer to mind ("Johnny Depp!").

retrieval cue External information that is associated with stored information and helps bring it to mind.

A particular light, odor, or melody can make a memory reappear vividly, with all its force and its precision, as if a window opened on the past.

DENISE KAPPA/DREAMSTIME.COM

Callahan

"I wonder if you'd mind giving me directions. I've never been sober in this part of town before."

Hints are one kind of retrieval cue, but they are not the only kind. The **encoding specificity principle** states that *a retrieval cue can serve as an effective reminder when it helps recreate the specific way in which information was initially encoded* (Tulving & Thomson, 1973). External contexts often make powerful retrieval cues. For example, in one study, divers learned some words on land and some other words underwater; they recalled the words best when they were tested in the same dry or wet environment in which they had initially learned them because the environment itself served as a retrieval cue (Godden & Baddely, 1975). Recovering alcoholics often experience a renewed urge to drink when visiting places in which they once drank because these places serve as retrieval cues. There may even be some wisdom to finding a seat in a classroom, sitting in it every day, and then sitting in it again when you take the test because the feel of the chair and the sights you see may help you remember the information you learned while you sat there.

● **Why might it be a good idea to sit in the same seat for an exam that you sat in during lecture?**

Retrieval cues need not be external contexts—they can also be inner states. **State-dependent retrieval** is *the tendency for information to be better recalled when the person is in the same state during encoding and retrieval.* For example, retrieving information when you are in a sad or happy mood increases the likelihood that you will retrieve sad or happy episodes (Eich, 1995), which is part of the reason it is so hard to "look on the bright side" when you're feeling low. Retrieval cues can even be thoughts themselves, as when one thought calls to mind another, related thought (Anderson et al., 1976).

The encoding specificity principle makes some unusual predictions. For example, you learned earlier that making semantic judgments about a word (e.g., "What does *orange* mean?") usually produces more durable memory for the word than does making rhyme judgments (e.g., "What rhymes with *orange*?"). So if you were asked to think of a word that rhymes with *brain* and your friend were asked to think about what *brain* means, we would expect your friend to remember the word better the next day if we simply asked you both, "Hey, what was that word you saw yesterday?" However, if instead of asking that question, we asked you both, "What was that word that rhymed with *train*?" we would expect you to remember it better than your friend did (Fisher & Craik, 1977). This is a fairly astounding finding. Semantic judgments almost always yield better memory than rhyme judgments. But in this case, the typical finding is turned upside down because the retrieval cue matched your encoding context better than it matched your friend's. The principle of **transfer-appropriate processing** states that *memory is likely to transfer from one situation to another when we process information in a way that is*

Culture & Community

Is Language a Factor in Memory Retrieval? A Study from Cornell University Indicates That It Is

In a memory retrieval experiment, bilingual Russian American college students were asked to relate memories that came to mind after hearing prompt words (Marian & Neisser, 2000). They were queried about four different stages of their lives. One part of the interview was conducted in English, and the other part was conducted in Russian. Participants were able to recall more events that took place in Russia when interviewed in Russian than in English, whereas they were able to recall more events that took place in the United States when interviewed in English than in Russian. Like other forms of context discussed in this section that are known to influence remembering, such as our moods or the external environment, this study shows that language can serve as a contextual cue that plays a significant role in determining what will be remembered.

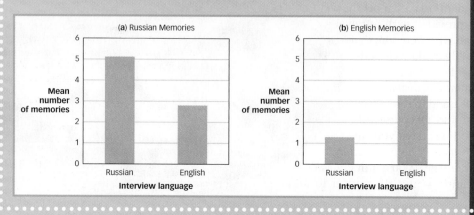

appropriate to the retrieval cues that will be available later (Morris, Bransford, & Franks, 1977; Roediger, Weldon, & Challis, 1989).

Separating the Components of Retrieval

Before leaving the topic of retrieval, let's look at how the process actually works. There is reason to believe that *trying* to recall an incident and *successfully* recalling one are fundamentally different processes that occur in different parts of the brain (Moscovitch, 1994; Schacter, 1996). For example, regions in the left frontal lobe show heightened activity when people *try* to retrieve information that was presented to them earlier (Shallice et al., 1994; Squire et al., 1992; Tulving et al., 1994). Many psychologists believe that this activity reflects the mental effort that people put forth when they struggle to dredge up the past event (Lepage et al., 2000). However, *successfully* remembering a past experience tends to be accompanied by activity in the hippocampal region (see **FIGURE 5.9**) and also in parts of the brain that play a role in processing the sensory features of an experience (Eldridge et al., 2000; Nyberg et al., 1996; Schacter et al., 1996a). For instance, recall of previously heard sounds is accompanied by activity in the auditory cortex (the upper part of the temporal lobe), whereas recall of previously seen pictures is accompanied by activity in the visual cortex (in the occipital lobe) (Wheeler, Petersen, & Buckner, 2000). Although retrieval may seem like a single process, brain studies suggest that separately identifiable processes are at work.

● **How is brain activity different when trying to recall versus successfully recalling?**

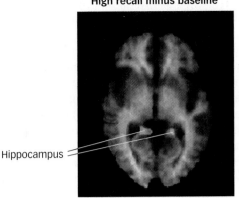
High recall minus baseline

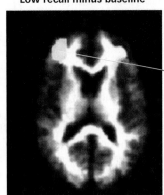
Low recall minus baseline

Left frontal lobe

Hippocampus

FIGURE 5.9 ● ● ● ● ● ● ● ● ● ● ● ● ● ● ●
PET Scans of Successful and Unsuccessful Recall *When people successfully remembered words they saw earlier in an experiment, achieving high levels of recall on a test, the hippocampus showed increased activity. When people tried but failed to recall words they had seen earlier, achieving low levels of recall on a test, the left frontal lobe showed increased activity (Schacter et al., 1996a).*

summary quiz [5.3]

9. You are more likely to recall a happy event in your life when you are in a happy mood. This illustrates
   a. state-dependent retrieval.
   b. transfer-appropriate processing.
   c. the encoding specificity principle.
   d. elaborative encoding.

10. Your textbook suggests that sitting in the same seat in a classroom every day, including exam day, may help you retrieve information learned in class when taking your exam. This illustrates
    a. state-dependent retrieval.
    b. transfer-appropriate processing.
    c. the encoding specificity principle.
    d. organizational encoding.

11. *Trying* to recall a melody involves the _____, whereas *successfully* recalling the melody involves the _____.
    a. left frontal lobe; hypothalamus and parietal lobe
    b. right frontal lobe; hippocampus and temporal lobe
    c. left frontal lobe; hypothalamus and temporal lobe
    d. right frontal lobe; amygdala and occipital lobe

encoding specificity principle The idea that a retrieval cue can serve as an effective reminder when it helps re-create the specific way in which information was initially encoded.

state-dependent retrieval The tendency for information to be better recalled when the person is in the same state during encoding and retrieval.

transfer-appropriate processing The idea that memory is likely to transfer from one situation to another when we process information in a way that is appropriate to the retrieval cues that will be available later.

explicit memory The act of consciously or intentionally retrieving past experiences.

implicit memory The influence of past experiences on later behavior and performance, even though people are not trying to recollect them and are not aware that they are remembering them.

procedural memory The gradual acquisition of skills as a result of practice, or "knowing how," to do things.

priming An enhanced ability to think of a stimulus, such as a word or object, as a result of a recent exposure to the stimulus.

Multiple Forms of Memory: How the Past Returns

Although Greg was unable to make new memories, some of the new things that happened to him seemed to leave a mark. For example, Greg did not recall learning that his father had died, but he did seem sad and withdrawn for years after hearing the news. Similarly, HM could not make new memories after his surgery, but if he played a game in which he had to track a moving target, his performance gradually improved with each round (Milner, 1962). Greg could not consciously remember hearing about his father's death, and HM could not consciously remember playing the tracking game, but both showed clear signs of having been permanently changed by experiences that they so rapidly forgot. In other words, these patients *behaved* as though they were remembering things while claiming to remember nothing at all. This suggests that there must be several kinds of memory, some of which are accessible to conscious recall and some that we cannot consciously access (Eichenbaum & Cohen, 2001; Schacter & Tulving, 1994; Schacter, Wagner, & Buckner, 2000; Squire & Kandel, 1999).

Explicit and Implicit Memory

The fact that people can be changed by past experiences without having any awareness of those experiences suggests that there must be at least two different classes of memory (**FIGURE 5.10**). **Explicit memory** occurs *when people consciously or intentionally retrieve past experiences*. Recalling last summer's vacation, incidents from a novel you just read, or facts you studied for a test all involve explicit memory. Indeed, anytime you start a sentence with "I remember . . . ," you are talking about an explicit memory. **Implicit memory** occurs when *past experiences influence later behavior and performance, even though people are not trying to recollect them and are not aware that they are remembering them* (Graf & Schacter, 1985; Schacter, 1987). Implicit memories are not consciously recalled, but their presence is "implied" by our actions. Greg's persistent sadness after his father's death, even though he had no conscious knowledge of the event, is an example of implicit memory. So is HM's improved performance on a tracking task that he didn't consciously remember doing. So is the ability to ride a bike or tie your shoelaces or play guitar: you may know how to do these things, but you probably can't describe how to do them. Such knowledge reflects a particular kind of implicit memory called **procedural memory**, which refers to *the gradual acquisition of skills as a result of practice, or "knowing how," to do things*.

One of the hallmarks of procedural memory is that the things you remember are automatically translated into actions. Sometimes you can explain how it is done ("Put one

● **What type of memory is it when you just "know how" to do something?**

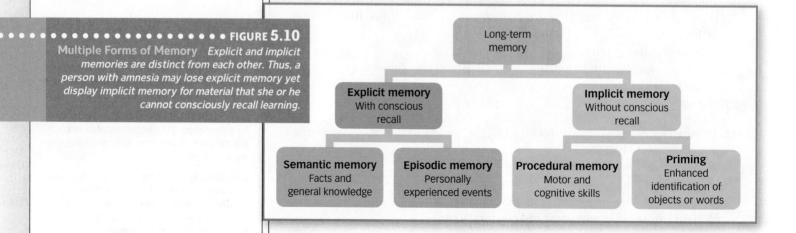

●●●●●●●●●●●●●●●●●●●● **FIGURE 5.10**
Multiple Forms of Memory *Explicit and implicit memories are distinct from each other. Thus, a person with amnesia may lose explicit memory yet display implicit memory for material that she or he cannot consciously recall learning.*

Long-term memory

Explicit memory With conscious recall

Implicit memory Without conscious recall

Semantic memory Facts and general knowledge

Episodic memory Personally experienced events

Procedural memory Motor and cognitive skills

Priming Enhanced identification of objects or words

finger on the third fret of the E string, one finger . . ."), and sometimes you can't ("Get on the bike and . . . well, uh . . . just balance"). The fact that people who have amnesia can acquire new procedural memories suggests that the hippocampal structures that are usually damaged in these patients may be necessary for explicit memory, but they aren't needed for implicit procedural memory. In fact, it appears that brain regions outside the hippocampal area (including areas in the motor cortex) are involved in procedural memory. Chapter 6 discusses this evidence further, where you will also see that procedural memory is crucial for learning various kinds of motor, perceptual, and cognitive skills.

Not all implicit memories are procedural or "how to" memories. For example, in one experiment, college students were asked to study a long list of words, including items such as *avocado, mystery, climate, octopus,* and *assassin* (Tulving, Schacter, & Stark, 1982). Later, explicit memory was tested by showing participants some of these words along with new ones they hadn't seen and asking them which words were on the list. To test implicit memory, participants received word fragments and were asked them to come up with a word that fit the fragment.

Try the test yourself:

ch——nk

o–t–p—

–og–y——

–l–m–te

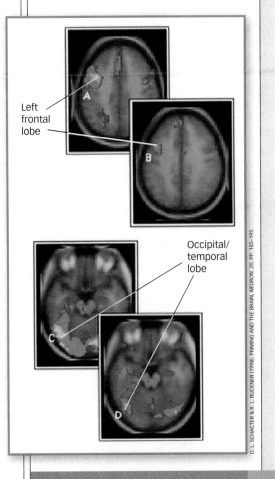

Left frontal lobe

Occipital/ temporal lobe

D. L. SCHACTER & R. L. BUCKNER (1998). PRIMING AND THE BRAIN, NEURON, 20, PP. 185–195.

You probably had difficulty coming up with the answers for the first and third fragments (*chipmunk, bogeyman*) but had little problem coming up with answers for the second and fourth (*octopus, climate*). Seeing *octopus* and *climate* on the original list made those words more accessible later, during the fill-in-the-blanks test. This is an example of **priming**, which refers to *an enhanced ability to think of a stimulus, such as a word or object, as a result of a recent exposure to the stimulus* (Tulving & Schacter, 1990). Just as priming a pump makes water flow more easily, priming the memory system makes some information more accessible. In the fill-in-the-blanks experiment, people showed priming for studied words even when they failed to consciously remember that they had seen them earlier. This suggests that priming is an example of implicit, not explicit memory. As such, you'd expect amnesic patients such as HM and Greg to show priming. In fact, many experiments have shown that amnesic patients can show substantial priming effects—often as large as healthy, nonamnesic people—even though they have no explicit memory for the items they studied. These and other similar results suggest that priming, like procedural memory, does not require the hippocampal structures that are damaged in cases of amnesia (Schacter & Curran, 2000).

● **How does priming make memory more efficient?**

If the hippocampal region isn't required for procedural memory and priming, what parts of the brain are involved? Experiments have revealed that priming is associated with *reduced* activity in various regions of the cortex that are activated when people perform an unprimed task. For instance, when research participants are shown the word stem *mot___* or *tab___* and are asked to provide the first word that comes to mind, parts of the occipital lobe involved in visual processing and parts of the frontal lobe involved in word retrieval become active. But if people perform the same task after being primed by seeing *motel* and *table,* there's less activity in these same regions (Buckner et al., 1995; Schacter, Dobbins, & Schnyer, 2004; Wiggs & Martin, 1998). Something similar happens when people see pictures of everyday objects on two different occasions. On the second exposure to a picture, there's less activity in parts of the visual cortex that were activated by seeing the picture initially. Priming seems to make it easier for parts of the cortex that are involved in perceiving a word or object to identify the item after a recent exposure to it. This suggests that the brain "saves" a bit of processing time after priming (**FIGURE 5.11**).

FIGURE 5.11 ● ● ● ● ● ● ● ● ● ● ● ● ● ● ● ● ● ●
Primed and Unprimed Processing of Stimuli *Priming is associated with reduced levels of activation in the cortex on a number of different tasks. In each pair of fMRIs, the images on the upper left (A, C) show brain regions in the frontal lobe (A) and occipital/temporal lobe (C) that are active during an unprimed task (in this case, providing a word response to a visual word cue). The images on the lower right within each pair (B, D) show reduced activity in the same regions during the primed version of the same task.*

semantic memory   A network of associated facts and concepts that make up our general knowledge of the world.

episodic memory   The collection of past personal experiences that occurred at a particular time and place.

Semantic and Episodic Memory

Consider these two questions: (a) Why do we celebrate on July 4? and (b) What is the most spectacular Fourth of July celebration you've ever seen? Every American knows the answer to the first question (we celebrate the signing of the Declaration of Independence on July 4, 1776), but we all have our own answers to the second. Although both of these questions required you to search your long-term memory and explicitly retrieve information that was stored there, one required you to dredge up a fact that every American schoolchild knows and that is not part of your personal autobiography and one required you to revisit a particular time and place—or episode—from your personal past. These memories are called *semantic* and *episodic* memories, respectively (Tulving, 1972, 1983, 1998). **Semantic memory** is *a network of associated facts and concepts that make up our general knowledge of the world,* whereas **episodic memory** is *the collection of past personal experiences that occurred at a particular time and place.*

● **What form of memory uses "mental time travel"?**

Episodic memory is special because it is the only form of memory that allows us to engage in "mental time travel," projecting ourselves into the past and revisiting events that have happened to us. This ability allows us to connect our pasts and our presents and construct a cohesive story of our lives. People who have amnesia can usually travel back in time and revisit episodes that occurred before they became amnesiac, but they are unable to revisit episodes that happened later. For example, Greg couldn't travel back to any time after 1969 because that's when he stopped being able to create new episodic memories. But can people with amnesia create new semantic memories?

Researchers have studied three young adults who suffered damage to the hippocampus during birth as a result of difficult deliveries that interrupted the oxygen supply to their brains (Vargha-Khadem et al., 1997). Their parents noticed that the children could not recall what happened during a typical day, had to be constantly reminded of appointments, and often became lost and disoriented. In view of their hippocampal damage, you might also expect that each of the three would perform poorly in school and might even be classified as learning disabled. Remarkably, however, all three children learned to read, write, and spell; developed normal vocabularies; and acquired other kinds of semantic knowledge that allowed them to perform well at school. Based on this evidence, researchers have concluded that the hippocampus is not necessary for acquiring new *semantic* memories.

This contestant on the game show Who Wants to Be a Millionaire? *is consulting her semantic memory to answer the question. The answer is B: Bulgaria.*

summary quiz [5.4]

12. Remembering how to ride a bike or tie your shoelaces illustrates
    a. iconic memory.
    b. procedural memory.
    c. explicit memory.
    d. priming.

13. An enhanced ability to think of a stimulus, such as a word or object, as a result of recent exposure to the stimulus, is called
    a. elaborative encoding.
    b. chunking.
    c. priming.
    d. state-dependent retrieval.

14. Almost all American schoolchildren know that July 4 celebrates the signing of the Declaration of Independence. This illustrates
    a. semantic memory.
    b. episodic memory.
    c. implicit memory.
    d. explicit memory.

Memory Failures: The Seven Sins of Memory

You probably haven't given much thought to breathing today, and the reason is that from the moment you woke up, you've been doing it effortlessly and well. But the moment breathing fails, you are reminded of just how important it is. Memory is like that. Every time we see, think, notice, imagine, or wonder, we are drawing on our ability to use information stored in our brains, but it isn't until this ability fails that we become acutely aware of just how much we should treasure it. Like a lot of human behavior, we can better understand how a process works correctly by examining what happens when it works incorrectly. We've seen in other contexts how an understanding of mind bugs—those foibles and errors of human thought and action—reveals the normal operation of various behaviors. Such memory mind bugs—the "seven sins" of memory—cast similar illumination on how memory normally operates and how often it operates well (Schacter, 1999, 2001b). We'll discuss each of the seven sins in detail.

1. Transience

The investigation and eventual impeachment of U.S. president Bill Clinton held the nation spellbound in the late 1990s. Aside from tabloid revelations about Clinton's relationship with White House intern Monica Lewinsky, the investigation also produced a lot of discussion about Clinton's claims to have forgotten a variety of things. For example, 3 weeks after a meeting with his good friend Vernon Jordan to discuss a sexual harassment lawsuit, the president claimed not to remember any of the important details of that discussion (Schacter, 2001b). Was that claim reasonable? Could a person simply forget such important information so quickly? Or, as Clinton's prosecutor argued, were these apparent memory lapses self-serving conveniences designed to avoid embarrassing admissions?

We may never know for sure. But certainly, memories can and do degrade with time. The culprit here is **transience**: *forgetting what occurs with the passage of time*. Transience

transience Forgetting what occurs with the passage of time.

APTV/AP PHOTO

President Clinton hugs Monica Lewinsky as he greets the crowd at a public appearance. Clinton's claims to have forgotten several incidents related to their affair may be an example of transience.

retroactive interference Situations in which later learning impairs memory for information acquired earlier.

proactive interference Situations in which earlier learning impairs memory for information acquired later.

absentmindedness A lapse in attention that results in memory failure.

prospective memory Remembering to do things in the future.

occurs during the storage phase of memory, after an experience has been encoded and before it is retrieved. You've already seen the workings of transience—rapid forgetting—in sensory storage and short-term storage. Transience also occurs in long-term storage, as was first illustrated in the late 1870s by Hermann Ebbinghaus, a German philosopher who measured his own memory for lists of nonsense syllables at different delays after studying them (Ebbinghaus, 1885/1964). Ebbinghaus charted his recall of nonsense syllables over time, creating the forgetting curve shown in **FIGURE 5.12**. Ebbinghaus noted a rapid drop-off in retention during the first few tests, followed by a slower rate of forgetting on later tests—a general pattern confirmed by many subsequent memory researchers (Wixted & Ebbesen, 1991). So, for example, when English speakers were tested for memory of Spanish vocabulary acquired during high school or college courses 1 to 50 years previously, there was a rapid drop-off in memory during the first 3 years after the students' last class, followed by tiny losses in later years (Bahrick, 1984, 2000). In all these studies, memories don't fade at a constant rate as time passes; most forgetting happens soon after an event occurs, with increasingly less forgetting as more time passes.

With the passage of time, the quality of our memories also changes. At early time points on the forgetting curve—minutes, hours, and days—memory preserves a relatively detailed record, allowing us to reproduce the past with reasonable if not perfect accuracy. But with the passing of time, we increasingly rely on our general memories for what usually happens and attempt to reconstruct the details by inference and even sheer guesswork. Transience involves a gradual switch from specific to more general memories (Brewer, 1996; Eldridge, Barnard, & Bekerian, 1994; Thompson et al., 1996). In one early study, British research participants read a brief Native American folktale that had odd imagery and unfamiliar plots in it, and then recounted it as best they could

● **How might general memories come to distort specific memories?**

after a delay (Bartlett, 1932). The readers made interesting but understandable errors, often eliminating details that didn't make sense to them or adding elements to make the story more coherent. As the specifics of the story slipped away, the general meaning of the events stayed in memory but usually with elaborations and embellishments that were consistent with the readers' worldview. Because the story was unfamiliar to the readers, they raided their stores of general information and patched together a reasonable recollection of what *probably* happened.

Yet another way that memories can be distorted is by interference from other memories. For example, if you carry out the same activities at work each day, by the time Friday rolls around, it may be difficult to remember what you did on Monday because later activities blend in with earlier ones. This is an example of **retroactive**

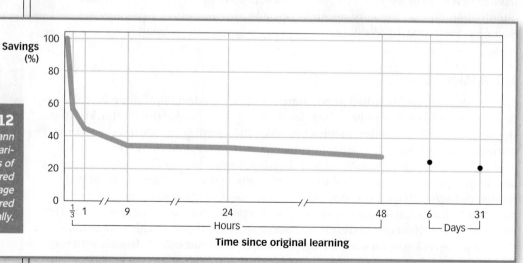

● **FIGURE 5.12**
The Curve of Forgetting *Hermann Ebbinghaus measured his retention at various delay intervals after he studied lists of nonsense syllables. Retention was measured in percent savings—that is, the percentage of time needed to relearn the list compared to the time needed to learn it initially.*

interference, which occurs when *later learning impairs memory for information acquired earlier* (Postman & Underwood, 1973). **Proactive interference**, in contrast, refers to situations in which *earlier learning impairs memory for information acquired later.* If you use the same parking lot each day at work or school, you've probably gone out to find your car and then stood there confused by the memories of having parked it on previous days.

2. Absentmindedness

The great cellist Yo-Yo Ma put his treasured $2.5 million instrument in the trunk of a taxicab in Manhattan and then rode to his destination. After a 10-minute trip, he paid the driver and left the cab, forgetting his cello. Minutes later, Ma realized what he had done and called the police. Fortunately, they tracked down the taxi and recovered the instrument within hours (Finkelstein, 1999). But how had the celebrated cellist forgotten about something so important that had occurred only 10 minutes earlier? Transience is not a likely culprit. As soon as Mr. Ma realized what he'd done with his instrument, he recalled where he had put it. This information had not disappeared from his memory (which is why he was able to tell the police where the cello was). Instead, Yo-Yo Ma was a victim of **absentmindedness**, which is *a lapse in attention that results in memory failure.*

What makes people absentminded? One common cause is lack of attention. Attention plays a vital role in encoding information into long-term memory. Without proper attention, material is much less likely to be stored properly, and recalled later. In studies of "divided attention," research participants are given materials to remember, such as a list of words, a story, or a series of pictures. At the same time, they are required to perform an additional task that draws their attention away from the material. For example, in one study, participants listened to lists of 15 words for a later memory test (Craik et al., 1996). They were allowed to pay full attention to some of the lists, but while they heard other lists, they simultaneously viewed a visual display containing four boxes and pressed different keys to indicate where an asterisk was appearing and disappearing. On a later test, participants recalled far fewer words from the list they had heard while their attention was divided.

What happens in the brain when attention is divided? In one study, volunteers tried to learn a list of word pairs while researchers scanned their brains with positron emission tomography (PET) (Shallice et al., 1994). Some people simultaneously performed a task that took little attention (they moved a bar the same way over and over), whereas other people simultaneously performed a task that took a great deal of attention (they moved a bar over and over but in a novel, unpredictable way each time). The researchers observed less activity in the participants' lower left frontal lobe when their attention was divided. As you saw earlier, greater activity in the lower left frontal region during encoding is associated with better memory. Dividing attention, then, prevents the lower left frontal lobe from playing its normal role in elaborative encoding, and the result is absentminded forgetting.

● **How is memory affected for someone whose attention is divided?**

Another common cause of absentmindedness is forgetting to carry out actions that we planned to do in the future. On any given day, you need to remember the times and places that your classes meet, you need to remember with whom and where you are having lunch, you need to remember which grocery items to pick up for dinner, and you need to remember which page of this book you were on when you fell asleep. In other words, you have to remember to remember, and this is called **prospective memory**, or *remembering to do things in the future* (Einstein & McDaniel, 1990).

Yo-Yo Ma with his $2.5 million cello. The famous cellist lost it when he absentmindedly forgot that he'd placed the instrument in a taxi's trunk minutes earlier.

TED THAI/GETTY IMAGES

"It says, 'Please disregard this reminder if your check is in the mail.'"

LEE LORENZ/CARTOONBANK.COM

● *Many people rely on memory aids such as calendars—and, more recently, personal digital assistants (PDAs) such as the iPhone—to help them remember to perform a particular activity in the future.*

🧠 **ONLY HUMAN**

MONEY TO BURN Chef Albert Grabham of the New House Hotel in Wales hid the restaurant's New Year's Eve earnings in the oven. He failed to remember that when he lit the same oven to prepare New Year's Day lunch.

blocking A failure to retrieve information that is available in memory even though you are trying to produce it.

Failures of prospective memory are a major source of absentmindedness. Avoiding these mind bugs often requires having a cue available at the moment you need to remember to carry out an action. For example, air traffic controllers must sometimes postpone an action, such as granting a pilot's request to change altitude, but remember to carry out that action a few minutes later when conditions change. In a simulated air traffic control experiment, researchers provided controllers with electronic signals to remind them to carry out a deferred request 1 minute later. The reminders were made available either during the 1-minute waiting period or at the time the controller needed to act on the deferred request. The controllers' memory for the deferred action improved only when the reminder was available at the time needed for retrieval. Providing the reminder during the waiting period did not help (Vortac, Edwards, & Manning, 1995). An early reminder, then, is no reminder at all.

3. Blocking

Have you ever tried to recall the name of a famous movie actor or a book you've read—and felt that the answer was "on the tip of your tongue," rolling around in your head *somewhere* but just out of reach it at the moment? This tip-of-the-tongue experience is a classic example of **blocking**, which is *a failure to retrieve information that is available in memory even though you are trying to produce it*. The sought-after information has been encoded and stored, and a cue is available that would ordinarily trigger recall of it. The information has not faded from memory, and you aren't forgetting to retrieve it. Rather, you are experiencing a full-blown retrieval failure, which makes this memory mind bug especially frustrating. It seems absolutely clear that you should be able to produce the information you seek, but the fact is that you can't. Researchers have described the tip-of-the-tongue state, in particular, as "a mild torment, something like [being] on the brink of a sneeze" (Brown & McNeill, 1966, p. 326).

Blocking occurs especially often for the names of people and places (Cohen, 1990; Valentine, Brennen, & Brédart, 1996). Why? Because their links to related concepts and knowledge are weaker than for common names. That somebody's last name is Baker doesn't tell us much about the person, but saying that he *is* a baker does. To illustrate this point, researchers

● **Why is Snow White's name easier to remember than Mary Poppins's?**

showed people pictures of cartoon and comic strip characters, some with descriptive names that highlight key features of the character (e.g., Grumpy, Snow White, Scrooge) and others with arbitrary names (e.g., Aladdin, Mary Poppins, Pinocchio) (Brédart & Valentine, 1998). Even though the two types of names were equally familiar to participants in the experiment, they blocked less often on the descriptive names than on the arbitrary names.

Although it's frustrating when it occurs, blocking is a relatively infrequent event for most of us. However, it occurs more often as we grow older, and it is a very common complaint among people in their 60s and 70s (Burke et al., 1991). Even more striking, some brain-damaged patients live in a nearly perpetual tip-of-the-tongue state. One patient could recall the names of only 2 of 40 famous people when she saw their photographs, compared to 25 of 40 for healthy volunteers in the control group (Semenza & Zettin, 1989). Yet she could still recall correctly the occupations of 32 of these people—the same number as healthy people could recall. This case and similar ones have given researchers important clues about what parts of the brain are involved in retrieving proper names. Name blocking usually results from damage to parts of the left temporal lobe on the surface of the cortex, most often as a result of a stroke. In fact, studies that show strong activation of regions within the temporal lobe when people recall proper names support this idea (Damasio et al., 1996; Tempini et al., 1998).

4. Memory Misattribution

Shortly after the devastating 1995 bombing of the federal building in Oklahoma City, police set about searching for two suspects they called John Doe 1 and John Doe 2. John Doe 1 turned out to be Timothy McVeigh, who was quickly apprehended and later convicted of the crime and sentenced to death. John Doe 2, who had supposedly accompanied McVeigh when he rented a van from Elliott's Body Shop, 2 days before the bombing, was never found. In fact, John Doe 2 had never existed; he was a product of the memory of Tom Kessinger, a mechanic at Elliott's Body Shop who was present when McVeigh rented the van. The day after, two other men had also rented a van in Kessinger's presence. The first man, like McVeigh, was tall and fair. The second man was shorter and stockier, was dark haired, wore a blue-and-white cap, and had a tattoo beneath his left sleeve—a match to the description of John Doe 2. Kessinger had confused his recollections of men he had seen on separate days in the same place. He was a victim of **memory misattribution:** *assigning a recollection or an idea to the wrong source* (**FIGURE 5.13**).

Memory misattribution errors are some of the primary causes of eyewitness misidentifications. The memory researcher Donald Thomson was accused of rape based on the victim's detailed recollection of his face, but he was eventually cleared when it turned out he had an airtight alibi. At the time of the rape, Thompson was giving a live television interview on the subject of distorted memories! The victim had been watching the show just before she was assaulted and misattributed her memory of Thomson's face to the rapist (Schacter, 1996; Thomson, 1988).

Part of memory is knowing where our memories came from. This is known as **source memory:** *recall of when, where, and how information was acquired* (Johnson, Hashtroudi, & Lindsay, 1993; Schacter, Harbluk, & McLachlan, 1984). People sometimes correctly recall a fact they learned earlier or accurately recognize a person or object they have seen before but misattribute the source of this knowledge—just as happened to Tom Kessinger and the rape victim in the Donald Thomson incident (Davies, 1988). Such misattribution could be the cause of déjà vu experiences, where you suddenly feel that you have been in a situation before even

● **What can explain a déjà vu experience?**

memory misattribution Assigning a recollection or an idea to the wrong source.

source memory Recall of when, where, and how information was acquired.

FIGURE 5.13 ● ● ● ● ● ● ● ● ● ● ● ● ● ● ● ● ● ● ●
Memory Misattribution *In 1995, the Murrah Federal Building in Oklahoma City was bombed in an act of terrorism. The police sketch shows "John Doe 2," who was originally thought to have been culprit Timothy McVeigh's partner in the bombing. It was later determined that the witness had confused his memories of different men whom he had encountered at Elliott's Body Shop on different days.*

Doonesbury

though you can't recall any details. A present situation that is similar to a past experience may trigger a general sense of familiarity that is mistakenly attributed to having been in the exact situation previously (Reed, 1988).

Patients with damage to the frontal lobes are especially prone to memory misattribution errors (Schacter et al., 1984; Shimamura & Squire, 1987). This is probably because the frontal lobes play a significant role in effortful retrieval processes, which are required to dredge up the correct source of a memory. These patients sometimes produce bizarre misattributions. In 1991, a British photographer in his mid-40s known as MR was overcome with feelings of familiarity about people he didn't know. He kept asking his wife whether each new passing stranger was "somebody"—a screen actor, television newsperson, or local celebrity. MR's feelings were so intense that he often could not resist approaching strangers and asking whether they were indeed famous celebrities. When given formal tests, MR recognized the faces of actual celebrities as accurately as did healthy volunteers in the control group. But MR also "recognized" more than 75% of unfamiliar faces, whereas healthy controls hardly ever did. Neurological exams revealed that MR suffered from multiple sclerosis, which had caused damage to his frontal lobes (Ward et al., 1999).

But we are all vulnerable to memory misattribution. Take the following test and there is a good chance that you will experience false recognition for yourself. First study the two lists of words presented in **TABLE 5.1** by reading each word for about 1 second. When you are done, return to the paragraph you were reading for more instructions, but don't look back at the table!

Now, try to recognize which of the following words appeared on the list you just studied: *taste, bread, needle, king, sweet,* and *thread.* If you think that *taste* and *thread* were on the lists you studied, you're right. And if you think that *bread* and *king* weren't on those lists, you're also right. But if you think that *needle* or *sweet* appeared on the lists, you're dead wrong.

Most people make exactly the same mistake, claiming with confidence that they saw *needle* and *sweet* on the list. This occurs because all the words in the lists are associated with *needle* or *sweet.* Seeing each word in the study list activates related words. Because *needle* and *sweet* are related to all of the associates, they become more activated than other words—so highly activated that only minutes later, people swear that they actually studied the words (Deese, 1959; Roediger & McDermott, 1995, 2000). In fact, brain scanning studies using PET and fMRI show that many of the same brain regions are active during false recognition and true recognition, including the hippocampus (Cabeza et al., 2001; Schacter et al., 1996b; Slotnick & Schacter, 2004) (**FIGURE 5.14**). It is possible, however, to reduce or avoid false recognition by presenting distinctive information, such as a picture of *thread,* and encouraging participants to require specific recollections of seeing the picture before they say "yes" on a recognition test (Schacter, Israel, & Racine, 1999). Unfortunately, we do not always demand specific recollections before we say that we encountered a word in an experiment or—more importantly—make a positive identification of a suspect. When people experience a strong sense

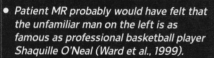

TABLE 5.1

False Recognition

Sour	Honey	Thread	Haystack
Candy	Soda	Pin	Pain
Sugar	Chocolate	Eye	Hurt
Bitter	Heart	Sewing	Injection
Good	Cake	Point	Syringe
Tooth	Tart	Prick	Cloth
Nice	Pie	Thimble	Knitting

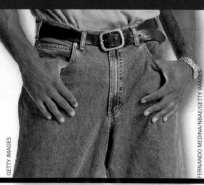

Patient MR probably would have felt that the unfamiliar man on the left is as famous as professional basketball player Shaquille O'Neal (Ward et al., 1999).

GETTY IMAGES

FERNANDO MEDINA/NBAE/GETTY IMAGES

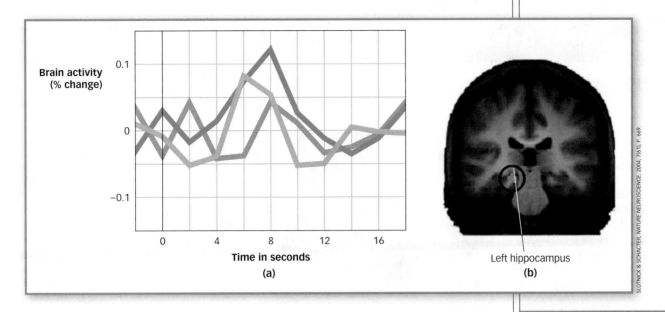

Brain activity
(% change)

0.1

0

−0.1

0   4   8   12   16

Time in seconds

(a)

Left hippocampus

(b)

SLOTNICK & SCHACTER, NATURE NEUROSCIENCE, 2004, 7(61), P. 669.

of familiarity about a person, object, or event but lack specific recollections, a potentially dangerous recipe for memory misattribution is in place. Understanding this point may be a key to reducing the dangerous consequences of misattribution in eyewitness testimony (see the Real World box on the next page).

5. Suggestibility

On October 4, 1992, an El Al cargo plane crashed into an apartment building in a southern suburb of Amsterdam, killing 39 residents and all 4 members of the airline crew. The disaster dominated news in the Netherlands for days as people viewed footage of the crash scene and read about the catastrophe. Ten months later, Dutch psychologists asked a simple question of university students: "Did you see the television film of the moment the plane hit the apartment building?" Fifty-five percent answered "yes." (Crombag et al., 1996). All of

FIGURE 5.14 • • • • • • • • • • • • • • •

Hippocampal Activity during True and False Recognition *Many brain regions show similar activation during true and false recognition, including the hippocampus. The figure shows results from an fMRI study of true and false recognition of visual shapes (Slotnick & Schacter, 2004). (a) A plot showing the activity level in the strength of the fMRI signal from the hippocampus over time. This shows that after a few seconds, there is comparable activation for true recognition of previously studied shapes (red line) and false recognition of similar shapes that were not presented (yellow line). Both true and false recognition show increased hippocampal activity compared with correctly classifying un-related shapes as new (purple line). (b) A region of the left hippocampus.*

In 1992, an El Al cargo plane crashed into an apartment building in a suburb of Amsterdam. When Dutch psychologists asked students if they'd seen the television film of the plane crashing, most said they had. In fact, no such footage exists (Crombag, Wagenaar, & Koppen, 1996).

ALBERT OVERBEEK/AP PHOTO

[THE REAL WORLD] •••

Deadly Misattributions

On July 25, 1984, a 9-year-old girl was found dead in the woods near Baltimore after being brutally beaten and sexually assaulted. A witness identified 23-year-old Kirk Bloodsworth as the killer, based on a sketch police generated from five other witness accounts. Although Bloodsworth passionately maintained his innocence, a jury convicted him of first-degree murder, and the judge sentenced him to death. After Bloodsworth spent 2 years on death row, the sentence was reduced to life in prison on an appeal. In 1993, DNA testing revealed that Bloodsworth was not the source of incriminating semen stains in the victim's underwear. He was released from prison after serving 9 years, later received a full pardon, and returned to his quiet life as a crab fisherman (Chebium, 2000; Connors, Lundregan, Miller, & McEwen, 1997; Wells et al., 1998). The witness's memory misattribution cost Bloodsworth a decade of his life, and his mother did not live to see him freed: She died of a heart attack several months before his release.

Bloodsworth is not alone. The first 40 cases in which DNA evidence led to the release of wrongfully imprisoned individuals revealed that 36 of the convictions—90%—were based partly or entirely on mistaken eyewitness identification (Wells et al., 1998). Fifty separate eyewitnesses were involved in these cases; they were all confident in their memories but seriously mistaken. These statistics are especially troubling because eyewitness testimony is frequently relied on in

TODD DUDEK/AP PHOTO

Kirk Bloodsworth spent 9 years behind bars for a crime he didn't commit. He was released after DNA evidence led to the reversal of his conviction based on mistaken eyewitness testimony. Here he holds up the book that tells his story, by author and attorney Tim Junkin.

the courtroom: Each year more than 75,000 criminal trials are decided on the basis of eyewitness testimony (Ross et al., 1994, p. 918). Common lineup identification practices may often promote misattribution because people are encouraged to rely on general familiarity (Wells et al., 1998, 2000). In standard lineup procedures, witnesses are shown several suspects; after seeing all of them, they attempt to identify the culprit. Under these conditions, witnesses tend to rely on "relative judgments": They choose

the person who, relative to the others in the lineup, looks most like the suspect. The problem is that even when the suspect is *not* in the lineup, witnesses still tend to choose the person who looks most like the suspect. Witnesses rely on general similarities between a face in a lineup and the actual culprit, even when they lack specific recollections of the culprit. There are ways to minimize reliance on relative judgments. For example, witnesses can be asked to make a "thumbs-up or thumbs-down" decision about each suspect immediately after seeing each face instead of waiting until all suspects' faces have been displayed (Wells et al., 1998, 2000). This procedure encourages people to examine their memories more carefully and evaluate whether the pictured suspect matches the details of their recollections.

One encouraging development is that law enforcement officials are listening to what psychologists have to say about the construction of lineups and other identification procedures that could promote inaccurate identification. In early 1998, then attorney general Janet Reno formed a working group of psychologists, police, and attorneys to develop guidelines for collecting eyewitness evidence. This group eventually published a set of guidelines based on rigorous psychological studies that provide law enforcement officials with specific steps to take when questioning witnesses or constructing lineups in order to reduce the likelihood of eyewitness errors (Wells et al., 2000).

---

suggestibility The tendency to incorporate misleading information from external sources into personal recollections.

this might seem perfectly normal except for one key fact: There was no television film of the moment when the plane actually crashed. The researchers had asked a suggestive question that implied that television film of the crash had been shown. Respondents may have viewed television film of the postcrash scene, and they may have read, imagined, or talked about what might have happened when the plane hit the building, but they most definitely did not see it. The suggestive question led participants to misattribute information from these or other sources to a film that did not exist. **Suggestibility** is the *tendency to incorporate misleading information from external sources into personal recollections.*

Research evidence of suggestibility abounds. For example, in one study, Elizabeth Loftus and her colleagues showed participants a videotape of an automobile accident involving a white sports car (Loftus, 1975; Loftus et al., 1978). Some participants were then asked how fast the car was going when it passed the barn. Nearly 20% of these

COURTESY OF ELIZABETH LOFTUS

In a classic experiment by Elizabeth Loftus, people were shown a videotape of a car at a stop sign. Those who later received a misleading suggestion that the car had stopped at a yield sign often claimed they had seen the car at a yield sign (Loftus et al., 1978).

individuals later recalled seeing a barn in the videotape—even though there was no barn (participants who weren't asked about a barn almost never recalled seeing one). In later experiments, Loftus showed that people who received a misleading suggestion that they had earlier seen a car stop at a yield sign (they had actually seen the car at a stop sign) often claimed later to remember seeing a yield sign. Misleading suggestions do not eliminate the original memory (Berkerian & Bowers, 1983; McCloskey & Zaragoza, 1985). Instead, they cause participants to make source memory errors: They have difficulty recollecting whether they actually saw a yield sign or only learned about it later.

Other researchers have also successfully implanted false memories of childhood experiences in a significant minority of participants (Hyman & Billings, 1998; Hyman & Pentland, 1996). In one study, college students were asked about several childhood events that, according to their parents, actually happened. But they were also asked about an event that never happened. For instance, the students were asked if they remembered a wedding reception they attended when they were 5, running around with some other kids and bumping into a table and spilling the punch bowl on the parents of the bride. Students remembered nearly all of the true events and initially reported no memory for the false events. However, with repeated probing, approximately 20% to 40% of the participants in different experimental conditions eventually came to describe some memory of the false event.

People develop false memories in response to suggestions for some of the same reasons memory misattribution occurs. We do not store all the details of our experiences in memory, making us vulnerable to accepting suggestions about what might have happened or should have happened. In addition, visual imagery plays an important role in constructing false memories (Goff & Roediger, 1998). Asking people to imagine an event like spilling punch all over the bride's parents at a wedding increases the likelihood that they will develop a false memory of it (Hyman & Pentland, 1996).

● Why can childhood memories be influenced by suggestion?

Suggestibility played an important role in a controversy that arose during the 1980s and 1990s concerning the accuracy of childhood memories that people recall during psychotherapy. One highly publicized example involved a woman named Diana Halbrooks. After a few months in psychotherapy, she began recalling disturbing incidents from her childhood—for example, that her mother had tried to kill her and that her father had abused her sexually. Although her parents denied that these events had ever occurred, her therapist encouraged her to believe in the reality of her memories. Had Halbrooks retrieved terrible memories of events that had actually occurred, or were the memories inaccurate, perhaps the result of suggestive probing during psychotherapy?

Several kinds of evidence suggest that many recovered memories are inaccurate. First, some people have recovered highly implausible memories of being abused repeatedly during bizarre practices in satanic cults, and yet there is no proof of these practices or even that the cults exist (Pendergrast, 1995; Wright, 1994). Second, a number of the techniques used by psychotherapists to try to pull up forgotten childhood memories are clearly suggestive. A survey of 145 therapists in the United States revealed that approximately 1 in 3 tried to help patients remember childhood sexual abuse by using hypnosis or by encouraging them to imagine incidents that might or might not have actually happened (Poole et al., 1995). Yet research has shown that imagining past events and hypnosis can help create false memories (Garry, Manning, Loftus, & Sherman, 1996; Hyman & Pentland, 1996; McConkey, Barnier, & Sheehan, 1998). Although some recovered memories (especially those that patients remember on their own) are probably accurate, those recovered using techniques such as visualization that are known to create false memories in the lab are probably suspect.

A growing number of patients eventually retracted their recovered memories after leaving therapy or returning to their families (McHugh, Lief, Freyd, & Fetkewicz, 2004). This is just what happened to Diana Halbrooks: She stopped therapy and eventually came to realize that the "memories" she had recovered were inaccurate. By the end of the 1990s, the number of new cases of disputed recovered memories of childhood sexual abuse had slowed to a trickle (McHugh et al., 2004). This probably occurred, at least in part, because some of the therapists who had been using suggestive procedures stopped doing so (McNally, 2003).

6. Bias

In 2000, the outcome of a very close presidential race between George W. Bush and Al Gore was decided by the Supreme Court 5 weeks after the election had taken place.

The day after the election (when the result was still in doubt), supporters of Bush and Gore were asked to predict how happy they would be after the outcome of the election was determined (Wilson, Meyers, & Gilbert, 2003). These same respondents reported how happy they felt with the outcome on the day after Al Gore conceded. And 4 months later, the participants recalled how happy they had been right after the election was decided.

Bush supporters, who eventually enjoyed a positive result (their candidate took office), were understandably happy on the day after the Supreme Court's decision. However, their retrospective accounts *over*estimated how happy they were at the time. Conversely, Gore supporters were not pleased with the outcome. But when polled 4 months after the election was decided, Gore supporters *under*estimated how happy they actually were at the time of the result. In both groups, recollections of happiness were at odds with existing reports of their actual happiness at the time (Wilson et al., 2003).

PAUL J. RICHARDS/AFP/GETTY IMAGES

DOUG MILLS/AP PHOTO

How happy do you think you'd be if the candidate you supported won an election? Do you think you'd accurately remember your level of happiness if you recalled it several months later? Chances are good that bias in the memory process would alter your recollection of your previous happiness. Indeed, 4 months after they heard the outcome of the 2000 presidential election, Bush supporters overestimated how happy they were, while Gore supporters underestimated how happy they were.

These results illustrate the problem of **bias**, which is *the distorting influences of present knowledge, beliefs, and feelings on recollection of previous experiences.* Sometimes what people remember from their pasts says less about what actually happened than about what they think, feel, or believe now.

Researchers have also found that our current moods can bias our recall of past experiences (Bower, 1981; Eich, 1995). So, in addition to helping you recall actual sad memories (as you saw earlier in this chapter), a sad mood can also bias your recollections of experiences that may

● **How does your current outlook color your memory of a past event?**

not have been so sad. *Consistency bias* is the bias to reconstruct the past to fit the present. One researcher asked people in 1973 to rate their attitudes toward a variety of

controversial social issues, including legalization of marijuana, women's rights, and aid to minorities (Marcus, 1986). They were asked to make the same rating again in 1982 and also to indicate what their attitudes had been in 1973. Researchers found that participants' recollections of their 1973 attitudes in 1982 were more closely related to what they believed in 1982 than to what they had actually said in 1973.

Whereas consistency bias exaggerates the similarity between past and present, *change bias* is the tendency to exaggerate differences between what we feel or believe now and what we felt or believed in the past. In other words, change biases also occur. For example, most of us would like to believe that our romantic attachments grow stronger over time. In one study, dating couples were asked, once a year for 4 years, to assess the present quality of their relationships and to recall how they felt in past years (Sprecher, 1999). Couples who stayed together for the 4 years recalled that the strength of their love had increased since they last reported on it. Yet their actual ratings at the time did not show any increases in love and attachment. Objectively, the couples did not love each other more today than yesterday. But they did from the subjective perspective of memory.

A special case of change bias is *egocentric bias,* the tendency to exaggerate the change between present and past in order to make ourselves look good in retrospect. For example, students sometimes remember feeling more anxious before taking an exam than they actually reported at the time (Keuler & Safer, 1998), and blood donors sometimes recall being more nervous about giving blood than they actually were (Breckler, 1994). In both cases, change biases color memory and make people feel that they behaved more bravely or courageously than they actually did. Similarly, when college students tried to remember high school grades and their memories were checked against actual transcripts, they were highly accurate for grades of A (89% correct) and extremely inaccurate for grades of D (29% correct) (Bahrick, Hall, & Berger, 1996). The students were remembering the past as they wanted it to be rather than the way it was.

The way each member of this happy ● ● ● ● ● ● ● ● ● ● ● couple recalls earlier feelings toward the other depends on how each currently views their relationship.

ANDERSEN ROSS/PHOTOLIBRARY

7. Persistence

The artist Melinda Stickney-Gibson awoke in her apartment to the smell of smoke. She jumped out of bed and saw black plumes rising through cracks in the floor. Raging flames had engulfed the entire building, and there was no chance to escape except by jumping from her third-floor window. Shortly after she crashed to the ground, the

bias The distorting influences of present knowledge, beliefs, and feelings on recollection of previous experiences.

BETTMANN/CORBIS

KATHY WILLENS/AP PHOTO

•••••••••• *Some events are so emotionally charged, such as the Kennedy assassination and the terrorist attack on the World Trade Center, that we form unusually detailed memories of when and where we heard about them. These flashbulb memories generally persist much longer than memories for more ordinary events.*

building exploded into a brilliant fireball. Although she survived the fire and the fall, Melinda became overwhelmed by memories of the fire. When she sat down in front of a blank canvas to start a new painting, her memories of that awful night intruded. Her paintings, which were previously bright, colorful abstractions, became dark meditations that included only black, orange, and ochre—the colors of the fire (Schacter, 1996).

Melinda Stickney-Gibson's experiences illustrate memory's seventh and most deadly sin: **persistence**, or *the intrusive recollection of events that we wish we could forget*. Melinda's experience is far from unique: Persistence frequently occurs after disturbing or traumatic incidents, such as the fire that destroyed her home. Although being able to quickly call up memories is usually considered a good thing, in the case of persistence, that ability mutates into a bedeviling mind bug.

● **How does emotional trauma affect memory?**

Intrusive memories are undesirable consequences of the fact that emotional experiences generally lead to more vivid and enduring recollections than nonemotional experiences do. One line of evidence comes from the study of **flashbulb memories**, which are *detailed recollections of when and where we heard about shocking events*. For example, most Americans can recall exactly where they were and how they heard about the September 11, 2001, terrorist attacks on the World Trade Center and the Pentagon— almost as if a mental flashbulb had gone off and recorded the event in long-lasting and vivid detail. Enhanced retention of flashbulb memories is partly attributable to the emotional arousal elicited by events such as the September 11 terrorist attacks. A key player in the brain's response to emotional events is a small almond-shaped structure called the amygdala, shown in **FIGURE 5.15**. The amygdala influences hormonal systems that kick into high gear when we experience an arousing event; these stress-related hormones, such as adrenaline and cortisol, mobilize the body in the face of threat—and they also enhance memory for the experience. Damage to the amygdala does not result in a general memory deficit. Patients with amygdala damage, however, do not remember emotional events any better than nonemotional events (Cahill & McGaugh, 1998).

For example, consider what happened when people viewed a series of photographic slides that began with a mother walking her child to school and later included an emotionally arousing event: the child being hit by a car. When tested later, the research participants remembered the arousing event better than the mundane ones. But patients

persistence The intrusive recollection of events that we wish we could forget.

flashbulb memories Detailed recollections of when and where we heard about shocking events.

with amygdala damage remembered the mundane and emotionally arousing events equally well (Cahill & McGaugh, 1998). PET and fMRI scans show that when healthy people view a slide sequence that includes an emotionally arousing event, the level of activity in their amygdalas at the time they see it is a good predictor of their subsequent memory for the slide. When there is heightened activity in the amygdala as people watch emotional events, there's a better chance that they will recall those events on a later test (Cahill et al., 1996; Kensinger & Schacter, 2005). And when people are given a drug that interferes with the amygdala-mediated release of stress hormones, their memory for the emotional sections is no better than their memory for the mundane sections.

In many cases, there are clear benefits to forming strong memories for highly emotional events—particularly those that are life-threatening. In the case of persistence, though, such memories may be too strong—strong enough to interfere with other aspects of daily life.

Hippocampus

Amygdala

Are the Seven Sins Vices or Virtues?

You may have concluded that evolution burdened us with an extremely inefficient memory system that is so prone to error that it often jeopardizes our well-being. Not so. The seven sins are the price we pay for the many benefits that memory provides (Schacter, 2001b). These mind bugs are the occasional result of the normally efficient operation of the human memory system.

Consider the seemingly buggy nature of transience, for example. Wouldn't it be great to remember all the details of every incident in your life, no matter how much time had passed? Not necessarily. It is helpful and sometimes important to forget information that isn't current, like an old phone number. If we didn't gradually forget information over time, our minds would be cluttered with details that we no longer need (Bjork & Bjork, 1988). Information that is used infrequently is less likely to be needed in the future than information that is used more frequently over the same period (Anderson & Schooler, 1991, 2000). Memory, in essence, makes a bet that when we haven't used information recently, we probably won't need it in the future. We win this bet more often than we lose it, making transience an adaptive property of memory. But we are acutely aware of the losses—the frustrations of forgetting—and are never aware of the wins. This is why people are often quick to complain about their memories: The drawbacks of forgetting are painfully evident, but the benefits of forgetting are hidden.

● **How are we better off with imperfect memories?**

Similarly, absentmindedness and blocking can be frustrating, but they are side effects of our memory's (usually successful) attempt to sort through incoming information, preserving details that are worthy of attention and recall, and discard those that are less worthy.

Memory misattribution and suggestibility both occur because we often fail to recall the details of exactly when and where we saw a face or learned a fact. This is because memory is adapted to retain information that is most likely to be needed in the environment in which it operates. We seldom need to remember all the precise contextual details of every experience. Our memories carefully record such details only when we think they may be needed later, and most of the time we are better off for it. Bias skews our memories so that we depict ourselves in an overly favorable light—but it can produce the benefit of contributing to our overall sense of contentment. Holding positive illusions about ourselves can lead to greater psychological well-being (Taylor, 1989). Although persistence can cause us to be haunted by traumas that we'd be better off forgetting, overall, it is probably adaptive to remember threatening or traumatic events that could pose a threat to survival.

Although each of the seven sins can cause trouble in our lives, they have an adaptive side as well. You can think of the seven sins as costs we pay for benefits that allow memory to work as well as it does most of the time.

summary quiz [5.5]

15. If you carry out the same activities at work each day, by the time Friday comes, it may be difficult to recall what you did on Monday, because late-week activities blend in with early-week ones. This illustrates
    a. retroactive interference.
    b. proactive interference.
    c. blocking.
    d. memory misattribution.

16. When trying to recall the name of a book you read last summer, you feel that the answer is "right on the tip of your tongue." This is a classic example of
    a. retroactive interference.
    b. proactive interference.
    c. blocking.
    d. memory misattribution.

17. In 1992, a cargo plane crashed into an apartment building near Amsterdam. When Dutch psychologists asked students if they'd seen the television film of the plane crashing, most said they did. In fact, no such film exists. This illustrates a memory failure called
    a. memory misattribution.
    b. suggestibility.
    c. bias.
    d. persistence.

18. Students sometimes remember feeling more anxious before taking an exam than they actually reported at the time. This illustrates the memory failure called
    a. consistency bias.
    b. persistence.
    c. memory misattribution.
    d. egocentric bias.

The Mystery of Childhood Amnesia

As you have seen, transience is a pervasive characteristic of memory. Nonetheless, you can easily recall many experiences from different times in your life, such as last summer's job or vacation, the sights and sounds of a favorite concert, or the most exciting sporting event you've ever attended. But there is one period of time from which you likely have few or no memories: the first few years of your life. This lack of memory for our early years is called *childhood amnesia or infantile amnesia.*

In the 1930s and 1940s, psychologists carried out systematic studies in which they asked large samples of individuals to report their earliest memories with the dates when they occurred. These studies revealed that, on average, an individual's earliest memory dates to about $3\frac{1}{2}$ years of age (Dudycha & Dudycha, 1933; Waldfogel, 1948). Later studies suggested that women report slightly earlier first memories (3.07 years of age) than men (3.4 years) (Howes, Siegel, & Brown, 1993). In one study, researchers asked individuals between 4 and 20 years old to recall as much as they could about a specific event: the birth of a younger sibling (Sheingold & Tenney, 1982). Participants who were at least 3 years old at the time of the birth remembered it in considerable detail, whereas participants who were younger than 3 years old at the time of the birth remembered little or nothing. A more recent study found that individuals can recall events surrounding the birth of a sibling that occurred when they were about 2.4 years old; some people even showed evidence of recall from ages 2.0 to 2.4 years, although these memories were very sketchy (Eacott & Crawley, 1998).

But such studies must be interpreted with caution. Memories of early events may be based on family conversations that took place long after the events occurred. An adult or a child who remembers having ice cream in the hospital as a 3-year-old when his baby sister was born may be recalling what his parents told him after the event. Consistent with this idea, cross-cultural studies have turned up an interesting finding. Individuals from cultures that emphasize talking about the past, such as North American culture, tend to report earlier first memories than individuals from cultures that place less emphasis on talking about the past, such as Korean and other Asian cultures (MacDonald, Uesilana, & Hayne, 2000; Mullen, 1994).

Recent research has examined whether the events that people say they remember from early childhood really are *personal recollections,* which involve conscious re-experiencing of some aspect of the event, or whether people *just know* about these events (perhaps from family photos and discussions), even though they don't truly possess personal recollections (Multhaup, Johnson, & Tetirick, 2005). Several experiments revealed that personal recollections tend to emerge later than memories based on "just knowing," with the transition from mostly "know" memories to mostly "recollect" memories occurring at 4.7 years.

Some events in your personal history are personal recollections. In other words, you actually remember the occurrence of the event.

Other events from your past are ones that you know happened but are not personal recollections. Instead, your knowledge of the event is based on an external source of information, perhaps your parents and/or other family members, friends, pictures, photo albums, diaries, or family stories. To find out about your own "recollected" versus "known" memories, complete the items listed here from the 2005 study by Multhaup et al.

Instructions	Event	Recollect	Know	Age	Don't Know
Please label each of the events listed as a personal "recollection" or as an event that you "know" happened but that is not a personal memory. If you neither "recollect" nor "know" the event (perhaps because you never experienced it), please label it as "don't know." For each event you "recollect" or "know," indicate your age at the time the event occurred, as best you can determine, with the year followed by month (e.g., 4.0 is 4 years old exactly, 4.6 is $4\frac{1}{2}$ years old, 4.9 is $4\frac{3}{4}$, and so forth).	You read your first book with chapters.	❏	❏	❏	❏
	You went to your first sleepover.	❏	❏	❏	❏
	You saw your first movie in a movie theater.	❏	❏	❏	❏
	You took your first swimming lesson.	❏	❏	❏	❏
	You joined your first organized sports team.	❏	❏	❏	❏
	You learned to write in cursive.	❏	❏	❏	❏
	You stopped taking naps.	❏	❏	❏	❏
	You learned to spell your name.	❏	❏	❏	❏
	You went to an amusement park for the first time.	❏	❏	❏	❏
	You were toilet trained.	❏	❏	❏	❏
	Your first permanent tooth came in.	❏	❏	❏	❏
	You learned to ride a bicycle (two wheels, no training wheels).	❏	❏	❏	❏
	You slept in a bed instead of a crib.	❏	❏	❏	❏

(Items are sampled from experiments 1 and 2 of Multhaup et al., 2005, p. 172.)

CHAPTER REVIEW

Summary

Encoding: Transforming Perceptions into Memories

- Encoding is the process of transforming information into a lasting memory.

- Most instances of spectacular memory performance reflect skillful use of encoding strategies, rather than so-called photographic memory.

- Elaborative encoding, visual imagery encoding, and organizational encoding are all strategies that increase memory and use different parts of the brain.

Storage: Maintaining Memories over Time

- There are several types of memory storage: sensory memory, which holds information for a second or two; short-term or working memory, which holds information for about 15 to 20 seconds; and long-term memory, which stores information from minutes to years or decades.

- The hippocampus and nearby structures play an important role in long-term memory storage, as shown by patients such as HM.

- Memory storage depends on changes in synapses, and long-term potentiation (LTP) increases synaptic connections.

Retrieval: Bringing Memories to Mind

- Retrieval cues, which help reinstate how information was encoded, can help trigger successful recall of that information.

- External contexts, as well as moods and inner states, can serve as retrieval cues.

- Retrieval can be separated into the effort we make while trying to remember (which may involve the right frontal lobe of the brain) and the successful recovery of stored information (which may involve the hippocampus and also cortical areas related to sensory aspects of the material being recalled).

Multiple Forms of Memory: How the Past Returns

- Long-term memory includes explicit memory (which can be consciously recalled) and implicit memory (the unconscious influences of past experiences on later behavior).

- Two examples of implicit memory are procedural memory, the acquisition of skills as a result of practice, and priming, a change in the ability to recognize information as the result of past exposure to that information.

- Patients with amnesia retain implicit memory, including procedural memory and priming, but lack explicit memory.

- Two subclasses of explicit memory are episodic memory, the collection of personal experiences from a particular time and place, and semantic memory, a network of general, impersonal knowledge of facts and concepts.

Memory Failures: The Seven Sins of Memory

- Memory's mind bugs can be classified into "seven sins."

- Some of these "sins" reflect failure to retrieve information we want: Transience refers to decay of memory over time; absentmindedness can reflect failures of attention and is often associated with forgetting to do things in the future; blocking occurs when stored information is temporarily inaccessible (such as tip-of-the-tongue experiences). In contrast, persistence is the intrusive recollection of events we wish we could forget.

- Other "sins" reflect errors in memory content. Memory misattribution involves mistaken recollection of the specifics of where and when an event occurred; suggestibility is the tendency to incorporate misleading information from external sources into personal recollection; bias reflects the influence of current knowledge, beliefs, and feelings on memory.

Key Terms

memory (p. 128)

encoding (p. 128)

storage (p. 128)

retrieval (p. 128)

elaborative encoding (p. 129)

visual imagery encoding (p. 131)

organizational encoding (p. 131)

memory storage (p. 133)

sensory memory store (p. 133)

iconic memory (p. 133)

echoic memory (p. 133)

short-term memory store (p. 133)

rehearsal (p. 134)

chunking (p. 134)

working memory (p. 134)

long-term memory store (p. 134)

anterograde amnesia (p. 135)

retrograde amnesia (p. 135)

long-term potentiation (LTP) (p. 136)

retrieval cue (p. 137)

encoding specificity principle (p. 138)

state-dependent retrieval (p. 138)

transfer-appropriate processing (p. 138)

explicit memory (p. 140)

implicit memory (p. 140)

procedural memory (p. 140)

priming (p. 141)

semantic memory (p. 142)

episodic memory (p. 142)

transience (p. 143)

retroactive interference (p. 144)

proactive interference (p. 145)

absentmindedness (p. 145)

prospective memory (p. 145)

blocking (p. 146)

memory misattribution (p. 147)

source memory (p. 147)

suggestibility (p. 150)

bias (p. 153)

persistence (p. 154)

flashbulb memories (p. 154)

Critical Thinking Questions

1. Elaborative encoding involves actively relating new information to facts you already know; visual imagery encoding involves storing new information by converting it into mental pictures.

   How might you use both kinds of encoding to help store a new fact, such as the date of a friend's birthday that falls on, say, November 1?

2. Retrieval cues are "hints" that help bring stored information to mind. How does this explain the fact that most students prefer multiple-choice exams to fill-in-the-blank exams?

3. Transience, absentmindedness, and blocking are three of the seven "sins" of memory, and they deal with ways that memories can be temporarily or permanently lost.

   Suppose that, mentally consumed by planning for a psychology test the next day, you place your keys in an unusual spot and later forget where you put them. Is this more likely to reflect the memory "sin" of transience, absentmindedness, or blocking?

4. Misattribution, suggestibility, and bias are three memory "sins" that involve memories that are not forgotten but distorted.

   When researchers ask romantically involved couples to rate their relationships and then ask again 2 months later, those couples whose relationships have since soured tend to recall their initial ratings as more negative than they really were. Is this more likely to reflect the memory "sin" of misattribution, suggestibility, or bias?

Answers to Summary Quizzes

Summary Quiz 5.1
1. c; 2. a; 3. b; 4. d

Summary Quiz 5.2
5. b; 6. c; 7. a; 8. d

Summary Quiz 5.3
9. a; 10. c; 11. b

Summary Quiz 5.4
12. b; 13. c; 14. a

Summary Quiz 5.5
15. a; 16. c; 17. b; 18. d

Need more help? Additional resources are located at the book's free companion Web site at:
www.worthpublishers.com/schacterbrief1e

CHAPTER SIX

Learning

ADAM AND TERI'S DAUGHTER, CARLY, celebrated her first birthday on September 11, 2001. The family happened to be living in Boston at the time, and they awoke that morning full of anticipation for a fun-filled day of birthday celebration.

What they got instead was a phone call from a friend in Texas, urging them to turn on the local news. Like many Americans, Adam and Teri watched with sadness and horror as terrorist attacks in New York, Pennsylvania, and the nation's capital took place before their eyes. American Airlines Flight 11, which crashed into the North Tower of the World Trade Center, had originated from Boston that morning, heightening the sense of uncertainty and anxiety that already had begun to define the day. Adam and Teri watched in shock as United Airlines Flight 175 crashed into the South Tower on live television. As the news reports filtered in throughout the day, each more disturbing than the last, the couple could scarcely avert their eyes from the television, and they ended up having CNN on all day long.

Yet through it all, young Carly played with her presents, blissfully unaware of the events unfolding on the TV screen. One gift, a small yellow soccer goal, turned out to be a favorite. When the ball hit the back of the net, it triggered a voice that yelled, "Goooooaaaallll!" and then played one of several songs at random. Carly loved to hear the music, and she would repeatedly whack the toy to make it play a song. In a surreal scene, fire, turmoil, and carnage were set to the strains of "John Jacob Jingleheimer Schmidt."

And that's what makes this a story about learning.

Quite a curious thing happened. As the weeks turned to months and 2001 turned to 2002, the immediate emotional impact of 9/11 faded for Adam. Carly grew and developed, and she continued to love playing with her soccer goal. Each time it played a song, though, Adam felt a chill run through his body and saw images of burning buildings in his mind's eye. It was as though John Jacob Jingleheimer Schmidt was a madman bent on bedeviling his life. Carly is much older now, and her baby toys have been put up on a shelf. But just the sight of that little yellow goal can still bring back a flood of sad memories

SEAN LOCKE/ISTOCKPHOTO

and call up a welter of unpleasant emotions for her parents.

What's at work here is a type of learning based on association. Adam and Teri came to associate a unique historical tragedy and a child's toy, and as a result, either of the two stimuli produced certain mental and emotional reactions. The fear and sadness that were triggered by watching the events of 9/11 came to be triggered by an innocuous plaything, and it was an effect that lasted for years. In this chapter, we'll consider this type of learning as well as other ways that knowledge is acquired and stored. ■

● As baby Carly played with her new soccer goal, television images showed the horrifying events of September 11, 2001. Carly's parents, Adam and Teri, learned an association that lasted for years between the baby's toy and the 9/11 events.

Defining Learning: Experience That Causes a Permanent Change

Learning is shorthand for a collection of different techniques, procedures, and outcomes that produce changes in an organism's behavior. Learning psychologists have identified and studied as many as 40 different kinds of learning. However, there is a basic principle at the core of all of them. **Learning** involves *some experience that results in a relatively permanent change in the state of the learner.* This definition emphasizes several key ideas: Learning is based on experience; learning produces changes in the organism; and these changes are relatively permanent. Think back to Adam and Teri's experiences on September 11, 2001—seeing the horrors of 9/11 unfold on their TV screen and hearing Carly's toy changed their response to what had been a harmless child's toy. Furthermore, the association they learned lasted for years.

Learning can be conscious and deliberate or unconscious. For example, memorizing the names of all the U.S. presidents is a conscious and deliberate activity, with an explicit awareness of the learning process as it is taking place. In comparison, the kind of learning that associated Carly's toy with images of horror is much more implicit. Adam and Teri certainly weren't aware of or consciously focused on learning as it was taking place. Some other forms of learning start out explicitly but become more implicit over time. When you first learned to drive a car, for example, you probably devoted a lot of attention to the many movements and sequences that needed to be carried out simultaneously ("Step lightly on the accelerator while you push the turn indicator, and look in the rearview mirror while you turn the steering wheel"). That complex interplay of motions is now probably quite effortless and automatic for you. Explicit learning has become implicit over time.

● **How are learning and memory linked?**

These distinctions in learning might remind you of similar distinctions in memory and for good reason. In Chapter 5, you read about the differences between *implicit* and *explicit* memories as well as *procedural*, *semantic*, and *episodic* memories. Do different forms of learning mirror different types of memory? It's not that simple, but it is true that learning and memory are inextricably linked. Learning produces memories; and conversely, the existence of memories implies that knowledge was acquired, that experience was registered and recorded in the brain, or that learning has taken place.

The Case of Habituation

If you've ever lived under the flight path of your local airport, near railroad tracks, or by a busy highway, you probably noticed the loud noises when you first moved in. You probably also noticed that after a while, the roar wasn't quite so deafening anymore and

learning Some experience that results in a relatively permanent change in the state of the learner.

habituation A general process in which repeated or prolonged exposure to a stimulus results in a gradual reduction in responding.

that eventually you ignored the sounds of the planes, trains, or automobiles in your vicinity.

Habituation is *a general process in which repeated or prolonged exposure to a stimulus results in a gradual reduction in responding.* For example, a car that backfires unexpectedly as you walk by will produce a startle response: You'll jump back; your eyes will widen; your muscles will tense; and your body will experience an increase in sweating, blood pressure, and alertness. If another car were to backfire a block later, you might show another startle response, but it would be less dramatic and subside more quickly. If a third backfire should occur, you would likely not respond at all. You would have become *habituated* to the sound of a car backfiring.

● **Why won't the noise from a highway near your home keep you awake at night?**

Habituation is a simple form of learning. An experience results in a change in the state of the learner: In the preceding example, you begin by reacting one way to a stimulus and, with experience, your reactions change. However, this kind of change usually isn't permanent. In most cases of habituation, a person will exhibit the original reaction if enough time has gone by. Thus, when you return home from a 2-week vacation, the roar of the jets passing over your home will probably sound just as loud as ever.

Learning and Behaviorism

As you'll recall from Chapter 1, a sizable chunk of psychology's history was devoted to a single dominant viewpoint. Behaviorism, with its insistence on measuring only observable, quantifiable behavior and its dismissal of mental activity as irrelevant and unknowable, was the major outlook of most psychologists working from the 1930s through the 1950s. This was also the period during which most of the fundamental work on learning theory took place. Most behaviorists argued that the "permanent change in experience" that resulted from learning could be demonstrated equally well in almost any organism: rats, dogs, pigeons, mice, pigs, or humans. From this perspective, behaviorists viewed learning as a purely behavioral, eminently observable activity that did not necessitate any mental activity.

As you'll see shortly, in many ways the behaviorists were right. Much of what we know about how organisms learn comes directly from the behaviorists' observations of behaviors. However, the behaviorists also overstated their case. Some important cognitive considerations—that is, elements of mental activity—need to be addressed in order to understand the learning process.

Living near a busy highway can be ● ● ● ● ● ● ● ● ● ● unpleasant. Most people who live near major highways become habituated to the sound of traffic.

MICHAEL KLINEC/ALAMY

summary quiz [6.1]

1. _____ is defined as an experience that results in a relatively permanent change in an organism's behavior.
   - a. Behaviorism
   - b. Learning
   - c. Habituation
   - d. Acquisition

2. Andi lives near the flight path of a large airport. At first, she was keenly aware of the loud roar of jets on the runway, but eventually, she no longer noticed the sound. This illustrates
   - a. habituation.
   - b. classical conditioning.
   - c. operant learning.
   - d. biological preparedness.

3. Most behaviorists in the mid-20th century argued that
   - a. elements of cognitive activity are involved in human learning.
   - b. habituation is not necessary for learning to occur.
   - c. all learning is an observable activity.
   - d. nonhuman animals learn in a fundamentally different way than humans.

Classical Conditioning: One Thing Leads to Another

You'll recall from Chapter 1 that the early behaviorists were greatly influenced by the work of Russian physiologist Ivan Pavlov, who had revealed the mechanics of one form of learning, which came to be called classical conditioning. **Classical conditioning** occurs *when a neutral stimulus evokes a response after being paired with a stimulus that naturally evokes a response.* In his classic experiments, Pavlov showed that dogs learned to salivate to neutral stimuli such as a bell or a tone after that stimulus had been associated with another stimulus that naturally evokes salivation, such as food.

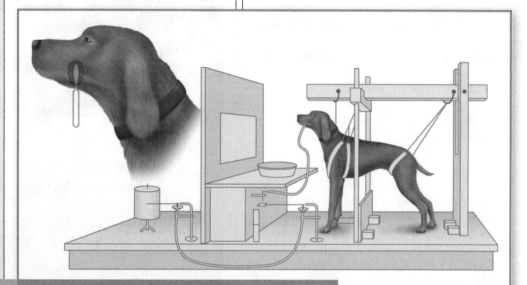

● **FIGURE 6.1**
Pavlov's Apparatus for Studying Classical Conditioning
Pavlov presented auditory stimuli to the animals using a bell or a tuning fork. Visual stimuli could be presented on the screen. The inset shows a close-up of the tube inserted in the dog's salivary gland for collecting saliva.

Pavlov's Experiments on Classical Conditioning

Pavlov's basic experimental setup involved cradling dogs in a harness to administer various kinds foods and to measure the salivary response to each, as shown in **FIGURE 6.1**. He noticed that dogs that previously had been in the experiment began to produce a kind of "anticipatory" salivary response as soon as they were put in the harness, before any food was presented. Pavlov and his colleagues regarded these responses as annoyances at first because they interfered with collecting naturally occurring salivary secretions. In reality, the dogs were exhibiting classical conditioning.

When the dogs were initially presented with a plate of food, they began to salivate. No surprise here—placing food in front of most animals will launch the salivary process. Pavlov called the presentation of food an **unconditioned stimulus (US)**, or *something that reliably produces a naturally occurring reaction in an organism.* He called the dogs' salivation an **unconditioned response (UR)**, or *a reflexive reaction that is reliably elicited by an unconditioned stimulus.*

Pavlov soon discovered that he could make the dogs salivate to stimuli that don't usually make animals salivate. In various experiments, Pavlov paired the presentation of food with the sound of a buzzer, the ticking of a metronome, the humming of a tuning fork, or the flash of a light (Pavlov, 1927). Sure enough, he found that the dogs salivated to the sound of a buzzer, the ticking of a metronome, the humming of a tuning fork, or the flash of a light, each of which had become a **conditioned stimulus (CS)**, or *a stimulus that is initially neutral and produces no reliable response in an organism* (see **FIGURE 6.2** on page 165). When dogs hear the sound of a buzzer in the wild, they're not known to salivate. However, when the buzzer (CS) is paired over time with the food (US), the animal will learn to associate food with the sound, and eventually the CS is sufficient to produce a response, or salivation. This response resembles the UR, but Pavlov called it the **conditioned response (CR)**, or *a reaction that resembles an unconditioned response but is produced by a conditioned stimulus.* As you can imagine, a range of stimuli might be used as a CS, and as we noted earlier, several different stimuli became the CS in Pavlov's experiment.

● **Why do some dogs seem to know when it's dinner time?**

Let's apply these four basic elements of the classical conditioning process—the US, UR, CS, and CR—to a real-world example. Consider your own dog (or cat). You probably

classical conditioning When a neutral stimulus evokes a response after being paired with a stimulus that naturally evokes a response.

unconditioned stimulus (US) Something that reliably produces a naturally occurring reaction in an organism.

unconditioned response (UR) A reflexive reaction that is reliably elicited by an unconditioned stimulus.

conditioned stimulus (CS) A stimulus that is initially neutral and produces no reliable response in an organism.

conditioned response (CR) A reaction that resembles an unconditioned response but is produced by a conditioned stimulus.

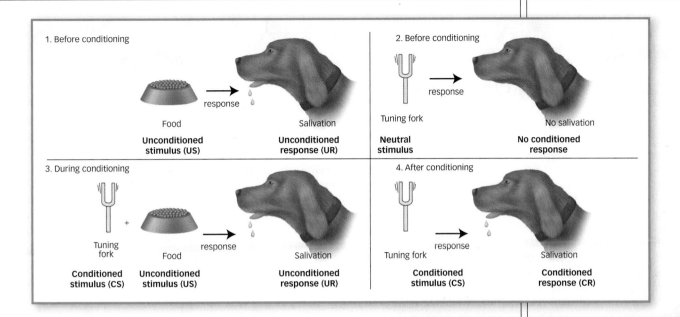

1. Before conditioning

Food
Unconditioned stimulus (US)

response

Salivation
Unconditioned response (UR)

2. Before conditioning

Tuning fork
Neutral stimulus

response

No salivation
No conditioned response

3. During conditioning

Tuning fork
Conditioned stimulus (CS)
+
Food
Unconditioned stimulus (US)

response

Salivation
Unconditioned response (UR)

4. After conditioning

Tuning fork
Conditioned stimulus (CS)

response

Salivation
Conditioned response (CR)

FIGURE 6.2 •
The Elements of Classical Conditioning *In classical conditioning, a previously neutral stimulus (e.g., the sound of a tuning fork) is paired with an unconditioned stimulus (e.g., the presentation of food). After several trials associating the two, the conditioned stimulus (the sound) alone can produce a conditioned response*

think you have the only dog that can tell time because she always knows when dinner's coming and gets ready to eat. Sorry to burst your bubble, but your dog is no clock-watching wonder hound. Instead, the presentation of food (the US) has become associated with a complex CS—your getting up, moving into the kitchen, opening the cabinet, working the can opener—such that the CS alone signals to your dog that food is on the way and therefore initiates the CR of her getting ready to eat.

As another example, think back to Adam and Teri's experiences on September 11, 2001. As they watched the World Trade Center collapsing on television, they felt sadness, fear, and anxiety. The images of devastation and horror were the US, and the negative feelings those images caused were the UR. However, Carly's soccer goal acted as the CS. The toy—and especially the songs it played—was an initially neutral stimulus that was associated with the US that day. As the horrific images flashed across the screen, "John Jacob Jingleheimer Schmidt" provided an endless sound track. Eventually the CS all by itself—the music played by the toy—was sufficient to produce the CR: feelings of sadness, fear, and anxiety.

When Pavlov's findings first appeared in the scientific and popular literature (Pavlov, 1923a, 1923b), they produced a flurry of excitement because psychologists now had demonstrable evidence of how conditioning produced learned behaviors. This was the kind of psychology that Watson and the behaviorists were proposing: An organism experiences events or stimuli that are observable and measurable, and changes in that organism can be directly observed and measured. Dogs learned to salivate to the sound of a buzzer, and there was no need to resort to explanations about why it had happened, what the dog wanted, or how the animal thought about the situation. In other words, there was no need to consider the mind in this classical conditioning paradigm, which appealed to Watson and the behaviorists. Pavlov also appreciated the significance of his discovery and embarked on a systematic investigation of the mechanisms of classical conditioning. (The Real World box on the next page shows how Pavlov's ideas help explain how drug overdoses occur.)

"I THINK MOM'S USING THE CAN OPENER."

Understanding Drug Overdoses

All too often, police are confronted with a perplexing problem: the sudden death of addicts from a drug overdose. These deaths are puzzling for at least three reasons: The victims are often experienced drug users, the dose taken is usually not larger than what they usually take, and the deaths tend to occur in unusual settings. Experienced drug users are just that: experienced! You'd think that if a heroin addict or crack cocaine user were ingesting a typical amount of a substance he or she had used many times before, the chances of an overdose would be *lower* than usual.

Classical conditioning provides some insight into how these deaths occur. First, when classical conditioning takes place, the CS is more than a simple bell or tone: It also includes the overall *context* within which the conditioning takes place. Indeed, Pavlov's dogs often began to salivate even as they approached the experimental apparatus. Second, many CRs are compensatory reactions to the US. In some of Pavlov's early experiments, he used a very mild acid solution as the US because it produces large amounts of saliva that dilute the acid in the dog's mouth. When that salivary response is eventually conditioned to the sound of a tone, in a way it represents the remnants of the body's natural reaction to the presentation of the US.

These two finer points of classical conditioning help explain what happens when someone takes a drug such as heroin (Siegel, 1984). When the drug is injected, the entire setting (the drug paraphernalia, the room, the lighting, the addict's usual companions) functions as the CS, and the addict's brain reacts to the heroin by secreting neurotransmitters that counteract its effects. Over time, this protective physiological response becomes part of the CR, and like all CRs, it occurs in the presence of the CS but prior to the actual administration of the drug. These compensatory physiological reactions are also what make drug abusers take increasingly larger doses to achieve the same effect; ultimately, these reactions produce *drug tolerance*, discussed in Chapter 8.

Based on these principles of classical conditioning, taking drugs in a new environment can be fatal for a longtime drug user. If an addict injects the usual dose in a setting that is sufficiently novel or where heroin has never been taken before, the CS is now altered. What's more, the physiological compensatory CR either does not occur or is substantially decreased. As a result, the addict's usual dose becomes an overdose, and death often results. This effect has also been shown experimentally: Rats that have had extensive experience with morphine in one setting were much more likely to survive dose increases in that same setting than in a novel one (Siegel, 1976).

The basic principles of classical conditioning help explain this real-world tragedy of drug overdose. Intuitively, addicts may stick with the crack houses, opium dens, or "shooting galleries" with which they're familiar for just this reason.

AP PHOTO/CHRIS GARDNER

Although opium dens and crack houses may be considered blight, it is often safer for addicts to use drugs there. The environment becomes part of the addict's CS, so ironically, busting crack houses may contribute to more deaths from drug overdose when addicts are pushed to use drugs in new situations.

---

acquisition The phase of classical conditioning when the CS and the US are presented together.

extinction The gradual elimination of a learned response that occurs when the US is no longer presented.

spontaneous recovery The tendency of a learned behavior to recover from extinction after a rest period.

generalization A process in which the CR is observed even though the CS is slightly different from the original one used during acquisition.

The Basic Principles of Classical Conditioning

Classical conditioning requires some period of association between the CS and US. This period is called **acquisition**, or *the phase of classical conditioning when the CS and the US are presented together*. During the initial phase of classical conditioning, typically there is a gradual increase in learning: It starts low, rises rapidly, and then slowly tapers off, as shown on the left side of **FIGURE 6.3** (on page 167). Pavlov's dogs gradually increased their amount of salivation over several trials of pairing a tone with the presentation of food, and similarly, your dog eventually learned to associate your kitchen preparations with the subsequent appearance of food. After learning has been established, the CS by itself will reliably elicit the CR.

After Pavlov and his colleagues had explored the process of acquisition extensively, they turned to the next logical question: What would happen if they continued to present

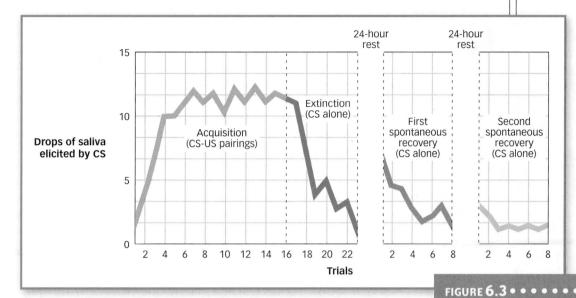

FIGURE 6.3 •
Acquisition, Extinction, and Spontaneous Recovery
In classical conditioning, the CS is originally neutral and produces no specific response. After several trials pairing the CS with the US, the CS alone comes to elicit the salivary response (the CR). Learning tends to take place fairly rapidly and then levels off as stable responding develops. In extinction, the CR diminishes quickly until it no longer occurs. A rest period, however, is typically followed by spontaneous recovery of the CR. In fact, a well-learned CR may show spontaneous recovery after more than one rest.

the CS (buzzer) but stopped presenting the US (food)? The result is just as you might imagine: As shown on the right side of the first panel in **FIGURE 6.3** (above), behavior declines abruptly and continues to drop until eventually the dog ceases to salivate to the sound of the buzzer. This process is called **extinction**, *the gradual elimination of a learned response that occurs when the CS is presented but no longer paired with the US.* Similarly, if you make noises in the kitchen without subsequently presenting a meaty plate of Alpo, eventually your dog will stop salivating or even getting aroused every time you walk into the kitchen.

Having established that he could produce learning through conditioning and then extinguish it, Pavlov wondered if this elimination of conditioned behavior was perma-

● **How does conditioned behavior change when the unconditioned stimulus is removed?**

nent. Is a single session of extinction sufficient to knock out the CR completely, or is there some residual change in the dog's behavior so that the CR might reappear?

To explore this question, Pavlov extinguished the classically conditioned salivation response and then allowed the dogs to have a short rest period. When they were brought back to the lab and presented with the CS again, they displayed **spontaneous recovery**, *the tendency of a learned behavior to recover from extinction after a rest period.* This phenomenon is shown in the middle panel in **FIGURE 6.3**. Notice that this recovery takes place even though there have not been any additional associations between the CS and US. Some spontaneous recovery of the conditioned response even takes place in what is essentially a second extinction session after another period of rest (see the right-hand panel in **FIGURE 6.3**). Clearly, extinction had not completely wiped out the learning that had been acquired. The ability of the CS to elicit the CR was weakened, but it was not eliminated. In fact, if the CS-US pairings are introduced again, the animal will show rapid conditioning, much more rapid than during the initial acquisition phase. This effect is known as *savings*, since it suggests that some underlying neural changes that occurred during the initial learning are "saved" no matter how many extinction trials are conducted, and it is a good illustration of the permanence of some kinds of learning.

Another important principle governing classical conditioning is **generalization**, in which *the CR is observed even though the CS is slightly different from the original one used during acquisition.* Suppose you decide to break down and buy a new can opener, replacing the crummy one that you've had for years. Let's say the new one makes a slightly different sound. Do you think your dog will be stumped,

Some people desire money as an end in itself to the extent that they will put others' welfare at risk in order to accumulate vast amounts of cash. Disgraced financier Bernard Madoff was sentenced to 150 years in prison after being convicted for defrauding hundreds of investors out of billions of dollars in order to create a vast fortune for himself. Individuals such as Madoff may be showing the effects of second-order conditioning.

unable to anticipate the presentation of her food? Will a whole new round of conditioning need to be established with this modified CS?

Probably not. It wouldn't be very adaptive for an organism if each little change in the CS-US pairing required an extensive regimen of new learning. Rather, your dog's conditioning to the sound of the old can opener will probably generalize to the sound of the new one. As you might expect, the more the new stimulus changes, the less conditioned responding is observed. If you replaced a hand-held can opener with an electric can opener, your dog would probably show a much weaker conditioned response (Pearce, 1987; Rescorla, 2006).

Some generalization studies used a 1,000-hertz (Hz) tone as the CS during the acquisition phase. The test stimuli used were tones of higher or lower pitches. As you might expect, an animal gives the maximum response to the original stimulus of 1,000 Hz, with a systematic drop-off as the pitch of the replacement stimulus is farther away from the original tone of 1,000 Hz regardless of whether the tone was higher or lower. Interestingly, when the stimulus is one of the octaves of the original stimulus (octaves in music are tones that are direct multiples of each other), either 500 Hz or 2,000 Hz, there is a slight increase in responding. In these cases, the rate of responding is lower than that of the original CS but higher than it is in other cases of dissimilar tones. The animals clearly show that they detect octaves just like we do, and in this case, responding has generalized to those octaves (see **FIGURE 6.4**, below).

● **How can changing can openers affect a conditioned dog's response?**

When an organism generalizes to a new stimulus, two things are happening. First, by responding to the new stimulus used during generalization testing, the organism demonstrates that it recognizes the similarity between the original CS and the new stimulus. Second, by displaying *diminished* responding to that new stimulus, it also tells us that it notices a difference between the two stimuli. In the second case, the organism shows **discrimination**, or *the capacity to distinguish between similar but distinct stimuli.*

Here's a true story about a talented golden retriever named Splash. Splash was very well trained to perform a number of behaviors when his name was called, as in "Go, Splash," to fetch a ball. The sound of his name was the CS, and running after a target was the US. Repeated attempts to trick him, by yelling, "Go, Splat!" or, "Go, Crash!" or even, "Go, Spla!" resulted in predictable outcomes. Splash would start to move, but then hesitate, showing that he discriminated between the appropriate stimulus ("Splash!") and the substituted ones ("Splat!").

Conceptually, generalization and discrimination are two sides of the same coin. The more organisms show one, the less they show the other, and training can modify the balance between the two.

•••••••••••••••••••••••••••• **FIGURE 6.4**

Stimulus Generalization *In this experiment, an animal was conditioned using a 1,000-Hz tone (the CS) and tested with a variety of tones of higher and lower pitches. As the pitches move farther away from the original CS, the strength of the CR drops off systematically. However, when the tone is an octave of the original (i.e., either 500 or 2,000 Hz), there is an increase in the CR.*

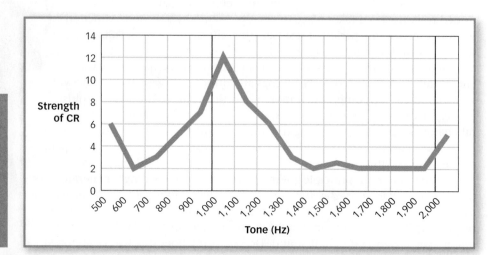

Conditioned Emotional Responses: The Case of Little Albert

Before you conclude that classical conditioning is merely a sophisticated way to train your dog, let's revisit the larger principles of Pavlov's work. Classical conditioning demonstrates that durable, substantial changes in behavior can be achieved simply by setting up the proper conditions. With the skillful association of a naturally occurring US with an appropriate CS, an organism can learn to perform a variety of behaviors, often after relatively few acquisition trials. There is no reference to an organism's *wanting* to learn the behavior, *willingness* to do it, *thinking* about the situation, or *reasoning* through the available options. We don't need to consider internal and cognitive explanations to demonstrate the effects of classical conditioning: The stimuli, the eliciting circumstances, and the resulting behavior are there to be observed by one and all.

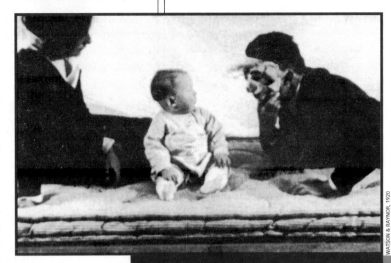

John Watson and Rosalie Rayner show Little Albert an unusual bunny mask. Why doesn't the mere presence of these experimenters serve as a conditioned stimulus in itself?

It was this kind of simplicity that appealed to behaviorists. In fact, Watson and his followers thought that it was possible to develop general explanations of pretty much *any* behavior of *any* organism based on classical conditioning principles.

As a step in that direction, Watson embarked on a controversial study with his research assistant Rosalie Rayner (Watson & Rayner, 1920). To support his contention that even complex behaviors were the result of conditioning, Watson enlisted the assistance of 9-month-old "Little Albert." Watson presented Little Albert with a variety of stimuli: a white rat, a dog, a rabbit, various masks, and a burning newspaper. Albert's reactions in most cases were curiosity or indifference, and he showed no fear of any of the items. Then Watson unexpectedly struck a large steel bar with a hammer, producing a loud noise. Predictably, this caused Albert to cry, tremble, and be generally displeased.

Watson and Rayner then led Little Albert through the acquisition phase of classical conditioning. Albert was presented with a white rat. As soon as he reached out to touch it, the steel bar was struck. This pairing occurred again and again over several trials. Eventually, the sight of the rat alone caused Albert to recoil in terror, crying and clamoring to get away from it. In this situation, a US (the loud sound) was paired with a CS (the presence of the rat) such that the CS all by itself was sufficient to produce the CR (a fearful reaction). Little Albert also showed stimulus generalization. The sight of a white rabbit, a seal-fur coat, and a Santa Claus mask produced the same kinds of fear reactions in the infant.

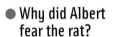

● **Why did Albert fear the rat?**

What was Watson's goal in all this? First, he wanted to show that a relatively complex reaction could be conditioned using Pavlovian techniques. Second, he wanted to show that emotional responses such as fear and anxiety could be produced by classical conditioning and therefore need not be the product of deeper unconscious processes or early life experiences as Freud and his followers had argued (see Chapter 1). Instead, Watson proposed that fears could be learned, just like any other behavior. Third, Watson wanted to confirm that conditioning could be applied to humans as well as to other animals. This study was controversial in its cavalier treatment of a young child, especially given that Watson and Rayner did not follow up with Albert or his mother during the ensuing years (Harris, 1979). Modern ethical guidelines that govern the treatment of research participants make sure that this kind of study could not be conducted today. At the time, however, it was consistent with a behaviorist view of psychology. As Watson (1930) summarized his position several years later:

> Give me a dozen healthy infants, well-formed, and my own specified world to bring them up in and I'll guarantee to take any one at random and train him to become any type of specialist I might select—doctor, lawyer, artist, merchant-chief and, yes, even beggar-man and thief, regardless of his talents, penchants, tendencies, abilities, vocations, and race of his ancestors. (p. 104)

discrimination The capacity to distinguish between similar but distinct stimuli.

Watson was promoting a staunch view that learning and the environment were responsible for determining behavior, more so than genetics or personality. He intended his statements to be extreme in order to shake up the young discipline of psychology and highlight the importance of acquired experiences in shaping behavior.

A Deeper Understanding of Classical Conditioning

As a form of learning, classical conditioning could be reliably produced, it had a simple set of principles, and it had applications to real-life situations. In short, classical conditioning offered a good deal of utility for psychologists who sought to understand the mechanisms underlying learning, and it continues to do so today.

Like a lot of strong starters, though, classical conditioning has been subjected to deeper scrutiny in order to understand exactly how, when, and why it works. Let's examine three areas that give us a closer look at the mechanisms of classical conditioning.

The Neural Elements of Classical Conditioning

Pavlov saw his research as providing insights into how the brain works. After all, he was trained in medicine, not psychology, and was a bit surprised when psychologists became excited by his findings. Recent research has clarified some of what Pavlov hoped to understand about conditioning and the brain.

For example, fear conditioning has been extensively studied in part because the brain substrates are particularly evident. In Chapter 3, you saw that the amygdala plays an important role in the experience of emotion, including fear and anxiety. So, it should come as no surprise that the amygdala, particularly an area known as the *central nucleus*, is also critical for emotional conditioning.

Consider a rat who is conditioned to a series of CS-US pairings where the CS is a tone and the US is a mild electric shock. When rats experience sudden painful stimuli in nature, they show a defensive reaction, known as *freezing*, where they crouch down and sit motionless. In addition, their autonomic nervous systems go to work: Heart rate and blood pressure increase, and various hormones associated with stress are released. When fear conditioning takes place, these two components—one behavioral and one physiological—occur, except that now they are elicited by the CS.

The central nucleus of the amygdala plays a role in producing both of these outcomes through two distinct connections with other parts of the brain. If connections linking the amygdala to the midbrain are disrupted, the rat does not exhibit the behavioral freezing response. If the connections between the amygdala and the hypothalamus are severed, the autonomic responses associated with fear cease (LeDoux et al., 1988). Hence, the action of the amygdala is an essential element in fear conditioning, and its links with other areas of the brain are responsible for producing specific features of conditioning. The amygdala is involved in fear conditioning in people as well as rats and other animals (Phelps & LeDoux, 2005).

● **What is the role of the amygdala in fear conditioning?**

The Cognitive Elements of Classical Conditioning

Pavlov's work was a behaviorist's dream come true. In this view, conditioning is something that *happens to* a dog, a rat, or a person, apart from what the organism thinks about the conditioning situation. However, eventually someone was bound to ask an important question: Why didn't Pavlov's dogs salivate to Pavlov? After all, he was instrumental in the arrival of the CS. If Pavlov delivered the food to the dogs, why didn't they form an association with him? Indeed, if Watson was present whenever the unpleasant US was sounded, why didn't Little Albert come to fear *him?*

Maybe classical conditioning isn't such an unthinking, mechanical process as behaviorists originally had assumed (Rescorla, 1966, 1988). Somehow, Pavlov's dogs were sensitive to the fact that Pavlov was not a *reliable* indicator of the arrival of food. Pavlov was linked with the arrival of food, but he was also linked with other activities that had nothing to do with food, including checking on the apparatus, bringing the dog from

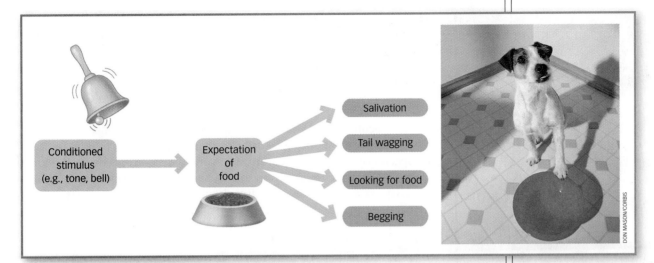

DON MASON/CORBIS

FIGURE 6.5 ● ● ● ● ● ● ● ● ● ● ● ● ● ● ● ● ●
Expectation in Classical Conditioning
In the Rescorla-Wagner model of classical conditioning, a CS serves to set up an expectation. The expectation in turn leads to an array of behaviors associated with the presence of the CS.

the kennel to the laboratory, and standing around and talking with his assistants. These observations suggest that perhaps cognitive components are involved in classical conditioning after all.

Robert Rescorla and Allan Wagner (1972) were the first to theorize that classical conditioning only occurs when an animal has learned to set up an *expectation* (see **FIGURE 6.5**). The sound of a tone, because of its systematic pairing with food, served to set up this cognitive state for the laboratory dogs; Pavlov, because of the lack of any reliable link with food, did not. Rescorla and Wagner predicted that conditioning would be easier when the CS was an *unfamiliar* event than when it was familiar. The reason is that familiar

● **How does familiarity with the stimulus hinder new conditioning?**

events, being familiar, already have expectations associated with them, making new conditioning difficult. For example, Adam didn't recoil in horror every time he saw his daughter Carly, even though she was present during the acquisition phase of 9/11. The familiarity of Carly in multiple contexts made her, thankfully, a poor CS for Adam's fear conditioning. In short, classical conditioning might appear to be a primitive and unthinking process, but it is actually quite sophisticated and incorporates a significant cognitive element.

The Evolutionary Elements of Classical Conditioning

In addition to this cognitive component, evolutionary mechanisms also play an important role in classical conditioning. As you learned in Chapter 1, evolution and natural selection go hand in hand with adaptiveness: Behaviors that are adaptive allow an organism to survive and thrive in its environment. In the case of classical conditioning, psychologists began to appreciate how this type of learning could have adaptive value. In fact, there are good reasons why animals may have evolved to condition to novel stimuli more easily than to familiar stimuli. An example comes from conditioning of food aversions and food preferences.

Under certain conditions, people ● ● ● ● ● ● ● ● ● ● may develop food aversions. This serving of hummus looks inviting and probably tastes delicious, but at least one psychologist avoids it like the plague.

You may think food preference is a matter of personal taste, but in fact food aversions can be classically conditioned. A psychology professor was once on a job interview in Southern California, and his hosts took him to lunch at a Middle Eastern restaurant. Suffering from a case of bad hummus, he was up all night long. Needless to say, he was in pretty rough shape the following day, and he didn't get the job offer.

This colleague developed a lifelong aversion to hummus. Why would one bad incident taint food preferences in such a lasting way? On the face of it, this looks like a case of classical conditioning. The hummus was the CS, its apparent toxicity was the US, and the resulting gastric distress was the UR. The UR (the nausea) became linked to the once-neutral CS (the hummus) and became a CR (an aversion to hummus). However, this case has several unusual aspects.

© PAUL COWAN
DREAMSTIME.COM

● Rats can be difficult to poison because of learned taste aversions, which are an evolutionarily adaptive element of classical conditioning. Here a worker tries his best in the sewers of France.

For starters, all of the psychologist's hosts also ate the hummus, yet none of them reported feeling ill. It's not clear, then, what the US was; it couldn't have been anything that was actually in the food. What's more, the time between the hummus and the distress was several hours; usually a response follows a stimulus fairly quickly. Most baffling, this aversion was cemented with a single acquisition trial. Usually it takes several pairings of a CS and US to establish learning.

These peculiarities are not so peculiar from an evolutionary perspective. What seems like a mindbug is actually the manifestation of an adaptive process. Any species that forages or consumes a variety of foods needs to develop a mechanism by which it can learn to avoid any food that once made it ill. To have adaptive value, this mechanism should have several properties.

First, there should be rapid learning that occurs in perhaps one or two trials. If learning takes more trials than this, the animal could die from eating a toxic substance. Second, conditioning should be able to take place over very long intervals, perhaps up to several hours. Toxic substances often don't cause illness immediately, so the organism would need to form an association between food and the illness over a longer term. Third, the organism should develop the aversion to the smell or taste of the food rather than its ingestion. It's more adaptive to reject a potentially toxic substance based on smell alone than it is to ingest it. Finally, learned aversions should occur more often with novel foods than familiar ones. It is not adaptive for an animal to develop an aversion to everything it has eaten on the particular day it got sick. Our psychologist friend didn't develop an aversion to the Coke he drank with lunch or the scrambled eggs he had for breakfast that day, only to the unfamiliar hummus.

John Garcia and his colleagues illustrated the adaptiveness of classical conditioning in a series of studies with rats (Garcia & Koelling, 1966). They paired a variety of CSs with a US, such as injection of a toxic substance, that caused nausea and vomiting hours later. If the CS was water laced with a harmless but distinctly flavored novel substance (such as strawberry), the rats developed a strong aversion to the smell and taste of strawberries. But if the CS was a familiar food that the animal had eaten before, the aversion was much less likely to develop.

This research had an interesting application. It led to the development of a technique for dealing with an unanticipated side effect of radiation and chemotherapy: Cancer patients who experience nausea from their treatments often develop aversions to foods they ate before the therapy. Broberg and Bernstein (1987) reasoned that, if the findings with rats generalized to humans, a simple technique should minimize the negative consequences of this effect. They gave their patients an unusual food (coconut or root beer–flavored candy) at the end of the last meal before undergoing treatment. Sure enough, the conditioned food aversions that the patients developed were overwhelmingly for one of the unusual flavors and not for any of the other foods in the meal. As a result, patients were spared developing aversions to more common foods that they are more likely to eat. Understanding the basis of mindbugs can have practical as well as theoretical value.

● How have cancer patients' discomfort been eased by our understanding of food aversions?

Studies such as these suggest that evolution has provided each species with a kind of **biological preparedness**, *a propensity for learning particular kinds of associations over others*, so that some behaviors are relatively easy to condition in some species but not others. For example, the taste and smell stimuli that produce food aversions in rats do not work with most species of birds. Birds depend primarily on visual cues for finding food and are relatively insensitive to taste and smell. However, it is relatively easy to produce a food aversion in birds using an unfamiliar visual stimulus as the CS, such as a brightly colored food (Wilcoxon, Dragoin, & Kral, 1971). Indeed, most researchers agree that conditioning works best with stimuli that are biologically relevant to the organism (Domjan, 2005).

biological preparedness A propensity for learning particular kinds of associations over others.

Culture & Community

Is It Possible That Humans Have an Innate Ability to Understand Geometry?

In a study (Dhaene et al. 2006) of the Munduruku, an isolated indigenous tribe located in the Amazon, Munduruku children and adults were compared to American children and adults on their basic comprehension of geometric shapes. In each test, the participants identified which figure among the series of six images presented to them did *not* belong in the group. Each series tested basic geometric concepts like parallels, shapes, distance, and symmetry.

All participants performed well above the level of chance, and only American adults showed a significant advantage. Before this study, it was largely believed that people must "learn" geometry through cultural interventions like maps, mathematical tools, or the terms used in geometry. In contrast, this study provides evidence that core knowledge of geometry is a universal intuition of the human mind.

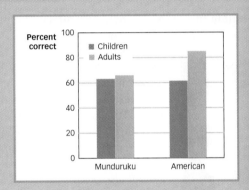

summary quiz [6.2]

4. When you make noise with your can opener in the kitchen, but no longer follow the noise with a bowl of dog food, your dog will stop running into the kitchen at the sound of the can opener. Your clever dog is displaying
   a. acquisition.
   c. discrimination.
   b. generalization.
   d. extinction.

5. Every time Little Albert reached out to touch the cute white rat, the experimenter startled Albert with a loud noise. Soon Little Albert feared not only the rat but also a white rabbit, a fur coat, and a Santa Claus mask. This phenomenon is called
   a. extinction.
   c. generalization.
   b. spontaneous recovery.
   d. discrimination.

6. The classical conditioning of fear involves which area of the brain?
   a. amygdala
   c. hippocampus
   b. hypothalamus
   d. temporal cortex

7. Jeff loved chili dogs, but one day he ate one and soon after became violently ill. After that, the mere sight or smell of a chili dog made Jeff nauseous. Jeff's nausea is an example of a(n)
   a. conditioned stimulus.
   c. unconditioned stimulus.
   b. conditioned response.
   d. unconditioned response.

operant conditioning A type of learning in which the consequences of an organism's behavior determine whether it will be repeated in the future.

law of effect The principle that behaviors that are followed by a "satisfying state of affairs" tend to be repeated and those that produce an "unpleasant state of affairs" are less likely to be repeated.

operant behavior Behavior that an organism produces that has some impact on the environment.

reinforcer Any stimulus or event that functions to increase the likelihood of the behavior that led to it.

punisher Any stimulus or event that functions to decrease the likelihood of the behavior that led to it.

Operant Conditioning: Reinforcements from the Environment

The learned behaviors you've seen so far share a common feature: They all occurred beyond the voluntary control of the organism. Most animals don't voluntarily salivate or feel spasms of anxiety; rather, these animals exhibit these responses involuntarily during the conditioning process. In fact, these reflexlike behaviors make up only a small portion of our behavioral repertoires. The remainder are behaviors that we voluntarily perform, behaviors that modify and change the environment around us. The study of classical conditioning is the study of behaviors that are *reactive*. We turn now to a different form of learning: **operant conditioning**, *a type of learning in which the consequences of an organism's behavior determine whether it will be repeated in the future*. The study of operant conditioning is the exploration of behaviors that are *active*.

The Early Days: The Law of Effect

The study of how active behavior affects the environment began at about the same time as classical conditioning. In fact, Edward L. Thorndike (1874–1949) first examined active behaviors back in the 1890s, before Pavlov published his findings. Thorndike's research focused on *instrumental behaviors*—that is, behavior that required an organism to *do* something, solve a problem, or otherwise manipulate elements of its environment (Thorndike, 1898). For example, Thorndike completed several experiments using a puzzle box, which was a wooden crate with a door that would open when a concealed lever was moved in the right way (see **FIGURE 6.6**). A hungry cat placed in a puzzle box would try various behaviors to get out—scratching at the door, meowing loudly, sniffing the inside of the box, putting its paw through the openings—but only one behavior opened the door and led to food: tripping the lever in just the right way. After this happened, Thorndike placed the cat back in the box for another round. Don't get the wrong idea. Thorndike probably really liked cats. Far from teasing them, he was after an important behavioral principle.

Fairly quickly, the cats became quite skilled at triggering the lever for their release. At first, the cats enacted any number of likely (but ultimately ineffective) behaviors, but only one behavior led to freedom and food. Over time, the ineffective behaviors became less and less frequent, and the one instrumental behavior (going right for the latch) became more frequent (see **FIGURE 6.7**, below).

YALE UNIVERSITY LIBRARY

● ● ● **FIGURE 6.6**
Thorndike's Puzzle Box
In Thorndike's original experiments, food was placed just outside the door of the puzzle box, where the cat could see it. If the cat triggered the appropriate lever, it would open the door and let the cat out.

● ● ● **FIGURE 6.7**
The Law of Effect *Thorndike's cats displayed trial-and-error behavior when trying to escape from the puzzle box. They made lots of irrelevant movements and actions until, over time, they discovered the solution. Once they figured out what behavior was instrumental in opening the latch, they stopped all other ineffective behaviors and escaped from the box faster and faster.*

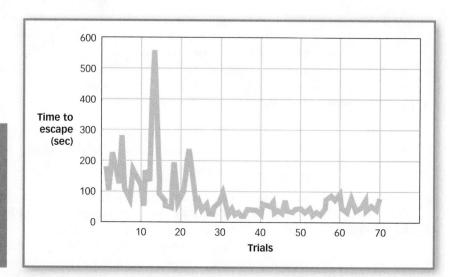

From these observations, Thorndike developed the **law of effect**, which states that *behaviors that are followed by a "satisfying state of affairs" tend to be repeated, and those that produce an "unpleasant state of affairs" are less likely to be repeated.*

The circumstances that Thorndike used to study learning were very different from those in studies of classical conditioning. Remember that in classical conditioning experiments, the US occurred on every training trial no matter what the animal did.

● **What is the relationship between behavior and reward?**

Pavlov delivered food to the dog whether it salivated or not. But in Thorndike's work, the behavior of the animal determined what happened next. If the behavior was "correct" (i.e., the latch was triggered), the animal was rewarded with food. Incorrect behaviors produced no results and the animal was stuck in the box until it performed the correct behavior. Although different from classical conditioning, Thorndike's work resonated with most behaviorists at the time: It was still observable, quantifiable, and free from explanations involving the mind (Galef, 1998).

DAVE KING/GETTY IMAGES

Reinforcement, Punishment, and the Development of Operant Conditioning

Several decades after Thorndike's work, B. F. Skinner (1904–1990) coined the term ***operant behavior*** to refer to *behavior that an organism produces that has some impact on the environment.* In Skinner's system, all of these emitted behaviors "operated" on the environment in some manner, and the environment responded by providing events that either strengthened those behaviors (i.e., they *reinforced* them) or made them less likely to occur (i.e., they *punished* them).

In order to study operant behavior scientifically, Skinner developed a variation on Thorndike's puzzle box. The *operant chamber,* or *Skinner box,* as it is commonly called (**FIGURE 6.8**), allows a researcher to study the behavior of small organisms in a controlled environment.

Skinner's approach to the study of learning focused on *reinforcement* and *punishment.* These terms, which have commonsense connotations, turned out to be rather difficult to define. For example, some people love roller coasters, whereas others find them horrifying; the chance to go on one will be a reinforcement for one group but a punishment for another. Dogs can be trained with praise and a good belly rub—procedures that are nearly useless for most cats. Skinner settled on a "neutral" definition that would characterize each term by its effect on behavior. Therefore, a **reinforcer** is *any stimulus or event that functions to increase the likelihood of the behavior that led to it,* whereas a **punisher** is *any stimulus or event that functions to decrease the likelihood of the behavior that led to it.*

WALTER DAWN/PHOTO RESEARCHERS

FIGURE 6.8 ● ● ● ● ● ● ● ● ●
Skinner Box *In a typical Skinner box, or operant conditioning chamber, a rat, pigeon, or other suitably sized animal is placed in this environment and observed during learning trials that use operant conditioning principles.*

Whether a particular stimulus acts as a reinforcer or punisher depends in part on whether it increases or decreases the likelihood of a behavior. Presenting food is usually reinforcing, producing an increase in the behavior that led to it; removing food is often punishing, leading to a decrease in the behavior. Turning on an electric shock is typically punishing (the behavior that led to it); turning it off is rewarding (and increases the behavior that led to it).

To keep these possibilities distinct, Skinner used the term *positive* for situations in which a stimulus was presented and *negative* for situations in which it was removed. Consequently, there is *positive reinforcement* (where something desirable is presented) and *negative reinforcement* (where something undesirable is removed), as well as *positive punishment* (where something unpleasant is administered) and *negative punishment* (where something desirable is removed). Here the words *positive* and *negative* mean, respectively, something that is *added* or something that is *taken away.* As you can see from **TABLE 6.1** (on page 176), positive and negative reinforcement increase the likelihood of the behavior and positive and negative punishment decrease the likelihood of the behavior.

COURTESY DAIRY QUEEN

TABLE 6.1

Reinforcement and Punishment

	Increases the Likelihood of Behavior	Decreases the Likelihood of Behavior
Stimulus is presented	Positive reinforcement	Positive punishment
Stimulus is removed	Negative reinforcement	Negative punishment

Negative reinforcement involves the removal of something undesirable from the environment. When Daddy stops the car, he gets a reward: His little monster stops screaming. However, from the child's perspective, this is positive reinforcement. The child's tantrum results in something positive added to the environment: stopping for a snack.

These distinctions can be confusing at first; after all, "negative reinforcement" and "punishment" both sound like they should be "bad" and produce the same type of behavior. There are a couple of ways to keep track of these distinctions. First, remember that *positive* and *negative* simply mean *presentation* or *removal,* and the terms don't necessarily mean "good" or "bad" as they do in everyday speech. Negative reinforcement, for example, involves something pleasant; it's the *removal* of something unpleasant, like a shock, and the absence of a shock is indeed pleasant.

Second, bear in mind that reinforcement is generally more effective than punishment in promoting learning. There are many reasons (Gershoff, 2002), but one reason is this: Punishment signals that an unacceptable behavior has occurred, but it doesn't specify what should be done instead. Spanking a young child for starting to run into a busy street certainly stops the behavior—which, in this case, is probably a good idea. But it doesn't promote any kind of learning about the desired behavior. Reinforcers and punishers often gain their functions from basic biological mechanisms.

● **Why is reinforcement more constructive than punishment in learning desired behavior?**

Food, comfort, shelter, and warmth are examples of *primary reinforcers* because they help satisfy biological needs. However, the vast majority of reinforcers or punishers in our daily lives have little to do with biology. Handshakes, verbal approval, an encouraging grin, a bronze trophy, or money all serve powerful reinforcing functions, yet none of them taste very good or help keep you warm at night. The point is, we learn to perform a lot of behaviors based on reinforcements that have little or nothing to do with biological satisfaction.

These *secondary reinforcers* derive their effectiveness from their associations with primary reinforcers through classical conditioning. For example, money starts out as a neutral CS that, through its association with primary USs, such as acquiring food or shelter, takes on a conditioned emotional element. Flashing lights, originally a neutral CS, acquire powerful negative elements through association with a speeding ticket and a fine. Under normal circumstances, as long as the CS-US link is maintained, the secondary reinforcers and punishers can be used to modify and control behavior. If the links are broken (i.e., if an extinction procedure is introduced), secondary reinforcers typically lose these functions. Money that is no longer backed by a solvent government quickly loses its reinforcing capacity and becomes worth no more than the paper it is printed on.

But as long as behaviors are linked with reinforcement, those behaviors should continue to occur, right? Actually, no. Sometimes, the presentation of rewards can cause the opposite effect: a decrease in performing the behavior. An example of such a mindbug is **overjustification effect**, *when external rewards can undermine the intrinsic satisfaction of performing a behavior.* In one study nursery school children were given colored pens and paper and were asked to draw whatever they wanted (Lepper & Greene, 1978). For a young child, the pleasures of drawing and creative expression are rewarding all by themselves. Some children, though, received a "Good Player Award" for their efforts at artwork, whereas other children did not. As you may have guessed, the Good Players spent more time at the task than the other children. As you may not have guessed, when the

THE NEW YORKER COLLECTION 1993 TOM CHENEY FROM CARTOONBANK.COM.

"Oh, not bad. The light comes on, I press the bar, they write me a check. How about you?"

experimenters stopped handing out the Good Player certificates to the first group, the amount of time the children spent drawing dropped significantly below that of the group that never received any external reinforcements.

This was a case of *over*justification, or too much reinforcement. The children who received the extrinsic reinforcement of the certificate came to view their task as one that gets rewards. The children who

● **Can rewards backfire?**

didn't receive the extrinsic reinforcement continued to perform the task for its own sake. When the extrinsic rewards were later removed, children in the first group found little reason to continue engaging in the task. Other researchers have found that when people are paid for tasks such as writing poetry, drawing, or finding solutions to economic and business problems, they tend to produce *less* creative solutions when monetary rewards are offered (Amabile, 1996). You can weigh in on these issues in the Where Do You Stand? box at the end of this chapter (on page 193).

Drawing pictures is fun. Drawing pictures for external rewards might, oddly enough, make drawing pictures seem like much less fun.

The Basic Principles of Operant Conditioning

After establishing how reinforcement and punishment produced learned behavior, Skinner and other scientists began to expand the parameters of operant conditioning. They started by investigating some phenomena that were well known in classical conditioning, such as discrimination, generalization, and extinction.

For example, if a pigeon is reinforced for pecking a key whenever a particular tone is sounded but never reinforced if the tone is absent, that tone will quickly become a *discriminative stimulus,* or a stimulus that is associated with reinforcement for key pecking in that situation. Pigeons, reinforced under these conditions, will quickly learn to engage in vigorous key pressing whenever the tone sounds but cease if it is turned off. The tone sets the occasion, or context, for the pigeon to emit the response.

You similarly modify your behavior based on what context you're in. We all take off our clothes at least once a day, but usually not in public. We scream at rock concerts but not in libraries. We say, "Please pass the gravy," at the dinner table but not in a classroom. Although these observations may seem like nothing more than common sense, Thorndike was the first to recognize the underlying message: Learning takes place *in contexts,* not in the free range of any plausible situation. As Skinner rephrased it later, most behavior is under *stimulus control,* which develops when a particular response only occurs when the appropriate stimulus is present.

Stimulus control, perhaps not surprisingly, shows both discrimination and generalization effects similar to those we saw with classical conditioning. To demonstrate this, researchers used either a painting by the French Impressionist Claude Monet or one of Pablo Picasso's paintings from his Cubist period for the discriminative stimulus (Watanabe, Sakamoto, & Wakita, 1995). Some participants were reinforced only if they responded when the Monet painting was present; others were reinforced for responding to the Picasso. Later, the participants were tested on new paintings, and they discriminated appropriately: Those trained with the Monet painting responded when other paintings by Monet were presented, and those trained with a Picasso painting reacted when other paintings by Picasso were shown. If these results don't seem particularly startling to you, it might help to know that the research participants were pigeons who were trained to key-peck to these various works of art. Stimulus control, and its ability to foster stimulus discrimination and stimulus generalization, is effective even if the stimulus has no meaning to the respondent.

As in classical conditioning, operant behavior undergoes extinction when the reinforcements stop. Pigeons cease pecking at a key if food is no longer presented following the behavior. You wouldn't put more money into a vending machine if it failed to give you its promised candy bar or soda. Warm smiles that are greeted with scowls and

overjustification effect Circumstances when external rewards can undermine the intrinsic satisfaction of performing a behavior.

shaping Learning that results from the reinforcement of successive approximations to a final desired behavior.

frowns will quickly disappear. On the surface, extinction of operant behavior looks like that of classical conditioning: The response rate drops off fairly rapidly, and, if a rest period is provided, spontaneous recovery is typically seen.

One important difference between classical and operant conditioning is that, in classical conditioning, responses are usually hardwired—behaviors that the animal already displays, such as salivation or fear. Classical conditioning only changes the conditions in which these behaviors are produced. By contrast, operant conditioning can produce brand-new behaviors. Have you ever been to AquaLand and wondered how the dolphins learn to jump up in the air, twist around, splash back down, do a somersault, and then jump through a hoop, all in one smooth motion? These behaviors are the result of **shaping**, or *learning that results from the reinforcement of successive approximations to a final desired behavior.* The outcomes of one set of behaviors shape the next set of behaviors

To illustrate the effects of shaping, Skinner noted that if you put a rat in a Skinner box and wait for it to press the bar, you could end up waiting a very long time; bar

● **How can operant conditioning produce complex behaviors?**

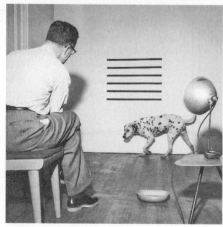
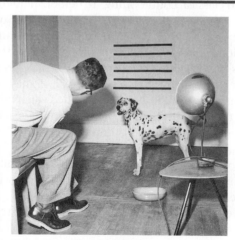
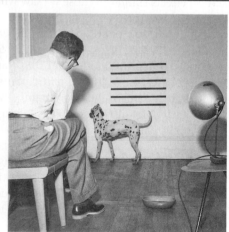

1 minute   4 minutes   8 minutes

pressing just isn't very high in a rat's natural hierarchy of responses. However, it is relatively easy to "shape" bar pressing. Watch the rat closely: If it turns in the direction of the bar, deliver a food reward. This will reinforce turning toward the bar, making such a movement more likely. Now wait for the rat to take a step toward the bar before delivering food; this will reinforce moving toward the bar. After the rat walks closer to the bar, wait until it touches the bar before presenting the food. Notice that none of these behaviors is the final desired behavior—reliably pressing the bar. Rather, each behavior is a *successive approximation* to the final product, or a behavior that gets incrementally closer to the overall desired behavior. In the dolphin example—and indeed, in many instances of animal training in which relatively simple animals seem to perform astoundingly complex behaviors—each smaller behavior is reinforced until the overall sequence of behavior gets performed reliably.

In shaping, complicated behaviors can be established by pairing responses with reinforcement. But what if reinforcement occurs, regardless of what the organism is doing? To find out, Skinner (1947) put several pigeons in Skinner boxes, set the food dispenser to deliver food every 15 seconds, and left the birds to their own devices. Later he returned and found the birds engaging in odd, idiosyncratic behaviors, such as pecking aimlessly in a corner or turning in cir-

● How would a behaviorist explain superstitions?

cles. He referred to these behaviors as "superstitious" and offered a behaviorist analysis of their occurrence. The pigeons, he argued, were simply repeating behaviors that had been accidentally reinforced. A pigeon that just happened to have pecked randomly in the corner when the food showed up had connected the delivery of food to that behavior. Because this pecking behavior was "reinforced" by the delivery of food, the pigeon was likely to repeat it. Now pecking in the corner was more likely to occur, and it was more likely to be reinforced 15 seconds later when the food appeared again.

For each pigeon, the behavior reinforced would be whatever the pigeon happened to be doing when the food was first delivered. Skinner's pigeons acted as though there was a causal relationship between their behaviors and the appearance of food when it was merely an accidental correlation. Superstitious behavior is not limited to pigeons, of course. Baseball players who enjoy several home runs on a day when they happened to have not showered are likely to continue that tradition, laboring under the belief that the accidental correlation between poor personal hygiene and a good day at bat is somehow causal. This "stench causes home runs" hypothesis is just one of many examples of human superstitions (Gilbert et al., 2000; Radford & Radford, 1949).

Why does Tiger Woods always wear his Sunday red shirt for the final round of a golf tournament? Some people think that he is engaging in superstitious behavior, but it's more than just that: Tiger feels more aggressive when wearing a red shirt, which helps him perform down the stretch.

JAMIE SQUIRE/GETTY IMAGES

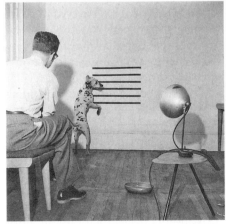

12 minutes

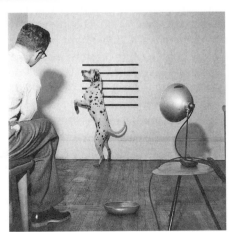

16 minutes

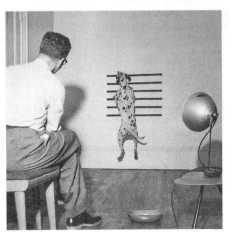

20 minutes

fixed interval schedule (FI) An operant conditioning principle in which reinforcements are presented at fixed time periods, provided that the appropriate response is made.

variable interval schedule (VI) An operant conditioning principle in which behavior is reinforced based on an average time that has expired since the last reinforcement.

fixed ratio schedule (FR) An operant conditioning principle in which reinforcement is delivered after a specific number of responses have been made.

variable ratio schedule (VR) An operant conditioning principle in which the delivery of reinforcement is based on a particular average number of responses.

intermittent reinforcement An operant conditioning principle in which only some of the responses made are followed by reinforcement.

Schedules of Reinforcement

The law of effect states that behaviors that are reinforced tend to occur more often. But how much more often? Partly, this depends on how often reinforcement is received.

Skinner was intrigued by this fact, and he explored dozens of what came to be known as *schedules of reinforcement* (Ferster & Skinner, 1957) (see **FIGURE 6.9** on page 181). The two most important are *interval schedules,* based on the time intervals between reinforcements, and *ratio schedules,* based on the ratio of responses to reinforcements.

Under a **fixed interval schedule (FI)**, *reinforcements are presented at fixed time periods, provided that the appropriate response is made.* For example, on a 2-minute fixed interval schedule, a response will be reinforced, but only after 2 minutes have expired since the last reinforcement. Pigeons in Skinner boxes produce predictable patterns of behavior under these schedules. They show little responding right after the presentation of reinforcement, but as the next time interval draws to a close, they show a burst of responding. If this pattern seems odd to you, consider how often undergraduates behave exactly like this. They do relatively little work until just before the upcoming exam, then engage in a burst of reading and studying—and then probably take a little time off after the exam before they start seriously preparing for the next test.

Under a **variable interval schedule (VI)**, a *behavior is reinforced based on an average time that has expired since the last reinforcement.* For example, on a 2-minute variable interval schedule, responses will be reinforced every 2 minutes *on average* but not after each 2-minute period. Variable interval schedules typically produce steady, consistent responding because the time until the next reinforcement is less predictable. For example, a radio station might advertise that they give away concert tickets every hour, which is true, but the DJs are likely to say, "Sometime this hour, I'll be giving away a pair of tickets to see the Arctic Monkeys in concert!" which is

● **How does a radio station use scheduled reinforcements to keep you listening?**

also true. The reinforcement—getting the tickets—might average out to once an hour across the span of the broadcasting day, but the presentation of the reinforcement is variable: It might come early in the 10 o'clock hour, later in the 11 o'clock hour, and so on. The result is to keep listeners tuned in steadily throughout the day, rather than just tuning in every hour on the hour for a chance to win those tickets.

Both fixed interval schedules and variable interval schedules tend to produce slow, methodical responding because the reinforcements follow a time scale that is independent of how many responses occur. It doesn't matter if a rat on a fixed interval schedule presses a bar 1 time during a 2-minute period or 100 times: The reinforcing food pellet won't drop out of the shoot until 2 minutes have elapsed, regardless of the number of responses.

● *Radio station promotions and giveaways often follow a variable interval schedule of reinforcement.*

Under a **fixed ratio schedule (FR)**, *reinforcement is delivered after a specific number of responses have been made.* One schedule might present reinforcement after every fourth response; a different schedule might present reinforcement after every 20 responses. The special case of presenting reinforcement after *each* response is called *continuous reinforcement.* There are many situations in which people find themselves being reinforced on a fixed ratio schedule. Book clubs often give you a "freebie" after a set number of regular purchases, pieceworkers get paid after making a fixed number of products, and some credit card companies return to their customers a percentage of the amount charged.

Under a **variable ratio schedule (VR)**, *the delivery of reinforcement is based on a particular average number of responses.* For example, under a 10-response variable ratio schedule, reinforcement follows every 10th response—on average. Slot machines in modern casinos pay off on variable ratio schedules that are determined by the random number generator that controls the play of the machines. A casino might advertise that they pay off on "every 100 pulls on average," which could be true. However, one player might hit a jackpot after 3 pulls on a slot machine, whereas another player might not hit until after 80 pulls. The ratio of responses to reinforcements is variable, which probably helps casinos stay in business.

These pieceworkers in a textile factory get paid following a fixed ratio schedule: They receive payment after some set number of shirts have been sewn.

All ratio schedules encourage high and consistent rates of responding because the number of rewards received is directly related to the number of responses made. Unlike a rat following a fixed interval schedule, where food is delivered at a specified time regardless of the number of responses, rats following a ratio schedule should respond quickly and often. Not surprisingly, variable ratio schedules produce slightly higher rates of responding than fixed ratio schedules primarily because there's always the possibility of a reward after the very next response—even if a reinforcement was just obtained.

● **How do ratio schedules work to keep you spending your money?**

All of these schedules of reinforcement provide **intermittent reinforcement**, meaning that *only some of the responses made are followed by reinforcement.* They all produce behavior that is much more resistant to extinction than a continuous reinforcement schedule. One way to think about this effect is to recognize that the more irregular and intermittent a schedule is, the more difficult it becomes for an organism to detect when it has actually been placed on extinction.

FIGURE 6.9 ● ● ● ● ● ● ● ● ● ● ● ● ●
Reinforcement Schedules *Different schedules of reinforcement produce different rates of responding. These lines represent the amount of responding that occurs under each type of reinforcement. The black slash marks indicate when reinforcement was administered. Notice that ratio schedules tend to produce higher rates of responding than do interval schedules, as shown by the steeper lines for fixed ratio and variable ratio.*

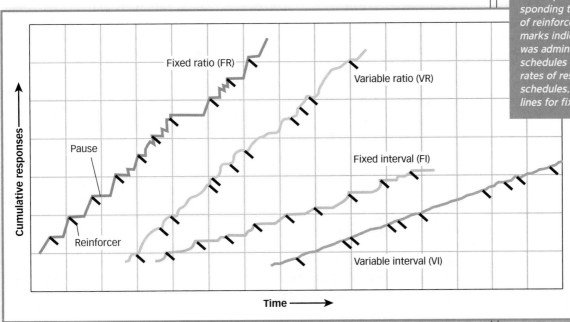

OTTMAR BIERWAGEN/SPECTRUM PHOTOFILE

● *Slot machines in casinos pay out following a variable ratio schedule. This helps explain why some gamblers feel incredibly lucky, whereas others (like this chap) can't believe they can play a machine for so long without winning a thing.*

For example, if you've just put a dollar into a soda machine that, unbeknownst to you, is broken, no soda comes out. Because you're used to getting your sodas on a continuous reinforcement schedule—one dollar produces one soda—this abrupt change in the environment is easily noticed, and you are unlikely to put additional money into the machine. In other words, you'd quickly show extinction. However, if you've put your dollar into a slot machine that, unbeknownst to you, is broken, do you stop after one or two plays? Almost certainly not. If you're a regular slot player, you're used to going for many plays in a row without winning anything, so it's difficult to tell that anything is out of the ordinary. Under conditions of intermittent reinforcement, all organisms will show considerable resistance to extinction and continue for many trials before they stop responding.

This relationship between intermittent reinforcement schedules and the robustness of the behavior they produce is called the **intermittent reinforcement effect**, *the fact that operant behaviors that are maintained under intermittent reinforcement schedules resist extinction better than those maintained under continuous reinforcement.* In one extreme case, Skinner gradually extended a variable ratio schedule until he managed to get a pigeon to make an astonishing 10,000 pecks at an illuminated key for one food reinforcer! Behavior maintained under a schedule like this is virtually immune to extinction.

A Deeper Understanding of Operant Conditioning

Like classical conditioning, operant conditioning also quickly proved powerful. It's difficult to argue this fact when a rat learns to perform relatively complex behaviors after only 20 minutes of practice, prompted by little more than the skillful presentation of rat chow. The results are evident: "Learning" in its most fundamental sense is a change in behavior brought about by experience. This observation was enough for the early behaviorists, who didn't include the mind in the analysis of an organism's actions. Skinner was satisfied to observe an organism perform the behavior; he didn't look for a deeper explanation of mental processes (Skinner, 1950). However, some research on operant conditioning digs deeper into the underlying mechanisms that produce the familiar outcomes of reinforcement. Let's examine three elements that expand our view of operant conditioning beyond strict behaviorism: the neural, cognitive, and evolutionary elements of operant conditioning.

The Neural Elements of Operant Conditioning

Soon after psychologists came to appreciate the range and variety of things that could function as reinforcers, they began looking for underlying brain mechanisms that might account for these effects. The first hint of how specific brain structures might contribute to the process of reinforcement came from the discovery of what came to be called *pleasure centers.* James Olds and his associates inserted tiny electrodes into different parts of a rat's brain and allowed the animal to control electric stimulation of its own brain by pressing a bar. They discovered that some brain areas, particularly those in the limbic system (see Chapter 3), produced what appeared to be intensely positive experiences: The rats would press the bar repeatedly to stimulate these structures. The researchers observed that these rats would ignore food, water, and other life-sustaining necessities for hours on end simply to receive stimulation directly in the brain. They then called these parts of the brain "pleasure centers" (Olds, 1956) (see **FIGURE 6.10**, on page 183).

● **Where are the brain's "pleasure centers"?**

In the years since these early studies, researchers have identified a number of structures and pathways in the brain that deliver rewards through stimulation (Wise, 1989, 2005). The neurons in the *medial forebrain bundle,* a pathway that meanders its way from the midbrain through the *hypothalamus* into the *nucleus accumbens,* are the most susceptible to stimulation that produces pleasure. This is not surprising as psychologists have identified this bundle of cells as crucial to behaviors that clearly involve pleasure, such as eating, drinking, and engaging in sexual activity. Second, the neurons along

intermittent reinforcement effect The fact that operant behaviors that are maintained under intermittent reinforcement schedules resist extinction better than those maintained under continuous reinforcement.

latent learning A condition in which something is learned but it is not manifested as a behavioral change until sometime in the future.

this pathway are *dopaminergic;* that is, they secrete the neurotransmitter *dopamine.* Remember from Chapter 3 that higher levels of dopamine in the brain are usually associated with positive emotions.

Researchers have found good support for this "reward center." First, as you've just seen, rats will work to stimulate this pathway at the expense of other basic needs (Olds & Fobes, 1981). However, if drugs that block the action of dopamine are administered to the rats, they cease stimulating the pleasure centers (Stellar, Kelley, & Corbett, 1983). Second, drugs such as cocaine, amphetamine, and opiates activate these pathways and centers (Moghaddam & Bunney, 1989), but dopamine-blocking drugs dramatically diminish their reinforcing effects (White & Milner, 1992). Third, fMRI studies (see Chapter 3) show increased activity in the nucleus accumbens in heterosexual men looking at pictures of attractive women (Aharon et al., 2001) and in individuals who believe they are about to receive money (Knutson et al., 2001). Finally, rats given primary reinforcers such as food or water or that are allowed to engage in sexual activity show increased dopamine secretion in the nucleus accumbens—but only if the rats are hungry, thirsty, or sexually aroused (Damsma et al., 1992). After all, food tastes a lot better when we are hungry, and sexual activity is more pleasurable when we are aroused. These biological structures underlying rewards and reinforcements probably evolved to ensure that species engaged in activities that helped survival and reproduction.

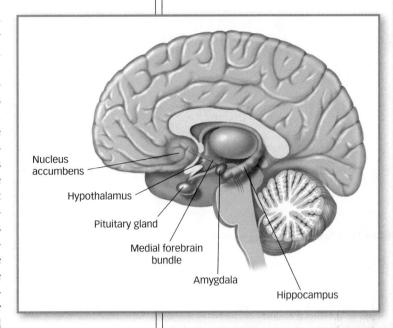

Nucleus accumbens

Hypothalamus

Pituitary gland

Medial forebrain bundle

Amygdala

Hippocampus

FIGURE **6.10** • • • • • • • • • • • • •
Pleasure Centers in the Brain *The nucleus accumbens, medial forebrain bundle, and hypothalamus are all major pleasure centers in the brain.*

The Cognitive Elements of Operant Conditioning

In addition to studying the brain substrates of operant conditioning, other researchers began to question Skinner's strictly behaviorist interpretation of learning and to suggest that cognition might play a role. Edward Chace Tolman (1886–1959) was the strongest early advocate of a cognitive approach to operant learning. Tolman argued that there was more to learning than just knowing the circumstances in the environment (the properties of the stimulus) and being able to observe a particular outcome (the reinforced response). Instead, Tolman focused less on the stimulus-response connection and more on what happens in the organism's mind when faced with the stimulus.

One phenomenon that suggested that simple stimulus-response interpretations of operant learning were inadequate was **latent learning**, in which *something is learned but it is not manifested as a behavioral change until sometime in the future.* Latent learning can easily be established in rats and occurs without any obvious reinforcement, a finding that posed a direct challenge to the then-dominant behaviorist position that all learning required some form of reinforcement (Tolman & Honzik, 1930b). Tolman gave three groups of rats access to a complex maze every day for over 2 weeks. The control group never received any reinforcement for navigating the maze. They were simply allowed to run around until they reached the goal box at the end of the maze. In **FIGURE 6.11** (on page 184) you can see that over the 2 weeks of the study, this group (in green) got a little better at finding their way through the maze but not by much. A second group of rats received regular reinforcements; when they reached the goal box, they found a small food reward there. Not surprisingly, these rats showed clear learning, as can be seen in blue in **FIGURE 6.11**. A third group was treated exactly like the control group for the first 10 days and then rewarded for the last 7 days. This group's behavior (in orange) was quite striking. For the first 10 days, they behaved like the rats in the control group. However, during the final 7 days, they behaved a lot like the rats in the second group that had been reinforced every day. Clearly, the rats in this third group had learned a lot about the maze and the location of the goal box during those first 10 days even though they had not received any reinforcements for their behavior. In other words, they showed evidence of latent learning.

Edward Chace Tolman advocated a • • •
cognitive approach to operant learning and provided evidence that in maze learning experiments, rats develop a mental picture of the maze, which he called a cognitive map.

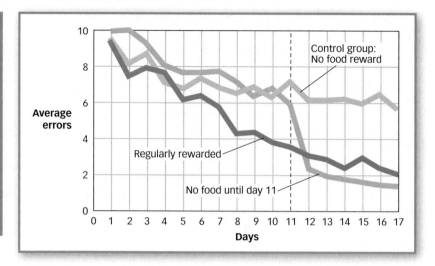

● FIGURE 6.11

Latent Learning *Rats in a control group that never received any reinforcement (in green) improved at finding their way through the maze over 17 days but not by much. Rats that received regular reinforcements (in blue) showed fairly clear learning; their error rate decreased steadily over time. Rats in the latent learning group (in orange) were treated exactly like the control group rats for the first 10 days and then like the regularly rewarded group for the last 7 days. Their dramatic improvement on day 12 shows that these rats had learned a lot about the maze and the location of the goal box even though they had never received reinforcements. Notice also that on the last 7 days, these latent learners actually seem to make fewer errors than their regularly rewarded counterparts.*

These results suggested to Tolman that beyond simply learning "start here, end here," his rats had developed a sophisticated mental picture of the maze. Tolman called this a **cognitive map**, or *a mental representation of the physical features of the environment.* One simple experiment provided support for Tolman's theories and wreaked havoc with the noncognitive explanations offered by staunch behaviorists. Tolman trained a group of rats in the maze shown in **FIGURE 6.12a**. As you can see, rats run down a straightaway, take a left, a right, a long right, and then end up in the goal box at the end of the maze.

After they had mastered the maze, Tolman changed things around a bit and put them in the maze shown in **FIGURE 6.12b**. The goal box was still in the same place relative to the start box. However, many alternative paths now spoked off the main platform, and

● What are "cognitive maps," and why are they a challenge to behaviorism?

the main straightaway that the rats had learned to use was blocked. Most behaviorists would predict that the rats in this situation—running down a familiar path only to find it blocked—would show stimulus generalization and pick the next closest path, such as

● FIGURE 6.12

Cognitive Maps *(a) Rats trained to run from a start box to a goal box in the maze on the left mastered the task quite readily. When these rats were then placed in the maze on the right (b), in which the main straightaway had been blocked, they did something unusual. Rather than simply backtrack and try the next closest runway (i.e., those labeled 8 or 9 in the figure), which would be predicted by stimulus generalization, the rats typically chose runway 5, which led most directly to where the goal box had been during their training. The rats had formed a cognitive map of their environment and so knew where they needed to end up, spatially, compared to where they began.*

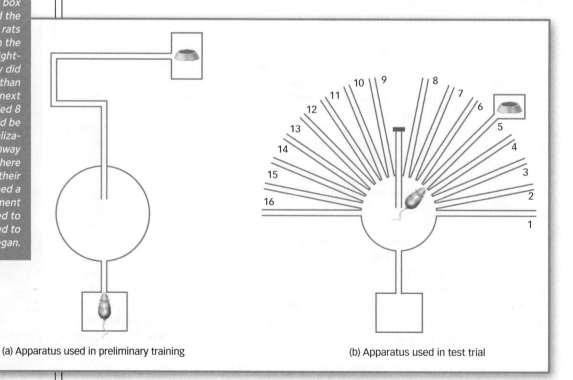

(a) Apparatus used in preliminary training   (b) Apparatus used in test trial

one immediately adjacent to the straightaway. This was not what Tolman observed. When faced with the blocked path, the rats instead ran all the way down the path that led directly to the goal box. The rats had formed a sophisticated cognitive map of their environment and behaved in a way that suggested they were successfully following that map after the conditions had changed. Latent learning and cognitive maps suggest that operant conditioning involves much more than an animal responding to a stimulus. Tolman's experiments strongly suggest that there is a cognitive component, even in rats, to operant learning.

The Evolutionary Elements of Operant Conditioning

As you'll recall, classical conditioning has an adaptive value that has been fine-tuned by evolution. Not surprisingly, we can also view operant conditioning from an evolutionary perspective. This viewpoint grew out of a set of curious observations from the early days of conditioning experiments. Several behaviorists were using simple T mazes like the one shown in **FIGURE 6.13**. If a rat found food in one arm of the maze on the first trial of the day, it typically ran down the *other* arm on the very next trial. A staunch behaviorist wouldn't expect the rats to behave this way. After all, the rats in these experiments were hungry, and they had just been reinforced for turning in a particular direction. According to operant conditioning, this should *increase* the likelihood of turning in that same direction, not reduce it. With additional trials the rats eventually learned to go to the arm with the food, but they had to learn to overcome this initial tendency to go "the wrong way." How can we explain this mindbug?

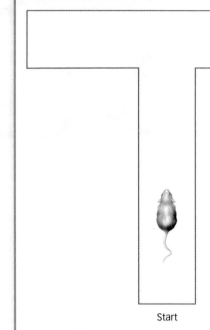

FIGURE 6.13 • • • • • • • • • • • • • • • • • •
A Simple T Maze *When rats find food in the right arm of a typical T maze, on the next trial, they will often run to the left arm of the maze. This contradicts basic principles of operant conditioning: If the behavior of running to the right arm is reinforced, it should be more likely to occur again in the future. However, this behavior is perfectly consistent with a rat's evolutionary preparedness. Like most foraging animals, rats explore their environments in search of food and seldom return to where food has already been found. Quite sensibly, if food has already been found in the right arm of the T maze, the rat will search the left arm next to see if more food is there.*

What was puzzling from a behaviorist perspective makes sense when viewed from an evolutionary perspective. Rats are foragers, and like all foraging species, they have evolved a highly adaptive strategy for survival. They move around in their environment looking for food. If they find it somewhere, they eat it (or store it) and then go look somewhere else for more. If they do not find food, they forage in another part of the environment. So, if the rat just found food in the *right* arm of a T maze, the obvious place to look next time is the *left* arm. The rat knows that there isn't any more food in the right arm because it just ate the food it found there! Indeed, foraging animals such as rats have well-developed spatial representations that allow them to search their environment efficiently. So, in this case it's not the rat who is the victim of a mindbug—it's the behaviorist theorist!

● **What explains a rat's behavior in a T-maze?**

Two of Skinner's former students, Keller Breland and Marian Breland, were among the first researchers to discover that it wasn't just rats in T mazes that presented a problem for behaviorists (Breland & Breland, 1961). For example, the Brelands, who made a career out of training animals for commercials and movies, often used pigs because pigs are surprisingly good at learning all sorts of tricks. However, they discovered that it was extremely difficult to teach a pig the simple task of dropping coins in a box. Instead of depositing the coins, the pigs persisted in rooting with them as if they were digging them up in soil, tossing them in the air with their snouts and pushing them around. The Brelands tried to train raccoons at the same task, with different but equally dismal results. The raccoons spent their time rubbing the coins between their paws instead of dropping them in the box.

Having learned the association between the coins and food, the animals began to treat the coins as stand-ins for food. Pigs are biologically predisposed to root out their food, and raccoons have evolved to clean their food by rubbing it with their paws is exactly what each species of animal did with the coins.

cognitive map A mental representation of the physical features of the environment.

The misbehavior of organisms: Pigs are biologically predisposed to root out their food, just as raccoons are predisposed to wash their food. Trying to train either species to behave differently can prove to be an exercise in futility.

The Brelands' work shows that each species, including humans, is biologically predisposed to learn some things more readily than others and to respond to stimuli in ways that are consistent with its evolutionary history (Gallistel, 2000). Such adaptive behaviors, however, evolved over extraordinarily long periods and in particular environmental contexts. If those circumstances change, some of the behavioral mechanisms that support learning can lead an organism astray. Raccoons that associated coins with food failed to follow the simple route to obtaining food by dropping the coins in the box; "nature" took over, and they wasted time rubbing the coins together. The point is that although much of every organism's behavior results from predispositions sharpened by evolutionary mechanisms, these mechanisms sometimes can have ironic consequences.

summary quiz [6.3]

8. Which of the following is an example of a secondary reinforcer?
  a. food   c. warmth
  b. shelter   d. money

9. Some college students do relatively little work until just before the upcoming exam, when they then engage in a burst of studying. After the exam, they take some time off before starting the cycle again. These students are operating under which schedule of reinforcement?
  a. fixed interval   c. fixed ratio
  b. variable interval   d. variable ratio

10. The neurons in the _____ are crucial to behaviors associated with pleasure, such as eating, drinking, and sexual activity.
  a. pituitary gland   c. hippocampus
  b. medial forebrain bundle   d. parietal lobe

11. _____ is a condition in which something is learned but not manifested in a behavioral change until sometime in the future.
  a. Latent learning   c. Implicit learning
  b. Observational learning   d. Successive approximation

Observational Learning: Look at Me

The guiding principle of operant conditioning is that reinforcement determines future behavior. That tenet fit well with behaviorism's insistence on observable action and the behaviorists' reluctance to consider what was going on in the mind. As we've already seen, however, cognition helps explain why operant conditioning doesn't always happen as behaviorists would expect. The next section looks at learning by keeping one's eyes and ears open to the surrounding environment and further chips away at strict behaviorist doctrine.

Learning without Direct Experience

Four-year-old Rodney and his 2-year-old sister Margie had always been told to keep away from the stove, and that's good advice for any child. Being a mischievous imp, however, Rodney decided one day to heat up a burner and place his hand over it . . . until the singeing of his flesh led him to recoil, shrieking in pain. Rodney was more scared than hurt, really—and no one hearing this story doubts that he learned something important that day. But little Margie, who stood by watching these events unfold, *also* learned the same lesson. Rodney's story is a behaviorist's textbook example: The administration of punishment led to a learned change in his behavior. But how can we explain Margie's learning? She received neither punishment nor reinforcement—indeed, she didn't even have direct experience with the wicked appliance—yet it's arguable that she's just as likely to keep her hands away from stoves in the future as Rodney is.

Margie's is a case of **observational learning**, in which *learning takes place by watching the actions of others*. Observational learning challenges behaviorism's reinforcement-based explanations of classical and operant conditioning, but there is no doubt that this type of learning produces changes in behavior. In all societies, appropriate social behavior is passed on from generation to generation largely through observation (Bandura, 1965), not only through deliberate training of the young but also through young people observing the patterns of behaviors of their elders. Tasks such as using chopsticks or learning to operate a TV's remote control are more easily acquired if we watch these activities being carried out before we try ourselves. Even complex motor tasks, such as performing surgery, are learned in part through extensive observation and imitation of models. And anyone who is about to undergo surgery is grateful for observational learning. Imagine if surgeons had to learn by trial-and-error or by Skinner's technique for shaping of successive approximations!

● Why might a younger sibling appear to learn faster than a first-born?

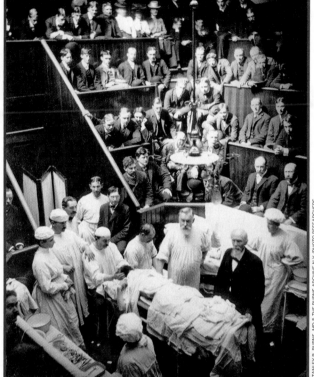

Observational learning plays an important role in surgical training, as illustrated by the medical students observing famed German surgeon Vincenz Czerny (beard and white gown) perform stomach surgery in 1901 at a San Francisco hospital.

STANLEY B. BURNS, MD & THE BURNS ARCHIVE N.Y./PHOTO RESEARCHERS

Observational Learning in Humans

In a series of studies that have become landmarks in psychology, Albert Bandura and his colleagues investigated the parameters of observational learning (Bandura, Ross, & Ross, 1961). The researchers escorted individual preschoolers into a play area, stocked with a number of desirable toys that 4-year-olds typically like: stickers, ink stamps, crayons. An adult *model,* someone whose behavior might serve as a guide for others, was then led into the room and seated in the opposite corner, where there were several toys including a Bobo doll, which is a large inflatable plastic toy with a weighted bottom that allows it to bounce back upright when knocked down. The adult played quietly for a bit but then started aggressing toward the Bobo doll, knocking it down, jumping on it, hitting it with the mallet, kicking it around the room, and yelling "Pow!" and "Kick him!" When the children who observed these actions were later allowed to play with a

observational learning A condition in which learning takes place by watching the actions of others.

● Video games have become a must-have device in many households. Research on observational learning suggests that seeing violent images—in video games, on television, or in movies—can increase the likelihood of enacting violent behavior.

ALEX SEGRE/ALAMY

variety of toys, including a Bobo doll, they were more than twice as likely to interact with it in an aggressive manner as a group of children who hadn't observed the aggressive model.

As **FIGURE 6.14** shows, the degree of imitation that the children showed was startling. In fact, the adult model purposely used novel behaviors such as hitting the doll with a mallet or throwing it up in the air so that the researchers could distinguish aggressive acts that were clearly the result of observational learning. The children in these studies also showed that they were sensitive to the consequences of the actions they observed. When they saw the adult models being punished for behaving aggressively, the children showed considerably less aggression. When the children observed a model being rewarded and praised for aggressive behavior, they displayed an increase in aggression (Bandura, Ross, & Ross, 1963).

● **What did the Bobo doll experiment show about children and aggressive behavior?**

The observational learning seen in Bandura's studies has implications for social learning, cultural transmission of norms and values, and psychotherapy, as well as moral and ethical issues (Bandura, 1977, 1994). For example, a recent review of the literature on the effects of viewing violence on subsequent behavior concluded that viewing media violence has both immediate and long-term effects in increasing the likelihood of aggressive and violent behavior among youth (Anderson et al., 2003). This conclusion

● FIGURE **6.14**

Beating Up Bobo *Children who were exposed to an adult model who behaved aggressively toward a Bobo doll were likely to behave aggressively themselves. This behavior occurred in the absence of any direct reinforcement. Observational learning was responsible for producing the children's behaviors.*

ALBERT BANDURA, DEPT. OF PSYCHOLOGY, STANFORD UNIVERSITY

speaks volumes about the impact of violence and aggression as presented on TV, in movies, and in video games on our society, but it is hardly surprising in light of Bandura's pioneering research more than 40 years earlier.

Observational Learning in Animals

Humans aren't the only creatures capable of learning through observing. A wide variety of species learns by observing. In one study, for example, pigeons watched other pigeons get reinforced for either pecking at the feeder or stepping on a bar. When placed in the box later, the pigeons tended to use whatever technique they had observed other pigeons using earlier (Zentall, Sutton, & Sherburne, 1996). In another series of studies, researchers showed that laboratory-raised rhesus monkeys that had never seen a snake would develop a fear of snakes simply by observing the fear reactions of other monkeys (Cook & Mineka, 1990; Mineka & Cook, 1988). These results also support our earlier discussion of how each species has evolved particular biological predispositions for specific behaviors. Virtually every rhesus monkey raised in the wild has a fear of snakes, which strongly suggests that such a fear is one of this species' predispositions.

Observational learning may involve a neural component as well. *Mirror neurons* are a type of cell found in the brains of primates (including humans). Mirror neurons fire when an animal performs an action, such as when a monkey reaches for a food item. More importantly, however, mirror neurons also fire when an animal watches someone *else* perform the same specific task (Rizzolatti & Craighero, 2004). Although this "someone else" is usually a fellow member of the same species, some research suggests that mirror neurons in monkeys also fire when they observe humans performing an action (Fogassi et al., 2005). For example, monkeys' mirror neurons fired when they observed humans grasping for a piece of food, either to eat it or to place it in a container.

● **What do mirror neurons do?**

Mirror neurons, then, may play a critical role in the imitation of behavior as well as the prediction of future behavior (Rizzolatti, 2004). If the neurons fire when another organism is seen performing an action, it could indicate an awareness of intentionality, or that the animal is anticipating a likely course of future actions. Both of these elements—rote imitation of well-understood behaviors and an awareness of how behavior is likely to unfold—contribute to observational learning.

summary quiz [6.4]

12. After watching her 4-year-old brother Anthony burn his hand on a hot stove, 2-year-old Isabel refused to even go near the stove. Her behavior is best explained by the concept of
   a. negative reinforcement.
   b. positive reinforcement.
   c. observational learning.
   d. punishment.

13. Which is true of observational learning?
   a. Although humans learn by observing others, nonhuman animals seem to lack this capability.
   b. If a child sees an adult being punished for engaging in a certain behavior, the child is less likely to imitate the behavior.
   c. Humans learn complex behaviors more readily by trial and error than by observation.
   d. Viewing media violence does not affect the likelihood of aggressive behavior among youth.

14. Mirror neurons in the brain fire
   a. when an individual performs an action, but not when the individual watches someone else perform that action.
   b. when an individual watches someone perform an action, but not when the individual performs the action.
   c. when an individual watches someone get punished, but not when the individual watches someone get rewarded.
   d. when an individual either performs an action or watches someone else perform that action.

Implicit Learning: Under the Wires

So far, we have covered a lot of what is known about learning with only the briefest consideration of *awareness* in the learning process. You may remember we distinguished between explicit learning and implicit learning at the beginning of the chapter. People often know that they are learning, are aware of what they're learning, and can describe what they know about a topic. If you have learned something concrete, such as doing arithmetic or typing on a computer keyboard, you know that you know it and you know *what* it is you know.

But did Pavlov's dogs *know* that they had been conditioned to salivate to a bell? Did Adam and Teri in our opening vignette understand that they had learned to associate their child's toy with an emotional event? Were Bandura's young research participants aware that the adult model was affecting their behavior? It certainly makes sense to ask whether these basic learning processes in humans require an awareness on the part of the learner.

For starters, it's safe to assume that people are sensitive to the patterns of events that occur in the world around them. Most people don't stumble through life thoroughly unaware of what's going on. But people usually are attuned to linguistic, social, emotional, or sensorimotor events in the world around them so much so that they gradually build up internal representations of those patterns that were acquired without explicit awareness. This process is often called **implicit learning**, or *learning that takes place largely independent of awareness of both the process and the products of information acquisition.* As an example, although children are often given explicit rules of social conduct ("Don't chew with your mouth open"), they learn how to behave in a civilized way through experience. They're probably not aware of when or how they learned a particular course of action and may not even be able to state the general principle underlying their behavior. Yet most kids have learned not to eat with their feet, to listen when they are spoken to, and not to kick the dog. Implicit learning is knowledge that sneaks in "under the wires."

● How can you learn something without being aware of it?

Ways to Study Implicit Learning

Early studies of implicit learning showed research participants 15- or 20-letter strings and asked them to memorize them. The letter strings, which at first glance look like nonsense syllables, were actually formed using a complex set of rules called an *artificial grammar*. Take a look at the letter strings shown in **FIGURE 6.15** (on page 191). The ones on the left are "correct" and follow the rules of the artificial grammar; the ones on the right all violated the rules. The differences are pretty subtle, and if you haven't been through the learning phase of the experiment, both sets look a lot alike. Participants were not told anything about the rules, but with experience, they gradually developed

implicit learning Learning that takes place largely independent of awareness of both the process and the products of information acquisition.

FIGURE 6.15 •
Artificial Grammar and Implicit Learning *These are examples of letter strings formed by an artificial grammar. Research participants are exposed to the rules of the grammar and are later tested on new letter strings. Participants show reliable accuracy at distinguishing the valid, grammatical strings from the invalid, nongrammatical strings even though they usually can't explicitly state the rule they are following when making such judgments. Using an artificial grammar is one way of studying implicit learning (Reber, 1996).*

Grammatical Strings	Nongrammatical Strings
VXJJ	VXTJJ
XXVT	XVTVVJ
VJTVXJ	VJTTVTV
VJTVTV	VJTXXVJ
XXXXVX	XXXVTJJ

a vague, intuitive sense of the "correctness" of particular letter groupings. These letter groups became familiar to the participants, and they processed these letter groupings more rapidly and efficiently than the "incorrect" letter groupings (Reber, 1967, 1996). Research participants were then asked to classify new letter strings based on whether they follow the rules of the grammar. People turn out to be quite good at this task (usually they get between 60% and 70% correct), but they are unable to provide much in the way of explicit awareness of the rules and regularities that they are using. The experience is like when you come across a sentence with a grammatical error—you are immediately aware that something is wrong, and you can certainly make the sentence grammatical. But unless you are a trained linguist, you'll probably find it difficult to articulate which rules of English grammar were violated or which rules you used to repair the sentence.

● **Why are tasks learned implicitly difficult to explain to others?**

Other studies of implicit learning have used a *serial reaction time* task (Nissen & Bullemer, 1987). Here research participants are presented with five small boxes on a computer screen. Each box lights up briefly; when it does, the person is asked to press the button that is just underneath that box as quickly as possible. As with the artificial grammar task, the sequence of lights appears to be random, but in fact it follows a pattern. Research participants eventually get faster with practice as they learn to anticipate which box is most likely to light up next. But, if asked, they are generally unaware that there is a pattern to the lights.

Implicit learning has some characteristics that distinguish it from explicit learning. For example, when asked to carry out implicit tasks, people differ relatively little from one another, but on explicit tasks, such as conscious problem solving, they show large individual-to-individual differences (Reber, Walkenfeld, & Hernstadt, 1991). Implicit learning also seems to be unrelated to IQ: People with high scores on standard intelligence tests are no better at implicit learning tasks, on average, than those whose scores are more modest (Reber & Allen, 2000). Implicit learning changes little across the life span. Eight-month-old infants can develop implicit learning of complex auditory patterns as well as college students (Saffran, Aslin, & Newport, 1996). At the other end of the life span, implicit learning abilities decline more slowly in old age than explicit learning abilities (Howard & Howard, 1997).

Implicit learning is remarkably resistant to various disorders that are known to affect explicit learning. A group of patients suffering from various psychoses were so severely impaired that they could not solve simple problems that college students had little difficulty with. Yet these patients were able to solve an artificial grammar learning task about as well as college students (Abrams & Reber, 1988). Other studies have found that profoundly amnesic patients not only show normal implicit memories but also display virtually normal implicit learning of artificial grammar (Knowlton, Ramus, & Squire, 1992). In fact, these patients made accurate judgments about novel letter strings even though they had essentially no explicit memory of having been in the learning phase of the experiment!

Does studying all night help • • • • • • • •
or hurt your chances on the morning's exam? The latest research shows that information is consolidated by the brain during sleep, strengthening learning and making you better prepared to take the test.

Implicit and Explicit Learning Use Distinct Neural Pathways

The fact that patients suffering from psychoses or amnesia show implicit learning strongly suggests that the brain structures that underlie implicit leaning are distinct from those that underlie explicit learning. What's more, it appears that distinct regions of the brain may be activated depending on how people approach a task.

For example, in one study, participants saw a series of dot patterns, each of which looked like an array of stars in the night sky (Reber et al., 2003). Actually, all the stimuli were constructed to conform to an underlying prototypical dot pattern. The dots, however, varied so much that it was virtually impossible for a viewer to guess that they all had this common structure. Before the experiment began, half of the participants were told about the existence of the prototype; in other words, they were given instructions that encouraged explicit processing. The others were given standard implicit learning instructions: They were told nothing other than to attend to the dot patterns.

● **What technology shows that implicit and explicit learning are associated with separate structures of the brain?**

The participants were then scanned as they made decisions about new dot patterns, attempting to categorize them into those that conformed to the prototype and those that did not. Interestingly, both groups performed equally well on this task, correctly classifying about 65% of the new dot patterns. However, the brain scans revealed that the two groups were making these decisions using very different parts of their brains (see **FIGURE 6.16**). Participants who were given the explicit instructions showed *increased* brain activity in the prefrontal cortex, parietal cortex, hippocampus, and a variety of other areas known to be associated with the processing of explicit memories. Those given the implicit instructions showed *decreased* brain activation primarily in the occipital region, which is involved in visual processing. This finding suggests that participants recruited distinct brain structures in different ways depending on whether they were approaching the task using explicit or implicit learning.

● **FIGURE 6.16**
Implicit and Explicit Learning Activate Different Brain Areas
Research participants were scanned with fMRI while engaged in either implicit or explicit learning about the categorization of dot patterns. The occipital region (in blue) showed decreased brain activity after implicit learning. The areas in yellow, orange, and red showed increased brain activity during explicit learning, including the left temporal lobe (far left), right frontal lobe (second from left and second from right), and parietal lobe (second from right and far right) (Reber et al., 2003).

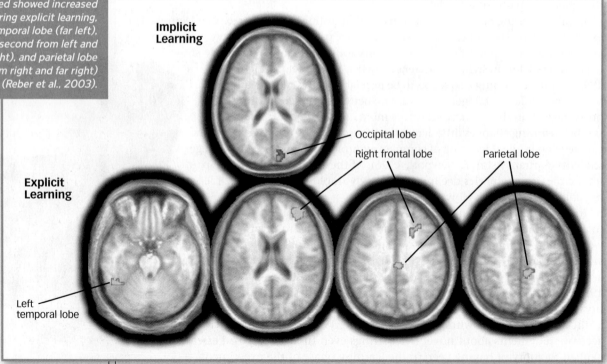

Implicit Learning

Occipital lobe

Right frontal lobe

Parietal lobe

Explicit Learning

Left temporal lobe

summary quiz [6.5]

15. Learning that takes place largely independent of awareness of both the process and the products of information acquisition is known as
   a. latent learning.
   b. implicit learning.
   c. unconscious learning.
   d. observational learning.

16. Which is true of implicit learning?
   a. People with high scores on intelligence tests are better implicit learners than those with low scores.
   b. Implicit learning decreases across the lifespan.
   c. People show large individual differences in implicit learning.
   d. Amnesic patients with *explicit* learning problems still show normal *implicit* learning.

17. Individuals who are given implicit instructions show *decreased* activity on which part of the brain?
   a. prefrontal cortex
   b. parietal cortex
   c. occipital region
   d. hippocampus

WhereDoYouStand?

Learning for Rewards or for Its Own Sake?

The principles of operant conditioning and the merits of reinforcement have more than found their way into mainstream culture. The least psychology-savvy parent intuitively understands that rewarding a child's good behavior should make that behavior more likely to occur in the future; the "law of effect" may mean nothing to this parent, but the principle and the outcome are readily appreciated nonetheless. If reward shapes good behavior, then more reward must be the pathway to exemplary behavior, often in the form of good grades, high test scores, and overall clean living. So, bring on the rewards!

Maybe, maybe not. As you learned earlier in this chapter, the *overjustification effect* predicts that sometimes too much external reinforcement for performing an intrinsically rewarding task can undermine future performance. Rewarding a child for getting good grades or high test scores might backfire: The child may come to see the behavior as directed toward the attainment of rewards rather than for its own satisfying outcomes. In short, learning should be fun for its own sake, not because new toys, new clothes, or cash are riding on a set of straight A's.

Many parents seem to think differently. You probably have friends whose parents shower them with gifts whenever a report card shows improvement; in fact, the website www.rewardsforgrades.com lists organizations that will give students external reinforcements for good grades, high test scores, perfect school attendance, and other behaviors that students are usually expected to produce just because they're students. Krispy Kreme offers a free doughnut for each A, Blockbuster gives free kids' movie rentals, and Limited Too offers a $5 discount on merchandise if you present a report card "with passing grades" (which, in many school districts, might mean all D's).

Or if you happen to be enrolled at Wichita State University, you already might be familiar with the Cash for Grades initiative (www.cashforgrades.com). The proposal is that an 8%-per-credit-hour increase to student fees would be used to then reward good student performance: $624 to a student with a 3.5 GPA at the end of a semester, $804 for straight A's.

Where do you stand on this issue? Is this much ado about nothing or too much of a good thing? On the one hand, some proponents of rewarding good academic performance argue that it mirrors the real world that, presumably, academic performance is preparing students to enter. After all, in most jobs, better performance is reinforced with better salaries, so why not model that in the school system? On the other hand, shouldn't the search for knowledge be reward enough? Is the subtle shift away from wanting to learn for its own sake to wanting to learn for a doughnut harmful in the long run?

CHAPTER REVIEW

Summary

Defining Learning: Experience That Causes a Permanent Change

- Learning creates a permanent change in the learner.

- Habituation is a simple form of learning that isn't permanent.

- Learning is a behavioral, observable activity, as the behaviorists proposed, but it is also a mental activity.

Classical Conditioning: One Thing Leads to Another

- In classical conditioning, a neutral stimulus (the conditioned stimulus, CS) is paired with a meaningful event (the unconditioned stimulus, US) until it elicits a response (the conditioned response, CR).

- Classical conditioning was embraced by the behaviorists, since it explained how behavior could be learned without having to invoke higher-level functions, such as thinking or awareness.

- If the CS is no longer paired with the US, the CR may decline or extinguish, but the CR often shows spontaneous recovery if the CS is presented again after a delay. Learned responses may generalize to other, similar stimuli—or the organism may discriminate stimuli by giving different responses to each.

- Even complex responses, such as emotional reactions, can be conditioned by pairing a neutral CS with a US that evokes fear or anxiety.

- The amygdala is an important brain substrate of classical fear conditioning; species may have evolved to prepared to condition quickly to biologically relevant stimuli, such as those that pose a threat to the organism's health or survival.

Operant Conditioning: Reinforcements from the Environment

- Operant conditioning is a process in which behaviors are modified according to their consequences: behaviors that are reinforced tend to increase in frequency, and behaviors that are punished tend to decrease in frequency.

- Operant conditioning shares many features with classical conditioning, including extinction, discrimination, and generalization. Complex behaviors may be achieved through shaping, and superstitious behaviors increase in frequency if they are paired with reinforcers—even though they do not "cause" those reinforcers to appear.

- Schedules of reinforcement define the relationship between response and reinforcement. Under interval schedules, reinforcements are presented for the first response that occurs after a time interval has expired. Under ratio schedules, organisms must perform a given number of responses to obtain reinforcement.

- Reinforcement may be associated with activity in "pleasure centers" in the brain, such as the nucleus accumbens, medial forebrain bundle, and hypothalamus.

- Although the strict behaviorists tried to explain operant conditioning without considering cognitive or evolutionary mechanisms, organisms behave as though they have expectations about the outcomes of their actions, and animal species may differ in terms of what they find hard or easy to learn.

Observational Learning: Look at Me

- Observational learning is a process by which organisms acquire information simply by watching other organisms behave.

- Complex behaviors can be acquired more quickly by observation than through shaping by successive approximation, and the harmful consequences of trial-and-error learning can be avoided.

- Animal studies suggest that observational learning may involve biological preparedness and may depend on mirror neurons in the brain, which fire when an individual performs an action or watches someone else perform that action.

Implicit Learning: Under the Wires

- Implicit learning is learning that occurs without explicit or conscious awareness on the part of the learner.

- Complex behaviors, such as grammar and social rules, can be learned through implicit learning. In the lab, implicit learning can be studied by asking participants to learn artificial grammars or motor tasks.

- Implicit and explicit learning differ from each other in a number of ways; for example, amnesic patients with explicit learning problems can exhibit intact implicit learning, and implicit and explicit learning recruit distinct brain structures.

Key Terms

learning (p. 162)

habituation (p. 163)

classical conditioning (p. 164)

unconditioned stimulus (US) (p. 164)

unconditioned response (UR) (p. 164)

conditioned stimulus (CS) (p. 164)

conditioned response (CR) (p. 164)

acquisition (p. 166)

extinction (p. 167)

spontaneous recovery (p. 167)

generalization (p. 167)

discrimination (p. 168)

biological preparedness (p. 172)

operant conditioning (p. 175)

law of effect (p. 175)

operant behavior (p. 175)

reinforcer (p. 175)

punisher (p. 175)

overjustification effect (p. 176)

shaping (p. 178)

fixed interval schedule (FI) (p. 180)

variable interval schedule (VI) (p. 180)

fixed ratio schedule (FR) (p. 180)

variable ratio schedule (VR) (p. 180)

intermittent reinforcement (p. 181)

intermittent reinforcement effect (p. 182)

latent learning (p. 183)

cognitive map (p. 184)

observational learning (p. 187)

implicit learning (p. 190)

Critical Thinking Questions

1. In habituation, repeated or prolonged exposure to a stimulus that initially evoked a response results in a gradual reduction of that response.

   How might psychologists use the concept of habituation to explain the fact that today's action movies tend to show much more graphic violence than movies of the 1980s, which in turn tended to show more graphic violence than movies of the 1950s?

2. Little Albert was exposed to the sight of a rat paired with a distressing loud noise; with repeated pairings of the rat and the noise, he began to show a CR to the rat—crying and trembling.

   Many people break into a cold sweat at the mere sound of a dentist's drill. How might this reaction be explained as a conditioned emotional response? (Hint: Assuming that human babies aren't born with a natural fear of drill sounds, then the cold sweat is a learned response [CR]. What are the CS and US?)

3. In operant conditioning, a reinforcer is a stimulus or event that increases the likelihood of the behavior that led to it, and a punisher is a stimulus or event that decreases the likelihood of the behavior that led to it.

   Suppose you are the mayor of a suburban town, and you want to institute some new policies to decrease the number of drivers who speed on residential streets. How might you use punishment to decrease the behavior you desire (speeding)? How might you use reinforcement to increase the behavior you desire (safe driving)? Based on the principles of operant conditioning you read about in this section, which approach do you think might be most fruitful?

4. In fixed ratio (FR) schedules, reinforcement is delivered after a specific number of responses have been made. In variable ratio (VR) schedules, reinforcement is delivered after an average number of responses on average. Both FR and VR are examples of intermittent reinforcement schedules, because only some responses are followed by reinforcement, and they are both more resistant to extinction than continuous reinforcement schedules, in which a reinforcement is delivered after every response.

   Imagine you own an insurance company, and you want to encourage your salespeople to sell as much merchandise as possible. You decide to give them bonuses, based on the number of items sold. How might you set up a system of bonuses using an FR schedule? Using a VR schedule? Which system do you think would encourage your salespeople to work harder, in terms of making more sales?

5. Observational learning takes place when one individual watches and learns from the actions of others. By contrast, in classical conditioning, learning takes place when an individual directly experiences the consequences (US) associated with a stimulus or event (CS).

   Monkeys can be classically conditioned to fear objects such as snakes or flowers, if those objects are paired with an aversive US, such as electric shock. Monkeys can also learn to fear snakes through observational learning, if they see another monkey reacting with fear to the sight of a snake. But monkeys cannot be trained to fear flowers through observational learning—no matter how many times they watch another monkey who has been conditioned to fear the same flower. How does the principle of biological preparedness account for this finding?

Answers to Summary Quizzes

Summary Quiz 6-1
1. b ; 2. a ; 3. c

Summary Quiz 6-2
4. d; 5. c; 6. a; 7. b

Summary Quiz 6-3
8. d; 9. a; 10. b; 11. a

Summary Quiz 6-4
12. c; 13. b; 14. d

Summary Quiz 6-5
15. b; 16. d; 17. c

Need more help? Additional resources are located at the book's free companion Web site at: www.worthpublishers.com/schacterbriefle

o very very large.
ale a powerful me
s an artist for ove
erience. Art and e
sider myself a self
me into this univer

Language, Thought, and Intelligence

AN ENGLISH BOY NAMED CHRISTOPHER showed an amazing talent for languages. By the age of 6, he had learned French from his sister's schoolbooks; he acquired Greek from a textbook in only 3 months. His talent was so prodigious that grown-up Christopher could converse fluently in 16 languages. When tested on English-French translations, he scored as well as a native French speaker. Presented with a made-up language, he figured out the complex rules easily, even though advanced language students found them virtually impossible to decipher (Smith & Tsimpli, 1995).

If you've concluded that Christopher is extremely smart, perhaps even a genius, you're wrong. His scores on standard intelligence tests are far below normal. He fails simple cognitive tests that 4-year-old children pass with ease, and he cannot even learn the rules for simple games like tic-tac-toe. Despite his dazzling talent, Christopher lives in a halfway house because he does not have the cognitive capacity to make decisions, reason, or solve problems in a way that would allow him to live independently.

Christopher's strengths and weaknesses offer compelling evidence that cognition is composed of distinct abilities. People who learn languages with lightning speed are not necessarily gifted at decision making or problem solving. People who excel at reasoning may have no special ability to master languages. In this chapter, you will learn about several higher cognitive functions that distinguish us as humans: acquiring and using language, forming concepts and categories, making decisions: the components of intelligence itself. ■

ROMAN SIGAEV/ISTOCKPHOTO

Christopher absorbed languages quickly from textbooks, yet he completely failed simple tests of other cognitive abilities

Language and Communication: Nothing's More Personal

Language is *a system for communicating with others using signals that convey meaning and are combined according to rules of grammar.* Language allows individuals to exchange information about the world, coordinate group action, and form strong social bonds. Most social species have systems of communication that allow them to transmit messages to each other. Honeybees communicate the location of food sources by means of a "waggle dance" that indicates both the direction and distance of the food source from the hive (Kirchner & Towne, 1994; Von Frisch, 1974). Vervet monkeys have three different warning calls that uniquely signal the presence of their main predators: a leopard, an eagle, and a snake (Cheney & Seyfarth, 1990). A leopard call provokes them to climb higher into a tree; an eagle call makes them look up into the sky. Each different warning call conveys a particular meaning and functions like a word in a simple language.

● *Honeybees communicate with each other about the location of food by doing a waggle dance that indicates the direction and distance of food from the hive.*

The Complex Structure of Human Language

Human language may have evolved from signaling systems used by other species. However, three striking differences distinguish human language from vervet monkey yelps, for example. First, the complex structure of human language distinguishes it from simpler signaling systems. Second, humans use words to refer to intangible things, such as *unicorn* or *democracy.* These words could not have originated as simple alarm calls. Third, we use language to name, categorize, and describe things to ourselves when we think. It's doubtful that honeybees consciously think, *I'll fly north today to find more honey so the queen will be impressed!*

● **What do all languages have in common?**

Compared with other forms of communication, human language is a relatively recent evolutionary phenomenon, emerging as a spoken system no more than 1 to 3 million years ago and as a written system as little as 6,000 years ago. There are approximately 4,000 human languages, which linguists have grouped into about 50 language families (Nadasdy, 1995). Despite their differences, all of these languages share a basic structure involving a set of sounds and rules for combining those sounds to produce meanings.

Basic Characteristics

The smallest unit of sound that is recognizable as speech rather than as random noise is the **phoneme.** For example, *b* and *p* are classified as phonemes in English, meaning that they can be used as building blocks for spoken language. Different languages use different phonemes. For example, the language spoken by the !Kung population of Namibia and Angola includes a clicking sound, a phoneme that does not appear in English.

Phonemes are combined to make **morphemes,** *the smallest meaningful units of language* (see **FIGURE 7.1** on page 199). For example, your brain recognizes the *p* sound you make at the beginning of *pat* as a speech sound, but it carries no particular meaning. The morpheme *pat,* in contrast, is recognized as an element of speech that carries meaning. Morphemes can be complete words (e.g., *pat,* or *eat*) or they can be elements that are combined to form words (e.g., *-ing* or *–ed*).

All languages have a **grammar,** *a set of rules that specifies how the units of language can be combined to produce meaningful messages.* These rules generally fall into two categories: *rules of morphology,* which indicate how morphemes can be combined to form words (for example, *eat* + *ing* = *eating*), and *rules of syntax,* which indicate how words can be combined to form phrases and sentences.

language A system for communicating with others using signals that convey meaning and are combined according to rules of grammar.

phoneme The smallest unit of sound that is recognizable as speech rather than as random noise.

morphemes The smallest meaningful units of language.

grammar A set of rules that specify how the units of language can be combined to produce meaningful messages.

deep structure The meaning of a sentence.

surface structure How a sentence is worded.

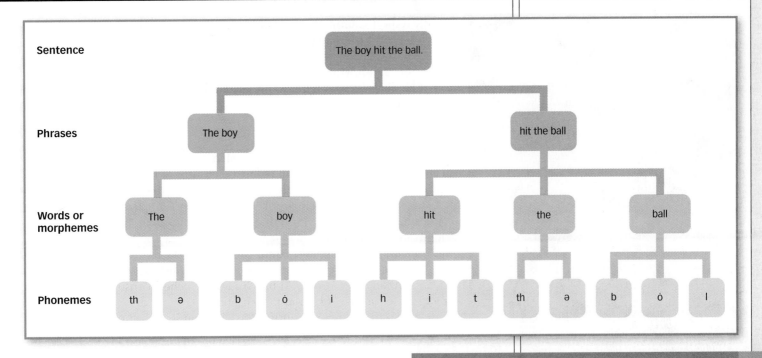

FIGURE 7.1 •

Units of Language A sentence—the largest unit of language—can be broken down into progressively smaller units: phrases, morphemes, and phonemes. In all languages, phonemes and morphemes form words, which can be combined into phrases and ultimately into sentences.

Deep Structure versus Surface Structure

Language, like other features of the human mind, is not perfect. Everyday experience shows us how often misunderstandings occur. These mindbugs sometimes result from differences between the deep structure of sentences and their surface structure (Chomsky, 1957). **Deep structure** refers to *the meaning of a sentence.* **Surface structure** refers to *how a sentence is worded.* The sentences "The dog chased the cat" and "The cat was chased by the dog" mean the same thing (they have the same deep structure) even though on the surface their structures are different.

To generate a sentence, you begin with a deep structure (the meaning of the sentence) and create a surface structure (the particular words) to convey that meaning. When you comprehend a sentence, you do the reverse, processing the surface structure in order to extract the deep structure. After the deep structure is extracted, the surface structure is usually forgotten (Jarvella, 1970, 1971). In one study, researchers played tape-recorded stories to volunteers and then asked them to pick the sentences they had heard (Sachs, 1967). Participants frequently confused sentences they heard with sentences that had the same deep structure but a different surface structure. For example, if they heard the sentence "He struck John on the shoulder," they often mistakenly claimed they had heard "John was struck on the shoulder by him." In contrast, they rarely misidentified "John struck him on the shoulder" because this sentence has a different deep structure from the original sentence.

● **Is the meaning or wording of a sentence more memorable?**
• • • • • • • • • • • • • • • • • • • •

Language Development

Language is a complex cognitive skill, yet we learn to speak and understand with little effort. We can carry on complex conversations with playmates and family before we begin school. Three characteristics of language development are worth bearing in mind. First, children learn language at an astonishingly rapid rate. The average 1-year-old has a vocabulary of 10 words. This tiny vocabulary expands to over *10,000* words in the next 4 years, requiring the child to learn, on average, about six or seven new words *every day.* Second, children make few errors while learning to speak, and the errors they do make

● *Infants enjoy sucking on pacifiers a lot more than you do. Psychologists figured out how to use this natural tendency to learn about speech processing.*

usually respect grammatical rules. This is an extraordinary feat. There are over 3 *million* ways to rearrange the words in any 10-word sentence, but only a few of these arrangements will be both grammatically correct and meaningful (Bickerton, 1990). Third, at every stage of development, children's *passive mastery* of language (their ability to understand) develops faster than their *active mastery* (their ability to speak).

Distinguishing Speech Sounds

At birth, infants can distinguish among all of the contrasting sounds that occur in all human languages. Within the first 6 months of life, they lose this ability and, like their parents, can only distinguish among the contrasting sounds in the language they hear being spoken around them. For example, two distinct sounds in English are the *l* sound and the *r* sound, as in *lead* and *read*. These sounds are not distinguished in Japanese; instead, the *l* and *r* sounds fall within the same phoneme. Japanese adults cannot hear the difference between these two phonemes, but American adults can distinguish between them easily— and so can Japanese infants. In one study, researchers constructed a tape of a voice saying "la-la-la" or "ra-ra-ra" repeatedly (Eimas et al., 1971). They rigged a pacifier so that whenever an infant sucked on it, a tape player that broadcasted the "la-la" tape was activated. When the *la-la* sound began playing in response to their sucking, the babies were delighted and kept sucking on the pacifier to keep the *la-la* sound playing. After a while, they began to lose interest, and sucking frequency declined to about half of its initial rate. At this point, the experiments switched the tape so that the voice now said "ra-ra-ra" repeatedly. The Japanese infants began sucking again with vigor, indicating that they could hear the difference between the old, boring *la* sound and the new, interesting *ra* sound.

● **What language ability do babies have that adults do not?**

Studies like these help explain why it is so difficult to learn a second language as an adult. You might not be able to even *hear* some of the speech sounds that carry crucial information in the language you want to learn, much less pronounce them properly. In a very real sense, your brain has become too specialized for your native language!

Infants can distinguish among speech sounds, but they cannot produce them reliably, relying mostly on cooing, cries, laughs, and other vocalizations to communicate. Between the ages of about 4 and 6 months, they begin to babble speech sounds. Regardless of the language they hear spoken, all infants go through the same babbling sequence. For example, *d* and *t* appear in infant babbling before *m* and *n*. Even deaf babies babble sounds they've never heard, and they do so in the same order as hearing babies do (Ollers & Eilers, 1988). This is evidence that babies aren't simply imitating the sounds they hear. Deaf babies don't babble as much, however, and their babbling is delayed relative to hearing babies (11 months rather than 6).

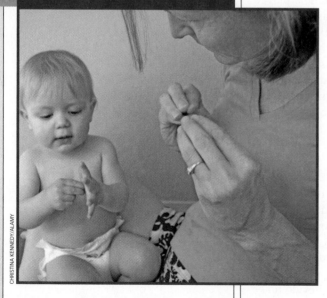

● *Deaf infants who learn sign language from their parents start babbling with their hands around the same time that hearing infants babble vocally.*

In order for vocal babbling to continue, however, babies must be able to hear themselves. In fact, delayed babbling or the cessation of babbling merits testing for possible hearing difficulties. Babbling problems can lead to speech impairments, but they do not necessarily prevent language acquisition. Deaf infants whose parents communicate using American Sign Language (ASL) begin to babble with their hands at the same age that hearing children begin to babble vocally—between 4 and 6 months (Petitto & Marentette, 1991). Their babbling consists of sign language syllables that are the fundamental components of ASL.

Language Milestones

At about 10 to 12 months of age, babies begin to utter (or sign) their first words. By 18 months, they can say about 50 words and can understand several times more than that. Toddlers generally learn nouns before verbs, and the nouns they learn first are names for everyday, concrete objects (e.g., chair, table, milk) (see **TABLE 7.1**). At about this time, their vocabularies undergo explosive growth. By the time the average child begins school, a vocabulary of 10,000 words is not unusual. By fifth grade, the average child knows the meanings of 40,000 words. By college, the average student's vocabulary is about 200,000 words. **Fast mapping**, in which *children map a word onto an underlying concept after only a single exposure,* enables them to learn at this rapid pace (Mervis & Bertrand, 1994). This astonishingly easy process contrasts dramatically with the effort required later to learn other concepts and skills, such as arithmetic or writing.

Around 24 months, children begin to form two-word sentences and phrases, such as "more milk" or "throw ball." Such sentences are referred to as *telegraphic speech* because they tend to consist of nouns and verbs, without the other elements, such as prepositions or articles, we normally use to link our speech together. Yet these two-word sentences tend to be grammatical; the words are ordered in a manner consistent with the syntactical rules of the language children are learning to speak. So, for example, toddlers will say "throw ball" rather than "ball throw" when they want you to throw the ball to them and "more milk" rather than "milk more" when they want you to give them more milk. With these seemingly primitive expressions, 2-year-olds show that they have already acquired an appreciation of the grammatical rules of the language they are learning.

TABLE 7.1

Language Milestones

Average Age	Language Milestones
0–4 months	Can tell the difference between speech sounds (phonemes). Cooing, especially in response to speech.
4–6 months	Babbles consonants.
6–10 months	Understands some words and simple requests.
10–12 months	Begins to use single words.
12–18 months	Vocabulary of 30–50 words (simple nouns, adjectives, and action words).
18–24 months	Two-word phrases ordered according to the syntactic rules. Vocabulary of 50–200 words. Understands rules.
24–36 months	Vocabulary of about 1,000 words. Production of phrases and incomplete sentences.
36–60 months	Vocabulary grows to more than 10,000 words; production of full sentences; mastery of grammatical morphemes (such as -ed for past tense) and function words (such as *the, and, but*). Can form questions and negations.

The Emergence of Grammatical Rules

Evidence of the ease with which children acquire grammatical rules comes from some interesting developmental mindbugs: errors that children make while forming sentences. If you listen to average 2- or 3-year-old children speaking, you may notice that they use the correct past-tense versions of common verbs, as in the expressions "I ran" and "You ate." By the age of 4 or 5, the same children will be using incorrect forms of these verbs, saying such things as "I runned" or "You eated"—forms most children are unlikely to have ever heard (Prasada & Pinker, 1993). The reason is that very young children memorize the particular sounds (i.e., words) that express what they want to communicate. But as children acquire the grammatical rules of their language, they tend to *overgeneralize.* For example, if a child overgeneralizes the rule that past tense is indicated by -*ed,* then *run* becomes *runned* instead of *ran.*

These errors show that language acquisition is not simply a matter of imitating adult speech. Instead, children acquire grammatical rules by listening to the speech around them and using the rules to create verbal forms they've never heard. They manage this without explicit awareness of the grammatical rules they've learned. In fact, few children or adults can articulate the grammatical rules of their native language, yet the speech they produce obeys these rules.

By about 3 years of age, children begin to generate complete simple sentences that include prepositions and articles (e.g., "Give me *the* ball" and "That belongs *to* me"). The sentences increase in complexity over the next 2 years. By the time the child is 4 to 5 years of age, many aspects of the language acquisition process are complete. As children

● **Why is it unlikely that children are using imitation to pick up language?**

fast mapping The fact that children can map a word onto an underlying concept after only a single exposure.

continue to mature, their language skills become more refined, with added appreciation of subtler communicative uses of language, such as humor, sarcasm, or irony.

Theories of Language Development

We know a good deal about how language develops, but the underlying acquisition processes have been the subject of considerable controversy and (at times) angry exchanges among theoreticians. As you learned in Chapter 1, Skinner used principles of reinforcement to argue that we learn language the way he thought we learn everything—through imitation, instruction, and trial-and-error learning. But in the 1950s, linguist Noam Chomsky published a blistering critique of this behaviorist explanation, arguing that language-learning capacities are built into the brain, which is specialized to rapidly acquire language through simple exposure to speech. Let's look at each theory and then examine more recent accounts of language development.

Behaviorist Explanations

According to behaviorists, children acquire language through simple principles of operant conditioning (Skinner, 1957), which you learned about in Chapter 6. As infants mature, they begin to vocalize. Those vocalizations that are not reinforced gradually diminish, and those that are reinforced remain in the developing child's repertoire. So, for example, when an infant gurgles "prah," most English-speaking parents are pretty indifferent. However, a sound that even remotely resembles "da-da" is likely to be reinforced with smiles, whoops, and cackles of "Good baby!" by doting parents. Maturing children also imitate the speech patterns they hear. Then parents or other adults shape those speech patterns by reinforcing those that are grammatical and ignoring or punishing those that are ungrammatical. "I no want milk" is likely to be squelched by parental clucks and titters, whereas "No milk for me, thanks" will probably be reinforced. According to Skinner, then, we learn to talk in the same way we learn any other skill: through reinforcement, shaping, extinction, and the other basic principles of operant conditioning.

The behavioral explanation is attractive because it offers a simple account of language development, but the theory cannot account for many fundamental characteristics of language development (Chomsky, 1986; Pinker, 1994; Pinker & Bloom, 1990).

- First, parents don't spend much time teaching their children to speak grammatically. So, for example, when a child expresses a sentiment such as "Nobody like me," his or her mother will typically respond with something like "Why do you think that?" rather than "Now, listen carefully and repeat after me: Nobody likes me" (Brown & Hanlon, 1970).

- Second, children generate many more grammatical sentences than they ever hear. This shows that children don't just imitate; they learn the rules for generating sentences.

- Third, as you read earlier in this chapter, the errors children make when learning to speak tend to be overgeneralizations of grammatical rules. The behaviorist explanation would not predict these overgeneralizations if children were learning through trial and error or simply imitating what they hear.

Nativist Explanations

Contrary to Skinner's behaviorist theory of language acquisition, Chomsky and others have argued that humans have a particular ability for language that is separate from general intelligence. This **nativist theory** holds that *language development is best explained as an innate, biological capacity*. According to Chomsky, the human brain is equipped with a **language acquisition device (LAD)**—*a collection of processes that facilitate language learning*. Language processes naturally emerge as the infant matures, provided the infant receives adequate input to maintain the acquisition process.

nativist theory The view that language development is best explained as an innate, biological capacity.

language acquisition device (LAD) A collection of processes that facilitate language learning.

genetic dysphasia A syndrome characterized by an inability to learn the grammatical structure of language despite having otherwise normal intelligence.

Christopher's story is consistent with the nativist view of language development: His genius for language acquisition, despite his low overall intelligence, indicates that language capacity can be distinct from other mental capacities. Other individuals show the opposite pattern: People with normal or near-normal intelligence can find certain aspects of human language difficult or impossible to learn. This condition is known **genetic dysphasia**, *a syndrome characterized by an inability to learn the grammatical structure of language despite having otherwise normal intelligence.* Consider some sentences generated by children with the disorder:

She remembered when she hurts herself the other day.

Carol is cry in the church.

Notice that the ideas these children are trying to communicate are intelligent. The problem lies in their inability to grasp syntactical rules. These problems persist even if the children receive special language training. When asked to describe what she did over the weekend, one child wrote, "On Saturday I watch TV." Her teacher corrected the sentence to "On Saturday, I watch*ed* TV," drawing attention to the *-ed* rule for describing past events. The following week, the child was asked to write another account of what she did over the weekend. She wrote, "On Saturday I wash myself and I watched TV and I went to bed." Notice that although she had memorized the past tense forms *watched* and *went,* she could not generalize the rule to form the past tense of another word (*washed*).

As predicted by the nativist view, studies of people with genetic dysphasia suggest that normal children learn the grammatical rules of human language with ease in part because they are "wired" to do so. Also consistent with the nativist view is evidence that language can be acquired only during a restricted period of development, as has been observed with songbirds. If young songbirds are prevented from hearing adult birds sing during a particular period in their early lives, they do not learn to sing. A similar mechanism seems to affect human language learning, as illustrated by the tragic case of Genie (Curtiss, 1977). At the age of 20 months, Genie was tied to a chair by her parents and kept in virtual isolation. Her father forbade Genie's mother and brother to speak to her, and he himself only growled and barked at her. She remained in this brutal state until the age of 13, when she was removed from the house. Genie's life improved substantially, and she received years of language instruction. But it was too late. Her language skills remained extremely primitive. She developed a basic vocabulary and could communicate her ideas, but she could not grasp the grammatical rules of English.

Similar cases have been reported, with a common theme: Once puberty is reached, acquiring language becomes extremely difficult (Brown, 1958). Data from studies of language acquisition in immigrants support this conclusion. In one study, researchers found that the proficiency with which immigrants spoke English depended not on how long they'd lived in the United States but on their age at immigration (Johnson & Newport, 1989). Those who arrived as children were the most proficient, whereas among those who immigrated after puberty, proficiency showed a significant decline regardless of the number of years in their new country. Given these data, it is unfortunate that most U.S. schools do not offer training in other languages until middle school or high school.

"Got Idea. Talk Better. Combine words. Make Sentences."

Immigrants who learn English as a second language are more proficient if they start to learn English before puberty rather than after.

Interactionist Explanations

Nativist theories are often criticized because they do not explain *how* language develops. A complete theory of

SUSAN MEISELAS/MAGNUM

● *A group of deaf children in Nicaragua created their own sign language, complete with grammatical rules, without receiving formal instruction. The language has evolved and matured over the past 25 years.*

language acquisition requires an explanation of the processes by which the innate, biological capacity for language combines with environmental experience. This is just what interactionist accounts of language acquisition do. Interactionists point out that parents tailor their verbal interactions with children in ways that simplify the language acquisition process: They speak slowly, enunciate clearly, and use simpler sentences than they do when speaking with adults (Bruner, 1983; Farrar, 1990). This observation supports the interactionist notion that although infants are born with an innate ability to acquire language, social interactions play a crucial role in language.

Further evidence of the interaction of biology and experience comes from a fascinating study of deaf children's creation of a new language (Senghas, Kita, & Ozyurek, 2004). Prior to about 1980, deaf children in Nicaragua stayed at home and usually had little contact with other deaf individuals. In 1981, some deaf children began to attend a new vocational school. At first, the school did not teach a formal sign language, and none of the children had learned to sign at home, but the children gradually began to communicate using hand signals that they invented.

Over the past 25 years, their sign language has developed considerably, and researchers have studied this new language for the telltale characteristics of languages that have evolved over much longer periods. For instance, mature languages typically break down experience into separate components. When we describe something in motion, such as a rock rolling down a hill, our language separates the type of movement

● **How does the interactionist theory of language acquisition differ from behaviorist and nativist theories?**

(rolling) and the direction of movement (down). If we simply made a gesture, however, we would use a single continuous downward movement to indicate this motion. This is exactly what the first children to develop the Nicaraguan sign language did. But younger groups of children, who have developed the sign language further, use separate signs to describe the direction and the type of movement—a defining characteristic of mature languages. That the younger children did not merely copy the signs from the older users suggests that a predisposition exists to use language to dissect our experiences. Thus, their acts of creation nicely illustrate the interplay of nativism (the predisposition to use language) and experience (growing up in an insulated deaf culture).

The Neurological Specialization That Allows Language to Develop

As the brain matures, specialization of specific neurological structures takes place, and this allows language to develop. In early infancy, language processing is distributed across many areas of the brain. But language processing gradually becomes more and more concentrated in two areas, sometimes referred to as the language centers of the brain. The first, *Broca's area,* is located in the left frontal cortex; it is involved in the production of the sequential patterns in vocal and sign languages (see **FIGURE 7.2**). The second, *Wernicke's area,* located in the left temporal cortex, is involved in language comprehension (whether spoken or signed). As the brain matures, these areas become increasingly specialized for

● **How does language processing change in the brain as the child matures?**

language, so much so that damage to them results in a serious condition called **aphasia,** defined as *difficulty in producing or comprehending language.*

As you saw in Chapter 1, patients with damage to Broca's area can understand language relatively well, although they have increasing comprehension difficulty as grammatical structures get more complex (Broca, 1861, 1863). But their real struggle is with speech production. Typically, they speak in short, staccato

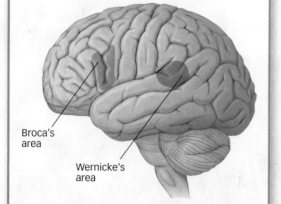

Broca's area

Wernicke's area

●●●●●●●●●●●●●●●●●●●●●● ● **FIGURE 7.2**

Broca's and Wernicke's Areas *Neuroscientists study people with brain damage in order to better understand how the brain normally operates. When Broca's area is damaged, patients have a hard time producing sentences. When Wernicke's area is damaged, patients can produce sentences, but they tend to be meaningless.*

phrases and grammatical structure is impaired. A person with the condition might say something like "Ah, Monday, uh, Casey park. Two, uh, friends, and, uh, 30 minutes."

In contrast, patients with damage to Wernicke's area can produce grammatical speech, but it tends to be meaningless, and they have considerable difficulty comprehending language (Wernicke, 1874). Such a patient might say something like "I feel very well. In other words, I used to be able to work cigarettes. I don't know how. Things I couldn't hear from are here."

In normal language processing, Wernicke's area is highly active when we make judgments about word meaning, and damage to this area impairs comprehension of spoken and signed language although the ability to identify non-language sounds is unimpaired. For example, Japanese can be written using symbols that, like the English alphabet, represent speech sounds, or by using pictographs that, like Chinese pictographs, represent ideas. Japanese patients who suffer from Wernicke's aphasia encounter difficulties in writing and understanding the symbols that represent speech sounds but not pictographs.

In normal language development, Broca's area and Wernicke's area become specialized for processing and producing language as long as the developing child is exposed to spoken or signed language. As the case of Genie shows, there is a critical period during which this specialization occurs; and if the developing brain does not receive adequate language input, this process can be permanently disrupted.

Culture & Community

Does Bilingual Education Slow Cognitive Development?

Question: What do you call someone who speaks more than one language?
Answer: A polygot.
Question: What do you call someone who speaks only one language?
Answer: An American.

In most of the world, bilingualism is the norm, not the exception. In fact nearly half of the world's population speaks more than one language (Hakuta, 1999). Despite this, bilingualism is the source of considerable controversy in the American educational system. Detractors argue that bilingual instruction can slow the cognitive development of children—a perspective supported by early research but contradicted in recent studies.

New findings show that monolingual and bilingual students show similar rates of language development. Bilingual students even exceed monolingual students in cognitive flexibility and analytic reasoning (Bialystok, 1999) and, in fact, show increased ability of the left parietal lobe to handle linguistic demands (Mechelli et al., 2004).

summary quiz [7.1]

1. The sentences "The dog chased the cat" and "The cat was chased by the dog" have _____ deep structure and _____ surface structure.
   a. different; different
   b. the same; different
   c. different; the same
   d. the same; the same

2. On the day 2 year-old Isabel helped her father build bookshelves, she added the words *board, measuring tape,* and *dowel* to her vocabulary after her first encounter with these objects. This is an example of
   a. a language acquisition device.
   b. fast mapping.
   c. telegraphic speed.
   d. linguistic relativity.

3. A collection of processes that facilitate language learning is called
   a. a language acquisition device.
   b. fast mapping.
   c. an exemplar.
   d. a deep structure.

4. Damage to Wernicke's area results in
   a. failure to produce grammatical speech.
   b. great difficulty in understanding language.
   c. genetic dysphasia.
   d. great difficulty in identifying nonlanguage sounds.

aphasia Difficulty in producing or comprehending language.

concept A mental representation that groups or categorizes shared features of related objects, events, or other stimuli.

category-specific deficit A neurological syndrome that is characterized by an inability to recognize objects that belong to a particular category while leaving the ability to recognize objects outside the category undisturbed.

family resemblance theory Members of a category have features that appear to be characteristic of category members but may not be possessed by every member.

Concepts and Categories: How We Think

A **concept** is a *mental representation that groups or categorizes shared features of related objects, events, or other stimuli*. For example, your concept of a chair might include such features as sturdiness, relative flatness, an object that you can sit on. That set of attributes defines a category of objects in the world including desk chairs, recliner chairs, flat rocks, bar stools, and so on.

● **Why are concepts useful to us?**

Concepts are fundamental to our ability to think and make sense of the world. As with other aspects of cognition, we can gain insight into how concepts are organized by looking at some instances in which they are rather disorganized. Some mindbugs in the form of unusual disorders help us understand how concepts are normally organized in the brain.

The Organization of Concepts and Category-Specific Deficits

Over 20 years ago, two neuropsychologists described a mindbug resulting from brain injury that had major implications for understanding how concepts are organized (Warrington & McCarthy, 1983). Their patient could not recognize a variety of human-made objects or retrieve any information about them, but his knowledge of living things and foods was perfectly normal. In the following year, the two neuropsychologists reported four patients who exhibited the reverse pattern: They could recognize information about human-made objects, but their ability to recognize information about living things and foods was severely impaired (Warrington & Shallice, 1984). Since the publication of these pioneering studies, over 100 similar cases have been reported (Martin & Caramazza, 2003). The syndrome is called **category-specific deficit**, *an inability to recognize objects that belong to a particular category while leaving the ability to recognize objects outside the category undisturbed.*

Category-specific deficits like these have been observed even when the brain trauma that produces them occurs shortly after birth. Two researchers reported the case of Adam, a 16-year-old boy who suffered a stroke a day after he was born (Farah & Rabinowitz, 2003). Adam has severe difficulty recognizing faces and other biological objects. When shown a picture of a cherry, he identified it as "a Chinese yo-yo." When shown a picture of a mouse, he identified it as an owl. He made errors like these on 79% of the animal pictures and 54% of the plant pictures he was shown. In contrast, he made only 15% errors when identifying pictures of nonliving things, such as spatulas, brooms, and cigars. The fact that 16-year-old Adam exhibited category-specific deficits despite suffering his stroke when he was only 1 day old strongly suggests that the brain is "prewired" to organize perceptual and sensory inputs into broad-based categories, such as living and nonliving things.

The type of category-specific deficit suffered depends on where the brain is damaged. Deficits usually result when an individual suffers a stroke or other trauma to areas in the left hemisphere of the cerebral cortex (Martin & Caramazza, 2003). Damage to the front part of the left temporal lobe results in difficulty identifying humans, damage to the lower left temporal lobe results in difficulty identifying animals, and damage to the region where the temporal lobe meets the occipital and parietal lobes impairs the ability to retrieve names of tools (Damasio et al., 1996). Similarly, imaging studies of healthy people have demonstrated that the same regions of the brain are more active during naming of tools than animals and vice versa, as shown in **FIGURE 7.3** (Martin & Chao, 2001).

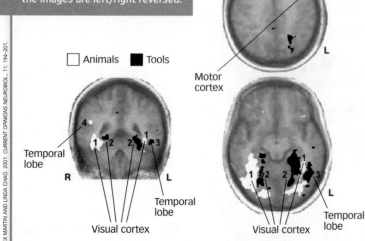

●●●●●●●●●●●●●●●●●●●● **FIGURE 7.3**

Brain Areas Involved in Category-Specific Processing *Participants were asked to silently name pictures of animals and tools while they were scanned with fMRI. The fMRIs revealed greater activity in the areas in white when participants named animals, and areas in black showed greater activity when participants named tools. Specific regions indicated by numbers include areas within the visual cortex (1, 2), parts of the temporal lobe (3, 4), and the motor cortex (5). Note that the images are left/right reversed.*

□ Animals ■ Tools

Motor cortex

Temporal lobe

Temporal lobe

Visual cortex

Visual cortex

Temporal lobe

ALEX MARTIN AND LINDA CHAO. 2001. CURRENT OPINIONS NEUROBIOL. 11: 194–201.

"Attention, everyone! I'd like to introduce the newest member of our family."

Cases of category-specific deficit provide new insights into how the brain organizes our concepts about the world, classifying them into categories based on shared similarities. Our category for "dog" may be something like "small, four-footed animal with fur

● **How does the brain organize our concepts of the world?**

that wags its tail and barks." Our category for "bird" may be something like "small, winged, beaked creature that flies." We form these categories in large part by noticing similarities among objects and events that we experience in everyday life. A stroke or trauma that damaged the particular place in your brain that stores your "dog" category would wipe out your ability to recognize dogs or remember anything about them.

Psychological Theories of Concepts and Categories

Psychologists have investigated the nature of human concepts, how they are acquired, and how they are used to make decisions and guide actions. For example, what is your definition of "dog"? Can you come up with a rule of "dogship" that includes all dogs and excludes all nondogs? Most people can't, but they still use the term *dog* intelligently, easily classifying objects as dogs or nondogs. Several theories seek to explain how people perform these acts of categorization.

Family Resemblance Theory

Eleanor Rosch developed a theory of concepts based on **family resemblance**—that is, *features that appear to be characteristic of category members but may not be possessed by every member* (Rosch, 1973, 1975; Rosch & Mervis, 1975; Wittgenstein, 1953/1999). For example, you and your brother may have your mother's eyes, although you and your sister may have your father's high cheekbones. There is a strong family resemblance among you, your parents, and your siblings despite the fact that there is no necessarily defining feature that you all have in common. Similarly, many members of the "bird" category have feathers and wings, so these are the characteristic features. Anything that has these features is likely to be classified as a bird because of this "family resemblance" to other members of the bird category. **FIGURE 7.4** illustrates family resemblance theory.

FIGURE 7.4 ● ● ● ● ● ● ● ● ● ● ● ●
Family Resemblance Theory *The family resemblance here is unmistakable, even though no two Smith brothers share all the family features. The prototype is brother 9. He has it all: brown hair, large ears, large nose, mustache, and glasses.*

Properties	Generic bird	Wren	Blue heron	Golden eagle	Domestic goose	Penguin
Flies regularly	✔	✔	✔	✔		
Sings	✔	✔	✔			
Lays eggs	✔	✔	✔	✔	✔	✔
is small	✔	✔				
Nests in trees	✔	✔				

● FIGURE **7.5**

Critical Features of a Category *We tend to think of a generic bird as possessing a number of critical features, but not every bird possesses all of those features. In North America, a wren is a "better example" of a bird than a penguin or an ostrich.*

Prototype Theory

Building on the idea of family resemblance, Rosch also proposed that psychological categories (those that we form naturally) are best described as organized around a **prototype**, which is *the "best" or "most typical member" of the category.* A prototype possesses most (or all) of the most characteristic features of the category. For North Americans, the prototype of the bird category would be something like a robin: a small animal with feathers and wings that flies through the air, lays eggs, and migrates (see **FIGURE 7.5**, above). (If you lived in Antarctica, your prototype of a bird might be a penguin: a small animal that has flippers, swims, and lays eggs.) According to *prototype theory,* if your prototypical bird is a robin, then a canary would be considered a better example of a bird than would an ostrich because a canary has more features in common with a robin than an ostrich does. People make category judgments by comparing new instances to the category's prototype. This contrasts with the classical approach to concepts in which something either is or is not an example of a concept (i.e., it either does or does not belong in the category "dog" or "bird").

Exemplar Theory

In contrast to prototype theory, **exemplar theory** holds that *we make category judgments by comparing a new instance with stored memories for other instances of the category* (Medin & Schaffer, 1978). Imagine that you're out walking in the woods, and from the corner of your eye you spot a four-legged animal that might be a wolf or coyote but that reminds you of your cousin's German shepherd. You figure it must be a dog and continue to enjoy your walk rather than fleeing in a panic. You probably categorized this new animal as a dog because it bore a striking resemblance to examples (or *exemplars*) of other dogs you've encountered. Exemplar theory does a better job than prototype theory in accounting for certain aspects of categorization, especially in that we recall not only what a *prototypical* dog looks like but also what *specific* dogs look like.

END IMAGES/SUPERSTOCK

There is family resemblance between family members despite the fact that there is no defining feature that they all have in common. Instead, there are shared common features. Someone who also shares some of those features may be categorized as belonging to the family.

Researchers have concluded that we use both prototypes and exemplars when forming concepts and categories. In other words, when we see a new four-legged animal, we decide whether it is a dog both by comparing it against our prototype of a generic dog and also by comparing it against specific exemplars of dogs we have encountered. Neuroimaging shows that the visual cortex is involved in forming prototypes, whereas the prefrontal cortex and basal ganglia are involved in learning exemplars (Ashby & Ell, 2001). This evidence suggests that exemplar-based learning involves analysis and decision making (prefrontal cortex), whereas prototype formation is a more holistic process involving image processing (visual cortex).

● **How do prototypes and exemplars relate to each other?**

summary quiz [7.2]

5. An inability to recognize objects that belong to a particular category while leaving the ability to recognize objects outside the category is called
  a. genetic dysphasia.
  c. category-specific deficit.
  b. Broca's aphasia.
  d. Wernicke's aphasia.

6. The "best" or "most typical member" of a category is called a(n)
  a. concept.
  c. exemplar.
  b. prototype.
  d. heuristic.

7. A theory of categorization that says we make category judgments by comparing a new instance with stored memories for other instances of the category is called
  a. exemplar theory.
  c. prototype theory.
  b. family resemblance theory.
  d. linguistic relativity hypothesis.

Judging, Valuing, and Deciding: Sometimes We're Logical, Sometimes Not

We use categories and concepts to guide the hundreds of decisions and judgments we make during the course of an average day. Some decisions are easy—what to wear, what to eat for breakfast, and whether to walk or ride to class—and some are more difficult— which car to buy, which apartment to rent, and which job to take after graduation.

Decision making, like other cognitive activities, is vulnerable to mindbugs—many of little consequence. Had you really thought through your decision to go out with Marge, you might instead have called Emily, who's a lot more fun, but all in all, your decision about the evening was okay. The same kinds of slips in the decision-making process can have tragic results, however. In one experiment, a large group of physicians were asked to predict the incidence of breast cancer among women whose mammogram screening tests showed possible evidence of breast cancer. The physicians were told to take into consideration the rarity of breast cancer (1% of the population at the time the study was done) and radiologists' record in diagnosing the condition (correctly recognized only 79% of the time and falsely diagnosed almost 10% of the time). Most of the physicians estimated the probability that cancer was present to be about 75%. The correct answer is 8%! The physicians apparently experienced difficulty taking so much information into account when making their decision (Eddy, 1982). Similar dismal results have been reported with a number of medical screening tests (Hoffrage & Gigerenzer, 1996; Windeler & Kobberling, 1986). Such mistakes can lead to tragic consequences: In one case, a well-meaning surgeon urged many of his "high-risk" female patients to undergo a mastectomy in order to avoid developing breast cancer— even though the vast majority of these women (85 out of 90) were not expected to develop breast cancer at all (Gigerenzer, 2002).

Before you conclude that humans are poorly equipped to make important decisions, note that our success rate often depends on the nature of the task. Let's find out why this is so.

Decision Making: Rational and Otherwise

Economists contend that if we are rational and free to make our own decisions, we will behave as predicted by **rational choice theory:** *We make decisions by determining how likely something is to happen, judging the value of the outcome, and then multiplying the two*

prototype The "best" or "most typical member" of a category.

exemplar theory A theory of categorization that argues that we make category judgments by comparing a new instance with stored memories for other instances of the category.

rational choice theory The classical view that we make decisions by determining how likely something is to happen, judging the value of the outcome, and then multiplying the two.

● People don't always make rational choices. When a lottery jackpot is larger than usual, more people will buy lottery tickets, thinking that they might well "win big." However, more people buying lottery tickets reduces the likelihood of any one person's winning the lottery. Ironically, people have a better chance at winning a lottery with a relatively small jackpot.

(Edwards, 1955). This means that our judgments will vary depending on the value we assign to the possible outcomes. Suppose, for example, you were asked to choose between a 10% opportunity to gain $500 and a 20% chance of gaining $2,000. The rational person would choose the second alternative because the expected payoff is $400 ($2,000 × 20%), whereas the first offers an expected gain of only $50 ($500 × 10%). Selecting the option with the highest expected value seems so straightforward that many economists accepted the basic ideas in rational choice theory. But how well does this theory describe decision making in our everyday lives? In many cases, the answer is "not very well."

As you learned earlier in the chapter, humans easily group events and objects into categories based on similarity, and they classify new events and objects by deciding how similar they are to categories that have already been learned. However, these strengths of human decision making can turn into weaknesses when certain tasks inadvertently activate these skills. In other words, the same principles that allow cognition to occur easily and accurately can pop up as mindbugs to bedevil our decision making. Here are three examples of such mindbugs.

● **How do we fail as rational decision makers?**

Judging Frequencies and Probabilities

Consider the following list of words:

> **block table block pen telephone block disk glass table block telephone block watch table candy**

You probably noticed that the words *block* and *table* occurred more frequently than the other words did. In fact, studies have shown that people are quite good at estimating the frequency with which things occur (Barsalou & Ross, 1986; Gallistel & Gelman, 1992; Hasher & Zacks, 1984).

This skill matters quite a bit when it comes to decision making. As you'll remember, physicians performed dismally when they were asked to estimate the true probability of breast cancer among women who showed possible evidence of the disease. However, dramatically different results were obtained when the study was repeated using *frequency* information instead of *probability* information. Stating the problem as "10 out of every 1,000 women actually have breast cancer" instead of "1% of women actually have breast cancer" led 46% of the physicians to derive the right answer, compared to only 8% who came up with right answer when the problem was presented using probabilities (Hoffrage & Gigerenzer, 1998). This finding suggests at a minimum that when seeking advice—even from a highly skilled decision maker—you'd be well served to make sure that your problem is described using frequencies rather than probabilities.

The Conjunction Fallacy

Consider the following description:

Linda is 31 years old, single, outspoken, and very bright. In college, she majored in philosophy. As a student, she was deeply concerned with issues of discrimination and social justice and also participated in antinuclear demonstrations.

ONLY HUMAN

NOW, LET ME CALCULATE HOW LIKELY IT IS WE'LL WALK AWAY FROM THIS. . . . Some of the 280 survivors (out of 340) of a Dutch charter plane that crashed in a wind gust in the resort town of Faro, Portugal, gathered to tell their stories to reporters. Wim Kodman, 27, who is a botanist, said he was trying to calm a friend during the wind turbulence by appealing to logic. Said Kodman, "I told him, 'I'm a scientist; we're objective.' I told him a crash was improbable. I was trying to remember the exact probability when we smashed into the ground."

conjunction fallacy When people think that two events are more likely to occur together than either individual event.

framing effects When people give different answers to the same problem depending on how the problem is phrased (or framed).

sunk-cost fallacy A framing effect in which people make decisions about a current situation based on what they have previously invested in the situation.

Which state of affairs is more probable?

a. Linda is a bank teller.

b. Linda is a bank teller and is active in the feminist movement.

In one study, 89% of participants rated option **b** as more probable than option **a** (Tversky & Kahneman, 1983), although that's logically impossible. This mindbug is called the **conjunction fallacy** because *people think that two events are more likely to occur together than either individual event.* In fact, the joint probability that *two* things are true is always mathematically less than the independent probability of each event; therefore, it's always *more* probable that any one state of affairs is true than is a set of events simultaneously (**FIGURE 7.6**).

Framing Effects

You've seen that, according to rational choice theory, our judgments will vary depending on the value we place on the expected outcome. So how effective are we at assigning value to our choices? Not surprisingly, a mindbug can affect this situation. Studies show that **framing effects**, which occur when *people give different answers to the same problem depending on how the problem is phrased (or framed),* can influence the assignment of value.

For example, if people are told that a particular drug has a 70% effectiveness rate, they're usually pretty impressed: 70% of the time the drug cures what ails you sounds like a good deal. Tell them instead that a drug has a 30% failure rate—30% of the time it does no good—and they typically perceive it as risky, potentially harmful, something to be avoided. Notice that the information is the same: A 70% effectiveness rate means that 30% of the time, it's ineffective. The way the information is framed, however, leads to substantially different conclusions (Tversky & Kahneman, 1981).

● **Why does a 70% success rate sound better than a 30% failure rate?**

One of the most striking framing effects is the **sunk-cost fallacy**, which occurs when *people make decisions about a current situation based on what they have previously invested in the situation.* Imagine waiting in line for 3 hours, paying $100 for a ticket to see your favorite bands, and waking on the day of the outdoor concert to find that it's bitterly cold and rainy. If you go, you'll feel miserable. But if you stay home, the $100 you paid for the ticket and the time you spent in line will have been wasted.

Notice that you have two choices: (1) spend $100 and stay comfortably at home or (2) spend $100 and endure many uncomfortable hours in the rain. The $100 is gone in either case; it's a sunk cost, irretrievable now. But the way you framed the problem creates a mindbug: Because you invested time and money, you probably feel obligated to follow through, even though it's something you no longer want. If you can turn off the mindbug and ask, "Would I rather spend $100 to be comfortable or spend it to be miserable?" the smart choice is clear: Stay home and listen to the podcast!

Even the National Basketball Association (NBA) is guilty of a sunk-cost fallacy. Coaches should play their most productive players and keep them on the team longer. But they don't. The most *expensive* players are given more time on court and are kept on the team longer than cheaper players, even if the costly players are not performing up to par (Staw & Hoang, 1995). Coaches act to justify their team's investment in an expensive player rather than recognize the loss. Mindbugs can be costly!

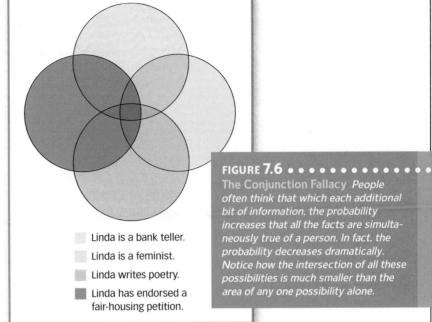

FIGURE 7.6 ● ● ● ● ● ● ● ● ● ●
The Conjunction Fallacy *People often think that with each additional bit of information, the probability increases that all the facts are simultaneously true of a person. In fact, the probability decreases dramatically. Notice how the intersection of all these possibilities is much smaller than the area of any one possibility alone.*

Linda is a bank teller.

Linda is a feminist.

Linda writes poetry.

Linda has endorsed a fair-housing petition.

Worth the cost? Sports teams sometimes ● ● ●
try to justify their investment in an expensive player who is underperforming—an example of a sunk-cost effect. Adrián Beltré is a highly paid baseball player, but his performance has not always lived up to his salary.

ANDY ALTENBURGER/ICON SMI

Prospect Theory

As you have seen, everyday decision making seems riddled with errors and shortcomings. Our decisions vary wildly depending on how a problem is presented (e.g., frequencies versus probabilities or framed in terms of losses rather than savings), and we seem to be prone to fallacies, such as the sunk-cost fallacy or the conjunction fallacy.

According to a totally rational model of inference, people should make decisions that maximize value; in other words, they should seek to increase what psychologists and economists call *expected utility*. We face decisions like this every day. If you are making a decision that involves money, and if money is what you value, then you should choose the outcome that is likely to bring you the most money. So, for example, when deciding which of two apartments to rent, you'd compare the monthly expenses for each and choose the one that leaves more money in your pocket.

● **Why will most people take more risks to avoid losses than to make gains?**

As you have seen, however, people often make decisions that are inconsistent with this simple principle. The question is, why? To explain these effects, Amos Tversky and Daniel Kahneman (1992) developed **prospect theory**, which argues that *people choose to take on risk when evaluating potential losses and avoid risks when evaluating potential gains*. These decision processes take place in two phases.

- First, people *simplify* available information. So, in a task like choosing an apartment, they tend to ignore a lot of potentially useful information because apartments differ in so many ways (the closeness of restaurants, the presence of a swimming pool, the color of the carpet, etc.). Comparing each apartment on each factor is simply too much work; focusing only on differences that matter is more efficient.

- In the second phase, people choose the prospect that they believe offers the *best value*. This value is personal and may differ from an objective measure of "best value." For example, you might choose the apartment with higher rent because you can walk to eight great bars and restaurants.

Prospect theory makes other assumptions that account for people's choice patterns. One assumption, called the *certainty* effect, suggests that when making decisions, people give greater weight to outcomes that are a sure thing. When deciding between playing a lottery with an 80% chance of winning $4,000 or receiving $3,000 outright, most people choose the $3,000, even though the expected value of the first choice is $200 more ($4,000 × 80% = $3,200)! Apparently, people weigh certainty much more heavily than expected payoffs when making choices.

Prospect theory also assumes that in evaluating choices, people compare them to a *reference point*. For example, suppose you're still torn between two apartments. The $400 monthly rent for apartment A is discounted $10 if you pay before the fifth of the month. A $10 surcharge is tacked onto the $390 per month rent for apartment B if you pay after the fifth of the month. Although the apartments are objectively identical in terms of cost, different reference points may make apartment A seem psychologically more appealing than B.

Prospect theory also assumes that people are *more willing to take risks to avoid losses than to achieve gains*. Given a choice between a definite $300 rebate on your first month's rent or spinning a wheel that offers an 80% chance of getting a $400 rebate, you'll most likely choose the lower sure payoff over the higher potential payoff ($400 × 80% = $320). However, given a choice between a sure fine of $300 for damaging an apartment or a spinning of a wheel that has an 80% chance of a $400 fine, most people will choose the higher potential loss over the sure loss. This asymmetry in risk preferences shows that we are willing to take on risk if we think it will ward off a loss, but we're risk-averse if we expect to lose some benefits.

prospect theory Proposes that people choose to take on risk when evaluating potential losses and avoid risks when evaluating potential gains.

intelligence A hypothetical mental ability that enables people to direct their thinking, adapt to their circumstances, and learn from their experiences.

summary quiz [7.3]

8. Consider the following description: Paula is 42 years old, married, and extremely intelligent. In college, she majored in English and served as a writing tutor. Which state of affairs is most probable?
   a. Paula works in a bookstore.
   b. Paula works in a bookstore and writes poetry.
   c. Paula works in a bookstore, writes poetry, and does crossword puzzles.
   d. Paula works in a bookstore, writes poetry, does crossword puzzles, and is active in the antiwar movement.

9. Claire spent $100 for a nonrefundable ticket to a play. Then she found out her granddaughter's first dance recital was that day. Claire really wanted to go to the recital but felt obligated to go to the play. She was displaying
   a. the representative heuristic.
   b. the sunk-cost fallacy.
   c. functional fixedness.
   d. the availability bias.

10. Which view states that people choose to take on risks when evaluating potential losses and avoid risks when evaluating potential gains?
   a. the frequency format hypothesis
   b. prospect theory
   c. means-end analysis
   d. belief bias

Intelligence

Let's return for a moment to Christopher, the boy who could learn languages but not tic-tac-toe. Would you call him intelligent? That's a difficult question. It seems odd to say that someone is intelligent when he or she can't master a simple game, but it seems equally odd to say that someone is unintelligent when he or she can master 16 languages. In a world of Albert Einsteins and Homer Simpsons, we'd have no trouble distinguishing the geniuses from the dullards. But ours is a world of people like Christopher and people like us—people who are sometimes brilliant, typically competent, and occasionally dimmer than broccoli. This forces us to ask hard questions: What exactly is intelligence? How can it be measured? Where does it come from? Can it be improved?

Psychologists have been asking such questions for more than a century. They agree that intelligence involves the ability to reason, plan, solve problems, think abstractly, comprehend complex ideas, and learn from experience. It not just the product of "book learning" but also the ability to "figure things out." Psychologists generally define **intelligence** as *a mental ability that enables people to direct their thinking, adapt to their circumstances, and learn from their experiences.* Clearly, intelligence is a good thing to have. So how do we measure it?

The Measurement of Intelligence: Highly Classified

Few things are more dangerous than a man with a mission. In the 1920s, psychologist Henry Goddard administered intelligence tests to arriving immigrants at Ellis Island and concluded that the overwhelming majority of Jews, Hungarians, Italians, and Russians were "feebleminded." Goddard also used his tests to identify feebleminded

When immigrants arrived at Ellis Island in the 1920s, they were given intelligence tests, which supposedly revealed that Jews, Hungarians, Italians, and Russians were "feebleminded."

NATIONAL PARK SERVICE

ratio IQ A statistic obtained by dividing a person's mental age by the person's physical age and then multiplying the quotient by 100 (see *deviation IQ*).

deviation IQ A statistic obtained by dividing a person's test score by the average test score of people in the same age group and then multiplying the quotient by 100 (see *ratio IQ*).

American families (who, he claimed, were largely responsible for the nation's social problems) and suggested that the government should segregate them in isolated colonies and "take away from these people the power of procreation" (Goddard, 1913, p. 107). The United States subsequently passed laws restricting the immigration of people from Southern and Eastern Europe, and 27 states passed laws requiring the sterilization of "mental defectives."

The Invention of IQ

From Goddard's day to our own, intelligence tests have been used to rationalize prejudice and legitimate discrimination against people of different races, religions, and nationalities. While intelligence testing has achieved many notable successes, its history is marred by more than its share of fraud and disgrace (Chorover, 1980; Lewontin, Rose, & Kamin, 1984). The fact that intelligence tests have occasionally been used to further detestable ends is especially ironic because such tests were originally developed for the noble purpose of helping poor children prosper, learn, and grow. When France instituted a sweeping set of education reforms in the 19th century that made a primary school education available to children of every social class, French classrooms were suddenly filled with a diverse group of children who differed dramatically in their readiness to learn. The French government called on psychologist Alfred Binet and physician Theophile Simon to create a test that would allow educators to develop remedial programs for those children who lagged behind their peers. "Before these children could be educated," Binet (1909) wrote, "they had to be selected. How could this be done?"

● **What was the original goal of the IQ test?**

Binet and Simon set out to develop an objective test that would provide an unbiased measure of a child's ability. They began, sensibly enough, by looking for tasks that the best students in a class could perform and that the worst students could not. The tasks they tried included solving logic problems; remembering words; copying pictures; distinguishing edible and inedible foods; making rhymes; and answering questions such as "When anyone has offended you and asks you to excuse him, what ought you to do?" Binet and Simon settled on 30 of these tasks and assembled them into a test that they claimed could measure a child's "natural intelligence," meaning a child's *aptitude* for learning independent of the child's prior educational *achievement*. Binet and Simon suggested that teachers could use their test to estimate a child's "mental age" simply by computing the average test score of children in different age groups and then finding the age group whose average test score was most like that of the child's. For example, a child who was 10 years old but whose score was about the same as the score of the average 8-year-old was considered to have a mental age of 8 and thus to need remedial education.

This simple idea became the basis for the most common measure of intelligence: the intelligence quotient. To measure the intelligence of a child, psychologists compute a ratio intelligence quotient (or **ratio IQ**) by *dividing the child's mental age by his or her physical age, and then multiplying by 100*. So a 10-year-old whose mental age is 10 has an IQ of $(10/10) \times 100 = 100$, but a 10-year-old who scores like an average 8-year-old and thus has a mental age of 8 has an IQ of $(8/10) \times 100 = 80$. This measure doesn't work well for adults (after all, there's nothing wrong with a 55-year-old who scores like a 45-year-old), and thus psychologists use a slightly different measure called the **deviation IQ**, which is computed by

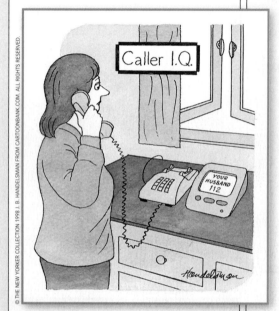

Caller I.Q.

YOUR HUSBAND 112

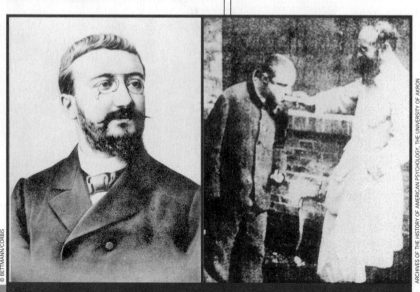

● *Alfred Binet (left, 1857–1911) and Theodore Simon (right, 1872–1961) developed the first intelligence test to identify children who needed remedial education.*

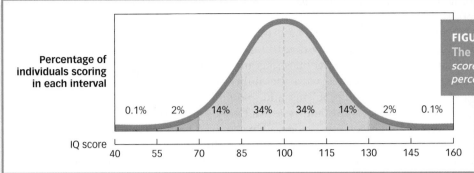

FIGURE **7.7** •
The Normal Curve of Intelligence *Deviation IQ scores produce a normal curve. This chart shows the percentage of people who score in each range of IQ.*

dividing the adult's test score by the average test score of people in the same age group, and then multiplying by 100. Thus, an adult who scores the same as others in the same age group has an IQ of 100. **FIGURE 7.7** (above) shows the percentage of people who typically score at each level of IQ on a standard intelligence test.

The Logic of Intelligence Testing

Binet and Simon's test did a good job of predicting a child's performance in school, and intelligence is surely one of the factors that contributes to that performance. But surely there are others. Affability, motivation, intact hearing, doting parents—all of these seem likely to influence a child's scholastic performance. Binet and Simon's test identified students who were likely to perform poorly in school, but was it a test of intelligence?

As you learned in Chapter 2, psychological research typically involves generating an operational definition of a hypothetical property that one wishes to measure. To design an intelligence test, we begin with the assumption that a *hypothetical property* called intelligence enables people to perform a wide variety of *consequential behaviors* such as getting good grades in school, becoming a group leader, earning a large income, finding the best route to the gym, or inventing a greaseless burrito (**FIGURE 7.8**, below). Because measuring how well people perform each of these consequential behaviors would be highly impractical, we instead devise an easily administered set of tasks (e.g., a geometric puzzle) and questions (e.g., "*Butterfly* is to *caterpillar* as *woman* is to ____") whose successful completion is known to be correlated with those behaviors. Now, instead of measuring the consequential behaviors (which is difficult to do), we can simply give people our test (which is easy to do). We

Is a Rubik's cube an intelligence test? *Intelligence is a hypothetical property that makes possible consequential behavior such as school achievement and job performance. People who can perform such behaviors can often solve puzzles like this one.*

© EMPIRE331 | DREAMSTIME.COM

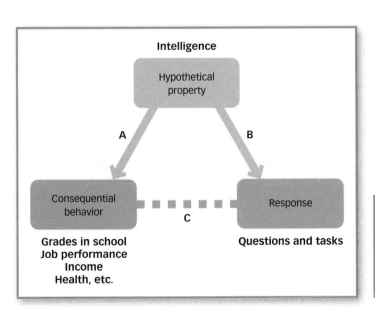

FIGURE **7.8** •
The Logic of Intelligence Testing *An intelligence test is a set of questions and tasks that elicit responses. These responses are correlated with numerous consequential behaviors (path C), presumably because the hypothetical property called intelligence causes both the responses (path B) and the consequential behaviors (path A).*

could call this "an intelligence test" as long as we understood that what we mean by that phrase is "a measurement of responses that are correlated with consequential behaviors that are correlated with intelligence." In other words, intelligence tests do not "measure" intelligence in the same way that thermometers measure temperature. Rather, they measure the ability to answer questions and perform tasks that are highly correlated with the ability to get good grades, solve real-world problems, and so on.

● **What do intelligence tests measure?**

Finding such questions and tasks isn't easy, and since Binet and Simon's day, psychologists have worked hard to construct intelligence tests that can predict a person's ability to perform the consequential behaviors that intelligence should make possible. Today the most widely used intelligence tests are the *Stanford-Binet* (a test that is based on Binet and Simon's original test but that has been modified and updated many times) and the *WAIS* (the Wechsler Adult Intelligence Scale). Both tests require respondents to answer a variety of questions and solve a variety of problems. For example, the WAIS's 13 subtests involve seeing similarities and differences, drawing inferences, working out and applying rules, remembering and manipulating material, constructing shapes, articulating the meaning of words, recalling general knowledge, explaining practical actions in everyday life, working with numbers, attending to details, and so forth.

So what are the consequential behaviors that the scores on these tests predict? Binet and Simon would be pleased to know that intelligence tests predict school performance

● **What do intelligence tests predict?**

better than they predict just about anything else. The correlation between a person's score on a standard intelligence test and his or her academic performance is roughly $r = .5$ across a wide range of people and situations. An intelligence test score is also the best predictor of the number of years of education an individual will receive, which is in part why these scores also predict a person's occupational status and income. For example, a person's score on an intelligence test taken in early adulthood correlates about $r = .4$ with the person's later occupational status (Jencks, 1979). One study of brothers found that the brother who exceeded his sibling by 15 IQ points had, on average, about 17% greater annual earnings. There is also a strong correlation between the average intelligence score of a nation and its overall economic status (Lynn & Vanhanen, 2002). An analysis of the data from thousands of studies revealed that intelligence test scores are among the best predictors of how well employees perform in their jobs (Hunter & Hunter, 1984), and job performance correlates more highly with intelligence ($r = .53$) than with factors such as performance during a job interview ($r = .14$) or education ($r = .10$).

But intelligence scores don't just predict success at school and work. Intelligence scores also do a reasonably good job of predicting a wide variety of behaviors that most of us think of as "smart" (see The Real World box on page 217). One study identified 320 people with extremely high intelligence test scores at age 13 and followed them for 10 years (Lubinski et al., 2001). Not only were they 50 times more likely than the general population to get graduate degrees and 500 times more likely than the general population to obtain a perfect score on the Graduate Record Examination, but also, at a time when fewer than a quarter of their peers had completed an undergraduate degree, they had already published scientific studies in peer-reviewed journals and stories in leading literary magazines, obtained prestigious scholastic fellowships, written operas, developed successful commercial products, and obtained patents. Intelligence test scores also predict people's performance on a variety of basic cognitive tasks. For instance, when people are briefly exposed to a pair of vertical lines and are asked to determine which is longer, people with high intelligence test

JEOPARDY PRODUCTIONS VIA GETTY IMAGES

● *Intelligence is highly correlated with income. Jeopardy contestant Ken Jennings finally lost on September 7, 2004, after becoming the biggest money winner in TV game show history at the time, earning $2,520,700 over a 74-game run.*

[THE REAL WORLD] •••••••••••••••••••••••••••••••••••••

Look Smart

Your interview is in 30 minutes. you've checked your hair twice, eaten your weight in breath mints, combed your résumé for typos, and rehearsed your answers to all the standard questions. Now you have to dazzle them with your intelligence whether you've got it or not. Because intelligence is one of the most valued of all human traits, we are often in the business of trying to make others think we're smart regardless of whether that's true. So we make clever jokes and drop the names of some of the longer books we've read in the hope that prospective employers, prospective dates, prospective customers,

and prospective in-laws will be appropriately impressed.

But are we doing the right things, and if so, are we getting the credit we deserve? Research shows that ordinary people are, in fact, reasonably good judges of other people's intelligence (Borkenau & Liebler, 1995). For example, observers can look at a pair of photographs and reliably determine which of the two people in them is smarter (Zebrowitz et al., 2002). When observers watch 1-minute videotapes of different people engaged in social interactions, they can accurately estimate which person has the highest IQ—even if they see the videos without sound (Murphy, Hall, & Colvin, 2003).

How do we do this amazing trick? We notice gaze. As it turns out, intelligent people hold the gaze of their conversation partners both when they are speaking and when they are listening, and observers seem to be tuned into this fact (Murphy et al., 2003). This is especially true when the observers are women (who tend to be better judges of intelligence) and the people being observed are men (whose intelligence tends to be easier to judge).

The bottom line? Breath mints are fine and a little gel on the cowlick certainly can't hurt, but when you get to the interview, don't forget to stare.

---

scores require less time to get the right answer (Deary & Stough, 1996; Grudnick & Kranzler, 2001; Nettleback & Lally, 1976). The same is true when people attempt to distinguish between colors or between tones (Acton & Schroeder, 2001). People with high intelligence test scores also have faster and less variable reaction times to almost any kind of stimulus (Deary, Der, & Ford, 2001). Clearly, intelligence scores predict many of the behaviors that we would expect intelligent people to perform (see **FIGURE 7.9**, below).

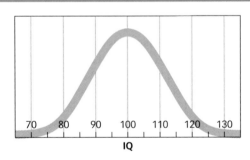

Population Percentages

Total population distribution	5	20	50	20	5
Out of labor force more than 1 month out of year (men)	22	19	15	14	10
Unemployed more than 1 month out of year (men)	12	10	7	7	2
Divorced in 5 years	21	22	23	15	9
Had children outside of marriage (women)	32	17	8	4	2
Lives in poverty	30	16	6	3	2
Ever incarcerated (men)	7	7	3	1	0
Chronic welfare recipient (mothers)	31	17	8	2	0
High school dropout	55	35	6	0.4	0

FIGURE 7.9 • • • • • • • • • • • • • • • • • •
Life Outcomes and Intelligence *People with lower intelligence test scores typically have poorer life outcomes. This chart shows the percentage of people at different levels of IQ who experience the negative life outcomes listed in the leftmost column. Adapted from Gottfredson (1998).*

factor analysis A statistical technique that explains a large number of correlations in terms of a small number of underlying factors.

two-factor theory of intelligence Spearman's theory suggesting that every task requires a combination of a general ability (which he called *g*) and skills that are specific to the task (which he called *s*).

fluid intelligence The ability to process information (see *crystallized intelligence*).

crystallized intelligence The accuracy and amount of information available for processing (see *fluid intelligence*).

The Nature of Intelligence: Pluribus or Unum?

During the 1990s, Michael Jordan won the National Basketball Association's Most Valuable Player award five times, led the Chicago Bulls to six league championships, and had the highest regular season scoring average in the history of the game. The Associated Press named him the second-greatest athlete of the century, and ESPN named him the first. So when Jordan quit professional basketball in 1993 to join professional baseball, he was as surprised as anyone to find that compared to his teammates, he—well, there's really no way to say this nicely—sucked. One of his teammates lamented that Jordan "couldn't hit a curveball with an ironing board," and a major league manager called him "a disgrace to the game" (Wulf, 1994).

Michael Jordan's brilliance on the court and his mediocrity on the diamond proved beyond all doubt that basketball and baseball require different abilities that are not necessarily possessed by the same individual. But if these two sports require different abilities, then what does it mean to say that someone is the greatest athlete of the century? Is *athleticism* a meaningless abstraction? The science of intelligence has grappled with a similar question for more than a hundred years. As we have seen, intelligence test scores predict consequential behaviors that hint at the existence of a hypothetical property called intelligence. But is there really such a property, or is intelligence just a meaningless abstraction?

General and Specific Abilities

Charles Spearman was a student of Wilhelm Wundt (who founded the first experimental psychology laboratory), and he set out to answer precisely this question. Spearman invented a technique known as **factor analysis**, which is *a statistical technique that explains a large number of correlations in terms of a small number of underlying factors.* Although Spearman's technique was complex, his reasoning was simple: If there really is a single, general ability called intelligence that enables people to perform a variety of intelligent behaviors, then those who have this ability should do well at just about everything and those who lack it should do well at just about nothing. In other words, if intelligence is a single, general ability, then there should be a very strong, positive correlation between people's performances on all kinds of tests.

To find out if there was, Spearman (1904) measured how well school-age children could discriminate small differences in color, auditory pitch, and weight, and he then correlated these scores with the children's grades in different academic subjects as well as with their teachers' estimates of their intellectual ability. His research revealed two things. First, it revealed that most of these measures were indeed positively correlated: Children who scored high on one measure—for example, distinguishing the musical note C-sharp from D—tended to score high on the other measures—for example, solving algebraic equations. Some psychologists have called this finding "the most replicated result in all of psychology" (Deary, 2000, p. 6). Second, Spearman's research revealed that although different measures were positively correlated, they were not perfectly correlated: The child who had the very highest score on one measure didn't necessarily have the very highest score on *every* measure. Spearman combined these two facts into a **two-factor theory of intelligence**, which suggested that *every task requires a combination of a general ability* (g) *and skills that are specific to the task* (s).

As sensible as Spearman's conclusions were, not everyone agreed with them. Louis Thurstone (1938) noticed that while scores on most tests were indeed positively correlated, scores on verbal tests were more highly correlated with scores on other verbal tests than they were with scores on perceptual tests. Thurstone took this "clustering

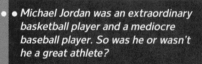

● Michael Jordan was an extraordinary basketball player and a mediocre baseball player. So was he or wasn't he a great athlete?

PATRICK MURPHY-RACEY/SPORTS ILLUSTRATED/GETTY IMAGES

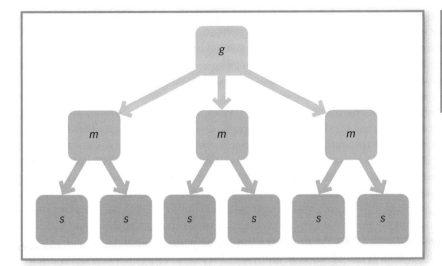

FIGURE 7.10 ● ● ● ● ● ● ● ● ● ● ● ●
A Three-Level Hierarchy *Most intelligence test data are best described by a three-level hierarchy with general intelligence (g) at the top, specific abilities (s) at the bottom, and a small number of middle-level abilities (m) (sometimes called group factors) in the middle.*

of correlations" to mean that there was actually no such thing as *g* and that there were instead a few stable and independent mental abilities such as perceptual ability, verbal ability, and numerical ability,

● **Why is the three-level hierarchy of abilities a useful way to think about intelligence?**

which he called the *primary mental abilities*. In essence, Thurstone argued that just as we have games called *baseball* and *basketball* but no game called *athletics,* so we have abilities such as verbal ability and perceptual ability but no general ability called intelligence.

As it turns out, both Spearman and Thurstone were right. More modern mathematical techniques have revealed that the correlations between scores on different mental ability tests are best described by a three-level hierarchy (see **FIGURE 7.10**, above) with a high-level ability or *general factor* (like Spearman's *g*) at the top, many low-level abilities or *specific factors* (like Spearman's *s*) at the bottom, and a few middle-level abilities or *group factors* (like Thurstone's primary mental abilities) in the middle (Gustafsson, 1984). As this hierarchy suggests, people have a very general ability called intelligence, which is made up of a small set of independent subabilities, which are made up of a large set of specific abilities that are unique to particular tasks.

Middle-Level Abilities

So what are these middle-level abilities? Some psychologists have taken a "bottom-up" approach to answering this question by examining the correlations between people's responses to different items on different intelligence tests, much as Spearman and Thurstone did. For example, psychologist John Carroll conducted a landmark analysis of intelligence test scores from nearly 500 studies conducted over a half century (Carroll, 1993), and he concluded that there are exactly eight independent middle-level abilities: *memory and learning, visual perception, auditory perception, retrieval ability, cognitive speediness, processing speed, crystallized intelligence,* and *fluid intelligence.* Although most of the abilities on this list are self-explanatory, the last two are not. **Fluid intelligence** refers to *the ability to process information,* and **crystallized intelligence**

● **Is fluid intelligence like a processing system or like data? What about crystallized intelligence?**

refers to *the accuracy and amount of information available for processing* (Horn & Cattell, 1966). If we think of the brain as a machine that uses old information ("Some spiders don't spin webs" and "All spiders eat insects") as raw material to produce new information ("That means some spiders must stalk their prey rather than trapping them"), then

Charles Spearman (left, 1863–1945) ● ● ● ● ● ● ● ● ●
discovered that people who did well on one ability test tended to do well on another, which he attributed to a hypothetical property called general intelligence, or g. Louis Thurstone (right, 1887– 1955) disagreed with Spearman's interpretation of the data and believed that people had several primary mental abilities and not a single ability called general intelligence.

"I don't have to be smart, because someday I'll just hire lots of smart people to work for me."

ONLY HUMAN

DON'T TELL PEOPLE THEIR IQ UNLESS THEY ASK In 1997, Daniel Long was fired from his job as a greeter at a Wal-Mart in Des Moines, Iowa, because he told a customer that she had to be "smarter than the cart" to get two shopping carts unstuck.

fluid intelligence refers to the way the machine runs, and crystallized intelligence refers to the information it uses and produces (Salthouse, 2000). Whereas crystallized intelligence is generally assessed by tests of vocabulary, factual information, and so on, fluid intelligence is generally assessed by tests that pose novel, abstract problems that must be solved under time pressure.

Other psychologists have taken a "top-down" approach to answering the question about the nature of middle-level abilities. Rather than starting with people's responses on standard intelligence tests, they have started with general theories about the nature of intelligence—some of which are not measured by standard tests. For example, psychologist Robert Sternberg (1988) believes that there are three kinds of intelligence, which he calls *analytic intelligence, creative intelligence,* and *practical intelligence.* Analytical intelligence is the ability to identify and define problems and to find strategies for solving them. Creative intelligence is the ability to generate solutions that other people do not. Practical intelligence is the ability to apply and implement these solutions in everyday settings. Some studies suggest that these different kinds of intelligence are independent. For example, workers at milk-processing plants develop complex strategies for efficiently combining partially filled cases of milk, and not only do they outperform highly educated white-collar workers, but their performance is also unrelated to their scores on intelligence tests, suggesting that practical and analytic intelligence are not the same thing (Scribner, 1984). Sternberg has argued that tests of practical intelligence are better than tests of analytic intelligence at predicting a person's job performance, though such claims have been severely criticized (Brody, 2003; Gottfredson, 2003).

Psychologist Howard Gardner also believes that standard intelligence tests fail to measure some important human abilities. His observations of ordinary people, people with brain damage, **prodigies** (*people of normal intelligence who have an extraordinary ability*), and **savants** (*people of low intelligence who have an extraordinary ability*) led him to conclude that there are eight distinct kinds of intelligence: *linguistic, logical-mathematical, spatial, musical, bodily-kinesthetic, interpersonal, intrapersonal,* and *naturalistic.* Although few data confirm the existence or independence of these eight abilities, Gardner's suggestions are intriguing. Moreover, he argues that standard intelligence tests measure only the first three of these abilities because they are the abilities most valued by Western culture but that other cultures may conceive of intelligence differently. For instance, the Confucian tradition

● **Why does intelligence seem to vary between cultures?**

emphasizes the ability to behave properly, the Taoist tradition emphasizes humility and self-knowledge, and the Buddhist tradition emphasizes determination and mental effort (Yang & Sternberg, 1997). Westerners regard people as intelligent when they speak quickly and often, but Africans regard

● The 5-year-old who drew the picture on the left is a savant, a "low-functioning" autistic child with a mental age of about 3 years. The picture on the right was drawn by a normal 5-year-old.

people as intelligent when they are deliberate and quiet (Irvine, 1978). Unlike Western societies, many African and Asian societies conceive of intelligence as including social responsibility and cooperativeness (Azuma & Kashiwagi, 1987; Serpell, 1974; White & Kirkpatrick, 1985), and the word for *intelligence* in Zimbabwe, *ngware,* means to be wise in social relationships.

summary quiz [7.4]

11. Isabel is 3 years old. Her mental age is 5. What is her ratio IQ?
    a. 100   b. 120   c. 60   d. 167

12. Intelligence tests predict _____ better than they predict anything else.
    a. occupational status   c. school performance
    b. income   d. creativity

13. The theory that every task requires combination of a general ability and skills that are specific to the task is known as the _____ theory.
    a. general and specific   c. primary mental abilities
    b. two-factor   d. fluid and crystallized intelligence

14. The accuracy and amount of information available for processing is called
    a. fluid intelligence.   c. creative intelligence.
    b. crystallized intelligence.   d. practical intelligence.

Unlike Americans, Africans describe people as intelligent when they are deliberate and quiet. "Thought is hallowed in the lean oil of solitude," wrote Nigerian poet Wole Soyinka, who won the Nobel Prize in Literature in 1986.

The Origins of Intelligence: From SES to DNA

Stanford professor Lewis Terman improved on Binet and Simon's work and produced the intelligence test now known as the Stanford-Binet. Among the things his test revealed was that Whites performed much better than non-Whites. "Are the inferior races really inferior, or are they merely unfortunate in their lack of opportunity to learn?" he asked, and then answered unequivocally: "Their dullness seems to be racial, or at least inherent in the family stocks from which they come." He went on to suggest that "children of this group should be segregated into separate classes . . . [because] they cannot master abstractions but they can often be made into efficient workers" (Terman, 1916).

Nearly a century later, these sentences make us cringe, and it is difficult to decide which of Terman's suggestions is the most repugnant. Is it the suggestion that a person's intelligence is a product of his or her genes? Is it the suggestion that members of some racial groups score better than others on intelligence tests? Or is it the suggestion that the groups that score best do so because they are genetically superior? If all of these suggestions seem repugnant to you, then you may be surprised to learn that the first and second suggestions are now widely accepted as facts by most scientists. Intelligence *is* influenced by genes, and some groups *do* perform better than others on intelligence tests. However, the last of Terman's suggestions—that genes *cause* some groups to outperform others—is not a fact. Indeed, it is a highly provocative claim that has been the subject of both passionate and acrimonious debate. Let's examine all three suggestions and see what the facts really are.

Intelligence and Genes

The notion that all people are not born equal is at least two millennia old. In *The Republic,* the philosopher Plato suggested that some people are naturally constituted to

prodigy A person of normal intelligence who has an extraordinary ability.

savant A person of low intelligence who has an extraordinary ability.

Sir Francis Galton (1822–1911) studied the physical and psychological traits that appeared to run in families. In his book Hereditary Genius, he concluded that intelligence was largely inherited.

Small genetic differences can make a big difference. A single gene on chromosome 15 determines whether a dog will be too small for your pocket or too large for your garage.

rule, others to be soldiers, and others to be tradesmen. But it wasn't until late in the 19th century that this suggestion became the subject of scientific inquiry. Sir Francis Galton was a half cousin of Charles Darwin, who became interested in the origins of intelligence (Galton, 1869). He did careful genealogical studies of eminent families, and he collected measurements that ranged from head size to the ability to discriminate tones from over 12,000 people. Based on these measurements, he concluded that intelligence was inherited. Was he right? Intelligence is clearly a function of how and how well the brain works, and given that brains are designed by genes, it would be rather remarkable if genes *didn't* play a role in determining a person's intelligence.

The importance of genes is easy to see when we compare the intelligence test scores of people who do and do not share genes. For example, brothers and sisters share (on average) 50% of their genes, and thus we should expect the intelligence test scores of siblings to be much more similar than the intelligence test scores of unrelated people. And they are—by a country mile. But there is a problem with this kind of comparison, which is that siblings share many things other than genes. For instance, siblings typically grow up in the same house, go to the same schools, read many of the same books, and have many of the same friends. Thus, the similarity of their intelligence test scores may reflect the similarity of their genes, or it may reflect the similarity of their experiences. To solve this problem, psychologists have studied the similarity of the intelligence test scores of people who share genes but not experiences, who share experiences but not genes, or who share both. Who are these people?

● **Why are siblings' intelligence test scores often so similar?**

Identical twins (also called *monozygotic twins*) are *twins who develop from the splitting of a single egg that was fertilized by a single sperm,* and **fraternal twins** (also called *dizygotic twins*) are *twins who develop from two different eggs that were fertilized by two different sperm.* Identical twins are genetic copies of each other, whereas fraternal twins are merely siblings who happened to have spent 9 months together in their mother's womb. Identical twins share 100% of their genes, and fraternal twins (like all siblings who have the same biological mother and father) share on average 50% of their genes. Studies show that the intelligence test scores of identical twins are correlated about *r* = .86 when the twins are raised in the same household and about *r* = .78 when they are raised in different households (e.g., when they are adopted by different families). As you'll notice from **TABLE 7.2** (on page 223), identical twins who are raised apart have more similar intelligence scores than do fraternal twins who are raised together. In other words, people who share all their genes have extremely similar intelligence test scores regardless of whether they share experiences. Indeed, the correlation between the intelligence test scores of identical twins who have never met is about the same as the correlation between the intelligence test scores of a single person who has taken the test twice! By comparison, the intelligence test scores of unrelated people raised in the same household (e.g., two siblings, one or both of whom were adopted) are correlated about *r* = .32 (Bouchard & McGue, 1981). These patterns of correlation clearly suggest that genes play an important role in determining intelligence. Of course, **TABLE 7.2** shows that shared environments play a role, too. Genetic influence can be seen by noting that identical twins raised apart are more similar than fraternal twins raised together, but environmental influence can be seen by noting that unrelated siblings raised together are more similar than related siblings raised apart.

Exactly how powerful is the effect of genes on intelligence? The **heritability coefficient** (commonly denoted as h^2) is *a statistic that describes the proportion of the difference between people's scores that can be explained by differences in their genetic makeup.* When the data from numerous studies of children and adults are analyzed together, the heritability of intelligence is roughly .5, which is to say that about 50% of the difference between people's intelligence test scores is due to genetic differences between them (Plomin & Spinath, 2004). This fact may tempt you to conclude that half your intelligence is due

TABLE 7.2

Intelligence Test Correlations between People with Different Relationships

Relationship	Shared Home?	% Shared Genes	Correlation between Intelligence Test Scores (r)
Twins			
Identical twins ($n = 4,672$)	Yes	100%	.86
Identical twins ($n = 93$)	No	100%	.78
Fraternal twins ($n = 5,533$)	Yes	50%	.60
Parents and Children			
Parent-biological child ($n = 8,433$)	Yes	50%	.42
Parent-biological child ($n = 720$)	No	50%	.24
Nonbiological parent-adopted child ($n = 1,491$)	Yes	0%	.19
Siblings			
Biological siblings (2 parents in common) ($n = 26,473$)	Yes	50%	.47
Nonbiological siblings (no parents in common) ($n = 714$)	Yes	0%	.32
Biological siblings (2 parents in common) ($n = 203$)	No	50%	.24

Source: Plomin et al., 2001a, p. 168.

identical twins (also called **monozygotic twins**) Twins who develop from the splitting of a single egg that was fertilized by a single sperm (see *fraternal twins*).

fraternal twins (also called **dizygotic twins**) Twins who develop from two different eggs that were fertilized by two different sperm (see *identical twins*).

heritability coefficient A statistic (commonly denoted as h^2) that describes the proportion of the difference between people's scores that can be explained by differences in their genetic makeup.

to your genes and half is due to your experiences, but that's not right. To understand why, consider the rectangles in **FIGURE 7.11** (below).

These rectangles clearly differ in size. If you were asked to say what percentage of the difference in their sizes is due to differences in their heights and what percentage is due to differences in their widths, you would quickly and correctly say that 100% of the difference in their sizes is due to differences in their widths and 0% is due to differences in their heights (which are, after all, identical). Good answer. Now, if you were asked to say how much of the size of rectangle A was due to its height and how much was due to its width, you would quickly and correctly say, "That's a dumb question." And it is a dumb question because the size of a single rectangle cannot be due more (or less) to height than to width. Only the *differences* in the sizes of rectangles can. Similarly, if you measured the intelligence of all the people in your psychology class and were then asked to say what percentage of the difference in their intelligences was due to differences in their genes and what percentage was due to differences in their experiences, you would quickly and correctly say that about half was due to each. That's what the heritability coefficient of .5 suggests. If you were next asked to say how much of a particular classmate's intelligence is due to her genes and how much is due to her experiences, you would (we hope) quickly and correctly say, "That's a dumb question." It is a dumb question because the intelligence of a single person cannot be due more (or less) to genes than to experience.

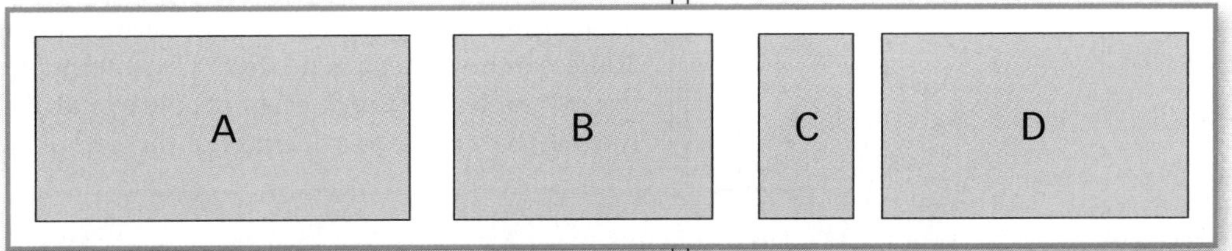

FIGURE 7.11

How to Ask a Dumb Question *These four rectangles differ in size. How much of the difference in their sizes is due to differences in their widths, and how much is due to differences in their heights? Answer: 100% and 0%, respectively. Now, how much of rectangle A's size is due to width, and how much is due to height? Answer: That's a dumb question.*

(LEFT: JEFF VINNICK/GETTY IMAGES (MIDDLE): © REUTERS/CORBIS (RIGHT): CLIVE BRUNSKILL/GETTY IMAGES

● *Identical twins (such as hockey players Daniel and Henrik Sedin) share 100% of their genes. Fraternal twins (such as swimmer Susie Maroney and her brother, Sean) share about 50% of their genes, as do non-twin siblings (such as tennis players Serena and Venus Williams).*

The heritability coefficient tells us why people in a particular group differ from one another, and thus its value can change depending on the particular group of people we measure. For example, the heritability of intelligence among wealthy children is about .72 and among poor children about .10 (Turkheimer et al., 2003). How can that be? Well, if we assume that wealthy children have fairly similar environments—that is, if they all have nice homes with books, plenty of free time, ample nutrition, and so on—then all the differences in their intelligence must be due to the one and only factor that distinguishes them from each other—namely, their genes. Conversely, if we assume that poor children have fairly different environments—that is, some have books and free time and ample nutrition, while others have some or none of these—then the difference in their intelligences may be due to either of the factors that distinguish them—namely, their genes and their environments.

● **Why is the heritability coefficient higher among children of the wealthy than among children of the poor?**

Heritability coefficients give us some sense of how large a role genes play in explaining differences in intelligence. But whether large or small, exactly *how* do genes play their role? It is tempting to imagine an "intelligence gene" that directly determines a person's brainpower at birth in the same way that, say, the hemoglobin beta gene found on chromosome 11p15.4 directly determines whether a person will be anemic. But a gene that influences intelligence is not necessarily an "intelligence gene" (Posthuma & de Geus, 2006). For instance, a gene that caused someone to enjoy the smell of library dust or to interact successfully with other people would almost surely make that person smarter, but it would be strange to call either of these an "intelligence gene." Although it is tempting to think of genes as the direct causes of traits, they may actually exert some of their most powerful influences by determining the nature of the social, physical, and intellectual environments in which people live their lives (Plomin et al., 2001a). This fact suggests that the distinction between genes and environments—between nature and nurture—is not just simple but simpleminded. Genes and environments interact in complex ways to make us who we are, and although psychologists do not yet know enough to say exactly how these interactions unfold, they do know enough to say that Terman's first suggestion was right: Intelligence is influenced by genes.

© VIVIANE MOOS/CORBIS

● *A river separates one of the richest and one of the poorest neighborhoods in Bombay, India. Research suggests that intelligence is more heritable in wealthy than poor neighborhoods.*

Intelligence and Groups

But what of Terman's second suggestion? Are some groups of people more intelligent than others? We should all hope so. If atomic scientists and neurosurgeons aren't a little bit smarter than average, then those of us who live near nuclear power plants or need spinal cord surgery have a lot to worry about. Between-group differences in intelligence are not inherently troubling. No one is troubled by the possibility that Nobel laureates are on average more intelligent than shoe salesmen, and that includes the shoe salesmen. But most of us are extremely troubled by the possibility that people of one gender, race, or nationality are more intelligent than people of another, because intelligence is a valuable commodity, and it just doesn't seem fair for a few groups to corner the market by accidents of birth or geography.

But fair or not, some groups do tend to outscore others on intelligence tests. For example, Asians routinely outscore Whites, who routinely outscore Latinos, who routinely outscore Blacks (Neisser et al., 1996; Rushton, 1995). Women routinely outscore men on tests that require rapid access to and use of semantic information, production and comprehension of complex prose, and fine motor skills, but men routinely outscore women on tests that require transformations in visual or spatial memory, certain motor skills, and fluid reasoning in abstract mathematical and scientific domains (Halpern, 1997). Indeed, group differences in performance on intelligence tests "are among the most thoroughly documented findings in psychology" (Suzuki & Valencia, 1997, p. 1104). Terman's second suggestion was clearly right: Some groups really do perform better than others on intelligence tests. The important questions that follow from this fact are (a) do group differences in intelligence test scores reflect group differences in actual intelligence, and (b) if so, what causes these group differences?

Intelligence tests are, of course, imperfect measures of intelligence. Could those imperfections create an advantage for one group over another? There is little doubt that the earliest intelligence tests were culturally biased; that is, they asked questions whose answers were more likely to be known by members of one culture (usually White Europeans) than another. When Binet and Simon asked students, "When anyone has offended you and asks you to excuse him, what ought you to do?" they were looking for answers such as "Accept the apology graciously." The answer "Demand three goats" would have been counted as wrong. But intelligence tests have come a long way in a century, and one would have to look awfully hard to find questions on a modern intelligence test that have a clear cultural bias (Suzuki & Valencia, 1997). Moreover, group differences emerge even on those portions of intelligence tests that measure nonverbal skills. In short, culturally biased tests are very unlikely to explain group differences in intelligence test scores.

● **How can the testing situation affect people's scores?**

But even when test *questions* are unbiased, testing *situations* may not be. For example, African American students perform more poorly on tests if they are asked to report their race at the top of the answer sheet, presumably because doing so causes them to feel anxious about confirming racial stereotypes, and this anxiety naturally interferes with their test performance (Steele & Aronson, 1995). European American students do not show the same effect when asked to report their race. When Asian American women are reminded of their gender, they perform unusually poorly on tests of mathematical skill, presumably because they are aware of stereotypes suggesting that women can't do math. But when the same women are instead reminded of their ethnicity, they perform unusually well on the same tests, presumably because they are aware of stereotypes suggesting that Asians are especially good at math (Shih, Pittinsky, & Ambady, 1999). Indeed, simply reading an essay suggesting that mathematical ability is strongly influenced by genes causes women to perform more poorly on subsequent tests of mathematical skill (Dar-Nimrod & Heine, 2006)! Findings such as these remind us that the situation in which intelligence tests are administered can affect members of different groups differently and may cause group differences in performance that do not reflect group differences in intelligence.

Research suggests that men tend to outperform women in abstract mathematical and scientific domains, and women tend to outperform men on production and comprehension of complex prose. Sonya Kovalevsky (1850–1891), who was regarded as one of the greatest mathematicians of her time, wrote, "It seems to me that the poet must see what others do not see, must look deeper than others look. And the mathematician must do the same thing. As for myself, all my life I have been unable to decide for which I had the greater inclination, mathematics or literature."

THE GRANGER COLLECTION

Can anxiety over racial and gender stereo-types affect individual student performance? Studies show that if these students are asked to list their ethnicities prior to taking the exam, the African American students will score poorer and the Asian American students will score higher than if neither group was asked to list their ethnicity. Interestingly, if Asian American women are asked to list their gender instead of their race, the opposite occurs, and the women will perform unusual-ly poorer than expected on math tests. What can these studies teach us about standard-ized testing?

MICHAEL J. DOOLITTLE/THE IMAGE WORKS

Situational biases may explain some of the between-group difference in intelligence test scores but surely not all. If we assume that some of these differences reflect real dif-ferences in the abilities that intelligence tests measure, then what could account for these ability differences? The obvious candidates are genes and experiences. Although scientists do not yet know enough about the complex interaction of these two candi-dates to say which is the more important determinant of between-group differences, this much is clear: Different groups *may* have different genes that influence intelligence, but they *definitely* have different experiences that influence intelligence. For example, in America, the average Black child has lower socioeconomic status (SES) than the av-erage White child. Black children often come from families with less income; attend worse schools; and have lower birth weights, poorer diets, higher rates of chronic illness, lower rates of treatment, and so on (Acevedo-Garcia et al., 2007; National Center for Health Statistics, 2004). All of these factors can affect intelligence. Indeed, for almost a century socioeconomic status has proved to be a better predictor than ethnicity of a child's intelligence test performance. Everyone agrees that *some* percentage of the between-group difference in intelligence is accounted for by experiential differences, and the only question is whether *any* of the between-group difference in intelligence is accounted for by genetic differences.

Some scientists believe that the answer to this question is yes, and others believe the answer is no. Perhaps because the question is so technically difficult to answer or per-haps because the answer has such important social and political repercussions, there is as yet no consensus among those who have carefully studied the data. When the American Psychological Association appointed a special task force to summarize what is known about the cause of the difference between the intelligence test scores of Black and White Americans, the task force concluded, "Culturally based explanations of the Black/White IQ differential have been proposed; some are plausible, but so far none has been conclusively supported. There is even less empirical support for a genetic in-terpretation. In short, no adequate explanation of the differential between the IQ means of Blacks and Whites is presently available" (Neisser et al., 1996, p. 97). Such is the state of the art.

Changing Intelligence

Americans believe that every individual should have an equal chance to succeed in life, and one of the reasons we bristle when we hear about genetic influences on intelligence is that we mistakenly believe that our genes are our destinies—that *genetic* is a synonym for *unchangeable*. In fact, traits that are influenced by genes are almost always modifiable.

The Dutch were renowned for being short in the 19th century but are now the second-tallest people in the world, and most scientists attribute their dramatic and rapid change in height to changes in diet. Yes, height is a highly heritable trait. But genes do not dictate a person's precise height so much as they dictate the range of heights that a person may achieve (Scarr & McCartney, 1983).

So is intelligence like height in this regard? Can intelligence change? Yes—it can and it does. For example, when people take intelligence tests many years apart, the people who get the best (or worst) scores when they take the test the first time tend to get the best (or worst) scores when they take it the second time. In other words, an individual's *relative intelligence* is likely to be stable over time, and the people who are the most intelligent at age 11 are likely to be the most intelligent at age 80 (Deary et al., 2000, 2004). On the other hand, an individual's *absolute intelligence* typically changes over the course of his or her lifetime (Owens, 1966; Schaie, 1996, 2005; Schwartzman, Gold, & Andres, 1987). How can a person's relative intelligence remain stable if his or her absolute intelligence changes? Well, the shortest person in your 1st grade class was probably not the tallest person in your 10th grade class, which is to say that the relative heights of your classmates probably stayed about the same as they aged. On the other hand, everyone got taller (we hope) between 1st and 10th grade, which is to say that everyone's absolute height changed. Intelligence is like that.

Not only does intelligence change across the lifespan, but it also tends to change across generations. The *Flynn effect* refers to the accidental discovery by James Flynn that the average intelligence test score has been rising by about 0.3% every year, which is to say that the average person today scores about 15 IQ points higher than the average person did 50 years ago (Dickens & Flynn, 2001; Flynn, 1984). Although no one is sure why, researchers have speculated that the effect is due to better nutrition, better parenting, better schooling, better test-taking ability, and even the visual and spatial demands of television and video games (Neisser, 1998).

Intelligence waxes and wanes naturally. But what about intentional efforts to improve it? Modern education is an attempt to do just that on a mass scale, and the correlation between the amount of formal education a person receives and his or her intelligence is quite high—somewhere in the range of $r = .55$ to $.90$ (Ceci, 1991; Neisser et al., 1996). But is this correlation so high because smart people tend to stay in school or because school makes people smart? The answer, it seems, is both. More intelligent people are indeed more likely to stay in high school and go on to college, but it also

Genetic does not mean "unchangeable." In the 19th century, Dutch men such as Vincent van Gogh were renowned for being short. Today the average Dutch man is 6 feet tall.

BURSTEIN COLLECTION/CORBIS

ANDY NELSON/CHRISTIAN SCIENCE MONITOR VIA GETTY IMAGES

Although their school was burned by attackers in 2006, the students at the Girls High School of Mondrawet in Afghanistan continue to attend. Studies show that education increases intelligence.

appears that staying in school can itself increase IQ (Ceci & Williams, 1997, p. 1052). For instance, the intelligence of schoolchildren declines during the summer, and these declines are most pronounced for children whose summers are spent on the least academically oriented activities (Hayes & Grether, 1983; Heyns, 1978). Furthermore, children born in the first 9 months of a calendar year typically start school an entire year earlier than those born in the last 3 months of the same year, and sure enough, students with late birthdays tend to have lower intelligence test scores than students with early birthdays (Baltes & Reinert, 1969). Although educational programs can reliably increase

● **Can intelligence be improved?**
∙∙∙∙∙∙∙∙∙∙∙∙∙∙∙∙∙∙∙∙∙∙∙∙∙∙∙∙∙

intelligence, studies suggest that such programs usually have only a minor impact, tend to enhance test-taking ability more than cognitive ability, and have effects that dwindle and vanish within a few years (Perkins & Grotzer, 1997). In other words, educational programs appear to produce increases in intelligence that are smaller, narrower, and shorter-lived than we might wish.

Education is a moderately effective way to increase intelligence, but it is also expensive and time-consuming. Not surprisingly, then, scientists are looking for cheaper, quicker, and more effective ways to boost the national IQ. *Cognitive enhancers* are drugs that produce improvements in the psychological processes that underlie intelligent behavior, such as memory, attention, and executive function. For example, conventional stimulants such as methylphenidate, or Ritalin (Elliott et al., 1997; Halliday et al., 1994; McKetin et al., 1999), can enhance cognitive performance, which is why there has been an alarming increase in their abuse by healthy students over the past few years. Although no one has yet developed a safe and powerful "smart pill," many experts believe that this is likely to happen in the next few years (Farah et al., 2004; Rose, 2002; Turner & Sahakian, 2006). Clearly, we are about to enter a brave new world.

What kind of world will it be? Because people who are above average in intelligence tend to have better health, longer lives, better jobs, and higher incomes than those who are below average, we may be tempted to conclude that the more intelligence we have, the better off we are. In general, this is probably true, but there are some reasons to be cautious. For example, although moderately gifted children (those with IQs of 130 to 150) are as well adjusted as their less intelligent peers, profoundly gifted children (with IQs of 180 or more) have a rate of social and emotional problems that is twice that of an average child (Winner, 1997). This is not all that surprising when you consider how out of step such children are with their peers. Furthermore, it is interesting to note that gifted children are rarely gifted in all departments. Rather, they tend to have very specialized gifts. For example, more than 95% of gifted children show a sharp disparity between their mathematical and verbal abilities (Achter, Lubinski, & Benbow, 1996), suggesting that those who are exceptionally talented in one domain are not quite so talented in the other. Some research suggests that what really distinguishes gifted children is the sheer amount of time they spend engaged in their domain of excellence (Ericsson & Charness, 1999). The essence of nature's "gift" may be the capacity for passionate devotion to a single activity.

summary quiz [7.5]

15. The genetic influence on intelligence is illustrated by the finding that
   a. unrelated siblings raised together are more similar than related siblings reared apart.
   b. identical twins reared apart are more similar than fraternal twins reared together.
   c. parents and biological children living together are more similar than parents and biological children living apart.
   d. identical twins living together are more similar than identical twins living apart.

16. Which statement is true?

  a. Half of your best friend's intelligence is due to her genes, and half is due to her experiences.

  b. The heritability of intelligence is about .5 for both poor and rich children.

  c. Across all populations, about 50% of the difference between people's intelligence test scores is due to genetic differences between them.

  d. The heritability coefficient tells us how much of each person's intelligence is due to environment and how much is due to heredity.

17. Female students who are asked their gender before a math test tend to perform more poorly than if they were not asked their gender. According to the textbook, this is because

  a. they are insulted.

  b. they want to please their teacher.

  c. they are reluctant to outperform the boys in their class, so deliberately don't do well.

  d. they feel anxious about confirming gender stereotypes that women can't do math, which interferes with their performance.

18. Which statement is true?

  a. Relative and absolute intelligence both are likely to remain stable over time.

  b. Relative and absolute intelligence both are likely to change over time.

  c. Relative intelligence is likely to be stable over time, whereas absolute intelligence is likely to change.

  d. Relative intelligence is likely to change over time, whereas absolute intelligence is likely to be stable.

WhereDoYouStand?

Making Kids Smart or Making Smart Kids?

Once upon a time, babies were a surprise. Until the day they were born, no one knew if Mom would deliver a girl, a boy, or perhaps one of each. Advances in medicine such as amniocentesis and ultrasound technology have allowed parents to look inside the womb and learn about the gender and health of their children long before they actually meet them. Now parents can do more than just look. For example, IVF (in vitro fertilization) involves creating dozens of human embryos in the laboratory, determining which have genetic abnormalities, and then implanting only the normal embryos in a woman's womb. Gene therapy involves replacing the faulty sections of an embryo's DNA with healthy sections. These and other techniques may (or may soon) be used to reduce a couple's chances of having a child with a devastating illness such as Tay-Sachs disease, early-onset Alzheimer's disease, sickle-cell disease, hemophilia, neurofibromatosis, muscular dystrophy, and Fanconi's anemia. But in the not-too-distant future, they may also enable a couple to increase the odds that their baby will have the traits they value—such as intelligence.

If scientists do find genes that are directly related to intelligence, IVF and gene therapy will provide methods of increasing a couple's chances of having an intelligent—perhaps even an extraordinarily intelligent—child. Those who oppose the selection or manipulation of embryos fear that there is no clear line that separates repairing or selecting genes that cause disease and repairing or deselecting genes that cause normal intelligence. This could ultimately lead to a lot of interesting people never being born. As Shannon Brownlee (2002) of the New America Foundation wryly noted, "Today, Tom Sawyer and Huck Finn would have been diagnosed with attention-deficit disorder and medicated. Tomorrow, they might not be allowed out of the petri dish."

People on the other side of this debate wonder what the fuss is about. After all, many couples are already selecting their offspring for high IQ by mating with the smartest people they can find. And once their babies are born, most parents will work hard to enhance their children's intelligence by giving them everything from vitamins to cello lessons. Science writer Ron Bailey predicted that parents will someday "screen embryos for desirable traits such as tougher immune systems, stronger bodies, and smarter brains. What horrors do such designer babies face? Longer, healthier, smarter, and perhaps even happier lives? It is hard to see any ethical problem with that" (Bailey, 2002).

Should parents be allowed to use genetic screening or gene therapy to increase the odds that they will have intelligent children? Where do you stand?

CHAPTER REVIEW

Summary

Language and Communication: Nothing's More Personal

- Human language is characterized by a complex organization from phonemes to morphemes to words to phrases and sentences.

- Most children follow a pattern of language development that includes milestones such as distinguishing speech sounds (phonemes), followed by babbling, followed by understanding and using single words, and, finally, attaining adult mastery.

- Children appear to be biologically predisposed to process language in ways that allow them to extract grammatical rules from the language they hear.

- In the brain, Broca's area is critical for language production, and Wernicke's area is critical for language comprehension.

Concepts and Categories: How We Think

- We organize knowledge about objects and events by creating concepts and categories.

- Studies of people with brain damage have shown that the brain organizes concepts into distinct categories, such as living things and human-made tools.

- When we encounter a new object, we assess how well it fits in with our existing categories; prototype theory holds that we compare new items against the most "typical" member of the category; exemplar theory holds that we compare new items against other examples from the category.

Judging, Valuing, and Deciding: Sometimes We're Logical, Sometimes Not

- Rational choice theory assumes that humans make decisions based on how likely something is to happen and on the expected value of the outcome.

- However, humans often depart from rational choice; they are much less accurate at judging probabilities than at judging

frequencies, and decision making can be led further astray by mindbugs such the conjunction fallacy, and framing effects.

- Prospect theory argues that people are biased to take on risk when evaluating potential losses but to avoid risk when evaluating potential gains.

Intelligence: Highly Classified

- Intelligence is a hypothetical mental ability that allows people to direct their thinking and learn from their experiences.

- Intelligence tests measure responses (to questions and on tasks) that are thought to be correlated with consequential behaviors that are made possible by intelligence. These behaviors include academic performance and job performance.

- Most researchers agree that between g (general intelligence) and s (specific abilities) are several middle-level abilities, but not all researchers agree about what they are.

The Origins of Intelligence: From SES to DNA

- Both genes and environment influence intelligence.

- The heritability coefficient describes the extent to which differences in the intelligence test scores of different people are due to differences in their genes. It does not describe the extent to which an individual's intelligence is inherited.

- Some ethnic groups score better than others on intelligence tests, but there is no compelling evidence to suggest that these differences are due to genetic factors.

- Intelligence changes naturally over time and can be changed by interventions. Education increases intelligence, though its impact is smaller, narrower, and more short-lived than we might wish.

Key Terms

language (p. 198)
phoneme (p. 198)
morphemes (p. 198)
grammar (p. 198)
deep structure (p. 199)
surface structure (p. 199)
fast mapping (p. 201)
nativist theory (p. 202)
language acquisition device (LAD) (p. 202)

genetic dysphasia (p. 203)
aphasia (p. 204)
concept (p. 206)
category-specific deficit (p. 206)
family resemblance theory (p. 207)
prototype (p. 208)
exemplar theory (p. 208)
rational choice theory (p. 209)
conjunction fallacy (p. 211)

framing effects (p. 211)
sunk-cost fallacy (p. 211)
prospect theory (p. 212)
intelligence (p. 213)
ratio IQ (p. 214)
deviation IQ (p. 214)
factor analysis (p. 218)
two-factor theory of intelligence (p. 218)
fluid intelligence (p. 219)

crystallized intelligence (p. 219)
prodigies (p. 220)
savants (p. 220)
identical twins (p. 222)
fraternal twins (p. 222)
heritability coefficient (p. 222)

Critical Thinking Questions

1. To create a sentence, you have to change the deep structure of an idea into the surface structure of a sentence. The one receiving the message translates the surface structure of the sentence back into the deep structure of the idea.

   With surface structure so important to communication, why are we able to communicate effectively when we quickly forget the surface structure of sentences? Why might this forgetfulness of the surface structure be an evolutionary benefit?

2. In this chapter you read about how deaf children at a school in Nicaragua developed their own sign language. Explain how this supports the interactionist explanation of language development.

3. Rational choice theory posits that people evaluate all options when making a decision and choose the alternative with the greatest benefit to them. However, psychological research shows us that this not always the case. Indeed, we are often forced to make decisions without all the information present. In these conditions, we are often fooled into making a different decision than we normally would because of how the options are presented to us.

   Think to a recent election. How might some political candidates use conjunction fallacy, framing effects, or prospect theory to influence voters' evaluations of their opponents or their opponents' views?

4. Intelligence tests were developed for a noble purpose, but early in their history, they were sometimes used to legitimate prejudice and discrimination. Intelligence test results can also be influenced by features of the testing situation. Given what you learned about what intelligence tests can measure, would you support or oppose the suggestion that intelligence tests should be given to all school children?

Answers to Summary Quizzes

Summary Quiz 7.1
1. b; 2. b; 3. a; 4. b

Summary Quiz 7.2
5. c; 6. b; 7. a

Summary Quiz 7.3
8. a; 9. b; 10. b

Summary Quiz 7.4
11. d; 12. c; 13. b; 14. b

Summary Quiz 7.5
15. b; 16. c; 17. d; 18. c

Need more help? Additional resources are located at the book's free companion Web site at:
www.worthpublishers.com/schacterbrief1e

Consciousness

UNCONSCIOUSNESS IS SOMETHING YOU don't really appreciate until you need it. Belle Riskin needed it one day on an operating table. She awoke just as doctors were pushing a breathing tube down her throat. She felt she was choking, but she couldn't see, breathe, scream, or move. Unable even to blink an eye, she couldn't signal to the surgeons that she was conscious. "I was terrified. . . . It was like being buried alive," she explained later. "I knew I was conscious, that something was going on during the surgery. I had just enough awareness to know I was being intubated" (Groves, 2004).

How could this happen? Anesthesia for surgery is supposed to leave the patient unconscious, "feeling no pain," and yet in this case—and in about one in a thousand other operations (Sandin et al., 2000)—the patient regains consciousness at some point and even remembers the experience. Some patients remember pain; others remember the clink of surgical instruments in a pan or the conversations of doctors and nurses. This is not how modern surgery is supposed to go, but the problem arises because muscle-relaxing drugs are used to keep the patient from moving during the operation. Then, when the drugs that are given to induce unconsciousness fail to do the job, the patient is unable to move or tell doctors that there is a problem.

Waking up in surgery sounds pretty rough all by itself, but this could cause additional complications. The conscious patient could become alarmed and emotional during the operation, spiking blood pressure and heart rate to dangerous levels. Fortunately, new methods of monitoring wakefulness are being developed. One system uses sensors attached to the person's head and gives readings on a scale from 0 (no electrical activity signaling consciousness in the brain) to 100 (fully alert), providing a kind of "consciousness meter." Anesthesiologists using this index deliver anesthetics to keep the patient in the recommended range of 40 to 65 during surgery; this

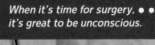
When it's time for surgery, it's great to be unconscious.

RICHARD RANSIER/CORBIS

consciousness The person's subjective experience of the world and the mind.

Cartesian theater (after philosopher René Descartes) A mental screen or stage on which things appear to be presented for viewing by the mind's eye.

phenomenology How things seem to the conscious person.

problem of other minds The fundamental difficulty we have in perceiving the consciousness of others.

system reduces postsurgical reports of consciousness and memory for the surgical experience (Sigl & Chamoun, 1994). One of these devices in the operating room might have helped Belle Riskin settle into the unconsciousness she so dearly needed. ■

Most of the time, of course, consciousness is something we cherish. How else could we experience a favorite work of art; the mellow strains of an oldie on the radio; the taste of a sweet, juicy peach; or the touch of a loved one's hand? **Consciousness** is *a person's subjective experience of the world and the mind.* Although you might think of consciousness as simply "being awake," the defining feature of consciousness is experience, which you have when you're not awake but experiencing a vivid dream. Conscious experience is essential to what it means to be human. The anesthesiologist's dilemma in trying to monitor Belle Riskin's consciousness is a stark reminder, though, that it is impossible for one person to experience another's consciousness. Your consciousness is utterly private, a world of personal experience that only you can know.

How can this private world be studied? One way to explore consciousness is to examine it directly, trying to understand what it is like. Another way to explore consciousness is to examine its altered states: the departures from normal, everyday waking that occur during alternate states such as sleep, intoxication with alcohol and other drugs, and hypnosis and meditation. Like the traveler who learns the meaning of *home* by roaming far away, we can learn the meaning of consciousness by exploring its exotic variations.

Conscious and Unconscious: The Mind's Eye, Open and Closed

What does it feel like to be you right now? It probably feels as though you are somewhere inside your head, looking out at the world through your eyes. You can feel your hands on this book, perhaps, and notice the position of your body or the sounds in the room when you orient yourself toward them. If you shut your eyes, you may be able to imagine things in your mind. The philosopher Daniel Dennett called this "place in your head" where "you" are the **Cartesian Theater** (after philosopher René Descartes), *a mental screen or stage on which things appear to be presented for viewing by your mind's eye* (Dennett, 1991). Unfortunately, the Cartesian Theater isn't available on DVD, making it difficult to share exactly what's on our mental screen with our friends, a researcher, or even ourselves in precisely the same way a second time. As you'll recall from Chapter 1, Wilhelm Wundt encountered similar problems when studying consciousness in the earliest days of psychology.

The Mysteries of Consciousness

Other sciences, such as physics, chemistry, and biology, have the great luxury of studying *objects,* things that we all can see. Psychology studies objects, too, looking at people and their brains and behaviors, but it has the unique challenge of also trying to make sense of *subjects.* A physicist is not concerned with what it is like to be a neutron, but psychologists hope to understand what it is like to be a human—that is, grasping the subjective perspectives of the people that they study. Psychologists hope to include an understanding of **phenomenology**, *how things seem to the conscious person,* in their understanding of mind and behavior. Phenomenology in psychology brings up mysteries pondered by

● **What are the great mysteries of consciousness?**

"We keep this section closed off."

great thinkers almost since the beginning of thinking. Let's look at two of the more vexing mysteries of consciousness: the problem of other minds and the mind/body problem.

The Problem of Other Minds

One great mystery is called the **problem of other minds**, *the fundamental difficulty we have in perceiving the consciousness of others*. How do you know that anyone else is conscious? People are often willing to describe in depth how they feel, how they think, and what they are experiencing. But perhaps they are just *saying* these things. There is no clear way to distinguish a conscious person from someone who might do and say all the same things as a conscious person but who is *not* conscious. Philosophers have called this hypothetical nonconscious person a "zombie," in reference to the living-yet-dead creatures of horror films (Chalmers, 1996). A philosopher's zombie could talk about experiences ("The lights are so bright!") and even seem to react to them (wincing and turning away) but might not be having any inner experience at all. No one knows whether there could be such a zombie, but then again, because of the problem of other minds, none of us will ever know for sure that another person is *not* a zombie.

Even the "consciousness meter" used by anesthesiologists falls short. It certainly doesn't give the anesthesiologist any special insight into what it is like to be the patient on the operating table; it only predicts whether patients will *say* they were conscious. We simply lack the ability to directly perceive the consciousness of others. In short, you are the only thing in the universe you will ever truly know what it is like to be.

The problem of other minds also means there is no way you can tell if another person's experience of anything is at all like yours. Although you know what the color red looks like to you, for instance, you cannot know whether it looks the same to other people. Maybe they're seeing what you see as blue and just *calling* it red. Of course, most people have come to trust each other in describing their inner lives, reaching the general assumption that other human minds are pretty much like their own. But they don't know this for a fact, and they can't know it directly. The perception of other minds is in fact something that happens in the mind of the perceiver.

How do people perceive other minds? Researchers conducting a large online survey asked people to compare the minds of 13 different targets, such as a baby, chimp, robot, man, and woman, on 18 different mental capacities, such as feeling pain, pleasure, hunger, and consciousness (see **FIGURE 8.1**, below) (Gray, Gray, & Wegner, 2007). The results suggested that people judge minds according to two major dimensions: the capacity for *experience* (such as the ability to feel pain, pleasure, hunger, consciousness, anger, or fear)

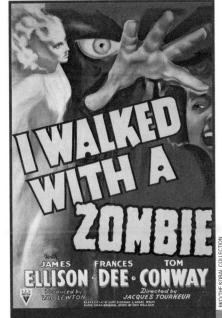

How would you know if you walked with a zombie? Could you perceive its lack of consciousness?

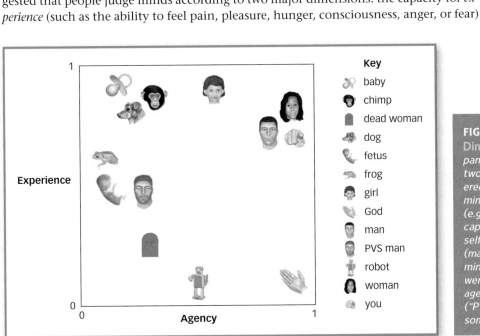

Key

🍼 baby
🐵 chimp
🗿 dead woman
🐕 dog
🫘 fetus
🐸 frog
👧 girl
🧔 God
👨 man
🧔 PVS man
🤖 robot
👩 woman
🖐 you

FIGURE 8.1

Dimensions of Mind Perception *When participants judged the mental capacities of 13 targets, two dimensions of mind perception were discovered (Gray et al., 2007). Participants perceived minds as varying in the capacity for experience (e.g., abilities to feel pain or pleasure) and in the capacity for agency (e.g., abilities to plan or exert self-control). They perceived normal adult humans (male, female, or "you," the respondent) to have minds on both dimensions, whereas other targets were perceived to have reduced experience or agency. The man in a persistent vegetative state ("PVS man"), for example, was judged to have only some experience and very little agency.*

NORELDO, THE MENTAL MARVEL, READS THE MIND OF HIS CAT, NED.

and the capacity for *agency* (such as the ability for self-control, planning, memory, or thought). As shown in **FIGURE 8.1** (on page 235), respondents rated some targets as having little experience or agency (the dead person), others as having experiences but little agency (the baby), and yet others as having both experience and agency (adult humans). Still others were perceived to have agency without experiences (the robot, God).

Ultimately, the problem of other minds is a problem for psychological science. As you'll remember from Chapter 2, the scientific method requires that any observation made by one scientist should, in principle, be available for observation by any other scientist. But if other minds aren't observable, how can consciousness be a topic of scientific study? One radical solution is to eliminate consciousness from psychology entirely and follow the other sciences into total objectivity by renouncing the study of *anything* mental. This was the solution offered by behaviorism, and it turned out to have its own shortcomings, as you saw in Chapter 1. Despite the problem of other minds, modern psychology has embraced the study of consciousness. The astonishing richness of mental life simply cannot be ignored.

The Mind/Body Problem

Another mystery of consciousness is the **mind/body problem**, *the issue of how the mind is related to the brain and body.* French philosopher and mathematician René Descartes (1596–1650) is famous, among other things, for proposing that the human body is a machine made of physical matter but that the human mind or soul is a separate entity made of a "thinking substance." He proposed that the mind has its effects on the brain and body through the pineal gland, a small structure located near the center of the brain (see **FIGURE 8.2**). In fact, the pineal gland is not even a nerve structure but rather is an endocrine gland quite poorly equipped to serve as a center of human consciousness. We now know that, far from the tiny connection between mind and brain in the pineal gland that was proposed by Descartes, the mind and brain are connected everywhere to each other! In other words, "the mind is what the brain does" (Minsky, 1986, p. 287).

But Descartes was right in pointing out the difficulty of reconciling the physical body with the mind. Most psychologists assume that mental events are intimately tied to brain events, such that every thought, perception, or feeling is associated with a particular pattern of activation of neurons in the brain (see Chapter 3). Thinking about a particular duck, for instance, occurs with a unique array of neural connections and activations. If the neurons repeat that pattern, then you must be thinking of the duck; conversely, if you think of the duck, the brain activity occurs in that pattern.

One telling set of studies, however, suggests that the brain's activities *precede* the activities of the conscious mind. The electrical activity in the brains of volunteers was measured using sensors placed on their scalps as they repeatedly decided when to move a hand (Libet, 1985). Participants were also asked to indicate exactly when they consciously chose to move by reporting the position of a dot moving rapidly around the face of a clock just at the point of the decision (**FIGURE 8.3a**, on page 237). As a rule, the

● **What comes first: brain activity or thinking?**

brain begins to show electrical activity around half a second before a voluntary action (535 milliseconds, to be exact). This makes sense since brain activity certainly seems to be necessary to get an action started. Surprisingly, though, the brain also started to show electrical activity before the person's conscious decision to move. As shown in **FIGURE 8.3b**, the brain becomes active more than 300 milliseconds before participants report that they are consciously trying to move. Although your personal intuition is that you *think* of an action and *then* do it, these experiments suggest that your brain is getting started before *either* the thinking or the doing, preparing the way for both thought and action. Quite simply, it may appear to us that our minds are leading our brains and bodies, but the order of events may be the other way around (Wegner, 2002).

● FIGURE 8.2
Seat of the Soul *Descartes imagined that the seat of the soul—and consciousness—might reside in the pineal gland located in the ventricles of the brain. This original drawing from Descartes (1662) shows the pineal gland (H) nicely situated for a soul, right in the middle of the brain.*

mind/body problem The issue of how the mind is related to the brain and body.

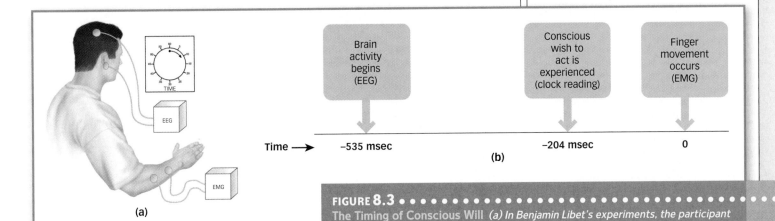

FIGURE 8.3 •
The Timing of Conscious Will *(a) In Benjamin Libet's experiments, the participant was asked to move fingers at will while simultaneously watching a dot move around the face of a clock to mark the moment at which the action was consciously willed. Meanwhile, EEG sensors timed the onset of brain activation and EMG sensors timed the muscle movement. (b) The experiment showed that brain activity (EEG) precedes the willed movement of the finger (EMG) but that the reported time of consciously willing the finger to move follows the brain activity.*

The Nature of Consciousness

How would you describe your own consciousness? Researchers examining people's descriptions suggest that consciousness has four basic properties—intentionality, unity, selectivity, and transience—that it occurs on different levels, and that it includes a range of different contents. Let's examine each of these points in turn.

Four Basic Properties

The first basic property of consciousness is *intentionality:* the quality of being directed toward an object. Consciousness is always *about* something. But how long can consciousness be directed toward a object, and how many objects can it consider? Researchers have found that conscious attention is limited. Despite all the lush detail you see in your mind's eye, the kaleidoscope of sights and sounds and feelings and thoughts, the object of your consciousness at any one moment is just a small part of all of this (see **FIGURE 8.4**).

The second basic property of consciousness is *unity,* or resistance to division. This property becomes clear when you try to attend to more than one thing at a time. You may wishfully think that you

FIGURE 8.4 •
Bellotto's *Dresden* **and Close-up** *The people on the bridge in the distance look very finely detailed in* View of Dresden with the Frauenkirche at Left, *by Bernardo Bellotto (1720–1780) (left). However, when you examine the detail closely (right), you find that the people are made of brushstrokes merely suggesting people—an arm here, a torso there. Consciousness produces a similar impression of "filling in," as it seems to consist of extreme detail even in areas that are peripheral (Dennett, 1991).*

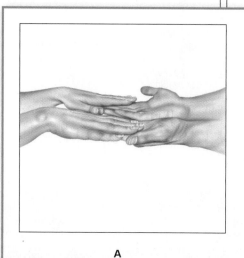
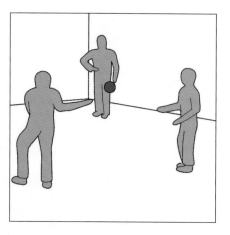
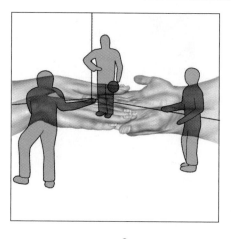

A   B   C

Divided Attention *Research participants presented with two different games (A and B) could easily follow each game separately. When participants tried to follow the action in the two different games simultaneously (C), they performed remarkably poorly (Neisser & Becklen, 1975).*

cocktail party phenomenon A phenomenon in which people tune in one message even while they filter out others nearby.

minimal consciousness A low-level kind of sensory awareness and responsiveness that occurs when the mind inputs sensations and may output behavior.

full consciousness Consciousness in which you know and are able to report your mental state.

self-consciousness A distinct level of consciousness in which the person's attention is drawn to the self as an object.

can study and watch TV simultaneously, for example, but research suggests not. One study had research participants divide their attention by reacting to two games superimposed on a television screen (see **FIGURE 8.5**). They had to push one button when one person slapped another's hands in the first game and push another button when a ball was passed in the second game. The participants were easily able to follow one game at

● **Why shouldn't you study and watch TV at the same time?**

a time, but their performance took a nosedive when they tried to follow both simultaneously. Their error rate when attending to the two tasks was eight times greater than when attending to either task alone (Neisser & Becklen, 1975). Your attempts to study, in other words, could seriously interfere with a full appreciation of your TV show.

The third property of consciousness is *selectivity,* the capacity to include some objects and not others. The conscious system is most inclined to select information of special interest to the person. For example, in what has come to be known as the **cocktail party phenomenon,** *people tune in one message even while they filter out others nearby.* Perhaps you have noticed how abruptly your attention is diverted from whatever conversation you are having when someone else within earshot at the party mentions your name. Selectivity is not only a property of waking consciousness, however; the mind works this way in other states. People are more sensitive to their own name than others' names, for example, even during sleep (Oswald, Taylor, & Triesman, 1960). This is why when you are trying to wake someone up, it is best to use the person's name (particularly if you want to sleep with that person again).

The fourth and final basic property of consciousness is *transience,* or the tendency to change. Consciousness wiggles and fidgets like that toddler in the seat behind you on the airplane. The mind wanders not just sometimes, but incessantly, from one "right now" to the next "right now" and then on to the next (Wegner, 1997). William James, whom you met way back in Chapter 1, famously described consciousness as a stream: "Consciousness . . . does not appear to itself chopped up in bits. Such words as 'chain' or 'train' do not describe it. . . . It is nothing jointed; it flows. A 'river' or a 'stream' are the metaphors by which it is most naturally described" (James, 1890, Vol. 1, p. 239).

The basic properties of consciousness are reminiscent of the "bouncing ball" that moves from word to word when the lyrics of a sing-along tune are shown on a karaoke machine. The ball always

● **How is consciousness like a karaoke "bouncing ball"?**

bounces on something (intentionality), there is only one ball (unity), the ball selects one target and not others (selectivity), and the ball keeps bouncing all the time (transience).

Levels of Consciousness

Consciousness can also be understood as having levels, ranging from minimal consciousness to full consciousness to self-consciousness. These levels of consciousness would probably all register as "conscious" on that wakefulness meter for surgery patients you read about at the beginning of the chapter. The levels of consciousness that psychologists distinguish are not a matter of degree of overall brain activity but instead involve different qualities of awareness of the world and of the self.

In its minimal form, consciousness is just a connection between the person and the world. When you sense the sun coming in through the window, for example, you might turn toward the light. Such **minimal consciousness** is *consciousness that occurs when the mind inputs sensations and may output behavior* (Armstrong, 1980). This level of consciousness is a kind of sensory awareness and responsiveness, something that could even happen when someone pokes you during sleep and you turn over. Something seems to register in your mind, at least in the sense that you experience it, but you may not think at all about having had the experience.

Now consider the glorious feeling of waking up on a spring morning as rays of sun stream across your pillow. It's not just that you are having this experience; you are also *aware* that you are having this experience. The critical ingredient that accompanies **full consciousness** is that you *know and are able to report your mental state*. When you have a hurt leg and mindlessly rub it, for instance, you may be minimally conscious of the pain. It is only when you realize that it hurts, though, that you become fully conscious of the pain. Full consciousness involves not only thinking about things but also thinking about the fact that you are thinking about things (Jaynes, 1976).

Full consciousness fluctuates over time, coming and going throughout the day. You've no doubt had experiences of reading and suddenly realizing that you have "zoned out" and are not processing what you read. When people are asked to report each time they zone out during reading, they report doing this every few minutes (Schooler, Reichle, & Halpern, 2001). When you're zoned out, you are minimally conscious of wherever your mind has wandered, and you return with a jolt into the full consciousness that your mind had drifted away.

● **What is "full consciousness"?**

It's easy to zone out while reading: ● ● ● ● ● ● ● ● ● ● ● *Your eyes continue to follow the print, but you're not processing the content and your mind has drifted elsewhere. Hello? Are you still paying attention while you're reading this?*

Full consciousness involves a certain consciousness of oneself; the person notices the self in a particular mental state ("Here I am, reading this sentence"). However, this is not quite the same thing as *self*-consciousness. Sometimes consciousness is entirely flooded with the self ("Gosh, I'm such a good reader!"), focusing on the self to the exclusion of almost everything else. William James (1890) and other theorists have suggested that **self-consciousness** is yet another distinct level of consciousness in which *the person's attention is drawn to the self as an object*. Most people report experiencing such self-consciousness when they are embarrassed, when they find themselves the focus of attention in a group, when someone focuses a camera on them, or when they catch sight of themselves in a mirror.

Most animals don't appear to have such self-consciousness. The typical dog, cat, or bird seems mystified by a mirror, ignoring it or acting as though there is some other critter back there. However, chimpanzees that have spent time with mirrors sometimes behave in ways that suggest they recognize themselves in a mirror. To examine this, researchers painted an odorless red dye over the eyebrow of an anesthetized chimp and then watched when the awakened chimp was presented with a mirror (Gallup, 1977). If the chimp interpreted the mirror image as a representation of some other chimp with an unusual approach to cosmetics, we would expect it just to look at the mirror or perhaps to reach toward it. But the chimp reached toward its *own eye* as it looked into the mirror—not the mirror image—suggesting that it recognized the image as a reflection of itself.

Besides chimps, few other animals—possibly dolphins (Reiss & Marino, 2001) and elephants (Plotnik, de Waal, & Reiss, 2006)—can recognize their own mirror images. Dogs, cats, birds, monkeys, and gorillas have been tested and don't seem to know they

A chimpanzee tried to wipe off the red ● ● ● ● ● ● ● ● *dye on its eyebrow in the Gallup experiment. This suggests that some animals recognize themselves in the mirror.*

● *Self-consciousness is a curse and a blessing. Looking in a mirror can make people evaluate themselves on deeper attributes such as honesty as well as superficial ones such as looks.*

are looking at themselves. Even humans don't have self-recognition right away. Infants don't recognize themselves in mirrors until they've reached about 18 months of age (Lewis & Brooks-Gunn, 1979). The experience of self-consciousness, as measured by self-recognition in mirrors, is limited to a few animals and to humans only after a certain stage of development.

Conscious Contents

What's on your mind? For that matter, what's on everybody's mind? One way to learn what is on people's minds is to ask them. For example, volunteers can be equipped with electronic beepers, and asked to record their current thoughts when beeped at random times throughout the day (Csikszentmihalyi & Larson, 1987). Such studies show that consciousness is dominated by the immediate environment, what the person is currently seeing, feeling, hearing, tasting, and smelling. Consciousness is also dominated by the person's *current concerns,* or what the person is thinking about repeatedly (Klinger, 1975). In one study, 175 college students were asked to report their current concerns; topics such as family relations, educational progress, health issues, and social activities (including dating) came up frequently (Goetzman, Hughes, & Klinger, 1994). Keep in mind that these concerns are ones the students didn't mind reporting to psychologists; their private preoccupations may have been different and probably far more interesting.

The current concerns that populate consciousness can sometimes get the upper hand, transforming everyday thoughts into rumination and worry. Thoughts that return again and again, or problem-solving attempts that never seem to succeed, can come to dominate consciousness. When this happens, people may exert **mental control**, *the attempt to change conscious states of mind.* For example, someone troubled by a recurring worry about the future ("What if I can't get a decent job when I graduate?") might choose to try not to think about this because it causes too much anxiety and uncertainty. Whenever this thought comes to mind, the person engages in **thought suppression**, the *conscious avoidance of a thought.* This may seem like a perfectly sensible strategy because it eliminates the worry and allows the person to move on to think about something else.

Or does it? The great Russian novelist Fyodor Dostoevsky (1863–1955) remarked on the difficulty of thought suppression: "Try to pose for yourself this task: not to think of a polar bear, and you will see that the cursed thing will come to mind every minute." Inspired by this observation, Daniel Wegner and his colleagues gave people this exact task in the laboratory (1987). Participants were asked to try not to think about a white bear for 5 minutes while they recorded all their thoughts aloud into a tape recorder. In addition, they were asked to ring a bell if the thought of a white bear came to mind. On average, they mentioned the white bear or rang the bell (indicating the thought) more than once per minute. Thought suppression simply didn't work and instead produced a flurry of returns of the unwanted thought. What's more, when some research participants later were specifically asked to change tasks and deliberately *think* about a white bear, they became oddly preoccupied with it.

● Look away from the book for a minute and try not to think about a white bear. Can you do it?

mental control The attempt to change conscious states of mind.

thought suppression The conscious avoidance of a thought.

rebound effect of thought suppression The tendency of a thought to return to consciousness with greater frequency following suppression.

ironic processes of mental control Mental processes that can produce ironic errors because monitoring for errors can itself produce them.

Dilbert

OKAY, LET ME THINK ALOUD FOR A MINUTE.

THE COST WILL BE $3,000...LOSING FOCUS...MONKEYS ARE FUNNY...MY TONGUE IS DIGESTING IN MY MOUTH.

THAT DIDN'T HELP AS MUCH AS I HAD HOPED.

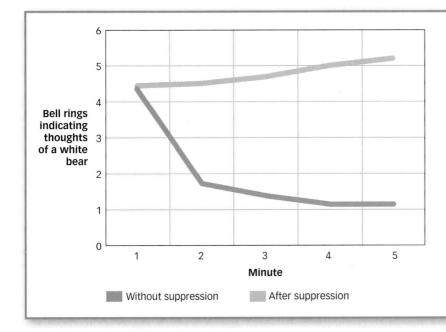

FIGURE 8.6 •

Rebound Effect *Research participants were first asked to try not to think about a white bear, and then they were asked to think about it and to ring a bell whenever it came to mind. Compared to those who were simply asked to think about a bear without prior suppression, those people who first suppressed the thought showed a rebound of increased thinking (Wegner et al., 1987).*

A graph of their bell rings in **FIGURE 8.6** shows that these participants had the white bear come to mind far more often than did people who had only been asked to think about the bear from the outset, with no prior suppression. This **rebound effect of thought suppression**, *the tendency of a thought to return to consciousness with greater frequency following suppression,* suggests that attempts at mental control may be difficult indeed. The act of trying to suppress a thought may itself cause that thought to return to consciousness in a robust way.

As with thought suppression, other attempts to "steer" consciousness in any direction can result in mental states that are precisely the opposite of those desired. How ironic: Trying to consciously achieve one task may produce precisely the opposite outcome! These ironic effects seem most likely to occur when the person is distracted or under stress. People who are distracted while they are trying to get into a good mood, for example, tend to become sad (Wegner, Erber, & Zanakos, 1993), and those who are distracted while trying to relax actually become more anxious than those who are not trying to relax (Wegner, Broome, & Blumberg, 1997). Likewise, an attempt not to overshoot a golf putt, undertaken during distraction, often yields the unwanted overshot (Wegner, Ansfield, & Pilloff, 1998). The theory of **ironic processes of mental control** proposes that such *ironic errors occur because the mental process that monitors errors can itself produce them* (Wegner, 1994a, 2009). In the attempt not to think of a white bear, for instance, a small part of the mind is ironically *searching* for the white bear (Wegner, 2004b).

Ironic processes are mental functions that are needed for effective mental control—they help in the process of banishing a thought from consciousness—but they can sometimes yield the very failure they seem designed to overcome. Ironic processes of mental control are among the mindbugs that the study of psychology holds up for examination. And because ironic processes occur outside consciousness, they remind us, too, that much of the mind's machinery may be hidden from our view, lying outside the fringes of our experience.

"Are you not thinking what I'm not thinking?"

The Unconscious Mind

Many mental processes are unconscious, in the sense that they occur without our experience of them. Just to put the role of consciousness in perspective, think for a moment about the mental processes involved in simple addition. What happens in consciousness between hearing a problem ("What's 4 plus 5?") and thinking of the

dynamic unconscious An active system encompassing a lifetime of hidden memories, the person's deepest instincts and desires, and the person's inner struggle to control these forces.

repression A mental process that removes unacceptable thoughts and memories from consciousness.

cognitive unconscious The mental processes that give rise to the person's thoughts, choices, emotions, and behavior even though they are not experienced by the person.

subliminal perception A thought or behavior that is influenced by stimuli that a person cannot consciously report perceiving.

answer ("9")? Probably nothing; the answer just appears in the mind. But this is a piece of calculation that must take at least a bit of thinking. After all, at a very young age you may have had to solve such problems by counting on your fingers. Now that you don't have to do that anymore (right?), the answer seems to pop into your head automatically, by virtue of a process that doesn't require you to be aware of any underlying steps and, for that matter, doesn't even *allow* you to be aware of the steps. The answer just suddenly appears. Nothing conscious seems to bridge this gap, but the answer comes from somewhere, and this emptiness points to the unconscious mind.

Freudian Unconscious

The true champion of the unconscious mind was Sigmund Freud. As you read in Chapter 1, Freud's psychoanalytic theory viewed conscious thought as the surface of a much deeper mind made up of unconscious processes. Far more than just a collection of hidden processes, Freud described a **dynamic unconscious**—*an active system encompassing a lifetime of hidden memories, the person's deepest instincts and desires, and the person's inner struggle to control these forces.* The dynamic unconscious might contain hidden sexual thoughts about one's parents, for example, or destructive urges aimed at a helpless infant—the kinds of thoughts people keep secret from others and may not even acknowledge to themselves. According to Freud's theory, the unconscious is a force to be held in check by **repression**, *a mental process that removes unacceptable thoughts and memories from consciousness and keeps them in the unconscious.* Without repression, a person might think, do, or say every unconscious impulse or animal urge, no matter how selfish or immoral. With repression, these desires are held in the recesses of the dynamic unconscious.

Freud looked for evidence of the unconscious mind in speech errors and lapses of consciousness, or what are commonly called "Freudian slips." Forgetting the name of someone you dislike, for example, is a mindbug that seems to have special meaning. Freud believed that such errors are not random and instead have some surplus meaning that may appear to have been created by an intelligent unconscious mind, even though the person consciously disavows them. For example, when Condoleezza Rice, serving as the National Security Advisor for President George W. Bush, was addressing an audience at a Washington, DC, dinner party, she reportedly said, "As I was telling my husba—" before breaking off and correcting herself: "As I was telling President Bush . . . ." Although no one seriously believes the single Rice and married Bush were an "item," you can almost hear her dynamic unconscious trumpeting the psychological intimacy they enjoyed.

● **What do Freudian slips tell us about the unconscious mind?**

Many of the meaningful errors Freud attributed to the dynamic unconscious were not predicted in advance and so seem to depend on clever after-the-fact interpretations. That's not so good. Suggesting a pattern to a series of random events is quite clever, but it's not the same as scientifically predicting and explaining when and why an event should happen. Anyone can offer a reasonable, compelling explanation for an event after it has already happened, but the true work of science is to offer testable hypotheses that are evaluated based on reliable evidence. Condi Rice's curious slip about being married to President Bush may have been a random error, only meaningful in the minds of news commentators who found it amusing and worthy of explanation.

Cognitive Unconscious

Modern psychologists share Freud's interest in the impact of unconscious mental processes on consciousness and on behavior. However, rather than Freud's vision of the unconscious as a teeming menagerie of animal urges and repressed thoughts, the current study of the unconscious mind views it as the factory that builds the products of conscious thought and behavior (Kihlstrom, 1987; Wilson, 2002). The **cognitive unconscious** includes *all the mental processes that are not experienced by the person but that give rise to the person's thoughts, choices, emotions, and behavior.*

One indication of the cognitive unconscious at work is when the person's thought or behavior is changed by exposure to information outside consciousness. This happens in **subliminal perception**, when *thought or behavior is influenced by stimuli that a person cannot consciously report perceiving*. Worries about the potential of subliminal influence were first provoked in 1957, when a marketer, James Vicary, claimed he had increased concession sales at a New Jersey theater by flashing the words "Eat Popcorn" and "Drink Coke" briefly on-screen during movies. It turns out his story was a hoax, and many attempts to increase sales using similar methods have failed. But the very idea of influencing behavior outside consciousness created a wave of alarm about insidious "subliminal persuasion" that still concerns people (Epley, Savitsky, & Kachelski, 1999; Pratkanis, 1992).

Subliminal perception does occur, but the degree of influence it has on behavior is not very large (Dijksterhuis, Aarts, & Smith, 2005). One set of studies examined whether beverage choices could be influenced by brief visual exposures to thirst-related words while subjects were performing a computer task (Strahan, Spencer, & Zanna, 2002). Although the exposure did have an effect, the effect was small and mainly affected participants who reported already being thirsty at the start of the experiment.

Unconscious influences on behavior are not limited to cases of subliminal persuasion—they can happen when you are merely reminded of an idea in passing. For example, the thought of getting old can make a person walk more slowly. John Bargh and his colleagues discovered this by having college students complete a survey that called for them to make sentences with various words (Bargh, Chen, & Burrows, 1996). The students were not informed that most of the words were commonly associated with aging (*Florida, gray, wrinkled*), and even afterward they didn't report being aware of this trend. In this case, the "aging" idea wasn't presented subliminally, just not very noticeably. As these research participants left the experiment, they were clocked as they walked down the hall. Compared with those not exposed to the aging-related words, these people walked more slowly! Just as with subliminal perception, a passing exposure to ideas can influence actions without conscious awareness.

● **What's an example of an idea that had an unconscious influence on you?**

President George W. Bush denied that Republican Party commercials used subliminal messages (which he called "subliminable") after Democrats complained that the word RATS subtly flashed on-screen in a TV spot criticizing his opponent Al Gore in the 2000 election. "One frame out of 900 hardly makes a conspiracy." he said in the ad's defense—although the ad was pulled off the air.

summary quiz [8.1]

1. The *cocktail party phenomenon*, in which people tune into one conversation while filtering out others nearby, illustrates which basic property of consciousness?
   a. intentionality
   b. unity
   c. selectivity
   d. transience

2. Watching your favorite TV show while studying could seriously interfere with your ability to master the material you are trying to study because of which basic property of consciousness?
   a. intentionality
   b. unity
   c. selectivity
   d. transience

3. When people are embarrassed or find themselves the focus of attention in a group, they are experiencing a state known as
   a. self-consciousness.
   b. full consciousness.
   c. minimal consciousness.
   d. unconsciousness.

4. All the mental processes that are not experienced by the person but that give rise to the person's thoughts and behaviors are known as
   a. repression.
   b. subliminal perception.
   c. the dynamic unconscious.
   d. the cognitive unconscious.

altered states of consciousness Forms of experience that depart from the normal subjective experience of the world and the mind.

circadian rhythm A naturally occurring 24-hour cycle.

REM sleep A stage of sleep characterized by rapid eye movements and a high level of brain activity.

Sleep and Dreaming: Good Night, Mind

What's it like to be asleep? Sometimes it's like nothing at all. Sleep can produce a state of unconsciousness in which the mind and brain apparently turn off the functions that create experience: The Cartesian Theater is closed. But this is an oversimplification because the theater actually seems to reopen during the night for special shows of bizarre cult films—in other words, dreams. Dream consciousness involves a transformation of experience that is so radical it is commonly considered an **altered state of consciousness**—*a form of experience that departs significantly from the normal subjective experience of the world and the mind.* Such altered states can be accompanied by changes in thinking, disturbances in the sense of time, feelings of the loss of control, changes in emotional expression, alterations in body image and sense of self, perceptual distortions, and changes in meaning or significance (Ludwig, 1966). The world of sleep and dreams, then, provides two unique perspectives on consciousness: a view of the mind without consciousness and a view of consciousness in an altered state.

● **Why are dreams considered an altered state of consciousness?**

Sleep

Consider a typical night. As you begin to fall asleep, the busy, task-oriented thoughts of the waking mind are replaced by wandering thoughts and images, odd juxtapositions, some of them almost dreamlike. Eventually, your presence of mind goes away entirely. Time and experience stop, you are unconscious, and in fact there seems to be no "you" there to have experiences. But then come dreams, whole vistas of a vivid and surrealistic consciousness you just don't get during the day, a set of experiences that occur with the odd prerequisite that there is nothing "out there" you are actually experiencing. More patches of unconsciousness may occur, with more dreams here and there. And finally, the glimmerings of waking consciousness return again in a foggy and imprecise form as you enter postsleep consciousness and then wake up, often with bad hair.

Sleep Cycle

The sequence of events that occurs during a night of sleep is part of one of the major rhythms of human life, the cycle of sleep and waking. This **circadian rhythm** is *a naturally occurring 24-hour cycle*—from the Latin *circa,* "about," and *dies,* "day." Even people who are sequestered in underground buildings without clocks and allowed to sleep whenever they want to, tend to have a rest-activity cycle of about 25.1 hours (Aschoff, 1965). This slight deviation from 24 hours is not easily explained (Lavie, 2001), but it may underlie the tendency many people have to want to stay up a little later each night and wake up a little later each day. We're 25.1-hour people living in a 24-hour world.

The sleep cycle is far more than a simple on/off routine, however, as many bodily and psychological processes ebb and flow in this rhythm. EEG (electroencephalograph) recordings of the human brain reveal a regular pattern of changes in electrical activity in the brain accompanying the circadian cycle. During waking, these changes involve alternation between high-frequency activity (called *beta waves*) during alertness and lower-frequency activity (*alpha waves*) during relaxation.

The largest changes in EEG occur during sleep. These changes show a regular pattern over the course of the night consisting of five sleep stages (see **FIGURE 8.7**, on page 245). In the first stage of

● Dreamers, *by Albert Joseph Moore (1879/1882). Without measuring REM sleep, it's hard to know whether Moore's "Dreamers" are actually dreaming.*

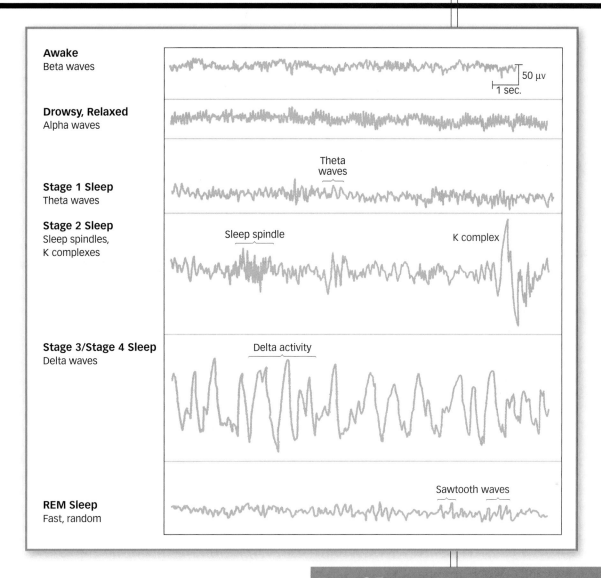

Awake
Beta waves

50 µv
1 sec.

Drowsy, Relaxed
Alpha waves

Theta waves

Stage 1 Sleep
Theta waves

Stage 2 Sleep
Sleep spindles,
K complexes

Sleep spindle

K complex

Stage 3/Stage 4 Sleep
Delta waves

Delta activity

Sawtooth waves

REM Sleep
Fast, random

FIGURE 8.7 •
EEG Patterns during the Stages of Sleep *The waking brain shows high-frequency beta wave activity, which changes during drowsiness and relaxation to lower-frequency alpha waves. Stage 1 sleep shows lower-frequency theta waves, which are accompanied in Stage 2 by irregular patterns called sleep spindles and K complexes. Stages 3 and 4 are marked by the lowest frequencies, delta waves. During REM sleep, EEG patterns return to higher-frequency sawtooth waves that resemble the beta waves of waking.*

sleep, the EEG moves to frequency patterns even lower than alpha waves (*theta waves*). In the second stage of sleep, these patterns are interrupted by short bursts of activity, and the sleeper becomes somewhat more difficult to awaken. The deepest stages of sleep are 3 and 4, known as slow-wave sleep, in which the EEG patterns show activity called *delta waves*.

During the fifth sleep stage, **REM sleep**, *a stage of sleep characterized by rapid eye movements and a high level of brain activity*, EEG patterns become high-frequency sawtooth waves, similar to beta waves, suggesting that the mind at this time is as active as it is during waking (see **FIGURE 8.7**, above). During REM sleep, the pulse quickens, blood pressure rises, and there are telltale signs of sexual arousal. At the same time, measurements of muscle movements indicate that the sleeper is very still, except for a rapid side-to-side movement of the eyes. (Watch someone sleeping and you may be able to see the REMs through their closed eyelids. Be careful doing this with strangers down at the bus depot.)

Although many people believe that they don't dream much (if at all), some 80% of people awakened during REM sleep report dreams. Some dreams are also reported in other sleep stages (non-REM sleep) but not as many—and the dreams that occur at these times are described as less wild than REM dreams and more like normal thinking.

Putting EEG and REM data together produces a picture of how a typical night's sleep progresses through cycles of sleep stages (see **FIGURE 8.8**, on page 246). In the first hour

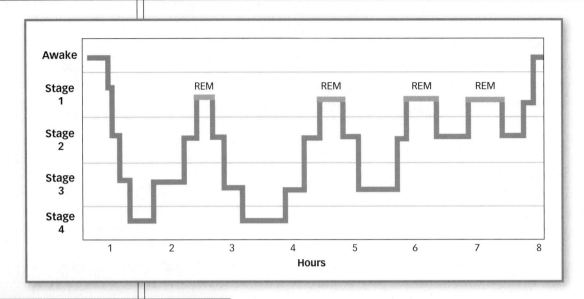

● **FIGURE 8.8**

Stages of Sleep during the Night *Over the course of the typical night, sleep cycles into deeper stages early on and then more shallow stages later. REM periods become longer in later cycles, and the deeper slow-wave sleep of stages 3 and 4 disappears halfway through the night.*

of the night, you fall all the way from waking to the fourth and deepest stage of sleep, the stage marked by delta waves. These slow waves indicate a general synchronization of neural firing, as though the brain is doing one thing at this time rather than many—the neuronal equivalent of "the wave" moving through the crowd at a stadium, as lots of individuals move together in synchrony. You then return to lighter sleep stages, eventually reaching REM and dreamland. You then continue to cycle between REM and slow-wave sleep stages every 90 minutes or so throughout the night. Periods of REM last longer as the night goes on, and lighter sleep stages predominate between these periods, with the deeper slow-wave stages 3 and 4 disappearing halfway through the night. Although you're either unconscious or dream-conscious at the time, your brain and mind cycle through a remarkable array of different states each time you have a night's sleep.

● **What are the stages in a typical night's sleep?**

Sleep Needs and Deprivation

How much do people sleep? The answer depends on the age of the sleeper (Dement, 1999). Newborns will sleep 6 to 8 times in 24 hours, often totaling more than 16 hours. The typical 6-year-old child might need 11 or 12 hours of sleep, and the progression to less sleep then continues into adulthood, when the average is about 7 to 7½ hours per night. With aging, people can get along with even a bit less sleep than that. Over a whole lifetime, we get about 1 hour of sleep for every 2 hours we are awake.

This is a lot of sleeping, and you might wonder whether, rather than sleeping our lives away, perhaps we can stay awake and enjoy life. The world record for staying awake belongs to Randy Gardner, who at age 17 stayed up for 264 hours and 12 minutes for a science project. Randy was followed around for much of the 11 days and nights by sleep researchers, who noted that he seemed remarkably chipper and easy to keep awake during the day—but that he struggled mightily at night, when fighting drowsiness required heroic measures. When Randy finally did go to sleep, he slept only 14 hours and 40 minutes and awakened essentially recovered (Dement, 1978).

● **What is the relationship between sleep and learning?**

Feats like this one suggest that sleep might be expendable. This is the theory behind the classic "all-nighter" that you may have tried on the way to a rough exam. But it turns out that this theory is mistaken. Robert Stickgold and his colleagues (2000b) found that when people learning a difficult perceptual task are kept up all night after they finished practicing the task, their learning of the task is wiped out. Even after two nights of catch-up sleep, they show little indication of their initial training on the task. Sleep following learning appears to be essential for memory consolidation (see Chapter 5). It is as though memories normally deteriorate unless sleep occurs to help keep them in place. Studying all night may help you cram for the exam, but it won't make the material stick—which pretty much defeats the whole point.

Sleep turns out to be a necessity rather than a luxury in other ways as well. At the extreme, sleep loss can be fatal. When rats are forced to break Randy Gardner's human waking record and stay awake even longer, they have trouble regulating their body temperature and lose weight although they eat much more than normal. Their bodily systems break down, and they die, on average, in 21 days (Rechsthaffen et al., 1983). In healthy young humans, even a few hours of sleep deprivation each night can have a cumulative detrimental effect: reducing mental acuity and reaction time, increasing irritability and depression, and increasing the risk of accidents and injury (Coren, 1997).

Some studies have deprived people of different sleep stages selectively by waking them whenever certain stages are detected. Studies of REM sleep deprivation indicate that this part of sleep is important psychologically, as memory problems and excessive aggression are observed in both humans and rats after only a few days of being wakened whenever REM activity starts (Ellman et al., 1991). Deprivation from slow-wave sleep (in stages 3 and 4), in turn, has more physical effects, with just a few nights of deprivation leaving people feeling tired, fatigued, and hypersensitive to muscle and bone pain (Lentz et al., 1999).

It's clearly dangerous to neglect the need for sleep. But why would we have such a need in the first place? Insects don't seem to sleep, but most "higher" animals do, including fish and birds. Giraffes sleep less than 2 hours daily, whereas brown bats snooze for almost 20 hours. These variations in sleep needs, and the very existence of a need, are hard to explain. Is the restoration that happens during the unconsciousness of sleep something that simply can't be achieved during consciousness? Sleep is, after all, potentially costly in the course of evolution. The sleeping animal is easy prey, so the habit of sleep would not seem to have developed so widely across species unless it had significant benefits that made up for this vulnerability. Theories of sleep have not yet determined why the brain and body have evolved to need these recurring episodes of unconsciousness.

Sleep deprivation can often be diagnosed without the help of any psychologists or brain-scanning equipment.

Sleep Disorders

In answer to the question "Did you sleep well?" comedian Stephen Wright said, "No, I made a couple of mistakes." Sleeping well is something everyone would love to do, but for many people, sleep disorders are mindbugs that can get in the way. Perhaps the most common sleep disorder is **insomnia**, *difficulty in falling asleep or staying asleep.* About 15% of adults complain of severe or frequent insomnia, and another 15% report having mild or occasional insomnia (Bootzin et al., 1993). Insomnia has many causes, including anxiety associated with stressful life events, so insomnia may sometimes be a sign of other emotional difficulties.

Insomnia can be exacerbated by worry about insomnia (Borkevec, 1982). No doubt you've experienced some nights on which sleeping was a high priority, such as before a class presentation or an important interview, and you've found that you were unable to fall asleep. In this situation, sleeping seems to be an emergency, and every wish to sleep takes you further from that goal. The desire to sleep initiates an ironic process of mental control—a heightened sensitivity to signs of sleeplessness—and this sensitivity can interfere with sleep (Ansfield, Wegner, & Bowser, 1996). The paradoxical solution for insomnia in some cases, then, may be to give up the pursuit of sleep and instead find something else to do.

Giving up on trying so hard to sleep is probably better than another common remedy—the use of sleeping pills. Although sedatives can be useful for brief sleep problems associated with emotional events, their long-term use is not effective. To begin with, most sleeping pills are addictive. People become dependent on the pills to sleep and may

insomnia Difficulty in falling asleep or staying asleep.

need to increase the dose over time to achieve the same effect. Even in short-term use, sedatives can interfere with the normal sleep cycle. Although they promote sleep, they reduce the proportion of time spent in REM and slow-wave sleep (Nishino, Mignot, & Dement, 1995), robbing people of dreams and their deepest sleep stages. As a result, the quality of sleep achieved with pills may not be high, and there may be side effects such as grogginess and irritability during the day. Finally, stopping the treatment suddenly can produce insomnia that is worse than before.

● **What are some problems caused by sleeping pills?**

Sleep apnea is *a disorder in which the person stops breathing for brief periods while asleep.* A person with apnea usually snores, as apnea involves an involuntary obstruction of the breathing passage. When episodes of apnea occur for over 10 seconds at a time and recur many times during the night, they may cause many awakenings and sleep loss or insomnia. Apnea occurs most often in middle-age overweight men (Partinen, 1994) and may go undiagnosed because it is not easy for the sleeper to notice. Bed partners may be the ones who finally get tired of the snoring and noisy gasping for air when the sleeper's breathing restarts. Therapies involving weight loss, drugs, or surgery may solve the problem.

Another common sleep disorder is **somnambulism,** commonly called sleepwalking, which occurs when *a person arises and walks around while asleep.* Sleepwalking is more common in children, peaking around the age of 11 or 12, with as many as 25% of children experiencing at least one episode (Empson, 1984). Sleepwalking tends to happen early in the night, usually in slow-wave sleep, and sleepwalkers may awaken during their walk or return to bed without waking, in which case they will probably not remember the episode in the morning. Sleepwalking is not usually linked to any additional problems and is only problematic in that sleepwalkers can hurt themselves, tripping over furniture or falling down stairs. Contrary to popular belief, it is safe to wake sleepwalkers or lead them back to bed.

● **Is it safe to wake a sleepwalker?**

Other sleep disorders are less common. **Narcolepsy** is *a disorder in which sudden sleep attacks occur in the middle of waking activities.* Narcolepsy involves the intrusion of a dreaming state of sleep (with REM) into waking and is often accompanied by unrelenting excessive sleepiness and uncontrollable sleep attacks lasting from 30 seconds to 30 minutes. This disorder appears to have a genetic basis, as it runs in families, and it can be treated effectively with medication. **Sleep paralysis** is *the experience of waking up unable to move* and is sometimes associated with narcolepsy. This eerie experience usually lasts only a few moments and may occur with an experience of pressure on the chest (Hishakawa, 1976). **Night terrors** (or sleep terrors) are *abrupt awakenings with panic and intense emotional arousal.* These terrors, which occur mainly in boys ages 3 to 7, happen most often in non-REM sleep early in the sleep cycle and do not usually have dream content the sleeper can report.

To sum up, there is a lot going on when we close our eyes for the night. Humans follow a pretty regular sleep cycle, going through five stages of non-REM and REM sleep during the night. Disruptions to that cycle, from either sleep deprivation or sleep disorders, can produce consequences for waking consciousness. But something else happens during a night's sleep that affects our consciousness, both while asleep and when we wake up. It's dreaming.

Dreams

Pioneering sleep researcher William C. Dement (1959) said, "Dreaming permits each and every one of us to be quietly and safely insane every night of our lives." Indeed, dreams do seem to have a touch of insanity about them. We experience crazy things in dreams, but even more

ONLY HUMAN

DUBIOUS TEENAGER EXCUSE #53
Authorities are investigating how a sleepwalking London teenager ended up asleep atop a 130-foot crane in the middle of the night. A passerby spotted the girl around 1:30 a.m. and called the police, thinking she was going to jump. A firefighter climbed up and inched along the beam to where the girl was sleeping. He was very cautious about startling her as he secured the unidentified teen in a safety harness. A special rescue truck was called, which deployed a hydraulic ladder to get the girl down after 2½ hours. The girl's parents were called to the scene and told police their daughter is a frequent sleepwalker (Sleepwalker found dozing high atop crane, 2005).

● *Sleepwalkers in cartoons have their arms outstretched and eyes closed, but that's just for cartoons. A real-life sleepwalker usually walks normally with eyes open, sometimes with a glassy look.*

ESTHALTO/MATTHIEU SPOHN/GETTY IMAGES

bizarre is the fact that we are the writers, producers, and directors of the crazy things we experience. Just what are these experiences, and how can the experiences be explained?

Dream Consciousness

Dreams depart dramatically from reality. You may dream of being naked in public, of falling from a great height, of sleeping through an important appointment, of your teeth being loose and falling out, of being chased, or even of flying (Holloway, 2001). These things don't happen much in reality unless you have a very bad life.

The quality of consciousness in dreaming is also altered significantly from waking consciousness. There are five major characteristics of dream consciousness that distinguish it from the waking state (Hobson, 1988). For one, we intensely feel *emotion*, whether it is bliss or terror or love or awe. Second, dream *thought* is illogical: The continuities of time, place, and person don't apply. You may find you are in one place and then another, for example, without any travel in between—or people may change identity from one dream scene to the next. Third, *sensation* is fully formed and meaningful; visual sensation is predominant, and you may also deeply experience sound, touch, and movement (although pain is very uncommon). A fourth aspect of dreaming is *uncritical acceptance,* as though the images and events were perfectly normal rather than bizarre. A final feature of dreaming is the *difficulty of remembering* the dream after it is over. People often remember dreams only if they are awakened during the dream and even then may lose recall for the dream within just a few minutes of waking. If waking memory were this bad, you'd be standing around half naked in the street much of the time, having forgotten your destination, clothes, and probably your lunch money.

Some of the most memorable dreams are nightmares, as these frightening dreams often wake up the dreamer. One set of daily dream logs from college undergraduates suggested that the average student has about 24 nightmares per year (Wood & Bootzin, 1990), although some people may have them as often as every night. Children have more nightmares than adults, and people who have experienced traumatic events are inclined to have nightmares that relive those events. Following the 1989 earthquake in the San Francisco Bay Area, for example, college students who had experienced the quake reported more nightmares than those who had not and often reported that the dreams were about the quake (Wood et al., 1992). This effect of trauma may not only produce dreams of the traumatic event: When police officers experience "critical

● **What distinguishes dream consciousness from the waking state?**

sleep apnea A disorder in which the person stops breathing for brief periods while asleep.

somnambulism (sleepwalking) Occurs when the person arises and walks around while asleep.

narcolepsy A disorder in which sudden sleep attacks occur in the middle of waking activities.

sleep paralysis The experience of waking up unable to move.

night terrors (or sleep terrors) Abrupt awakenings with panic and intense emotional arousal.

• The Nightmare, by Henry Fuseli (1790). Fuseli depicts not only a mare in this painting but also an incubus—an imp perched on the dreamer's chest that is traditionally associated with especially horrifying nightmares.

incidents" of conflict and danger, they tend to have more nightmares in general (Neylan et al., 2002).

Not all of our dreams are fantastic and surreal, however. We also dream about mundane topics that reflect prior waking experiences or "day residue." Current conscious concerns pop up (Nikles et al., 1998), along with images from the recent past. A dream may even incorporate sensations experienced during sleep, as when sleepers in one study were led to dream of water when drops were sprayed on their faces during REM sleep (Dement & Wolpert, 1958). The day residue does not usually include episodic memories—that is, complete daytime events replayed in the mind. Rather, dreams that reflect the day's experience tend to single out sensory experiences or objects from waking life. One study had research participants play the computer game Tetris and found that participants often reported dreaming about the Tetris geometric figures falling down—even though they seldom reported dreams about being in the experiment or playing the game (Stickgold et al., 2001). Even severely amnesic patients who couldn't recall playing the game at all reported Tetris-like images appearing in their dreams (Stickgold et al., 2000b). The content of dreams takes snapshots from the day rather than retelling the stories of what you have done or seen. This means that dreams often come without clear plots or storylines, so they may not make a lot of sense.

Dream Theories

Dreams are puzzles that cry out to be solved. How could you *not* want to make sense out of these experiences? Dreams are emotionally riveting, filled with vivid images from your own life, and they seem very real. The search for dream meaning goes all the way back to biblical figures, who interpreted dreams and looked for prophecies in them. In the Old Testament, the prophet Daniel (a favorite of the authors of this book) curried favor with King Nebuchadnezzar of Babylon by interpreting the king's dream. Unfortunately, the meaning of dreams is usually far from obvious.

In the first psychological theory of dreams, Freud (1900/1965) proposed that dreams are confusing and obscure because the dynamic unconscious creates them precisely *to be* confusing and obscure. According to Freud's theory, dreams represent wishes, and some of these wishes are so unacceptable, taboo, and anxiety producing that the mind can only express them in disguised form. For example, a dream about a tree burning down in the park across the street from where a friend once lived might represent a camouflaged wish for the death of the friend. In this case, wishing for the death of a friend is unacceptable, so it is disguised as a tree on fire. The problem with this approach is that any dream can have an infinite number of potential interpretations, and finding the correct one is a matter of guesswork—and of convincing the dreamer that one interpretation is superior to the others.

Although dreams may not represent elaborately hidden wishes, evidence indicates that they do feature the return of suppressed thoughts. Researchers asked volunteers to think of a personal acquaintance and then to spend 5 minutes before going to bed writing down whatever came to mind (Wegner, Wenzlaff, & Kozak, 2004). Some participants were asked to suppress thoughts of this person as they wrote, others were asked to focus on thoughts of the person, and yet others were asked just to write freely about anything. The next morning, participants wrote dream reports. Overall, all participants mentioned dreaming more about the person they had named than about other people. But they most often dreamed of the person they named if they were in the group that had been assigned to suppress thoughts of the person the night before. This finding suggests that Freud was right to suspect that dreams harbor unwanted thoughts. Perhaps this is why actors dream of forgetting their lines, travelers dream of getting lost, and football players dream of fumbling the ball.

Another key theory of dreaming is the **activation-synthesis model** (Hobson & McCarley, 1977). This theory proposes that *dreams are produced when the mind attempts to make sense of random neural activity that occurs in the brain during sleep.* During waking

● **What is the evidence that we dream about our suppressed thoughts?**

activation-synthesis model The theory that dreams are produced when the brain attempts to make sense of activations that occur randomly during sleep.

Culture & Community

What Do Dreams Mean to Us Around the World?

A recent study (Morewedge & Norton, 2009) assessed how people from three different cultures evaluate their dreams. Participants were asked to rate different theories of dreaming on a scale of 1 (do not agree at all) to 7 (agree completely).

A significant majority of students from the United States, South Korea, and India agreed with the Freudian theory that dreams have meanings. Only small percentages believed the other options, that dreams provide a means to solve problems, promote learning, or are by-products of unrelated brain activity.

The figure to the right illustrates the findings across all three cultural participants. It appears that in many parts of the world, people have an intuition that dreams contain something deep and relevant.

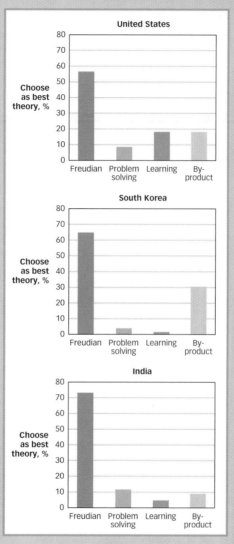

consciousness, the mind is devoted to interpreting lots of information that arrives through the senses. You figure out that the odd noise you're hearing during class is your cell phone vibrating, for example, or you realize that the strange smell in the hall outside your room must be from burned popcorn. In the dream state, the mind doesn't have access to external sensations, but it keeps on doing what it usually does: interpreting information. Because that information now comes from neural activations that occur without the continuity provided by the perception of reality, the brain's interpretive mechanisms can run free (see the Hot Science box on the next page). This might be why, for example, a person in a dream can sometimes change into someone else. There is no actual person being perceived to help the mind keep a stable view. In the mind's effort to perceive and give meaning to brain activation, the person you view in a dream about a grocery store might seem to be a clerk but then change to be your favorite teacher when the dream scene moves to

[HOT SCIENCE]

Dreaming and the Brain

What happens in the brain when we dream? Several studies have made fMRI scans of people's brains during sleep, focusing on the areas of the brain that show changes in activation during REM periods. These studies show that the brain changes that occur during REM sleep correspond clearly with certain alterations of consciousness that occur in dreaming. The figure shows some of the patterns of activation and deactivation found in the dreaming brain (Schwartz & Maquet, 2002).

One notable feature that distinguishes dreams from waking consciousness, for instance, is their scariness. Nightmares by definition are terrifying, but even your common, run-of-the-mill dream is often populated with anxiety-producing images (Neilson, Deslauriers, & Baylor, 1991). There are heights to look down from, dangerous people lurking, the occasional monster, lots of minor worries, and at least once in a while that major exam you've forgotten about until you walk into class. These thoughts suggest that the brain areas responsible for fear or emotion somehow work overtime in dreams. And indeed, the amgydala—which is involved in responding to threatening or stressful events—is quite active during REM sleep.

The typical dream is also a visual wonderland, with visual events present in almost all dreams. This dream "picture show" doesn't involve actual perception, of course, just the imagination of visual events. It turns out that the areas of the brain responsible for visual perception are *not* activated during dreaming, whereas the visual association areas in the occipital lobe that are responsible for visual imagery *do* show activation (Braun et al., 1998), as shown in the figure. Your brain is smart enough to realize that it's not really seeing bizarre images but acts instead as though it's imagining bizarre images.

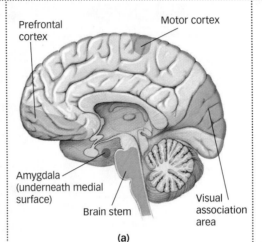

(a)

(b)

Brain activation and deactivation during REM sleep. Brain areas shaded red are activated during REM sleep; those shaded blue are deactivated. (a) The medial view shows the activation of the amygdala, the visual association areas, the motor cortex, and the brain stem and the deactivation of the prefrontal cortex. (b) The ventral view shows the activation of other visual association areas and the deactivation of the prefrontal cortex (Schwartz & Maquet, 2002).

During REM, the prefrontal cortex shows relatively less arousal than it usually does during waking consciousness. What does this mean for the dreamer? As a rule, the prefrontal areas are associated with planning and executing actions, and often dreams seem to be unplanned and rambling. Perhaps this is why dreams often don't have very sensible storylines; they've been scripted by an author whose ability to plan is inactive.

Another odd fact of dreaming is that while the eyes are moving rapidly, the body is otherwise very still. During REM sleep, the motor cortex is activated, but spinal neurons running through the brain stem inhibit the expression of this motor activation (Lai & Siegal, 1999). This turns out to be a useful property of brain activation in dreaming; otherwise, you might get up and act out every dream! In fact, when this inhibitory area is lesioned in cats, they become highly active during REM sleep (Jouvet & Mounier, 1961). Normally, the brain inhibits movement during dreams, perhaps to keep us from hurting ourselves.

Brain scans may also someday help solve the intriguing question of whether people can be aware that they are dreaming. Some people report that they sometimes know they are dreaming while the dream is ongoing—they experience the dream equivalent of full consciousness. Such *lucid dreaming*, the awareness of dreaming during the dream, has been described often (LaBerge & Rheingold, 1990) but is still a matter of controversy because evidence of such dreams comes only from these descriptions reported by the dreamers. One goal of brain imaging research is to examine how the brain may be involved in the creation of such elusive states of mind. Researchers have not yet established whether there are differences in brain activation between minimal consciousness and full consciousness during waking, but perhaps if they do, brain research can corroborate the reports of lucid dreamers.

your school. The great interest people have in interpreting their dreams the next morning may be an extension of the interpretive activity they've been doing all night.

The Freudian theory and the activation-synthesis theory differ in the significance they place on the meaning of dreams. Dream research has not yet sorted out whether one of these theories or yet another might be the best account of the meaning of dreams.

summary quiz [8.2]

5. Dreaming is most likely to occur during which stage(s) of sleep?
   a. the first stage, as we begin to drift off into sleep
   b. the second stage, marked by short bursts of electric activity in the brain
   c. the third and fourth stages, which are the deepest stages of sleep
   d. the fifth stage, characterized by rapid eye movements and a high level of brain activity

6. The sleep disorder in which a person stops breathing for brief periods while asleep is called
   a. insomnia.
   c. somnambulism.
   b. sleep apnea.
   d. narcolepsy.

7. One of the characteristics of dream consciousness that distinguishes it from the waking state is
   a. our emotions are muted.
   b. our sensations are weaker.
   c. we uncritically accept bizarre images and events as normal.
   d. dream thought is more logical and consistent.

8. The theory of dreaming that proposes that dreams are produced when the mind attempts to make sense of random neural activity that occurs in the brain during sleep is called
   a. the activation-synthesis model.
   c. the altered state of consciousness model.
   b. Freud's psychoanalytic theory.
   d. the cognitive unconscious theory.

psychoactive drug A chemical that influences consciousness or behavior by altering the brain's chemical message system.

Drugs and Consciousness: Artificial Inspiration

The author of the antiutopian novel *Brave New World*, Aldous Huxley, once wrote of his experiences with the drug mescaline. His essay "The Doors of Perception" described the intense experience that accompanied his departure from normal consciousness. He described "a world where everything shone with the Inner Light, and was infinite in its significance. The legs, for example, of [a] chair—how miraculous their tubularity, how supernatural their polished smoothness! I spent several minutes—or was it several centuries?—not merely gazing at those bamboo legs, but actually *being* them" (Huxley, 1954).

Being the legs of a chair? This is better than being a seat cushion, but it still sounds like an odd experience. Still, some people seek out such experiences, often through using drugs. **Psychoactive drugs** are *chemicals that influence consciousness or behavior by altering the brain's chemical message system*. As you read in Chapter 3, information is communicated in the brain through neurotransmitters that convey neural impulses to neighboring neurons. Drugs alter these neural connections by preventing the bonding of neurotransmitters to sites in the postsynaptic neuron or by inhibiting the reuptake of or enhancing the bonding and transmission of neurotransmitters. Different drugs can intensify or dull transmission patterns, creating changes in brain electrical activity that mimic natural operations of the brain. For example, a drug such as Valium (benzodiazepine) induces sleep but prevents dreaming and so creates a state similar to naturally occurring slow-wave sleep. Other drugs prompt patterns of brain activity that do not occur naturally, however, and their influence on consciousness can be dramatic. Like

The seat of consciousness. ● ● ● ● ● ● ● ● ● ●

BRENT MADSON

Huxley experiencing himself becoming the legs of a chair, people using drugs can have experiences unlike any they might find in normal waking consciousness or even in dreams.

Drug Use and Abuse

Why do children sometimes spin around until they get dizzy and fall to the ground? There is something strangely attractive about states of consciousness that depart from the norm, and people throughout history have sought out these altered states by dancing, fasting, chanting, meditating, and ingesting a bizarre assortment of chemicals to intoxicate themselves (Tart, 1969). People pursue altered consciousness even when there are costs, from the nausea that accompanies dizziness to the life-wrecking obsession with a drug that can come with addiction. In this regard, the pursuit of altered consciousness can be a malicious mindbug.

Often, drug-induced changes in consciousness begin as pleasant and spark an initial attraction. Researchers have measured the attractiveness of psychoactive drugs by seeing how much laboratory animals will work to get them. In one study, researchers

● **What is the allure of altered consciousness?**

allowed rats to intravenously administer cocaine to themselves by pressing a lever (Bozarth & Wise, 1985). Rats given free access to cocaine increased their use over the course of the 30-day study. They not only continued to self-administer at a high rate but also occasionally binged to the point of giving themselves convulsions. They stopped grooming themselves and eating until they lost on average almost a third of their body weight. About 90% of the rats died by the end of the study.

Rats are not tiny humans, of course, so such research is not a firm basis for understanding human responses to cocaine. But these results do make it clear that cocaine is addictive and that the results of such addiction can be dire. Studies of self-administration of drugs in laboratory animals show that animals will work to obtain not only cocaine but also alcohol, amphetamines, barbiturates, caffeine, opiates (e.g., morphine and heroin), nicotine, phenylcycladine (PCP), MDMA (ecstasy), and THC (tetrahydrocannabinol, the active ingredient in marijuana).

People usually do not become addicted to a psychoactive drug the first time they use it. They may experiment a few times, then try again, and eventually find that their tendency to use the drug increases over time due to several factors, such as drug tolerance, physical dependence, and psychological dependence. **Drug tolerance** is *the tendency for larger drug doses to be required over time to achieve the same effect*. Physicians who prescribe morphine to control pain in their patients are faced with

● **What problems arise with morphine prescriptions?**

tolerance problems because steadily greater amounts of the drug may be needed to dampen the same pain. With increased tolerance comes the danger of drug overdose; users find they need to use more and more of a drug to produce the same high. But then, if a new batch of heroin or cocaine is more concentrated than usual, the "normal" amount the user takes to achieve the same high can be fatal.

Self-administration of addictive drugs can also be prompted by withdrawal symptoms, which result when the drug is abruptly discontinued. Some withdrawal symptoms signal *physical dependence,* when pain, convulsions, hallucinations, or other unpleasant symptoms accompany withdrawal. A common example is the "caffeine headache" some people complain of when they haven't had their daily jolt of java. Other withdrawal symptoms result from *psychological dependence,* a strong desire to return to the drug even when physical withdrawal symptoms are gone. Drugs can create an emotional need over time that continues to prey on the mind, particularly in

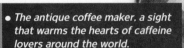
The antique coffee maker, a sight that warms the hearts of caffeine lovers around the world.

JOHN LANDER/ALAMY

circumstances that are reminders of the drug. Some ex-smokers report longing wistfully for an after-dinner smoke, for example, even years after they've successfully quit the habit.

Drug addiction reveals a human mindbug: our inability to look past the immediate consequences of our behavior. Although we would like to think that our behavior is guided by a rational analysis of future consequences, there is something intensely inviting about the prospect of a soon-to-be-had pleasure and something pale, hazy, and distant about the costs this act might bring at some future time. The immediate satisfaction associated with taking most drugs may outweigh a rational analysis of the later consequences that can result from taking those drugs, such as drug addiction.

The psychological and social problems stemming from addiction are major. For many people, drug addiction becomes a way of life, and for some, it is a cause of death. But a life of addiction is not the only possible endpoint of drug use. Stanley Schachter (1982) suggested that the visibility of addiction is misleading and that in fact many people overcome addictions. He found that 64% of a sample of people who had a history of cigarette smoking had quit successfully, although many had to try again and again to achieve their success. One study of soldiers who became addicted to heroin in Vietnam found that 3 years after their return, only 12% remained addicted (Robins et al., 1980). Although addiction is dangerous, it may not be incurable.

It may not be accurate to view all recreational drug use under the umbrella of "addiction." Many people at this point in the history of Western society, for example, would not call the repeated use of caffeine an addiction, and some do not label the use of alcohol, tobacco, or marijuana in this way. In other times and places, however, each of these has been considered a terrifying addiction worthy of prohibition and public censure. In the early 17th century, for example, tobacco use was punishable by death in Germany, by castration in Russia, and by decapitation in China (Corti, 1931). Not a good time to be traveling around waving a cigar. By contrast, cocaine, heroin, marijuana, and amphetamines have each been popular and even recommended as medicines at several points throughout history (Inciardi, 2001). Rather than viewing *all* drug use as a problem, it is important to consider the costs and benefits of such use and to establish ways to help people choose behaviors that are informed by this knowledge (Parrott et al., 2004).

People will often endure significant • • • • • • • • • • • inconveniences to maintain their addictions.

"Hi. My name is Barry, and I check my E-mail two to three hundred times a day."

Types of Psychoactive Drugs

Four in five North Americans use caffeine in some form every day, but not all psychoactive drugs are this familiar. To learn how both the well-known and lesser-known drugs influence the mind, let's consider several broad categories of drugs: depressants, stimulants, narcotics, hallucinogens, and marijuana. **TABLE 8.1** (on page 256) summarizes what is known about the potential dangers of these different types of drugs.

Depressants

Depressants are *substances that reduce the activity of the central nervous system.* Depressants have a sedative or calming effect, tend to induce sleep in high doses, and can arrest breathing in extremely high doses. Depressants can produce both physical and psychological dependence.

drug tolerance The tendency for larger doses of a drug to be required over time to achieve the same effect.

depressants Substances that reduce the activity of the central nervous system.

TABLE 8.1

Dangers of Drugs

Drug	Dangers		
	Overdose	Physical Dependence	Psychological Dependence
	(Can taking too much cause death or injury?)	(Will stopping use make you sick?)	(Will you crave it when you stop using it?)
Depressants			
Alcohol	X	X	X
Barbiturates/benzodiazepines	X	X	X
Toxic inhalants	X	X	X
Stimulants			
Amphetamines	X	X	X
MDMA (Ecstasy)	X		?
Cocaine	X	X	X
Narcotics (opium, heroin, morphine, methadone, codeine)	X	X	X
Hallucinogens (LSD, mescaline, psilocybin, PCP, ketamine)	X		?
Marijuana			?

Alcohol is "king of the depressants," with its worldwide use beginning in prehistory, its easy availability in most cultures, and its widespread acceptance as a socially approved substance. Fifty-two percent of Americans over 12 years of age report having had a drink in the past month, and 15% have binged on alcohol (over five drinks in succession) in that time. Young adults (ages 18 to 25) have even higher rates, with 60% reporting a drink last month and 31% reporting a binge (*Health, United States,* 2001; National Center for Health Statistics, 2001). Drinking while driving is a main cause of auto accidents, contributing to 32% of crash fatalities in 2006 (U.S. Department of Transportation, 2008). A survey of undergraduates revealed that alcohol contributes to as many as 90% of rapes and 95% of violent crimes on campus (Wechsler et al., 1994).

Alcohol's initial effects, euphoria and reduced anxiety, feel pretty positive. As it is consumed in greater quantities, drunkenness results, bringing slowed reactions, slurred speech, poor judgment, and other reductions in the effectiveness of thought and action. The exact way in which alcohol influences neural mechanisms is still not understood, but like other depressants, alcohol increases activity of the neurotransmitter GABA (De Witte, 1996). As you read in Chapter 3, GABA normally inhibits the transmission of neural impulses, so one effect of alcohol is as a disinhibitor—a chemical that lets transmissions occur that otherwise would be held in check. But there are many contradictions. Some people using alcohol become loud and aggressive, others become emotional and weepy, others become sullen, and still others turn giddy—and the same person can experience each of these effects in different circumstances. How can one drug do this? Two theories have been offered to account for these variable effects: *expectancy theory* and *alcohol myopia.*

Expectancy theory suggests that *alcohol effects are produced by people's expectations of how alcohol will influence them in particular situations* (Marlatt & Rohsenow, 1980). So, for instance, if you've watched friends or family drink at weddings and notice that this often produces hilarity and gregariousness, you could well experience these effects yourself should you drink alcohol on a similarly festive occasion. Seeing people getting drunk and fighting in bars, in turn, might lead to aggression after drinking.

● **Why do people experience being drunk differently?**

expectancy theory The idea that alcohol effects can be produced by people's expectations of how alcohol will influence them in particular situations.

alcohol myopia A condition that results when alcohol hampers attention, leading people to respond in simple ways to complex situations.

stimulants Substances that excite the central nervous system, heightening arousal and activity levels.

Another approach to the varied effects of alcohol is the theory of **alcohol myopia**, which proposes that *alcohol hampers attention, leading people to respond in simple ways to complex situations* (Steele & Josephs, 1990). This theory recognizes that life is filled with complicated pushes and pulls, and our behavior is often a balancing act. Imagine that you are really attracted to someone who is dating your friend. Do you make your feelings known or focus on your friendship? The myopia theory holds that when you drink alcohol, your fine judgment is impaired. It becomes hard to appreciate the subtlety of these different options, and the inappropriate response is to veer full-tilt one way or the other. So, alcohol might lead you to make a wild pass at your friend's date or perhaps just cry in your beer over your timidity—depending on which way you happened to tilt in your myopic state.

Compared to alcohol, the other depressants are much less popular but still are widely used and abused. *Barbiturates* such as Seconal or Nembutal are prescribed as sleep aids and as anesthetics before surgery. *Benzodiazepines* such as Valium and Xanax are also called minor tranquilizers and are prescribed as antianxiety drugs. These drugs are prescribed by physicians to treat anxiety or sleep problems, but they are dangerous when used in combination with alcohol. Physical dependence is possible because withdrawal from long-term use can produce severe symptoms (including convulsions), and psychological dependence is common as well.

Finally, *toxic inhalants* are perhaps the most alarming substances in this category. These drugs are easily accessible even to children in the vapors of glue, gasoline, or propane. Sniffing or "huffing" these vapors can promote temporary effects that resemble drunkenness, but overdoses are sometimes lethal, and continued use holds the potential for permanent brain damage (Fornazzari et al., 1983).

"Hey, what is this stuff? It makes everything I think seem profound."

Stimulants

The **stimulants** are *substances that excite the central nervous system, heightening arousal and activity levels.* They include caffeine, amphetamines, nicotine, cocaine, and ecstasy (MDMA) and sometimes have a legitimate pharmaceutical purpose. *Amphetamines* (also called "speed"), for example, were originally prepared for medicinal uses and as diet drugs; however, amphetamines such as Methedrine and Dexedrine are widely abused, causing insomnia, aggression, and paranoia with long-term use. Stimulants increase the levels of dopamine and norepinephrine in the brain, thereby inducing higher levels of activity in the brain circuits that depend on these neurotransmitters. As a result, they increase alertness and energy in the user, often producing a euphoric sense of confidence and a kind of agitated motivation to get things done. All stimulants produce physical and psychological dependence, and their withdrawal symptoms involve depressive effects such as fatigue and negative emotions.

Ecstasy is an amphetamine derivative also known as MDMA, "X," or "e." It is a stimulant, but it has added effects somewhat like those of hallucinogens. (We'll talk about those shortly.) Ecstasy is particularly known for making users feel empathic and close to those around them. It is used often as a party drug to enhance the group feeling at dances or raves, but it has dangerous side effects such as interfering with the regulation of body temperature, making users highly susceptible to heatstroke and exhaustion. Although ecstasy is not as likely as some other drugs to cause physical or psychological dependence, it nonetheless can lead to some dependence. Ecstasy's potentially toxic effect on serotonin-activated neurons in the human brain is under intense debate, and a good deal of research attention is being devoted to studying the effects of this drug on humans.

Cocaine is derived from leaves of the coca plant, which has been cultivated by indigenous peoples of the Andes for millennia and chewed as a medication. Yes, the urban legend is true: Coca-Cola contained cocaine until 1903 and still may use coca leaves (with cocaine removed) as a flavoring—although the company's not telling. (Pepsi-Cola never contained cocaine and is probably made from something brown.) Freud tried

● Coca-Cola has been a popular product for more than 100 years. In the early days, one of the fatigue-relieving ingredients was a small amount of cocaine.

cocaine and wrote effusively about it for a while. Cocaine (usually snorted) and crack cocaine (smoked) produce exhilaration and euphoria and are seriously addictive, both for humans and the rats you read about earlier in this chapter. Withdrawal takes the form of an unpleasant "crash," cravings are common, and antisocial effects like those generated by amphetamines—aggressiveness and paranoia—are frequent with long-term use. Although cocaine has enjoyed popularity as a "party drug," its extraordinary potential to create dependence should be taken very seriously.

Narcotics

Opium, which comes from poppy seeds, and its derivatives *heroin*, morphine, methadone, and codeine (as well as prescription drugs such as Demerol and Oxycontin), are known as **narcotics** or **opiates**, *drugs derived from opium that are capable of relieving pain*. Narcotics induce a feeling of well-being and relaxation that is enjoyable but can also induce stupor and lethargy. The addictive properties of narcotics are powerful, and long-term use produces both tolerance and dependence. Because these drugs are often administered with hypodermic syringes, they also introduce the danger of diseases such as HIV when users share syringes. Unfortunately, these drugs are especially alluring because they are external mimics of the brain's own internal relaxation and well-being system.

The brain produces **endorphins** or **endogenous opioids**, which are *neurotransmitters that are closely related to opiates*. Endorphins play a role in how the brain copes internally with pain and stress. These substances reduce the experience of pain naturally. When you exercise for a while and start to feel your muscles burning, for example, you may also find that there comes a time when the pain eases—sometimes even *during* the exercise. Endorphins are secreted in the pituitary gland and other brain sites as a response to injury or exertion, creating a kind of natural remedy (like the so-called runner's high) that subsequently reduces pain and increases feelings of well-being. When people use narcotics, the brain's endorphin receptors are artificially flooded, however, reducing receptor effectiveness and possibly also depressing the production of endorphins. When external administration of narcotics stops, withdrawal symptoms are likely to occur.

● **Why are narcotics especially alluring?**

Hallucinogens

The drugs that produce the most extreme alterations of consciousness are the **hallucinogens**, *drugs that alter sensation and perception, often causing hallucinations*. These include LSD (lysergic acid diethylamide), or acid; mescaline; psilocybin; PCP (phencycladine); and ketamine (an animal anesthetic). Some of these drugs are derived from plants (mescaline from peyote cactus, psilocybin or "shrooms" from mushrooms) and have been used by people since ancient times. For example, the ingestion of peyote plays a prominent role in some Native American religious practices. The other hallucinogens are largely synthetic. LSD was first made by chemist Albert Hofman in 1938, leading to a rash of experimentation with hallucinogens that influenced popular culture in the 1960s.

The experiment was not a great success. These drugs produce profound changes in perception. Sensations may seem unusually intense, objects may seem to move or change, patterns or colors may appear, and these perceptions may be accompanied by exaggerated emotions ranging from blissful transcendence to abject terror. These are the "I've become the legs of a chair!" drugs. But the effects of hallucinogens are dramatic and unpredictable, creating a psychological roller-coaster ride that some people find intriguing but others find deeply disturbing. Hallucinogens are the main class of drugs that animals *won't* work to self-administer, so it is not surprising that in humans these

narcotics or **opiates** Highly addictive drugs derived from opium that relieve pain.

endorphins or **endogenous opiates** Neurotransmitters that have a similar structure to opiates and that appear to play a role in how the brain copes internally with pain and stress.

hallucinogens Drugs that alter sensation and perception and often cause visual and auditory hallucinations.

marijuana The leaves and buds of the hemp plant.

drugs are unlikely to be addictive. Hallucinogens do not induce significant tolerance or dependence, and overdose deaths are rare. Although hallucinogens still enjoy a marginal popularity with people interested in experimenting with their perceptions, they have been more a cultural trend than a dangerous attraction.

Marijuana

Marijuana is derived from the *leaves and buds of the hemp plant.* When smoked or eaten, either as is or in concentrated form as *hashish,* this drug produces an intoxication that is mildly hallucinogenic. Users describe the experience as euphoric, with heightened senses of sight and sound and the perception of a rush of ideas. Marijuana affects judgment and short-term memory and impairs motor skills and coordination—making driving a car or operating heavy equipment a poor choice during its use ("Where did I leave the darn bulldozer?"). The active ingredient in marijuana is known as THC, and researchers have found that receptors in the brain that respond to THC (Stephens, 1999) are normally activated by a neurotransmitter called *anandamide* that is naturally produced in the brain (Wiley, 1999). Anandamide is involved in the regulation of mood, memory, appetite, and pain perception and has been found temporarily to stimulate overeating in laboratory animals, much as marijuana does in humans (Williams & Kirkham, 1999). Some chemicals found in dark chocolate also mimic anandamide, although very weakly, perhaps accounting for the well-being some people claim they enjoy after a "dose" of chocolate.

● **What are the risks of marijuana use?**

The addiction potential of marijuana is not strong; tolerance does not seem to develop, and physical withdrawal symptoms are minimal. Psychological dependence is possible, however, and some people do become chronic users. Marijuana use has been widespread throughout the world for recorded history, both as a medicine for pain and/or nausea and as a recreational drug, but its use remains controversial. States such as California and Oregon have passed legislation favoring medical uses, as has British Columbia in Canada, but the U.S. federal government classifies marijuana as a "Schedule I Controlled Substance," recognizing no medical use and maintaining that marijuana has the same high potential for abuse as heroin. All told, it seems that the greatest danger of marijuana is that its use is illegal.

Psychedelic art and music of the 1960s were inspired by some visual and auditory effects of drugs such as LSD.

MARTIN SHARP © PRIVATE COLLECTION/THE BRIDGEMAN ART LIBRARY

summary quiz [8.3]

9. The tendency for larger drug doses to be required over time to achieve the same effect is known as
   - a. psychological dependence.
   - b. drug tolerance.
   - c. physical dependence.
   - d. drug addiction.

10. Which class of depressants is prescribed to treat anxiety?
    - a. benzodiazepines
    - b. toxic inhalants
    - c. amphetamines
    - d. barbiturates

11. Which of the following stimulants increases alertness and energy but can lead to insomnia, aggression, and paranoia?
    - a. cocaine
    - b. ecstasy
    - c. marijuana
    - d. amphetamines

12. Neurotransmitters produced by the brain that are closely related to opiates and that increase feelings of well-being are called
    - a. dopamines.
    - b. serotonins.
    - c. endorphins.
    - d. GABAs.

Hypnosis: Open to Suggestion

You may have never been hypnotized, but you have probably heard or read about it. Its wonders are often described with an air of amazement, and demonstrations of stage hypnosis make it seem very powerful and mysterious. When you think of hypnosis, you may envision people down on all fours acting like farm animals or perhaps "regressing" to early childhood and talking in childlike voices. Some of what you might think is true, but many of the common beliefs about hypnosis are false. **Hypnosis** is *an altered state of consciousness characterized by suggestibility and the feeling that one's actions are occurring involuntarily.* In other words, it is mainly a state of mind in which people follow instructions readily and feel that their actions are things that are happening to them rather than things they are doing (Lynn, Rhue, & Weekes, 1990).

Induction and Susceptibility

The essence of hypnosis is in leading people to expect that certain things will happen to them that are outside their conscious will (Wegner, 2002). To induce hypnosis, then, a hypnotist may ask the person to be hypnotized to sit quietly and focus on some item (e.g., a spot on the wall) and then suggest to the person what effects hypnosis will have ("Your eyelids are slowly closing" or "Your arms are getting heavy"). These are "suggestions," ideas the hypnotist mentions to the volunteer about what the volunteer will do. Some of these ideas seem to cause the actions—just thinking about their eyelids slowly closing, for instance, may make many people shut their eyes briefly or at least blink. Just as you may find yawning contagious when you see someone else yawning, many different behaviors can be made more common just by concentrating on them. In hypnosis, a series of behavior suggestions can induce in some people a state of mind that makes them susceptible to even very unusual suggestions, such as getting down on all fours and sniffing in the corner.

Not everyone is equally hypnotizable. Susceptibility varies greatly, such that some hypnotic "virtuosos" are strongly influenced, most people are only moderately influenced, and some people are entirely unaffected. One of the best indicators of a person's susceptibility is the person's own judgment. So, if you think you might be hypnotizable, you may well be (Hilgard, 1965). People with active, vivid imaginations, or who are easily absorbed in activities such as watching a movie, are also somewhat more prone to be good candidates for hypnosis (Sheehan, 1979; Tellegen & Atkinson, 1974).

● **What makes someone easy to hypnotize?**

Hypnotic Effects

Hypnotists often claim that their volunteers can perform great feats not possible when the volunteers are fully conscious. One of the claims for superhuman strength involves asking a hypnotized person to become "stiff as a board" and lie unsupported with shoulders on one chair and feet on another. However, many people can do this without hypnosis. Similarly, the claim that people will perform extreme actions when hypnotized fails to take into account that people will also perform these actions when they are simply under a lot of social pressure. Some early studies reported, for instance, that hypnotized people could be led to throw what they thought was a flask of acid in an experimenter's face (Rowland, 1939; Young, 1948). In further examinations of this phenomenon, participants who were not hypnotized were asked to *simulate* being hypnotized (Orne & Evans, 1965). They were instructed to be so convincing in faking

AP PHOTO/MARSHALL INDEPENDENT, GREG DEVEREAX

Stage hypnotists often perform an induction on a whole audience and then bring some of the more susceptible members onstage for further demonstrations. This hypnotist seems to think it is entertaining to see people slump over.

hypnosis An altered state of consciousness characterized by suggestibility and the feeling that one's actions are occurring involuntarily.

hypnotic analgesia The reduction of pain through hypnosis in people who are susceptible to hypnosis.

their hypnosis that they would fool the experimenter. These people, just like the hypnotized participants, threw what they thought was acid in the experimenter's face! Clearly, hypnotic induction was not a necessary requirement to produce this behavior in the research participants.

Hypnosis also has been touted as a cure for lost memory. The claim that hypnosis helps people unearth memories that they are not able to retrieve in normal consciousness seems to have surfaced because hypnotized people often make up memories to satisfy the hypnotist's suggestions. For example, Paul Ingram, a sheriff's deputy accused of sexual abuse by his daughters in the 1980s, was asked by interrogators in session after session to relax and imagine having committed the crimes. He emerged from these sessions having confessed to dozens of horrendous acts of "satanic ritual abuse." These confessions were called into question, however, when independent investigator Richard Ofshe used the same technique to ask Ingram about a crime that Ofshe had simply made up out of thin air, something of which Ingram had never been accused. Ingram produced a three-page handwritten confession, complete with dialogue (Ofshe, 1992). Still, prosecutors in the case accepted Ingram's guilty plea, and he was only released in 2003 after a public outcry and years of work on his defense. After a person claims to remember something, even under hypnosis, it is difficult to convince others that the memory was false (Loftus & Ketchum, 1994).

A hypnotist stands on a subject who has been rendered "stiff as a board" by hypnosis.

Although all the preceding claims for hypnosis are somewhat debatable, one well-established effect is **hypnotic analgesia**, *the reduction of pain through hypnosis in people who are hypnotically susceptible.* For example, one study (see **FIGURE 8.9**, below) found that for pain induced in volunteers in the laboratory, hypnosis was more effective than morphine, diazepam (Valium), aspirin, acupuncture, or placebos (Stern et al., 1977).

● Why do some argue that hypnosis is indeed a different state of consciousness?

For people who are hypnotically susceptible, hypnosis can be used to control pain in surgeries and dental procedures, in some cases more effectively than any form of anesthesia (Druckman & Bjork, 1994; Kihlstrom, 1985). Evidence for pain control supports the idea that hypnosis is a different state of consciousness and not entirely a matter of skillful role-playing on the part of highly motivated people.

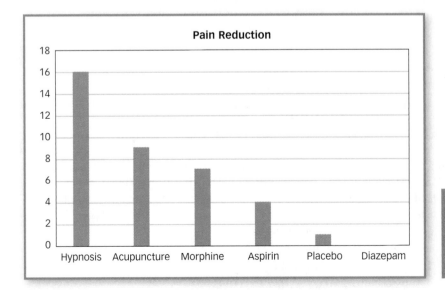

Pain Reduction

FIGURE 8.9
Hypnotic Analgesia *The degree of pain reduction reported by people using different techniques for the treatment of laboratory-induced pain. Hypnosis wins. From Stern et al., 1977.*

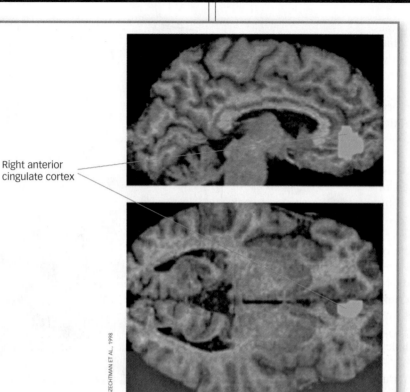

Right anterior cingulate cortex

SZECHTMAN ET AL., 1998

(b)

Brain Activity during Hypnosis
Researchers found right anterior cingulate cortex activation in hypnotized research participants both when they were hearing a target sentence and when they were following the suggestion to hallucinate the sentence. The right anterior cingulated cortex is involved in the regulation of attention. The brain is viewed here in two cross-sectional scans: (a) upright and (b) horizontal.

The conscious state of hypnosis is accompanied by unique patterns of brain activation. In one study, researchers prescreened highly hypnotizable people for their ability to hallucinate during hypnosis (Szechtman et al., 1998). After a standard hypnotic induction, participants' brains were scanned while they performed each of three tasks: perception, imagination, and hypnotic hallucination. For the perception task, participants heard a recording of the sentence "The man did not speak often, but when he did, it was worth hearing what he had to say." For the imagination task, they were asked to imagine hearing this line again. For the hypnotic hallucination task, they listened as the hypnotist suggested that the tape was playing once more (although it was not). The researchers expected this last suggestion to prompt an auditory hallucination of the line, and participants indeed reported thinking they heard it.

The PET scan revealed that the right anterior cingulate cortex, an area involved in the regulation of attention, was just as active while the participants were hallucinating as when they were actually hearing the line. However, there was less activation in this brain area when participants were merely imagining the sentence. **FIGURE 8.10** shows where the right anterior cingulate area was activated in the hypnotizable participants both during hearing and hallucinating. This pattern of activation was not found in people who were not highly hypnotizable. The researchers concluded that hypnosis stimulated the brain to register the hallucinated voice as real rather than as imagined.

summary quiz [8.4]

13. Which of the following four individuals is *least* likely to be a good candidate for hypnosis?
    a. Jake, who spends lots of time watching movies
    b. Ava, who is convinced she is easily hypnotizable
    c. Evan, who has an active, vivid imagination
    d. Isabel, who loves to play sports

14. One well-established effect of hypnosis is
    a. retrieving lost memories.
    b. reducing pain.
    c. giving people the physical strength to lie unsupported with shoulders on one chair and feet on another.
    d. making people perform extreme actions such as throwing acid in someone's face.

15. Your textbook describes research in which highly hypnotizable individuals were given standard hypnotic induction instructions. They were then asked to listen to a voice on tape, and then were told that the tape was playing again (although it was not). What brain area was activated during both tasks?
    a. right anterior cingulate cortex
    b. medial forebrain bundle
    c. auditory association area
    d. amygdala

Meditation and Religious Experiences: Higher Consciousness

meditation The practice of intentional contemplation.

Some altered states of consciousness occur without hypnosis, without drugs, and without other external aids. In fact, the altered states of consciousness that occur naturally or through special practices such as meditation can provide some of the best moments in life. Abraham Maslow (1962) described these "peak experiences" as special states of mind in which you feel fully alive and glad to be human. Sometimes these come from simple pleasures—a breathtaking sunset or a magical moment of personal creativity—and other times they can arise through meditative or religious experiences.

Meditation

Meditation is *the practice of intentional contemplation.* Techniques of meditation are associated with a variety of religious traditions and are also practiced outside religious contexts. The techniques vary widely. Some forms of meditation call for attempts to clear the mind of thought, others involve focusing on a single thought (e.g., thinking about a candle flame), and still others involve concentration on breathing or on a mantra, a repetitive sound such as *om.* At a minimum, the techniques have in common a period of quiet.

Why would someone meditate? The time spent meditating can be restful and revitalizing, and according to meditation enthusiasts, the repeated practice of meditation can enhance psychological well-being. Meditation temporarily influences brain

● **What are some positive outcomes of meditation?**

activation, usually producing patterns known as *alpha waves* that are associated with relaxation (Dillbeck & Orme-Johnson, 1987). A brain-scanning study of Buddhist practitioners during meditation found especially low levels of activation in the posterior superior parietal lobe (Newberg et al., 2001). This area is normally associated with judging physical space and orienting oneself in space—knowing angles, distances, and the physical landscape and distinguishing between the self and other objects in space. When this area is deactivated during meditation, its normal function of locating the self in space may subside to yield an experience of immersion and a loss of self.

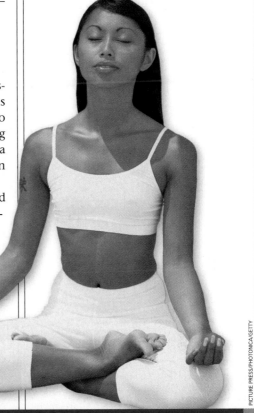

Meditation can confer physical and psychological ● ● ● ● ● ● ● ● ● ● benefits on its practitioners, but research has not yet determined how it might work.

Ecstatic Religious Experiences

In some religious traditions, people describe personal experiences of altered consciousness—feelings of ecstasy, rapture, conversion, or mystical union. Members of a religious group may "speak in tongues," or the celebrants may go into trances, report seeing visions, or feel as though they are possessed by spirits. These altered states may happen during prayer or worship or without any special religious activity. Altered states of consciousness of one sort or another are associated with religious practices around the world (Bourguignon, 1968).

Like meditation, certain brain activation patterns are associated with ecstatic religious experiences. Some people who experience religious fervor show the same type of brain activation that occurs in some cases of

● **What is the relationship between religious fervor and epilepsy?**

epilepsy. Several prophets, saints, and founders of religions have been documented as having epilepsy—Joan of Arc, for example, had symptoms of epilepsy accompanying the religious visions that inspired her and her followers (Saver & Rabin, 1997). People asked to describe what it is like to have a seizure, in turn, sometimes report feeling what they call a religious "aura." One patient described his seizures as consisting of feelings of incredible contentment, detachment, and fulfillment, accompanied by the visualization

PICTURE PRESS/PHOTONICA/GETTY

Whirling dervishes of the Mevlevi order of Sufism perform the Sema, a spiritual ceremony that aids in their quest for divine illumination.

of a bright light and soft music; sometimes he also saw a bearded man he assumed was Jesus Christ (Morgan, 1990). Surgery to remove a tumor in the patient's right anterior temporal lobe eliminated the seizures but also stopped his religious ecstasies. Cases such as this suggest the right anterior temporal lobe might be involved when people without epilepsy experience profound religious feelings. The special moments of connection that people feel with God or the universe may depend on the way in which brain activation promotes a religious state of consciousness.

The states of religious ecstasy and meditation are just two of the intriguing varieties of experience that consciousness makes available to us. Our consciousness ranges from the normal everyday awareness of walking, thinking, or gazing at a picture to an array of states that are far from normal or everyday—sleep, dreams, drug intoxication, hypnosis, and beyond. These states of mind stand as a reminder that the human mind is not just something that students of psychology can look at and study. The mind is something each of us looks *through* at the world and at ourselves.

summary quiz [8.5]

16. According to the textbook, meditation and ecstatic religious experience are altered states of consciousness that occur
    a. naturally.
    b. through hypnosis.
    c. by taking certain drugs.
    d. in the zone between sleeping and waking.

17. Meditation usually produces what kind of brain activity?
    a. delta waves   c. beta waves
    b. alpha waves   d. theta waves

18. Ecstatic religious experiences may have a basis in the same brain region associated with
    a. somnambulism.   c. epilepsy.
    b. meditation.   d. hypnotic analgesia.

WhereDoYouStand?

Drugs and the Regulation of Consciousness

Why does everyone have an opinion about drug use? Given that it's not possible to perceive what happens in anyone else's mind (that pesky "other minds" mystery of consciousness), why does it matter so much to us what people do to their own consciousness? Is consciousness something that governments should be able to legislate, or should people be free to choose their own conscious states (McWilliams, 1993)? After all, how can a "free society" justify regulating what people do inside their own heads?

Individuals and governments alike answer these questions by pointing to the costs of drug addiction, both to the addict and to the society that must "carry" unproductive people, pay for their welfare, and often even take care of their children. Drug users appear to be troublemakers and criminals, the culprits behind all those "drug-related" shootings, knifings, robberies, and petty thefts you see in the news day after day. It makes sense that their behavior appears to be caused by drug use, and widespread anger about the drug problem has surfaced in the form of the "War on Drugs," a federal government program that has focused on drug use as a criminal offense and has attempted to stop drug use through the imprisonment of users.

Social commentators such as economist Milton Friedman and psychiatrist Thomas Szasz believe that the War on Drugs is much like the era of Prohibition, the federal government's 1920–1933 ban on alcohol (Trebach & Zeese, 1992). This famous experiment failed because the harm produced by the policy outweighed the damage produced by legal alcohol consumption. Illegal alcohol became wildly expensive, and the promise of large profits led to the rapid growth of organized criminal suppliers, an entire criminal subculture complete with gang killings and turf wars over distribution rights. With the huge jump in organized crime came a parallel wave of crime by "users"; illegal alcohol was so expensive that people who were dependent on it begged, stole, or sold anything to

In the Netherlands, marijuana use is not prosecuted. The drug is sold in "coffee shops" to those over 18.

get money to buy it. The current War on Drugs has led to the same buildup of criminal supply systems, along with an increase in crimes committed by users to get drug money. These observations bring up the question of whether it is the drug use that causes social problems or the *prohibition* of drug use that causes these problems.

What should be done? One possibility is the *harm reduction approach,* a response to high-risk behaviors that focuses on reducing the harm such behaviors have on *people's lives* (Marlatt, 1998). This approach (which originated in the Netherlands and England) focuses on reducing drug harm rather than reducing drug use. Harm reduction involves tactics such as providing intravenous drug users with sterile syringes to help them avoid contracting HIV and other infections from shared needles. A harm reduction idea for alcoholics, in turn, is to allow moderate drinking; the demand to be cold sober may keep many alcoholics on the street and away from any treatment at all (Marlatt et al., 1993). Harm reduction strategies may not always find public support because they challenge the popular idea that the solution to drug and alcohol problems must always be prohibition: stopping use entirely.

Harm reduction seems to be working in the Netherlands. The Netherlands Ministry of Justice (1999) reported that the decriminalization of marijuana there in 1979 has not led to increased use and that the use of other drugs remains at a level far below that of other European countries and the United States. A comparison of drug users in Amsterdam and San Francisco revealed that the city in which marijuana is criminalized—San Francisco—had higher rates of drug use for both marijuana and other drugs (Reinarman, Cohen, & Kaal, 2004).

Should the United States, like the Netherlands, legalize use of psychoactive drugs? If yes, which ones? What about caffeine and alcohol? Should there be restrictions on when or where these substances are used? For a legal drug, should there be age limits restricting use? Where do you stand?

Prohibition was an attempt to legislate self-control that eventually produced so many problems that people campaigned in the streets to repeal the law.

CHAPTER REVIEW

Summary

Conscious and Unconscious: The Mind's Eye, Open and Closed

- Consciousness is a mystery of psychology because other people's minds cannot be perceived directly and because the relationship between mind and body is perplexing.

- Consciousness has four basic properties: intentionality, unity, selectivity, and transience. It can also be understood in terms of levels: minimal consciousness, full consciousness, and self-consciousness.

- Unconscious processes influence a person's conscious thoughts and behaviors without that person's awareness.

Sleep and Dreaming: Good Night, Mind

- Sleep and dreaming present a view of the mind with an altered state of consciousness.

- During a night's sleep, the brain passes in and out of five stages of sleep; most dreaming occurs in the REM sleep stage.

- Sleep can be disrupted through various disorders; deprivation from sleep and dreams has psychological and physiological costs.

- In dreaming, the dreamer uncritically accepts changes in emotion, thought, and sensation but poorly remembers the dream on awakening.

- Theories of dreaming include Freud's psychoanalytic theory and more current views such as the activation-synthesis model.

Drugs and Consciousness: Artificial Inspiration

- Psychoactive drugs influence consciousness by altering the brain's chemical messaging system.

- Drug tolerance can result in overdose, and physical and psychological dependence can lead to addiction.

- Major types of psychoactive drugs include depressants, stimulants, narcotics, hallucinogens, and marijuana.

Hypnosis: Open to Suggestion

- Hypnosis is an altered state of consciousness characterized by suggestibility.

- Although many claims for hypnosis overstate its effects, hypnosis can create the experience that one's actions are occurring involuntarily, create analgesia, and even change brain activations in ways that suggest that hypnotic experiences are more than imagination.

Meditation and Religious Experiences: Higher Consciousness

- Meditation and religious ecstasy can be understood as altered states of consciousness.

- Meditation involves contemplation that may focus on a specific thought, sound or action, or it may be an attempt to avoid any focus; it promotes relaxation.

- Ecstatic religious experiences may have a basis in the same brain region—the right anterior temporal lobe—associated with some forms of epilepsy.

Key Terms

consciousness (p. 234)

Cartesian Theater (p. 234)

phenomenology (p. 234)

problem of other minds (p. 235)

mind/body problem (p. 236)

cocktail party phenomenon (p. 238)

minimal consciousness (p. 239)

full consciousness (p. 239)

self-consciousness (p. 239)

mental control (p. 240)

thought suppression (p. 240)

rebound effect of thought suppression (p. 241)

ironic processes of mental control (p. 241)

dynamic unconscious (p. 242)

repression (p. 242)

cognitive unconscious (p. 242)

subliminal perception (p. 243)

altered state of consciousness (p. 244)

circadian rhythm (p. 244)

REM sleep (p. 245)

insomnia (p. 247)

sleep apnea (p. 248)

somnambulism (p. 248)

narcolepsy (p. 248)

sleep paralysis (p. 248)

night terrors (p. 248)

activation-synthesis model (p. 250)

psychoactive drugs (p. 253)

drug tolerance (p. 254)

depressants (p. 255)

expectancy theory (p. 256)

alcohol myopia (p. 257)

stimulants (p. 257)

narcotics or opiates (p. 258)

endorphins or endogenous opiates (p. 258)

hallucinogens (p. 258)

marijuana (p. 259)

hypnosis (p. 260)

hypnotic analgesia (p. 261)

meditation (p. 263)

Critical Thinking Questions

1. Freud theorized that dreams represent unacceptable or anxiety-producing wishes that the mind can only express in disguised form. A different theory of dreaming, the activation-synthesis model, proposes that dreams are produced when the mind attempts to make sense of random neural activity that occurs in the brain during sleep.

    Suppose a man is expecting a visit from his mother-in-law; the night before her arrival, he dreams that he comes home from work to find that his mother-in-law has driven a bus through the living room window of his house. How might Freud have interpreted such a dream? How might the activation-synthesis model interpret such a dream?

2. Alcohol has many effects, which can differ from person to person and from situation to situation. Expectancy theory suggests that alcohol's effects are influenced by people's expectations of how alcohol will influence them. The theory of alcohol myopia proposes that alcohol hampers attention, leading people to respond in simple ways to complex situations.

    Which one of these theories views a person's response to alcohol as being (at least partially) learned, through a process similar to observational learning?

3. Psychoactive drugs are chemicals that, when ingested, influence consciousness or behavior by altering the brain's chemical message system. Stimulant drugs can influence brain activity and often produce a sense of euphoria and well-being. Meditation is the practice of internal contemplation, and it can also temporarily influence brain activity and enhance the sense of well-being.

    Why do you think many cultures view psychoactive drugs as dangerous but meditation as healthful?

Answers to Summary Quizzes

Summary Quiz 8.1
1. c; 2. b; 3. a; 4. d

Summary Quiz 8.2
5. d; 6. b; 7. c; 8. a

Summary Quiz 8.3
9. b; 10. a; 11. d; 12. c

Summary Quiz 8.4
13. d; 14. b; 15. a

Summary Quiz 8.5
16. a; 17. b; 18. c

Need more help? Additional resources are located at the book's free companion Web site at:
www.worthpublishers.com/schacterbrief1e

Emotion and Motivation

AT 6:02 P.M. ON OCTOBER 2, 2002, James Martin was walking across the Shoppers Food Warehouse parking lot in Wheaton, Maryland, with a bag of groceries in his arms. As Martin approached his truck, there was a sudden, loud pop, and a bullet from a Bushmaster XM15 semiautomatic rifle severed his spinal cord and perforated his aorta. He crumpled to the pavement and bled to death.

James Martin was the first, but he would not be the last. The next day, in a period of less than 90 minutes, James Buchanan was shot while mowing the lawn, Premkumar Walekar was shot while pumping gas, Sarah Ramos was shot while sitting at a bus stop, Lori Ann Lewis-Rivera was shot while vacuuming her car, and Pascal Charlot was shot while taking a walk. The serial killer whom the media called the "Beltway Sniper" seemed to select his victims at random and shoot them from afar. The authorities received a note demanding $10 million to stop the killings, and that note provided clues that led to the arrest of two men: 42-year-old John Allen Muhammad and 17-year-old Lee Boyd Malvo.

Why did these men ride around in a car for 22 days, slaughtering innocent people at random? Everyone had a different answer. The authorities discovered that Muhammad and Malvo had made the decision to ask for $10 million only *after* they had killed most of their victims. Prosecutors claimed that Muhammad had come to Maryland to kill his ex-wife and that when he was unable to locate her, he went mad and "began shooting people around her" (Ahlers, 2003). Muhammad's attorney argued that his client was a troubled veteran for whom "something went terribly wrong. He came back from Desert Storm a different man" (Sipe, 2006). A psychologist described Muhammad as a "very, very

STEVE HELBER/AFP/GETTY IMAGES

AP PHOTO/SUSAN WALSH, FILE

What motivated John Allen Muhammad (left) and Lee Boyd Malvo (right), to spend 22 days killing people at random?

angry individual," but added, "Of course there are a lot of angry people who don't explode. So there must have been something in his social interaction—in his marriage or his military career—that pulled the trigger" (Leonard, 2002). To further complicate matters, the teenage Malvo claimed that he had not wanted to kill anyone and that he'd participated in the slaughter only to please Muhammad, whom he called "Father."

Not everyone believed that the two men were motivated by greed, by rage, or by filial loyalty. "Muhammad might have seen himself as a foot soldier in the jihad against the United States and he took up arms to terrorize Americans," wrote one commentator (Pipes, 2002). "In a society that celebrates celebrity above all, they were seeking to enter the Hall of Fame in the only category where they stood a chance, as criminals and serial killers," wrote another (Buchanan, 2002). ∎

"**W**hy? Why? Why? Why? That's the question I think everyone is asking," said Malvo's brother (Pipes, 2002). And indeed it was. Serial killers fascinate us—not only because of our morbid curiosity, but because we are fascinated by people whose motives we can't fathom and whose emotions we can't comprehend. What could have led Muhammad to select another human being at random and put a bullet through his heart? What could have compelled Malvo to take aim at a pregnant woman simply because his surrogate father told him to? How could these men have pulled the triggers of their rifles; watched helpless people fall to the ground, and then driven away calmly? How could they not have felt sadness, remorse, or disgust?

When we ask why people feel and act as they do, we are asking questions about their emotions and motivations. As you will see, emotions and motivations are intimately connected, and understanding their connection allows us to answer the "Why?" question that everyone is asking.

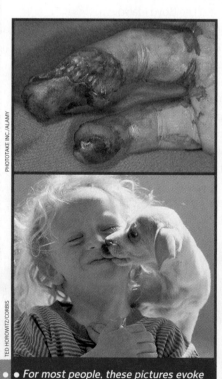

PHOTOTAKE INC./ALAMY

TED HOROWITZ/CORBIS

● *For most people, these pictures evoke emotional experiences. Having these experiences is easy, but describing them is difficult.*

Emotional Experience: The Feeling Machine

Trying to describe love to someone who had never experienced it would be a bit like trying to describe green to someone who was born blind. You could tell them about its sources ("It's that feeling you get when you see your sweetheart across the room"), and you could describe its physiological correlates ("It makes your pupils dilate"), but in the end, your descriptions would largely miss the point because the essential feature of love—like the essential feature of all emotions—is the *experience*. It *feels* like something to love, and what it feels like is love's defining attribute.

What Is Emotion?

What can we do when we want to study something whose defining attribute resists description? Psychologists have developed a clever technique that capitalizes on the fact that while people can't always say what an emotional experience feels like ("Love is . . . um . . . uh . . ."), they can usually say how similar it is to another ("Love is more like happiness than like anger"). By asking people to rate the similarity of dozens of emotional experiences, psychologists have been able to map those experiences using a sophisticated technique known as *multidimensional scaling*. The mathematics behind this technique is complex, but the logic is simple. If you listed the distances between a dozen U.S. cities and then handed the list to a friend and challenged him to draw a map on which every city was the listed distance from every other, your friend would be forced to draw a map of the United

● **What is the logic behind** *multidimensional scaling*?

States because there is no other map that allows every city to appear at precisely the right distance from every other.

The same logic can be used to generate a map of the emotional landscape. If you listed the similarity of a dozen emotional experiences (assigning smaller "distances" to those that were conceptually "close" to each other and larger "distances" to those that are conceptually "far away" from each other) and then challenged a friend to draw a map on which every experience was the listed "distance" from every other, your friend would draw a map like the one shown in **FIGURE 9.1**, below. This is the unique map that allows every emotional experience to be precisely the right "distance" from every other. What good is this map? As it turns out, maps don't just show how close things are to each other: They also reveal the *dimensions* on which those things vary. For example, the emotion map in **FIGURE 9.1** reveals that emotional experiences differ on two dimensions that are called *valence* (how positive or negative the experience is) and *arousal* (how active or passive the experience is), and every emotional experience can be described by its unique coordinates in this two-dimensional space (Russell, 1980; Watson & Tellegen, 1985).

This map of emotional experience suggests that any definition of emotion must include two things: first, the fact that emotional experiences are always good or bad, and second, the fact that these experiences are associated with characteristic levels of bodily arousal. As such, **emotion** can be defined as *a positive or negative experience that is associated with a particular pattern of physiological activity*. As you are about to see, the first step in understanding emotion involves understanding how experience and physiological activity are related.

emotion A positive or negative experience that is associated with a particular pattern of physiological activity.

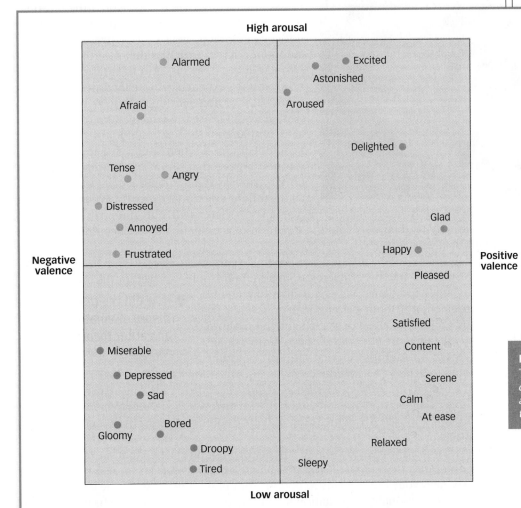

High arousal

Alarmed   Excited
Astonished
Aroused
Afraid
Delighted
Tense   Angry
Distressed
Annoyed   Glad
Frustrated   Happy

Negative valence   **Positive valence**

Pleased
Satisfied
Miserable   Content
Depressed   Serene
Sad   Calm
Bored   At ease
Gloomy
Droopy   Relaxed
Tired   Sleepy

Low arousal

FIGURE 9.1 ● ● ● ● ● ● ● ● ● ● ● ● ● ● ●
Two Dimensions of Emotion *Just as cities can be mapped by their longitude and latitude, emotions can be mapped by their arousal and valence.*

"I never realized they had feelings."

The Emotional Body

You probably think that if you walked into your kitchen right now and saw a bear nosing through the cupboards, you would feel fear, your heart would start to pound, and the muscles in your legs would prepare you for running away. But William James and Carl Lange suggested that the events that produce an emotion might actually happen in the opposite order (Lange & James, 1922). The **James-Lange theory** of emotion asserts that *stimuli trigger activity in the autonomic nervous system, which in turn produces an emotional experience in the brain.* In other words, first you see the bear, then your heart starts pounding and your leg muscles contract, and *then* you experience fear, which is simply your experience of your body's activity. James saw emotional experience as the consequence—and not the cause—of our physiological reactions to objects and events in the world.

But James's former student, Walter Cannon, disagreed, and together with *his* student, Philip Bard, Cannon proposed an alternative to James's theory. The **Cannon-Bard theory** of emotion suggested that *a stimulus simultaneously triggers activity in the autonomic nervous system and emotional experience in the brain* (Bard, 1934; Cannon, 1927). Cannon favored his own theory over the James-Lange theory for several reasons. First, the autonomic nervous system reacts too slowly to account for the rapid onset of emotional experience. For example, a blush is an autonomic response to embarrassment that takes 15 to 30 seconds to occur, and yet one can feel embarrassed long before that, so how could the blush be the cause of the feeling? Second, people often have difficulty accurately detecting changes in their own autonomic activity, such as their heart rates. If people cannot detect increases in their heart rates, then how can they experience those increases as an emotion? Third, if nonemotional stimuli—such as temperature—can cause the same pattern of autonomic activity that emotional stimuli do, then why don't people feel afraid when they get a fever? Finally, Cannon argued that there simply weren't enough unique patterns of autonomic activity to account for all the unique emotional experiences people have. If many different emotional experiences are associated with the same pattern of autonomic activity, then how could that pattern of activity be the sole determinant of the emotional experience?

England's Prince William blushes with embarrassment as he arrives at his hotel and finds a throng of adoring female fans. Because the experience of embarrassment precedes blushing by up to 30 seconds, it is unlikely that blushing is the cause of the experience.

These are all good questions, and about 30 years after Cannon asked them, psychologists Stanley Schachter and Jerome Singer supplied some answers (Schachter & Singer, 1962). James and Lange were right, they claimed, to equate emotion with the perception of one's bodily reactions. Cannon and Bard were also right, they claimed, to note that there are not nearly enough distinct bodily reactions to account for the wide variety of emotions

● **How did the *two-factor theory* of emotion expand on earlier theories?**

that human beings can experience. Whereas James and Lange had suggested that different emotions are *different experiences* of *different patterns* of bodily activity, Schachter and Singer claimed that different emotions are merely *different interpretations* of *a single pattern* of bodily activity, which they called "undifferentiated physiological arousal" (see **FIGURE 9.2**).

Schachter and Singer's **two-factor theory** of emotion claimed that *emotions are inferences about the causes of undifferentiated physiological arousal.* When you see a bear in your kitchen, your heart begins to pound. Your brain quickly scans the environment, looking for a reasonable explanation for all that pounding, and finds a bear. Your brain

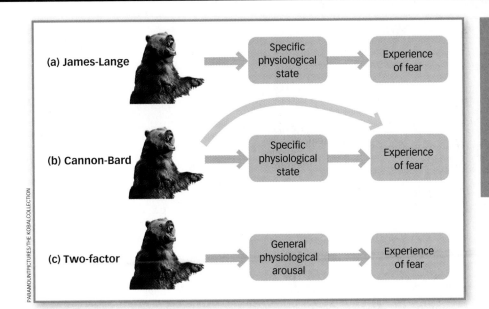

FIGURE 9.2 •••••••••••••••••••••••••••••••
Classic Theories of Emotion *Classic theories make different claims about the origins of emotion. (a) The James-Lange theory suggests that stimuli trigger specific physiological states, which are then experienced as emotions. (b) The Cannon-Bard theory suggests that stimuli trigger both specific physiological states and emotional experiences independently. (c) The two-factor theory suggests that stimuli trigger general physiological arousal whose cause the brain interprets, and this interpretation leads to emotional experience.*

(a) James-Lange → Specific physiological state → Experience of fear

(b) Cannon-Bard → Specific physiological state → Experience of fear

(c) Two-factor → General physiological arousal → Experience of fear

then does what brains do so well: It puts two and two together, and interprets your arousal as fear. In other words, when people are physiologically aroused in the presence of something that they think should scare them, they label their arousal as *fear*. But if they have precisely the same bodily response in the presence of something that they think should delight them, they may label that arousal as *excitement*. According to Schachter and Singer, people have the same physiological reaction to all emotional stimuli, but they interpret that reaction differently on different occasions.

Schachter and Singer sought to support their theory with an experiment in which they gave participants an injection of epinephrine, a neurotransmitter that mimics the action of the sympathetic nervous system, causing increases in blood pressure, heart rate, blood flow to the brain, blood sugar levels, and respiration. Participants then interacted with another person who (unbeknownst to them) was a confederate of the experimenter. Schachter and Singer predicted that those participants who experienced epinephrine-induced arousal, but who hadn't been informed of the injection's effects, would seek an explanation for their arousal—and that the confederate's behavior would supply it. In fact, that's what happened. When the confederate acted goofy, the participants concluded that they themselves were feeling *happy*; when the confederate acted nasty, they concluded that they themselves were feeling *angry*. These and other studies suggest that people can indeed misattribute their arousal to other stimuli in their environments and that the inferences people draw about the causes of their arousal can influence their emotional experience.

● **Why is it difficult to identify the origin of an emotional experience?**

Research has not been so kind to another part of the two-factor model, however. One of the theory's central claims is that all emotional experiences derive from the same pattern of bodily activity, namely, undifferentiated physiological arousal. Paul Ekman and colleagues (1983) measured participants' physiological reactions during six different emotions and found that anger, fear, and sadness each produced a higher heart rate than disgust; that fear and disgust produced higher galvanic skin response (sweating) than did sadness or anger; and that anger produced a larger increase in finger temperature than did fear (see **FIGURE 9.3**, on page 274).

So it now appears that James and Lange were right when they suggested that patterns of physiological response are not the same for all emotions. But it appears that Cannon and Bard were right when they suggested that people are not perfectly sensitive to these patterns of response, which is why people must sometimes make inferences about what they are feeling. Our bodily activity and our mental activity are both the causes and the

James-Lange theory A theory about the relationship between emotional experience and physiological activity suggesting that stimuli trigger activity in the autonomic nervous system, which in turn produces an emotional experience in the brain.

Cannon-Bard theory A theory about the relationship between emotional experience and physiological activity suggesting that a stimulus simultaneously triggers activity in the autonomic nervous system and emotional experience in the brain.

two-factor theory A theory about the relationship between emotional experience and physiological activity suggesting that emotions are inferences about the causes of undifferentiated physiological arousal.

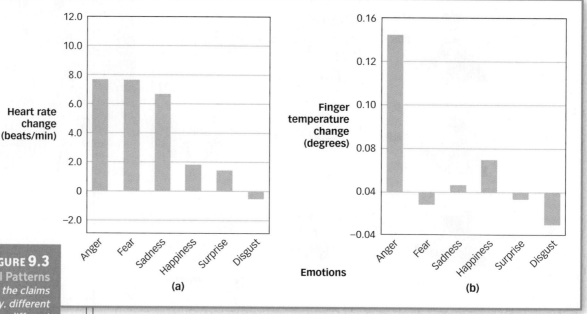

(a)

(b)

Emotions

● **FIGURE 9.3**

Different Physiological Patterns of Emotion *Contrary to the claims of the two-factor theory, different emotions do seem to have different underlying patterns of physiological arousal. (a) Anger, fear, and sadness all produce higher heart rates compared to happiness, surprise, and disgust. (b) Anger produces a much larger increase in finger temperature than any other emotion.*

● ● ● ● ● ● ● ● ● *Animals with Klüver-Bucy syndrome become hypersexual and will attempt to mate with members of different species and even inanimate objects.*

appraisal An evaluation of the emotion-relevant aspects of a stimulus that is performed by the amygdala.

consequences of our emotional experience. The precise nature of their interplay is not yet fully understood, but as you are about to see, much progress has been made over last few decades by following the trail of emotion from the beating heart to the living brain.

The Emotional Brain

Psychologist Heinrich Klüver and the physician Paul Bucy were studying the effects of hallucinogenic drugs in rhesus monkeys when they made an accidental discovery that Klüver would later call "the most striking behavior changes ever produced by a brain operation in animals" (Klüver, 1951, p. 151). After surgically removing a particular monkey's temporal lobe, they noticed that she would eat just about anything and have sex with just about anyone or anything—as though she could no longer distinguish between good and bad food or good and bad mates. But the most striking thing about her was her extraordinary lack of fear. She were eerily calm when being handled by experimenters or being confronted by snakes, both of which rhesus monkeys typically find alarming (Klüver & Bucy, 1937, 1939). This constellation of behaviors became known as "temporal lobe syndrome" or "Klüver-Bucy syndrome."

What explained this behavior? As it turned out, Klüver and Bucy's surgery damaged several brain regions including the amygdala, a brain structure that we now know plays a key role in the production of emotion, particularly in **appraisal**, which is *an evaluation of the emotion-relevant aspects of a stimulus* (Arnold, 1960; Lazarus, 1984; Roseman, 1984; Roseman & Smith, 2001; Scherer, 1999, 2001) (**FIGURE 9.4**, page 275). Klüver and Bucy's monkey was calm in the presence of a snake because her amygdala had been damaged, so the sight of a snake was no longer coded as threatening. Research on human beings has reached a similar conclusion. For example, normal people have superior memory for emotionally evocative words such as *death* or *crap,* but people whose amygdalae are damaged (LaBar & Phelps, 1998) or who take drugs that temporarily impair neurotransmission in the amygdala (van Stegeren et al., 1998) do not.

The amygdala's job is to make a very rapid appraisal of a stimulus, and thus it does not require much information (Zajonc, 1980, 1984). When people are shown fearful faces at speeds so fast that they are unaware of having seen them, their amygdalae show

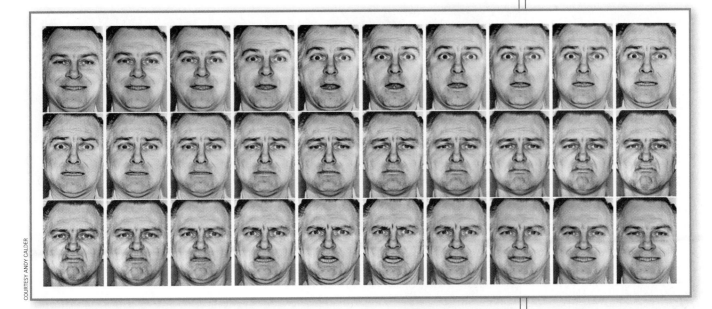

COURTESY ANDY CALDER

increased activity (Whalen et al., 1998). Psychologist Joseph LeDoux (2000) mapped the route that information about a stimulus takes through the brain and found that it is transmitted simultaneously along two distinct routes: the "fast pathway," which goes from the thalamus directly to the amygdala, and the "slow pathway," which goes from the thalamus to the cortex and *then* to the amygdala (see **FIGURE 9.5**). This means that while the cortex is slowly using the information to conduct a full-scale investigation of the stimulus's identity and importance ("This seems to be an animal . . . probably a mammal . . . perhaps a member of the genus *Ursus* . . ."), the amygdala has already received the information directly from the thalamus and is making one very fast and very simple decision: "Is this potentially bad for me?" If the amygdala's answer to that question is yes, it initiates the neural processes that ultimately produce the bodily reactions and conscious experience that we call fear.

When the cortex finally finishes processing the information, it sends a signal to the amygdala telling it to maintain fear ("We've now analyzed all the data up here, and sure enough, that thing is a bear—and bears bite!") or decrease it ("Relax, it's just some guy in a bear costume"). When people are asked to *experience* emotions such as happiness, sadness, fear, and anger, they show increased activity in the limbic system and decreased activity in the cortex (Damasio et al., 2000); but when people are asked to *inhibit* these emotions, they show increased cortical activity and decreased limbic activity (Ochsner et al., 2002). In a sense, the amygdala presses the emotional gas pedal and the cortex then hits the brakes. That's why adults with cortical damage and children (whose cortices are not well developed) have difficulty inhibiting their emotions (Stuss & Benson, 1986).

FIGURE 9.4 ·

Emotion Recognition and the Amygdala *Facial expressions of emotion were morphed into a continuum that ran from happiness to surprise to fear to sadness to disgust to anger and back to happiness. This sequence was shown to a patient with bilateral amygdala damage and to a group of 10 people without brain damage. Although the patient's recognition of happiness, sadness, and surprise was generally in line with that of the undamaged group, her recognition of anger, disgust, and fear was impaired. (Calder et al., 1996)*

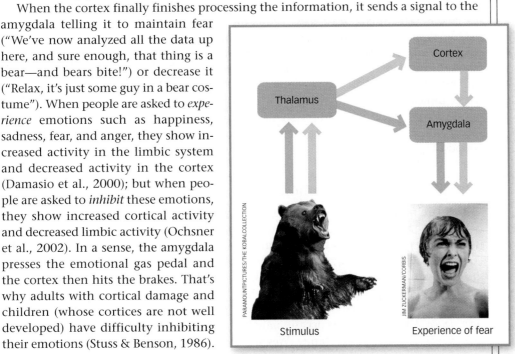

PARAMOUNTPICTURES/THE KOBALCOLLECTION

JIM ZUCKERMAN/CORBIS

Stimulus   Experience of fear

FIGURE 9.5 · · · · · · · · · · · · · · · · · ·

The Fast and Slow Pathways of Fear *According to Joseph LeDoux, information about a stimulus takes two routes simultaneously: the "fast pathway" (shown in pink), which goes from the thalamus directly to the amygdala, and the "slow pathway" (shown in green), which goes from the thalamus to the cortex and then to the amygdala. Because the amygdala receives information from the thalamus before it receives information from the cortex, people can be afraid of something before they know what it is.*

Culture & Community

Do We Really Fear People from Other Cultures More Than Our Own?

While people are able to recognize the meaning behind facial expressions across cultures, a recent study sheds new light on the relationship between fear response and culture (Chiao et al., 2009).

Using fMRI (a brain imaging technique), psychologists measured the amygdala response of young Americans and young Japanese as they looked at angry, fearful, happy, and neutral faces from both cultures. As the bar graphs here show, amygdala response was greater when participants saw fearful faces of someone from their own culture. Fear perceived in the face of one's own cultural group may more clearly indicate threat and therefore may be more likely to trigger the amygdala response associated with fear.

Right Amygdala

Percent signal change

■ Own culture
■ Other culture

Anger   Fear   Happy   Neutral

Left Amygdala

Percent signal change

■ Own culture
■ Other culture

Anger   Fear   Happy   Neutral

Studies of the brain confirm what psychologists have long suspected: Emotion is a primitive system that prepares us to react rapidly and on the basis of little information to things that are relevant to our survival and well-being. While our newly acquired cortex identifies a stimulus, considers what it knows about it, and carefully plans a response, our ancient limbic system does what it has done so well for all those millennia before the cortex evolved: It makes a split-second decision about the significance of the objects and events in our environment and, when necessary, prepares our hearts and our legs to get our butts out of the woods.

● **Why is emotion considered a primitive system?**

The Regulation of Emotion

People are never agnostic about their own emotional experience. We may not care whether we have cereal or eggs for breakfast, whether we play cricket or cards this afternoon, or whether we spend a few minutes thinking about hedgehogs, earwax, or the War of 1812. But we always care whether we are feeling happy or fearful, angry or relaxed, joyful or disgusted. Because we care so much about our emotional experiences, we take an active role in determining which ones we will have. **Emotion regulation** refers to *the cognitive and behavioral strategies people use to influence their own emotional experience.* Although people occasionally feel a bit too chipper for their own good and seek ways to "cheer down" (Erber, Wegner, & Therriault, 1996; Parrott, 1993), emotion

emotion regulation The use of cognitive and behavioral strategies to influence one's emotional experience.

reappraisal A strategy that involves changing one's emotional experience by changing the meaning of the emotion-eliciting stimulus.

regulation is more often an attempt to turn negative emotions into positive ones. A patient who is feeling depressed may whistle a silly song while waiting for his doctor, and a doctor who is feeling silly may think a few depressing thoughts before entering the room to give the patient bad news. Both are regulating their emotional experience.

Nine out of 10 people report that they attempt to regulate their emotional experience at least once a day (Gross, 1998), and they describe more than a thousand different strategies for doing so (Parkinson & Totterdell, 1999). Some of these are behavioral strategies (e.g., avoiding situations that trigger unwanted emotions, doing distracting activities, or taking drugs), and some are cognitive strategies (e.g., trying not to think about the cause of the unwanted emotion or recruiting memories that trigger the desired emotion). Research suggests that one of the most effective strategies for emotion regulation is **reappraisal**, which involves *changing one's emotional experience by changing the meaning of the emotion-eliciting stimulus*. How people think about an event can determine how they feel about it. For example, participants who watched a circumcision that was described as a joyous religious ritual had slower heart rates, had lower skin conductance levels, and reported less distress than did participants who watched the circumcision but did not hear the same description (Lazarus & Alfert, 1964).

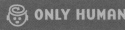

Taking heroin and singing in church would seem to have little in common, but both can be forms of emotion regulation.

In another study, participants' brains were scanned as they saw photos that induced negative emotions, such as a photo of a woman crying during a funeral. Some participants were then asked to reappraise the picture, for example, by imagining that the woman in the photo was at a wedding rather than a funeral. The results showed that when participants initially saw the photo, their amygdalae became active. But as they reappraised the picture, several key areas of the cortex became active, and moments later, their amygdalae were deactivated (Ochsner et al., 2002). In other words, participants consciously and willfully turned down the activity of their own amygdalae simply by thinking about the photo in a different way.

● **How does reappraisal of an event change emotional experience?**

Studies such as these demonstrate at the neural level what psychologists have observed for centuries at the behavioral level: Because emotions are reactions to the appraisals of an event and not to the event itself, changes in appraisal bring about changes in emotional experience. As you will learn in Chapter 14, therapists often attempt to alleviate depression and distress by helping people find new ways to think about the events that happen to them. Indeed, reappraisal appears to be important for both mental and physical health (Davidson, Putnam, & Larson, 2000), and the inability to reappraise events lies at the heart of psychiatric disorders, such as depression (Gross & Munoz, 1995).

ONLY HUMAN

WHO ENFORCES THE EMOTION REGULATION? In 1991, the mayor of Sund, Norway, proposed a resolution to the town council that banned crankiness and required people to be happy and think positively. The resolution contained an exemption for those who had a good reason to be unhappy.

summary quiz [9.1]

1. _____ is a positive or negative experience that is associated with a particular pattern of physiological activity.
   a. Motivation   b. Emotion   c. Valence   d. Arousal

2. "Emotions are inferences about the causes of undifferentiated physiological arousal." This is a statement of
   a. the James-Lange theory.   c. Schachter and Singer's two-factor theory.
   b. the Cannon-Bard theory.   d. the Klüver-Bucy syndrome.

3. A structure involved in the rapid appraisal of the emotional relevance of stimuli is the
   a. amygdala.   b. cortex.   c. hypothalamus.   d. thalamus.

4. An effective cognitive strategy for regulating one's emotional experiences is
   a. arousal.   b. valence.   c. appraisal.   d. reappraisal.

Emotional Communication: Msgs w/o Wrds

Emotions may be private events, but the "bodily reactions" they produce are not. An **emotional expression** is *an observable sign of an emotional state,* and human beings exhibit many such signs. For example, people's emotional states influence the way they talk—from intonation and inflection to loudness and duration—and research shows that listeners can infer a speaker's emotional state from vocal cues alone with better-

● **How are we "walking, talking advertisements" of our inner states?**

than-chance accuracy (Banse & Scherer, 1996; Frick, 1985). The voice is not the only clue to a person's emotional state. In fact, observers can often estimate a person's emotional state from the direction of the person's gaze, gait, posture, and even from a person's touch (Dittrich et al., 1996; Keltner & Shiota, 2003; Wallbott, 1998). In some sense, we are walking, talking advertisements for what's going on inside us.

No part of the body is more exquisitely designed for communicating emotion than the face. Underneath every face lie 43 muscles that are capable of creating more than 10,000 unique configurations, which enables a face to convey information about its owner's emotional state with an astonishing degree of subtlety and specificity (Ekman, 1965). Psychologists Paul Ekman and Wallace Friesen (1978) spent years cataloguing the muscle movements of which the human face is capable. They isolated 46 unique movements, which they called *action units,* and they gave each one a number and a memorable name, such as "cheek puffer" and "dimpler" and "nasolabial deepener" (all of which, oddly enough, are also the names of heavy metal bands). Research has shown that combinations of these action units are reliably related to specific emotional states (Davidson et al., 1990). For example, when someone feels happy, the movements of the *zygomatic major* (a muscle that pulls the lip corners up) and the *obicularis oculi* (a muscle that crinkles the outside edges of the eyes) produce a unique facial expression that psychologists describe as "action units 6 and 12" and that the rest of us simply call smiling (Ekman & Friesen, 1982; Frank, Ekman, & Friesen, 1993; Steiner, 1986).

Communicative Expression

Why are our emotions written all over our faces? In 1872, Charles Darwin published a book titled *The Expression of the Emotions in Man and Animals,* in which he speculated about the evolutionary significance of emotional expression (Darwin, 1872/1998). Darwin noticed that people and animals seem to share certain facial and postural expressions, and he suggested that these expressions are a means by which organisms communicate information about their internal states to each other. If a dominant animal can bare its teeth and communicate the message "I am angry at you," and if a subordinate animal can lower its head and communicate the message "I am afraid of you," then the two may be able to establish a pecking order without actually spilling blood. Emotional expressions are a convenient way for one animal to let another animal know how it is feeling and hence how it is prepared to act. In this sense, emotional expressions are a bit like the words or phrases of a nonverbal language.

emotional expression Any observable sign of an emotional state.

universality hypothesis The hypothesis that emotional expressions have the same meaning for everyone.

Some animals looking soothed, angry, and sulky, according to Charles Darwin.

The Universality of Expression

Of course, a language only works if everybody speaks the same one, and that fact led Darwin to develop the **universality hypothesis**, which suggests that *emotional expressions have the same meaning for everyone*. In other words, every human being expresses happiness with a smile, and every human being understands that a smile signifies happiness. Two lines of evidence suggest that Darwin was largely correct. First, people are quite accurate at judging the emotional expressions of members of other cultures (Boucher & Carlson, 1980; Ekman & Friesen, 1971; Ekman et al., 1987; Elfenbein & Ambady, 2002; Frank & Stennet, 2001; Haidt & Keltner, 1999; Izard, 1971; McAndrew, 1986; Shimoda, Argyle, & Ricci-Bitt, 1978). In the 1950s, researchers showed photographs of people expressing anger, disgust, fear, happiness, sadness, and surprise to members of the South Fore, a people who lived a Stone Age existence in the highlands of Papua New Guinea and who had had little contact with the outside world. The researchers discovered that the Fore could recognize the emotional expressions of Americans about as accurately as Americans could and vice versa. The one striking exception to this rule was that the Fore had trouble distinguishing expressions of surprise from expressions of fear, perhaps because for people who live in the wild, surprises are rarely pleasant.

An Israeli woman cries at the funeral of a relative who was killed in a suicide attack in 2005. The universality hypothesis suggests that any human being who looks at this picture will know what she is feeling.

The second line of evidence in favor of the universality hypothesis is that people who have never seen a human face make the same facial expressions as those who have.

● **Which facial expressions are considered universal?** For instance, congenitally blind people make all the facial expressions associated with the basic emotions (Galati, Scherer, & Ricci-Bitt, 1997), and 2-day-old infants (who have had virtually no exposure to human faces) react to sweet tastes with a smile and to bitter tastes with an expression of disgust (Steiner, 1973, 1979). In short, a good deal of evidence suggests that the facial displays of at least six emotions—*anger, disgust, fear, happiness, sadness, and surprise*—are universal. Recent evidence suggests that some other emotions, such as embarrassment, amusement, guilt, or shame, may have a universal pattern of facial expression as well (Keltner, 1995; Keltner & Buswell, 1996; Keltner & Haidt, 1999; Keltner & Harker, 1998).

The Cause and Effect of Expression

Why do so many people seem to express so many emotions in the same ways? After all, people in different cultures don't speak the same languages, so why do they smile the same smiles and frown the same frowns? The answer is that words are *symbols* and facial

Why is Stevie Wonder smiling? Perhaps it's the 22 Grammy Awards he's won since 1974. Research shows that people who are born blind express emotion on their faces in the same ways that sighted people do.

On September 19, 1982, Scott Fahlman posted a message to an Internet user's group that read, "I propose the following character sequence for joke markers: :-) Read it sideways." And so the emoticon was born. Fahlman's smile (above left) is a sign of happiness, whereas his emoticon is a symbol.

expressions are *signs*. Symbols are arbitrary designations that have no causal relationship with the things they symbolize. We English speakers use the word *cat* to indicate a particular animal, but there is nothing about felines that actually causes this particular sound to pop out of our mouths, and we aren't surprised when other human beings make different sounds—such as *popoki* or *gatto*—to indicate the same thing. Facial expressions, in contrast, are not arbitrary symbols of emotion. They are signs of emotion, and signs are *caused* by the things they signify. The feeling of happiness *causes* the contraction of the zygomatic major and thus its contraction is a sign of that feeling in the same way a footprint in the snow is a sign that someone walked there.

Although emotional experiences cause emotional expressions, sometimes the causal path runs in the other direction. The **facial feedback hypothesis** (Adelmann & Zajonc, 1989; Izard, 1971; Tomkins, 1981) suggests that *emotional expressions can cause the emotional experiences they signify*. For instance, people feel happier when they are asked to make the sound of a long *e* or to hold a pencil in their teeth (both of which cause contraction of the zygomatic major) than when they are asked to make the sound of a long *u* or to hold a pencil in their lips (Strack, Martin, & Stepper, 1988; Zajonc, 1989) (see **FIGURE 9.6**). Some researchers believe that this happens because the muscle contractions of a smile change the temperature of the brain, which in turn brings about a pleasant affective state (Zajonc, 1989). Others believe that the smile and the feeling of happiness become so strongly associated through experience that one always brings about the other. Although no one is sure why it happens, smiling does seem to be a cheap cure for the blues.

The fact that emotional expressions can cause the emotional experiences they signify may help explain why people are generally so good at recognizing the emotional expressions of others. Some studies suggest that observers unconsciously mimic the body postures and facial expressions of the people they are watching (Chartrand & Bargh, 1999; Dimberg, 1982). When we see someone lean forward and smile, we lean very slightly and slightly contract our zygomatic major. What purpose does this subtle mimicry serve? If making a facial expression brings about the feeling it signifies, then one can tell what others are feeling simply by imitating their expressions and thereby experiencing their feelings oneself (Lipps, 1907). If this is actually what happens, then we would expect people who have trouble experiencing emotions to have trouble recognizing the emotional expressions of others. In fact, people with amygdala damage are typically quite poor at recognizing facial expressions of fear and anger (Adolphs, Russell, & Tranel, 1999), and this is especially true if their brain damage was sustained early in life (Adolphs et al., 1997). This suggests that our emotional expressions play an important role in both sending and receiving information (see the Real World box on page 281).

● Why are people so good at recognizing other's expressions?

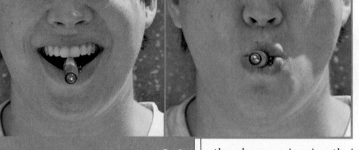

FIGURE 9.6
The Facial Feedback Hypothesis
Research shows that people who hold a pen in their teeth feel happier than those who hold a pen in their lips. Holding a pen in the teeth contracts the zygomatic major muscles of the face in the same way a smile does.

facial feedback hypothesis The hypothesis that emotional expressions can cause the emotional experiences they signify.

display rules Norms for the control of emotional expression.

Deceptive Expression

Given how important emotional expressions are, it's no wonder that people have learned to use them to their advantage. Because you can control most of the muscles in your face, you don't have to display the emotion you are actually feeling or actually feel the emotion you are displaying. When your roommate makes a sarcastic remark about your haircut, you may make the facial expression for contempt (accompanied, perhaps, by a reinforcing hand gesture), but when your boss makes the same remark, you probably swallow hard and display a pained smile. Your expressions are moderated by your knowledge that it is permissible to show contempt for your peers but not for your superiors. **Display rules** are *norms for the control of emotional expression* (Ekman, 1972; Ekman & Friesen, 1968), and following them requires using several techniques:

[THE REAL WORLD] •

That's Gross!

If you want to feel one of the most powerful, most irrational, and most poorly understood of all emotions, just spit in a glass of water. Then drink it. Despite the fact that the spit is yours and despite the fact that it was in your mouth just a moment ago, you will probably experience disgust.

Psychologist Paul Rozin has spent a lifetime disgusting people in order to understand the nature of this emotion, which is produced by the prospect of incorporating an offensive substance into one's body (Rozin & Fallon, 1987). The disgust reaction is characterized by feelings of nausea, a facial expression marked by distinct actions of the nose and mouth, and an etymology meaning "bad taste" (Rozin, Haidt, & McCauley, 1999). In this sense, disgust is a kind of defensive response that ensures that improper substances do not enter our bodies through our mouths, noses, or other orifices. For Americans, these improper substances include certain animals (e.g., rats and roaches), certain body products (e.g., vomit, feces, or blood), and certain foods (e.g., dog meat). The thought of eating a sumptuous meal of stewed monkey brains or of biting into an apple teeming with maggots makes most Americans feel nauseated, despite the fact that people in many other countries find both dishes quite palatable.

Disgust plays an important role, but it can be quite irrational, and its irrationality seems to follow two rules. The first is the rule of *contagion*, which suggests that any two things that were once in contact will continue to share their properties. So, for example, would you be willing to lick raisins off a flyswatter? Of course not. The flyswatter may have invisible traces of roach legs and fly guts on it, and those things can make you sick. Okay, then, what if the flyswatter were washed in alcohol, heated to within a degree

San Francisco's Exploratorium features an exhibit on disgust that invites visitors to drink clean water from a toilet. Casual observation suggests that 5-year-olds are generally willing and 55-year-olds are not.

COURTESY ALAN SWINKELS

of melting, and cooled to within a degree of breaking, making it the most sterile and hygienic thing in your entire house? Would you lick raisins off it then? Most people still say no (Rozin, Millman, & Nemeroff, 1986b). And the reason is that the swatter once touched a bug and thus it will forever have a disgusting essence of "bugginess" that cannot be cleansed away.

The second irrational rule is the rule of *similarity*, which suggests that things that share appearances also share properties. If someone whipped up a batch of fudge that was shaped to look convincingly like dog poop, chances are you'd turn down the opportunity to sample it. Fudge is fudge, of course, and its shape shouldn't matter, but most people still balk at this proposition (Rozin et al., 1986b)—most people, that is, except children. Children under 2 years of age will readily put any number of disgusting things in their mouths, which suggests that disgust (unlike many emotions) develops late in life (Rozin et al., 1986a). A 4-year-old will avoid eating human hair because it doesn't taste very good, but a 10-year-old child will avoid eating it because . . . well, it's haaaaaaaaair—and that's gross!

If you want to observe the irrationality of disgust for yourself, just offer your friends some guacamole in a disposable diaper or some lemonade in a bedpan. And make sure to stir it with a comb.

■ *Intensification* involves exaggerating the expression of one's emotion, as when a person pretends to be more surprised by a gift than she really is.

■ *Deintensification* involves muting the expression of one's emotion, as when the loser of a contest tries to look less distressed than he really is.

■ *Masking* involves expressing one emotion while feeling another, as when a poker player tries to look distressed rather than delighted as she examines a hand with four aces.

■ *Neutralizing* involves feeling an emotion but displaying no expression, as when judges try not to betray their leanings while lawyers make their arguments.

Although people in different cultures all use the same techniques, they use them in the service of different display rules. For example, in one study, Japanese and American college students watched an unpleasant film of car accidents and amputations (Ekman, 1972;

Can you tell what this woman is feeling? She hopes not. Helen Duann is a champion poker player who knows how to keep a "poker face," which is a neutral expression that provide little information about her emotional state.

FIGURE 9.7

Genuine and Fake Smiles Both spontaneous smiles (left) and voluntary smiles (right) raise the corners of the mouth, but only a spontaneous smile crinkles the corners of the eye.

Friesen, 1972). When the students didn't know that the experimenters were observing them, Japanese and American students made similar expressions of disgust, but when they realized that they were being observed, the Japanese students (but not the American students) masked their disgust with pleasant expressions. Many Asian societies have a strong cultural norm against displaying negative emotions in the presence of a respected person, and people in these societies may mask or neutralize their expressions.

● **Do people attempt to control their emotional expression in the same way across cultures?**

Our attempts to obey our culture's display rules don't always work out so well. Darwin (1898/1998) noted that "those muscles of the face which are least obedient to the will, will sometimes alone betray a slight and passing emotion" (p. 79). Despite our best attempts to smile bravely when we receive a poor grade on an exam, our voices, bodies, and faces are "leaky" instruments that may betray our emotional states even when we don't want them to. Four sets of features can allow a careful observer to tell whether our emotional expression is sincere (Ekman, 2003a):

■ *Morphology:* Certain facial muscles tend to resist conscious control, and for a trained observer, these so-called *reliable muscles* are quite revealing. For example, the zygomatic major raises the corners of the mouth, and this happens when people smile spontaneously or when they force themselves to smile. But only a genuine, spontaneous smile engages the obicularis oculi, which crinkles the corners of the eyes (see **FIGURE 9.7**).

■ *Symmetry:* Sincere expressions are a bit more symmetrical than insincere expressions. A slightly lopsided smile is less likely to be genuine than is a perfectly even one.

■ *Duration:* Sincere expressions tend to last between a half second and 5 seconds, and expressions that last for shorter or longer periods are more likely to be insincere.

■ *Temporal patterning:* Sincere expressions appear and disappear smoothly over a few seconds, whereas insincere expressions tend to have more abrupt onsets and offsets.

Given the reliable differences between sincere and insincere expressions, you might think that people would be quite good at telling one from the other. In fact, studies show that human lie detection ability is fairly awful. Under most conditions, most people score barely better than chance (DePaulo, Stone, & Lassiter, 1985; Ekman, 1992; Zuckerman, DePaulo, & Rosenthal, 1981; Zuckerman & Driver, 1985). One reason for this is that people have a strong bias toward believing that others are sincere. In everyday life, most people are sincere most of the time, so it makes sense

● **Why are people such poor lie detectors?**

that we are predisposed to believe what we see and hear. This may explain why people tend to mistake liars for truth tellers but not the other way around (Gilbert, 1991). A second reason why people are such poor lie detectors is that they don't seem to know which pieces of information to attend to and which to ignore. People seem to think that certain things—such as whether a person speaks quickly or averts her gaze—are associated with lying when, in fact, they are not.

When people can't do something well (e.g., adding numbers or picking up 10-ton rocks), they typically turn the job over to machines (see **FIGURE 9.8** on page 283). Can machines detect lies better than we can? The answer is yes, but that's not saying much. The most widely used lie detection machine is the *polygraph,* which measures a variety of physiological responses that are associated

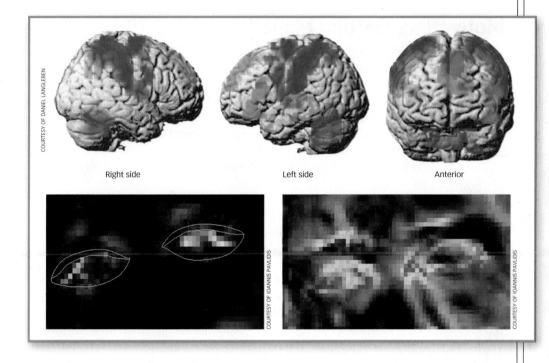

Right side   Left side   Anterior

COURTESY OF DANIEL LANGLEBEN

COURTESY OF IOANNIS PAVLIDIS

FIGURE 9.8 • • • • • • • • • • • • • • •
Lie Detection Machines *Some researchers hope to replace the polygraph with more accurate machines, such as those that measure changes in blood flow in the brain and the face. As the top panel shows, some areas of the brain are more active when people tell lies than when they tell the truth (shown in red), and some are more active when people tell the truth than when they tell lies (shown in blue) (Langleben et al., 2005). The bottom panel shows images taken by a thermal camera that detects the heat caused by blood flow to different parts of the face. The images show a person's face before (left) and after (right) telling a lie (Pavlidus, Eberhardt, & Levine, 2002). Although neither of these new techniques is extremely accurate, that could soon change.*

with stress, which people often feel when they are afraid of being caught in a lie. In fact, the machine is so widely used by governments and businesses that the National Research Council recently met to consider all the scientific evidence on its validity. After much study, it concluded that the polygraph can indeed detect lies at a rate that is significantly better than chance (National Research Council, 2003). However, it also concluded that "almost a century of research in scientific psychology and physiology provides little basis for the expectation that a polygraph test could have extremely high accuracy" (p. 212). In short, neither people nor machines are particularly good at lie detection, which is why lying continues to be a staple of human social interaction.

summary quiz [9.2]

5. Which of the following findings does *not* support the universality hypothesis?
    a. Congenitally blind people make the facial expressions associated with the basic emotions.
    b. People feel happier when asked to hold a pencil in their teeth.
    c. Infants react to bitter tastes with an expression of disgust.
    d. People are quite accurate at judging emotional expressions of happiness, sadness, anger, and fear in members of other cultures.

6. According to the facial feedback hypothesis,
    a. people unconsciously mimic the facial expressions of others.
    b. people often feel one emotion but display another.
    c. emotional expressions can cause emotional experiences.
    d. emotional experiences can cause emotional expressions.

7. Your roommate asks if you like her new outfit. You think it's hideous but smile broadly and say, "I love it!" This is an example of
    a. masking.
    b. intensification.
    c. deintensification.
    d. neutralizing.

Motivation: Getting Moved

You now know something about how emotions are produced, experienced, and communicated. But what in the world are they *for*? Emotions have several functions, and one of the most important is that they motivate behavior. **Motivation** refers to *the purpose for or cause of an action,* and it is no coincidence that the words *emotion* and *motivation* share a common linguistic root that means "to move." We act because our emotions move us to do so, and they move us in two different ways. First, emotions provide us with *information* about the world; second, emotions are the *objectives* toward which we strive. Let's examine each of these in turn.

The Function of Emotion

The first function of emotion is to provide us with information about the world. For example, most people report being more satisfied with their lives when they are asked the question on a sunny day rather than a rainy day. Why? Because people feel happier on sunny days, and they use their happiness as information about the quality of their lives (Schwarz & Clore, 1983). We all know that satisfying lives and bright futures make us feel good—so when we feel good, we naturally conclude that our lives must be satisfying and our futures must be bright. Because the world influences our emotions, our emotions provide information about the world (Schwarz, Mannheim, & Clore, 1988).

Indeed, this information is often critical. When neurologist Antonio Damasio was asked to examine a patient with an unusual form of brain damage, he asked the patient to choose between two dates for an appointment. It sounds like a simple decision, but for the next half hour, the patient enumerated reasons for and against each of the two possible dates, completely unable to decide in favor of one option or the other (Damasio, 1994). The problem wasn't any impairment of the patient's ability to think or reason. On the contrary, he could think and reason all too well. What he couldn't do was feel. The patient's injury had left him unable to experience emotion, and thus when he entertained one option ("If I come next Tuesday, I'll have to cancel my lunch with Fred"), he didn't feel any better or any worse than when he entertained another ("If I come next Wednesday, I'll have to get up early to catch the bus"). And because he *felt* nothing when he thought about an option, he couldn't decide which was better.

The second function of emotions is to give us something to strive for. People strongly prefer to experience positive rather than negative emotions, and the emotional experiences that we call happiness, satisfaction, pleasure, and joy are often the goals that our behavior is meant to accomplish. The **hedonic principle** is *the notion that all people are motivated to experience pleasure and avoid pain,* and some very smart folks have argued that this single principle can explain all human behavior. For example, Aristotle (350 BC/1998) observed that the pursuit of pleasure and the avoidance of pain "is a first principle, for it is for the sake of this that we all do all that we do."

This may sound a bit extreme, but it isn't hard to convince yourself that Aristotle was on to something. If a friend asked you why you went to the mall, you might explain that you wanted to buy a new pair of mittens. If your friend then asked why you wanted to buy a new pair of mittens, you might explain that you wanted to keep your hands warm. If your friend then asked why you wanted to keep your hands warm, you might explain that warm hands are a pleasure and cold hands are a pain. But if your friend then asked why you wanted to experience pleasure instead of pain, you'd find yourself tongue-tied. There is no answer to this question because there is no other motivation on which the desire for pleasure rests. People want many things, of course,

● *It is easy to explain why you want mittens, but can you explain why you want pleasure?*

● **How do emotions give us something to strive for?**

motivation The purpose for or cause of an action.

hedonic principle The notion that all people are motivated to experience pleasure and avoid pain.

from peace and prosperity to health and security, but the reason they want them is that these things promote pleasure and avert pain.

According to the hedonic principle, then, our emotional experience can be thought of as a gauge that ranges from bad to good, and our primary motivation—perhaps even our *sole* motivation—is to keep the needle on the gauge as close to *good* as possible. Even when we voluntarily do things that tilt the needle in the opposite direction, such as letting the dentist drill our teeth or waking up early for a boring class, we are doing these things because we believe that they will nudge the needle toward *good* in the future and keep it there longer.

The Conceptualization of Motivation

The hedonic principle sets the stage for an understanding of motivation but leaves many questions unanswered. For example, if our primary motivation is to keep the needle on *good,* so to speak, then which things push the needle in that direction and which things push it away? The answers lie in our *instincts* and *drives*.

Instincts

When a newborn baby is given a drop of sugar water, it smiles; but when it is given a check for $10,000, it acts like it couldn't care less. By the time the baby gets into college, these responses pretty much reverse. It seems clear that nature endows us with certain motivations and that experience endows us with others. William James (1890) called the inherited tendency to seek a particular goal an *instinct,* which he defined as "the faculty of acting in such a way as to produce certain ends, without foresight of the ends, and without previous education in the performance" (p. 383). According to James, nature hardwired penguins, parrots, puppies, and people to want certain things without training and to execute the behaviors that produce these things without thinking.

But by 1930, the concept of instinct had fallen out of fashion. The problem was that it flew in the face of American psychology's newest and most unstoppable force: behaviorism. Behaviorists rejected the concept of instinct on two grounds. First, they believed that behavior should be explained by the external stimuli that evoke it and not by reference to the hypothetical internal states on which it depends. Second, behaviorists wanted nothing to do with the notion of inherited behavior because for them all complex behavior was learned. Because instincts were inherited tendencies that resided inside the organism, behaviorists considered the concept doubly repugnant.

Drives

But within a few decades, some behaviorists began to realize that the strict prohibition against the mention of internal states made certain phenomena difficult to explain. For example, if all behavior is a response to an external stimulus, then why does a rat that is sitting still in its cage at 9:00 a.m. start wandering around and looking for food by noon? Nothing in the cage has changed, so why has the rat's behavior changed? What visible, measurable external stimulus is the wandering rat responding to? The obvious answer (obvious, at least, to any ordinary person) is that the rat is responding to something inside itself, which meant that one should look inside the rat if one wanted to explain its wandering.

● **How do we regulate our bodies like thermostats?**

These behaviorists began by noting that bodies are like thermostats. When thermostats detect that the room is too cold, they send signals that initiate corrective actions such as turning on a furnace. Similarly, when bodies detect that they are underfed, they

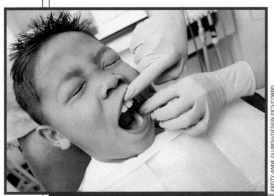

Many people voluntarily do things that cause them pain. According to the hedonic principle, people would not visit the dentist unless the pain of having dental work was ultimately outweighed by the pleasure of having had it done.

All animals are born with both the motivation and the ability to perform certain complex behaviors. Spiders don't teach their offspring how to build elaborate webs, but their offspring build them nonetheless.

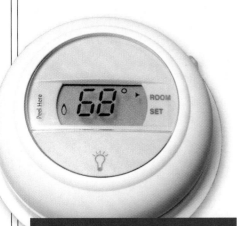

Bodies are a bit like thermostats: they sense when something is wrong and then take action to make it right.

• *All mammals experience sex drives and hunger drives. This one seems to experience Sunday drives as well.*

send signals that initiate corrective actions such as eating. To survive, an organism needs to maintain precise levels of nutrition, warmth, and so on; when these levels depart from an optimal point, the organism receives a signal to take corrective action. That signal is called a **drive**, which is *an internal state generated by departures from physiological optimality.* According to this view, it isn't food per se that organisms find rewarding; it is the reduction of the drive for food. Hunger is a drive, a drive is an internal state, and when organisms eat, they are attempting to change their internal state.

The words *instinct* and *drive* are no longer widely used in psychology, but the concepts remain part of the modern conception of motivation. The concept of instinct reminds us that nature endows organisms with a tendency to seek certain things, and the concept of drive reminds us that this seeking is initiated by an internal state. Modern psychologists are more likely to talk in terms of the "needs" that motivate organisms to take action.

So what are these needs? Abraham Maslow (1954) attempted to organize the list of human needs in a meaningful way (see **FIGURE 9.9**). He noted that some needs (e.g., the need to eat) must be satisfied before others (e.g., the need to mate), and he built a hierarchy of needs that had the strongest and most immediate needs at the bottom and the weakest and most deferrable needs at the top. Maslow suggested that as a rule, people will not experience a need until all the needs below it are met. So when people are hungry or thirsty or exhausted, they will not seek intellectual fulfillment or moral clarity, which is to say that philosophy is a luxury of the well fed. Although many aspects of Maslow's theory failed to win empirical support (e.g., a person on a hunger strike may value her principles more than her physical needs; see Wahba & Bridwell, 1976), the idea that some needs take precedence over others is clearly right. And although there are exceptions, those that typically take precedence are those that we share with

FIGURE 9.9
Maslow's Hierarchy of Needs *Humans are motivated to satisfy a variety of needs. Psychologist Abraham Maslow thought these needs formed a hierarchy, with lower-order needs forming a base and self-actualization needs forming a pinnacle. He suggested that people don't experience higher needs until the needs below them have been met.*

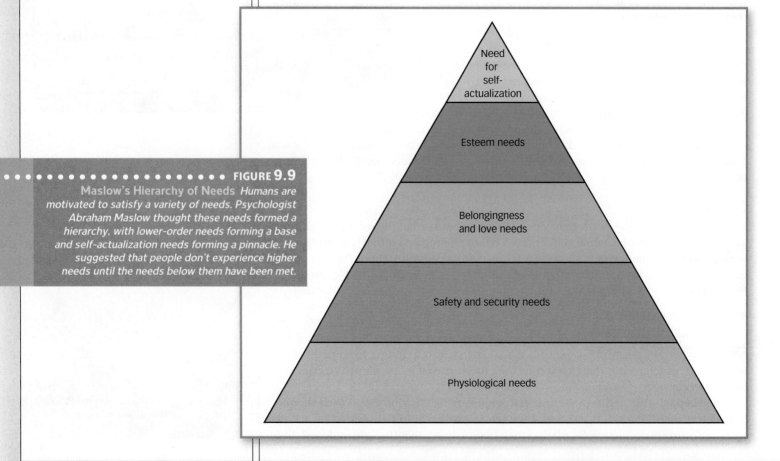

other mammals and that are related to our common biology. Two of these needs—the need to eat and the need to mate—are among the most powerful and well studied, so let's see how they work.

Eating

Hunger tells an organism to eat. But how does hunger arise? At every moment, your body is sending signals to your brain about its current energy state. If your body needs energy, it sends a signal to tell your brain to switch hunger on, and if your body has sufficient energy, it sends a signal to tell your brain to switch hunger off (Gropp et al., 2005). No one knows precisely what these signals are or how they are sent and received,

● **Which chemical switches hunger on, and which switches it off?**

but research has identified a variety of candidates. For example, *ghrelin* is a chemical that is produced in the stomach, and it appears to be a signal that tells the brain to switch hunger on (Inui, 2001; Nakazato et al., 2001); when people are injected with ghrelin, they become intensely hungry and eat about 30% more than usual (Wren et al., 2001). *Leptin* is a chemical secreted by fat cells, and it appears to be a signal that tells the brain to switch hunger off. Some researchers believe that there is no general state called hunger but rather that there are many different hungers, each of which is a response to a unique nutritional deficit and each of which is switched on by a unique chemical messenger (Rozin & Kalat, 1971). For example, rats that are deprived of protein will turn down fats and carbohydrates and specifically seek proteins, suggesting that they are experiencing a specific "protein hunger" and not a general hunger (Rozin, 1968).

Whether hunger is one signal or many, the primary receiver of these signals is the hypothalamus. Different parts of the hypothalamus receive different signals (see **FIGURE 9.10**). The *lateral hypothalamus* receives hunger signals, and when it is destroyed, animals sitting in a cage full of food will starve themselves to death. The *ventromedial hypothalamus* receives satiety signals, and when it is destroyed, animals will gorge themselves to the point of illness and obesity (Miller, 1960; Steinbaum & Miller, 1965). These two structures were once thought to be the "hunger center" and "satiety center" of the brain, but recent research has shown that this view is far too simple. Hypothalamic structures play an important role in turning hunger on and off, but the way they execute these functions is complex and poorly understood (Stellar & Stellar, 1985).

drive An internal state generated by departures from physiological optimality.

"Never get a tattoo when you're drunk and hungry."

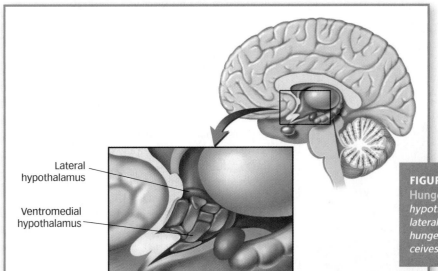

Lateral hypothalamus

Ventromedial hypothalamus

FIGURE 9.10 ●
Hunger, Satiety, and the Hypothalamus *The hypothalamus comprises many parts. In general, the lateral hypothalamus receives the signals that turn hunger on and the ventromedial hypothalamus receives the signals that turn hunger off.*

● Although people who suffer from anorexia are dangerously thin, they typically see themselves as fat. Sixteen-year-old Hannah Hartney has been suffering from anorexia since she was 9 years old.

Eating Disorders

Feelings of hunger tell us when to eat and when to stop. But for the 10 to 30 million Americans who have eating disorders, eating is a much more complicated affair (Hoek & van Hoeken, 2003). For instance, **bulimia nervosa** is *a disorder characterized by binge eating followed by purging.* Individuals with bulimia typically ingest large quantities of food in a relatively short period and then take laxatives or induce vomiting to purge the food from their bodies. These people are caught in a cycle: They eat to ameliorate negative emotions such as sadness and anxiety, but then concern about weight gain leads them to experience negative emotions such as guilt and self-loathing, and these emotions then lead them to purge.

Anorexia nervosa is *a disorder characterized by an intense fear of being fat and severe restriction of food intake.* Individuals with anorexia tend to have a distorted body image that leads them to believe they are fat when they are actually emaciated. They tend to be high-achieving perfectionists who see their severe control of eating as a triumph of will over impulse. Contrary to what you might expect, people with anorexia have extremely *high* levels of ghrelin in their blood, which suggests that their bodies are trying desperately to switch hunger on but that hunger's call is being suppressed, ignored, or overridden (Ariyasu et al., 2001). Like most eating disorders, anorexia strikes more women than men, and 40% of newly identified cases of anorexia are among females who are 15 to 19 years old. Individuals with anorexia believe that thinness equals beauty, and it isn't hard to understand why. The average American woman is 5'4" tall and weighs 140 pounds, but the average American fashion model is 5'11" tall and weighs 117 pounds. Indeed, most college-age women want to be thinner than they are (Rozin, Trachtenberg, & Cohen, 2001), and nearly one in five reports being *embarrassed* to buy a chocolate bar (Rozin, Bauer, & Catanese, 2003).

● **How do people with anorexia respond to their bodies' attempts to turn hunger on?**

Obesity

America's newest, most pernicious, and most pervasive eating-related problem is obesity, which is defined as having a body mass index of 30 or greater. **TABLE 9.1** (on page 281) allows you to compute your body mass index, and the odds are that you won't like what you learn. Approximately 3 million Americans die each year from obesity-related illnesses (Allison et al., 1999), and that number is growing fast. Obese people are viewed negatively by others, have lower self-esteem, and have a lower quality of life (Hebl & Heatherton, 1997; Kolotkin, Meter, & Williams, 2001). Indeed, the stigma of obesity is so powerful that average-weight people are viewed negatively if they even have a relationship with someone who is obese (Hebl & Mannix, 2003).

● Prejudice against obese people is powerful and widespread. In this photo, members of the self-proclaimed "Bod Squad" protest against weight loss surgery in front of a San Francisco hospital.

Obesity can result from biochemical abnormalities, and it seems to have a strong genetic component, but overeating is often a part of its cause. If the brain has a complex system of on and off switches that regulate hunger, why does anyone overeat? Hunger is just one of the reasons why people eat—and not always the most important one. For example, people often eat to reduce negative emotions such as sadness or anxiety, and they often eat out of habit ("It's noon") or obligation ("Everyone else is ordering lunch"), all of which can cause people to eat more than they should.

Moreover, nature seems to have designed us for overeating. For most of our evolutionary history, the main food-related problem facing our ancestors was starvation. Their brains and bodies evolved two strategies to avoid it. First, they developed a strong attraction to foods that provide large amounts of energy per bite—in other words, foods that are calorically rich—which is why most of us prefer hamburgers and milk shakes to celery

TABLE 9.1

Body Mass Index Table

	Normal						Overweight					Obese									Extremely Obese															
BMI	19	20	21	22	23	24	25	26	27	28	29	30	31	32	33	34	35	36	37	38	39	40	41	42	43	44	45	46	47	48	49	50	51	52	53	54
Height (Inches)													Body Weight (pounds)																							
58	91	96	100	105	110	115	119	124	129	134	138	143	148	153	158	162	167	172	177	181	186	191	196	201	205	210	215	220	224	229	234	239	244	248	253	258
59	94	99	104	109	114	119	124	128	133	138	143	148	153	158	163	169	173	178	183	188	193	198	203	208	212	217	222	227	232	237	242	247	252	257	262	267
60	97	102	107	112	116	123	128	133	138	143	148	153	156	163	168	174	179	184	189	194	199	204	209	215	220	225	230	235	240	245	250	256	261	266	271	278
61	100	108	111	116	122	127	132	137	143	148	153	156	164	169	174	180	186	190	195	201	206	211	217	222	227	232	238	243	248	254	259	264	269	275	280	285
62	104	109	115	120	126	131	138	142	147	153	158	164	169	175	180	186	191	196	202	207	213	218	224	229	235	240	248	251	258	262	267	273	278	264	289	295
63	107	113	118	124	130	135	141	148	152	158	163	169	175	180	188	191	197	203	208	214	220	225	231	237	242	248	254	260	265	270	278	282	287	293	299	304
64	110	118	122	128	134	140	145	151	157	163	169	174	180	188	192	197	204	209	215	221	227	232	238	244	250	258	262	267	273	279	285	291	298	302	308	314
65	114	120	128	132	138	144	150	156	162	168	174	180	186	192	193	204	210	218	222	228	234	240	246	252	258	264	270	278	282	288	294	300	308	312	318	324
66	118	124	130	138	142	148	155	161	167	173	179	186	192	198	204	210	216	223	229	235	241	247	253	260	266	272	278	284	291	297	303	309	315	322	328	334
67	121	127	134	140	146	153	159	166	172	178	185	191	198	204	211	217	223	230	238	242	249	256	261	268	274	280	287	293	299	308	312	319	325	331	338	344
68	125	131	138	144	151	158	164	171	177	184	190	197	203	210	216	223	230	236	243	249	256	262	269	278	282	289	295	302	303	315	322	328	335	341	348	354
69	128	135	142	149	155	162	169	178	182	189	195	203	209	218	223	230	236	243	250	257	263	270	277	284	291	297	304	311	318	324	331	338	345	351	358	365
70	132	139	146	153	160	167	174	181	188	195	202	209	216	222	229	236	243	250	257	264	271	278	285	292	299	308	313	320	327	334	341	348	355	362	369	378
71	138	143	150	157	166	172	179	186	193	200	208	215	222	229	235	243	250	257	265	272	279	288	293	301	308	315	322	329	338	343	351	358	365	372	379	388
72	140	147	154	162	169	177	184	191	199	208	213	221	228	235	242	250	258	265	272	279	287	294	302	309	316	324	331	338	346	353	361	368	375	383	390	397
73	144	151	159	166	174	182	189	197	204	212	219	227	236	242	250	257	266	272	280	288	295	302	310	318	326	333	340	348	355	363	371	378	388	393	401	408
74	148	155	163	171	179	188	194	202	210	218	225	233	241	249	258	264	272	280	287	295	303	311	319	328	334	342	350	358	365	373	381	389	398	404	412	420
75	152	160	166	178	184	192	200	208	216	224	232	240	248	256	264	272	279	287	295	303	311	319	327	335	343	351	359	367	375	383	391	399	407	415	423	431
76	158	164	172	180	189	197	205	213	221	230	238	246	254	263	271	279	287	295	304	312	320	328	338	344	353	361	369	377	385	394	402	410	418	428	436	443

Source: Adapted from National Institutes of Health, 1998, *Clinical Guidelines on the Identification, Evaluation, and Treatment of Overweight and Obesity in Adults: The Evidence Report.* This and other information about overweight and obesity can be found at www.nhlbi.nih.gov/guidelines/obesity/ob_home.htm.

and water. Second, they developed an ability to store excess food energy in the form of fat, which enabled them to eat more than they needed when food was plentiful and then live off their reserves when food was scarce. We are beautifully engineered for a world in which food is generally low cal and scarce, and the problem is that we don't live in that world anymore.

● **How do our bodies react when we try to diet?**

It is all too easy for most of us to overeat and become overweight or obese, and it is all too difficult to reverse course. The human body resists weight loss in two ways. First, when we gain weight, we experience an increase in both the size and the number of fat cells in our bodies (usually in our abdomens if we are male and in our thighs and buttocks if we are female). But when we lose weight, we experience a decrease in the size of our fat cells but no decrease in their number. Once our bodies have added a fat cell, that cell is pretty much there to stay. It may become thinner when we diet, but it is unlikely to die. Second, our bodies respond to dieting by decreasing our **metabolism**, which is *the rate at which energy is used*. When our bodies sense that we are living through a famine (which is what they conclude when we refuse to feed them), they find more efficient ways to turn food into fat—a great trick for our ancestors but a real nuisance for us. Indeed, when rats are overfed, then put on diets, then overfed again and put on diets again, they gain weight faster and lose it more slowly the second time around, which suggests that with each round of dieting, their bodies become increasingly efficient at converting food to fat (Brownell et al., 1986). The bottom line is that avoiding obesity is much easier than overcoming it.

Mating

Food motivates us more strongly than sex because food is essential to our survival. But sex is essential to our DNA's survival, and thus evolution has ensured that a healthy desire for sex is wired deep into the brain of every mammal. In some ways, that wiring scheme is simple: Glands secrete hormones that travel through the blood to the brain and stimulate sexual desire. But which hormones, which parts of the brain, and what triggers the launch in the first place?

bulimia nervosa An eating disorder characterized by binge eating followed by purging.

anorexia nervosa An eating disorder characterized by an intense fear of being fat and severe restriction of food intake.

metabolism The rate at which energy is used by the body.

"Come back, young man. He needs a booster shot."

Sexual Interest

A hormone called dihydroepiandosterone (DHEA) seems to be involved in the initial onset of sexual desire. Both males and females begin producing this hormone at about the age of 6, which may explain why boys and girls both experience their initial sexual interest at about the age of 10 despite the fact that boys reach puberty much later than girls. Two other hormones have more gender-specific effects. Both males and females produce testosterone and estrogen, but males produce more of the former and females produce more of the latter. As you will learn in Chapter 11, these two hormones are largely responsible for the physical and psychological changes that characterize puberty.

The females of most mammalian species—for example, dogs, cats, and rats—have little or no interest in sex except when their estrogen levels are high, which happens when they are ovulating (i.e., when they are "in estrus" or "in heat"). In other words, estrogen regulates both ovulation and sexual interest in these mammals. But female human beings can be interested in sex at any point in their monthly cycles. Although the level of estrogen in a woman's body changes dramatically over the course of her monthly menstrual cycle, studies suggest that sexual desire changes little if at all. Somewhere in the course of our evolution, it seems, women's sexual interest became independent of their ovulation. Some theorists have speculated that the advantage of this independence was that it made it more difficult for males to know whether a female was in the fertile phase of her monthly cycle. Male mammals often guard their mates jealously when their mates are ovulating but go off in search of other females when their mates are not. If a male cannot use his mate's sexual receptivity to tell when she is ovulating, then he has no choice but to stay around and guard her all the time. For females who are trying to keep their mates at home so that they will contribute to the rearing of children, sexual interest that is continuous and independent of fertility may be an excellent strategy.

If estrogen is not the hormonal basis of women's sex drives, then what is? Two pieces of evidence suggests that the answer is testosterone—the same hormone that drives male sexuality. First, when women are given testosterone, their sex drives increase.

● **The red coloration on the female gelada's chest indicates she is in estrus and thus amenable to sex. The sexual interest of female human beings is not limited to a particular time in their monthly cycle. and they do not clearly advertise their fertility.**

● **What hormone regulates the sex drive in both men and women?**

Second, men naturally have more testosterone than women do, and they clearly have a stronger sex drive. Men are more likely than women to think about sex, have sexual fantasies, seek sex and sexual variety (whether positions or partners), masturbate, want sex at an early point in a relationship, sacrifice other things for sex, have permissive attitudes toward sex, and complain about low sex drive in their partners (Baumeister, Cantanese, & Vohs, 2001, pp. 263–264). All of this suggests that testosterone may be the hormonal basis of sex drive in both men and women.

Sexual Activity

Men and women may have different levels of sexual drive, but their physiological responses during sex are fairly similar. Prior to the 1960s, data on human sexual behavior consisted primarily of people's answers to questions about their sex lives—and you may have noticed that this is a topic about which people don't always tell the truth. William Masters and Virginia Johnson changed all that by conducting groundbreaking studies in which they actually measured the physical responses of many hundreds of volunteers as they masturbated or had sex in the laboratory (Masters & Johnson, 1966). Their work led to many discoveries, including a better understanding of the **human sexual response cycle**, which refers to *the stages of physiological arousal during sexual activity* (see **FIGURE 9.11** on page 291). Human sexual response has four phases:

● **Why was the work of Masters and Johnson considered revolutionary?**

- During the *excitement phase,* muscle tension and blood flow increase in and around the sexual organs, heart and respiration rates increase, and blood pressure rises. Both men and women may experience erect nipples and a "sex flush" on the skin of the upper body and face. A man's penis typically becomes erect or partially erect and his testicles draw upward, while a woman's vagina typically becomes lubricated and her clitoris becomes swollen.

- During the *plateau phase,* heart rate and muscle tension increase further. A man's urinary bladder closes to prevent urine from mixing with semen, and muscles at the base of his penis begin a steady rhythmic contraction. A woman's clitoris may withdraw slightly, and her vagina may become more lubricated. Her outer vagina may swell, and her muscles may tighten and reduce the diameter of the opening of the vagina.

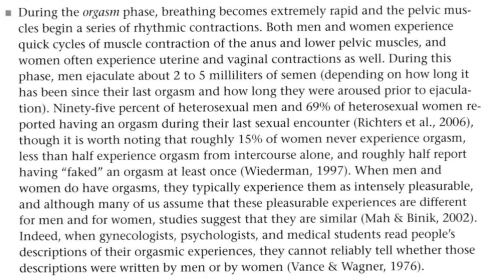

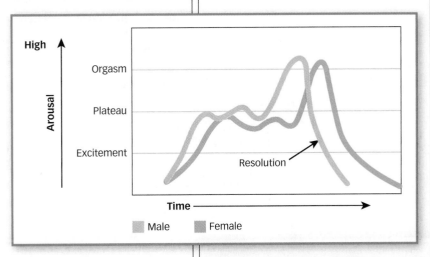

- During the *orgasm* phase, breathing becomes extremely rapid and the pelvic muscles begin a series of rhythmic contractions. Both men and women experience quick cycles of muscle contraction of the anus and lower pelvic muscles, and women often experience uterine and vaginal contractions as well. During this phase, men ejaculate about 2 to 5 milliliters of semen (depending on how long it has been since their last orgasm and how long they were aroused prior to ejaculation). Ninety-five percent of heterosexual men and 69% of heterosexual women reported having an orgasm during their last sexual encounter (Richters et al., 2006), though it is worth noting that roughly 15% of women never experience orgasm, less than half experience orgasm from intercourse alone, and roughly half report having "faked" an orgasm at least once (Wiederman, 1997). When men and women do have orgasms, they typically experience them as intensely pleasurable, and although many of us assume that these pleasurable experiences are different for men and for women, studies suggest that they are similar (Mah & Binik, 2002). Indeed, when gynecologists, psychologists, and medical students read people's descriptions of their orgasmic experiences, they cannot reliably tell whether those descriptions were written by men or by women (Vance & Wagner, 1976).

- During the *resolution phase,* muscles relax, blood pressure drops, and the body returns to its resting state. Most men and women experience a *refractory period,* during which further stimulation does not produce excitement. This period may last from minutes to days and is typically longer for men than for women.

Men and women are similar in their responses during sexual activity, and they are also similar in their reasons for engaging in sexual activity in the first place. Sex is necessary for reproduction, of course, but the vast majority of sexual acts are performed for other reasons, which include experiencing pleasure, coping with negative emotions, increasing emotional intimacy between partners, pleasing one's partner, impressing one's friends, and reassuring oneself of one's own attractiveness (Cooper, Shapiro, & Powers, 1998). It is worth noting that not all sex is motivated by one of these reasons: About half of college-age women and a quarter of college-age men report having unwanted sexual activity in a dating relationship (O'Sullivan & Allegeier, 1998). We will have much more to say about sexual attraction and relationships in Chapter 15.

Kinds of Motivation

Eating and mating are two things that human beings are strongly motivated to do—but what are the others, and how do they relate to each other? Alas, there is no widely accepted list of human motivations, which has made it difficult for psychologists to

FIGURE 9.11 • • • • • • • • • • • • • • • • •
The Human Sexual Response Cycle
The pattern of the sexual response cycle is quite similar for men and for women. Both men and women go through the excitement, plateau, orgasm, and resolutions phases, though the timing of their response may differ.

human sexual response cycle The stages of physiological arousal during sexual activity.

develop theories about where motivations come from and how they operate. Nonetheless, psychologists have made initial progress by identifying several of the dimensions on which motivations differ. Three of those dimensions are especially important.

Intrinsic versus Extrinsic

Taking a psychology exam is not like eating a french fry. One makes you tired and the other makes you fat, one requires that you move your lips and one requires that you don't, and so on. But the key difference between these activities is that one is a means to an end and one is an end in itself. An **intrinsic motivation** is *a motivation to take actions that are themselves rewarding.* When we eat a french fry because it tastes good, exercise because it feels good, or listen to music because it sounds good, we are intrinsically motivated. These activities don't have to *have* a payoff because they *are* a payoff. An **extrinsic motivation** is *a motivation to take actions that lead to reward.* When we floss our teeth so we can avoid gum disease (and get dates), when we work hard for money so we can pay our rent (and get dates), and when we take an exam so we can get a college degree (and get money to get dates), we are extrinsically motivated. None of these things directly brings pleasure, but all may lead to pleasure in the long run.

Extrinsic motivation gets a bad rap. Americans tend to feel sorry for or disdainful of students who choose courses just to please their parents and parents who choose jobs just to earn a lot of money. But the fact is that our ability to engage in behaviors that are unrewarding in the present because we believe they will bring greater rewards in the future is one of our species' most significant talents, and no other species can do it as well as we can (Gilbert, 2006). In research on the ability to delay gratification, people are typically faced with a choice between getting something they want right now (e.g., a scoop of ice cream) or waiting and getting more of what they want later (e.g., two scoops of ice cream). Studies show that 4-year-old children who can delay gratification are judged to be more intelligent and socially competent 10 years later and that they have higher SAT scores when they enter college (Mischel, Shoda, & Rodriguez, 1989). In fact, the ability to delay gratification is a better predictor of a child's grades in school than is the child's IQ (Duckworth & Seligman, 2005). Apparently there is something to be said for extrinsic motivation.

There is a lot to be said for intrinsic motivation, too. People work harder when they are intrinsically motivated, they enjoy what they do more, and they do it more creatively. Both kinds of motivation have advantages, which is why many of us try to build lives in which we are both intrinsically and extrinsically motivated by the same activity—lives in which we are paid the big bucks for doing exactly what we like to do best. Who hasn't fantasized about becoming a professional artist, a professional athlete, or a professional chocolatier? Alas, research suggests that it is difficult to eat your chocolate and have it too because extrinsic rewards can undermine intrinsic rewards (Deci, Koestner, & Ryan, 1999; Henderlong & Lepper, 2002). For example, in one study, college students who were intrinsically interested in a puzzle either were paid to complete it or completed it for free, and those who were paid were less likely to play with the puzzle later on (Deci, 1971). It appears that under some circumstances, people take rewards to indicate that an activity isn't inherently pleasurable ("If they had to pay me to do that puzzle, it couldn't have been a very fun one"), and thus rewards can cause people to lose their intrinsic motivation.

● **Why do we often engage in behavior that won't benefit us until much later?**

● **When do rewards backfire?**

Conscious versus Unconscious

When prizewinning artists or scientists are asked to explain their achievements, they typically say things like "I wanted to liberate color from form" or "I wanted to cure

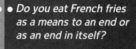

● *Do you eat French fries as a means to an end or as an end in itself?*

FOODFOLIO/ALAMY

KIRK WEDDLE PHOTOGRAPHY

● *Will this child enjoy swimming when he grows up? Studies suggest that extrinsic motivators, such as money, can undermine a person's intrinsic interest in performing activities such as swimming.*

diabetes." They almost never say, "I wanted to exceed my father's accomplishments, thereby proving to my mother that I was worthy of her love." A **conscious motivation** is *a motivation of which one is aware,* and an **unconscious motivation** is *a motivation of which one is not aware.*

A person who is shopping for mittens may be simultaneously motivated to increase her happiness, to keep her hands warm, and to find the mitten aisle in the store—so which of these motives will be conscious and which will be unconscious? Notice that some of these motivations are quite general (increasing happiness) and some are quite specific (looking for mittens). Robin Vallacher and Daniel Wegner have suggested that people tend to be aware of their general motivations unless the complexities of executing an action force them to become aware of their specific motivations (Vallacher & Wegner, 1985, 1987). For example, if a person is changing a lightbulb and is asked about her motivation, she may say something like "I'm helping my dad out." But the moment the lightbulb gets stuck, her answer will change to "I'm trying to get these threads aligned." The person has both motivations, of course, but she is conscious of her more general motivation when her action is easy and of her more specific motivation when her action is difficult.

● **When are people likely to be aware of their motivations?**

Approach versus Avoidance

The poet James Thurber (1956) wrote, "All men should strive to learn before they die / what they are running from, and to, and why." "Running to" corresponds to what psychologists call an **approach motivation**, which is *a motivation to experience a positive outcome,* and "running from" corresponds to an **avoidance motivation**, which is *a motivation not to experience a negative outcome.* These are not just two ways of saying the same thing: Pleasure and pain are independent phenomena that occur in different parts of the brain (Davidson et al., 1990).

Research suggests that, all else being equal, avoidance motivations tend to be more powerful than approach motivations. As you learned in Chapter 4, most people will turn down a chance to bet on a coin flip that would pay them $10 if it came up heads but would require them to pay $8 if it came up tails because they believe that the pain of losing $8 will be more intense than the pleasure of winning $10 (Kahneman & Tversky, 1979).

Although avoidance motivation tends to be stronger than approach motivation overall, there are people who naturally favor one or the other. For instance, in one study, participants were given an anagram task. Some were told that they would be paid $4 for the experiment, but they could earn an extra dollar by finding 90% or more of all the possible words. Others were told that they that they would be paid $5 for the experiment, but they could avoid losing a dollar by not missing more than 10% of all the possible words. People who naturally tended to think in terms of achieving gains performed better in the first case than in the second. But people who naturally tended to think in terms of avoiding losses performed better in the second case than in the first (Shah, Higgins, & Friedman, 1998).

intrinsic motivation A motivation to take actions that are themselves rewarding.

extrinsic motivation A motivation to take actions that are not themselves rewarding but that lead to reward.

conscious motivation A motivation of which one is aware.

unconscious motivation A motivation of which one is not aware.

approach motivation A motivation to experience positive outcomes.

avoidance motivation A motivation not to experience negative outcomes.

MICHAELBROWN/GETTYIMAGES

People are motivated to avoid losses and achieve gains, but whether an outcome is seen as a loss or a gain often depends on how it is described. Smart retailers refer to price discrepancies such as this one as a "cash discount" rather than a "credit card surcharge."

summary quiz [9.3]

8. The notion that organisms are motivated to approach pleasure and avoid pain is known as
   a. the hedonic principle.   c. drive theory.
   b. Maslow's hierarchy of needs. d. the instinct principle.

9. According to Maslow, the weakest and most deferrable need(s) is (are)
   a. belongingness and love needs. c. esteem needs.
   b. need for self-actualization.   d. safety and security needs.

10. Which is true of human sexual drives?
   a. Men and women experience different sequences of physiological arousal.
   b. Women's sex drives are regulated by estrogen, whereas men's are regulated by testosterone.
   c. Men and women engage in sex for very different reasons.
   d. Boys and girls both experience their initial sexual interest at about the same age.

11. When we floss our teeth to avoid gum disease or get a job so we can pay our rent, we are displaying what kind of motivation?
   a. unconscious motivation   c. extrinsic motivation
   b. intrinsic motivation   d. achievement motivation

WhereDoYouStand?

Here Comes the Bribe

Americans prize their right to vote. They talk about it, they sing about it, and they die for it. They just don't use it very much.

The U.S. Census Bureau estimates that about 60% of American citizens who are eligible to vote in a presidential election actually do so, and the numbers are significantly lower for "off-year" elections. Not all countries have this problem. Belgium, for instance, has a voter turnout rate close to 100% because for the better part of a century, failing to vote in Belgium has been illegal. (If you failed to vote in Belgium, don't worry; this only applies to Belgians.) Belgians who fail to vote may be fined; and if they fail to vote several times in a row, they may be "legally disenfranchised," which makes it difficult for them to get a job. Although some people have suggested that America should join the long list of countries that have compulsory voting, Americans generally don't like the threat of punishment.

But they sure do love the possibility of reward—and that's what led Arizona ophthalmologist Mark Osterloh to propose the Arizona Voter Reward Act, which would have awarded $1 million to a randomly selected voter in every election. As soon as Osterloh announced his idea, people lined up against it. An editorial in the *Yuma Sun* summed up the opposition: "A jackpot is not the right motivator for voting. . . . People should vote because they want to and because they think it is important. . . . Bribing people to vote is a superficial approach that will have no beneficial outcome to the process, except to make some people feel good that the turnout numbers are higher" (Editorial, 2006). Nonetheless, 185,902 of Osterloh's fellow Arizonans thought his idea had merit, and they signed their names to get his proposed measure on the ballot.

In November 2006, Arizonans defeated the measure by a sound margin, but Osterloh wasn't dejected. "I believe somebody is eventually going to bring this back and get this approved somewhere around the world, and it's going to spread," he said days after the election. "If anybody has a better idea of how to get people to vote, let me know and I will support it" (Rotstein, 2006).

Should our government motivate people to vote with extrinsic rewards or punishments? We know where Arizonans stand on this issue. How about you?

CHAPTER REVIEW

Summary

Emotional Experience: The Feeling Machine
- Emotion has two underlying dimensions: arousal and valence.
- The James-Lange theory suggests that physiological reactions precede emotional experience; the Cannon-Bard theory suggests that emotional experiences and physiological reactions occur simultaneously. Two-factor theory suggests that a stimulus causes physiological arousal that people then interpret as emotion in a given context.

- The amygdala is a key structure in producing emotion, particularly in rapid appraisal of the emotional relevance of stimuli.
- People can use strategies such as reappraisal to regulate their own emotions.

Emotional Communication: Msgs w/o Wrds
- The voice, the body, and the face all communicate information about a person's emotional state.

- Emotional expressions are the same for all people and are universally understood.

- Not all emotional expressions are sincere; people use display rules to help them decide which emotions to express. People are generally poor at determining when an expression is sincere.

Motivation: Getting Moved

- Emotions motivate us by providing information about the world and by giving us something to strive for.

- The hedonic principle suggests that organisms approach pleasure and avoid pain and that this basic motivation underlies all others.

- When the body experiences a deficit, we experience a drive to remedy it; hunger and mating are two powerful biological drives.

- Motivations may be classified in many ways, including intrinsic versus extrinsic, conscious versus unconscious, and approach versus avoidance.

Key Terms

emotion (p. 271)

James-Lange theory (p. 272)

Cannon-Bard theory (p. 272)

two-factor theory (p. 272)

appraisal (p. 274)

emotion regulation (p. 276)

reappraisal (p. 277)

emotional expression (p. 278)

universality hypothesis (p. 279)

facial feedback hypothesis (p. 280)

display rules (p. 280)

motivation (p. 284)

hedonic principle (p. 284)

drive (p. 286)

bulimia nervosa (p. 288)

anorexia nervosa (p. 288)

metabolism (p. 289)

human sexual response cycle (p. 290)

intrinsic motivation (p. 292)

extrinsic motivation (p. 292)

conscious motivation (p. 293)

unconscious motivation (p. 293)

approach motivation (p. 293)

avoidance motivation (p. 293)

Critical Thinking Questions

1. More than two millennia ago, Roman emperor Marcus Aurelius wrote, "If you are distressed by anything external, the pain is not due to the thing itself, but to your estimate of it; and this you have the power to revoke at any moment." Does research support this claim? What about your personal experience? Have you ever had a painful emotion that you were able to revoke?

2. Although a wide variety of human languages are spoken across the globe, evidence suggests that facial displays of at least six emotions—anger, disgust, fear, happiness, sadness, and surprise—are universal. How can you explain this?

3. The hedonic principle is the notion that all people are motivated to experience pleasure and avoid pain. According to Aristotle, *all* other motivations rest on this one. If this is true, then how can you explain the fact that people go to war?

Answers to Summary Quizzes

Summary Quiz 9.1
1. b; 2. c; 3. a; 4. d

Summary Quiz 9.2
5. b; 6. c; 7. a

Summary Quiz 9.3
8. a; 9. b; 10. d; 11. c

Need more help? Additional resources are located at the book's free companion Web site at: www.worthpublishers.com/schacterbriefle

Development

HIS MOTHER CALLED HIM ADI AND showered him with affection, but his father was not so kind. As his sister later recalled, "Adi challenged my father to extreme harshness and got his sound thrashing every day." Although his father wanted him to become a civil servant, Adi's true love was art, and his mother encouraged that gentler interest. Adi was just 18 years old when his mother was diagnosed with terminal cancer, and he was heartbroken when she died. Even her physician remarked that "in all my career, I have never seen anyone so prostrate with grief."

But Adi had little time for grieving. As he wrote, "Poverty and hard reality compelled me to make a quick decision. I was faced with the problem of somehow making my own living." Adi resolved to make his living as an artist. He moved to the city and applied to art school, but he was flatly rejected. Motherless and penniless, Adi wandered the city streets for 5 long years, sleeping on park benches, living in homeless shelters, and eating in soup kitchens, all the while trying desperately to sell his sketches and watercolors. Ten years later, Adi had achieved the fame he so desired—but not as an artist. Indeed, most of us know him not by the nickname Adi, but by his full legal name: Adolf Hitler. ■

One of Adi's paintings, The Church of Preux-Au-Bois, sold at auction in 2006 for just under $20,000.

AP PHOTO/BARRY GOMER

From infancy to childhood to adolescence to adulthood, people exhibit both continuity and change.

DANIEL GILBERT

THE SEVEN AGES OF MAN

SLEEPY   HAPPY   DOPEY

BASHFUL   DOC   SNEEZY   GRUMPY

W hy is it so difficult to imagine the greatest mass murderer of the 20th century as a gentle child who loved to draw, as a compassionate adolescent who cared for his ailing mother, or as a dedicated young adult who suffered cold and hunger for the sake of art? After all, none of us began as the people we are now, and few of us will end up that way. From birth to infancy, from childhood to adolescence, from young adulthood to old age, one of the most obvious facts about human beings is that they change over time. Their development includes both dramatic transformations and striking consistencies in the way they look, think, feel, and act. **Developmental psychology** is *the study of continuity and change across the life span,* and every human being exhibits both. In the last century, psychologists have made some remarkable discoveries about how we acquire our first understanding of ourselves and our worlds; about what we seem to know at birth, what we must learn along the way, and what we never seem to get quite right; about the emotional bonds between us and our parents and, later, between us and our children; about how we develop our sense of right and wrong; and about the radical transformations of adolescence, the subtle transformations of adulthood, and the surprising delights of old age.

Prenatality: A Womb with a View

You probably calculate your age by counting your birthdays, but the fact is that when you were born, you were already 9 months old. The *prenatal stage* of development ends with birth, but it begins 9 months earlier when about 200 million sperm begin a hazardous journey from a woman's vagina, through her uterus, and on to her fallopian tubes. Many of these sperm have defects that prevent them from swimming vigorously enough to make progress, and others get stuck in the spermatazoidal equivalent of a traffic jam. Of those that manage to make their way through the uterus, many take a wrong turn and end up in the fallopian tube that does not contain an egg. A mere 200 or so of the original 200 million sperm manage to find the right fallopian tube and get close enough to an egg to release digestive enzymes that erode the egg's protective outer layer. As soon as one of these sperm manages to penetrate the coating, the egg quickly releases a chemical that seals the coating and keeps all the remaining sperm from entering. After triumphing over massive odds, the one successful sperm sheds its tail and fertilizes the egg. In about 12 hours, the nuclei of the sperm and the egg merge, and the prenatal development of a unique human being begins.

YORGOS NIKAS/WELLCOME TRUST

This electron micrograph shows a false-color image of several human sperm, one of which is fertilizing an egg.

Prenatal Development

A **zygote** is *a fertilized egg that contains chromosomes from both a sperm and an egg.* From the first moment of its existence, a zygote has one thing in common with the person it will ultimately become: gender. Each human sperm cell and each human egg cell contain 23 *chromosomes* that contain *genes,* which provide the blueprint for all biological development. One of these chromosomes (the 23rd) can come in two variations: X or Y. Some sperm carry an X chromosome, and others carry a Y chromosome. If the egg is fertilized by a sperm that carries a Y chromosome, then the zygote is male; if the egg is fertilized by a sperm that carries an X chromosome, the zygote is female.

The 2-week period that begins at conception is known as the **germinal stage,** and it is during this stage that the one-celled zygote begins to divide—into two cells which divide into four, which divide into eight, and so on. By the time of birth, the zygote has divided into trillions of cells, each of which contains exactly one set of 23 chromosomes from the sperm and one set of 23 chromosomes from the egg. During the germinal stage, the zygote migrates back down the fallopian tube and implants itself in the wall of the uterus. This is a difficult journey, and about half of all zygotes do not complete it, either because they are defective or because they implant themselves in an inhospitable part of the uterus.

When the zygote implants itself on the uterine wall, a new stage of development begins. The **embryonic stage** is *a period that lasts from the second week until about the eighth week* (see **FIGURE 10.1**). During this stage, the zygote continues to divide and its cells begin to differentiate. The zygote at this stage is known as an *embryo,* and although it is just an inch long, it already has a beating heart and other body parts, such as arms and legs. Embryos that have one X chromosome and one Y chromosome begin to produce a hormone called testosterone, which masculinizes their reproductive organs, and embryos that have two X chromosomes do not. Without testosterone, the embryo continues developing as a female. In a sense, then, males are a specialized form of females.

What distinguishes an embryo from a zygote and a fetus?

The **fetal stage** is *a period that lasts from the ninth week until birth.* The embryo at this stage is known as a *fetus,* and it has a skeleton and muscles that make it capable of movement. During the last 3 months of the fetal stage, the size of the fetus increases rapidly. It develops a layer of insulating fat beneath its skin, and its digestive and respiratory systems mature. The cells that ultimately become the brain divide very quickly around the third and fourth week after conception. During the fetal stage, these brain cells begin to generate axons and dendrites (which permit communication with other brain cells). They also begin to undergo a process known as **myelination**—which is *the formation of a fatty sheath around the axons of a brain cell.* Just as plastic sheathing insulates a wire, myelin insulates a brain cell and prevents the leakage of neural signals

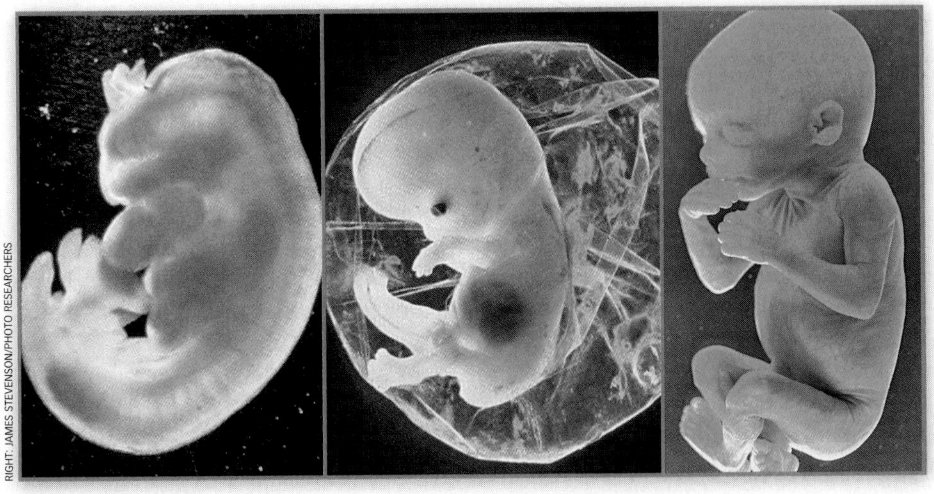

LEFT: CLAUDE EDELMANN/PHOTO RESEARCHERS
CENTER: BIOPHOTO ASSOCIATES/PHOTO RESEARCHERS
RIGHT: JAMES STEVENSON/PHOTO RESEARCHERS

FIGURE 10.1 **Prenatal Development** *Human beings undergo amazing development in the 9 months of prenatal development. These images show an embryo at 30 days, an embryo at 8 to 9 weeks, and a fetus at 5 months.*

developmental psychology The study of continuity and change across the life span.

zygote A single cell that contains chromosomes from both a sperm and an egg.

germinal stage The 2-week period of prenatal development that begins at conception.

embryonic stage The period of prenatal development that lasts from the second week until about the eighth week.

fetal stage The period of prenatal development that lasts from the ninth week until birth.

myelination The formation of a fatty sheath around the axons of a brain cell.

that travel along the axon. The process of myelination does not occur at a constant rate across all areas; for example, the myelination of the cortex continues into adulthood.

Although the brain undergoes rapid and complex growth during the fetal period, at birth it is nowhere near its adult size. Whereas a newborn chimp's brain is nearly 60% of its adult size, a newborn human's brain is only 25% of its adult size, which is to say that 75% of the brain's development occurs outside the womb. Why are human beings born with such underdeveloped brains when other primates are not? There are at least two reasons. First, the human brain has nearly tripled in size in just 2 million years of evolution, and bigger brains require bigger heads to house them. If a newborn's head were closer to its adult size, the baby could not pass through its mother's birth canal. Second, one of our species' greatest talents is its ability to adapt to a wide range of novel environments that differ in terms of climate, social structure, and so on. Rather than arriving in the world with a fully developed brain that may or may not meet the requirements of its environment, human beings arrive with brains that do much of their developing *within* the very environments in which they will function. The fact that our underdeveloped brains are specifically shaped by the unique social and physical environment into which we are born allows us to be exceptionally adaptable.

Prenatal Environment

It is natural to assume that genes influence development from the moment of conception and that the environment influences development from the moment of birth. But that's not so. Even before birth, the womb is an environment that influences development in a multitude of ways. For example, the *placenta* is the organ that physically links the bloodstreams of the mother and the developing embryo or fetus and permits the exchange of materials. As such, the foods a woman eats during pregnancy can affect fetal development. Toward the end of World War II, the Nazis imposed a food embargo on large Dutch cities, and many pregnant women suffered severe food deprivation. Subsequent research on their children's development demonstrated that food deprivation during the first 6 months of pregnancy caused the children to have both physical and psychological problems (Neugebauer, Hoek, & Susser, 1999; Stein et al., 1975; Susser, Brown, & Matte, 1999).

These effects are not unique to food. Almost anything that a woman eats, drinks, inhales, injects, or otherwise comes into contact with can pass through the placenta and affect the development of her fetus. *Agents that damage the process of development* are called **teratogens**, which literally means "monster makers." Alcohol is a particularly popular teratogen. **Fetal alcohol syndrome** is *a developmental disorder that stems from heavy alcohol use by the mother during pregnancy,* and it increases the risk of birth defects, especially with respect to the shape and size of the head and the structure of the brain. Children with fetal alcohol syndrome frequently exhibit mental retardation and have more problems with academic achievement than other children (Carmichael Olson et al., 1997; Streissguth et al., 1999). Tobacco is another popular teratogen. Babies whose mothers smoke tobacco have lower birth weights (Horta et al., 1997) and are more likely to have perceptual and attentional problems in childhood (Fried & Watkinson, 2000). As far as scientists can tell, there are no "safe amounts" of alcohol and tobacco for pregnant women. Other teratogens include lead in the water, paint dust in the air, and mercury in fish.

The prenatal environment is rich with chemicals, but it is also rich with information. The developing fetus can sense stimulation—and can learn. Wombs are dark, because

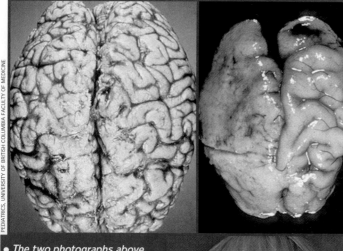

COURTESY OF STERLING K. CLARREN, MD CLINICAL PROFESSOR OF PEDIATRICS, UNIVERSITY OF BRITISH COLUMBIA FACULTY OF MEDICINE

GEORGE STEINMETZ

The two photographs above show the brains of a normal 6-week-old child (left) and a 6-week-old child born with fetal alcohol syndrome (FAS) (right). The child in the photo at right has the telltale facial features associated with FAS: short eye openings, a flat midface, an indistinct or flat ridge under the nose, and a thin upper lip. Children with FAS may also have tiny folds of tissue along the eye opening, a low nasal ridge, an underdeveloped jaw, and minor ear anomalies.

only the brightest light can filter through the mother's abdomen, but they are not quiet. High-frequency sounds tend to be muffled, but low-frequency sounds such as human voices can penetrate the mother's abdomen. Newborns who are just 2 hours old will suck a nipple more vigorously when they hear the sound of their mother's voice than

● **Can a fetus learn?**

when they hear the voice of a female stranger (Querleu et al., 1984), which suggests that they became familiar with their mother's voice while they were developing inside her. In one study, researchers arranged for some women to read aloud a short passage from *The Cat in the Hat* repeatedly during the last 6 weeks of pregnancy. Once the babies were born, the researchers tested their reactions to this passage as well as passages from other stories. Babies whose mothers had read aloud reacted to the passage from *The Cat in the Hat* differently than they reacted to an unfamiliar passage, whereas infants whose mothers had not read aloud reacted to both passages similarly (DeCasper & Spence, 1986). Clearly, the fetus is listening.

summary quiz [10.1]

1. Developmental psychology is the study of
   a. the child, from birth to adolescence.
   b. adulthood, from the 20s through old age.
   c. prenatal growth, from conception until birth.
   d. continuity and change across the life span.

2. During the embryonic stage, which of the following occurs?
   a. An insulating layer of fat develops below the skin.
   b. The digestive and respiratory systems mature.
   c. The embryo grows to the length of six inches.
   d. The heart begins to beat.

3. Which is true of vulnerability to teratogens?
   a. Vulnerability is greatest early in the pregnancy.
   b. Vulnerability is greatest in the late stages of pregnancy.
   c. The central nervous systems is most vulnerable late in pregnancy.
   d. Small amounts of alcohol and tobacco will not harm the fetus.

Infancy and Childhood: Becoming a Person

Newborns may appear to be capable of little more than squalling and squirming, but in the last decade, researchers have discovered that they are actually more sophisticated than anyone suspected. **Infancy** is *the stage of development that begins at birth and lasts between 18 and 24 months,* and as you will see, much more happens during this stage than meets the untrained eye.

Perceptual and Motor Development

New parents like to stand around the crib and make goofy faces at the baby because they think the baby will be amused. In fact, newborns have a rather limited range of vision, but when visual stimuli are close enough to be seen, newborns are quite responsive to them. Newborns in one study were shown a circle with diagonal stripes, and they initially stared at it for quite some time. But as the circle was presented again and again, the infants stared less and less each time (Slater, Morison, & Somers, 1988). Recall from

teratogens Agents that damage the process of development, such as drugs and viruses.

fetal alcohol syndrome A developmental disorder that stems from heavy alcohol use by the mother during pregnancy.

infancy The stage of development that begins at birth and lasts between 18 and 24 months.

ONLY HUMAN

NO OFFENSE TAKEN In December 1996, officials at the Wellington City Art Gallery in New Zealand denied entry to a 9-day-old baby whose mother sought to buy a ticket. Director Paula Savage said she was strictly enforcing the gallery's policy of not permitting minors to see the sexually explicit work of controversial photographer Robert Mapplethorpe.

Some children develop motor skills earlier than others.

QILAI SHEN/PANOS PICTURES

Chapter 6 that *habituation* is the tendency for organisms to respond less intensely to a stimulus as the frequency of exposure to that stimulus increases, and babies habituate just like the rest of us do.

Interestingly, newborns seem to be especially attuned to social stimuli. For example, newborns in one study were shown a blank disk, a disk with scrambled facial features, or a disk with a regular face. When one of the disks was moved across their fields of vision, the newborns tracked the disk by moving both their heads and their eyes. Moreover, they tracked the disk with the regular face longer than they tracked the other disks (Johnson et al., 1991). But newborns don't merely track social stimuli with their eyes; they respond to them in other surprising ways. Researchers in one study stood close to some newborns while sticking out their tongues and stood close to other newborns while pursing their lips. Newborns in the first group stuck out their own tongues more often than those in the second group did, and newborns in the second group pursed their lips more often than those in the first group did (Meltzoff & Moore, 1977). Indeed, newborns have been shown to mimic facial expressions in their very first *hour* of life (Reissland, 1988).

● **How do newborns respond to social stimuli?**

Although infants can use their eyes right away, they must spend considerably more time learning how to use most of their other parts. **Motor development** is *the emergence of the ability to execute physical actions* such as reaching, grasping, crawling, and walking. Infants are born with a small set of **reflexes,** which are *specific patterns of motor response that are triggered by specific patterns of sensory stimulation.* For example, the *rooting reflex* is the tendency for infants to move their mouths toward any object that touches their cheek, and the *sucking reflex* is the tendency to suck any object that enters their mouths. These two reflexes allow newborns to find their mother's nipple and begin feeding—a behavior so vitally important that nature took no chances and hardwired it into every one of us. Interestingly, these and other reflexes that are present at birth seem to disappear in the first few months as children learn to execute more sophisticated motor behavior.

The development of these more sophisticated behaviors tends to obey two general rules. The first is the **cephalocaudal rule** (or the "top-to-bottom" rule), which describes *the tendency for motor skills to emerge in sequence from the head to the feet.* Infants tend to gain control over their heads first, their arms and trunks next, and their legs last. The second rule is the **proximodistal rule** (or the "inside-to-outside" rule), which describes *the tendency for motor skills to emerge in sequence from the center to the periphery.* Babies learn to control their trunks before their elbows and knees, and they learn to control their elbows and knees before their hands and feet (see **FIGURE 10.2**, on page 303). Motor skills generally emerge in an orderly sequence that corresponds to these rules, but they do not emerge on a strict timetable. Rather, the timing of these skills is influenced by many factors, such as the baby's incentive for reaching, body weight, muscular development, and general level of activity. In one study, babies who had visually stimulating mobiles hanging above their cribs began reaching for objects 6 weeks earlier than babies who did not (White & Held, 1966). Furthermore, different infants seem to acquire the same skill in different ways. One study examined how children learn to reach by closely following the development of four infants (Thelen et al., 1993). Two of the infants were especially energetic and initially produced large circular movements of both arms. To reach accurately, these infants had to learn to dampen these large circular movements by holding their arms rigid at the elbow and swiping at an object. The other two infants were less energetic and did not produce large, circular movements. Thus, their first step in learning to reach involved learning to lift their arms against the force of gravity and extend them forward. Detailed observations such as these suggest that while all infants learn skills such as reaching, different infants accomplish this goal in different ways (Adolph & Avoilio, 2000).

● **In what order do motor skills develop?**

Infants mimic the facial expressions of adults. And vice versa.

CARLOS E. SANTA MARIA/SHUTTERSTOCK.COM

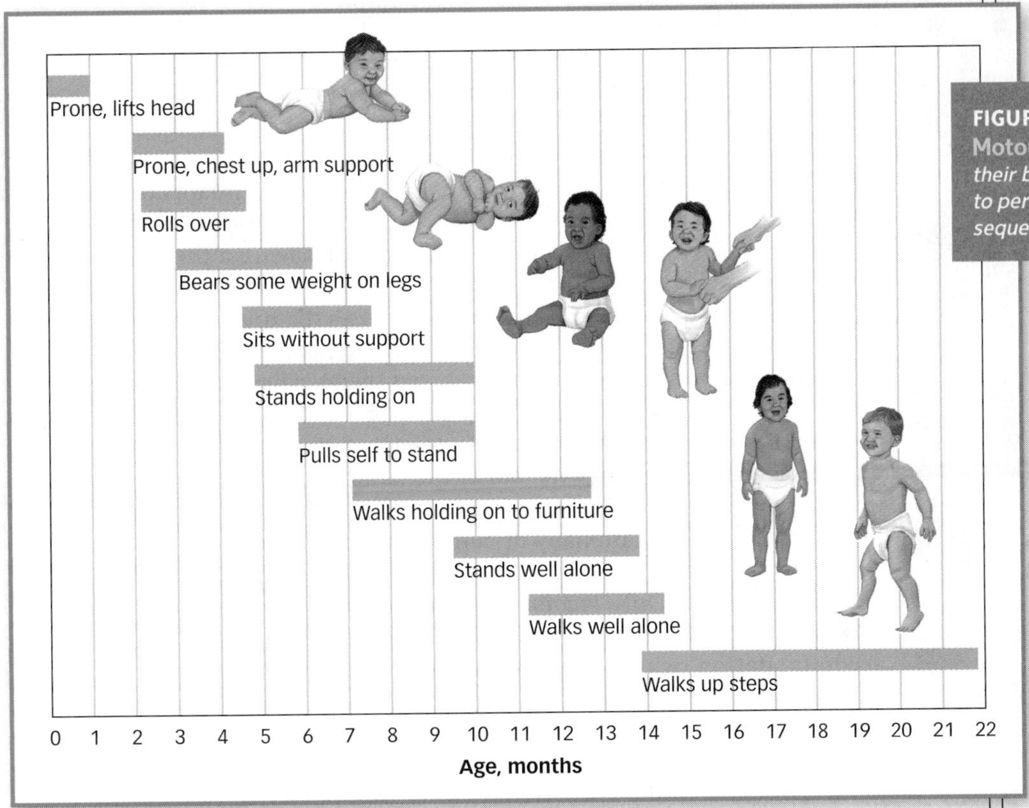
Prone, lifts head
Prone, chest up, arm support
Rolls over
Bears some weight on legs
Sits without support
Stands holding on
Pulls self to stand
Walks holding on to furniture
Stands well alone
Walks well alone
Walks up steps
0 1 2 3 4 5 6 7 8 9 10 11 12 13 14 15 16 17 18 19 20 21 22
Age, months

FIGURE 10.2 **Motor Development** *Infants learn to control their bodies from head to feet and from center to periphery. These skills emerge in a strict sequence.*

Cognitive Development

Infants can see. But what exactly do they make of the visual stimuli to which their eyes respond? In the first half of the 20th century, a Swiss biologist named Jean Piaget was following up work by Alfred Binet, who had pioneered the development of intelligence tests for children. To his surprise, Piaget found that when children in the same age group were confronted with difficult problems, they made the same mistakes—mistakes that virtually disappeared when these children graduated to the next age group. The similarity and the age specificity of children's mistakes led Piaget to suspect that as children grow, they move through several stages of **cognitive development**—which refers to *the emergence of the ability to understand the world.* Piaget proposed that children pass through four sequential stages, which he called the *sensorimotor* stage, the *preoperational* stage, the *concrete operational* stage, and the *formal operational* stage (Piaget, 1954a; see **TABLE 10.1**).

TABLE 10.1

Piaget's Four Stages of Cognitive Development

Stage	Characteristics
Sensorimotor (Birth–2 years)	Infant experiences world through movement and senses, develops schemas, begins to act intentionally, and shows evidence of understanding object permanence.
Preoperational (2–6 years)	Child acquires motor skills but does not understand conservation of physical properties. Child begins this stage by thinking egocentrically but ends with a basic understanding of other minds.
Concrete operational (6–11 years)	Child can think logically about physical objects and events and understands conservation of physical properties.
Formal operational (11 years and up)	Child can think logically about abstract propositions and hypotheticals.

motor development The emergence of the ability to execute physical action.

reflexes Specific patterns of motor response that are triggered by specific patterns of sensory stimulation.

cephalocaudal rule The "top-to-bottom" rule that describes the tendency for motor skills to emerge in sequence from the head to the feet.

proximodistal rule The "inside-to-outside" rule that describes the tendency for motor skills to emerge in sequence from the center to the periphery.

cognitive development The emergence of the ability to understand the world.

Jean Piaget (1896–1980) is widely considered to be the father of modern developmental psychology.

FARRELL GREHAN/CORBIS

Discovering Our Worlds

The first of Piaget's four stages is the **sensorimotor stage**, which is *a stage of development that begins at birth and lasts through infancy.* As the word *sensorimotor* suggests, infants at this stage use their ability to *sense* and their ability to *move* to acquire information about the world in which they live. By actively exploring their environments with their eyes, mouths, and fingers, infants begin to construct **schemas**, which are *theories about or models of the way the world works.*

As every scientist knows, the key advantage of having a theory is that one can use it to predict and control what will happen in novel situations. If an infant learns that tugging at a stuffed animal causes the toy to come closer, then that observation is incorporated into the infant's theory about how physical objects behave, and the infant can later use that theory when he or she wants a different object to come closer, such as a rattle or a ball. Piaget called this process **assimilation**, which occurs when *infants apply their schemas in novel situations.* Of course, if the infant tugs the tail of the family cat, the cat is likely to sprint in the opposite direction. Infants' theories about the world ("Things come closer if I pull them") are occasionally disconfirmed, and thus infants must occasionally adjust their schemas in light of their new experiences ("Aha! Only *inanimate* things come closer when I pull them"). Piaget called this process **accommodation**, which occurs when *infants revise their schemas in light of new information.*

● **How are infants like scientists when they learn about the world?**

What kinds of schemas do infants develop, apply, and revise? Piaget suggested that infants do not have—and hence must acquire—some very basic understandings about the physical world. For example, when you put a pair of socks away, you know that the socks exist even after you close the drawer, and you would be quite surprised if you opened the drawer a moment later and found it empty. But according to Piaget, this would not surprise an infant because infants do not have a theory of **object permanence**, which is *the idea that objects continue to exist even when they are not visible.* Piaget noted that in the first few months of life, infants act as though objects stop existing the moment they are out of sight. For instance, he observed that a 2-month-old infant will track a moving object with her eyes, but once the object leaves her visual field, she will not search for it.

Was Piaget right? Recent research suggests that when infants are tested in other ways, they demonstrate a sense of object permanence much earlier than Piaget realized. For instance, in one study, infants were shown a miniature drawbridge that flipped up and down. Once the babies got used to this, they watched as a box was placed behind the drawbridge—in its path but out of their sight. Some infants then saw a *possible* event: The drawbridge began to flip and then suddenly stopped, as if impeded by the box that the infants could not see. Other infants saw an *impossible* event: The drawbridge began to flip and then continued, as if unimpeded by the box (see **FIGURE 10.3**, on page 305). What did infants do? Four-month-old infants stared longer at the impossible event than at the possible event, suggesting that they were puzzled by it (Baillargeon, Spelke, & Wasserman, 1985). The fact that the infants were puzzled by the impossible event suggests that they knew the box existed even when they could not see it (Fantz, 1964).

Studies such as these suggest that infants do have some understanding of object permanence. Clearly, infants do not think of the world only in terms of its visible parts, and at some level they must "know" that when objects continue to exist even when they are out of sight. Although infants seem to have a better understanding of the physical world than Piaget claimed, it is still not clear just how much they know or how and when they come to know it. As Piaget (1977/1927) wrote: "The child's first year of life is unfortunately still an abyss of

MICHAEL HAGEDORN/CORBIS

During the sensorimotor stage, infants explore with their hands and mouths, learning important lessons about the physical world such as "No matter how hard you try you can't actually swallow silverware."

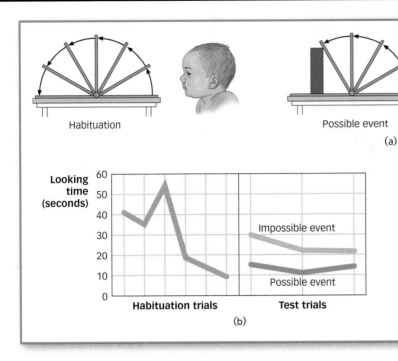

Habituation   Possible event   Impossible event

(a)

Looking time (seconds)

Impossible event

Possible event

Habituation trials   Test trials

(b)

FIGURE 10.3

The Possible and the Impossible Event *(a) In the habituation trials, infants watched a drawbridge flip back and forth with nothing in its path until they grew bored. Then a box was placed behind the drawbridge and the infants were shown one of two events: In the possible event, the box kept the drawbridge from flipping all the way over; in the impossible event, it did not. (b) The graph shows the infants' "looking time" during the habituation and the test trials. During the test trials, their interest was reawakened by the impossible event but not by the possible event (Baillargeon et al., 1985).*

mysteries for the psychologist. If only we could know what is going on in a baby's mind while observing him in action, we could certainly understand everything there is to psychology."

Discovering Our Minds

The long period following infancy is called **childhood,** which is *the stage of development that begins at about 18 to 24 months and lasts until adolescence, which begins between 11 and 14 years.*

According to Piaget, childhood consists of two stages. The first is a **preoperational stage,** which is *the stage of development that begins at about 2 years and ends at about 6 years,* during which the child learns about physical (or "concrete") objects. Next is the **concrete operational stage,** which is *the stage of development that begins at about 6 years and ends at about 11 years,* during which the child can perform "concrete operations" which means that the child learns how actions (or "operations") can affect or transform objects. A key difference between children in the preoperational stage and children in the concrete operational stage is that only the latter understand that the number of objects doesn't change when those objects are rearranged. For example, in

● **What do children come to understand at the concrete-operational stage?**

one study, Piaget showed children a row of cups and asked them to place an egg in each. Preoperational children were able to do this, and afterward they readily agreed that there were just as many eggs as there were cups. Then Piaget removed the eggs and spread them out in a long line that extended beyond the row of cups. Preoperational children incorrectly claimed that there were now more eggs than cups because the row of eggs was longer than the row of cups. Concrete-operational children, on the other hand, correctly reported that the number of eggs did not change when those eggs were spread out in a longer line. They understood that *quantity* is a property of a set of objects that does not change when an operation such as *spreading out* alters the set's appearance (Piaget, 1954b). Piaget called this insight **conservation,** which is *the notion that the quantitative properties of an object are stable despite changes in the object's appearance.*

Why don't preoperational children seem to grasp the notion of conservation? One reason is that preoperational children do not fully grasp the fact that they have *minds*

sensorimotor stage A stage of development that begins at birth and lasts through infancy in which infants acquire information about the world by sensing it and moving around within it.

schemas Theories about or models of the way the world works.

assimilation The process by which infants apply their schemas in novel situations.

accommodation The process by which infants revise their schemas in light of new information.

object permanence The idea that objects continue to exist even when they are not visible.

childhood The stage of development that begins at about 18 to 24 months and lasts until adolescence.

preoperational stage The stage of development that begins at about 2 years and ends at about 6 years, in which children have a preliminary understanding of the physical world.

concrete operational stage The stage of development that begins at about 6 years and ends at about 11 years, in which children acquire a basic understanding of the physical world and a preliminary understanding of their own and others' minds.

conservation The notion that the quantitative properties of an object are invariant despite changes in the object's appearance.

When preoperational children are shown two equal-size glasses filled with equal amounts of liquid, they correctly say that neither glass "has more." But when the contents of one glass are poured into a taller, thinner glass, they incorrectly say that the taller glass now "has more." Concrete operational children don't make this mistake because they recognize that operations such as pouring change the appearance of the liquid but not its actual volume.

LAURA DWIGHT/PHOTOEDIT

and that these minds contain *mental representations* of the world. As adults, we all distinguish between the subjective and the objective, between appearances and realities, between things in the mind and things in the world. We realize that things aren't always as they seem—that a wagon can *be* red but *look* gray at dusk, a highway can *be* dry but *look* wet in the heat. We make a distinction between the way things *are* and the way we *see* them. But preoperational children don't make this distinction so easily. When something *looks* gray or wet, they tend to assume it *is* gray or wet. As children develop into the concrete operational stage, they begin to realize that the way the world *appears* is not necessarily the way the world really *is*. Once children understand that brains represent—and hence can misrepresent—objects in the world, they are in a better position to solve a variety of problems that require them to ignore an object's subjective appearance while attempting to understand its objective properties.

For example, children who are in the concrete operational stage understand that when water is poured from a short, wide beaker into a tall, thin cylinder, it is still the same amount of water despite the fact that the water level in the cylinder is higher. But it isn't until these children move on to the **formal operational stage**, which is *the stage of development that begins around the age of 11 and lasts through adulthood,* that they can solve nonphysical problems with similar ease. Childhood ends when formal operations begin, and people who move on to this stage are able to reason systematically about abstract concepts such as *liberty* and *love* and about events that *will* happen, that *might have* happened, and that *never* happened. There are no tangible objects in the world to which words such as *liberty* or *love* refer, and yet people at the formal operational stage can think and reason about such concepts in a systematic way. The ability to generate, consider, reason about, or otherwise operate on abstract objects is the hallmark of formal operations.

RICHARD B. LEVINE

At the preoperational stage, children generally do not distinguish between the way things look and the way things are. They do not realize that when a friendly adult wears a scary mask, he is still a friendly adult.

Discovering Other Minds

As children develop, they discover their own minds. They also discover the minds of others. Because preoperational children don't fully grasp the fact that they have minds that mentally represent objects, they also don't fully grasp the fact that other people have minds that may mentally represent the same objects in different ways. Hence, they generally expect others to see the world as they do. **Egocentrism** is *the failure to understand that the world appears differently to different observers.* When 3-year-old children are asked what a person on the opposite side of a table is seeing, they typically claim that the other person sees what they see.

Just as 3-year-old children have trouble understanding that others may not see what they see, so too do they have trouble understanding that others may not know what they know. In one study using the *false belief test,* children saw a puppet named Maxi deposit some chocolate in a cupboard and then leave the room. A second puppet arrived a moment later, found the chocolate, and moved it to a different cupboard. The children were then asked where Maxi would look for the chocolate when he returned—in the first cupboard where he had initially put it or in the second cupboard where the children knew it was currently. Most 5-year-olds realized that Maxi would search the first cupboard because, after all, Maxi had not seen the chocolate being moved. But 3-year-olds typically claimed that Maxi would look in the second cupboard because, after all, that's where *the children* knew the chocolate really was (Wimmer & Perner, 1983). Children all over the world pass and fail the false belief test at about the same age (Callaghan et al., 2005; see **FIGURE 10.4**, on page 307).

● What does the *false belief test* show?

ONLY HUMAN

VOTE EARLY, VOTE OFTEN In August 1991, the government of Finland proposed having a referendum on the age at which children should start school and suggested that children as young as 5 should be allowed to vote on the measure. The "preliterate" voters would be presented three drawings of birthday cakes with 5, 6, and 7 candles and would be asked to circle one of them.

Only when the child understands the concept of mental representation can she understand that different people sometimes have different beliefs. Although we all ultimately achieve this insight, research suggests that even adults have trouble believing that others see the world differently than they do (Gilovich, Kruger, & Savitsky, 1999; Royzman, Cassidy, & Baron, 2003). It seems that egocentrism goes away, but it doesn't go very far.

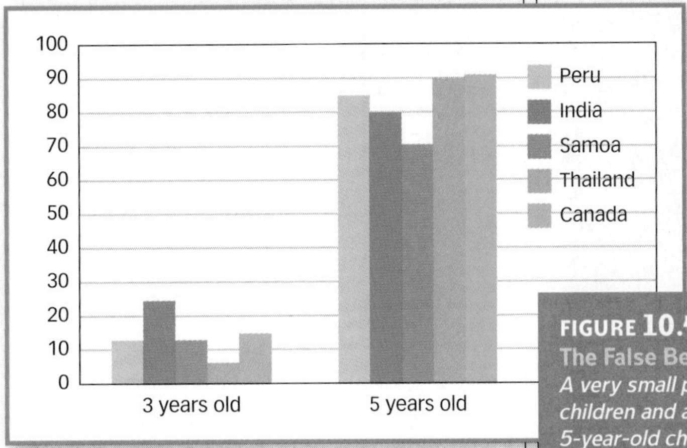

Different people have different perceptions and beliefs, but they also have different desires and emotions. Surprisingly, even very young children (who cannot understand that others have different perceptions or beliefs) seem to understand that other people have different desires. For example, a 2-year-old who likes dogs can understand that other children don't and can correctly predict that other children will avoid dogs that she herself would approach. When 18-month-old toddlers see an adult express disgust while eating a food that the toddlers enjoy, they hand the adult a different food, as if they understand that different people have different tastes (Repacholi & Gopnik, 1997).

Children take quite a long time, however, to understand that other people may have emotional reactions unlike their own. When 5-year-olds hear a story in which Little Red Riding Hood knocks on her grandmother's door, unaware that a wolf is inside waiting to devour her, they realize that Little Red Riding Hood does not know what they know. Nonetheless, they expect Little Red Riding Hood to feel afraid (Bradmetz & Schneider, 2004; DeRosnay et al., 2004; Harris et al., 1989). It is only at about 6 years of age that children come to understand that because they and others have different knowledge, they and others may also experience different emotions in the same situation.

Clearly, children have a whole lot to learn about how the mind works—and most of them eventually do. The vast majority of children ultimately come to understand that they and others have minds and that these minds represent the world in different ways. Once children understand these things, they are said to have acquired a **theory of mind**, which is *the idea that human behavior is guided by mental representations*. But two groups of children lag far behind their peers in acquiring this understanding. *Autism* is a relatively rare disorder that affects approximately 1 in 2,500 children (Frith, 2003). Children with autism typically have difficulty communicating with other people and making friends, and some psychologists have suggested that this is because these children fail to acquire a theory of mind. Although children with autism are typically normal—and sometimes far *better* than normal—on most intellectual dimensions, they have difficulty understanding other people. Specifically, they do not seem to understand that other people can have false beliefs (Baron-Cohen, Leslie, & Frith, 1985), belief-based emotions (Baron-Cohen, 1991), or self-conscious emotions such as embarrassment and shame (Heerey, Keltner, & Capps, 2003). Deaf children who are born

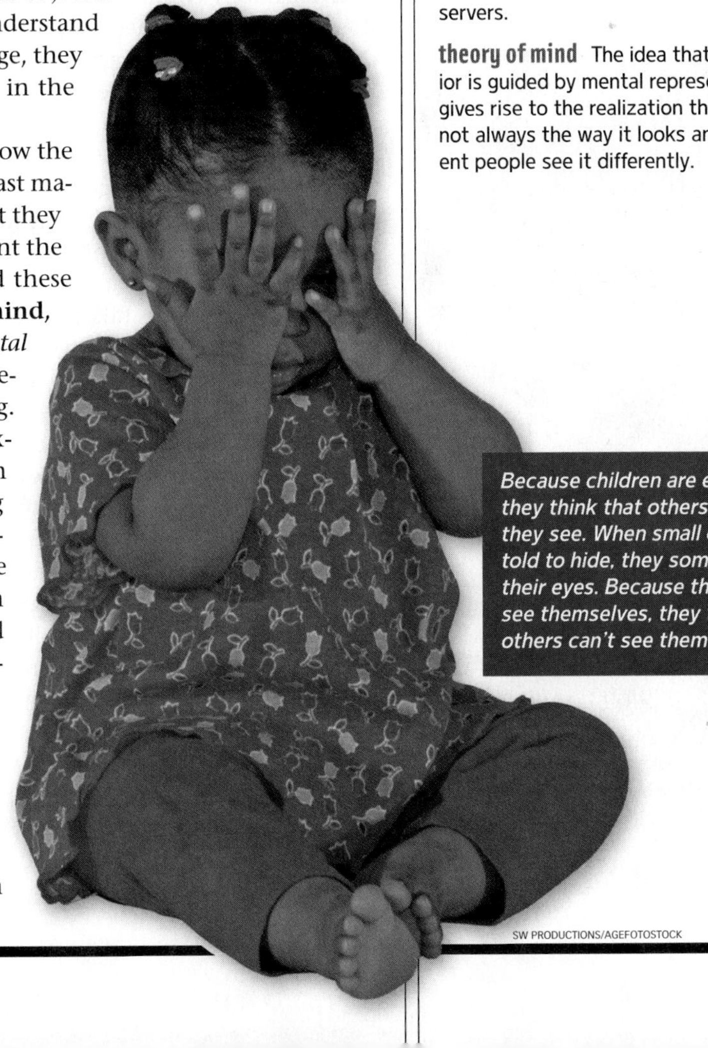

FIGURE 10.4 •
The False Belief Test across Cultures
A very small percentage of 3-year-old children and a very large percentage of 5-year-old children give the correct response in the false belief test. Research shows that this transition happens at about the same time in a wide variety of cultures (Callaghan et al., 2005).

formal operational stage The stage of development that begins around the age of 11 and lasts through adulthood, in which children gain a deeper understanding of their own and others' minds and learn to reason abstractly.

egocentrism The failure to understand that the world appears differently to different observers.

theory of mind The idea that human behavior is guided by mental representation, which gives rise to the realization that the world is not always the way it looks and that different people see it differently.

Because children are egocentric, • • • • • • • • •
they think that others see what they see. When small children are told to hide, they sometimes cover their eyes. Because they cannot see themselves, they think that others can't see them either.

● *Daniel Tammet is an autistic man who cannot drive a car or tell left from right. But he recently broke a European record by spending 5 hours, 9 minutes, and 24 seconds reciting the first 22,514 digits of pi from memory. "I just wanted to show people that disability needn't get in the way," he said (Johnson, 2005). Although only 10% of autistic people have extraordinary abilities such as this, they are 10 times more likely to have such abilities than are nonautistic people. No one knows why.*

"You're five. How could you possibly understand the problems of a five-and-a-half-year-old?"

● *Prior to the 18th century, children were thought of as "faulty small adults" and were typically portrayed with adult features, proportions, gestures, and dress. But modern research reveals that children and adults are remarkably different and that they think about the world in fundamentally different ways. These two boys are George Villiers, Second Duke of Buckingham, and his brother, Lord Francis Villiers, painted by Van Dyke in 1635.*

to hearing parents who do not know sign language also seem to lag behind their peers in acquiring a theory of mind. These children are slow to learn to communicate because they do not have ready access to any form of conventional language, and this restriction seems to slow the development of their understanding of other minds. Like children with autism, these deaf children display difficulties in understanding false beliefs even at 5 or 6 years of age (DeVilliers, 2005; Peterson & Siegal, 1999).

Even among children with no obvious disabilities, there is considerable variability in the rate at which a theory of mind is acquired. What causes this variability? A variety of factors have been examined, including the number of siblings that a child has, the frequency with which the child engages in pretend play, whether the child has an imaginary companion, and the socioeconomic status of the child's family. Of all the factors researchers have studied, language seems to be the most important (Astington & Baird, 2005). Children's language skills are an excellent predictor of how well they perform on false belief tests (such as the one in which Maxi looks for chocolate), and the likelihood of correctly completing this test increases with verbal ability (Happe, 1995). This is true both for children with and without autism.

The way caregivers talk to children is also a good predictor of their success at these tests. Children whose caregivers frequently talk about thoughts and feelings tend to be good at understanding beliefs and belief-based emotions. Some psychologists speculate that children benefit from hearing psychological words such as *want, think, know,* and *sad;* others suggest that children benefit from the grammatically complex sentences that typically contain these psychological words; and some believe that caregivers

● **How does language influence the child's understanding of the mind?**

who use psychological words are also more effective in getting children to reflect on mental states. Whatever the explanation, it is clear that language—and especially language about thoughts and feelings—is an important tool for helping children make sense of their own and others' minds (Harris, de Rosnay, & Pons, 2005).

Cognitive development—from the sensorimotor stage to formal operations—is a complex journey, and Piaget's ideas about it were nothing less than groundbreaking. Although many of these ideas have held up quite well, in the last few decades, psychologists have discovered two important qualifications. First, Piaget thought that children graduated from one stage to another in the same way that they graduated from kindergarten to first grade: A child is in kindergarten *or* first grade, he is never in both, and there is a particular moment of transition to which everyone can point. Modern psychologists see development as a more continuous and less steplike progression than Piaget believed. Children who are transitioning between stages may perform more mature behaviors one day and less mature behaviors the next.

A second qualification of Piaget's claims is that children acquire many of the abilities that Piaget described much *earlier* than he realized. For example, Piaget suggested that infants had no sense of object permanence because they did not actively search for objects that were moved out of their sight. But when researchers use experimental procedures that allow infants to "show what they know," even 4-month-olds display a sense of object permanence. Every year, it seems, research lowers the age at which babies can demonstrate their ability to perform sophisticated cognitive tasks.

Discovering Our Cultures

Piaget saw the child as a lone scientist who made observations through interactions with objects, developed theories, and then revised those theories in light of new observations. And yet, most scientists don't start from scratch. Rather, they receive training from more experienced scientists and they inherit the theories and methods of their disciplines. According to Russian psychologist Lev Vygotsky, children do much the same thing. Unlike Piaget, Vygotsky believed that cognitive development was largely the result of children's interaction with members of their own cultures rather than interaction with objects. He noted that *cultural tools,* such as language and counting systems, exert a strong influence on cognitive development (Vygotsky, 1978).

For example, in both Chinese and English, the numbers beyond 20 are named by a decade (twenty) that is followed by a digit (one) and their names follow a logical pattern (twenty-one, twenty-two, twenty-three, etc.). In Chinese, the numbers from 11 to 19 are similarly constructed (ten-one, ten-two, ten-three . . .). But in English, the names of the numbers between 11 and 19 are constructed differently than the others. They either

● **How does language influence a child's ability to do math?**

reverse the order of the decade and the digit (sixteen, seventeen) or they are entirely arbitrary (eleven, twelve). The difference in the regularity of these two systems makes a big difference to the

children who must learn them. It is obvious to a Chinese child that 12—which is called "ten-two"—can be decomposed into 10 and 2, but it is not so obvious to an American child who calls the number "twelve" (see **FIGURE 10.5**). In one study, children from many countries were asked to hand an experimenter a certain number of bricks. Some of the bricks were single, and some were glued together in strips of 10. When Asian children were asked to hand the experimenter 26 bricks, they tended to hand over two strips of

Lev Vygotsky (pictured here with his daughter) was a Soviet developmental psychologist whose theories emphasized the role that social life—rather than individual experience—plays in cognitive development.

JAMES V. WERTSCH/WASHINGTON UNIVERSITY

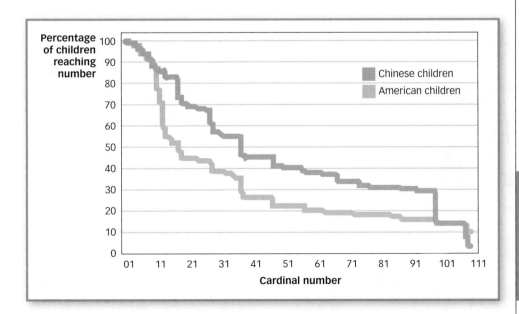

FIGURE 10.5 ● ● ● ● ● ● ● ● ● ● ● ● ● ●
Twelve or Two-Teen? *As this graph shows, the percentage of American children who can count through the cardinal numbers drops off suddenly when they hit the number 11, whereas the percentage of Chinese children shows a more gradual decline (Miller, Smith, & Zhu, 1995).*

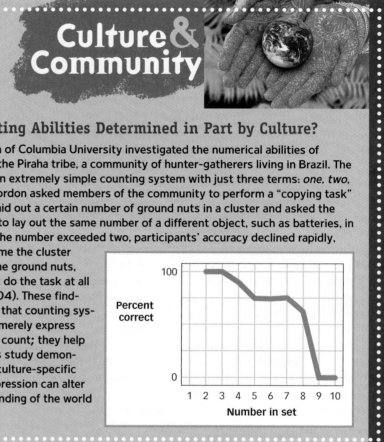

Are Counting Abilities Determined in Part by Culture?

Peter Gordon of Columbia University investigated the numerical abilities of members of the Piraha tribe, a community of hunter-gatherers living in Brazil. The Piraha have an extremely simple counting system with just three terms: *one, two,* and *many.* Gordon asked members of the community to perform a "copying task" in which he laid out a certain number of ground nuts in a cluster and asked the participants to lay out the same number of a different object, such as batteries, in a line. Once the number exceeded two, participants' accuracy declined rapidly, and by the time the cluster contained nine ground nuts, they couldn't do the task at all (Gordon, 2004). These findings suggest that counting systems do not merely express our ability to count; they help create it. This study demonstrates how culture-specific means of expression can alter our understanding of the world around us.

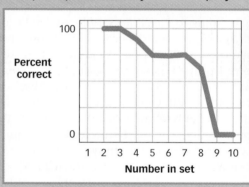

10 plus six singles. Non-Asian children tended to use the clumsier strategy of counting out 26 single bricks (Miura et al., 1994). Results such as these suggest that the regularity of the counting system that children inherit can promote or discourage their discovery of the fact that two-digit numbers can be decomposed.

Vygotsky believed that at any age, a child was capable of acquiring a range of skills, and he called this range the child's *zone of proximal development* (Vygotsky, 1978). He suggested that children who interacted with teachers tended to acquire skills toward the top of this range, whereas children who did not tended to acquire skills toward the bottom. The ability to acquire skills from others requires some basic communicative abilities. For example, communication requires that infants look at adults to gauge their reactions, a phenomenon known as *social referencing.* It also requires that infants and adults focus on the same object and not just on each other. Babies will look at an adult's eyes quite early, but it isn't until around 9 to 15 months that they begin looking at the point in space to which an adult's eyes are directed, a phenomenon known as *joint attention.* These two abilities prepare human infants to learn from more skilled members of their species.

Children are not lone explorers who discover the world for themselves but members of families, communities, and societies that teach them much of what they need to know.

Social Development

Unlike baby turtles, baby humans cannot survive without caregivers. But what exactly do caregivers provide? The obvious answers are warmth, safety, and food, and those obvious answers are right. But caregivers also provide something else that is every bit as essential to an infant's development.

During World War II, psychologists studied infants who were living in orphanages while awaiting adoption. Although these children were warm, safe, and well fed, many were physically and developmentally retarded, and nearly two out of five died before they could be adopted (Spitz, 1949). Shortly thereafter, psychologist Harry Harlow (1958; Harlow & Harlow, 1965) discovered that baby rhesus monkeys that were warm, safe, and well fed but were allowed no social contact for the first 6 months of their lives developed a variety of pathologies. The socially isolated monkeys turned out to be incapable of communicating with or learning from others of their kind, and when the females matured and became mothers, they ignored, rejected, and sometimes even attacked their own babies. Harlow also discovered that when socially isolated monkeys were put in a cage with two "artificial mothers"—one that was made of wire and dispensed food and one that was made of cloth and dispensed no food—they spent most of their time clinging to the soft cloth mother despite the fact that the wire mother was the source of their nourishment. Clearly, infants of all these species require something more from their caregivers than mere sustenance. But what?

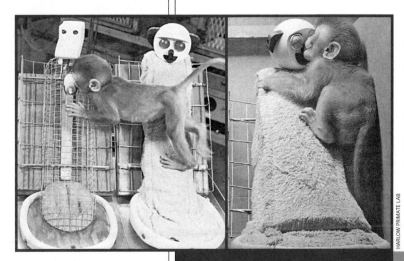

Harlow's monkeys preferred the comfort and warmth of a terry-cloth mother (right) to the wire mother (left) even when the wire mother was associated with food.

Becoming Attached

Psychiatrist John Bowlby was fascinated by the studies of rhesus monkeys reared in isolation and children in orphanages, and he sought to understand how human infants form attachments to their caregivers (Bowlby, 1969, 1973, 1980). Bowlby noted that from the moment they are born, monkeys cling to their mothers' furry chests because they must stay close to their caregivers to survive. Newly hatched ducks and geese show a related tendency to follow after their mother from the minute they are born. Indeed, this tendency is so strong that newly hatched geese can be "tricked" into faithfully following the first moving object they see—even if that object is a human being or a tennis ball. The ethologist Konrad Lorenz called this *imprinting* and theorized that the first moving object a hatchling saw was somehow imprinted on its bird brain as "the thing I must always stay near" (Lorenz, 1952).

Human babies, Bowlby suggested, have a similar need, but they are much less physically developed than goslings or monkeys and hence cannot waddle or cling. Because they cannot stay close to their caregivers, human babies have developed a different strategy: they do things that cause their caregivers to stay close to them. When a baby cries, gurgles, coos, makes eye contact, or smiles, most adults reflexively move toward the baby, and Bowlby claimed that this is *why* the baby emits these "come hither" signals.

● **How and why do infants form attachments?**

Bowlby claimed that babies begin their lives by sending these signals to anyone within range to receive them, but during their first 6 months, they begin to keep a mental tally of who responds most often and most promptly, and they soon begin to target their signals to the best responder or *primary caregiver*. This person quickly becomes the emotional center of the infant's universe. Infants feel secure in the primary caregiver's presence and will happily crawl around, exploring their environments with their eyes, ears, fingers, and mouths. But if their primary caregiver gets too far away, infants begin to feel insecure, and they take

Like goslings, human babies need to stay close to their mothers to survive. Unlike goslings, human babies know how to get their mothers to come to them rather than the other way around.

● *It doesn't take a psychologist to see that this child is securely attached.*

JEFF GREENBERG/OMNI PHOTO

action to decrease the distance between themselves and their primary caregiver, perhaps by crawling toward their caregiver or by crying until their caregiver moves toward them. Bowlby believed that all this happens because evolution has equipped human infants with a social reflex that is every bit as basic as the physical reflexes that cause them to suck and to grasp. Human infants, Bowlby suggested, are predisposed to form an **attachment**—that is, *an emotional bond*—with a primary caregiver.

Given the fundamental importance of attachment, it is not surprising that infants who are deprived of the opportunity to become attached suffer a variety of social and emotional deficits (O'Connor & Ruter, 2000; Rutter, O'Connor, & the English and Romanian Adoptees Study Team, 2004). Furthermore, even when attachment does happen, it can happen in ways that are more or less successful (Ainsworth et al., 1978). Psychologist Mary Ainsworth developed the Strange Situation test to measure a child's attachment style. The test involves bringing a child and his or her primary caregiver (usually the child's mother) to a laboratory room and then staging a series of episodes, including ones in which the primary caregiver briefly leaves the room and then returns. Research shows that infants' reactions tend to fit one of four attachment styles.

Among American infants, the majority (about 60%) show a secure attachment style, meaning that, when the caregiver returns, infants who had been distressed by the caregiver's absence go to her and are calmed by her proximity, while those who had not been distressed acknowledge her return with a glance or greeting. Another 20% of American infants display an avoidant attachment style, meaning that they are generally not distressed when their caregiver leaves the room, and they generally do not acknowledge her when she returns. About 15% of American infants display an *ambivalent* attachment style, meaning that they are almost always distressed when their caregiver leaves the room; but then rebuff their caregiver's attempt to calm them when she returns, arching their backs and squirming to get away. And a very few American infants (5% or fewer) display a *disorganized* attachment style, with no consistent pattern of responses when their caregiver leaves or returns.

Research has shown that a child's behavior in the Strange Situation test correlates fairly well with his or her behavior at home (Solomon & George, 1999) and in the laboratory (see **FIGURE 10.6**). Nonetheless, it is not unusual for a child's attachment style to change over time (Lamb, Sternberg, & Prodromidis, 1992). And while some aspects of attachment styles appear to be stable across cultures—secure attachment is the most common style in just about every country that has ever been studied (van IJzendoorn & Kroonenberg, 1988)—other attachment styles vary across cultures. For example, German children (whose parents tend to foster independence) are more likely to have avoidant than ambivalent attachment styles, whereas Japanese children (whose mothers typically stay home) are more likely to have ambivalent than avoidant attachment styles (Takahashi, 1986).

● ● ● ● ● ● ● ● ● ● ● ● ● ● ● **FIGURE 10.6**

Attachment Style and Memory
We often remember best those events that fit with our view of the world. Researchers assessed 1-year-old children's attachment styles with the strange situation test. Two years later, the same group of children were shown a puppet show in which some happy events (e.g., the puppet got a present) or unhappy events (e.g., the puppet spilled his juice) occurred. Securely attached children later remembered more of the happy events than the unhappy ones, but insecurely attached children showed the opposite pattern (Belsky. Spritz, & Crnic. 1996).

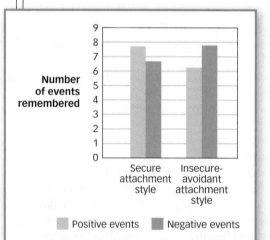

Number of events remembered

Secure attachment style | Insecure-avoidant attachment style

☐ Positive events   ■ Negative events

attachment The emotional bond that forms between newborns and their primary caregivers.

internal working model of attachment A set of expectations about how the primary caregiver will respond when the child feels insecure.

temperaments Characteristic patterns of emotional reactivity.

Working Models

Why do different infants have different attachment styles? The capacity for attachment may be innate, but the quality of that attachment is influenced by the child, the primary caregiver, and their interaction. Infants seem to keep track of the responsiveness of their primary caregiver and use this information to create an **internal working model of**

attachment, which is *a set of expectations about how the primary caregiver will respond when the child feels insecure.* Infants with different attachment styles appear to have different working models. Specifically, infants with a secure attachment style seem to be

● **How do caregivers influence the quality of a child's attachment?**

certain that their primary caregiver will respond, infants with an avoidant attachment style seem to be certain that their primary caregiver will not respond, and infants with an ambivalent attachment style seem to be uncertain about whether their primary caregiver will respond. Infants with a disorganized attachment style seem to be confused about their caregivers, which has led some psychologists to speculate that this style primarily characterizes children who have been abused (Carolson, 1998; Cicchetti & Toth, 1998).

Attachment is an interaction between two people, and thus both of them—the primary caregiver and the child—play a role in determining the nature of the child's working model (see **FIGURE 10.7**). Different children are born with different **temperaments**, or *characteristic patterns of emotional reactivity* (Thomas & Chess, 1977). These differences in temperament seem to emerge from stable differences in biology (Kagan, 1997). For example, 10% to 15% of infants have highly reactive limbic systems that produce an "inhibited" temperament. These infants thrash and cry when shown a new toy or a new person; they grow into children who tend to avoid novel people, objects, and situations; and they ultimately become quiet, cautious, and sometimes shy adults (Schwartz et al., 2003). These studies suggest that from the earliest moments of life, some infants are prone to feel insecure when their primary caregiver leaves a room and are inconsolable when she returns.

A caregiver's behavior also has an important influence on the infant's working model and attachment style. Studies have shown that mothers of securely attached infants tend to be especially sensitive to signs of their child's emotional state, especially good at detecting their infant's "request" for reassurance, and especially responsive to that request (Ainsworth et al., 1978; De Wolff & van IJzendoorn, 1997). Mothers of infants with an ambivalent attachment style tend to respond inconsistently, only sometimes attending to their infants when they show signs of distress. Mothers of infants with an avoidant attachment style are typically indifferent to their child's need for reassurance and may even reject their attempts at physical closeness (Isabelle, 1993). Another study found that when mothers think of their babies as unique individuals with emotional lives rather than as creatures with urgent physical needs, their infants end up more securely attached (Meins, 2003; Meins et al., 2001). In short, a child's social development may reflect not just innate temperament and biological differences, but also social interaction with the caregiver (see the Real World box on the next page).

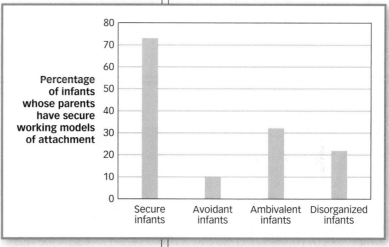

FIGURE 10.7 ● ● ● ● ● ● ● ● ● ● ● ● ● ●
Parents' Attachment Styles Affect Their Children's Attachment Styles
Studies suggest that securely attached infants tend to have parents who have secure working models of attachment (van IJzendoorn, 1995).

Moral Development

From the moment of birth, human beings can make one distinction quickly and well, and that's the distinction between pleasure and pain. Before babies hit their very first diapers, they can tell when something feels good, they can tell when something feels bad, and they strongly prefer the former to the latter. But as they mature, they begin to notice that their pleasures ("Throwing food is fun") don't always please others ("Throwing food makes Mom mad"). This is a problem. Human beings need each other to survive and thrive, and when we make other people feel bad, those others tend to avoid us, exclude us, or retaliate against us. We are social animals, and it is in our own selfish interests to learn how to balance our needs and the needs of others. We do this by developing a

How do children learn to decide ● ● ● ● ● what is right and what is wrong?

©SEAN JUSTICE/CORBIS

[THE REAL WORLD] •••••••••••••••••••••••••••••••••••••••

The Truth about Day Care

In 1975, about 37% of married American women with children under age 6 worked outside the home. In 1998, that figure had risen to 64%. The majority of working parents entrust their children's care to someone else for some part of the day, and that someone else is often a day care provider. While liberals applaud the economic liberation of women, conservatives lament the emotional toll that they believe day care takes on children. Researchers at the National Institute for Child Health and Development have been trying to approach the matter scientifically by conducting a large-scale study of the effects of day care on approximately 1,300 children living in a wide variety of settings in North America. So far, the results of the study suggest that day care has little effect on the quality of the attachment that children establish with their primary caregivers. While the attachment styles of infants and toddlers are strongly influenced by their mother's sensitivity and responsiveness, attachment styles are generally not influenced by the quality, amount, age of entry, stability, or type of day care the children receive (NICHD Early Child Care Research Network, 1997).

But the results were not all good news. Although day care had no large, direct effects on children's attachments, there was evidence of a subtle interaction between a child's experience at home and at day care. Specifically, 15-month-old infants were likely to be

Would these children in day care be better off at home with their mothers?

insecurely attached if their mothers were low in sensitivity *and* the infants (a) attended a poor-quality day care, (b) spent more than 10 hours a week in day care, or (c) had more than one day care arrangement. This suggests that day care itself does not increase the risk of emotional insecurity, but certain kinds of day care can do so when combined with the stress of having a mother who is unresponsive and insensitive. A similar effect was observed among toddlers who were 24 and 36 months old (NICHD Early Child Care Research Network, 1999). It is also important to note that while the quality of day care does not have a powerful influence on emotional attachment, it does influence a child's cognitive and social competence (NICHD Early Child Care Research Network, 2002).

In short, the best evidence to date suggests that day care does not put children at risk, but that *bad* day care puts *some* children at risk. This may not be the all-or-none conclusion that spinmeisters on both the left and right want to hear, but it has the redeeming quality of being true.

new distinction—the distinction between right and wrong. "Bad behavior" usually involves the gratification of our own desires at the expense of someone else's, and most moral systems are a set of recommendations for balancing different people's competing needs.

Knowing What's Right

How do children think about right and wrong? Piaget spent time playing marbles with children and quizzing them about how they came to know the rules of the game and what they thought should happen to children who broke them. By listening carefully to what children said, Piaget noticed that their moral thinking changed systematically over time in three important ways (Piaget, 1932/1965):

■ First, Piaget noticed that children's moral thinking tends to shift *from realism to relativism*. Very young children regard moral rules as real, inviolable truths about the world. Young children generally don't believe that a bad action, such as hitting someone, can be good even if everyone agreed to allow it. As they mature, children begin to realize that some moral rules (e.g., wives should obey their husbands) are inventions and that groups of people can therefore agree to adopt them, change them, or abandon them entirely.

■ Second, Piaget noticed that children's moral thinking tends to shift *from prescriptions to principles*. Young children think of moral rules as guidelines for specific actions in specific situations ("Children should take turns playing marbles"). As they mature, children come to see that rules are expressions of more general principles, such as fairness and equity, which means that rules can be abandoned or modified when they fail to serve the general principle ("If a child missed his turn, then it would be fair to give him two turns").

■ Finally, Piaget noticed that children's moral thinking tends to shift *from outcomes to intentions*. For the young child, an unintentional action that causes great harm seems "more wrong" than an intentional action that causes slight harm because young children tend to judge the morality of an action by its outcome rather than by what the actor intended (cf. Yuill & Perner, 1988). As they mature, children begin to see that the morality of an action is critically dependent on the actor's state of mind.

Psychologist Lawrence Kohlberg picked up where Piaget left off and offered a more detailed theory of the development of moral reasoning (Kohlberg, 1963, 1986). According to Kohlberg, moral reasoning proceeds through three major stages. Kohlberg based his theory on people's responses to a series of moral dilemmas such as this one:

A woman was near death from a special kind of cancer. There was one drug that the doctors thought might save her. It was a form of radium that a druggist in the same town had recently discovered. The drug was expensive to make, but the druggist was charging 10 times what the drug cost him to make. He paid $200 for the radium and charged $2,000 for a small dose of the drug. The sick woman's husband, Heinz, went to everyone he knew to borrow the money, but he could only get together about $1,000, which is half of what it cost. He told the druggist that his wife was dying and asked him to sell it cheaper or let him pay later. But the druggist said, "No, I discovered the drug, and I'm going to make money from it." So Heinz got desperate and broke into the man's store to steal the drug for his wife. Should the husband have done that?

● **According to Kohlberg, how does a child's moral thinking develop?**

On the basis of their responses, Kohlberg concluded that most children are at the **preconventional stage**, *a stage of moral development in which the morality of an action is primarily determined by its consequences for the actor*. Immoral actions are those for which one is punished, and the appropriate resolution to any moral dilemma is to choose the behavior with the least likelihood of punishment. For example, children at this stage often base their moral judgment of Heinz on the relative costs of one decision ("It would be bad if he got blamed for his wife's death") and another ("It would be bad if he went to jail for stealing").

Kohlberg argued that older children move to the **conventional stage**, which is *a stage of moral development in which the morality of an action is primarily determined by the extent to which it conforms to social rules*. Children at this stage believe that everyone should uphold the generally accepted norms of their cultures, obey the laws of society, and fulfill their civic duties and familial obligations. They believe that Heinz must weigh the dishonor he will bring upon himself and his family by stealing (i.e., breaking a law) against the guilt he will feel if he allows his wife to die (i.e., failing to fulfill a duty).

Finally, Kohlberg believed that some adults move to the **postconventional stage**, which is *a stage of moral development at which the morality of an action is determined by a set of general principles that reflect core values*, such as the right to life, liberty, and the pursuit of happiness. When a behavior violates these principles, it is immoral; and if a law requires these principles to be violated, then it should be disobeyed. For a person who has reached the postconventional

preconventional stage A stage of moral development in which the morality of an action is primarily determined by its consequences for the actor.

conventional stage A stage of moral development in which the morality of an action is primarily determined by the extent to which it conforms to social rules.

postconventional stage A stage of moral development at which the morality of an action is determined by a set of general principles that reflect core values.

After World War II, Lawrence Kohlberg served in the Merchant Marine, and volunteered to help smuggle Jewish refugees into British-controlled Palestine. He spent his life trying to understand how people determine what is right and what is wrong.

stage, a woman's life is always more important than a shopkeeper's profits, so stealing the drug is not only a moral behavior—it is a moral obligation.

Research supports Kohlberg's general claim that moral reasoning shifts from an emphasis on punishment to an emphasis on social rules and finally to an emphasis on ethical principles (Walker, 1988). But research also suggests that these stages are not quite as discrete as Kohlberg thought. For instance, a single person may use preconventional, conventional, and postconventional thinking in different circumstances, which suggests that the developing person does not "reach a stage" so much as "acquires a skill" that may or may not be used on a particular occasion. Because Kohlberg developed his theory by studying a sample of American boys, some critics of Kohlberg's theory have suggested that it does not describe the development of moral thinking in girls (Gilligan, 1982) or non-Westerners (Simpson, 1974). Other critics have noted that the correlation between a child's level of moral reasoning and that same child's degree of moral behavior is not particularly strong (Blasi, 1980; Haidt, 2001; Thoma et al., 1999). These critics suggest that how people reason about morality may be interesting in the abstract, but it has little to do with how people actually behave in their everyday lives.

Feeling What's Right

Research on moral reasoning portrays children as little jurists who use rational analysis—sometimes simple and sometimes sophisticated—to distinguish between right and wrong. But moral dilemmas don't just make us think. They also make us *feel*. Consider the following scenario.

You are standing on a bridge. Below you can see a runaway trolley hurtling down the track toward five people who will be killed if it remains on its present course. You are sure that you can save these people by flipping a lever that will switch the trolley onto a different track, where it will kill just one person instead of five. Is it morally permissible to divert the trolley and prevent five deaths at the cost of one?

Now consider a slightly different version of this problem:

You and a large man are standing on a bridge. Below you can see a runaway trolley hurtling down the track toward five people who will be killed if it remains on its present course. You are sure that you can save these people by pushing the large man onto the track, where his body will be caught up in the trolley's wheels and stop it before it kills the five people. Is it morally permissible to push the large man and thus prevent five deaths at the cost of one?

If you are like most people, you believe that it is morally permissible to sacrifice one person for the sake of five in the first case but not in the second case. And if you are like most people, you can't say why. Indeed, you probably didn't reach this conclusion by moral reasoning at all. Rather, you had a negative emotional reaction to the thought of pushing another human being into the path of an oncoming trolley, and that reaction was sufficient to convince you that pushing him would be wrong. You may have come up with a few good arguments to support this position, but those arguments probably followed rather than preceded your conclusion (Greene et al., 2001).

The way people respond to cases such as these has convinced some psychologists that our moral judgments are the consequences—and not the causes—of our emotional reactions (Haidt, 2001). According to this *moral intuitionist* perspective, we have evolved to react emotionally to a small family of events that are particularly relevant to reproduction and survival, and we have developed the distinction between right and wrong as a way of labeling and explaining these emotional reactions. According to the moral intuitionist perspective, the reason most people consider it permissible to stop a trolley by pulling a switch but not by pushing someone

• Most people are upset by the suffering of others, and research suggests that even young children have this response, which may be the basis of their emerging morality.

© CREASOURCE/CORBIS

onto the tracks is that people have negative emotional reactions to other people's physical pain (Greene et al., 2001). This aversion to others' suffering begins early in childhood. Even very young children distinguish between actions that are wrong because they violate a social rule and actions that are wrong because they cause suffering. When asked whether it would be okay to leave toys on the floor in a school that allowed such

● **How do emotions influence our moral judgments?**

behavior, young children tend to say it would. But when asked whether it would be okay to hit another child in a school that allowed such behavior, young children tend to say it would not (Smetana, 1981; Smetana & Braeges, 1990).

Children clearly think about transgressions that cause others to be observably distressed (e.g., hitting) differently from transgressions that do not (e.g., leaving toys on the floor). Why might that be? One possibility is that observing distress automatically triggers an empathic reaction in the brain of the observer. Recent research has shown that some of the same brain regions that are activated when people experience an unpleasant emotion are also activated when people see someone else experience that emotion (Carr et al., 2003). (See the discussion of mirror neurons in Chapter 3.) Studies such as these suggest that our brains respond to other people's *expressions* of distress by creating within us the *experience* of distress, and this mechanism may have evolved because it allows us to know instantly what others are feeling. The fact that we can actually *feel* another person's distress may explain why even a small child who is incapable of sophisticated moral reasoning still considers it wrong to inflict distress on others.

summary quiz [10.2]

4. In terms of motor development, babies gain control over their _____ before they gain control over their _____.
   a. extremities; trunk
   b. legs; arms
   c. head; trunk
   d. arms; shoulders

5. Little Isabel sees a butterfly and exclaims "Bird!" "No, that's a butterfly," says her grandmother. The next time Isabel sees a butterfly, she says "Butterfly." According to Piaget, Isabel has just shown
   a. habituation.
   b. concrete operations.
   c. assimilation.
   d. accommodation.

6. Baby Maria plays without a fuss when her mother leaves and, upon her return, ignores her. Maria is demonstrating which type of attachment style?
   a. avoidant
   b. ambivalent
   c. disorganized
   d. secure

7. For Lawrence Kohlberg, the sequence of moral development unfolds in the following order: emphasis on _____, then emphasis on _____, and finally, emphasis on _____.
   a. social roles; consequences; ethical principles
   b. ethical principles; social roles; consequences
   c. social roles; ethical principles; consequences
   d. consequences; social roles; ethical principles

adolescence The period of development that begins with the onset of sexual maturity (about 11 to 14 years of age) and lasts until the beginning of adulthood (about 18 to 21 years of age).

puberty The bodily changes associated with sexual maturity.

primary sex characteristics Bodily structures that are directly involved in reproduction.

secondary sex characteristics Bodily structures that change dramatically with sexual maturity but that are not directly involved in reproduction.

• *Early puberty is big news.*

• *Some cultures skip adolescence entirely. When a Krobo female menstruates for the first time, older women take her into seclusion for 2 weeks and teach her about sex, birth control, and marriage. Afterward, a public ceremony called the durbar is held, and the young female who that morning was regarded as a child is thereafter regarded as an adult.*

Adolescence: Minding the Gap

Between childhood and adulthood is an extended developmental stage that may not qualify for a hood of its own but that is clearly distinct from the stages that come before and after. **Adolescence** is *the period of development that begins with the onset of sexual maturity (about 11 to 14 years of age) and lasts until the beginning of adulthood (about 18 to 21 years of age).* Unlike the transition from embryo to fetus or from infant to child, this transition is both sudden and clearly marked. In just 3 or 4 years, the average adolescent gains about 40 pounds and grows about 10 inches. Girls' growth rates begin to accelerate around the age of 10, and they reach their full heights at around 15½ years. Boys experience an equivalent growth spurt about 2 years later and reach their full heights at around 17½ years. The growth spurt signals the onset of **puberty**, which refers to *the bodily changes associated with sexual maturity.* These changes involve **primary sex characteristics,** which are *bodily structures that are directly involved in reproduction,* for example, the onset of menstruation in girls and the emergence of the capacity for ejaculation in boys. They also involve **secondary sex characteristics,** which are *bodily structures that change dramatically with sexual maturity but that are not directly involved in reproduction,* for example, the enlargement of the breasts and the widening of the hips in girls and the appearance of facial hair, pubic hair, underarm hair, and the lowering of the voice in both genders. This pattern of changes is caused by increased production of sex-specific hormones: estrogen in girls and testosterone in boys.

Just as the body changes during adolescence, so too does the brain. An infant's brain forms many more new synapses than it actually needs, and by the time a child is 2 years old, she has about 15,000 synapses per neuron—which is twice as many as the average adult (Huttenlocher, 1979). This early period of synaptic proliferation is followed by a period of synaptic pruning in which the synapses that are not frequently used are eliminated. This is a clever system that allows our brain's wiring to be determined both by our genes and our experiences: Our genes "offer" a very large set of synaptic connections to the environment, which then "chooses" which ones to keep. Scientists used to think that this process ended early in life, but recent evidence suggests that some brain areas including the prefrontal cortex undergo a second round of synaptic proliferation just before puberty and a second round of synaptic pruning during adolescence (Giedd et al., 1999). Clearly, the adolescent brain is a work in progress.

● **How does experience change the structure of the brain?**

The Protraction of Adolescence

Although the onset of puberty is largely determined by a genetic program, there is considerable variation across individuals (e.g., people tend to reach puberty at about the

same age as their same-sexed parent did) and across cultures (e.g., African American girls tend to reach puberty before European American girls do) (see **FIGURE 10.8**, on page 319). There is also considerable variation across generations (Malina, Bouchard, & Beunen, 1988). For example, in Scandinavia, the United Kingdom, and the United States, the age of first menstruation was between 16 and 17 years in the 19th century but was approximately 13 years in 1960. Currently, about a third of all boys in the United States show some signs of genital maturity by the age of 9 (Reiter & Lee, 2001). The decrease in the age of the onset of puberty is due at least in part to changes in the environment (Ellis & Garber, 2000). For

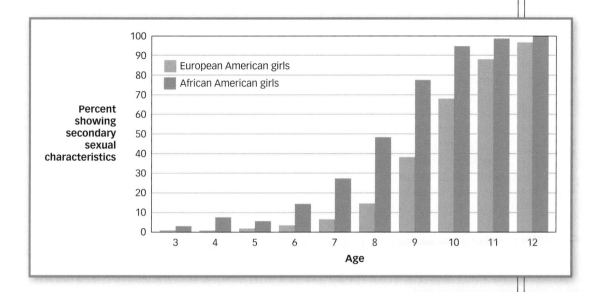

FIGURE **10.8** •
Secondary Sexual Characteristics *The graph shows the percentage of girls in each age group who show breast and/or pubic hair development. These characteristics appear earlier in African American than European American girls. There is no evidence that African American boys mature earlier than European American boys (Herman-Giddens et al., 1997).*

example, both body fat and stress hormones hasten the onset of puberty (Kim & Smith, 1998), and there is reason to suspect that both factors have increased over the last century in the industrialized world.

The increasingly early onset of puberty has important psychological consequences. Just two centuries ago, the gap between childhood and adulthood was relatively brief because people became physically adult at roughly the same time that they were ready to accept adult roles in society. But in modern societies, people typically spend 3 to 10 years in school after they reach puberty. Thus, while the age at which people become physically mature has decreased, the age at which they are recognized by society as adults has increased, and so the period between childhood and adulthood has become extended or *protracted*. What are the consequences of a protracted adolescence?

Adolescence is often characterized as a time of internal turmoil and external recklessness, and some psychologists have speculated that the protraction of adolescence is in part to blame for its bad reputation (Moffitt, 1993). According to these theorists, adolescents are adults who have temporarily been denied a place in adult society. As such, they feel especially compelled to do things to demonstrate their adulthood, such as smoking, drinking, using drugs, having sex, and committing crimes. In a sense, adolescents are people who are forced to live in the gap between two worlds, and the so-called storm and stress of adolescence may be understood in part as a consequence of this dilemma.

● **What does research say about the popular view of stormy adolescence?**
●●●●●●●●●●●●●●●●●●●●●●●●●●●●●●

Although many adolescents experiment • • • • • • • • • • *with various forms of reckless behavior, few continue to behave recklessly as adults.*

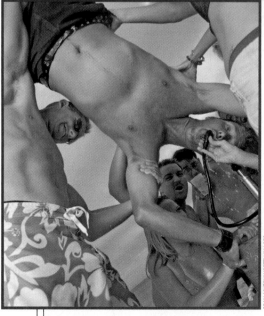

With that said, it is important to note that the storm and stress of adolescence is not quite as intense as all those coming-of-age movies would have us believe (Steinberg & Morris, 2001). Research suggests that the "moody adolescent" who is a victim of "raging hormones" is largely a myth. In fact, adolescents are no moodier than children (Buchanan, Eccles, & Becker, 1992), and fluctuations in their hormone levels have only a tiny impact on their moods (Brooks-Gunn, Graber, & Paikoff, 1994). The common stereotype of adolescents as "reckless rebels" is also more than a little misleading. The vast majority of adolescents do dabble in misbehavior, but their experiments appear to have few long-term consequences, and most adolescents who try drugs or break the law end up becoming sober, law-abiding adults (Steinberg, 1999). In short, adolescence is not a terribly troubled time for most people, and adolescents typically "age out" of the troubles they get themselves into (Sampson & Laub, 1995).

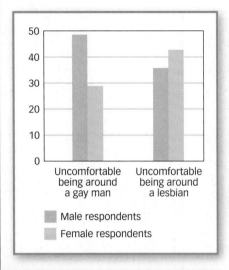

Male respondents

Female respondents

•••••••••••••••••••••• **FIGURE 10.9**

Heterosexuals' Attitudes toward Homosexuals *It isn't surprising that homosexual adolescents are reluctant to reveal their sexual orientations. As a recent public opinion survey shows, a sizable percentage of heterosexual men and women say that they feel "somewhat or very uncomfortable" being around a gay man or a lesbian (Herek, 2002).*

• *Sex education does not increase the likelihood that teenagers will have sex, but it does decrease the likelihood that they will have babies. Teenage mothers and their children fare quite poorly on most measures of success and well-being.*

Sexuality

Puberty is not an easy time for anyone, but it is especially difficult for some. Boys who reach puberty later than their peers often find this period especially stressful because immature boys may be less athletic and may feel less "manly" than their peers (Petersen, 1985). Among girls, those who reach puberty earlier than their peers are most likely to experience a variety of negative consequences, ranging from distress (Peskin, 1973) to delinquency (Caspi & Moffitt, 1991). Early-maturing girls don't have as much time as their peers do to develop the skills necessary to cope with adolescence (Petersen & Grockett, 1985), but because they appear to be mature, others expect them to act like adults. Early-maturing girls also tend to receive attention from older men, who may lead them into a variety of unhealthy activities (Ge, Conger, & Elder, 1996). Some research suggests that the timing of puberty has a greater influence on emotional and behavioral problems than does the occurrence of puberty itself (Buchanan et al., 1992).

For some adolescents, puberty is additionally complicated by the fact that they are attracted to members of the same sex. Not only does this make them different from the majority of their peers, but with few exceptions, human cultures tend to disapprove of homosexual behavior and react to it with responses that range from snickering to beheading (see **FIGURE 10.9**). What determines whether a person is sexually oriented toward the same or the opposite sex? In the past, psychologists believed that a person's sexual orientation depended entirely on his or her upbringing. For example, psychoanalytic theorists suggested that boys who grow up with a domineering mother and a submissive father are less likely to identify with their father and are thereby more likely to become homosexual. However, scientific research has failed to identify *any* aspect of parenting that has a significant impact on sexual orientation (Bell, Weinberg, & Hammersmith, 1981), and indeed, children raised by homosexual couples and heterosexual couples are equally likely to become heterosexual adults (Patterson, 1995). There is also little support for the idea that a person's early sexual encounters have a lasting impact on his or her sexual orientation (Bohan, 1996).

In contrast, considerable evidence suggests that genetics plays a role in determining sexual orientation. Gay men and lesbians tend to have a larger proportion of gay and lesbian siblings than do heterosexuals (Bailey et al., 1999). Furthermore, the identical twin of a gay man (with whom he shares 100% of his genes) has a 50% chance of being gay, whereas the fraternal twin or nontwin brother of a gay man (with whom he shares 50% of his genes) has only a 15% chance (Bailey & Pillard, 1991; Gladue, 1994). A similar pattern has emerged in studies of women (Bailey et al., 1993). In addition, some evidence suggests that the fetal environment may play a role in determining sexual orientation and that high levels of androgens predispose the fetus—whether male or female—later to develop a sexual preference for women (Ellis & Ames, 1987; Meyer-Bahlberg et al., 1995). Although the science of sexual orientation is still young and fraught with conflicting findings, one fact is clear: Sexual orientation is not a simple matter of choice.

● **Is sexual orientation simply a choice people make?**

But *having* sex is a matter of choice, and American teenagers typically choose it. More than 65% of American women report having had sexual intercourse by age 18 and 90% by age 21 (Hogan, Sun, & Cornwell, 2000). Unfortunately, teenagers' interest in sex often surpasses their knowledge about it. A quarter of American teenagers have had four or more sexual partners by their senior year in high school, but only about half report using a condom during their last intercourse (CDC, 2002). The United States has one of the highest rates of teen pregnancy of all modern industrialized nations (Darroch et al., 2001), not because American teens have more sex than others but because they are less knowledgeable about it. Most American parents do not talk to their children extensively about sex (Ansuini, Fiddler-Woite, & Woite, 1996), and those who do start too late (Jaccard, Dittus, & Gordon, 1998). Despite what some people may believe, sex education lowers the likelihood that teenagers will get pregnant or catch a sexually transmitted disease, and does not increase the likelihood that they will have sex in the first place (Satcher, 2001).

Parents and Peers

Adolescents spend a lot of time trying to figure out what they want, what they believe, and what they *should* want and believe. The child's view of herself and her world is tightly tied to the views of her parents, but puberty creates a new set of needs that begins to snip away at these bonds by orienting the adolescent toward peers rather than parents. The psychologist Erik Erikson characterized each stage of life by the major task confronting the individual at that stage, and he suggested that the major task of adolescence was the development of an adult identity (see **TABLE 10.2**). Whereas children define themselves almost entirely in terms of their relationships with parents and siblings, adolescence marks a shift in emphasis from family relations to peer relations.

Two things can make this shift difficult. First, children cannot choose their parents, but adolescents can choose their peers. As such, adolescents have the power to shape themselves by joining groups that will lead them to develop new values, attitudes, beliefs, and perspectives. In a sense, adolescents have the opportunity to invent the adults they will soon become, and the responsibility this opportunity entails can be overwhelming. Second, as adolescents strive for greater autonomy, their parents naturally rebel. For instance, parents and adolescents tend to disagree about the age at which

TABLE 10.2

Erikson's Stages of Human Development

Stage	Ages	Crisis	Key Event	Positive Resolution
1. Oral-sensory	Birth to 12 to 18 months	Trust vs. mistrust	Feeding	Child develops a belief that the environment can be counted on to meet his or her basic physiological and social needs.
2. Muscular-anal	18 months to 3 years	Autonomy vs. shame/doubt	Toilet training	Child learns what he or she can can control and develops a sense of free will and corresponding sense of regret and sorrow for inappropriate use of self-control.
3. Locomotor	3 to 6 years	Initiative vs. guilt	Independence	Child learns to begin action, to explore, to imagine, and to feel remorse for actions.
4. Latency	6 to 12 years	Industry vs. inferiority	School	Child learns to do things well or correctly in comparison to a standard or to others.
5. Adolescence	12 to 18 years	Identity vs. role confusion	Peer relationships	Adolescent develops a sense of self in relationship to others and to own internal thoughts and desires.
6. Young adulthood	19 to 40 years	Intimacy vs isolation	Love relationships	Person develops the ability to give and receive love; begins to make long-term commitment to relationships.
7. Middle adulthood	40 to 65 years	Generativity vs. stagnation	Parenting	Person develops interest in guiding the development of the next generation.
8. Maturity	65 to death	Ego integrity vs. despair	Reflection on and acceptance of one's life	Person develops a sense of acceptance of life as it was lived and the importance of the people and relationships that developed over the life span.

"So I blame you for everything—whose fault is that?"

certain adult behaviors, such as staying out late or having sex, become permissible, and you don't need a psychologist to tell you which position each party tends to hold (Holmbeck & O'Donnell, 1991). Because adolescents and parents often have different ideas about who should control the adolescent's behavior, their relationships may become more conflictive and less close and their interactions briefer and less frequent (Larson & Richards, 1991).

But these conflicts and tensions are not as dramatic, pervasive, and inevitable as movies might lead us to believe. For example, adolescents tend to have aspirations and values that are quite similar to those of their parents (Elder & Conger, 2000). Familial bickering tends to be about much smaller issues, such as dress and language (Caspi et al., 1993). Furthermore, in cultures that emphasize the importance of duty and obligation, parents and adolescents may show few if any signs of tension and conflict (Greenfield et al., 2003).

As adolescents pull away from their parents, they move toward their peers. Studies show that across a wide variety of cultures, historical epochs, and even species, peer relations evolve in a similar way (Dunphy, 1963; Weisfeld, 1999). Young adolescents initially form groups or "cliques" (Brown, Mory, & Kinney, 1994) with others of their own gender. Next, male cliques and female cliques begin to meet in public places, such as town squares or shopping malls, and they begin to interact—but only in groups and only in public. After a few years, the older members of these single-sex cliques "peel off" and form smaller, mixed-sex cliques, which may assemble in private as well as in public but usually assemble as a group. Finally, couples "peel off" from the small mixed-sex clique and begin romantic relationships.

● **What factors contribute to parent-child conflict in adolescence?**

Studies show that throughout adolescence, people spend increasing amounts of time with opposite-sex peers while maintaining the amount of time they spend with same-sex peers (Richards et al., 1998), and they accomplish this by spending less time with their parents (Larson & Richards, 1991). Although peers exert considerable influence on the adolescent's beliefs and behaviors—both for better and for worse—this influence generally occurs because adolescents respect, admire, and like their peers and not because their peers pressure them (Susman et al., 1994). Acceptance by peers is of tremendous importance to adolescents, and those who are rejected by their peers tend to be

● ● ● ● ● ● ● ● *Adolescents form same-sex cliques that meet opposite-sex cliques in public places. Eventually, these people will form mixed-sex cliques, pair off into romantic relationships, get married, and have children who will take their places at the mall.*

withdrawn, lonely, and depressed (Pope & Bierman, 1999). Fortunately for those of us who were seventh-grade nerds, individuals who are unpopular in early adolescence can become popular in later adolescence as their peers become less rigid and more tolerant (Kinney, 1993).

adulthood The stage of development that begins around 18 to 21 years and ends at death.

summary quiz [10.3]

8. Which of the following is a primary sex characteristic?
   a. onset of menstruation
   b. breast enlargement
   c. appearance of pubic hair
   d. lowering of the voice

9. Over the past few generations, the age of onset of puberty has _____, and the age at which young people take on adult responsibilities has _____.
   a. increased; increased
   b. decreased; decreased
   c. decreased; increased
   d. increased; decreased

10. Reaching puberty earlier than one's peers
   a. is especially stressful for boys.
   b. can lead to negative consequences, such as distress and delinquency, in girls.
   c. is beneficial for both girls and boys.
   d. is associated with negative consequences for both girls and boys.

11. Throughout adolescence, young people spend _____ time with other-sex peers, _____ time with same-sex peers, and _____ time with parents.
   a. less; more; more
   b. more; less; the same amount of
   c. more; the same amount of; less
   d. the same amount of; more; less

Adulthood: The Short Happy Future

It takes fewer than 7,000 days for a single-celled zygote to become a registered voter. The speed of this radical transformation is astonishing, but it slows considerably when a person reaches **adulthood**, which is *the stage of development that begins around 18 to 21 years and ends at death.* Because observable physical change slows from a gallop to a crawl, we sometimes have the sense that adulthood is a destination to which development delivers us and that, once we've arrived, our journey is complete. But that's not so. Although they are more gradual and less noticeable, many physical, cognitive, and emotional changes take place between our first legal beer and our last legal breath.

Changing Abilities

The early 20s are the peak years for health, stamina, vigor, and prowess, and because our psychology is so closely tied to our biology, these are also the years during which most of our cognitive abilities are at their sharpest. At this very moment you see further, hear better, remember more, and weigh less than you ever will again. Enjoy it. Somewhere between the ages of 26 and 30, you will begin the slow and steady decline that does not end until you do. A mere 10 or 15 years after puberty, your body will begin to deteriorate

At the annual family reunion, the changes in children are usually more obvious than the changes in adults. But the fact is that development occurs throughout the entire lifespan.

BLEND IMAGES/ALAMY

in almost every way: Your muscles will be replaced by fat, your skin will become less elas-tic, your hair will thin and your bones will weaken, your sensory abilities will become less acute, and your brain cells will die at an accelerated rate. Eventually, if you are a woman, your ovaries will stop producing eggs and you will become infertile; if you are a man, your erections will be fewer and further between.

As these physical changes accumulate, they will begin to have measurable psycho-logical consequences. For instance, as your brain ages, your prefrontal cortex and its associated subcortical connections will deteriorate more quickly than will the other areas of your brain (Raz, 2000). Recall from Chapter 3 that your prefrontal cortex is re-sponsible for *controlled processing*, which means that you will experience the most no-ticeable cognitive decline on tasks that require effort, initiative, or strategy. For example, older adults show a much more pronounced decline on tests of working memory (the ability to hold information "in mind") than on tests of long-term memory (the ability to retrieve information), a much more pronounced decline on tests of episodic memory (the ability to remember particular past events) than on tests of semantic memory (the ability to remember general information such as the meanings of words), and a much more pronounced decline on tests of retrieval (the ability to "go find" information in memory) than on tests of recognition (the ability to decide whether information was encountered before).

And yet, while the cognitive machinery gets rustier with age, research suggests that the operators of that machinery often compensate by using it more skillfully (Bäckman & Dixon, 1992; Salthouse, 1987). Although older chess players *remember* chess positions more poorly than younger players do, they *play* as well as

● **How do we compensate for our aging brains?**

younger players because they search the board more efficiently (Charness, 1981). Although older typists *react* more slowly than younger typists do, they *type* as quickly and accurately as younger typists because they are better at anticipating the next word (Salthouse, 1984). Older airline pilots are considerably worse than younger pilots when it comes to keeping a list of words in short-term memory, but this age difference disappears when those words are the "heading commands" that pilots receive from the control tower every day (Morrow et al., 1994). These patterns of error suggest that older adults are somehow compensating for age-related declines in memory and attention.

How do they do it? When young adults try to keep verbal information in working memory, the left prefrontal cortex is more strongly activated than the right, and when young adults try to keep spatial information in working memory, the right prefrontal cortex is more strongly activated than the left (Smith & Jonides, 1997). But this *bilateral asymmetry* is not seen among older adults, and some scientists take this to mean that

● Although young chess players can remember the positions of pieces better than older players can, older players search the board more efficiently.

IMAGESBAZAAR

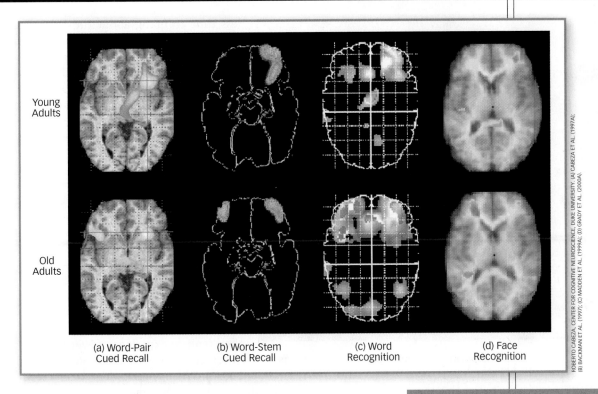

Young
Adults

Old
Adults

(a) Word-Pair
Cued Recall

(b) Word-Stem
Cued Recall

(c) Word
Recognition

(d) Face
Recognition

older brains compensate for the declining abilities of one neural structure by calling on other neural structures to help out (Cabeza, 2002; see **FIGURE 10.10**). The young brain can be characterized as a group of specialists, but as these specialists becomes older and less able, they begin to work together on tasks that each once handled independently. In short, the machinery of body and brain do break down with age, but a seasoned driver in an old jalopy can often hold his own against a rookie in a hot rod.

Changing Orientations

One reason why Grandpa can't find his car keys is that his prefrontal cortex doesn't function like it used to. But another reason is that the location of car keys just isn't the sort of thing that grandpas spend their precious time memorizing. According to *socioemotional selectivity theory* (Carstensen & Turk-Charles, 1994), younger adults are generally oriented toward the acquisition of information that will be useful to them in the future (e.g., reading the newspaper), whereas older adults are generally oriented toward information that brings emotional satisfaction in the present (e.g., reading novels). Because

young people have such long futures, they *invest* their time attending to, thinking about, and remembering potentially *useful information* that may serve them well in the many days to come. But older people have shorter futures and so they *spend* their time attending to, thinking about, and remembering *positive information* that serves them well in the moment (see **FIGURE 10.11**). Interestingly, this basic change in orientation toward information also occurs among younger people whose futures are sadly shortened by terminal illness (Carstensen & Fredrickson, 1998). Although people spend

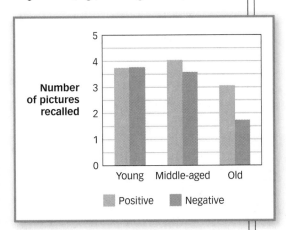

FIGURE 10.10
Bilaterality in Older and Younger Brains *Across a variety of tasks, older adult brains show bilateral activation, and young adult brains show unilateral activation. One possible explanation for this is that older brains compensate for the declining abilities of one neural structure by calling on other neural structures for help (Cabeza, 2002).*

FIGURE 10.11
Memory for Pictures *Memory declines with age in general, but the ability to remember negative information such as unpleasant pictures declines much more quickly than the ability to remember positive information (Carstensen et al., 2000).*

● As people age, they prefer to spend time with family and a few close friends rather than large circles of acquaintances. Some grandfathers will even dress like ducks to impress important members of their small social networks.

DANIEL GILBERT

less time thinking about the future as they age, they do not spend more time thinking about the past (Carstensen, Isaacowitz, & Charles, 1999). Rather, they spend more time thinking about the present.

This change in older people's orientation toward information influences much more than memory. Not only are older adults less likely than younger adults to attend to or remember negative information, but they are also less likely to be emotionally influenced by it. Whereas younger adults show activation of the amygdala when they see both pleasant and unpleasant pictures, older adults show greater activation when they see pleasant pictures than when they see unpleasant pictures (Mather et al., 2004). Studies also reveal that as people age, they tend to experience fewer negative emotions and more complex emotions (Carstensen et al., 2000; Charles, Reynolds, & Gatz, 2001; Mroczek & Spiro, 2005; see **FIGURE 10.12**). What's more, older people seem better able than younger people to sustain their positive emotional experiences and to curtail their negative ones (Lawton et al., 1992).

These changes influence the activities in which older people choose to engage. Psychologists have long known that social networks get smaller as people age, and they have assumed that this happens because friends die at an accelerating rate. Some of this shrinkage is indeed due to loss, but it now appears that much of it is a matter of choice: in general, older adults become more selective about their interaction partners, choosing to spend time

● **Why are older people generally happier than younger people?**

with family and a few close friends rather than with a large circle of acquaintances. A study of older adults who ranged in age from 69 to 104 found that the oldest adults had fewer peripheral social partners than the younger adults did, but they had just as many emotionally close partners whom they identified as member of their "inner circle" (Lang & Carstensen, 1994).

Together, these changes tend to produce emotional satisfaction. In one survey, 38% of people over 65 described themselves

● **FIGURE 10.12**

Happiness and Age *Despite what our youth-oriented culture would have you believe, people's overall happiness generally increases with age. As this graph shows, people experience a small decrease in positive affect beginning around age 55, but this is more than compensated for by the large decrease in negative affect that begins around the age of 15 and continues through middle age (Charles et al., 2001).*

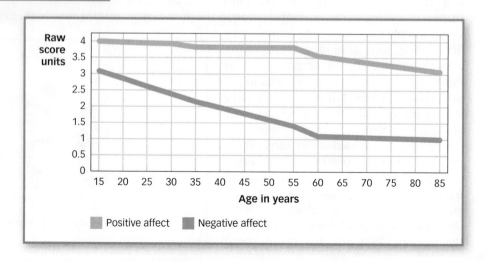

as very happy, but only 28% of 18- to 29-year-olds said the same (Pew Research Center for the People & the Press, 1997). Although Western culture values youth (which is why Westerners spend billions of dollars every year trying appear younger than they are), research suggests that one of the best ways to increase one's share of happiness in life is simply to get older. The machinery may not work as well, but the passengers seem to enjoy the ride more.

Changing Roles

The psychological separation from parents that begins in adolescence becomes a physical separation in adulthood. In virtually all human societies, young adults eventually leave their parents' home, get married, and have children of their own. Marriage and parenthood are two of the most significant aspects of adult life, and most people experience both of them. The average college-aged American will get married around the age of 27, have approximately 1.8 children, and consider their marriage and children to be their greatest sources of happiness. Indeed, in one survey, a whopping 93% of American mothers said that their children were a source of happiness all or most of the time (Pew Research Center, 1997).

But do marriage and children really make us happy? Research has consistently shown that married people live longer (see **FIGURE 10.13**), have more frequent sex (and enjoy that sex more), and earn several times as much money as unmarried people do (Waite, 1995). Given these differences, it is no surprise that married people report being happier than unmarried people—whether those unmarried people are single, widowed, divorced, or

"Two Stones tickets, please, senior discount."

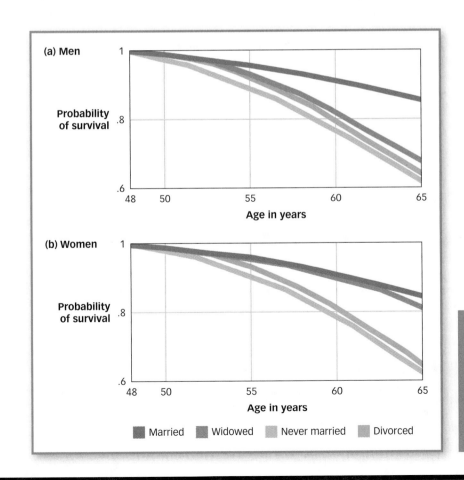

cohabiting (Johnson & Wu, 2002). But some researchers suggest that married people may be happier because happy people may be more likely to get married and that marriage may be the consequence—and not the cause—of happiness (Lucas et al., 2003). The general consensus among scientists seems to be that both of these positions are right: Even before marriage, people who end up married tend to be happier than those who never marry, but marriage does seem to confer further benefits.

Children are another story. In general, research suggests that children slightly decrease rather than increase their parents' happiness (DiTella, MacCulloch, & Oswald, 2003). For example, parents typically report lower marital satisfaction than do nonparents—and the more children they have, the less satisfaction they report (Twenge, Campbell, & Foster, 2003). Studies of marital satisfaction at different points in the life span reveal an interesting pattern of peaks and valleys: Marital satisfaction starts out high, plummets at about the time that the children are in diapers, begins to recover, plummets again when the children are in adolescence, and returns to its premarital levels only when children leave home (see **FIGURE 10.14**). A study that measured the moment-to-moment happiness of American women as they went about their daily activities found that women were less happy when taking care of their children than when eating, exercising, shopping, napping, or watching television and only slightly happier than when they were doing housework (Kahneman et al., 2004). *Thinking* about children is a delight, but *raising* children is hard work. Perhaps that's why when women in a national survey were asked to name a mother's most important quality, mothers of grown children were most likely to name "love," whereas mothers of young children were most likely to name "patience" (Pew Research Center, 1997).

● **Are children really bundles of joy?**

Does all of this mean that people would be happier if they didn't have children? Not necessarily. Because researchers cannot randomly assign people to be parents or nonparents, studies of the effects of parenthood are necessarily correlational. People who want children and have children may be somewhat less happy than people who neither want them nor have them, but it is possible that people who want children would be even less happy if they didn't have them. What seems clear is that raising children is a challenging job that most people find to be meaningful and rewarding—especially when it's over.

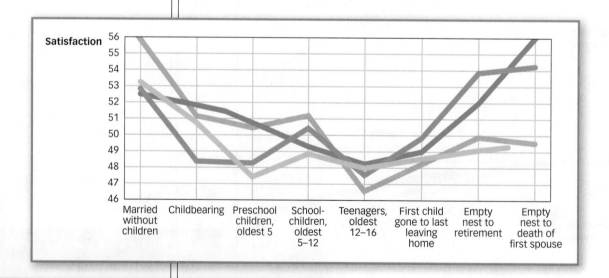

FIGURE 10.14

Marital Satisfaction over the Life Span *This graph shows the results of four independent studies of marital satisfaction among men and women. All four studies suggest that marital satisfaction is highest before children are born and after they leave home (Walker, 1977).*

summary quiz [10.4]

12. The peak years for health, stamina, and vigor are the
   a. early 20s.
   b. late 20s.
   c. early 30s.
   d. late 30s.

13. According to socioemotional selectivity theory, older adults are
   a. more likely to remember negative information than positive information.
   b. more likely than young adults to seek potentially useful information.
   c. less likely than young adults to seek emotionally satisfying information.
   d. increasingly likely to think about the present.

14. Which is true of marital satisfaction over the life span?
   a. It increases steadily.
   b. It decreases steadily.
   c. It is remarkably stable.
   d. It shows peaks and valleys, corresponding to the presence and ages of children.

WhereDoYouStand?

Licensing Parents

Common law states that "when practice of a profession or calling requires special knowledge or skill and intimately affects public health, morals, order or safety, or general welfare, legislature may prescribe reasonable qualifications for persons desiring to pursue such professions or calling and require them to demonstrate possession of such qualifications by examination." Most of us would probably agree that this is reasonable and that people who want to operate automobiles, use firearms, pilot airplanes, or perform surgeries should be required to demonstrate their proficiency and obtain a license. After all, if people were allowed to practice law or build bridges without first demonstrating their knowledge and skill, the public welfare would be gravely compromised.

So why not apply this logic to parenting? Why not outlaw reproduction by citizens who can't qualify for a parenting license? Because this suggestion sounds so outrageous, you may be surprised to learn that it has become the subject of serious debate among ethicists who are trying to decide how best to balance the interests of parents against the damage that bad parenting can do (Tittle, 2004; Warnock, 2003). The arguments *against* parental licensing are all too obvious: People have a fundamental right to reproduce; people have different definitions of "good parenting"; a licensing system would invite abuse by governments that want to limit the reproduction of citizens who have the wrong genes, the wrong skin color, or the wrong political beliefs. Americans are naturally suspicious of governmental intrusion into private affairs, and what could be more private than the decision to have a child?

For most people, parental licensing is a ridiculous and dangerous idea. And yet some of the arguments in its favor are not easily dismissed. Consider a few:

- Bad flossing is a private affair. Bad parenting is not. Every one of us pays the price when parents abuse, neglect, or fail to educate their children. Bad parents impose significant social and economic burdens on the rest of society—not to mention on their own children. Society has a clear interest in *preventing* (and not just punishing) abusive and negligent parenting.

- Licensing is not meant to prevent potentially bad parents from having children; it is meant to make potentially bad parents into good ones. Driver's education turns potentially bad drivers into good ones, but most people wouldn't sign up for such training if they didn't have to do so in order to qualify for a driver's license. Parental licensing would motivate people to learn the things that every parent should know.

- If we demand that people meet certain standards before they are allowed to *adopt* children, then why should we not demand that they meet the same standards before being allowed to bear children? Are our biological children worth less than our adopted ones?

Anyone who has read George Orwell's *1984* or Aldous Huxley's *Brave New World* will find the notion of parental licensing more than a little frightening. And yet, bad parenting can have devastating consequences for children and for society. Is parental licensing the right solution, or is it a bad answer to a good question? Where do you stand?

CHAPTER REVIEW

Summary

Prenatality: A Womb with a View

- Developmental psychology studies continuity and change across the life span.

- During the prenatal stage of development, a fertilized egg (zygote) develops into an embryo and then a fetus.

- The environment has important physical and psychological influences on the fetus.

Infancy and Childhood: Becoming a Person

- Infants slowly develop perceptual and motor skills that allow them to start to develop theories about how the world works.

- Piaget proposed that a child's cognitive development occurs in four stages: the sensorimotor stage, the preoperational stage, the concrete operational stage, and the formal operational stage.

- Cognitive development also reflects social development, as children form attachments to caregivers and are given tools for understanding that have been developed by their cultures.

- Humans also develop moral principles; Piaget conceived the development of moral thinking as a shift from realism to relativism, from prescriptions to principles, and from consequences to principles. Kohlberg conceived the development of moral reasoning as occurring in three stages: the preconventional stage, the conventional stage, and the postconventional stage; later researchers have noted that moral behavior depends on feeling as much as on abstract reasoning.

Adolescence: Minding the Gap

- Adolescence, the stage between childhood and adulthood, begins with the onset of puberty.

- Puberty is occurring earlier than ever before, while the entrance of young people into adult society is occurring later.

- During puberty, sexual interest intensifies and, in some cultures, sexual activity begins.

- As adolescents seek to develop their adult identities, they seek increasing autonomy from their parents and become more peer oriented.

Adulthood: The Short Happy Future

- Gradual physical decline begins early in adulthood.

- Older adults show declines in working memory, episodic memory, and retrieval tasks, but they often develop strategies to compensate.

- Older people are more oriented toward emotionally satisfying information, which influences their basic cognitive performance, the size and structure of their social networks, and their general happiness.

- People who get married are typically happier than people who do not, but children and the responsibilities that parenthood entails present a significant challenge.

Key Terms

developmental psychology (p. 298)

zygote (p. 299)

germinal stage (p. 299)

embryonic stage (p. 299)

fetal stage (p. 299)

myelination (p. 299)

teratogens (p. 300)

fetal alcohol syndrome (p. 300)

infancy (p. 301)

motor development (p. 302)

reflexes (p. 302)

cephalocaudal rule (p. 302)

proximodistal rule (p. 302)

cognitive development (p. 303)

sensorimotor stage (p. 304)

schemas (p. 304)

assimilation (p. 304)

accommodation (p. 304)

object permanence (p. 304)

childhood (p. 305)

preoperational stage (p. 305)

concrete operational stage (p. 305)

conservation (p. 305)

formal operational stage (p. 306)

egocentrism (p. 306)

theory of mind (p. 307)

attachment (p. 312)

internal working model of attachment (p. 312–313)

temperaments (p. 313)

preconventional stage (p. 315)

conventional stage (p. 315)

postconventional stage (p. 315)

adolescence (p. 318)

puberty (p. 318)

primary sex characteristics (p. 318)

secondary sex characteristics (p. 318)

adulthood (p. 323)

Critical Thinking Questions

1. Perceptual and motor development tend to obey the proximodistal rule, meaning that motor skills tend to emerge in sequence from center to periphery. Piaget proposed that cognitive development also passes through stages.

    Might the stages of cognitive development be thought of as also following a proximodistal rule?

2. Adolescence is a period of transition, as the body reaches sexual maturity and the individual prepares to take an adult role in society. In modern industrialized societies, puberty is coming earlier than ever before, while the entry into adult roles is delayed.

    In what ways might the protraction of adolescence influence the rates of teenage sexual activity and teenage pregnancy?

3. As we age, portions of our brain deteriorate and cognitive function may decline, but older adults can often compensate by recruiting additional brain areas to help. Also as we age, we are more likely to experience and remember positive emotions than negative ones.

    Could this emotional selectivity be a side effect of cognitive decline? Or might it be a compensation mechanism?

Answers to Summary Quizzes

Summary Quiz 10.1
1. d; 2. d; 3. a

Summary Quiz 10.2
4. c; 5. d; 6. a; 7. d

Summary Quiz 10.3
8. a; 9. c; 10. b; 11. c

Summary Quiz 10.4
12. a; 13. d; 14. d

Need more help? Additional resources are located at the book's free companion Web site at:
www.worthpublishers.com/schacterbrief1e

Personality

AMY WINEHOUSE IS A SINGER known for her personality. Her music has personality, yes—a bluesy, boozy, contralto that seems carefully composed to sound as though she doesn't care. The songs she chooses have personality, too, like the memorable "Rehab" ("They tried to make me go to rehab, I said 'No, no, no'"). Her life, at least as it's portrayed in gossip magazines and websites, is an expression of personality as well. If you believe all you read, she's had boyfriend troubles, drug troubles, drinking troubles, family troubles, international diplomacy troubles, and more. On top of all that, she's collected enough bad tattoos to rival the Sunday comics. How much of this is real and how much is a show we don't know. But she's one of a kind. Amy Winehouse has personality in an important sense—she has qualities that make her psychologically different from other people. ■

Personality is *an individual's characteristic style of behaving, thinking, and feeling.* Winehouse's personal troubles, her melodramatic styles of song and life, her way of drawing attention to herself by embracing things others might call tacky, are all parts of her personality. In this chapter, we will explore personality, first by looking at what it is and how it is measured and then by focusing on each of four main approaches to understanding personality—trait-biological, psychodynamic, humanistic-existential, and social cognitive. (Psychologists have personalities, too, so their different approaches, even to the topic of personality, shouldn't be that surprising.) At the end of the chapter, we will discuss the psychology of self to see how our views of what we are like can shape and define our personality.

Singer Amy Winehouse arrives at the MTV Movie Awards in Los Angeles, 2007.

AP PHOTO/KEVORK DJANSEZIAN

Personality: What It Is and How It Is Measured

If someone said, "You have no personality," how would you feel? Like a cookie-cutter person, a grayish lump, probably a bore to boot, who should go out and get a personality as soon as possible? People don't usually strive for a personality; one seems to develop naturally as we travel through life. As psychologists have tried to understand the process of personality development, they have pondered questions of description (How do people differ?), explanation (Why do people differ?), and the more quantitative question of measurement (How can personality be assessed?).

Describing and Explaining Personality

Like early biology studies, the descriptive aspect of personality psychology is taxonomic in approach. The first biologists earnestly attempted to classify all plants and animals—whether lichens or ants or fossilized skunks. Similarly, personality psychologists began by labeling and describing different personalities. And just as biology came of age with Darwin's theory of evolution, which *explained* how differences among species arose, the maturing study of personality has also developed explanations of the basis for psychological differences among people.

● **What does it mean to say that personality is in the eye of the beholder?**

Most personality psychologists focus on specific, psychologically meaningful individual differences—characteristics such as honesty or anxiousness or moodiness. Still, personality is often in the eye of the beholder. There is usually a high degree of similarity among any one individual's descriptions of many different people ("Jason thinks that Bob is considerate, Jeff is kind, and Gina is nice to others"). In contrast, resemblance is quite low when many people describe one person ("Bob thinks Jason is smart, Jeff thinks he is competitive, and Gina thinks he has a good sense of humor") (Dornbusch et al., 1965). As you will see, theorists also differ in their views on the characteristics of personality worth describing.

In general, explanations of personality differences are concerned with (1) *prior events* that can shape an individual's personality or (2) *anticipated events* that might motivate the person to reveal particular personality characteristics. Thus, on the one hand, Amy

● *How would you describe each of these personalities?*

ZUMA PRESS/NEWSCOM

BETTMANN/CORBIS

Winehouse's genes and prior experiences may have led her to a life of problem behavior; on the other hand, she expected to find happiness in drugs and alcohol, and those motives also might explain her behavior. Understanding the puzzle that is Winehouse's life—or the life of any ordinary woman or man—also depends on insights into the interaction between the past and future. Personality psychologists study questions of how our personalities are determined by the forces in our minds and in our personal history of heredity and environment, and by the choices we make and the goals we seek.

Measuring Personality

Of all the things psychologists have set out to measure, personality must be one of the toughest. How do you capture the uniqueness of a person—like a moonbeam in a jar? Different traditions have tended to favor different measurement techniques. The general personality measures can be classified broadly into personality inventories and projective techniques.

Personality Inventories

To learn about an individual's personality, you could follow the person around and, clipboard in hand, record every single thing the person does, says, thinks, and feels—including how long this goes on before the person calls the police. Some observations might involve your own impressions ("Day 5: seems to be getting irritable"); others would involve objectively observable events that anyone could verify ("Day 7: grabbed my pencil and broke it in half, then bit my hand").

Psychologists have figured out ways to obtain objective data on personality without driving their subjects to distraction. The most popular technique is the **self-report**—*a series of answers to a questionnaire that asks people to indicate the extent to which sets of statements or adjectives accurately describe their own behavior or mental state*. The respondent typically produces a self-description by circling a number on a scale or indicating whether an item is true or false. The researcher then combines the answers to get a general sense of the individual's personality with respect to a particular domain.

Perhaps the best-known self-report measure is the **Minnesota Multiphasic Personality Inventory (MMPI)**, *a well-researched clinical questionnaire used to assess personality and psychological problems*. The MMPI consists of more than 500 descriptive statements—for example, "I often feel like breaking things," "I think the world is a dangerous place," and "I'm good at socializing"—to which the respondent answers "true," "false," or "cannot say," depending on whether the item applies to him or her. Its 10 main subscales measure different personality characteristics which are thought to represent personality difficulties when demonstrated to an extreme degree (Hathaway & McKinley, 1951). Like many early psychological tests, the original items were generated by studying how specific groups of people, as compared to the general population, completed a variety of items and then creating the scales from the items that these groups answered differently.

In addition to assessing tendencies toward clinical problems—for example, depression, hypochondria, anxiety, paranoia, and unconventional ideas or bizarre thoughts and beliefs—the MMPI measures some relatively general personality characteristics, such as degree of masculine and feminine gender role identification, sociability versus social inhibition, and impulsivity. The MMPI also includes *validity scales* that assess a person's attitudes toward test taking and any tendency to try to distort the results by faking answers.

● **What are some limitations of personality inventories?**

Personality inventories such as the MMPI are easy to administer: Just give someone a pencil and away they go. The person's scores can be calculated by a computer and compared with the average ratings of thousands of other test takers. Because no interpretation of the responses is needed, biases are minimized. Of course, an accurate reading of personality will only occur if people provide honest responses—especially about characteristics that might be

personality An individual's characteristic style of behaving, thinking, and feeling.

self-report A series of answers to a questionnaire that asks people to indicate the extent to which sets of statements or adjectives accurately describe their own behavior or mental state.

Minnesota Multiphasic Personality Inventory (MMPI) A well-researched clinical questionnaire used to assess personality and psychological problems.

projective techniques A standard series of ambiguous stimuli designed to elicit unique responses that reveal inner aspects of an individual's personality.

Rorschach Inkblot Test A projective personality test in which individual interpretations of the meaning of a set of unstructured inkblots are analyzed to identify a respondent's inner feelings and interpret his or her personality structure.

Thematic Apperception Test (TAT) A projective personality test in which respondents reveal underlying motives, concerns, and the way they see the social world through the stories they make up about ambiguous pictures of people.

unflattering—and if they don't always agree or always disagree—a phenomenon known as *response style*. The validity scales help detect these problems but cannot take them away altogether.

Another drawback is related to the actual characteristics being measured. Certain personality factors may function largely outside consciousness, and so asking people to tell us about them makes little sense. (For example, would someone know if he or she were conceited?) Despite potential drawbacks, however, personality inventories remain an efficient and effective means of testing, classifying, and researching a wide range of personality characteristics.

Projective Techniques

The second major class of tools for evaluating personality, the **projective techniques**, consist of *a standard series of ambiguous stimuli designed to elicit unique responses that reveal inner aspects of an individual's personality.* The developers of projective tests assumed that people will project personality factors that are out of awareness—wishes, concerns, impulses, and ways of seeing the world—onto ambiguous stimuli and will not censor these responses. As an example of such projection, consider the game of cloud watching. If you and a friend were looking at the sky one day and she suddenly became seriously upset because one cloud looked to her like a flesh-eating monster, her response would reveal a lot more about her inner conflicts than her explicit answer to a direct question about the kind of things that frighten her.

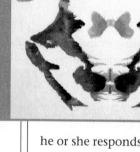

• **FIGURE 11.1**
Sample Rorschach Inkblot *Test takers are shown a card such as this sample and asked, "What might this be?" What they perceive, where they see it, and why it looks that way are assumed to reflect unconscious aspects of their personality. (Behn-Rorschach Test, Verlag Hans Huber, Bern, Switzerland, 1941.)*

Probably the best-known and mostly widely used technique is the **Rorschach Inkblot Test**, *a projective personality test in which individual interpretations of the meaning of a set of unstructured inkblots are analyzed to identify a respondent's inner feelings and interpret his or her personality structure.* An example inkblot is shown in **FIGURE 11.1**. Responses are scored according to complicated systems (derived in part from research with patients) that classify *what* is seen (content), *where* it is seen (location), and *why* it is seen that way (determinants). For example, most people who look at **FIGURE 11.1** report seeing birds or people. Someone who is unable to see obvious items when he or she responds to a blot may be described as having difficulty perceiving the world as others do and as seeing things according to his or her unique perspective (Exner, 1993; Rapaport, 1946).

Can psychologists using the Rorschach test discover aspects of personality that are usually hidden, even from the person taking the test? Critics argue that although the Rorschach captures some of the more complex and private aspects of personality, the test is open to the subjective interpretation and theoretic biases of the examiner. In fact, to have value, a test of personality should permit prediction of a person's behavior, but evidence is sparse that Rorschach test scores have such predictive value (Dawes, 1994; Fowler, 1985; Wood, Nezworski, & Stejskal, 1996; Wood et al., 2003). Many psychologists still use the technique, but it is losing its popularity (Garb, 1999; Widiger, 2001).

Another widely used test is the **Thematic Apperception Test (TAT)**, *a projective personality test in which respondents reveal underlying motives, concerns, and the way they see the social world through the stories they make up about ambiguous pictures of people.* To get a sense of the test, look at **FIGURE 11.2** on page 337. Who are those people, and what are they doing and thinking? What led them to this moment, and what will happen next? Different people tell very different stories about this image. In creating the stories, the test taker is thought to identify with the main characters and to project his or her view of others and the world onto the other details in the drawing. Psychologists who use the TAT look for repeated themes and their relationship across a large number of cards, typically 10.

ONLY HUMAN

RORSCHACH TEST WITH TOMATO SAUCE? In March 1991, motorists in Stone Mountain, Georgia, reported seeing the image of Christ in a forkful of spaghetti on a Pizza Hut billboard. One woman said the image caused her to abandon plans to quit her church choir.

Many of the TAT drawings tend to elicit a consistent set of themes, such as successes and failures, competition and jealousy, conflict with parents and siblings, feelings about intimate relationships, aggression and sexuality. The sample card shown in **FIGURE 11.2** tends to elicit themes regarding mother-daughter relationships, aging, and concerns regarding femininity and women's roles (Murray, 1943). Here is one young woman's response to the

● **Why might a projective test like the TAT story be less than reliable?**

drawing—one that seems to reveal her own personal internal situation and a conflict between her wish for independence and fear that this is wrong and is punishable by a tragic loss: "The old lady in the background seems angry and thinks the younger one is making a big mistake. Maybe they're related. . . . Everything the young woman does is wrong in her mother's eyes. The daughter just wants to get away and live her own life but is too guilty to leave her mother's side, thinking it will hurt her. In the end, hmm? The girl does leave and the mother dies."

Projective tests remain controversial in psychology. Critics argue that such tests are open to the subjective interpretation and theoretic biases of the examiner. Although a TAT story like the above may *seem* revealing, the examiner must always add an interpretation (was this about the client's actual mother, about her own conflicted desires for independence, about trying to be funny or creative or oddball?), and that interpretation could well be the scorer's *own* projection into the mind of the test taker. Thus, despite the rich picture of a personality and the insights into an individual's motives that these tests offer, projective tests should be understood primarily as a way in which a psychologist can get to know someone personally and intuitively (McClelland et al., 1953). When measured by rigorous scientific criteria, the TAT, like the Rorschach and other projective tests, has not been found to be reliable or valid in predicting behavior (Lilienfeld, Lynn, & Lohr, 2003).

FIGURE 11.2 ● ● ● ● ● ● ● ● ● ● ● ● ● ● ● ● ●

Sample TAT Card *Test takers are shown cards with ambiguous scenes such as this sample and are asked to tell a story about what is happening in the picture. The main themes of the story, the thoughts and feelings of the characters, and how the story develops and resolves are considered useful indices of unconscious aspects of an individual's personality (Murray, 1943).*

summary quiz [11.1]

1. Which of the following is *not* a drawback of self-report personality measures such as the MMPI?
   a. People may respond in ways that put themselves in a flattering light.
   b. Some people tend to always agree or always disagree with the statements on the test.
   c. Responses do not need to be interpreted.
   d. People are unaware of some of their personality characteristics and thus cannot answer accurately.

2. Rorschach tests are losing popularity because
   a. there is little evidence that they have predictive value.
   b. personality factors may function outside of consciousness.
   c. their results are scored by computers.
   d. projective techniques have become more popular.

3. Which of the following is an accurate statement about projective techniques?
   a. They are easy to administer and score.
   b. They are open to subjective interpretation by the examiner.
   c. The method of scoring eliminates theoretical biases of the examiner.
   d. They are the most reliable and valid of the personality tests.

The Trait Approach: Identifying Patterns of Behavior

Imagine writing a story about the people you know. To capture their special qualities, you might describe their traits: Lulu is *friendly, aggressive,* and *domineering;* Seth is *flaky, humorous,* and *superficial.* The trait approach to personality uses such trait terms to characterize differences among individuals. In attempting to create manageable and meaningful sets of descriptors, trait theorists face two significant challenges: narrowing down the almost infinite set of adjectives, and answering the more basic question of why people have particular traits—whether they arise from biological or hereditary foundations.

Traits as Behavioral Dispositions and Motives

Gordon Allport (1937), one of the first trait theorists, proposed that personality can best be understood as a combination of traits. A **trait** is *a relatively stable disposition to behave in a particular and consistent way.* For example, a person who keeps his books organized alphabetically in bookshelves, hangs his clothing neatly in the closet, knows the schedule for the local bus, keeps a clear agenda in a daily planner, and lists birthdays of friends and family in his calendar can be said to have the trait of *orderliness.* This trait consistently manifests itself in a variety of settings.

The "orderliness" trait, of course, describes a person but doesn't explain his or her behavior. *Why* does the person behave in this way? There are two basic ways in which a trait might serve as an explanation—the trait may be a preexisting disposition of the person that causes the person's behavior, or it may be a motivation that guides the person's behavior. Allport saw traits as preexisting dispositions, causes of behavior that reliably trigger the behavior. The person's orderliness, for example, is an inner property of the person that will cause the person to straighten things up and be tidy in a wide array of situations.

● **How might traits both describe people and explain their behavior?**

Henry Murray, a trait theorist interested in motivation, suggested instead that traits reflect needs or desires. Just as a hunger motive might explain someone's many trips to the snack bar, a need for orderliness might explain the neat closet, organized calendar, and familiarity with the bus schedule (Murray & Kluckhohn, 1953). As a rule, researchers examining traits as causes have used personality inventories to measure them, whereas those examining traits as motives have more often used projective tests.

● *A closet isn't just a place for clothes. In some cases, it's a personality test.*

COURTESY MICHIGAN SHELF DISTRIBUTORS, INC.

MICHAEL NEWMAN/PHOTOEDIT

The Search for Core Traits

Picking a single trait such as orderliness and studying it in depth doesn't get us very far in the search for the core of human character—for the basic set of traits that define how humans differ from one another. How have researchers tried to discover such core traits?

Classification Using Language

The study of core traits began with an exploration of how personality is represented in the store of wisdom we call language. Generation after generation, people have described people with words, so early psychologists proposed that core traits could be discerned by finding the main themes in all the adjectives used to describe personality. In one such analysis, a painstaking count of relevant words in a dictionary of English resulted in a list of over 18,000 potential traits (Allport & Odbert, 1936)!

Although narrowing down such a list isn't too difficult because so many words are synonyms—for example, *giving, generous,* and *bighearted* all mean more or less the same thing—the process is too subjective to permit development of a true set of core of traits. Just looking at traitlike words that seemed to represent motives, for instance, led Murray (1938) to propose over 40 basic motivations in addition to the need for orderliness.

More recently, researchers have used the computational procedure called *factor analysis,* described in Chapter 7, which sorts trait terms into a small number of underlying dimensions, or "factors," based on how people use the traits to rate themselves. In a typical study using factor analysis, hundreds of people rate themselves on hundreds of adjectives, indicating how accurately each one describes their personality. The researcher then calculates the patterns to determine similarities in the raters' usage—whether, for example, people who describe themselves as *responsible* also describe themselves as *careful* but not *negligent* or *careless*. Factor analysis can also reveal which adjectives are unrelated. For example, if people who describe themselves as *responsible* are neither more nor less likely to describe themselves as *creative* or *innovative,* the factor analysis would reveal that responsibility and creativity/innovation represent different factors.

Using the factor analysis technique, Hans Eysenck (1967) developed a model of personality with only two (later expanded to three) major traits. He identified one dimension that distinguished people who are sociable and active (extraverts) from those who are relatively introspective and quiet (introverts). His analysis also identified a second dimension ranging from the tendency to be very neurotic or emotionally unstable to the tendency to be more emotionally stable. He believed that many behavioral tendencies could be understood in terms of their relation to these core traits. **FIGURE 11.3** suggests that these two dimensions may not be an oversimplified view; the two central dimensions seem to capture a much larger number of specific traits.

The Big Five Dimensions of Personality

Today many factor analysis researchers agree that personality is best captured by five factors (John & Srivastava, 1999; McCrae & Costa, 1999). The **Big Five,** as they are affectionately called, are *the traits of the five-factor model: conscientiousness, agreeableness, neuroticism, openness to experience,* and *extraversion* (see **TABLE 11.1**). The five-factor model is now widely preferred for several reasons. First, modern factor analysis techniques confirm that this set of five factors strikes the right balance between accounting for as much variation in personality as possible while avoiding overlapping traits. Second, in a large number of studies using different kinds of data—people's descriptions of their own personalities, other people's descriptions of their personalities, interviewer checklists, and behavioral observation—the same five factors

trait A relatively stable disposition to behave in a particular and consistent way.

Big Five The traits of the five-factor model: conscientiousness, agreeableness, neuroticism, openness to experience, and extroversion.

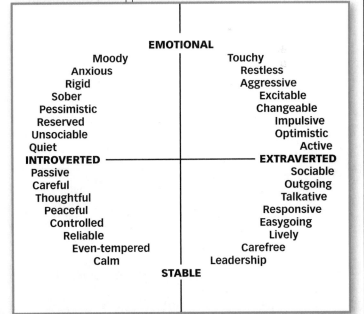

FIGURE 11.3 • • • • • • • • • • • • • • • •
Eysenck's Depiction of Trait Dimensions *The trait dimensions shown here can be combined to describe a great deal of the variability in human personality. If you look at the adjectives between any two of the four possible points on the grid, you'll see a interesting range of possible surface characteristics (Eysenck & Eysenck, 1985).*

TABLE 11.1

The Big Five Factor Model

Conscientiousness	organized . . . . disorganized
	careful . . . . careless
	self-disciplined . . . . weak-willed
Agreeableness	softhearted . . . . ruthless
	trusting . . . . suspicious
	helpful . . . . uncooperative
Neuroticism	worried . . . . calm
	insecure . . . . secure
	self-pitying . . . . self-satisfied
Openness to experience	imaginative . . . . down-to-earth
	variety . . . . routine
	independent . . . . conforming
Extraversion	social . . . . retiring
	fun loving . . . . sober
	affectionate . . . . reserved

Source: McCrae & Costa, 1999, 1990.

have emerged. Third, and perhaps most important, the basic five-factor structure seems to show up across a wide range of participants, including children, adults in other cultures, and even among those who use other languages, suggesting that the Big Five may be universal (John & Srivastava, 1999).

Research on the Big Five has shown that people's personalities tend to remain stable through their lifetime, scores at one time in life correlating strongly with scores at later dates, even later decades (Caspi, Roberts, & Shiner, 2005). Some variability is typical in childhood, with less in adolescence and then greater stability in adulthood. As William James put it: "It is well for the world that in most of us, by the age of thirty, the character has set like plaster, and will never soften again" (James, 1890, p. 121).

● **What are the strengths of the five-factor model?**

Traits as Biological Building Blocks

Can we explain *why* a person has a stable set of personality traits? On the one hand, many trait theorists have argued that immutable brain and biological processes produce the remarkable stability of traits over the life span.

On the other hand, brain damage certainly can produce personality change, as the classic case of Phineas Gage so vividly demonstrates (see Chapter 3). You may recall that after the blasting accident that blew a steel rod through his frontal lobes, Gage showed a dramatic loss of social appropriateness and conscientiousness (Damasio, 1994). In fact, when someone experiences a profound change in personality, testing often reveals the presence of such brain pathologies as Alzheimer's disease, stroke, or brain tumor (Feinberg, 2001). The administration of antidepressant medication and other pharmaceutical treatments that change brain chemistry can also trigger personality changes, making people, for example, somewhat more extraverted and less neurotic (Bagby et al., 1999; Knutson et al., 1998).

Genes, Traits, and Personality

Some of the most compelling evidence for the importance of biological factors in personality comes from the domain of behavioral genetics. Like researchers studying genetic influences on intelligence (see Chapter 7), personality psychologists have looked at correlations between the traits in monozygotic, or identical, twins who share the same genes and dizygotic, or fraternal, twins (who on average share only half of their genes). The evidence has been generally consistent: In one review of studies involving over 24,000 twin pairs, for example, identical twins proved markedly more similar to each other in personality than did fraternal twins (Loehlin, 1992).

Simply put, the more genes you have in common with someone, the more similar your personalities are likely to be. Genetics seems to influence most personality traits, and current estimates place the average genetic component of personality in the range of .40 to .60. These heritability coefficients, as you learned in Chapter 7, indicate that roughly half the variability among individuals results from genetic factors (Bouchard & Loehlin, 2001). Genetic factors do

● *Austin, Texas, protester marches to call for an end to capital punishment. Many of our opinions and attitudes, such as our view of capital punishment, appear to be shaped by our genes—so odds are that this protest is something that his family would approve.*

not account for everything, certainly—the remaining half of the variability in personality remains to be explained by differences in life experiences and other factors—but they appear to be remarkably influential.

As in the study of intelligence, potential confounding factors must be ruled out to ensure that effects are truly due to genetics and not to environmental experiences. Are identical twins treated more similarly, and do they have a greater *shared environment* than fraternal twins? As children, were they dressed in the same snappy outfits and placed on the same Little League teams, and could this somehow have produced similarities in their personalities? Studies of identical twins reared far apart in adoptive families—an experience that pretty much eliminates the potential effect of shared environmental factors—suggest that shared environments have little impact: Reared-apart identical twins end up at least as similar in personality as those who grow up together (McGue & Bouchard, 1998; Tellegen et al., 1988).

Researchers have also assessed specific behavioral and attitude similarities in twins, and the evidence for heritability in these studies is often striking. When 3,000 pairs of identical and fraternal twins were asked their opinions on political and social issues, such as the death penalty, censorship, and nudist camps, significantly high heritability estimates were obtained for these and many other attitudes—for example, the score for views on the death penalty was approximately .50 (Martin et al., 1986).

● **What do studies of twins tell us about personality?**

A specific gene directly responsible for attitudes on the death penalty or any other specific behavior or attitude is extremely unlikely. Rather, a set of genes—or, more likely, many sets of genes interacting—may produce a specific physiological characteristic such as a tendency to have a strong fear reaction in anticipation of punishment. This biological factor may then shape the person's belief about a range of social issues, perhaps including whether the fear of punishment is effective in deterring criminal behavior (Tesser, 1993).

Traits in the Brain

But what neurophysiological mechanisms influence the development of personality traits? In his personality model, Eysenck (1967) speculated that individual differences in levels of cortical arousal might underlie differences between extraverts and introverts. Extroverts pursue stimulation because their *reticular formation*—the part of the brain that regulates arousal, or alertness (as described in Chapter 3)—is not easily stimulated. To achieve greater cortical arousal and feel fully alert, Eysenck argued, extroverts are drawn to activities such as listening to loud music and having a lot of social contact. In contrast, introverts may prefer reading or quiet activities because their cortex is very easily stimulated to a point higher than optimal.

Teaching is a fine profession for an extrovert.

Behavioral and physiological research generally supports Eysenck's view. When introverts and extroverts are presented with a range of intense stimuli, introverts respond more strongly, including salivating more when a drop of lemon juice is placed on their tongues and reacting more negatively to electric shocks or loud noises (Bartol & Costello, 1976; Stelmack, 1990). This reactivity has an impact on the ability to concentrate: Extroverts tend to perform well at tasks that are done in a noisy, arousing context—such as bartending or teaching—whereas introverts are better at tasks that require concentration in tranquil contexts—such as the work of a librarian or nighttime security guard (Geen, 1984; Lieberman & Rosenthal, 2001; Matthews & Gilliland, 1999).

● **What neurological differences explain why extraverts pursue more stimulation than introverts?**

psychodynamic approach An approach that regards personality as formed by needs, strivings, and desires, largely operating outside of awareness motives that can also produce emotional disorders.

id The part of the mind containing the drives present at birth; it is the source of our bodily needs, wants, desires, and impulses, particularly our sexual and aggressive drives.

ego The component of personality, developed through contact with the external world, that enables us to deal with life's practical demands.

superego The mental system that reflects the internalization of cultural rules, mainly learned as parents exercise their authority.

summary quiz [11.2]

4. One of the first theorists to propose that personality consisted of a combination of traits and that these traits were preexisting dispositions of the individual was
   a. Hans Eysenck.
   b. Gordon Allport.
   c. Henry Murray.
   d. Phineas Gage.

5. Which of the following is *not* one of the Big Five personality factors?
   a. openness to experience
   b. agreeableness
   c. self-esteem
   d. conscientiousness

6. Probably the most compelling evidence for the importance of biological factors in personality is the marked similarity in personality of
   a. fraternal twins reared apart.
   b. adopted children and their adoptive parents.
   c. identical twins reared together.
   d. identical twins reared apart.

7. The idea that individual differences in levels of cortical arousal may underlie differences between extroverts and introverts was proposed by
   a. Hans Eysenck.
   b. Gordon Allport.
   c. Henry Murray.
   d. Paul Broca.

The Psychodynamic Approach: Forces That Lie beneath Awareness

Rather than trying to understand personality in terms of broad theories for describing individual differences, Freud looked for personality in the details—the meanings and insights revealed by careful analysis of the tiniest blemishes in a person's thought and behavior. Working with patients who came to him with disorders that did not seem to have any physical basis, he began by interpreting the origins of their common mind-bugs, errors that have come to be called "Freudian slips."

Freud used the term *psychoanalysis* to refer to both his theory of personality and his method of treating patients. Freud's ideas were the first of many theories building on his basic idea that personality is a mystery to the person who "owns" it because we can't know our own deepest motives. The theories of Freud and his followers (discussed in Chapter 13) are referred to as the **psychodynamic approach**. According to this approach, *personality is formed by needs, strivings, and desires largely operating outside of awareness—motives that can produce emotional disorders.*

The Structure of the Mind: Id, Ego, and Superego

To explain the emotional difficulties that beset his patients, Freud proposed that the mind consists of three independent, interacting, and often conflicting systems: the id, the ego, and the superego.

The most basic system, the **id**, is *the part of the mind containing the drives present at birth; it is the source of our bodily needs, wants, desires, and impulses, particularly our sexual and aggressive drives.* The id operates according to the *pleasure principle*, the psychic force that motivates the tendency to seek immediate gratification of any impulse. If governed

• Sigmund Freud was the first psychology theorist to be honored with his own bobble-head doll. Let's hope he's not the last.

Sigmund Freud

The id, ego, and superego go to Hollywood. Freud's themes of the wild id, the gray flannel ego, and the superego saying no show up in the movies, just as they do in life.

by the id alone, you would never be able to tolerate the buildup of hunger while waiting to be served at a restaurant but would simply grab food from tables nearby.

All that the id can do is wish. The **ego** is *the component of personality, developed through contact with the external world, that enables us to deal with life's practical demands.* The ego operates according to the *reality principle,* the regulating mechanism that enables the individual to delay gratifying immediate needs and function effectively in the real world. The ego helps you resist the impulse to snatch others' food and also finds the restaurant and pays the check.

The final system of the mind is the **superego**, *the mental system that reflects the internalization of cultural rules, mainly learned as parents exercise their authority.* The superego consists of a set of guidelines, internal standards, and other codes of conduct that regulate and control our behaviors, thoughts, and fantasies. It acts as a kind of conscience, punishing us when it finds we are doing or thinking something wrong (by producing guilt or other painful feelings) and rewarding us (with feelings of pride or self-congratulation) for living up to ideal standards.

According to Freud, the relative strength of the interactions among the three systems of mind—that is, which system is usually dominant—determines an individual's basic personality structure. The id force of personal needs, the superego force of social pressures to quell those needs, and the ego force of reality's demands together create constant controversy, almost like a puppet theater or a bad play.

Dealing with Inner Conflict

According to Freud, the dynamics between the id, ego, and superego are largely governed by *anxiety,* an unpleasant feeling that arises when unwanted thoughts or feelings occur—such as when the id seeks a gratification that the ego thinks will

● **How is personality shaped by the interaction of the id, ego, and superego?**

lead to real-world dangers or the superego sees as eliciting punishment. When the ego receives an "alert signal" in the form of anxiety, it launches into a defensive position in an attempt to ward off the anxiety. According to Freud, it first tries *repression,* which, as you read in Chapter 8, is a mental process that removes painful experiences and unacceptable impulses from the conscious mind. Repression is sometimes referred to as "motivated forgetting." Indeed, functional imaging studies suggest the repression of memories may involve decreased activation of the hippocampus—a region (as discussed in Chapter 5) that is central to memory (Anderson et al., 2004) (see **FIGURE 11.4**).

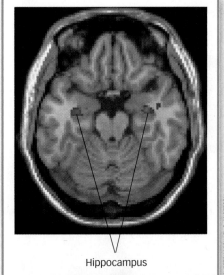

Hippocampus

FIGURE 11.4
Decreased Hippocampal Activity during Memory Suppression *The fMRI scans of people intentionally trying to forget a list of words reveal reduced activation (shown in blue) in the left and right hippocampal areas. (From Anderson et al., 2004.)*

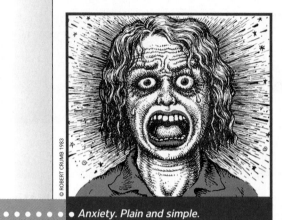

© ROBERT CRUMB 1983

● *Anxiety. Plain and simple.*

Repression may not be adequate to keep unacceptable drives from entering consciousness. When such material begins to surface, the ego can employ other means of self-deception, called **defense mechanisms**, which are *unconscious coping mechanisms that reduce anxiety generated by threats from unacceptable impulses.* Anna Freud (1936), Freud's daughter and a psychodynamic theorist, identified a number of defense mechanisms and detailed how they operate. Let's look at a few of the most common.

■ **Rationalization** is *a defense mechanism that involves supplying a reasonable-sounding explanation for unacceptable feelings and behavior to conceal (mostly from oneself) one's underlying motives or feelings.* For example, someone who drops a class after having failed an exam might tell herself that she is quitting because poor ventilation in the classroom made it impossible to concentrate.

■ **Reaction formation** is *a defense mechanism that involves unconsciously replacing threatening inner wishes and fantasies with an exaggerated version of their opposite.* Examples include being excessively nice to someone you dislike, finding yourself very worried and protective about a person you have thoughts of hurting, or being cold and indifferent toward someone to whom you are strongly attracted.

■ **Projection** is *a defense mechanism that involves attributing one's own threatening feelings, motives, or impulses to another person or group.* For example, people who think that they themselves are overly rigid or dishonest may have a tendency to judge other people as having the same qualities (Newman, Baumeister, & Duff, 1995).

■ **Regression** is *a defense mechanism in which the ego deals with internal conflict and perceived threat by reverting to an immature behavior or earlier stage of development,* a time when things felt safer and more secure. Examples of regression include the use of baby talk or whining in a child (or adult) who has already mastered appropriate speech or a return to thumb sucking, teddy bear cuddling, or watching cartoons in response to something distressing.

■ **Displacement** is *a defense mechanism that involves shifting unacceptable wishes or drives to a neutral or less threatening alternative.* Displacement should be familiar to you if you've ever slammed a door, thrown a textbook across a room, or yelled at your roommate or your cat when you were really angry at your boss.

■ **Identification** is *a defense mechanism that helps deal with feelings of threat and anxiety by enabling us unconsciously to take on the characteristics of another person who seems more powerful or better able to cope.* A child whose parent bullies or severely punishes her may later take on the characteristics of that parent and begin bullying others.

■ **Sublimation** is *a defense mechanism that involves channeling unacceptable sexual or aggressive drives into socially acceptable and culturally enhancing activities.* Football, rugby, and other contact sports, for example, may be construed as culturally sanctioned and valued activities that channel our aggressive drives.

● *Through reaction formation, a person defends against underlying feelings, such as covering hostility with an exaggerated display of affection. Maybe there's more to this sibling squeeze than love?*

TODD WARNOCK/GETTY IMAGES

Defense mechanisms are useful mindbugs: They help us overcome anxiety and engage effectively with the outside world. The ego's capacity to use defense mechanisms in a healthy and flexible fashion may depend on the nature of early experiences with caregivers, the defense mechanisms they used, and possibly some biological and temperamental factors as well (McWilliams, 1994). Our characteristic style of defense becomes our signature in dealing with the world—and an essential aspect of our personality.

● **How can our defense mechanisms be useful?**

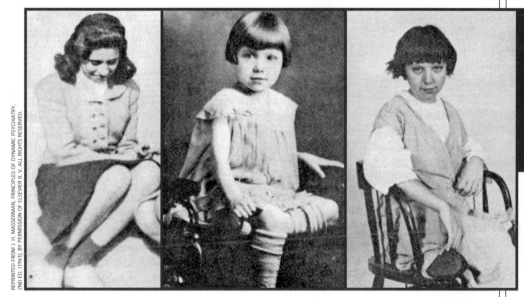

The young woman shown in the photograph on the left grew up under harsh circumstances: family strife, instability, and substance abuse, among other horrors. At age 17, she discovered a photograph of herself taken when she was 5 years old (middle) after which she adopted the look and mannerisms of a 5-year-old. The image on the right shows the same woman after regression (Masserman, 1961).

Psychosexual Stages and the Development of Personality

Freud had a great talent for coming up with troubling, highly controversial ideas. People in Victorian society did not openly discuss how much fun it is to suck on things, or the frustrations of their own toilet training, or their childhood sexual desire for their mother. Many consider Freud's views on personality development to be fanciful, and they are no longer widely held because little research evidence supports them; nevertheless, people find this part of his legacy oddly fascinating.

Freud believed that a person's basic personality is formed before 6 years of age during a series of sensitive periods, or life stages, when experiences influence all that will follow. Freud called these periods **psychosexual stages,** defined as *distinct early life stages through which personality is formed as children experience sexual pleasures from specific body areas and as caregivers redirect or interfere with those pleasures.* He argued that as a result of adult interference with pleasure-seeking energies, the child experiences conflict. At each stage, a different bodily region, or *erotogenic* zone, dominates the child's subjective experience—for example, during the oral stage, pleasure centers on the mouth. Each region represents a battleground between the child's id impulses and the adult external world. **TABLE 11.2** provides a summary of the psychosexual stages.

TABLE 11.2

The Psychosexual Stages

Stage	Oral	Anal	Phallic	Latency	Genital
Age	0–18 months	2–3 years	3–5 years	5–13 years	Adulthood
Erotogenic zone	Mouth	Anus/urethra	Penis/clitoris	—	Penis/vagina
Areas of conflict with caregiver	Feeding, weaning	Toileting	Masturbation (Oedipus conflict)	—	Adult responsibilities
Associated personality features	Talkative, dependent, addictive, needy	Orderly, controlling, disorganized, sloppy	Flirtatious, vain, jealous, competitive	—	Authentic investments in love and work; capacity for healthy adult relationships

defense mechanisms Unconscious coping mechanisms that reduce anxiety generated by threats from unacceptable impulses.

rationalization A defense mechanism that involves supplying a reasonable-sounding explanation for unacceptable feelings and behavior to conceal (mostly from oneself) one's underlying motives or feelings.

reaction formation A defense mechanism that involves unconsciously replacing threatening inner wishes and fantasies with an exaggerated version of their opposite.

projection A defense mechanism that involves attributing one's own threatening feelings, motives, or impulses to another person or group.

regression A defense mechanism in which the ego deals with internal conflict and perceived threat by reverting to an immature behavior or earlier stage of development.

displacement A defense mechanism that involves shifting unacceptable wishes or drives to a neutral or less threatening alternative.

identification A defense mechanism that helps deal with feelings of threat and anxiety by enabling us unconsciously to take on the characteristics of another person who seems more powerful or better able to cope.

sublimation A defense mechanism that involves channeling unacceptable sexual or aggressive drives into socially acceptable and culturally enhancing activities.

psychosexual stages Distinct early life stages through which personality is formed as children experience sexual pleasures from specific body areas and caregivers redirect or interfere with those pleasures.

Problems and conflicts encountered at any psychosexual stage, Freud believed, will influence personality in adulthood. Conflict resulting from a person's being deprived or, paradoxically, overindulged at a given stage could result in **fixation**, meaning that the *person's pleasure-seeking drives become stuck, or arrested, at that psychosexual stage*. Freud described particular personality traits as being derived from fixations at the different psychosexual stages. Here's how he explained the effects of fixation.

In the first year and a half of life, the infant is in the **oral stage**, *during which experience centers on the pleasures and frustrations associated with the mouth, sucking, and being fed.* Infants who are deprived of pleasurable feeding or indulgently overfed may develop an oral personality; that is, their lives will center on issues related to fullness and emptiness and what they can "take in" from others and the environment. When angry, such people may express themselves with "biting" sarcasm and "mouth off" at others—referred to as *oral aggression*. Personality traits associated with the oral stage include depression, lack of trust, envy, and demandingness.

Between 2 and 3 years of age, the child moves on to the **anal stage**, *during which experience is dominated by the pleasures and frustrations associated with the anus, retention and expulsion of feces and urine, and toilet training.* From the toddler's perspective, the soiling of one's diapers is a wonderful convenience that can feel pretty good. But sooner or later caregivers begin to disagree, and their opinions are voiced more strongly as the child gets older. Individuals who have had difficulty negotiating this conflict may develop a rigid personality and remain preoccupied with issues of control of others and of themselves and their emotions. They may be preoccupied with their possessions, money, issues of submission and rebellion, and concerns about cleanliness versus messiness.

MARTHA HOLMES/TIME LIFE PICTURES/GETTY IMAGES

● *One of the id's desires is to make a fine mess, a desire that is often frustrated early in life, perhaps during the anal stage. Famous painter Jackson Pollack found a way to make extraordinarily fine messes, behavior that at some level all of us envy.*

Between the ages of 3 and 5 years, the child is in the **phallic stage**, *during which experience is dominated by the pleasure, conflict, and frustration associated with the phallic-genital region as well as coping with powerful incestuous feelings of love, hate, jealousy, and conflict.* In part, parental concerns about the child's developing awareness of the genital region set off the conflict: The child may touch his or her genitals in public or explore masturbation and may be curious about the parent's genitals.

According to Freud, boys in the phallic stage experience the **Oedipus conflict**, *a developmental experience in which a child's conflicting feelings toward the opposite sex parent is (usually) resolved by identifying with the same sex parent.* (In Greek myth, Oedipus was a young man who, unknowingly, killed his father and ended up marrying his mother.) Freud thought that, around age 4 or 5, boys wonder about their love affair with Mommy, noticing she has positive feelings for someone else (Daddy)—and experiencing jealousy. Freud believed individuals must give up their Oedipal desires if they are to be able to move on and build a life with a partner in the future. Males who are unable to resolve the Oedipus conflict and who get stuck in the phallic stage tend to be unusually preoccupied with issues of seduction, jealousy, competition, power, and authority. Females stuck in this phase, Freud thought, would display seductiveness, flirtatiousness, and jealousy.

A more relaxed period in which children are no longer struggling with the power of their sexual and aggressive drives occurs between the ages of 5 and 13, as children experience the **latency stage**, *in which the primary focus is on the further development of intellectual, creative, interpersonal, and athletic skills.* Because Freud believed that the most significant aspects of personality development occur during the first three psychosexual stages (before the age of 5 years), psychodynamic psychologists do not speak of fixation at the latency period. Simply making it to the latency period relatively undisturbed by conflicts of the earlier stages is a sign of healthy personality development.

At puberty and thereafter, the fifth and final stage of personality development occurs. This, the **genital stage**, is *the time for the coming together of the mature adult personality with a capacity to love, work, and relate to others in a mutually satisfying and reciprocal manner.* The degree to which the individual is encumbered by unresolved conflicts at the earlier stages will impact whether he or she will be able to achieve a genital level of development. Freud believed that people who are fixated in a prior stage fail in developing healthy adult sexuality and a well-adjusted adult personality.

What should we make of all this? On the one hand, the psychoanalytic theory of psychosexual stages offers an intriguing picture of early family relationships and the extent to which they allow the child to satisfy basic needs and wishes. The theory picks up on themes that seem to ring true in many cases; you may very well know people who seem to be "oral" or "anal," for example, or who have issues about sexuality that seem to have had a great influence on their personalities. On the other hand, critics argue that psychodynamic explanations are too complex and tend to focus on after-the-fact

● **Why do critics say Freud's psychosexual stages are more interpretation than explanation?**

interpretation rather than testable prediction. Describing a person fixated at the oral stage as "biting," for example, seems just so much

"Don't worry—it's just a phase."

wordplay—not the basis of a scientific theory. And, for example, the control issues that preoccupy an adult with a so-called anal character might reflect an inborn headstrong and controlling temperament and have nothing to do with a parental style of toilet training. The psychosexual stage theory offers a compelling set of story plots for interpreting lives once they have unfolded but has not generated the kinds of clear-cut predictions that inspire research.

summary quiz [11.3]

8. Which of Freud's systems helps you to find a restaurant and to resist the temptation to snatch food off other people's plates?
  a. id
  b. ego
  c. superego
  d. pleasure principle

9. Your professor singled you out for criticism in class, which made you very angry. When you got home, you slammed the door and yelled at your roommate. Freud would say you are using which defense mechanism?
  a. reaction formation
  b. sublimation
  c. displacement
  d. projection

10. Your roommate has a rigid personality and is preoccupied with possessions, money, and issues of controlling others. According to Freud, your roommate is fixated at the _____ stage.
  a. oral
  b. anal
  c. phallic
  d. genital

11. According to Freud, psychological problems in adulthood are primarily a result of
  a. making unhealthy choices when faced with difficult decisions.
  b. experiencing considerable punishment and few rewards during childhood.
  c. having a poor self-concept because of rejection by others.
  d. having unresolved conflicts during one or more stages of psychosexual development.

fixation A phenomenon in which a person's pleasure-seeking drives become psychologically stuck, or arrested, at a particular psychosexual stage.

oral stage The first psychosexual stage, in which experience centers on the pleasures and frustrations associated with the mouth, sucking, and being fed.

anal stage The second psychosexual stage, which is dominated by the pleasures and frustrations associated with the anus, retention and expulsion of feces and urine, and toilet training.

phallic stage The third psychosexual stage, during which experience is dominated by the pleasure, conflict, and frustration associated with the phallic-genital region as well as powerful incestuous feelings of love, hate, jealousy, and conflict.

Oedipus conflict A developmental experience in which a child's conflicting feelings toward the opposite-sex parent is (usually) resolved by identifying with the same-sex parent.

latency stage The fourth psychosexual stage, in which the primary focus is on the further development of intellectual, creative, interpersonal, and athletic skills.

genital stage The final psychosexual stage, a time for the coming together of the mature adult personality with a capacity to love, work, and relate to others in a mutually satisfying and reciprocal manner.

The Humanistic-Existential Approach: Personality as Choice

In the 1950s and 1960s, psychologists began to try to understand personality from a viewpoint quite different from trait theory's biological determinism and Freud's focus on unconscious drives from unresolved child experiences. These new humanistic and existential theorists turned attention to how humans make *healthy choices* that create their personalities. *Humanistic psychologists* emphasized a positive, optimistic view of human nature that highlights people's inherent goodness and their potential for personal growth. *Existentialist psychologists* focused on the individual as a responsible agent who is free to create and live his or her life while negotiating the issue of meaning and the reality of death. The *humanistic-existential approach* integrates these insights with a focus on how a personality can become optimal.

Human Needs and Self-actualization

Humanists see the **self-actualizing tendency**, *the human motive toward realizing our inner potential*, as a major factor in personality. The pursuit of knowledge, the expression of one's creativity, the quest for spiritual enlightenment, and the desire to give to society are all examples of self-actualization. As you saw in Chapter 9, the noted humanistic theorist Abraham Maslow (1970) proposed a *hierarchy of needs,* a model of essential human needs arranged according to their priority, in which basic physiological and safety needs must be sat-

● **What is it to be self-actualized?**

isfied before a person can afford to focus on higher-level psychological needs. Only when these basic needs are satisfied can you pursue higher needs, culminating in *self-actualization*—the need to be good, to be fully alive, and to find meaning in life.

Humanist psychologists explain individual personality differences as arising from the various ways that the environment facilitates—or blocks—attempts to satisfy psychological needs. Like a wilting plant deprived of water, sunshine, and nutrients, an individual growing up in an arid social environment can fail to develop his or her unique potential. For example, someone with the inherent potential to be a great scientist, artist, parent, or teacher might never realize these talents if his or her energies and resources are instead directed toward meeting basic needs of security, belongingness, and the like. Research indicates that when people shape their lives around goals that do not match their true nature and capabilities, they are less likely to be happy than those whose lives and goals do match (Ryan & Deci, 2000).

CHARLES QUIGG/AMHERST COLLEGE PUBLIC AFFAIRS

● *In the seminar States of Poverty held at Amherst College, student Tony Jack asked, "Has anyone here ever actually seen a food stamp?" Tony had seen food stamps and more and would never have been able to afford an elite education if Amherst hadn't provided extra help with a full scholarship and a start-up grant and job. Tony was provided with conditions for growth—and graduated with honors in May 2007.*

Personality as Existence

Existentialists agree with humanists about many of the features of personality but focus on challenges to the human condition that are more profound than the lack of a nurturing environment. Rollo May (1983) and Victor Frankl (2000), for example, argued that specific aspects of the human condition, such as awareness of our own existence and the ability to make choices about how to behave, have a double-edged quality: They bring an extraordinary richness and dignity to human life, but they also force us to confront realities that are difficult to face, such as the prospect of our own death. The **existential approach** *regards personality as governed by an individual's ongoing choices and decisions in the context of the realities of life and death.*

● **What is angst, and how is it created?**

According to the existential perspective, the difficulties we face in finding meaning in life and in accepting the responsibility of making free choices provoke a type of anxiety existentialists call *angst* (the anxiety of fully being). The human ability to consider limitless numbers of goals and actions is exhilarating, but it can also open the door to profound questions such as "Why am I here?" and "What is the meaning of my life?"

Thinking about the meaning of existence also can evoke an awareness the inevitability of death. What, then, should we do with each moment? What is the purpose of living if life as we know it will end one day, perhaps even today? Alternatively, does life have more meaning given that it is so temporary?

Existential theorists do not suggest that people consider these profound existential issues on a day-to-day and moment-to-moment basis. Rather than ruminate about death and meaning, people typically pursue superficial answers that help them deal with the angst and dread they experience, and the defenses they construct form the basis of their personalities (Binswanger, 1958; May, 1983).

Unfortunately, security-providing defense mechanisms can be self-defeating and stifle the potential for personal growth. The pursuit of superficial relationships can make possible the avoidance of real intimacy. A fortress of consumer goods can provide a false sense of security. Immersion in drugs or addictive behaviors such as compulsive web browsing, video gaming, or television watching can numb the mind to existential realities.

If defenses are so thin and pointless, how do you deal with existence? For existentialists, the solution is to face the issues square-on and learn to accept and tolerate the pain of existence. Indeed, being fully human means confronting existential realities rather than denying them or embracing comforting illusions. This requires the courage to accept the inherent anxiety and the dread of nonbeing that is part of being alive. Such courage may be facilitated by developing supportive relationships with others who can supply unconditional positive regard. There's something about being loved that helps take away the angst.

self-actualizing tendency The human motive toward realizing our inner potential.

existential approach A school of thought that regards personality as governed by an individual's ongoing choices and decisions in the context of the realities of life and death.

summary quiz [11.4]

12. The view that personality is governed by an inherent striving toward self-actualization and the development of our unique potentials was proposed by
a. Abraham Maslow.
b. Rollo May.
c. Victor Frankl.
d. Albert Bandura.

13. Which approach regards personality as governed by an individual's choices in the context of the realities of life and eventual death?
a. humanistic
b. existential
c. psychodynamic
d. social cognitive

14. According to Rollo May and Victor Frankl, a major aspect of personality development involves
a. the importance of a nurturing environment.
b. gratifying basic physiological needs.
c. actualizing one's full potential.
d. questioning the meaning of life.

The Social Cognitive Approach: Personalities in Situations

What is it like to be a person? The **social cognitive approach** *views personality in terms of how the person thinks about the situations encountered in daily life and behaves in response to them.* Bringing together insights from social psychology, cognitive psychology, and learning theory, this approach emphasizes how the person experiences and construes situations (Bandura, 1986; Mischel & Shoda, 1999; Ross & Nisbett, 1991; Wegner & Gilbert, 2000).

The idea that situations cause behavior was a fundamental principle of behaviorism, as you read in Chapter 6. Consider how a behaviorist such as B. F. Skinner would explain your behavior right now. If you have been reinforced in the past by getting good grades when studying only the night before an exam, he would have predicted that you are in fact reading these words for the first time the night before the test! If you have been reinforced for studying well in advance, he would have predicted that you are reading this chapter with plenty of time to spare. For a behaviorist, then, differences in behavior reflect differences in how the behaviors have been rewarded in past situations.

Researchers in social cognition agree that the situation and learning history are key determinants of behavior, but they go much further than Skinner would have in looking inside the psychological "black box" of the mind to examine the thoughts and feelings that come between the situation and the person's response to it. Because human "situations" and "reinforcements" are radically open to interpretation, social cognitive psychologists focus on how people *perceive* their environments. People think about their goals, the consequences of their behavior, and how they might achieve certain things in different situations (Lewin, 1951). The social cognitive approach looks at how personality and situation interact to cause behavior, how personality contributes to the way people construct situations in their own minds, and how people's goals and expectancies influence their responses to situations.

Consistency of Personality across Situations

Although social cognitive psychologists attribute behavior both to the individual's personality and to his or her situation, situation can often trump personality. For example, a person would have to be pretty strange to act exactly the same way at a memorial service and a toga party. At the core of the social cognitive approach is a natural puzzle, the **person-situation controversy**, which focuses on *the question of whether behavior is caused more by personality or by situational factors.*

● **Does a person's behavior in one situation allow us to predict future behaviors?**

This controversy began in earnest when Walter Mischel (1968) argued that measured personality traits often do a poor job of predicting individuals' behavior. Mischel reviewed decades of research that compared scores on standard personality tests with actual behavior, looking at evidence from studies asking questions such as "Does a person with a high score on a test of introversion actually spend more time alone than someone with a low score?" Mischel's disturbing conclusion: The average correlation between trait and behavior is only about .30. This is certainly better than zero (i.e., chance) but not very good when you remember that a perfect prediction is represented by a correlation of 1.0.

Even knowing how a person will behave in one situation is not particularly helpful in predicting the person's behavior in another situation. For example, in classic studies, Hartshorne and May (1928) assessed children's honesty by examining their willingness to cheat on a test and found that such dishonesty was not consistent from one situation to another. The assessment of a child's trait of honesty

● *Is this student, cheating on a test, more likely than others to steal candy or lie to her grandmother? Social cognitive research indicates that behavior in one situation does not necessarily predict behavior in a different situation.*

VEER

in a cheating situation was of almost no use in predicting whether the child would act honestly in a different situation—such as when given the opportunity to steal money. Mischel proposed that measured traits do not predict behaviors very well because behaviors are determined more by situational factors than personality theorists were willing to acknowledge.

Is there no personality, then? Do we all just do what situations require? The person-situation controversy has inspired many studies in the years since Mischel's critique, and it turns out that information about both personality and situation are necessary to predict behavior. Although people may not necessarily act the same way across situations, they often do act in a similar manner within the same type of situation (Mischel & Shoda, 1999). A person who is outgoing at parties but withdrawn at the office would be difficult to characterize as an extravert or an introvert, but if he is *always* outgoing at parties and *always* withdrawn at the office, personality consistency within situations has been demonstrated.

Among the children in Hartshorne and May's studies, cheating versus not cheating on a test was actually a fairly good predictor of cheating on a test later—as long as the situation was similar (Hartshorne & May, 1928). Personality consistency, then, appears to be a matter of when and where a certain kind of behavior tends to be shown. Social cognitive theorists believe these patterns of personality consistency in response to situations arise from the way different people construe situations and from the ways different people pursue goals within situations.

Personal Constructs

How can we understand differences in the way situations are interpreted? Recall our notion of personality often existing "in the eye of the beholder." Situations may exist "in the eye of the beholder" as well. One person's gold mine may be another person's hole in the dirt. George Kelly (1955) long ago realized that these differences in perspective could be used to understand the *perceiver's* personality. He suggested that people view the social world from differing perspectives and that these different views arise through the application of **personal constructs**, *dimensions people use in making sense of their experiences.* Consider, for example, different individuals' personal constructs of a clown: One person may see him as a source of fun, another as a tragic figure, and yet another as so frightening that the circus is off-limits.

● **Why doesn't everyone love clowns?**

Here's how Kelly assessed personal constructs about social relationships: He'd ask people to (1) list the people in their life, (2) consider three of the people and state a way in which two of them were similar to each other and different from the third, and (3) repeat this for other triads of people to produce a list of the dimensions used to classify friends and family. One respondent might focus on the degree to which people (self included) are lazy or hardworking, for example; someone else might attend to the degree to which people are sociable or unfriendly.

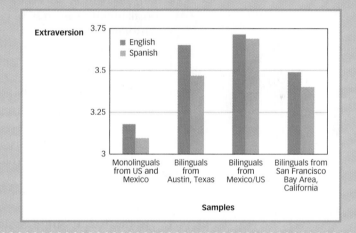

Culture & Community

Does Your Personality Change According to Which Language You're Speaking?

The personalities of people in groups speaking different languages often can diverge. A study revealed that personality tests taken by English-speaking Americans and Spanish-speaking Mexicans differ reliably: The Americans were found to be more extroverted, more agreeable, and more conscientious than the Mexicans (Ramirez-Esparza et al., 2006).

But why? To see if language might play a role in this difference, the researchers then sought out Spanish-English bilinguals in Texas, California, and Mexico and gave them the personality scale in each language. And in fact, language was a key: Scores of the bilingual participants were more extraverted, agreeable, and conscientious when they took the test in English than when they took it in Spanish. Personality may be influenced by the group you belong to because of the language you are speaking.

social cognitive approach An approach that views personality in terms of how the person thinks about the situations encountered in daily life and behaves in response to them.

person-situation controversy The question of whether behavior is caused more by personality or by situational factors.

personal constructs Dimensions people use in making sense of their experiences.

Kelly proposed that different personal constructs (*construals*) are the key to personality differences—that is, that different construals lead to disparate behaviors. Taking a long break from work for a leisurely lunch might seem lazy to you. To your friend, the break might seem an ideal opportunity for catching up with friends, so he will wonder why you always choose to eat at your desk. Social cognitive theory explains different responses to situations with the idea that people see things in different ways.

Personal Goals and Expectancies

Social cognitive theories also recognize that a person's unique perspective on situations is reflected in his or her personal goals, which are often conscious. In fact, people can usually tell you their goals, whether they are to "find a date for this weekend," "get a good grade in psych," "establish a fulfilling career," or just "get this darn bag of chips open."

People translate goals into behavior in part through **outcome expectancies,** *a person's assumptions about the likely consequences of a future behavior.* Just as a laboratory rat learns that pressing a bar releases a food pellet, we learn that "if I am friendly toward people, they will be friendly in return" or "if I ask people to pull my finger, they will withdraw from me." So we learn to perform behaviors that we expect will have the outcome of moving us closer to our goals.

Outcome expectancies combine with a person's goals to produce the person's characteristic style of behavior. An individual with the goal of making friends and the expectancy that being kind will produce warmth in return is likely to behave very differently from an individual whose goal is to achieve fame at any cost and who believes that shameless self-promotion is the route to fame. We do not all want the same things from life, clearly, and our personalities largely reflect the goals we pursue and the expectancies we have about the best ways to pursue them.

People differ in their generalized expectancy for achieving goals. Some people seem to feel that they are fully in control of what happens to them in life, whereas others feel that the world doles out rewards and punishments to them irrespective of their actions. Julian Rotter (1966) defined a person's **locus of control** as *the person's tendency to perceive the control of rewards as internal to the self or external in the environment.* People who believe they control their own destiny are said to have an *internal* locus of control, whereas those who believe that outcomes are random, determined by luck, or controlled by other people are

● **What is the advantage of an internal locus of control?**

described as having an *external* locus of control. These beliefs translate into individual differences in emotion and behavior. For example, people with an internal locus of control tend to be less anxious, achieve more, and cope better with stress than do people with an external orientation (Lefcourt, 1982).

summary quiz [11.5]

15. The psychologist who noted that personality traits often do a poor job of predicting an individual's behavior was
    a. George Kelly.
    b. Walter Mischel.
    c. Julian Rotter.
    d. B. F. Skinner.

16. Dimensions that people use in making sense of their experiences are called
    a. social cognitions.
    b. outcome expectancies.
    c. personal constructs.
    d. locuses of control.

17. Tyler has been getting poor evaluations at work. He attributes this to having a mean boss who always assigns him the hardest tasks. According to Julian Rotter, Tyler would be said to have
    a. external locus of control.
    b. internal locus of control.
    c. high performance anxiety.
    d. poorly developed personal constructs.

The Self: Personality in the Mirror

Imagine that you wake up tomorrow morning, drag yourself into the bathroom, look into the mirror, and don't recognize the face looking back at you. This was the plight of a patient studied by neurologist Todd Feinberg (2001). The woman, married for 30 years and the mother of two grown children, one day began to respond to her mirror image as if it were a different person. She talked to and challenged the person in the mirror. When there was no response, she tried to attack it as if it were an intruder. Her husband, shaken by this bizarre behavior, brought her to the neurologist, who was gradually able to convince her that the image in the mirror was in fact herself.

Most of us are pretty familiar with the face that looks back at us from every mirror. We developed the ability to recognize ourselves in mirrors by 18 months of age (as discussed in Chapter 8), and we share this skill with chimps and other apes who have been raised in the presence of mirrors. Self-recognition in mirrors signals our amazing capacity for reflexive thinking, for directing attention to our own thoughts, feelings, and actions—an ability that enables us to construct ideas about our own personality. Unlike a cow, which will never know that it has a poor sense of humor, or a cat, which will never know that it is awfully friendly (for a cat), humans have rich and detailed self-knowledge.

Admittedly, none of us know all there is to know about our own personality (or psychodynamic psychologists would be out of work). But we do have enough self-knowledge to reliably respond to personality inventories and report on our traits and behaviors. These observations draw on our **self-concept**, *a person's explicit knowledge of his or her own behaviors, traits, and other personal characteristics*, and our **self-esteem**, *the extent to which an individual likes, values, and accepts the self*. Self-concept and self-esteem are critically important facets of personality, not just because they reveal how people see their own personalities, but because they also guide how people think others will see them.

outcome expectancies A person's assumptions about the likely consequences of a future behavior.

locus of control A person's tendency to perceive the control of rewards as internal to the self or external in the environment.

self-concept A person's explicit knowledge of his or her own behaviors, traits, and other personal characteristics.

self-esteem The extent to which an individual likes, values, and accepts the self.

What do these self-portraits of Frida Kahlo, M. C. Escher, Norman Rockwell, Salvador Dali, Wanda Wulz, and Jean-Michel Basquiat reveal about each artist's self-concept?

Self-concept

Almost everyone has a place for memorabilia, a drawer or box somewhere that holds all those sentimental keepsakes—photos, yearbooks, cards and letters, maybe that scrap of the old security blanket—all memories of "life as *Me*." Perhaps you've wanted to organize these things sometime but have never gotten around to it. Fortunately, the knowledge of ourselves that we store in our *autobiographical memory* seems to be organized naturally in two ways: as narratives about episodes in our lives and in terms of traits (as would be suggested by the distinction between episodic and semantic memory discussed in Chapter 5).

Self-concept Organization

The aspect of the self-concept that is a *self-narrative*—a story that we tell about ourselves—can be brief or very lengthy. Your life story could start with your birth and upbringing, describe a series of defining moments, and end where you are today. You could select specific events and experiences, goals and life tasks, and memories of places and people that have influenced you. Self-narrative organizes the highlights and low blows of your life into a story in which you are the leading character and binds them together into your self-concept (McAdams, 1993).

Self-concept is also organized in a more abstract way, in terms of personality traits. Just as you can judge an object on its attributes ("Is this apple green?"), you are able to judge yourself on any number of traits—whether you are considerate or smart or lazy or active or, for that matter, green—and do so quite reliably, making the same rating on multiple occasions. One person might define herself as independent, for example, whereas another might not care much about her level of independence but instead emphasize her sense of style.

● **What is your life story as you see it— your self-narrative?**

self-verification The tendency to seek evidence to confirm the self-concept.

How do our behavior self-narratives and trait self-concepts compare? These two methods of self-conceptualization don't always match up. You may think of yourself as an honest person, for example, but also recall that time you nabbed a handful of change from your parents' dresser and conveniently forgot to replace it. The traits we use to describe ourselves are generalizations, and not every episode in our life stories may fit. In fact, research suggests that the stores of knowledge about our behaviors and traits are not very well integrated (Kihlstrom & Klein, 1994). In people who develop amnesia, for example, memory for behaviors can be lost even though the trait self-concept remains stable (Klein, 2004). People can have a pretty strong sense of who they are even though they may not remember a single example of when they acted that way.

A key element in personality involves the stories, myths, and fairy tales we tell ourselves about our lives. Are you living the story of the prince or princess in a castle, or are you the troll in the woods?

Causes and Effects of Self-concept

How do self-concepts arise, and how do they affect us? Although we can gain self-knowledge in private moments of insight, we more often arrive at our self-concepts through interacting with others. Young children in particular receive plenty of feedback from their parents, teachers, siblings, and friends about their characteristics, and this helps them to form an idea of who they are. Even adults would find it difficult to hold a view of the self as "kind" or "smart" if no one else ever shared this impression. The sense of self, then, is largely developed and maintained in relationships with others.

Over the course of a lifetime, however, we become less and less impressed with what others have to say about us. As a result, the person who says you're a jerk may upset you momentarily, but you bounce back, secure in the knowledge that you're not truly a jerk. And just as we might argue vehemently with someone who tried to tell us a refrigerator is a pair of underpants or that up is actually down and to the left, we are likely to defend our self-concept against anyone whose view of us departs from our own.

Because it is so stable, a major effect of the self-concept is to promote consistency in behavior across situations (Lecky, 1945). As existential theorists emphasize, people derive a comforting sense of familiarity and stability from knowing who they are. We tend to engage in what William Swann (1983) called **self-verification,** *the tendency to seek evidence to confirm the self-concept,* and we find it disconcerting if someone sees us quite differently from the way we see ourselves. In one study, Swann (1983) gave people who considered themselves submissive feedback that they seemed very dominant and forceful. Rather than accepting this discrepant information, they went out of their way to act in an extremely submissive manner. Our tendency to project into the world our concept of the self contributes to personality coherence. This talent for self-reflection enables the personality to become self-sustaining.

Self-esteem

On the whole, whereas self-concept defines what we think of ourselves, self-esteem is the extent to which we generally like (or dislike) that portrait of ourselves. When our friend Amy Winehouse sang "You know I'm no good," she was telling us something about her self-esteem. Researchers who study self-esteem typically ask participants to fill out a self-esteem questionnaire that asks people to evaluate themselves in terms of statements such as "On the whole, I am satisfied with myself," or "At times, I feel I am no good at all" (Rosenberg, 1965). People who strongly agree with the positive statements about themselves and strongly disagree with the negative statements are considered to have high self-esteem; people who show the opposite pattern are considered to have low self-esteem.

In general, compared with people with low self-esteem, those with high self-esteem tend to live happier and healthier lives, cope better with

Implicit Egotism: Liking Ourselves without Knowing It

What's your favorite letter of the alphabet? About 30% of people answer by picking what just happens to be the first letter of their first name. Could this choice indicate that some people think so highly of themselves that they base judgments of seemingly unrelated topics on how much it reminds them of themselves?

This *name-letter effect* was discovered some years ago (Nuttin, 1985), but only recently have researchers gone on to discover how broad the egotistic bias in preferences can be. Brett Pelham and his colleagues have found subtle yet systematic biases toward this effect when people choose their home cities, streets, and even occupations (Pelham, Mirenberg, & Jones, 2002). When the researchers examined the rolls of people moving into several southern states, for example, they found people named George were more likely than those with other names to move to Georgia. The same was true for Florences (Florida), Kenneths (Kentucky), and Louises (Louisiana). You can guess where the Virginias tended to relocate. The name effect seems to work for occupations as well: Slightly more people named Dennis and Denise chose dentistry and Lauras and Lawrences chose law compared with other occupations. Although the biases are small (if your name is Wally, you don't *have* to move to Walla Walla), they are consistent across many tests of the hypothesis.

These biases have been called expressions of *implicit egotism* because people are not

What's your favorite letter?

typically aware that they are influenced by the wonderful sound of their own names (Pelham, Carvallo, & Jones, 2005). When Buffy moves to Buffalo, she is not likely to volunteer that she did so because it matched her name. Yet people who show this egotistic bias in one way also tend to show it in others: People who strongly prefer their own name letter also are likely to pick their birth date as their favorite number (Koole, Dijksterhuis, & van Knippenberg, 2001). And people who like their name letter were also found to evaluate themselves positively on self-ratings of personality traits. This was especially true when the self-ratings were made in response to instructions to work *quickly*. The people who

preferred their name letter made snap judgments of themselves that leaned in a positive direction—suggesting that their special self-appreciation was an automatic response.

At some level, of course, a bit of egotism is probably good for us. It's sad to meet someone who hates her own name or whose snap judgment of self is "I'm worthless." Yet in another sense, implicit egotism is a curiously subtle mindbug—a tendency to make biased judgments of what we will do and where we will go in life just because we happen to have a certain name. Yes, the bias is only a small one. But your authors wonder: Should we have considered writing with a colleague whose name wasn't Dan?

stress, and be more likely to persist at difficult tasks. In contrast, individuals with low self-esteem are more likely—for example—to perceive rejection in ambiguous feedback from others and to develop eating disorders than those with high self-esteem (Baumeister et al., 2003).

Sources of Self-esteem

Some psychologists contend that high self-esteem arises primarily from being accepted and valued by significant others (Brown, 1993). Other psychologists focus on the influence of specific self-evaluations, judgments about one's value or competence in specific domains such as appearance, athletics, or scholastics.

An important factor is whom people choose for comparison. For example, James (1890) noted that an accomplished athlete who is the second best in the world should feel pretty proud, but this athlete might not if the standard of comparison involves

Silver medalist Duje Draganja of Croatia, gold medalist G. Hall Jr. of the United States, and bronze medalist Roland Schoeman of South Africa show off their medals following their 50-meter swimming final. Notice the expression on Draganja's face compared to those of the gold and bronze medalists.

being best in the world. In fact, athletes in the 1992 Olympics who had won silver medals looked less happy during the medal ceremony than those who had won bronze (Medvec et al., 1995). If the actual self is seen as falling short of the ideal self—the person that they would like to be—people tend to feel sad or dejected; when they become aware that the actual self is inconsistent with the self they have a duty to be, they are likely to feel anxious or agitated (Higgins, 1987).

Self-esteem is also affected by what kinds of domain we consider most important in our self-concept. One person's self-worth might be entirely contingent on, for example, how well she does in school, whereas another's self-worth might be based on his physical attractiveness (Crocker & Wolfe, 2001; Pelham, 1985). The first person's self-esteem might receive a big boost when she gets an A on an exam, but much less of a boost when she's complimented on her new hairstyle—and this effect might be exactly reversed in the second person (see the Hot Science box on page 356).

The Desire for Self-esteem

What's so great about self-esteem? Why do people want to see themselves in a positive light and avoid seeing themselves negatively?

One theory suggests that self-esteem feels good because it reflects our degree of social dominance or status. People with high self-esteem seem to carry themselves in a way that is similar to high-status animals of other social species. Dominant male gorillas, for example, appear confident and comfortable and not anxious or withdrawn. Perhaps

High self-esteem in humans may reflect the same sort of social status and respect that dominant male gorillas enjoy.

self-serving bias People's tendency to take credit for their successes but downplay responsibility for their failures.

narcissism A trait that reflects a grandiose view of the self combined with a tendency to seek admiration from and exploit others.

ONLY HUMAN

SPECIAL, SO VERY SPECIAL Furious at a rush-hour accident that blocked traffic in the Boston suburb of Weymouth, motorist (and software engineer) Anna Gitlin, 25, went ballistic at a police officer and then allegedly bumped him with her car, screaming, "I don't care who [expletive deleted by the *Boston Globe*] died. I'm more important!"

high self-esteem in humans reflects high social status or suggests that the person is worthy of respect, and this perception triggers natural affective responses (Barkow, 1980; Maslow, 1937).

Another approach, based on evolutionary theory, holds that early humans who managed to survive to pass on their genes were those able to maintain good relations with others rather than being cast out to fend for themselves. Self-esteem could have evolved as an inner gauge of how much a person feels included by others at any given moment (Leary & Baumeister, 2000).

● **How might self esteem have played a role in evolution?**

A third major theory is consistent with the existential and psychodynamic approaches to personality and suggests that the source of distress underlying negative self-esteem is ultimately the fear of death (Solomon, Greenberg, & Pyszczynski, 1991). In this view, humans find it anxiety provoking, in fact terrifying, to contemplate their own mortality, and so they try to defend against this awareness by immersing themselves in activities (e.g., earning money or dressing up to appear attractive) that their culture defines as meaningful and valuable. The higher our self-esteem, the less anxious we feel with the knowledge that someday we will no longer exist.

Whatever the reason that low self-esteem feels so bad and high self-esteem feels so good, people are generally motivated to see themselves positively. In fact, we often process information in a biased manner in order to feel good about the self. Research on the **self-serving bias** shows that *people tend to take credit for their successes but downplay responsibility for their failures.* You may have noticed this tendency in yourself, particularly in terms of the attributions you make about exams when you get a good grade ("I studied really intensely, and I'm good at that subject") or a bad grade ("The test was ridiculously tricky, and the professor is a nimnutz").

On the whole, most people satisfy the desire for high self-esteem and maintain a reasonably positive view of self by engaging in the self-serving bias. In fact, if people are asked to rate themselves across a range of characteristics, they tend to see themselves as better than the average person in most domains (Alicke et al., 1995). For example, 90% of drivers describe their driving skills as better than average, and 86% of workers rate their performance on the job as above average. These kinds of judgments simply cannot be accurate, statistically speaking, since the average of a group of people has to be the average, not better than average! This mindbug may be adaptive, however. People who do not engage in this self-serving bias to boost their self-esteem tend to be more at risk for depression, anxiety, and related health problems (Taylor & Brown, 1988).

At the same time, a few people take positive self-esteem to the extreme. **Narcissism**, *a grandiose view of the self combined with a tendency to seek admiration from and exploit others,* is considered a personality disorder (see Chapter 13). Healthy self-esteem seems to lie between these extremes: where people employ a self-serving bias—without letting it get out of control.

The self is the part of personality that the person knows and can report about. Some of the personality measures we have seen in this chapter—such as personality inventories based on self-reports—are really no different from measures of self-concept. Both depend on the person's perceptions and memories of the self's behavior and traits. But personality runs deeper than this as well. The unconscious forces identified in psychodynamic approaches provide themes for behavior, and sources of mental disorder, that are not accessible for self-report. The humanistic and existential approaches remind us of the profound concerns we humans face and the difficulties we may have in understanding all the forces that shape our self-views. Finally, in emphasizing how personality shapes our perceptions of social life, the social cognitive approach brings the self back to center stage. The self, after all, is the hub of each person's social world.

"I got into the stupidest thing with my reflection this morning."

summary quiz [11.6]

18. If you are like many college students, you attribute your good exam grades to your ability and effort, and attribute your bad exam grades to an unfair teacher or the extreme difficulty of the test. This is known as

a. self-narrative.

b. self-verification.

c. self-serving bias.

d. self-esteem.

19. Which is true of self-narratives and trait self-concepts?

a. Both are aspects of the self-concept.

b. The two are highly consistent with each other.

c. When people develop amnesia, they lose their memory for both their past behaviors and their trait self-concept.

d. Self-narratives are the assessments we make of our personality traits.

20. Which of the following is *not* one of the theories that attempts to explain the benefits of high self-esteem?

a. It reflects high status.

b. It reflects a narcissistic view of the self.

c. It reflects being accepted by others.

d. It reflects a defense against the awareness of death.

21. William Swann developed the concept known as

a. self-narrative.

b. self-serving bias.

c. narcissism.

d. self-verification.

WhereDoYouStand?

Personality Testing for Fun and Profit

Many people enjoy filling out personality tests. In fact, dozens of Web sites, magazine articles, and popular books offer personality tests to complete as well as handy summaries of test scores. Unfortunately, many personality tests are no more than a collection of questions someone has put together to offer entertainment to test takers. These tests yield a sense of self-insight that is no more valid than what you might get from the random "wisdom" of a fortune cookie or your daily horoscope.

The personality tests discussed in this chapter are more valid, of course: They have been developed and refined to offer reliable predictions of a person's tendencies. Still, the validity of many personality tests, particularly the projective tests, remains controversial, and critics question whether personality tests should be used for serious purposes.

In fact, business, government, and the military often use personality tests in hiring. And vocational counselors use the Myers-Briggs Type Indicator personality test (which primarily assesses the individual's standing on the extraversion/introversion personality dimension) to direct people toward occupations that match their strengths. Although such tests have been criticized for their flimsy theoretical and research foundations (Paul, 2004), businesses have not abandoned them. The possibility also exists that such tests might be someday used to predict whether criminals behind bars have been rehabilitated or might return to crime if released. If tests could be developed that would predict with certainty whether a person would be likely to commit a violent crime or become a terrorist or a sexual predator, do you think such tests should be used to make decisions about people's lives?

Think of all you have learned about the different approaches to personality, the strengths and weaknesses of different kinds of tests, the person-situation controversy, and the fact that personality measures do correlate significantly (although not perfectly) with a person's behaviors. Are personality tests useful for making decisions about people now? If such tests were perfected, should they be used in the future? Where do you stand?

CHAPTER REVIEW

Summary

Personality: What It Is and How It Is Measured

- In psychology, personality refers to a person's characteristic style of behaving, thinking, and feeling.
- Personality psychologists attempt to find the best ways to describe personality, to explain how personalities come about, and to measure personality.
- Two general classes of personality tests are personality inventories, such as the MMPI, and projective techniques, such as the Rorschach Inkblot Test and the TAT.

The Trait Approach: Identifying Patterns of Behavior

- The trait approach tries to identify personality dimensions that can be used to characterize an individual's behavior.
- Many personality psychologists currently focus on the Big Five personality factors: conscientiousness, agreeableness, neuroticism, openness to experience, and extroversion.
- To address the question of why traits arise, trait theorists often adopt a biological perspective, construing personality largely as the result of genetic influences on brain mechanisms.

The Psychodynamic Approach: Forces That Lie beneath Awareness

- Freud believed that the personality results from a complex interplay among id, ego, and superego.
- Defense mechanisms are methods the mind may use to reduce anxiety generated from unacceptable impulses.
- Freud also believed that the developing person passes through a series of psychosexual stages and that individuals who fail to progress beyond one of the stages have corresponding personality traits.

The Humanistic-Existential Approach: Personality as Choice

- The humanistic-existential approach to personality grew out of philosophical traditions that are at odds with most of the assumptions of the trait and psychoanalytic approaches.
- Humanists see personality as directed by an inherent striving toward self-actualization and development of our unique human potentials.
- Existentialists focus on angst and the defensive response people often have to questions about the meaning of life and the inevitability of death.

The Social Cognitive Approach: Personalities in Situations

- The social cognitive approach focuses on personality as arising from individuals' behavior in situations.
- According to social cognitive personality theorists, the same person may behave differently in different situations, but should behave consistently in similar situations.
- People translate their goals into behavior through outcome expectancies, their assumptions about the likely consequences of future behaviors.

The Self: Personality in the Mirror

- The self-concept is a person's knowledge of his or her behaviors, traits, and other characteristics.
- People's self-concept develops through social feedback, and people often act to try to confirm these views.
- Self-esteem is a person's evaluation of self, and is derived from being accepted by others, as well as by how we evaluate ourselves by comparison to others.

Key Terms

personality (p. 333)

self-report (p. 335)

Minnesota Multiphasic Personality Inventory (MMPI) (p. 335)

projective techniques (p. 336)

Rorschach Inkblot Test (p. 336)

Thematic Apperception Text (TAT) (p. 336)

trait (p. 338)

Big Five (p. 339)

psychodynamic approach (p. 342)

id (p. 342)

ego (p. 343)

superego (p. 343)

defense mechanisms (p. 344)

rationalization (p. 344)

reaction formation (p. 344)

projection (p. 344)

regression (p. 344)

displacement (p. 344)

identification (p. 344)

sublimation (p. 344)

psychosexual stages (p. 345)

fixation (p. 346)

oral stage (p. 346)

anal stage (p. 346)

phallic stage (p. 346)

Oedipus conflict (p. 346)

latency stage (p. 346)

genital stage (p. 346)

self-actualizing tendency (p. 348)

existential approach (p. 348)

social cognitive approach (p. 350)

person-situation controversy (p. 350)

personal constructs (p. 351)

outcome expectancies (p. 352)

locus of control (p. 352)

self-concept (p. 353)

self-esteem (p. 353)

self-verification (p. 355)

self-serving bias (p. 358)

narcissism (p. 358)

Critical Thinking Questions

1. A school librarian is exhausted after the third grade class has spent an hour in the library. At the same time, the gym teacher dreads running the quiet study hall. What is the neurological explanation for both of their reactions?

2. Research on men who report *homophobia*—the dread of gay men and lesbians—revealed an interesting result (Adams, Wright, & Lohr, 1996). Homophobic participants, heterosexual men who agreed with statements such as "I would feel nervous being with a group of homosexuals," and a comparison group of nonhomophobic men were shown videos of sexual activity, including heterosexual, gay male, and lesbian segments. Each man's sexual arousal was then assessed by means of a device that measures penile tumescence. Curiously, the homophobic men showed greater arousal to the male homosexual images than did men in a control group. The

psychoanalytic interpretation seems clear: Men troubled by their own homosexual arousal formed opposite reactions to this unacceptable feeling, turning their unwanted attraction into "dread."

   Do these results imply that homophobia is a defense mechanism? If so, which one?

3. The text says, "There's something about being loved that helps take away the angst."

   According to a humanist or existentialist, what are some specific ways love could lessen angst?

4. The text discusses how behavior self-narratives and trait self-concepts don't always match up.

   Think about your own self-narrative and self-concept. Are there areas that don't match up? How might you explain that?

Answers to Summary Quizzes

Summary Quiz 11.1
1. c; 2. a; 3. b

Summary Quiz 11.2
4. b; 5. c; 6. d; 7. a

Summary Quiz 11.3
8. b; 9. c; 10. b; 11. d

Summary Quiz 11.4
12. a; 13. b; 14. d

Summary Quiz 11.5
15. b; 16. c; 17. a

Summary Quiz 11.6
18. c; 19. a; 20. b; 21. d

Need more help? Additional resources are located at the book's free companion Web site at: www.worthpublishers.com/schacterbrief1e

Psychological Disorders

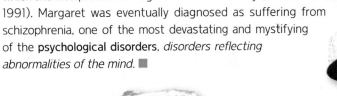

MARGARET, A 39-YEAR-OLD MOTHER, believed that God was punishing her for marrying a man she did not love and bringing two children into the world. As her punishment, God had made her and her children immortal so that they would have to suffer in their unhappy home life forever—a realization that came to her one evening when she was washing dishes and saw a fork lying across a knife in the shape of a cross. Margaret found further support for her belief in two pieces of evidence. First, a local TV station was rerunning old episodes of *The Honeymooners*, a 1950s situation comedy in which the main characters often argue and shout at each other. She saw this as a sign from God that her own marital conflict would go on forever. Second, she believed (falsely) that the pupils of her children's eyes were fixed in size and would neither dilate nor contract—which she interpreted as a sign of their immortality (Oltmanns, Neale, & Davison, 1991). Margaret was eventually diagnosed as suffering from schizophrenia, one of the most devastating and mystifying of the **psychological disorders**, *disorders reflecting abnormalities of the mind.* ■

LEONARD MCCOMBE/TIME LIFE PICTURES/GETTY IMAGES

Is a bitter argument on TV a sign from God? Probably not, but for a viewer troubled by a mental disorder like schizophrenia, excess meaning may be found all around.

psychological disorders Disorders reflecting abnormalities of the mind.

medical model The conceptualization of psychological abnormalities as diseases that, like biological diseases, have symptoms and causes and possible cures.

Psychological disorders (sometimes called mental disorders) are hard to define and explain. Psychiatrists and psychologists agree that a psychological disorder is not, say, extreme anxiety before a chemistry test or deep sadness at the death of a beloved pet. To qualify as a psychological disorder, thoughts, feelings, and emotions must be persistent, harmful to the person experiencing them, and uncontrollable. Approximately 40% of people will develop some type of psychological disorder during the course of their lives—at a substantial cost in health, productivity, and happiness (Kessler et al., 1994; Narrow et al., 2002; Regier et al., 1993; Robins & Regier, 1991). Data compiled by the Global Burden of Disease Study reveal that, after cardiovascular disease, psychological disorders are the second-greatest contributor to a loss of years of healthy life (Murray & Lopez, 1996). Problems of the head are nearly as great a plague on humanity as problems of the heart.

Psychologists who study mental disorders seek to uncover ways to understand, treat, and prevent such human misery. And because the mindbugs they uncover reveal the mind's limits and functions, the study of mental disorders offers insights into the nature of normal mental functioning. This chapter goes deeper into the study of mindbugs than does any other chapter of the book because it is devoted to the psychological problems that are so persistent and intense that they interfere with people's lives. In discovering what goes wrong in psychological disorder, we learn what the mind must do in order to run trouble-free.

The study of psychological disorders can be unsettling because you may well see yourself mirrored in the various conditions. Like medical students who come to worry about their own symptoms with each new disease they examine, students of abnormal psychology can catch their own version of "medical students' disease," noticing personal oddities as they read about the peculiarities of others (Woods, Natterson, & Silverman, 1966). Is your late-night frenzy to finish an assignment a kind of mania? Is your fear of snakes a phobia? Does forgetting where you left your keys qualify you for diagnosis with a dissociative disorder? Please relax. You may not always avoid self-diagnosis, but you're not alone. Studying mental disorders heightens everyone's sensitivity to his or her own eccentricities. In fact, you would be "abnormal" if studying mental disorders *didn't* make you reflect on yourself.

In this chapter, we first consider the question, "What is abnormal?" The enormously complicated human mind can produce behaviors, thoughts, and emotions that change radically from moment to moment. How do psychologists decide that a particular mind is disordered? We will examine the key factors that must be weighed in making such a decision. Our exploration of psychological disorders will then focus on each of several major forms of mental disorder, including anxiety disorders, dissociative disorders, mood disorders, schizophrenia, and personality disorders. As we view each of these problems, we will look at how they can influence thought and behavior, and at what is known about their prevalence and their causes.

Identifying Psychological Disorders: What Is Abnormal?

The idea of a *psychological disorder* is a relatively recent invention, historically speaking. People who act strangely or report bizarre thoughts or emotions have been known since ancient times, but their difficulties were often understood in the context of religion or the supernatural. In some cultures and religious traditions, madness is still interpreted as possession by animal spirits or demons, as enchantment by a witch or shaman, or as God's punishment for wrongdoing. In many societies, including our own, people with

SPENCER 1929

WISE   IGNORANT   INSANE   IDIOTIC

psychological disorders have been feared and ridiculed, and often treated as criminals—punished, imprisoned, or put to death for their "crime" of deviating from the normal.

Over the past 200 years, these ways of looking at psychological abnormalities have largely been replaced in industrialized areas of the world by a **medical model**, *the conceptualization of psychological disorders as diseases that, like biological diseases, have symptoms and causes and possible cures.* Treating abnormal behavior in the way we treat illness suggests that a first step is to determine the nature of the problem through *diagnosis.* In diagnosis, clinicians seek to determine the nature of the patient's mental disease by assessing *symptoms*—behaviors, thoughts, and emotions suggestive of an underlying abnormal *syndrome,* a coherent cluster of symptoms usually due to a single cause. So, for example, just as a fever, sniffles, and cough are symptoms of a cold, Margaret's delusions, paranoia and irrational beliefs can be viewed as symptoms of her schizophrenia.

● **What's the first step in helping someone with a psychological disorder?**

As useful as the medical model can be, it should nonetheless be viewed with some skepticism. Every action or thought suggestive of abnormality cannot be traced to an underlying disease (American Psychiatric Association, 2000; Keisler, 1999; Persons, 1986). And, as you will discover in Chapter 13, some of the most successful treatments for abnormal behavior or thought focus on simply eliminating the behavior or thought; no effort is made to treat the root "syndrome." Nevertheless, the medical model is still a vast improvement over older alternatives—such as viewing psychological disorders as the work of witchcraft or as punishment for sin. Viewing psychological disorders as medical problems reminds us that people who are suffering deserve care and treatment, not condemnation.

To understand how psychological disorders are defined and diagnosed, we'll first consider definitions of normal and abnormal behavior. Then we'll look at how mental disorders are categorized into groups, how the causes and cures of disorders are viewed in the medical model, and what consequences can occur—for better or for worse—when such disorders are diagnosed.

ARCHIVO ICONOGRAFICO, S.A./CORBIS

Interior of a Madhouse, Francisco de Goya (1746–1828), 1815–1819. Early treatment of mental disorders amounted to little more than imprisonment.

DSM-IV-TR (Diagnostic and Statistical Manual of Mental Disorders [Fourth Edition, Text Revision]) A classification system that describes the features used to diagnose each recognized mental disorder and indicates how the disorder can be distinguished from other, similar problems.

Classification of Psychological Disorders

To facilitate diagnosis, psychologists have generally adopted an approach developed by psychiatrists—physicians concerned with treatment of mental disorders—who use a system for classifying mental disorders. In 1952, in recognition of the need to have a consensual diagnostic system for therapists and researchers, the first version of the *Diagnostic and Statistical Manual of Mental Disorders* (*DSM*) was published, followed by a revision in 1968 (*DSM-II*). These early versions provided a common language for talking about disorders, but the diagnostic criteria were still often vague and based on tenuous theoretical assumptions.

The most current version of this manual is the *Diagnostic and Statistical Manual of Mental Disorders* (*Fourth Edition, Text Revision*), or *DSM-IV-TR* (American Psychiatric Association, 2000). The **DSM-IV-TR** is *a classification system that describes the features used to diagnose each recognized mental disorder and indicates how the disorder can be distinguished from other, similar problems*. Each disorder is named and classified as though it were a distinct illness. The major mental disorders distinguished in the *DSM-IV-TR* are shown in **TABLE 12.1** on page 367.

A major misconception is the idea that a mental disorder can be defined entirely in terms of deviation from the average, the typical, or "healthy." Yes, people who have mental

● **Why is mental disease more than simply a departure from the norm?**

disorders may behave, think, or experience emotions in unusual ways, but simple departure from the norm can't be the whole picture, or we'd rapidly be diagnosing mental disorders in the most creative and visionary people—anyone whose ideas deviate from those around them.

The *DSM-IV-TR* definition takes these concerns into account by focusing on three key elements that must be present for a cluster of symptoms to qualify as a potential mental disorder:

■ A disorder is manifested in symptoms that involve *disturbances in behavior, thoughts, or emotions*.

■ The symptoms are associated with significant *personal distress or impairment*.

■ The symptoms stem from an *internal dysfunction* (biological, psychological, or both).

So, on the one hand, if someone experiences extreme sadness and distress after the death of a loved one, for example, this would not be indicative of a mental disorder because bereavement is a normal, expected response that does not originate from internal dysfunction. On the other hand, a prolonged period of unremitting sadness that interferes with a person's

● **Why is it difficult to make reliable diagnoses?**

ability to perform the activities of everyday life might indeed indicate depression, which is an example of a mood disorder, as shown in **TABLE 12.1**.

As these examples suggest, determining the degree to which a person has a psychological disorder is always difficult. Psychological disorder exists along a continuum from normal to abnormal without a bright line of separation. The *DSM-IV-TR* recognizes this explicitly by recommending that diagnoses include a *global assessment of functioning,* a 0 to 100 rating of the person, with more severe disorders indicated by lower numbers and more effective functioning by higher numbers.

Even so, the path to reliable diagnosis remains thorny. In general, the *DSM-IV-TR* produces better diagnostic reliability than did earlier *DSM* versions, but critics argue that considerable room for improvement remains. Numerous diagnostic categories continue to depend on interpretation-based criteria rather than on observable behavior, and

● *Some atypical behavior may be based on ulterior motives, like making a statement about recycling*

DAVID GROSSMAN/ALAMY

TABLE 12.1

Main *DSM-IV-TR* Categories of Mental Disorders

1. **Disorders usually first diagnosed in infancy, childhood, or early adolescence:** These include mental retardation, bed-wetting, etc.

2. **Delirium, dementia, amnestic, and other cognitive disorders:** These are disorders of thinking caused by Alzheimer's, human immunodeficiency virus (HIV) and acquired immunodeficiency syndrome (AIDS), Parkinson's disease, etc.

3. **Mental disorders due to a general medical condition not elsewhere classified:** These include problems caused by physical deterioration of the brain due to disease, drug use, etc.

4. **Substance-related disorders:** These problems are caused by dependence on alcohol, cocaine, tobacco, and so forth [see Chapter 8].

5. **Schizophrenia and other psychotic disorders:** This is a group of disorders characterized by major disturbances in perception, language and thought, emotion, and behavior [this chapter].

6. **Mood disorders:** These are problems associated with severe disturbances of mood, such as depression, mania, or alternating episodes of both [this chapter].

7. **Anxiety disorders:** These include problems associated with severe anxiety, such as phobias and obsessive-compulsive disorder [this chapter], and posttraumatic stress disorder [see Chapter 15].

8. **Somatoform disorders:** These are problems related to unusual preoccupation with physical health or physical symptoms with no physical cause [see Chapter 15].

9. **Factitious disorders:** These are disorders that the individual adopts to satisfy some economic or psychological need [see Chapter 15].

10. **Dissociative disorder:** In these types of disorders, the normal integration of consciousness, memory, or identity is suddenly and temporarily altered, such as amnesia and dissociative identity disorder [this chapter].

11. **Sexual and gender identity disorders:** These include problems related to unsatisfactory sexual activity, finding unusual objects or situations arousing, gender identity problems, and so forth.

12. **Eating disorders:** These are problems related to food, such as anorexia nervosa and bulimia nervosa [see Chapter 10].

13. **Sleep disorders:** These include serious disturbances of sleep, such as insomnia, sleep terrors, or hypersomnia [see Chapter 8].

14. **Impulse control disorder not elsewhere classified:** These problems include kleptomania, pathological gambling, and pyromania.

15. **Adjustment disorders:** These problems are related to specific stressors such as divorce, family discord, and economic concern.

16. **Personality disorders:** These problems are related to lifelong behavior patterns such as self-centeredness, overdependency, and antisocial behaviors [this chapter].

17. **Other conditions that may be a focus of clinical attention:** These include problems related to physical or sexual abuse, relational problems, and occupational problems.

Source: From the DSM-IV-TR (American Psychiatric Association, 2000).

diagnosis continues to focus on patient self-reports (which are susceptible to censorship and distortion). Levels of agreement among different diagnosticians can vary depending on the diagnostic category (Bertelsen, 1999; Nathan & Lagenbucher, 1999). Agreement among diagnosticians on, say, whether a patient has schizophrenia may even depend on the clinic setting. Such disagreement may not reflect differences in the prevalence of schizophrenia in various localities but rather in the array of symptoms that the clinicians were trained to expect in people with the disease (Keller et al., 1995).

"First off, you're not a nut. You're a legume."

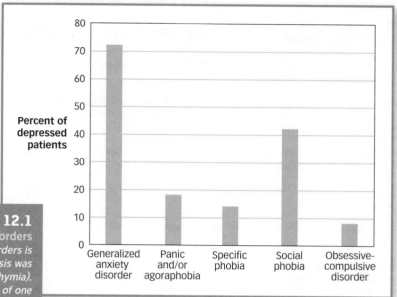

●●●●●●●●●●●●●●●●●●●●●●●●●● **FIGURE 12.1**
Comorbidity of Depression and Anxiety Disorders
The comorbidity of depression and anxiety disorders is substantial. Of 102 patients whose primary diagnosis was depression (major depressive disorder or dysthymia), large percentages also had a secondary diagnosis of one or more anxiety disorders. (Brown et al., 2001.)

● *The Mad Hatter in Alice in Wonderland was Lewis Carroll's portrayal of a mental disorder common among hatmakers in the 1800s. Hatters could become "mad as a hatter" because they unwittingly exposed themselves to a mercury compound with serious side effects when they processed fur into felt for hats.*

Diagnostic difficulty is further increased when a person suffers from more than one disorder. As shown in **FIGURE 12.1**, for example, people with depression (a mood disorder) often have secondary diagnoses of anxiety disorders. *The co-occurrence of two or more disorders in a single individual* is referred to as **comorbidity** and is relatively common in patients seen within the *DSM* diagnostic system (Kessler et al., 1994). Comorbidity raises a host of confusing possibilities: A person could be depressed because a phobia makes social situations impossible, or the person could be phobic about showing a despairing mood in public, or the disorders could be unrelated but co-occurring. Diagnosticians try hard to solve the problem of comorbidity because understanding the underlying basis for a person's disorder may suggest methods of treatment.

Causation of Psychological Disorders

The medical model of psychological disorder suggests that knowing a person's diagnosis is useful because any given category of mental illness is likely to have a distinctive cause. In other words, just as different viruses, or bacteria, or types of trauma, or genetic abnormalities cause different physical illnesses, so a specifiable pattern of causes (or *etiology*) may exist for different psychological disorders. The medical model also suggests that each category of psychological disorder is likely to have a common *prognosis*, a typical course over time and susceptibility to treatment and cure. Unfortunately, this basic medical model is usually an oversimplification; it is rarely useful to focus on a *single cause* that is *internal* to the person and that suggests a *single cure.*

"Mad Hatter syndrome," first described in the 1800s in workers who used a mercury compound in making felt hats, was one of those rare single-cause disorders. The symptoms: trembling, loss of memory and coordination, slurred speech, depression, and anxiety. The cause: mercury poisoning. The cure: getting out of the hat business. Things are seldom so simple, however, and a full explanation of all the different ways in which the mind can become disordered needs to take into account multiple levels of causation.

An integrated perspective that incorporates biological, psychological, and environmental factors offers the most comprehensive and useful framework for understanding most psychological disorders. On the biological side, the focus is on genetic influences, biochemical imbalances, and structural abnormalities of the brain. The psychological perspective focuses on maladaptive learning and coping, cognitive biases, dysfunctional

● **Why does assessment require looking at a number of factors?**
●●●●●●●●●●●●●●●●●●●●●●●●●●●

attitudes, and interpersonal problems. Environmental factors include poor socialization, stressful life circumstances, and cultural and social inequities. The complexity of causation suggests that different individuals can experience a similar psychological disorder (e.g., depression) for different reasons. A person might fall into depression as a result of biological causes (e.g., genetics, hormones), psychological causes (e.g., faulty beliefs, hopelessness, poor strategies for coping with loss), environmental causes (e.g., stress or loneliness), or (more likely) as a result of some combination of these factors. And, of course, multiple causes mean there may not be single cures.

The observation that most disorders have both internal (biological and psychological) *and* external (environmental) causes has given rise to a theory known as the **diathesis-stress model**, which suggests that *a person may be predisposed for a psychological disorder that remains unexpressed until triggered by stress*. The diathesis is the internal predisposition, which could be genetic, and the stress is the external trigger. For example, most people were able to cope with their strong emotional reactions to the terrorist attack of September 11, 2001. However, for some who had a predisposition to negative emotions or were already contending with major life stressors, the horror of the events may have overwhelmed their ability to cope, thereby precipitating a psychological disorder. Although diastheses can be inherited, it's important to remember that heritability is not destiny. A person who inherits a diathesis may never encounter the precipitating stress, whereas someone with little genetic propensity to a dis-

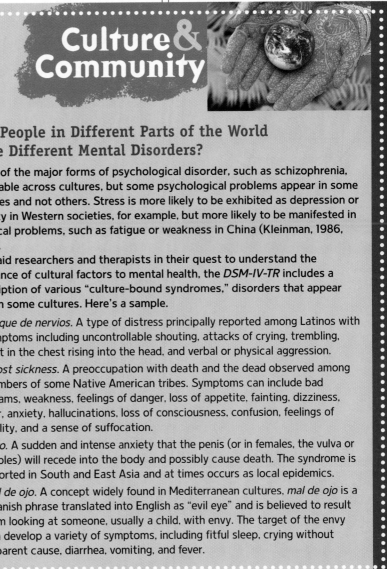

Culture & Community

Can People in Different Parts of the World Have Different Mental Disorders?

Many of the major forms of psychological disorder, such as schizophrenia, are stable across cultures, but some psychological problems appear in some cultures and not others. Stress is more likely to be exhibited as depression or anxiety in Western societies, for example, but more likely to be manifested in physical problems, such as fatigue or weakness in China (Kleinman, 1986, 1988).

To aid researchers and therapists in their quest to understand the relevance of cultural factors to mental health, the *DSM-IV-TR* includes a description of various "culture-bound syndromes," disorders that appear only in some cultures. Here's a sample.

- *Ataque de nervios*. A type of distress principally reported among Latinos with symptoms including uncontrollable shouting, attacks of crying, trembling, heat in the chest rising into the head, and verbal or physical aggression.

- *Ghost sickness*. A preoccupation with death and the dead observed among members of some Native American tribes. Symptoms can include bad dreams, weakness, feelings of danger, loss of appetite, fainting, dizziness, fear, anxiety, hallucinations, loss of consciousness, confusion, feelings of futility, and a sense of suffocation.

- *Koro*. A sudden and intense anxiety that the penis (or in females, the vulva or nipples) will recede into the body and possibly cause death. The syndrome is reported in South and East Asia and at times occurs as local epidemics.

- *Mal de ojo*. A concept widely found in Mediterranean cultures, *mal de ojo* is a Spanish phrase translated into English as "evil eye" and is believed to result from looking at someone, usually a child, with envy. The target of the envy can develop a variety of symptoms, including fitful sleep, crying without apparent cause, diarrhea, vomiting, and fever.

order may come to suffer from it given the right pattern of stress. The tendency to oversimplify mental disorders by attributing them to single, internal causes is nowhere more evident than in the interpretation of the role of the brain in psychological disorders. Brain scans of people with and without disorders can give rise to an unusually strong impression

● What are the limitations of using brain scans for diagnosing?

that psychological problems are internal—after all, there it is!—and perhaps also permanent, inevitable, and even untreatable. Brain influences and processes are fundamentally important for knowing the full story of psychological disorders but are not the only chapter in that story.

Searching for the biological causes of psychological disorders in the brain and body also tends to invite a particular error in explanation—the *intervention-causation fallacy*. This fallacy involves the assumption that if a treatment is effective, it must address the cause of the problem. This may sometimes be true, but it is certainly not a general rule. To get a sense of the error in this logic, imagine that you've spent sleepless night after sleepless night worrying about a loved one who was recently hospitalized with a serious illness. You discover that taking a sleeping medicine before bed helps you sleep. On the basis of your favorable response, should we conclude that your insomnia was caused by a deficiency of sleeping pills—that a part of your brain needed the

comorbidity The co-occurrence of two or more disorders in a single individual.

diathesis-stress model A model suggesting that a person may be predisposed for a mental disorder that remains unexpressed until triggered by stress.

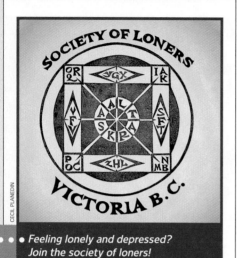

● *Feeling lonely and depressed? Join the society of loners!*

chemicals in the pills? Of course not. Your anxiety and sleeplessness were due to your loved one's illness, not to the absence of a pill. Be cautious about drawing inferences about causality based on responsiveness to treatment; the cure does not necessarily point to the cause.

The diagnosis and classification of mental disorders is a useful basis for exploring causes and cures of psychological problems. At the same time, these tools make it all too easy to assume that the problems arise from single, internal causes that are inherited and involve brain dysfunction—and that therefore can be dispelled with an intervention that simply eliminates the cause. Psychological problems are usually more challenging and complicated than this ideal model would suggest.

Consequences of Labeling

An important complication in the diagnosis and classification of psychological disorders is the effect of labeling. Psychiatric labels can have negative consequences, since many of these labels carry the baggage of negative stereotypes and stigma, such as the idea that mental disorder is a sign of personal weakness, or the idea that psychiatric patients are dangerous. The stigma associated with mental disorders may explain why nearly 70% of people with diagnosable psychological disorders do not seek treatment (Kessler et al., 1996; Regier et al., 1993; Sussman, Robins, & Earls, 1987).

Unfortunately, educating people about mental disorders does not dispel the stigma borne by those with these diseases (Phelan et al., 1997). In fact, expectations created by psychiatric labels can sometimes even compromise the judgment of mental health professionals (Garb, 1998; Langer & Abelson, 1974; Temerlin & Trousdale, 1969). In a classic demonstration of this phenomenon, psychologist David Rosenhan and six associates reported to different mental hospitals complaining of "hearing voices"—a symptom sometimes found in people with schizophrenia. Each was

● **Why might someone avoid seeking help?**

admitted to a hospital, and each promptly reported that the symptom had ceased. Even so, hospital staff were reluctant to identify these "patients" as normal: it took an average of 19 days for these "patients" to secure their release, and even then they were released with the diagnosis of "schizophrenia in remission" (Rosenhan, 1973). Apparently, once hospital staff had labeled these "patients" as having a psychological disease, the label stuck.

Labeling may even affect how the labeled person views him- or herself; persons given such a label may come to view themselves not just as mentally disordered, but as hopeless or worthless. Such a view may cause these persons to develop an attitude of defeat and, as a result, to fail to work toward their own recovery. As one small step toward counteracting such consequences, clinicians have adopted the important practice of applying labels to the disorder and not to the person with the disorder. For example, a patient might be described as "a person with schizophrenia," not as "a schizophrenic." You'll notice that we follow this model in the text.

"We don't use the word 'crazy' in this office, Mr. Channing. Everywhere else, sure, but not here."

summary quiz [12.1]

1. The view that a person may be predisposed for a psychological disorder that remains unexpressed until triggered by external causes is called
   a. the medical model.
   b. the diathesis-stress model.
   c. the comorbidity model.
   d. the intervention causation fallacy.

2. The assumption that if a treatment is effective, it must address the cause of the problem is called
   a. the medical model.
   b. the diathesis-stress model.
   c. the comorbidity model.
   d. the intervention causation fallacy.

3. Which of the following individuals is most likely to have a psychological disorder, according to the *DSM-IV-TR*?
   a. Brittany feels very anxious before she takes exams, even though she always performs well on them.
   b. Jeff was grief-stricken when his beloved dog died 5 years ago, and he still is not ready to get another dog.
   c. Since being demoted at her job 2 years ago, Jill has become hostile toward her colleagues and preoccupied with undermining their work performance while neglecting her own job responsibilities.
   d. Kyle was laid off 6 months ago when his company down-sized, and he has been unable to find work since. Lately, he has been feeling a great deal of distress.

Anxiety Disorders: When Fears Take Over

"Okay, time for a pop quiz that will be half your grade for this class!" If your instructor had actually said that, you would probably have experienced a wave of anxiety and dread. Your reaction would be appropriate, and—no matter how intense the feeling—it would not be a sign that you have a psychological disorder. In fact, situation-related anxiety is normal and can be adaptive—in this case, perhaps by reminding you to keep up with your textbook assignments so you are prepared for pop quizzes. When anxiety arises that is out of proportion to real threats and challenges, however, it is maladaptive. It can take hold of people's lives, stealing their peace of mind and undermining their ability to function normally. Pathological anxiety is expressed as an **anxiety disorder**, *the class of psychological disorder in which anxiety is the predominant feature*. People commonly experience more than one type of anxiety disorder at a given time, and there is significant comorbidity between anxiety and depression (Brown & Barlow, 2002). Among the anxiety disorders recognized in the *DSM-IV-TR* are *generalized anxiety disorder, phobic disorders, panic disorder,* and *obsessive-compulsive disorder*.

● **When is anxiety harmful, and when is it helpful?**

Generalized Anxiety Disorder

Terry, a 31-year-old man, began to experience debilitating anxiety during his first year as medical resident. The 36-hour on-call periods were grueling, and he became concerned that he and other interns were making too many errors and oversights. He worried incessantly for a year and finally resigned his position. However, he continued to be plagued with anxiety about making mistakes—self-doubt that extended to his personal relationships. When he eventually sought treatment, he described himself as "worthless" and unable to control his debilitating anxiety, and he complained of headaches and constant fatigue (Vitkus, 1996).

Terry's symptoms are typical of **generalized anxiety disorder (GAD)**—called *generalized* because the unrelenting worries are not focused on any particular threat; they are, in fact, often exaggerated and irrational. In people suffering from GAD, *chronic excessive*

anxiety disorder The class of mental disorder in which anxiety is the predominant feature.

generalized anxiety disorder (GAD) A disorder characterized by chronic excessive worry accompanied by three or more of the following symptoms: restlessness, fatigue, concentration problems, irritability, muscle tension, and sleep disturbance.

phobic disorders Disorders characterized by marked, persistent, and excessive fear and avoidance of specific objects, activities, or situations.

specific phobia A disorder that involves an irrational fear of a particular object or situation that markedly interferes with an individual's ability to function.

social phobia A disorder that involves an irrational fear of being publicly humiliated or embarrassed.

preparedness theory The idea that people are instinctively predisposed toward certain fears.

worry is accompanied by three or more of the following symptoms: restlessness, fatigue, concentration problems, irritability, muscle tension, and sleep disturbance. The uncontrollable worrying produces a sense of loss of control that can so erode self-confidence that simple decisions seem fraught with dire consequences. For example, Terry needed to buy a new suit for a special occasion but began shaking and sweating when he approached a clothing store because he was afraid of choosing the "wrong" suit. He became so anxious that he could not even enter the store.

About 5% of North Americans are estimated to suffer from GAD at some time in their lives (Kessler et al., 1994). Research suggests that both biological and psychological factors contribute to the risk of GAD. GAD occurs more frequently in lower-socioeconomic groups than in middle- and upper-income groups (Blazer et al., 1991) and is approximately twice as common in women as in men (Eaton et al., 1994). The condition is especially prevalent among people who have low incomes, are living in large cities, or are trapped in environments rendered unpredictable by political and economic strife.

● **What factors contribute to GAD?**

The causes of GAD are unknown; some patients with GAD respond to treatment with drugs that appear to stimulate the neurotransmitter gamma-aminobutyric acid (GABA), but as you read in the previous section, just because a drug remediates the symptoms, this does not necessarily mean that GAD is caused by an imbalance in GABA. Some research suggests that unpredictable traumatic experiences in childhood increase the risk of developing GAD, which supports the idea that environmental stressors play a role (Torgensen, 1986). Moreover, major life changes (new job, new baby, personal loss, physical illness, etc.) often immediately precede the development of GAD (Blazer, Hughes, & George, 1987). The relatively high rates of GAD among women may also be related to stress because women are more likely than men to live in poverty, experience discrimination, or be subjected to sexual or physical abuse (Koss, 1990; Strickland, 1991). Still, many people who might be expected to develop GAD don't, supporting the diathesis-stress notion that biological and/or genetic vulnerability must also be a key factor in this disorder.

● *Potential anxiety victims? Generalized anxiety disorder is more common for women and children living below the poverty line than for others.*

 **ONLY HUMAN**

DON'T LOOK DOWN! A 1992 *Los Angeles Times* story on fear of heights featured an interview with the psychotherapist who heads the Anxiety Disorders Association. He reported that one of his patients could cross the 200-foot-high Chesapeake Bay Bridge in Maryland only if his wife drove the car and locked him in the trunk.

Phobic Disorders

Unlike the generalized anxiety of GAD, anxiety in a phobic disorder is more specific. The *DSM-IV-TR* describes **phobic disorders** as characterized by *marked, persistent, and excessive fear and avoidance of specific objects, activities, or situations.* An individual with a phobic disorder recognizes that the fear is irrational but cannot prevent it from interfering with everyday functioning. Consider Mary, a 47-year-old mother of three, who sought treatment for *claustrophobia*—an intense fear of enclosed spaces. She traced her fear to childhood, when her older siblings would scare her by locking her in closets and confining her under blankets. Her own children grown, she wanted to find a job but could not because of a terror of elevators and other confined places that, she felt, shackled her to her home (Carson, Butcher, & Mineka, 2000). Many people feel anxious in enclosed spaces, but Mary's fears were abnormal and dysfunctional because they were wildly disproportional to any actual risk and because they imposed unwanted restrictions on her life.

Phobic disorders can be divided into two major classes. A **specific phobia** is *an irrational fear of a particular object or situation that markedly interferes with an individual's ability to function.* Specific phobias fall into five categories: (1) animals (e.g., dogs, cats, rats, snakes, spiders); (2) natural environments (e.g., heights, darkness, water, storms); (3) situations (e.g., bridges, elevators, tunnels, enclosed places); (4) blood, injections, and injury; and (5) other phobias, including illness and death. Approximately 11% of people in the United States will develop a specific phobia during their lives and—for unknown reasons—the risk seems to be increasing in younger generations (Magee et al., 1996). With few exceptions (e.g., fear of heights), specific phobias are much more common among women than among men, with a ratio of about 4 to 1 (Kessler et al., 1994, 1996).

The second major class of phobic disorder is **social phobia**, which is *an irrational fear of being publicly humiliated or embarrassed*. Social phobia can be restricted to situations such as public speaking, eating in public, or urinating in a public bathroom, or the fear can be generalized to a variety of social situations that involve being observed or interacting with unfamiliar people. Individuals with social phobia try to avoid situations where unfamiliar people might evaluate them, and they experience intense anxiety and distress when public exposure is unavoidable. Social phobia can develop in childhood, but it typically emerges between early adolescence and the age of 25 (Schneier et al., 1992). Many people experience social phobia; about 11% of men and 15% of women qualify for diagnosis at some time in their lives (Kessler et al., 1994). Even higher rates are found among people who are undereducated, have low incomes, or both (Magee et al., 1996).

Why are phobias so common? The high rates of both specific and social phobias suggest a predisposition to be fearful of certain objects and situations. Indeed, most of

● **Why might we be predisposed to certain phobias?**

the situations and objects of people's phobias could pose a real threat—for example, falling from a high place or being attacked by a vicious dog or poisonous snake or spider. Social situations have their own dangers. A roomful of strangers may not attack or bite, but they could form impressions that affect your prospects for friends, jobs, or marriage. And of course, in some very rare cases, they could attack or bite.

Observations such as these are the basis for the **preparedness theory** of phobia, which maintains that *people are instinctively predisposed toward certain fears* (Seligman, 1971). The preparedness theory is supported by research showing that both humans and monkeys can quickly be conditioned to have a fear response for stimuli such as snakes and spiders but not for neutral stimuli such as flowers or toy rabbits (Cook & Mineka, 1989; Öhman, Dimberg, & Ost, 1985). This research raises the possibility that phobias can be classically conditioned: thus, for example, a person might develop an irrational fear of all dogs after experiencing a bite from one dog. However, conditioning isn't a complete explanation of phobias: Not everyone bitten by a dog develops a phobia, and people who do have phobias are no more likely than people without phobias to recall personal experiences with the feared object (Craske, 1999; McNally & Steketec, 1985).

Other factors must also predispose individuals to develop phobias. Genetics probably plays a role; for example, over 30% of first-degree relatives (parents, siblings, or children) of patients with specific phobias also have a phobia (Fryer et al., 1990). Temperament may also play a role in vulnerability to phobias: infants who display excessive shyness and inhibition are at an increased risk for developing a phobic behavior later in life (Hirschfeld et al., 1992; Morris, 2001; Stein, Chavira, & Jang, 2001). And neurobiological factors may also play a role: Abnormalities in the

No fear of heights here. Construction workers eat their lunches atop a steel beam 800 feet above ground during the 1932 construction of the RCA Building (now the GE Building) in Rockefeller Center in Manhattan.

BETTMANN/CORBIS

To someone with a phobia of dogs, there are no best friends in the park.

THOMAS NORTHCUT/GETTY IMAGES

neurotransmitters serotonin and dopamine are more common in individuals who report phobias than among people who don't (Stein, 1998), and individuals with phobias sometimes show abnormally high levels of activity in the amygdala, an area of the brain linked with the development of emotional associations (discussed in Chapter 9 and in Hirschfeld et al., 1992; LeDoux, 1998; Morris, 2001; Ninan, 1999; Stein et al., 2001).

Panic Disorder

If you suddenly found yourself in danger of death, a wave of panic might wash over you. People who suffer panic attacks are frequently overwhelmed by such intense fears and by powerful physical symptoms of anxiety—in the absence of actual danger. Mindy, a 25-year-old art director, had been having panic attacks with increasing frequency, often two or three times a day, when she finally sought help at a clinic. The attacks began with a sudden wave of "horrible fear" that seemed to come out of nowhere, often accompanied by trembling, nausea, and a tightening of the chest. The attacks began when she was in high school and had continued intermittently ever since. During an episode, Mindy feared that she would do something crazy (Spitzer et al., 1994, pp. 201–202).

Mindy's condition, called **panic disorder**, is characterized by *the sudden occurrence of multiple psychological and physiological symptoms that contribute to a feeling of stark terror*. The acute symptoms of a panic attack typically last only a few minutes and include shortness of breath, heart palpitations, sweating, dizziness, and a fear that one is going crazy or about to die. Not surprisingly, panic attacks often send people rushing to emergency rooms or their physicians' offices for what they believe is a heart attack or other medical emergency (Hirschfeld, 1996).

Approximately 8% to 12% of the U.S. population reports having an occasional panic attack, typically during a period of intense stress (Norton et al., 1985; Salge, Beck, & Logan, 1988; Telch, Lucas, & Nelson, 1989). An occasional episode is not sufficient for a diagnosis of panic disorder. According to *DSM-IV-TR* criteria, panic disorder is only diagnosed if the individual experiences recurrent unexpected attacks and also reports significant dread and anxiety about having another attack. When this criterion is applied, approximately 3.5% of people will have diagnosable panic disorder sometime in their lives; of those, about three out of seven will also develop **agoraphobia**, *a specific phobia involving a fear of venturing into public places* (Kessler et al., 1994). These people are not afraid of public places in themselves; rather they are afraid of having a panic attack in a public place or around strangers. Panic disorder is especially prevalent among women, who are twice as likely to be diagnosed with it as are men (Weissman et al., 1997).

● **What is it about public places that many agoraphobics fear?**

Family studies suggest a modest hereditary component to panic disorder. If one identical twin has the disorder, the likelihood of the other twin having it is about 30% (Crowe, 1990; Kendler et al., 1995; Torgensen, 1983). Psychological factors may also play a role: People who experience panic attacks may be hypersensitive to physiological signs of anxiety, which they interpret as having disastrous consequences for their well-being. Supporting this cognitive explanation is research showing that people who are high in anxiety sensitivity (i.e., they believe that bodily arousal and other symptoms of anxiety can have dire consequences) have an elevated risk for experiencing panic attacks (Schmidt, Lerew, & Jackson, 1997; Telch et al., 1989). Thus, panic attacks may be traceable to the fear of fear itself. Understanding this psychological link may be key in developing therapies to treat patients who suffer from this disorder.

Obsessive-Compulsive Disorder

Karen, a 34-year-old with four children, experienced intrusive, repetitive thoughts in which she imagined that one or more of her children was having a serious accident. In addition, an extensive series of protective counting rituals hampered her daily routine. For example, when grocery shopping, Karen had the feeling that if she selected the first

● *In panic disorder with agoraphobia, the fear of having a panic attack in public may prevent the person from going outside.*

item (say, a box of cereal) on a shelf, something terrible would happen to her oldest child. If she selected the second item, some unknown disaster would befall her second child, and so on for the four children. Karen's preoccupation with numbers extended to other activities, most notably the pattern in which she smoked cigarettes and drank coffee: if she had one, she felt that she had to have at least four in a row or one of her children would be harmed in some way. She acknowledged that her counting rituals were irrational, but she found that she became extremely anxious when she tried to stop (Oltmanns et al., 1991).

Karen's symptoms are typical of **obsessive-compulsive disorder (OCD)**, in which *repetitive, intrusive thoughts (obsessions) and ritualistic behaviors (compulsions) designed to fend off those thoughts interfere significantly with an individual's functioning.* Anxiety plays a role in this disorder because the obsessive thoughts typically produce anxiety, and the compulsive behaviors are performed to reduce this anxiety. It is not uncommon for people to have occasional intrusive thoughts that prompt ritualistic behavior (e.g., double- or triple-checking to be sure the garage door is

● **How effective is willful effort at curing OCD?**

closed or the oven is off), but the obsessions and compulsions of OCD are intense, frequent, and experienced as irrational and excessive. Attempts to cope with the obsessive thoughts by trying to suppress or ignore them are of little or no benefit. In fact (as discussed in Chapter 8), thought suppression can backfire, increasing the frequency and intensity of the obsessive thoughts (Wegner, 1994a; Wenzlaff & Wegner, 2000).

Approximately 2.5% of people will develop OCD sometime in their lives, with similar rates across different cultures (Gibbs, 1996; Karno & Golding, 1991; Robins & Regier, 1991). Women tend to be more susceptible than men, but the difference is not large (Karno & Golding, 1991). The most common obsessions involve contamination, aggression, death, sex, disease, orderliness, and disfigurement (Jenike, Baer, & Minichiello, 1986; Rachman & DeSilva, 1978). Compulsions typically take the form of cleaning, checking, repeating, ordering/arranging, and counting (Antony, Downie, & Swinson, 1998). Although compulsive behavior is always excessive, it can vary considerably in intensity and frequency. For example, fear of contamination may lead to 15 minutes of hand washing in some individuals, while others may need to spend hours with disinfectants and extremely hot water, scrubbing their hands until they bleed.

Family studies indicate a moderate genetic heritability for OCD: Identical twins show a higher concordance than do fraternal twins. Relatives of individuals with OCD may not have the disorder themselves, but they are at greater risk for other types of anxiety disorders than are members of the general public (Billet, Richter, & Kennedy, 1998). Researchers have not determined the biological mechanisms that may contribute to OCD, but some evidence implicates heightened neural activity in the caudate nucleus of the basal ganglia (discussed in Chapter 3), a brain region known to be involved in the initiation of intentional actions (Kronig et al., 1999). Drugs that increase the activity of the neurotransmitter serotonin in the brain can inhibit the activity of the caudate nucleus and relieve some of the symptoms of obsessive-compulsive disorder (Hansen et al., 2002). However, this finding does not indicate that overactivity of the caudate nucleus is the cause of OCD. It could also be an effect of the disorder: Patients with OCD often respond favorably to psychotherapy and show a corresponding reduction in activity in the caudate nucleus (Baxter et al., 1992).

panic disorder A disorder characterized by the sudden occurrence of multiple psychological and physiological symptoms that contribute to a feeling of stark terror.

agoraphobia An extreme fear of venturing into public places.

obsessive-compulsive disorder (OCD) A disorder in which repetitive, intrusive thoughts (obsessions) and ritualistic behaviors (compulsions) designed to fend off those thoughts interfere significantly with an individual's functioning.

STEVE SMITH/SUPERSTOCK

Hand washing is a good idea whether you are an employee or not. But the feeling that one "must wash hands" can come to mind many dozens of times a day in some people with obsessive-compulsive disorder, leading to compulsive washing and even damage to the skin.

🌐 **ONLY HUMAN**

YOU NEVER KNOW WHEN YOU MIGHT NEED ONE OF THESE In May 1996, Stanford University won the right over the University of California at Berkeley to house the literary legacy of the late Pulitzer- and Oscar-winning writer William Saroyan, apparently because it also agreed to take custody of Saroyan's nonliterary property. Because Saroyan was a compulsive collector, his nonliterary archives include, among other things, hundreds of boxes of rocks, matchbook covers, old newspapers (numbering in the thousands), labels peeled off cans, and a plastic bag filled with about 10,000 rubber bands.

summary quiz [12.2]

4. Katie experiences intense anxiety and distress whenever she has to interact with unfamiliar people. She probably is suffering from
   a. generalized anxiety disorder.   c. specific phobia.
   b. social phobia.   d. panic disorder.

5. People develop phobias of certain objects, such as spiders and snakes, much more easily than objects such as flowers or stuffed animals. This fact is best explained by which theory?
   a. preparedness   c. observational learning
   b. classical conditioning   d. diathesis-stress

6. Agoraphobia often develops in a person who suffers from
   a. generalized anxiety disorder.   c. obsessive-compulsive disorder.
   b. social phobia.   d. panic disorder.

7. Symptoms of obsessive-compulsive disorder can be relieved by medications that increase the activity of the neurotransmitter
   a. GABA.   c. serotonin.
   b. dopamine.   d. epinephrine.

Dissociative Disorders: Going to Pieces

Mary, a 35-year-old social worker being treated with hypnosis for chronic pain in her forearm, mentioned to her doctor that she often found her car low on fuel in the morning despite her having filled it with gas the day before. Overnight the odometer would gain 50 to 100 miles, even though she had no memory of driving the car. During one hypnotic session, Mary suddenly blurted out in a strange voice, "It's about time you knew about me." In the new voice, she identified herself as "Marian" and described the drives that she took at night, which were retreats to the nearby hills to "work out problems." Mary knew nothing of "Marian" and her nighttime adventures. Marian was as abrupt and hostile as Mary was compliant and caring. In the course of therapy, six other personalities emerged—including one who claimed to be a 6-year-old child (Spitzer et al., 1994).

Mary suffers from a type of **dissociative disorder,** *a condition in which normal cognitive processes are severely disjointed and fragmented, creating significant disruptions in memory, awareness, or personality that can vary in length from a matter of minutes to many years.* To some extent, a bit of dissociation, or "splitting," of cognitive processes is normal. For example, research on implicit memory shows that we often retain and are influenced by information that we do not consciously remember (discussed in Chapter 5). Moreover, we can engage in more than one activity or mental process while maintaining only dim awareness of the perceptions and decisions that guide other behaviors (such as talking while driving a car). Our ordinary continuity of memory and awareness of our personal identity contrasts with Mary's profound cognitive fragmentation and blindness to her own mental processes and states.

Dissociative Identity Disorder

Dissociative identity disorder (DID) is characterized by *the presence within an individual of two or more distinct identities that at different times take control of the individual's behavior.* (The disorder was once called "multiple personality disorder.") When the original

dissociative disorder A condition in which normal cognitive processes are severely disjointed and fragmented, creating significant disruptions in memory, awareness, or personality that can vary in length from a matter of minutes to many years.

dissociative identity disorder (DID) The presence within an individual of two or more distinct identities that at different times take control of the individual's behavior.

dissociative fugue The sudden loss of memory for one's personal history, accompanied by an abrupt departure from home and the assumption of a new identity.

dissociative amnesia The sudden loss of memory for significant personal information.

personality, or host personality, is dominant, the individual often is unaware of the alternate personalities or "alters" (as in Mary's case). However, the alters typically know about the host personality and about each other. The number of distinct identities can range considerably, with some cases numbering more than 100. Sometimes alters share certain characteristics; sometimes they are dissimilar—assuming different vocal patterns, dialects, ages, morals, and even gender identities.

Prior to 1970, DID was considered rare, with only about 100 cases reported in the professional literature worldwide. However, since that time, the number of reported cases has grown enormously. Recent estimates are that between 0.5% and 1% of the general population suffers from the disorder, with a female-to-male prevalence of about 9 to 1 (Maldonado & Butler, 1998). Most patients are diagnosed when they are in their 20s or 30s, although the actual age of onset is probably during childhood (Maldonado & Butler, 1998; Putnam et al., 1986). The strange transition of DID—from a rare disorder to a minor epidemic—has raised concerns that the disorder is a matter of faking or fashion (Spanos, 1994). The most common explanation targets psychotherapists who, though often well meaning, are said to have created the disorder in patients who are vulnerable to their suggestive procedures. Accounts of how therapists treat DID, often using hypnosis, have revealed some cajoling and coaxing

PARAMOUNT PICTURES/PHOTOFEST

Robert Louis Stevenson's 1886 portrayal of dissociative disorder has become so well known that "Jekyll and Hyde" is popular as a synonym for a radically changing personality. This poster is from a 1931 film version.

● **What accounts for the increase in DID diagnoses?**

of clients into reporting evidence of alternate personalities (Acocella, 1999).

Most patients with DID report a history of severe childhood abuse and trauma (Coons, 1994; Putnam et al., 1986), and that evidence supports a popular explanation rooted in psychodynamic theory. From this viewpoint, the helpless child, confronted with intolerable abuse and trauma, responds with the primitive psychological defense of splitting or dissociating to escape the pain and horror. Because the child cannot escape the situation, she essentially escapes from herself. Once the dissociation takes hold, it can set into motion a psychological process that may lead to the development of multiple identities (Kluft, 1984, 1991). Critics of the psychodynamic explanation of DID note that, in most cases, the determination of childhood trauma is based on self-reported memories, which can be susceptible to errors and distortions (Dorahy, 2001). Furthermore, early abuse and trauma are especially prevalent in low-income households, while cases of multiple personality occur almost exclusively among people of middle income (Acocella, 1999). In short, dissociative identity disorder is poorly understood and deep questions exist about what it is, how it arises, and how it can be treated.

Dissociative Amnesia and Dissociative Fugue

"Burt," a 42-year-old short-order cook in a small town, came to the attention of police when he got into a heated altercation with another man in the diner. When the police took Burt to the hospital, they discovered that he had no identification documents, and he claimed that he couldn't remember his name, his address, or any other personal information. Eventually, the police matched his description to that of Gene Saunders, a resident of a city 200 miles away, who had disappeared a month earlier. When Gene Saunders's wife came to identify him, he denied knowing her and his real identity. Before he disappeared, Gene Saunders had been experiencing considerable difficulties at home and at work and had become withdrawn and irritable. Two days before he left, he had a violent argument with his 18-year-old son, who accused him of being a failure (Spitzer et al., 1994, pp. 254–255).

Burt's case is an example of **dissociative fugue**, which involves *the sudden loss of memory for one's personal history, accompanied by an abrupt departure from home and the assumption of a new identity*. A related, but less severe, condition is **dissociative amnesia**, *the sudden loss of memory for significant personal information*. Whereas patients with dissociative fugue lose their whole identity, patients with dissociative amnesia retain their identity but lose memories for a period that typically spans a specific event or period of time but can involve extended periods (months or years) of a person's life (Kihlstrom, 2005).

● *Call me "Al." A man identified only by the name "Al" gave a news conference in Denver in 2006 in hopes that someone might be able to tell him more about himself. A victim of a dissociative fugue state, he had no memory of his identity or his life. His fiancée recognized him on TV and confirmed his identity as Jeffrey Alan Ingram, an unemployed machinist from Olympia, Washington.*

Both dissociative amnesia and dissociative fugue rarely occur before adulthood or after the age of 50 (Sackeim & Devanand, 1991). In both conditions, the memory loss is too extensive, and the information forgotten too vital, to be the result of normal forgetting. Dissociative fugue states may last for a few hours or for years; they usually end rather abruptly, and victims typically recover their memories and personal identities. Dissociative amnesia may also be temporary: People have lost significant personal memories and then recovered them later (Brenneis, 2000; Schooler, Bendiksen, & Ambadar, 1997).

Both dissociative fugue and dissociative amnesia differ from other kinds of memory impairments— such as the anterograde amnesia you read about in Chapter 5—in that they cannot be attributed to brain injury, drug use, or another mental disorder. The underlying causes of dissociative fugue and dissociative amnesia remain a mystery, although episodes may be triggered by stressful life circumstances.

● **How do dissociative fugue and dissociative amnesia differ from other kinds of memory impairments?**

summary quiz [12.3]

8. Pat was involved in a severe auto accident and is unable to recall the event. Pat is displaying
    a. dissociative amnesia.   c. dissociative identity disorder.
    b. dissociative fugue.   d. split personality.

9. Alex woke up one morning in a motel. He could not recall his name or anything about his past life. Alex was showing the symptoms of
    a. dissociative amnesia.   c. dissociative identity disorder.
    b. dissociative fugue.   d. split personality.

10. Which is an accurate statement about dissociative identity disorder?
    a. It is much less common today than it was prior to 1970.
    b. It occurs almost exclusively among people in low-income households.
    c. Most patients with the disorder report a history of severe childhood abuse and trauma.
    d. The original or "host" personality usually is aware of the alters.

mood disorders Mental disorders that have mood disturbance as their predominant feature.

major depressive disorder A disorder characterized by a severely depressed mood that lasts 2 weeks or more and is accompanied by feelings of worthlessness and lack of pleasure, lethargy, and sleep and appetite disturbances.

dysthymia A disorder that involves the same symptoms as in depression only less severe, but the symptoms last longer, persisting for at least 2 years.

double depression A moderately depressed mood that persists for at least 2 years and is punctuated by periods of major depression.

seasonal affective disorder (SAD) Depression that involves recurrent depressive episodes in a seasonal pattern.

Mood Disorders: At the Mercy of Emotions

You're probably in a mood right now. Maybe you're happy that it's almost time to get a snack or saddened by something you heard on the radio—or you may feel good or bad without having a clue why. As you learned in Chapter 9, moods are relatively long-lasting, nonspecific emotional states—and *nonspecific* means we often may have no idea what has caused a mood. Changing moods lend variety to our experiences, like different-colored lights shining on the stage as we play out our lives. However, for people with mood disorders, moods can become so intense that they are pulled or pushed into life-threatening actions. **Mood disorders**—*mental disorders that have mood disturbance as their predominant feature*—take two main forms: depressive disorders and bipolar disorder.

Depressive Disorders

Most people occasionally feel depressed, pessimistic, and unmotivated. But these periods are relatively short-lived and mild. Depression is much more than such sadness. The experience of R. A., a 58-year-old man who visited his primary care physician for

The Blue Devils. *George Cruikshank (1806–1877) portrays a depressed man tormented by demons offering him methods of suicide, appearing as bill collectors, and making a funeral procession.*

treatment of his diabetes, is fairly typical. During the visit, he mentioned difficulties falling asleep and staying asleep that left him chronically fatigued. He complained that over the past 6 months, he'd stopped exercising and gained 12 pounds and had

● **What is the difference between depression and sadness?**

lost interest in socializing. Nothing he normally enjoyed, including sexual activity, could give him pleasure anymore; he had trouble concentrating and was forgetful, irritable, impatient, and frustrated (Lustman, Caudle, & Clouse, 2002). R. A.'s sense of hopelessness and weariness

and his lack of normal pleasures goes far beyond normal sadness; it is also different from the normal responses of sorrow and grief that accompany a tragic situation such as the death of a loved one (Bowlby, 1980). Instead, depressive mood disorders are dysfunctional, chronic, and fall outside the range of socially or culturally expected responses.

Major depression, also known as unipolar depression, is characterized by *a severely depressed mood that lasts 2 or more weeks and is accompanied by feelings of worthlessness and lack of pleasure, lethargy, and sleep and appetite disturbances*. The bodily symptoms in major depression may seem contrary—sleeping too much or sleeping very little, for example, or overeating or failing to eat. Great sadness or despair is not always present, although intrusive thoughts of failure or ending one's life are not uncommon. **Dysthymia** is a related condition in which *the same cognitive and bodily problems as in depression are present, but they are less severe and last longer—persisting for at least 2 years*. Patients who suffer from dysthymia punctuated by periods of major depression are said to have **double depression**. Another variant, **seasonal affective disorder (SAD)**, involves *recurrent depressive episodes in a seasonal pattern*; usually, the episodes begin in fall or winter and remit in spring, although recurrent summer depressive episodes are not unknown.

On average, an episode of major depression lasts about 6 months (Beck, 1967; Robins & Guze, 1972). However, without treatment, approximately 80% of individuals will experience at least one recurrence of the disorder (Judd, 1997; Mueller et al., 1999). Compared with people who have a single episode, individuals with recurrent depression have more severe symptoms, higher rates of depression in their families, more suicide attempts, and higher rates of divorce (Merikangas, Wicki, & Angst, 1994). The median lifetime risk for depression of about 16% seems to be increasing in younger generations (Lavori et al., 1987; Wittchen, Knauper, & Kessler, 1994). For example, a large international

A time for seasonal affective disorder. When the sun goes away, sadness can play.

● *Actress Brooke Shields experienced severe postpartum depression and wrote a book about it.*

DESIREE NAVARRO/GETTY IMAGES

study found evidence of a substantial global increase in the risk for depression across the past century (Cross-National Collaborative Research Group, 1992).

This situation is especially dire for women because they are diagnosed with depression at a rate twice that of men (Kessler et al., 1996; Lavori et al., 1987; Robins et al.,

● **What are some reasons more women than men experience depression?**

1984; Wittchen et al., 1994). Socioeconomic standing has been invoked as an explanation for women's heightened risk: Their incomes are lower than those of men, and poverty could cause depression. Sex differences in hormones are another possibility: Estrogen, androgen, and progesterone influence depression; some women experience *postpartum depression* (depression following childbirth) due to changing hormone balances. It is also possible that the higher rate of depression in women reflects greater willingness by women to face their depression and seek out help, leading to higher rates of diagnosis.

A number of factors probably contribute to development of depression. One factor is genetics. Heritability estimates for major depression typically range from 33% to 45% (Plomin et al., 1997; Wallace, Schnieder, & McGuffin, 2002), and heritability is probably much higher for "severe" major depression (defined as three or more episodes) than for "less severe" major depression (defined as one or two episodes) (Bertelsen, Harvald, & Hauge, 1977; Katz & McGuffin, 1993; Plomin et al., 1997; Roth & Mountjoy, 1997).

Biological factors also play a role. Drugs that increase levels of the neurotransmitters norepinephrine and serotonin can sometimes reduce depression, which might suggest that depression may be caused by a depletion of these neurotransmitters. But some studies have found *increases* in norepinephrine activity among depressed patients (Thase & Howland, 1995). Moreover, even though the antidepressant medications change neurochemical transmission in less than a day, they typically take at least 2 weeks to relieve depressive symptoms. So biochemistry cannot be the whole story. Brain abnormalities may also play a role. Individuals with major depression often show diminished activity in the left prefrontal cortex and increased activity in the right prefrontal cortex (see **FIGURE 12.2**)—areas of the brain involved in the processing of emotions (Davidson, 2004;

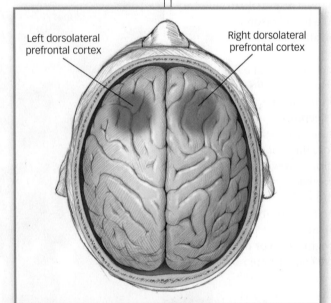

Left dorsolateral prefrontal cortex

Right dorsolateral prefrontal cortex

Davidson et al., 2002). But again, the story is complicated. These abnormal activity patterns may be effects of the mood disturbance, or they may cause people to be more susceptible to depression in the face of stress or trauma.

Psychological factors may also predispose individuals to develop depression. One of the first theorists to emphasize the role of thought in depression, Aaron Beck (1967), noted that his depressed patients distorted perceptions of their experiences and embraced dysfunctional attitudes that promoted and maintained negative mood states. Elaborating on this idea, **helplessness theory** maintains that *individuals who are prone to depression automatically attribute negative experiences to causes that are internal (i.e., their own fault), stable (i.e., unlikely to change), and global (i.e., widespread)* (Abramson, Seligman, & Teasdale, 1978). For example, a student at risk for depression might view a bad grade on a math test as a sign of low intelligence (internal) that will never change (stable) and that will lead to failure in all his or her future endeavors (global). In contrast, a student without this tendency might have the opposite response, attributing the grade to something external (poor teaching), unstable (a missed study session), and/or specific (boring subject).

Under normal conditions, individuals at risk for depression may work hard to suppress

● **What is helplessness theory?**

such thoughts that threaten their emotional well-being. But when cognitive demands arise (time pressures, distraction, stress, etc.), individuals who are at risk for depression often display heightened levels of negative thinking (Wenzlaff &

● **FIGURE 12.2**

Brain and Depression *Reduced activation in the left dorsolateral prefrontal cortex (blue) and increased activation in the right dorsolateral prefrontal cortex (red) have been found to be linked with depression in several studies.*

Bates, 1998; Wenzlaff & Eisenberg, 2001). They may worry about failures, think that people are avoiding them, or wonder whether anything is worthwhile. This breakdown in mental control may explain why stressful life events such as a prolonged illness or the loss of a loved one often precede a descent into depression (Kessler, 1997). Ironically, thought suppression itself may intensify depressive thoughts and ultimately contribute to relapse (Rude et al., 2002; Wenzlaff, 2005; Wenzlaff & Bates, 1998; see the Real World box on the next page).

Bipolar Disorder

If depression is bad, would the opposite be better? Not for Julie, a 20-year-old college sophomore. When first seen by a clinician, Julie had gone 5 days without sleep and was extremely active and expressing bizarre thoughts and ideas. She proclaimed to friends that she did not menstruate because she was "of a third sex, a gender above the two human sexes," that she had switched souls with a senator from her state, and that she was capable of saving the world from nuclear destruction (Vitkus, 1999). Julie's periods of abnormally high mood and activity would alternate with periods of crushing depression.

The diagnostic label for this constellation of symptoms is **bipolar disorder**—*an unstable emotional condition characterized by cycles of abnormal, persistent high mood (mania) and low mood (depression)*. In about two thirds of patients, manic episodes immediately precede or immediately follow depressive episodes (Whybrow, 1997). The depressive phase of bipolar disorder is often clinically indistinguishable from major depression (Perris, 1992). In the manic phase, which must last at least a week to meet *DSM-IV-TR* requirements, mood can be elevated, expansive, or irritable. Other prominent symptoms of the manic phase include grandiosity, decreased need for sleep, talkativeness, racing thoughts, distractibility, and reckless behavior (e.g., compulsive gambling, sexual indiscretions, and unrestrained spending sprees). Psychotic features such as hallucinations (erroneous perceptions) and delusions (erroneous beliefs) may be present, and so the disorder can be misdiagnosed as schizophrenia.

The lifetime risk for bipolar disorder is about 1.3% for both men and women (Wittchen et al., 1994). Bipolar disorder is typically a recurrent condition, with approximately 90% of afflicted people suffering from several episodes over a lifetime (Coryell et al., 1995). About 10% of cases have *rapid cycling bipolar disorder,* characterized by at least four mood episodes (either manic or depressive) every year. Rapid cycling is more common in women than in men and is sometimes precipitated by taking certain kinds of antidepressant drugs (Liebenluft, 1996; Whybrow, 1997). Unfortunately, bipolar disorder tends to be persistent. In one study, 24% of patients had relapsed within 6 months of recovery from an episode, and 77% had at least one new episode within 4 years of recovery (Coryell et al., 1995).

Among the various mental disorders, bipolar disorder has the highest rate of heritability, with concordance as high as 80% for identical twins and 16% for fraternal twins (Bertelsen et al., 1977). Close relatives of an individual with bipolar disorder are also at heightened risk for unipolar depression (Bertelsen et al., 1977)—a finding that raises the possibility that the genetic transmission of bipolar disorder is connected to the genetic transmission of unipolar depression. Thus, bipolar disorder may be *polygenic,* arising from the action of many genes in an additive or interactive fashion.

Biochemical imbalances may be involved in bipolar disorder, but specific neurotransmitters have not been identified. Some researchers have suggested that low levels of serotonin and norepinephrine may

Man Ray (1890–1976) offered a caricature of sadness as art in Tears, 1930–1932.

helplessness theory The idea that individuals who are prone to depression automatically attribute negative experiences to causes that are internal (i.e., their own fault), stable (i.e., unlikely to change), and global (i.e., widespread).

bipolar disorder An unstable emotional condition characterized by cycles of abnormal, persistent high mood (mania) and low mood (depression).

Winston Churchill made a pet of his bipolar illness, calling his depression the "black dog" that followed him around.

[THE REAL WORLD] ●

Suicide Risk and Prevention

Overall, suicide is the 11th leading cause of death in the United States and the third most common form of death among high school and college students (King, 1997). In 2000, 10.6 out of 100,000 Americans died by suicide—a total of 29,350 in the nation that year (National Institute of Mental Health, 2003). Although people have various reasons for taking their own lives, approximately 50% kill themselves during the recovery phase of a depressive episode (Isacsson & Rich, 1997). The lifetime risk of suicide in people with mood disorders is about 4%, compared to a risk of only 0.5% in the general population (Bostwick & Pankratz, 2000). In the United States, women attempt suicide about three to four times more often than men. However, because men typically use more lethal methods than do women (e.g., guns versus pills), men are three to four times more likely to actually kill themselves than are women (Canetto & Lester, 1995). The tragic effects of suicide extend beyond the loss of life, compounding the grief of families and loved ones who must contend with feelings of abandonment, guilt, shame, and futility.

Researchers have identified a variety of motives for suicide, including a profound sense of alienation, intolerable psychological or physical suffering or both, hopelessness, an escape from feelings of worthlessness, and a desperate cry for help (Baumeister & Tice, 1990; Durkheim, 1951; Joiner, 2006). Studies show an increased risk of suicide among family members with a relative who committed suicide (Kety, 1990; Mann et al., 1999). This elevated risk may be a function of biological factors in depression, or suicide could be contagious, with exposure making it a more salient option during desperate times. Contagious effects are suggested by the occasional "clusters" of suicides in which several people—usually teenagers—attempt to kill themselves following a highly publicized case (Gould, 1990). In fact, suicide in the United States has been found to increase after nationally televised news or feature stories about suicide (Phillips & Carstensen, 1986).

How can you tell if someone is at risk for suicide? Unfortunately, definitive prediction is impossible, but a variety of warning signs can suggest an increased risk (Substance Abuse

Over 1,218 people have jumped from the Golden Gate Bridge since its completion in 1937, a jump 98% likely to be fatal. The city of San Francisco continues to debate whether to install a suicide barrier (Guthmann, 2005).

DAVID SANGER PHOTOGRAPHY/ALAMY

and Mental Health Services Administration, 2005). Any one sign is a cause for concern, and the risk is especially serious when several occur together.

- Talk about suicide. About 90% of people who are suicidal discuss their intentions, so this obvious warning sign should not be dismissed as simply a means of getting attention. Although most people who threaten suicide do not actually attempt it, they are at greater risk than those who do not talk about it.

- An upturn in mood following a prolonged depressive episode. Surprisingly, suicide risk increases at this point. In fact, a sudden lifting of mood may reflect relief at the prospect that suicide will end the emotional suffering.
- A failed love interest or loss of a loved one through separation or death.
- A severe, stressful event that is especially shameful or humiliating.
- A family history of suicide.
- Unusual reckless or risky behavior, seemingly carried out without thinking.
- An unexplained decline in school or workplace performance.
- Withdrawal from friends, family, and regular activities.
- Expressing feelings of being trapped, as though there's "no way out."
- "Cleaning house" by giving away prized possessions.
- Increased alcohol or drug use. Substance abuse is associated with approximately 25% to 50% of suicides and is especially associated with adolescent suicides (Conwell et al., 1996; Woods et al., 1997).

Anyone who is potentially suicidal should be encouraged to seek professional help. Colleges and universities have student counseling centers, and most cities have suicide prevention centers with 24-hour hotlines and walk-in emergency counseling. The U.S. National Suicide Prevention Lifeline is 1-800-273-TALK.

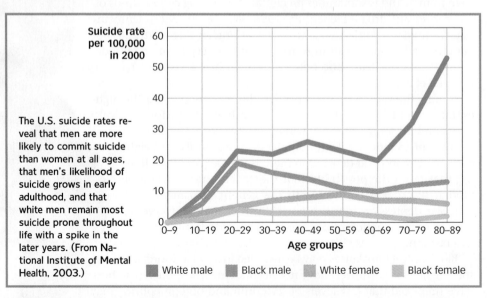

The U.S. suicide rates reveal that men are more likely to commit suicide than women at all ages, that men's likelihood of suicide grows in early adulthood, and that white men remain most suicide prone throughout life with a spike in the later years. (From National Institute of Mental Health, 2003.)

Suicide rate per 100,000 in 2000

■ White male   ■ Black male   ■ White female   ■ Black female

contribute to the emotional roller coaster that characterizes bipolar disorder (Whybrow, 1997). This notion is not well substantiated and doesn't explain why lithium, a chemical unrelated to these neurotransmitters, often helps stabilize both the depressive and manic symptoms associated with bipolar disorder (see Chapter 14). Psychological factors may also contribute. Stressful life experiences often precede manic and depressive episodes (Ellicot et al., 1990; Hammen, 1995). One study found that severely stressed patients took an average of three times longer to recover from an episode than did patients not affected by stress (Johnson & Miller, 1997). Personality characteristics such as neuroticism and conscientiousness have also been found to predict increases in bipolar symptoms over time (Lozano & Johnson, 2001). Finally, patients living with family members who are hostile toward or critical of the patient are more likely to relapse than patients with supportive families (Miklowitz et al., 1988). These data are consistent with a stress-diathesis model, in which environmental stressors can trigger the disorder in persons with preexisting vulnerability.

● **How does stress relate to manic depressive episodes?**

summary quiz [12.4]

11. Major depression is characterized by _____, whereas bipolar disorder is characterized by _____.
   a. mania only; alternating periods of mania and depression
   b. alternating periods of mania and depression; mania and depression occurring at the same time
   c. depression only; alternating periods of mania and depression
   d. alternating periods of mania and depression; depression only

12. The condition in which the same cognitive and bodily problems as in depression are present, but are less severe and last longer, is called
   a. dysthymia.
   b. double depression.
   c. seasonal affective disorder.
   d. bipolar disorder.

13. Which is true of depression in women and men?
   a. Men are twice as likely as women to be diagnosed with depression.
   b. Women are twice as likely as men to be diagnosed with depression.
   c. Among young adults, women are more depressed than men; among older adults, men are more depressed than women.
   d. Women and men are equally likely to be diagnosed with depression.

14. Which of the following is true regarding factors associated with mood disorders?
   a. People with mood disorders show abnormally high levels of norepinephrine and serotonin.
   b. People who attribute their failures to external and unstable causes are more prone to depression.
   c. People with major depression often show increased activity in the left frontal cortex and diminished activity in the right prefrontal cortex.
   d. Close relatives of individuals with mood disorders have a heightened risk for developing mood disorders themselves, indicating that heredity plays a role.

schizophrenia A disorder characterized by the profound disruption of basic psychological processes; a distorted perception of reality; altered or blunted emotion; and disturbances in thought, motivation, and behavior.

delusion A patently false belief system, often bizarre and grandiose, that is maintained in spite of its irrationality.

hallucination A false perceptual experience that has a compelling sense of being real despite the absence of external stimulation.

Schizophrenia: Losing the Grasp on Reality

In the opening vignette of this chapter, you read about Margaret, the woman who believed God was punishing her and who saw evidence of this punishment in everyday events: reading arcane meanings into the way objects were positioned in the sink and

● **What is schizophrenia?**

the programs that were playing on the television. Margaret suffered from **schizophrenia**, a psychological disorder characterized by *the profound disruption of basic psychological processes; a distorted perception of reality; altered or blunted emotion;, and disturbances in thought, motivation, and behavior.* Traditionally, schizophrenia was regarded primarily as a disturbance of thought and perception, in which the sense of reality becomes severely distorted and confused. However, this condition is now understood to take different forms affecting a wide range of functions.

Symptoms and Types of Schizophrenia

According to the *DSM-IV-TR,* schizophrenia is diagnosed when two or more of the following symptoms emerge during a continuous period of at least 1 month with signs of the disorder persisting for at least 6 months: *delusion, hallucination, disorganized speech, grossly disorganized behavior* or *catatonic behavior,* and *negative symptoms.* Let's consider each symptom in detail.

■ **Delusion** is *a patently false belief system, often bizarre and grandiose, that is maintained in spite of its irrationality.* For example, an individual with schizophrenia may believe that he or she is Jesus Christ, Napoleon, Joan of Arc, or some other famous person. Delusions of persecution are also common, such as believing that the CIA, demons, extraterrestrials, or other malevolent forces are conspiring to harm or control the patient. People with schizophrenia have little or no insight into their disordered perceptual and thought processes. Because they cannot understand that they have lost control of their own minds, delusions that attribute control to external agents (e.g., demons or the CIA) may represent the patients' attempts to make sense of the tormenting delusions (Roberts, 1991).

■ **Hallucination** is *a false perceptual experience that has a compelling sense of being real despite the absence of external stimulation.* The perceptual disturbances associated with schizophrenia can include hearing, seeing, or smelling things that are not there or having tactile sensations in the absence of relevant sensory stimulation. Among people with schizophrenia, some 65% report hearing voices (Frith & Fletcher, 1995),

● The Clown Voice, *2003. Artist Elizabeth Autumn Daniels writes, "When I was about 17, I started hallucinating and thinking people were out to get me. . . . I thought that people were going to bomb my house. I was hearing 10 voices in my head nonstop. . . . Turns out I am paranoid schizophrenic. . . . But finally the past couple of months I have found the right medication. . . . I have been drawing and painting since I was 5 years old. . . . And now it is helping me heal. I drew this because the clown is what I saw when I heard one of the voices in my head."*

ELIZABETH AUTUMN DANIELS/THE SURVIVOR ART GALLERY

sometimes scolding or commanding or ridiculing. One patient reported a voice saying, "He's getting up now. He's going to wash. It's about time" (Frith & Fletcher, 1995). British psychiatrist Henry Maudsley (1886) long ago proposed that these voices are in fact produced in the mind of the schizophrenic individual, and recent research substantiates his idea. In one PET imaging study, auditory hallucinations were accompanied by activation in Broca's area—the part of the brain (as discussed in Chapters 3 and 7) associated with the production of language (McGuire, Shah, & Murray, 1993).

- **Disorganized speech** is *a severe disruption of verbal communication in which ideas shift rapidly and incoherently from one to another unrelated topic.* The abnormal speech patterns in schizophrenia reflect difficulties in organizing thoughts and focusing attention. Responses to questions are often irrelevant, ideas are loosely associated, and words are used in peculiar ways. For example, asked by her doctor, "Can you tell me the name of this place?" one patient with schizophrenia responded, "I have not been a drinker for 16 years. I am taking a mental rest after a 'carter' assignment of 'quill.' You know, a 'penwrap.' I had contracts with Warner Brothers Studios and Eugene broke phonograph records but Mike protested. I have been with the police department for 35 years. I am made of flesh and blood—see, Doctor" [pulling up dress] (Carson et al., 2000, p. 474).

- **Grossly disorganized behavior** is *behavior that is inappropriate for the situation or ineffective in attaining goals, often with specific motor disturbances.* A patient might exhibit constant childlike silliness, improper sexual behavior (e.g., masturbating in public), disheveled appearance, or loud shouting or swearing. Specific motor disturbances might include strange movements, rigid posturing, odd mannerisms, bizarre grimacing, or hyperactivity. Some patients show **catatonic behavior,** *a marked decrease in all movement or an increase in muscular rigidity and overactivity.* These patients may actively resist movement (when someone is trying to move them) or become completely unresponsive and unaware of their surroundings.

- **Negative symptoms** of schizophrenia include *emotional and social withdrawal; apathy; poverty of speech; and other indications of the absence or insufficiency of normal behavior, motivation, and emotion.* These negative symptoms refer to things missing in people with schizophrenia; in contrast, the other symptoms (e.g., hallucinations and delusions) are called "positive symptoms," because they appear more in people with schizophrenia than in other people.

The various symptoms of schizophrenia do not all occur in every case. Recent editions of the DSM have identified five subtypes of schizophrenia (see **TABLE 12.2** on page 386). Three of these types—paranoid, catatonic, and disorganized—depend primarily on the relative prominence of various symptoms. The paranoid type involves preoccupation with delusions and hallucinations; the catatonic type involves immobility and stupor or agitated, purposeless motor activity; the disorganized type is often the most severe, featuring disorganized speech and behavior and flat or inappropriate emotion. The *DSM-IV-TR* reserves the undifferentiated type for cases that do not neatly fall into these three categories and the residual type for individuals who have substantially recovered from at least one schizophrenic episode but still have lingering symptoms.

Schizophrenia occurs in about 1% of the population and is about equally common in men and women (Gottesman, 1991; Jablensky, 1997). The first episode typically occurs during late adolescence or early adulthood (Gottesman, 1991), although females usually have a later onset than do males (Iacono & Beiser, 1992; Marcus et al., 1993). Despite its relatively low frequency, schizophrenia is the primary diagnosis for nearly 40% of all admissions to state and county mental hospitals; it is the second most frequent diagnosis for inpatient psychiatric admission at other types of institutions (Rosenstein, Milazzo-Sayre, & Manderscheid, 1990). The disproportionate rate of hospitalization for schizophrenia is a testament to the devastation it causes in people's lives.

A patient suffering from catatonic schizophrenia may assume an unusual posture and fail to move for hours.

● **What are the characteristics of schizophrenia?**

disorganized speech A severe disruption of verbal communication in which ideas shift rapidly and incoherently from one to another unrelated topic.

grossly disorganized behavior Behavior that is inappropriate for the situation or ineffective in attaining goals, often with specific motor disturbances.

catatonic behavior A marked decrease in all movement or an increase in muscular rigidity and overactivity.

negative symptoms Emotional and social withdrawal; apathy; poverty of speech; and other indications of the absence or insufficiency of normal behavior, motivation, and emotion.

TABLE 12.2

Types of Schizophrenia

Types	Characteristics
Paranoid type	Symptoms dominated by absurd, illogical, and changeable delusions, frequently accompanied by vivid hallucinations, with a resulting impairment of critical judgment and erratic, unpredictable, and occasionally dangerous behaviors. In chronic cases, there is usually less disorganization of behavior than in other types of schizophrenia and less extreme withdrawal from social interaction.
Catatonic type	Often characterized by alternating periods of extreme withdrawal and extreme excitement, although in some cases one or the other reaction predominates. In the withdrawal reaction, there is a sudden loss of all animation and a tendency to remain motionless for hours or even days in a single position. The person may undergo an abrupt change, with excitement coming on suddenly; the person may talk or shout incoherently, pace rapidly, and engage in uninhibited, impulsive, and frenzied behavior. In this state, an individual may be dangerous.
Disorganized type	Usually occurs at an earlier age than most other types of schizophrenia and represents a more severe disintegration of the personality. Emotional distortion and blunting typically are manifested in inappropriate laughter and silliness, peculiar mannerisms, and bizarre, often obscene behavior.
Undifferentiated type	A pattern of symptoms in which there is a rapidly changing mixture of all or most of the primary indicators of schizophrenia. Commonly observed are indications of perplexity, confusion, emotional turmoil, delusions, excitement, dreamlike autism, depression, and fear. Most often this picture is seen in patients who are in the process of breaking down and developing schizophrenia. It is also seen, however, when major adjustment demands impinge on a person with an already-established schizophrenic psychosis. In such cases, it frequently foreshadows an impending change to another primary schizophrenic subtype.
Residual type	Mild indication of schizophrenia shown by individuals in remission following a schizophrenic episode.

Biological and Psychological Factors Associated with Schizophrenia

Although schizophrenia is a dizzyingly complex disorder, many biological factors have been identified that contribute to the disease. Genetics play a key role. Family studies indicate that the closer a person's genetic relatedness to a person with schizophrenia, the greater the likelihood of developing the disorder (Gottesman, 1991). As shown in **FIGURE 12.3** (on page 387), concordance rates increase dramatically with biological relatedness. The rates are estimates and vary considerably from study to study, but almost every study finds the average concordance rates higher for identical twins (48%) than for fraternal twins (17%), which suggests a genetic component for the disorder (Torrey et al., 1994).

Identical twins may share more than their genes. Considerable evidence suggests that the prenatal and perinatal environments may also affect concordance rates in identical twins (Jurewicz, Owen, & O'Donovan, 2001; Thaker, 2002; Torrey et al., 1994). For example, because approximately 70% of identical twins share the same prenatal blood supply, toxins in the mother's blood could contribute to the high concordance rate. When one twin develops schizophrenia and the other twin does not, birth records often show that the afflicted twin is second born and had a lower birth weight (Wahl, 1976). In addition, people with late winter or early spring birth dates have about a 20% greater risk of schizophrenia than do those born in late summer or early fall (DeLisi, Crow, & Hirsch, 1986), raising the possibility that viral exposure during a

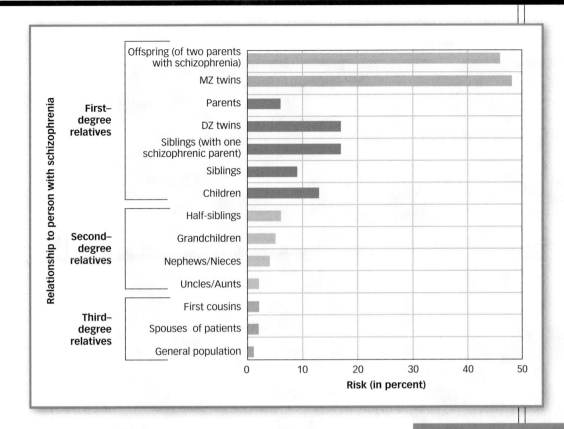

FIGURE 12.3 ●
Average Risk of Developing Schizophrenia *The risk of schizophrenia among biological relatives is greater for those with greater degrees of relatedness. An identical (MZ) twin of a twin with schizophrenia has a 48% risk of developing schizophrenia, for example, and offspring of two parents with schizophrenia have a 46% risk of developing the disorder. (Adapted from Gottesman, 1991.)*

critical period for brain development may contribute to the risk of schizophrenia (Rothermundt, Arolt, & Bayer, 2001). Further support for this idea comes from studies showing that maternal influenza in the second trimester of pregnancy is associated with an increased risk of schizophrenia (Wright et al., 1995).

As with other psychological disorders, biochemical factors may play a role in schizophrenia. During the 1950s, major tranquilizers were discovered that could reduce the symptoms of schizophrenia by lowering levels of the neurotransmitter dopamine. This finding suggested the **dopamine hypothesis,** the *idea that schizophrenia involves an excess of dopamine activity.* The hypothesis is attractive, but considerable evidence suggests that things are not quite so simple (Csermansky & Grace, 1998; Grace & Moore, 1998). For example, many individuals with schizophrenia do not respond favorably to dopamine-blocking drugs (e.g., major tranquilizers), and those who do seldom show a complete remission of symptoms. Moreover, the drugs block dopamine receptors very rapidly, yet individuals with schizophrenia typically do not show a beneficial response for weeks. Finally, research has implicated other neurotransmitters in schizophrenia, suggesting that the disorder may involve a complex interaction among a host of different biochemicals (Benes, 1998; Lewis et al., 1999; Sawa & Snyder, 2002). In sum, the precise role of neurotransmitters in schizophrenia has yet to be determined.

Finally, recent neuroimaging studies provide evidence of a variety of brain abnormalities in schizophrenia. Paul Thompson and his colleagues (2001) examined changes in the brains of adolescents whose MRI scans could be traced sequentially from the onset of schizophrenia. Over the years, the brains showed progressive tissue loss beginning in the parietal lobe and eventually encompassing much of the brain (see **FIGURE 12.4** on page 388). All adolescents lose some gray matter over time in a kind of normal "pruning" of the brain, but in the case of those developing schizophrenia, the loss was dramatic enough to seem pathological. Of course, because these brain scans were obtained from adolescents who had already been diagnosed with schizophrenia, it isn't clear whether these biological changes are a cause, or an effect, of the disease.

dopamine hypothesis The idea that schizophrenia involves an excess of dopamine activity.

Side views   Top view

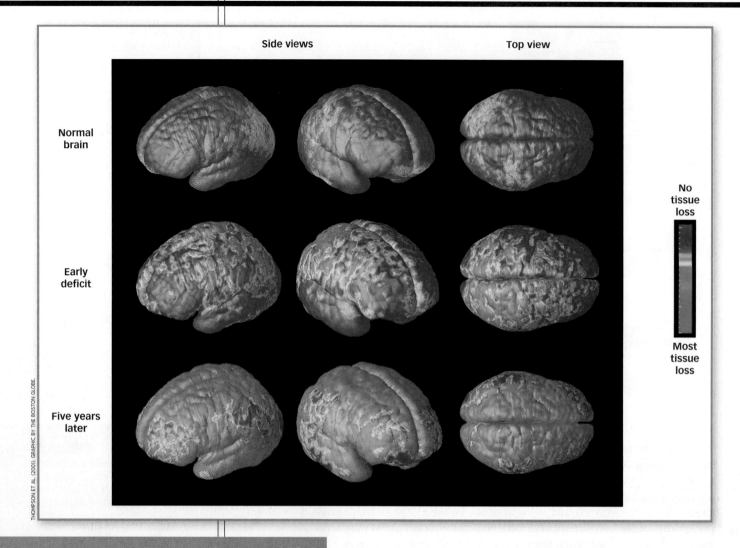

THOMPSON ET AL. (2001). GRAPHIC BY THE BOSTON GLOBE.

Normal brain

Early deficit

Five years later

No tissue loss

Most tissue loss

● FIGURE **12.4**

Brain Tissue Loss in Adolescent Schizophrenia
MRI scan composites reveal brain tissue loss in adolescents diagnosed with schizophrenia. Normal brains (top) show minimal loss due to "pruning." Early deficit scans (middle) reveal loss in the parietal areas. Patients at this stage may experience symptoms such as hallucinations or bizarre thoughts. Scans 5 years later (bottom) reveal extensive tissue loss over much of the cortex. Patients at this stage are likely to suffer from delusions, disorganized speech and behavior, and negative symptoms such as social withdrawal. (From Thompson et al., 2001.)

With all these potential biological contributors to schizophrenia, you might think there would be few psychological or social causes of the disorder. However, several studies do suggest that environment plays a role in the development of and recovery from the condition. One large-scale study compared the risk of schizophrenia in children adopted into healthy families and those adopted into severely disturbed families (Tienari et al., 2004). (Disturbed families were defined as those with extreme conflict, lack of communication, or chaotic relationships.) Among children whose biological mothers had schizophrenia, the disturbed environment increased the likelihood of developing schizophrenia—an outcome that was not found among children who were also reared in disturbed families but whose biological mothers did *not* have schizophrenia. This finding provides support for the diathesis-stress model described earlier. However, conclusions about the role of family functioning in the risk of schizophrenia must be tempered by the realization that the studies in this area are correlational and that a basic association between characteristics does not indicate that one causes the other (see Chapter 2). Thus, although dysfunction in families may contribute to schizophrenia, the reverse may also be true. The dysfunctional and bizarre behavior of a family member with schizophrenia may in itself be a source of stress that promotes dysfunctional communications and interactions among family members.

● What are the roles of genetics and environment in schizophrenia?

summary quiz [12.5]

15. Schizophrenia affects about ___% of the population, and it accounts for nearly ___ % of admissions to state and county mental hospitals.
    a. 1; 1   b. 1; 40   c. 5; 5   d. 5; 20

16. Amy believes that God is punishing her, and she sees evidence of this punishment in everyday events such as the way objects are positioned in the sink and the programs that are playing on TV. Amy would most likely be diagnosed with _____ schizophrenia.
    a. paranoid   c. disorganized
    b. catatonic   d. undifferentiated

17. Keith believes that he is Richard the Lionheart, who has been given the mission to lead a crusade against the heathens. Keith is showing
    a. hallucinations.   c. delusions.
    b. disorganized speech.   d. grossly disorganized behavior.

personality disorder Disorder characterized by deeply ingrained, inflexible patterns of thinking, feeling, or relating to others or controlling impulses that cause distress or impaired functioning.

antisocial personality disorder (APD) A pervasive pattern of disregard for and violation of the rights of others that begins in childhood or early adolescence and continues into adulthood.

Personality Disorders: Going to Extremes

Henri Desiré Landru began using the personal columns to attract a woman "interested in matrimony" in Paris in 1914, and he succeeded in seducing 10 women. He bilked them of their savings, poisoned them, and cremated them in his stove, also disposing of a boy and two dogs along the way. He recorded his murders in a notebook and maintained a marriage and a mistress all the while. The gruesome actions of serial killers such as Landru leave us frightened and wondering; however, bullies, compulsive liars, and even drivers who regularly speed through a school zone share the same shocking blindness to human pain. The *DSM-IV-TR* suggests that this pattern of extreme disregard for other people should be considered a disorder and offers the category **antisocial personality disorder (APD)**, defined as *a pervasive pattern of disregard for and violation of the rights of others that begins in childhood or early adolescence and continues into adulthood.*

More generally, **personality disorders** are *disorders characterized by deeply ingrained, inflexible patterns of thinking, feeling, or relating to others or controlling impulses that cause distress or impaired functioning.* Let's look at the types of personality disorders and then take a closer look at antisocial personality disorder.

THREE LIONS/GETTY IMAGES

Henri Desiré Landru (1869–1922), a serial killer who met widows through ads he placed in newspapers' lonely hearts columns. After obtaining enough information to embezzle money from them, he murdered 10 women and the son of one of the women. He was executed for serial murder in 1922.

Types of Personality Disorders

The *DSM-IV-TR* lists 10 personality disorders (see **TABLE 12.3** on page 390), which can range from the relatively mild to the extreme and dangerous. You might think you recognize some of these descriptions as relating to people you know: schizotypal personality disorder might remind you of the oddly dressed spaceball who sits next to you in math class; obsessive-compulsive personality disorder might sound just like your perfectionist, neat-freak roommate, and so on. But don't rush to judgment. Having an odd personality is not the same thing as having a psychological disorder; the *DMS-IV-TR* specifically notes that a diagnosis of personality disorder requires that the symptoms cause distress or impaired functioning. Still, the array of personality disorders suggests that there are multiple ways an individual's gift of a unique personality could become a burden.

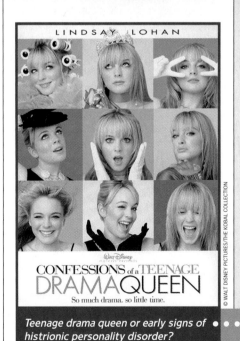

© WALT DISNEY PICTURES/THE KOBAL COLLECTION

CONFESSIONS of a TEENAGE DRAMAQUEEN
So much drama. so little time.

Teenage drama queen or early signs of histrionic personality disorder?

TABLE 12.3

Clusters of Personality Disorders

Cluster	Personality Disorder	Characteristics
A. Odd/ Eccentric	Schizotypal	Peculiar or eccentric manners of speaking or dressing. Strange beliefs. "Magical thinking" such as belief in ESP or telepathy. Difficulty forming relationships. May react oddly in conversation, not respond, or talk to self. Speech elaborate or difficult to follow. (Possibly a mild form of schizophrenia.)
	Paranoid	Distrust in others, suspicion that people have sinister motives. Apt to challenge the loyalties of friends and read hostile intentions into others' actions. Prone to anger and aggressive outbursts but otherwise emotionally cold. Often jealous, guarded, secretive, overly serious.
	Schizoid	Extreme introversion and withdrawal from relationships. Prefers to be alone, little interest in others. Humorless, distant, often absorbed with own thoughts and feelings, a daydreamer. Fearful of closeness, with poor social skills, often seen as a "loner."
B. Dramatic/ Erratic	Antisocial	Impoverished moral sense or "conscience." History of deception, crime, legal problems, impulsive and aggressive or violent behavior. Little emotional empathy or remorse for hurting others. Manipulative, careless, callous. At high risk for substance abuse and alcoholism.
	Borderline	Unstable moods and intense, stormy personal relationships. Frequent mood changes and anger, unpredictable impulses. Self-mutilation or suicidal threats or gestures to get attention or manipulate others. Self-image fluctuation and a tendency to see others as "all good" or "all bad."
	Histrionic	Constant attention seeking. Grandiose language, provocative dress, exaggerated illnesses, all to gain attention. Believes that everyone loves them. Emotional, lively, overly dramatic, enthusiastic, and excessively flirtatious. Shallow and labile true emotions. "Onstage."
	Narcissistic	Inflated sense of self-importance, absorbed by fantasies of self and success. Exaggerates own achievement, assumes others will recognize they are superior. Good first impressions but poor longer-term relationships. Exploitative of others.
C. Anxious/ Inhibited	Avoidant	Socially anxious and uncomfortable unless they are confident of being liked. In contrast with schizoid person, yearns for social contact. Fears criticism and worries about being embarrassed in front of others. Avoids social situations due to fear of rejection.
	Dependent	Submissive, dependent, requiring excessive approval, reassurance, and advice. Clings to people and fears losing them. Lacking self-confidence. Uncomfortable when alone. May be devastated by end of close relationship or suicidal if breakup is threatened.
	Obsessive-compulsive	Conscientious, orderly, perfectionist. Excessive need to do everything "right." Inflexibly high standards and caution can interfere with their productivity. Fear of errors can make them strict and controlling. Poor expression of emotions. (*Not* the same as obsessive-compulsive disorder.)

Source: From *DSM-IV-TR* (American Psychiatric Association, 2000).

Personality disorders are the most controversial classifications in the *DSM-IV-TR* for several reasons. First, critics question whether having a problem personality is really a disorder, given that 14.8% of the U.S. population has a personality disorder that fits a *DSM-IV-TR* description (Grant et al., 2004). Another question is whether personality problems correspond to "disorders" or whether such problems might be better understood as extreme values on trait dimensions such as the Big Five traits discussed in Chapter 12 (Trull & Durrett, 2005). Finally, definitions of many personality problems share characteristics with the major disorders and may be mild versions of these conditions. Overall, for example, roughly half of people with an anxiety or mood disorder have a comorbid personality disorder (Van Velzen & Emmelkamp, 1996). Research is ongoing on these various questions (Oldham, Skodol, & Bender, 2005).

● **Why is self-reporting a problem in diagnosing personality disorders?**

A further diagnostic complication is that personality measurement depends largely on self-reports. Not incidentally, people with exaggerated personalities often seem blind to the high impact their personalities can have. For example, people suffering from paranoid personality disorder are likely to be suspicious of anyone who accuses them of paranoia; similarly, people with narcissistic personality disorder are likely to see comments on their personality as mere jealousy. It's difficult to see a troubled personality from the inside.

To solve this problem, researchers have turned to *peer nomination* measures, reports by others who know the person. Research on peer nominations in college sororities and fraternities and in groups of military recruits reveals that groups arrive at remarkably homogeneous assessments of their personality-disordered members (Oltmanns & Turkheimer, 2006). Through gossip or through personal experience, everybody in the group seems to know who among them is paranoid, dependent, avoidant, or unusual in some other way. Peer nominations using basic reports of the behavior of people in a group can predict which members will have further problems—such as dropping out of college or being discharged early from the military (Fiedler, Oltmanns, & Turkheimer, 2004).

Military recruits going through basic training develop knowledge of one another's personalities. Their judgments of one another at the end of training produce valid predictions of who will later receive early discharge from the military.

The common feature of personality disorders is a failure to take other people's perspectives, particularly on the self. People with personality disorders often blame others, society, or the universe for their difficulties, distorting their perceptions of the world in a way that makes the personality disorder seem perfectly normal—at least to them. In many of the personality disorders, this blindness perpetuates the disorder and so hurts the person who suffers from it: People with personality disorders are often unhappy or depressed. Antisocial personality disorder, however, is particularly likely to go beyond harm to self and to exact a cost on anyone who knows the person—because the individual with antisocial personality disorder also lacks insight into what it means to hurt others.

Antisocial Personality Disorder

Adults with a diagnosis of antisocial personality disorder typically have a history of *conduct disorder* before the age of 15—problems such as aggression, destruction of property, rule violations, and deceitfulness, lying, or stealing. Early fire setting and cruelty to animals often predict antisocial tendencies. In adulthood, the diagnosis of APD is given to individuals who show three or more of a set of seven diagnostic signs: illegal behavior, deception, impulsivity, physical aggression, recklessness, irresponsibility, and a lack of

● **What are some of the factors that contribute to APD?**

remorse for wrongdoing. About 3.6% of the general population has antisocial personality disorder, and the rate of occurrence in men is three times the rate in women (Grant et al., 2004). Many people with APD commit crimes, and many are caught because of the frequency and flagrancy of their infractions. Among 22,790 prisoners in one study, 47% of the men and 21% of women were diagnosed with antisocial personality disorder (Fazel & Danesh, 2002). Statistics such as these support the notion of a "criminal personality," a person born to be wild.

Both the early onset of conduct problems and the lack of success in treatment suggest that career criminality has an internal cause (Lykken, 1995). Evidence of brain abnormalities in people with APD is also accumulating (Blair, Peschardt, & Mitchell, 2005). One line of investigation has looked at sensitivity to fear in psychopaths and individuals who show no such psychopathology. For example, criminal psychopaths who are shown negative emotional words such as *hate* or *corpse* exhibit less activity in the amygdala and hippocampus than do noncriminals (Kiehl et al., 2001). The two brain areas are involved in the process of fear conditioning (Patrick, Cuthbert, & Lang, 1994), so their relative inactivity in such studies suggests that psychopaths are less sensitive to fear than are other people. Violent psychopaths can target their aggression toward the self as well as others, often behaving in reckless ways that lead to violent ends. It might seem peaceful to go through life "without fear," but perhaps fear is useful in keeping people from the extremes of antisocial behavior.

The psychological disorders we have examined in this chapter represent a tragic loss of human potential. The contentment, peace, and love that people could be enjoying are crowded out by pain and suffering when the mind goes awry (see the Hot Science box).

[HOT SCIENCE]

Positive Psychology: Exterminating the Mindbugs

You are now familiar with some of the most difficult challenges we face—profound, painful mental problems that can cause great unhappiness. Although the downside of human experience has always been part of the domain of psychology, psychologists' interests go beyond the negative aspects of life, including a flourishing movement known as *positive psychology*—an approach that seeks to understand what makes our lives pleasant, good, and meaningful. Martin E. P. Seligman has championed this movement, organizing the field of positive psychology by suggesting that human happiness and virtue deserve the same careful study usually devoted to mental disorders (and all the other mindbugs). In contrast to the classification of mental disorders in the *DSM*, for example, Seligman and his colleagues (Peterson & Seligman, 2004) introduced a complementary system for classifying, *Character Strengths and Virtues*, the *CSV*, which lists virtues such as wisdom and knowledge, courage, humanity, justice, and temperance. These positive qualities of humans are seldom mentioned in the *DSM*, of course, as they show the mind in good order rather than in disorder.

In line with the *CSV* system's positive approach, no individual is expected to have every strength or virtue, and individuals are not supposed to "keep score" by measuring themselves with this list. Rather, the list illustrates our potential to build personal strengths that help to make us happy and human. Listing positive characteristics of people makes for a kind of celebration, an appreciation of what being a person can be.

The positive psychology movement has been particularly effective in stimulating research on happiness. Each of us claims to be something of an expert on what will make us happy (Chocolate, please, lots of it, and on the

double! No, wait, I'd like servants, that's it—servants! Or should I request world peace? No, no, a speedboat . . .), but it is often surprising just how mistaken we can be about what will bring us the joy we desire (Gilbert, 2006). Research supplies some happy facts:

- Money can buy happiness, but only a little. Wealthy people are only the tiniest bit happier than the average person (Diener, Horwitz, & Emmons, 1985), although extreme poverty is associated with less happiness—particularly in cultures where such poverty is rare (Diener & Biswas-Diener, 2002).

- Friends make you happy. People report that the main source of their happiness is relationships—with their friends, spouses, and children (*Time* poll, 2005).

- Some people do "live happily ever after." Married people are happier than singles, especially right after getting married and then again when their children are grown (Coombs, 1991). Their greater happiness may be, however, because they were happier to begin with (Lucas et al., 2003).

- Happiness is born, not made. Twin studies reveal that as much as 50% of variability in happiness is due to genetic factors (Lykken & Tellegen, 1996). Ideally, try to be born happy.

- Happy times may not last. People regularly overestimate the degree to which positive events such as winning the lottery will make them happy. They fail to appreciate their own tendency to adjust psychologically to emotional experiences and "get over it," no matter what "it" is (Gilbert, 2006; Wilson & Gilbert, 2003).

- Happiness dispels the blues. Happiness undermines negative emotions such as anger, fear, and sadness, acting to neutralize these feelings and enhance mental health (Fredrickson, 2001).

- Happiness comes from goodness. Doing good deeds or seeing them done can lead to feelings of elevation and happiness (Haidt, 2006).

More happy facts are surfacing every day, as many researchers have joined the movement toward positive psychology (Gable & Haidt, 2005). This movement provides a useful balance to the more common focus of the field on the negative—the disorders, the illusions, the errors, and, yes, the mindbugs. Knowing about mindbugs does aid in understanding how the mind works: As you have seen at many points in the text, you can learn a lot about a mechanism by seeing how it breaks down. All too often, though, the focus in studying psychological disorders and errors can be too gloomy, a constant reminder of the perils of being "only human." Like the good physician who brings to a patient's bedside both an analytical appreciation of the patient's disorder and a warm smile to help the patient through the rough times, the field of psychology must temper the bitter with the sweet. Psychological science can be most effective when it unites the problem-solving approach of studying disorders with the ideals and optimism of studying wellness.

A scientific approach to psychological disorders that views them through a medical model is beginning to sort out their symptoms and causes. As we will see in the next chapter, this approach already offers treatments for some disorders that are remarkably effective and for other disorders offers hope that pain and suffering can be alleviated in the future.

summary quiz [12.6]

18. Nina has an inflated sense of self-importance, is preoccupied with success fantasies, and assumes that others will recognize her superior achievements. Nina most likely would be diagnosed as having _____ personality disorder.

   a. histrionic   c. borderline

   b. narcissistic   d. antisocial

19. The common feature of personality disorders is

   a. excessive fear of rejection or embarrassment.

   b. unstable moods and stormy personal relationships.

   c. a failure to take other people's perspectives, particularly on the self.

   d. excessive attention seeking, through being overly dramatic.

20. Jim was diagnosed as having antisocial personality disorder based on the fact that he

   a. is emotionally distant, suspicious of others, and has an intense fear of rejection.

   b. avoids social interaction, has very poor social skills, and is often seen as a "loner."

   c. is very peculiar in his speech and dress and has difficulty forming relationships.

   d. is manipulative, impulsive, and shows little emotional empathy.

WhereDoYouStand?

Normal or Abnormal

In the course of learning about mental disorders, you may have found yourself thinking about how they relate to your own experience. On the one hand, imagining the experience of those with anxiety disorders or depression is fairly easy because you know what it feels like to be tense or blue. On the other hand, severe disorders may seem more foreign because they involve extreme distortions of reality reflected by hallucinations and bizarre delusions. But just how unusual are these severe symptoms?

Some of these symptoms are at least moderately common. In one study of 375 college students, 71% of participants reported hearing brief, occasional hallucinated voices during periods of wakefulness, and 39% had heard their own thoughts spoken aloud (Linszen et al., 1997; Posey & Losch, 1983). A study of 586 college students found that 30% to 40% had heard voices when no one was present, and of those, almost half heard voices at least once a month (Barrett & Etheridge, 1992). Reports of verbal hallucinations were not associated with measures of overt or incipient psychopathology. Apparently, hallucinatory experiences—at least of an auditory type—may not be as abnormal as you might have guessed.

What about delusional thinking? Beliefs about scientifically unverified, paranormal experiences may be pretty common. For example, in a survey of 60,000 adults, 50% expressed a belief in thought transference between two people, 25% said they believe in ghosts, and 25% in reincarnation (Cox & Cowling, 1989). Formal diagnostic interviews with a cross section of ordinary U.S. residents revealed that approximately 8% had delusions that met criteria for paranoia (Eaton et al., 1991).

So what is normal or abnormal? Where do you stand? Each of us may have some personal quirks that others would surely find abnormal—and we can certainly identify some of the things our friends do as pretty peculiar as well. As we have tried to demonstrate in this chapter, however, questions of what is normal or abnormal hinge more on what causes difficulty in people's lives than on simple counts of what behaviors are common or uncommon.

CHAPTER REVIEW

Summary

Identifying Psychological Disorders: What Is Abnormal?

- The study of psychological disorders follows a medical model in which symptoms are understood to indicate an underlying disorder.

- The *DSM-IV-TR* is a classification system that defines a psychological disorder as occurring when the person experiences disturbances of thought, emotion, or behavior that produce distress or impairment and that arise from internal sources.

- Many psychological disorders arise from multiple causes or as a result of the interaction of diathesis (internal predisposition) and stress. It is a common error to assume that an intervention that cures a disorder reflects the cause of the disorder.

Anxiety Disorders: When Fears Take Over

- People with anxiety disorders have irrational worries and fears that undermine their ability to function normally.

- Generalized anxiety disorder (GAD) involves a chronic state of anxiety, whereas phobic disorders involve anxiety tied to a specific object or situation.

- People who suffer from panic disorder experience recurring sudden and intense attacks of anxiety.

- People with obsessive-compulsive disorder experience recurring, anxiety-provoking thoughts that compel them to engage in ritualistic, irrational behavior.

Dissociative Disorders: Going to Pieces

- Dissociative disorders involve severely disjointed and fragmented cognitive processes reflected in significant disruptions in memory, awareness, or personality.

- People with dissociative identity disorder (DID) shift between two or more identities that are distinctive from each other in terms of personal memories, behavioral characteristics, and attitudes.

- Dissociative amnesia and dissociative fugue involve significant memory loss that is too extensive to be the result of normal forgetting and cannot be attributed to brain injury, drugs, or another mental disorder.

Mood Disorders: At the Mercy of Emotions

- Mood disorders are mental disorders in which a disturbance in mood is the predominant feature.

- Major depression (or unipolar depression) is characterized by a severely depressed mood lasting at least 2 weeks; symptoms include excessive self-criticism, guilt, difficulty concentrating, suicidal thoughts, sleep and appetite disturbances, and lethargy. Dysthymia, a related disorder, involves less severe symptoms that persist for at least 2 years.

- Bipolar disorder is an unstable emotional condition involving extreme mood swings of depression and mania. The manic phase is characterized by periods of abnormally and persistently elevated, expansive, or irritable mood, lasting at least 1 week.

Schizophrenia: Losing the Grasp on Reality

- Schizophrenia is a severe psychological disorder involving hallucinations, disorganized thoughts and behavior, and emotional and social withdrawal.

- Schizophrenia affects only 1% of the population, but it accounts for a disproportionate share of psychiatric hospitalizations.

- Risks for developing schizophrenia include genetic factors, biochemical factors (perhaps a complex interaction among many neurotransmitters), brain abnormalities, and a stressful home environment.

Personality Disorders: Going to Extremes

- Personality disorders are deeply ingrained, inflexible patterns of thinking, feeling, relating to others, or controlling impulses that cause distress or impaired functioning.

- Antisocial personality disorder is associated with a lack of moral emotions and behavior; people with antisocial personality disorder can be manipulative, dangerous, and reckless, often hurting others and sometimes hurting themselves.

Key Terms

psychological disorders (p. 363)
medical model (p. 365)
DSM-IV-TR (p. 366)
comorbidity (p. 368)
diathesis-stress model (p. 369)
anxiety disorder (p. 371)
generalized anxiety disorder (GAD) (p. 371)
phobic disorders (p. 372)
specific phobia (p. 372)

social phobia (p. 373)
preparedness theory (p. 373)
panic disorder (p. 374)
agoraphobia (p. 374)
obsessive-compulsive disorder (OCD) (p. 375)
dissociative disorder (p. 376)
dissociative identity disorder (DID), (p. 376)
dissociative fugue (p. 377)
dissociative amnesia (p. 377)

mood disorders (p. 378)
major depression (p. 379)
dysthymia (p. 379)
double depression (p. 379)
seasonal affective disorder (SAD), (p. 379)
helplessness theory (p. 380)
bipolar disorder (p. 381)
schizophrenia (p. 384)
delusion (p. 384)

hallucination (p. 384)
disorganized speech (p. 385)
grossly disorganized behavior (p. 385)
catatonic behavior (p. 385)
negative symptoms (p. 385)
dopamine hypothesis (p. 387)
antisocial personality disorder (APD), (p. 389)
personality disorders (p. 389)

Critical Thinking Questions

1. Psychological disorders can be caused by biological, psychological, and environmental factors. The diathesis-stress model suggests that a person may be predisposed for a psychological disorder that remains unexpressed until triggered by stress.

   Suppose that identical twins (with the same genetic profile) grow up in the same household (sharing the same parents, the same basic diet, the same access to television, etc.). As a teenager, one twin but not the other develops a mental disorder such as schizophrenia. How could this be?

2. Phobias are anxiety disorders that involve excessive and persistent fear of a specific object, activity or situation. Some phobias may be learned through classical conditioning, in which a conditioned stimulus (CS) that is paired with an anxiety-evoking stimulus (US) itself comes to elicit a fear response (CR).

   Suppose a friend of yours has a phobia of dogs which is so intense that he is afraid to go outside in case one of his neighbors' dogs barks at him. Using the principles of classical conditioning you learned in Chapter 5, how might you help him overcome his fear?

3. Major depression (also known as unipolar depression) is characterized by a severely depressed mood, accompanied by feelings of worthlessness and lack of pleasure, and by sleep and appetite disturbances. To be characterized as major depression, the episode must last at least 2 weeks, but on average episodes last about 6 months.

   Both seasonal affective disorder (SAD) and bipolar disorder involve shorter, but cyclically recurring, depressive episodes. If you have a friend who experiences recurring periods of severe depression, how would you determine whether she is suffering from SAD or bipolar disorder?

Answers to Summary Quizzes

Summary Quiz 12.1
1. b; 2. d; 3. c

Summary Quiz 12.2
4. b; 5. a; 6. d; 7. c

Summary Quiz 12.3
8. a; 9. b; 10. c

Summary Quiz 12.4
11. c; 12. a; 13. b; 14. d

Summary Quiz 12.5
15. b; 16. a ; 17. c

Summary Quiz 12.6
18. b; 19. c; 20. d

Need more help? Additional resources are located at the book's free companion Web site at:
www.worthpublishers.com/schacterbriefle

Treatment of Psychological Disorders

THE PLANE WAS STILL AT THE GATE, BUT Lisa was buckled in her seat with her hands tightly squeezing the armrests, her knuckles white. She glanced out the window, swallowed hard, and then stole a look at the people across the aisle. They seemed calm, but she didn't feel calm at all. Her heart was pounding, and then she noticed that the plane was starting to move. She was deathly afraid of flying, but she hoped that this flight might be easier. After all, she wasn't really in a plane. Instead, she was seated in a psychologist's office, wearing virtual

ROZA/DREAMSTIME.COM

reality goggles that projected the sights and sounds of the flight all around her. She was in therapy.

Psychological therapy takes many forms. In this case, Lisa's fear was being treated with a relatively new technique called *virtual reality therapy*. The therapist sat nearby during the virtual flight and encouraged Lisa to progress at her own pace through the stages of air travel that made her anxious—sitting on a plane with the engines off, sitting on a plane with the engines on, taxiing on the runway, a smooth takeoff and a smooth flight, a smooth landing, a close pass similar to a missed landing, a rough landing, a turbulent flight, and a rough takeoff. Lisa came back for six sessions over several weeks, and at the end of her virtual travels she reported feeling no anxiety about any of these virtual events. With the therapist's encouragement, she soon took the step of flying in a real plane (Rothbaum et al., 1996). ■

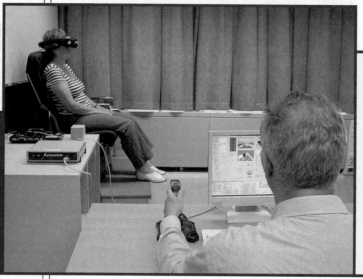

● Virtual reality therapy offers new possibilities for treating people with psychological disorders, especially phobias. Clients can practice engaging in "virtual experiences" before tackling the real-life experiences they fear. On the left is a therapist conducting a virtual flight, on the right, the client's virtual "view" out the "plane" window.

There are a number of ways to treat most psychological disorders, with the goal of changing a person's thoughts, behaviors, emotions, or coping skills. Treatments requiring a person to wear wraparound video goggles are not yet commonplace, but the variety and ingenuity of goggle-free treatment techniques is remarkable. In this chapter, we will explore the most common approaches to psychological treatment. We will examine why people need to seek psychological help in the first place, and then explore how psychotherapy for individuals is built on the major theories of the causes and cures of disorders—including psychoanalytic, behavioral, cognitive, and humanistic/existential theories—and explore how psychotherapy can be conducted for people in groups as well. We'll look into medical and biological approaches to treatment that focus on understanding the brain's role in disorders. Finally, we will discuss whether treatment works, as well as how we know that treatment works.

Treatment: Getting Help to Those Who Need It

Estimates suggest that almost one in five people suffers from some type of mental disorder (Narrow et al., 2002). The personal costs of these disorders involve anguish to the sufferers as well as interference in their ability to carry on the activities of daily life. Think about Lisa, our fearful flyer. If she did not (or could not) seek treatment, she would be unable to take advantage of air travel—but there's more. Some people with fear of airplanes develop difficulty with simple day-to-day tasks due to a disabling fear of encountering anything that could even remind them of airplanes. Watching an airplane trip on television might be too much to bear, and even the sound of airplanes flying overhead could be so frightening as to keep the person at home all the time.

Beyond the personal costs, the social burdens associated with mental disorders are also enormous. For example, people with anxiety disorders report levels of impairment in their daily lives that are comparable to or higher than those

● **What are some of the personal, social, and financial costs of mental illness?**

of people with chronic medical illnesses, such as multiple sclerosis or end-stage renal disease (Antony, Roth, et al., 1998). Impairment is widespread, affecting family life, the ability to work, maintenance of friendships, and more. A person with schizophrenia or severe depression may be unable to hold down a job or even get organized enough to collect a welfare check, and people with many disorders stop getting along with family or people who are trying to help. At the extreme, victims of some disorders can become violent and dangerous to themselves or others.

There are financial costs, too. One set of calculations found that the annual financial burden of anxiety disorders alone in the United States was $42.3 billion, or $1,542 per sufferer, including costs of treatment, diminished productivity, and absenteeism in the workplace (Greenberg et al., 1999). If we add in similar figures for schizophrenia, mood disorders, substance abuse, and all the other psychological problems, the overall costs are astronomical. In addition to the personal benefits of treatment, then, society also stands to benefit from the effective treatment of psychological disorders.

Cho Seung-Hui slaughtered 32 people at Virginia Tech University in 2007 and then killed himself. He sent an angry, rambling manifesto and videos of himself to the media. Posing with guns, he said, "Jesus was crucifying me. When the time came, I did it. I had no choice. . . . This didn't have to happen." Cho was clearly mentally ill, and effective treatment might have saved these lives.

Why People Cannot or Will Not Seek Treatment

Despite the high prevalence of psychological problems in the general population, most people who suffer from such problems do not receive help. One national survey of more than 1,600 adults diagnosed with depression or an anxiety disorder found that only 30% received appropriate treatment for the problem—despite the fact that 83% had seen a health care provider in the previous year (in most cases, a family doctor) (Young et al., 2001). People may fail to get treatment because of three major problems:

● **What are the obstacles to help/treatment for the mentally ill?**

1. *People may not realize that their disorder needs to be treated.* Mental illness is often not taken nearly as seriously as physical illness, perhaps because the origin of mental illness is "hidden" and usually cannot be diagnosed by a blood test or x-ray. The stigma of mental illness often includes beliefs that mental problems can be solved by "mind over matter." In other words, some people believe that mental illness is a sign of personal weakness or that people suffering from mental illness are not trying hard enough to help themselves.

2. *There may be barriers to treatment, such as beliefs and circumstances that keep people from getting help.* Individuals may believe that they should be able to handle things themselves. In some cases, families discourage their loved ones from seeking help because the public acknowledgment of a psychological disorder may be seen as an embarrassment to the family. In other cases, there may be financial obstacles to getting treatment, such as lack of medical insurance that covers treatment for mental health disorders. Barriers may even arise from treatment providers or facilities themselves, including such factors as long waiting lists, lack of funding for adequate staffing, or lack of staff education about the most up-to-date treatments. Cultural and gender factors may also affect who seeks treatment and who does not. For example, one study of college students found that being male predicted negative attitudes toward seeking psychological help, suggesting that men may be less likely than women to seek psychological services (Komiya, Good, & Sherrod, 2000).

3. *Even people who acknowledge they have a problem may not know where to look for services.* Like finding a good lawyer or plumber, finding the right psychologist can be more difficult than simply flipping through the yellow pages or searching online. This confusion is understandable given the plethora of different types of treatments available.

Even when people seek and find help, they sometimes do not receive the most effective treatments, which further complicates things (see the Real World box on page 400). For example, although cognitive and behavioral therapies yield the best results for treating anxiety disorders, most people do not receive these treatments. In one study, most individuals seeking help in a clinic specializing in anxiety disorders reported having previously received treatments other than cognitive or behavioral therapy for their anxiety problems even though there is little evidence

There's nothing funny about depression.

[THE REAL WORLD] •

Types of Psychotherapists

Therapists have widely varying backgrounds and training, and this affects the kinds of services they offer. There are several major "flavors":

- **Psychologist** A psychologist who practices psychotherapy holds a doctorate with specialization in clinical psychology (a Ph.D. or Psy.D.). This degree takes about 5 years to complete, and the psychologist will have extensive training in therapy, the assessment of psychological disorders, and research. The psychologist will sometimes have a specialty, such as working with adolescents or helping people overcome sleep disorders, and will usually conduct therapy that involves talking. Psychologists must be licensed by the state, and most states require candidates to complete about 2 years of supervised practical training and a competency exam.

- **Psychiatrist** A psychiatrist is a medical doctor who has completed an M.D. with specialized training in assessing and treating mental disorders. Psychiatrists can prescribe medications, and some also practice psychotherapy. General practice physicians can also prescribe medications for mental disorders and often are the first to see people with such disorders because people consult them for a wide range of health problems. However, general practice physicians do not typically receive much specialized training in the diagnosis or treatment of mental disorders, and they do not practice psychotherapy.

- **Social worker** A social worker has a master's degree in social work and has training in working with people in dire life situations such as poverty, homelessness, or family conflict. Clinical or psychiatric social workers also receive special training to help people in these situations who have mental disorders. Social workers often work in government or private social service agencies, and they also may work in hospitals or have a private practice.

- **Counselor** Counselors have a wide range of training. To be a counseling psychologist, for example, requires a doctorate and practical training; the title uses that key term *psychologist* and is regulated by state laws. But states vary in how they define *counselor*. In some cases, a counselor must have a master's degree and extensive training in therapy, whereas in others, this person may have minimal training or relevant education. Counselors who work in schools usually have a master's degree and specific training in counseling in educational settings.

Some people offer therapy under made-up terms that sound professional—"mind/body healing therapist," for example, or "marital adjustment adviser." Often these terms are simply invented to mislead clients and avoid licensing boards, and the "therapist" may have no training or expertise at all. And, of course, there are a few people who claim to be licensed practitioners who are not: Louise Wightman, who had once worked as stripper "Princess Cheyenne," was convicted of fraud in 2007 after conducting psychotherapy as a psychologist with dozens of clients. She claimed she didn't know the Ph.D. degree she had purchased over the Internet was bogus (Associated Press, 2007).

People who offer therapy may be well meaning and even helpful, but they could do harm too. For these reasons, it's important that a person seeking therapy shops wisely for a therapist whose training and credentials reflect expertise and inspire confidence. Such therapists can be found by referral from a general practice physician or school counselor, by visiting a college clinic or hospital, or by contacting an Internet site of an organization such as the American Psychological Association that offers referrals to licensed mental health care providers.

The therapist's personality and approach can sometimes be as important as his or her background or training. If you are shopping for a therapist, you should seek out someone who is willing and open to answer questions, who has a clear understanding about the type of problem leading you to seek therapy, and who shows general respect and empathy for you. A therapist is someone you are entrusting with your mental health, and you should only enter into such a relationship when you and the therapist have good rapport.

Which one? Finding the right psychotherapist can seem like finding the best watermelon: You won't really know until you've had a taste. Shoppers sometimes thump melons on the theory that the sweetest ones sound different, but no one quite knows how a good one will sound. In the case of psychotherapists, fortunately, no thumping is required. You can find out about their qualifications in advance and even talk to several to see which one seems right.

for the effectiveness of these other approaches for anxiety disorders. Only about a third of people reported previously receiving the treatment approaches most strongly supported by prior research (Rowa et al., 2000). Clearly, before choosing or prescribing a therapy, we need to know what kinds of treatments are available and understand which treatments are best for particular disorders.

Approaches to Treatment

Treatments can be divided broadly into two kinds: psychotherapy, in which a person interacts with a psychotherapist, and medical or biological treatments, in which the mental disorder is treated with drugs or surgery. In some cases, both psychotherapy *and* biological treatments are used. Lisa's fear of flying, for example, might be treated not only with the virtual reality therapy you read about (a form of psychotherapy) in preparation for the real flight but also with antianxiety medications in the hours before the actual takeoff. For many years, psychotherapy was the main form of treatment for psychological disorders because few medical or biological options were available. But alongside psychotherapy, there have always been folk remedies that depend on biology. As we learn more about the biology and chemistry of the brain, approaches to mental health that begin with the brain are becoming increasingly widespread. As you'll see later in the chapter, often the most effective treatments combine both psychotherapy and medications.

Culture & Community

Is Psychotherapy the Same around the World?

Not at all. Some psychotherapies are indigenous to particular cultures. For example, two well-known therapies influenced by Buddhism originated in Japan: Morita therapy and Naikan therapy (Sato, 2001).

Morita therapy instructs patients that feelings cannot be changed and are to be accepted. Actions can be taken to achieve goals, in spite of feelings, and these actions may in turn increase positive feelings. In Naikan, patients are asked to think about what they can do for others. They examine instances of care and benevolence they received from another person, recollect memories of what they returned to that person, and recall any trouble or worries they have given to that person. The goal of Naikan therapy is to have patients realize their indebtedness to their significant others, their mothers, in particular.

COURTESY OF REN ADAMS

summary quiz [13.1]

1. Which of the following statements is true?
   a. Mental illness is very rare, with only 1 person in 100 suffering from a psychological disorder.
   b. The majority of individuals with psychological disorders seek treatment.
   c. Women and men are equally likely to seek treatment for psychological disorders.
   d. Mental illness is often not taken as seriously as physical illness.

2. Your textbook lists three reasons why people may fail to get treatment for psychological disorders. Which of the following is *not* one of these reasons?
   a. People may be unaware that they have a problem.
   b. People may be aware that most treatments are ineffective.
   c. People face obstacles to getting treatment.
   d. People may not know where to look for treatment.

3. The most effective treatment for psychological disorders often is
   a. psychotherapy.
   b. medication.
   c. a combination of psychotherapy and medication.
   d. doing nothing, since most people improve anyway.

COURTESY OF MISSOURI STATE ARCHIVES

Patients in steam cabinets, about 1910. Without a clue about how to proceed, early mental health workers gave patients steam baths as a form of treatment for psychological disorders in the forlorn hope that something might work.

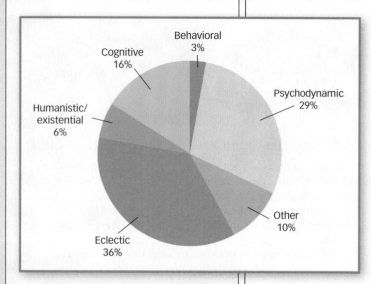

•••••••••••••••••• **FIGURE 13.1**

Approaches to Psychotherapy in the 21st Century *This chart shows the percentage of psychologists (from among 1,000 members of the American Psychological Association's Division of Psychotherapy) who have various primary psychotherapy orientations (adapted from Norcross et al., 2002).*

Psychological Therapies: Healing the Mind through Interaction

Psychological therapy, or **psychotherapy**, is *an interaction between a therapist and someone suffering from a psychological problem, with the goal of providing support or relief from the problem.* Currently over 400 different systems of psychotherapy exist. Although there are similarities among all the psychotherapies, each approach is unique in its goals, aims, and methods. A recent survey of 1,000 psychotherapists asked them to describe their main theoretical orientation (Norcross, Hedges, & Castle, 2002; see **FIGURE 13.1**). Over a third reported using **eclectic psychotherapy**, a form of psychotherapy that involves *drawing on techniques from different forms of therapy, depending on the client and the problem.* This allows the therapists to apply an appropriate theoretical perspective that is suited to the problem at hand rather than adhering to a single theoretical perspective for all clients and all types of problems. Nevertheless, as **FIGURE 13.1** shows, the majority of psychotherapists use a single approach, such as psychodynamic therapy, behavioral and cognitive therapies, humanistic and existential therapies, or group therapy. We'll examine each of those four major branches of psychotherapy in turn.

Psychodynamic Therapy

Psychodynamic psychotherapy has its roots in Freud's psychoanalytically oriented theory of personality (see Chapter 11). **Psychodynamic psychotherapies** *explore childhood events and encourage individuals to use this understanding to develop insight into their psychological problems.* There are a number of different psychodynamic therapies that can vary substantially, but they all share the belief that the path to overcoming psychological problems is to develop insight into the unconscious memories, impulses, wishes, and conflicts that are assumed to underlie these problems. Psychodynamic therapies include psychoanalysis and modern psychodynamic therapy, such as interpersonal psychotherapy.

● **What is the commonly held belief behind all psychodynamic therapies?**

Psychoanalysis

As you saw in Chapter 11, *psychoanalysis* assumes that humans are born with aggressive and sexual urges that are repressed during childhood development through the use of defense mechanisms. Psychoanalysts encourage their clients to bring these repressed conflicts into consciousness so that the clients can understand them and reduce their unwanted influences. Psychoanalysts focus a great deal on early childhood events because they believe that urges and conflicts were likely to be repressed during this time.

Traditional psychoanalysis takes place over an average of 3 to 6 years, with four or five sessions per week (Ursano & Silberman, 2003). During a session, the client reclines on a couch, facing away from the analyst, and is asked to express whatever thoughts and feelings come to mind. Occasionally, the analyst may comment on some of the information presented by the client, but the analyst does not express his or her values and judgments. The stereotypic image you might have of psychological therapy—a person lying on a couch talking to a person sitting in a chair—springs from this approach.

How to Develop Insight

The goal of psychoanalysis is for the client to understand the unconscious in a process Freud called developing insight. A psychoanalyst can use several key techniques to help the client develop insight, including these:

In traditional psychoanalysis, the patient lies on a couch, with the therapist sitting behind, out of the patient's view. This also happens in the comics.

Free association. In free association, the client reports every thought that enters the mind, without censorship or filtering. This strategy allows the stream of consciousness to flow unimpeded. If the client stops, the therapist prompts further associations ("And what does that make you think of?"). The therapist may then look for themes that recur during therapy sessions.

Dream analysis. Psychoanalysis treats dreams as metaphors that symbolize unconscious conflicts or wishes, and that contain disguised clues that the therapist can help the client understand. A psychoanalytic therapy session might begin with an invitation for the client to recount a dream, after which the client might be asked to participate in the interpretation by freely associating to the dream.

Interpretation. This is the process by which the therapist deciphers the meaning (e.g., unconscious impulses or fantasies) underlying what the client says and does. Interpretation is used throughout therapy, during free association, dream analysis, and in other aspects of the treatment. During the process of interpretation, the analyst suggests possible meanings to the client, looking for signs that the correct meaning has been discovered. Unfortunately, a correct interpretation is usually not accompanied by giant flashing neon lights. The analyst could overinterpret the client's thoughts and emotions and sometimes even contribute interpretations that are far from the truth. For example, the discovery that a client had a traumatic sexual experience with a visiting relative as a child might seem so important to the analyst that it could suggest a way of understanding many of the client's dreams and associations. But this particular event actually might *not* be the basis of the client's unconscious conflicts, in which case the therapist would be directing the client to an insight that is really no insight at all.

Analysis of resistance. In the process of "trying on" different interpretations of the client's thoughts and actions, the analyst may suggest an interpretation that the client finds particularly unacceptable. **Resistance** is *a reluctance to cooperate with treatment for fear of confronting unpleasant unconscious material.* For example, the therapist might suggest that the client's problem with obsessive health worries could be traced to a childhood rivalry with her mother for her father's love and attention. The client could find the suggestion insulting and fervently resist the interpretation. Curiously, the analyst might interpret this resistance as a signal not that the interpretation is wrong but instead that the interpretation is on the right track. If a client always shifts the topic of discussion away from a particular idea, that might signal to the therapist that this is indeed an issue on which the client could be directed to confront in order to develop insight.

● **What might a client's resistance signal to a therapist?**

"I'll say a normal word, then you say the first sick thing that pops into your head."

ONLY HUMAN

PSYCHO-BEAR-APY? The Central Park Zoo revealed in 1994 that it had paid an animal behaviorist $25,000 for psychotherapy for Gus, its 9-year-old polar bear who was involved in various repetitive behaviors, which the zoo director said could have been a mild neurosis. The behaviorist recommended creating games to make Gus's life less monotonous.

The Process of Transference

These psychoanalytic techniques may be used over the course of an intensive and lengthy process of analysis. During this process, the client and psychoanalyst often develop a close relationship. Freud noticed this relationship developing in his analyses and was at first troubled by it: Clients would develop an unusually strong attachment to him, almost as though they were viewing him as a parent or lover, and he worried that this could interfere with achieving the goal of insight. Over time, however, he came to believe that the development and resolution of this relationship was a key process of psychoanalysis.

Transference occurs *when the analyst begins to assume a major significance in the client's life and the client reacts to the analyst based on unconscious childhood fantasies.* Successful psychoanalysis involves analyzing the transference so that the client understands this reaction and why it occurs. In fact, insight, the ultimate goal of psychoanalysis, may be enhanced because interpretations of the client's interaction with the therapist also have implications for the client's past and future relationships (Andersen & Berk, 1998).

psychotherapy An interaction between a therapist and someone suffering from a psychological problem, with the goal of providing support or relief from the problem.

eclectic psychotherapy Treatment that draws on techniques from different forms of therapy, depending on the client and the problem.

psychodynamic psychotherapies A general approach to treatment that explores childhood events and encourages individuals to develop insight into their psychological problems.

resistance A reluctance to cooperate with treatment for fear of confronting unpleasant unconscious material.

transference An event that occurs in psychoanalysis when the analyst begins to assume a major significance in the client's life and the client reacts to the analyst based on unconscious childhood fantasies.

FREUD MUSEUM, LONDON

● *Sigmund Freud, with his mother, Amalia, on her 90th birthday.*

Beyond Psychoanalysis

Although Freud's insights and techniques are fundamental, modern psychodynamic theory reflects the contributions of many who followed, including several of Freud's students who broke away from him and developed their own approaches to psychotherapy. Carl Jung (1875–1961) and Alfred Adler (1870–1937) agreed with Freud that insight was a key therapeutic goal but disagreed that insight usually involves unconscious conflicts about sex and aggression (Arlow, 2000). Instead, Jung emphasized what he called the *collective unconscious,* the culturally determined symbols and myths that are shared among all people that, he argued, could serve as a basis for interpretation beyond sex or aggression. Adler believed that emotional conflicts are the result of perceptions of inferiority and that psychotherapy should help people overcome problems resulting from inferior social status, sex roles, and discrimination.

● **In what common ways do other psychodynamic theories differ from Freudian analysis?**

Other analysts to break with Freud were Melanie Klein (1882–1960), who believed that primitive fantasies of loss and persecution (e.g., worrying about a parent dying or about being bullied) were important factors underlying mental illness, and Karen Horney (1885–1952), who disagreed with Freud about inherent differences in the psychology of men and women and traced such differences to society and culture rather than biology. All of these approaches to psychotherapy stress that the individual is part of a larger society and that conflicts can reflect the individual's role in that society.

These social themes have been developed most explicitly in **interpersonal psychotherapy (IPT),** *a form of psychotherapy that focuses on helping clients improve current relationships* (Weissman, Markowitz, & Klerman, 2000). Therapists using IPT try to focus treatment on the person's interpersonal behaviors and feelings. They pay particular attention to the client's grief (an exaggerated reaction to the loss of a loved one), role disputes (conflicts with a significant other), role transitions (changes in life status, such as starting a new job, getting married, or retiring), or interpersonal deficits (lack of the necessary skills to start or maintain a relationship). The treatment focuses on interpersonal functioning with the assumption that, as interpersonal relations improve, symptoms will subside.

Behavioral and Cognitive Therapies

Unlike psychodynamic psychotherapy, which emphasizes early developmental processes as the source of psychological dysfunction, behavioral and cognitive treatments emphasize the current factors that contribute to the problem—maladaptive behaviors and dysfunctional thoughts.

Behavior Therapy

The idea of focusing treatment on the client's behavior rather than the client's unconscious was inspired by behaviorism. As you read in Chapter 1, behaviorists rejected theories that posited "invisible" mental properties that were difficult to test and impossible to observe. Behaviorists found psychoanalytic ideas particularly hard to test: How do you know whether a person has an unconscious conflict or whether insight has occurred? Behavioral principles, in contrast, focused solely on behaviors that could be observed (e.g., avoidance of a feared object, such as refusing to get on an airplane). **Behavior therapy** assumes that *disordered behavior is learned and that symptom relief is achieved through changing overt maladaptive behaviors into more constructive behaviors.* A variety of behavior therapy techniques have been developed for many disorders, based on the learning principles you encountered in Chapter 6—including operant conditioning procedures (which focus on reinforcement and punishment) and classical conditioning procedures (which focus on extinction). Here are three examples of behavior therapy techniques in action:

● **What primary problem did behaviorists have with psychoanalytic ideas?**

interpersonal psychotherapy (IPT) A form of psychotherapy that focuses on helping clients improve current relationships.

behavior therapy A type of therapy that assumes that disordered behavior is learned and that symptom relief is achieved through changing overt maladaptive behaviors into more constructive behaviors.

token economy A form of behavior therapy in which clients are given "tokens" for desired behaviors, which they can later trade for rewards.

exposure therapy An approach to treatment that involves confronting an emotion-arousing stimulus directly and repeatedly, ultimately leading to a decrease in the emotional response.

systematic desensitization A procedure in which a client relaxes all the muscles of his or her body while imagining being in increasingly frightening situations.

cognitive therapy A form of psychotherapy that involves helping a client identify and correct any distorted thinking about self, others, or the world.

Eliminating unwanted behaviors. How would you change a 3-year-old boy's habit of throwing tantrums at the grocery store? A behavior therapist might investigate what happens after the tantrum: Did the child get candy to "shut him up"? Did the mortified parent provide a lot of attention, begging the child to be quiet? The study of operant conditioning shows that behavior can be predicted by its *consequences* (the reinforcing or punishing events that follow). Adjusting these might help change the behavior. Making the consequences less reinforcing (no candy) and more punishing (a period of time-out in the car while the parent watches from nearby rather than providing a rush of attention) could eliminate the problem behavior.

Promoting desired behaviors. In a psychiatric hospital, patients may sometimes become unresponsive and apathetic, withdrawing from social interaction and failing to participate in treatment programs. A behavior therapy technique sometimes used in such cases is the **token economy**, which involves *giving clients "tokens" for desired behaviors, which they can later trade for rewards*. Tokens for behaviors such as cleaning their rooms, getting exercise, or helping other patients signal positive reinforcement because they can be exchanged for rewards such as time away from the hospital, television privileges, and special foods. Token economies have proven to be effective while the system of rewards is in place, but the learned behaviors are not usually maintained when the reinforcements are discontinued (Glynn, 1990). Similar systems used in classrooms to encourage positive behaviors may work temporarily but can undermine students' interest in these behaviors when the reinforcements are no longer available (Lepper & Greene, 1976). A child who is rewarded for controlling his temper in class may become an ogre on the playground when no teacher is present to offer rewards for good behavior.

Reducing unwanted emotional responses. One of the most powerful ways to reduce fear is by gradual *exposure* to the feared object or situation, a behavioral method originated by psychiatrist Joseph Wolpe (1958). **Exposure therapy** involves *confronting an emotion-arousing stimulus directly and repeatedly, ultimately leading to a decrease in the emotional response*. This technique depends on the processes of habituation and response extinction that were originally discovered in the study of classical conditioning (see Chapter 6). Wolpe called his form of treatment **systematic desensitization,** *a procedure in which a client relaxes all the muscles of his or her body while imagining being in increasingly frightening situations*. For example, a client who fears snakes might first imagine seeing a photo of a snake, followed by imagining seeing a snake that is inside an aquarium,

● **How might exposure therapy help treat a phobia or fear of a specific object?**

followed eventually by imagining holding a large snake, all while engaging in exercises that relax the muscles of the body. It's now known that *in vivo exposure*, or live exposure, is more effective than imaginary exposure (Emmelkamp & Wessels, 1975; Stern & Marks, 1973). In other words, if a person fears social situations, it is better for that person to practice social interaction than to merely imagine it. Behavioral therapists use an exposure hierarchy to expose the client gradually to the feared object or situation. Easier situations are practiced first, and as fear decreases, the client progresses to more difficult or frightening situations.

Cognitive Therapy

Whereas behavior therapy doesn't take into account a person's thoughts and feelings, and instead focuses on an individual's behavior, **cognitive therapy** focuses on *helping a client identify and correct any distorted thinking about self, others, or the world* (e.g., Beck & Weishaar, 2000). For example, behaviorists might explain a phobia as the outcome of a classical conditioning experience such as being bitten by a dog, where the dog bite leads to the development of a dog phobia through the simple association of the dog with the experience of pain. Cognitive theorists might instead emphasize the *meaning*

A behavioral therapist might treat this temper tantrum with an analysis of the antecedents, behavior, and consequences of the act.

Exposure therapy is a powerful treatment for overcoming fear. Up to 90% of individuals with animal phobias are able to overcome their fears in as little as one session lasting 2 to 3 hours. Eventually, almost anyone could handle a snake.

"Don't make me come over there!"

of the event. It might not be the event itself that caused the fear, but rather the individual's beliefs and assumptions about the event and the feared stimulus. In the case of a dog bite, cognitive theorists might focus on a person's new or strengthened belief that dogs are dangerous to explain the fear.

Cognitive therapies use a principal technique called **cognitive restructuring**, which involves *teaching clients to question the automatic beliefs, assumptions, and predictions that often lead to negative emotions and to replace negative thinking with more realistic and positive beliefs.* Specifically, clients are taught to examine the evidence for and against a particular belief or to be more accepting of outcomes that may be undesirable yet still manageable. For example, a depressed client may believe that she is stupid and will never pass her college courses—all on the basis of one poor grade. In this situation, the therapist would work with the client to examine the validity of this belief. The therapist would consider relevant evidence such as grades on previous exams, performance on other coursework, and examples of intelligence outside school. It may be that the client has never failed a course before and has achieved good grades in this particular course in the past. In this case, the therapist would encourage the client to consider all this information in determining whether she is truly "stupid."

● **How might a client restructure a negative self image into a positive one?**

Some forms of cognitive therapy include techniques for coping with unwanted thoughts and feelings, techniques that resemble meditation (see Chapter 8). Clients may be encouraged to attend to their troubling thoughts or emotions or be given meditative techniques that allow them to gain a new focus. One such technique, called **mindfulness meditation**, *teaches an individual to be fully present in each moment; to be aware of his or her thoughts, feelings, and sensations; and to detect symptoms before they become a problem.* Researchers have found mindfulness meditation to be helpful for preventing relapse in depression. In one study, people recovering from depression were about half as likely to relapse during a 60-week assessment period if they received mindfulness meditation–based cognitive therapy than if they received treatment as usual (Teasdale, Segal, & Williams, 2000).

▶ *Western cognitive therapy meets the Eastern Buddhist meditation tradition as Aaron Beck greets his holiness the Dalai Lama at the International Congress for Cognitive Psychotherapy in 2005. Beck's approach to psychotherapy helps people change maladaptive thinking patterns in a direct and rational approach, whereas the practice of Buddhism expressed by the Lama aims to create mental peace through meditation. Here they seem to be amused by each other's choice of clothing.*

Cognitive Behavioral Therapy

Historically, cognitive and behavioral therapies were considered distinct systems of therapy, and some people continue to follow this distinction, using solely behavioral *or* cognitive techniques. Today, the extent to which therapists use cognitive versus behavioral techniques depends on the individual therapist as well as the type of problem being treated. Most therapists working with anxiety and depression use *a blend of cognitive and behavioral therapeutic strategies,* often referred to as **cognitive behavioral therapy**, or **CBT.** In a way, this technique acknowledges that there may be behaviors that people cannot control through rational thought but also that there are ways of helping people think more rationally when thought does play a role. In contrast to traditional behavior therapy and cognitive therapy, CBT is "problem focused," meaning that it is undertaken for specific problems (e.g., reducing the frequency of panic attacks or returning to work after a bout of depression), and "action oriented," meaning that the therapist tries to

● **Why do most therapists use a blend of cognitive and behavioral strategies?**

cognitive restructuring A therapeutic approach that teaches clients to question the automatic beliefs, assumptions, and predictions that often lead to negative emotions and to replace negative thinking with more realistic and positive beliefs.

mindfulness meditation A form of cognitive therapy that teaches an individual to be fully present in each moment; to be aware of his or her thoughts, feelings, and sensations; and to detect symptoms before they become a problem.

cognitive behavioral therapy (CBT) A blend of cognitive and behavioral therapeutic strategies.

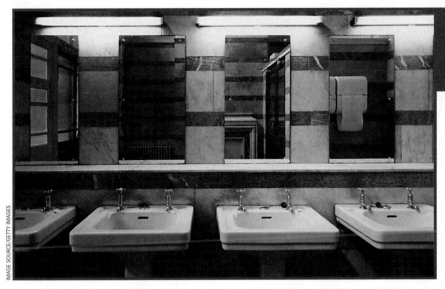

The cognitive behavior therapy (CBT) client with obsessive-compulsive disorder who fears contamination in public restrooms might be given "homework" to visit three such restrooms in a week not necessarily to touch anything, but just to look.

assist the client in selecting specific strategies to help address those problems. The client is expected to *do* things, such as practice relaxation exercises or use a diary to monitor relevant symptoms (e.g., the severity of depressed mood, panic attack symptoms). This is in contrast to psychodynamic or other therapies where goals may not be explicitly discussed or agreed on and the client's only necessary action is to attend the therapy session.

CBT also contrasts with psychodynamic approaches in its assumptions about what the client can know. CBT is *transparent* in that nothing is withheld from the client. By the end of the course of therapy, most clients have a very good understanding of the treatment they have received as well as the specific techniques that are used to make the desired changes. For example, clients with obsessive-compulsive disorder who fear contamination would feel confident in knowing how to confront feared situations such as public washrooms and why confronting this situation is helpful. In this way, the CBT model of therapy differs from the more mystical relationship between the therapist and client in psychodynamic psychotherapy, in which the therapist serves almost as a kind of spiritual guide urging the client toward insight.

"That's Eleanor. She's a fact checker."

Humanistic and Existential Therapies

Humanistic and existential therapies emerged in the middle of the 20th century, in part as a reaction to the negative views that psychodynamic psychotherapies hold about human nature. Psychodynamic approaches emphasize unconscious drives toward sex and aggression, as we noted earlier. Humanistic and existential therapies assume that human nature is generally positive, and they emphasize the natural tendency of each individual to strive for personal improvement. Humanistic and existential therapies share the assumption that psychological problems stem from feelings of alienation and loneliness—and that these feelings can be traced to failures to reach one's potential (in the humanistic approach) or from failures to find meaning in life (in the existential approach). Although interest in these approaches peaked in the 1960s and 1970s, some therapists continue to use these approaches today. Two well-known types are person-centered therapy (a humanistic approach) and Gestalt therapy (an existential approach).

● **How does a humanistic view of human nature differ from a psychodynamic view?**

person-centered therapy An approach to therapy that assumes all individuals have a tendency toward growth and that this growth can be facilitated by acceptance and genuine reactions from the therapist.

Gestalt therapy An existentialist approach to treatment with the goal of helping the client become aware of his or her thoughts, behaviors, experiences, and feelings and to "own" or take responsibility for them.

group therapy Therapy in which multiple participants (who often do not know one another at the outset) work on their individual problems in a group atmosphere.

Person-Centered Therapy

Person-centered therapy (also known as *client-centered therapy*) *assumes that all individuals have a tendency toward growth and that this growth can be facilitated by acceptance and genuine reactions from the therapist* (Rogers, 1951). Person-centered therapy assumes that each individual is qualified to determine his or her own goals for therapy, such as feeling more confident or making a career decision, and even the frequency and length of therapy. In this type of *nondirective* treatment, the therapist tends not to provide advice or suggestions about what the client should be doing. Instead, the therapist paraphrases the client's words, mirroring the client's thoughts and sentiments (e.g., "I think I hear you saying . . ."). Person-centered therapists believe that with adequate support, the client will recognize the right things to do.

Person-centered therapists strive to demonstrate three basic qualities: congruence, empathy, and unconditional positive regard. *Congruence* refers to openness and honesty in the therapeutic relationship and ensuring that the therapist communicates the same message at all levels. For example, the same message must be communicated in the therapist's words, the therapist's facial expression, and the therapist's body language. Saying, "I think your concerns are valid," while smirking would simply not do. *Empathy* refers to the continuous process of trying to understand the client by getting inside his or her way of thinking, feeling, and understanding the world. Seeing the world from the client's perspective enables the therapist to better appreciate the client apprehensions, worries, or fears. Finally, the therapist must treat the client with *unconditional positive regard* by providing a nonjudgmental, warm, and accepting environment in which the client can feel safe expressing his or her thoughts and feelings.

In person-centered therapy, the goal of therapy sessions is not to uncover repressed conflicts, as in psychodynamic therapy, or to challenge unrealistic thoughts, as in cognitive behavior therapy. Instead, the person-centered therapist tries to understand the client's experience and reflect that experience back to in a supportive way, encouraging the client's natural tendency toward growth. This style of therapy is a bit reminiscent of psychoanalysis in its way of encouraging the client toward the free expression of thoughts and feelings, although humanistic therapies clearly start from a set of assumptions about human nature that differ diametrically from psychodynamic theories.

Gestalt Therapy

Gestalt therapy *has the goal of helping the client become aware of his or her thoughts, behaviors, experiences, and feelings and to "own" or take responsibility for them.* Gestalt therapists are encouraged to be enthusiastic and warm toward their clients, an approach they share in common with person-centered therapists. Gestalt therapy emphasizes the experiences and behaviors that are occurring at that particular moment in the therapy session. For example, if a client is talking about something stressful that occurred during the previous week, the therapist might shift the attention to the client's current experience by asking, "How do you feel as you describe what happened to you?" This technique is known as *focusing*. Clients are also encouraged to put their feelings into action. One way to do this is the *empty chair technique*, in which the client imagines that another person (e.g., a spouse, a parent, a coworker) is in an empty chair, sitting directly across from the client. The client then moves from chair to chair, alternating from role playing what he or she would say to the other person and what he or she imagines the other person would respond. In this type of therapy, the goal is to facilitate awareness of the client's thoughts, feelings, behaviors, and experiences in the "here and now," with the assumption that greater awareness will clear a path to living more fully and meaningfully.

As part of Gestalt therapy, clients are encouraged to imagine that another person is sitting across from them in a chair. The client then moves from chair to chair, role-playing what he or she would say to the imagined person and what that person would answer.

PHOTOALTO/ALAMY

Groups in Therapy

It is natural to think of psychopathology as an illness that affects only the individual. A particular person "is depressed," for example, or "has anxiety." Yet each person lives in a world of other people, and interactions with others may intensify and even create disorders. A depressed person may be lonely after moving away from friends and loved ones, or an anxious person could be worried about pressures from parents. These ideas suggest that people might be able to recover from disorders in the same way they got into them—not just as an individual effort, but through social processes.

● **When is group therapy the best option?**

Couples and Family Therapy

When a couple is "having problems," neither individual may be suffering from any psychopathology. Rather, it may be the relationship itself that is disordered. *Couples therapy* is when a married, cohabitating, or dating couple is seen together in therapy to work on problems usually arising within the relationship. A traditional use of couples therapy might involve a couple seeking help because they are unhappy with their relationship. In this scenario, both members of the couple are expected to attend therapy sessions and the problem is seen as arising from their interaction rather than from the problems of one half of the couple. Treatment strategies would target changes in *both* parties, focusing on ways to break their repetitive dysfunctional pattern (Watzlawick, Beavin, & Jackson, 1967).

Families enter therapy for many reasons, sometimes to help particular members and other times because there are problems in one or more of the relationships in the family.

There are cases when therapy with even larger groups is warranted. An individual may be having a problem—say, an adolescent is abusing alcohol—but the source of the problem is in the individual's relationships with family members; perhaps the mother is herself an alcoholic who subtly encourages the adolescent to drink and the father travels and neglects the family. In this case, it could be useful for the therapist to work with the whole group at once in *family therapy*—psychotherapy involving members of a family. In family therapy, the "client" is the entire family. Family therapists believe that problem behaviors exhibited by a particular family member are the result of a dysfunctional family. For example, an adolescent girl suffering from bulimia might be treated in therapy with her mother, father, and older brother. The therapist would work to understand how the family members relate to one another, how the family is organized, and how it changes over time. In discussions with the family, the therapist might discover that the parents' excessive enthusiasm about her brother's athletic career led the girl to try to gain their approval by controlling her weight to become "beautiful." Both couples and family therapy involve more than one person attending therapy together, and the problems and solutions are seen as arising from the *interaction* of these individuals rather than simply from any one individual.

Group Therapy

Taking these ideas one step further, if individuals (or families) can benefit from talking with a psychotherapist, perhaps they can also benefit from talking with other clients who are talking with the therapist. This is **group therapy**, *a technique in which multiple participants (who often do not know one another at the outset) work on their individual problems in a group atmosphere*. The therapist in group therapy serves more as a discussion leader than as a personal therapist, conducting the sessions both by talking with individuals and by encouraging them to talk with one another. Group therapy is often used for people who have a common problem, such as substance abuse, but it can also be used for those with differing problems.

● **What are the pros and cons of a group therapy approach?**

"So, does anyone in the group feel like responding to what Richard has just shared with us?"

Why do people choose group therapy? One advantage is that groups provide a context in which clients can practice relating to others. People in group therapy have a "built-in" set of peers whom they have to talk to and get along with on a regular basis. This can be especially helpful for clients who are otherwise socially isolated. Second, attending a group with others who have similar problems shows clients that they are not alone in their suffering. Third, group members model appropriate behaviors for one another and share their insights about how to deal with their problems.

Group therapy also has disadvantages. It may be difficult to assemble a group of individuals who have similar needs. This is particularly an issue with CBT, which tends to focus on specific problems such as depression or panic disorder. Group therapy may become a problem if one or more members undermine the treatment of other group members. This can occur if some group members dominate the discussions, threaten other group members, or make others in the group uncomfortable (e.g., attempting to date other members). Finally, clients in group therapy get less attention than they might in individual psychotherapy. As a result, those who tend to participate less in the group may not benefit as much as those who participate more.

Self-Help and Support Groups

An important offshoot of group therapy is the concept of *self-help groups* and *support groups*, which are discussion or Internet chat groups that focus on a particular disorder or difficult life experience and are often run by peers who have themselves struggled with the same issues. The most famous self-help and support groups are Alcoholics Anonymous (AA), Gamblers Anonymous, and Al-Anon (a program for the family and friends of those with alcohol problems). Other self-help groups offer support to cancer survivors or to parents of children with autism or to people with mood disorders, eating disorders, substance abuse

> ● **What are pros and cons of self-help support groups?**

• *Self-help groups are a cost-effective, time-effective, and treatment-effective solution for dealing with some types of psychological problems.*

problems, and self-harming disorders—in fact, self-help and support groups exist for just about every psychological disorder. In addition to being cost effective, self-help and support groups allow people to realize that they are not the only ones with a particular problem and give them the opportunity to offer guidance and support to each other based on personal experiences of success.

In some cases, though, self-help and support groups can do more harm than good. Some members may be disruptive or aggressive or encourage one another to engage in behaviors that are countertherapeutic (e.g., avoiding feared situations or using alcohol to cope). People with moderate problems may be exposed to others with severe problems and may become oversensitized to symptoms they might otherwise have not found disturbing. Because self-help and support groups are usually not led by trained therapists, mechanisms to evaluate these groups or to ensure their quality are rarely in place.

Today, AA has more than 2 million members in the United States, with 185,000 group meetings that occur around the world (Mack, Franklin, & Frances, 2003).Members are encouraged to follow "12 steps" to reach the goal of lifelong abstinence from all drinking, and the steps include believing in a higher power, practicing prayer and meditation, and making amends for harm to others. Most members attend group meetings several times per week, and between meetings they receive additional support from their "sponsor." A few studies examining the effectiveness of AA have been conducted, and it appears that individuals who participate tend to overcome problem drinking with greater success than those who do not participate in AA (Fiorentine, 1999; Morgenstern et al., 1997). However, several tenets of the AA philosophy are not supported by the research. We know that the general AA program is useful, but questions about which parts of this program are most helpful have yet to be studied.

Considered together, the many social approaches to psychotherapy reveal how important interpersonal relationships are for each of us. It may not always be clear how psychotherapy works, whether one approach is better than another, or what particular theory should be used to understand how problems have developed. What is clear, however, is that social interactions between people—both in individual therapy and in all the different forms of therapy in groups—can be useful in treating psychological disorders.

summary quiz [13.2]

4. Which type of psychotherapy emphasizes helping clients gain insight into their unconscious conflicts?
   a. humanistic
   b. Gestalt
   c. cognitive
   d. psychodynamic

5. Which type of therapy aims at challenging irrational thoughts?
   a. Gestalt
   b. existential
   c. cognitive
   d. person-centered

6. Which type of therapy would likely work best to eliminate a person's fear of snakes?
   a. psychodynamic
   b. behavioral
   c. cognitive
   d. humanistic

7. Which type of therapy aims to help clients become aware of their thoughts, feelings, and behaviors in the present moment?
   a. Gestalt
   b. person-centered
   c. cognitive
   d. behavioral

Medical and Biological Treatments: Healing the Mind through the Brain

Ever since someone discovered that a whack to the head can affect the mind, people have suspected that direct brain interventions might hold the keys to a cure for psychological disorders. Archeological evidence, for example, indicates that the occasional human thousands of years ago was "treated" for some malady by the practice of trepanning—drilling a hole in the skull, perhaps in the belief that this would release evil spirits that were affecting the mind (Alt et al., 1997). Surgery for psychological disorders is a last resort nowadays, and treatments that focus on the brain usually involve interventions that are less dramatic. The use of drugs to influence the brain was also discovered in prehistory (alcohol, for example, has been around for a long time). Since then, drug treatments have grown in variety and effectiveness to become what is now the most common medical approach in treating psychological disorders.

This is a trepanned skull from a Stone Age burial site (about 5900–6200 BCE) in the Alsace region of France. Two holes were drilled in the skull, and the patient lived afterward, as shown by the regrowth of bone covering the holes (from Alt et al., 1997). Don't try this at home.

DR. KURT W. ALT

● *People with schizophrenia are two to three times more likely to smoke tobacco than the average person (Kelly & McCreadie, 2000). Several explanations are being tested for this, including the possibility that people with schizophrenia seek out nicotine to reduce their symptoms. If this is true, their "self-medication" may point the way toward new drug treatments for the disorder that might be more helpful and less harmful than smoking.*

Antipsychotic Medications

The story of drug treatments for severe psychological disorders starts in the 1950s, with chlorpromazine (brand name Thorazine), which was originally developed as a sedative but which, when administered to people with schizophrenia, often left them euphoric and docile when they had formerly been agitated and incorrigible (Barondes, 2003). Chlorpromazine was the first in a series of **antipsychotic drugs**, which *treat schizophrenia and related psychotic disorders*, and which completely changed the way schizophrenia was managed. Other related medications, such as thioridazine (Mellaril) and haloperidol (Haldol) followed. Before the introduction of antipsychotic drugs, people with schizophrenia often exhibited bizarre symptoms and were sometimes so disruptive and difficult to manage that the only way to protect them (and other people) was to keep them in asylums. In the period following the introduction of these drugs, the number of people in psychiatric hospitals decreased by more than two thirds. Antipsychotic drugs made possible the deinstitutionalization of hundreds of thousands of people and gave a major boost to the field of **psychopharmacology**, *the study of drug effects on psychological states and symptoms*.

● **What do antipsychotic drugs do?**

Antipsychotic medications are believed to block dopamine receptors in parts of the brain such as the mesolimbic area, an area between the tegmentum (in the midbrain) and various subcortical structures (see Chapter 3). The medication reduces dopamine activity in these areas. As you read in Chapter 12, the effectiveness of schizophrenia medications led to the "dopamine hypothesis," suggesting that schizophrenia may be caused by excess dopamine in the synapse. Research has indeed found that dopamine overactivity in the mesolimbic areas of the brain is related to the more bizarre positive symptoms of schizophrenia, such as hallucinations and delusions (Marangell et al., 2003).

Although antipsychotic drugs work well for positive symptoms, it turns out that negative symptoms of schizophrenia, such as emotional numbing and social withdrawal, may be related to dopamine *under* activity in the mesocortical areas of the brain (connections between parts of the tegmentum and the cortex). This may help explain why antipsychotic medications do not relieve negative symptoms well. Instead of a medication that blocks dopamine receptors, negative symptoms require a medication that *increases* the amount of dopamine available at the synapse. This is a good example of how medical treatments can have broad psychological effects but not target specific psychological symptoms.

After the introduction of antipsychotic medications, there was little change in the available treatments for schizophrenia for more than a quarter of a century. However, in the 1990s, a new class of antipsychotic drugs was introduced. These newer drugs, which include clozapine (Clozaril), risperidone (Risperidal), and olanzepine (Zyprexa), have become known as *atypical antipsychotics* (the older drugs are now often referred to as *conventional* or *typical* antipsychotics). Unlike the older antipsychotic medications, these newer drugs appear to affect both the dopamine and serotonin systems, blocking both types of receptors. The ability to block serotonin receptors appears to be a useful addition since enhanced serotonin activity in the brain has been implicated in some of the core difficulties in schizophrenia, such as cognitive and perceptual disruptions, as well as mood disturbances. This may explain why atypical antipsychotics work at least as well as older drugs for the positive symptoms of schizophrenia but also work fairly well for negative symptoms (Bradford, Stroup, & Lieberman, 2002).

● **What are the advantages of the newer, atypical antipsychotic medications?**

Like most medications, antipsychotic drugs have side effects. The side effects can be sufficiently unpleasant that some people "go off their meds," preferring their symptoms to the drug. One side effect that often occurs with long-term use is *tardive dyskinesia*, a condition of involuntary movements of the face, mouth, and extremities. In fact, patients often need to take another medication to treat the unwanted side effects of the conventional antipsychotic drugs. Side effects of the newer medications tend to be milder than those of the older antipsychotics. For that reason, the atypical antipsychotics are now usually the front-line treatments for schizophrenia (Marangell et al., 2003).

Antianxiety Medications

Antianxiety medications are *drugs that help reduce a person's experience of fear or anxiety.* The most commonly used antianxiety medications are the *benzodiazepines,* a type of tranquilizer that works by facilitating the action of the neurotransmitter gamma-aminobutyric acid (GABA). As you read in Chapter 3, GABA inhibits certain neurons in the brain, producing a calming effect for the person. Commonly prescribed benzodiazepines include diazepam (Valium), lorazepam (Ativan), and alprazolam (Xanax). The benzodiazepines typically take effect in a matter of minutes and are effective for reducing symptoms of anxiety disorders (Roy-Byrne & Cowley, 2002).

Nonetheless, these days doctors are relatively cautious when prescribing benzodiazepines. One concern is that these drugs have the potential for abuse. They are often associated with the development of *tolerance,* which is the need for higher dosages over time to achieve the same effects following long-term use (see Chapter 8). Furthermore, after people become tolerant of the drug, they risk significant withdrawal symptoms following discontinuation.

● **What are some reasons for caution when prescribing antianxiety medications?**

Some withdrawal symptoms include increased heart rate, shakiness, insomnia, agitation, and anxiety—the very symptoms the drug was taken to eliminate! Another consideration when prescribing benzodiazepines is their side effects. The most common side effect is drowsiness, although benzodiazepines can also have negative effects on coordination and memory.

A newer drug, buspirone (Buspar), has been shown to reduce anxiety among individuals who suffer from generalized anxiety disorder (GAD). Buspirone is not as effective as the benzodiazepines for anxiety disorders other than GAD, but it doesn't produce the drowsiness and withdrawal symptoms associated with benzodiazepines (Roy-Byrne & Cowley, 2002). Gabapentin (Neurontin), an antiseizure medication, has also been recently studied as a remedy for anxiety. Preliminary results suggest that this drug may be useful for treating social anxiety and panic disorder (Pande et al., 1999, 2000).

Antidepressants and Mood Stabilizers

Antidepressants are *a class of drugs that help lift people's mood.* They were first introduced in the 1950s, when iproniazid, a drug that was used to treat tuberculosis, was found to elevate mood (Selikoff, Robitzek, & Ornstein, 1952). Iproniazid is a *monoamine oxidase inhibitor (MAOI),* a medication that prevents the enzyme monoamine oxidase from breaking down neurotransmitters such as norepinephrine, serotonin, and dopamine. However, despite their effectiveness, MAOIs are rarely prescribed anymore. MAOI side effects such as dizziness and loss of sexual interest are often difficult to tolerate, and these drugs interact with many different medications, including over-the-counter cold medicines. They also can cause dangerous increases in blood pressure when taken with foods that contain tyramine, a natural substance formed from the breakdown of protein in certain cheeses, beans, aged meats, soy products, and draft beer.

A second category of antidepressants is the *tricyclic antidepressants,* which were also introduced in the 1950s. These include drugs such as imipramine (Tofranil) and amitriptyline (Elavil). These medications block the reuptake of norepinephrine and serotonin,

WHAT'S NEW IN PHARMACOLOGY
by Maira Kalman and Rick Meyerowitz

ASK YOUR DOCTOR

Dysplosives	**Nostalgics**	**Antipepsodines**	**Pandemonics**
Preventidrool	Nothin	Theatrical (overactin)	Hypochondriax
Revoltin	Miketycin	Monrodoctrin	Credenza
Cucumberdil	Neo-sufferin	Espresso bismol	Hydrocortidrek
Dixichixil	Pseudointellectuol	Ibuproblem	Relapsin
Preventafit	Benumbitussin	Phenaminafenafinaphen	Schwarzeneggra
Krazyglucosamine	Trafficort	Globbinlarynx	Thatsol

antipsychotic drugs Medications that are used to treat schizophrenia and related psychotic disorders.

psychopharmacology The study of drug effects on psychological states and symptoms.

antianxiety medications Drugs that help reduce a person's experience of fear or anxiety.

antidepressants A class of drugs that help lift people's mood.

thereby increasing the amount of neurotransmitter in the synaptic space between neurons. The most common side effects of tricyclic antidepressants include dry mouth, constipation, difficulty urinating, blurred vision, and racing heart (Marangell et al., 2003). Although these drugs are still prescribed, they are used much less frequently than they were in the past because of these side effects.

Among the most commonly used antidepressants today are the *selective serotonin reuptake inhibitors,* or SSRIs, which include drugs such as fluoxetine (Prozac), citalopram (Celexa), and paroxetine (Paxil). The SSRIs work by blocking the reuptake of serotonin in the brain, which makes more serotonin available in the synaptic space between neurons. The greater availability of serotonin in the synapse gives the neuron a better chance of "recognizing" and using this neurotransmitter in sending the desired signal.

● **What are the most common antidepressants used today? How do they work?**

The SSRIs were developed based on hypotheses that low levels of serotonin are a causal factor in depression (see Chapter 12). Supporting this hypothesis, SSRIs are effective for depression, as well as for a wide range of other problems. SSRIs are called "selective" because, unlike the tricyclic antidepressants, which work on the serotonin and norepinephrine systems, SSRIs work more specifically on the serotonin system (see **FIGURE 13.2**).

Finally, in the past several years, a number of new antidepressants such as Effexor and Wellbutrin have been introduced. Effexor is an example of a serotonin and norepineprhine reuptake inhibitor (SNRI); whereas SSRIs act only on serotonin, SNRIs act on both serotonin and norepinephrine. Wellbutrin, in contrast, is a norepinephrine and dopamine reuptake inhibitor. These and other newly developed antidepressants appear to have fewer side effects than the tricyclic antidepressants and MAOIs.

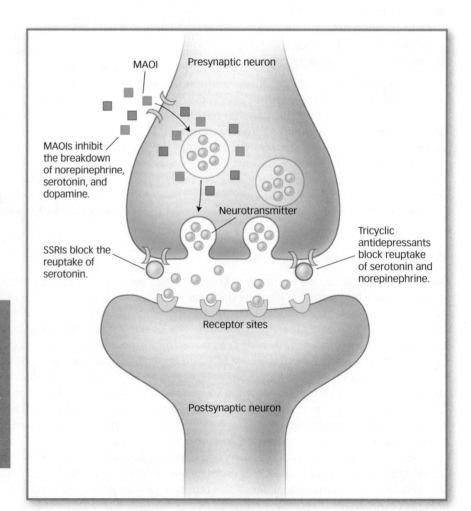

·················· **FIGURE 13.2**

Antidepressant Drug Actions *Antidepressant drugs, such as MAOIs, SSRIs, and tricyclic antidepressants, act on neurotransmitters such as serotonin, dopamine, and norepinephrine by inhibiting their breakdown and blocking reuptake. These actions make more of the neurotransmitter available for release and leave more of the neurotransmitter in the synaptic gap to activate the receptor sites on the postsynaptic neuron. These drugs relieve depression and often alleviate anxiety and other disorders.*

Most antidepressants take from a few weeks to more than a month before they start to have an effect. Besides relieving symptoms of depression, almost all of the antidepressants effectively treat anxiety disorders, and many of them can resolve other problems, such as eating disorders. In fact, several companies that manufacture SSRIs have recently marketed their drugs as treatments for anxiety disorders rather than for their antidepressant effects. The general improvement in mood and outlook produced by antidepressants is attractive not only to people who are clinically depressed or anxious but also to many others seeking to level out the emotional hills and valleys of everyday life. Prozac is widely prescribed for people who are not suffering from specific disorders, and there is considerable debate about whether antidepressants should be used in this way to contribute to the well-being of people who are not sick (Kramer, 1997).

Although antidepressants are effective in treating major depression, they are not recommended for treating bipolar disorder, which is characterized by manic or hypomanic episodes (see Chapter 12). Antidepressants are not prescribed because they might actually trigger a manic

● **Why aren't antidepressants prescribed for bipolar disorder?**

episode in a person with bipolar disorder. Instead, bipolar disorder is treated with *mood stabilizers,* which are medications used to

suppress swings between mania and depression. Commonly used mood stabilizers include lithium and valproate. Even in unipolar depression, lithium is sometimes effective when combined with traditional antidepressants in people who do not respond to antidepressants alone.

Lithium has been associated with possible long-term kidney and thyroid problems, so people taking lithium must monitor their blood levels of lithium on a regular basis. Furthermore, lithium has a precise range in which it is useful for each person—another reason it should be closely monitored with blood tests. Valproate, in contrast, does not require such careful blood monitoring. Although valproate may have side effects of nausea and weight gain, it is currently the most commonly prescribed drug in the United States for bipolar disorder (Schatzberg, Cole, & DeBattista, 2003). In sum, although the antidepressants are effective for a wide variety of problems, mood stabilizers may be required when a person's symptoms include extreme swings between highs and lows, such as experienced with bipolar disorder.

Herbal and Natural Products

In a survey of more than 2,000 Americans, 7% of those suffering from anxiety disorders and 9% of those suffering from severe depression reported using alternative "medications" such as herbal medicines, megavitamins, homeopathic remedies, or naturopathic remedies to treat these problems (Kessler et al., 2001). Major reasons people use these products are that they are easily available over the counter, are less expensive, and are perceived as "natural" alternatives to "drugs." Are herbal and natural products effective in treating mental health problems, or are they just so much "snake oil"?

The answer to this question isn't simple. Herbal products are not considered medications by regulatory agencies (e.g., the U.S. Food and Drug Administration)

● **Why are herbal remedies used? Are they actually effective?**

and are exempt from rigorous research to establish their safety and effectiveness. Instead, herbal products are classified as nutritional supplements and regulated in the same way as

foods. There is little scientific information about herbal products, including possible interactions with other medications, possible tolerance and withdrawal symptoms, side effects, appropriate dosages, how they work, or even *whether* they work—and the purity

"More lithium."

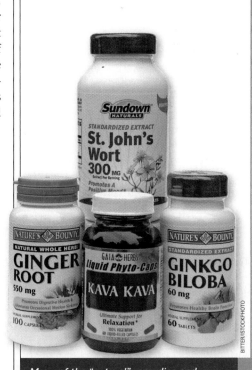

Many of the "natural" remedies and treatments available at health food and supplement stores come with little or no evidence of effectiveness and no claims for any specific benefit on the label, but the price tag is usually quite clear.

of these products often varies from brand to brand (Kressmann, Muller, & Blume, 2002). Although herbal medications and treatments are worthy of continued research, these products should be closely monitored and used judiciously until more is known about their safety and effectiveness.

Combining Medication and Psychotherapy

Psychologists looking for effective ways to treat psychological disorders get pretty excited about the progress of drug therapy. New drugs appear with some regularity, improving on prior medications and suggesting even greater improvements to come. At the same time, as we have seen, drugs can be blunt instruments as treatment devices, producing general changes in mood or relieving unpleasant symptoms—but leaving specific problems untreated. How can we bring medication and psychotherapy together to produce comprehensive treatments?

Many studies have compared psychological treatments, medication, and combinations of these approaches for addressing psychological disorders. The results of these studies often depend on the particular problem being considered. For example, in the cases of schizophrenia and bipolar disorder, researchers have found that medication is a necessary part of treatment, and studies have tended to examine whether adding psychotherapeutic treatments such as social skills training or cognitive behavioral treatment can be helpful. In the case of anxiety disorders, medication and psychotherapy may be about equally effective. One study compared cognitive behavior therapy, imipramine (the antidepressant also known as Tofranil), and the combination of these treatments (CBT plus imipramine) with a placebo (administration of an inert medication) for the treatment of panic disorder (Barlow et al., 2000). After 12 weeks of treatment, either CBT alone or imipramine alone was found to be superior to a placebo. For the CBT-plus-imipramine condition, the response rate also exceeded the placebo one but was not significantly better than that for either CBT or imipramine alone. In other

● **Do therapy and medications work through similar mechanisms?**

words, either treatment was better than nothing, but the combination of treatments was not significantly more effective than one or the other (see **FIGURE 13.3**).

Given that both therapy and medications are effective, one question is whether they work through similar mechanisms. A recent study of people with social phobia examined patterns of cerebral blood flow following treatment using either citalopram (an SSRI) or CBT (Furmark et al., 2002). Patients in both groups were alerted to the possibility that they would soon have to speak in public. In both groups, those who responded to treatment showed similar reductions in activation in the amygdala, hippocampus, and neighboring cortical areas during this challenge. As you'll recall from Chapter 5, the amygdala and hippocampus play significant roles in memory for emotional information.

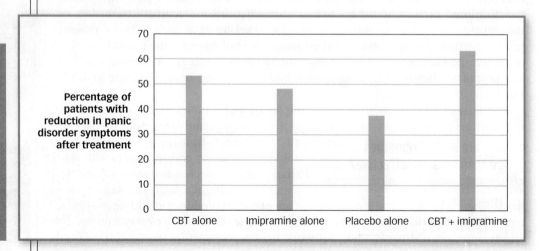

······ ● ● ● ● ● ● ● **FIGURE 13.3**
The Effectiveness of Medication and Psychotherapy for Panic Disorder *One study of CBT and medication (imipramine) for panic disorder found that the effects of CBT, medication, and treatment that combined CBT and medication were not significantly different over the short term, though all three were superior to the placebo condition (Barlow et al., 2000).*

Percentage of patients with reduction in panic disorder symptoms after treatment

CBT alone   Imipramine alone   Placebo alone   CBT + imipramine

These findings suggest that both therapy and medication affect the brain in regions associated with a reaction to threat. Although it might seem that events that influence the brain should be physical—after all, the brain is a physical object—both the physical administration of a drug and the psychological application of psychotherapy produce similar influences on the brain.

One complication in combining medication and psychotherapy is that these treatments are often provided by different people. Psychiatrists are trained in the administration of medication in medical school (and they may also provide psychotherapy), whereas psychologists provide psychotherapy but not medication. This means that the coordination of treatment often requires cooperation between psychologists and psychiatrists.

The question of whether psychologists should be licensed to prescribe medications has been a source of debate among physicians as well as among psychologists (Heiby, 2002; Lavoie & Fleet, 2002; Sammons, Paige, & Levant, 2003). Opponents argue that psychologists do not have the medical training to understand how medications interact with other drugs. On the other hand, proponents of prescription privileges argue that patient safety would not be compromised as long as rigorous training procedures were established. This issue remains a focus of debate, so at present, the coordination of medication and psychotherapy usually involves a team effort of psychiatry and psychology.

Biological Treatments beyond Medication

Although medication can be an effective biological treatment, for some people medications do not work or side effects are intolerable. If this group of people doesn't respond to psychotherapy, either, what other options do they have to achieve symptom relief? Some additional avenues of help are available, but some are risky or poorly understood.

● **Where do people turn if medication and therapy are unsuccessful?**

One example is **electroconvulsive therapy (ECT)**, more commonly known as "shock therapy," which is *a treatment that involves inducing a mild seizure by delivering an electrical shock to the brain.* The shock is applied to the person's scalp for less than a second. ECT is primarily used to treat severe depression, although it may also be useful for treating mania (Mukherjee, Sackeim, & Schnur, 1994). Patients are pretreated with muscle relaxants and are under general anesthetic, so they are not conscious of the procedure. The main side effect of ECT is impaired short-term memory, which usually improves over the first month or two after the end of treatment. In addition, patients undergoing this procedure sometimes report headaches and muscle aches afterward (Marangell et al., 2003). Despite these side effects, the treatment can be effective: About half the individuals who do not respond to medication alone may find ECT helpful in treating their depression (Prudic et al., 1996).

Another biological approach that does not involve medication is **transcranial magnetic stimulation (TMS)**, *a treatment that involves placing a powerful pulsed magnet over a person's scalp, which alters neuronal activity in the brain* (George, Lisanby, & Sackeim, 1999). As a treatment for depression, the magnet is placed just above the right or left eyebrow in an effort to stimulate the right or left prefrontal cortex—areas of the brain implicated in depression. TMS is an exciting development because it is noninvasive and has fewer side effects than ECT (see Chapter 2). Side effects are minimal; they include mild headache and small risk of seizure, but TMS has no impact on memory or concentration. TMS may be particularly useful in treating depression that is unresponsive to medication (Fitzgerald et al., 2003; Kauffmann, Cheema, & Miller,

electroconvulsive therapy (ECT) A treatment that involves inducing a mild seizure by delivering an electrical shock to the brain.

transcranial magnetic stimulation (TMS) A treatment that involves placing a powerful pulsed magnet over a person's scalp, which alters neuronal activity in the brain.

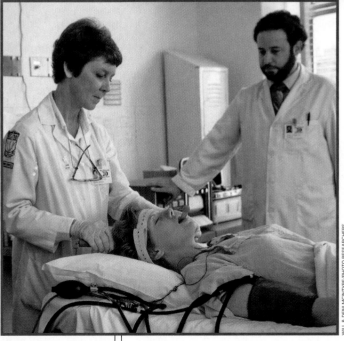

Electroconvulsive therapy (ECT) can be an effective treatment for severe depression. To reduce the side effects, it is administered under general anesthesia.

WILL & DENI MCINTYRE/PHOTO RESEARCHERS

● *Rosemary Kennedy, sister of President John F. Kennedy, was intellectually challenged from childhood and had violent tantrums and rages that began in her early 20s. Her family agreed to her treatment with a lobotomy at St. Elizabeth's Hospital in Washington, DC, in 1942, but it went very wrong. She became permanently paralyzed on one side, incontinent, and unable to speak coherently, and she spent the rest of her life in institutions.*

2004). In fact, a recent study comparing TMS to ECT found that both procedures were effective, with no significant differences between them (Janicak et al., 2002). Other studies have investigated the utility of TMS for problems such as hallucinations, and early results are promising (Hoffman et al., 2003).

In very rare cases, **psychosurgery**, *the surgical destruction of specific brain areas,* is used to treat certain psychological disorders, such as obsessive-compulsive disorder (OCD). Psychosurgery has a controversial history, beginning in the 1930s with the invention of the lobotomy to calm violent or agitated human patients. Lobotomies involved inserting an instrument into the brain through the patient's eye socket or through holes drilled in the side of the head. The objective was to sever connections between the frontal lobes and inner brain structures such as the thalamus, known to be involved in emotion. Although some lobotomies produced highly successful results, many patients were devastated by significant and permanent side effects such as extreme lethargy or childlike impulsivity.

Today, psychosurgeries are far more precise than lobotomies of the 1930s and 1940s in targeting particular brain areas to lesion. This increased precision has produced better results. For example, patients suffering from obsessive-compulsive disorder who fail to respond to treatment (including several trials of medications and cognitive behavioral treatment) may benefit from specific surgical procedures called *cingulotomy* and *anterior capsulotomy.* Cingulotomy involves destroying part of the cingulate gyrus and corpus callosum (see Chapter 3). Anterior capsulotomy involves creating small lesions to disrupt the pathway between the caudate nucleus and putamen. Long-term follow-up studies suggest that more than a quarter of patients with OCD who do not respond to standard treatments report significant benefit following psychosurgery, with relatively few side effects (Baer et al., 1995; Cumming et al., 1995; Hay et al., 1993). However, due to the intrusive nature of psychosurgery and a lack of controlled studies, these procedures are currently reserved for the most severe cases.

summary quiz [13.3]

8. Medications called *atypical antipsychotics*
   a. affect only the dopamine system.
   b. affect only the serotonin system.
   c. affect both the dopamine and serotonin systems.
   d. do not work as well as typical antipsychotics.

9. Which is true of the benzodiazepines?
   a. They work by facilitating the action of the neurotransmitter dopamine.
   b. They are the most commonly used antianxiety medications.
   c. They typically take several weeks before they start to have an effect.
   d. They are recommended for treating bipolar disorders.

10. Among the most commonly used antidepressants today are the
    a. selective serotonin reuptake inhibiters.
    b. monoamine oxidase inhibitors.
    c. tricyclic antidepressants.
    d. mood stabilizers.

11. Electroconvulsive therapy is primarily used to treat
    a. severe anxiety.
    b. schizophrenia.
    c. obsessive-compulsive disorder.
    d. depression.

Treatment Effectiveness: For Better or for Worse

Think back to our fearful flyer Lisa at the beginning of the chapter. What if, instead of virtual reality therapy, Lisa had been assigned by her therapist to a drug treatment or to psychosurgery? For that matter, what if her therapy was to walk around for a week wearing a large false nose? Could these alternatives have been just as effective for treating her phobia? Through this chapter, we have explored various psychological and biomedical treatments that may help people with psychological disorders. But do these treatments actually work, and which ones work better than the others?

As you learned in Chapter 2, this can be a difficult detective exercise. The detection is made even more difficult because people may approach treatment evaluation very unscientifically, often by simply noticing an improvement (or no improvement or that dreaded decline) and reaching a conclusion based on that sole observation. Treatment evaluation can be susceptible to illusions—mindbugs in how people process information about treatment effects—and these illusions can only be overcome by scientific evaluation of the effectiveness of treatments.

Treatment Illusions

Imagine you're sick and the doctor says, "Take a pill." You follow the doctor's orders, and you get better. To what do you attribute your improvement? If you're like most people, you reach the conclusion that the pill cured you. How could this be an illusion? There are at least three ways: Maybe you would have gotten better anyway; maybe the pill wasn't the active ingredient in your cure; or maybe after you're better, you mistakenly remember having been more ill than you really were. These possibilities point to three potential illusions of treatment—illusions produced by natural improvement, by nonspecific treatment effects, and by reconstructive memory.

Natural improvement is the tendency of symptoms to return to their mean or average level, a process sometimes called *regression to the mean.* The illusion in this case happens when you conclude mistakenly that a treatment has made you better when you would have gotten better anyway. People typically turn to therapy or medication when their symptoms are at their worst, so they start their personal "experiment" to see if treatment makes them improve at a time when things couldn't get much worse. When this is the case, the client's symptoms will often improve regardless of

● **What are three kinds of treatment illusions?**

whether there was any treatment at all; when you're at rock bottom, there's nowhere to move but up. In most cases, for example, depression that becomes severe enough to make a person a candidate for treatment will tend to lift in several months. A person who enters therapy for depression may develop an illusion that the therapy works because the therapy coincides with the typical course of the illness and the person's natural return to health.

Another treatment illusion occurs when a client or therapist attributes the client's improvement to a feature of treatment, although that feature wasn't really the active element that caused improvement. Recovery could be produced by *nonspecific treatment effects* that are not related to the specific mechanisms by which treatment is supposed to be working. For example, the doctor prescribing the medication might simply be a pleasant and hopeful individual who gives the client a sense that

● **What is the placebo effect?**

things will improve. Client and doctor alike might attribute the client's improvement to the effects of medication on the brain, whereas the true active ingredient was the warm relationship with the good doctor.

Simply knowing that you are getting a treatment can be a nonspecific treatment effect. These instances include the positive influences that can be produced by a **placebo**, *an inert substance or procedure that has been applied with the expectation that a healing response will be produced.* For

psychosurgery Surgical destruction of specific brain areas.

placebo An inert substance or procedure that has been applied with the expectation that a healing response will be produced.

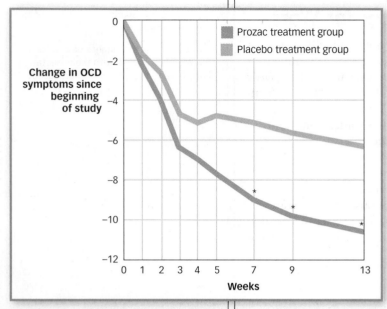

INSADCO PHOTOGRAPHY/ALAMY

•••••••••••••••••••••• **FIGURE 13.4**

The Placebo Effect *Two groups of patients were given pills to treat OCD. The first group was given Prozac, an antidepressant, and the second group was given an inert sugar pill, a placebo. Interestingly, both groups showed significant improvement in their OCD symptoms until week 7, when the benefits of taking the placebo leveled off. As shown by the asterisks (*), Prozac reduced symptoms significantly more than did placebo pills by weeks 7, 9, and 13 (Geller et al., 2001).*

•••••••• *When you feel you've come a long way, you may remember where you started as farther down than it was. People who feel they have improved from a treatment program may reconstruct memories of the past that exaggerate their pretreatment problems.*

example, if you take a sugar pill that does not contain any painkiller for a headache thinking it is Tylenol or aspirin, this pill is a placebo. Placebos can have profound effects in the case of psychological treatments. Research shows that a large percentage of individuals with anxiety, depression, and other emotional problems experience significant improvement after a placebo treatment. Chapter 15 further discusses how placebo effects may occur as well as their influence on the brain.

One study compared the decrease in symptoms of obsessive-compulsive disorder between adolescents taking Prozac (fluoxetine) and those taking a placebo (Geller et al., 2001). Participants receiving medication showed a dramatic decrease in symptoms over the course of the 13-week study. Those taking a placebo also showed a reduction in symptoms, and the difference between the Prozac and placebo groups only became significant in the seventh week of treatment (see **FIGURE 13.4**). In fact, some psychologists estimate that up to 75% of the effects shown by antidepressant medications are due to the placebo effect (Kirsch & Sapirstein, 1998).

A third treatment illusion can come about when the client's motivation to get well causes errors in *reconstructive memory* for the original symptoms. You might think that you've improved because of a treatment when in fact you're simply misremembering—mistakenly believing that your symptoms before treatment were worse than they actually were. This tendency was first observed in research examining the effectiveness of a study skills class (Conway & Ross, 1984). Some students who wanted to take the class were enrolled, while others were randomly assigned to a waiting list until the class could be offered again. When their study abilities were measured afterward, those students who took the class were no better at studying than their wait-listed counterparts. However, those who took the class *said* that they had improved. How could this be? Those participants recalled their study skills before the class as being worse than they actually had been. This motivated reconstruction of the past was dubbed by the researchers "getting what you want by revising what you had" (Conway & Ross, 1984). A client who forms a strong expectation of success in therapy might conclude later that even a useless treatment had worked wonders—by recalling past symptoms and troubles as worse than they were and thereby making the treatment seem effective.

A person who enters treatment is often anxious to get well and so may be especially likely to succumb to errors and illusions in assessing the effectiveness of the treatment. Treatments can look as if they worked when mindbugs lead us to ignore natural improvement, to overlook nonspecific treatment effects (e.g., the placebo effect), and to reconstruct our pretreatment history as worse than it was. Such treatment illusions can be overcome by using scientific methods to evaluate treatments—rather than trusting only our potentially faulty personal skills of observation.

Treatment Studies

How can treatment be evaluated in a way that allows us to choose treatments that work and not waste time with procedures that may be useless or even harmful? Treatment studies depend generally on the research design concepts covered in Chapter 2 but also depend on some ideas that are unique to the evaluation of psychological treatments.

There are two main types of treatment studies: outcome studies and process studies. *Outcome studies* are designed to evaluate *whether* a particular treatment works, often in relation to some other treatment or a control condition. For example, to study the outcome of treatment for depression, researchers might compare the self-reported moods and symptoms of two groups of people who were initially depressed—those who had received a treatment for 6 weeks and a control group who had also been selected for the study but had been assigned to a waiting list for later treatment and were simply tested 6 weeks after their selection. The outcome study could determine whether this treatment had any benefit.

Process studies are designed to answer questions regarding *why* a treatment works or under what circumstances a treatment works. For example, process researchers might examine whether a treatment for depression is more effective for certain clients than others. Process studies also can examine whether some parts of the treatment are particularly helpful, whereas others are irrelevant to the treatment's success. Process studies can refine therapies and target their influence to make them more effective.

Both outcome and process studies can be plagued by treatment illusions, so scientists usually design their research to overcome them. For example, the treatment illusions caused by natural improvement and reconstructive memory happen when people compare their symptoms before treatment to their symptoms after treatment. To avoid this, researchers typically compare an treatment (or experimental) group and a control group need to be randomly selected from the same population of patients before the study and then compared at the end of treatment. That way, natural improvement or motivated reconstructive memory can't cause illusions of effective treatment.

But what should happen to the control group during the treatment? If they simply stay home waiting until they can get treatment later (a wait-list control group), they won't receive the nonspecific effects of the treatment that the treatment group enjoys (such as visiting the comforting therapist or taking a medication). So, ideally, a treatment should be assessed in a *double-blind experiment*—a study in which both the patient and the researcher/therapist are uninformed about which treatment the patient

● **Why is a double-blind experiment so important in assessing treatment effectiveness?**

is receiving (see Chapter 2). In the case of drug studies, this isn't hard to arrange because active drugs and placebos can be made to look alike to both the patients and the researchers during the study. Keeping both patients and researchers "in the dark" is much harder in the study of psychotherapy; in fact,

it may even be impossible. Both the patient and the therapist can easily notice the differences in treatments such as psychoanalysis and behavior therapy, for example, so there's no way to keep the beliefs and expectations of both patient and therapist out of the picture in evaluating psychotherapy effectiveness.

Many psychological disorders don't play favorites with one gender or the other, but anxiety and depression are more common for women than men.

Which Treatments Work?

The distinguished psychologist Hans Eysenck (1916–1997) reviewed the relatively few studies of psychotherapy effectiveness available in 1957 and raised a furor among therapists by concluding that psychotherapy—particularly psychoanalysis—

● **What is the current thinking about the effectiveness of psychotherapy?**

not only was ineffective but seemed to *impede* recovery (Eysenck, 1957). Much larger numbers of studies have been examined statistically since then, and they support a more optimistic conclusion: The typical psychotherapy client is better off than three quarters of untreated individuals (Seligman, 1995; Smith, Glass, & Miller, 1980). Although critiques of psychotherapy continue to point out weaknesses in how patients are tested, diagnosed, and treated (Dawes, 1994), strong evidence generally supports the effectiveness of many treatments. The key question then becomes, Which treatments are effective for which problems (Hunsley & Di Giulio, 2002)?

One of the most enduring debates in clinical psychology concerns how the various psychotherapies compare to one another. Some psychologists have argued for years that evidence supports the conclusion

"Well, I do have this recurring dream that one day I might see some results."

St. Panacea was a shepherdess born in Italy in 1378. The name Panacea means "all healing," and a remedy for all that ails us is something we all would love. But a treatment that heals everything could be too much of a wish come true. Psychotherapy researchers worry that if any version of psychotherapy is effective for any mental disorder, the "active ingredient" of psychotherapy may be so general that the treatment could be meaningless.

that most psychotherapies work about equally well. In this view, it is the nonspecific factors shared by all forms of psychotherapy, such as contact with and empathy from a professional, that contribute to change (Luborsky et al., 2002; Luborsky & Singer, 1975). In contrast, others have argued that there are important differences between therapies and that certain treatments are more effective than others, especially for treating particular types of problems (Beutler, 2002; Hunsley & Di Giulio, 2002). Yet others have noted that some treatments such as long-term psychodynamic therapy are not easily studied, because of the difficulty of establishing a control group, and because the therapy typically takes a long time—but this doesn't mean that psychotherapy may not be effective nonetheless.

Even trickier than the question of establishing whether a treatment works is whether a psychotherapy or medication might actually do damage. The dangers of drug treatment should be clear to anyone who has read a magazine ad for a drug—and studied the fine print with its list of side effects, potential drug interactions, and complications. Many drugs used for psychological treatment may be addictive, creating long-term dependency with serious withdrawal symptoms. The strongest critics of drug treatment claim that drugs do no more than trade one unwanted symptom for another—trading depression for sexual disinterest, anxiety for intoxication, or agitation for lethargy and dulled emotion (see, e.g., Breggin, 2000).

The dangers of psychotherapy are more subtle, but one is clear enough in some cases that there is actually a name for it: **Iatrogenic illness** is *a disorder or symptom that occurs as a result of a medical or psychotherapeutic treatment itself* (e.g., Boisvert & Faust, 2002). Such an illness might arise, for example, when a psychotherapist becomes convinced that a client has a disorder that in fact the client does not have. As a result, the therapist works to help the client accept that diagnosis and participate in psychotherapy to treat that disorder. Being treated for a disorder can, under certain conditions, make a person show signs of that very disorder—and so an iatrogenic illness is born.

There are cases of patients who have been influenced through hypnosis and repeated suggestions in therapy to believe that they have dissociative identity disorder (even coming to express multiple personalities) or to believe that they were subjected to traumatic events as a child and "recover" memories of such events when investigation reveals no evidence for these problems prior to therapy (Acocella, 1999; McNally, 2003; Ofshe & Watters, 1994). There are people who have entered therapy with a vague sense that something odd has happened to them and who emerge after hypnosis or other imagination-enhancing techniques with the conviction that their therapist's theory was right: They were abducted by space aliens (Clancy, 2005). Needless to say,

a therapy that leads patients to develop such bizarre beliefs is doing more harm than good.

To regulate the potentially powerful influence of therapies, psychologists hold themselves to a set of ethical standards for the treatment of people with mental disorders (American Psychological Association, 2002). Adherence to these standards is required for membership in the American Psychological Association, and state licensing boards also monitor adherence to ethical principles in therapy. These ethical standards include (1) striving to benefit clients and taking care to do no harm; (2) establishing relationships of trust with clients; (3) promoting accuracy, honesty, and truthfulness; (4) seeking fairness in treatment and taking precautions to avoid biases; and (5) respecting the dignity and worth of all people. When people suffering from mental disorders come to psychologists for help, adhering to these guidelines is the least that psychologists can do. Ideally, in the hope of relieving this suffering, they can do much more.

"First, I'd like to thank everyone who believed in me."

summary quiz [13.4]

12. Joe attributes the lessening of his depression to the medication he took. But in fact, his improvement was the result of positive interactions with his pleasant, supportive therapist. This phenomenon illustrates a treatment illusion called
    a. regression to the mean.
    b. nonspecific treatment effects.
    c. natural improvement.
    d. error in reconstructive memory.

13. Dr. Carolyn Johnson is studying whether Drug X is more effective in treating anxiety in women than in men. Her research is an example of a(n)
    a. double-blind experiment.
    b. placebo control.
    c. outcome study.
    d. process study.

14. Which statement is true regarding treatments for psychological disorders?
    a. Receiving psychotherapy does not lead to any more improvement than no treatment at all.
    b. Drug treatments for psychological problems are prescribed only if there are no known side effects.
    c. A disorder or symptom may occur as a result of the treatment itself.
    d. Treatments that take a long time, such as psychodynamic therapy, are usually ineffective.

iatrogenic illness A disorder or symptom that occurs as a result of a medical or psychotherapeutic treatment.

WhereDoYouStand?

Should Drugs Be Used to Prevent Traumatic Memories?

Medication can be an effective means of treating the symptoms of psychological disorders. Is medication also an effective way of *preventing* psychological disorders? Psychiatrist Roger Pitman's controversial studies of posttraumatic stress disorder (PTSD; see Chapter 15) focus on the use of the drug propranolol to prevent the consolidation of distressing memories after traumatic events. One of the key symptoms of PTSD is the presence of vivid and intrusive memories of a traumatic event such as a car accident or being the victim of a physical or sexual assault. If these memories are such prominent symptoms of PTSD, can we avoid the

disorder if we prevent these memories from being associated with unpleasant emotions?

The idea that the emotional consequences of traumatic memories might be blocked is based on the role of brain structures and chemicals in the consolidation of emotional memories. Researchers have confirmed that the amygdala and the hippocampus are involved in emotional memory (McNally, 2003). Propranolol is a drug that dampens emotional arousal by blocking beta-adrenergic receptors in the peripheral and central nervous system; this weakens the effects of chemicals such as adrenaline on receptors in these brain areas. If arousal cues were dampened by the administration of propranolol immediately after the trauma, perhaps the memories of the event would not be linked so strongly with the emotional response to the trauma.

To test this hypothesis, Pitman and his colleagues gave people who had experienced a traumatic event either propranolol or a placebo (sugar pill) when they arrived in an emergency room right after the trauma. On follow-up, the researchers found that the group given propranolol was significantly less physiologically reactive later when listening to a tape about their accident than those given the placebo (Pitman et al., 2002). This medication does not prevent memories from forming, but it seems to prevent them from becoming associated with upsetting emotions.

Some people question whether researchers should be tampering with memory at all. A *New York Times Magazine* article argued that our painful memories are essential in shaping us into caring human beings with empathy toward others (Henig, 2004). Opponents of such research also point out that our memories, good and bad, make us who we are. Proponents of the approach note that the treatment is not meant to *remove* unpleasant memories, only to reduce the emotional arousal which, in PTSD patients, leads to such debilitating symptoms.

Where do you stand? Should people be given drugs to reduce the influence of traumatic events on their memories? Would you want to take such a drug if you suffered a trauma? By taking such a drug, do you feel you might be losing an experience that makes you you?

CHAPTER REVIEW

Summary

Treatment: Getting Help to Those Who Need It

- Mental illness is often misunderstood, and because of this, it too often goes untreated.

- Untreated mental illness can be extremely costly, affecting an individual's ability to function and also causing social and financial burdens.

- Many people who suffer from mental illness do not get the help they need; they may be unaware that they have a problem, they may face obstacles to getting treatment, and they simply may not know where to turn.

- Treatments include psychotherapy, which focuses on the mind, and medical and biological methods, which focus on the brain and body.

Psychological Therapies: Healing the Mind through Interaction

- Psychodynamic therapies, including psychoanalysis, emphasize helping clients gain insight into their unconscious conflicts.

- Behavior therapy applies learning principles to specific behavior problems; cognitive therapy aims at challenging irrational thoughts. Cognitive behavior therapy (CBT) merges these approaches.

- Humanistic approaches (e.g., person-centered therapy) and existential approaches (e.g., Gestalt therapy) focus on helping people to develop a sense of personal worth.

- Group therapies target couples, families, or groups of clients brought together for the purpose of therapy.

Medical and Biological Treatments: Healing the Mind through the Brain

- Medications have been developed to treat many psychological disorders, including antipsychotic medications (used to treat schizophrenia and psychotic disorders), antianxiety medications (used to treat anxiety disorders), and antidepressants (used to treat depression and related disorders).

- Medications are often combined with psychotherapy.

- Other biomedical treatments include electroconvulsive therapy (ECT), transcranial magnetic stimulation (TMS), and psychosurgery—this last used in extreme cases, when other methods of treatment have been exhausted.

Treatment Effectiveness: For Better or for Worse

- Observing improvement during treatment does not necessarily mean that the treatment was effective; it might instead reflect natural improvement, nonspecific treatment effects (e.g., the placebo effect), and reconstructive memory processes.

- Treatment studies focus on both treatment outcomes and processes, using scientific research methods such as double-blind techniques and placebo controls.

- Treatments for psychological disorders are generally more effective than no treatment at all, but some are more effective than others for certain disorders, and both medication and psychotherapy have dangers that ethical practitioners must consider carefully.

Key Terms

psychotherapy (p. 402)

eclectic psychotherapy (p. 402)

psychodynamic psychotherapies (p. 402)

resistance (p. 403)

transference (p. 403)

interpersonal psychotherapy (IPT) (p. 404)

behavior therapy (p. 404)

token economy (p. 405)

exposure therapy (p. 405)

systematic desensitization (p. 405)

cognitive therapy (p. 405)

cognitive restructuring (p. 406)

mindfulness mediation (p. 406)

cognitive behavioral therapy (CBT) (p. 406)

person-centered therapy (p. 408)

Gestalt therapy (p. 408)

group therapy (p. 409)

antipsychotic drugs (p. 412)

psychopharmacology (p. 412)

antianxiety medications (p. 413)

antidepressants (p. 413)

electroconvulsive therapy (ECT) (p. 417)

transcranial magnetic stimulation (TMS) (p. 417)

psychosurgery (p. 418)

placebo (p. 419)

iatrogenic illness (p. 422)

Critical Thinking Questions

1. Psychodynamic psychotherapies focus on exploring childhood events to understand current psychological problems. In contrast, behavioral therapy assumes that disordered behavior is learned and that symptom relief is achieved through changing behaviors, sometimes through conditioning principles, while cognitive therapies use cognitive restructuring to teach clients to replace negative thinking with more realistic and positive beliefs.

   Suppose a young man comes to visit a therapist, reporting that he's been extremely depressed since the death of his mother, who raised him single-handedly after his father died. It's been over a year since her death, but the man is still experiencing extreme sadness and hopelessness, as well as loss of appetite and trouble sleeping.

   How might a psychologist who follows each of the above systems begin therapy?

2. Some antidepressant medications, called benzodiazepines, work by facilitating the action of the neurotransmitter GABA, which inhibits certain types of neurons in the brain.

   Back in Chapter 8, you read about a widely used, legally available psychoactive drug that also increases GABA. What was it? How are the effects of this drug similar to those of the benzodiazepines?

3. Treatment illusions are mindbugs in which an individual's improvement is mistakenly attributed to a treatment for a mental disorder.

   Suppose you experience a severe panic attack every time you walk into your organic chemistry class; the symptoms are so bad that you can't concentrate on the lesson, and you're sure you'll fail the class. You visit a psychiatrist, who prescribes an antianxiety medication. The next time you attend the class, you feel much calmer and more confident. Possibly, the medication is causing chemical changes in your brain that are resulting in a reduction of anxiety. But name three other ways in which treatment illusions could be responsible for your reduction in symptoms.

Answers to Summary Quizzes

Summary Quiz 13.1
1. d; 2. b; 3. c

Summary Quiz 13.2
4. d; 5. c; 6. b; 7. a

Summary Quiz 13.3
8. c; 9. b; 10. a; 11. d

Summary Quiz 13.4
12. b; 13. d; 14. c

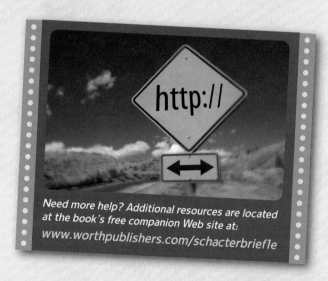

Need more help? Additional resources are located at the book's free companion Web site at: www.worthpublishers.com/schacterbriefle

Stress and Health

THE 53-YEAR-OLD PATIENT WAS SEMICOMATOSE with severe bronchial asthma when admitted to a hospital on July 13, 1960. Mr. X (fortunately, not his real name) was treated and discharged symptom free after a few days and went directly to his mother's home—where, in a matter of hours, he was wheezing so badly that he arrived back at the hospital in near-terminal condition. After two more severe attacks at his mother's house, a psychotherapist recommended that he not visit his mother again. A month later, Mr. X phoned his mother. He was found an hour later blue and gasping for breath and was pronounced dead shortly thereafter.

How did Mr. X die? The autopsy report cited heart damage from lack of oxygen as the cause of death, but interviews with his family and doctors revealed a more complicated story (Mathis, 1964). His first asthma attack had occurred shortly after he received a profitable offer for the family business and told his mother he wanted to sell. His mother was upset, but, urged on by his wife, he decided to take the offer. In an angry confrontation, his mother said, "Do this and something dire will happen to you." Two days later he had his first incident of mild wheezing. His asthma became much worse after the business was sold, and during his many hospitalizations, Mr. X came to recognize that his troubles might be due to fear of his mother's curse. On the day of his death, he expressed the belief that he was "allergic" to his mother and worried that her past predictions had been infallible. In the telephone conversation that preceded his death, he told his mother that he thought he was getting better. She replied by repeating her warning of "dire results." ■

Imagine that someone ordered an authentic voodoo doll from New Orleans, named it after you, and started sticking it with pins in your presence. Even if you didn't believe in curses at all, might this be stressful?

C an a person literally be frightened to death? Perhaps. The case of Mr. X resembles the phenomenon of "voodoo death" examined by physiologist Walter B. Cannon (1942). Cannon reviewed reports from around the world—often from traditional cultures in which death curses are taken very seriously—and found evidence for a profound connection between mind and body. Just as physical trauma can cause reduced blood pressure, rapid shallow pulse, and the deprivation of oxygen to the body's vital organs, so great fear can evoke physiological reactions that eventually result in death. Although such deaths are rare and their causes are always open to interpretation, the case of Mr. X shows how harm to the mind may provoke illness of the body.

Now, on an average day, you probably don't get a death curse from your mom. But modern life can present a welter of frights, bothers, and looming disasters that might make a nasty call from a loved one almost a relief. A wild driver may challenge your rights as a pedestrian, a band of evil professors may impose impossible project deadlines, or a fire may leave you out on the street. Perhaps it's just the really, really awful weather. Life has its **stressors**, *specific events or chronic pressures that place demands on a person or threaten the person's well-being.* Although such stressors rarely result in sudden death, they do have both immediate and cumulative effects that can influence health.

In this chapter, we'll look at what psychologists and physicians have learned about the kinds of life events that produce **stress**, *the physical and psychological response to internal or external stressors;* typical responses to such stressors; and ways to manage stress. Because sickness and health are not merely features of the physical body, we then consider the more general topic of **health psychology**, *the subfield of psychology concerned with ways psychological factors influence the causes and treatment of physical illness and the maintenance of health.* You will see how perceptions of illness can affect its course and how health-promoting behaviors can improve the quality of people's lives.

Sources of Stress: What Gets to You

First of all, what are the sources of stress? A natural catastrophe, such as a hurricane, earthquake, or volcanic eruption, is an obvious source. But, for most of us, stressors are personal events that affect the comfortable pattern of our lives, and little annoyances that bug us day after day. Let's look at the life events that can cause stress, chronic sources of stress, and the relationship between lack of perceived control and the impact of stressors.

Stressful Events

People often seem to get sick after major life events. In pioneering work, Thomas Holmes and Richard Rahe (1967) followed up on this observation, proposing that major life changes cause stress and that increased stress causes illness. To test their idea, they asked people to rate the magnitude of readjustment required by each of many events found to be associated with the onset of illness (Rahe et al., 1964). The resulting list of life events is remarkably predictive: Simply adding up the degree of life change for a person is a significant indicator of the person's future illness (Miller, 1996). A person who is divorced and loses a job and has a friend die all in a year, for example, is more likely to get sick than one who escapes the year with only a divorce.

A version of this list adapted for the life events of college students (and sporting the snappy acronym CUSS, for College Undergraduate Stress Scale) is shown in **TABLE 14.1** (on page 429). To assess your stressful events, check off any events that have happened to you in the past year and sum your point total. In a large sample of students in an introductory psychology class, the average was 1,247 points, ranging from 182 to 2,571 (Renner & Mackin, 1998).

Looking at the list, you may wonder why positive events are included. Stressful life events are unpleasant, right? Why would getting married be stressful? Isn't a wedding

● **Where are you on the stress scale?**
····························

stressors Specific events or chronic pressures that place demands on a person or threaten the person's well-being.

stress The physical and psychological response to internal or external stressors.

health psychology The subfield of psychology concerned with ways psychological factors influence the causes and treatment of physical illness and the maintenance of health.

TABLE 14.1

College Undergraduate Stress Scale

Event	Stress Rating	Event	Stress Rating
Being raped	100	Lack of sleep	69
Finding out that you are HIV positive	100	Change in housing situation (hassles, moves)	69
Being accused of rape	98	Competing or performing in public	69
Death of a close friend	97	Getting in a physical fight	66
Death of a close family member	96	Difficulties with a roommate	66
Contracting a sexually transmitted disease (other than AIDS)	94	Job changes (applying, new job, work hassles)	65
Concerns about being pregnant	91	Declaring a major or concerns about future plans	65
Finals week	90	A class you hate	62
Concerns about your partner being pregnant	90	Drinking or use of drugs	61
Oversleeping for an exam	89	Confrontations with professors	60
Flunking a class	89	Starting a new semester	58
Having a boyfriend or girlfriend cheat on you	85	Going on a first date	57
Ending a steady dating relationship	85	Registration	55
Serious illness in a close friend or family member	85	Maintaining a steady dating relationship	55
Financial difficulties	84	Commuting to campus or work or both	54
Writing a major term paper	83	Peer pressures	53
Being caught cheating on a test	83	Being away from home for the first time	53
Drunk driving	82	Getting sick	52
Sense of overload in school or work	82	Concerns about your appearance	52
Two exams in one day	80	Getting straight A's	51
Cheating on your boyfriend or girlfriend	77	A difficult class that you love	48
Getting married	76	Making new friends; getting along with friends	47
Negative consequences of drinking or drug use	75	Fraternity or sorority rush	47
Depression or crisis in your best friend	73	Falling asleep in class	40
Difficulties with parents	73	Attending an athletic event	20
Talking in front of class	72		

Source: Renner and Mackin (1998).

Note: To compute your personal life change score, sum the stress ratings for all events that have happened to you in the last year.

supposed to be fun? Research has shown that compared with negative events, positive events produce less psychological distress and fewer physical symptoms (McFarlane et al., 1980), and the happiness can sometimes even counteract the effects of negative events (Fredrickson, 2000). However, positive events often require readjustment and preparedness that many people find extremely stressful (e.g., Brown & McGill, 1989), so these events are included in computing life-change scores.

Chronic Stressors

Life would be simpler if an occasional stressful event such as a wedding or a lost job were the only pressure we faced. At least each event would be limited in scope, with a beginning, a middle, and, ideally, an end. But unfortunately, life brings with it continued exposure to **chronic stressors,** *sources of stress that occur continuously or repeatedly.* Strained relationships, long lines at the supermarket, nagging relatives, overwork, money troubles—small stressors that may be easy to ignore if they happen only occasionally can accumulate to produce distress and illness. People who report having a lot of daily hassles also report more psychological symptoms (Kanner et al., 1981) and physical symptoms (Delongis et al., 1982), and these effects often have a greater and longer-lasting impact than major life events.

Many chronic stressors are linked to particular environments. For example, features of city life—noise, traffic, crowding, pollution, and even the threat of violence—provide particularly insistent sources of chronic stress. Rural areas have their own chronic stressors, of course, especially isolation and lack of access to amenities such as health care. The realization that chronic stressors are linked to environments has spawned the subfield *environmental psychology,* the scientific study of environmental effects on behavior and health.

● **What are some examples of environmental factors that cause chronic stress?**

● *Crazy-busy? The daily hassle of more work than time can become a significant stressor. Also a fire hazard.*

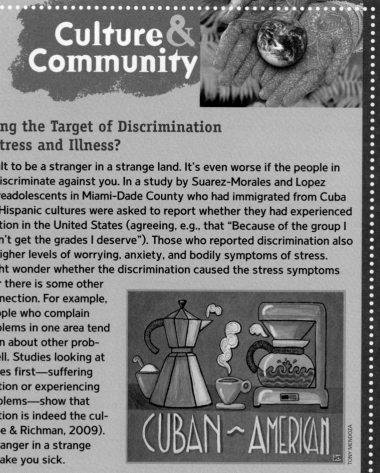

Culture & Community

Can Being the Target of Discrimination Cause Stress and Illness?

It is difficult to be a stranger in a strange land. It's even worse if the people in this land discriminate against you. In a study by Suarez-Morales and Lopez (2009), preadolescents in Miami-Dade County who had immigrated from Cuba and other Hispanic cultures were asked to report whether they had experienced discrimination in the United States (agreeing, e.g., that "Because of the group I am in, I don't get the grades I deserve"). Those who reported discrimination also reported higher levels of worrying, anxiety, and bodily symptoms of stress.

You might wonder whether the discrimination caused the stress symptoms or whether there is some other causal connection. For example, maybe people who complain about problems in one area tend to complain about other problems as well. Studies looking at which comes first—suffering discrimination or experiencing health problems—show that discrimination is indeed the culprit (Pascoe & Richman, 2009). Being a stranger in a strange land can make you sick.

chronic stressor A source of stress that occurs continuously or repeatedly.

When the "Theme Building" was designed for Los Angeles International Airport in the early '60s to celebrate the modern age, few probably anticipated that it would someday be shown in a textbook as a reminder of the stress of airplane noise on children living nearby.

In one study of the influence of noise on children, environmental psychologists looked at the impact of attending schools under the flight path to Los Angeles International Airport. Did the noise of more than 300 jets flying overhead each day have an influence beyond making kids yell to be heard? Compared with children matched for race, economic background, and ethnicity who attended nearby schools away from the noise, children going to school in the flight path had higher blood pressure and gave up more easily when working on difficult problems and puzzles (Cohen et al., 1980). Next time you fly into LA, please try to do so more quietly for the children.

Perceived Control over Stressful Events

What do death curses, catastrophes, stressful life changes, and daily hassles have in common? Right off the bat, of course, their threat to the person or the status quo is easy to see. Stressors challenge you to *do something*—to take some action to eliminate or overcome the stressor.

Paradoxically, events are most stressful when there is *nothing to do*—no way to deal with the challenge. Expecting that you will have control over what happens to you is associated with effectiveness in dealing with stress. Researchers David Glass and Jerome Singer (1972), in classic studies of *perceived control,* looked at the aftereffects of loud noise on people who could or could not control it. Participants were asked to solve puzzles and proofread in a quiet room or in a room filled with noise as loud as that in classrooms under the LA flight path. Glass and Singer found that bursts of such noise hurt people's performance on the tasks after the noise was over. However, this dramatic decline in performance was prevented among participants who were told during the noise period that they could stop the noise just by pushing a button. They didn't actually take this option, but access to the "panic button" shielded them from the detrimental effects of the noise.

● **Why is the ability to control the source of stress so important?**

Subsequent studies have found that a lack of perceived control underlies other stressors, too. The stressful effects of crowding, for example, appear to stem from the feeling that you can't control getting away from the crowded conditions (Sherrod, 1974). Being jammed into a crowded dormitory room may be easier to handle, after all, the moment you learn of the button that drops open the trapdoor under your roommate's chair.

When the cabin attendant announces that "we have a full cabin on this flight," conditions can be stressful not so much because of the crowding, but because there is no obvious control over the crowding. Taking control, for example, by keeping busy or wearing headphones to decrease contact with others or even by talking with people and getting to know them may help decrease the stress.

fight-or-flight response An emotional and physiological reaction to an emergency that increases readiness for action.

general adaptation syndrome (GAS) A three-stage physiological response that appears regardless of the stressor that is encountered.

summary quiz [14.1]

1. According to the College Undergraduate Stress Scale, which of the following events is most stressful?
   a. concerns about your appearance
   b. getting married
   c. getting sick
   d. confrontations with professors

2. A person living in an area where there is considerable traffic, noise, crowding, and pollution is exposed to what kinds of stressors?
   a. chronic stressors
   b. intermittent stressors
   c. positive stressors
   d. controllable stressors

3. Two groups are exposed to loud noise while trying to solve puzzles. Group A is instructed they can stop the noise by pushing a button, whereas Group B is told nothing. Group A's puzzle-solving performance will
   a. be unaffected by the instruction.
   b. become slightly worse than Group B's.
   c. become much worse than Group B's.
   d. become better than Group B's.

Stress Reactions: All Shook Up

An accident at the Three Mile Island nuclear plant near Harrisburg, Pennsylvania, on March 28, 1979, created a near meltdown in the reactor and released radioactivity into the air and into the Susquehanna River. The situation was out of control for 2 days, on the brink of a major disaster that was averted only when plant operators luckily made the right decision to repressurize the coolant system. Local residents fled the area. Most eventually returned when the danger had subsided, but they suffered lasting effects of the stress associated with this potentially deadly event.

A study conducted a year and a half later compared area residents with people from unaffected areas (Fleming et al., 1985). The local group showed physical signs of stress: They had relatively high levels of *catecholamines* (biochemicals indicating the activation

A near meltdown occurred at the Three Mile Island nuclear plant near Harrisburg, Pennsylvania, on March 28, 1979.

JOHN S. ZEEDICK/GETTY IMAGES

of emotional systems), and they had fewer white blood cells available to fight infection (Schaeffer et al., 1985). The residents also suffered psychological effects, including higher levels of anxiety, depression, and alienation compared with people from elsewhere. Even on a simple proofreading task, residents performed more poorly than did people from unaffected areas. Because the radiation released was not sufficient to account for any of these effects, they were attributed to the aftermath of stress. In short, stress can produce changes in every system of the body, influencing how people feel and how they act.

Physical Reactions

Before he became interested in voodoo death, Walter Cannon (1929) coined a phrase to describe the body's response to any threatening stimulus: the **fight-or-flight response**, *an emotional and physiological reaction to an emergency that increases readiness for action.* The mind asks, "Should I stay and battle this somehow, or should I run like mad?" And the body prepares to react. If you're a cat at this time, your hair stands on end. If you're a human, your hair stands on end, too, but not as visibly. Cannon recognized this common response across species and suspected that it might be the body's first mobilization to

● **How does the body react to a flight-or-flight situation?**

any threat. Research conducted since Cannon's discovery has revealed what is happening in the brain and body during this reaction.

Brain activation in response to threat occurs in the hypothalamus, stimulating the nearby pituitary gland, which in turn releases a hormone known as ACTH (short for adrenocorticotropic hormone). ACTH travels through the bloodstream and stimulates the adrenal glands atop the kidneys (see **FIGURE 14.1**). In this cascading response of the *HPA axis* (for *h*ypothalamus, *p*ituitary, *a*drenal), the adrenal glands are then stimulated to release hormones, including the *catecholamines* mentioned earlier (epinephrine and norepinephrine), which increase sympathetic nervous system activation (and therefore increase heart rate, blood pressure, and respiration rate) and decrease parasympathetic activation (see Chapter 3). The increased respiration and blood pressure make more oxygen available to the muscles to energize attack or to initiate escape. The adrenal glands also release *cortisol*, a hormone that increases the concentration of glucose in the blood to make fuel available to the muscles. Everything is prepared for a full-tilt response to the threat.

General Adaptation Syndrome

What might have happened to Three Mile Island's neighbors if the sirens had wailed again and again for days or weeks at a time? Starting in the 1930s, Hans Selye, a Canadian physician, undertook a variety of experiments that looked at the physiological consequences of severe threats to well-being. He subjected rats to heat, cold, infection, trauma, hemorrhage, and other prolonged stressors, making few friends among the rats or their sympathizers but learning a lot about stress. His stressed-out rats developed physiological responses that included an enlarged adrenal cortex, shrinking of the lymph glands, and ulceration of the stomach. Noting that many different kinds of stressors caused similar patterns of physiological change, he called the reaction **general adaptation syndrome (GAS)**, which he defined as *a three-stage physiological stress response that appears regardless of the stressor that is encountered.* The GAS is *nonspecific*; that is, the response doesn't vary, no matter what the source of the repeated stress.

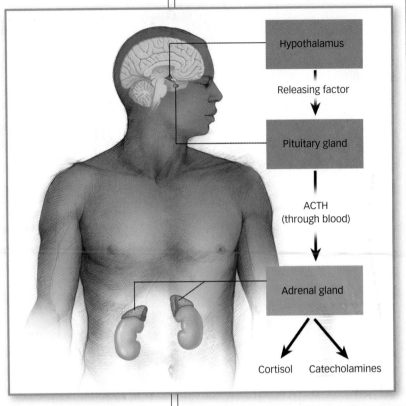

Hypothalamus

Releasing factor

Pituitary gland

ACTH (through blood)

Adrenal gland

Cortisol   Catecholamines

FIGURE 14.1 • • • • • • • • • • • • • •

HPA Axis *Just a few seconds after a fearful stimulus is perceived, the hypothalamus activates the pituitary gland to release adrenocorticotropic hormone (ACTH). The ACTH then travels through the bloodstream to activate the adrenal glands to release catecholamines and cortisol, which energize the fight-or-flight response.*

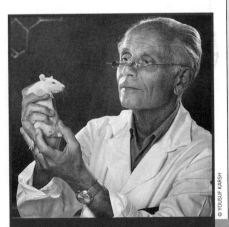

Hans Selye with rat. Given all the stress Selye put rats under, this one looks surprisingly calm.

······························· ● **FIGURE 14.2**
Selye's Three Phases of Stress Response
*In Selye's theory, resistance to stress builds over time
but then can only last so long before exhaustion sets in.*

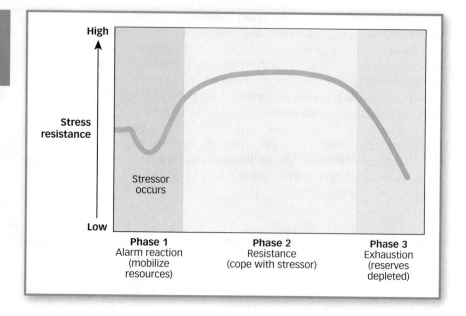

None of this is very good news. Although Friedrich Nietzsche once said, "What does not kill me makes me stronger," Selye found that severe stress takes a toll on the body. He saw the GAS as occurring in three phases (see **FIGURE 14.2**):

● **What are the three phases of GAS?**

■ First comes the *alarm phase*, in which the body rapidly mobilizes its resources to respond to the threat. Energy is required, and the body calls on its stored fat and muscle. The alarm phase is equivalent to Cannon's fight-or-flight response.

■ Next, in the *resistance phase,* the body adapts to its high state of arousal as it tries to cope with the stressor. Continuing to draw on resources of fat and muscle, it shuts down unnecessary processes: digestion, growth, and sex drive stall; menstruation stops; production of testosterone and sperm decrease. The body is being taxed to generate resistance, and all the fun stuff is put on hold.

■ If the GAS goes on for long enough, the *exhaustion phase* sets in. The body's resistance collapses. Many of the resistance-phase defenses create gradual damage as they operate, leading to costs for the body that can include susceptibility to infection, tumor growth, aging, irreversible organ damage, or death.

Stress Effects on the Immune Response

The **immune system** is *a complex response system that protects the body from bacteria, viruses, and other foreign substances.* The system includes white blood cells such as **lymphocytes** (including T cells and B cells), *cells that produce antibodies that fight infection.* The immune system is remarkably responsive to psychological influences. *Psychoneuroimmunology* is the study of how the immune system responds to psychological variables, such as the presence of stressors. Stressors can cause hormones such as gluco-

● **How does stress affect the immune system?**

corticoids to flood the brain, wearing down the immune system and making it less able to fight invaders.

For example, in one study, medical student volunteers agreed to receive small wounds to the roof of the mouth. Researchers observed that these wounds healed more slowly during exam periods than during summer vacation (Marucha, Kiecolt-Glaser, & Favagehi, 1998). In another study, a set of selfless, healthy volunteers permitted researchers to swab common cold virus in their noses (Cohen et al., 1998). You might think that a direct application of the virus would be like exposure to a massive full-facial sneeze and that all the participants would catch colds. The researchers observed, though, that some people got colds and others didn't—and stress helped account for the difference. Volunteers who had experienced

immune system A complex response system that protects the body from bacteria, viruses, and other foreign substances.

lymphocytes White blood cells that produce antibodies that fight infection.

Type A behavior pattern The tendency toward easily aroused hostility, impatience, a sense of time urgency, and competitive achievement strivings.

chronic stressors (lasting a month or longer) were especially likely to suffer colds. In particular, participants who had lost a job or who were going through extended interpersonal problems with family or friends were most susceptible to the virus. Brief stressful life events (those lasting less than a month) had no impact.

The effect of stress on immune response may help to explain why social status is related to health. Studies of British civil servants beginning in the 1960s found that mortality varied precisely with civil service grade: the higher the classification, the lower the rates of death, regardless of cause (Marmot et al., 1991). One explanation is that people in lower-status jobs more often engage in unhealthy behavior such as smoking and drinking alcohol, and there is evidence of this. But there is also evidence that the stress of living life at the bottom levels of society increases risk of infections by weakening the immune system. People who perceive themselves as low in social status are more prone to suffer from respiratory infections, for example, than those who do not bear this social burden—and the same holds true for low-status male monkeys (Cohen, 1999).

"I'd like to get your arrow count down."

Stress and Cardiovascular Health

The heart and circulatory system are also sensitive to stress. For example, for several days after Iraq's 1991 missile attack on Israel, heart attack rates went up markedly among citizens in Tel Aviv (Meisel et al., 1991). The full story of how stress affects the cardiovascular system starts earlier than the occurrence of a heart attack, however: Chronic stress creates changes in the body that increase later vulnerability to this condition.

The main cause of coronary heart disease is *atherosclerosis,* a gradual narrowing of the arteries that occurs as fatty deposits, or plaque, build up on the inner walls of the arteries. Narrowed arteries result in a reduced blood supply and, eventually, when an artery is blocked by a blood clot or by detached plaque, in a heart attack. Although smoking, a sedentary lifestyle, and a diet high in fat and cholesterol can cause coronary heart disease, chronic

● **How does chronic stress increase the chance of a heart attack?**

stress is a major contributor (Krantz & McCeney, 2002). As a result of stress-activated arousal of the sympathetic nervous system, blood pressure goes up and stays up, and this gradually damages the blood vessels. The damaged vessels accumulate plaque, and the more plaque, the greater the likelihood of coronary heart disease.

In the 1950s, cardiologists Meyer Friedman and Ray Rosenman (1974) conducted a revolutionary study that demonstrated a link between work-related stress and coronary heart disease. They interviewed and tested 3,000 healthy middle-age men and then tracked their subsequent cardiovascular health. Based on their research, Friedman and Rosenman developed the concept of the **Type A behavior pattern**, which is characterized by *a tendency toward easily aroused hostility, impatience, a sense of time urgency, and competitive achievement strivings,* and they compared Type A individuals to those with a less driven behavior pattern (sometimes called *Type B*). The Type A men were identified not only by their answers to questions in the interview (agreeing that they walk and talk fast, work late, set goals for themselves, work hard to win, and easily get frustrated and angry at others) but also by the pushy and impatient way in which they answered the questions. They watched the clock, barked back answers, and interrupted the interviewer, at some points even slapping him with a fish. Okay, the part about the fish is wrong, but you get the idea: These people were intense. The researchers found that of the 258 men who had heart attacks in the 9 years following the interview, over two thirds had been classified as Type A, and only one third had been classified as Type B.

Road rage starts to make sense when you believe that all the other drivers on the road are trying to kill you.

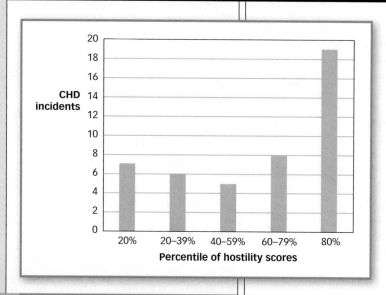

A later study of stress and anger tracked medical students for up to 48 years to see how their behavior while they were young related to their later susceptibility to coronary problems (Chang et al., 2002). Students who responded to stress with anger and hostility were found to be three times more likely later to develop premature heart disease and six times more likely to have an early heart attack than were students who did not respond with anger. Hostility, particularly in men, predicts heart disease better than any other major causal factor, such as smoking, high caloric intake, or even high levels of LDL cholesterol (Niaura et al., 2002; see also **FIGURE 14.3**). Stress affects the cardiovascular system to some degree in everyone but is particularly harmful in those people who respond to stressful events with hostility.

● **What causal factor most predicts heart attacks?**

FIGURE 14.3
Hostility and Coronary Heart Disease
Of 2,280 men studied over the course of 3 years, 45 suffered coronary heart disease (CHD) incidents, such as heart attack. Many more of these incidents occurred in the group who had initially scored above the 80th percentile in hostility (Niaura et al., 2002).

Psychological Reactions

The body's response to stress is intertwined with responses of the mind. Perhaps the first thing the mind does is try to sort things out—to interpret whether an event is threatening or not and, if it is, whether something can be done about it.

Stress Interpretation

The interpretation of a stimulus as stressful or not is called *primary appraisal* (Lazarus & Folkman, 1984). Primary appraisal allows you to realize that a small dark spot on your shirt is a stressor ("Spider!") or that a 70-mile-per-hour drop from a great height in a small car full of screaming people is not a stressor ("Roller coaster!").

In a demonstration of the importance of interpretation, researchers used a gruesome film of a subincision—a kind of genital surgery that is part of some tribal initiation rites—to severely stress volunteer participants (Speisman et al., 1964). Self-reports and participants' autonomic arousal (heart rate and skin conductance level) were the measures of stress. Before viewing the film, one group heard an introduction that downplayed the pain and emphasized the coming-of-age aspect of the initiation. This interpretation markedly reduced the film viewers' stress compared with another group whose viewing was preceded by a lecture accentuating the pain and trauma.

● **What is the difference between a threat and a challenge?**

The next step in interpretation is *secondary appraisal*—determining whether the stressor is something you can handle or not—that is, whether you have control over the event (Lazarus & Folkman, 1984). Interestingly, the body responds differently depending on whether the stressor is perceived as a *threat* (a stressor you believe you might *not* be able to overcome) or a *challenge* (a stressor you feel fairly confident you can control) (Blascovich & Tomaka, 1996). The same midterm exam could be a challenge if you were well prepared and a threat if you neglected to study.

Stress Disorders

Psychological reactions to stress can lead to stress disorders. For example, a person who lives through a terrifying and uncontrollable experience may develop **posttraumatic stress disorder** (PTSD), a disorder characterized by *chronic physiological arousal, recurrent unwanted thoughts or images of the trauma, and avoidance of things that call the traumatic event to mind.*

Psychological scars left by traumatic events are nowhere more apparent than in war. Many soldiers returning from combat have PTSD symptoms, including flashbacks of battle, exaggerated anxiety and startle reactions, and even medical conditions that do

posttraumatic stress disorder (PTSD) A disorder characterized by chronic physiological arousal, recurrent unwanted thoughts or images of the trauma, and avoidance of things that call the traumatic event to mind.

not arise from physical damage (e.g., paralysis or chronic fatigue). Most of these symptoms are normal, appropriate responses to horrifying events; and for most people, the symptoms subside with time. In PTSD, the symptoms can last much longer. For example, the Centers for Disease Control (1988) found that even 20 years after the Vietnam War, 15% of veterans who had seen combat continued to report lingering symptoms. This long-term psychological response is now recognized not only among the victims, witnesses, and perpetrators of war but also among ordinary people who are traumatized by any of life's terrible events. At some time over the course of their lives, about 8% of Americans are estimated to suffer from PTSD (Kessler et al., 1995).

Not everyone who is exposed to a traumatic event develops PTSD, suggesting that people differ in their degree of sensitivity to trauma. Research using magnetic resonance imaging (MRI) to examine brain structures has found one possible indication of such sensitivity. In some studies comparing people without and with PTSD, the hippocampus was found to be smaller in volume among individuals with PTSD (Stein et al., 1997). This raises an important question: Does the reduced hippocampal volume reflect a preexisting condition that makes the brain sensitive to stress, or does the traumatic stress itself somehow kill nerve cells? One study suggests that

● **What structure in the brain might be an indicator for susceptibility to PTSD?**

although a group of combat veterans with PTSD showed reduced hippocampal volume, so do the identical (monozygotic) twins of those men (**FIGURE 14.4**, below)—even though those twins had never had any combat exposure or developed PTSD (Gilbertson et al., 2002). This suggests that the veterans' reduced hippocampal volumes weren't caused by the combat exposure; instead, both these veterans and their twin brothers might have had a smaller hippocampus to begin with, a preexisting condition that made them susceptible to developing PTSD, when they were later exposed to trauma.

The traumatic events of war leave many suffering symptoms of PTSD.

MATT CARDY/GETTY IMAGES

Burnout

Did you ever take a class from an instructor who had lost interest in the job? The syndrome is easy to spot: The teacher looks distant and blank, almost robotic, giving predictable and humdrum lessons each day—as if it doesn't matter whether anyone is listening. Now imagine *being* this instructor. You decided to teach because you wanted to shape young minds. You worked hard, and for a while things were great. But one day, you look up to see a roomful of miserable students who are bored and don't care about anything you have to say. They text-message while you talk and start shuffling papers and putting things away long before the end of class. You're happy at work only

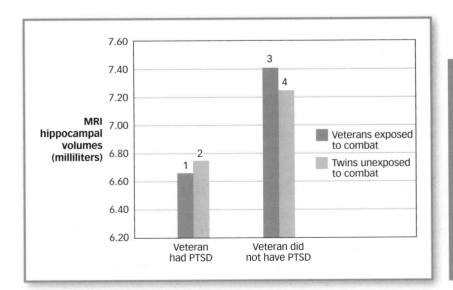

FIGURE 14.4 ● ● ● ● ● ● ● ● ● ● ●
Hippocampal Volumes of Vietnam Veterans and Their Identical Twins *Average hippocampal volumes for four groups of participants: (1) combat-exposed veterans who developed PTSD; (2) their combat-unexposed twins with no PTSD themselves; (3) combat-exposed veterans who never developed PTSD; and (4) their unexposed twins, also with no PTSD. Smaller hippocampal volumes were found both for the combat-exposed veterans with PTSD (group 1) and their twins who had not been exposed to combat (group 2) in comparison to veterans without PTSD (group 3) and their twins (group 4). This pattern of findings suggests that an inherited smaller hippocampus may make some people sensitive to conditions that cause PTSD (Gilbertson et al., 2002).*

BETTMANN/CORBIS

• *An automatic nurse might be one solution to the problem of burnout among members of health professions. This "nursing table" patented in 1869 was to take care of the sick with minimal human intervention.*

when you're not in class. When people feel this way, especially about their jobs or careers, they are suffering from **burnout**, *a state of physical, emotional, and mental exhaustion created by long-term involvement in an emotionally demanding situation and accompanied by lowered performance and motivation.*

Burnout is a particular problem in the helping professions (Freudenberger, 1974; Pines & Aronson, 1988). Teachers, nurses, clergy, doctors, dentists, psychologists, social workers, police officers, and others who repeatedly encounter emotional turmoil on the job may only be able to work productively for a limited time. Eventually, many succumb to symptoms of burnout: over-whelming exhaustion, a deep cynicism and detachment from the job, and a sense of ineffectiveness and lack of accomplishment (Maslach, 2003). Their unhappiness can even spread to others; people with burnout tend to become disgruntled employees who revel in their coworkers' failures and ignore their coworkers' successes (Brenninkmeijer, Vanyperen, & Buunk, 2001).

● **Why is burnout a problem especially in the helping professions?**

What causes burnout? One theory suggests that the culprit is using your job to give meaning to your life (Pines, 1993). If you define yourself only by your career and gauge your self-worth by success at work, you risk having nothing left when work fails. For example, a teacher in danger of burnout might do well to invest time in family, hobbies, or other self-expressions. Others argue that some emotionally stressful jobs lead to burnout no matter how they are approached and active efforts to overcome the stress before burnout occurs are important. The stress management techniques discussed in the next section may be lifesavers for people in such jobs.

summary quiz [14.2]

4. When a person feels threatened, a chain of events occurs within the nervous and endocrine systems to prepare the body for action. This reaction starts in the
   a. adrenal glands.   c. pituitary gland.
   b. hypothalamus.   d. amygdala.

5. In Hans Selye's general adaptation syndrome, the alarm phase is equivalent to
   a. the Type A behavior pattern.   c. the fight-or-flight response.
   b. primary appraisal.   d. posttraumatic stress disorder.

6. Development of heart disease is linked to which psychological characteristic?
   a. competitive achievement strivings   c. a sense of time urgency
   b. impatience   d. hostility

7. A person who is experiencing physical, emotional, and mental exhaustion and reduced performance and motivation due to long-term involvement in an emotionally demanding situation is experiencing
   a. burnout.   c. Type A behavior pattern.
   b. posttraumatic stress disorder.   d. the fight-or-flight response.

burnout A state of physical, emotional, and mental exhaustion created by long-term involvement in an emotionally demanding situation and accompanied by lowered performance and motivation.

repressive coping Avoiding situations or thoughts that are reminders of a stressor and maintaining an artificially positive viewpoint.

rational coping Facing a stressor and working to overcome it.

Stress Management: Dealing with It

Most college students (92%) say they occasionally feel overwhelmed by the tasks they face, and over a third say they have dropped courses or received low grades in response to severe stress (Deuenwald, 2003). No doubt you are among the lucky 8% who are entirely cool and report no stress. But just in case you're not, you may appreciate our exploration of stress management techniques—ways to counteract psychological and physical stress reactions directly by managing your mind and body and ways to sidestep stress by managing your situation. These techniques resemble some of the forms of cognitive behavior therapy we explored in Chapter 13, but they are strategies people often exercise on their own, without the help of a therapist.

Mind Management

Stressful events are magnified in the mind. If you fear public speaking, for example, just the thought of an upcoming presentation to a group can create anxiety. And if you do break down during a presentation—going blank, for example, or blurting out something embarrassing—intrusive memories of this stressful event could echo in your mind afterward. A significant part of stress management, then, is control of the mind.

Repressive Coping

Controlling your thoughts isn't easy, but some people do seem to be able to banish unpleasant thoughts from mind. This style of dealing with stress, called **repressive coping**, is *characterized by avoiding situations or thoughts that are reminders of a stressor and maintaining an artificially positive viewpoint.* Everyone has *some* problems, of course, but repressors are good at deliberately ignoring them (Barnier, Levin, & Maher, 2004). So, for example, when repressors suffer a heart attack, they are less likely than other people to report intrusive thoughts of their heart problems in the days and weeks that follow (Ginzburg, Solomon, & Bleich, 2002).

● **When is it useful to avoid stressful thoughts and when is avoidance a problem?**

Like Mr. X, who was persuaded to avoid his mother's home as a way of keeping her frightening threats out of mind, people often rearrange their lives in order to avoid stressful situations. Many victims of rape, for example, move away from home, and they typically avoid the place where the rape occurred (Ellis, 1983). Anticipating and attempting to avoid reminders of the traumatic experience, they become wary of strangers, especially men who resemble the assailant, and they check doors, locks, and windows more frequently than before. Although it may make sense to try to avoid stressful thoughts and situations when stress is at its peak, research indicates that longer-term use of such strategies can be harmful (Suls & Fletcher, 1985; Wegner & Pennebaker, 1993). The avoidance of thoughts and situations makes your world a bit smaller each day; a better approach is to come to grips with fears or problems. This is the basic idea of rational coping.

Rational Coping

Rational coping involves *facing the stressor and working to overcome it.* This strategy is the opposite of repressive coping and so may seem to be the most unpleasant and unnerving thing you could do when faced with stress. It requires approaching rather than avoiding a stressor in order to lessen its longer-term negative impact (Hayes, Strosahl, & Wilson, 1999). Rational coping is a three-step process: *acceptance,* coming to realize that the stressor exists and cannot be wished away; *exposure,* attending to the stressor, thinking about it, and even seeking it out; and *understanding,* working to find the meaning of the stressor in your life.

● **What are the three steps in rational coping?**

When the trauma is particularly intense, rational coping may be difficult to undertake. In rape trauma, for example, even accepting that the rape happened takes time and effort; the initial impulse is to deny the event and try to live as though it had never occurred. Psychotherapy may help during the exposure step by helping victims to confront and think about what happened. Using a technique called

Actor Heath Ledger's death in 2008 was ruled an accident: An autopsy revealed he had taken a potent array of painkillers, sleeping pills, and antianxiety drugs. It is impossible to know just what happened, but some guess that he was engaged in repressive coping—using the drugs to erase anxiety from his mind.

ALESSANDRA BENEDETTI/CORBIS

● *How do you cope with a tidal wave? This survivor of the devastating 2004 Tsunami south of Madras, India, looks for her belongings in the wreckage.*

"prolonged exposure," rape survivors relive the traumatic event in their imagination by recording a verbal account of the event and then listening to the recording daily. In one study, rape survivors were instructed to seek out objectively safe situations that caused them anxiety or that they had avoided. This sounds like bitter medicine indeed, but it is remarkably effective, producing significant reductions in anxiety and PTSD symptoms compared to no therapy and compared to other therapies that promote more gradual and subtle forms of exposure (Foa et al., 1999).

The third element of rational coping involves coming to an understanding of the meaning of the stressful events. A trauma victim may wonder again and again, "Why me?" or, "How did it happen?" or, "Why?" Survivors of incest frequently voice the desire to make sense of their trauma (Silver, Boon, & Stones, 1983)—a process that is difficult, even impossible, during bouts of suppression and avoidance.

Reframing

Changing the way you think is another way to cope with stressful thoughts. **Reframing** involves *finding a new or creative way to think about a stressor that reduces its threat.* If you experience anxiety at the thought of public speaking, for example, you might reframe by shifting from thinking of an audience as evaluating you to thinking of yourself as evaluating them, and this might make speech giving easier.

Reframing can be an effective way to prepare for a moderately stressful situation, but if something like public speaking is so stressful that you can't bear to think about until you absolutely must, the technique may be not be usable. **Stress inoculation training (SIT)** is *a reframing technique that helps people to cope with stressful situations by developing positive ways to think about the situation.* For example, in one study, people who had difficulty controlling their anger were trained to rehearse thoughts such as "Just roll with the punches; don't get bent out of shape." Participants who practiced these thoughts were less likely to become physiologically aroused in response to laboratory-based provocations, both imaginary and real. Subsequent research on SIT has revealed that it can be useful, too, for helping people who have suffered prior traumatic events to become more comfortable living with those events (Foa & Meadows, 1997).

● **How has writing about stressful events shown to be helpful?**

Reframing apparently can take place spontaneously if people are given the opportunity to spend time thinking and writing about stressful events. In an important series of studies, Jamie Pennebaker (1989) found that the physical health of a group of college students improved after they spent a few hours writing about their deepest thoughts and feelings. Compared with students who had written about something else, members of the self-disclosure group were less likely in subsequent months to visit the student health center; they also used less aspirin and achieved better grades (Pennebaker & Beall, 1986; Pennebaker, Colder, & Sharp, 1990). In fact, engaging in such expressive writing was found to improve immune function (Pennebaker, Kiecolt-Glaser, & Glaser, 1988), while suppressing emotional topics weakened it (Petrie, Booth, & Pennebaker, 1998). The positive effect of self-disclosing writing may reflect its usefulness in reframing trauma and reducing stress.

● *Perhaps Ganesh, the Hindu god of wisdom, finds it therapeutic to write about his thoughts and feelings from time to time.*

Body Management

Stress can express itself as tension in your neck muscles, back pain, a knot in your stomach, sweaty hands, or the harried face you glimpse in the mirror. Because stress so often manifests itself through bodily symptoms, bodily techniques such as relaxation, biofeedback, and aerobic exercise are useful in its management.

Relaxation

Imagine for a moment that you are scratching your chin. Don't actually do it; just think about it and notice that your body participates by moving ever so slightly, tensing and relaxing in the sequence of the imagined action. Our bodies respond to all the things we think about doing every day. These thoughts create muscle tension even when we think we're doing nothing at all. **Relaxation therapy** is *a technique for reducing tension by consciously relaxing muscles of the body.* A person in relaxation therapy may be asked to relax specific muscle groups one at a time or to imagine warmth flowing through the body or to think about a relaxing situation. Meditation, hypnosis, yoga, and prayer have some elements in common with relaxation therapy (see Chapter 8). These activities all draw on a **relaxation response**, *a condition of reduced muscle tension, cortical activity, heart rate, breathing rate, and blood pressure* (Benson, 1990). Basically, as soon as you get in a comfortable position, quiet down, and focus on something repetitive or soothing that holds your attention, you relax.

● **What do meditation, hypnosis, yoga, and prayer have in common?**

Relaxing on a regular basis can reduce symptoms of stress (Carlson & Hoyle, 1993) and even reduce blood levels of cortisol, the biochemical marker of the stress response (McKinney et al., 1997). For example, in patients who are suffering from tension headache, relaxation reduces the tension that causes the headache; in people with cancer, relaxation makes it easier to cope with stressful treatments; in people with stress-related cardiovascular problems, relaxation can reduce the high blood pressure that puts the heart at risk (Mandle et al., 1996).

Biofeedback

Wouldn't it be nice if, instead of having to learn to relax, you could just flip a switch and relax as fast as possible? **Biofeedback**, *the use of an external monitoring device to obtain information about a bodily function and possibly gain control over that function,* was developed with this goal of high-tech relaxation in mind.

Biofeedback can help people control physiological functions they are not likely to become aware of in other ways. For example, you probably have no idea right now what brain-wave patterns you are producing. In the late 1950s, Joe Kamiya (1969), a psychologist using the electroencephalograph (also called the EEG and discussed in Chapter 3), initiated a brain-wave biofeedback revolution when he found that people could change their brain waves from alert beta patterns to relaxed alpha patterns and back again when they were permitted to monitor their own EEG readings.

● **How does biofeedback work?**

Recent studies suggest that EEG biofeedback (or neurofeedback) is moderately successful in treating brain-wave abnormalities in disorders such as epilepsy (Yucha & Gilbert, 2004). Often, however, the use of biofeedback to produce relaxation in the brain turns out to be a bit of technological overkill and may not be much more effective than simply having the person stretch out in a hammock and hum a happy tune. Unfortunately, biofeedback is not a magic bullet that gives people control over stress-induced health troubles, but it has proven useful as a technique for pursuing the benefits of relaxation (Moss et al., 2002). People who find that they cannot relax successfully through relaxation therapy may find that biofeedback provides a useful alternative.

reframing Finding a new or creative way to think about a stressor that reduces its threat.

stress inoculation training (SIT) A therapy that helps people to cope with stressful situations by developing positive ways to think about the situation.

relaxation therapy A technique for reducing tension by consciously relaxing muscles of the body.

relaxation response A condition of reduced muscle tension, cortical activity, heart rate, breathing rate, and blood pressure.

biofeedback The use of an external monitoring device to obtain information about a bodily function and possibly gain control over that function.

MICHAEL NEWMAN/PHOTOEDIT

Biofeedback gives people access to visual or audio feedback showing levels of psychophysiological functions such as heart rate, breathing, or skin temperature that they would otherwise be unable to sense directly.

Exercise is helpful for the reduction of stress and even better if you get to carry the Olympic torch.

Aerobic Exercise

A jogger nicely decked out in a neon running suit bounces back and forth in place at the crosswalk and then springs away when the signal changes. It is tempting to assume this jogger is the picture of psychological health—happy, unstressed, and even downright exuberant. It is also a bit tempting, if you're driving a car, to run up on the curb and mow the jogger down. As it turns out, the stereotype is true: Studies indicate that *aerobic exercise* (exercise that increases heart rate and oxygen intake for a sustained period) is associated with psychological well-being (Hassmen, Koivula, & Uutela, 2000). But does exercise *cause* psychological well-being, or does psychological well-being cause people to exercise? Perhaps general happiness is what inspires the jogger's bounce. Or could some unknown third factor (neon pants?) cause both the need to exercise and the sense of well-being? As we've mentioned many times, correlation does not always imply causation.

To try to tease apart causal factors, researchers have randomly assigned people to aerobic exercise activities and no-exercise comparison groups and have found that exercise actually does promote stress relief and happiness. In one experiment, mildly depressed college women were randomly placed in a 10-week program of aerobic exercise (1 hour, twice each week), a program of relaxation, or no treatment. The exercise group became less depressed over the course of the program, improving more than the relaxation group and the control group (McCann & Holmes, 1984). Subsequent studies have found that as little as 10 minutes of exercise at a time can yield a positive mood boost (Hanson, Stevens, & Coast, 2001).

The reasons for this positive effect are unclear. Researchers have suggested that the effect results from increases in the body's production of neurotransmitters such as serotonin, which can have a positive effect on mood (as discussed in Chapter 3) or to increases in the production of endorphins—the endogenous opioids discussed in Chapters 3 and 8 (Jacobs, 1994).

Beyond boosting positive mood, exercise also stands to keep you healthy into the future. Current U.S. government recommendations suggest that 30 minutes of moderately vigorous exercise per day will reduce the risk of chronic illness (Dietary Guidelines Advisory Committee, 2005). Perhaps the simplest thing you can do to improve your happiness and health, then, is to regularly participate in an aerobic activity. Pick something you find fun: Sign up for a dance class, get into a regular basketball game, or start paddling a canoe—anything that will keep you coming back for more. If all else fails, park the car, get out a big foam rubber bat, and chase down the next bouncy jogger you see.

● **What are the benefits of exercise?**

Situation Management

After you have tried to manage stress by managing your mind and managing your body, what's left to manage? Look around and you'll notice a whole world out there. Perhaps that could be managed as well. Situation management involves changing your life situation as a way of reducing the impact of stress on your mind and body. Ways to manage your situation can include seeking out social support and finding a place for humor in your life.

Social Support

The wisdom of the National Safety Council's first rule—"Always swim with a buddy"—is obvious when you're in water over your head, but people often don't realize that the same principle applies whenever danger threatens. Other people can offer help in times of stress. **Social support** is *aid gained through interacting with others.* One of the more self-defeating things you can do in life is to fail to connect to people in this way. Just failing to get married, for example, is bad for your health. Unmarried individuals have an elevated risk of mortality from cardiovascular disease, cancer, pneumonia and influenza, chronic obstructive pulmonary disease, and liver disease and cirrhosis

social support The aid gained through interacting with others.

(Johnson et al., 2000). More generally, good ongoing relationships with friends and family and participation in social activities and religious groups can be as healthy for you as exercising and avoiding smoking (House, Landis, & Umberson, 1988).

Social support is helpful on many levels:

- An intimate partner can help you remember to get your exercise and follow your doctor's orders, and together you'll probably follow a more healthy diet than you would all alone with your snacks.

- Talking about problems with friends and family can offer many of the benefits of professional psychotherapy, usually without the hourly fees.

- Sharing tasks and helping each other when times get tough can reduce the amount of work and worry in each other's lives.

The helpfulness of strong social bonds, though, transcends mere convenience. Lonely people are more likely than others to be stressed and depressed (Baumeister & Leary, 1995), and they can be more susceptible to illness because of lower-than-normal levels of immune functioning (Kiecolt-Glaser et al., 1984).

Many first-year college students experience something of a crisis of social support. No matter how outgoing and popular they were in high school, newcomers typically find the task of developing satisfying new social relationships quite daunting. New friendships can seem shallow, connections with teachers may be perfunctory and even threatening, and social groups that are encountered can seem like islands of lost souls ("Hey, we're forming a club to investigate the lack of clubs on campus—want to join?"). Not surprisingly, research shows that students reporting the greatest feelings of isolation also show reduced immune responses to flu vaccinations (Pressman et al., 2005). Time spent getting to know people in new social situations can be an investment in your own health.

● **Why is the hormone oxytocin a health advantage for women?**

The value of social support in protecting against stress may be very different for women and men: Whereas women seek support under stress, men do not. The fight-or-flight response to stress may be largely a male reaction, according to research on sex differences by Shelley Taylor (2002). Taylor suggests that the female response to stress is to *tend-and-befriend* by taking care of people and bringing them together. Like males, human females respond to stressors with sympathetic nervous system arousal and the release of epinephrine and norepinephrine; but unlike males, they also release the hormone *oxytocin*, a hormone secreted by the pituitary gland in pregnant and nursing mothers. In the presence of estrogen, oxytocin triggers social responses—a tendency to seek out social contacts, nurture others, and create and maintain cooperative groups. After a hard day at work, a man may come home frustrated and worried about his job and end up drinking a beer and fuming alone. A woman under the same type of stress may instead play with her kids or talk to friends on the phone. The tend-and-befriend response to stress may help to explain why women are healthier and have a longer life span than do men. The typical male response amplifies the unhealthy effects of stress, whereas the female response takes a lesser toll on her mind and body—and provides social support for the people around her as well.

Humor

Wouldn't it be nice to laugh at your troubles and move on? Most of us recognize that humor can diffuse unpleasant situations and bad feelings, and it makes sense that bringing some fun into your life could help to reduce stress. The extreme point of view on

There's really no need for escape; getting married can often be good for your health.

BURKE/TRIOLO PRODUCTIONS/GETTY IMAGES

"I don't think it's anything serious."

PERCIVAL/CARTOONSTOCK.COM

this topic is staked out in self-help books with titles such as *Health, Healing, and the Amuse System* and *How Serious Is This? Seeing Humor in Daily Stress.* Is laughter truly the best medicine? Should we close down the hospitals and send in the clowns?

There is a kernel of truth to the theory that humor can help us cope with stress. For example, humor can reduce sensitivity to pain and distress, as researchers found when they subjected volunteers to an overinflated blood pressure cuff. Participants were more tolerant of the pain during a laughter-inducing comedy audiotape than during a neutral tape or instructed relaxation (Cogan et al., 1987).

● **How does humor mitigate stress?**

Humor can also reduce the time needed to calm down after a stressful event. For example, men viewing a highly stressful film about three industrial accidents were asked to narrate the film aloud either by describing the events seriously or by making their commentary as funny as possible. Although men in both groups reported feeling tense while watching the film and showed increased levels of sympathetic nervous arousal (increased heart rate and skin conductance, decreased skin temperature), those looking for humor in the experience bounced back to normal arousal levels more quickly than did those in the serious-story group (Newman & Stone, 1996).

summary quiz [14.3]

8. Avoiding situations or thoughts that are reminders of a stressor, and maintaining an artificially positive viewpoint, is called
   a. rational coping.
   b. repressive coping.
   c. reframing.
   d. situation management.

9. If you experience anxiety at the thought of public speaking, a recommended technique is to picture the audience sitting there with no clothes on. This is an example of
   a. rational coping.
   b. repressive coping.
   c. reframing.
   d. situation management.

10. According to the research of Shelley Taylor, a woman is *least* likely to respond to stress by doing which of the following?
   a. taking a long drive by herself
   b. playing with her child
   c. talking to a friend on the phone
   d. visiting an elderly relative

11. A hormone that appears to be involved in the tend-and-befriend response to stress is
   a. serotonin.
   b. dopamine.
   c. epinephrine.
   d. oxytocin.

The Psychology of Illness: When It's in Your Head

One of the mind's main influences on the body's health and illness is the mind's sensitivity to bodily symptoms. No doubt Mr. X, the poor victim of "voodoo death" discussed at the beginning of this chapter, had his attention radically reoriented toward his body by his mother's repeated warning that something bad would happen. This sensitivity may have then amplified his fear of dying and so aggravated his asthma. Noticing what is wrong with the body can be helpful when it motivates a search for treatment, but sensitivity can also lead to further problems when it snowballs into a preoccupation with illness that itself can cause harm.

Recognizing Illness and Seeking Treatment

You probably weren't thinking about your breathing a minute ago, but now that you're reading this sentence, you notice it. Sometimes we are very attentive to our bodies. At other times, the body seems to be on "automatic," running along unnoticed until specific symptoms announce themselves or are pointed out by an annoying textbook writer.

Directing attention toward the body or away from it can influence the symptoms we perceive. When people are bored, for example, they have more attention available to direct toward their bodies and so focus more on physical symptoms. Pennebaker (1980) audiotaped classrooms and found that people are more likely to cough when someone else has just coughed—but that such psychological contagion is much more likely at boring points in a lecture. Interestingly, coughing is not something people do on purpose (as Pennebaker found when he recorded clusters of coughs among sleeping firefighters). Thus, awareness and occurrence of physical symptoms can be influenced by psychological factors beyond our control.

Headache, as envisioned by caricaturist George Cruikshank (1792–1878).

People differ substantially in the degree to which they attend to and report bodily symptoms. People who report many physical symptoms tend to be negative in other ways as well—describing themselves as anxious, depressed, and under stress (Watson & Pennebaker, 1989). Do people with many symptom complaints truly have a lot of problems or are they just high-volume complainers? To answer this question, researchers used fMRI brain scans to compare severity of reported symptoms with degree of activation in brain areas usually associated with pain experience. Volunteers underwent several applications of a thermal stimulus (of 110° to 120° F) to the leg, and, as you might expect, some of the participants found it more painful than did others. Scans during the painful events revealed that the anterior cingulate cortex, somatosensory cortex, and prefrontal cortex (areas known to respond to painful body stimulation) were particularly active in those participants who reported higher levels of pain experience. Because other brain areas sensitive to pain such as the thalamus were not particularly active (see **FIGURE 14.5**), the researchers concluded that more reporting of pain is suggestive of greater activation but only of some of the brain areas linked with pain (Coghill, McHaffie, & Yen, 2003; see the Hot Science box on page 447).

● **What is the relationship between pain and activity in the brain?**

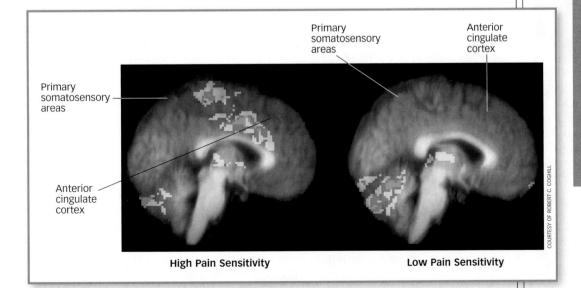

High Pain Sensitivity   **Low Pain Sensitivity**

Primary somatosensory areas

Anterior cingulate cortex

Primary somatosensory areas

Anterior cingulate cortex

FIGURE 14.5 ● ● ● ● ● ● ● ● ● ● ● ● ● ● ●
The Brain in Pain *fMRI scans of brain activation in high- (left) and low-pain-sensitive (right) individuals during painful stimulation. The anterior cingulate cortex and primary somatosensory areas show greater activation in high-pain-sensitive individuals. Levels of activation are highest in yellow and red, then light blue and dark blue (Coghill, McHaffie, & Yen, 2003).*

"Instead of an expensive, invasive procedure, we've decided to beat it out of you."

In contrast to complainers are those who underreport symptoms and pain or ignore or deny the possibility that they are sick. Insensitivity to symptoms comes with costs: It can delay the search for treatment, sometimes with serious repercussions. Of 2,404 patients in one study who had been treated for a heart attack, 40% had delayed going to the hospital for over 6 hours from the time they first noticed suspicious symptoms (Gurwitz et al., 1997). Severe chest pain or a history of prior heart surgery did send people to the hospital in a hurry. Those with more subtle symptoms often waited around for hours, however, not calling an ambulance or their doctor, just hoping the problem would go away—which was not a good idea because many of the treatments that can reduce the damage of a heart attack are most useful when provided early. When it comes to your own health, protecting your mind from distress through the denial of illness is a mindbug that can result in exposing your body to great danger.

Somatoform Disorders

The flip side of denial is excessive sensitivity to illness, and it turns out that sensitivity also has its perils. Indeed, hypersensitivity to symptoms or to the possibility of illness is a mindbug that underlies a variety of psychological problems and can also undermine physical health. Psychologists studying **psychosomatic illness,** *an interaction between mind and body that can produce illness,* explore ways in which mind (psyche) can influence body (soma) and vice versa. The study of mind-body interactions focuses on psychological disorders called **somatoform disorders,** in which *the patient displays physical symptoms not fully explained by a general medical condition.*

● **How can hypersensitivity to symptoms undermine health?**

The best-known somatoform disorder is **hypochondriasis,** *a psychological disorder in which a person is preoccupied with minor symptoms and develops an exaggerated belief that the symptoms signify a life-threatening illness.* You may know people who constantly worry about their health, and these poor souls can mentally turn every cough into tuberculosis and every headache into a brain tumor. It is said that fairy-tale author Hans Christian Andersen (1805–1875) was a hypochondriac, talking about his ailments and their possible meaning with anyone who would listen. It is also said that he had a morbid fear of being buried alive and placed a note by his bed each night as he slept explaining, "I only *appear* to be dead." For a hypochondriac, the tendency to catastrophize symptoms by imagining their worst-possible interpretation can become a chronic source of anxiety.

Somatoform disorders fascinated Sigmund Freud and other physicians early in the history of psychology because they demonstrated that the mind could produce physical illnesses without any physiological cause. Current theories focus on the idea that such symptoms occur as a result of breakdowns in the psychological processes underlying voluntary movement and attention (Hallett et al., 2005).

● *Is sickness a role we play? Michael Jackson's life was tragic, a story of amazing talent, personal eccentricity, and untimely death played out in the public eye. In the midst of a trial for child molestation, of which he was acquitted, he complained of severe back pain. Although the facts are still unclear, his use of illness to procure benefits—including painkilling drugs—may have played a role in his demise.*

On Being a Patient

Getting sick is more than a change in physical state; it can involve a transformation of identity. This change can be particularly profound with a serious illness: A kind of cloud settles over you, a feeling that you are now different, and this transformation can influence everything you feel and do in this new world of illness. You even take on a new role in life: a **sick role**—*a socially recognized set of rights and obligations linked with illness.* The sick person is absolved of responsibility for many everyday obligations and enjoys exemption from normal activities. For example, in addition to skipping school and homework and staying on the couch all day, a sick child can watch TV and avoid eating

[HOT SCIENCE]

Why Sickness Feels Bad: Psychological Effects of Immune Response

Why does it feel so bad to be sick? You notice scratchiness in your throat or the start of sniffles, and you think you might be coming down with something. And in just a few short hours, you're achy all over, energy gone, no appetite, feverish, feeling dull and listless. You're sick. The question is, why does it have to be like this? Why couldn't it feel good? As long as you're going to have to stay at home and miss out on things anyway, couldn't sickness be less of a pain?

Sickness makes you miserable for good reason. Misery is part of the *sickness response,* a coordinated, adaptive set of reactions to illness organized by the brain (Hart, 1988; Maier & Watkins, 1998; Watkins & Maier, 2005). Feeling sick keeps you home, where you'll spread germs to fewer people. More importantly, the sickness response makes you withdraw from activity and lie still, conserving the energy for fighting illness that you'd normally expend on other behavior. Appetite loss is similarly helpful: The energy spent on digestion is conserved. Thus, the behavioral changes that accompany illness are not random side effects; they help the body fight disease.

How does the brain know it should do this? The immune response to an infection begins with one of the components of the immune response, the activation of white blood cells that "eat" microbes, and also release *cytokines,* proteins that circulate through the body and communicate among the other white blood cells—and also communicate the sickness response to the brain (Maier & Watkins, 1998). Administration of cytokines to an animal can artificially create the sickness response, and administration of drugs that oppose the action of cytokines can block the sickness response even during an ongoing infection. Cytokines do not enter the brain, but they activate the vagus nerve that runs from the intestines, stomach, and chest to the brain and induce the "I am infected" message (Goehler et al., 2000). Perhaps this is why we often feel sickness in the "gut," a gnawing discomfort in the very center of the body.

Interestingly, the sickness response can be prompted without any infection at all—merely by the introduction of stress. The stressful presence of a predator's odor, for instance, can produce the sickness response of lethargy in an animal—along with symptoms of infection such as fever and increased white blood cell count (Maier & Watkins, 2000). In humans, the connection between sickness response, immune reaction, and stress is illustrated in depression, a condition in which all the sickness machinery runs at full speed. So in addition to fatigue and malaise, depressed people show signs characteristic of infection, including high levels of cytokines circulating in the blood (Maes, 1995).

Just as illness can make you feel a bit depressed, severe depression seems to recruit the brain's sickness response and make you feel ill (Watkins & Maier, 2005).

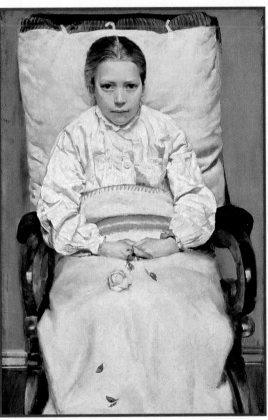

Sickness not only feels bad but it also shows. The pain of being ill has an emotional wallop like mild depression.

SICK GIRL, BY CHRISTIAN KROHG/NASJONALGALLERIET, OSLO, NORWAY/THE BRIDGEMAN ART LIBRARY

---

anything unpleasant at dinner. At the extreme, the sick person can get away with being rude, lazy, demanding, and picky. In return for these exemptions, the sick role also incurs obligations. The properly "sick" individual cannot appear to enjoy the illness or reveal signs of wanting to be sick and must also take care to pursue treatment to end this "undesirable" condition.

● **What benefits might come from being ill?**

Some people feign medical or psychological symptoms to achieve something they want, a type of behavior called *malingering.* Because many symptoms of illness cannot be faked—even facial expressions of pain are difficult to simulate (Williams, 2002)—malingering is possible only with a restricted number of illnesses. Faking illness is suspected when the secondary gains of illness—such as the ability to rest, to be freed from performing unpleasant tasks, or to be helped by others—outweigh the costs. Such gains can be very subtle, as when a child

psychosomatic illness An interaction between mind and body that can produce illness.

somatoform disorders The set of psychological disorders in which the person displays physical symptoms not fully explained by a general medical condition.

hypochondriasis A psychological disorder in which a person is preoccupied with minor symptoms and develops an exaggerated belief that the symptoms signify a life-threatening illness.

sick role A socially recognized set of rights and obligations linked with illness.

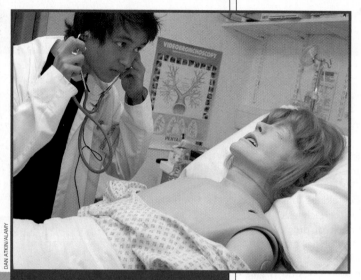

● Doctor and patient have two modes of interaction, the technical and the interpersonal. Medical training with robot patients may help doctors learn the technical side of health care, but it is likely to do little to improve the interpersonal side.

stays in bed because of the comfort provided by an otherwise distant parent, or they can be obvious, as when insurance benefits turn out to be a cash award for Best Actor. Some behaviors that may lead to illness may not be under the patient's control; for example, self-starvation may be part of an uncontrollable eating disorder. For this reason, malingering can be difficult to diagnose and treat (Feldman, 2004).

Patient-Practitioner Interaction

Medical care usually occurs through a strange interaction. On one side is a patient, often miserable, who expects to be questioned and examined and possibly prodded, pained, or given bad news. On the other side is a health care provider, who hopes to obtain useful information from the patient, help in some way, cope with the emotional part of the interaction, and achieve all of this as efficiently as possible because more patients are waiting. Seems less like a time for healing than an occasion for major awkwardness.

One of the keys to an effective medical care interaction is physician empathy (Spiro et al., 1994). To offer successful treatment, the physician must simultaneously understand the patient's physical state and psychological state. Physicians often err on the side of failing to acknowledge patients' emotions, focusing instead on technical issues of the case (Suchman et al., 1997). This is particularly unfortunate because a substantial percentage of patients who seek medical care do so for treatment of psychological and emotional problems (Taylor, 1986). As the Greek physician Hippocrates wrote in the fourth century BCE, "Some patients, though conscious that their condition is perilous, recover their health simply through their contentment with the goodness of the physician." The best physician treats the patient's mind as well as the patient's body.

● **Why is it important that a physician be empathic?**

Another important part of the medical care interaction is motivating the patient to follow the prescribed regimen of care (Cohen, 1979). When researchers check compliance by counting the pills remaining in a patient's bottle after a prescription has been under way, they find that patients often do an astonishingly poor job of following doctors' orders (see **FIGURE 14.6**). Compliance deteriorates when the treatment must be *frequent,* as when eyedrops for glaucoma are required every few hours, or *inconvenient* or *painful,* such as drawing blood or performing injections in managing diabetes. Finally, compliance decreases *as the number of treatments increases.* This is a worrisome problem especially for older patients, who may have difficulty remembering when to take which pill. Failures in medical care may stem from the failure of health care providers to recognize mindbugs in the psychological processes that are involved in self-care. Helping people to follow doctors' orders involves psychology, not medicine, and is an essential part of promoting health.

● **FIGURE 14.6**
Antacid Intake *A scatter plot of antacid intake measured by bottle count plotted against patient's stated intake for 116 patients. When the actual and stated intakes are the same, the point lies on the diagonal line; when stated intake is greater than actual, the point lies above the line. Most patients exaggerated their intake (Roth & Caron, 1978).*

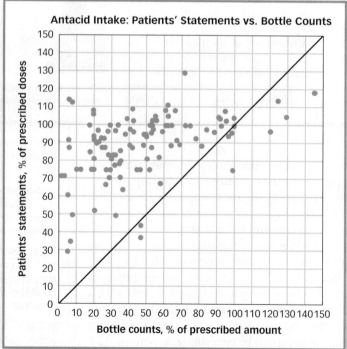

Antacid Intake: Patients' Statements vs. Bottle Counts

y-axis: Patients' statements, % of prescribed doses (0 to 150)
x-axis: Bottle counts, % of prescribed amount (0 to 150)

summary quiz [14.4]

12. A person who is preoccupied with minor symptoms and believes they signify a life-threatening illness is likely to be diagnosed with
 a. somatization disorder.
 b. hypochondriasis.
 c. posttraumatic stress disorder.
 d. repressive coping.

13. Some people pretend they are sick to achieve something they want. This behavior is called
 a. the sick role.
 b. Type B behavior.
 c. malingering.
 d. somatoform disorder.

14. The successful health care provider
 a. is empathic.
 b. must understand the patient's physical state and psychological state.
 c. must be time efficient because other patients are usually waiting.
 d. all of the above.

The Psychology of Health: Feeling Good

Two types of psychological factors influence personal health: health-relevant personality traits and health behavior. Personality can influence health through relatively enduring traits that make some people particularly susceptible to health problems or stress while sparing or protecting others. The Type A behavior pattern is an example. Because personality is not typically something we choose ("I'd like a bit of that sense of humor and extroversion over there, please, but hold the whininess"), this source of health can be outside personal control. In contrast, engaging in positive health behaviors is something anyone can do, at least in principle.

Personality and Health

Different health problems seem to plague different social groups. For example, men are more susceptible to heart disease than are women, and African Americans are more susceptible to asthma than are Asian or European Americans. Beyond these general social categories, personality turns out to be a factor in wellness, with individual differences in optimism and hardiness important influences.

Optimism

Pollyanna is one of literature's most famous optimists. Eleanor H. Porter's 1913 novel portrayed Pollyanna as a girl who greeted life with boundless good cheer even when she was orphaned and sent to live with her cruel aunt. Her response to a sunny day was to remark on the good weather, of course—but her response to a gloomy day was to point out how lucky it is that not every day is gloomy! Her crotchety Aunt Polly had exactly the opposite attitude, somehow managing to turn every happy moment into an opportunity for strict correction. A person's level of optimism or pessimism tends to be fairly stable over time, and research comparing the personalities of twins reared together versus those reared apart suggests that this stability arises because these traits are moderately heritable (Plomin et al., 1992). Perhaps Pollyanna and Aunt Polly were each "born that way."

An optimist who believes that "in uncertain times, I usually expect the best" is likely to be healthier than a pessimist who believes that "if something can go wrong for me, it will." In a study of 309 patients who had undergone coronary artery bypass surgery, for example, researchers found that initial levels of optimism were related to patients' postoperative health (Scheier et al., 1999). Patients with higher levels of overall optimism (not merely optimism about the particular surgery) were less likely than other patients after their surgery to need rehospitalization for complications such as infection, heart attacks, or further surgery.

Optimism seems to aid in the maintenance of psychological health in the face of physical health problems. When sick, optimists are more likely than pessimists to maintain positive emotions, avoid negative emotions such as anxiety and depression, stick to medical regimens their caregivers have prescribed, and keep up their relationships with others. Among women who have surgery for breast cancer, for example, optimists are less likely to experience distress and fatigue after treatment than are pessimists, largely because they keep up social contacts and recreational activities during their treatment (Carver, Lehman, & Antoni, 2003).

● **Who's healthier, the optimist or the pessimist? Why?**

The benefits of optimism raise an important question: If the traits of optimism and pessimism are stable over time—even resistant to change—can pessimists ever hope to gain any of the advantages of optimism (Heatherton & Weinberger, 1994)? Research has shown that even die-hard pessimists can be trained to become significantly more optimistic and that this training can improve their psychosocial health outcomes. For example, pessimistic breast cancer patients who received 10 weeks of training in stress management techniques became more optimistic and were less likely than those who received only relaxation exercises to suffer distress and fatigue during their cancer treatments (Antoni et al., 2001).

Hardiness

Some people seem to be thick-skinned, somehow able to take stress or abuse that could be devastating to others. Are there personality traits that contribute to such resilience and offer protection from stress-induced illness? To identify such traits, Suzanne Kobasa (1979) studied a group of stress-resistant business executives. These individuals reported high levels of stressful life events but had histories of relatively few illnesses compared with a similar group who succumbed to stress by getting sick. The stress-resistant group

● **What traits define *hardiness*?**

(Kobasa called them *hardy*) shared several traits, all conveniently beginning with the letter *C*. They showed a sense of *commitment,* an ability to become involved in life's tasks and encounters rather than just dabbling. They exhibited a belief in *control,* the expectation that their actions and words have a causal influence over their lives and environment. And they were willing to accept *challenge,* undertaking change and accepting opportunities for growth.

Can just anyone develop hardiness? Researchers have attempted to teach hardiness with some success. In one such attempt, participants attended 10 weekly "hardiness training" sessions, in which they were encouraged to examine their stresses, develop action plans for dealing with them, explore their bodily reactions to stress, and find ways to compensate for unchangeable situations without falling into self-pity. Compared with control groups (who engaged in relaxation and meditation training or in group discussions about stress), the hardiness-training group reported greater reductions in their perceived personal stress as well as fewer symptoms of illness (Maddi, Kahn, & Maddi, 1998). The long-term effect of such training is not clear, but the possibility that some of the traits may be within anyone's reach is encouraging.

Health-Promoting Behaviors and Self-regulation

Even without changing our personalities at all, we can do certain things to be healthy. The importance of healthy eating, safe sex, and giving up smoking are common knowledge. But we don't seem to be acting on the basis of this knowledge. At the turn of the

● *A club badge distributed to members of the Polly Anna Club in the United Kingdom, circa 1913.*

21st century, 21% of Americans are obese (Mokdad et al., 2003). The prevalence of unsafe sex is difficult to estimate, but 65 million Americans currently suffer from an incurable sexually transmitted disease (STD), while 15 million contract one or more new STDs each year (Centers for Disease Control, 2000b)—and another million live with human immunodeficiency virus/acquired immune deficiency syndrome (HIV/AIDS), which is usually contracted through unprotected sex with an infected partner (Centers for Disease Control, 2006). And despite endless warnings, 29.5% of Americans use tobacco on a regular basis (National Household Survey on Drug National Household Survey on Drug Abuse, 2001). What's going on?

Self-regulation

Doing what is good for you is not necessarily easy. Mark Twain once remarked, "The only way to keep your health is to eat what you don't want, drink what you don't like, and do what you'd druther not." Engaging in health-promoting behaviors involves **self-regulation**, *the exercise of voluntary control over the self to bring the self into line with preferred standards.* When you decide on a salad rather than a cheeseburger, for instance, you control your impulse and behave in a way that will help to make you the kind of person you would prefer to be—a healthy one. Self-regulation often involves putting off immediate gratification for longer-term gains, one of those life tasks that is so difficult it qualifies as a mindbug (see Chapter 8).

Self-regulation requires a kind of inner strength or willpower. One theory suggests that self-control is a kind of strength that can be fatigued (Schmeichel & Baumeister, 2004). In other words, trying to exercise control in one area may exhaust self-control, leaving behavior in other areas unregulated. To test this theory, researchers seated hungry volunteers near a batch of fresh, hot, chocolate chip cookies. They asked some participants to leave the cookies alone but help themselves to a healthy snack of radishes,

● **Why is it difficult to achieve and maintain self-control?**

whereas others were allowed to indulge. When later challenged with an impossibly difficult figure-tracing task, the self-control group was more likely than the self-indulgent group to abandon the difficult task—behavior interpreted as evidence that they had depleted their pool of self-control (Baumeister et al., 1998). The take-home message from this experiment is that to control behavior successfully, we need to choose our battles, exercising self-control mainly on the personal weaknesses that are most harmful to health.

Sometimes, though, self-regulation is less a matter of brute force than of strategy. Martial artists claim that anyone can easily overcome a large attacker with the use of the right moves, and overcoming our own unhealthy impulses may also be a matter of finesse. Let's look carefully at healthy approaches to some key challenges for self-regulation—eating, safe sex, and smoking—to learn what "smart moves" can aid us in our struggles.

Eating Wisely

In many Western cultures, the weight of the average citizen is increasing alarmingly. One explanation is based on our evolutionary history: In order to ensure their survival, our ancestors found it useful to eat well in times of plenty to store calories for leaner times. In postindustrial societies in the 21st century, however, there are no leaner times, and people can't burn all of the calories they consume (Pinel, Assanand, & Lehman, 2000). But why, then, isn't obesity endemic throughout the Western world? Why are people in France leaner on average than Americans even though their foods are high in fat? One reason has to do with average portion, which is far smaller in France than in the United States. Activity level in France is also greater. Research by Paul Rozin and his colleagues finds that the time people spend eating differs between cultures as well. At a McDonald's in France, meals take an average of 22 minutes, whereas in the United States, they take under 15 minutes (Rozin et al., 2003). Right now Americans seem to be involved in some kind of national eating contest.

Short of moving to France, what can you do? Studies indicate that dieting doesn't always work because the process of conscious self-regulation can be easily undermined by

JEAN SANDLER/FEATUREPICS

*Nobody ever said self-control was ● ● ● ● ● ● ● ● ● ● ● ●
easy. Probably the only reason you're
able to keep yourself from eating this
cookie is that it's just a picture of a
cookie. Really. Don't eat it.*

self-regulation The exercise of voluntary control over the self to bring the self into line with preferred standards.

Is eating a contest? Joey Chestnut, of San Jose, California, is on the way to eating 68 hot dogs to win his third consecutive world record on July 4, 2009. North American culture makes excessive eating almost a competition, but it's hard to find winners.

stress, leading people who are trying to control themselves to lose control by overindulging in the very behavior they had been trying to overcome. This may remind you of a general principle discussed in Chapter 8: Trying hard not to do something can often directly produce the unwanted behavior (Wegner, 1994a, 1994b).

The restraint problem may be inherent in the very act of self-control (Polivy & Herman, 1992). Rather than dieting, then, heading toward normal weight should involve a new emphasis on exercise and nutrition (Prochaska & Sallis, 2004). In emphasizing what is good to eat, the person can freely think about food rather than trying to suppress thoughts about it. A focus on increasing activity rather than reducing food intake, in turn, gives people another positive and active goal to pursue. Self-regulation is more effective when it focuses on what to do rather than on what not to do (Wegner & Wenzlaff, 1996).

● **Why is exercise a more effective weight loss choice than dieting?**

Avoiding Sexual Risks

People put themselves at risk when they have unprotected vaginal, oral, or anal intercourse with many sexual partners or with partners who themselves have many sexual partners, exhibit symptoms of STDs, are HIV positive, or are intravenous drug users. Sexually active adolescents and adults are usually aware of such risks, not to mention the risk of unwanted pregnancy, and yet many behave in risky ways nonetheless.

Why doesn't awareness translate into avoidance? Risk takers harbor an *illusion of unique invulnerability,* a systematic bias toward believing that they are less likely to fall victim to the problem than are others (Perloff & Fetzer, 1986). For example, a study of sexually active female college students found that respondents judged their own likelihood of getting pregnant in the next year as under 10% but estimated the average for other females at the university to be 27% (Burger & Burns, 1988). Paradoxically, this illusion was *even stronger* among women in the sample who reported using inadequate or no contraceptive techniques. The tendency to think, *It won't happen to me,* may be most pronounced when it probably will.

Risky sex is often the impulsive result of last-minute emotions. When thought is further blurred by alcohol or recreational drugs, people often fail to use the latex condoms that can reduce their exposure to the risks of pregnancy, HIV, and many other STDs. Like other forms of self-regulation, the avoidance of sexual risk requires the kind of planning that can be easily undone by circumstances that hamper the ability to think ahead. One approach to reducing sexual risk taking, then, is simply finding ways to help people plan ahead. Sex education programs offer adolescents just such a chance by encouraging them at a time when they have not had much sex experience to think about what they might do when they will need to make decisions. Although sex education is sometimes criticized as increasing adolescents' awareness of and interest in sex, the research evidence is clear: Sex education reduces the likelihood that adolescents will engage in unprotected sexual activity and benefits their health (American Psychological Association, 2005). The same holds true for adults.

● **Why does planning ahead reduce sexual risk taking?**

Not Smoking

One in two smokers dies prematurely from smoking-related diseases such as lung cancer, heart disease, emphysema, and cancer of the mouth and throat. Lung cancer itself kills more people than any other form of cancer, and smoking causes 80% of lung cancers. Although the overall rate of smoking in the United States is declining, new smokers abound, and many can't seem to stop. College students are puffing away along with everyone else, with 28.5% of students currently smoking (Wechsler et al., 1998). In the face of all the devastating health consequences, why don't people quit?

Nicotine, the active ingredient in cigarettes, is addictive, and so smoking is difficult to stop once the habit is established (discussed in Chapter 8). As in other forms of self-regulation, the resolve to quit smoking is fragile and seems to break down under stress. In the months following 9/11, for example, cigarette sales jumped 13% in Massachusetts (Phillips, 2002). And for some time after quitting, ex-smokers remain sensitive to cues in the environment: Eating or drinking, a bad mood, anxiety, or just seeing someone else smoking is enough to make them want a cigarette (Shiffman et al., 1996). The good news is that the urge decreases and people become less likely to relapse the longer they've been away from nicotine.

Psychological programs and techniques to help people kick the habit include nicotine replacement systems such as gum and skin patches, counseling programs, and hypnosis—but these programs are not always successful. Trying

● **To quit smoking forever, how many times do you need to quit?**

again and again in different ways is apparently the best approach (Schachter, 1982). After all, to quit smoking forever, you only need to quit one more time than you start up. But like the self-regulation of eating and sexuality, the self-regulation of smoking can require effort and thought. The ancient Greeks blamed self-control problems on *akrasia*, or "weakness of will." Modern psychology focuses less on blaming a person's character for poor self-regulation and points instead toward the difficulty of the task. Keeping healthy by behaving in healthy ways is one of the great challenges of life.

Some people like to smoke because it enhances their overall "look."

IMAGESHOP/ALAMY

summary quiz [14.5]

15. When sick, optimists are more likely than pessimists to
    a. avoid people.
    b. not follow the medical regimens prescribed by caregivers.
    c. avoid negative emotions.
    d. experience stress and fatigue after treatment.

16. Which of the following traits are found in hardy individuals?
    a. tendency to avoid taking on challenging tasks
    b. spending considerable time in outdoor activities
    c. exhibiting a belief in their control over their lives and environments
    d. dealing with stress through rational coping

17. People are leaner in France than in the United States. One reason seems to be that
    a. French foods are much lower in fat.
    b. the French typically eat one very large meal per day, but very little else.
    c. the French eat much more quickly than Americans.
    d. the activity level in France is greater than in the United States.

18. Which is true of smoking and health?
    a. The overall rate of smoking in the United States is increasing.
    b. Lung cancer, which is strongly influenced by smoking, kills more people than any other form of cancer.
    c. One out of 10 smokers dies prematurely from smoking-related diseases.
    d. The percent of college students who currently smoke has dropped sharply, to about 10%.

WhereDoYouStand?

Consider Yourself Warned

Just 6 months after the terrorist attack of September 11, 2001, President George W. Bush created the Homeland Security Advisory System. This official gauge of the danger of a new attack provides color codes for "threat conditions" from low (green) through guarded (blue), elevated (yellow), high (orange), and severe (red). The Presidential Directive creating the system described it as a "comprehensive and effective means to disseminate information regarding the risk of terrorist acts to Federal, State, and local authorities and to the American people" (Office of the Press Secretary, 2002).

Since that time, the warning level has never been below yellow. Although it has been raised to red only once (and just for flights from the United Kingdom to the United States), it has been orange eight times. The higher threat conditions prompt warnings for citizens "to be vigilant, take notice of their surroundings, and report suspicious items or activities to local authorities immediately." These are probably good ideas no matter what the threat conditions, so it is unclear whether this warning system is a useful response to terrorist threat. Certainly, if the level is raised to red, people could

respond by avoiding travel or through other emergency actions that could protect them. But as long as the warning gauge merely wavers between yellow and orange, psychologist Philip Zimbardo argues, the system does nothing more than put citizens under constant stress (Zhang, 2004).

We are surrounded every day with silly warnings—the steam iron label that warns "Do not use while wearing clothing" or the matchbook that says "Warning: Contents may catch fire." Are there times when we warn ourselves needlessly? Should we limit warnings such as the Homeland Security Advisory System to a more specific function, only telling us when there is a known threat rather than triggering stress about vague possibilities? Or is ongoing warning about terrorism a good idea, something that keeps all of us on our toes? Should we always know how worried we should be? Where do you stand?

The Homeland Security Advisory System communicates U.S. government estimates of terrorist "threat conditions" on a color-coded scale.

··CHAPTER REVIEW

Summary

Sources of Stress: What Gets to You
- Stressors are events and threats that place specific demands on a person or threaten well-being.
- Sources of stress include major life events (even the happy ones), catastrophic events, and chronic hassles—some of which can be traced to an environment.
- Events are most stressful when we perceive that there is no way to control or deal with the challenge.

Stress Reactions: All Shook Up
- The body responds to stress with an initial fight-or-flight reaction, which activates the hypothalamus-pituitary-adrenal (HPA) axis and prepares the body to face the threat or run away from it. Chronic stress can overtax the body, causing susceptibility to infection, aging, tumors and organ damage, and death.
- The psychological response to stress can, if prolonged, lead to anxiety disorders such as PTSD or to burnout.

Stress Management: Dealing with It
- The management of stress involves strategies for influencing the mind, the body, and the situation.
- People try to manage their minds by trying to suppress stressful thoughts or avoid the situations that produce them, by rationally coping with the stressor, and by reframing.
- Body management strategies involve attempting to reduce stress symptoms through relaxation, biofeedback, and aerobic exercise.
- Overcoming stress by managing your situation can involve seeking out social support or attempting to find humor in stressful events.

The Psychology of Illness: When It's in Your Head
- The psychology of illness concerns how sensitivity to the body leads people to recognize illness and seek treatment.
- Somatoform disorders, such as hypochondriasis, can stem from too much sensitivity.

- The sick role is a set of rights and obligations linked with illness; some people fake illness in order to accrue those rights.
- Successful health care providers interact with their patients to understand both the physical state and the psychological state.

The Psychology of Health: Feeling Good
- The connection between mind and body can be revealed through the influences of personality and self-regulation of behavior on health.

- The personality traits of optimism and hardiness are associated with reduced risk for illnesses, perhaps because people with these traits can fend off stress.
- The self-regulation of behaviors such as eating, sexuality, and smoking is difficult for many people because self-regulation is easily disrupted by stress; strategies for maintaining self-control can pay off with significant improvements in health and quality of life.

Key Terms

stressors (p. 428)

stress (p. 428)

health psychology (p. 428)

chronic stressor (p. 430)

fight-or-flight response (p. 433)

general adaptation syndrome (GAS) (p. 433)

immune system (p. 434)

lymphocytes (p. 434)

Type A behavior pattern (p. 435)

posttraumatic stress disorder (PTSD) (p. 436)

burnout (p. 438)

repressive coping (p. 439)

rational coping (p. 439)

reframing (p. 440)

stress inoculation training (SIT) (p. 440)

relaxation therapy (p. 441)

relaxation response (p. 441)

biofeedback (p. 441)

social support (p. 442)

psychosomatic illness (p. 446)

somatoform disorders (p. 446)

hypochondriasis (p. 446)

sick role (p. 446)

self-regulation (p. 451)

Critical Thinking Questions

1. Review the events in the stress scale (**TABLE 14.1** on page 429), and evaluate which of them are something a person has control over and which are not. How does the potential for control of an event relate to the stress rating?

2. Have you ever experienced burnout? If so, what coping techniques worked for you? What are some of the characteristics of burnout that make it something that must be handled on a individual basis?

3. Have you ever ridden on public transportation sitting next to a person with a hacking cough? We are bombarded by

advertisements for medicines designed to suppress symptoms of illness, so we can keep going. Is staying home with a cold socially acceptable or considered malingering? How does this jibe with the concept of the "sick role," *a socially recognized set of rights and obligations linked with illness?*

4. One of the reasons given in the text for the fact that people in France are leaner than people in the United States is that the average fast-food meal in France is 22 minutes, while in the U.S. it's 15 minutes. How could the length of the average meal influence an individual's body weight?

Answers to Summary Quizzes

Summary Quiz 14.1
1. b; 2. a; 3. d

Summary Quiz 14.2
4. b; 5. c; 6. d; 7. a

Summary Quiz 14.3
8. b; 9. c; 10. a; 11. d

Summary Quiz 14.4
12. b; 13. c; 14. d

Summary Quiz 14.5
15. c; 16. c; 17. d; 18. b

Need more help? Additional resources are located at the book's free companion Web site at:
www.worthpublishers.com/schacterbriefle

Social Psychology

IN 1999, 16 MEN AND WOMEN VOLUNTEERED for one of the most unusual psychology experiments ever conducted. They agreed to leave their homes, their jobs, their families and friends and to be flown to an uninhabited island off the coast of Borneo, where they would be left to survive on their own. The rules of the experiment were simple: The volunteers would meet every few days and vote to evict one of them, and the last volunteer to remain would receive $1 million. One of the things that made this psychology experiment so unusual was that it was captured on film and broadcast as a national television show called *Survivor*.

The volunteers faced many challenges but none more daunting than each other. Indeed, for 13 weeks, television viewers watched a remarkable interpersonal drama unfold as each volunteer tried to avoid being eliminated by the others. Some volunteers tried to make themselves essential by becoming expert at construction or fishing; others tried to make themselves liked by telling jokes and helping others. In the very first week, coalitions began to form: The two Black volunteers agreed never to vote against each other, and the women agreed to vote against the men. But within a short time, the nature of these alliances began to shift as the volunteers formed new bonds based on personalities, abilities, and romantic attractions rather than ethnicity or gender. Finally, after 3 months of backstabbing, treachery, and mosquito bites, 51 million viewers watched as a 39-year-old corporate trainer named Richard Hatch won the prize by a single vote. ■

MONTY BRINTON / CBS/SHNS/PHOTOS/NEWSCOM

Study this chapter carefully. Richard Hatch earned a million dollars by knowing more about social psychology than anyone else on his island.

How did Mr. Hatch manage to be the last survivor? "The first hour on the island I stepped into my strategy and thought, 'I'm going to focus on how to establish an alliance with four people early on.' I spend a lot of time thinking about who people are and why they interact the way they do" (CBS, 2000).

Although you won't be receiving any money for your efforts, in this chapter, you too will spend time thinking about who people are and why they interact the way they do, because when stripped to its bare essentials, the game of life is not unlike the game of *Survivor*. People have many needs—for food and shelter, for love and meaning—and they satisfy those needs by harming each other and helping each other (*social behavior*); by influencing others to think, feel, and act in a particular way (*social influence*); and by figuring out what others are like and why they behave as they do (*social cognition*). As you will see, *social psychology*—the study of the causes and consequences of interpersonal behavior—is critical for understanding how our species has managed to become the ultimate survivor on this island we call Earth.

"Selective breeding has given me an aptitude for the law, but I still love fetching a dead duck out of freezing water."

Social Behavior: Interacting with People

On any given day, most of us interact with a wide variety of people—such as friends, coworkers, family members, and strangers—in a variety of contexts—such as work, school, commerce, and recreation. We confide, conflict, cajole, carouse, criticize, and collaborate. We make dates; we make friends; we make lunch; we make love. We marry each other, we murder each other, and we do just about everything in between. Indeed, social behavior is so diverse and multifaceted that one of the challenges facing the psychologists who wish to understand it is to find a single framework within which all of the many forms of social behavior can be organized and understood.

The theory of evolution by natural selection provides one such framework (Dawkins, 1976). As you learned in Chapter 3, parents pass along some of their genes to their children, who in turn pass along some of *their* genetic material to their children, and so on. It's convenient to think of ourselves as people who happen to have genes inside them, but the evolutionary perspective suggests that we are really vehicles for our genes and that much of our social behavior revolves around the two fundamental tasks of *survival* and *reproduction*.

Survival: The Struggle for Resources

For most animals, survival is a struggle because the resources that life requires—food, water, and shelter—are scarce. Human beings engage in social behaviors that range from hurting each other to helping each other. *Hurting* and *helping* are antonyms, so you might expect them to have little in common. But as you will see, these opposite forms of social behavior are often different solutions to the same problem of scarce resources.

Aggression

The simplest way to solve the problem of scarce resources is to take what you want and smack the stripes off of anyone who tries to stop you. **Aggression** is *behavior whose purpose is to harm another,* and a quick glance at the front page of the newspaper reveals that human beings are as capable of aggression as any other animal and better at it than most (Anderson & Bushman, 2002; Geen, 1998). Sometimes people engage in *premeditated aggression,* which occurs when people consciously decide to use aggression to achieve their goals. The bank robber who threatens a teller wants to be wealthier, the zealot who assassinates a politician wants the government to change its policies, and the fighter pilot who

● How does aggression increase the odds of survival?

aggression Behavior whose purpose is to harm another.

frustration-aggression principle A principle stating that people aggress when their goals are thwarted.

bombs an enemy wants his or her nation to win a war. Each of these individuals has a goal, and each inflicts harm in order to achieve it. However, this harm does not necessarily entail violence: Check forgers and computer hackers can aggress with the stroke of a pen or the stroke of a key. The idea that aggression can be a means to an end is captured by the **frustration-aggression principle**, which suggests that *people aggress when their goals are thwarted* (Berkowitz, 1989; Dollard et al., 1939). The robber's goal of having money is thwarted by the clerk who is standing in front of the cash register, and so the robber aggresses in order to eliminate that obstacle.

Aggression is a way of attaining a goal by harming others. The unknown robber on the left engaged in violence, which is just one of many ways to aggress. When Tyco CEO Dennis Kozlowski (right) defrauded shareholders and stole hundreds of millions of dollars, he aggressed without engaging in violence.

But the newspaper stories that make us shake our heads in disbelief are those that describe *impulsive aggression,* which occurs when people aggress spontaneously and without premeditation. Impulsive aggression is rarely about scarce resources. Studies of violent crime suggest that about a third of all murders begin with a quarrel over a trivial matter (Daly & Wilson, 1988), and the stabbings, beatings, lootings, and shootings that make headlines are not calculated attempts to achieve a goal. Rather, impulsive aggression is a response to an unpleasant internal state, such as frustration, anger, or pain (Berkowitz, 1990). When a laboratory rat is given a painful electric shock, it will attack anything in its cage, including other animals, stuffed dolls, or even tennis balls (Berkowitz, 1993). In the natural environment, the source of an animal's pain is often nearby, such as a predator or a bush full of prickly thorns, and thus impulsive aggression may have evolved as a way to eliminate sources of pain.

Some human aggression is also a response to an unpleasant internal state. For instance, when people feel hot and bothered, they tend to behave aggressively (Anderson, 1989; Anderson, Bushman, & Groom, 1997). The correlation between a city's average daytime temperature and its rate of violent crime is so strong that we can predict with confidence that if the average temperature in the United States were to increase by just 2 degrees Fahrenheit (which is what you should expect from global warming in your lifetime), we would observe about 50,000 more violent crimes per year (**FIGURE 15.1**). What's notable about these instances of impulsive aggression is that they are often directed toward people who are not responsible for the unpleasant state, and as such, they have little chance of alleviating it. Like a shocked rat that attacks the tennis ball in its cage, people who feel frustrated, hurt, or angry often aggress against others simply because they are nearby.

Not everyone aggresses when they are hot and bothered. So who does, and when and why? The single best predictor of impulsive aggression is gender (Wrangham & Peterson, 1997). Crimes such as assault, battery, and murder are almost exclusively perpetrated by men—and especially by young men—who were responsible for 97% of the same-sex murders in the United States, Britain, and Canada (Archer, 1994). Although most societies encourage males to be more aggressive than females, male aggressiveness is not merely the product of socialization. Many studies show that impulsive aggression is strongly correlated with the presence of testosterone, which is typically higher in men than in women (see Chapter 10), in young men than in older men, and in violent criminals than in nonviolent criminals (Dabbs et al., 1995).

● **Are men more aggressive than women?**

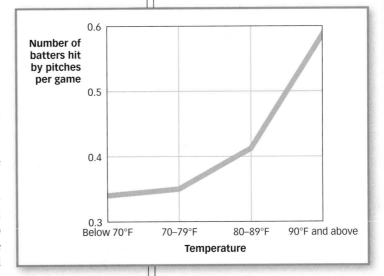

Number of batters hit by pitches per game

Temperature: Below 70°F | 70–79°F | 80–89°F | 90°F and above

FIGURE 15.1 ● ● ● ● ● ● ● ● ● ● ● ●
Temper and Temperature *Professional pitchers have awfully good aim, so when they hit batters with the baseball, it's safe to assume that it wasn't an accident. This figure shows the average number of batters who were hit by pitcher per game during the 1986–1988 major league baseball seasons. As you can see, the temperature on the field was highly correlated with the likelihood of being beaned.*

"What's amazing to me is that this late in the game we <u>still</u> have to settle our differences with rocks."

When men aggress, it is often in response to perceived challenges or threats—not to their lives or their resources, but to their dominance and their status. Indeed, three quarters of all murders can be classified as "status competitions" or "contests to save face" (Daly & Wilson, 1988). Contrary to popular wisdom, men with unrealistically *high* self-regard—and not *low* self-regard—are most prone to violence because such men are especially likely to perceive others' actions as a challenge to their inflated sense of their own status (Baumeister, Smart, & Boden, 1996).

Although women can be just as aggressive as men, their aggression tends to be more premeditated than impulsive and more likely to be focused on attaining or protecting a resource than on attaining or protecting their status. Women are *much* less likely than men to aggress without provocation or to aggress in ways that cause physical injury, but they are only *slightly* less likely than men to aggress when provoked or to aggress in ways that cause psychological injury (Bettencourt & Miller, 1996; Eagly & Steffen, 1986). Indeed, women may even be *more* likely than men to aggress by causing social harm—for example, by ostracizing others or by spreading malicious rumors about them (Crick & Grotpeter, 1995).

Cooperation

Physical prowess may enable individuals to win conflicts over resources, but when individuals work together, they can often attain more resources for themselves than either could have attained alone. **Cooperation** is *behavior by two or more individuals that leads to mutual benefit* (Deutsch, 1949; Pruitt, 1998), and it is one of our species' greatest achievements—right up there with language, fire, and opposable thumbs (Axelrod, 1984; Axelrod & Hamilton, 1981). Every roadway and supermarket, every television and compact disc, every ballet and surgery is the result of cooperation, and it is difficult to think of an important human achievement that could have occurred without it.

If the benefits of cooperation are plentiful and clear, then why don't people cooperate all the time? The answer is that cooperation is *risky*, as a simple game called *the prisoner's dilemma* illustrates. Imagine that you and your friend have been arrested for bank robbery and are being interrogated separately. The detectives tell you that if you and your friend both confess, you'll each get 10 years in prison, and if you both refuse to confess, you'll each get 1 year in prison. However, if one of you confesses and the other doesn't, then the one who confesses will go free and the one who doesn't confess will be put away for 30 years. What should you do? If you study **FIGURE 15.2**, you'll see that you and your friend would be wise to cooperate. If you trust your friend and refuse to confess and if your friend trusts you and does the same, then you will both get a light sentence. But if you refuse to confess and your friend betrays you by confessing, then your friend gets to go home and wash his car while you spend the next few decades making license plates.

● **What are the risks of cooperating?**

	COOPERATION (B does not confess)	NONCOOPERATION (B confesses)
COOPERATION (A does not confess)	A gets 1 year B gets 1 year	A gets 30 years B gets 0 years
NONCOOPERATION (A confesses)	A gets 0 years B gets 30 years	A gets 10 years B gets 10 years

● ● ● ● **FIGURE 15.2**
The Prisoner's Dilemma Game *The prisoner's dilemma game illustrates the benefits and costs of cooperation. Players A and B receive benefits whose size depends on whether they independently decide to cooperate. Mutual cooperation leads to a relatively moderate benefit to both players, but if only one player cooperates, then the cooperator gets no benefit and the noncooperator gets a large benefit.*

The prisoner's dilemma is interesting because it mirrors the risks and benefits of cooperation in everyday life. For example, if everyone pays his or her taxes, then the tax rate stays low and everyone enjoys the benefits of sturdy bridges and first-rate museums. If no one pays taxes, then the bridges fall down and the museums shut their doors. There is clearly a *moderate* benefit to everyone if everyone pays taxes, but there is a *huge* benefit to the few noncooperators who don't pay taxes while everyone else does because they get to use the bridges and enjoy the museums while keeping their entire incomes. This dilemma makes it difficult for people to decide whether to pay taxes and risk being

cooperation Behavior by two or more individuals that leads to mutual benefit.

altruism Behavior that benefits another without benefiting oneself.

reciprocal altruism Behavior that benefits another with the expectation that those benefits will be returned in the future.

chumps or to cheat and risk having the bridges collapse and the museums shut down. If you are like most people, you would be perfectly willing to cooperate in this sort of dilemma but worry that others won't do the same. Indeed, even nonhuman primates object to being cheated by an experimenter. In one study, monkeys were willing to work for a slice of cucumber before—but not after—they saw the experimenter give another monkey a more delicious food for doing less work (Brosnan & DeWaal, 2003).

Altruism

When people cooperate, they can realize great benefits. But is cooperation always driven by self-interest? Although human beings and other animals appear to engage in **altruism**, which is *behavior that benefits another without benefiting oneself,* such behavior often benefits the apparent altruist in subtle ways. For example, birds and squirrels give "alarm calls" when they see a predator, which puts them at increased risk of being eaten but allows their fellow birds and squirrels to escape. Ants and bees spend their lives caring for the offspring of the queen rather than bearing offspring of their own. Although such behaviors may appear to be altruistic, they are actually self-interested because individuals who promote the survival of their relatives are promoting the survival of their own genes (Hamilton, 1964).

Not all cooperation takes place between closely related individuals. For example, male baboons will risk injury to help an unrelated baboon win a fight, and monkeys will spend time grooming unrelated monkeys when they could be looking out for themselves. Such behaviors may appear to be instances of noble generosity, but careful studies of primates have revealed that the individuals who perform such favors tend to receive favors in return. **Reciprocal altruism** is *behavior that benefits another with the expectation that those benefits will be returned in the future,* and despite the second word in its name, it isn't very altruistic at all (Trivers, 1972a). Indeed, reciprocal altruism is merely cooperation extended over long periods of time.

So what about people? Like other animals, people are generally willing to contribute to the benefit of others in direct proportion to their degree of relatedness (Burnstein, Crandall, & Kitayama, 1994). Unlike other animals, however, human beings are also willing to provide benefits to complete strangers who will never be able to return the favor (Batson, 2002). As the World Trade Center burned on the morning of September 11, 2001, civilians in sailboats headed *toward* the destruction rather than away from it, initiating the largest waterborne

● **Are human beings genuinely altruistic?**

evacuation in the history of the United States. As one observer remarked, "If you're out on the water in a pleasure craft and you see those buildings on fire, in a strictly rational sense you should head to New Jersey. Instead, people went into potential danger and rescued strangers. That's social" (Dreifus, 2003). Indeed, heroism may be uncommon but it is not unheard of, which is to say that human beings are clearly capable of genuine altruism. Some studies even suggest that we tend to underestimate just how altruistic most people really are (Miller & Ratner, 1998).

Groups

People benefit from cooperation, but how does cooperation ever get started in the first place? After all, cooperation requires that someone take an initial risk by benefiting an individual and *trusting* that that individual will someday repay the favor. Human beings have developed a remarkably inventive way to

Kevin Hart owns the Gator Motel in Fargo, Georgia, which he runs on an honor system: Guests arrive, stay as long as they like, and leave their payment on the dresser. If just a few people cheated, it would not affect the room rates, but if too many cheated, then prices would have to rise. How would you decide whether to pay or to cheat? Before answering this question, please notice the large dog.

Ground squirrels put themselves in danger when they warn others about predators, but those they warn share their genes, so the behavior is not truly altruistic. In contrast, Christine Karg-Palreiro anonymously donated her kidney to an unrelated individual in 2003 and later remarked, "If I had a spare, I'd do it again." The United Network for Organ Sharing reports that in the past 20 years, more than 100 people have made anonymous organ donations to strangers.

In 1935, Rubin Stacy was lynched by a mob of masked men after allegedly assaulting a White woman. What effect might wearing masks have on members of a mob?

Groups can lead people to feel deindividuated and hence less responsible for their actions. What are the chances that any of these individuals would stroll through the mall naked if they were alone?

group A collection of two or more people who believe they have something in common.

prejudice A positive or negative evaluation of another person based on his or her group membership.

discrimination Positive or negative behavior toward another person based on his or her group membership.

deindividuation A phenomenon that occurs when immersion in a group causes people to become less aware of their individual values.

minimize the risk of initial cooperation, and it is called the **group**, which is *a collection of two or more people who believe they have something in common.* Every one of us is a member of many such groups. We refer to the smaller ones as families and teams, and we refer to the larger ones as religions and nations.

Although there are profound differences between such groups, they all seem to have one thing in common: The people in them tend to display **prejudice**, which is *a positive or negative evaluation of another person based on his or her group membership,* and **discrimination**, which is *positive or negative behavior toward another person based on his or her group membership.* Specifically, people tend to be positively prejudiced toward members of their own groups, they tend to discriminate in favor of their own groups, and they tend to expect that their fellow group members will do the same for them in the future (see the Where Do You Stand? box on page 487 at the end of the chapter). Because people favor members of their own groups, group membership allows people to know in advance who is most and least likely to repay their efforts to cooperate, and this knowledge reduces the risks of cooperation.

It doesn't take much to create this kind of favoritism. In one set of studies, participants were shown abstract paintings by two artists and were then divided into two groups based on their preference for one artist or the other (Tajfel, 1970; Tajfel et al., 1971). When participants were subsequently asked to allocate money to other participants, they consistently allocated more money to those in their group (Brewer, 1979). Indeed, participants show positive prejudice and discrimination even when they are randomly assigned to completely meaningless groups such as "Group X" and "Group Y" (Hodson & Sorrentino, 2001; Locksley, Ortiz, & Hepburn, 1980). In other words, just knowing that "I'm one of *us* and not one of *them*" seems sufficient to produce this kind of favoritism.

Prejudice and discrimination may sound bad, but groups are capable of much worse things, such as riots, lynchings, gang rapes, and stampedes (Milgram & Toch, 1968). If we take death and destruction as our measure, then a group of humans is clearly among the most dangerous of all natural phenomena. Why do people in groups do dreadful things that they would never do alone? This is a particularly compelling mindbug: Law-abiding, rational individuals often behave differently when they start hanging around together in a group. There are at least three reasons for this:

● **How does being in a group change an individual's behavior?**

■ **Deindividuation** occurs *when immersion in a group causes people to become less aware of their individual values.* We all have urges and impulses that we hold in check. We may want to slap the guy who blasts his music on the elevator, grab the Rolex from the jeweler's window, or plant a kiss on the attractive stranger in the library, but we don't do these things because we have self-control and scruples. Research has shown that people are most likely to exert self-control and adhere to their scruples when their attention is focused on themselves (Wicklund, 1975); when people assemble in groups, their attention is naturally drawn to others and *away* from themselves, and thus they are less likely to abide by their own moral values (Mullen, 1986; Mullen, Chapman, & Peaugh, 1989; Wegner & Schaefer, 1978).

■ **Diffusion of responsibility** occurs when *individuals feel diminished responsibility for their actions because they are surrounded by others who are acting the same way.* For example, *social loafing* occurs when people expend less effort when in a group than alone. People applaud less loudly when they are in a large audience than a small one (Latané, Williams, & Harkins, 1979), and athletes exert less effort in team events than in solo events (Williams et al., 1989). People in groups leave worse tips at restaurants (Freeman et al., 1975), donate less money to charitable causes (Wiesenthal, Austrom, & Silverman, 1983), and are less likely to respond when someone says hello (Jones & Foshay, 1984).

- **Group polarization** is *the tendency for a group's initial leaning to get stronger over time* (Lamm & Myers, 1978). You might expect that mixing people who have one opinion with people who have the opposite opinion would lead a group to have a moderate view, but, in fact, mixing often makes everyone's initial position stronger. In addition, group leaders can be extraordinarily influential despite the fact that they are not necessarily well informed (Hollander, 1964). After a bit of group discussion, an initial opinion of "That's a pretty good idea" becomes "This is the greatest idea we've ever had!"

In the 1957 film **Twelve Angry Men**, a jury is prepared to convict an innocent teenager of murder until one lone juror bravely voices his disagreement and ultimately changes the other jurors' minds. Alas, it is all too rare for group members who hold minority opinions to change or even to try to change the decision of a group.

The misbehavior of groups is so well documented that we might wonder if people would be better off without them. Prob-

● **What do people gain from groups?**

ably not. One of the very best predictors of a person's general happiness and life satisfaction is the quality and extent of their social relationships and group memberships (Myers & Diener, 1995), and people who are excluded from groups are invariably anxious, lonely, depressed, and at increased risk for illness and premature death (Cacioppo, Hawkley, & Berntson, 2003; Cohen, 1988; Leary, 1990). Indeed, recent studies reveal that being excluded from a group activates areas of the brain that are normally activated by physical pain (**FIGURE 15.3**; Eisenberger,

Anterior cingulate cortex

Right ventral prefrontal cortex

(a)   (b)

FIGURE 15.3 ● ● ● ● ● ● ● ● ● ● ● ● ● ● ● ● ● ● ●
A recent study revealed that when people are excluded from a social group, (a) the anterior cingulate cortex (ACC) and (b) the right ventral prefrontal cortex (RVPC) become active. Interestingly, the ACC is commonly associated with the experience of physical pain and the RVPC is commonly associated with pain relief. Apparently, social exclusion causes people to feel pain and to make an effort to diminish it.
Eisenberger, N. I., Lieberman, M. D., & Williams, K. D. (2003). Science, 302, 290–292.

Lieberman, & Williams, 2003). Belonging is not just a source of psychological and physical well-being but also a source of identity (Tajfel & Turner, 1986), which is why people typically describe themselves by listing the groups of which they are members ("I'm a Canadian, an architect, and a mother of two"). Groups are a way to lower the risks of cooperation and increase the odds of survival, but they are more than that. We are not merely *in* our groups: We *are* our groups.

Reproduction: The Quest for Immortality

Survival matters. But from an evolutionary point of view, survival only matters because it is a prerequisite for reproduction. A vehicle for genes must stay alive in order to build the next vehicle, so it is not surprising that our urge to reproduce—which involves everything from having sex to raising children—is every bit as strong as our urge to stay alive. Indeed, a great deal of our social behavior can be understood in terms of our basic reproductive drive (Buss & Kenrick, 1998).

diffusion of responsibility The tendency for individuals to feel diminished responsibility for their actions when they are surrounded by others who are acting the same way.

group polarization The tendency for a group's initial leaning to get stronger over time.

Selectivity

Survival is the first step on the road to reproduction, but the second step involves finding someone of the opposite sex. You need only look around whatever room you are in to know that not just anyone will do. People *select* their reproductive and sexual partners, and perhaps the most striking fact about this selection is that women are more selective than men (Feingold, 1992a). In one study, an attractive person (who was working for the experimenters) approached an opposite-sex stranger on a college campus and asked one of two questions: "Would you go out tonight?" or "Would you go to bed with me?" About half of the men and women who were approached agreed to go out with the attractive person. Although *none* of the women agreed to go to bed with the person, *three quarters* of the men did (Clark & Hatfield, 1989).

One explanation for this difference is that males and females have different reproductive biology (Buss & Schmitt, 1993; Trivers, 1972b). Men produce billions of sperm in their lifetimes, their ability to conceive a child tomorrow is not inhibited by having conceived one today, and conception has no significant physical costs. In contrast, women produce a small number of eggs in their lifetimes, conception eliminates their ability to conceive again for at least 9 more months,

> ● **What makes women the choosier sex?**

and pregnancy produces physical changes that increase their nutritional requirements and put them at risk of illness and death. Therefore, if a man makes an "evolutionary mistake" by mating with a woman whose genes do not produce healthy offspring or who won't do her part to raise them, he has lost nothing except a few sperm. But if a woman makes the same mistake by mating with a man whose genes do not produce healthy offspring or who won't do his part to raise them, she has lost a precious egg, borne the costs of pregnancy, risked her life in childbirth, and missed at least 9 months of other reproductive opportunities. Women are naturally more selective because reproduction is much more costly for women than for men.

Although reproductive biology makes sex a more expensive proposition for women than for men, it is important to note two things. First, women are more selective than men *on average,* but there is still tremendous variability *among* men and *among* women (Gangestad & Simpson, 2000). We've described the typical reproductive strategies of *most* women and men but certainly not the strategy of any particular woman or man. Second, like biology, social norms can also make sex differentially expensive for women and men and can thereby increase or decrease gender differences in selectivity (Eagly & Wood, 1999). For example, in cultures that glorify promiscuous men as *playboys* and disparage promiscuous women as *sluts,* women are likely to be much more selective than men because the reputational costs of sex are much higher. When cultures lower the costs of sex for women by providing access to effective birth control, by promoting the financial independence of women, or by adopting communal styles of child rearing, women do indeed become less selective (Kasser & Sharma, 1999). Similarly, when sex is expensive for men—for example, when they are choosing a long-term mate for a monogamous relationship rather than a short-term mate for a weekend in Vermont—they can be every bit as selective as women (Kenrick et al., 1990). Our basic biology generally makes sex a more expensive proposition for women than for men, but social forces can exaggerate, equalize, or reverse those costs. The higher the costs, the greater the selectivity.

Attraction

For most of us, there are a very small number of people with whom we are willing to have sex, an even smaller number of people with whom we are willing to have children, and a staggeringly large number of people with whom we are unwilling to have either. So when we meet someone new, how do we decide which of these categories that person belongs in? Many things go into choosing a date, a lover, or a partner for life, but perhaps none is more important than the simple feeling we call *attraction* (Berscheid & Reiss, 1998). Research suggests that attraction is caused by a wide range of factors that

If men could become pregnant, how might their behavior change? Among seahorses, it is the male that carries the young, and not coincidentally, males are more selective than are females.

DR. PAUL ZAHL/PHOTO RESEARCHERS

CREATAS/JUPITER IMAGES

mere exposure effect The tendency for liking to increase with the frequency of exposure.

can be roughly divided into the situational, the physical, and the psychological.

Situational factors. One of the best predictors of any kind of interpersonal relationship is the physical proximity of the people involved (Nahemow & Lawton, 1975). For example, in one study, students who had been randomly assigned to university housing were asked to name their three closest friends; nearly half named their next-door neighbor (Festinger, Schachter, & Back, 1950). Proximity provides not only the opportunity for attraction but also the motivation. People naturally work hard to like those with whom they expect to have social interactions (Darley & Berscheid, 1967). When new neighbors move into the apartment next door, you know your day-to-day existence will be better if you like them than if you detest them, and so you make every effort to like them. In fact, the closer they live, the more effort you make.

Proximity provides something else as well. Every time we encounter a person, that person becomes a bit more familiar to us, and people—like other animals—generally prefer familiar to novel stimuli. *The tendency for liking to increase with the frequency of exposure* is called the **mere exposure effect** (Bornstein, 1989; Zajonc, 1968). For instance, in some experiments, geometric shapes, faces, or alphabetical characters were flashed on a computer screen so quickly that participants were unaware of

● **Why do people generally like their neighbors?**

having seen them. These participants were then shown some of the "old" stimuli that had been flashed across the screen as well as some "new" stimuli that had not. Although they could not reliably tell which stimuli were old and which were new, participants tended to *like* the old stimuli better than the new ones (Monahan, Murphy, & Zajonc, 2000). In other words, the mere act of being exposed to some things (rather than others) in the environment led to increased liking for those things.

Physical factors. Once people are in the same place at the same time, they can begin to learn about each other's personal qualities, and in most cases, the first quality they learn about is the other person's appearance. Research suggests that this influence is stronger than most of us might suspect. In one study, researchers arranged a dance for first-year university students and randomly assigned each student to an opposite-sex partner. Midway through the dance, the students confidentially reported how much they liked their partners, how attractive they thought their partners were, and how much

● **What is the role of beauty in attraction?**

they would like to see their partners again. The researchers measured many of the students' attributes—from their attitudes to their personalities—and they found that the partner's physical appearance was the *only* attribute that influenced the students' feelings of attraction (Walster et al., 1966). Field studies have revealed the same thing. For instance, one study found that a man's height and a woman's weight were among the best predictors of how many responses a personal ad received

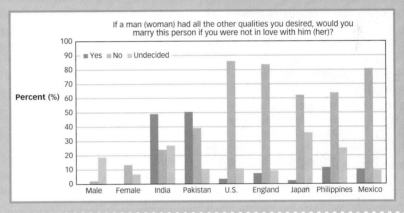

Culture & Community

Does Love = Marriage Around the World?

Would you marry someone you didn't love? When students from 11 different countries were asked this question (Levine et al., 1995), the majority of Pakistani students said yes and the majority of Americans said no. Although students from different cultures disagreed about whether love was necessary to get married, they tended to agree that it was not necessary to stay married. When asked whether a couple who fell out of love should get divorced, about a third of Pakistani and American students said yes. It appears that some ideas about the importance of romantic love are more universal than others.

If a man (woman) had all the other qualities you desired, would you marry this person if you were not in love with him (her)?

Chart: Percent (%) vs. categories (Male, Female, India, Pakistan, U.S., England, Japan, Philippines, Mexico) with legend: Yes, No, Undecided.

In 2003, actress Carol Channing (then 82) married the boy next door—her childhood sweetheart, Harry Kullijian (then 83). Research on proximity and attraction suggests that Carol and Harry had a good chance of ending up together, though in this case it seems to have taken a while.

The woman pictured here prefers the photograph on the right, but her husband prefers the one on the left. Why? The photograph on the left is printed normally and the one on the right is printed in reverse. Because we tend to see ourselves mostly in the mirror, reverse-printed photographs look to us more like the image we are used to seeing (Mita, Dermer, & Knight, 1977). Because of the mere exposure effect, people tend to favor reverse-printed photographs of themselves.

Research on how people misinterpret their arousal may help explain why Brandon Harding proposed marriage (and why Melani Dino said yes) right after they finished skydiving in Snohomish, Washington.

In a commercial for Pantene hair products, model Kelly LeBrock pleaded with viewers, "Don't hate me because I'm beautiful." Research on the power of physical attractiveness suggests that there was not much danger of that happening.

(Lynn & Shurgot, 1984), and another study found that physical attractiveness was the *only* factor that predicted the online dating choices of both women and men (Green, Buchanan, & Heuer, 1984).

Physical beauty is important in just about every interpersonal context (Etcoff, 1999; Langlois et al., 2000). Beautiful people have more friends, more dates, more sex, and more fun than the rest of us do (Curran & Lippold, 1975), and they can even expect to earn 10% more money over the course of their lives (Hamermesh & Biddle, 1994). People tend to believe that beautiful people have superior personal qualities (Dion, Berscheid, & Walster, 1972; Eagly et al., 1991), and in some cases they actually do. For instance, because beautiful people have more friends and more opportunities for social interaction, they tend to have better social skills than do less beautiful people (Feingold, 1992b). Beauty is so powerful that it even influences how mothers treat their own children: Mothers of attractive children are more affectionate and playful with their children compared to mothers of less attractive children (Langlois et al., 1995). It is interesting to note that although men and women are equally influenced by the beauty of their potential partners, men are more likely than women to acknowledge this fact (Feingold, 1990).

So it pays to be beautiful. But what exactly constitutes beauty? Although standards of beauty do indeed vary from person to person and culture to culture, many aspects of physical appearance seem to be universally appreciated or disdained (Cunningham et al., 1995). For example:

- Male bodies are considered most attractive when they approximate an *inverted triangle* (i.e., broad shoulders with a narrow waist and hips), and female bodies are considered most attractive when they approximate an *hourglass* (i.e., broad shoulders and hips with a narrow waist). In fact, the most attractive female body across many cultures seems to be the "perfect hourglass" in which the waist is precisely 70% the size of the hips (Singh, 1993).

- Human faces and human bodies are generally considered more attractive when they are *bilaterally symmetrical*—that is, when the left half is a mirror image of the right (Perrett et al., 1999).

- Characteristics such as large eyes, high eyebrows, and a small chin make people look *immature* or "baby-faced" (Berry & McArthur, 1985). As a general rule, female faces are considered more attractive when they have immature features, but male faces are considered more attractive when they have mature features (Cunningham, Barbee, & Pike, 1990; Zebrowitz & Montepare, 1992).

Is there any rhyme or reason to this list of scenic attractions? The evolutionary perspective suggests that we should be attracted to people who have the *genes* and the propensity for *parental behavior* that will enable our children to grow, prosper, and become parents themselves. In other words, the things we find attractive in others should be reasonably reliable indicators of their genetic qualities and parental tendencies. Are they?

- Testosterone causes male bodies to become "inverted triangles" just as estrogen causes female bodies to become "hourglasses." Men who are high in testosterone tend to be socially dominant and therefore have more resources to devote to their offspring, whereas women who are high in estrogen tend to be especially fertile and potentially have more offspring to make use of those resources.

- Asymmetrical features can be signs of genetic mutation, prenatal exposure to pathogens, or susceptibility to disease (Jones et al., 2001; Thornhill & Gangestad, 1993), so physical symmetry is an indicator of overall health.

- Younger women are generally more fertile than older women, whereas older men generally have more resources than younger men. Thus, a youthful appearance is a signal of a woman's ability to bear children, just as a mature appearance is a signal of a man's ability to raise them. Studies have shown that across a wide variety of human cultures women prefer older men and men prefer younger women (Buss, 1989).

Artists have been sculpting and painting the Three Graces for thousands of years, and the body types they depict show how standards of beauty change across time. Nonetheless, research suggests that even as the size of the ideal female changes across time, the ideal hip-to-waist ratio remains constant (Singh, 1993).

The evolutionary perspective suggests that the feeling we call *attraction* is simply our genes' way of telling us that we are in the presence of a person who has both the genes and the propensity toward parental behavior to make those genes immortal. It is no coincidence that people in different epochs and people in different cultures appreciate many of the same features in the opposite sex (see the Hot Science box on page 468).

[HOT SCIENCE]

Beautifully Average

If someone described you as "average-looking," you might not be insulted, but odds are that your mother would be furious. Tell Mom to relax. Psychologists have recently learned that when it comes to faces, average-looking is awfully hard to beat.

A face can be beautiful for many reasons, but research shows that faces are considered especially beautiful when their features approximate the average of the human population. In a clever series of studies, researchers digitized the photographs of many college students and then used a computer program to "morph" those faces together (Langlois & Roggman, 1990; Langlois, Roggman, & Musselman, 1994). Specifically, the program averaged the value of each pixel in the digitized photographs, producing a "composite face" that was the average of its components. The composite face and the component faces were then shown to participants, who rated the attractiveness of each. The participants tended to rate the composite as more attractive than the component faces. Interestingly, the more components that went into making a composite, the more attractive that composite was judged to be: The average of 100 faces is more attractive than the average of 10.

Why do people find averageness so attractive? Nature experiments with organisms by generating mutations and seeing which ones work. Some mutations prove so valuable that those who have them out-reproduce those who don't, and soon the entire species has the mutation too. But *most* of nature's experiments are failures, and most mutations are unimportant at best and harmful at worst. The mutations that make some people vulnerable to certain diseases are good examples. One reason why we are attracted to averageness might be that people who look like everyone else are unlikely to carry a mutant gene. If this speculation is true, then our preference for averageness shouldn't be something we have to learn. In fact, research shows that people in a variety of cultures prefer composites to components (Rhodes et al., 2001). Perhaps even more startling is the fact that newborn babies seem to have the same preference (Langlois, Roggman, & Rieser-Danner, 1990; Rubenstein, Kalakanis, & Langlois, 1999).

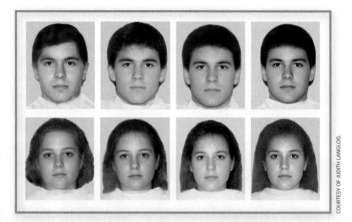

Most people find the composite faces more attractive when more faces are used to make the composite. From left to right, the faces above are composites of 4 faces, 8 faces, 16 faces, and 32 faces.
Langlois, J. H., & Roggman, L. A. (1990). Psychological Science, 1, 115-121.

Remember that averageness is just one of the many things we find attractive in a face, and it's not always the most important one. Many movie stars whom we would all consider extremely attractive have unusual facial features. Nonetheless, research shows that even if an average face isn't more attractive than every face, it's more attractive than most faces picked at random. In other words, tell Mom not to beat anyone up just yet.

Psychological factors. If attraction is all about big biceps and high cheekbones, then why don't we just skip the small talk and pick our mates from photographs? Physical attributes may determine who draws our attention and quickens our pulse, but after people begin interacting, they quickly go beyond appearances (Cramer, Schaefer, & Reid, 1996; Regan, 1998). People's *inner* qualities—personalities, points of view, attitudes, beliefs, values, ambitions, and abilities—play an important role in determining their sustained interest in each other, and there isn't much mystery about the kinds of inner qualities that people find most attractive. For example, intelligence, sense of humor, sensitivity, and ambition are high on just about everybody's list (Daniel et al., 1985).

● **What are the nonphysical attributes that determine attraction?**

Although we may be attracted to the person with the quickest wit and the highest IQ, research suggests that we typically interact with people whose standing on these dimensions is roughly *similar* to our own (Byrne, Ervin, & Lamberth, 1970; Byrne & Nelson, 1965; Hatfield & Rapson, 1992; Neimeyer & Mitchell, 1988). We marry people with similar levels of education, religious backgrounds, ethnicities, socioeconomic statuses, and personalities (Botwin, Buss, & Shackelford, 1997; Buss, 1985; Caspi & Herbener, 1990), and some research even suggests that we are unusually likely to marry someone whose surname starts with the same letter of the alphabet that ours does (Jones et al., 2004).

Why is similarity so attractive? First, it's easy to interact with people who are similar to us because we can instantly agree on a wide range of issues, such as what to eat, where to live, how to raise children, and how to spend our money. Second, when someone shares our attitudes and beliefs, we feel a bit more confident that those attitudes and beliefs are correct (Byrne & Clore, 1970). Indeed, research shows that when the accuracy of a person's attitudes and beliefs is challenged, similarity becomes an even more important determinant of their attraction to others (Greenberg et al., 1990; Hirschberger, Florian, & Mikulincer, 2002). Third, if we like people who share our attitudes and beliefs, then we can reasonably expect them to like us for the same reason—and *being* liked is a powerful source of attraction (Aronson & Worchel, 1966; Backman & Secord, 1959; Condon & Crano, 1988).

Relationships

Selecting an attractive mate is the beginning of the reproductive process, but the real work consists of bearing and raising children. For human beings, that work is ordinarily done in the context of committed, long-term, romantic relationships such as a marriage. Only a few animals have relationships of this kind, so why are we among them? The an-

● **What are the survival benefits of long-term relationships?**

swer is that we're born too soon. Human beings have large heads to house their large brains, and thus a fully developed human infant could not pass through its mother's birth canal. As such, human infants are *born before they are fully developed* and thus need a great deal of care—often more than one parent can provide. If human infants were more like tadpoles—ready at birth to swim, find food, and escape predators—then their parents might not need to form and maintain relationships. But human infants are remarkably helpless creatures that require years of intense care before they can fend for themselves, and so human adults do almost all of their reproducing in the context of committed, long-term relationships. (By the way, some baby birds also require more food than one adult caretaker can provide, and the adults of those species also tend to form long-term relationships.)

About 90% of Americans marry, and about 80% of those who divorce marry a second time (Norton, 1987). How do we decide whom to marry? The evolutionary perspective suggests that marriage is all about making and raising babies, but if you're like most people, *you* think that marriage is all about love. So you may be surprised to learn that love-based marriage is a rather recent invention (Brehm, 1992; Fisher, 1993; Hunt, 1959). Throughout history and across cultures, marriage has traditionally served a variety of economic (and decidedly unromantic) functions, ranging from cementing agreements between clans to paying back debts. Ancient Greeks and Romans married, but they considered love a form of madness. Twelfth-century Europeans married but thought of love as a game to be played by knights and ladies of the court (who happened to be

After the 1992 presidential election, Bill Clinton's chief strategist, James Carville, married George H. W. Bush's chief strategist, Mary Matalin. Despite the occasional odd couple, most people are attracted to those with similar attitudes and beliefs. Perhaps this couple's shared passion for politics outweighed their party affiliations.

Are people more like cattle or robins? In most ways, we are more like any mammal than we are like any bird, but songbirds and people do share one thing that cattle don't: Their young are helpless at birth and thus require significant parental care. Interestingly, adult robins and adult human beings (but not adult cattle) have enduring relationships. And sing.

social exchange The hypothesis that people remain in relationships only as long as they perceive a favorable ratio of costs to benefits.

equity A state of affairs in which the cost-benefit ratios of two partners are roughly equal.

married, but not to the knights). Indeed, it wasn't until the 17th century that Westerners began seriously considering the possibility that love might actually be a *reason* to get married.

But is it? Most people who get married expect to stay married, and in this respect, most people are wrong. About 65% of marriages in the United States end in permanent separation or divorce (Castro-Martin & Bumpass, 1989). Although many reasons account for this (Gottman, 1994; Karney & Bradbury, 1995), one is that couples don't always have a clear understanding of what love is. Indeed, a language that uses the same word to describe the deepest forms of intimacy ("I love Emily") and the most shallow forms of satisfaction ("I love ketchup") is bound to confuse the people who speak it. Psychologists distinguish two basic kinds of love—*passionate love*, which is an experience involving feelings of euphoria, intimacy, and intense sexual attraction, and *companionate love*, which is an experience involving affection, trust, and concern for a partner's well-being (Hatfield, 1988; Rubin, 1973; Sternberg, 1986). The ideal romantic relationship gives rise to both types of love, but the speeds, trajectories, and durations of the two experiences are markedly different (**FIGURE 15.4**).

● What are the two basic types of love?

Passionate love has a rapid onset, reaches its peak quickly, and begins to diminish within just a few months. Companionate love takes some time to get started, grows slowly, and need never stop. As such, the love we feel early in a relationship is not the same love we feel later. When people marry for passionate love, they may not choose a partner with whom they can easily develop companionate love, and if they don't understand how quickly passionate love cools, they may blame their partners when it does. In many cultures, parents try to keep children from making these mistakes by choosing their marriage partners for them. Some studies suggest that arranged marriages yield greater satisfaction over the long term than do "love matches" (Yelsma & Athappilly, 1988), but other studies suggest just the opposite (Xiaohe & Whyte, 1990). If there *are* any benefits to arranged marriage, they may derive from the

● ● ● ● ● ● ● ● ● ● ● ● ● ● **FIGURE 15.4**
Passionate and Companionate Love
Companionate and passionate love have different time courses and trajectories. Passionate love begins to cool within just a few months, but companionate love can grow slowly but steadily over years.

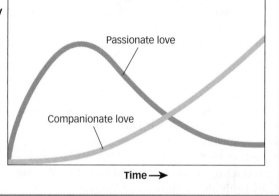

Intensity

Passionate love

Companionate love

Time →

● ● ● ● ● ● ● ● *As relationships endure, passionate love fades and companionate love grows. Ronald Reagan and Nancy Davis were "crazy" about each other when they met in 1951, but after many decades, what they valued most about their marriage was the fact that they were "best friends."*

fact that parents are less likely to pick partners on the basis of passionate love and more likely to pick partners who have a high potential for companionate love (Haidt, 2006).

We've examined some of the factors that draw people into intimate relationships, but what determines when people will be drawn out? **Social exchange** is *the hypothesis that people remain in relationships only as long as they perceive a favorable ratio of costs to benefits* (Homans, 1961; Thibaut & Kelley, 1959). The costs of a relationship include the time, money, and affection that have to be poured into a relationship to make it work—as well as the inability to form a new (and possibly more satisfying) relationship with someone else instead. A relationship that provides an acceptable level of benefits at a reasonable cost would probably be maintained. What is acceptable? Surprisingly, research suggests that most people seek **equity**, which is *a state of affairs in which the cost-benefit ratios of two partners are roughly equal* (Messick & Cook, 1983; Walster, Walster, & Berscheid, 1978). For example, spouses are more distressed when their respective cost-benefit ratios are *different* than when their cost-benefit ratios are *unfavorable*—and this is true even when their cost-benefit ratio is *more* favorable than their partner's (Schafer & Keith, 1980).

"This next one goes out to all those who have ever been in love, then become engaged, gotten married, participated in the tragic deterioration of a relationship, suffered the pains and agonies of a bitter divorce, subjected themselves to the fruitless search for a new partner, and ultimately resigned themselves to remaining single in a world full of irresponsible jerks, noncommittal weirdos, and neurotic misfits."

summary quiz [15.1]

1. The CEO of a major company defrauded shareholders and stole hundreds of millions of dollars. This CEO displayed what kind of behavior?
   a. social loafing
   b. deindividuation
   c. aggression
   d. cognitive dissonance

2. The prisoner's dilemma game illustrates
   a. the hypothesis-confirming bias.
   b. the benefits and costs of cooperation.
   c. the diffusion of responsibility.
   d. group polarization.

3. People in a mob situation are more likely to stray from their own moral values. This is an example of
   a. group polarization.
   b. social loafing.
   c. deindividuation.
   d. bystander effect.

4. Isabel was voted the "Best-Looking Girl" in her high school graduating class. According to the text, Isabel, compared to her peers, also is likely to
   a. have more friends.
   b. have fewer dates, because boys are afraid of being turned down if they ask her out.
   c. engage in less sex, because she is highly selective of her sexual partners.
   d. spend less time in sports because of her many social commitments.

social influence The control of one person's behavior by another.

observational learning Learning that occurs when one person observes another person being rewarded or punished.

norms A customary standard for behavior that is widely shared by members of a culture.

normative influence A phenomenon whereby one person's behavior is influenced by another person's behavior because the latter provides information about what is appropriate.

norm of reciprocity The norm that people should benefit those who have benefited them.

door-in-the-face technique A strategy that uses reciprocating concessions to influence behavior.

Social Influence: Controlling People

Those of us who grew up watching Wonder Woman and Superman cartoons on Saturday mornings have usually thought a bit about which of the standard superpowers we'd most like to have. Superstrength and superspeed have obvious benefits, invisibility and x-ray vision could be interesting as well as lucrative, and there's a lot to be said for flying. But when it comes right down to it, the ability to control other people would probably be more useful. After all, who needs to leap tall buildings, change the course of mighty rivers, or bend steel in their bare hands if you can get someone else to do it for you? The things we want from life—gourmet food, interesting jobs, big houses, fancy cars—can be given to us by others, and the things we want most—loving families, loyal friends, admiring children, appreciative employers—cannot be had in any other way.

Social influence is *the control of one person's behavior by another,* and those who know how to exert such influence can have and be just about anything they please (Cialdini & Trost, 1998). Human beings are not unique in their exercise of—or susceptibility to—social influence. Indeed, influence is the fundamental force that binds the individual members of any social species together, and without it there could be no groups, no cooperation, and no altruism. All social animals wield and yield to social influence, but human beings have raised influence to the status of an art, developing subtle and complex techniques not observed anywhere else in the natural world.

How does social influence work? If you want others to give you their time, money, allegiance, or affection, you'd be wise to consider first what it is *they* want. People have three basic wants that make them susceptible to social influence. First, people have a *hedonic motive,* or a desire to experience pleasure and avoid pain. Second, people have an *approval motive,* or a desire to be accepted and to avoid being rejected. Third, people have an *accuracy motive,* or a desire to believe what is true and to avoid believing what is false. Most forms of social influence appeal to one or more of these motives.

● **What makes people susceptible to influence?**

The Hedonic Motive: The Power of Pleasure

Pleasure seeking is probably the most fundamental of all motives, and social influence often involves creating situations in which others can achieve more pleasure by doing what we want them to do than by doing something else. Parents, teachers, governments, and businesses constantly try to influence our behavior by offering rewards and threatening punishments. There's nothing mysterious about these influence attempts, and they are often quite effective. When the Republic of Singapore warned its citizens in 1992 that anyone caught chewing gum in public would face a year in prison and a $5,500 fine, the rest of the world seemed either outraged or amused. When all the criticism and chuckling subsided, though, it was hard to ignore the fact that the incidence of felonious gum chewing in Singapore had fallen to an all-time low.

You'll recall from Chapter 5 that even a sea slug will repeat behaviors that are followed by rewards and avoid behaviors that are followed by punishments. Reward and punishment are sometimes *more effective* influences on human than nonhuman behavior because people are especially good at **observational learning,** which is *the process of learning by observing others being rewarded and punished.* In a classic study, children who saw an adult behave aggressively were more likely to behave aggressively themselves if they observed the adult being rewarded rather than punished for this behavior (Bandura, 1965). This method of social influence can be effective even when rewards and punishments are quite subtle. For instance, toddlers in one study watched their mothers being exposed to a rubber snake (Gerull & Rapee, 2002). Those who saw their mothers frown were more likely to avoid the snake than were those who saw their mothers smile.

At the same time, however, social influence attempts that are based on reward and punishment can also backfire because people don't always take kindly to being

● *Spectators watch as convicted criminal Meya Gul is hanged in front of a hotel in Kabul, Afghanistan, on September 23, 2000. Whether or not public punishment is ethical, research on observational learning suggests that it can be effective.*

AP PHOTO/AMIR SHAH

● **When can influence based on rewards and punishments backfire?**

manipulated. In one study, researchers placed signs in two restrooms on a college campus. One sign read, "Please don't write on these walls," and the other read, "Do not write on these walls under any circumstances." Two weeks later, the walls in the second restroom had more graffiti than the walls in the first restroom did, presumably because students didn't appreciate the threatening tone of the second sign and thus wrote on the walls just to prove that they could (Pennebaker & Sanders, 1976).

The Approval Motive: The Power of Social Acceptance

Other people stand between us and starvation, predation, loneliness, and all the other things that make getting shipwrecked such a bad idea. We depend on others for safety, sustenance, and solidarity, all of which become conspicuous by their absence. Social rejection is not just a blow to our self-esteem but also a hazard to our health. Indeed, being isolated and lonely makes people susceptible to a wide variety of physical illnesses (Pressman et al., 2005). Having others like us, accept us, and approve of us is a powerful human motive (Baumeister & Leary, 1995; Leary et al., 1995), and like any motive, it leaves us vulnerable to social influence. This influence comes in several different forms.

Normative Influence

You probably know that you are supposed to face forward in an elevator and that you shouldn't talk to the person next to you even if you were talking to that person before you got on the elevator unless you are the only two people on the elevator, in which case, it's okay to talk and face sideways but still not backward. What's so interesting about rules such as these is that they are both elaborate and unwritten. No one ever taught you this complicated elevator etiquette, but you nonetheless managed to pick

● **How do we learn such things as elevator etiquette?**

it up along the way. The unwritten rules that govern social behavior are called **norms**, which are *customary standards for behavior that are widely shared by members of a culture* (Miller & Prentice, 1996). We learn norms with exceptional ease and we obey them with exceptional fidelity because we know that if we don't, others won't approve of us.

Our slavish devotion to norms provides a powerful lever for influence. **Normative influence** occurs when *one person's behavior is influenced by another person's behavior because the latter provides information about what is appropriate*. For example, every human culture has a **norm of reciprocity**, which is *the unwritten rule that people should benefit those who have benefited them* (Gouldner, 1960). Thus, when a friend pays for lunch, you probably feel an immediate urge to repay the favor, perhaps even offering, "My treat next time," or words to that effect. Indeed, the norm of reciprocity is so strong that when researchers randomly pulled the names of strangers from a telephone directory and sent them all Christmas cards, they received Christmas cards back from most (Kunz & Woolcott, 1976). Some social influence techniques trade on this norm of reciprocity. For example, waiters and waitresses get bigger tips when they give customers a piece of candy along with the bill because customers feel obligated to do "a little extra" for those who have done "a little extra" for them (Strohmetz et al., 2002).

The norm of reciprocity always involves swapping, but the swapping doesn't always involve favors. The **door-in-the-face technique** is *a strategy that uses reciprocating concessions to influence behavior*.

Attention Dog Guardians
Pick up after your dogs - Thank you.
Attention Dogs
Grrrr, bark, woof. Good dog.

District of North Vancouver
Bylaw 5981-11(i)

People (and other social animals) are ● ● ● ● ● ● ● ●
*motivated by a need for approval,
which leads them to obey norms.*

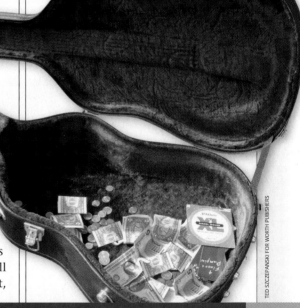

Have you ever wondered which big spender left the bill as a tip? In ● ● ● ● ● ● ●
fact, the bills are often put there by the very people you are tipping because they know that the presence of paper money will suggest to you that others are leaving big tips and that it would be socially appropriate for you to do the same. By the way, the customary gratuity for someone who writes a textbook for you is 15%. But most students send more.

Here's how it works: You ask someone for something more valuable than you really want, you wait for that person to refuse (to "slam the door in your face"), and then you ask the person for what you really want. This technique works like a charm. In one study, researchers asked college students to volunteer to supervise adolescents who were going on a field trip, and only 17% of the students agreed. But when the researchers first asked students to commit to spending 2 hours per week for 2 years working at a youth detention center (to which every one of the students said no) and *then* asked them if they'd be willing to supervise the field trip, 50% of the students agreed (Cialdini et al., 1975). There's a mindbug at work: People were more likely to endorse the second request *because* they refused the first request, although most people would balk at the second request if they heard it all by itself. How does this technique involve the norm of reciprocity? The researchers began by asking for a large favor, which the student firmly refused. They then made a concession by asking for a smaller favor. Because the researchers made a concession, the norm of reciprocity demanded that the student make one, too.

● ● ● ● *The perplexed research participant (center), flanked by confederates (who are "in" on the experiment), is on the verge of conformity in one of Solomon Asch's line-judging experiments.*

Conformity

People can influence us by invoking familiar norms. But if you've ever found yourself sneaking a peek at the diner next to you, hoping to discover whether the little fork is supposed to be used for the shrimp or the salad, then you know that other people can also influence us by defining *new* norms in ambiguous, confusing, or novel situations. **Conformity** is *the tendency to do what others do simply because others are doing it,* and it results in part from normative influence.

In a classic study, Solomon Asch had participants sit in a room with seven other people who appeared to be ordinary participants but who were actually trained actors (Asch, 1951, 1956). An experimenter explained that the participants would be shown cards with three

● **How can normative influence occur if we don't know the norms?**

Standard

A B C

FIGURE 15.5 ● ● ● ● ● ● ● ● ● ● ● ● ● ● ● ●
Asch's Conformity Study *If you were asked which of the lines on the right—A, B, or C—matches the standard line on the left, what would you say? Research on conformity suggests that your answer would depend, in part, on how other people in the room answered the same question.*

lines printed on them and that their job was to state which of the three lines matched a "standard line" that was printed on another card (**FIGURE 15.5**). The experimenter held up a card and then went around the room, asking each person to answer aloud in turn. The real participant was among the last to be called on. Everything was normal on the first two trials, but on the third trial, something odd happened: The actors all began giving the same wrong answer! What did the real participant do? Results showed that 75% of them conformed and announced the wrong answer on at least one trial. Participants didn't actually misperceive the length of the lines; that'd be pretty difficult for someone with normal vision to do. Rather, they merely said something they didn't believe in order to gain social approval.

Obedience

Other people's behavior can provide information about norms, but in most situations there are a few people whom we all recognize as having special authority both to define and enforce the norms. The usher at a movie theater may be an underpaid high school student who isn't allowed to drink, drive, vote, or stay up past 10 on a school night, but in the context of the theater, the usher is the authority. So when the usher asks you to take your feet off the seat in front of you, you obey. **Obedience** is *the tendency to do what authorities tell us to do simply because they tell us to do it.*

Authorities can influence us by threatening punishment and promising reward, but research suggests that much of their influence is *normative* (Tyler, 1990).

● **Why do we obey authorities?**

Stanley Milgram demonstrated this in one of psychology's most infamous experiments (Milgram, 1963). The participants in this experiment met a middle-aged man who was introduced as another participant but who was actually a trained actor. An experimenter in a lab coat explained that the participant would play the role of *teacher* and the actor would play the role of *learner*. The teacher and learner would sit in different rooms, the teacher would read words to the learner over a microphone, and the learner would then repeat the words back to the teacher. If the learner made a mistake, the teacher would press a button that delivered an electric shock to the learner. Each time the learner made an error, the teacher would increase the level of shock (**FIGURE 15.6**). The shock-generating machine (which wasn't actually hooked up, of course) offered 30 levels of shock, ranging from 15 volts (labeled "slight shock") to 450 volts (labeled "Danger: Severe shock").

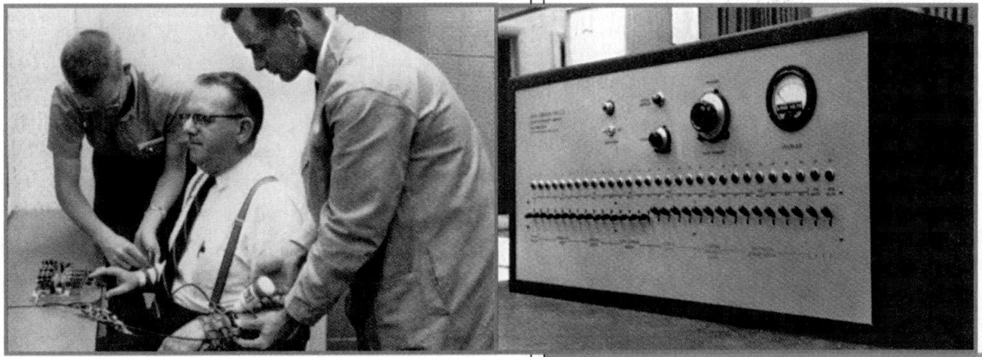

After the learner was strapped into his chair, the experiment began. When the learner made his first mistake, the participant dutifully delivered a 15-volt shock. As the learner made more mistakes, he received more shocks. When the participant delivered the 75-volt shock, the learner cried out in pain. At 150 volts, the learner screamed, "Get me out of here. I told you I have heart trouble. . . . I refuse to go on. Let me out!" With every shock, the learner's screams became more agonized as he pleaded pitifully for his freedom. Then, after receiving the 330-volt shock, the learner stopped responding altogether. Participants were naturally upset by all of this, and they typically asked the experimenter to stop the experiment. But the experimenter simply replied, "You have no choice; you must go on." The experimenter never threatened the participant with punishment of any kind. Rather, he just stood there with his

In 2005, Private Lynndie England was convicted for her role in the abuse of Iraqi prisoners at the Abu Ghraib prison. When the judge asked her why she had abused the prisoners, she implicated her fellow soldiers. "I refused at first . . . [but] they were being very persistent, bugging me, so I said, 'Okay, whatever.'" Then she added, "I was yielding to peer pressure."

FIGURE 15.6
Milgram's Obedience Studies *The learner (left) being hooked up to the shock generator (right) that was used in Stanley Milgram's obedience studies.*

conformity The tendency to do what others do simply because others are doing it.

obedience The tendency to do what authorities tell us to do simply because they tell us to do it.

● ● ● *Is this the face of a monster? In this photo, Nazi war criminal Adolph Eichmann sits before the District Court of Jerusalem. Eichmann acknowledged that he sent millions of Jews to their deaths but argued that he was merely obeying authority. He was sentenced to death and hanged in 1962.*

clipboard in hand and calmly instructed the participant to continue. Eighty percent of the participants continued to shock the learner even after he screamed, complained, pleaded, and then fell silent. And 62% of the participants went all the way, delivering the highest possible voltage.

Were these people psychopathic sadists? Would a normal person electrocute a stranger just because some guy in a lab coat told them to? The answer, it seems, is yes, because being *normal* means being sensitive to and respectful of social norms. The participants in this experiment knew that hurting others is *often* wrong but not *always* wrong. Doctors give painful injections, and teachers give painful exams. In many situations it is permissible—and even desirable—to cause someone to suffer in the service of a higher goal. The experimenter's calm demeanor and persistent instruction suggested that he, and not the participant, knew what was appropriate in this particular situation. Subsequent research confirmed that participants' obedience was due to normative pressure. When the experimenter's authority to define the norm was undermined—for exam-

"Sure, I follow the herd—not out of brainless obedience, mind you, but out of a deep and abiding respect for the concept of community."

ple, when a second experimenter appeared to disagree with the first or when the instructions were given by a person who wasn't wearing a lab coat—participants rarely obeyed the instructions (Milgram, 1974; Miller, 1986).

The Accuracy Motive: The Power of Being Right

Just about every action relies on an **attitude**, which is *an enduring positive or negative evaluation of an object or event,* and a **belief,** which is *an enduring piece of knowledge about an object or event.* When we are hungry, we open the refrigerator and grab an apple because our attitudes tell us that apples taste good and our beliefs tell us that those good-tasting apples are to be found in the refrigerator. In a sense, attitudes tell us what we should do ("Eat an apple") and beliefs tell us how we should do it ("Start by opening the fridge"). If attitudes or beliefs are inaccurate—that is, if we don't know what is good and we don't know what is true—then our actions are fruitless. Because we rely so heavily on our attitudes and beliefs to guide our actions, it isn't surprising that we want to have the right ones. We are motivated to be accurate, and like any motive, this one leaves us vulnerable to social influence.

Informational Influence

Other human beings have pretty much the same sensory apparatus that we do, and thus we rely on their reactions to the world to tell us about the world. If everyone in a movie theater suddenly jumped up and ran screaming for the exit, you'd probably join them—not because you were afraid that they'd think less of you if you didn't, but because their behavior would suggest that there was something worth running from. **Informational influence** occurs when *a person's behavior is influenced by another person's behavior because the latter provides information about what is good or true.* You can demonstrate the power of informational influence by standing in the middle of the sidewalk, tilting back your head, and staring at the top of a tall building. Research shows that within just a few minutes, other people will begin stopping

attitude An enduring positive or negative evaluation of an object or event.

belief An enduring piece of knowledge about an object or event.

informational influence A phenomenon whereby a person's behavior is influenced by another person's behavior because the latter provides information about what is good or true.

persuasion A phenomenon that occurs when a person's attitudes or beliefs are influenced by a communication from another person.

systematic persuasion A change in attitudes or beliefs that is brought about by appeals to reason.

heuristic persuasion A change in attitudes or beliefs that is brought about by appeals to habit or emotion.

and staring, too, believing that you must know something they don't (Milgram, Bickman, & Berkowitz, 1969).

You are the constant target of informational influence. Advertisements that refer to soft drinks as "popular" or books as "best sellers" are reminding you that other people are buying these particular sodas and novels, which suggests that they know something you don't and that you'd be wise to follow their example. Situation comedies provide "laugh tracks" because the producers know that when you hear other people laughing, you will mindlessly assume that something must be funny

The behavior of others provides information about the world to which they are reacting. When a social animal flees, others tend to follow.

● **How do informational influence and normative influence differ?**

(Nosanchuk & Lightstone, 1974). Bars and nightclubs may waive the cover charge for the first group of patrons because they know that when a club looks full, passersby will assume that others spent money to get into the club and that the club must be worth the expense. In short, the world is full of objects and events that we know little about, and we can often cure our ignorance by paying attention to the way in which others are acting toward them. Alas, the very thing that makes us open to information leaves us open to manipulation as well.

Persuasion

When the next presidential election rolls around, two things will happen. First, the candidates will say that they intend to win your vote by making arguments that focus on the issues. Second, the candidates will then avoid arguments, ignore issues, and attempt to win your vote with a variety of cheap tricks. What the candidates promise to do and what they actually do reflect two basic forms of **persuasion**, which occurs when *a person's attitudes or beliefs are influenced by a communication from another person* (Petty & Wegener, 1998). The candidates will promise to persuade you by demonstrating that

Is McDonald's trying to keep track of sales from the parking lot? Probably not. Rather, they want you to know that other people are buying their hamburgers, which suggests that they are worth buying, which in turn suggests that you just might want to stop and have one yourself right about now.

● **In what ways do politicians appeal to emotion?**

their positions on the issues are the most practical, intelligent, fair, and beneficial. Having made that promise, they will then devote most of their financial resources to persuading you by other means—for example, by dressing nicely and smiling a lot, by surrounding themselves with famous athletes and movie stars, by repeatedly pairing their opponent's name with words and images that nobody much cares for, and so on. In other words, the candidates will promise to engage in **systematic persuasion**, which refers to *a change in attitudes or beliefs that is brought about by appeals to reason,* but they will spend most of their time and money engaged in **heuristic persuasion**, which refers to *a change in attitudes or beliefs that is brought about by appeals to habit or emotion* (Chaiken, 1980; Petty & Cacioppo, 1986).

How do these two forms of persuasion work? *Systematic persuasion* appeals to logic and reason. People should be more persuaded when evidence and arguments are strong rather than weak. Although this is often true, many rhetorical devices can make arguments and evidence seem stronger than they actually are. For example, people generally pay more attention to the argument they hear first but remember best the argument they hear last. As such, a candidate may prefer to speak first if the debate is being held 1 day before the election but may prefer to speak last if the debate is being held 1 month before the election (Miller & Campbell, 1959).

Heuristic persuasion appeals to habit and emotion. Rather than weighing evidence and analyzing arguments, people often use *heuristics*—which are simple shortcuts or "rules of thumb"—to help them decide whether to believe a communication (see Chapter 7). For instance, participants in one study read the statement, "When a

The order in which information is presented can have an influence on the persuasiveness of a communication.

Systematic and heuristic persuasion have long been the staples of advertising. The automobile advertisement on the left presents facts about the car and invites you to "see for yourself," whereas the advertisement on the right tells you only that most people choose this ketchup. Can you guess why advertisers include more facts when selling cars than ketchup? Answer: Cars are more expensive (and thus people are strongly motivated to consider evidence for or against buying them), but ketchup is cheap.

government becomes oppressive, it is the right of the people to abolish it." Those who were told that the remark had been made by Abraham Lincoln were more persuaded by it than were those who were told that the remark had been made by Communist leader Vladimir Lenin (Lorge, 1936). (In case you're wondering, the sentence paraphrases a statement in the U.S. Declaration of Independence.) Rather than analyzing the content of the remark, participants used a simple heuristic ("Always trust Honest Abe" or "Never trust a Commie") to help them decide whether to accept the communication.

Consistency

If a friend told you that rabbits had just staged a coup in Antarctica and were halting all carrot exports, you probably wouldn't turn on CNN to see if it was true. You'd know right away that your friend was joking because the statement is logically inconsistent with other things that you know are true—for example, that rabbits rarely foment revolution and that Antarctica does not export carrots. People evaluate the accuracy of new beliefs by assessing their *consistency* with old beliefs, and although this is not a foolproof method for determining whether something is true, it provides a pretty good approximation. Most people have a desire for accuracy, and because consistency is a rough measure of accuracy, most of us have a desire for consistency as well (Cialdini, Trost, & Newsom, 1995).

● **How can people's desire for consistency be used as a tool of persuasion?**

Our desire for consistency can leave us vulnerable to social influence. For example, the **foot-in-the-door technique** is *a strategy that uses a person's desire for consistency to influence that person's behavior* (Burger, 1999). In one study, experimenters went to a neighborhood, knocked on doors, and asked homeowners if they would install in their front yards a large, unsightly sign that said, "Drive Carefully." Only 17% of the homeowners agreed to install the sign. The experimenters asked some other homeowners to sign a petition urging the state legislature to promote safe driving, which almost all agreed to do, and *then* asked those homeowners if they would install the unsightly sign. Fifty-five percent of *these* homeowners agreed to install the sign (Freedman & Fraser, 1966)!

Why would a homeowner be more likely to grant two requests than one? They had just signed a petition stating that safe driving was important to them, and they knew that refusing to install the sign would be inconsistent with that action. As they wrestled with these facts, they probably began to experience a feeling called **cognitive dissonance**, which is *an unpleasant state that arises when a person recognizes the inconsistency of his or her actions, attitudes, or beliefs* (Festinger, 1957). When people experience the unpleasant state of cognitive dissonance, they naturally try to alleviate it, and one way to alleviate cognitive dissonance is to change one's actions, attitudes, or beliefs in order to restore consistency among them (Aronson, 1969; Cooper & Fazio, 1984).

foot-in-the-door technique A strategy that uses a person's desire for consistency to influence that person's behavior.

cognitive dissonance An unpleasant state that arises when a person recognizes the inconsistency of his or her actions, attitudes, or beliefs.

We desire consistency, but occasions inevitably arise when we just can't help but be inconsistent—for example, when we tell a friend that her new hairstyle is "unusually trendy" when it actually resembles a wet skunk after an unfortunate encounter with a blender. Why don't we experience cognitive dissonance under such circumstances and come to believe our own lies? Because telling a friend that her hairstyle is trendy is inconsistent with the belief that her hairstyle is hideous, but it is perfectly consistent with the belief that one should be nice to one's friends. When small inconsistencies are *justified* by large consistencies, cognitive dissonance does not occur.

For example, participants in one study were asked to perform a dull task that involved turning knobs one way, then the other, and then back again. After the participants were sufficiently bored, the experimenter explained that he desperately needed a few more people to volunteer for the study, and he asked the participants to go into the hallway, find another person, and tell that person that the knob-turning task was great fun. The experimenter offered some participants $1 to tell this lie, and he offered other participants $20. All participants agreed to tell the lie, and after they did so, they were asked to report their true enjoyment of the knob-turning task. The results showed that participants liked the task *more* when they were paid $1 than $20 to lie about it (Festinger & Carlsmith, 1959). Why? Because the belief that *the knob-turning task was dull* was inconsistent with the belief that *I recommended the task to that person in the hallway*, but the latter belief was perfectly consistent with the belief that *$20 is a lot of money*. For some participants, the large payment justified the lie, so only those people who received the small payment experienced cognitive dissonance. As such, only the participants who received $1 felt the need to restore consistency by changing their beliefs about the enjoyableness of the task (**FIGURE 15.7**).

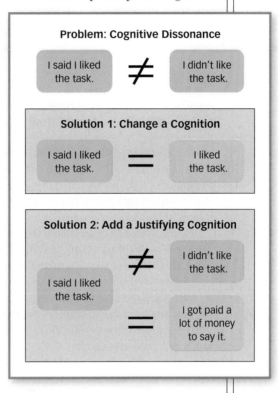

Problem: Cognitive Dissonance

I said I liked the task. ≠ I didn't like the task.

Solution 1: Change a Cognition

I said I liked the task. = I liked the task.

Solution 2: Add a Justifying Cognition

I said I liked the task. ≠ I didn't like the task.

= I got paid a lot of money to say it.

FIGURE 15.7 ● ● ● ● ● ● ● ● ● ● ● ● ● ● ●
Reducing Cognitive Dissonance *Behaving in ways that are inconsistent with your attitudes and beliefs can cause cognitive dissonance. One way to eliminate that dissonance is to change your attitude or belief. Another way is to add a justification.*

summary quiz [15.2]

5. Yasmine took her cousin Jade out to lunch, and picked up the tab. Jade replied, "Thanks. My turn next time." Jade's response demonstrates what principle?
   a. common courtesy
   b. observational learning
   c. diffusion of responsibility
   d. norm of reciprocity

6. The tendency to do what authorities tell us to do simply because they tell us to do it is known as
   a. persuasion.
   b. the self-fulfilling prophecy.
   c. conformity.
   d. obedience.

social cognition The processes by which people come to understand others.

stereotyping The process by which people draw inferences about others based on their knowledge of the categories to which others belong.

7. Andrea and Jeff had to wait in line for over an hour to get into an exclusive restaurant. Despite being served a mediocre meal, they glowingly praised the restaurant to their friends. This behavior was probably a result of
   a. conformity.
   b. the norm of reciprocity.
   c. perceptual confirmation.
   d. cognitive dissonance.

Social Cognition: Understanding People

"Now, what's with Big Tom? Can he really be as clueless as he appears? He seems to still just be trying to float and hope for the best. . . . I can't quite make out what Jenna's trying to do, either. She knows from experience that she yaps far too much and I would have thought she would have tempered that trait by now. Rob's . . . personality is humorous, but he's created animosity in several of the others . . . so he could be in serious trouble."

These words aren't great poetry. They're not even grammatical prose. But they are worth a million bucks because they represent the musings of Richard Hatch, who won the game of *Survivor* by thinking long and hard about the other people on his island—about who they were, what they did, and why (Hatch, 2005). Hatch was an informal specialist in **social cognition**, which refers to *the processes by which people come to understand other.* Most of us specialize in precisely the same subject—drawing inferences about other people's thoughts and feelings, their beliefs and desires, their abilities and aspirations, their intentions, needs, and characters—because other people can provide us with the greatest benefits and exact from us the greatest costs.

As it turns out, the inferences we draw about other people are based on the categories to which they belong and on the things they say and do. Let's examine these two kinds of inferences in turn.

● **How do we draw inferences about other people?**

Stereotyping: Drawing Inferences from Categories

You'll recall from Chapter 7 that *categories* are classes of related stimuli. Once we have identified a novel stimulus as a member of a category ("That's a textbook"), we can then use our knowledge of the category to make educated guesses about the properties of the novel stimulus ("It's probably expensive") and act accordingly ("I think I'll borrow it from the library"). The same is true of people. **Stereotyping** is *the process by which people draw inferences about others based on their knowledge of the categories to which others belong.* The moment we categorize a person as an adult, a male, a baseball player, and a Russian, we can use our knowledge of those categories to make some educated guesses about him—for example, that he shaves his face but not his legs, that he understands the infield fly rule, and that he knows more about Chekhov than we do. As these examples suggest, stereotyping is a very useful process (Allport, 1954). And yet, ever since the word was coined in 1936, it has had a distasteful connotation. Why? Because stereotyping is a useful process that can often produce harmful results, and it does so because stereotypes can be inaccurate, overused, self-perpetuating, and automatic.

● ● ● *These photos show a former basketball player who was recently elected to the city council in Athens, Greece, and a Brazilian poet who wrote, "To not contemplating, I prefer eternal blindness." Despite what your stereotypes might suggest, Thiago de Mello (left) is the Brazilian poet and Yvette Jarvis (right) is the former basketball player and Greek politician.*

RENO MASSOLA/LATINPHOTO.ORG

Stereotypes Can Be Inaccurate

The inferences we draw about individuals are only as accurate as our stereotypes about the categories to which they belong. There are only two ways to acquire a belief about anything: to see for yourself or to take somebody else's word for it. In fact, most of what we know about the members of human categories is hearsay—stuff we picked up from friends and uncles, from novels and newspapers, from jokes and movies and late-night television. In the process of inheriting the wisdom of our culture, it is inevitable that we also will inherit its ignorance.

But even direct observation can produce inaccurate stereotypes. For example, research participants in one study were shown a long series of positive and negative behaviors and were told that each behavior had been performed by a member of one

● **How can direct observation produce inaccurate stereotypes?**

of two groups: Group A or Group B (**FIGURE 15.8**). There were more positive than negative behaviors in the series, and there were more members of Group A than of Group B. The series of behaviors was carefully arranged so that each group behaved negatively exactly one third of the time. After seeing the series, participants correctly remembered that Group A had behaved negatively one third of the time. However, they incorrectly remembered that Group B had behaved negatively more than *half* the time (Hamilton & Gifford, 1976).

Why did this happen? Bad behavior was rare and being a member of Group B was rare; thus participants were especially likely to notice when the two co-occurred ("Aha! There's one of those unusual Group B people doing an unusually awful thing again"). These findings help explain why members of majority groups tend to overestimate the number of crimes (which are relatively rare events) committed by members of minority groups (who are relatively rare people; that's why they're in the minority). Even when we directly observe people, we can end up with inaccurate beliefs about the groups to which they belong. This mindbug has the potential to create disastrous consequences for societies and for social relationships.

Stereotypes Can Be Overused

Because all thumbtacks are pretty much alike, our beliefs about thumbtacks ("small, cheap, painful when chewed") are quite useful, and we will rarely be mistaken if we

generalize from one thumbtack to another. Human categories, however, are so variable that our stereotypes may offer only the vaguest of clues about the individuals who populate those categories. You probably believe that men have greater upper body strength than women do, and this belief is right *on average*. But the upper body strength of individuals *within* each of these categories is so varied that you cannot easily predict how much weight a particular person can lift simply by knowing that person's gender. The inherent variability of human categories makes stereotypes much less useful than they might otherwise be. In our quest to define the forest, we often miss the uniqueness of each tree.

Alas, we don't always recognize this because the mere act of categorizing a stimulus tends to warp our perceptions of

● **How does categorizing something change our perception of it?**

that category's variability. For instance, participants in some studies were shown a series of lines of different lengths (**FIGURE 15.9**; McGarty & Turner, 1992; Tajfel & Wilkes, 1963). For one group of

participants, the longest lines were labeled *A* and the shortest lines were labeled *B*, as they are on the right side of **FIGURE 15.9**.

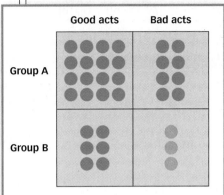

FIGURE 15.8 ● ● ● ● ● ● ● ● ● ● ● ●
Illusory Correlation *Group A and Group B each perform two-thirds good acts and one-third bad acts. However, "Group B" and "bad acts" are both rare, leading people to notice and remember their co-occurrence, which leads them to perceive a correlation between group membership and behavior that isn't really there.*

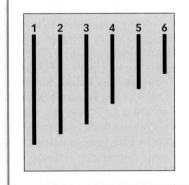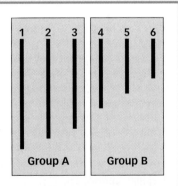

FIGURE 15.9 ● ● ● ● ● ● ● ● ● ● ● ● ● ● ● ● ● ● ●
Assimilation and Contrast *People who see the lines on the right tend to overestimate the similarity of lines 1 and 3 and underestimate the similarity of lines 3 and 4. Simply labeling lines 1 through 3 "Group A" and lines 4 through 6 "Group B" causes the lines within a group to seem more similar to each other than they really are and the lines in different groups to seem more different from each other than they really are.*

> ● ● *They may all look alike to you, but if you confuse the harmless snake on the left with the deadly snake on the right, you won't be around to do it a second time.*

For the second group of participants, the lines were shown without these category labels, as they are on the left side of **FIGURE 15.9**. Interestingly, those participants who saw the category labels *overestimated* the similarity of the lines that shared a label and *underestimated* the similarity of lines that did not.

You've probably experienced this phenomenon yourself. For instance, we all identify colors as members of categories such as *blue* or *green,* which leads us to overestimate the similarity of colors that share a category label and to underestimate the similarity of colors that do not. This is why we see discrete *bands* of color when we look at rainbows, which are actually a smooth continuum of colors. This is also why we tend to underestimate the distance between cities that are in the same country, such as Memphis, Tennessee, and Pierre, South Dakota, and overestimate the distance between cities that are in different countries, such as Memphis, Tennessee, and Toronto, Canada (Burris & Branscombe, 2005). What's true of colors and distances is true of people as well. The mere act of categorizing people as Blacks or Whites, Jews or Gentiles, artists or accountants can cause us to underestimate the variability within those categories ("All artists are wacky") and to overestimate the variability between them ("Artists are much wackier than accountants"). When we underestimate the variability of a human category, we feel justified in using our stereotypes.

Stereotypes Can Be Self-Perpetuating

When we meet a man who likes ballet more than football or a senior citizen who likes hip-hop more than easy-listening, why don't we recognize that our stereotypes are inaccurate? Stereotypes are a bit like viruses, and once they take up residence inside us, they perpetuate themselves and resist even our most concerted efforts to eradicate them. Here are three mindbugs that contribute to self-perpetuating stereotypes.

● **How is a stereotype like a virus?**

- **Perceptual confirmation** is *the tendency for observers to perceive what they expect to perceive.* In one study, participants listened to a radio broadcast of a college basketball game and were asked to evaluate the performance of one of the players. Although all participants heard the same prerecorded game, some were led to believe that the player was Black and others were led to believe that the player was White. Participants' stereotypes led them to expect different performances from athletes of different ethnic origins. In fact, the participants perceived just what they expected. Those who believed the player was Black thought he had exhibited greater athletic ability but less intelligence than did those who thought he was White (Stone, Perry, & Darley, 1997). Stereotypes perpetuate themselves in part by biasing our perception of individuals, leading us to believe that those individuals have confirmed our stereotypes when, in fact, they have not (Fiske, 1998).

- **Self-fulfilling prophecy** is *a phenomenon whereby observers bring about what they expect to perceive.* When people know that observers have a negative stereotype about them, they may experience *stereotype threat,* or fear of confirming an observer's stereotype. Ironically, this fear can cause people to behave in precisely the

perceptual confirmation A phenomenon that occurs when observers perceive what they expect to perceive.

self-fulfilling prophecy A phenomenon whereby observers bring about what they expect to perceive.

subtyping The process of creating a modification to a stereotype, rather than abandoning it altogether, when confronted with evidence that clearly disconfirms that stereotype evidence.

way that the stereotype predicts. In one study, American students of African or European ancestry were given a test, and half of the students in each group were asked to list their race at the top of the exam. Students who were not asked to list their race performed as well as their SAT scores suggested they should (Steele & Aronson, 1995). But when students were asked to list their races, African American students performed more poorly than their SAT scores suggested they should (**FIGURE 15.10**). Similarly, observers tend to seek information that confirms rather than disconfirms their stereotypes (Snyder & Swann, 1978). When a man asks a woman, "Do you like cooking more than sewing?" he is giving her very little opportunity to explain that she actually prefers sumo wrestling to both. Stereotypes perpetuate themselves in part by causing the stereotyped individual to behave in ways that confirm the stereotype.

- **Subtyping** is *the process of creating a modification to a stereotype, rather than abandoning it altogether, when confronted with evidence that clearly disconfirms that stereotype* (Weber & Crocker, 1983). For example, people tend to believe that public relations agents are sociable. In one study, participants learned about a PR agent who was *slightly* unsociable, and the results showed that their stereotypes about PR agents shifted a bit to accommodate this new information. But when participants learned about a PR agent who was *extremely* unsociable, their stereotypes did not change at all (Kunda & Oleson, 1997). Instead, they tended to think of the extremely unsociable PR agent as "an exception to the rule" and thereby preserve their stereotypes about PR agents in general. Subtyping is a powerful method for preserving our stereotypes in the face of contradictory evidence.

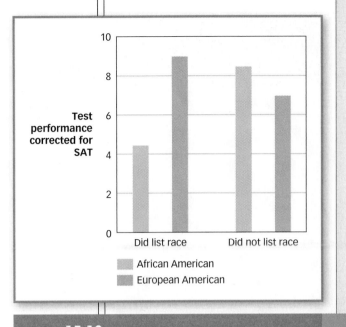

FIGURE 15.10 •••••••••••••••••••••••••••••••
Stereotype Threat and Exam Performance *When asked to indicate their race before starting a test, African American students perform more poorly than their SAT scores suggest they should. (Steele & Aronson, 1995)*

Stereotyping Can Be Automatic

If stereotypes are inaccurate and self-perpetuating, then why don't we just stop using them? Stereotyping can happen *unconsciously* (which means that we don't always know we are using them) and *automatically* (which means that we often cannot avoid using them even when we try). For example, in one study, photos of Black or White men holding guns or cameras were flashed on a computer screen for less than 1 second each. Participants earned money by pressing a button labeled "shoot" whenever the man on the screen was holding a gun but lost money if they shot a man holding a camera. The participants made some mistakes, of course, but the kinds of mistakes they made were quite disturbing: Participants were more likely to shoot a man holding a gun when that man was Black and less likely to shoot a man holding a camera when that man was White (Correll et al., 2002). Although the photos appeared on the screen so quickly that participants did not have enough time to consciously consult their stereotypes, those stereotypes worked unconsciously, causing them to mistake a camera for a gun when it was in the hands of a Black man and a gun for a camera when it was in the hands of a White man. Interestingly, Black participants were just as likely to make this pattern of errors as were White participants.

Many of us think that nuns are traditional and proper. Does this photo of Sister Rosa Elena nailing Sister Amanda de Jesús with a snowball change your stereotype, or are you tempted to subtype them instead?

Stereotypes comprise all the information that we have absorbed over the years about members of different human categories, for better or for worse, and we can't *decide* not to use that information any more than we can *decide* not to see the color green. In fact, trying not to use stereotypes can make matters worse instead of better. Participants in one study were shown a photograph of a tough-looking male "skinhead" and were asked to write an essay describing a typical day in his life. Some of the participants were told that they should not allow their stereotypes about skinheads to influence their essays, and others were given no such instructions. Next, the experimenter brought each participant to a room with eight empty chairs. The first chair had a jacket draped over

Ahmed Amadou Diallo was gunned down at his home in the Bronx on February 4, 1999. Four White police officers fired 41 shots at Diallo, who had no police record and was unarmed. Diallo was hit 19 times and died instantly. The officers testified that Diallo had gestured with his hands, leading them to believe that he was reaching for a gun.

it, and the experimenter explained that it belonged to the person in the photograph, who had gone to use the restroom. Where did participants choose to sit? Participants who had been told not to let their stereotypes influence their essays sat farther away from the skinhead's jacket than did participants who had been given no instructions (Macrae et al., 1994).

Why did this happen? As you learned in Chapter 8, attempts to suppress a thought can increase the likelihood that people will experience the very thought they are trying to suppress (Wegner et al., 1987). Stereotypical thoughts are no exception. Although stereotyping is often unconscious and automatic, it is not inevitable (Blair, 2002). We cannot stop using stereotypes with the flick of a mental switch, but research shows that stereotyping effects can be reduced (and sometimes eliminated) by a variety of factors ranging from educational programs (Kawakami et al., 2000; Rudman, Ashmore, & Gary, 2001) to damage to the prefrontal cortex (Milne & Grafman, 2001). Education is probably the better social policy.

● **How can stereotyping be reduced or eliminated?**

Attribution: Drawing Inferences from Actions

In 1963, Dr. Martin Luther King Jr. gave a speech in which he described his vision for America. "I have a dream that my four children will one day live in a nation where they will not be judged by the color of their skin but by the content of their character." Research on stereotyping demonstrates that Dr. King's concerns were well justified. We do indeed judge others by the color of their skin—as well as by their gender, nationality, religion, age, and occupation—and in so doing, we sometimes make tragic errors. But are we any better at judging people by the content of their character? If we could "turn off" our stereotypes and treat each person as an individual, would we judge these individuals accurately?

Not necessarily. Treating a person as an individual means judging that person by his or her own words and deeds. This is more difficult than it sounds because the relationship between what a person *is* and what a person *says or does* is not always straightforward. An honest person may lie to save a friend from embarrassment, and a dishonest person may tell the truth to bolster her credibility. Happy people have some rotten days, polite people can be rude in traffic, and people who despise us can be flattering when they need a favor. In short, people's behavior *sometimes* tells us about the kind of people they are, but sometimes it simply tells us about the kind of situation they happen to be in.

● **What does a person's behavior tell us about them?**

SAM GROSS/CARTOONBANK.COM

"For God's sake, think! Why is he being so nice to you?"

To judge people accurately we need to know not only *what* they did but also *why* they did it. Is the batter who hit the home run a talented slugger, or was the wind blowing in just the right direction? Is the politician who gave the pro-life speech really opposed to abortion, or was she just trying to win the conservative vote? When we answer questions such as these, we are making **attributions**, which are *inferences about the causes of people's behaviors* (Gilbert, 1998; Heider, 1958; Jones & Davis, 1965; Kelley, 1967). We make *situational attributions* when we decide that a person's behavior was caused by some temporary aspect of the situation in which it happened ("He was lucky that the wind carried the ball into the stands"), and we make *dispositional attributions* when we decide that a person's behavior was caused by his or her relatively enduring tendency to think, feel, or act in a particular way ("He's got a great eye and a powerful swing").

attribution An inference about the cause of a person's behavior.

correspondence bias The tendency to make a dispositional attribution even when a person's behavior was caused by the situation.

Research suggests that people often fall prey to the **correspondence bias**, which is *the tendency to make a dispositional attribution even when a person's behavior was caused by the situation* (Gilbert & Malone, 1995; Jones & Harris, 1967; Ross, 1977). This bias is one of the most commonly observed mind-bugs, which is why the psychologist Lee Ross has called it the *fundamental attribution error*. For example, volunteers in one experiment played a trivia game in which one participant acted as the "quizmaster" and made up a list of unusual questions, another participant acted as the "contestant" and tried to answer those questions, and a third participant acted as the "observer" and simply watched the game. The quizmasters tended to ask tricky questions based on their own idiosyncratic knowledge, and contestants were generally unable to answer them. After watching the game, the observers were asked to decide how knowledgeable the quizmaster and the contestant were. Although the quizmasters had asked good questions and the contestants had given bad answers, it should have been clear to the observers that all this asking and answering was a product of the roles they had been assigned to play and that the contestant would have asked equally good questions and the quizmaster would have given equally bad answers had their roles been reversed. And yet observers tended to rate the quizmaster as more knowledgeable than the contestant (Ross, Amabile, & Steinmetz, 1977) and were more likely to choose the quizmaster as their own partner in an upcoming game (Quattrone, 1982). Even when we know that a successful athlete had a home field advantage or that a successful entrepreneur had family connections, we tend to attribute their success to talent and tenacity. Why do we make dispositional attributions even when we shouldn't?

First, the situational causes of behavior are often invisible (Ichheiser, 1949). For example, professors tend to assume that fawning students really do admire them in spite of the strong incentive for students to suck up to those who control their grades. The problem is that professors can literally *see* the student laughing at witless jokes and applauding after boring lectures, but they cannot *see* "control over grades." Situations are not as tangible or visible as behaviors, so it is all too easy to ignore them (Taylor & Fiske, 1978). Second, even when situations are too obvious to ignore, situational attributions tend to be more complex and require more time and attention, which means that they are less likely to be made in the busy world of everyday life. Information about situations is hard to get and hard to use, and thus we are prone to believe that others' actions are caused by their dispositions.

We are more prone to correspondence bias when judging others than when judging ourselves. The **actor-observer effect** is *the tendency to make situational attributions for our*

PHILIP G. ZIMBARDO, INC.

Do abusive people seek power, or does power lead people to be abusive? In Philip Zimbardo's infamous "Stanford Prison Experiment," researchers built a simulated prison in the basement of the psychology department and randomly assigned volunteers to play the role of prisoner or guard. The study had to be abandoned when many of the "guards" began abusing the "prisoners." In a situation where ordinary people were given the power to harm, they used it. The researchers wrote, "If these reactions had been observed within the confines of an existing penal institution, it is probable that a dispositional hypothesis [or attribution] would be invoked as an explanation" (Haney, Banks, & Zimbardo, 1973). Indeed, more than 30 years later, the prisoner abuse and torture at Abu Ghraib in Iraq was officially denounced as the work of "a few bad apples."

The Kennedy brothers (Senator Robert, Senator Ted, and President John) and the Bush brothers (Governor Jeb and President George) were all very successful men with very successful fathers. Was their success due to the content of their characters or to the money and fame that came with their family names?

AP PHOTO

actor-observer effect The tendency to make situational attributions for our own behaviors while making dispositional attributions for the identical behavior of others.

own behaviors while making dispositional attributions for the identical behavior of others (Jones & Nisbett, 1972). When college students were asked to explain why they and their friends had chosen their majors, they tended to explain their own choices in terms of situations ("I chose economics because my parents told me I have to support myself as soon as I'm done with college") but tended to explain their friends' choices in terms of dispositions ("Norma chose economics because she's materialistic") (Nisbett et al., 1973). The actor-observer effect occurs because people typically have *more information* about the situations that caused their own behavior than about the situations that caused other people's behavior. We can remember getting the please-major-in-something-practical lecture from our parents, but we weren't at Norma's house to see her get the same lecture.

summary quiz [15.3]

8. A common occupational stereotype is that lawyers are manipulative. Most people who subscribe to this stereotype
   a. believe that the stereotype applies to *all* lawyers.
   b. believe that the stereotype actually applies to just a small percentage of lawyers.
   c. believe that lawyers are more likely than others to have this characteristic.
   d. would not be likely to misperceive lawyers whom they actually met.

9. Professor Rogers, who believes that women are innately unsuited for science, is much more likely to notice the mistakes of his female lab assistants than his male lab assistants. This is an example of
   a. correspondence bias.
   b. the self-fulfilling prophecy.
   c. perceptual confirmation.
   d. actor-observer effect.

10. Which statement best describes the concept of stereotype threat?
   a. Your expectations about someone may lead that person to act in ways that confirm your expectation.
   b. If you belong to a group that is negatively stereotyped and are reminded of your group membership, you may become anxious and your performance may suffer.
   c. People tend to have negative perceptions of individuals who deviate from gender stereotypes.
   d. When a person clearly disconfirms an observer's stereotype, the observer may create a new subcategory in order to retain the stereotype.

11. Brittany says, "I'm majoring in finance because my parents expect me to join the family business when I graduate, but my friend Abigail is majoring in finance because she's materialistic." This statement illustrates
   a. the self-fulfilling prophecy.
   b. the actor-observer effect.
   c. cognitive dissonance.
   d. unconscious stereotyping.

WhereDoYouStand?

Are You Prejudiced?

The satirist Ambrose Bierce (1911) defined a *bigot* as "one who is obstinately and zealously attached to an opinion that you do not entertain." Indeed, most of us think of prejudice as a bad habit whose defining feature is that other people do it and we don't. Not so fast. Recent research using the *implicit association test* (IAT) suggests that even people who think of themselves as egalitarian can harbor unconscious prejudices.

In one study, White participants were asked to classify a series of words (Greenwald et al., 1998). Some of the words were names such as *Greg* or *Jamal*, and others were related to a dislikable category such as *insects* or to a likable category such as *flowers*. When one of these words appeared on the computer screen, the participant's job was to press a button as quickly as possible to indicate whether it was a flower, an insect, a predominantly White name, or a predominantly Black name.

Now comes the interesting part. Although the participants were asked to classify the words as belonging to one of four categories, the experimental apparatus only had two buttons! On the *consistent* trials, participants were told to press the right-hand button if the word was either an insect or a Black name and to press the left-hand button if the word was a flower or a White name. On the *inconsistent* trials, participants were told to press the left-hand button if the word was a flower or a Black name and to press the right-hand button if the word was an insect or a White name (see the figure). Why did the experimenters arrange and rearrange the apparatus this way? Because previous research has shown that a classification task of this sort is much easier if the dislikable words (or the likable words) share a single button. Thus, if White participants disliked Black names, they should have found the classification task easier when Black names and insects shared one button and White names and flowers shared the other. And, in fact, White participants were indeed much faster on the consistent than the inconsistent trials.

Do these results mean that these White participants were a bunch of hate-mongers? Probably not. Psychologists since Freud have recognized that people can consciously think one thing while unconsciously feeling another. Whites who honestly believe in tolerance, diversity, and racial equality and who harbor no conscious prejudice toward Blacks may still show evidence of unconscious prejudice on the IAT (Greenwald & Nosek, 2001). In fact, Black participants also show unconscious prejudice against Blacks on this test (Lieberman et al., 2005).

How can our conscious and unconscious attitudes be so different? You know from Chapter 6 that if an experimenter repeatedly exposed you to the word *democracy* while administering an electric shock, you would eventually develop a negative association with that word. Yet if the experimenter explicitly asked you how you felt about democracy, you would probably say you liked it. In other words, you would have

both a negative unconscious attitude toward democracy that was based on the pairing of the word with electric shock and a positive conscious attitude toward democracy that was based on your knowledge of world politics (Wilson, Lindsey, & Schooler, 2000). Similarly, Whites who have positive conscious attitudes toward Blacks may nonetheless develop negative unconscious attitudes simply by watching movies and reading newspapers that pair Black names and faces with negative concepts, such as *poverty* and *crime*. Because all Americans are exposed to the same media, Blacks have the same unconscious attitudes toward their own group that Whites do (Greenwald et al., 2002).

This research has potentially profound social, moral, legal, and ethical implications. For instance, in the United States, employers are not allowed to discriminate against applicants on the basis of gender or race (among other things), and they face severe legal repercussions if they are found to have done so. Yet, if people have prejudices that they don't know about and can't control—if they consciously believe all the right things but unconsciously believe some of the wrong ones—then how can they be held accountable for any ill actions that their prejudices may produce? Before you decide where you stand on this issue, you might want to take the IAT yourself at https://implicit.harvard.edu/implicit/demo/.

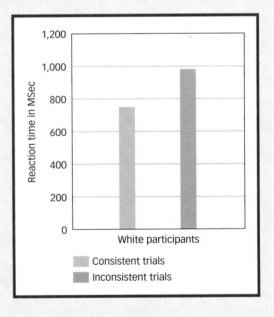

Results of an IAT Experiment In this IAT experiment, White participants responded faster on consistent trials when a likable object was paired with a White name. The reaction time on inconsistent trials was considerably slower. (Greenwald et al., 1998)

CHAPTER REVIEW AND QUIZ ANSWERS

Summary

Social Behavior: Interacting with People

- Evolutionary pressures have made survival and reproduction two fundamental challenges for humans and other animals.

- Survival requires competing against others for access to scarce resources, and two ways of gaining such access are through aggression and through cooperation.

- Reproduction requires choosing the right mate. Mates are chosen based on physical, psychological, and situational attraction, and (for humans) reproduction is usually accomplished within the context of a committed, long-term relationship.

Social Influence: Controlling People

- Social influence exploits basic hedonic, approval, and accuracy motives.

- Social influence exploits hedonic motives by creating situations in which others experience pleasure by doing what we want them to do.

- It exploits approval motives by encouraging others to do what we do, to conform to group behaviors, and to obey authority.

- It exploits accuracy motives by informational influences, persuasion, and the need to feel that we are consistent in our beliefs and our actions.

Social Cognition: Understanding People

- We make inferences about people based on the categories to which they belong, which is the basis of stereotyping.

- Although some stereotypes are useful, they can be inaccurate, they can be overused, they can be self-perpetuating, and they can operate unconsciously and automatically which makes it difficult to avoid using them.

- We also make inferences about people based on their behavior, assuming that they act as they do because of the situations in which they find themselves or because of their own dispositions.

Key Terms

aggression (p. 458)

frustration-aggression principle (p. 459)

cooperation (p. 460)

altruism (p. 461)

reciprocal altruism (p. 461)

group (p. 462)

prejudice (p. 462)

discrimination (p. 462)

deindividuation (p. 462)

diffusion of responsibility (p. 462)

group polarization (p. 463)

mere exposure effect (p. 465)

social exchange (p. 471)

equity (p. 471)

social influence (p. 472)

observational learning (p. 472)

norms (p. 473)

normative influence (p. 473)

norm of reciprocity (p. 473)

door-in-the-face technique (p. 473)

conformity (p. 474)

obedience (p. 475)

attitude (p. 476)

belief (p. 476)

informational influence (p. 476)

persuasion (p. 477)

systematic persuasion (p. 477)

heuristic persuasion (p. 477)

foot-in-the-door technique (p. 478)

cognitive dissonance (p. 478)

social cognition (p. 480)

stereotyping (p. 480)

perceptual confirmation (p. 482)

self-fulfilling prophecy (p. 482)

subtyping (p. 483)

attributions (p. 484)

correspondence bias (p. 484)

actor-observer effect (p. 485)

Critical Thinking Questions

1. Although aggression is part of our evolutionary past, does it have to be part of our future? Why or why not?

2. Of what groups are you a member? Have you experienced prejudice or discrimination of a positive or negative nature because of your group membership? How might understanding the dynamics of groups change how you participate in them?

3. Explain how the candidates in the 2008 presidential election attempted to persuade the American public with their campaign slogans: Obama, "Yes We Can"; McCain, "Country First." Why were these slogans effective or ineffective?

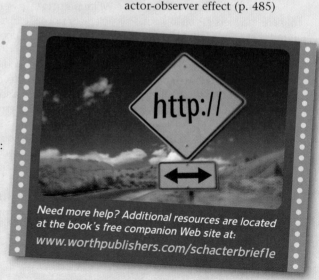

Need more help? Additional resources are located at the book's free companion Web site at:
www.worthpublishers.com/schacterbrief1e

Answers to Summary Quizzes

Summary Quiz 15.1
1. c; 2. b; 3. c; 4. a

Summary Quiz 15.2
5. d; 6. d; 7. d

Summary Quiz 15.3
8. c; 9. c; 10. b; 11. b

APPENDIX

Statistics for Psychology

The Law of Large Numbers

If you sat down and started picking cards from a deck, you would expect to pick as many red cards as black cards over the long run. But *only* over the long run. You would not be surprised if you picked just two cards and they both turned out to be red, but you *would* be surprised if you picked just 20 cards and they all turned out to be red. Your intuition tells you that when the number of cards you pick is small, you really can't expect your hand to have the same proportion of red and black cards as does the full deck.

Your intuition is exactly right. Remember from Chapter 2 that a *population* is the complete collection of objects or events that might be measured, and a *sample* is the partial collection of objects or events that is measured. In this case, the full deck is a population, and the cards in your hand are a sample of that population. Your intuition about the cards is captured by the **law of large numbers**, which states that as sample size increases, the attributes of the sample more closely reflect the attributes of the population from which the sample was drawn. In plain English, the more cards you pick, the more likely it is that half the cards in your hand will be red and half will be black.

Precisely the same logic informs the methods of psychology. For example, if we wanted to know how happy people are in Florida, we would begin with an operational definition of happiness. For the sake of simplicity, we might define happiness as a person's belief about his or her own emotional state. Then we'd develop a way to measure that belief, for example, by asking the person to make a checkmark on a 10-point rating scale. If we used this measure to measure the happiness of just one Floridian, our lone observation would tell us little about the happiness of the roughly 19 million people who actually live in that state. However, if we were to measure the happiness of a hundred Floridians, or a thousand Floridians, or even a million Floridians, the average of our measurements would begin to approximate the average happiness of all Floridians. The law of large numbers suggests that as the size of our sample increases, the average happiness of the people in our sample becomes a better approximation of the average happiness of the people in the population.

Averaging

If we have chosen a representative and sufficiently large sample, the average happiness of that sample can tell us about the average happiness of the population from which it was drawn. But the average cannot tell us about the happiness of particular individuals in that population. For example,

law of large numbers States that as sample size increases, the attributes of the sample more closely reflect the attributes of the population from which the sample was drawn.

On average, men have more upper-body strength than women, but there are still many women with more upper-body strength than many men.

when psychologists claim that women have better fine motor skills than men (and they do), or that men have better spatial ability than women (and they do), or that children are more suggestible than adults (and they are), their claims are not true—and are not meant to be true—of every individual in these populations. Rather, when psychologists say that women have better fine motor skills than men, they mean that when the fine motor skills of a large sample of women and men are measured, the average of the women's measurements is reliably higher than the average of the men's.

FIGURE A.1 illustrates this point with hypothetical observations that are arranged in a pair of **frequency distributions**, which are graphic representations of the measurements of a sample that are arranged by the number of times each measurement as observed. These frequency distributions display every possible score on a fine motor skills test on the horizontal axis and display the number of times (or the frequency with which) each score was observed among a sample of men and women on the vertical axis. A frequency distribution can have any shape, but it commonly takes the shape known as a normal distribution (sometimes also called a bell curve). A **normal distribution** is a frequency distribution in which most measurements are concentrated around the mean and fall off toward the tails, and the two sides of the distribution are symmetrical. As you can see in FIGURE A.1, normal distributions are symmetrical (i.e., the left half is a mirror image of the right half), have a peak in the middle, and trail off at either end. Most scores can be found toward the center of a normal distribution, with fewer scores at the extremes. In fact, the point at the very center of a normal distribution is where you'll find the average.

•••••••••••••••••••••••••••••• FIGURE **A.1**

Frequency Distributions *This graph shows the hypothetical scores of a sample of men and women who took a test of fine motor skills. The scores are represented along the horizontal axis, and the frequency of each score is represented along the vertical axis. As you can see, the average score of women is a bit higher than the average score of men. Both distributions are examples of normal distributions.*

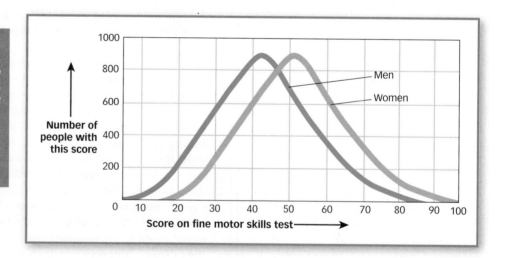

Descriptive Statistics

A frequency distribution depicts every measurement in a sample and thus provides a full and complete picture of that sample. But like most full and complete pictures, it is a terribly cumbersome way to communicate information. When we ask a friend how she's been, we don't want her to show us a graph depicting her happiness on each day of the previous six months. Rather, we want a brief summary statement that captures the essential information that such a graph would provide—for example, "I'm doing pretty well" or "I've been having some ups and downs lately." In psychology, brief summary statements that capture the essential information from a frequency distribution are called *descriptive statistics*. There are two important kinds of descriptive statistics:

■ *Descriptions of central tendency* are summary statements about the value of the measurements that lie near the center or midpoint of a frequency distribution. When a friend says that she has been "doing pretty well," she is describing the central tendency (or approximate location of the midpoint) of the frequency distribution of her happiness measurements. The three most common descriptions of central tendency are the **mode** (the value of the most frequently observed measurement), the **mean** (the average value of all the measurements), and the **median** (the value that is greater than or equal to the values of half the measurements and less than or equal to half the values of the measurements). In a normal distribution, the mean, median, and mode are all the same value, but when the distribution departs from normality, these three descriptive statistics can differ. **FIGURE A.2** shows how each of these descriptive statistics is calculated.

■ *Descriptions of variability* are statements about the extent to which the measurements in a frequency distribution differ from each other. When a friend says that she has been having some "ups and downs" lately, she is offering a brief summary statement that describes how the measurements in the frequency distribution of her happiness scores over the past six months tend to differ from one another. A mathematically simple description of variability is the **range**, which is the value of the largest measurement minus the value of the smallest measurement (**FIGURE A.2**). There are several other common descriptions of variability, such as the *variance* and the *standard deviation*, but all such descriptions give us a sense of how similar or different the scores in a distribution tend to be.

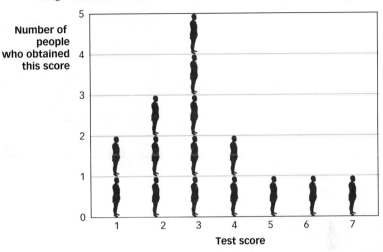

- Mode = 3 because there are five 3s and only three 2s, two 1s, two 4s, one 5, one 6, and one 7.
- Mean = 3.27 because (1 + 1 + 2 + 2 + 2 + 3 + 3 + 3 + 3 + 3 + 4 + 4 + 5 + 6 + 7)/15 = 3.27
- Median = 3 because 10 scores are ≥ 3 and 10 scores are ≤ 3
- Range = 6 because 7 − 1 = 6

FIGURE A.2 • • • • • • • • • • • • •
Some Descriptive Statistics *This frequency distribution shows the scores of 15 individuals on a seven-point test. Descriptive statistics include measures of central tendency (such as the mean, median, and mode) and measures of variability (such as the range).*

frequency distributions Graphic representations of the measurements of a sample that are arranged by the number of times each measurement was observed.

normal distribution A frequency distribution in which most measurements are concentrated around the mean and fall off toward the tails, and the two sides of the distribution are symmetrical.

mode The value of the most frequently observed measurement.

mean The average value of all the measurements.

median The value that is greater than or equal to the values of half the measurements and less than or equal to half the values of the measurements.

range The value of the largest measurement minus the value of the smallest measurement.

correlation coefficient A measure of the direction and strength of a correlation, and it is symbolized by the letter *r* (as in "relationship").

Measuring Correlation

Every correlation can be described in two equally reasonable ways. A positive correlation describes a relationship between two variables in "more-more" or "less-less" terms. When we say that *more age* is associated with *more height* or that *less age* is associated with *less height*, we are describing a positive correlation. A negative correlation describes a relationship between two variables in "more-less" or "less-more" terms. When we say that *more cholesterol* is associated with *less longevity* or that *less cholesterol* is associated with *more longevity*, we are describing a negative correlation. How we choose to describe any particular correlation is usually just a matter of simplicity and convenience.

Of course, just because two variables are correlated doesn't mean that every single individual follows the "more-more" or "more-less" rule. There is a correlation between age and height, and most children are shorter than most adults. But not in every case. There are *some* tall kids and some *short* adults. The **correlation coefficient** is a measure of the direction and strength of a correlation, and it is symbolized by the letter *r* (as in "relationship"). Like most measures, the correlation coefficient has a limited range. If you were to measure the number of hours of sunshine per day in your hometown, that measure would have a range of 24 because it could only have a value from 0 to

When children line up by age, they also tend to line up by height. The pattern of variation in age (from youngest to oldest) is synchronized with the pattern of variation in height (from shortest to tallest).

PETER TURNLEY/CORBIS

24. Values such as −7 and 36.8 would be meaningless. Similarly, the value of *r* can range from −1 to 1, and numbers outside that range are meaningless. What, then, do the numbers *inside* that range mean?

■ When *r* = 1, the relationship between the variables is called a *perfect positive correlation*, which means that every time the value of one variable increases by a certain amount, the value of the second variable always increases by a certain amount, too. If every increase in age of one year was associated with an increase in height of, say, three inches, then age and height would be perfectly positively correlated (**FIGURE A.3a**).

■ When *r* = −1, the relationship between the variables is called a *perfect negative correlation*, which means that as the value of one variable increases by a certain amount, the value of the second variable *decreases* by a certain amount, and this happens without exception. If every increase in age of one year were associated with a decrease in height of, say, one inch, then age and height would be perfectly negatively correlated (**FIGURE A.3b**).

■ When *r* = 0, there is no systematic relationship between the variables, which are said to be *uncorrelated*. This means that the pattern of variation of one variable is not synchronized in any way with the pattern of variation of the other. If increases in age of one year were sometimes associated with a large increase in height, sometimes with a small increase in height, and sometimes with no increase at all—or even a decrease—then age and height would be uncorrelated (**FIGURE A.3c**).

● ● ● ● ● ● ● ● ● ● ● ● ● ● ● ● ● ● ● **FIGURE A.3**
Three Kinds of Correlations   *This figure illustrates pairs of variables that have (a) a perfect positive correlation (r = 1), (b) a perfect negative correlation (r = −1), and (c) no correlation (r = 0).*

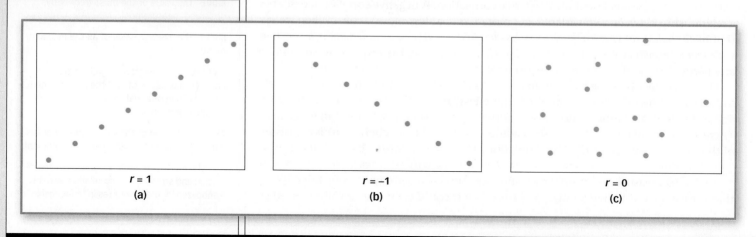

r = 1	*r* = −1	*r* = 0
(a)	(b)	(c)

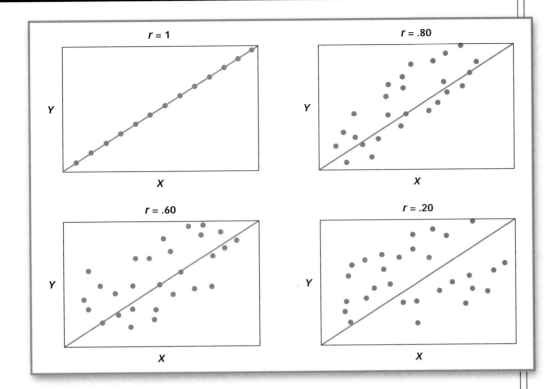

FIGURE A.4 • • • • • • • • • • • • • • • •
Positive Correlations of
Different Strengths *These
graphs represent different
degrees of positive correlation
between two variables. Scores
that are on the line adhere strictly
to the rule X = Y. The more
exceptions there are to this rule,
the weaker the correlation is.*

Perfect negative and positive correlations, such as those in **FIGURES A.3a** and **A.3b**, are extremely rare in real life. Age and height are correlated, but they are imperfectly correlated; that is, exceptions to the "more-more" rule clearly do exist. The more exceptions there are, the closer to zero r will be. **FIGURE A.4** shows four cases in which two variables are positively correlated but have different numbers of exceptions, and as you can see, the number of exceptions changes the value of r quite dramatically. Two variables can have a perfect correlation ($r = 1$), a strong correlation (e.g., $r = .80$), a moderate correlation (e.g., $r = .60$), or a weak correlation (e.g., $r = .20$). The correlation coefficient, then, is a measure of both the *direction* and *strength* of the relationship between two variables. The sign of r (positive or negative) tells us the direction of the relationship, and the absolute value of r (between 0 and 1) tells us about the number of exceptions to the rule.

Statistical Significance

The correlation coefficient r gives us a way to assess the strength of a correlation between two variables. But it tells us nothing about the causal relationship between these two variables. How do we tell if a change in one variable is actually *causing* the change in another? In Chapter 2, you learned that the way to do this was by conducting an experiment that involves manipulating an independent variable (thereby creating an experimental group and a control group) and then measuring a dependent variable. If the average measurement in the two groups differs, then you can conclude that this difference was caused by the manipulation.

There's just one small problem with this conclusion, and that's that every once in a while, differences are caused by chance. How can we tell if the differences we observed in an experiment were caused by chance? Unfortunately, we can't tell for sure. But we can calculate the *odds* that they were caused by chance. A sophisticated mathematical technique allows psychologists to calculate p, which is the likelihood that a measured difference between two groups was caused by chance. If $p < .05$, then the odds are less than 5% that differences between the experimental and control groups were caused by chance. Psychologists do not accept the results of an experiment unless $p < .05$, and when it is, the result is said to be *statistically significant*.

Glossary

absentmindedness A lapse in attention that results in memory failure. (p. 145)

absolute threshold The minimal intensity needed to just barely detect a stimulus. (p. 92)

accommodation The process by which infants revise their schemas in light of new information. (p. 304)

acquisition The phase of classical conditioning when the CS and the US are presented together. (p. 166)

action potential An electric signal that is conducted along an axon to a synapse. (p. 59)

activation-synthesis model The theory that dreams are produced when the brain attempts to make sense of activations that occur randomly during sleep. (p. 250)

actor-observer effect The tendency to make situational attributions for our own behaviors while making dispositional attributions for the identical behavior of others. (p. 485)

adolescence The period of development that begins with the onset of sexual maturity (about 11 to 14 years of age) and lasts until the beginning of adulthood (about 18 to 21 years of age). (p. 318)

adulthood The stage of development that begins around 18 to 21 years and ends at death. (p. 323)

aggression Behavior whose purpose is to harm another. (p. 458)

agoraphobia An extreme fear of venturing into public places. (p. 374)

alcohol myopia A condition that results when alcohol hampers attention, leading people to respond in simple ways to complex situations. (p. 257)

altered states of consciousness Forms of experience that depart from the normal subjective experience of the world and the mind. (p. 244)

altruism Behavior that benefits another without benefiting oneself. (p. 461)

amygdala A part of the subcortical system that plays a central role in many emotional processes, particularly the formation of emotional memories. (p. 70)

anal stage The second psychosexual stage, which is dominated by the pleasures and frustrations associated with the anus, retention and expulsion of feces and urine, and toilet training. (p. 346)

anorexia nervosa An eating disorder characterized by an intense fear of being fat and severe restriction of food intake. (p. 288)

anterograde amnesia The inability to transfer new information from the short-term store into the long-term store. (p. 135)

antianxiety medications Drugs that help reduce a person's experience of fear or anxiety. (p. 413)

antidepressants A class of drugs that help lift people's mood. (p. 413)

antipsychotic drugs Medications that are used to treat schizophrenia and related psychotic disorders. (p. 412)

antisocial personality disorder (APD) A pervasive pattern of disregard for and violation of the rights of others that begins in childhood or early adolescence and continues into adulthood. (p. 389)

anxiety disorder The class of mental disorder in which anxiety is the predominant feature. (p. 371)

aphasia Difficulty in producing or comprehending language. (p. 204)

apparent motion The perception of movement as a result of alternating signals appearing in rapid succession in different locations. (p. 109)

appraisal An evaluation of the emotion-relevant aspects of a stimulus that is performed by the amygdala. (p. 274)

approach motivation A motivation to experience positive outcomes. (p. 293)

area A1 A portion of the temporal lobe that contains the primary auditory cortex. (p. 113)

area V1 The part of the occipital lobe that contains the primary visual cortex. (p. 102)

assimilation The process by which infants apply their schemas in novel situations. (p. 304)

association areas Areas of the cerebral cortex that are composed of neurons that help provide sense and meaning to information registered in the cortex. (p. 71)

attachment The emotional bond that forms between newborns and their primary caregivers. (p. 312)

attitude An enduring positive or negative evaluation of an object or event. (p. 476)

attribution An inference about the cause of a person's behavior. (p. 484)

autonomic nervous system (ANS) A set of nerves that carries involuntary and automatic commands that control blood vessels, body organs, and glands. (p. 65)

avoidance motivation A motivation not to experience negative outcomes. (p. 293)

axon The part of a neuron that transmits information to other neurons, muscles, or glands. (p. 57)

basilar membrane A structure in the inner ear that undulates when vibrations from the ossicles reach the cochlear fluid. (p. 112)

behavior Observable actions of human beings and nonhuman animals. (p. 2)

behavior therapy A type of therapy that assumes that disordered behavior is learned and that symptom relief is achieved through changing overt maladaptive behaviors into more constructive behaviors. (p. 404)

behavioral neuroscience An approach to psychology that links psychological processes to activities in the nervous system and other bodily processes. (p. 20)

behaviorism An approach that advocates that psychologists restrict themselves to the scientific study of objectively observable behavior. (p. 15)

belief An enduring piece of knowledge about an object or event. (p. 476)

bias The distorting influences of present knowledge, beliefs, and feelings on recollection of previous experiences. (p. 153)

Big Five The traits of the five-factor model: conscientiousness, agreeableness, neuroticism, openness to experience, and extroversion. (p. 339)

binocular disparity The difference in the retinal images of the two eyes that provides information about depth. (p. 107)

biofeedback The use of an external monitoring device to obtain information about a bodily function and possibly gain control over that function. (p. 441)

biological preparedness A propensity for learning particular kinds of associations over others. (p. 172)

bipolar disorder An unstable emotional condition characterized by cycles of abnormal, persistent high mood (mania) and low mood (depression). (p. 381)

blind spot An area of the retina that contains neither rods nor cones and therefore has no mechanism to sense light. (p. 99)

blocking A failure to retrieve information that is available in memory even though you are trying to produce it. (p. 146)

bulimia nervosa An eating disorder characterized by binge eating followed by purging. (p. 288)

burnout A state of physical, emotional, and mental exhaustion created by long-term involvement in an emotionally demanding situation and accompanied by lowered performance and motivation. (p. 438)

Cannon-Bard theory A theory about the relationship between emotional experience and physiological activity suggesting that a stimulus simultaneously triggers activity in the autonomic nervous system and emotional experience in the brain. (p. 272)

Cartesian Theater (after philosopher René Descartes) A mental screen or stage on which things appear to be presented for viewing by the mind's eye. (p. 234)

case method A method of gathering scientific knowledge by studying a single individual. (p. 37)

catatonic behavior A marked decrease in all movement or an increase in muscular rigidity and overactivity. (p. 385)

category-specific deficit A neurological syndrome that is characterized by an inability to recognize objects that belong to a particular category while leaving the ability to recognize objects outside the category undisturbed. (p. 206)

cell body The part of a neuron that coordinates information-processing tasks and keeps the cell alive. (p. 57)

central nervous system (CNS) The part of the nervous system that is composed of the brain and spinal cord. (p. 64)

cephalocaudal rule The "top-to-bottom" rule that describes the tendency for motor skills to emerge in sequence from the head to the feet. (p. 302)

cerebellum A large structure of the hindbrain that controls fine motor skills. (p. 69)

cerebral cortex The outermost layer of the brain, visible to the naked eye and divided into two hemispheres. (p. 70)

childhood The stage of development that begins at about 18 to 24 months and lasts until adolescence. (p. 305)

chromosomes Strands of DNA wound around each other in a double-helix configuration. (p. 75)

chronic stressor A source of stress that occurs continuously or repeatedly. (p. 430)

chunking Combining small pieces of information into larger clusters or chunks that are more easily held in short-term memory. (p. 134)

circadian rhythm A naturally occurring 24-hour cycle. (p. 244)

classical conditioning When a neutral stimulus evokes a response after being paired with a stimulus that naturally evokes a response. (p. 164)

cochlea A fluid-filled tube that is the organ of auditory transduction. (p. 112)

cocktail party phenomenon A phenomenon in which people tune in one message even while they filter out others nearby. (p. 238)

cognitive behavioral therapy (CBT) A blend of cognitive and behavioral therapeutic strategies. (p. 406)

cognitive development The emergence of the ability to understand the world. (p. 304)

cognitive dissonance An unpleasant state that arises when a person recognizes the inconsistency of his or her actions, attitudes, or beliefs. (p. 478)

cognitive map A mental representation of the physical features of the environment. (p. 184)

cognitive neuroscience A field that attempts to understand the links between cognitive processes and brain activity. (p. 21)

cognitive psychology The scientific study of mental processes, including perception, thought, memory, and reasoning. (p. 19)

cognitive restructuring A therapeutic approach that teaches clients to question the automatic beliefs, assumptions, and predictions that often lead to negative emotions and to replace negative thinking with more realistic and positive beliefs. (p. 406)

cognitive therapy A form of psychotherapy that involves helping a client identify and correct any distorted thinking about self, others, or the world. (p. 405)

cognitive unconscious The mental processes that give rise to the person's thoughts, choices, emotions, and behavior even though they are not experienced by the person. (p. 242)

comorbidity The co-occurrence of two or more disorders in a single individual. (p. 368)

concept A mental representation that groups or categorizes shared features of related objects, events, or other stimuli. (p. 206)

concrete operational stage The stage of development that begins at about 6 years and ends at about 11 years, in which children acquire a basic understanding of the physical world and a preliminary understanding of their own and others' minds. (p. 305)

conditioned response (CR) A reaction that resembles an unconditioned response but is produced by a conditioned stimulus. (p. 164)

conditioned stimulus (CS) A stimulus that is initially neutral and produces no reliable response in an organism. (p. 164)

cones Photoreceptors that detect color, operate under normal daylight conditions, and allow us to focus on fine detail. (p. 98)

conformity The tendency to do what others do simply because others are doing it. (p. 474)

conjunction fallacy When people think that two events are more likely to occur together than either individual event. (p. 211)

conscious motivation A motivation of which one is aware. (p. 293)

consciousness A person's subjective experience of the world and the mind. (pp. 6, 234)

conservation The notion that the quantitative properties of an object are invariant despite changes in the object's appearance. (p. 305)

control group One of the two groups of participants created by the manipulation of an independent variable in an experiment that is not exposed to the stimulus being studied. (p. 45)

conventional stage A stage of moral development in which the morality of an action is primarily determined by the extent to which it conforms to social rules. (p. 315)

cooperation Behavior by two or more individuals that leads to mutual benefit. (p. 460)

corpus callosum A thick band of nerve fibers that connects large areas of the cerebral cortex on each side of the brain and supports communication of information across the hemispheres. (p. 70)

correlated The "co-relationship" or pattern of covariation between two variables, each of which has been measured several times. (p. 41)

correspondence bias The tendency to make a dispositional attribution even when a person's behavior was caused by the situation. (p. 484)

crystallized intelligence The accuracy and amount of information available for processing (see *fluid intelligence*). (p. 219)

cultural psychology The study of how cultures reflect and shape the psychological processes of their members. (p. 24)

debriefing A verbal description of the true nature and purpose of a study that psychologists provide to people after they have participated in the study. (p. 49)

deep structure The meaning of a sentence. (p. 199)

defense mechanisms Unconscious coping mechanisms that reduce anxiety generated by threats from unacceptable impulses. (p. 344)

deindividuation A phenomenon that occurs when immersion in a group causes people to become less aware of their individual values. (p. 462)

delusion A patently false belief system, often bizarre and grandiose, that is maintained in spite of its irrationality. (p. 384)

demand characteristics Those aspects of an observational setting that cause people to behave as they think an observer wants or expects them to behave. (p. 37)

dendrites The part of a neuron that receives information from other neurons and relays it to the cell body. (p. 57)

dependent variable The variable that is measured in a study. (p. 45)

depressants Substances that reduce the activity of the central nervous system. (p. 255)

developmental psychology The study of continuity and change across the life span. (p. 298)

deviation IQ A statistic obtained by dividing a person's test score by the average test score of people in the same age group and then multiplying the quotient by 100 (see *ratio IQ*). (p. 214)

diathesis-stress model A model suggesting that a person may be predisposed for a mental disorder that remains unexpressed until triggered by stress. (p. 369)

diffusion of responsibility The tendency for individuals to feel diminished responsibility for their actions when they are surrounded by others who are acting the same way. (p. 462)

discrimination Positive or negative behavior toward another person based on his or her group membership. (p. 462)

discrimination The capacity to distinguish between similar but distinct stimuli. (p. 168)

disorganized speech A severe disruption of verbal communication in which ideas shift rapidly and incoherently from one to another unrelated topic. (p. 385)

displacement A defense mechanism that involves shifting unacceptable wishes or drives to a neutral or less threatening alternative. (p. 344)

display rules Norms for the control of emotional expression. (p. 280)

dissociative amnesia The sudden loss of memory for significant personal information. (p. 377)

dissociative disorder A condition in which normal cognitive processes are severely disjointed and fragmented, creating significant disruptions in memory, awareness, or personality that can vary in length from a matter of minutes to many years. (p. 376)

dissociative fugue The sudden loss of memory for one's personal history, accompanied by an abrupt departure from home and the assumption of a new identity. (p. 377)

dissociative identity disorder (DID) The presence within an individual of two or more distinct identities that at different times take control of the individual's behavior. (p. 376)

door-in-the-face technique A strategy that uses reciprocating concessions to influence behavior. (p. 473)

dopamine hypothesis The idea that schizophrenia involves an excess of dopamine activity. (p. 387)

double depression A moderately depressed mood that persists for at least 2 years and is punctuated by periods of major depression. (p. 379)

double-blind observation An observation whose true purpose is hidden from the researcher as well as from the participant. (p. 39)

drive An internal state generated by departures from physiological optimality. (p. 286)

drug tolerance The tendency for larger doses of a drug to be required over time to achieve the same effect. (p. 254)

DSM-IV-TR (Diagnostic and Statistical Manual of Mental Disorders [Fourth Edition, Text Revision]) A classification system that describes the features used to diagnose each recognized mental disorder and indicates how the disorder can be distinguished from other, similar problems. (p. 366)

dynamic unconscious An active system encompassing a lifetime of hidden memories, the person's deepest instincts and desires, and the person's inner struggle to control these forces. (p. 242)

dysthymia A disorder that involves the same symptoms as in depression only less severe, but the symptoms last longer, persisting for at least 2 years. (p. 379)

echoic memory A fast-decaying store of auditory information. (p. 133)

eclectic psychotherapy Treatment that draws on techniques from different forms of therapy, depending on the client and the problem. (p. 402)

ego The component of personality, developed through contact with the external world, that enables us to deal with life's practical demands. (p. 343)

egocentrism The failure to understand that the world appears differently to different observers. (p. 306)

elaborative encoding The process of actively relating new information to knowledge that is already in memory. (p. 129)

electroconvulsive therapy (ECT) A treatment that involves inducing a mild seizure by delivering an electrical shock to the brain. (p. 417)

electromyograph (EMG) A device that measures muscle contractions under the surface of a person's skin. (p. 35)

embryonic stage The period of prenatal development that lasts from the second week until about the eighth week. (p. 299)

emotion A positive or negative experience that is associated with a particular pattern of physiological activity. (p. 271)

emotion regulation The use of cognitive and behavioral strategies to influence one's emotional experience. (p. 276)

emotional expression Any observable sign of an emotional state. (p. 278)

empiricism Originally a Greek school of medicine that stressed the importance of observation, and now generally used to describe any attempt to acquire knowledge by observing objects or events. (p. 34)

encoding The process by which we transform what we perceive, think, or feel into an enduring memory. (p. 128)

encoding specificity principle The idea that a retrieval cue can serve as an effective reminder when it helps re-create the specific way in which information was initially encoded. (p. 138)

endorphins or **endogenous opiates** Neurotransmitters that have a similar structure to opiates and that appear to play a role in how the brain copes internally with pain and stress. (p. 258)

episodic memory The collection of past personal experiences that occurred at a particular time and place. (p. 142)

equity A state of affairs in which the cost-benefit ratios of two partners are roughly equal. (p. 471)

evolutionary psychology A psychological approach that explains mind and behavior in terms of the adaptive value of abilities that are preserved over time by natural selection. (p. 21)

exemplar theory A theory of categorization that argues that we make category judgments by comparing a new instance with stored memories for other instances of the category. (p. 208)

existential approach A school of thought that regards personality as governed by an individual's ongoing choices and decisions in the context of the realities of life and death. (p. 348)

expectancy theory The idea that alcohol effects can be produced by people's expectations of how alcohol will influence them in particular situations. (p. 256)

experiment A technique for establishing the causal relationship between variables. (p. 44)

experimental group One of the two groups of participants created by the manipulation of an independent variable in an experiment; the experimental group is exposed to the stimulus being studied and the *control group* is not. (p. 45)

explicit memory The act of consciously or intentionally retrieving past experiences. (p. 140)

exposure therapy An approach to treatment that involves confronting an emotion-arousing stimulus directly and repeatedly, ultimately leading to a decrease in the emotional response. (p. 405)

external validity A characteristic of an experiment in which the independent and dependent variables are operationally defined in a normal, typical, or realistic way. (p. 46)

extinction The gradual elimination of a learned response that occurs when the US is no longer presented. (p. 167)

extrinsic motivation A motivation to take actions that are not themselves rewarding but that lead to reward. (p. 292)

facial feedback hypothesis The hypothesis that emotional expressions can cause the emotional experiences they signify. (p. 280)

factor analysis A statistical technique that explains a large number of correlations in terms of a small number of underlying factors. (p. 218)

family resemblance theory Members of a category have features that appear to be characteristic of category members but may not be possessed by every member. (p. 207)

fast mapping The fact that children can map a word onto an underlying concept after only a single exposure. (p. 201)

fetal alcohol syndrome A developmental disorder that stems from heavy alcohol use by the mother during pregnancy. (p. 300)

fetal stage The period of prenatal development that lasts from the ninth week until birth. (p. 299)

fight-or-flight response An emotional and physiological reaction to an emergency that increases readiness for action. (p. 433)

fixation A phenomenon in which a person's pleasure-seeking drives become psychologically stuck, or arrested, at a particular psychosexual stage. (p. 346)

fixed interval schedule (FI) An operant conditioning principle in which reinforcements

are presented at fixed time periods, provided that the appropriate response is made. (p. 180)

fixed ratio schedule (FR) An operant conditioning principle in which reinforcement is delivered after a specific number of responses have been made. (p. 180)

flashbulb memories Detailed recollections of when and where we heard about shocking events. (p. 154)

fluid intelligence The ability to process information (see *crystallized intelligence*). (p. 218)

foot-in-the-door technique A strategy that uses a person's desire for consistency to influence that person's behavior. (p. 478)

formal operational stage The stage of development that begins around the age of 11 and lasts through adulthood, in which children gain a deeper understanding of their own and others' minds and learn to reason abstractly. (p. 306)

fovea An area of the retina where vision is the clearest and there are no rods at all. (p. 98)

framing effects When people give different answers to the same problem depending on how the problem is phrased (or framed). (p. 211)

fraternal twins (also called dizygotic twins) Twins who develop from two different eggs that were fertilized by two different sperm (see *identical twins*). (p. 222)

frontal lobe A region of the cerebral cortex that has specialized areas for movement, abstract thinking, planning, memory, and judgment. (p. 71)

frustration-aggression principle A principle stating that people aggress when their goals are thwarted. (p. 459)

full consciousness Consciousness in which you know and are able to report your mental-state. (p. 239)

functionalism The study of the purpose mental processes serve in enabling people to adapt to their environment. (p. 8)

gate-control theory A theory of pain perception based on the idea that signals arriving from pain receptors in the body can be stopped, or *gated,* by interneurons in the spinal cord via feedback from two directions. (p. 117)

gene The unit of hereditary transmission. (p. 75)

general adaptation syndrome (GAS) A three-stage physiological response that appears regardless of the stressor that is encountered. (p. 433)

generalization A process in which the CR is observed even though the CS is slightly different from the original one used during acquisition. (p. 167)

generalized anxiety disorder (GAD) A disorder characterized by chronic excessive

worry accompanied by three or more of the following symptoms: restlessness, fatigue, concentration problems, irritability, muscle tension, and sleep disturbance. (p. 371)

genetic dysphasia A syndrome characterized by an inability to learn the grammatical structure of language despite having otherwise normal intelligence. (p. 203)

genital stage The final psychosexual stage, a time for the coming together of the mature adult personality with a capacity to love, work, and relate to others in a mutually satisfying and reciprocal manner. (p. 346)

germinal stage The 2-week period of prenatal development that begins at conception. (p. 299)

Gestalt psychology A psychological approach that emphasizes that we often perceive the whole rather than the sum of the parts. (p. 12)

Gestalt therapy An existentialist approach to treatment with the goal of helping the client become aware of his or her thoughts, behaviors, experiences, and feelings and to "own" or take responsibility for them. (p. 408)

glial cells Support cells found in the nervous system. (p. 57)

grammar A set of rules that specify how the units of language can be combined to produce meaningful messages. (p. 198)

grossly disorganized behavior Behavior that is inappropriate for the situation or ineffective in attaining goals, often with specific motor disturbances. (p. 385)

group A collection of two or more people who believe they have something in common. (p. 462)

group polarization The tendency for a group's initial leaning to get stronger over time. (p. 463)

group therapy Therapy in which multiple participants (who often do not know one another at the outset) work on their individual problems in a group atmosphere. (p. 409)

habituation A general process in which repeated or prolonged exposure to a stimulus results in a gradual reduction in responding. (p. 163)

hair cells Specialized auditory receptor neurons embedded in the basilar membrane. (p. 112)

hallucination A false perceptual experience that has a compelling sense of being real despite the absence of external stimulation. (p. 384)

hallucinogens Drugs that alter sensation and perception and often cause visual and auditory hallucinations. (p. 258)

haptic perception The active exploration of the environment by touching and grasping objects with our hands. (p. 115)

health psychology The subfield of psychology concerned with ways psychological factors influence the causes and treatment of physical illness and the maintenance of health. (p. 428)

hedonic principle The notion that all people are motivated to experience pleasure and avoid pain. (p. 284)

helplessness theory The idea that individuals who are prone to depression automatically attribute negative experiences to causes that are internal (i.e., their own fault), stable (i.e., unlikely to change), and global (i.e., widespread). (p. 380)

heritability coefficient A statistic (commonly denoted as h^2) that describes the proportion of the difference between people's scores that can be explained by differences in their genetic makeup. (p. 222)

heuristic persuasion A change in attitudes or beliefs that is brought about by appeals to habit or emotion. (p. 477)

hindbrain An area of the brain that coordinates information coming into and out of the spinal cord. (p. 68)

hippocampus A structure critical for creating new memories and integrating them into a network of knowledge so that they can be stored indefinitely in other parts of the cerebral cortex. (p. 70)

human sexual response cycle The stages of physiological arousal during sexual activity. (p. 290)

humanistic psychology An approach to understanding human nature that emphasizes the positive potential of human beings. (p. 14)

hypochondriasis A psychological disorder in which a person is preoccupied with minor symptoms and develops an exaggerated belief that the symptoms signify a life-threatening illness. (p. 446)

hypothalamus A subcortical structure that regulates body temperature, hunger, thirst, and sexual behavior. (p. 70)

hypothesis A specific and testable prediction that is usually derived from a *theory*. (p. 46)

hysteria A temporary loss of cognitive or motor functions, usually as a result of emotionally upsetting experiences. (p. 12)

iatrogenic illness A disorder or symptom that occurs as a result of a medical or psychotherapeutic treatment. (p. 422)

iconic memory A fast-decaying store of visual information. (p. 133)

id The part of the mind containing the drives present at birth; it is the source of our bodily needs, wants, desires, and impulses, particularly our sexual and aggressive drives. (p. 342)

identical twins (also called monozygotic twins) Twins who develop from the splitting of a single egg that was fertilized by a single sperm (see *fraternal twins*). (p. 222)

identification A defense mechanism that helps deal with feelings of threat and anxiety by enabling us unconsciously to take on the characteristics of another person who seems more powerful or better able to cope. (p. 344)

illusions Errors of perception, memory, or judgment in which subjective experience differs from objective reality. (p. 10)

immune system A complex response system that protects the body from bacteria, viruses, and other foreign substances. (p. 434)

implicit learning Learning that takes place largely independent of awareness of both the process and the products of information acquisition. (p. 190)

implicit memory The influence of past experiences on later behavior and performance, even though people are not trying to recollect them and are not aware that they are remembering them. (p. 140)

independent variable The variable that is manipulated in an experiment. (p. 45)

infancy The stage of development that begins at birth and lasts between 18 and 24 months. (p. 301)

informational influence A phenomenon whereby a person's behavior is influenced by another person's behavior because the latter provides information about what is good or true. (p. 476)

informed consent A written agreement to participate in a study made by a person who has been informed of all the risks that participation may entail. (p. 49)

insomnia Difficulty in falling asleep or staying asleep. (p. 247)

intelligence A hypothetical mental ability that enables people to direct their thinking, adapt to their circumstances, and learn from their experiences. (p. 213)

intermittent reinforcement An operant conditioning principle in which only some of the responses made are followed by reinforcement. (p. 181)

intermittent reinforcement effect The fact that operant behaviors that are maintained under intermittent reinforcement schedules resist extinction better than those maintained under continuous reinforcement. (p. 182)

internal validity The characteristic of an experiment that allows one to draw accurate inferences about the causal relationship between an independent and dependent variable. (p. 45)

internal working model of attachment A set of expectations about how the primary caregiver will respond when the child feels insecure. (p. 312)

interneurons Neurons that connect sensory neurons, motor neurons, or other interneurons. (p. 57)

interpersonal psychotherapy (IPT) A form of psychotherapy that focuses on helping clients improve current relationships. (p. 404)

intrinsic motivation A motivation to take actions that are themselves rewarding. (p. 292)

introspection The subjective observation of one's own experience. (p. 7)

ironic processes of mental control Mental processes that can produce ironic errors because monitoring for errors can itself produce them. (p. 241)

James-Lange theory A theory about the relationship between emotional experience and physiological activity suggesting that stimuli trigger activity in the autonomic nervous system, which in turn produces an emotional experience in the brain. (p. 272)

just noticeable difference (JND) The minimal change in a stimulus that can just barely be detected. (p. 93)

language A system for communicating with others using signals that convey meaning and are combined according to rules of grammar. (p. 198)

language acquisition device (LAD) A collection of processes that facilitate language learning. (p. 202)

latency stage The fourth psychosexual stage, in which the primary focus is on the further development of intellectual, creative, interpersonal, and athletic skills. (p. 346)

latent learning A condition in which something is learned but it is not manifested as a behavioral change until sometime in the future. (p. 183)

law of effect The principle that behaviors that are followed by a "satisfying state of affairs" tend to be repeated and those that produce an "unpleasant state of affairs" are less likely to be repeated. (p. 175)

learning Some experience that results in a relatively permanent change in the state of the learner. (p. 162)

locus of control A person's tendency to perceive the control of rewards as internal to the self or external in the environment. (p. 352)

long-term memory store A place in which information can be kept for hours, days, weeks, or years. (p. 134)

long-term potentiation (LTP) Enhanced neural processing that results from the strengthening of synaptic connections. (p. 136)

loudness A sound's intensity. (p. 111)

lymphocytes White blood cells that produce antibodies that fight infection. (p. 434)

major depression A disorder characterized by a severely depressed mood that lasts 2 weeks or more and is accompanied by feelings of worthlessness and lack of pleasure, lethargy, and sleep and appetite disturbances. (p. 379)

marijuana The leaves and buds of the hemp plant. (p. 259)

matched pairs An observational technique that involves matching each participant in the experimental group with a specific participant in the control group in order to eliminate the possibility that a third variable (and not the independent variable) caused changes in the dependent variable. (p. 42)

matched samples An observational technique that involves matching the average of the participants in the experimental and control groups in order to eliminate the possibility that a third variable (and not the independent variable) caused changes in the dependent variable. (p. 42)

measure A device that can detect the measurable events to which an operational definition refers. (p. 35)

medical model The conceptualization of psychological abnormalities as diseases that, like biological diseases, have symptoms and causes and possible cures. (p. 365)

meditation The practice of intentional contemplation. (p. 263)

medulla An extension of the spinal cord into the skull that coordinates heart rate, circulation, and respiration. (p. 68)

memory misattribution Assigning a recollection or an idea to the wrong source. (p. 147)

memory The ability to store and retrieve information over time. (p. 128)

memory storage The process of maintaining information in memory over time. (p. 133)

mental control The attempt to change conscious states of mind. (p. 240)

mere exposure effect The tendency for liking to increase with the frequency of exposure. (p. 465)

metabolism The rate at which energy is used by the body. (p. 289)

method A set of rules and techniques for observation that allow researchers to avoid the illusions, mistakes, and erroneous conclusions that simple observation can produce. (p. 34)

mind Our private inner experience of perceptions, thoughts, memories, and feelings. (p. 2)

mind/body problem The issue of how the mind is related to the brain and body. (p. 236)

mindfulness meditation A form of cognitive therapy that teaches an individual to be fully present in each moment; to be aware of his or her thoughts, feelings, and sensations; and to detect symptoms before they become a problem. (p. 406)

minimal consciousness A low-level kind of sensory awareness and responsiveness that occurs when the mind inputs sensations and may output behavior. (p. 239)

Minnesota Multiphasic Personality Inventory (MMPI) A well-researched clinical questionnaire used to assess personality and psychological problems. (p. 335)

monocular depth cues Aspects of a scene that yield information about depth when viewed with only one eye. (p. 106)

mood disorders Mental disorders that have mood disturbance as their predominant feature. (p. 378)

morphemes The smallest meaningful units of language. (p. 198)

motivation The purpose for or cause of an action. (p. 284)

motor development The emergence of the ability to execute physical action. (p. 302)

motor neurons Neurons that carry signals from the spinal cord to the muscles to produce movement. (p. 57)

myelin sheath An insulating layer of fatty material. (p. 57)

myelination The formation of a fatty sheath around the axons of a brain cell. (p. 299)

narcissism A trait that reflects a grandiose view of the self combined with a tendency to seek admiration from and exploit others. (p. 358)

narcolepsy A disorder in which sudden sleep attacks occur in the middle of waking activities. (p. 248)

narcotics or **opiates** Highly addictive drugs derived from opium that relieve pain. (p. 258)

nativism The philosophical view that certain kinds of knowledge are innate or inborn. (p. 4)

nativist theory The view that language development is best explained as an innate, biological capacity. (p. 202)

natural selection Charles Darwin's theory that the features of an organism that help it survive and reproduce are more likely than other features to be passed on to subsequent generations. (p. 8)

naturalistic observation A method of gathering scientific knowledge by unobtrusively observing people in their natural environments. (p. 37)

negative symptoms Emotional and social withdrawal; apathy; poverty of speech; and other indications of the absence or insufficiency of normal behavior, motivation, and emotion. (p. 385)

nervous system An interacting network of neurons that conveys electrochemical information throughout the body. (p. 64)

neurons Cells in the nervous system that communicate with one another to perform information-processing tasks. (p. 56)

neurotransmitters Chemicals that transmit information across the synapse to a receiving neuron's dendrites. (p. 60)

night terrors (or sleep terrors) Abrupt awakenings with panic and intense emotional arousal. (p. 248)

norm of reciprocity The norm that people should benefit those who have benefited them. (p. 473)

normative influence A phenomenon whereby one person's behavior is influenced by another person's behavior because the latter provides information about what is appropriate. (p. 473)

norms A customary standard for behavior that is widely shared by members of a culture. (p. 473)

obedience The tendency to do what authorities tell us to do simply because they tell us to do it. (p. 474)

object permanence The idea that objects continue to exist even when they are not visible. (p. 304)

observational learning A condition in which learning takes place by watching the actions of others. (p. 187)

observational learning Learning that occurs when one person observes another person being rewarded or punished. (p. 472)

obsessive-compulsive disorder (OCD) A disorder in which repetitive, intrusive thoughts (obsessions) and ritualistic behaviors (compulsions) designed to fend off those thoughts interfere significantly with an individual's functioning. (p. 375)

occipital lobe A region of the cerebral cortex that processes visual information. (p. 71)

Oedipus conflict A developmental experience in which a child's conflicting feelings toward the opposite-sex parent is (usually) resolved by identifying with the same-sex parent. (p. 346)

olfactory bulb A brain structure located above the nasal cavity beneath the frontal lobes. (p. 120)

olfactory receptor neurons (ORNs) Receptor cells that initiate the sense of smell. (p. 119)

operant behavior Behavior that an organism produces that has some impact on the environment. (p. 175)

operant conditioning A type of learning in which the consequences of an organism's behavior determine whether it will be repeated in the future. (p. 175)

operational definition A description of an abstract property in terms of a concrete condition that can be measured. (p. 35)

oral stage The first psychosexual stage, in which experience centers on the pleasures and frustrations associated with the mouth, sucking, and being fed. (p. 346)

organizational encoding The act of categorizing information by noticing the relationships among a series of items. (p. 131)

outcome expectancies A person's assumptions about the likely consequences of a future behavior. (p. 352)

overjustification effect Circumstances when external rewards can undermine the intrinsic satisfaction of performing a behavior. (p. 176)

panic disorder A disorder characterized by the sudden occurrence of multiple psychological and physiological symptoms that contribute to a feeling of stark terror. (p. 374)

parasympathetic nervous system A set of nerves that helps the body return to a normal resting state. (p. 65)

parietal lobe A region of the cerebral cortex whose functions include processing information about touch. (p. 71)

perception The organization, identification, and interpretation of a sensation in order to form a mental representation. (p. 90)

perceptual confirmation A phenomenon that occurs when observers perceive what they expect to perceive. (p. 482)

perceptual constancy A perceptual principle stating that even as aspects of sensory signals change, perception remains consistent. (p. 104)

peripheral nervous system (PNS) The part of the nervous system that connects the central nervous system to the body's organs and muscles. (p. 64)

persistence The intrusive recollection of events that we wish we could forget. (p. 154)

personal constructs Dimensions people use in making sense of their experiences. (p. 351)

personality disorder Disorder characterized by deeply ingrained, inflexible patterns of thinking, feeling, or relating to others or controlling impulses that cause distress or impaired functioning. (p. 389)

personality An individual's characteristic style of behaving, thinking, and feeling. (p. 333)

person-centered therapy An approach to therapy that assumes all individuals have a tendency toward growth and that this growth can be facilitated by acceptance and genuine reactions from the therapist. (p. 408)

person-situation controversy The question of whether behavior is caused more by personality or by situational factors. (p. 350)

persuasion A phenomenon that occurs when a person's attitudes or beliefs are influenced by a communication from another person. (p. 477)

phallic stage The third psychosexual stage, during which experience is dominated by the pleasure, conflict, and frustration associated with the phallic-genital region as well as powerful incestuous feelings of love, hate, jealousy, and conflict. (p. 346)

phenomenology How things seem to the conscious person. (p. 234)

pheromones Biochemical odorants emitted by other members of their species that can affect an animal's behavior or physiology. (p. 120)

philosophical empiricism The philosophical view that all knowledge is acquired through experience. (p. 5)

phobic disorders Disorders characterized by marked, persistent, and excessive fear and avoidance of specific objects, activities, or situations. (p. 372)

phoneme The smallest unit of sound that is recognizable as speech rather than as random noise. (p. 198)

phrenology A now defunct theory that specific mental abilities and characteristics, ranging from memory to the capacity for happiness, are localized in specific regions of the brain. (p. 5)

physiology The study of biological processes, especially in the human body. (p. 6)

pitch How high or low a sound is. (p. 111)

pituitary gland The "master gland" of the body's hormone-producing system, which releases hormones that direct the functions of many other glands in the body. (p. 70)

place code The cochlea encodes different frequencies at different locations along the basilar membrane. (p. 114)

placebo An inert substance or procedure that has been applied with the expectation that a healing response will be produced. (p. 419)

pons A brain structure that relays information from the cerebellum to the rest of the brain. (p. 69)

population The complete collection of participants who might possibly be measured. (p. 37)

postconventional stage A stage of moral development at which the morality of an action is determined by a set of general principles that reflect core values. (p. 315)

posttraumatic stress disorder (PTSD) A disorder characterized by chronic physiological arousal, recurrent unwanted thoughts or images of the trauma, and avoidance of things that call the traumatic event to mind. (p. 436)

power The tendency for a measure to produce different results when it is used to measure different things. (p. 36)

preconventional stage A stage of moral development in which the morality of an action is primarily determined by its consequences for the actor. (p. 315)

prejudice A positive or negative evaluation of another person based on his or her group membership. (p. 462)

preoperational stage The stage of development that begins at about 2 years and ends at about 6 years, in which children have a preliminary understanding of the physical world. (p. 305)

preparedness theory The idea that people are instinctively predisposed toward certain fears. (p. 373)

primary sex characteristics Bodily structures that are directly involved in reproduction. (p. 318)

priming An enhanced ability to think of a stimulus, such as a word or object, as a result of a recent exposure to the stimulus. (p. 141)

proactive interference Situations in which earlier learning impairs memory for information acquired later. (p. 145)

problem of other minds The fundamental difficulty we have in perceiving the consciousness of others. (p. 235)

procedural memory The gradual acquisition of skills as a result of practice, or "knowing how," to do things. (p. 140)

prodigy A person of normal intelligence who has an extraordinary ability. (p. 221)

projection A defense mechanism that involves attributing one's own threatening feelings, motives, or impulses to another person or group. (p. 344)

projective techniques A standard series of ambiguous stimuli designed to elicit unique responses that reveal inner aspects of an individual's personality. (p. 336)

prospect theory Proposes that people choose to take on risk when evaluating potential losses and avoid risks when evaluating potential gains. (p. 212)

prospective memory Remembering to do things in the future. (p. 145)

prototype The "best" or "most typical member" of a category. (p. 208)

proximodistal rule The "inside-to-outside" rule that describes the tendency for motor skills to emerge in sequence from the center to the periphery. (p. 302)

psychoactive drug A chemical that influences consciousness or behavior by altering the brain's chemical message system. (p. 253)

psychoanalysis A therapeutic approach that focuses on bringing unconscious material into conscious awareness to better understand psychological disorders. (p. 13)

psychoanalytic theory Sigmund Freud's approach to understanding human behavior that emphasizes the importance of unconscious mental processes in shaping feelings, thoughts, and behaviors. (p. 13)

psychodynamic approach An approach that regards personality as formed by needs, strivings, and desires, largely operating outside of awareness motives that can also produce emotional disorders. (p. 342)

psychodynamic psychotherapies A general approach to treatment that explores childhood events and encourages individuals to develop insight into their psychological problems. (p. 402)

psychological disorders Disorders reflecting abnormalities of the mind. (p. 363)

psychology The scientific study of mind and behavior. (p. 2)

psychopharmacology The study of drug effects on psychological states and symptoms. (p. 412)

psychophysics Methods that measure the strength of a stimulus and the observer's sensitivity to that stimulus. (p. 92)

psychosexual stages Distinct early life stages through which personality is formed as children experience sexual pleasures from specific body areas and caregivers redirect or interfere with those pleasures. (p. 345)

psychosomatic illness An interaction between mind and body that can produce illness. (p. 446)

psychosurgery Surgical destruction of specific brain areas. (p. 418)

psychotherapy An interaction between a therapist and someone suffering from a psychological problem, with the goal of providing support or relief from the problem. (p. 402)

puberty The bodily changes associated with sexual maturity. (p. 318)

punisher Any stimulus or event that functions to decrease the likelihood of the behavior that led to it. (p. 175)

random sampling A technique for choosing participants that ensures that every member of a population has an equal chance of being included in the sample. (p. 47)

ratio IQ A statistic obtained by dividing a person's mental age by the person's physical age and then multiplying the quotient by 100 (see *deviation IQ*). (p. 214)

rational choice theory The classical view that we make decisions by determining how likely something is to happen, judging the value of the outcome, and then multiplying the two. (p. 209)

rational coping Facing a stressor and working to overcome it. (p. 439)

rationalization A defense mechanism that involves supplying a reasonable-sounding explanation for unacceptable feelings and be-

havior to conceal (mostly from oneself) one's underlying motives or feelings. (p. 344)

reaction formation A defense mechanism that involves unconsciously replacing threatening inner wishes and fantasies with an exaggerated version of their opposite. (p. 344)

reaction time The amount of time taken to respond to a specific stimulus. (p. 6)

reappraisal A strategy that involves changing one's emotional experience by changing the meaning of the emotion-eliciting stimulus. (p. 277)

rebound effect of thought suppression The tendency of a thought to return to consciousness with greater frequency following suppression. (p. 241)

receptive field The region of the sensory surface that, when stimulated, causes a change in the firing rate of that neuron. (p. 100)

receptors Parts of the cell membrane that receive the neurotransmitter and initiate a new electric signal. (p. 60)

reciprocal altruism Behavior that benefits another with the expectation that those benefits will be returned in the future. (p. 461)

referred pain The feeling of pain when sensory information from internal and external areas converge on the same nerve cells in the spinal cord. (p. 116)

reflexes Specific patterns of motor response that are triggered by specific patterns of sensory stimulation. (p. 302)

refractory period The time following an action potential during which a new action potential cannot be initiated. (p. 60)

reframing Finding a new or creative way to think about a stressor that reduces its threat. (p. 440)

regression A defense mechanism in which the ego deals with internal conflict and perceived threat by reverting to an immature behavior or earlier stage of development. (p. 344)

rehearsal The process of keeping information in short-term memory by mentally repeating it. (p. 134)

reinforcement The consequences of a behavior that determine whether it will be more likely that the behavior will occur again. (p. 16)

reinforcer Any stimulus or event that functions to increase the likelihood of the behavior that led to it. (p. 175)

relaxation response A condition of reduced muscle tension, cortical activity, heart rate, breathing rate, and blood pressure. (p. 441)

relaxation therapy A technique for reducing tension by consciously relaxing muscles of the body. (p. 441)

reliability The tendency for a measure to produce the same result whenever it is used to measure the same thing. (p. 36)

REM sleep A stage of sleep characterized by rapid eye movements and a high level of brain activity. (p. 245)

repression A mental process that removes unacceptable thoughts and memories from consciousness. (p. 242)

repressive coping Avoiding situations or thoughts that are reminders of a stressor and maintaining an artificially positive viewpoint. (p. 439)

resistance A reluctance to cooperate with treatment for fear of confronting unpleasant unconscious material. (p. 403)

response An action or physiological change elicited by a stimulus. (p. 16)

resting potential The difference in electric charge between the inside and outside of a neuron's cell membrane. (p. 59)

reticular formation A brain structure that regulates sleep, wakefulness, and levels of arousal. (p. 68)

retina Light-sensitive tissue lining the back of the eyeball. (p. 97)

retrieval cue External information that is associated with stored information and helps bring it to mind. (p. 137)

retrieval The process of bringing to mind information that has been previously encoded and stored. (p. 128)

retroactive interference Situations in which later learning impairs memory for information acquired earlier. (p. 144)

retrograde amnesia The inability to retrieve information that was acquired before a particular date, usually the date of an injury or operation. (p. 135)

rods Photoreceptors that become active only under low-light conditions for night vision. (p. 98)

Rorschach Inkblot Test A projective personality test in which individual interpretations of the meaning of a set of unstructured inkblots are analyzed to identify a respondent's inner feelings and interpret his or her personality structure. (p. 336)

sample The partial collection of people who actually were measured in a study. (p. 37)

savant A person of low intelligence who has an extraordinary ability. (p. 220)

schemas Theories about or models of the way the world works. (p. 304)

schizophrenia A disorder characterized by the profound disruption of basic psychological processes; a distorted perception of reality; altered or blunted emotion; and disturbances in thought, motivation, and behavior. (p. 384)

seasonal affective disorder (SAD) Depression that involves recurrent depressive episodes in a seasonal pattern. (p. 379)

secondary sex characteristics Bodily structures that change dramatically with sexual maturity but that are not directly involved in reproduction. (p. 318)

self-actualizing tendency The human motive toward realizing our inner potential. (p. 348)

self-concept A person's explicit knowledge of his or her own behaviors, traits, and other personal characteristics. (p. 353)

self-consciousness A distinct level of consciousness in which the person's attention is drawn to the self as an object. (p. 239)

self-esteem The extent to which an individual likes, values, and accepts the self. (p. 353)

self-fulfilling prophecy A phenomenon whereby observers bring about what they expect to perceive. (p. 482)

self-regulation The exercise of voluntary control over the self to bring the self into line with preferred standards. (p. 451)

self-report A series of answers to a questionnaire that asks people to indicate the extent to which sets of statements or adjectives accurately describe their own behavior or mental state. (p. 335)

self-serving bias People's tendency to take credit for their successes but downplay responsibility for their failures. (p. 358)

self-verification The tendency to seek evidence to confirm the self-concept. (p. 355)

semantic memory A network of associated facts and concepts that make up our general knowledge of the world. (p. 142)

sensation Simple awareness due to the stimulation of a sense organ. (p. 90)

sensorimotor stage A stage of development that begins at birth and lasts through infancy in which infants acquire information about the world by sensing it and moving around within it. (p. 304)

sensory adaptation Sensitivity to prolonged stimulation tends to decline over time as an organism adapts to current conditions. (p. 94)

sensory memory store The place in which sensory information is kept for a few seconds or less. (p. 133)

sensory neurons Neurons that receive information from the external world and convey this information to the brain via the spinal cord. (p. 57)

shaping Learning that results from the reinforcement of successive approximations to a final desired behavior. (p. 178)

short-term memory store A place where nonsensory information is kept for more than a few seconds but less than a minute. (p. 133)

sick role A socially recognized set of rights and obligations linked with illness. (p. 446)

signal detection theory An observation that the response to a stimulus depends both on a person's sensitivity to the stimulus in the presence of noise and on a person's response criterion. (p. 93)

sleep apnea A disorder in which the person stops breathing for brief periods while asleep. (p. 248)

sleep paralysis The experience of waking up unable to move. (p. 248)

social cognition The processes by which people come to understand others. (p. 480)

social cognitive approach An approach that views personality in terms of how the person thinks about the situations encountered in daily life and behaves in response to them. (p. 350)

social exchange The hypothesis that people remain in relationships only as long as they perceive a favorable ratio of costs to benefits. (p. 471)

social influence The control of one person's behavior by another. (p. 472)

social phobia A disorder that involves an irrational fear of being publicly humiliated or embarrassed. (p. 373)

social psychology A subfield of psychology that studies the causes and consequences of interpersonal behavior. (p. 22)

social support The aid gained through interacting with others. (p. 442)

somatic nervous system A set of nerves that conveys information into and out of the central nervous system. (p. 64)

somatoform disorders The set of psychological disorders in which the person displays physical symptoms not fully explained by a general medical condition. (p. 446)

somnambulism (sleepwalking) Occurs when the person arises and walks around while asleep. (p. 248)

source memory Recall of when, where, and how information was acquired. (p. 147)

specific phobia A disorder that involves an irrational fear of a particular object or situation that markedly interferes with an individual's ability to function. (p. 372)

spinal reflexes Simple pathways in the nervous system that rapidly generate muscle contractions. (p. 67)

spontaneous recovery The tendency of a learned behavior to recover from extinction after a rest period. (p. 167)

state-dependent retrieval The tendency for information to be better recalled when the person is in the same state during encoding and retrieval. (p. 138)

stereotyping The process by which people draw inferences about others based on their knowledge of the categories to which others belong. (p. 480)

stimulants Substances that excite the central nervous system, heightening arousal and activity levels. (p. 257)

stimulus Sensory input from the environment. (p. 6)

storage The process of maintaining information in memory over time. (p. 128)

stress The physical and psychological response to internal or external stressors. (p. 428)

stress inoculation training (SIT) A therapy that helps people to cope with stressful situations by developing positive ways to think about the situation. (p. 440)

stressors Specific events or chronic pressures that place demands on a person or threaten the person's well-being. (p. 428)

structuralism The analysis of the basic elements that constitute the mind. (p. 7)

subcortical structures Areas of the forebrain housed under the cerebral cortex near the very center of the brain. (p. 70)

sublimation A defense mechanism that involves channeling unacceptable sexual or aggressive drives into socially acceptable and culturally enhancing activities. (p. 344)

subliminal perception A thought or behavior that is influenced by stimuli that a person cannot consciously report perceiving. (p. 243)

subtyping The process of creating a modification to a stereotype, rather than abandoning it altogether, when confronted with evidence that clearly disconfirms that stereotype evidence. (p. 483)

suggestibility The tendency to incorporate misleading information from external sources into personal recollections. (p. 150)

sunk-cost fallacy A framing effect in which people make decisions about a current situation based on what they have previously invested in the situation. (p. 211)

superego The mental system that reflects the internalization of cultural rules, mainly learned as parents exercise their authority. (p. 343)

surface structure How a sentence is worded. (p. 199)

sympathetic nervous system A set of nerves that prepares the body for action in threatening situations. (p. 65)

synapse The junction or region between the axon of one neuron and the dendrites or cell body of another. (p. 57)

systematic desensitization A procedure in which a client relaxes all the muscles of his or her body while imagining being in increasingly frightening situations. (p. 405)

systematic persuasion A change in attitudes or beliefs that is brought about by appeals to reason. (p. 477)

taste buds The organ of taste transduction. (p. 121)

tectum A part of the midbrain that orients an organism in the environment. (p. 69)

tegmentum A part of the midbrain that is involved in movement and arousal. (p. 69)

temperaments Characteristic patterns of emotional reactivity. (p. 313)

temporal code The cochlea registers low frequencies via the firing rate of action potentials entering the auditory nerve. (p. 114)

temporal lobe A region of the cerebral cortex responsible for hearing and language. (p. 71)

teratogens Agents that damage the process of development, such as drugs and viruses. (p. 300)

terminal buttons Knoblike structures that branch out from an axon. (p. 60)

thalamus A subcortical structure that relays and filters information from the senses and transmits the information to the cerebral cortex. (p. 70)

Thematic Apperception Test (TAT) A projective personality test in which respondents reveal underlying motives, concerns, and the way they see the social world through the stories they make up about ambiguous pictures of people. (p. 336)

theory A hypothetical account of how and why a phenomenon occurs, usually in the form of a statement about the causal relationship between two or more properties. Theories lead to *hypotheses*. (p. 46)

theory of mind The idea that human behavior is guided by mental representation, which gives rise to the realization that the world is not always the way it looks and that different people see it differently. (p. 307)

third-variable correlation The fact that two variables may be correlated only because they are both caused by a third variable. (p. 42)

third-variable problem The fact that the causal relationship between two variables cannot be inferred from the correlation between them because of the ever-present possibility of third-variable correlation. (p. 43)

thought suppression The conscious avoidance of a thought. (p. 240)

timbre A listener's experience of sound quality or resonance. (p. 111)

token economy A form of behavior therapy in which clients are given "tokens" for desired behaviors, which they can later trade for rewards. (p. 405)

trait A relatively stable disposition to behave in a particular and consistent way. (p. 338)

transcranial magnetic stimulation (TMS) A treatment that involves placing a powerful pulsed magnet over a person's scalp, which alters neuronal activity in the brain. (p. 417)

transduction What takes place when many sensors in the body convert physical signals from the environment into neural signals sent to the central nervous system. (p. 91)

transfer-appropriate processing The idea that memory is likely to transfer from one situation to another when we process information in a way that is appropriate to the retrieval cues that will be available later. (p. 138)

transference An event that occurs in psychoanalysis when the analyst begins to assume a major significance in the client's life and the client reacts to the analyst based on unconscious childhood fantasies. (p. 403)

transience Forgetting what occurs with the passage of time. (p. 143)

two-factor theory A theory about the relationship between emotional experience and physiological activity suggesting that emotions are inferences about the causes of undifferentiated physiological arousal. (p. 272)

two-factor theory of intelligence Spearman's theory suggesting that every task requires a combination of a general ability (which he called *g*) and skills that are specific to the task (which he called *s*). (p. 218)

Type A behavior pattern The tendency toward easily aroused hostility, impatience, a sense of time urgency, and competitive achievement strivings. (p. 435)

unconditioned response (UR) A reflexive reaction that is reliably elicited by an unconditioned stimulus. (p. 164)

unconditioned stimulus (US) Something that reliably produces a naturally occurring reaction in an organism. (p. 164)

unconscious The part of the mind that operates outside of conscious awareness but influences conscious thoughts, feelings, and actions. (p. 13)

unconscious motivation A motivation of which one is not aware. (p. 293)

universality hypothesis The hypothesis that emotional expressions have the same meaning for everyone. (p. 278)

validity The characteristic of an observation that allows one to draw accurate inferences from it. (p. 36)

variable A property whose value can vary or change. (p. 41)

variable interval schedule (VI) An operant conditioning principle in which behavior is reinforced based on an average time that has expired since the last reinforcement. (p. 180)

variable ratio schedule (VR) An operant conditioning principle in which the delivery of reinforcement is based on a particular average number of responses. (p. 180)

vestibular system The three fluid-filled semicircular canals and adjacent organs located next to the cochlea in each inner ear. (p. 118)

visual acuity The ability to see fine detail. (p. 96)

visual imagery encoding The process of storing new information by converting it into mental pictures. (p. 131)

visual-form agnosia The inability to recognize objects by sight. (p. 105)

Weber's law The just noticeable difference of a stimulus is a constant proportion despite variations in intensity. (p. 93)

working memory Active maintenance of information in short-term storage. (p. 134)

zygote A single cell that contains chromosomes from both a sperm and an egg. (p. 299)

References

Abel, T., Alberini, C., Ghirardi, M., Huang, Y.-Y., Nguyen, P., & Kandel, E. R. (1995). Steps toward a molecular definition of memory consolidation. In D. L. Schacter (Ed.), *Memory distortion: How minds, brains and societies reconstruct the past* (pp. 298–328). Cambridge, MA: Harvard University Press.

Abrams, M., & Reber, A. S. (1988). Implicit learning: Robustness in the face of psychiatric disorders. *Journal of Psycholinguistic Research, 17,* 425–439.

Abramson, L. Y., Seligman, M. E. P., & Teasdale, J. D. (1978). Learned helplessness in humans: Critique and reformulation. *Journal of Abnormal Psychology, 87,* 49–74.

Acevedo-Garcia, D., McArdle, N., Osypuk, T. L., Lefkowitz, B., & Krimgold, B. K. (2007). *Children left behind: How metropolitan areas are failing America's children.* Boston: Harvard School of Public Health.

Achter, J. A., Lubinski, D., & Benbow, C. P. (1996). Multipotentiality among the intellectually gifted: "It was never there and already it's vanishing." *Journal of Counseling Psychology, 43,* 65–76.

Acocella, J. (1999). *Creating hysteria: Women and multiple personality disorder.* San Francisco: Jossey-Bass.

Acton, G. S., & Schroeder, D. H. (2001). Sensory discrimination as related to general intelligence. *Intelligence, 29,* 263–271.

Adams, H. E., Wright, L. W., Jr., & Lohr, B. A. (1996). Is homophobia associated with homosexual arousal? *Journal of Abnormal Psychology, 105,* 440–445.

Addis, D. R., Wong, A. T., & Schacter, D. L. (2007). Remembering the past and imagining the future: Common and distinct neural substrates during event construction and elaboration. *Neuropsychologia, 45,* 1363–1377.

Adelmann, P. K., & Zajonc, R. B. (1989). Facial efference and the experience of emotion. *Annual Review of Psychology, 40,* 249–280.

Adolph, K. E., & Avoilio, A. M. (2000). Walking infants adapt locomotion to changing body dimensions. *Journal of Experimental Psychology: Human Perception and Performance, 26,* 1148–1166.

Adolphs, R., Cahil, L., Schul, R., & Babinsky, R. (1997). Impaired declarative memory for emotional material following bilateral amygdala damage in humans. *Learning and Memory, 4,* 291–300.

Adolphs, R., Russell, J. A., & Tranel, D. (1999). A role for the human amygdala in recognizing emotional arousal from unpleasant stimuli. *Psychological Science, 10,* 167–171.

Aharon, I., Etcoff, N., Ariely, D., Chabris, C. F., O'Conner, E., & Breiter, H. C. (2001). Beautiful faces have variable reward value: fMRI and behavioral evidence. *Neuron, 32,* 537–551.

Ahlers, M. (2003, September 23). Bitter divorce blamed for sniper shootings. *CNN.com.* Retrieved September 15, 2007, from http://www.cnn.com/2003/LAW/09/23/sprj.dcsp.sniper.hearing/index.html

Ainsworth, M. D. S., Blehar, M. C., Waters, E., & Wall, S. (1978). *Patterns of attachment: A psychological study of the strange situation.* Hillsdale, NJ: Erlbaum.

Albee, E. (1962). *Who's afraid of Virginia Woolf?* New York: Atheneum.

Alicke, M. D., Klotz, M. L., Breitenbecher, D. L., Yurak, T. J., & Vredenburg, D. S. (1995). Personal contact, individuation, and the better-than-average effect. *Journal of Personality and Social Psychology, 68,* 804–824.

Allison, D. B., Fontaine, K. R., Manson, J. E., Stevens, J., & VanItallie, T. B. (1999). Annual deaths attributable to obesity in the United States. *Journal of the American Medical Association, 282,* 1530–1538.

Allport, G. W. (1937). *Personality: A psychological interpretation.* New York: Holt.

Allport, G. W. (1954). *The nature of prejudice.* Cambridge, MA: Addison-Wesley.

Allport, G. W., & Odbert, H. S. (1936). Trait-names: A psycholexical study. *Psychological Monographs, 47,* 592.

Alt, K. W., Jeunesse, C., Buitrago-Téllez, C. H., Wächter, R., Boës, E., & Pichler, S. L. (1997). Evidence for stone age cranial surgery. *Nature, 387,* 360.

Amabile, T. M. (1996). *Creativity in context.* Boulder, CO: Westview Press.

American Psychiatric Association. (2000). *Diagnostic and statistical manual of mental disorders DSM-IV-TR* (4th ed.). Washington, DC: American Psychiatric Press.

American Psychological Association. (2002). *Ethical principles of psychologists and code of conduct.* Washington, DC: Author.

American Psychological Association. (2005). Resolution in favor of empirically supported sex education and HIV prevention programs for adolescents. Washington, DC.

Andersen, S. M., & Berk, J. S. (1998). Transference in everyday experience: Implications of experimental research for relevant clinical phenomena. *Review of General Psychology, 2,* 81–120.

Anderson, C. A. (1989). Temperature and aggression: Ubiquitous effects of heat on occurrence of human violence. *Psychological Bulletin, 106,* 74–96.

Anderson, C. A., Berkowitz, L., Donnerstein, E., Huesmann, L. R., Johnson, J. D., Linz, D., et al. (2003). The influence of media violence on youth. *Psychological Science in the Public Interest, 4,* 81–110.

Anderson, C. A., & Bushman, B. J. (2002). Human aggression. *Annual Review of Psychology, 53,* 27–51.

Anderson, C. A., Bushman, B. J., & Groom, R. W. (1997). Hot years and serious and deadly assault: Empirical tests of the heat hypothesis. *Journal of Personality and Social Psychology, 73,* 1213–1223.

Anderson, J. R., & Schooler, L. J. (1991). Reflections of the environment in memory. *Psychological Science, 2,* 396–408.

Anderson, J. R., & Schooler, L. J. (2000). The adaptive nature of memory. In E. Tulving & F. I. M. Craik (Eds.), *The Oxford handbook of memory* (pp. 557–570). Oxford: Oxford University Press.

Anderson, M. C., Ochsner, K. N., Kuhl, B., Cooper, J., Robertson, E., Gabrieli, S. W., et al. (2004). Neural systems underlying the suppression of unwanted memories. *Science, 303,* 232–235.

Anderson, R. C., Pichert, J. W., Goetz, E. T., Schallert, D. L., Stevens, K. V., & Trollip, S. R. (1976). Instantiation of general terms. *Journal of Verbal Learning and Verbal Behavior, 15,* 667–679.

Andrewes, D. (2001). *Neuropsychology: From theory to practice.* Hove, England: Psychology Press.

Angier, N. (1997, December 23). Joined for life, and living life to the full. *New York Times,* p. F1.

Ansfield, M., Wegner, D. M., & Bowser, R. (1996). Ironic effects of sleep urgency. *Behavior Research and Therapy, 34,* 523–531.

Ansuini, C. G., Fiddler-Woite, J., & Woite, R. S. (1996). The source, accuracy, and impact of initial sexuality information on lifetime wellness. *Adolescence, 31,* 283–289.

Antoni, M. H., Lehman, J. M., Klibourn, K. M., Boyers, A. E., Culver, J. L., Alferi, S. M., et al. (2001). Cognitive-behavioral stress management intervention decreases the prevalence of depression and enhances benefit finding among women under treatment for early-stage breast cancer. *Health Psychology, 20,* 20–32.

Antony, M. M., Downie, F., & Swinson, R. (1998). Diagnostic issues and epidemiology in obsessive-compulsive disorder. In R. Swinson, M. Antony, S. Rachman, & M. Richter (Eds.), *Obsessive-compulsive disorder: Theory, research, and treatment* (pp. 3–32). New York: Guilford Press.

Antony, M. M., Roth, D., Swinson, R. P., Huta, V., & Devins, G. M. (1998). Illness intrusiveness in individuals with panic disorder, obsessive compulsive disorder, or social phobia. *Journal of Nervous and Mental Disease, 186,* 311–315.

Archer, J. E. (Ed.). (1994). *Male violence.* London: Routledge.

Aristotle. (1998). *The Nichomachean ethics* (D. W. Ross, Trans.). Oxford: Oxford University Press. (Original work published 350 BC)

Ariyasu, H., Takaya, K., Tagami, T., Ogawa, Y., Hosoda, K., Akamizu, T., et al. (2001). Stomach is a major source of circulating ghrelin, and feeding state determines plasma ghrelin-like immunoreactivity levels in humans. *Journal of Clinical Endocrinology and Metabolism, 86,* 4753–4758.

Arlow, J. A. (2000). Psychoanalysis. In R. J. Corsini & D. Wedding (Eds.), *Current psychotherapies* (6th ed., pp. 16–53). Itasca, IL: Peacock.

Armstrong, D. M. (1980). *The nature of mind.* Ithaca, NY: Cornell University Press.

Arnold, M. B. (Ed.). (1960). *Emotion and personality: Psychological aspects* (Vol. 1). New York: Columbia University Press.

Aronson, E. (1969). The theory of cognitive dissonance: A current perspective. In L. Berkowitz (Ed.), *Advances in experimental social psychology* (Vol. 4, pp. 1–34): Academic Press.

Aronson, E., & Worchel, P. (1966). Similarity versus liking as determinants of interpersonal attractiveness. *Psychonomic Science, 5,* 157–158.

Asch, S. E. (1951). Effects of group pressure on the modification and distortion of judgments. In H. Guetzkow (Ed.), *Groups, leadership, and men* (pp. 177–190). Pittsburgh: Carnegie Press.

Asch, S. E. (1956). Studies of independence and conformity: 1 A minority of one against a unanimous majority. *Psychological Monographs: General and Applied, 70,* 1–70.

Aschoff, J. (1965). Circadian rhythms in man. *Science, 148,* 1427–1432.

Ashby, F. G., & Ell, S. W. (2001). The neurobiology of human category learning. *Trends in Cognitive Sciences, 5,* 204–210.

Associated Press. (2007). Former stripper guilty of posing as psychologist. *BostonHerald.com.*

Astington, J. W., & Baird, J. (2005). *Why language matters for theory of mind.* Oxford: Oxford University Press.

Axelrod, R. (1984). *The evolution of cooperation.* New York: Basic Books.

Axelrod, R., & Hamilton, W. D. (1981). The evolution of cooperation. *Science, 211,* 1390–1396.

Azuma, H., & Kashiwagi, K. (1987). Descriptors for an intelligent person: A Japanese study. *Japanese Psychological Research, 29,* 17–26.

Baars, B. J. (1986). The cognitive revolution in psychology. New York: Guilford Press.

Backman, C. W., & Secord, P. F. (1959). The effect of perceived liking on interpersonal attraction. *Human Relations, 12,* 379–384.

Bäckman, L., & Dixon, R. A. (1992). Psychological compensation: A theoretical framework. *Psychological Bulletin, 112,* 259–283.

Baddeley, A. D., & Hitch, G. J. (1974). Working memory. In S. Dornic (Ed.), *Attention and performance.* Hillsdale, NJ: Erlbaum.

Baer, L., Rauch, S. L., Ballantine, H. T., Jr., Martuza, R., Cosgrove, R., Cassem, E., et al. (1995). Cingulotomy for intractable obsessive-compulsive disorder: Prospective long-term follow-up of 18 patients. *Archives of General Psychiatry, 52,* 384–392.

Bagby, R. M., Levitan, R. D., Kennedy, S. H., Levitt, A. J., & Joffe, R. T. (1999). Selective alteration of personality in response to nor-adrenergic and serotonergic antidepressant medication in depressed sample: Evidence of non-specificity. *Psychiatry Research, 86,* 211–216.

Bahrick, H. P. (1984). Semantic memory content in permastore: 50 years of memory for Spanish learned in school. *Journal of Experimental Psychology: General, 113,* 1–29.

Bahrick, H. P. (2000). Long-term maintenance of knowledge. In E. Tulving & F. I. M. Craik (Eds.), *The Oxford handbook of memory* (pp. 347–362). New York: Oxford University Press.

Bahrick, H. P., Hall, L. K., & Berger, S. A. (1996). Accuracy and distortion in memory for high school grades. *Psychological Science, 7,* 265–271.

Bailey, J. M., & Pillard, R. C. (1991). A genetic study of male sexual orientation. *Archives of General Psychiatry, 48,* 1089–1096.

Bailey, J. M., Pillard, R. C., Dawood, K., Miller, M. B., Farrer, L. A., Trivedi, S., et al. (1999). A family history study of male sexual orientation using three independent samples. *Behavior Genetics, 29,* 79–86.

Bailey, J. M., Pillard, R. C., Neale, M. C., & Agyes, Y. (1993). Heritable factors influence sexual orientation in women. *Archives of General Psychiatry, 50,* 217–223.

Bailey, R. (2002, March 6). Hooray for designer babies! *Reason.com.* Retrieved September 30, 2007, from http://www.reason.com/news/show/34776.html

Baillargeon, R., Spelke, E. S., & Wasserman, S. (1985). Object permanence in 5-month-old infants. *Cognition, 20,* 191–208.

Baler, R. D., & Volkow, N. D. (2006). Drug addiction: the neurobiology of disrupted self-control. *Trends in Molecular Medicine 12,* 559–566.

Baltes, P. B., & Reinert, G. (1969). Cohort effects in cognitive development of children as revealed by cross-sectional sequences. *Developmental Psychology, 1,* 169–177.

Bandura, A. (1965). Influence of models' reinforcement contingencies on the acquisition of imitative responses. *Journal of Social and Personality Psychology, 1,* 589–595.

Bandura, A. (1977). *Social learning theory.* Englewood Cliffs, NJ: Prentice Hall.

Bandura, A. (1986). *Social foundations of thought and action: A social cognitive theory.* Englewood Cliffs, NJ: Prentice Hall.

Bandura, A. (1994). Social cognitive theory of mass communication. In J. Bryant & D. Zillmann (Eds.), *Media effects: Advances in theory and research* (pp. 61–90). Hillsdale, NJ: Erlbaum.

Bandura, A., Ross, D., & Ross, S. (1961). Transmission of aggression through imitation of adult models. *Journal of Abnormal and Social Psychology, 63,* 575–582.

Bandura, A., Ross, D., & Ross, S. (1963). Vicarious reinforcement and imitative learning. *Journal of Abnormal and Social Psychology, 67,* 601–607.

Banse, R., & Scherer, K. R. (1996). Acoustic profiles in vocal emotion expression. *Journal of Personality and Social Psychology, 70,* 614–636.

Bard, P. (1934). On emotional experience after decortication with some remarks on theoretical views. *Psychological Review, 41,* 309–329.

Bargh, J. A., Chen, M., & Burrows, L. (1996). The automaticity of social behavior: Direct effects of trait concept and stereotype activation on action. *Journal of Personality and Social Psychology, 71,* 230–244.

Barker, A. T., Jalinous, R., & Freeston, I. L. (1985). Noninvasive magnetic stimulation of the human motor cortex. *Lancet, 2,* 1106–1107.

Barkow, J. (1980). Prestige and self-esteem: A biosocial interpretation. In D. R. Omark, F. F. Stayer, & D. G. Freedman (Eds.), *Dominance relations* (pp. 319–322). New York: Garland.

Barlow, D. H., Gorman, J. M., Shear, M. K., & Woods, S. W. (2000). Cognitive-behavioral therapy, imipramine, or their combination for panic disorder: A randomized controlled trial. *Journal of the American Medical Association, 283*(19), 2529–2536.

Barnier, A. J., Levin, K., & Maher, A. (2004). Suppressing thoughts of past events: Are repressive copers good suppressors? *Cognition and Emotion, 18,* 457–477.

Baron-Cohen, S. (1991). Do people with autism understand what causes emotion? *Child Development, 62,* 385–395.

Baron-Cohen, S., Leslie, A., & Frith, U. (1985). Does the autistic child have a "theory of mind"? *Cognition, 21,* 37–46.

Barondes, S. (2003). *Better than Prozac.* New York: Oxford University Press.

Barrett, T. R., & Etheridge, J. B. (1992). Verbal hallucinations in normals: I: People who hear voices. *Applied Cognitive Psychology, 6,* 379–387.

Barsalou, L. W., & Ross, B. H. (1986). The roles of automatic and strategic processing in sensitivity to superordinate and property frequency. *Journal of Experimental Psychology: Learning, Memory, & Cognition, 12,* 116–134.

Bartlett, F. C. (1932). *Remembering.* Cambridge: Cambridge University Press.

Bartol, C. R., & Costello, N. (1976). Extraversion as a function of temporal duration of electric shock: An exploratory study. *Perceptual and Motor Skills, 42,* 1174.

Bartoshuk, L. M., & Beauchamp, G. K. (1994). Chemical senses. *Annual Review of Psychology, 45,* 419–445.

Batson, C. D. (2002). Addressing the altruism question experimentally. In S. G. Post & L. G. Underwood (Eds.), *Altruism & altruistic love: Science, philosophy, & religion in dialogue* (pp. 89–105). London: Oxford University Press.

Baumeister, R. F., Bratslavsky, E., Muraven, M., & Tice, D. M. (1998). Ego depletion: Is the active self a limited resource? *Journal of Personality and Social Psychology, 74,* 1252–1265.

Baumeister, R. F., Campbell, J. D., Krueger, J. I., & Vohs, K. D. (2003). Does high self-esteem cause better performance, interpersonal success, happiness, or healthier lifestyles? *Psychological Science in the Public Interest, 4,* 1–44.

Baumeister, R. F., Cantanese, K. R., & Vohs, K. D. (2001). Is there a gender difference in strength of sex drive? Theoretical views, conceptual distinctions, and a review of relevant evidence. *Personality and Social Psychology Review, 5,* 242–273.

Baumeister, R. F., & Leary, M. R. (1995). The need to belong: Desire for interpersonal attachments as a fundamental human motivation. *Psychological Bulletin, 117,* 497–529.

Baumeister, R. F., Smart, L., & Boden, J. M. (1996). Relation of threatened egotism to violence and aggression: The dark side of high self-esteem. *Psychological Review, 103,* 5–33.

Baumeister, R. F., & Tice, D. M. (1990). Anxiety and social exclusion. *Journal of Social and Clinical Psychology, 9,* 165–195.

Baxter, L. R., Schwartz, J. M., Bergman, K. S., Szuba, M. P., Guze, B. H., Mazziotta, J. C., Alazraki, A., et al. (1992). Caudate glucose metabolic rate changes with both drug behavior therapy for obsessive-compulsive disorder. *Archives of General Psychiatry, 49,* 681–689.

Bayley, P. J., Gold, J. J., Hopkins, R. O., & Squire, L. R. (2005). The neuroanatomy of remote memory. *Neuron, 46,* 799–810.

Beck, A. T. (1967). *Depression: Causes and treatment.* Philadelphia: University of Pennsylvania Press.

Beck, A. T., & Weishaar, M. (2000). Cognitive therapy. In R. J. Corsini & D. Wedding (Eds.), *Current psychotherapies* (6th ed., pp. 241–272). Itasca, IL: F. E. Peacock.

Beckers, G., & Zeki, S. (1995). The consequences of inactivating areas V1 and V5 on visual motion perception. *Brain, 118,* 49–60.

Bell, A. P., Weinberg, M. S., & Hammersmith, S. K. (1981). *Sexual preference: Its development in men and women.* Bloomington: Indiana University Press.

Belsky, J., Spritz, B., & Crnic, K. (1996). Infant attachment security and affective-cognitive information processing at age 3. *Psychological Science, 7,* 111–114.

Benes, F. M. (1998). Model generation and testing to probe neural circuitry in the cingulated cortex of postmortem schizophrenia brain. *Schizophrenia Bulletin, 24,* 219–230.

Benjamin, L. T., Jr. (Ed.). (1988). *A history of psychology: Original sources and contemporary research.* New York: McGraw-Hill.

Benson, H. (Ed.). (1990). *The relaxation response.* New York: Harper Torch.

Berglund, H., Lindstrom, P., & Savic, I. (2006). Brain response to putative pheromones in lesbian women. *Proceedings of the National Academy of Sciences, 103,* 8269–8274.

Berkerian, D. A., & Bowers, J. M. (1983). Eyewitness testimony: Were we misled? *Journal of Experimental Psychology: Learning, Memory, and Cognition, 9,* 139–145.

Berkowitz, L. (1990). On the formation and regulation of anger and aggression: A cognitive-neoassociationistic analysis. *American Psychologist, 45,* 494–503.

Berkowitz, L. (1993). Pain and aggression: Some findings and implications. *Motivation and Emotion, 17,* 277–293.

Berry, D. S., & McArthur, L. Z. (1985). Some components and consequences of a babyface. *Journal of Personality and Social Psychology, 48,* 312–323.

Berry, J. W., Poortinga, Y. H., Segall, M. H., & Dasen, P. R. (1992). *Cross-cultural psychology: Research and applications.* New York: Cambridge University Press.

Berscheid, E., & Reiss, H. T. (1998). Interpersonal attraction and close relationships. In D. T. Gilbert, S. T. Fiske, & G. Lindzey (Eds.), *The handbook of social psychology* (4th ed., Vol. 2, pp. 193–281). New York: McGraw-Hill.

Bertelsen, A. (1999). Reflections on the clinical utility of the ICD-10 and DSM-IV classifications and their diagnostic criteria. *Australian and New Zealand Journal of Psychiatry, 33,* 166–173.

Bertelsen, B., Harvald, B., & Hauge, M. (1977). A Danish twin study of manic-depressive disorders. *British Journal of Psychiatry, 130,* 330–351.

Bertenthal, B. I., Rose, J. L., & Bai, D. L. (1997). Perception-action coupling in the development of visual control of posture. *Journal of Experimental Psychology: Human Perception & Performance, 23,* 1631–1643.

Bettencourt, B. A., & Miller, N. (1996). Gender differences in aggression as a function of provocation: A meta-analysis. *Psychological Bulletin, 119,* 422–447.

Beutler, L. E. (2002). The dodo bird is extinct. *Clinical Psychology: Science and Practice, 9,* 30–34.

Bialystok, E. (1999). Cognitive complexity and attentional control in the bilingual mind. *Child Development, 70,* 636–644.

Bickerton, D. (1990). *Language and species.* Chicago: Chicago University Press.

Bierce, A. (1911). *The devil's dictionary.* New York: A. & C. Boni.

Billet, E., Richter, J., & Kennedy, J. (1998). Genetics of obsessive-compulsive disorder. In R. Swinson, M. Anthony, S. Rachman & M. Richter (Eds.), *Obsessive-compulsive disorder: Theory, research, and treatment* (pp. 181–206). New York: Guilford Press.

Binet, A. (1909). *Les idées modernes sur les enfants.* Paris: Flammarion.

Binswanger, L. (1958). The existential analysis school of thought. In R. May (Ed.), *Existence: A new dimension in psychiatry and psychology.* New York: Basic Books.

Bjork, D. W. (1983). *The compromised scientist: William James in the development of American psychology.* New York: Columbia University Press.

Bjork, R. A., & Bjork, E. L. (1988). On the adaptive aspects of retrieval failure in autobiographical memory. In M. M. Gruneberg, P. E. Morris, R. N. Sykes (Eds.), *Practical aspects of memory: Current research and issues* (pp. 283–288). Chichester, England: Wiley.

Blair, I. V. (2002). The malleability of automatic stereotypes and prejudice. *Personality and Social Psychology Review, 6,* 242–261.

Blair, J., Peschardt, K., & Mitchell, D. R. (2005). *Psychopath: Emotion and the brain.* Oxford: Blackwell.

Blascovich, J., & Tomaka, J. (1996). The biopsychosocial model of arousal regulation. In M. P. Zanna (Ed.), *Advances in experimental social psychology* (Vol. 28, pp. 1–51). San Diego, CA: Academic Press.

Blasi, A. (1980). Bridging moral cognition and moral action: A critical review of the literature. *Psychological Bulletin, 88,* 1–45.

Blazer, D. G., Hughes, D., & George, L. D. (1987). Stressful life events and the onset of a generalized anxiety syndrome. *American Journal of Psychiatry, 144,* 1178–1183.

Blazer, D. G., Hughes, D. J., George, L. K., Swartz, M., & Boyer, R. (1991). Generalized anxiety disorder. In L. N. Robins & D. A. Regier (Eds.), *Psychiatric disorders in America* (Vol. 180–203). New York: Free Press.

Bliss, T. V. P. (1999). Young receptors make smart mice. *Nature, 401,* 25–27.

Bliss, T. V. P., & Lømo, W. T. (1973). Long-lasting potentiation of synaptic transmission in the dentate area of the anesthetized rabbit following stimulation of the perforant path. *Journal of Physiology, 232,* 331–356.

Bohan, J. S. (1996). *Psychology and sexual orientation: Coming to terms.* New York: Routledge.

Boisvert, C. M., & Faust, D. (2002). Iatrogenic symptoms in psychotherapy: A theoretical exploration of the potential impact of labels, language, and belief systems. *American Journal of Psychotherapy, 56,* 244–259.

Boomsma, D., Busjahn, A., & Peltonen, L. (2002). Classical twin studies and beyond. *Nature Reviews Genetics, 3,* 872–882.

Bootzin, R. R., Manber, R., Perlis, M. L., Salvio, M. A., & Wyatt, J. K. (1993). Sleep disorders. In P. B. Sutker & H. E. Adams (Eds.), *Comprehensive handbook of psychopathology* (2nd ed.). New York: Plenum Press.

Borkenau, P., & Liebler, A. (1995). Observable attributes as manifestations and cues of personality and intelligence. *Journal of Personality, 63,* 1–25.

Borkevec, T. D. (1982). Insomnia. *Journal of Consulting and Clinical Psychology, 50,* 880–895.

Born, R. T., & Bradley, D. C. (2005). Structure and function of visual area MT. *Annual Review of Neuroscience, 28,* 157–189.

Bornstein, R. F. (1989). Exposure and affect: Overview and meta-analysis of research, 1968–1987. *Psychological Bulletin, 106,* 265–289.

Bostwick, J. M., & Pankratz, S. (2000). Affective disorders and suicide risk: A reexamination. *American Journal of Psychiatry, 157,* 1925–1932.

Botwin, M. D., Buss, D. M., & Shackelford, T. K. (1997). Personality and mate preferences: Five factors in mate selection and marital satisfaction. *Journal of Personality, 65,* 107–136.

Bouchard, T. J., & Loehlin, J. C. (2001). Genes, evolution, and personality. *Behavioral Genetics, 31,* 243–273.

Bouchard, T. J., & McGue, M. (1981). Familial studies of intelligence: A review. *Science, 212,* 1055–1059.

Boucher, J. D., & Carlson, G. E. (1980). Recognition of facial expressions in three cultures. *Journal of Cross-Cultural Psychology, 11,* 263–280.

Bourguignon, E. (1968). World distribution and patterns of possession states. In R. Prince (Ed.), *Trance and possession states* (pp. 3–34). Montreal, Canada: R. M. Burke Memorial Society.

Bower, G. H. (1981). Mood and memory. *American Psychologist, 36,* 129–148.

Bower, G. H., Clark, M. C., Lesgold, A. M., & Winzenz, D. (1969). Hierarchical retrieval schemes in recall of categorical word lists. *Journal of Verbal Learning and Verbal Behavior, 8,* 323–343.

Bowlby, J. (1969). *Attachment and loss: Vol. 1. Attachment.* New York: Basic Books.

Bowlby, J. (1973). *Attachment and loss: Vol. 2. Separation.* New York: Basic Books.

Bowlby, J. (1980). *Attachment and loss: Vol. 3. Loss: Sadness and depression.* New York: Basic Books.

Bozarth, M. A., & Wise, R. A. (1985). Toxicity associated with long-term intravenous heroin and cocaine self-administration in the rat. *Journal of the American Medical Association, 254,* 81–83.

Bradford, D., Stroup, S., & Lieberman, J. (2002). Pharmacological treatments for schizophrenia. In P. E. Nathan & J. M. Gorman (Eds.), *A guide to treatments that work* (2nd ed., pp. 169–199). New York: Oxford University Press.

Bradmetz, J., & Schneider, R. (2004). The role of the counterfactually satisfied desire in the lag between false-belief and false-emotion attributions in children aged 4–7. *British Journal of Developmental Psychology, 22,* 185–196.

Braun, A. R., Balkin, T. J., Wesensten, N. J., Gwadry, F., Carson, R. E., Varga, M., et al. (1998). Dissociated pattern of activity in visual cortices and their projections during rapid eye movement sleep. *Science, 279,* 91–95.

Breckler, S. J. (1994). Memory for the experiment of donating blood: Just how bad was it? *Basic and Applied Social Psychology, 15*, 467–488.

Brédart, S., & Valentine, T. (1998). Descriptiveness and proper name retrieval. *Memory, 6*, 199–206.

Breggin, P. R. (2000). *Reclaiming our children.* Cambridge, MA: Perseus Books.

Brehm, S. S. (1992). *Intimate relationships* (2nd ed.). New York: McGraw-Hill.

Breland, K., & Breland, M. (1961). The misbehavior of organisms. *American Psychologist, 16*, 681–684.

Brennan, P. A., & Zufall, F. (2006). Pheromonal communication in vertebrates. *Nature, 444*, 308–315.

Brenneis, C. B. (2000). Evaluating the evidence: Can we find authenticated recovered memory? *Journal of the American Psychoanalytic Association, 17*, 61–77.

Brenninkmeijer, V., Vanyperen, N. W., & Buunk, B. P. (2001). I am not a better teacher, but others are doing worse: Burnout and perceptions of superiority among teachers. *Social Psychology of Education, 4*(3–4), 259–274.

Brewer, M. B. (1979). In-group bias in the minimal intergroup situation: A cognitive-motivational analysis. *Psychological Bulletin, 86*, 307–324.

Brewer, W. F. (1996). What is recollective memory? In D. C. Rubin (Ed.), *Remembering our past: Studies in autobiographical memory* (pp. 19–66). New York: Cambridge University Press.

Broberg, D. J., & Bernstein, I. L. (1987). Candy as a scapegoat in the prevention of food aversions in children receiving chemotherapy. *Cancer, 60*, 2344–2347.

Broca, P. (1861). Remarques sur le siège de la faculté du langage articulé; suivies d'une observation d'aphemie (perte de la parole). *Bulletin de la société anatomique de Paris, 36*, 330–357.

Broca, P. (1863). Localisation des fonction cerebrales: Siège du langage articulé. *Bulletin de la société d'anthropologie de Paris, 4*, 200–202.

Brody, N. (2003). Construct validation of the Sternberg Triarchic Abilities Test: Comment and reanalysis. *Intelligence, 31*(4), 319–329.

Brooks-Gunn, J., Graber, J. A., & Paikoff, R. L. (1994). Studying links between hormones and negative affect: Models and measures. *Journal of Research on Adolescence, 4*, 469–486.

Brosnan, S. F., & DeWaal, F. B. M. (2003). Monkeys reject unequal pay. *Nature, 425*, 297–299.

Brown, B. B., Mory, M., & Kinney, D. (1994). Casting crowds in a relational perspective: Caricature, channel, and context. In G. A. R. Montemayor & T. Gullotta (Eds.), *Advances in adolescent development: Personal relationships during adolescence* (Vol. 5, pp. 123–167). Newbury Park, CA: Sage.

Brown, J. D. (1993). Self-esteem and self-evaluation: Feeling is believing. In J. M. Suls (Ed.), *The self in social perspective: Psychological perspectives on the self* (Vol. 4, pp. 27–58). Hillsdale, NJ: Erlbaum.

Brown, J. D., & McGill, K. L. (1989). The cost of good fortune: When positive life events produce negative health consequences. *Journal of Personality & Social Psychology, 57*, 1103–1110.

Brown, R. (1958). *Words and things.* New York: Free Press.

Brown, R., & Hanlon, C. (1970). Derivational complexity and order of acquisition in child speech. In J. R. Hayes (Ed.), *Cognition and the development of language* (pp. 11–53). New York: Wiley.

Brown, R., & McNeill, D. (1966). The "tip-of-the-tongue" phenomenon. *Journal of Verbal Learning and Verbal Behavior, 5*, 325–337.

Brown, S. C., & Craik, F. I. M. (2000). Encoding and retrieval of information. In E. Tulving & F. I. M. Craik (Eds.), *The Oxford handbook of memory* (pp. 93–107). New York: Oxford University Press.

Brown, T. A., & Barlow, D. H. (2002). Classification of anxiety and mood disorders. In D. H. Barlow (Ed.), *Anxiety and its disorders: The nature and treatment of anxiety and panic* (2nd ed.). New York: Guilford Press.

Brown, T. A., Campbell, L. A., Lehman, C. L., Grisham, J. R., & Mancill, R. B. (2001). Current and lifetime comorbidity of the *DSM-IV* anxiety and mood disorders in a large clinical sample. *Journal of Abnormal Psychology, 110*, 585–599.

Brownell, K. D., Greenwood, M. R. C., Stellar, E., & Shrager, E. E. (1986). The effects of repeated cycles of weight loss and regain in rats. *Physiology and Behavior, 38*, 459–464.

Brownlee, S. (2002, March). Designer babies. *The Washington Monthly.*

Bruner, J. S. (1983). Education as social invention. *Journal of Social Issues, 39*, 129–141.

Buchanan, C. M., Eccles, J. S., & Becker, J. B. (1992). Are adolescents the victims of raging hormones? Evidence for activational effects of hormones on moods and behavior at adolescence. *Psychological Bulletin, 111*, 62–107.

Buchanan, P. J. (2002, October 30). The Beltway sniper and the media. Retrieved September 15, 2006, from http://www.townhall.com/columnists/PatrickJBuchanan/2002/10/30/the_beltway_sniper_and_the_media

Buckner, R. L., Petersen, S. E., Ojemann, J. G., Miezin, F. M., Squire, L. R., & Raichle, M. E. (1995). Functional anatomical studies of explicit and implicit memory retrieval tasks. *Journal of Neuroscience, 15*, 12–29.

Burger, J. M. (1999). The foot-in-the-door compliance procedure: A multiple-process analysis and review. *Personality and Social Psychology Review, 3*, 303–325.

Burger, J. M., & Burns, L. (1988). The illusion of unique invulnerability and the use of effective contraception. *Personality and Social Psychology Bulletin, 14*, 264–270.

Burke, D., MacKay, D. G., Worthley, J. S., & Wade, E. (1991). On the tip of the tongue: What causes word failure in young and older adults? *Journal of Memory and Language, 30*, 237–246.

Burnstein, E., Crandall, C., & Kitayama, S. (1994). Some neo-Darwinian decision rules for altruism: Weighing cues for inclusive fitness as a function of the biological importance of the decision. *Journal of Personality & Social Psychology, 67*, 773–789.

Burris, C. T., & Branscombe, N. R. (2005). Distorted distance estimation induced by a self-relevant national boundary. *Journal of Experimental Social Psychology, 41*, 305–312.

Buss, D. M. (1985). Human mate selection. American Scientist, 73, 47–51.

Buss, D. M. (1989). Sex differences in human mate preferences: Evolutionary hypotheses tested in 37 cultures. *Behavioral and Brain Sciences, 12*, 1–49.

Buss, D. M. (1999). *Evolutionary psychology: The new science of the mind.* Boston: Allyn and Bacon.

Buss, D. M. (2000). *The dangerous passion: Why jealousy is as necessary as love and sex.* New York: Free Press.

Buss, D. M., Haselton, M. G., Shackelford, T. K., Bleske, A. L., & Wakefield, J. C. (1998). *Adaptations, exaptations, and spandrels. American Psychologist, 53*, 533–548.

Buss, D. M., & Kenrick, D. T. (1998). Evolutionary social psychology. In D. T. Gilbert, S. T. Fiske, & G. Lindzey (Eds.), *The handbook of social psychology* (4th ed., pp. 982–1026). New York: McGraw-Hill.

Buss, D. M., & Schmitt, D. P. (1993). Sexual strategies theory: An evolutionary perspective on human mating. *Psychological Review, 100*, 204–232.

Byrne, D., & Clore, G. L. (1970). A reinforcement model of evaluative responses. *Personality: An International Journal, 1*, 103–128.

Byrne, D., Ervin, C. R., & Lamberth, J. (1970). Continuity between the experimental study of attraction and real-life computer dating. *Journal of Personality and Social Psychology, 16*, 157–165.

Byrne, D., & Nelson, D. (1965). Attraction as a linear function of proportion of positive reinforcements. *Journal of Personality and Social Psychology, 1*, 659–663.

Cabeza, R. (2002). Hemispheric asymmetry reduction in older adults: The HAROLD model. *Psychology and Aging, 17*, 85–100.

Cabeza, R., Rao, S., Wagner, A. D., Mayer, A., & Schacter, D. L. (2001). Can medial temporal lobe regions distinguish true from false? An event-related fMRI study of veridical and illusory recognition memory. *Proceedings of the National Academy of Sciences (USA), 98*, 4805–4810.

Cacioppo, J. T., Hawkley, L. C., & Berntson, G. G. (2003). The anatomy of loneliness. *Current Directions in Psychological Science, 12*, 71–74.

Cahill, L., Haier, R. J., Fallon, J., Alkire, M. T., Tang, C., Keator, D., et al. (1996). Amygdala activity at encoding correlated with long-term, free recall of emotional information. *Proceedings of the National Academy of Sciences (USA), 93*, 8016–8021.

Cahill, L., & McGaugh, J. L. (1998). Mechanisms of emotional arousal and lasting declarative memory. *Trends in Neurosciences, 21*, 294–299.

Calder, A. J., Young, A. W., Rowland, D., Perrett, D. I., Hodges, J. R., & Etcoff, N. L. (1996). Facial emotion recognition after bilateral amygdala damage: Differentially severe impairment of fear. *Cognitive Neuropsychology, 13*, 699–745.

Calkins, M. W. (Ed.). (1930). *Mary Whiton Calkins* (Vol. 1). Worcester, MA: Clark University Press.

Callaghan, T., Rochat, P., Lillard, A., Claux, M. L., Odden, H., Itakura, S., et al. (2005). Synchrony in the onset of mental-state reasoning: Evidence from five cultures. *Psychological Science, 16*, 378–384.

Canetto, S., & Lester, D. (1995). Gender and the primary prevention of suicide mortality. *Suicide and Life Threatening Behavior, 25*, 85–89.

Cannon, W. B. (1927). The James-Lange theory of emotion: A critical examination and alternate theory. *American Journal of Psychology, 39*, 106–124.

Cannon, W. B. (1929). *Bodily changes in pain, hunger, fear, and rage: An account of recent research into the function of emotional excitement* (2nd ed.). New York: Appleton-Century-Crofts.

Cannon, W. B. (1942). "Voodoo" death. *American Anthropologist, 44*, 182–190.

Caplan, A. L. (Ed.). (1992). *When medicine went mad: Bioethics and the Holocaust.* Totowa, NJ: Humana Press.

Carlson, C., & Hoyle, R. (1993). Efficacy of abbreviated progressive muscle relaxation training: A quantitative review of behavioral medicine research. *Journal of Consulting & Clinical Psychology, 61*, 1059–1067.

Carmichael Olson, H., Streissguth, A. P., Sampson, P. D., Barr, H. M., Bookstein, F. L., & Thiede, K. (1997). Association of prenatal alcohol exposure with behavioral and learning problems in early adolescence. *Journal of the American Academy of Child and Adolescent Psychiatry, 36*, 1187–1194.

Carolson, E. A. (1998). A prospective longitudinal study of attachment disorganization/disorientation. *Child Development, 69*, 1107–1128.

Carr, L., Iacoboni, M., Dubeau, M., Mazziotta, J. C., & Lenzi, G. L. (2003). Neural mechanisms of empathy in humans: A relay from neural systems for imitation to limbic areas. *Proceedings of the National Academy of Sciences, 100*, 5497–5502.

Carroll, J. B. (1993). *Human cognitive abilities.* Cambridge: Cambridge University Press.

Carson, R. C., Butcher, J. N., & Mineka, S. (2000). *Abnormal psychology and modern life* (11th ed.). Boston: Allyn and Bacon.

Carstensen, L. L., & Fredrickson, B. L. (1998). Influence of HIV status and age on cognitive representations of others. *Health Psychology, 17*, 1–10.

Carstensen, L. L., Isaacowitz, D. M., & Charles, S. T. (1999). Taking time seriously: A theory of socioemotional selectivity. *American Psychologist, 54*, 165–181.

Carstensen, L. L., Pasupathi, M., Mayr, U., & Nesselroade, J. R. (2000). Emotional experience in everyday life across the adult life span. *Journal of Personality & Social Psychology, 79*, 644–655.

Carstensen, L. L., & Turk-Charles, S. (1994). The salience of emotion across the adult life span. *Psychology and Aging, 9*, 259–264.

Carver, C. S., Lehman, J. M., & Antoni, M. H. (2003). Dispositional pessimism predicts illness-related disruption of social and recreational activities among breast cancer patients. *Journal of Personality & Social Psychology, 84*, 813–821.

Caspi, A., & Herbener, E. S. (1990). Continuity and change: Assortative marriage and the consistency of personality in adulthood. *Journal of Personality and Social Psychology, 58*, 250–258.

Caspi, A., Lynam, D., Moffitt, T. E., & Silva, P. A. (1993). Unraveling girls' delinquency: Biological, dispositional, and contextual contributions to adolescent misbehavior. *Developmental Psychology, 29*, 19–30.

Caspi, A., & Moffitt, T. E. (1991). Individual differences are accentuated during periods of social change: The sample case of girls at puberty. *Journal of Personality and Social Psychology, 61*, 157–168.

Caspi, A., Roberts, B. W., & Shiner, R. L. (2005). Personality development: Stability and change. *Annual Review of Psychology, 56*, 453–484.

Castro-Martin, T., & Bumpass, L. (1989). Recent trends in marital disruption. *Demography, 26*, 37–51.

CBS. (2000). *Survivor.* Retrieved July 2, 2003, from http://www.cbs.com/primetime/survivor

Ceci, S. J. (1991). How much does schooling influence general intelligence and its cognitive components? A reassessment of the evidence. *Developmental Psychology, 27*, 703–722.

Ceci, S. J., DeSimone, M., & Johnson, S. (1992). Memory in context: A case study of "Bubbles P.," a gifted but uneven memorizer. In D. J. Herrmann, H. Weingartner, A. Searleman, & C. McEvoy (Eds.), *Memory improvement: Implications for memory theory* (pp. 169–186). New York: Springer-Verlag.

Ceci, S. J., & Williams, W. M. (1997). Schooling, intelligence, and income. *American Psychologist, 52*, 1051–1058.

Centers for Disease Control (CDC). (1988). Health status of Vietnam veterans: I. Psychosocial characteristics. *Journal of the American Medical Association, 259*, 2701–2708.

Centers for Disease Control (CDC). (August 18, 2000a). Surveillance for characteristics of health education among secondary schools—Secondary school education profiles, 1998. *Surveillance Summary, 49* (No. SS-8). Washington, DC: Author.

Centers for Disease Control (CDC). (2000b). *Tracking the hidden epidemics.* Washington, DC: Author.

Centers for Disease Control (CDC). (June 28, 2002). *Surveillance Summary, 51* (No. SS-54). Washington, DC: Author.

Centers for Disease Control (CDC). (2006). Epidemiology of HIV/AIDS—United States, 1981–2005. *Morbidity and Mortality Weekly Report, 55*, 589–592.

Chaiken, S. (1980). Heuristic versus systematic information processing and the use of source versus message cues in persuasion. *Journal of Personality and Social Psychology, 39,* 752–766.

Chalmers, D. (1996). *The conscious mind: In search of a fundamental theory.* New York: Oxford University Press.

Chandrashekar, J., Hoon, M. A., Ryba, N. J., & Zuker, C. S. (2006). The receptors and cells for human tastes. *Nature, 444,* 288–294.

Chang, P. P., Ford, D. E., Meoni, L. A., Wang, N., & Klag, M. J. (2002). Anger in young men and subsequent premature cardiovascular disease. *Archives of Internal Medicine, 162,* 901–906.

Charles, S. T., Reynolds, C. A., & Gatz, M. (2001). Age-related differences and change in positive and negative affect over 23 years. *Journal of Personality and Social Psychology, 80,* 136–151.

Charness, N. (1981). Aging and skilled problem solving. *Journal of Experimental Psychology: General, 110,* 21–38.

Chartrand, T. L., & Bargh, J. A. (1999). The chameleon effect: The perception-behavior link and social interaction. *Journal of Personality and Social Psychology, 76,* 893–910.

Chebium, R. (2000). Kirk Bloodsworth, twice convicted of rape and murder, exonerated by DNA evidence. *CNN.com.* Retrieved June 20, 2000, from http://www.cnn.com/2000/LAW/06/20/bloodsworth.profile

Chen, C., Burton, M., Greenberger, E., & Dmitrieva, J. (1999). Population migration and the variation of dopamine D4 receptor (DRD4) allele frequencies around the globe. *Evolution and Human Behavior, 20,* 309–324.

Cheney, D. L., & Seyfarth, R. M. (1990). *How monkeys see the world.* Chicago: University of Chicago Press.

Chiao, J. Y., Iidaka, T., Gordon, H. L., Nogawa, J., Bar, M., Aminoff, E., Sadato, N., & Nalini Ambady, N. (2008). Cultural specificity in amygdala response to fear faces, *Journal of Cognitive Neuroscience, 20,* 2167–2174.

Chomsky, N. (1957). *Syntactic structures.* The Hague: Mouton.

Chomsky, N. (1959). A review of *Verbal Behavior* by B. F. Skinner. *Language, 35,* 26–58.

Chorover, S. L. (1980). *From Genesis to genocide : The meaning of human nature and the power of behavior control.* Cambridge, MA: MIT Press.

Cialdini, R. B., & Trost, M. R. (1998). Social influence: Social norms, conformity, and compliance. In D. T. Gilbert, S. T. Fiske, & G. Lindzey (Eds.), *The handbook of social psychology* (4th ed., Vol. 2, pp. 151–192). New York: McGraw-Hill.

Cialdini, R. B., Trost, M. R., & Newsom, J. T. (1995). Preference for consistency: The development of a valid measure and the discovery of surprising behavioral implications. *Journal of Personality and Social Psychology, 69,* 318–328.

Cialdini, R. B., Vincent, J. E., Lewis, S. K., Catalan, J., Wheeler, D., & Darby, B. L. (1975). Reciprocal concessions procedure for inducing compliance: The door-in-the-face technique. *Journal of Personality and Social Psychology, 31,* 206–215.

Cicchetti, D., & Toth, S. L. (1998). Perspectives on research and practice in developmental psychopathology. In I. E. Sigel & K. A. Renninger (Eds.), *Handbook of child psychology: Vol. 4. Child psychology in practice* (5th ed., pp. 479–583). New York: Wiley.

Clancy, S. A. (2005). *Abducted: How people come to believe they were kidnapped by aliens.* Cambridge. MA: Harvard University Press.

Clark, R. D., & Hatfield, E. (1989). Gender differences in receptivity to sexual offers. *Journal of Psychology and Human Sexuality, 2,* 39–55.

Cogan, R., Cogan, D., Waltz, W., & McCue, M. (1987). Effects of laughter and relaxation on discomfort thresholds. *Journal of Behavioral Medicine, 10,* 139–144.

Coghill, R. C., McHaffie, J. G., & Yen, Y. (2003). Neural correlates of individual differences in the subjective experience of pain. *Proceedings of the National Academy of Sciences (USA), 100,* 8538–8542.

Cohen, G. (1990). Why is it difficult to put names to faces? *British Journal of Psychology, 81,* 287–297.

Cohen, S. (1988). Psychosocial models of the role of social support in the etiology of physical disease. *Health Psychology, 7,* 269–297.

Cohen, S., Evans, G. W., Krantz, D. S., & Stokols, D. (1980). Physiological, motivational, and cognitive effects of aircraft noise on children. *American Psychologist, 35,* 231–243.

Cohen, S., Frank, E., Doyle, W. J., Skoner, D. P., Rabin, B. S., & Gwaltney, J. M., Jr. (1998). Types of stressors that increase susceptibility to the common cold in healthy adults. *Health Psychology, 17,* 214–223.

Cohen, S. J. (Ed.). (1979). *New directions in patient compliance.* Lexington, MA: Heath.

Cole, M. (1996). *Cultural psychology: A once and future discipline.* Cambridge, MA: Belknap Press of Harvard University Press.

Condon, J. W., & Crano, W. D. (1988). Inferred evaluation and the relation between attitude similarity and interpersonal attraction. *Journal of Personality and Social Psychology, 54,* 789–797.

Connors, E., Lundregan, T., Miller, N., & McEwen, T. (1997). *Convicted by juries, exonerated by science: Case studies in the use of DNA evidence to establish innocence after trial.* Collingdale, PA: Diane Publishing.

Conway, M., & Ross, M. (1984). Getting what you want by revising what you had. *Journal of Personality and Social Psychology, 47,* 738–748.

Conwell, Y., Duberstein, P. R., Cox, C., Hermmann, J. H., Forbes, N. T., & Caine, E. D. (1996). Relationships of age and axis I diagnoses in victims of completed suicide: A psychological autopsy study. *American Journal of Psychiatry, 153,* 1001–1008.

Cook, M., & Mineka, S. (1989). Observational conditioning of fear to fear-relevant versus fear-irrelevant stimuli in rhesus monkeys. *Journal of Abnormal Psychology, 98,* 448–459.

Cook, M., & Mineka, S. (1990). Selective associations in the observational conditioning of fear in rhesus monkeys. *Journal of Experimental Psychology: Animal Behavior Process, 16,* 372–389.

Coombs, R. H. (1991). Marital status and personal well-being: A literature review. *Family Relations, 40,* 97–102.

Coons, P. M. (1994). Confirmation of childhood abuse in child and adolescent cases of multiple personality disorder and dissociative disorder not otherwise specified. *Journal of Nervous and Mental Disease, 182,* 461–464.

Cooper, J., & Fazio, R. H. (1984). A new look at dissonance theory. In L. Berkowitz (Ed.), *Advances in experimental social psychology* (Vol. 17, pp. 229–266). New York: Academic Press.

Cooper, J. R., Bloom, F. E., & Roth, R. H. (2003). *Biochemical basis of neuropharmacology.* New York: Oxford University Press.

Cooper, M. L., Shapiro, C. M., & Powers, A. M. (1998). Motivations for sex and risky sexual behavior among adolescents and young adults: A functional perspective. *Journal of Personality and Social Psychology, 75,* 1528–1558.

Coren, S. (1997). *Sleep thieves.* New York: Free Press.

Corkin, S. (1984). Lasting consequences of bilateral medial temporal lobectomy: Clinical course and experimental findings in H. M. *Seminars in Neurology, 4,* 249–259.

Corkin, S. (2002). What's new with the amnesic patient HM? *Nature Reviews Neuroscience, 3,* 153–160.

Correll, J., Park, B., Judd, C. M., & Wittenbrink, B. (2002). The police officer's dilemma: Using ethnicity to disambiguate potentially threatening individuals. *Journal of Personality and Social Psychology, 83,* 1314–1329.

Corti, E. (1931). *A history of smoking* (P. England, Trans.). London: Harrap.

Coryell, W., Endicott, J., Maser, J. D., Mueller, T., Lavori, P., & Keller, M. (1995). The likelihood of recurrence in bipolar affective disorder:

The importance of episode recency. *Journal of Affective Disorders, 33,* 201–206.

Cox, D., & Cowling, P. (1989). *Are you normal?* London: Tower Press.

Coyne, J. A. (2000, April 3). Of vice and men: Review of R. Tornhill and C. Palmer, *A natural history of rape. The New Republic,* 27–34.

Craik, F. I. M., Govoni, R., Naveh-Benjamin, M., & Anderson, N. D. (1996). The effects of divided attention on encoding and retrieval processes in human memory. *Journal of Experimental Psychology: General, 125,* 159–180.

Craik, F. I. M., & Tulving, E. (1975). Depth of processing and the retention of words in episodic memory. *Journal of Experimental Psychology: General, 104,* 268–294.

Cramer, R. E., Schaefer, J. T., & Reid, S. (1996). Identifying the ideal mate: More evidence for male-female convergence. *Current Psychology: Developmental, Learning, Personality, Social, 15,* 157–166.

Craske, M. G. (1999). *Anxiety disorders: Psychological approaches to theory and treatment.* Boulder, CO: Westview.

Crick, N. R., & Grotpeter, J. K. (1995). Relational aggression, gender, and social-psychological adjustment. *Child Development, 66,* 710–722.

Crocker, J., & Wolfe, C. T. (2001). Contingencies of self-worth. *Psychological Review, 108*(3), 593–623.

Crombag, H. F. M., Wagenaar, W. A., & Van Koppen, P. J. (1996). Crashing memories and the problem of "source monitoring." *Applied Cognitive Psychology, 10,* 95–104.

Cross-National Collaborative Research Group. (1992). The changing rate of major depression: Cross-national comparison. *Journal of the American Medical Association, 268,* 3098–3105.

Crowe, R. (1990). Panic disorder: Genetic considerations. *Journal of Psychiatric Researchers, 24,* 129–134.

Csermansky, J. G., & Grace, A. A. (1998). New models of the pathophysiology of schizophrenia: Editor's introduction. *Schizophrenia Bulletin, 24,* 185–187.

Csikszentmihalyi, M., & Larson, R. (1987). Validity and reliability of the experience-sampling method. *Journal of Nervous & Mental Disease, 175,* 526–536.

Cumming, S., Hay, P., Lee, T., & Sachdev, P. (1995). Neuropsychological outcome from psychosurgery for obsessive-compulsive disorder. *Australian and New Zealand Journal of Psychiatry, 29,* 293–298.

Cunningham, M. R., Barbee, A. P., & Pike, C. L. (1990). What do women want? Facialmetric assessment of multiple motives in the perception of male facial physical attractiveness. *Journal of Personality & Social Psychology, 59,* 61–72.

Cunningham, M. R., Roberts, A. R., Barbee, A. P., Druen, P. B., & Wu, C.-H. (1995). "Their ideas of beauty are, on the whole, the same as ours": Consistency and variability in the cross-cultural perception of female physical attractiveness. *Journal of Personality and Social Psychology, 68,* 261–279.

Curran, J. P., & Lippold, S. (1975). The effects of physical attraction and attitude similarity on attraction in dating dyads. *Journal of Personality, 43,* 528–539.

Curtiss, S. (1977). Genie: A psycholinguistic study of a modern-day "wild-child." New York: Academic Press.

Dabbs, J. M., Carr, T. S., Frady, R. L., & Riad, J. K. (1995). Testosterone, crime, and misbehavior among 692 male prison inmates. *Personality and Individual Differences, 18,* 627–633.

Dalton, P. (2003). Olfaction. In H. Pashler & S. Yantis (Eds.), *Stevens' handbook of experimental psychology: Vol. 1. Sensation and perception* (3rd ed., pp. 691–746). New York: Wiley.

Daly, M., & Wilson, M. (1988). Evolutionary social psychology and family homicide. *Science, 242,* 519–524.

Damasio, A. R. (1989). Time-locked multiregional retroactivation: A systems-level proposal for the neural substrates of recall and recognition. *Cognition, 33,* 25–62.

Damasio, A. R. (1994). *Descartes' error: Emotion, reason, and the human brain.* New York: Putnam.

Damasio, A. R. (2005). *Descartes' error: Emotion, reason, and the human brain.* (ppbk. ed). New York: Penguin.

Damasio, A. R., Grabowski, T. J., Bechara, A., Damasio, H., Ponto, L. L. B., Parvisi, J., et al. (2000). Subcortical and cortical brain activity during the feeling of self-generated emotions. *Nature Neuroscience, 3,* 1049–1056.

Damasio, H., Grabowski, T. J., Tranel, D., Hichwa, R. D., & Damasio, A. R. (1996). A neural basis for lexical retrieval. *Nature, 380,* 499–505.

Damsma, G., Pfaus, J. G., Wenkstern, D., Phillips, A. G., & Fibiger, H. C. (1992). Sexual behavior increases dopamine transmission in the nucleus accumbens and striatum of male rats: Comparison with novelty and locomotion. *Behavioral Neurosciences, 106,* 181–191.

Daniel, H. J., O'Brien, K. F., McCabe, R. B., & Quinter, V. E. (1985). Values in mate selection: A 1984 campus survey. *College Student Journal, 19,* 44–50.

Darley, J. M., & Berscheid, E. (1967). Increased liking caused by the anticipation of interpersonal contact. *Human Relations, 10,* 29–40.

Dar-Nimrod, I., & Heine, S. J. (2006). Exposure to scientific theories affects women's math performance. *Science, 314,* 435.

Darroch, J. E., Singh, S., Frost, J. J., & Study Team. (2001). Differences in teenage pregnancy rates among five developed countries: The roles of sexuality and contraceptive use. *Family Planning Perspectives, 33,* 244–250.

Darwin, C. (1998). *The expression of the emotions in man and animals.* (P. Ekman, Ed.) New York: Oxford University Press. (Originally published in 1872)

Darwin, C. J., Turvey, M. T., & Crowder, R. G. (1972). An auditory analogue of the Sperling partial report procedure: Evidence for brief auditory storage. *Cognitive Psychology, 3,* 255–267.

Davidson, R. J. (2004). What does the prefrontal cortex "do" in affect: Perspectives on frontal EEG asymmetry research. *Biological Psychology, 67,* 219–233.

Davidson, R. J., Ekman, P., Saron, C., Senulis, J., & Friesen, W. V. (1990). Emotional expression and brain physiology I: Approach/withdrawal and cerebral asymmetry. *Journal of Personality and Social Psychology, 58,* 330–341.

Davidson, R. J., Pizzagalli, D., Nitschke, J. B., & Putnam, K. (2002). Depression: Perspectives from affective neuroscience. *Annual Review of Psychology, 53,* 545–574.

Davidson, R. J., Putnam, K. M., & Larson, C. L. (2000). Dysfunction in the neural circuitry of emotion regulation—a possible prelude to violence. *Science, 289,* 591–594.

Davies, G. (1988). Faces and places: Laboratory research on context and face recognition. In G. M. Davies & D. M. Thomson (Eds.), *Memory in context: Context in memory* (pp. 35–53). New York: Wiley.

Dawes, R. M. (1994). *House of cards: Psychology and psychotherapy built on myth.* New York: Free Press.

Dawkins, R. J. (1976). *The selfish gene.* Oxford: Oxford University Press.

De Witte, P. (1996). The role of neurotransmitters in alcohol dependency. *Alcohol & Alcoholism, 31*(Suppl. 1), 13–16.

De Wolff, M., & van IJzendoorn, M. H. (1997). Sensitivity and attachment: A meta-analysis on parental antecedents of infant attachment. *Child Development, 68,* 571–591.

Deary, I. J. (2000). *Looking down on human intelligence: From psychometrics to the brain.* New York: Oxford University Press.

Deary, I. J., Der, G., & Ford, G. (2001). Reaction time and intelligence differences: A population based cohort study. *Intelligence, 29,* 389–399.

Deary, I. J., & Stough, C. (1996). Intelligence and inspection time: Achievements, prospects, and problems. *American Psychologist, 51,* 599–608.

Deary, I. J., Whalley, L. J., Lemmon, H., Crawford, J. R., & Starr, J. M. (2000). The stability of individual differences in mental ability from childhood to old age: Follow-up of the 1932 Scottish Mental Survey. *Intelligence, 28,* 49–55.

Deary, I. J., Whiteman, M. C., Starr, J. M., Whalley, L. J., & Fox, H. C. (2004). The impact of childhood intelligence on later life: Following up the Scottish mental surveys of 1932 and 1947. *Journal of Personality and Social Psychology, 86,* 130–147.

DeCasper, A. J., & Spence, M. J. (1986). Prenatal maternal speech influences newborns' perception of speech sounds. *Infant Behavior and Development, 9,* 133–150.

Deci, E. L. (1971). Effects of externally mediated rewards on intrinsic motivation. *Journal of Personality and Social Psychology, 18,* 105–115.

Deci, E. L., Koestner, R., & Ryan, R. M. (1999). A meta-analytic review of experiments examining the effects of extrinsic rewards on intrinsic motivation. *Psychological Bulletin, 125,* 627–668.

Deese, J. (1959). On the prediction of occurrence of particular verbal intrusions in immediate recall. *Journal of Experimental Psychology, 58,* 17–22.

Dehaene, S., Izard, V., Pica, P., & Spelke, E. (2006). Core knowledge of geometry in an Amazonian indigene group. *Science, 311* (January 20).

DeLisi, L. E., Crow, T. J., & Hirsch, S. R. (1986). The third biannual workshops on schizophrenia. *Archives of General Psychiatry, 43,* 706–711.

Delongis, A., Coyne, J. C., Dakof, G., Folkman, S., & Lazarus, R. S. (1982). Relationship of daily hassles, uplifts, and major life events to health status. *Health Psychology, 1,* 119–136.

Demb, J. B., Desmond, J. E., Wagner, A. D., Vaidya, C. J., Glover, G. H., & Gabrieli, J. D. E. (1995). Semantic encoding and retrieval in the left inferior prefrontal cortex: A functional MRI study of task difficulty and process specificity. *Journal of Neuroscience, 15,* 5870–5878.

Dement, W. C. (1999). *The promise of sleep.* New York: Delacorte Press.

Dement, W. C., & Wolpert, E. (1958). Relation of eye movements, body motility, and external stimuli to dream content. *Journal of Experimental Psychology, 55,* 543–553.

Dennett, D. (1991). *Consciousness explained.* New York: Basic Books.

DePaulo, B. M., Stone, J. I., & Lassiter, G. D. (1985). Deceiving and detecting deceit. In B. R. Schlenker (Ed.), *The self and social life* (pp. 323–370). New York: McGraw-Hill.

DeRosnay, M., Pons, F., Harris, P. L., & Morrell, J. M. B. (2004). A lag between understanding false belief and emotion attribution in young children: Relationships with linguistic ability and mothers' mental-state language. *British Journal of Developmental Psychology,* 197–218.

Deuenwald, M. (2003, June 12). Students find another staple of campus life: Stress. *New York Times.*

Deutsch, M. (1949). A theory of cooperation and competition. *Human Relations, 2,* 129–152.

DeVilliers, P. (2005). The role of language in theory-of-mind development: What deaf children tell us. In J. W. Astington & J. A. Baird (Eds.), *Why language matters for theory of mind* (pp. 266–297). Oxford: Oxford University Press.

Dickens, W. T., & Flynn, J. R. (2001). Heritability estimates versus large environmental effects: The IQ paradox resolved. *Psychological Review, 108,* 346–369.

Diener, E., & Biswas-Diener, R. (2002). Will money increase subjective well-being? *Social Indicators Research, 57,* 119–169.

Diener, E., Horwitz, J., & Emmons, R. A. (1985). Happiness of the very wealthy. *Social Indicators Research, 16,* 263–274.

Dietary Guidelines Advisory Committee. (2005). Dietary guidelines for Americans 2005. Retrieved October 15, 2007, from http://www.health.gov/dietaryguidelines

Dijksterhuis, A., Aarts, H., & Smith, P. K. (2005). The power of the subliminal: On subliminal persuasion and other potential applications. In J. S. U. R. Hassin & J. A. Bargh (Eds.), *The new unconscious* (pp. 77–106). New York: Oxford University Press.

Dillbeck, M. C., & Orme-Johnson, D. W. (1987). Physiological differences between Transcendental Meditation and rest. *American Psychologist, 42,* 879–881.

Dimberg, U. (1982). Facial reactions to facial expressions. *Psychophysiology, 19,* 643–647.

Dion, K., Berscheid, E., & Walster, E. (1972). What is beautiful is good. *Journal of Personality and Social Psychology, 24,* 285–290.

DiTella, R., MacCulloch, R. J., & Oswald, A. J. (2003). The macroeconomics of happiness. *Review of Economics and Statistics, 85,* 809–827.

Dittrich, W. H., Troscianko, T., Lea, S., & Morgan, D. (1996). Perception of emotion from dynamic point-light displays represented in dance. *Perception, 25,* 727–738.

Dollard, J., Doob, L. W., Miller, N. E., Mowrer, O. H., & Sears, R. R. (1939). *Frustration and aggression.* Oxford: Yale University Press.

Domjan, M. (2005). Pavlovian conditioning: A functional perspective. *Annual Review of Psychology, 56,* 179–206.

Dorahy, M. J. (2001). Dissociative identity disorder and memory dysfunction: The current state of experimental research and its future directions. *Clinical Psychology Review, 21,* 771–795.

Dornbusch, S. M., Hastorf, A. H., Richardson, S. A., Muzzy, R. E., & Vreeland, R. S. (1965). The perceiver and perceived: Their relative influence on categories of interpersonal perception. *Journal of Personality and Social Psychology, 1,* 434–440.

Dorus, S., Vallender, E. J., Evans, P. D., Anderson, J. R., Gilbert, S. L., Mahowald, M., et al. (2004). Accelerated evolution of nervous system genes in the origin of *Homo sapiens. Cell, 119,* 1027–1040.

Draguns, J. G. (1980). Psychological disorders of clinical severity. In H. C. Triandis & J. G. Draguns (Eds.), *Handbook of cross-cultural psychology* (Vol. 6, pp. 99–174). Boston: Allyn and Bacon.

Dreger, A. D. (1998). The limits of individuality: Ritual and sacrifice in the lives and medical treatment of conjoined twins. *Studies in History and Philosophy of Biological and Biomedical Sciences, 29,* 1–29.

Dreifus, C. (2003, May 20). Living one disaster after another, and then sharing the experience. *New York Times,* p. D2.

Drigotas, S. M., & Rusbult, C. E. (1992). Should I stay or should I go? A dependence model of breakups. *Journal of Personality and Social Psychology, 62,* 62–87.

Druckman, D., & Bjork, R. A. (1994). *Learning, remembering, believing: Enhancing human performance.* Washington, DC: National Academy Press.

Duchaine, B. C., Yovel, G., Butterworth, E. J., & Nakayama, K. (2006). Prosopagnosia as an impairment to face-specific mechanisms: Elimination of the alternative hypotheses in a developmental case. *Cognitive Neuropsychology, 23,* 714–747.

Duckworth, A. L., & Seligman, M. E. P. (2005). Self-discipline outdoes IQ in predicting academic performance of adolescents. *Psychological Science, 16,* 939–944.

Dudycha, G. J., & Dudycha, M. M. (1933). Some factors and characteristics of childhood memories. *Child Development, 4,* 265–278.

Dunphy, D. C. (1963). The social structure of urban adolescent peer groups. *Sociometry, 26,* 230–246.

Durkheim, E. (1951). *Suicide: A study in sociology* (G. Simpson, Trans.). New York: Free Press.

Eacott, M. J., & Crawley, R. A. (1998). The offset of childhood amnesia: Memory for events that occurred before age 3. *Journal of Experimental Psychology: General, 127,* 22–33.

Eagly, A. H., Ashmore, R. D., Makhijani, M. G., & Longo, L. C. (1991). What is beautiful is good, but . . . : A meta-analytic review of research on the physical attractiveness stereotype. *Psychological Bulletin, 110,* 109–128.

Eagly, A. H., & Steffen, V. J. (1986). Gender and aggressive behavior: A meta-analytic review of the social psychological literature. *Psychological Bulletin, 100,* 309–330.

Eagly, A. H., & Wood, W. (1999). The origins of sex differences in human behavior: Evolved dispositions versus social roles. *American Psychologist, 54,* 408–423.

Eaton, W. W., Kessler, R. C., Wittchen, H. U., & McGee, W. J. (1994). Panic and panic disorder in the United States. *American Journal of Psychiatry, 151,* 413–420.

Eaton, W. W., Romanoski, A., Anthony, J. C., & Nestadt, G. (1991). Screening for psychosis in the general population with a self-report interview. *Journal of Nervous and Mental Disease, 179,* 689–693.

Ebbinghaus, H. (1964). *Memory: A contribution to experimental psychology.* New York: Dover. (Original work published 1885)

Eddy, D. M. (1982). Probabilistic reasoning in clinical medicine: Problems and opportunities. In D. Kahneman, P. Slovic, & A. Tversky (Eds.), *Judgments under uncertainty: Heuristics and biases* (pp. 249–267). Cambridge, MA: Cambridge University Press.

Editorial. (2006, May 31). Bribing people to vote will not benefit system. *Yuma Sun.* Available: http://www.yumasun.com/articles/people-21362-vote-voting.html.

Edwards, W. (1955). The theory of decision making. *Psychological Bulletin, 51,* 201–214.

Eich, J. E. (1995). Searching for mood dependent memory. *Psychological Science, 6,* 67–75.

Eichenbaum, H., & Cohen, N. J. (2001). *From conditioning to conscious recollection: Memory systems of the brain.* New York: Oxford University Press.

Eimas, P. D., Siqueland, E. R., Jusczyk, P., & Vigorito, J. (1971). Speech perception in infants. *Science, 171,* 303–306.

Einstein, G. O., & McDaniel, M. A. (1990). Normal aging and prospective memory. *Journal of Experimental Psychology: Learning, Memory, and Cognition, 16,* 717–726.

Eisenberger, N. I., Lieberman, M. D., & Williams, K. D. (2003). Does rejection hurt? An fMRI study of social exclusion. *Science, 302,* 290–292.

Ekman, P. (1965). Differential communication of affect by head and body cues. *Journal of Personality and Social Psychology, 2,* 726–735.

Ekman, P. (1972). Universals and cultural differences in facial expressions of emotion. In J. K. Cole (Ed.), *Nebraska Symposium on Motivation, 1971* (pp. 207–283). Lincoln: University of Nebraska Press.

Ekman, P. (1992). *Telling lies.* New York: Norton.

Ekman, P. (2003). Darwin, deception, and facial expression. *Annals of the New York Academy of Science, 1000,* 205–221.

Ekman, P., & Friesen, W. V. (1968). Nonverbal behavior in psychotherapy research. In J. M. Shlien (Ed.), *Research in psychotherapy* (Vol. 3, pp. 179–216). Washington, DC: American Psychological Association.

Ekman, P., & Friesen, W. V. (1971). Constants across cultures in the face and emotion. *Journal of Personality and Social Psychology, 17,* 124–129.

Ekman, P., & Friesen, W. V. (1978). *The Facial Action Coding System.* Palo Alto, CA: Consulting Psychologists Press.

Ekman, P., & Friesen, W. V. (1982). Felt, false, and miserable smiles. *Journal of Nonverbal Behavior, 6,* 238–252.

Ekman, P., Friesen, W. V., O'Sullivan, M., Chan, A., Diacoyanni-Tarlatzis, I., Heider, K., et al. (1987). Universals and cultural differences in the judgments of facial expressions of emotion. *Journal of Personality and Social Psychology, 53,* 712–717.

Ekman, P., Levenson, R. W., & Friesen, W. V. (1983). Autonomic nervous system activity distinguishes among emotions. *Science, 221,* 1208–1210.

Elder, G. H., & Conger, R. D. (2000). *Children of the land: Adversity and success in rural America.* Chicago: University of Chicago Press.

Eldridge, L. L., Knowlton, B. J., Furmanski, C. S., Bookheimer, S. Y., & Engel, S. A. (2000). Remembering episodes: A selective role for the hippocampus during retrieval. *Nature Neuroscience, 3,* 1149–1152.

Eldridge, M. A., Barnard, P. J., & Bekerian, D. A. (1994). Autobiographical memory and daily schemas at work. *Memory, 2,* 51–74.

Elfenbein, H. A., & Ambady, N. (2002). On the universality and cultural specificity of emotion recognition: A meta-analysis. *Psychological Bulletin, 128,* 203–235.

Ellicot, A., Hammen, C., Gitlin, M., Brown, G., & Jaminson, K. (1990). Life events and course of bipolar disorder. *American Journal of Psychiatry, 147,* 1194–1198.

Elliott, R., Sahakian, B. J., Matthews, K., Bannerjea, A., Rimmer, J., & Robbins, T. W. (1997). Effects of methylphenidate on spatial working memory and planning in healthy young adults. *Psychopharmacology, 131,* 196–206.

Ellis, A. (2000). Rational emotive behavior therapy. In R. J. Corsini & D. Wedding (Eds.), *Current psychotherapies* (6th ed., pp. 168–204). Itasca, IL: F. E. Peacock.

Ellis, B. J., & Garber, J. (2000). Psychosocial antecedents of variation in girls' pubertal timing: Maternal depression, stepfather presence, and marital and family stress. *Child Development, 71,* 485–501.

Ellis, E. M. (1983). A review of empirical rape research: Victim reactions and response to treatment. *Clinical Psychology Review, 3,* 473–490.

Ellis, L., & Ames, M. A. (1987). Neurohormonal functioning in sexual orientation: A theory of homosexuality-heterosexuality. *Psychological Bulletin, 101,* 233–258.

Ellman, S. J., Spielman, A. J., Luck, D., Steiner, S. S., & Halperin, R. (1991). REM deprivation: A review. In S. J. Ellman & J. S. Antrobus (Eds.), *The mind in sleep: Psychology and psychophysiology* (2nd ed., pp. 329–376). New York: Wiley.

Emerson, R. C., Bergen, J. R., & Adelson, E. H. (1992). Directionally selective complex cells and the computation of motion energy in cat visual cortex. *Vision Research, 32,* 203–218.

Emmelkamp, P. M. G., & Wessels, H. (1975). Flooding in imagination vs. flooding in vivo: A comparison with agoraphobics. *Behaviour Research and Therapy, 13,* 7–15.

Empson, J. A. (1984). Sleep and its disorders. In R. Stevens (Ed.), *Aspects of consciousness.* New York: Academic Press.

Enns, J. T. (2004). *The thinking eye, the seeing brain.* New York: Norton.

Epley, N., Savitsky, K., & Kachelski, R. A. (1999). What every skeptic should know about subliminal persuasion. *Skeptical Inquirer, 23,* 40–45, 58.

Erber, R., Wegner, D. M., & Therriault, N. (1996). On being cool and collected: Mood regulation in anticipation of social interaction. *Journal of Personality and Social Psychology, 70,* 757–766.

Erickson, E. (1959). *Identity and the life cycle: Selected papers.* New York: International Universities Press.

Ericsson, K. A., & Charness, N. (1999). Expert performance: Its structure and acquisition. In S. J. Ceci & W. M. Williams (Eds.), *The nature-nurture debate: The essential readings* (pp. 200–256). Oxford: Blackwell.

Etcoff, N. (1999). *Survival of the prettiest: The science of beauty.* New York: Doubleday.

Evans, P. D., Gilbert, S. L, Mekel-Bobrov, N., Vallender, E. J., Anderson, J. R., Vaez-Azizi, L. M., et al. (2005). Microcephalin, a gene regulating brain size, continues to evolve adaptively in humans. *Science, 309,* 1717–1720.

Eysenck, H. J. (1957). The effects of psychotherapy: An evaluation. *Journal of Consulting Psychology, 16,* 319–324.

Eysenck, H. J. (1967). *The biological basis of personality.* Springfield, IL: Charles C. Thomas.

Eysenck, S. B. G., & Eysenck, H. J. (1985). *Personality and individual differences: A natural science approach.* New York: Plenum Press.

Fancher, R. E. (1979). *Pioneers of psychology.* New York: Norton.

Fantz, R. L. (1964). Visual experience in infants: Decreased attention to familiar patterns relative to novel ones. *Science, 164,* 668–670.

Farah, M. J., Illes, J. Cook-Deegan, R., Gardner, H., Kandel, E., King, P., et al. (2004). Neurocognitive enhancement: What can we do and what should we do? *Nature Reviews Neuroscience, 5,* 421–426.

Farah, M. J., & Rabinowitz, C. (2003). Genetic and environmental influences on the organization of semantic memory in the brain: Is "living things" an innate category? *Cognitive Neuropsychology, 20,* 401–408.

Farrar, M. J. (1990). Discourse and the acquisition of grammatical morphemes. *Journal of Child Language, 17,* 607–624.

Fazel, S., & Danesh, J. (2002). Serious mental disorder in 23,000 prisoners: A review of 62 surveys. *Lancet, 359,* 545–550.

Fechner, G. T. (1966). *Elements of psychophysics.* (H. E. Alder, Trans.). New York: Holt, Reinhart and Wilson. (Original work published 1860)

Feinberg, T. E. (2001). *Altered egos: How the brain creates the self.* New York: Oxford University Press.

Feingold, A. (1990). Gender differences in effects of physical attractiveness on romantic attraction: A comparison across five research paradigms. *Journal of Personality and Social Psychology, 59,* 981–993.

Feingold, A. (1992a). Gender differences in mate selection preferences: A test of the parental investment model. *Psychological Bulletin, 112,* 125–139.

Feingold, A. (1992b). Good-looking people are not what we think. *Psychological Bulletin, 111,* 304–341.

Feldman, M. D. (2004). *Playing sick.* New York: Brunner-Routledge.

Ferster, C. B., & Skinner, B. F. (1957). *Schedules of reinforcement.* New York: Appleton-Century-Crofts.

Festinger, L. (1957). *A theory of cognitive dissonance.* Stanford, CA: Stanford University Press.

Festinger, L., & Carlsmith, J. M. (1959). Cognitive consequences of forced compliance. *Journal of Abnormal and Social Psychology, 58,* 203–210.

Festinger, L., Schachter, S., & Back, K. (1950). *Social pressures in informal groups: A study of human factors in housing.* Oxford: Harper & Row.

Fiedler, E. R., Oltmanns, T. F., & Turkheimer, E. (2004). Traits associated with personality disorders and adjustment to military life: Predictive validity of self and peer reports. *Military Medicine, 169,* 32–40.

Finkelstein, K. E. (1999, October 17). Yo-Yo Ma's lost Stradivarius is found after wild search. *New York Times,* p. 34.

Fiorentine, R. (1999). After drug treatment: Are 12-step programs effective in maintaining abstinence? *American Journal of Drug and Alcohol Abuse, 25,* 93–116.

Fisher, H. E. (1993). *Anatomy of love: The mysteries of mating, marriage, and why we stray.* New York: Fawcett.

Fisher, R. P., & Craik, F. I. M. (1977). The interaction between encoding and retrieval operations in cued recall. *Journal of Experimental Psychology: Human Learning and Perception, 3,* 153–171.

Fiske, S. T. (1998). Stereotyping, prejudice, and discrimination. In D. T. Gilbert, S. T. Fiske, & G. Lindzey (Eds.), *The handbook of social psychology* (4th ed., Vol. 2, pp. 357–411). New York: McGraw-Hill.

Fitzgerald, P. B., Brown, T. L., Marston, N. A. U., Daskalakis, Z. J., de Castella, A., Kulkarni, J., et al. (2003). Transcranial magnetic stimulation in the treatment of depression: A double-blind, placebo-controlled trial. *Archives of General Psychiatry, 60,* 1002–1008.

Fleming, R., Baum, A., Gisriel, M. M., & Gatchel, R. J. (1985). Mediating influences of social support on stress at Three Mile Island. In A. Monat & R. S. Lazarus (Eds.), *Stress and coping: An anthology* (2nd ed.) (pp. 95–106). New York: Columbia University Press.

Fletcher, P. C., Shallice, T., & Dolan, R. J. (1998). The functional roles of prefrontal cortex in episodic memory. I. Encoding. *Brain, 121,* 1239–1248.

Flynn, J. R. (1984). The mean IQ of Americans: Massive gains 1932 to 1978. *Psychological Bulletin, 95,* 29–51.

Foa, E. B., Dancu, C. V., Hembree, E. A., Jaycox, L. H., Meadows, E. A., & Street, G. P. (1999). A comparison of exposure therapy, stress inoculation training, and their combination for reducing posttraumatic stress disorder in female assault victims. *Journal of Consulting & Clinical Psychology, 67,* 194–200.

Foa, E. B, & Meadows, E. A. (1997). Psychosocial treatments for posttraumatic stress disorder: A critical review. *Annual Review of Psychology, 48,* 449–480.

Fogassi, L., Ferrari, P. F., Gesierich, B., Rozzi, S., Chersi, F., & Rizzolatti, G. (2005). Parietal lobe: From action organization to intention understanding. *Science, 308,* 662–667.

Fornazzari, L., Wilkinson, D. A., Kapur, B. M., & Carlen, P. L. (1983). Cerebellar, cortical and functional impairment in toluene abusers. *Acta Neurologica Scandinavica, 67,* 319–329.

Fowler, D. (1985). Landmarks in computer-assisted psychological assessment. *Journal of Consulting and Clinical Psychology, 53,* 748–759.

Frank, M. G., Ekman, P., & Friesen, W. V. (1993). Behavioral markers and recognizability of the smile of enjoyment. *Journal of Personality and Social Psychology, 64,* 83–93.

Frank, M. G., & Stennet, J. (2001). The forced-choice paradigm and the perception of facial expressions of emotion. *Journal of Personality and Social Psychology, 80,* 75–85.

Frankl, V. (2000). *Man's search for meaning.* New York: Beacon Press.

Fredrickson, B. L. (2000). Cultivating positive emotions to optimize health and well-being. *Prevention and Treatment, 3.*

Fredrickson, B. L. (2001). The role of positive emotions in positive psychology: The broaden-and-build theory of positive emotions. *American Psychologist, 56,* 218–226.

Freedman, J. L., & Fraser, S. C. (1966). Compliance without pressure: The foot-in-the-door technique. *Journal of Personality and Social Psychology, 4,* 195–202.

Freeman, S., Walker, M. R., Borden, R., & Latané, B. (1975). Diffusion of responsibility and restaurant tipping: Cheaper by the bunch. *Personality and Social Psychology Bulletin, 1,* 584–587.

Freud, A. (1936). *The ego and the mechanisms of defense.* New York: International Universities Press.

Freud, S. (1938). The psychopathology of everyday life. In A. A. Brill (Ed.), *The basic writings of Sigmund Freud.* New York: Basic Books. (Original work published 1901)

Freud, S. (1952). *A general introduction to psychoanalysis.* New York: Pocket Books. (Original work published 1920)

Freud, S. (1953). Three essays on the theory of sexuality. In J. Strachey (Ed.), *The standard edition of the complete psychological works of Sigmund Freud* (Vol. 7, pp. 135–243). London: Hogarth Press. (Original work published 1905)

Freud, S. (1965). *The interpretation of dreams* (J. Strachey, Trans.). New York: Avon. (Original work published 1900)

Freudenberger, H. J. (1974). Staff burnout. *Journal of Social Issues, 30,* 159–165.

Frick, R. W. (1985). Communicating emotion: The role of prosodic features. *Psychological Bulletin, 97,* 412–429.

Fried, P. A., & Watkinson, B. (2000). Visuoperceptual functioning differs in 9- to 12-year-olds prenatally exposed to cigarettes and marijuana. *Neurotoxicology and Teratology, 22,* 11–20.

Friedman, M., & Rosenman, R. H. (1974). *Type A behavior and your heart.* New York: Knopf.

Friesen, W. V. (1972). Cultural differences in facial expressions in a social situation: An experimental test of the concept of display rules. Unpublished doctoral dissertation, University of California, San Francisco.

Frith, C. D., & Fletcher, P. (1995). Voices from nowhere. *Critical Quarterly, 37,* 71–83.

Frith, U. (2001). Mind blindness and the brain in autism. *Neuron, 32,* 969–979.

Frith, U. (2003). *Autism: Explaining the enigma.* Oxford: Blackwell.

Fryer, A. J., Mannuzza, S., Gallops, M. S., Martin, L. Y., Aaronson, C., Gorman, J. M., et al. (1990). Familial transmission of simple phobias and fears: A preliminary report. *Archives of General Psychiatry, 47,* 252–256.

Furmark, T., Tillfors, M., Marteinsdottir, I., Fischer, H., Pissiota, A., Långström, B., et al. (2002). Common changes in cerebral blood flow in patients with social phobia treated with citalopram or cognitive-behavioral therapy. *Archives of General Psychiatry, 59*(5), 425–433.

Fuster, J. M. (2003). *Cortex and mind.* New York: Oxford University Press.

Gable, S. L., & Haidt, J. (2005). What (and why) is positive psychology? *Review of General Psychology, 9,* 102–110.

Gais, S., & Born, J. (2004). Low acetylcholine during slow-wave sleep is critical for declaratived memory consolidation. *Proceedings of the National Academy of Sciences (USA), 101,* 2140–2144.

Galanter, E. (1962). Contemporary psychophysics. In R. Brown, E. Galanter, E. H. Hess, & G. Mandler (Eds.), *New directions in psychology* (pp. 87–156). New York: Holt, Rinehart, & Winston.

Galati, D., Scherer, K. R., & Ricci-Bitt, P. E. (1997). Voluntary facial expression of emotion: Comparing congenitally blind with normally sighted encoders. *Journal of Personality and Social Psychology, 73,* 1363–1379.

Galef, B. (1998). Edward Thorndike: Revolutionary psychologist, ambiguous biologist. *American Psychologist, 53,* 1128–1134.

Gallistel, C. R. (2000). The replacement of general-purpose learning models with adaptively specialized learning modules. In M. S. Gazzaniga (Ed.), *The new cognitive neurosciences* (pp. 1179–1191). Cambridge, MA: MIT Press.

Gallistel, C. R., & Gelman, R. (1992). Preverbal and verbal counting and computation. *Cognition,* Special issue: *Numerical Cognition, 44,* 43–74.

Gallup, G. G. (1997). On the rise and fall of self-conception in primates. *Annals of the New York Academy of Sciences, 818,* 73–84.

Galton, F. (1869). *Hereditary genius: An inquiry into its laws and consequences.* London: Macmillan/Fontana.

Gangestad, S. W., & Simpson, J. A. (2000). On the evolutionary psychology of human mating: Trade-offs and strategic pluralism. *Behavioral and Brain Sciences, 23,* 573–587.

Garb, H. N. (1998). *Studying the clinician: Judgment research and psychological assessment.* Washington, DC: American Psychological Association.

Garb, H. N. (1999). Call for a moratorium on the use of the Rorschach inkblot test in clinical and forensic settings. *Assessment, 6,* 313–315.

Garcia, J. (1981). Tilting at the windmills of academe. *American Psychologist, 36,* 149–158.

Garcia, J., & Koelling, R. A. (1966). Relation of cue to consequence in avoidance learning. *Psychonomic Science, 4,* 123–124.

Garry, M., Manning, C., Lofts, E. F., & Sherman, S. J. (1996). Imagination inflation: Imagining a childhood event inflates confidence that it occurred. *Psychonomic Bulletin and Review, 3,* 208–214.

Gazzaniga, M. S. (Ed.). (2000). *The new cognitive neurosciences.* Cambridge, MA: MIT Press.

Gazzaniga, M. S. (2006). Forty-five years of split brain research and still going strong. *Nature Reviews Neuroscience, 6,* 653–659.

Ge, X. J., Conger, R. D., & Elder, G. H. (1996). Coming of age too early: Pubertal influences on girls' vulnerability to psychological distress. *Child Development, 67,* 3386–3400.

Geen, R. G. (1984). Preferred stimulation levels in introverts and extraverts: Effects on arousal and performance. *Journal of Personality and Social Psychology, 46,* 1303–1312.

Geen, R. G. (1998). Aggression and antisocial behavior., *The handbook of social psychology* (4th ed., Vol. 2, pp. 317–356). New York: McGraw-Hill.

Geller, D. A., Hoog, S. L., Heiligenstein, J. H., Ricardi, R. K., Tamura, R., Kluszynski, S., Jacobson, J. G., et al. (2001). Fluoxetine treatment for obsessive-compulsive disorder in children and adolescents: A placebo-controlled clinical trial. *Journal of the American Academy of Child and Adolescent Psychiatry, 40,* 773–779.

George, D. (1981). *Sweet man: The real Duke Ellington.* New York: Putnam.

George, M. S., Lisanby, S. H., Sackeim, H. A. (1999), Transcranial magnetic stimulation: Applications in neuropsychiatry. *Archives of General Psychiatry, 56,* 300–311.

Gershoff, E. T. (2002). Corporal punishment by parents and associated child behaviors and experiences: A meta-analytic and theoretical review. *Psychological Bulletin, 128,* 539–579.

Gerull, F. C., & Rapee, R. M. (2002). Mother knows best: The effects of maternal modelling on the acquisition of fear and avoidance behaviour in toddlers. *Behaviour Research and Therapy, 40,* 279–287.

Gibbs, N. A. (1996). Nonclinical populations in research on obsessive-compulsive disorder: A critical review. *Clinical Psychology Review, 16,* 729–773.

Giedd, J. N., Blumenthal, J., Jeffries, N. O., Castellanos, F. X., Liu, H., Zijdenbos, A., et al. (1999). Brain development during childhood and adolescence: A longitudinal MRI study. *Nature Neuroscience, 2,* 861–863.

Gigerenzer, G. (2002). *Calculated risks: How to know when numbers deceive you.* New York: Simon & Schuster.

Gilbert, D. T. (1991). How mental systems believe. *American Psychologist, 46,* 107–119.

Gilbert, D. T. (1998). Ordinary personology. In D. T. Gilbert, S. T. Fiske, & G. Lindzey (Eds.), *The handbook of social psychology* (4th ed., Vol. 2, pp. 89–150). New York: McGraw-Hill.

Gilbert, D. T. (2006). *Stumbling on happiness.* New York: Knopf.

Gilbert, D. T., Brown, R. P., Pinel, E. C., & Wilson, T. D. (2000). The illusion of external agency. *Journal of Personality and Social Psychology, 79,* 690–700.

Gilbert, D. T., Gill, M. J., & Wilson, T. D. (2002). The future is now: Temporal correction in affective forecasting. *Organizational Behavior and Human Decision Processes, 88,* 430–444.

Gilbert, D. T., & Malone, P. S. (1995). The correspondence bias. *Psychological Bulletin, 117,* 21–38.

Gilbertson, M. W., Shenton, M. E., Ciszewski, A., Kasai, K., Lasko, N. B., Orr, S. P., et al. (2002). Smaller hippocampal volume predicts pathological vulnerability to psychological trauma. *Nature Neuroscience, 5,* 1242–1247.

Gilligan, C. (1982). *In a different voice: Psychological theory and women's development.* Cambridge, MA: Harvard University Press.

Gilovich, T., Kruger, J., & Savitsky, K. (1999). Everyday egocentrism and everyday interpersonal problems. In R. M. Kowalski & M. R. Leary (Eds.), *The social psychology of emotional and behavioral problems: Interfaces of social and clinical psychology* (pp. 69–95). Washington, DC: American Psychological Association.

Ginzburg, K., Solomon, Z., & Bleich, A. (2002). Repressive coping style, acute stress disorder, and posttraumatic stress disorder after myocardial infarction. *Psychosomatic Medicine, 64,* 748–757.

Gladue, B. A. (1994). The biopsychology of sexual orientation. *Current Directions in Psychological Science, 3,* 150–154.

Glynn, S. M. (1990). Token economy approaches for psychiatric patients: Progress and pitfalls over 25 years. *Behavior Modification, 14,* 383–407.

Goddard, H. H. (1913). *The Kallikak family: A study in the heredity of feeble-mindedness.* New York: Macmillan.

Godden, D. R., & Baddeley, A. D. (1975). Context-dependent memory in two natural environments: On land and underwater. *British Journal of Psychology, 66,* 325–331.

Goehler, L. E., Gaykema, R. P. A., Hansen, M. K., Anderson, K., Maier, S. F., & Watkins, L. R. (2000). Vagal immune-to-brain communication: A visceral chemosensory pathway. *Autonomic Neuroscience: Basic and Clinical, 85,* 49–59.

Goetzman, E. S., Hughes, T., & Klinger, E. (1994). *Current concerns of college students in a midwestern sample.* Unpublished report, University of Minnesota, Morris.

Goff, L. M., & Roediger, H. L., III. (1998). Imagination inflation for action events—Repeated imaginings lead to illusory recollections. *Memory & Cognition, 26,* 20–33.

Gordon, P. (2004). Numerical cognition without words: Evidence from Amazonia. *Science, 306,* 496–499.

Gottesman, I. I. (1991). *Schizophrenia genesis: The origins of madness.* New York: Freeman.

Gottfredson, L. S. (1998). The general intelligence factor. *Scientific American Presents, 9,* 24–29.

Gottfredson, L. S. (2003). Dissecting practical intelligence theory: Its claims and evidence. *Intelligence, 31(4),* 343–397.

Gottman, J. M. (1994). *What predicts divorce? The relationship between marital processes and marital outcomes.* Hillsdale, NJ: Erlbaum.

Gould, M. S. (1990). Suicide clusters and media exposure. In S. J. Blumenthal & D. J. Kupfer (Eds.), *Suicide over the life cycle: Risk factors, assessment, and treatment of suicidal patients* (pp. 517–532). Washington, DC: American Psychiatric Press.

Gouldner, A. W. (1960). The norm of reciprocity. *American Sociological Review, 25,* 161–178.

Grace, A. A., & Moore, H. (1998). Regulation of information flow in the nucleus accumbens: A model for the pathophysiology of schizophrenia. In M. F. Lanzenweger & R. H. Dworkin (Eds.), *Origins and development of schizophrenia* (pp. 123–160). Washington, DC: American Psychological Association.

Graf, P., & Schacter, D. L. (1985). Implicit and explicit memory for new associations in normal subjects and amnesic patients. *Journal of Experimental Psychology: Learning, Memory, and Cognition, 11,* 501–518.

Grant, B. F., Hasin, D. S., Stinson, F. S., Dawson, D. A., Chou, S. P., & Ruan, W. J. (2004). Prevalence, correlates, and disability of personality disorders in the U.S.: Results from the National Epidemiologic Survey on Alcohol and Related Conditions. *Journal of Clinical Psychiatry, 65,* 948–958.

Gray, H. M., Gray, K., & Wegner, D. M. (2007). Dimensions of mind perception. *Science, 315,* 619.

Green, D. A., & Swets, J. A. (1966). *Signal detection theory and psychophysics.* New York: Wiley.

Green, S. K., Buchanan, D. R., & Heuer, S. K. (1984). Winners, losers, and choosers: A field investigation of dating initiation. *Personality & Social Psychology Bulletin, 10,* 502–511.

Greenberg, J., Pyszczynski, T., Solomon, S., Rosenblatt, A., Veeder, M., Kirkland, S., et al. (1990). Evidence for terror management theory II: The effects of mortality salience on reactions to those who threaten or bolster the cultural worldview. *Journal of Personality and Social Psychology, 58,* 308–318.

Greenberg, P. E., Sisitsky, T., Kessler, R. C., Finkelstein, S. N., Berndt, E. R., Davidson, J. R. T., et al. (1999). The economic burden of anxiety disorders in the 1990s. *Journal of Clinical Psychiatry, 60,* 427–435.

Greene, J. D., Sommerville, R. B., Nystrom, L. E., Darley, J. M., & Cohen, J. D. (2001). An fMRI investigation of emotional engagement in moral judgment. *Science, 293,* 2105–2108.

Greenfield, P. M., Keller, H., Fuligni, A., & Maynard, A. (2003). Cultural pathways through universal development. *Annual Review of Psychology, 54,* 461–490.

Greenwald, A. G., Banaji, M. R., Rudman, L. A., Farnham, S. D., Nosek, B. A., & Mellott, D. S. (2002). A unified theory of implicit attitudes, stereotypes, self-esteem, and self-concept. *Psychological Review, 109,* 3–25.

Greenwald, A. G., McGhee, D. E., & Schwartz, J. L. K. (1998). Measuring individual differences in implicit cognition: The implicit association test. *Journal of Personality & Social Psychology, 74,* 1464–1480.

Greenwald, A. G., & Nosek, B. A. (2001). Health of the Implicit Association Test at age 3. *Zeitschrift für Experimentelle Psychologie, 48,* 85–93.

Gropp, E., Shanabrough, M., Borok, E., Xu, A. W., Janoschek, R., Buch, T., et al. (2005). Agouti-related peptide-expressing neurons are mandatory for feeding. *Nature Neuroscience, 8,* 1289–1291.

Gross, J. J. (1998). Antecedent- and response-focused emotion regulation: Divergent consequences for experience, expression, and physiology. *Journal of Personality and Social Psychology, 74,* 224–237.

Gross, J. J., & Munoz, R. F. (1995). Emotion regulation and mental health. *Clinical Psychology: Science and Practice, 2,* 151–164.

Groves, B. (2004, August 2). Unwelcome awareness. *The San Diego Union-Tribune,* p. 24.

Grudnick, J. L., & Kranzler, J. H. (2001). Meta-analysis of the relationship between intelligence and inspection time. *Intelligence, 29,* 523–535.

Gurwitz, J. H., McLaughlin, T. J., Willison, D. J., Guadagnoli, E., Hauptman, P. J., Gao, X., et al. (1997). Delayed hospital presentation in patients who have had acute myocardial infarction. *Annals of Internal Medicine, 126,* 593–599.

Gustafsson, J.-E. (1984). A unifying model for the structure of intellectual abilities. *Intelligence, 8,* 179–203.

Guthmann, E. (2005, October 31). *San Francisco Chronicle.*

Guthrie, R. V. (2000). Kenneth Bancroft Clark (1914–). In A. E. Kazdin (Ed.), *Encyclopedia of Psychology* (Vol. 2, p. 91). Washington, DC: American Psychological Association.

Haidt, J. (2001). The emotional dog and its rational tail: A social intuitionist approach to moral judgment. *Psychological Review, 108,* 814–834.

Haidt, J. (2006). *The happiness hypothesis: Finding modern truth in ancient wisdom.* New York: Basic Books.

Haidt, J., & Keltner, D. (1999). Culture and facial expression: Open-ended methods find more expressions and a gradient of recognition. *Cognition and Emotion, 13,* 225–266.

Hakuta, K. (1999). The debate on bilingual education. *Journal of Developmental and Behavioral Pediatrics, 20,* 36–37.

Hallett, M. (2000). Transcranial magnetic stimulation and the human brain. *Nature, 406,* 147–150.

Hallett, M., Cloninger, C. R., Fahn, S., & Jankovic, J. J. (Eds.). (2005). *The psychogenic movement disorders: Neurology and neuropsychiatry.* Philadelphia: Lippincott, Williams & Wilkins.

Halliday, R., Naylor, H., Brandeis, D., Callaway, E., Yano, L., & Herzig, K. (1994). The effect of D-amphetamine, clonidine, and yohimbine on human information processing. *Psychophysiology, 31,* 331–337.

Halpern, B. (2002). Taste. In H. Pashler & S. Yantis (Eds.), *Stevens' handbook of experimental psychology: Vol. 1. Sensation and perception* (3rd ed., pp. 653–690). New York: Wiley.

Halpern, D. F. (1997). Sex differences in intelligence: Implications for education. *American Psychologist, 52,* 1091–1102.

Hamermesh, D. S., & Biddle, J. E. (1994). Beauty and the labor market. *American Economic Review, 84,* 1174–1195.

Hamilton, D. L., & Gifford, R. K. (1976). Illusory correlation in interpersonal perception: A cognitive basis of stereotypic judgements. *Journal of Experimental Social Psychology, 12,* 392–407.

Hamilton, W. D. (1964). The genetical evolution of social behaviour. *Journal of Theoretical Biology, 7,* 1–16.

Hammen, C. L. (1995). Stress and the course of unipolar disorders. In C. M. Mazure (Ed.), *Does stress cause psychiatric illness?* Washington, DC: American Psychiatric Press.

Hammersla, J. F., & Frease-McMahan, L. (1990). University students' priorities: Life goals vs. relationships. *Sex Roles, 23,* 1–14.

Haney, C., Banks, C., & Zimbardo, P. G. (1973). Interpersonal dynamics in a simulated prison. *International Journal of Criminology and Penology, 1,* 69–97.

Hansen, E. S., Hasselbalch, S., Law, I., & Bolwig, T. G. (2002). The caudate nucleus in obsessive-compulsive disorder. Reduced metabolism following treatment with paroxetine: A PET study. *International Journal of Neuropsychopharmacology, 5,* 1–10.

Hanson, C. J., Stevens, L. C., & Coast, J. R. (2001). Exercise duration and mood state: How much is enough to feel better? *Health Psychology, 20,* 267–275.

Happe, F. G. E. (1995). The role of age and verbal ability in the theory-of-mind performance of subjects with autism. *Child Development, 66,* 843–855.

Harlow, H. F. (1958). The nature of love. *American Psychologist, 13,* 573–685.

Harlow, H. F., & Harlow, M. L. (1965). The affectional systems. In A. M. Schrier, H. F. Harlow, & F. Stollnitz (Eds.), *Behavior of nonhuman primates* (Vol. 2). New York: Academic Press.

Harris, B. (1979). Whatever happened to Little Albert? *American Psychologist, 34,* 151–160.

Harris, P. L., de Rosnay, M., & Pons, F. (2005). Language and children's understanding of mental states. *Current Directions in Psychological Science, 14,* 69–73.

Harris, P. L., Johnson, C. N., Hutton, D., Andrews, G., & Cooke, T. (1989). Young children's theory of mind and emotion. *Cognition and Emotion, 3,* 379–400.

Hart, B. L. (1988). Biological basis of the behavior of sick animals. *Neuroscience and Biobehavioral Reviews, 12,* 123–137.

Hartshorne, H., & May, M. (1928). *Studies in deceit.* New York: Macmillan.

Hasher, L., & Zacks, R. T. (1984). Automatic processing of fundamental information: The case of frequency of occurrence. *American Psychologist, 39,* 1372–1388.

Hasselmo, M. E. (2006). The role of acetylcholine in learning and memory. *Current Opinion in Neurobiology, 16,* 710–715.

Hassmen, P., Koivula, N., & Uutela, A. (2000). Physical exercise and psychological well-being: A population study in Finland. *Preventive Medicine, 30,* 17–25.

Hasson, U., Hendler, T., Bashat, D. B., & Malach, R. (2001). Vase or face? A neural correlate of shape-selective grouping processes in the human brain. *Journal of Cognitive Neuroscience, 13,* 744–753.

Hatch, R. (2005). *Richard Hatch homepage.* Retrieved August 24, 2005, from http://www.richardhatch.com

Hatfield, E. (1988). Passionate and companionate love. In R. J. Sternberg & M. L. Barnes (Eds.), *The psychology of love* (pp. 191–217). New Haven, CT: Yale University Press.

Hatfield, E., & Rapson, R. L. (1992). Similarity and attraction in close relationships. *Communication Monographs, 59,* 209–212.

Hathaway, S. R., & McKinley, J. C. (1951). *Minnesota Multiphasic Personality Inventory manual.* New York: Psychological Corporation.

Hausser, M. (2000). The Hodgkin-Huxley theory of the action potential. *Nature Neuroscience, 3,* 1165.

Haxby, J. V., Gobbini, M. I., Furey, M. L. Ishai, A., Schouten, J. L., & Pietrini, P. (2001). Distributed and overlapping representations of faces and objects in ventral temporal cortex. *Science, 293,* 2425–2430.

Hay, P., Sachdev, P., Cumming, S., Smith, J. S., Lee, T., Kitchener, P., et al. (1993). Treatment of obsessive-compulsive disorder by psychosurgery. *Acta Psychiatrica Scandinavica, 87,* 197–207.

Hayes, D. P., & Grether, J. (1983). The school year and vacations: When do students learn? *Cornell Journal of Social Relations, 17,* 56–71.

Hayes, S. C., Strosahl, K., & Wilson, K. G. (1999). *Acceptance and commitment therapy: An experiential approach to behavior change.* New York: Guilford Press.

Health, United States. (2001). Hyattsville, MD: National Center for Health Statistics.

Heatherton, T. F., & Weinberger, J. L. (Eds.). (1994). *Can personality change?* Washington, DC: American Psychological Association.

Hebb, D. O. (1949). *The organization of behavior.* New York: Wiley.

Hebl, M. R., & Heatherton, T. F. (1997). The stigma of obesity in women: The difference is Black and White. *Personality and Social Psychology Bulletin, 24,* 417–426.

Hebl, M. R., & Mannix, L. M. (2003). The weight of obesity in evaluating others: A mere proximity effect. *Personality and Social Psychology Bulletin, 29,* 28–38.

Heerey, E. A., Keltner, D., & Capps, L. M. (2003). Making sense of self-conscious emotion: Linking theory of mind and emotion in children with autism. *Emotion, 3,* 394–400.

Heiby, E. M. (2002). Prescription privileges for psychologists: Can differing views be reconciled? *Journal of Clinical Psychology, 58,* 589–597.

Heider, F. (1958). *The psychology of interpersonal relations.* New York: Wiley.

Henderlong, J., & Lepper, M. R. (2002). The effects of praise on children's intrinsic motivation: A review and synthesis. *Psychological Bulletin, 128,* 774–795.

Henig, R. M. (2004, April 4). The quest to forget. *New York Times Magazine,* 32–37.

Herek, G. M. (2002). Gender gaps in public opinion about lesbians and gay men. *Public Opinion Quarterly, 66,* 40–67.

Herman-Giddens, M. E., Slora, E. J., Wasserman, R. C., Bourdony, C. J., Bhapkar, M. V., Koch, G. G., et al. (1997). Secondary sexual characteristics and menses in young girls seen in office practice: A study from the pediatric research in office settings network. *Pediatrics and Perinatal Epidemiology, 99,* 505–512.

Herrmann, D. J., Raybeck, D., & Gruneberg, M. (2002). *Improving memory and study skills: Advances in theory and practice.* Seattle: Hogrefe and Huber.

Herrnstein, R. J. (1977). The evolution of behaviorism. *American Psychologist, 32,* 593–603.

Herrnstein, R. J., & Murray, C. (1994). *The bell curve.* New York: Free Press.

Heyns, B. (1978). *Summer learning and the effects of schooling.* New York: Academic Press.

Higgins, E. T. (1987). Self-discrepancy theory: A theory relating self and affect. *Psychological Review, 94,* 319–340.

Hilgard, E. R. (1965). *Hypnotic susceptibility.* New York: Harcourt, Brace and World.

Hilts, P. (1995). *Memory's ghost: The strange tale of Mr. M and the nature of memory.* New York: Simon & Schuster.

Hirschberger, G., Florian, V., & Mikulincer, M. (2002). The anxiety buffering function of close relationships: Mortality salience effects on the readiness to compromise mate selection standards. *European Journal of Social Psychology, 32,* 609–625.

Hirschfeld, D. R., Rosenbaum, J. F., Biederman, J., Bolduc, E. A., Faraone, S. V., Snidman, N., et al. (1992). Stable behavioral inhibition and its association with anxiety disorder. *Journal of the American Academy of Child and Adolescent Psychiatry, 31,* 103–111.

Hirschfeld, R. M. A. (1996). Panic disorder: Diagnosis, epidemiology, and clinical course. *Journal of Clinical Psychiatry, 57,* 3–8.

Hishakawa, Y. (1976). Sleep paralysis. In C. Guilleminault, W. C. Dement, & P. Passouant (Eds.), *Narcolepsy: Advances in sleep research* (Vol. 3, pp. 97–124). New York: Spectrum.

Hobson, J. A. (1988). *The dreaming brain.* New York: Basic Books.

Hobson, J. A., & McCarley, R. W. (1977). The brain as a dream-state generator: An activation-synthesis hypothesis of the dream process. *American Journal of Psychiatry, 134,* 1335–1368.

Hodgkin, A. L., & Huxley, A. F. (1939). Action potential recorded from inside a nerve fibre. *Nature, 144,* 710–712.

Hodson, G., & Sorrentino, R. M. (2001). Just who favors in in-group? Personality differences in reactions to uncertainty in the minimal group paradigm. *Group Dynamics, 5,* 92–101.

Hoek, H. W., & van Hoeken, D. (2003). Review of the prevalence and incidence of eating disorders. *International Journal of Eating Disorders, 34,* 383–396.

Hoffman, R. E., Hawkins, K. A., Gueorguieva, R., Boutros, N. N., Rachid, F., Carroll, K., et al. (2003). Transcranial magnetic stimulation of left temporoparietal cortex and medication-resistant auditory hallucinations. *Archives of General Psychiatry, 60,* 49–56.

Hoffrage, U., & Gigerenzer, G. (1996). The impact of information representation on Bayesian reasoning. In G. Cottrell (Ed.), *Proceedings of the Eighteenth Annual Conference of the Cognitive Science Society* (pp. 126–130). Mahwah, NJ: Erlbaum.

Hoffrage, U., & Gigerenzer, G. (1998). Using natural frequencies to improve diagnostic inferences. *Academic Medicine, 73,* 538–540.

Hogan, D. P., Sun, R., & Cornwell, G. T. (2000). Sexual and fertility behaviors of American females age 15–19 years: 1985, 1990 and 1995. *American Journal of Public Health, 90,* 1421–1425.

Hollander, E. P. (1964). *Leaders, groups, and influence.* Oxford: Oxford University Press.

Holloway, G. (2001). *The complete dream book: What your dreams tell about you and your life.* Naperville, IL: Sourcebooks.

Holmbeck, G. N., & O'Donnell, K. (1991). Discrepancies between perceptions of decision making and behavioral autonomy. In R. L. Paikoff (Ed.), *New directions for child development: No. 51. Shared views in the family during adolescence.* San Francisco: Jossey-Bass.

Holmes, T. H., & Rahe, R. H. (1967). The social readjustment rating scale. *Journal of Psychosomatic Research, 11,* 213–318.

Homans, G. C. (1961). *Social behavior.* New York: Harcourt, Brace and World.

Horn, J. L., & Cattell, R. B. (1966). Refinement and test of the theory of fluid and crystallized general intelligences. *Journal of Educational Psychology, 5,* 253–270.

Horta, B. L., Victoria, C. G., Menezes, A. M., Halpern, R., & Barros, F. C. (1997). Low birthweight, preterm births and intrauterine growth retardation in relation to maternal smoking. *Pediatrics and Perinatal Epidemiology, 11,* 140–151.

House, J., Landis, K., & Umberson, D. (1988). Social relationships and health. *Science, 241,* 540–545.

Hovland, C. I., Lumsdaine, A. A., & Sheffield, F. D. (1949). *Experiments on mass communications.* Princeton, NJ: Princeton University Press.

Howard, I. P. (2002). Depth perception. In S. Yantis & H. Pashler (Eds.), *Stevens' handbook of experimental psychology: Vol. 1. Sensation and perception* (3rd ed., pp. 77–120). New York: Wiley.

Howard, J. H., Jr., & Howard, D. V. (1997). Age differences in implicit learning of higher order dependencies in serial patterns. *Psychology and Aging, 12,* 634–656.

Howes, M., Siegel, M., & Brown, F. (1993). Early childhood memories—accuracy and affect. *Cognition, 47,* 95–119.

Hsu, L. K. G. (1990). *Eating disorders.* New York: Guilford Press.

Hubbard, E. M., & Ramachandran, V. S. (2003). Refining the experimental lever. *Journal of Consciousness Studies, 10,* 77–84.

Hubbard, E. M., & Ramachandran, V. S. (2005). Neurocognitive mechanisms of synesthesia. *Neuron, 48,* 509–520.

Hubel, D. H. (1988). *Eye, brain, and vision.* New York: Freeman.

Hubel, D. H., & Wiesel, T. N. (1962). Receptive fields, binocular interaction and functional architecture in the cat's visual cortex. *Journal of Physiology, 160,* 106–154.

Hubel, D. H., & Wiesel, T. N. (1998). Early exploration of the visual cortex. *Neuron, 20,* 401–412.

Huesmann, L. R., Moise-Titus, J., Podolski, C.-L., & Eron, L. D. (2003). Longitudinal relations between children's exposure to TV violence and their aggressive and violent behavior in young adulthood: 1977–1992. *Developmental Psychology, 39*, 201–221.

Hunsley, J., & Di Giulio, G. (2002). Dodo bird, phoenix, or urban legend? The question of psychotherapy equivalence. *Scientific Review of Mental Health Practice, 1*, 13–24.

Hunt, M. (1959). *The natural history of love.* New York: Knopf.

Hunter, J. E., & Hunter, R. F. (1984). Validity and utility of alternative predictors of job performance. *Psychological Bulletin, 96*, 72–98.

Huttenlocher, P. R. (1979). Synaptic density in human frontal cortex—developmental changes and effects of aging. *Brain Research, 163*, 195–205.

Huxley, A. (1954). *The doors of perception.* New York: Harper & Row.

Hyman, I. E., Jr., & Billings, F. J. (1998). Individual differences and the creation of false childhood memories. *Memory, 6*, 1–20.

Hyman, I. E., Jr., & Pentland, J. (1996). The role of mental imagery in the creation of false childhood memories. *Journal of Memory and Language, 35*, 101–117.

Iacoboni, M., & Dapretto, M. (2006). The mirror neuron system and the consequences of its dysfunction. *Nature Reviews Neuroscience, 7*, 942–951.

Iacoboni, M., Molnar-Szakacs, I., Gallese, V., Buccino, G., Mazziotta, J. C., & Rizzolatti, G. (2005). Grasping the intentions of others with one's own mirror neuron system. *PLoS Biology, 3*, 529–535.

Iacono, W. G., & Beiser, M. (1992). Where are women in first-episode studies of schizophrenia? *Schizophrenia Bulletin, 18*, 471–480.

Ichheiser, G. (1949). Misunderstandings in human relations: A study in false social perceptions. *American Journal of Sociology, 55* (Part 2): 1–70.

Inciardi, J. A. (2001). *The war on drugs III.* New York: Allyn and Bacon.

Ingram, R. E., Miranda, J., & Segal, Z. V. (1998). *Cognitive vulnerability to depression.* New York: Guilford Press.

Inui, A. (2001). Ghrelin: An orexigenic and somatotrophic signal from the stomach. *Nature Reviews Neuroscience, 2*, 551–560.

Irvine, J. T. (1978). Wolof magical thinking: Culture and conservation revisited. *Journal of Cross Cultural Psychology, 9*, 300–310.

Isabelle, R. A. (1993). Origins of attachment: Maternal interactive behavior across the first year. *Child Development, 64*, 605–621.

Isacsson, G., & Rich, C. L. (1997). Depression and antidepressants, and suicide: Pharmacoepidemiological evidence for suicide prevention. In R. W. Maris, M. M. Silverman, & S. S. Canetton (Eds.), *Review of suicidology* (pp. 168–201). New York: Guilford Press.

Ittelson, W. H. (1952). *The Ames demonstrations in perception.* Princeton, NJ: Princeton University Press.

Izard, C. E. (1971). *The face of emotion.* New York: Appleton-Century-Crofts.

Jablensky, A. (1997). The 100-year epidemiology of schizophrenia. *Schizophrenia Research, 28*, 111–125.

Jaccard, J., Dittus, P. J., & Gordon, V. V. (1998). Parent-adolescent congruency in reports of adolescent sexual behavior and in communications about sexual behavior. *Child Development, 69*, 247–261.

Jacobs, B. L. (1994). Serotonin, motor activity, and depression-related disorders. *American Scientist, 82*, 456–463.

James, T. W., Culham, J., Humphrey, G. K., Milner, A. D., & Goodale, M. A. (2003). Ventral occipital lesions impair object recognition but not object-directed grasping: An fMRI study. *Brain, 126*, 2463–2475.

James, W. (1884). What is an emotion? *Mind, 9*, 188–205.

James, W. (1890). *The principles of psychology.* Cambridge, MA: Harvard University Press.

James, W. (1902). *The varieties of religious experience: A study in human nature.* New York: Longman.

James, W. (1911). *Memories and studies.* New York: Longman.

Janicak, P. G., Dowd, S. M., Martis, B., Alam, D., Beedle, D., Krasuski, J., et al. (2002). Repetitive transcranial magnetic stimulation versus electroconvulsive therapy for major depression: Preliminary results of a randomized trial. *Biological Psychiatry, 51*, 659–667.

Jarvella, R. J. (1970). Effects of syntax on running memory span for connected discourse. *Psychonomic Science, 19*, 235–236.

Jarvella, R. J. (1971). Syntactic processing of connected speech. *Journal of Verbal Learning & Verbal Behavior, 10*, 409–416.

Jaynes, J. (1976). *The origin of consciousness in the breakdown of the bicameral mind.* London: Allen Lane.

Jencks, C. (1979). *Who gets ahead? The determinants of economic success in America.* New York: Wiley.

Jenike, M. A., Baer, L., & Minichiello, W. E. (1986). *Obsessive-compulsive disorders: Theory and management.* Littleton, MA: PSG Publishing.

John, O. P., & Srivastava, S. (1999). The Big Five trait taxonomy: History, measurement, and theoretical perspectives. In L. A. Pervin & O. P. John (Eds.), *Handbook of personality: Theory and research* (2nd ed., pp. 102–138). New York: Guilford Press.

Johnson, D. H. (1980). The relationship between spike rate and synchrony in responses of auditory-nerve fibers to single tones. *Journal of the Acoustical Society of America, 68*, 1115–1122.

Johnson, D. R., & Wu, J. (2002). An empirical test of crisis, social selection, and role explanations of the relationship between marital disruption and psychological distress: A pooled time-series analysis of four-wave panel data. *Journal of Marriage and the Family, 64*, 211–224.

Johnson, J. S., & Newport, E. L. (1989). Critical period effects in second language learning: The influence of maturational state on the acquisition of English as a second language. *Cognitive Psychology, 21*, 60–99.

Johnson, K. (2002). Neural basis of haptic perception. In H. Pashler & S. Yantis (Eds.), *Stevens' handbook of experimental psychology: Vol. 1. Sensation and perception* (3rd ed., pp. 537–583). New York: Wiley.

Johnson, M. H., Dziurawiec, S., Ellis, H. D., & Morton, J. (1991). Newborns' preferential tracking of face-like stimuli and its subsequent decline. *Cognition, 40*, 1–19.

Johnson, M. K., Hashtroudi, S., & Lindsay, D. S. (1993). Source monitoring. *Psychological Bulletin, 114*, 3–28.

Johnson, N. J., Backlund, E., Sorlie, P. D., & Loveless, C. A. (2000). Marital status and mortality: The National Longitudinal Mortality Study. *Annual Review of Epidemiology, 10*, 224–238.

Johnson, R. (2005, February 12). A genius explains. *The Guardian.*

Johnson, S. (2004). *Mind wide open: Your brain and the neuroscience of everyday life.* New York: Scribner.

Johnson, S. L., & Miller, I. (1997). Negative life events and time to recover from episodes of bipolar disorder. *Journal of Abnormal Psychology, 106*, 449–457.

Joiner, T. E., Jr. (2006). *Why people die by suicide.* Cambridge, MA: Harvard University Press.

Jones, B. C., Little, A. C., Penton-Voak, I. S., Tiddeman, B. P., Burt, D. M., & Perrett, D. I. (2001). Facial symmetry and judgements of apparent health: Support for a "good genes" explanation of the attractiveness-symmetry relationship. *Evolution and Human Behavior, 22*, 417–429.

Jones, E. E., & Davis, K. E. (1965). From acts to dispositions: The attribution process in person perception. In L. Berkowitz (Ed.), *Advances in experimental social psychology* (Vol. 2, pp. 219–266). New York: Academic Press.

Jones, E. E., & Harris, V. A. (1967). The attribution of attitudes. *Journal of Experimental Social Psychology, 3,* 1–24.

Jones, E. E., & Nisbett, R. E. (1972). The actor and the observer: Divergent perceptions of the causes of behavior. In E. E. Jones, D. E. Kanouse, H. H. Kelley, R. E. Nisbett, S. Valins, & B. Weiner (Eds.), *Attribution: Perceiving the causes of behavior* (pp. 79–94). Morristown, NJ: General Learning Press.

Jones, J. T., Pelham, B. W., Carvallo, M., & Mirenberg, M. C. (2004). How do I love thee? Let me count the Js: Implicit egotism and interpersonal attraction. *Journal of Personality and Social Psychology, 87,* 665–683.

Jones, L. M., & Foshay, N. N. (1984). Diffusion of responsibility in a nonemergency situation: Response to a greeting from a stranger. *Journal of Social Psychology, 123,* 155–158.

Jouvet, M., & Mounier, D. (1961). Identification of the neural structures responsible for rapid cortical activity during normal sleep. *Journal de Physiologie, 53,* 379–380.

Joyce, J. (1994). *Ulysses: The 1922 Text.* Introduction and notes by Jeri Johnson. New York: Oxford University Press.

Judd, L. L. (1997). The clinical course of unipolar major depressive disorders. *Archives of General Psychiatry, 54,* 989–991.

Jurewicz, I., Owen, R. J., & O'Donovan, M. C. (2001). Searching for susceptibility genes in schizophrenia. *European Neuropsychopharmacology, 11,* 395–398.

Kaas, J. H. (1991). Plasticity of sensory and motor maps in adult mammals. *Annual Review of Neuroscience, 14,* 137–167.

Kagan, J. (1997). Temperament and the reactions to unfamiliarity. *Child Development, 68,* 139–143.

Kahneman, D., Krueger, A. B., Schkade, D. A., Schwarz, N., & Stone, A. A. (2004). A survey method for characterizing daily life experience: The day reconstruction method. *Science, 306,* 1776–1780.

Kahneman, D., & Tversky, A. (1979). Prospect theory: An analysis of decision under risk. *Econometrica, 47,* 263–291.

Kamiya, J. (1969). Operant control of the EEG alpha rhythm and some of its reported effects on consciousness. In C. S. Tart (Ed.), *Altered states of consciousness* (pp. 519–529). Garden City, NY: Anchor Books.

Kandel, E. R. (2000). Nerve cells and behavior. In E. R. Kandel, G. H. Schwartz, & T. M. Jessell (Eds.), *Principles of neural science* (pp. 19–35). New York. McGraw-Hill.

Kanner, A. D., Coyne, J. C., Schaefer, C., & Lazarus, R. S. (1981). Comparison of two modes of stress management: Daily hassles and uplifts versus major life events. *Journal of Behavioral Medicine, 4,* 1–39.

Kanwisher, N. (2000). Domain specificity in face perception. *Nature Neuroscience, 3,* 759–763.

Kanwisher, N., McDermott, J., & Chun, M. M. (1997). The fusiform face area: A module in human extrastriate cortex specialized for face perception. *Journal of Neuroscience, 17,* 4302–4311.

Kanwisher, N., & Yovel, G. (2006). The fusiform face area: A cortical region specialized for the perception of faces. *Philosophical Transactions of the Royal Society (B), 361,* 2109–2128.

Kapur, S., Craik, F. I. M., Tulving, E., Wilson, A. A., Houle, S., & Brown, G. M. (1994). Neuroanatomical correlates of encoding in episodic memory: Levels of processing effects. *Proceedings of the National Academy of Sciences (USA), 91,* 2008–2011.

Karney, B. R., & Bradbury, T. N. (1995). The longitudinal course of marital quality and stability: A review of theory, methods, and research. *Psychological Bulletin, 118,* 3–34.

Karno, M., & Golding, J. M. (1991). Obsessive-compulsive disorder. In L. N. Robins & D. A. Regier (Eds.), *Psychiatric disorders in America: The epidemiologic catchment area study.* New York: Free Press.

Kasser, T., & Sharma, Y. S. (1999). Reproductive freedom, educational equality, and females' preference for resource-acquisition characteristics in mates. *Psychological Science, 10,* 374–377.

Katz, R., & McGuffin, P. (1993). The genetics of affective disorders. In J. P. Chapman & D. C. Fowles (Eds.), *Progress in experimental personality and psychopathology research* (Vol. 16). New York: Springer.

Kauffmann, C. D., Cheema, M. A., & Miller, B. E. (2004). Slow right prefrontal transcranial magnetic stimulation as a treatment for medication-resistant depression: A double-blind, placebo-controlled study. *Depression and Anxiety, 19,* 59–62.

Kawakami, K., Dovidio, J. F., Moll, J., Hermsen, S., & Russin, A. (2000). Just say no (to stereotyping): Effects of training in the negation of stereotypic associations on stereotype activation. *Journal of Personality and Social Psychology, 78,* 871–888.

Keefe, F. J., Abernathy, A. P., & Campbell, L. C. (2005). Psychological approaches to understanding and treating disease-related pain. *Annual Review of Psychology, 56,* 601–630.

Keefe, F. J., Lumley, M., Anderson, T., Lynch, T., & Carson, K. L. (2001). Pain and emotion: New research directions. *Journal of Clinical Psychology, 57,* 587–607.

Keisler, D. J. (1999). *Beyond the disease model of mental disorders.* New York: Praeger.

Keller, M. B., Klein, D. N., Hirschfeld, R. M., Kocsis, J. H., McCullough, J. P., Miller, I., et al. (1995). Results of the *DSM-IV* mood disorders field trial. *American Journal of Psychiatry, 152,* 843–849.

Kelley, H. H. (1967). Attribution theory in social psychology. In D. Levine (Ed.), *Nebraska Symposium on Motivation.* (Vol. 15, pp. 192–238). Lincoln: University of Nebraska Press.

Kelly, C., & McCreadie, R. (2000). Cigarette smoking and schizophrenia. *Advances in Psychiatric Treatment, 6,* 327–331.

Kelly, G. (1955). *The psychology of personal constructs.* New York: Norton.

Keltner, D. (1995). Signs of appeasement: Evidence for the distinct displays of embarrassment, amusement, and shame. *Journal of Personality and Social Psychology, 68,* 441–454.

Keltner, D., & Buswell, B. N. (1996). Evidence for the distinctness of embarrassment, shame, and guilt: A study of recalled antecedents and facial expressions of emotion. *Cognition and Emotion, 10,* 155–171.

Keltner, D., & Haidt, J. (1999). Social functions of emotions at four levels of analysis. *Cognition and Emotion, 13,* 505–521.

Keltner, D., & Harker, L. A. (1998). The forms and functions of the nonverbal signal of shame. In P. Gilbert & B. Andrews (Eds.), *Shame: Interpersonal behavior, psychopathology, and culture* (pp. 78–98). New York: Oxford University Press.

Keltner, D., & Shiota, M. N. (2003). New displays and new emotions: A commentary on Rozin and Cohen (2003). *Emotion, 3,* 86–91.

Kendler, K. S., Walters, E. E., Neale, M. C., Kessler, R. C., Heath, A. C., & Eaves, L. J. (1995). The structure of the genetic and environmental risk factors for six major psychiatric disorders in women: Phobia, generalized anxiety disorder, panic disorder, bulimia, major depression, and alcoholism. *Archives of General Psychiatry, 52,* 374–383.

Kenrick, D. T., Sadalla, E. K., Groth, G., & Trost, M. R. (1990). Evolution, traits, and the stages of human courtship: Qualifying the parental investment model. *Journal of Personality, 58,* 97–116.

Kensinger, E. A., & Schacter, D. L. (2005). Emotional content and reality monitoring ability: fMRI evidence for the influence of encoding processes. *Neuropsychologia, 43,* 1429–1443.

Kessler, R. C. (1997). The effects of stressful life events on depression. *Annual Review of Psychology, 48,* 191–214.

Kessler, R. C., McGonagle, K. A., Zhao, S., Nelson, C. B., Hughes, M., Eshleman, S., et al. (1994). Lifetime and 12-month prevalence of *DSM-III-R* psychiatric disorders in the United States: Results from the National Comorbidity Study. *Archives of General Psychiatry, 51,* 8–19.

Kessler, R. C., Nelson, C. B., McGonagle, K. A., Liu, J., Swartz, M., & Blazer, D. (1996). Comorbidity of *DSM-III-R* major depressive disorder in the general population: Results from the U.S. national comorbidity survey. *British Journal of Psychiatry, 168,* 17–30.

Kessler, R. C., Sonnega, A., Bromet, E., Hughes, M., & Nelson, C. B. (1995). Posttraumatic stress disorder in the National Comorbidity Survey. *Archives of General Psychiatry, 52,* 1048–1060.

Kessler, R. C., Soukup, J., Davis, R. B., Foster, D. F., Wilkey, S. A., Van Rompay, M. I., et al. (2001). The use of complementary and alternative therapies to treat anxiety and depression in the United States. *American Journal of Psychiatry, 158,* 289–294.

Kety, S. S. (1990). Genetic factors in suicide: Family, twin, and adoption studies. In S. J. Blumenthal & D. J. Kupfer (Eds.), *Suicide over the life cycle: Risk factors, assessment, and treatment of suicidal patients* (pp. 127–133). Washington, DC: American Psychiatric Press.

Keuler, D. J., & Safer, M. A. (1998). Memory bias in the assessment and recall of pre-exam anxiety: How anxious was I? *Applied Cognitive Psychology, 12,* S127–S137.

Kiecolt-Glaser, J. K., Garner, W., Speicher, C., Penn, G., & Glaser, R. (1984). Psychosocial modifiers of immunocompetence in medical students. *Psychosomatic Medicine, 46,* 7–14.

Kiehl, K. A., Smith, A. M., Hare, R. D., Mendrek, A., Forster, B. B., Brink, J., et al. (2001). Limbic abnormalities in affective processing by criminal psychopaths as revealed by functional magnetic resonance imaging. *Biological Psychiatry, 50,* 677–684.

Kihlstrom, J. F. (1985). Hypnosis. *Annual Review of Psychology, 36,* 385–418.

Kihlstrom, J. F. (1987). The cognitive unconscious. *Science, 237,* 1445–1452.

Kihlstrom, J. F. (2005). Dissociative disorders. *Annual Review of Clinical Psychology, 1,* 227–253.

Kihlstrom, J. F., & Klein, S. B. (1994). The self as a knowledge structure. In R. S. Wyer & T. K. Srull (Eds.), *Handbook of social cognition* (2nd ed., Vol. 1, pp. 153–208). Hillsdale, NJ: Erlbaum.

Kim, K., & Smith, P. K. (1998). Childhood stress, behavioural symptoms and mother-daughter pubertal development. *Journal of Adolescence, 21,* 231–240.

King, C. A. (1997). Suicidal behavior in adolescence. In R. W. Maris, M. M. Silverman, & S. S. Canetton (Eds.), *Review of suicidology, 1997* (pp. 61–95). New York: Guilford Press.

King, F. (1990). *Lump it or leave it.* New York: St. Martin's Press.

Kinney, D. A. (1993). From nerds to normals—The recovery of identity among adolescents from middle school to high school. *Sociology of Education, 66,* 21–40.

Kirchner, W. H., & Towne, W. F. (1994). The sensory basis of the honeybee's dance language. *Scientific American, 270*(6), 74–80.

Kirsch, I., & Sapirstein, G. (1998). Listening to Prozac but hearing placebo: A meta-analysis of antidepressant medication. *Prevention and Treatment, 1,* Article 0002. Retrieved May 18, 2007, from www.journals. apa.org/pt/prevention/volume1/pre0010002a.html

Kitayama, S., Duffy, S., Kawamura, T., & Larsen, J. T. (2003). Perceiving an object and its context in different cultures: A cultural look at new look. *Psychological Science, 14,* 201–206.

Klein, S. B. (2004). The cognitive neuroscience of knowing one's self. In M. Gazzaniga (Ed.), *The cognitive neurosciences* (3rd ed.). Cambridge, MA: MIT Press.

Kleinman, A. M. (1986). *Social origins of distress and disease: Depression, neurasthenia and pain in modern China.* New Haven, CT: Yale University Press.

Kleinman, A. M. (1988). *Rethinking psychiatry: From cultural category to personal experience.* New York: Free Press.

Klinger, E. (1975). Consequences of commitment to and disengagement from incentives. *Psychological Review, 82,* 1–25.

Kluft, R. P. (1984). Treatment of multiple personality. *Psychiatric Clinics of North America, 7,* 9–29.

Kluft, R. P. (1991). Multiple personality disorder. In A. Tasman & S. M. Goldfinger (Eds.), *American Psychiatric Press Review of Psychiatry* (Vol. 10, pp. 161–188). Washington, DC: American Psychiatric Press.

Klüver, H. (1951). Functional differences between the occipital and temporal lobes with special reference to the interrelations of behavior and extracerebral mechanisms. In L. A. Jeffress (Ed.), *Cerebral mechanisms in behavior* (pp. 147–199). New York: Wiley.

Klüver, H., & Bucy, P. C. (1937). "Psychic blindness" and other symptoms following bilateral temporary lobectomy in rhesus monkeys. *American Journal of Physiology, 119,* 352–353.

Klüver, H., & Bucy, P. C. (1939). Preliminary analysis of functions of the temporal lobes in monkeys. *Archives of Neurology and Psychiatry, 42,* 979–1000.

Knowlton, B. J., Ramus, S. J., & Squire, L. R. (1992). Intact artificial grammar learning in amnesia: Dissociation of classification learning and explicit memory for specific instances. *Psychological Science, 3,* 173–179.

Knutson, B., Adams, C. M., Fong, G. W., & Hommer, D. (2001). Anticipation of increasing monetary reward selectively recruits nucleus accumbens. *Journal of Neurosciences, 21,* 1–5.

Knutson, B., Wolkowitz, O. M., Cole, S. W., Chan, T., Moore, E. A., Johnson, R. C., et al. (1998). Selective alteration of personality and social behavior by serotonergic intervention. *American Journal of Psychiatry, 155,* 373–379.

Kobasa, S. (1979). Stressful life events, personality, and health: An inquiry into hardiness. *Journal of Personality and Social Psychology, 37,* 1–11.

Koffka, K. (1935). *Principles of Gestalt psychology.* New York: Harcourt, Brace and World.

Kohlberg, L. (1963). Development of children's orientation towards a moral order (Part I). Sequencing in the development of moral thought. *Vita Humana, 6,* 11–36.

Kohlberg, L. (1986). A current statement on some theoretical issues. In S. Modgil & C. Modgil (Eds.), *Lawrence Kohlberg.* Philadelphia: Falmer.

Kolb, B., & Whishaw, I. Q. (2003). *Fundamentals of human neuropsychology* (5th ed.). New York: Worth.

Kolotkin, R. L., Meter, K., & Williams, G. R. (2001). Quality of life and obesity. *Obesity Reviews,* 219–229.

Komiya, N., Good, G. E., & Sherrod, N. B. (2000). Emotional openness as a predictor of college students' attitudes toward seeking psychological help. *Journal of Counseling Psychology, 47,* 138–143.

Koole, S. L., Dijksterhuis, A., & van Knippenberg, A. (2001). What's in a name: Implicit self-esteem and the automatic self. *Journal of Personality and Social Psychology, 80,* 669–685.

Koss, M. P. (1990). The women's mental health research agenda: Violence against women. *American Psychologist, 45,* 374–380.

Kosslyn, S. M., Alpert, N. M., Thompson, W. L., Chabris, C. F., Rauch, S. L., & Anderson, A. K. (1993). Visual mental imagery activates topographically organized visual cortex: PET investigations. *Journal of Cognitive Neuroscience, 5,* 263–287.

Kramer, R. M. (1998). Revisiting the Bay of Pigs and Vietnam decisions 25 years later: How well has the groupthink hypothesis stood the test of time? *Organizational Behavior and Human Decision Processes, 73,* 236–271.

Krantz, D. S., & McCeney, M. K. (2002). Effects of psychological and social factors on organic disease: A critical assessment of research on coronary heart disease. *Annual Review of Psychology, 53,* 341–369.

Kressmann, S., Muller, W. E., & Blume, H. H. (2002). Pharmaceutical quality of different Ginkgo biloba brands. *Journal of Pharmacy and Pharmacology, 54,* 661–669.

Kroeze, W. K., & Roth, B. L. (1998). The molecular biology of serotonin receptors: Therapeutic implications for the interface of mood and psychosis. *Biological Psychiatry, 44,* 1128–1142.

Kronig, M. H., Apter, J., Asnis, G., Bystritsky, A., Curtis, G., Ferguson, J., et al. (1999). Placebo-controlled multicenter study of sertraline treatment for obsessive-compulsive disorder. *Journal of Clinical Psychopharmacology, 19,* 172–176.

Kubovy, M. (1981). Concurrent-Pitch segregation and the theory of indispensable attributes. In M. Kubovy & J. R. Pomerantz (Eds.), *Perceptual organization* (pp. 55–96). Hillsdale, NJ: Erlbaum.

Kuffler, S. W. (1953). Discharge patterns and function organization of mammalian retina. *Journal of Neurophysiology, 16,* 37–68.

Kunda, Z., & Oleson, K. C. (1997). When exceptions prove the rule: How extremity of deviance determines the impact of deviant examples on stereotypes. *Journal of Personality and Social Psychology, 72,* 965–979.

Kunz, P. R., & Woolcott, M. (1976). Season's greetings: From my status to yours. *Social Science Research, 5,* 269–278.

LaBar, K. S., & Phelps, E. A. (1998). Arousal-mediated memory consolidation: Role of the medial temporal lobe in humans. *Psychological Science, 9,* 490–493.

LaBerge, S., & Rheingold, H. (1990). *Exploring the world of lucid dreaming.* New York: Ballantine.

Lackner, J. R., & DiZio, P. (2005). Vestibular, proprioceptive, and haptic contributions to spatial orientation. *Annual Review of Psychology, 56,* 115–147.

Lai, Y., & Siegal, J. (1999). Muscle atonia in REM sleep. In B. Mallick & S. Inoue (Eds.), *Rapid eye movement sleep* (pp. 69–90). New Delhi, India: Narosa Publishing House.

Lamb, M. E., Sternberg, K. J., & Prodromidis, M. (1992). Nonmaternal care and the security of infant/mother attachment: A reanalysis of the data. *Infant Behavior & Development, 15,* 71–83.

Lamm, H., & Myers, D. G. (1978). Group-induced polarization of attitudes and behavior. *Advances in Experimental Social Psychology, 11,* 145–195.

Landauer, T. K., & Bjork, R. A. (1978). Optimum rehearsal patterns and name learning. In M. M. Gruneberg, P. E. Morris, & R. N. Sykes (Eds.), *Practical aspects of memory.* (pp. 625–632). New York: Academic Press.

Lang, F. R., & Carstensen, L. L. (1994). Close emotional relationships in late life: Further support for proactive aging in the social domain. *Psychology and Aging, 9,* 315–324.

Lange, C. G., & James, W. (1922). *The emotions.* Baltimore: Williams and Wilkins.

Langer, E. J., & Abelson, R. P. (1974). A patient by any other name . . . : Clinician group difference in labeling bias. *Journal of Consulting & Clinical Psychology, 42,* 4–9.

Langleben, D. D., Loughead, J. W., Bilker, W. B., Ruparel, K., Childress, A. R., Busch, S. I., et al. (2005). Telling truth from lie in individual subjects with fast event-related fMRI. *Human Brain Mapping 26,* 262–272.

Langlois, J. H., Kalakanis, L., Rubenstein, A. J., Larson, A., Hallam, M., & Smoot, M. (2000). Maxims or myths of beauty? A meta-analytic and theoretical review. *Psychological Bulletin, 126,* 390–423.

Langlois, J. H., Ritter, J. M., Casey, R. J., & Sawin, D. B. (1995). Infant attractiveness predicts maternal behaviors and attitudes. *Developmental Psychology, 31,* 464–472.

Langlois, J. H., & Roggman, L. A. (1990). Attractive faces are only average. *Psychological Science, 1,* 115–121.

Langlois, J. H., Roggman, L. A., & Musselman, L. (1994). What is average and what is not average about attractive faces? *Psychological Science, 5,* 214–220.

Langlois, J. H., Roggman, L. A., & Rieser-Danner, L. A. (1990). Infants' differential social responses to attractive and unattractive faces. *Developmental Psychology, 26,* 153–159.

Langston, J. W. (1995). *The case of the frozen addicts.* New York: Pantheon.

Larson, R., & Richards, M. H. (1991). Daily companionship in late childhood and early adolescence—changing developmental contexts. *Child Development, 62,* 284–300.

Lashley, K. S. (1960). In search of the engram. In F. A. Beach, D. O. Hebb, C. T. Morgan, & H. W. Nissen (Eds.), *The neuropsychology of Lashley.* New York: McGraw-Hill.

Latané, B., Williams, K., & Harkins, S. (1979). Many hands make light the work: The causes and consequences of social loafing. *Journal of Personality and Social Psychology, 37,* 822–832.

Laureys, S., Giacino, J. T., Schiff, N. D., Schabus, M., & Owen, A. M. (2006). How should functional imaging of patients with disorders of consciousness contribute to their clinical rehabilitation needs? *Current Opinion in Neurology, 19,* 520–527.

Lavie, P. (2001). Sleep-wake as a biological rhythm. *Annual Review of Psychology, 52,* 277–303.

Lavoie, K. L., & Fleet, R. P. (2002). Should psychologists be granted prescription privileges? A review of the prescription privilege debate for psychiatrists. *Canadian Journal of Psychiatry, 47*(5), 443–449.

Lavori, P. W., Klerman, G. L., Keller, M. B., Reich, T., Rice, J., & Endicott, J. (1987). Age-period-cohort analysis of secular trends in onset of major depression: Findings in siblings of patients with major affective disorder. *Journal of Psychiatric Researchers, 21,* 23–25.

Lawton, M. P., Kleban, M. H., Rajagopal, D., & Dean, J. (1992). The dimensions of affective experience in three age groups. *Psychology and Aging, 7,* 171–184.

Lazarus, R. S. (1984). On the primacy of cognition. *American Psychologist, 39,* 124–129.

Lazarus, R. S., & Alfert, E. (1964). Short-circuiting of threat by experimentally altering cognitive appraisal. *Journal of Abnormal and Social Psychology, 69,* 195–205.

Lazarus, R. S., & Folkman, S. (1984). *Stress, appraisal, and coping.* New York: Springer.

Leary, M. R. (1990). Responses to social exclusion: Social anxiety, jealousy, loneliness, depression, and low self-esteem. *Journal of Social and Clinical Psychology, 9,* 221–229.

Leary, M. R., & Baumeister, R. F. (2000). The nature and function of self-esteem: Sociometer theory. In M. P. Zanna (Ed.), *Advances in experimental social psychology* (Vol. 32, pp. 1–62). San Diego: Academic Press.

Leary, M. R., Tambor, E. S., Terdal, S. K., & Downs, D. L. (1995). Self-esteem as an interpersonal monitor: The sociometer hypothesis. *Journal of Personality and Social Psychology, 68,* 518–530.

Lecky, P. (1945). *Self-consistency: A theory of personality.* New York: Island Press.

LeDoux, J. E. (1998). Fear and the brain: Where have we been, and where are we going? *Biological Psychiatry, 153,* 1229–1238.

LeDoux, J. E. (2000). Emotion circuits in the brain. *Annual Review of Neuroscience, 23,* 155–184.

LeDoux, J. E., Iwata, J., Cicchetti, P., & Reis, D. J. (1988). Different projections of the central amygdaloid nucleus mediate autonomic and behavioral correlates of conditioned fear. *Journal of Neuroscience, 8,* 2517–2529.

Lee, D. N., & Aronson, E. (1974). Visual proprioceptive control of standing in human infants. *Perception & Psychophysics, 15,* 529–532.

Lefcourt, H. M. (1982). *Locus of control: Current trends in theory and research* (2nd ed.). Hillsdale, NJ: Erlbaum.

Lentz, M. J., Landis, C. A., Rothermel, J., & Shaver, J. L. (1999). Effects of selective slow wave sleep disruption on musculoskeletal pain and fatigue in middle aged women. *Journal of Rheumatology, 26,* 1586–1592.

Leonard, M. (2002, October 27). Arrest in sniper case; sniper suspect defies profile. *Boston Globe,* p. A1.

Lepage, M., Ghaffar, O., Nyberg, L., & Tulving, E. (2000). Prefrontal cortex and episodic memory retrieval mode. *Proceedings of the National Academy of Sciences (USA), 97,* 506–511.

Lepper, M. R., & Greene, D. (1978). Overjustification research and beyond: Toward a means-end analysis of intrinsic and extrinsic motivation. In M. R. Lepper & D. Greene (Eds.), *The hidden costs of reward: New perspectives on the psychology of human motivation.* New York: Wiley.

Levine, R. V., Norenzayan, A., & Philbrick, K. (2001). Cross-cultural differences in helping strangers. *Journal of Cross-Cultural Psychology, 32,* 543–560.

Levine, R., Sato, S., Hashimoto, T., & Verma, J. (1995). Love and marriage in eleven cultures. *Journal of Cross-Cultural Psychology, 26*(5), 554–571.

Lewin, K. (1951). Behavior and development as a function of the total situation. In K. Lewin, *Field theory in social science: Selected theoretical papers* (pp. 791–843). New York: Harper & Row.

Lewis, M., & Brooks-Gunn, J. (1979). *Social cognition and the acquisition of self.* New York: Plenum Press.

Lewis, R., Kapur, S., Jones, C., DaSilva, J., M. Brown, G. M., Wilson, A. A., et al. (1999). Serotonin 5-HT-sub-2 receptors in schizophrenia: A PET study using [-sup-1-sup-8F] setoperone in neuroleptic-naive patients and normal subjects. *American Journal of Psychiatry, 156,* 72–78.

Lewontin, R., Rose, S., & Kamin, L. J. (1984). *Not in our genes.* New York: Pantheon.

Li, H. Z., & Browne, A. J. (2000). Defining mental illness and accessing mental health services: Perspectives of Asian Canadians. *Canadian Journal of Community Mental Health, 19,* 143–159.

Li, W., Lexenberg, E., Parrish, T., & Gottfried, J. A. (2006). Learning to smell the roses: Experience-dependent neural plasticity in human piriform and orbitofrontal cortices. *Neuron, 52,* 1097–1108.

Libet, B. (1985). Unconscious cerebral initiative and the role of conscious will in voluntary action. *Behavioral and Brain Sciences, 8,* 529–566.

Liebenluft, E. (1996). Women with bipolar illness: Clinical and research issues. *American Journal of Psychiatry, 153,* 163–173.

Lieberman, M. D., Hariri, A., Jarcho, J. M., Eisenberger, N. I., & Bookheimer, S. Y. (2005). An fMRI investigation of race-related amygdala activity in African American and Caucasian-American individuals. *Nature Neuroscience, 8,* 720–722.

Lieberman, M. D., & Rosenthal, R. (2001). Why introverts can't always tell who likes them: Multitasking and nonverbal decoding. *Journal of Personality and Social Psychology, 80,* 294–310.

Lilienfeld, S. O., Lynn, S. J., & Lohr, J. M. (Eds.). (2003). *Science and pseudoscience in clinical psychology.* New York: Guilford Press.

Lillard, L. A., & Waite, L. J. (1995). 'Til death do us part: Marital disruption and mortality. *American Journal of Sociology, 100,* 1131–1156.

Lindstrom, M. (2005). *Brand sense: How to build powerful brands through touch, taste, smell, sight and sound.* London: Kogan Page.

Linszen, D. H., Dingemans, P. M., Nugter, M. A., Van der Does, A. J., Scholte, W. F., & Lenoir, M. A. (1997). Patient attributes and expressed emotion as risk factors for psychotic relapse. *Schizophrenia Bulletin, 23,* 119–130.

Lipps, T. (1907). Das Wissen von fremden Ichen. In T. Lipps (Ed.), *Psychologische Untersuchungen* (Vol. 1, pp. 694–722). Leipzig: Engelmann.

Locksley, A., Ortiz, V., & Hepburn, C. (1980). Social categorization and discriminatory behavior: Extinguishing the minimal intergroup discrimination effect. *Journal of Personality and Social Psychology, 39,* 773–783.

Loehlin, J. C. (1992). *Genes and environment in personality development.* Newbury Park, CA: Sage.

Loftus, E. F. (1975). Leading questions and eyewitness report. *Cognitive Psychology, 7,* 560–572.

Loftus, E., & Ketchum, K. (1994). *The myth of repressed memory.* New York: St. Martin's Press.

Loftus, E. F., Miller, D. G., & Burns, H. J. (1978). Semantic integration of verbal information into a visual memory. *Journal of Experimental Psychology: Human Learning and Memory, 4,* 19–31.

Lorenz, K. (1952). *King Solomon's ring.* New York: Crowell.

Lorge, I. (1936). Prestige, suggestion, and attitudes. *Journal of Social Psychology, 7,* 386–402.

Lozano, B. E., & Johnson, S. L. (2001). Can personality traits predict increases in manic and depressive symptoms? *Journal of Affective Disorders, 63,* 103–111.

Lubinski, D., Webb, R. M., Morelock, M. J., & Benbow, C. P. (2001). Top 1 in 10,000: A 10-year follow-up of the profoundly gifted. *Journal of Applied Psychology, 86,* 718–729.

Luborsky, L., Rosenthal, R., Diguer, L., Andrusyna, T. P., Berman, J. S., Levitt, J. T., et al. (2002). The dodo bird verdict is alive and well—mostly. *Clinical Psychology: Science and Practice, 9,* 2–12.

Luborsky, L., & Singer, B. (1975). Comparative studies of psychotherapies: Is it true that "everyone has one and all must have prizes"? *Archives of General Psychiatry, 32*(8), 995–1008.

Lucas, R. E., Clark, A. E., Georgellis, Y., & Diener, E. (2003). Reexamining adaptation and the set point model of happiness: Reactions to changes in marital status. *Journal of Personality and Social Psychology, 84,* 527–539.

Ludwig, A. M. (1966). Altered states of consciousness. *Archives of General Psychiatry, 15,* 225–234.

Lustman, P. J., Caudle, M. L., & Clouse, R. E. (2002). Case study: Nondysphoric depression in a man with type 2 diabetes. *Clinical Diabetes, 20,* 122–123.

Lykken, D. T. (1995). *The antisocial personalities.* Hillsdale, NJ: Erlbaum.

Lykken, D. T., & Tellegen, A. (1996). Happiness is a stochastic phenomenon. *Psychological Science, 7,* 186–189.

Lynn, M., & Shurgot, B. A. (1984). Responses to lonely hearts advertisements: Effects of reported physical attractiveness, physique, and coloration. *Personality and Social Psychology Bulletin, 10,* 349–357.

Lynn, R., & Vanhanen, T. (2002). *IQ and the wealth of nations.* Westport, CT: Praeger/Greenwood.

Lynn, S. J., Rhue, J. W., & Weekes, J. R. (1990). Hypnotic involuntariness: A social cognitive analysis. *Psychological Review, 97,* 169–184.

MacDonald, S., Uesiliana, K., & Hayne, H. (2000). Cross-cultural and gender differences in childhood amnesia. *Memory, 8*, 365–376.

Mack, A. H., Franklin, J. E., Jr., & Frances, R. J. (2003). Substance use disorders. In R. E. Hales & S. C. Yudofsky (Eds.), *The American Psychiatric Publishing textbook of clinical psychiatry* (4th ed., pp. 309–377). Washington, DC: American Psychiatric Publishing.

Mackinnon, A., & Foley, D. (1996). The genetics of anxiety disorders. In H. G. Westenberg, J. A. Den Boer & D. L. Murphy (Eds.), *Advances in the neurobiology of anxiety disorders* (pp. 39–59). Chichester, England: Wiley.

Macmillan, N. A., & Creelman, C. D. (2005). *Detection theory.* Mahwah, NJ: Erlbaum.

Macrae, C. N., Bodenhausen, G. V., Milne, A. B., & Jetten, J. (1994). Out of mind but back in sight: Stereotypes on the rebound. *Journal of Personality and Social Psychology, 67*, 808–817.

Maddi, S. R., Kahn, S., & Maddi, K. L. (1998). The effectiveness of hardiness training. *Consulting Psychology Journal: Practice and Research, 50*, 78–86.

Maes, M. (1995). Evidence for an immune response in major depression: A review and hypothesis. *Progress in Neuro-Psychopharmacology and Biological Psychiatry, 19*, 11–38.

Magee, W. J., Eaton, W. W., Wittchen, H.-U., McGonagle, K. A., & Kessler, R. C. (1996). Agoraphobia, simple phobia, and social phobia in the National Comorbidity Survey. *Archives of General Psychiatry, 53*, 159–168.

Maguire, E. A., Woollett, K., & Spiers, H. J. (2006). London taxi drivers and bus drivers: A structural MRI and neuropsychological analysis. *Hippocampus, 16*, 1091–1101.

Mah, K., & Binik, Y. M. (2002). Do all orgasms feel alike? Evaluating a two-dimensional model of the orgasm experience across gender and sexual context. *Journal of Sex Research, 39*, 104–113.

Maldonado, J. R., & Butler, L. D. (1998). *Treatments for dissociative disorders.* New York: Oxford University Press.

Malina, R. M., Bouchard, C., & Beunen, G. (1988). Human growth: Selected aspects of current research on well-nourished children. *Annual Review of Anthropology, 17*, 187–219.

Mandle, C. L., Jacobs, S. C., Arcari, P. M., & Domar, A. D. (1996). The efficacy of relaxation response interventions with adult patients: A review of the literature. *Journal of Cardiovascular Nursing, 10*, 4–26.

Mandler, G. (1967). Organization and memory. In K. W. Spence & J. T. Spence (Eds.), *The psychology of learning and motivation* (Vol. 1, pp. 327–372). New York: Academic Press.

Mann, J. J., Waternaux, C., Haas, G. L, & Malone, K. M. (1999). Toward a clinical model of suicidal behavior in psychiatric patients. *American Journal of Psychiatry, 156*, 181–189.

Marangell, L. B., Silver, J. M., Goff, D. M., & Yudofsky, S. C. (2003). Psychopharmacology and electroconvulsive therapy. In R. E. Hales & S. C. Yudofsky (Eds.), *The American Psychiatric Publishing textbook of clinical psychiatry* (4th ed., pp. 1047–1149). Washington, DC: American Psychiatric Publishing.

Marcus, J., Hans, S. L., Auerbach, J. G., & Auerbach, A. G. (1993). Children at risk for schizophrenia: The Jerusalem infant development study: II. Neurological deficits at school age. *Archives of General Psychiatry, 50*, 797–809.

Marian, V., & Neisser, U. (2000). Language-dependent recall of autobiographical memories. *Journal of Experimental Psychology, 129*, 361–368.

Marlatt, G. A. (Ed.). (1998). *Harm reduction: Pragmatic strategies for managing high-risk behaviors.* New York: Guilford Press.

Marlatt, G. A., Larimer, M. E., Baer, J. S., & Quigley, L. A. (1993). Harm reduction for alcohol problems: Moving beyond the controlled drinking controversy. *Behavior Therapy, 24*, 461–504.

Marlatt, G. A., & Rohsenow, D. (1980). Cognitive processes in alcohol use: Expectancy and the balanced placebo design. In N. K. Mello (Ed.), *Advances in substance abuse: Behavioral and biological research* (pp. 159–199). Greenwich, CT: JAI Press.

Marmot, M. G., Stansfeld, S., Patel, C., North, F., Head, J., White, L., et al. (1991). Health inequalities among British civil servants: The Whitehall II study. *Lancet, 337*, 1387–1393.

Martin, A. (2007). The representation of object concepts in the brain. *Annual Review of Psychology, 58*, 25–45.

Martin, A., & Caramazza, A. (2003). Neuropsychological and neuroimaging perspectives on conceptual knowledge: An introduction. *Cognitive Neuropsychology, 20*, 195–212.

Martin, A., & Chao, L. L. (2001). Semantic memory and the brain: Structure and processes. *Current Opinion in Neurobiology, 11*, 194–201.

Martin, N. G., Eaves, L. J., Geath, A. R., Jarding, R., Feingold, L. M., & Eysenck, H. J. (1986). Transmission of social attitudes. *Proceedings of the National Academy of Sciences (USA), 83*, 4364–4368.

Marucha, P. T., Kiecolt-Glaser, J. K., & Favagehi, M. (1998). Mucosal wound healing is impaired by examination stress. *Psychosomatic Medicine, 60*, 362–365.

Maslach, C. (2003). Job burnout: New directions in research and intervention. *Current Directions in Psychological Science, 12*, 189–192.

Maslow, A. H. (1937). Dominance-feeling, behavior, and status. In R. J. Lowry (Ed.), *Dominance, self-esteem, self-actualization: Germinal papers by A. H. Maslow.* Monterey, CA: Brooks-Cole.

Maslow, A. H. (1954). *Motivation and personality.* New York: Harper & Row.

Maslow, A. H. (1962). *Toward a psychology of being.* New York: Van Nostrand Reinhold.

Masserman, J. H. (1961). *Principles of dynamic psychiatry* (2nd ed.). Philadelphia: W. B. Saunders.

Masters, W. H., & Johnson, V. E. (1966). *Human sexual response.* Boston: Little, Brown.

Mather, M., Canli, T., English, T., Whitfield, S., Wais, P., Ochsner, K., et al. (2004). Amygdala responses to emotionally valenced stimuli in older and younger adults. *Psychological Science, 15*, 259–263.

Mathis, J. L. (1964). A sophisticated version of voodoo death. *Psychosomatic Medicine, 26*, 104–107.

Matthews, G., & Gilliland, K. (1999). The personality theories of H. J. Eysenck and J. A. Gray: A comparative review. *Personality and Individual Differences, 26*, 583–626.

Maudsley, H. (1886). *Natural causes and supernatural seemings.* London: Kegan Paul, Trench.

May, R. (1983). *The discovery of being: Writings in existential psychology.* New York: Norton.

McAdams, D. (1993). *The stories we live by: Personal myths and the making of the self.* New York: Morrow.

McAndrew, F. T. (1986). A cross-cultural study of recognition thresholds for facial expression of emotion. *Journal of Cross-Cultural Psychology, 17*, 211–224.

McCann, I. L., & Holmes, D. S. (1984). Influence of aerobic exercise on depression. *Journal of Personality and Social Psychology, 46*, 1142–1147.

McClelland, D. C., Atkinson, J. W., Clark, R. A., & Lowell, E. L. (1953). *The achievement motive.* New York: Appleton-Century-Crofts.

McCloskey, M., & Zaragoza, M. (1985). Misleading postevent information and memory for events: Arguments and evidence against memory impairment hypotheses. *Journal of Experimental Psychology: General, 114*, 1–16.

McConkey, K. M., Barnier, A. J., & Sheehan, P. W. (1998). Hypnosis and pseudomemory: Understanding the findings and their implications. In S. J. Lynn & K. M. McConkey (Eds.), *Truth in memory* (pp. 227–259). New York: Guilford Press.

McCrae, R. R., & Costa, P. T. (1990). *Personality in adulthood.* New York: Guilford Press.

McEvoy, S. P., Stevenson, M. R., McCartt, A. T., Woodward, M., Haworth, C., Palamara, P., et al. (2005). Role of mobile phones in motor vehicle crashes resulting in hospital attendance: A case-crossover study. *British Medical Journal, 331*, 428–430.

McFall, R. M., & Treat, T. A. (1999). Quantifying the information value of clinical assessments with signal detection theory. *Annual Review of Psychology, 50*, 215–241.

McFarlane, A. H., Norman, G. R., Streiner, D. L., Roy, R., & Scott, D. J. (1980). A longitudinal study of the influence of the psychosocial environment on health status: A preliminary report. *Journal of Health and Social Behavior, 21*, 124–133.

McGarty, C., & Turner, J. C. (1992). The effects of categorization on social judgement. *British Journal of Social Psychology, 31*, 253–268.

McGue, M., & Bouchard, T. J. (1998). Genetic and environmental influences on human behavioral differences. *Annual Review of Neuroscience, 21*, 1–24.

McGuire, P. K., Shah, G. M., & Murray, R. M. (1993). Increased blood flow in Broca's area during auditory hallucinations in schizophrenia. *Lancet, 342*, 703–706.

McHugh, P. R., Lief, H. I., Freyd, P. P., & Fetkewicz, J. M. (2004). From refusal to recollection: Family relationships after an accusation based on recovered memories. *Journal of Nervous and Mental Disease, 192*, 525–532.

McKetin, R., McLaren, J., Lubman, D. I., & Hides, L. (2006). The prevalence of psychotic symptoms among methamphetamine users. *Addiction, 101*, 1473–1478.

McKetin, R., Ward, P. B., Catts, S. V., Mattick, R. P., & Bell, J. R. (1999). Changes in auditory selective attention and event-related potentials following oral administration of D-amphetamine in humans. *Neuropsychopharmacology*, 380–390.

McKinney, C. H., Antoni, M. H., Kumar, M., Tims, F. C., & McCabe, P. M. (1997). Effects of guided imagery and music (GIM) therapy on mood and cortisol in healthy adults. *Health Psychology, 16*, 390–400.

McNally, R. J. (2003). *Remembering trauma.* Cambridge, MA: Belknap Press/Harvard University Press.

McNally, R. J., & Steketee, G. S. (1985). Etiology and maintenance of severe animal phobias. *Behavioral Research and Therapy, 23*, 431–435.

McNamara, B., Ray, J. L., Arthurs, O. J., & Boniface, S. (2001). Transcranial magnetic stimulation for depression and other psychiatric disorders. *Psychological Medicine, 31*, 1141–1146.

McWilliams, N. (1994). *Psychoanalytic diagnosis: Understanding personality structure in the clinical process.* New York: Guilford Press.

McWilliams, P. (1993). *Ain't nobody's business if you do: The absurdity of consensual crimes in a free society.* Los Angeles: Prelude Press.

Mead, M. (1968). *Sex and temperament in three primitive societies.* New York: Dell. (Original work published 1935)

Mechelli, A., Crinion, J. T., Noppeney, U., O'Doherty, J., Ashburner, J., Frackowiak, R. S., et al. (2004). Neurolinguistics: Structural plasticity in the human brain. *Nature, 431*, 757.

Medin, D. L., & Schaffer, M. M. (1978). Context theory of classification learning. *Psychological Review, 85*, 207–238.

Medvec, V. H., Madey, S. F., & Gilovich, T. (1995). When less is more: Counterfactual thinking and satisfaction among Olympic medalists. *Journal of Personality and Social Psychology, 69*, 603–610.

Meins, E. (2003). Emotional development and attachment relationships. In A. Slater & G. Bremner (Eds.), *An introduction to developmental psychology* (pp. 141–164). Malden, MA: Blackwell.

Meins, E., Fernyhough, C., Fradley, E., & Tuckey, M. (2001). Rethinking maternal sensitivity: Mothers' comments on infants' mental processes predict security of attachment at 12 months. *Journal of Child Psychology & Psychiatry & Allied Disciplines, 42*, 637–648.

Meisel, S. R., Dayan, K. I., Pauzner, H., Chetboun, I., Arbel, Y., David, D., et al. (1991). Effect of Iraqi missile war on incidence of acute myocardial infarction and sudden death in Israeli citizens. *Lancet, 338*, 660–661.

Mekel-Bobrov, N., Gilbert, S. L., Evans, P. D., Vallender, E. J., Anderson, J. R., Hudson, R. R., et al. (2005). Ongoing adaptive evolution of ASPM, a brain size determinant in *Homo sapiens. Science, 309*, 1720–1722.

Meltzoff, A. N., & Moore, M. K. (1977). Imitation of facial and manual gestures by human neonates. *Science, 198*, 75–78.

Melzack, R., & Wall, P. D. (1965). Pain mechanisms: A new theory. *Science, 150*, 971–979.

Merikangas, K. R., Wicki, W., & Angst, J. (1994). Heterogeneity of depression: Classification of depressive subtype by longitudinal course. *British Journal of Psychiatry, 164*, 342–348.

Mervis, C. B., & Bertrand, J. (1994). Acquisition of the "Novel Name" Nameless Category (N3C) principle. *Child Development, 65*, 1646–1662.

Merzenich, M. M., Recanzone, G. H., Jenkins, W. M., & Grajski, K. A. (1990). Adaptive mechanisms in cortical networks underlying cortical contributions to learning and nondeclarative memory. *Cold Spring Harbor Symposia on Quantitative Biology, 55*, 873–887.

Messick, D. M., & Cook, K. S. (1983). *Equity theory: Psychological and sociological perspectives.* New York: Praeger.

Meyer-Bahlberg, H. F. L., Ehrhardt, A. A., Rosen, L. R., & Gruen, R. S. (1995). Prenatal estrogens and the development of homosexual orientation. *Developmental Psychology, 31*, 12–21.

Miklowitz, D. J., Goldstein, M. J., Nuechterlein, K. H., Snyder, K. S., & Mintz, J. (1988). Family factors and the course of bipolar affective disorder. *Archives of General Psychiatry, 45*, 225–231.

Milgram, S. (1963). Behavioral study of obedience. *Journal of Abnormal and Social Psychology, 67*, 371–378.

Milgram, S. (1974). *Obedience to authority.* New York: Harper & Row.

Milgram, S., Bickman, L., & Berkowitz, O. (1969). Note on the drawing power of crowds of different size. *Journal of Personality and Social Psychology, 13*, 79–82.

Milgram, S., & Toch, H. (1968). Collective behavior: Crowds and social movements. In G. Lindzey & E. Aronson (Eds.), *The handbook of social psychology* (2nd ed., Vol. 4, pp. 507–610). Reading, MA: Addison-Wesley.

Miller, A. J. (1986). *The obedience experiments: A case study of controversy in social science.* New York: Praeger.

Miller, D. T., & Prentice, D. A. (1996). The construction of social norms and standards. In E. T. Higgins, & A. W. Kruglanski (Ed.), *Social psychology: Handbook of basic principles* (pp. 799–829). New York: Guilford Press.

Miller, D. T., & Ratner, R. K. (1998). The disparity between the actual and assumed power of self-interest. *Journal of Personality and Social Psychology, 74*, 53–62.

Miller, G. A. (1956). The magical number seven, plus or minus two: Some limits on our capacity for processing information. *Psychological Review, 63*, 81–96.

Miller, K. F., Smith, C. M., & Zhu, J. (1995). Preschool origins of cross-national differences in mathematical competence: The role of number-naming systems. *Psychological Science, 6*, 56–60.

Miller, N. E. (1960). Motivational effects of brain stimulation and drugs. *Federation Proceedings, 19,* 846–854.

Miller, N. E. (1978a). Biofeedback and visceral learning. *Annual Review of Psychology, 29,* 373–404.

Miller, N. E., & Campbell, D. T. (1959). Recency and primacy in persuasion as a function of the timing of speeches and measurements. *Journal of Abnormal & Social Psychology, 59,* 1–9.

Miller, T. W. (Ed.). (1996). *Theory and assessment of stressful life events.* Madison, CT: International Universities Press.

Miller, W. R. (1978b). Behavioral treatment of problem drinkers: A comparative outcome study of three controlled drinking therapies. *Journal of Consulting and Clinical Psychology, 46,* 74–86.

Milne, E., & Grafman, J. (2001). Ventromedial prefrontal cortex lesions in humans eliminate implicit gender stereotyping. *Journal of Neuroscience, 21,* 1–6.

Milner, B. (1962). Laterality effects in audition. In V. B. Mountcastle (Ed.), *Interhemispheric relations and cerebral dominance* (pp. 177–195). Baltimore: Johns Hopkins University Press.

Mineka, S., & Cook, M. (1988). Social learning and the acquisition of snake fear in monkeys. In T. Zentall & B. G. Galef, Jr. (Eds.), *Social learning* (pp. 51–73). Hillsdale, NJ: Erlbaum.

Minsky, M. (1986). *The society of mind.* New York: Simon & Schuster.

Mischel, W. (1968). *Personality and assessment.* New York: Wiley.

Mischel, W., & Shoda, Y. (1999). Integrating dispositions and processing dynamics within a unified theory of personality: The Cognitive-Affective Personality System. In L. A. Pervin & O. P. John (Eds.), *Handbook of personality: Theory and research.* New York: Guilford Press.

Mischel, W., Shoda, Y., & Rodriguez, M. L. (1989). Delay of gratification in children. *Science, 244,* 933–938.

Mita, T. H., Dermer, M., & Knight, J. (1977). Reversed facial images and the mere-exposure hypothesis. *Journal of Personality and Social Psychology, 35,* 597–601.

Miura, I. T., Okamoto, Y., Kim, C. C., & Chang, C. M. (1994). Comparisons of children's cognitive representation of number: China, France, Japan, Korea, Sweden and the United States. *International Journal of Behavioral Development, 17,* 401–411.

Moffitt, T. E. (1993). Adolescence-limited and life-course-persistent antisocial behavior: A developmental taxonomy. *Psychological Review, 100,* 674–701.

Moghaddam, B., & Bunney, B. S. (1989). Differential effect of cocaine on extracellular dopamine levels in rat medial prefrontal cortex and nucleus accumbens: Comparison to amphetamine. *Synapse, 4,* 156–161.

Mokdad, A. H. P., Ford, E. S., Bowman, B. A., Dietz, W. H., Vinicor, F., Bales, V. S., et al. (2003). Prevalence of obesity, diabetes, and obesity-related health risk factors, 2001. *Journal of the American Medical Association, 289*(1), 76–79.

Monahan, J. L., Murphy, S. T., & Zajonc, R. B. (2000). Subliminal mere exposure: Specific, general, and diffuse effects. *Psychological Science, 11,* 462–466.

Mook, D. G. (1983). In defense of external invalidity. *American Psychologist, 38,* 379–387.

Morewedge, C. K., & Norton, M. I. (2009). When dreaming is believing: The (motivated) interpretation of dreams. J*ournal of Personality and Social Psychology, 96,* 249–264.

Morgan, H. (1990). Dostoevsky's epilepsy: A case report and comparison. *Surgical Neurology, 33,* 413–416.

Morgenstern, J., Labouvie, E., McCrady, B. S., Kahler, C. W., & Frey, R. M. (1997). Affiliation with Alcoholics Anonymous after treatment:

A study of its therapeutic effects and mechanisms of action. *Journal of Consulting and Clinical Psychology, 65,* 768–777.

Morris, C. D., Bransford, J. D., & Franks, J. J. (1977). Levels of processing versus transfer-appropriate processing. *Journal of Verbal Learning and Verbal Behavior, 16,* 519–533.

Morris, R. G., Anderson, E., Lynch, G. S., & Baudry, M. (1986). Selective impairment of learning and blockade of long-term potentiation by an N-methyl-D-aspartate receptor antagonist, AP5. *Nature, 319,* 774–776.

Morris, T. L. (2001). Social phobia. In M. W. Vasey & M. R. Dadds (Eds.), *The developmental psychopathology of anxiety* (pp. 435–458). New York: Oxford University Press.

Morrow, D., Leirer, V., Altiteri, P., & Fitzsimmons, C. (1994). When expertise reduces age differences in performance. *Psychology and Aging, 9,* 134–148.

Moscovitch, M. (1994). Memory and working-with-memory: Evaluation of a component process model and comparisons with other models. In D. L. Schacter & E. Tulving (Eds.), *Memory systems 1994* (pp. 269–310). Cambridge, MA: MIT Press.

Moscovitch, M., Nadel, L., Winocur, G., Gilboa, A., & Rosenbaum, R. S. (2006). The cognitive neuroscience of remote episodic, semantic and spatial memory. *Current Opinion in Neurobiology, 16,* 179–190.

Moss, D., McGrady, A., Davies, T., & Wickramasekera, I. (2002). *Handbook of mind-body medicine for primary care.* Newbury Park, CA: Sage.

Mroczek, D. K., & Spiro, A. (2005). Change in life satisfaction during adulthood: Findings from the Veterans Affairs Normative Aging Study. *Journal of Personality and Social Psychology, 88,* 189.

Mueller, T. I., Leon, A. C., Keller, M. B., Solomon, D. A., Endicott, J., Coryell, W., et al. (1999). Recurrence after recovery from major depressive disorder during 15 years of observational follow-up. *American Journal of Psychiatry, 156,* 1000–1006.

Muenter, M. D., & Tyce, G. M. (1971). L-dopa therapy of Parkinson's disease: Plasma L-dopa concentration, therapeutic response, and side effects. *Mayo Clinic Proceedings, 46,* 231–239.

Mukherjee, S., Sackeim, H. A., & Schnur, D. B. (1994). Electroconvulsive therapy of acute manic episodes: a review of 50 years' experience. *American Journal of Psychiatry, 151,* 169–176.

Mullen, B. (1986). Atrocity as a function of lynch mob composition: A self-attention perspective. *Personality and Social Psychology Bulletin, 12,* 187–197.

Mullen, B., Chapman, J. G., & Peaugh, S. (1989). Focus of attention in groups: A self-attention perspective. *Journal of Social Psychology, 129,* 807–817.

Mullen, M. K. (1994). Earliest recollections of childhood: A demographic analysis. *Cognition, 52,* 55–79.

Multhaup, K. S., Johnson, M. D., & Tetirick, J. C. (2005). The wane of childhood amnesia for autobiographical and public event memories. *Memory, 13,* 161–173.

Murphy, N. A., Hall, J. A., & Colvin, C. R. (2003). Accurate intelligence assessments in social interactions: Mediators and gender effects. *Journal of Personality, 71,* 465–493.

Murray, C. J. L., & Lopez, A. D. (1996). *The global burden of disease: A comprehensive assessment of mortality and disability from diseases, injuries, and risk factors in 1990 and projected to 2020.* Cambridge, MA: Harvard School of Public Health.

Murray, H. A. (1938). *Explorations in personality.* New York: Oxford University Press.

Murray, H. A. (1943). *Thematic Apperception Test Manual.* Cambridge, MA: Harvard University Press.

Murray, H. A., & Kluckhohn, C. (1953). Outline of a conception of personality. In C. Kluckhohn, Murray, H. A., & Schneider, D. M. (Eds.), *Personality in nature, society, and culture* (2nd ed., pp. 3–52). New York: Knopf.

Myers, D. G., & Diener, E. (1995). Who is happy? *Psychological Science, 6*, 10–19.

Nadasdy, A. (1995). Phonetics, phonology, and applied linguistics. *Annual Review of Applied Linguistics, 15*, 68–77.

Nagasako, E. M., Oaklander, A. L., & Dworkin, R. H. (2003). Congenital insensitivity to pain: An update. *Pain, 101*, 213–219.

Nahemow, L., & Lawton, M. P. (1975). Similarity and propinquity in friendship formation. *Journal of Personality and Social Psychology, 32*, 205–213.

Nakazato, M., Murakami, N., Date, Y., Kojima, M., Matsuo, H., Kangawa, K., et al. (2001). A role for ghrelin in the central regulation of feeding. *Nature, 409*, 194–198.

Narrow, W. E., Rae, D. S., Robins, L. N., & Regier, D. A. (2002). Revised prevalence estimates of mental disorders in the United States: Using a clinical significance criterion to reconcile 2 surveys' estimates. *Archives of General Psychiatry, 59*, 115–123.

Nathan, P. E., & Lagenbucher, J. W. (1999). Psychopathology: Description and classification. *Annual Review of Psychology, 50*, 79–107.

National Center for Health Statistics. (2001). *Health, United States.* Hyattsville, MD: National Center for Health Statistics.

National Center for Injury Prevention and Control. (2001–2002). *Injury Fact Book.* Atlanta, GA: Centers for Disease Control and Prevention.

National Household Survey on Drug Abuse. (2001). Washington, DC: Substance Abuse and Mental Health Services Administration.

National Institute of Mental Health. (2003). In harm's way (NIH Publication No. 03-4594). Washington, DC: National Institutes of Health, U.S. Department of Health and Human Services.

National Research Council. (2003). *The polygraph and lie detection.* Washington, DC: National Academies Press.

Neilson, T. A., Deslauriers, D., & Baylor, G. W. (1991). Emotions in dream and waking event reports. *Dreaming, 1*, 287–300.

Neimeyer, R. A., & Mitchell, K. A. (1988). Similarity and attraction: A longitudinal study. *Journal of Social and Personal Relationships, 5*, 131–148.

Neisser, U. (Ed.). (1998). *The rising curve: Long-term gains in IQ and related measures.* Washington, DC: American Psychological Association.

Neisser, U., & Becklen, R. (1975). Selective looking: Attending to visually significant events. *Cognitive Psychology, 7*, 480–494.

Neisser, U., Boodoo, G., Bouchard, T. J., Jr., Boykin, A. W., Brody, N., Ceci, S. J., et al. (1996). Intelligence: Knowns and unknowns. *American Psychologist, 51*, 77–101.

Netherlands Ministry of Justice. (1999). *Fact Sheet: Dutch Drugs Policy.* Utrecht: Trimbos Institute, Netherlands Institute of Mental Health and Addiction.

Nettleback, T., & Lally, M. (1976). Inspection time and measured intelligence. *British Journal of Psychology, 67*, 17–22.

Neugebauer, R., Hoek, H. W., & Susser, E. (1999). Prenatal exposure to wartime famine and development of antisocial personality in early adulthood. *Journal of the American Medical Association, 282*, 455–462.

Newberg, A., Alavi, A., Baime, M., Pourdehnad, M., Santanna, J., & d'Aquili, E. (2001). The measurement of regional cerebral blood flow during the complex cognitive task of meditation: A preliminary SPECT study. *Psychiatry Research: Neuroimaging, 106*, 113–122.

Newman, A. J., Bavelier, D., Corina, D., Jezzard, P., & Neville, H. J. (2002). A critical period for right hemisphere recruitment in American Sign Language processing. *Nature Neuroscience, 5*, 76–80.

Newman, L. S., Baumeister, R. F., & Duff, K. J. (1995). A new look at defensive projection: Thought suppression, accessibility, and biased person perception, *Journal of Personality and Social Psychology, 72*, 980–1001.

Newman, M. G., & Stone, A. A. (1996). Does humor moderate the effects of experimentally induced stress? *Annals of Behavioral Medicine, 18*, 101–109.

Newsome, W. T., & Paré, E. B. (1988). A selective impairment of motion perception following lesions of the middle temporal visual area (MT). *Journal of Neuroscience, 8*, 2201–2211.

Neylan, T. C., Metzler, T. J., Best, S. R., Weiss, D. S., Fagan, J. A., Libermans, A., et al. (2002). Critical incident exposure and sleep quality in police officers. *Psychosomatic Medicine, 64*, 345–352.

Niaura, R., Todaro, J. F., Stroud, L., Spiro III, A., Ward, K. D., Weiss, S., et al. (2002). Hostility, the metabolic syndrome, and incident coronary heart disease. *Health Psychology, 21*, 588–593.

NICHD Early Child Care Research Network. (1997). The effects of infant child care on infant-mother attachment security: Results of the NICHD study of early child care. *Child Development, 68*, 860–879.

NICHD Early Child Care Research Network. (1999). Child care and mother-infant interaction in the first three years of life. *Developmental Psychlogy, 35*, 1399–1413.

NICHD Early Child Care Research Network. (2002). Child-care structure to process to outcome: Direct and indirect effects of child-care quality on young children's development. *Psychological Science, 13*, 199–206.

Nikles, C. D., II, Brecht, D. L., Klinger, E., & Bursell, A. L. (1998). The effects of current concern- and nonconcern-related waking suggestions on nocturnal dream content. *Journal of Personality and Social Psychology, 75*, 242–255.

Ninan, P. T. (1999). The functional anatomy, neurochemistry, and pharmacology of anxiety. *Journal of Clinical Psychiatry, 60*, 12–17.

Nisbett, R. E., Caputo, C., Legant, P., & Maracek, J. (1973). Behavior as seen by the actor and as seen by the observer. *Journal of Personality and Social Psychology, 27*, 154–164.

Nishino, S., Mignot, E., & Dement, W. C. (1995). Sedative-hypnotics. In A. F. Schatzberg & C. B. Nemeroff (Eds.), *American Psychiatric Press textbook of psychopharmacology* (pp. 405–416). Washington, DC: American Psychiatric Press.

Nissen, M. J., & Bullemer, P. (1987). Attentional requirements of learning: Evidence from performance measures. *Cognitive Psychology, 19*, 1–32.

Norcross, J. C., Hedges, M., & Castle, P. H. (2002). Psychologists conducting psychotherapy in 2001: A study of the Division 29 membership. *Psychotherapy: Theory/Research/Practice/Training, 39*, 97–102.

Norton, A. J. (1987). Families and children in the year 2000. *Children Today,* July–August, 6–9.

Norton, G. R., Harrison, B., Hauch, J., & Rhodes, L. (1985). Characteristics of people with infrequent panic attacks. *Journal of Abnormal Psychology, 94*, 216–221.

Nosanchuk, T. A., & Lightstone, J. (1974). Canned laughter and public and private conformity. *Journal of Personality & Social Psychology, 29*, 153–156.

Nunn, J. A., Gregory, L. J., & Brammer, M. (2002). Functional magnetic resonance imaging of synesthesia: Activation of V4/V8 by spoken words. *Nature Neuroscience, 5*, 371–375.

Nuttin, J. M. (1985). Narcissism beyond Gestalt and awareness: The name letter effect. *European Journal of Social Psychology, 15*, 353–361.

Nyberg, L., McIntosh, A. R., Houle, S., Nilsson, L.-G., & Tulving, E. (1996). Activation of medial temporal structures during episodic memory retrieval. *Nature, 380*, 715–717.

O'Connor, T. G., & Ruter, M. (2000). Attachment disorder following early severe deprivation: Extension and longitudinal follow-up. *Journal of the American Academy of Child and Adolescent Psychiatry, 39,* 703–712.

O'Sullivan, L. F., & Allegeier, E. R. (1998). Feigning sexual desire: Consenting to unwanted sexual activity in heterosexual dating relationships. *Journal of Sex Research, 35,* 234–243.

Ochsner, K. N., Bunge, S. A., Gross, J. J., & Gabrieli, J. D. E. (2002). Rethinking feelings: An fMRI study of the cognitive regulation of emotion. *Journal of Cognitive Neuroscience, 14,* 1215–1229.

Office of the Press Secretary. (2002, July 21). Homeland Security presidential directive 3. Retrieved August 2007 from http://www.whitehouse.gov/news/releases/2002/03/20020312-5.html

Ofshe, R. J. (1992). Inadvertent hypnosis during interrogation: False confession due to dissociative state, misidentified multiple personality, and the satanic cult hypothesis. *International Journal of Clinical and Experimental Hypnosis, 40,* 125–126.

Ofshe, R., & Watters, E. (1994). *Making monsters: False memories, psychotherapy, and sexual hysteria.* New York: Scribner/Macmillan.

Öhman, A., Dimberg, U., & Öst, L. G. (1985). Animal and social phobias: Biological constraints on learned fear responses. In S. Reiss & R. Bootzin (Eds.), *Theoretical issues in behavior therapy* (pp. 123–175). New York: Academic Press.

Öhman, A., & Mineka, S. (2001). Fears, phobias, and preparedness: Toward an evolved model of fear and fear learning. *Psychological Review, 108,* 483–522.

Oldham, J. M., Skodol, A. E., & Bender, D. S. (2005). *The American Psychiatric Publishing textbook of personality disorders.* Washington, DC: American Psychiatric Publishing.

Olds, J. (1956, October). Pleasure center in the brain. *Scientific American, 195,* 105–116.

Olds, J., & Fobes, J. I. (1981). The central basis of motivation: Intracranial self-stimulation studies. *Annual Review of Psychology, 32,* 523–574.

Ollers, D. K., & Eilers, R. E. (1988). The role of audition in infant babbling. *Child Development, 59,* 441–449.

Oltmanns, T. F., Neale, J. M., & Davison, G. C. (1991). *Case studies in abnormal psychology* (3rd ed.). New York: Wiley.

Oltmanns, T. F., & Turkheimer, E. (2006). Perceptions of self and others regarding pathological personality traits. In R. Kreuger & J. Tackett (Eds.), *Personality and psychopathology* (pp. 71–111). New York: Guilford Press.

Orban, G. A., Van Essen, D., & Vanduffel, W. (2004). Comparative mapping of higher visual areas in monkeys and humans. *Trends in Cognitive Sciences, 8,* 315–324.

Orne, M. T., & Evans, F. J. (1965). Social control in the psychological experiment: Antisocial behavior and hypnosis. *Journal of Personality and Social Psychology, 1,* 189–200.

Oswald, L., Taylor, A. M., & Triesman, M. (1960). Discriminative responses to stimulation during human sleep. *Brain, 83,* 440–453.

Owen, A. M., Coleman, M. R., Boly, M., Davis, M. H., Laureys, S., & Pickard, J. D. (2006). Detecting awareness in the vegetative state. *Science, 313,* 1402.

Owens, W. A. (1966). Age and mental abilities: A second adult follow-up. *Journal of Educational Psychology, 57,* 311–325.

Paivio, A. (1971). *Imagery and verbal processes.* New York: Holt, Reinhart and Winston.

Paivio, A. (1986). *Mental representations: A dual coding approach.* New York: Oxford University Press.

Palmieri, R. M., Ingersoll, C. D., & Stone, M. B. (2002). Center-of-pressure parameters used in the assessment of postural control. *Journal of Sport Rehabilitation, 11,* 51–66.

Pande, A. C., Davidson, J. R. T., Jefferson, J. W., Janney, C. A., Katzelnick, D. J., Weisler, R. H., et al. (1999). Treatment of social phobia with gabapentin: A placebo-controlled study. *Journal of Clinical Psychopharmacology, 19,* 341–348.

Pande, A. C., Pollack, M. H., Crockatt, J., Greiner, M., Chouinard, G., R. Bruce Lydiard, R., et al. (2000). Placebo-controlled study of gabapentin treatment of panic disorder. *Journal of Clinical Psychopharmacology, 20,* 467–471.

Parkinson, B., & Totterdell, P. (1999). Classifying affect-regulation strategies. *Cognition and Emotion, 13,* 277–303.

Parrott, A. C., Morinan, A., Moss, M., & Scholey, A. (2004). *Understanding drugs and behavior.* Chichester, England: Wiley.

Parrott, W. G. (1993). Beyond hedonism: Motives for inhibiting good moods and for maintaining bad moods. In D. M. Wegner & J. W. Pennebaker (Eds.), *Handbook of mental control* (pp. 278–308). Englewood Cliffs, NJ: Prentice Hall.

Partinen, M. (1994). Epidemiology of sleep disorders. In M. H. Kryger, T. Roth, & W. C. Dement (Eds.), *Principles and practice of sleep medicine* (2nd ed.). Philadelphia: Saunders.

Pascoe, E. A., & Richman, L. S. (2009). Perceived discrimination and health: A meta-analytic review. *Psychological Bulletin, 135,* 531–554.

Pascual-Leone, A., Houser, C. M., Reese, K., Shotland, L. I., Grafman, J., Sato, S., et al. (1993). Safety of rapid-rate transcranial magnetic stimulation in normal volunteers. *Electroencephalography and Clinical Neurophysiology, 89,* 120–130.

Patrick, C. J., Cuthbert, B. N., & Lang, P. J. (1994). Emotion in the criminal psychopath: Fear image processing. *Journal of Abnormal Psychology, 103,* 523–534.

Patterson, C. J. (1995). Lesbian mothers, gay fathers, and their children. In A. R. D'Augelli & C. J. Patterson (Eds.), *Lesbian, gay and bisexual identities across the lifespan: Psychological perspectives* (pp. 262–290). New York: Oxford University Press.

Paul, A. M. (2004). *The cult of personality testing.* New York: Free Press.

Pavlidis, I., Eberhardt, N. L., & Levine, J. A. (2002). Human behaviour: Seeing through the face of deception. *Nature, 415,* 35.

Pavlov, I. P. (1923a). New researches on conditioned reflexes. *Science, 58,* 359–361.

Pavlov, I. P. (1923b, July 23). Pavloff. *Time, 1*(21), 20–21.

Pavlov, I. P. (1927). *Conditioned reflexes.* Oxford: Oxford University Press.

Pawlowski, B., Dunbar, R. I. M., & Lipowicz, A. (2000). Tall men have more reproductive success. *Nature, 362,* 156.

Pearce, J. M. (1987). A model of stimulus generalization for Pavlovian conditioning. *Psychological Review, 84,* 61–73.

Pelham, B. W. (1985). Self-investment and self-esteem: Evidence for a Jamesian model of self-worth. *Journal of Personality and Social Psychology, 69,* 1141–1150.

Pelham, B. W., Carvallo, M., & Jones, J. T. (2005). Implicit egotism. *Current Directions in Psychological Science, 14,* 106–110.

Pelham, B. W., Mirenberg, M. C., & Jones, J. T. (2002). Why Susie sells seashells by the seashore: Implicit egotism and major life decisions. *Journal of Personality and Social Psychology, 82,* 469–487.

Pendergrast, M. (1995). *Victims of memory: Incest accusations and shattered lives.* Hinesburg, VT: Upper Access.

Penfield, W., & Rasmussen, T. (1950). *The cerebral cortex of man: A clinical study of localization of function.* New York: Macmillan.

Pennebaker, J. W. (1980). Perceptual and environmental determinants of coughing. *Basic and Applied Social Psychology, 1,* 83–91.

Pennebaker, J. W. (1989). Confession, inhibition, and disease. *Advances in Experimental Social Psychology, 22,* 211–244.

Pennebaker, J. W., Colder, M., & Sharp, L. K. (1990). Accelerating the coping process. *Journal of Personality and Social Psychology, 58,* 528–537.

Pennebaker, J. W., Kiecolt-Glaser, J. K., & Glaser, R. (1988). Disclosure of traumas and immune function: Health implications for psychotherapy. *Journal of Consulting and Clinical Psychology, 56,* 239–245.

Pennebaker, J. W., & Sanders, D. Y. (1976). American graffiti: Effects of authority and reactance arousal. *Personality and Social Psychology Bulletin, 2,* 264–267.

Perkins, D. N., & Grotzer, T. A. (1997). Teaching intelligence. *American Psychologist, 52,* 1125–1133.

Perloff, L. S., & Fetzer, B. K. (1986). Self-other judgments and perceived vulnerability to victimization. *Journal of Personality and Social Psychology, 50,* 502–510.

Perrett, D. I., Burt, D. M., Penton-Voak, I. S., Lee, K. J., Rowland, D. A., & Edwards, R. (1999). Symmetry and human facial attractiveness. *Evolution and Human Behavior, 20,* 295–307.

Perrett, D. I., Rolls, E. T., & Caan, W. (1982). Visual neurons responsive to faces in the monkey temporal cortex. *Experimental Brain Research, 47,* 329–342.

Perris, C. (1992). *Bipolar-unipolar distinction* (2nd ed.). New York: Guilford Press.

Persons, J. B. (1986). The advantages of studying psychological phenomena rather than psychiatric diagnoses. *American Psychologist, 41,* 1252–1260.

Peskin, H. (1973). Influence of the developmental schedule of puberty on learning and ego functioning. *Journal of Youth and Adolescence, 2,* 273–290.

Petersen, A. C. (1985). Pubertal development as a cause of disturbance—Myths, realities, and unanswered questions. *Genetic Social and General Psychology Monographs, 111,* 205–232.

Petersen, A. C., & Grockett, L. (1985). Pubertal timing and grade effects on adjustment. *Journal of Youth and Adolescence, 14,* 191–206.

Peterson, C., & Seligman, M. E. P. (2004). *Character strengths and virtues: A handbook and classification.* Washington, DC: American Psychological Association.

Peterson, C., & Siegal, M. (1999). Representing inner worlds: Theory of mind in autistic, deaf and normal hearing children. *Psychological Science, 10,* 126–129.

Peterson, L. R., & Peterson, M. J. (1959). Short-term retention of individual verbal items. *Journal of Experimental Psychology, 58,* 193–198.

Peterson, S. E., Fox, P. T., Posner, M. I., Mintun, M. A., & Raichle, M. E. (1989). Positron emission tomographic studies of the processing of single words. *Journal of Cognitive Neuroscience, 1,* 154–170.

Petitto, L. A., & Marentette, P. F. (1991). Babbling in the manual mode: Evidence for the ontogeny of language. *Science, 251,* 1493–1496.

Petrie, K. P., Booth, R. J., & Pennebaker, J. W. (1998). The immunological effects of thought suppression. *Journal of Personality and Social Psychology, 75,* 1264–1272.

Petty, R. E., & Cacioppo, J. T. (1986). The elaboration likelihood model of persuasion. In L. Berkowitz (Ed.), *Advances in experimental social psychology* (Vol. 19, pp. 123–205). New York: Academic Press.

Petty, R. E., & Wegener, D. T. (1998). Attitude change: Multiple roles for persuasion variables. In D. T. Gilbert, S. T. Fiske, & G. Lindzey (Eds.), *The handbook of social psychology* (4th ed., Vol. 1, pp. 323–390). Boston: McGraw-Hill.

Pew Research Center for the People & the Press. (1997). Motherhood today: A tougher job, less ably done. Pew Research Center: Author.

Pew Research Center for the People & the Press. (2006). Attitudes toward homosexuality in African countries. Pew Research Center: Author.

Phelan, J., Link, B., Stueve, A., & Pescosolido, B. (2000). Public conceptions of mental illness in 1950 and 1996: What is mental illness and is it to be feared? *Journal of Health and Social Behavior, 41,* 188–207.

Phelps, E. A. (2006). Emotion and cognition: Insights from studies of the human amygdala. *Annual Review of Psychology, 24,* 27–53.

Phelps, E. A., & LeDoux, J. L. (2005). Contributions of the amygdala to emotion processing: From animal models to human behavior. *Neuron, 48,* 175–187.

Phillips, D. P., & Carstensen, L. L. (1986). Clustering of teenage suicides after television news stories about suicide. *New England Journal of Medicine, 315,* 685–689.

Phillips, F. (2002, January 24). Jump in cigarette sales tied to Sept. 11 attacks. *Boston Globe,* p. B1.

Piaget, J. (1954a). *The child's concept of number.* New York: Norton.

Piaget, J. (1954b). *The construction of reality in the child.* New York: Basic Books.

Piaget, J. (1977). The first year of life of the child. In H. E. Gruber & J. J. Voneche (Eds.), *The essential Piaget: An interpretative reference and guide* (pp. 198–214). New York: Basic Books. (Work originally published 1927)

Piaget, J., & Inhelder, B. (1969). *The psychology of the child* (H. Weaver, Trans.). New York: Basic Books.

Pinel, J. P. J., Assanand, S., & Lehman, D. R. (2000). Hunger, eating, and ill health. *American Psychologist, 55,* 1105–1116.

Pines, A. M. (1993). Burnout: An existential perspective. In W. B. Schaufeli, C. Maslach & T. Marek (Eds.), *Professional burnout: Recent developments in theory and research* (pp. 33–51). Washington, DC: Taylor & Francis.

Pines, A., M., & Aronson, E. (1988). *Career burnout: Causes and cures* (2nd ed.). New York: Free Press.

Pinker, S. (1994). *The language instinct.* New York: Morrow.

Pinker, S. (1997a). Evolutionary psychology: An exchange. *New York Review of Books, 44,* 55–58.

Pinker, S. (1997b). *How the mind works.* New York: Norton.

Pinker, S., & Bloom, P. (1990). Natural language and natural selection. *Behavioral & Brain Sciences, 13,* 707–784.

Pipes, D. (2002, October 29). The snipers: Crazy or jihadis? *New York Post.* Retrieved September 15, 2007, from http://www.danielpipes.org/article/493

Pitman, R. K., Sanders, K. M., Zusman, R. M., Healy, A. R., Cheema, F., Lasko, N. B., Cahill, L., et al. (2002). Pilot study of secondary prevention of posttraumatic stress disorder with propranolol. *Biological Psychiatry, 51,* 189–192.

Plato. (1956). *Protagoras* (O. Jowett, Trans.). New York: Prentice Hall.

Plomin, R., De Fries, J. C., McClearn, G. E., & Rutter, M. (1997). *Behavior genetics* (3rd ed.). New York: Freeman.

Plomin, R., DeFries, J. C., McClearn, G. E., & McGuffin, P. (2001a). *Behavioral genetics.* (4th ed.). New York: Freeman.

Plomin, R., Hill, L., Craig, I. W., McGuffin, P., Purcell, S., Sham, P., et al. (2001b). A genome-wide scan of 1842 DNA markers for allelic associations with general cognitive ability: A five-stage design using DNA pooling and extreme selected groups. *Behavior Genetics, 31,* 497–509.

Plomin, R., Scheier, M. F., Bergeman, C. S., Pedersen, N. L., Nesselroade, J. R., & McClearn, G. E. (1992). Optimism, pessimism, and mental health: A twin/adoption analysis. *Personality and Individual Differences, 13,* 921–930.

Plomin, R., & Spinath, F. M. (2004). Intelligence: Genetics, genes, and genomics. *Journal of Personality and Social Psychology, 86,* 112–129.

Plotnik, J. M., de Waal, F. B. M., & Reiss, D. (2006). Self-recognition in an Asian elephant. *Proceedings of the National Academy of Science, 103,* 17053–17057.

Poole, D. A., Lindsay, S. D., Memon, A., & Bull, R. (1995). Psychotherapy and the recovery of memories of childhood sexual abuse: U.S. and British practitioners' opinions, practices, and experiences. *Journal of Consulting and Clinical Psychology, 63,* 426–487.

Pope, A. W., & Bierman, K. L. (1999). Predicting adolescent peer problems and antisocial activities: The relative roles of aggression and dysregulation. *Developmental Psychology, 35,* 335–346.

Posey, T. B., & Losch, M. E. (1983). Auditory hallucinations of hearing voices in 375 normal subjects. *Imagination, Cognition and Personality, 3,* 99–113.

Posner, M. I., & Raichle, M. E. (1994). *Images of mind.* New York: Freeman.

Posthuma, D., & de Geus, E. J. C. (2006). Progress in the molecular-genetic study of intelligence. *Current Directions in Psychological Science, 15,* 151–155.

Postman, L., & Underwood, B. J. (1973). Critical issues in interference theory. *Memory & Cognition, 1,* 19–40.

Prasada, S., & Pinker, S. (1993). Generalizations of regular and irregular morphology. *Language and Cognitive Processes, 8,* 1–56.

Pratkanis, A. R. (1992). The cargo-cult science of subliminal persuasion. *Skeptical Inquirer, 16,* 260–272.

Pressman, S. D., Cohen, S., Miller, G. E., Barkin, A., Rabin, B. S., & Treanor, J. J. (2005). Loneliness, social network size, and immune response to influenza vaccination in college freshmen. *Health Psychology, 24,* 297–306.

Prochaska, J. J., & Sallis, J. F. (2004). A randomized controlled trial of single versus multiple health behavior change: Promoting physical activity and nutrition among adolescents. *Health Psychology, 23,* 314–318.

Prudic, J., Haskett, R. F., Mulsant, B., Malone, K. M., Pettinati, H. M., Stephens, S., et al. (1996). Resistance to antidepressant medications and short-term clinical response to ECT. *American Journal of Psychiatry, 153,* 985–992.

Pruitt, D. G. (1998). Social conflict. In D. T. Gilbert, S. T. Fiske, & G. Lindzey (Eds.), *The handbook of social psychology* (4th ed., Vol. 2, pp. 470–503). New York: McGraw-Hill.

Putnam, F. W., Guroff, J. J., Silberman, E. K., Barban, L., & Post, R. M. (1986). The clinical phenomenology of multiple personality disorder: Review of 100 recent cases. *Journal of Clinical Psychiatry, 47,* 285–293.

Quattrone, G. A. (1982). Behavioral consequences of attributional bias. *Social Cognition, 1,* 358–378.

Querleu, D., Lefebvre, C., Titran, M., Renard, X., Morillon, M., & Crepin, G. (1984). Réactivité de nouveau-né de moins de deux heures de vie á la voix maternelle. *Journal de Gynecologie Obstetrique et de Biologie de la Reproduction, 13,* 125–134.

Quiroga, R. Q., Reddy, L., Kreiman, G., Koch, C., & Fried, I. (2005). Invariant visual representation by single neurons in the human brain. *Nature, 435,* 1102–1107.

Rachman, S. J., & DeSilva, P. (1978). Abnormal and normal obsessions. *Behavioral Research and Therapy, 16,* 223–248.

Radford, E., & Radford, M. A. (1949). *Encyclopedia of superstitions.* New York: Philosophical Library.

Rahe, R. H., Meyer, M., Smith, M., Klaer, G., & Holmes, T. H. (1964). Social stress and illness onset. *Journal of Psychosomatic Research, 8,* 35–44.

Raichle, M. E., & Mintun, M. A. (2006). Brain work and brain imaging. Annual Review of Neuroscience, *29,* 449–476.

Ramachandran, V. S., & Hubbard, E. M. (2003). Hearing colors, tasting shapes. *Scientific American, 288,* 52–59.

Ramirez-Esparza, N., S. D. Gosling, V. Benet-Martinez, J. P. Potter, & J. W. Pennebaker. (2006). Do bilinguals have two personalities? A special case of cultural frame switching. *Journal of Research in Personality 40,* 99–120.

Raz, N. (2000). Aging of the brain and its impact on cognitive performance: Integration of structural and functional findings. In F. I. M. Craik & T. A. Salthouse (Eds.), *The handbook of aging and cognition* (pp. 1–90). Mahwah, NJ: Erlbaum.

Read, K. E. (1965). *The high valley.* London: Allen and Unwin.

Reason, J., & Mycielska, K. (1982). *Absent-minded? The psychology of mental lapses and everyday errors.* Englewood Cliffs: Prentice-Hall.

Reber, A. S. (1967). Implicit learning of artificial grammars. *Journal of Verbal Learning and Verbal Behavior, 6,* 855–863.

Reber, A. S. (1996). *Implicit learning and tacit knowledge: An essay on the cognitive unconscious.* New York: Oxford University Press.

Reber, A. S., & Allen, R. (2000). Individual differences in implicit learning. In R. G. Kunzendorf & B. Wallace (Eds.), *Individual differences in conscious experience.* Philadelphia: John Benjamins.

Reber, A. S., Walkenfeld, F. F., & Hernstadt, R. (1991). Implicit learning: Individual differences and IQ. *Journal of Experimental Psychology: Learning, Memory, and Cognition, 17,* 888–896.

Reber, P. J., Gitelman, D. R., Parrish, T. B., & Mesulam, M. M. (2003). Dissociating explicit and implicit category knowledge with fMRI. *Journal of Cognitive Neuroscience, 15,* 574–583.

Rechsthaffen, A., Gilliland, M. A., Bergmann, B. M., & Winter, J. B. (1983). Physiological correlates of prolonged sleep deprivation in rats. *Science, 221,* 182–184.

Reed, G. (1988). *The psychology of anomalous experience* (Rev. ed.). Buffalo, NY: Prometheus Books.

Regan, P. C. (1998). What if you can't get what you want? Willingness to compromise ideal mate selection standards as a function of sex, mate value, and relationship context. *Personality and Social Psychology Bulletin, 24,* 1294–1303.

Regier, D. A., Narrow, W. E., Rae, D. S., Manderscheid, R. W., Locke, B. Z., & Goodwin, F. K. (1993). The de facto US mental and addictive disorders service system: Epidemiologic Catchment Area prospective 1-year prevalence rates of disorders and services. *Archives of General Psychiatry, 41,* 934–941.

Reinarman, C., Cohen, P. D. A., & Kaal, H. L. (2004). The limited relevance of drug policy: Cannabis in Amsterdam and San Francisco. *American Journal of Public Health, 94,* 836–842.

Reiss, D., & Marino, L. (2001). Mirror self-recognition in the bottlenose dolphin: A case of cognitive convergence. *Proceedings of the National Academy of Sciences, 98,* 5937–5942.

Reissland, N. (1988). Neonatal imitation in the first hour of life: Observations in rural Nepal. *Developmental Psychology, 24,* 464–469.

Reiter, E. O., & Lee, P. A. (2001). Have the onset and tempo of puberty changed? *Archives of Pediatrics and Adolescent Medicine, 155,* 988–989.

Renner, M. J., & Mackin, R. (1998). A life stress instrument for classroom use. *Teaching of Psychology, 25,* 46–48.

Repacholi, B. M., & Gopnik, A. (1997). Early reasoning about desires: Evidence from 14- and 18-month-olds. *Developmental Psychology, 33,* 12–21.

Rescorla, R. A. (1966). Predictability and number of pairings in Pavlovian fear conditioning. *Psychonomic Science, 4,* 383–384.

Rescorla, R. A. (1988). Classical conditioning: It's not what you think it is. *American Psychologist, 43,* 151–160.

Rescorla, R. A. (2006). Stimulus generalization of excitation and inhibition. *Quarterly Journal of Experimental Psychology, 59,* 53–67.

Rescorla, R. A., & Wagner, A. R. (1972). A theory of Pavlovian conditioning: Variations in effectiveness of reinforcement and nonreinforcement.

In A. Black & W. F. Prokasky, Jr. (Eds.), *Classical conditioning II.* New York: Appleton-Century-Crofts.

Ressler, K. J., & Nemeroff, C. B. (1999) Role of norepinephrine in the pathophysiology and treatment of mood disorders. *Biological Psychiatry, 46,* 1219–1233.

Rhodes, G., Yoshikawa, S., Clark, A., Lee, K., McKay, R., & Akamatsu, S. (2001). Attractiveness of facial averageness and symmetry in non-Western cultures: In search of biologically based standards of beauty. *Perception, 30,* 611–625.

Richards, M. H., Crowe, P. A., Larson, R., & Swarr, A. (1998). Developmental patterns and gender differences in the experience of peer companionship during adolescence. *Child Development, 69,* 154–163.

Richters, J., de Visser, R., Rissel, C., & Smith, A. (2006). Sexual practices at last heterosexual encounter and occurrence of orgasm in a national survey. *Journal of Sex Research, 43,* 217–226.

Rieber, R. W. (Ed.). (1980). *Wilhelm Wundt and the making of scientific psychology.* New York: Plenum Press.

Rizzolatti, G. (2004). The mirror-neuron system and imitation. In S. Hurley & N. Chater (Eds.), *Perspectives on imitation: From mirror neurons to memes* (pp. 55–76). Cambridge, MA: MIT Press.

Rizzolatti, G., & Craighero, L. (2004.) The mirror-neuron system. *Annual Review of Neuroscience, 27,* 169–192.

Roberts, G. A. (1991). Delusional belief and meaning in life: A preferred reality? *British Journal of Psychiatry, 159,* 20–29.

Robins, E., & Guze, S. B. (1972). Classification of affective disorders: The primary-secondary, the endogenous-reactive, and the neurotic-psychotic concepts. In T. A. Williams, M. M. Katz & J. A. Shields (Eds.), *Recent advances in the psychobiology of depressive illnesses* (pp. 283–293). Washington, DC: U.S. Government Printing Office.

Robins, L. N., Helzer, J. E., Hesselbrock, M., & Wish, E. (1980). Vietnam veterans three years after Vietnam. In L. Brill & C. Winick (Eds.), *The yearbook of substance use and abuse* (Vol. 11). New York: Human Sciences Press.

Robins, L. N., Helzer, J. E., Weissman, M. M., Orvaschel, H., Gruenberg, E., Burke, J. D., et al. (1984). Lifetime prevalence of specific psychiatric disorders in three sites. *Archives of General Psychiatry, 41,* 949–958.

Robins, L. N., & Regier, D. A. (1991). *Psychiatric disorders in America.* New York: Free Press.

Robinson, A., & Clinkenbeard, P. R. (1998). Giftedness: An exceptionality examined. *Annual Review of Psychology, 49,* 117–139.

Robinson, D. N. (1995). *An intellectual history of psychology.* Madison: University of Wisconsin Press.

Roediger III, H. L. (2000). Why retrieval is the key process to understanding human memory. In E. Tulving (Ed.), *Memory, consciousness, and the brain: The Tallinn conference* (pp. 52–75). Philadelphia: Psychology Press.

Roediger III, H. L., & McDermott, K. B. (1995). Creating false memories: Remembering words not presented in lists. *Journal of Experimental Psychology: Learning, Memory, and Cognition, 21,* 803–814.

Roediger III, H. L., & McDermott, K. B. (2000). Tricks of memory. *Current Directions in Psychological Science, 9,* 123–127.

Rogers, C. R. (1951). *Client-centered therapy: Its current practice, implications, and theory.* Boston: Houghton Mifflin.

Rogers, C. R. (1961). *On becoming a person.* Boston: Houghton Mifflin.

Rosch, E. H. (1973). Natural categories. *Cognitive Psychology, 4,* 328–350.

Rosch, E. H. (1975). Cognitive representations of semantic categories. *Journal of Experimental Psychology: General, 104,* 192–233.

Rosch, E. H., & Mervis, C. B. (1975). Family resemblances: Studies in the internal structure of categories. *Cognitive Psychology, 7,* 573–605.

Rose, S. P. R. (2002). Smart drugs: Do they work? Are they ethical? Will they be legal? *Nature Reviews Neuroscience 3,* 975–979.

Roseman, I. J. (1984). Cognitive determinants of emotion: A structural theory. *Review of Personality and Social Psychology, 5,* 11–36.

Roseman, I. J., & Smith, C. A. (2001). Appraisal theory: Overview, assumptions, varieties and controversies. In K. R. Scherer, A. Schorr, & T. Johnstone (Eds.), *Appraisal processes in emotion: Theory, methods, research* (pp. 3–19). New York: Oxford University Press.

Rosenberg, M. (1965). *Society and the adolescent self-image.* Princeton, NJ: Princeton University Press.

Rosenhan, D. (1973). On being sane in insane places. *Science, 179,* 250–258.

Rosenstein, M. J., Milazzo-Sayre, L. J., & Manderscheid, R. W. (1990). Characteristics of persons using specifically inpatient, outpatient, and partial care programs in 1986. In M. A. Sonnenschein (Ed.), *Mental health in the United States* (pp. 139–172). Washington, DC: U.S. Government Printing Office.

Rosenthal, R., & Fode, K. L. (1963). The effect of experimenter bias on the performance of the albino rat. *Behavioral Science, 8,* 183–189.

Ross, L. (1977). The intuitive psychologist and his shortcomings: Distortions in the attribution process. *Advances in Experimental Social Psychology, 10,* 173–220.

Ross, L., Amabile, T. M., & Steinmetz, J. L. (1977). Social roles, social control, and biases in social-perception processes. *Journal of Personality and Social Psychology, 35,* 485–494.

Ross, L., & Nisbett, R. E. (1991). *The person and the situation.* New York: McGraw-Hill.

Roth, H. P., & Caron, H. S. (1978). Accuracy of doctors' estimates and patients' statements on adherence to a drug regimen. *Clinical Pharmacology and Therapeutics, 23,* 361–370.

Roth, M., & Mountjoy, C. Q. (1997). The need for the concept of neurotic depression. In G. B. C. H. S. Akiskal (Ed.), *Dysthymia and the spectrum of chronic depressions* (pp. 96–129). New York: Guilford Press.

Rothbaum, B. O., Hodges, L., Watson, B. A., Kessler, G. D., & Opdyke, D. (1996). Virtual reality exposure therapy in the treatment of fear of flying: A case report. *Behaviour Research & Therapy, 34,* 477–481.

Rothermundt, M., Arolt, V., & Bayer, T. A. (2001). Review of immunological and immunopathological findings in schizophrenia. *Brain, Behavior, and Immunity, 15,* 319–339.

Rotstein, A. H. (2006, November 11). Despite 2–1 defeat on Election Day, backer of $1 million voter lottery still likes the idea. *Associated Press.*

Rotter, J. B. (1966). Generalized expectancies for internal versus external locus of control of reinforcement. *Psychological Monographs: General and Applied, 80.* 1–28.

Rowa, K., Antony, M. M., Brar, S., Summerfeldt, L. J., & Swinson, R. P. (2000). Treatment histories of patients with three anxiety disorders. *Depression and Anxiety, 12,* 92–98.

Rowland, L. W. (1939). Will hypnotized persons try to harm themselves or others? *Journal of Abnormal and Social Psychology, 34,* 114–117.

Roy-Byrne, P. P., & Cowley, D. (1998). *Pharmacological treatment of panic, generalized anxiety, and phobic disorders.* New York: Oxford University Press.

Royzman, E. B., Cassidy, K. W., & Baron, J. (2003). "I know, you know": Epistemic egocentrism in children and adults. *Review of General Psychology, 7,* 38–65.

Rozin, P. (1968). Are carbohydrate and protein intakes separately regulated? *Journal of Comparative and Physiological Psychology, 65,* 23–29.

Rozin, P., Bauer, R., & Catanese, D. (2003). Food and life, pleasure and worry, among American college students: Gender differences and regional similarities. *Journal of Personality and Social Psychology, 85,* 132–141.

Rozin, P., & Fallon, A. E. (1987). A perspective on disgust. *Psychological Review, 94,* 23–41.

Rozin, P., Haidt, J., & McCauley, C. R. (1999). Disgust: The body and soul emotion. In T. Dalgleish & M. J. Power (Eds.), *Handbook of cognition and emotion* (pp. 429–445). New York: Wiley.

Rozin, P., Hammer, L., Oster, H., Horowitz, T., & Marmora, V. (1986a). The child's concept of food: Differentiation of categories of rejected substances in the 1.4 to 5 years range. *Appetite, 7,* 141–151.

Rozin, P., Kabnick, K., Pete, E., Fischler, C., & Schields, C. (2003). The ecology of eating: Smaller portion sizes in France than in the United States help explain the French paradox. *Psychological Science, 14,* 450–454.

Rozin, P., & Kalat, J. W. (1971). Specific hungers and poison avoidance as adaptive specializations of learning. *Psychological Review, 78,* 459–486.

Rozin, P., Millman, L., & Nemeroff, C. (1986b). Operation of the laws of sympathetic magic in disgust and other domains. *Journal of Personality and Social Psychology, 50,* 703–712.

Rozin, P., Trachtenberg, S., & Cohen, A. B. (2001). Stability of body image and body image dissatisfaction in American college students over about the last 15 years. *Appetite, 37,* 245–248.

Rubenstein, A. J., Kalakanis, L., & Langlois, J. H. (1999). Infant preferences for attractive faces: A cognitive explanation. *Developmental Psychology, 35,* 848–855.

Rubin, Z. (1973). *Liking and loving.* New York: Holt, Reinhart and Winston.

Rude, S. S., Wenzlaff, R. M., Gibbs, B., Vane, J., & Whitney, T. (2002). Negative processing biases predict subsequent depressive symptoms. *Cognition and Emotion, 16,* 423–440.

Rudman, L. A., Ashmore, R. D., & Gary, M. L. (2001). "Unlearning" automatic biases: The malleability of implicit prejudice and stereotypes. *Journal of Personality and Social Psychology, 81,* 856–868.

Rushton, J. P. (1995). Asian achievement, brain size, and evolution: Comment on A. H. Yee. *Educational Psychology Review, 7,* 373–380.

Russell, J. A. (1980). A circumplex model of affect. *Journal of Personality and Social Psychology, 39,* 1161–1178.

Rutter, M., O'Connor, T. G., & the English and Romanian Adoptees Study Team (2004). Are there biological programming effects for psychological development? Findings from a study of Romanian adoptees. *Developmental Psychology, 40,* 81–94.

Ryan, R. M., & Deci, E. L. (2000). Self-determination theory and the facilitation of intrinsic motivation, social development, and well-being. *American Psychologist, 55,* 68–78.

Sachs, J. S. (1967). Recognition of semantic, syntactic, and lexical changes in sentences. *Psychonomic Bulletin, 1,* 17–18.

Sackeim, H. A., & Devanand, D. P. (1991). Dissociative disorders. In M. Hersen & S. M. Turner (Eds.), *Adult psychopathology and diagnosis* (2nd ed., pp. 279–322). New York: Wiley.

Sacks, O. (1995). *An anthropologist on Mars.* New York: Knopf.

Salge, R. A., Beck, J. G., & Logan, A. (1988). A community survey of panic. *Journal of Anxiety Disorder, 2,* 157–167.

Salthouse, T. A. (1984). Effects of age and skill in typing. *Journal of Experimental Psychology: General, 113,* 345–371.

Salthouse, T. A. (1987). Age, experience, and compensation. In C. Schooler & K. W. Schaie (Eds.), *Cognitive functioning and social structure over the life course* (pp. 142–150). New York: Ablex.

Salthouse, T. A. (2000). Pressing issues in cognitive aging. In D. Park & N. Schwartz (Eds.), *Cognitive aging: A primer.* Philadelphia: Psychology Press.

Sammons, M. T., Paige, R. U., & Levant, R. F. (Eds.). (2003). *Prescriptive authority for psychologists: A history and guide.* Washington, DC: American Psychological Association.

Sampson, R. J., & Laub, J. H. (1995). Understanding variability in lives through time: Contributions of life-course criminology. *Studies of Crime Prevention, 4,* 143–158.

Sandin, R. H., Enlund, G., Samuelsson, P., & Lenmarken, C. (2000). Awareness during anesthesia: A prospective case study. *The Lancet, 355,* 707–711.

Sarris, V. (1989). Max Wertheimer on seen motion: Theory and evidence. *Psychological Research, 51,* 58–68.

Sarter, M. (2006). Preclinical research into cognition enhancers. *Trends in Pharmacological Sciences, 27,* 602–608.

Satcher, D. (2001). *The Surgeon General's call to action to promote sexual health and responsible sexual behavior.* Washington, DC: U.S. Government Printing Office.

Sato, S. (2001). Autonomy and relatedness in psychopathology and treatment: A cross-cultural formulation. *Genetic, Social, and General Psychology Monographs, 127,* 89–127.

Savage, C. R., Deckersbach, T., Heckers, S., Wagner, A. D., Schacter, D. L., Alpert, N. M., et al. (2001). Prefrontal regions supporting spontaneous and directed application of verbal learning strategies: Evidence from PET. *Brain, 124,* 219–231.

Saver, J. L., & Rabin, J. (1997). The neural substrates of religious experience. *Journal of Neuropsychiatry and Clinical Neurosciences, 9,* 498–510.

Savic, I., Berglund, H., & Lindstrom, P. (2005). Brain response to putative pheromones in homosexual men. *Proceedings of the National Academy of Sciences, 102,* 7356–7361.

Sawa, A., & Snyder, S. H. (2002). Schizophrenia: Diverse approaches to a complex disease. *Science, 295,* 692–695.

Sawyer, T. F. (2000). Francis Cecil Sumner: His views and influence on African American higher education. *History of Psychology, 3*(2), 122–141.

Scarborough, E., & Furumoto, L. (1987). *Untold lives: The first generation of American women psychologists.* New York: Columbia University Press.

Scarr, S., & McCartney, K. (1983). How people make their own environments: A theory of genotype-to-environment factors. *Child Development, 54,* 424–435.

Schachter, S. (1982). Recidivism and self-cure of smoking and obesity. *American Psychologist, 37,* 436–444.

Schachter, S., & Singer, J. E. (1962). Cognitive, social, and psychological determinants of emotional state. *Physiological Review, 69,* 379–399.

Schacter, D. L. (1987). Implicit memory: History and current status. *Journal of Experimental Psychology: Learning, Memory, and Cognition, 13,* 501–518.

Schacter, D. L. (1996). *Searching for memory: The brain, the mind, and the past.* New York: Basic Books.

Schacter, D. L. (1999). The seven sins of memory: Insights from psychology and cognitive neuroscience. *American Psychologist, 54*(3), 182–203.

Schacter, D. L. (2001a). *Forgotten ideas, neglected pioneers: Richard Semon and the story of memory.* Philadelphia: Psychology Press.

Schacter, D. L. (2001b). *The seven sins of memory: How the mind forgets and remembers.* Boston: Houghton Mifflin.

Schacter, D. L., Alpert, N. M., Savage, C. R., Rauch, S. L., & Albert, M. S. (1996a). Conscious recollection and the human hippocampal formation: Evidence from positron emission tomography. *Proceedings of the National Academy of Sciences (USA) 93,* 321–325.

Schacter, D. L., & Curran, T. (2000). Memory without remembering and remembering without memory: Implicit and false memories. In M. S. Gazzaniga (Ed.), *The new cognitive neurosciences* (2nd ed.). Cambridge, MA: MIT Press.

Schacter, D. L., Dobbins, I. G., & Schnyer, D. M. (2004). Specificity of priming: A cognitive neuroscience perspective. *Nature Reviews Neuroscience, 5,* 853–862.

Schacter, D. L., Harbluk, J. L., & McLachlan, D. R. (1984). Retrieval without recollection: An experimental analysis of source amnesia. *Journal of Verbal Learning and Verbal Behavior, 23,* 593–611.

Schacter, D. L., Israel, L., & Racine, C. A. (1999). Suppressing false recognition in younger and older adults: The distinctiveness heuristic. *Journal of Memory and Language, 40,* 1–24.

Schacter, D. L., & Moscovitch, M. (1984). Infants, amnesics, and dissociable memory systems. In M. Moscovitch (Ed.), *Infant memory* (pp. 173–216). New York: Plenum Press.

Schacter, D. L., Reiman, E., Curran, T., Yun, L. S., Bandy, D., McDermott, K. B., et al. (1996b). Neuroanatomical correlates of veridical and illusory recognition memory: Evidence from positron emission tomography. *Neuron, 17,* 267–274.

Schacter, D. L., & Tulving, E. (1994). *Memory systems 1994.* Cambridge, MA: MIT Press.

Schacter, D. L., Wagner, A. D., & Buckner, R. L. (2000). Memory systems of 1999. In E. Tulving & F. I. M. Craik (Eds.), *The Oxford handbook of memory.* New York: Oxford University Press.

Schaeffer, M. A., McKinnon, W., Baum, A., Reynolds, C. P., Rikli, P., & Davidson, L. M. (1985). Immune status as a function of chronic stress at Three-Mile Island [Abstract]. *Psychosomatic Medicine, 47,* 85.

Schafer, R. B., & Keith, P. M. (1980). Equity and depression among married couples. *Social Psychology Quarterly, 43,* 430–435.

Schaie, K. W. (1996). *Intellectual development in adulthood: The Seattle longitudinal study.* New York: Cambridge University Press.

Schaie, K. W. (2005). *Developmental influences on adult intelligence: The Seattle longitudinal study.* New York: Oxford University Press.

Schatzberg, A. F., Cole, J. O., & DeBattista, C. (2003). *Manual of clinical psychopharmacology* (4th ed.). Washington, DC: American Psychiatric Publishing.

Scheier, M. F., Matthews, K. A., Owens, J. F., Schulz, R., Bridges, M. W., Magovern, Sr., G. J., et al. (1999). Optimism and rehospitalization after coronary artery bypass graft surgery. *Archives of Internal Medicine, 159,* 829–835.

Scherer, K. R. (1999). Appraisal theory. In T. Dalgleish & M. Power (Eds.), *Handbook of cognition and emotion* (pp. 637–663). New York: Wiley.

Scherer, K. R. (2001). The nature and study of appraisal: A review of the issues. In K. R. Scherer, A. Schorr, & T. Johnstone (Eds.), *Appraisal processes in emotion: Theory, methods, research* (pp. 369–391). New York: Oxford University Press.

Schmeichel, B. J., & Baumeister, R. F. (2004). Self-regulatory strength. In R. F. Baumeister & K. D. Vohs (Eds.), *Handbook of self-regulation* (pp. 84–98). New York: Guilford Press.

Schmidt, N. B., Lerew, D. R., & Jackson R. J. (1997). The role of anxiety sensitivity in the pathogenesis of panic: Prospective evaluation of spontaneous panic attacks during acute stress. *Journal of Abnormal Psychology, 106,* 355–365.

Schnapf, J. L., Kraft, T. W., & Baylor, D. A. (1987). Spectral sensitivity of human cone photoreceptors. *Nature, 325,* 439–441.

Schneider, B. H., Atkinson, L., & Tardif, C. (2001). Child-parent attachment and children's peer relations: A quantitative review. *Developmental Psychology, 37,* 86–100.

Schneier, F., Johnson, J., Hornig, C. D., Liebowitz, M. R., & Weissman, M. M. (1992). Social phobia: Comorbidity and morbidity in an epidemiologic sample. *Archives of General Psychiatry, 49,* 282–288.

Schnorr, J. A., & Atkinson, R. C. (1969). Repetition versus imagery instructions in the short- and long-term retention of paired associates. *Psychonomic Science, 15,* 183–184.

Schooler, J. W., Bendiksen, M., & Ambadar, Z. (1997). Taking the middle line: Can we accommodate both fabricated and recovered memories of sexual abuse? In M. A. Conway (Ed.), *Recovered memories and false memories* (pp. 251–292). Oxford: Oxford University Press.

Schooler, J. W., Reichle, E. D., & Halpern, D. V. (2001). *Zoning-out during reading: Evidence for dissociations between experience and meta-consciousness.* Paper presented at the Annual Meeting of the Psychonomic Society, Orlando, FL.

Schouwenburg, H. C. (1995). Academic procrastination: Theoretical notions, measurement, and research. In J. R. Ferrari, J. L. Johnson, & W. G. McCown (Eds.), *Procrastination and task avoidance: Theory, research, and treatment.* New York: Plenum Press.

Schreiner, C. E., Read, H. L., & Sutter, M. L. (2000). Modular organization of frequency integration in primary auditory cortex. *Annual Review of Neuroscience, 23,* 501–529.

Schultz, D. P., & Schultz, S. E. (1987). *A history of modern psychology* (4th ed.). San Diego: Harcourt Brace Jovanovich.

Schwartz, C. E., Wright, C. I., Shin, L. M., Kagan, J., & Rauch, S. L. (2003). Inhibited and uninhibited infants "grown up": Adult amygdalar response to novelty. *Science, 300,* 1952–1953.

Schwartz, J. H., & Westbrook, G. L. (2000). The cytology of neurons. In E. R. Kandel, G. H. Schwartz, & T. M. Jessell (Eds.), *Principles of neural science* (pp. 67–104). New York: McGraw-Hill.

Schwartz, S., & Maquet, P. (2002). Sleep imaging and the neuropsychological assessment of dreams. *Trends in Cognitive Sciences, 6,* 23–30.

Schwartzman, A. E., Gold, D., & Andres, D. (1987). Stability of intelligence: A 40-year follow-up. *Canadian Journal of Psychology, 41,* 244–256.

Schwarz, N., & Clore, G. L. (1983). Mood, misattribution, and judgments of well-being: Informative and directive functions of affective states. *Journal of Personality and Social Psychology, 45,* 513–523.

Schwarz, N., Mannheim, Z., & Clore, G. L. (1988). How do I feel about it? The informative function of affective states. In K. Fiedler & J. Forgas (Eds.), *Affect cognition and social behavior: New evidence and integrative attempts* (pp. 44–62). Toronto: C. J. Hogrefe.

Scoville, W. B., & Milner, B. (1957). Loss of recent memory after bilateral hippocampal lesions. *Journal of Neurology, Neurosurgery, and Psychiatry, 20,* 11–21.

Scribner, S. (1975). Recall of classical syllogisms: A cross-cultural investigation of errors on logical problems. In R. J. Falmagne (Ed.), *Reasoning: Representation and process in children and adults.* Hillsdale, NJ: Erlbaum.

Segall, M. H., Campbell, D. T., & Herskovits, M. J. (1963). Cultural differences in the perception of geometric illusions. *Science, 139,* 769–771.

Segall, M. H., Lonner, W. J., & Berry, J. W. (1998). Cross-cultural psychology as a scholarly discipline: On the flowering of culture in behavioral research. *American Psychologist, 53*(10), 1101–1110.

Seligman, M. E. P. (1971). Phobias and preparedness. *Behavior Therapy, 2,* 307–320.

Seligman, M. E. P. (1995). The effectiveness of psychotherapy: The consumer reports study. *American Psychologist, 48,* 966–971.

Selikoff, I. J., Robitzek, E. H., & Ornstein, G. G. (1952). Toxicity of hydrazine derivatives of isonicotinic acid in the chemotherapy of human tuberculosis. *Quarterly Bulletin of SeaView Hospital, 13,* 17–26.

Selye, H. (1956). *The stress of life.* New York: McGraw-Hill.

Semenza, C., & Zettin, M. (1989). Evidence from aphasia from proper names as pure referring expressions. *Nature, 342,* 678–679.

Senghas, A., Kita, S., & Ozyurek, A. (2004). Children create core properties of language: Evidence from an emerging sign language in Nicaragua. *Science, 305,* 1782.

Serpell, R. (1974). Aspects of intelligence in a developing country. *African Social Research, 17,* 578–596.

Shah, J., Higgins, E. T., & Friedman, R. S. (1998). Performance incentives and means: How regulatory focus influences goal attainment. *Journal of Personality and Social Psychology, 74,* 285–293.

Shallice, T., Fletcher, P., Frith, C. D., Grasby, P., Frackowiak, R. S. J., & Dolan, R. J. (1994). Brain regions associated with acquisition and retrieval of verbal episodic memory. *Nature, 368,* 633–635.

Sheehan, P. (1979). Hypnosis and the process of imagination. In E. Fromm & R. S. Shor (Eds.), *Hypnosis: Developments in research and new perspectives.* Chicago: Aldine.

Sheingold, K., & Tenney, Y. J. (1982). Memory for a salient childhood event. In U. Neisser (Ed.), *Memory observed* (pp. 201–212). New York: Freeman.

Shepherd, G. M. (1988). *Neurobiology.* New York: Oxford University Press.

Sherrod, D. (1974). Crowding, perceived control, and behavioral aftereffects. *Journal of Applied Social Psychology, 4,* 171–186.

Shiffman, S., Gnys, M., Richards, T. J., Paty, J. A., & Hickcox, M. (1996). Temptations to smoke after quitting: A comparison of lapsers and maintainers. *Health Psychology, 15,* 455–461.

Shih, M., Pittinsky, T. L., & Ambady, N. (1999). Stereotype susceptibility: Identity salience and shifts in quantitative performance. *Psychological Science, 10,* 80–83.

Shimamura, A. P., & Squire, L. R. (1987). A neuropsychological study of fact memory and source amnesia. *Journal of Experimental Psychology: Learning, Memory, and Cognition, 13,* 464–473.

Shimoda, K., Argyle, M., & Ricci-Bitt, P. E. (1978). The intercultural recognition of emotional expressions by three national racial groups: English, Italian, and Japanese. *European Journal of Social Psychology, 8,* 169–179.

Shomstein, S., & Yantis, S. (2004). Control of attention shifts between vision and audition in human cortex. *Journal of Neuroscience, 24,* 10702–10706.

Shweder, R. A. (1991). *Thinking through cultures: Expeditions in cultural psychology.* Cambridge, MA: Harvard University Press.

Shweder, R. A., & Sullivan, M. A. (1993). Cultural psychology: Who needs it? *Annual Review of Psychology, 44,* 497–523.

Siegel, B. (1988, October 30). Can evil beget good? Nazi data: A dilemma for science. *Los Angeles Times.*

Siegel, S. (1976). Morphine analgesia tolerance: Its situational specificity supports a Pavlovian conditioning model. *Science, 193,* 323–325.

Siegel, S. (1984). Pavlovian conditioning and heroin overdose: Reports by overdose victims. *Bulletin of the Psychonomic Society, 22,* 428–430.

Sigl, J. C., & Chamoun, N. (1994). An introduction to bispectral analysis for the electroencephalogram. *Journal of Clinical Monitoring, 10,* 392–404.

Silver, R. L., Boon, C., & Stones, M. H. (1983). Searching for meaning in misfortune: Making sense of incest. *Journal of Social Issues, 39,* 81–102.

Simon, L. (1998). *Genuine reality: A life of William James.* New York: Harcourt Brace.

Simpson, E. L. (1974). Moral development research: A case study of scientific cultural bias. *Human Development, 17,* 81–106.

Singh, D. (1993). Adaptive significance of female physical attractiveness: Role of waist-to-hip ratio. *Journal of Personality and Social Psychology, 65,* 293–307.

Sipe, K. (2006). Muhammad trial journal. Retrieved September 15, 2007, from http://home.hamptonroads.com/guestbook/journal.cfm?startrow=11&question=1&id=53

Skinner, B. F. (1938). *The behavior of organisms: An experimental analysis.* New York: Appleton-Century-Crofts.

Skinner, B. F. (1947). "Superstition" in the pigeon. *Journal of Experimental Psychology, 38,* 168–172.

Skinner, B. F. (1986). *Walden II.* Englewood Cliffs, NJ: Prentice Hall. (Original work published 1948)

Skinner, B. F. (1950). Are theories of learning necessary? *Psychological Review, 57,* 193–216.

Skinner, B. F. (1957). *Verbal behavior.* New York: Appleton-Century-Crofts.

Skinner, B. F. (1958). Teaching machines. *Science, 129,* 969–977.

Skinner, B. F. (1971). *Beyond freedom and dignity.* New York: Bantam Books.

Slater, A., Morison, V., & Somers, M. (1988). Orientation discrimination and cortical function in the human newborn. *Perception, 17,* 597–602.

Sleepwalker found dozing high atop crane. (2005, July 6). Retrieved March 3, 2007, from http://www.accessmylibrary.com

Slotnick, S. D., & Schacter, D. L. (2004). A sensory signature that distinguished true from false memories. *Nature Neuroscience, 7,* 664–672.

Smetana, J. G. (1981). Preschool children's conceptions of moral and social rules. *Child Development, 52,* 1333–1336.

Smetana, J. G., & Braeges, J. L. (1990). The development of toddler's moral and conventional judgments. *Merrill-Palmer Quarterly, 36,* 329–346.

Smith, E. E., & Jonides, J. (1997). Working memory: A view from neuroimaging. *Cognitive Psychology, 33,* 5–42.

Smith, M. L., Glass, G. V., & Miller, T. I. (1980). *The benefits of psychotherapy.* Baltimore: Johns Hopkins University Press.

Smith, N., & Tsimpli, I-M. (1995). *The mind of a savant.* Oxford: Oxford University Press.

Snyder, M., & Swann, W. B., Jr. (1978). Hypothesis testing processes in social interaction. *Journal of Personality and Social Psychology, 36,* 1202–1212.

Solomon, J., & George, C. (1999). The measurement of attachment security in infancy and childhood. In J. Cassidy & P. R. Shaver (Eds.), *Handbook of attachment: Theory, research and clinical applications* (pp. 287–316). New York: Guilford Press.

Solomon, S., Greenberg, J., & Pyszczynski, T. (1991). A terror management theory of social behavior: The psychological functions of self-esteem and cultural worldviews. In M. P. Zanna (Ed.), *Advances in experimental social psychology* (Vol. 24, pp. 93–159). New York: Academic Press.

Spanos, N. P. (1994). Multiple identity enactments and multiple personality disorder: A sociocognitive perspective. *Psychological Bulletin, 116,* 143–165.

Spearman, C. (1904). "General intelligence," objectively determined and measured. *American Journal of Psychology, 15,* 201–293.

Speisman, J. C., Lazarus, R. S., Moddkoff, A., & Davison, L. (1964). Experimental reduction of stress based on ego-defense theory. *Journal of Abnormal and Social Psychology, 68,* 367–380.

Sperling, G. (1960). The information available in brief visual presentations. *Psychological Monographs, 74* (Whole No. 48).

Spiro, H. M., McCrea Curnan, M. G., Peschel, E., & St. James, D. (1994). *Empathy and the practice of medicine: Beyond pills and the scalpel.* New Haven, CT: Yale University Press.

Spitz, R. A. (1949). Motherless infants. *Child Development, 20,* 145–155.

Spitzer, R. L., Gibbon, M., Skodol, A. E., Williams, J. B. W., & First, M. B. (1994). DSM-IV Casebook: *A learning companion to the diagnostic & statistical manual of mental disorders* (4th ed.). Washington, DC: American Psychiatric Press.

Sprecher, S. (1999). "I love you more today than yesterday": Romantic partners' perceptions of changes in love and related affect over time. *Journal of Personality and Social Psychology, 76,* 46–53.

Squire, L. R. (1992). Memory and the hippocampus: A synthesis from findings with rats, monkeys, and humans. *Psychological Review, 99,* 195–231.

Squire, L. R., & Kandel, E. R. (1999). *Memory: From mind to molecules.* New York: Scientific American Library.

Squire, L. R., Ojemann, J. G., Miezin, F. M., Petersen, S. E., Videen, T. O., & Raichle, M. E. (1992). Activation of the hippocampus in normal humans: A functional anatomical study of memory. *Proceedings of the National Academy of Sciences (USA), 89,* 1837–1841.

Staw, B. M., & Hoang, H. (1995). Sunk costs in the NBA: Why draft order affects playing time and survival in professional basketball. *Administrative Science Quarterly 40,* 474–494.

Steele, C. M., & Aronson, J. (1995). Stereotype threat and the intellectual test performance of African Americans. *Journal of Personality and Social Psychology, 69,* 797–811.

Steele, C. M., & Josephs, R. A. (1990). Alcohol myopia: Its prized and dangerous effects. *American Psychologist, 45,* 921–933.

Stein, M. B. (1998). Neurobiological perspectives on social phobia: From affiliation to zoology. *Biological Psychiatry, 44,* 1277–1285.

Stein, M. B., Chavira, D. A., & Jang, K. L. (2001). Bringing up bashful baby: Developmental pathways to social phobia. *Psychiatric Clinics of North America, 24,* 661–675.

Stein, M. B., Koverola, C., Hanna, C., Torchia, M. G., & McClarty, B. (1997). Hippocampal volume in women victimized by childhood sexual abuse. *Psychological Medicine, 27,* 951–959.

Stein, Z., Susser, M., Saenger, G., & Marolla, F. (1975). *Famine and development: The Dutch hunger winter of 1944–1945.* Oxford: Oxford University Press.

Steinbaum, E. A., & Miller, N. E. (1965). Obesity from eating elicited by daily stimulation of hypothalamus. *American Journal of Physiology, 208,* 1–5.

Steinberg, L. (1999). *Adolescence* (5th ed.). Boston: McGraw-Hill.

Steinberg, L., & Morris, A. S. (2001). Adolescent development. *Annual Review of Psychology, 52,* 83–110.

Steiner, F. (1986). Differentiating smiles. In E. Branniger-Huber & F. Steiner (Eds.), *FACS in psychotherapy research* (pp. 139–148). Zurich: Department of Clinical Psychology, Universität Zürich.

Steiner, J. E. (1973). The gustofacial response: Observation on normal and anencephalic newborn infants. In J. F. Bosma (Ed.), *Fourth symposium on oral sensation and perception: Development in the fetus and infant* (pp. 254–278). Bethesda, MD: U.S. Department of Heath, Education, and Welfare (DHEW 73-546).

Steiner, J. E. (1979). Human facial expressions in response to taste and smell stimulation. *Advances in Child Development and Behavior, 13,* 257–295.

Steinman, R. B., Pizlo, Z., & Pizlo, F. J. (2000). Phi is not beta, and why Wertheimer's discovery launched the Gestalt revolution. *Vision Research, 40,* 2257–2264.

Stellar, J. R., Kelley, A. E., & Corbett, D. (1983). Effects of peripheral and central dopamine blockade on lateral hypothalamic self-stimulation: Evidence for both reward and motor deficits. *Pharmacology, Biochemistry, and Behavior, 18,* 433–442.

Stellar, J. R., & Stellar, E. (1985). *The neurobiology of motivation and reward.* New York: Springer-Verlag.

Stelmack, R. M. (1990). Biological bases of extraversion: Psychophysiological evidence. *Journal of Personality, 58,* 293–311.

Stephens, R. S. (1999). Cannabis and hallucinogens. In B. S. McCrady & E. E. Epstein (Eds.), *Addictions: A comprehensive guidebook.* New York: Oxford University Press.

Sterelny, K., & Griffiths, P. E. (1999). *Sex and death: An introduction to philosophy of biology.* University of Chicago Press.

Stern, J. A., Brown, M., Ulett, A., & Sletten, I. (1977). A comparison of hypnosis, acupuncture, morphine, valium, aspirin, and placebo in the management of experimentally induced pain. In W. E. Edmonston (Ed.), *Conceptual and investigative approaches to hypnosis and hypnotic phenomena* (Vol. 296, pp. 175–193). New York: Annals of the New York Academy of Sciences.

Stern, R., & Marks, I. (1973). Brief and prolonged flooding: A comparison in agoraphobic patients. *Archives of General Psychiatry, 28,* 270–276.

Sternberg, R. J. (1986). A triangular theory of love. *Psychological Review, 93,* 119–135.

Sternberg, R. J. (1988). *The triarchic mind: A new theory of human intelligence.* New York: Viking.

Stevens, G., & Gardner, S. (1982). *The women of psychology* (Vol. 1). Rochester: Schenkman Books.

Stevens, J. (1988). An activity approach to practical memory. In M. M. Gruneberg, P. E. Morris, & R. N. Sykes (Eds.), *Practical aspects of memory: Current research and issues* (Vol. 1, pp. 335–341). New York: Wiley.

Stickgold, R., Hobson, J. A., Fosse, R., & Fosse, M. (2001). Sleep, learning, and dreams: Off-line memory reprocessing. *Science, 294,* 1052–1057.

Stickgold, R., James, L., & Hobson, J. A. (2000a). Visual discrimination learning requires post-traiing sleep. *Nature Neuroscience, 3,* 1237–1238.

Stickgold, R., Malia, A., Maguire, D., Roddenberry, D., & O'Connor, M. (2000b). Replaying the game: Hypnagogic images in normals and anmesics. *Science, 290,* 350–353.

Stigler, J. W., Shweder, R., & Herdt, G. (Eds.). (1990). *Cultural psychology: Essays on comparative human development.* Cambridge: Cambridge University Press.

Stone, J., Perry, Z. W., & Darley, J. M. (1997). "White men can't jump": Evidence for the perceptual confirmation of racial stereotypes following a basketball game. *Basic and Applied Social Psychology, 19,* 291–306.

Strack, F., Martin, L. L., & Stepper, S. (1988). Inhibiting and facilitating conditions of the human smile: A nonobtrusive test of the facial feedback hypothesis. *Journal of Personality and Social Psychology, 54,* 768–777.

Strahan, E. J., Spencer, S. J., & Zanna, M. P. (2002). Subliminal priming and persuasion: Striking while the iron is hot. *Journal of Experimental Social Psychology, 38,* 556–568.

Strayer, D. L., Drews, F. A., & Johnston, W. A. (2003). Cell phone induced failures of visual attention during simulated driving. *Journal of Experimental Psychology: Applied, 9,* 23–32.

Streissguth, A. P., Barr, H. M., Bookstein, F. L., Sampson, P. D., & Carmichael Olson, H. (1999). The long-term neurocognitive consequences of prenatal alcohol exposure: A 14-year study. *Psychological Science, 10,* 186–190.

Strickland, L. H. (1991). Russian and Soviet social psychology. *Canadian Psychology, 32,* 580–595.

Strohmetz, D. B., Rind, B., Fisher, R., & Lynn, M. (2002). Sweetening the till: The use of candy to increase restaurant tipping. *Journal of Applied Social Psychology, 32,* 300–309.

Stuss, D. T., & Benson, D. F. (1986). *The frontal lobes.* New York: Raven Press.

Suarez-Morales, L., & Lopez, B. (2009). The impact of acculturative stress and daily hassles on pre-adolescent psychological adjustment: Examining anxiety symptoms. *Journal of Primary Prevention, 30,* 335–349.

Substance Abuse and Mental Health Services Administration. (2005). *Suicide warning signs.* Washington, DC: U.S. Department of Health and Human Services.

Suchman, A. L., Markakis, K., Beckman, H. B., & Frankel, R. (1997). A model of empathic communication in the medical interview. *Journal of the American Medical Association, 277,* 678–682.

Sulloway, F. J. (1992). *Freud, biologist of the mind.* Cambridge, MA: Harvard University Press.

Suls, J., & Fletcher, B. (1985). The relative efficacy of avoidant and nonavoidant coping strategies: A meta-analysis. *Health Psychology, 4,* 249–288.

Susman, S., Dent, C., McAdams, L., Stacy, A., Burton, D., & Flay, B. (1994). Group self-identification and adolescent cigarette smoking: a 1-year prospective study. *Journal of Abnormal Psychology, 103,* 576–580.

Susser, E. B., Brown, A., & Matte, T. D. (1999). Prenatal factors and adult mental and physical health. *Canadian Journal of Psychiatry, 44*(4) 326–334.

Sussman, L. K., Robins, L. N., & Earls, F. (1987). Treatment-seeking for depression by black and white Americans. *Social Science and Medicine, 24,* 187–196.

Suzuki, L. A., & Valencia, R. R. (1997). Race-ethnicity and measured intelligence: Educational implications. *American Psychologist, 52,* 1103–1114.

Swann, W. B. (1983). Self-verification: Bringing social reality into harmony with the self. In J. M. Suls & Greenwald, A. G. (Eds.), *Psychological perspectives on the self* (Vol. 2, pp. 33–66). Hillsdale, NJ: Erlbaum.

Swets, J. A., Dawes, R. M., & Monahan, J. (2000). Psychological science can improve diagnostic decisions. *Psychological Science in the Public Interest, 1,* 1–26.

Szechtman, H., Woody, E., Bowers, K. S., & Nahmias, C. (1998). Where the imaginal appears real: A positron emission tomography study of auditory hallucinations. *Proceedings of the National Academy of Sciences, 95,* 1956–1960.

Szpunar, K. K., Watson, J. M., & McDermott, K. B. (2007). Neural substrates of envisioning the future. *Proceedings of the National Academy of Sciences (USA), 104,* 642–647.

Tajfel, H. (1970). Experiments in intergroup discrimination. *Scientific American, 223,* 96–102.

Tajfel, H., Billig, M. G., Bundy, R. P., & Flament, C. (1971). Social categorization and intergroup behaviour. *European Journal of Social Psychology, 1,* 149–178.

Tajfel, H., & Turner, J. C. (1986). The social identity theory of intergroup behavior. In S. Worchel & W. G. Austin (Eds.), *Psychology of intergroup relations* (pp. 7–24). Chicago: Nelson.

Tajfel, H., & Wilkes, A. L. (1963). Classification and quantitative judgement. *British Journal of Psychology, 54,* 101–114.

Takahashi, K. (1986). Examining the strange-situation procedure with Japanese mothers and 12-month-old infants. *Developmental Psychlogy, 22,* 265–270.

Tamminga, C. A., Nemeroff, C. B., Blakely, R. D., Brady, L., Carter, C. S., Davis, K. L, Dingledine, R., et al. (2002). Developing novel treatments for mood disorders: Accelerating discovery. *Biological Psychiatry, 52,* 589–609.

Tart, C. T. (Ed.). (1969). *Altered states of consciousness.* New York: Wiley.

Taylor, E. (2001). *William James on consciousness beyond the margin.* Princeton, NJ: Princeton University Press.

Taylor, S. E. (1986). *Health psychology.* New York: Random House.

Taylor, S. E. (1989). *Positive illusions.* New York: Basic Books.

Taylor, S. E. (2002). *The tending instinct: How nurturing is essential to who we are and how we live.* New York: Times Books.

Taylor, S. E., & Brown, J. D. (1988). Illusion and well-being: A social psychological perspective on mental health. *Psychological Bulletin, 103,* 193–210.

Taylor, S. E., & Fiske, S. T. (1978). Salience, attention, and attribution: Top of the head phenomena. In L. Berkowitz (Ed.), *Advances in experimental social psychology* (Vol. 11, pp. 249–288). New York: Academic Press.

Teasdale, J. D., Segal, Z. V., & Williams, J. M. G. (2000). Prevention of relapse/recurrence in major depression by Mindfulness-Based Cognitive Therapy. *Journal of Consulting and Clinical Psychology, 68,* 615–623.

Telch, M. J., Lucas, J. A., & Nelson, P. (1989). Non-clinical panic in college students: An investigation of prevalence and symptomology. *Journal of Abnormal Psychology, 98,* 300–306.

Tellegen, A., & Atkinson, G. (1974). Openness to absorbing and self-altering experiences ("absorption"), a trait related to hypnotic susceptibility. *Journal of Abnormal Psychology, 83,* 268–277.

Tellegen, A., Lykken, D. T., Bouchard, T. J., Wilcox, K., Segal, N., & Rich, A. (1988). Personality similarity in twins reared together and apart. *Journal of Personality and Social Psychology, 54,* 1031–1039.

Temerlin, M. K., & Trousdale, W. W. (1969). The social psychology of clinical diagnosis. *Psychotherapy: Theory, Research & Practice, 6,* 24–29.

Tempini, M. L., Price, C. J., Josephs, O., Vandenberghe, R., Cappa, S. F., Kapur, N., et al. (1998). The neural systems sustaining face and proper-name processing. *Brain, 121,* 2103–2118.

Terman, L. M. (1916). *The measurement of intelligence.* Boston: Houghton Mifflin.

Tesser, A. (1993). The importance of heritability in psychological research: The case of attitudes. *Psychological Review, 100,* 129–142.

Teyler, T. J., & DiScenna, P. (1986). The hippocampal memory indexing theory. *Behavioral Neuroscience, 100,* 147–154.

Thase, M. E., & Howland, R. H. (1995). Biological processes in depression: An updated review and integration. In E. E. Beckham & W. R. Leber (Eds.), *Handbook of depression* (2nd ed., pp. 213–279). New York: Guilford Press.

Thelen, E., Corbetta, D., Kamm, K., Spencer, J. P., Schneider, K., & Zernicke, R. F. (1993). The transition to reaching: Mapping intention and intrinsic dynamics. *Child Development, 64,* 1058–1098.

Thibaut, J. W., & Kelley, H. H. (1959). *The social psychology of groups.* New Brunswick, NJ: Transaction Publishers.

Thoma, S. J., Narvaez, D., Rest, J., & Derryberry, P. (1999). Does moral judgment development reduce to political attitudes or verbal ability? Evidence using the defining issues test. *Educational Psychology Review,* 325–341.

Thomas, A., & Chess, S. (1977). *Temperament and development.* New York: Brunner/Mazel.

Thompson, C. P., Skowronski, J., Larsen, S. F., & Betz, A. (1996). *Autobiographical memory: Remembering what and remembering when.* Mahwah, NJ: Erlbaum.

Thompson, P. M., Vidal, C., Giedd, J. N., Gochman, P., Blumenthal, J., Nicolson, R., et al. (2001). Accelerated gray matter loss in very early-onset schizophrenia. *Proceedings of the National Academy of Science (USA), 98,* 11650–11655.

Thomson, D. M. (1988). Context and false recognition. In G. M. Davies & D. M. Thomson (Eds.), *Memory in context: Context in memory* (pp. 285–304). Chichester, England: Wiley.

Thorndike, E. L. (1898). Animal intelligence: An experimental study of associative processes in animals. *Psychological Review Monograph Supplements, 2*, 4–160.

Thornhill, R., & Gangestad, S. W. (1993). Human facial beauty: Averageness, symmetry, and parasite resistance. *Human Nature, 4*, 237–269.

Thurber, J. (1956). *Further fables of our time.* New York: Simon & Schuster.

Thurstone, L. L. (1938). *Primary mental abilities.* Chicago: University of Chicago Press.

Tice, D. M., & Baumeister, R. F. (1997). Longitudinal study of procrastination, performance, stress, and health: The costs and benefits of dawdling. *Psychological Science, 8*(6), 454–458.

Tienari, P., Wynne, L. C., Sorri, A., Lahti, I., Läksy, K., Moring, J., et al. (2004). Genotype-environment interaction in schizophrenia-spectrum disorder: Long-term follow-up study of Finnish adoptees. *British Journal of Psychiatry, 184*, 216–222.

Time poll. (2005, January 17). Just how happy are we? *Time*, A4.

Tittle, P. (Ed.). (2004). *Should parents be licensed? Debating the issues.* New York: Prometheus Books.

Tolman, E. C., & Honzik, C. H. (1930a). "Insight" in rats. *University of California Publications in Psychology, 4*, 215–232.

Tolman, E. C., & Honzik, C. H. (1930b). Introduction and removal of reward and maze performance in rats. *University of California Publications in Psychology, 4*, 257–275.

Tomkins, S. S. (1981). The role of facial response in the experience of emotion. *Journal of Personality and Social Psychology, 40*, 351–357.

Tooby, J., & Cosmides, L. (2000). Mapping the evolved functional organization of mind and brain. In M. S. Gazzaniga (Ed.), *The cognitive neurosciences* (pp. 1185–1198). Cambridge, MA: MIT Press.

Tootell, R. B. H., Reppas, J. B., Dale, A. M., Look, R. B., Sereno, M. I., Malach, R., et al. (1995). Visual-motion aftereffect in human cortical area MT revealed by functional magnetic resonance imaging. *Nature, 375*, 139–141.

Torgensen, S. (1983). Genetic factors in anxiety disorders. *Archives of General Psychiatry, 40*, 1085–1089.

Torgensen, S. (1986). Childhood and family characteristics in panic and generalized anxiety disorder. *American Journal of Psychiatry, 143*, 630–639.

Torrey, E. F., Bower, A. E., Taylor, E. H., & Gottesman, I. I. (1994). *Schizophrenia and manic-depressive disorder: The biological roots of mental illness as revealed by the landmark study of identical twins.* New York: Basic Books.

Trebach, A. S., & Zeese, K. B. (Eds.). (1992). *Friedman and Szasz on liberty and drugs: Essays on the free market and prohibition.* Washington, DC: Drug Policy Foundation Press.

Treede, R. D., Kenshalo, D. R., Gracely, R. H., & Jones, A. K. (1999). The cortical representation of pain. *Pain, 79*, 105–111.

Trivers, R. L. (1972a). The evolution of reciprocal altruism. *The Quarterly Review of Biology, 46*, 35–57.

Trivers, R. L. (1972b). Parental investment and sexual selection. In B. Campbell (Ed.), *Sexual selection and the descent of man, 1871–1971* (pp. 139–179). Chicago: Aldine.

Trull, T. J., & Durrett, C. A. (2005). Categorical and dimensional models of personality disorder. *Annual Review of Clinical Psychology, 1*, 355–380.

Tulving, E. (1972). Episodic and semantic memory. In E. Tulving & W. Donaldson (Eds.), *Organization of memory* (pp. 381–403). New York: Academic Press.

Tulving, E. (1983). *Elements of episodic memory.* Oxford: Clarendon Press.

Tulving, E. (1998). Neurocognitive processes of human memory. In C. von Euler & I. Lundberg & R. Llins (Eds.), *Basic mechanisms in cognition and language* (pp. 261–281). Amsterdam: Elsevier.

Tulving, E., Kapur, S., Craik, F. I. M., Moscovitch, M., & Houle, S. (1994). Hemispheric encoding/retrieval asymmetry in episodic memory: Positron emission tomography findings. *Proceedings of the National Academy of Sciences (USA), 91*, 2016–2020.

Tulving, E., & Pearlstone, Z. (1966). Availability versus accessibility of information in memory for words. *Journal of Verbal Learning & Verbal Behavior, 5*, 381–391.

Tulving, E., & Schacter, D. L. (1990). Priming and human memory systems. *Science, 247*, 301–306.

Tulving, E., Schacter, D. L., & Stark, H. (1982). Priming effects in word-fragment completion are independent of recognition memory. *Journal of Experimental Psychology: Learning, Memory, and Cognition, 8*, 336–342.

Tulving, E., & Thompson, D. M. (1973). Encoding specificity and retrieval processes in episodic memory. *Psychological Review, 80*, 352–373.

Turkheimer, E., Haley, A., Waldron, M., D'Onofrio, B., & Gottesman, I. I. (2003). Socioeconomic status modifies heritability of IQ in young children. *Psychological Science, 14*, 623–628.

Turner, D. C., & Sahakian, B. J. (2006). Neuroethics of cognitive enhancement. *BioSocieties, 1*, 113–123.

Tversky, A., & Kahneman, D. (1981). The framing of decisions and the psychology of choice. *Science, 211*, 453–458.

Tversky, A., & Kahneman, D. (1983). Extensional versus intuitive reasoning: The conjunction fallacy in probability judgment. *Psychological Review, 90*, 293–315.

Tversky, A., & Kahneman, D. (1992). Advances in prospect theory: Cumulative representation of uncertainty. *Journal of Risk and Uncertainty, 5*, 297–323.

Twenge, J. M., Campbell, W. K., & Foster, C. A. (2003). Parenthood and marital satisfaction: A meta-analytic review. *Journal of Marriage and Family, 65*, 574–583.

Tyler, T. R. (1990). *Why people obey the law.* New Haven, CT: Yale University Press.

Ursano, R. J., & Silberman, E. K. (2003). Psychoanalysis, psychoanalytic psychotherapy, and supportive psychotherapy. In R. E. Hales & S. C. Yudofsky (Eds.), *The American Psychiatric Publishing textbook of clinical psychiatry* (4th ed., pp. 1177–1203). Washington, DC: American Psychiatric Publishing.

U.S. Department of Transportation, National Highway Traffic Safety Administration (NHTSA). (2008). *Traffic safety facts 2006: Alcohol-impaired driving.* Washington, DC: NHTSA. Available: http://www-nrd.nhtsa.dot.gov/Pubs/810801.pdf

Valentine, T., Brennen, T., & Brédart, S. (1996). *The cognitive psychology of proper names: On the importance of being Ernest.* London: Routledge.

Vallacher, R. R., & Wegner, D. M. (1985). *A theory of action identification.* Hillsdale, NJ: Erlbaum.

Vallacher, R. R., & Wegner, D. M. (1987). What do people think they're doing? Action identification and human behavior. *Psychological Review, 94*, 3–15.

Van Essen, D. C., Anderson, C. H., & Felleman, D. J. (1992). Information processing in the primate visual system: An integrated systems perspective. *Science, 255*, 419–423.

van IJzendoorn, M. H. (1995). Adult attachment representations, parental responsiveness, and infant attachment: A meta-analysis on the predictive validity of the Adult Attachment Interview. *Psychological Bulletin, 117,* 387–403.

van IJzendoorn, M. H., & Kroonenberg, P. M. (1988). Cross-cultural patterns of attachment: A meta-analysis of the strange situation. *Child Development, 59,* 147–156.

van Stegeren, A. H., Everaerd, W., Cahill, L., McGaugh, J. L., & Gooren, L. J. G. (1998). Memory for emotional events: Differential effects of centrally versus peripherally acting blocking agents. *Psychopharmacology, 138,* 305–310.

Van Velzen, C. J. M., & Emmelkamp, P. M. G. (1996). The assessment of personality disorders: Implications for cognitive and behavior therapy. *Behaviour Research and Therapy, 34,* 655–668.

Vance, E. B., & Wagner, N. N. (1976). Written descriptions of orgasm: A study of sex differences. *Archives of Sexual Behavior, 5,* 87–98.

Vargha-Khadem, F., Gadian, D. G., Watkins, K. E., Connelly, A., Van Paesschen, W., & Mishkin, M. (1997). Differential effects of early hippocampal pathology on episodic and semantic memory. *Science, 277,* 376–380.

Vitkus, J. (1996). *Casebook in abnormal psychology* (3rd ed.). New York: McGraw-Hill.

Vitkus, J. (1999). *Casebook in abnormal psychology* (4th ed.). New York: McGraw-Hill.

Von Frisch, K. (1974). Decoding the language of the bee. *Science, 185,* 663–668.

Vortac, O. U., Edwards, M. B., & Manning, C. A. (1995). Functions of external cues in prospective memory. *Memory, 3,* 201–219.

Vygotsky, L. S. (1978). *Mind in society: The development of higher psychological processes.* Cambridge, MA: Harvard University Press.

Wagner, A. D., Schacter, D. L., Rotte, M., Koutstaal, W., Maril, A., Dale, A. M., et al. (1998). Remembering and forgetting of verbal experiences as predicted by brain activity. *Science, 281,* 1188–1190.

Wahba, M. A., & Bridwell, L. G. (1976). Maslow reconsidered: A review of research on the need hierarchy theory. *Organizational Behavior & Human Performance, 15,* 212–240.

Wahl, O. F. (1976). Monozygotic twins discordant for schizophrenia: A review. *Psychological Bulletin, 83,* 91–106.

Waite, L. J. (1995). Does marriage matter? *Demography, 32,* 483–507.

Waldfogel, S. (1948). The frequency and affective character of childhood memories. *Psychological Monographs, 62* (Whole No. 291).

Walker, C. (1977). Some variations in marital satisfaction. In R. C. J. Peel (Ed.), *Equalities and inequalities in family life* (pp. 127–139). London: Academic Press.

Walker, L. J. (1988). The development of moral reasoning. *Annals of Child Development, 55,* 677–691.

Wallace, J., Schnieder, T., & McGuffin, P. (2002). Genetics of depression. In I. H. Gottlieb & C. L. Hammen (Eds.), *Handbook of depression* (pp. 169–191). New York: Guilford Press.

Wallbott, H. G. (1998). Bodily expression of emotion. *European Journal of Social Psychology, 28,* 879–896.

Walster, E., Aronson, V., Abrahams, D., & Rottmann, L. (1966). Importance of physical attractiveness in dating behavior. *Journal of Personality and Social Psychology, 4,* 508–516.

Walster, E., Walster, G. W., & Berscheid, E. (1978). *Equity: Theory and research.* Boston: Allyn and Bacon.

Wang, L. H., McCarthy, G., Song, A. W., & LaBar, K. S. (2005). Amygdala activation to sad pictures during high-field (4 tesla) functional magnetic resonance imaging. *Emotion, 5,* 12–22.

Ward, J., Parkin, A. J., Powell, G., Squires, E. J., Townshend, J., & Bradley, V. (1999). False recognition of unfamiliar people: "Seeing film stars everywhere." *Cognitive Neuropsychology, 16,* 293–315.

Warnock, M. (2003). *Making babies: Is there a right to have children?* Oxford: Oxford University Press.

Warrington, E. K., & McCarthy, R. A. (1983). Category specific access dysphasia. *Brain, 106,* 859–878.

Warrington, E. K., & Shallice, T. (1984). Category specific semantic impairments. *Brain, 107,* 829–854.

Watanabe, S., Sakamoto, J., & Wakita, M. (1995). Pigeons' discrimination of painting by Monet and Picasso. *Journal of the Experimental Analysis of Behavior, 63,* 165–174.

Watkins, L. R., & Maier, S. F. (2005). Immune regulation of central nervous system functions: From sickness responses to pathological pain. *Journal of Internal Medicine, 257,* 139–155.

Watson, D., & Pennebaker, J. W. (1989). Health complaints, stress, and distress: Exploring the central role of negative affectivity. *Psychological Review, 96,* 234–254.

Watson, D., & Tellegen, A. (1985). Toward a consensual structure of mood. *Psychological Bulletin, 98,* 219–235.

Watson, J. B. (1930). *Behaviorism* (Rev. ed.). Chicago: University of Chicago Press.

Watson, J. B., & Rayner, R. (1920). Conditioned emotional reactions. *Journal of Experimental Psychology, 3,* 1–14.

Watson, R. I. (1978). *The great psychologists.* New York: Lippincott.

Watzlawick, P., Beavin, J., & Jackson, D. D. (1967). *Pragmatics of human communication: A study of interactional patterns, pathologies, and paradoxes.* New York: Norton.

Weber, R., & Crocker, J. (1983). Cognitive processes in the revision of stereotypic beliefs. *Journal of Personality and Social Psychology, 45,* 961–977.

Wechsler, H., Davenport, A., Dowdall, G., Moeykens, B., & Castillo, S. (1994). Health and behavioral consequences of binge drinking in college: A national survey of students at 140 campuses. *Journal of the American Medical Association, 272,* 1672–1677.

Wechsler, H., Rigotti, N. A., Gledhill-Hoyt, J., & Lee, H. (1998). Increased levels of cigarette use among college students: A cause for national concern. *Journal of the American Medical Association, 280,* 1673–1678.

Wegner, D. M. (1994a). Ironic processes of mental control. *Psychological Review, 101,* 34–52.

Wegner, D. M. (1994b). *White bears and other unwanted thoughts: Suppression, obsession, and the psychology of mental control.* New York: Guilford Press.

Wegner, D. M. (1997). Why the mind wanders. In J. D. Cohen & J. W. Schooler (Eds.), *Scientific approaches to consciousness* (pp. 295–315). Mahwah, NJ: Erlbaum.

Wegner, D. M. (2002). *The illusion of conscious will.* Cambridge, MA: MIT Press.

Wegner, D. M. (2009). How to think, say, or do precisely the worst thing for any occasion. *Science, 325,* 48–51.

Wegner, D. M., Ansfield, M., & Pilloff, D. (1998). The putt and the pendulum: Ironic effects of the mental control of action. *Psychological Science, 9,* 196–199.

Wegner, D. M., Broome, A., & Blumberg, S. J. (1997). Ironic effects of trying to relax under stress. *Behavior Research and Therapy, 35,* 11–21.

Wegner, D. M., Erber, R. E., & Zanakos, S. (1993). Ironic processes in the mental control of mood and mood-related thought. *Journal of Personality and Social Psychology, 65,* 1093–1104.

Wegner, D. M., & Gilbert, D. T. (2000). Social psychology: The science of human experience. In H. Bless & J. Forgas (Eds.), *The message within: Subjective experience in social cognition and behavior* (pp. 1–9). Philadelphia: Psychology Press.

Wegner, D. M., & Pennebaker, J. W. (Eds.). (1993). *Handbook of mental control*. Englewood Cliffs, NJ: Prentice Hall.

Wegner, D. M., & Schaefer, D. (1978). The concentration of responsibility: An objective self-awareness analysis of group size effects in helping situations. *Journal of Personality and Social Psychology, 36*, 147–155.

Wegner, D. M., Schneider, D. J., Carter, S. R., & White, T. L. (1987). Paradoxical effects of thought suppression. *Journal of Personality and Social Psychology, 53*, 5–13.

Wegner, D. M., & Wenzlaff, R. M. (1996). Mental control. In E. T. Higgins & A. Kruglanski (Eds.), *Social psychology: Handbook of basic mechanisms and processes* (pp. 466–492). New York: Guilford Press.

Wegner, D. M., Wenzlaff, R. M., & Kozak, M. (2004). Dream rebound: The return of suppressed thoughts in dreams. *Psychological Science, 15*, 232–236.

Weisfeld, G. (1999). *Evolutionary principles of human adolescence*. New York: Basic Books.

Weissman, M. M., Bland, R. C., Canino, G. J., Faravelli, C., Greenwald, S., Hwu, H. G., et al. (1997). The cross-national epidemiology of panic disorder. *Archives of General Psychiatry, 54*, 305–309.

Weissman, M. M., Markowitz, J. C., & Klerman, G. L. (2000). *Comprehensive guide to interpersonal psychotherapy*. New York: Basic Books.

Wells, G. L., Malpass, R. S., Lindsay, R. C. L., Fisher, R. P., Turtle, J. W., & Fulero, S. M. (2000). From the lab to the police station: A successful application of eyewitness research. *American Psychologist, 55*, 581–598.

Wenzlaff, R. M. (2005). Seeking solace but finding despair: The persistence of intrusive thoughts in depression. In D. A. Clark (Ed.), *Intrusive thoughts in clinical disorders: Theory, research, and treatment* (pp. 54–85). New York: Guilford Press.

Wenzlaff, R. M., & Bates, D. E. (1998). Unmasking a cognitive vulnerability to depression: How lapses in mental control reveal depressive thinking. *Journal of Personality and Social Psychology, 75*, 1559–1571.

Wenzlaff, R. M., & Eisenberg, A. R. (2001). Mental control after dysphoria: Evidence of a suppressed, depressive bias. *Behavior Therapy, 32*, 27–45.

Wenzlaff, R. M., & Wegner, D. M. (2000). Thought suppression. In S. T. Fiske (Ed.), *Annual Review of Psychology* (Vol. 51, pp. 51–91). Palo Alto, CA: Annual Reviews.

Wernicke, K. (1874). *Der Aphasische Symptomenkomplex*. Breslau: Cohn and Weigart.

Whalen, P. J., Rauch, S. L., Etcoff, N. L., McInerney, S. C., Lee, M. B., & Jenike, M. A. (1998). Masked presentations of emotional facial expressions modulate amygdala activity without explicit knowledge. *Journal of Neuroscience, 18*, 411–418.

Wheeler, M. A., Petersen, S. E., & Buckner, R. L. (2000). Memory's echo: Vivid recollection activates modality-specific cortex. *Proceedings of the National Academy of Sciences (USA), 97*, 11125–11129.

White, B. L., & Held, R. (1966). Plasticity of motor development in the human infant. In J. F. Rosenblith & W. Allinsmith (Eds.), *The cause of behavior* (pp. 60–70). Boston: Allyn and Bacon.

White, F. J. (1996). Synaptic regulation of mesocorticolimbic dopamine neurons. *Annual Review of Neuroscience, 19*, 405–436.

White, G. M., & Kirkpatrick, J. (Eds.). (1985). *Person, self, and experience: Exploring pacific ethnopsychologies*. Berkeley: University of California Press.

White, N. M., & Milner, P. M. (1992). The psychobiology of reinforcers. *Annual Review of Psychology, 41*, 443–471.

Whybrow, P. C. (1997). *A mood apart*. New York: Basic Books.

Wicklund, R. (1975). Objective self-awareness. In L. Berkowitz (Ed.), *Advances in experimental social psychology* (Vol. 8, pp. 233–275). New York: Academic Press.

Widiger, T. A. (2001). The best and the worst of us? *Clinical Psychology: Science and Practice, 8*, 374–377.

Widiger, T. A., & Sankis, L. M. (2000). Adult psychopathology: Issues and controversies. *An Annual Review of Psychology, 51*, 377–404.

Wiederman, M. W. (1997). Pretending orgasm during sexual intercourse: Correlates in a sample of young adult women. *Journal of Sex & Marital Therapy, 23*, 131–139.

Wiener, D. N. (1996). *B. F. Skinner: Benign anarchist*. Boston: Allyn and Beacon.

Wiesenthal, D. L., Austrom, D., & Silverman, I. (1983). Diffusion of responsibility in charitable donations. *Basic and Applied Social Psychology, 4*, 17–27.

Wiggs, C. L., & Martin, A. (1998). Properties and mechanisms of perceptual priming. *Current Opinion in Neurobiology, 8*, 227–233.

Wilcoxon, H. C., Dragoin, W. B., & Kral, P. A. (1971). Illness-induced aversions in rats and quail: Relative salience of visual and gustatory cues. *Science, 171*, 826–828.

Wiley, J. L. (1999). Cannabis: Discrimination of "internal bliss"? *Pharmacology, Biochemistry, & Behavior, 64*, 257–260.

Williams, A. C. (2002). Facial expression of pain: An evolutionary account. *Behavioral and Brain Sciences, 25*, 439–488.

Williams, C. M., & Kirkham, T. C. (1999). Anandamide induces overeating: Mediation by central cannabinoid (CB1) receptors. *Psychopharmacology, 143*, 315–317.

Williams, K. D., Nida, S. A., Baca, L. D., & Latané, B. (1989). Social loafing and swimming: Effects of identifiability on individual and relay performance of intercollegiate swimmers. *Basic and Applied Social Psychology, 10*, 73–81.

Wilson, T. D. (2002). *Strangers to ourselves: Discovering the adaptive unconscious*. Cambridge, MA: Harvard University Press.

Wilson, T. D., & Gilbert, D. T. (2003). Affective forecasting. In M. P. Zanna (Ed.), *Advances in experimental social psychology* (Vol. 35, pp. 345–411). New York: Elsevier.

Wilson, T. D., Lindsey, S., & Schooler, T. Y. (2000). A model of dual attitudes. *Psychological Review, 107*, 101–126.

Wilson, T. D., Meyers, J., & Gilbert, D. T. (2003). "How happy was I, anyway?" A retrospective impact bias. *Social Cognition, 21*, 421–446.

Wimmer, H., & Perner, J. (1983). Beliefs about beliefs: Representations and constraining function of wrong beliefs in young children's understanding of deception. *Cognition, 13*, 103–128.

Windeler, J., & Kobberling, J. (1986). Empirische Untersuchung zur Einschatzung diagnostischer Verfahren am Beispiel des Haemoccult-Tests. [An empirical study of the value of diagnostic procedures using the example of the hemoccult test.] *Klinische Wochenscrhrift, 64*, 1106–1112.

Winner, E. (1997). Exceptionally high intelligence and schooling. *American Psychologist, 52*, 1070–1081.

Winterer, G., & Weinberger, D. R. (2004). Genes, dopamine and cortical signal-to-noise ratio in schizophrenia. *Trends in Neuroscience, 27*, 683–690.

Wise, R. A. (1989). Brain dopamine and reward. *Annual Review of Psychology, 40*, 191–225.

Wise, R. A. (2005). Forebrain substrates of reward and motivation. *Journal of Comparative Neurology, 493*, 115–121.

Wittchen, H., Knauper, B., & Kessler, R. C. (1994). Lifetime risk of depression. *British Journal of Psychiatry, 165*, 16–22.

Wittgenstein, L. (1999). *Philosophical investigations*. Upper Saddle River, NJ: Prentice Hall. (Original work published 1953)

Wixted, J. T., & Ebbensen, E. (1991). On the form of forgetting. *Psychological Science, 2*, 409–415.

Wolf, J. (2003, May 18). Through the looking glass. *The New York Times Magazine*, p. 120.

Wolpe, J. (1958). *Psychotherapy by reciprocal inhibition*. Stanford, CA: Stanford University Press.

Wong, D. T., Bymaster, F. P., & Engleman, E. A. (1995). Prozac (fluoxetine, Lilly 110140), the first selective serotonin uptake inhibitor and an antidepressant drug: Twenty years since its first publication. *Life Sciences, 57*, 411–441.

Wood, J. M., & Bootzin, R. R. (1990). Prevalence of nightmares and their independence from anxiety. *Journal of Abnormal Psychology, 99*, 64–68.

Wood, J. M., Bootzin, R. R., Rosenhan, D., Nolen-Hoeksema, S., & Jourden, F. (1992). Effects of the 1989 San Francisco earthquake on frequency and content of nightmares. *Journal of Abnormal Psychology, 101*, 219–224.

Wood, J. M., Nezworski, M. T., Lilienfeld, S. O., & Garb, H. N. (2003). *What's wrong with the Rorschach? Science confronts the controversial inkblot test*. New York: Wiley.

Wood, J. M., Nezworski, M. T., & Stejskal, W. J. (1996). The comprehensive system for the Rorschach: A critical examination. *Psychological Science, 7*, 3–10.

Woods, E. R., Lin, Y. G., Middleman, A., Beckford, P., Chase, L., & DuRant, R. H. (1997). The associations of suicide attempts in adolescents. *Pediatrics, 99*, 791–796.

Woods, S. C., Seeley, R. J., Porte, D., Jr., & Schwartz, M. W. (1998). Signals that regulate food intake and energy homeostasis. *Science, 280*, 1378–1383.

Woods, S. M., Natterson, J., & Silverman, J. (1966). Medical students' disease: hypochondriasis in medical education. *Journal of Medical Education, 41*, 785–790.

Wrangham, R., & Peterson, D. (1997). *Demonic males: Apes and the origin of human violence*. New York: Mariner.

Wren, A. M., Seal, L. J., Cohen, M. A., Brynes, A. E., Frost, G. S., Murphy, K. G., et al. (2001). Ghrelin enhances appetite and increases food intake in humans. *Journal of Clinical Endocrinology and Metabolism, 86*, 5992–5995.

Wrenn, C. C., Turchi, J. N., Schlosser, S., Dreiling, J. L., Stephenson, D. A., Crawley, J. N. (2006). Performance of galanin transgenic mice in the 5-choice serial reaction time attentional task. *Pharmacology Biochemistry and Behavior, 83*, 428–440.

Wright, L. (1994). *Remembering Satan: A case of recovered memory and the shattering of an American family*. New York: Knopf.

Wright, P., Takei, N., Rifkin, L., & Murray, R. M. (1995). Maternal influenza, obstetric complications, and schizophrenia. *American Journal of Psychiatry, 152*, 1714–1720.

Wulf, S. (1994, March 14). Err Jordan. *Sports Illustrated*.

Xiaohe, X., & Whyte, K. J. (1990). Love matches and arranged marriages: A Chinese replication. *Journal of Marriage and the Family, 52*, 709–722.

Yamaguchi, S. (1998). Basic properties of umami and its effects in humans. *Physiology and Behavior, 49*, 833–841.

Yang, S., & Sternberg, R. J. (1997). Conceptions of intelligence in ancient Chinese philosophy. *Journal of Theoretical and Philosophical Psychology, 17*, 101–119.

Yelsma, P., & Athappilly, K. (1988). Marital satisfaction and communication practices: Comparisons among Indian and American couples. *Journal of Comparative Family Studies, 19*, 37–53.

Yin, R. K. (1970). Face recognition by brain-injured patients: A dissociable ability. *Neuropsychologia, 8*, 395–402.

Young, A. S., Klap, R., Sherbourne, C. D., & Wells, K. B. (2001). The quality of care for depressive and anxiety disorders in the United States. *Archives of General Psychiatry, 58*, 55–61.

Young, P. C. (1948). Antisocial uses of hypnosis. In L. M. LeCron (Ed.), *Experimental hypnosis* (pp. 376–409). New York: Macmillan.

Young, R. M. (1990). *Mind, brain, and adaptation in the nineteenth century: Cerebral localization and its biological context from Gall to Ferrier*. New York: Oxford University Press.

Yucha, C., & Gilbert, C. D. (2004). *Evidence-based practice in biofeedback and neurofeedback*. Colorado Springs, CO: Association for Applied Psychophysiology and Biofeedback.

Yuill, N., & Perner, J. (1988). Intentionality and knowledge in children's judgments of actor's responsibility and recipient's emotional reaction. *Developmental Psychology, 24*, 358–365.

Zajonc, R. B. (1968). Attitudinal effects of mere exposure. *Journal of Personality and Social Psychology, 9*, 1–27.

Zajonc, R. B. (1980). Feeling and thinking: Preferences need no inferences. *American Psychologist, 35*, 151–175.

Zajonc, R. B. (1984). On the primacy of affect. In K. R. Scherer & P. Ekman (Eds.), *Approaches to emotion* (pp. 259–270). Hillsdale, NJ: Erlbaum.

Zajonc, R. B. (1989). Feeling the facial efference: Implications of the vascular theory of emotion. *Psychological Review, 96*, 395–416.

Zebrowitz, L. A., Hall, J. A., Murphy, N. A., & Rhodes, G. (2002). Looking smart and looking good: Facial cues to intelligence and their origins. *Personality and Social Psychology Bulletin, 28*, 238–249.

Zebrowitz, L. A., & Montepare, J. M. (1992). Impressions of baby-faced individuals across the life span. *Developmental Psychology, 28*, 1143–1152.

Zeki, S. (1993). *A vision of the brain*. London: Blackwell Scientific Publications.

Zentall, T. R., Sutton, J. E., & Sherburne, L. M. (1996). True imitative learning in pigeons. *Psychological Science, 7*, 343–346.

Zhang, J. (2004, October 2). Prof. Zimbardo faults Rumsfeld for Abu Ghraib. *Stanford Daily*. Retrieved August 2007 from http://daily.stanford.edu/article/2004/10/29/profZimbardoFaultsRumsfeldForAbuGhraib.

Zihl, J., von Cramon, D., & Mai, N. (1983). Selective disturbance of movement vision after bilateral brain damage. *Brain 106*, 313–340.

Zuckerman, M., DePaulo, B. M., & Rosenthal, R. (1981). Verbal and nonverbal communication of deception. In L. Berkowitz (Ed.), *Advances in experimental social psychology* (Vol. 14, pp. 1–59). New York: Academic Press.

Zuckerman, M., & Driver, R. E. (1985). Telling lies: Verbal and nonverbal correlates of deception. In W. Seigman & S. Feldstein (Eds.), *Multichannel integrations of nonverbal behavior* (pp. 129–147). Hillsdale, NJ: Erlbaum.

Name Index

Subject Index

Note: Page numbers followed by f indicate figures; those followed by t indicate tables.